# Women's Experiences
## A Psychological Perspective

Frances Elaine Donelson
*Michigan State University*

D1383423

Mayfield Publishing Company
Mountain View, California
London ◆ Toronto

**Library of Congress Cataloging-in-Publication Data**
Donelson, Frances Elaine.
    Women's experiences : a psychological perspective / Frances Elaine
Donelson.
        p.   cm.
    Includes bibliographical references and index.
    ISBN 0-7674-0043-7
    1. Women—Psychology.    2. Sex role—Psychological aspects.
I. Title.
HQ1206.D66   1999
155.6'33—dc21                                                            97-45772
                                                                          CIP

Manufactured in the United States of America
10  9  8  7  6  5  4  3  2  1

Mayfield Publishing Company
1280 Villa Street
Mountain View, California 94041

Sponsoring editor, Franklin C. Graham; developmental editors, Elaine Silverstein and Kathleen Engelberg; production editor, April Wells-Hayes; manuscript editor, Judith Brown; design manager, Susan Breitbard; text designer, Terri Wright; cover designer, Laurie Anderson; art editor, Robin Mouat; illustrators: Joan Carol, Robin Mouat, and Judy Waller; photo editor, Brian Pecko; manufacturing manager, Randy Hurst. The text was set in 10/12 Janson by Thompson Type and printed on 45# Custom LG by The Banta Book Group.

Cover image: Jane A. Sassaman, *Information Radiation*. Quilt, 65" × 65". Copyright © 1989 Jane A. Sassaman.

Focus on Research boxes courtesy of Jill Borchert and Nancy Cobb. Text and illustration credits continue at the back of the book on pages C-1–C-3, which constitute an extension of the copyright page.

# BRIEF CONTENTS

# CONTENTS

**Chapter 2    *Images and Stereotypes of Women    39***

## Chapter 3    *Gender-Related Views of Self and Others*   76

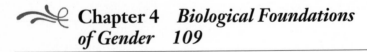 **Chapter 4   *Biological Foundations
of Gender   109***

**Chapter 5    *Development of Gender Role Behavior    145***

**Chapter 6   *Women's Experiences of Menstruation*   188**

**Chapter 7    *Development of Achievement
Motivation in Women*    224**

## Chapter 8   *Development of Cognitive Abilities and Moral Reasoning in Women   259*

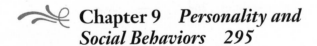

## Chapter 9   *Personality and Social Behaviors   295*

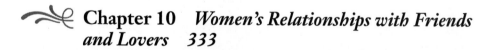 **Chapter 10    *Women's Relationships with Friends and Lovers    333***

## Chapter 11    *Women's Sexuality    372*

**Development of Sexuality in the Early Years    373**

**Chapter 12   *Women's Decisions About Reproductive Experiences   413***

# Chapter 13   *Women at Work and Working at Home*   447

## Chapter 14   *Adult Development in Women*   486

# Chapter 15    *Women's Experiences of Violence*    525

**Chapter 16    *Women's Mental Health*    566**

## Chapter 17  *Challenges, Religion, and Anger*   *603*

*To students who teach
and teachers who learn—
especially my parents,
Louella Tramel Donelson
and
Fred Wayne Donelson*

# PREFACE

## *Some Background*

In 1970, I taught a senior personality theory course to a group of students who have stood out in my mind ever since—and especially now, as I think about this book. At the end of that course, one student told me: "You're always criticizing psychology, but you don't fool me for a minute; I know you love it!" Of course, the student was right. Like other authors who have written on the psychology of women, I am often critical of a discipline that has neglected, even maligned, the women who constitute much of its subject matter. But I am a psychologist by choice and dedicated to correcting the discipline and sharing its information.

Most of all, I remember Elizabeth Santos, a courageous and determined woman. That fall and spring, my colleagues often commented that they had gone home after a hard day of classes and turned on their televisions, only to find Elizabeth on the local news, leading a protest. "There she is again," they would say. Elizabeth had been after me from the beginning of the term to teach a course on women. As an untenured faculty member, I resisted, fearing to offend my colleagues. But Ms. Santos kept after me. The more I listened, the more sense she made. By the end of the term, I was a convert—and had also managed to convert one of my tenured colleagues.

The first Psychology of Women course at Michigan State University was offered for the Spring 1971 term. A small group of us—two instructors and two graduate students—started designing the course. At that time, there was no field called "psychology of women," nor were there any relevant undergraduate textbooks. We sought out colleagues in the department and asked them, as guest lecturers, to focus their areas of competence on women. We got word of a new book by Judith Bardwick; the publisher provided us with the galley proofs to review, and by the first day of class we had her book in hand and guest lecturers lined up.

Over the years my commitment to a psychology of women has grown. I am fascinated by the challenges and demands the field makes upon the knowledge generated in other areas of psychology and in other behavioral and social disciplines as well. Those of us who are concerned with women's studies no longer must meet informally in homes or unused classrooms to plan our strategy for advocating the cause, seeing women within the whole of academia. We now schedule the Dean's conference room for meetings, and the Dean often attends.

In the years since Elizabeth Santos first talked me into teaching Psychology of Women, two lessons have stayed as fresh as when I learned them. One is the value of a commitment, shared with other scholars, to see things not as they are handed down by others but in the light of facts and women's understandings. As a scholar and a feminist, I lay out the facts as I see them. For the many who have insisted that traditional psychology did not ignore women, that there was—and is—no problem, there is simply too much information for us to accept the status quo. The second lesson is that teachers should always listen to students, even if at first what they are saying doesn't seem to make good sense. Because, in 1970, I didn't see Ms. Santos' point immediately, I can better understand those who in the late 1990s do not always see the problems women face in understanding their lives.

## The Field and the Book

The scope of Psychology of Women is now defined as the entire life span, from prenatal development through childhood, adolescence, adulthood, and old age. It covers women's development and experiences: physical experiences, early learning about gender, exploring sexuality, being employed, dealing with sexism and violence, enjoying life as a senior citizen, and facing the challenges of life's different phases. I also add explicit discussions of religion and of anger. These topics, often neglected by psychologists, give an additional chance for students to relate the facts in the text to their own lives and experiences.

Most people involved with Psychology of Women are social psychologists, who are concerned with environmental variables and social action, while I am a personality psychologist. Although social psychology and personality psychology are intertwined, so that I share concern for social contextual factors and social activism, I have incorporated into this book some perspectives of personality psychology. For example, I include material on ego development (Loevinger) as applied to gender identity, discussions of power motivation and intimacy motivation, and a person-oriented treatment of achievement motivation. The topics of religion and anger I also see as highly influenced by personality variables as well as by social ones. Attention to personality does not exclude the social influence and situational variation emphasized by social psychologists; in fact, personality psychologists are very sensitive to the contexts in which personality is shaped and manifested and do not assume rigid personality traits impervious to situational factors. Personality psychology is also relatively more open about biological contributors to human behavior, while at the same time remaining very clear about the interaction of biological contributors and social context. Typically, the data about social influences are clearer and/or stronger than the data about biological influences, though it must not be forgotten that the human being is a bio-psycho-social-spiritual being.

The challenge for both author and student is a major one. The human being is complicated, and many professional disciplines are relevant to our understanding. This text is called a general survey. At times students may be frustrated that I have not said more about a topic; however, in most cases, I have provided enough recent references as well as "oldies but goodies" to enable the interested student to develop a sound research foothold in areas of special concern.

## Features and Study Aids

A number of features and study aids are provided to help students master the content. Near the beginning of each chapter is a list of questions for personal thought. These are meant to stimulate a sense of personal relatedness to the material discussed in the chapter. At the end of each chapter are "Some Final Comments"—my more personalized summaries, which call attention to some big themes in the chapter. These are followed by more straightforward summaries, in which are listed the Key Terms in the text along with Key Points. The Key Terms and Key Points are intended as prompts— to memory, to recall, to understanding. They are not a substitute for reading the chapter and thinking about it. The Integrative Questions at the close of each chapter are intended to stimulate readers to think about what they have read, whether as students of psychology or as laypersons.

Many of the study aids are designed to maximize personal involvement with the material. Students who have become involved are likely to find something that captures their attention and encourages processing the text material in an individual way. There is no better way to understand academic material than to relate to it in ways that are personally meaningful, whether from individual experience or sheer intellectual curiosity.

Two kinds of boxes are included to highlight special material. "A Closer Look" boxes add depth to the text with such material as quotes and excerpts from primary sources, descriptions of personal experiences, profiles of prominent individuals, and sample items from assessment instruments and inventories. "Focus on Research" boxes, written by Jill Borchert of Midway College and Nancy Cobb of California State University, Los Angeles, bring selected research and methodology issues to the fore in each chapter. Each of these boxes highlights a key research study related to the chapter topic and examines it both for its research findings and for its exemplification of a particular research method.

## Acknowledgments

Writing a book is always much harder than one anticipates. Fortunately, I have had a great deal of support.

Students have been enormously helpful—even those who have only said, "Right on!" when they heard of my efforts. To those who have contributed their services, I owe special thanks: Domini Castelano, Carol Hodge, Alex Lukas, Lorraine McKelzey, Deborah Shapiro, Lauri VanEgrin, and Melissa Huber Yoder. My colleagues, too, have given time, information, and support: Hiram Fitzgerald, Lauren Harris, Linda

Jackson, Jackie Lerner, Roy Matthews, Ellen A. Strommen, and Chris Sullivan. Vickie Alexander, Janet Besow, Debbie Caine, Seika Reimsig, and especially Sondra Higbee, have all given invaluable assistance with the actual preparation of the book.

I also thank Jill Borchert of Midway College and Patricia L. Donat of Mississippi University for Women for their insightful reviews of the manuscript. And, finally, I thank the following people at Mayfield Publishing Company: my editor, Frank Graham; Judith Brown, Kate Engelberg, Marty Granahan, Ken King (who first encouraged me to do this book), and April Wells-Hayes.

An Eastern saying goes, "Life is not a puzzle to be solved, but a mystery to be experienced." I have been fortunate to have people to live the mystery with me while providing some solutions to many puzzles. I hope we have given some answers to the puzzles, but, more important, challenged the reader to experience the mystery.

## *Chapter 1*

# *The Psychology of Women*

*T*he main focus in a course or text on psychology of women obviously is women and understanding women—both for personal and practical purposes and for intellectual and academic purposes. Ultimately, understanding the experiences of women or of any group of people requires understanding the cultural context in which they live. There-fore, the psychology of women involves the study of women in school, at home, in the workplace, and in society at large. It includes women's biology and their physical and psychological development, but it also includes many other topics that affect women's lives: not only childbearing and equality in the workplace but also motivation to suc-ceed, sexuality, and power. Therefore, in this book we will consider how women think, what motivates them to succeed (or hampers them from succeeding), how they see personal relationships, and how they react to societal problems such as sexism, ageism, violence, and depression. These topics are relevant to men, but in this book we will look at them from the special focus of women's perspectives. It is necessary to shift perspectives toward women because a male perspective—specifically a white male perspective—has dominated psychological considerations until recently.

For some readers, the question Why study women? is the same as Why study yourself? Many women feel that their experiences and values are missing from the psychology courses they take, and they would like to know more about themselves. Some also simply want the chance to be heard. Women have been neglected in psy-chology and their voices unheard. Both women and men notice that, and both want to understand women better. They want to be informed about specific people they care about and about the approximately half of the population who generally are neglected in other courses. Students often comment that they think they will become better professionals if they understand women. Some of these students are planning to be psychologists, of course, but some are going to be personnel directors, lawyers, health care professionals, teachers, architects, engineers, and other professionals—all of whom will benefit from a deeper knowledge of women's experiences.

Before continuing, consider these questions for personal thought:

◆ Why are you taking a Psychology of Women course, or for what other reasons are you reading this book? What hopes and fears do you have about learning about the psychology of women? What have other people said to you about the topic? How did you feel about that?

◆ How do you think women have been portrayed throughout history? How many important women can you name in the history of the United States? In the history of psychology? How comfortable are you with your current knowledge about important women?

◆ What image comes to mind when you hear that a woman is a feminist? What image comes to mind when you hear that a man is a feminist?

◆ How have feminism and feminists contributed to your life?

◆ How are women of color the same as white women? How are they different?

◆ Does an ideological belief system such as feminism have a place in the science of psychology?

## *Historical Context*

Although women's lives are inextricably intertwined with those of other members of society, in a sense women's history is unwritten. Most written histories have been concerned with public events, and in most Western societies, the actors in those events have been men. When written histories have included women, it has often been to claim inferiority of their thoughts, feelings, and bodies. Thus, "Women's history is indispensable and essential to the emancipation of women" (Lerner, 1986, p. 3). Women are in the process of reclaiming their history and their bond with each other.

Women have long been portrayed negatively by male intellectual leaders of Western civilization (e.g., see Bohan, 1990; Hunter College Women's Studies Collective, 1983). Women have been seen as imperfect men or as reproducers without sufficient intellect to do more than reproduce and serve. Aristotle (384–322 B.C.) portrayed women as deformed (Aristotle, trans. 1953). An early Greek anatomist, Herophilus of Alexandria, assumed that women were unperfected men and managed to "see" in his dissections of human bodies that women had testes with seminal ducts connected to the bladder, just as men did (Laqueur, 1990). What he in fact saw we now know to be ovaries and Fallopian tubes, which do not connect to the bladder.

Saint Augustine and Martin Luther both defined women in terms of their bodily nature. Augustine allowed that women could be respected and admired and could be friends of men to the extent that they denied their bodies, but he warned that women were to be avoided and abhorred in their bodily nature (Ruether, 1983). Martin Luther believed that, although women often died in childbirth, they were created to do so. Jean Jacques Rousseau (1762/1966) thought that nature intended women to obey and please men. Friedrich Nietzsche (1886/1966) saw women as possessions predestined for service. Charles Darwin (1881/1971) wrote that men's intellectual powers enabled them to attain higher eminence than women in whatever they took up, and another 19th century scientist, Allen Grant, noted that "All that is distinctly human is man; all that is truly woman is merely reproductive" (Grant, 1889, p. 263, cited in Bohan, 1990, p. 213).

Some men have countered the trend. Plato (c. 427–347 B.C.), Aristotle's teacher, considered women less competent than men, but he recognized variation, so that some women were more competent than some men and more suitable than men as leaders (Plato, trans. 1955). Cotton Mather, an early American minister, wrote in 1692 that women were the more religious sex because they were more likely to turn to God for comfort. True, women were more vulnerable to fears of death because of their child-bearing abilities, but in emphasizing their religiosity, Mather and others like him turned the "curse of Eve" into a blessing (Cott, 1977). John Stuart Mill (1869/1970), husband of feminist Harriet Taylor, wrote that women should have equal rights, be able to own property and vote, be educated, and choose professions. He noted that there was no way of knowing what women were like until they were asked and allowed to speak.

Psychology has long been identified with philosophy and in many ways has perpetuated most philosophers' negative views of women. Psychologists through the years often have claimed to try to understand women but have not really listened to women. In his 1968 book, *Developing Women's Potential*, Edwin Lewis comments that women cannot be objective about women, but he can be objective because he is a man. His logic is that he is a psychologist first and a man second, whereas women writers are emotional and biased because they are women first. In an important article published that same year, "Psychology Constructs the Female," Naomi Weisstein writes that psychology has nothing to say about what women are really like, what they need, and what they want, essentially because psychology does not know (Weisstein, 1968). Researchers have tested theoretical models based on men by using men as research participants. For example, when women did not give results consistent with a model of motivation for achievement, they were no longer studied, as explained in a footnote in a lengthy book about achievement (chapter 7). Women have continually spoken out, both in society generally and in psychology specifically, and have acted on their strengths even when few heard their voices.

In spite of the continual stream of negative views of women in Western civilization, there have always been some groups that favored equality and discouraged dominance (Mead, 1935; Sanday, 1981). In some groups of the original inhabitants of North America, women had value, status, and power (Almquist, 1989; LaFromboise, Heyle, & Ozer, 1990; Lips, 1993; Norton, 1980; Woloch, 1984). The Iroquois declared that women were the progenitors of the nation and that women would own the land (Sanday, 1981). The women of the Seneca controlled all tribal land, had the final say over distribution of surplus food, and had strong influence over tribal decisions about warfare and peace (Jensen, 1990). The Hopi and Navajo also had strong traditions of women's power (O'Kelly & Carney, 1986). Part of the colonization efforts by the Europeans who came to this country was to pressure the Native Americans to adopt the European values of women's subordination (Almquist, 1989; Jensen, 1990).

In spite of the Western deprecation of women, we have been gifted with many strong women as inspirational models who contributed to some change, however small, in thinking about women. This is not the place for a review of women's accomplishments throughout history, but it is appropriate to call attention to some strong women and major events they have worked for in the United States (Table 1.1). For example, Sojourner Truth (1797?–1883), an African American evangelist, abolitionist, feminist, and former slave, appeared at a women's rights convention in Akron, Ohio, in 1851. Men were defining women as delicate creatures leading sheltered lives. Sojourner electrified the audience as she exposed her muscled arm and proclaimed the widely quoted words, "Ar'nt I a woman!" (See A Closer Look 1.1, p. 8) Elizabeth Blackwell (1821–1910) persisted in her desire to become a physician and became the first woman in the United States to graduate from a medical school in 1849. And she was first in her class! Antoinette Browne became the first ordained minister of a mainline denomination in 1853. (Women's achievements in religion are listed in chapter 17.) Women in the profession of psychology also have faced discrimination and have worked for women's causes, our next topic.

## Women in the History of Psychology

Women faced many barriers in entering scientific fields at the beginning of the 20th century (Bohan, 1990). Psychologists urged that women not be allowed into higher education because of the mediocrity of their intellectual potential (G. S. Hall, 1906; E. L. Thorndike, 1906). Nonetheless, women were reasonably prominent in the early psychological establishment and are becoming so again (Hogan & Sexton, 1991; Lott, 1991). There were no women among the 18 men attending the first annual meeting of the **American Psychological Association (APA)** in 1892. The following year, however, Mary Whiton Calkins and Christine Ladd-Franklin were among the 14 newly elected members, and Mary Floy Washburn was elected the following year (Hogan & Sexton, 1991). In 1903, all three women were cited as among the most famous psychologists in America. In 1905, Calkins became the first woman president of the APA, the 14th president. By 1917, women were 13% of the APA membership, a greater percentage than in other scientific organizations (Lott, 1991). Considering the few women with advanced degrees and the small size of the APA, women got off to a decent beginning in the young professional organization. In 1921, Washburn became the second woman to be president of the APA, the 30th president.

No woman was president for the next 51 years (Hogan & Sexton, 1991). Anne Anastasi was president in 1972, followed the next year by Leona Tyler. Since then, three other women have served in that role: Florence Denmark (1980), Janet Taylor Spence (1984), and Bonnie R. Strickland (1987). While some women have achieved prominence, their numbers are few considering the fact that more women than men have received doctorate degrees in psychology since 1984 (Howard et al., 1986). In the early 1990s, nearly half (46%) of the members of APA boards and committees were women, but only two women were on the 12-member Board of Directors (Hogan & Sexton, 1991). Nonetheless, contemporary women have pursued women's issues that were recognized by their predecessors.

**Table 1.1**  Notable Events in the History of American Women

| Year | Event |
| --- | --- |
| 1777 | Abigail Adams wrote to her husband, John Adams, "Do not put such unlimited power into the hands of the husbands. Remember all men would be tyrants if they could." |
| 1804 | Sacajawea, a young Indian woman, accompanied the Lewis and Clark expedition and is credited with helping to make the exploration a success. |
| 1821 | Emma Willard founded the first secondary school for women at Troy, New York. |
| 1833 | Prudence Crandall opened a school for African American girls in her home in Connecticut, but the resultant violence forced her to close it. |
| 1837 | The first national gathering of women organized for action without the assistance of men, the Anti-Slavery Convention of American Women, met. |
| 1848 | The first Women's Rights Convention was held in Seneca Falls, New York, led by Lucretia Mott and Elizabeth Cady Stanton. |
| 1849 | Elizabeth Blackwell received her medical degree at Geneva, New York—the first woman doctor in the United States. |
| 1851 | Sojourner Truth spoke in Akron, Ohio. |
| 1865 | Vassar College opened with the first college-level curriculum for women. |
| 1866 | Elizabeth Cady Stanton was the first woman candidate for Congress, although women could not vote. |
| 1868 | The first proposal for women's suffrage was introduced. Another proposal, introduced in 1878, came to be known as the Anthony Amendment. |
| 1890 | Elizabeth Cady Stanton was elected the first president of the unified suffrage organization, the National American Woman Suffrage Association. |
| 1893 | Hannah Greenbaum Solomon invited Jewish women to attend a conference, resulting in the National Council of Jewish Women. |
| 1896 | The National Association for Colored Women was established; Mary Church Terrell was the first president. |
| 1904 | Mary McLeod Bethune founded Bethune-Cookman College in Daytona Beach, Florida. |
| 1908 | The poem, "The New Colossus," written by Emma Lazarus (who died in 1887), was inscribed on a tablet at the Statue of Liberty, "Give me your tired, your poor . . ." |
| 1909 | The first significant strike of working women was conducted by shirtwaist makers in New York to protest low wages and long working hours. |
| 1914 | The Alaska Native Sisterhood was formed. |
| 1917 | Jeannette Rankin, a Republican from Montana, was the first woman elected to serve in Congress. |
| 1920 | The 19th Amendment was ratified, August 26, giving women the legal right to vote. |
| 1923 | The Equal Rights Amendment was introduced in Congress. |
| 1925 | Discrimination against women intensified. Medical schools placed a quota of 5% on women to be admitted. Columbia and Harvard law schools refused to consider women. |
| 1933 | Frances Perkins became the first woman to hold a cabinet post, the Department of Labor. |
| 1935 | The National Council of Negro Women was founded, with Mary McLeod Bethune as president. |
| 1955 | Rosa Parks was arrested for refusing to give up her bus seat to a white man, touching off the Montgomery, Alabama, bus boycott. |
| 1963 | The Equal Pay Act was passed. |
| 1963 | *The Feminine Mystique*, by Betty Friedan, was published. |
| 1968 | Women liberationists picketed the Miss America beauty pageant in Atlantic City. They did *not* burn bras. |
| 1969 | Shirley Chisholm, Democrat of New York City, was the first African American woman elected to Congress. |

*(continued)*

**Table 1.1**   Notable Events in the History of American Women    *(continued)*

| Year | Event |
| --- | --- |
| 1970 | Women's Equity Action League officer, Dr. Bernice Sandler, filed the first formal charges of sex discrimination. Women professors had filed charges against more than 300 colleges by the end of 1971. |
| 1970 | The Women's Affairs Division of the League of United Latin American Citizens was organized, with Julia Zozoya and Ada Pena leading the way. |
| 1970 | Native American women from 43 tribes met and organized the North American Indian Women's Association. |
| 1970 | Patsy Mink, Democrat of Hawaii, was the first Asian woman elected to Congress. Democrat Bella Abzug of New York was the first woman elected to Congress on a women's rights platform. |
| 1971 | A preview issue of *Ms.* magazine, with Gloria Steinem as editor, was published. |
| 1972 | The Equal Rights Amendment (ERA) was overwhelmingly approved by Congress and submitted to the states for ratification. |
| 1972 | Title 9 of the education amendments of 1972 was passed, prohibiting discrimination on the basis of sex. |
| 1972 | The National Conference of Puerto Rican Women was organized, with Carmen Maymi and Paquito Vivo in leading roles. |
| 1973 | The U.S. Supreme Court ruled in *Roe v. Wade* that during the first trimester of pregnancy, the decision to have an abortion is left solely to a woman and her physician. |
| 1973 | The National Black Feminists Organization was formed, led in part by Eleanor Holmes Norton. |
| 1973 | Billie Jean King beat Bobby Riggs in straight sets in the "Battle of the Sexes" tennis match. |
| 1974 | The Mexican American Women's Association was founded. |
| 1974 | Ella Grasso was elected Governor of Connecticut—the first woman governor elected in her own right. |
| 1977 | The National Women's Conference met in Houston, Texas. |
| 1978 | Col. Margaret A. Brewer was nominated as the first female general of the Marine Corps. Also, sea duty was opened to Navy women. |
| 1979 | Diana Nyad made a 60-mile swim from the Bahamas to Florida. |
| 1980 | The first women graduated from military service academies. |
| 1981 | The first woman Supreme Court justice, Sandra Day O'Connor, was appointed. |

The pioneer women psychologists addressed the scholarly biases in faulty claims about women; women late in the century are still doing the same. Dominant claims have been that women are inferior to men and, especially, are victims of their reproductive system (Lott, 1991; Sherif, 1979). In 1885 Mary Calkins and her student, Cordelia Nevers, provided data that refuted the claims (by Sir Francis Galton and Joseph Jastrow) that women were inferior to men in all capacities (Furumoto, 1980). Later, Calkins, sometimes called the foremother of a feminist social psychology, asserted that differences in environmental experiences began in infancy and continued, so that it was fruitless to claim that biology was responsible for differences between women and men (Lott, 1991). Women have continually tried to get people to recognize this.

Helen Thompson Wooley's 1903 dissertation at the University of Chicago was a sophisticated critique of the methodology used in assessing differences between

**Table 1.1**     *(continued)*

| Year | Event |
|------|-------|
| 1983 | The first woman in the United States to travel in space was Sally Ride. |
| 1983 | The House of Representatives defeated a plan to revive the ERA. |
| 1984 | Representative Geraldine A. Ferraro became the first female nominee of a major political party for national office. |
| 1989 | The Supreme Court, in *Webster v. Reproductive Health Services*, gutted many of the abortion rights given women by *Roe v. Wade*. |
| 1989 | The Supreme Court ruled that Price Waterhouse had discriminated against Ann B. Hopkins in denying her partnership in the firm because she was not sufficiently feminine. |
| 1989 | Rosabeth Moss Kanter took over the top editorial job at the *Harvard Business Review*, the first woman in the post. |
| 1989 | Eve Atkinson was named Athletic Director of Lafayette College, becoming the first woman to head a combined men's and women's athletic program at an NCAA Division 1 institution with a 1-AA football program. Merrily Dean Baker was named the first athletic director of a Big Ten University, Michigan State University, in 1992. |
| 1990 | Elizabeth M. Watson became the first woman to head the police force of one of the country's 20 largest cities, Houston, Texas. |
| 1990 | Martha S. Pope became the first woman to be named Sergeant-at-Arms of the U.S. Senate. |
| 1991 | Gertrude Belle Elion was the first woman inducted into the National Inventors Hall of Fame; she won a Nobel Prize in 1988 for pioneering DNA research. |
| 1991 | One of the nation's first female neurosurgeons, Dr. Frances Conley, announced her resignation as a tenured professor at Stanford Medical School in protest of sexual harassment; she stated that she felt guilty for not protesting earlier. |
| 1993 | Janet Reno became the first woman Attorney General of the United States. |
| 1995 | Eileen Collins was the first woman to pilot a U.S. spaceship; she had been the second woman to be an Air Force test pilot. |
| 1997 | Madeleine Albright was appointed the first woman U.S. Secretary of State. |

From *The Spirit of Houston: The First National Women's Conference*. An official report of the President of the Congress and the people of the United States, March, 1978. Washington, DC: National Commission on the Observance of International Women's Year, U.S. Department of State, 1978. And Kim Blankenship in S. Ruth, 1998, *Issues in feminism*. Mountain View, CA: Mayfield.

women and men and showed the importance of environmental influences (Lott, 1991; Sherif, 1979). Mary Putman Jacobi's Harvard dissertation in 1876 refuted the notion that women needed special mental and physical rest during menstruation (Sherif, 1979). Leta Hollingworth concluded in her 1914 dissertation that the menstrual cycle did not prevent women from achieving intellectual eminence (Lott, 1991; Sherif, 1979). She had women report their feelings daily instead of only reporting about their menstrual cycles generally; her methodological innovation was neglected until the 1970s (chapter 6).

In the 1920s and 1930s, psychoanalysts Karen Horney and Clara Thompson were writing critically of bias in psychoanalytic theory, presaging the critiques that reappeared in the 1960s and 1970s. Joining them in emphasizing the social factors that shape the development of women and men were Alfred Adler and Erich Fromm, both of whom rejected biologically based views of women. Karen Horney later founded her

## A Closer Look

### 1.1    Sojourner Truth: Early Feminist

The woman who came to be known as Sojourner Truth was born into slavery in New York about 1797 and freed by the Abolition Law of New York State, 1827. She felt called to spread the word of God, and she felt in need of a new name. The name, which she considered given by God, was Sojourner Truth. In spite of her lack of education and in spite of continued discrimination against her as a black, she proved herself strong in debates about abolitionism and women's rights. At age 70, she attended the Women's Rights Convention in New York in 1867 and warned the women to get going because she did not intend to die until she voted. She did die before she voted, but she did not die before she left a lasting impact on the American feminist, abolitionist, and religious landscapes.

In 1851 Sojourner Truth attended the Women's Convention in Akron, Ohio, and became annoyed that men were trying to undermine the feminist struggle by claiming women's inferiority in reasoning, strength, and morality (being descendants of Eve). Her intense impromptu speech, called "Ain't I a Woman," still inspires many. Her comments sometimes are translated into standard English rather than being left as they originally were. With some conflict, I have chosen to present her words as originally recorded, in part because the original language adds to the miracle of her success—her words and her personality swayed the ruling whites in the

North who did not speak her language but responded to her message. The words were recorded by Frances Gage, and the commentary is hers.

"Nobody eber help me into carriages, or ober mud puddles, or gives me any best

place and ar'nt I a woman? Look at me! Look at my arm! I have plowed, and planted, and gathered into barns, and no man could head me—and ar'nt I a woman? I could work as much and eat as much as a man (when I could get it) and bear de lash as well—and ar'nt I a woman? I have borne thirteen chlern and seen 'em mos' all sold off into slavery, and when I cried out with a mother's grief, none but Jesus heard—and ar'nt I a woman? Den dey talks 'bout dis thing in de head—what dis dey call it? ('Intellect,' whispered some one near.) Dat's it honey. What's dat got to do with women's rights or niggers' rights? If my cup won't hold but a pint and yourn holds a quart, wouldn't ye be mean not to let me have my little half-measure full?" And she pointed her significant finger and sent a keen glance at the minister who had made the argument. The cheering was long and loud.

"Den dat little man in black dar [Sojourner was about 6 feet tall], he say women can't have much rights as man, 'cause Christ wa'nt a woman. Whar did your Christ come from? From God and a woman. Man had nothing to do with him!"

"If de fust woman God ever made was strong enough to turn the world upside down, all 'lone,' den together

(and she glanced her eye over us), ought to be able to turn it back and get it right side up again, and now dey is asking to do it, de men better let em." There was much cheering, and Sojourner continued, "Bleeged to ye for hearing on me, and now ole Sojourner hasn't got nothing more to say."

Amid roars of applause, she turned to her corner, leaving more than one of us with streaming eyes and hearts beating with gratitude. She had taken us up to her strong arms and carried us safely over the slough of difficulty, turning the whole tide in our favor. I have never in my life seen anything like the magical influence that subdued the mobbish spirit of the day and turned the jibes and sneers of an excited crowd into notes of respect and admiration.

---

NOTE: Some translations use the word *ain't*, but *ar'nt* was used by Gage.

The extract is from *History of Woman Suffrage* (2nd ed., Vol. 1), edited by E. Cady Stanton, S. B. Anthony, and M. J. Gage, 1889, Rochester, NY: Charles Mann, as reprinted in *Issues in feminism* (2nd ed.), by S. Ruth, 1998, Mountain View, CA: Mayfield.

Also in W. Martin, 1972, *The American sisterhood, Writings of the feminist movement from colonial times to the present*. New York: Harper & Row.

own analytic institute because her ideas were too deviant for her to be accepted at the established psychoanalytic institutes, and Fromm joined her (A Closer Look 1.2).

## Recent Activism: The 1970s

There was no organized effort in psychology on behalf of women until the 1940s. Then, upset that women in psychology were being neglected by the men in their preparations for contributing to World War II efforts, women in the APA formed the National Council of Women Psychologists in 1942, renamed the International Council of Women Psychologists in 1946 (Hogan & Sexton, 1991). They dropped *women* from the name in 1959 in hopes that it would help them gain affiliation with the APA. The strategy did not work. Women continued their efforts to change their second-class status, and those efforts came to some fruition in the 1970s.

Efforts for women had a rebirth in 1969 when, once again, women in the APA tired of their treatment by the establishment and formed the Association for Women in Psychology (AWP—originally called Association of Women Psychologists) (Mednick & Urbanski, 1991; Tiefer, 1991). This time, the women's group had long-lasting influence, and it continues today, independent of the APA, though cooperative with it. The group exposed discrimination against women and called for the APA to address women's issues. In response, the APA appointed a task force on the status of women in psychology (chaired by Helen Astin). The study by the task force documented the disadvantaged status of women psychologists and psychologists' lack of knowledge about women. The Committee on Women in Psychology (Martha Mednick, chair) developed guidelines for nonsexist language and research and recommended the formation of what became Division 35, Psychology of Women, in 1973.

The division's journal, *Psychology of Women Quarterly*, was first published in fall 1976. The journal *Sex Roles* had begun publication the previous year, as had *Signs: Journal of Women in Culture and Society*. With division status and supporting journals, psychology of women was recognized as a legitimate area of psychology. Division 35 currently is the 12th largest division of the APA, with women constituting 92% to 96% of the membership, making it the division with the most women as members (Hogan & Sexton, 1991). The divisions next most populated by women are Developmental Psychology (51%) and Psychoanalysis (50%).

In 1973, only 32 psychology departments had courses in psychology of women; I am pleased that my department was among those few. The number had increased dramatically by the mid-1980s, to 209 departments, though still being only 23% of 896 departments surveyed (Walsh, 1985). Now, half of psychology departments have undergraduate courses, and about a third have graduate courses in psychology of women (Women's Programs Office, 1991). During three years in the mid-1970s (1974–1976), nine new general books on psychology of women appeared. The prestigious *Annual Review of Psychology* included a chapter on psychology of women for the first time (Mednick & Weissman, 1975).

Important critiques of psychological approaches to women's issues also were published and proved important in stimulating improved research. Anne Constantinople (1973) criticized standard ways of thinking about and measuring masculinity and

## A Closer Look

### 1.2 Karen Horney: Challenger of Freudian Orthodoxy

Karen Danielson was born in a small town near Hamburg, Germany, in 1885. Her father was a sea captain and a constant critic. He was a stern man convinced of the superiority of men. Karen's mother, 18 years younger than the captain, was his second wife. Karen was never close to her father but was close to her mother, who supported her against her father. Karen was convinced that she was not pretty (though that is doubted), so she decided that if she could not be pretty, she would be smart. And she did excel at her studies. After an experience with a kindly physician, she decided to become a physician herself. At the time, 1899, no universities in Germany admitted women, and there was not a Gymnasium course for girls in Hamburg to give her the training necessary for university admission. This changed 2 years later, and Karen entered the Gymnasium, against her father's objections and with her mother's support. In 1906 she became one of the first women in Germany to study medicine. She met student Oskar Horney and later married him, but the marriage was tumultuous. They separated in 1924 and later divorced.

After the separation, Karen Horney became intensely involved with her profession and with caring for three daughters (born within a five-year period). Her papers began to show important differences with Freudian theory. She thought that culture was responsible for differences between women and men, not anatomy as Freud and his orthodox fol-

lowers maintained. Freud's negative reaction only made her more outspoken. Horney came to the United States in 1932.

Horney increasingly was dissatisfied with Freud's theory and had no hesitancy about saying so. She became a leader of the Freudian opposition because she advocated abandoning the instinct theory and emphasizing ego and social influences on women's and men's development. In 1941 the established leaders of the New York Psychoanalytic Institute could take no more challenge and disqualified her. This was not the end for the determined Horney. She helped found the rival Association for the Advancement of Psychoanalysis, later renamed the Karen Horney Psychoanalytic Institute. The Karen Horney Clinic was founded in 1952. Both organizations continue.

A reviewer of psychoanalytic history considered Karen Horney an astute clinician, commenting that readers could see themselves or someone they knew on every page of her writings (Munroe, 1955). Her works include *Neurotic Personality of Our Times* (1937), *Self-Analysis* (1942), *Our Inner Conflicts* (1945), and *Neurosis and Human Growth* (1950). Horney died in 1952. She still is a model to women who see things differently from the way the establishment does.

SOURCE: Quinn, S. (1987). *A mind of her own: The life of Karen Horney.* New York: Summit Books.

femininity, pointing out that they are not opposites stemming from biology (chapter 3). Mary Brown Parlee (1973) criticized the biases in menstrual research, showing that the researchers' procedures focused on and encouraged reports of only negative experiences (chapter 6). Ellen Lenney (1977) critiqued the conclusion that women are less self-confident than men (chapter 7). Rowenna Helson (1972) challenged the biased views that career women are maladjusted (chapter 13). Nancy Chodorow (1978) gave impetus to feminist approaches to psychoanalysis (chapters 9, 14, 16). This small sampling of activities should suffice to point to the enthusiasm and effectiveness of women in the 1970s. Growth continues.

The growth of the study of women from women's points of view has occurred in many disciplines. Psychology does not exist apart from society outside of academia nor apart from other academic fields. Psychology of Women is part of Women's Studies, which, like psychology of women, started in the early 1970s. Today, over 600 schools have women's studies programs (Stake, Roades, Rose, Ellis, & West, 1994). The scholarship of women's studies tends to be more interdisciplinary and aware of ethnic and class differences than other programs (Hunter College Women's Studies Collective, 1983; Ruth, 1998). Psychology of women specifically aims for that scope, but progress has been slow (Lott, 1991; Mednick, 1991).

## Terminology: Sex and Gender

Before continuing, we need to pause and clarify some important terms. There has been much discussion about the terms **sex** and **gender,** with varying rules suggested about their use. One common convention is to use *sex* to refer to innate or biologically based attributes, so that *sex differences* would mean differences between males and females that are inherent. In contrast, *gender* refers to the nonbiological aspects of being a female or male, such as the cultural expectations for femininity and masculinity. A statement of *gender differences* refers to differences that result from experience (e.g., see Unger, 1979; Unger & Crawford, 1996).

For example, having a clitoris or penis is a sex difference, but wearing pink or blue booties is a gender difference. The distinction often is blurred because sex and gender obviously are intertwined. Adults respond to the sex of an infant and choose pink or blue booties because of their understandings of gender—what sex means in a social context. Then other adults assume sex on the basis of the "gender color" and interact with the infant on the basis of gender. Judgments based on female or male are matters of sex. Judgments based on *assumptions* about differences between male and female are matters of gender (Unger & Crawford, 1996). The distinction helps bring into focus the fact that many differences between women and men do not spring automatically from biological differences (Lips, 1997).

The distinction often is blurry also because we do not always know the reasons for observed differences or because biology and learning are highly intertwined. Even for experiences that clearly are biological—menstruation, giving birth—the social meaning of the experiences often goes beyond the implications necessitated by biology. Biological "facts" occur in a social context and have their implications for human experience within a social context. Unfortunately, *sex* calls attention to an actual or claimed biological basis, so that social elaboration may be neglected. Indeed, the biological "facts" are shaped by the social context; seeing the Fallopian tubes as connected to the bladder is a case in point. Because women have so long been seen as victims of their bodies, to the neglect of social conditions, some writers prefer to avoid *sex*. *Gender* calls attention to the social elaboration, so that biological bases may be neglected. I will use *gender* as the more inclusive term. The distinction is not meant to disallow biological bases to gender but to emphasize that any biological factor must be seen in its cultural context, and the cultural context often influences biology (chapters 4, 8).

Some standard terms still are stated in terms of *sex*. The journal *Sex Roles* really deals with gender roles. And, paradoxically, a dominant measure of adoption of gender roles is called a measure of sex roles (Bem Sex Role Inventory, chapter 3). Differences in social behaviors (chapter 9) have long been called sex differences, though they seem to be gender differences. Discrimination on the basis of sex is learned, so it should be *genderism*. However, *sexism* and *sex bias* are standard terms still used by some authorities who otherwise prefer *gender* (e.g., Hyde, 1991). The term *reverse sexism* also is used when, for example, a man is discriminated against for a job in favor of a woman. The term should be *sexism*. To add *reverse* is to suggest that sex discrimination against women is normal.

While talking about terminology, I also offer the caution that there is a difference between *feminine* and *feminist*. *Feminine* refers to characteristics assumed to be associated with women, while *feminists* are particular people who may or may not be women. When I am asked for a feminine perspective, I feel that I am being asked to say something warm and fuzzy at best, or demure and coy at worst. When I am asked for a feminist comment, I feel I am being asked for a strong, competent response at best, or a strident, nasty one at worst. Because of the intricate interplay of feminism with the psychology of women, as well as with other disciplines of women's studies, feminism deserves special attention.

## Feminism and the Psychology of Women

Some students taking psychology of women courses state a fear that the course will be feminist, while others are afraid it will not be. Estimates of how many college students are feminists vary from 16% to a third (DeFilippo & Wexler, 1991; Geyer, 1989; Lott, 1994; Renzetti, 1987). What is clear is that although many men are stronger feminists than many women are, women are much more likely to consider themselves feminists than men are and generally more likely to be supportive of feminism (Jackson, Fleury, & Lewandowski, 1996). However, among college students, both women and men are generally more positive toward feminism than opposed to it. When asked to give their own definitions of feminism, most (71%) gave favorable definitions (e.g., "working toward better rights"); few (6%) were negative (e.g., lashing out, opposing chivalry). Others (23%) were mixed. Similarly, students have described feminists, both women and men, in positive terms such as logical, knowledgeable, intelligent, caring, independent, and open-minded (Berryman-Fink & Verderber, 1985; Buhl, 1989). Although college students may not identify as feminist, they are supportive of the women's movement (Renzetti, 1987).

Why do college students not consider themselves feminists? Two general reasons have been suggested. First, some students still tend to see feminists as angry "bra burners," man-haters, or lesbians. Incidentally, the image of bra burners comes from a women's meeting in Atlantic City where women did put their bras in a garbage can, but they did not burn them (National Commission, 1978). Second, initial reluctance to adopt feminism may be due to perceptions that things are all OK for women now and that women can succeed as individuals without collective efforts (Katz, 1996). It takes a while to understand the misperceptions and to see a personal relevance of feminism (Faludi, 1991; Friedan, 1991). Feminism appears to grow during the college years. This may be due, in part, to a general liberalizing of attitudes during college, but personal experiences of sex discrimination seem to serve as a special catalyst for the development of a feminist perspective (Renzetti, 1987).

## What Is Feminism?

Who are the feminists? One woman at the turn of the century noted that she had never been able to find out what feminism is, but that she was called a feminist "whenever I express sentiments that differentiate me from a doormat" (Rebecca West, 1913, cited in Kramarae & Treichler, 1985). More recent statements voice much the same sentiment; for example, what women want from feminism is "respect for women as full and equal members of the human race" (K. Pollit, 1990, p. 12). One pointed, simple definition is that feminism is a movement to end sexism and sexist oppression (hooks, 1984). Some other comments about feminism are given in A Closer Look 1.3.

A **feminist** has been defined as a person whose beliefs, values, and attitudes reflect a high regard for women as human beings (Hunter College Women's Studies Collective, 1983). It is important that women are valued not for attributes imposed on them by others, but for those attributes that exist in women and are chosen by women. Gloria Steinem (1994) saw feminism as a belief in the full social, political, and economic equality for women. I like to add "and is willing to work for equality." Notice that a feminist is not necessarily a woman, nor are women necessarily feminists. You may know some men who are stronger feminists than some women. Notice also that the definitions say nothing about attitudes toward men. Feminism is not an anti-man movement, it is a pro-woman movement. It can also be seen as a pro-men movement because men as well as women are locked by stereotype into a "psychological straitjacket for both sexes" (Komarovsky, 1953/1993, p. 348). Gloria Steinem (1995) noted that men could add four years to their lives by reducing the stress associated with traditional male roles.

The understanding of what feminism is can be extended by knowing what feminists have done and are doing. Feminism and the woman's movement have a long history. Considering the woman's movement as women moving toward greater strength and freedom in awareness and in sociopolitical position, it has been an ongo-

*A Closer Look*

## 1.3 On Feminism . . .

Feminism may be a perspective, a world view, a political theory, a spiritual focus, or a kind of activism.
—Sheila Ruth, *Issues in Feminism*, 1998

[Feminism] begins but cannot end with the discovery by an individual of her self-consciousness as a woman. . . . Feminism means finally that we renounce our obedience to the fathers and recognize the world they have described is not the whole world.
—Adrienne Rich, *Of Woman Born*, 1976

Feminism is the political theory and practice to free all women; women of color, working-class women, poor women, physically challenged women, lesbians, old women, as well as white economically privileged heterosexual women. Anything less than this is not feminism, but merely female self-aggrandizement.
—Barbara Smith in Cherrie Moraga and Gloria Anzaldua, *This Bridge Called My Back*, 1981

[Feminism is] a method of analysis as well as a discovery of new material. It asks new questions as well as coming up with new answers. Its central concern is with the social distinction between men and women, with the fact of this distinction, with its meanings, and with its causes and consequences.
—Juliet Mitchell and Anne Oakley, *The Rights and Wrongs of Women*, 1976

[Feminism] is an entire world view or gestalt, not just a laundry list of "women's issues." Feminist theory provides a basis for understanding every area of our lives, and a feminist perspective can affect the world politically, culturally, economically, and spiritually.
—Charlotte Bunch, *Learning Our Way*, 1983

I became a feminist as an alternative to becoming a masochist.
—Sally Kempton in E. Partnow, *The New Quotable Woman*, 1993

ing process through the centuries (Ruth, 1998). The first stirrings of what is thought of as the women's movement were felt when Mary Wollstonecraft, in England, published *A Vindication of the Rights of Women* in 1792. A focal point for the beginning of women's rights activities in the United States was the first convention, July 19, 1848, at Seneca Falls, New York, planned by Elizabeth Cady Stanton and Lucretia Mott. Following 1920, when women attained the vote, women's issues submerged in public consciousness for a while. Then, in 1963, a suburban housewife with three little children described what she saw as the condition of American women. In so doing, she launched the new wave of American feminism of the 20th century. She was Betty Friedan; her book was *The Feminine Mystique*.

*Feminists of the 19th century were willing to march, picket, and demonstrate for equal rights. They laid the groundwork for many of the advances won by the women's movement of the 1970s and 1980s.*

The problem lay buried, unspoken, for many years in the minds of American women. It was a strange stirring, a sense of dissatisfaction, a yearning that women suffered in the middle of the 20th century in the United States. Each suburban wife struggled with it alone. As she made the beds, shopped for groceries, matched slipcover material, ate peanut butter sandwiches with her children, chauffeured Cub Scouts and Brownies, lay beside her husband at night, she was afraid to ask, even of herself, the silent question— "Is this all?" (Friedan, 1963/1983, p. 15)

Women have long asked, "Is this all?" and answered with activities to claim more for women. Women today owe more to the women of the previous century than most people realize. Women today also owe more to contemporary feminists than many realize (Friedan, 1991). The early feminists of the 19th century wanted the right to vote, the right to an education, the right to equal pay, the right to follow a profession of their own choosing, the right to regulate reproduction, and the right not to be used sexually. Women today have the right to vote. They also have in recent years been using educational institutions more than men have (chapter 13). But they still face discrimination in the classroom (chapter 7) and then on the job (chapter 13). Women's pay still lags behind men's (chapter 13). Reproductive decisions are not entirely under women's control, and birth control research in the United States is not advancing at a rapid pace (chapter 12). Children and women still often are used sexually (chapters 11, 16).

In working for what they wanted, the early feminists wrote articles and books, talked to women and to men, petitioned legislatures, held conferences, opened schools for women, pushed for women's access to professional training, and published newspapers (e.g., see Berg, 1978; Cott, 1977). They also stood outside brothels to note the men using them and published the names of the men in the newspaper. Today's feminists are doing much the same. Although they may not try to call attention to the men who use prostitutes, they have picketed beauty pageants and "nudie bars." New colleges for women have not been opening, but existing ones have become more popular. And contemporary feminists are working as the earlier feminists did for better health care.

## Varieties of Feminism

Feminism is a big umbrella term covering many varieties of feminists, and those varieties have been defined in many ways. Here we distinguish five kinds of feminism. Other distinctions are possible, and some people see more than one label as relevant to themselves. The variations have been well described as different lenses for viewing the experiences of women, each useful for seeing some phenomena better than others (Unger & Crawford, 1996).

**Liberal feminists** emphasize the equality of women and men and the principle that women and men, boys and girls, would behave the same if given equal environments and opportunities. **Cultural feminists,** on the other hand, value differences and stress that the attributes associated with women's culture (e.g., caring, relationships) have not been sufficiently valued and honored. Liberal feminists often are seen as minimalists and cultural feminists as maximalists (Hare-Mustin & Marecek, 1988; Lott, 1991; Mednick, 1991; Unger, 1989). Minimalists minimize gender differences, while maximalists (e.g., Chodorow, 1978; Gilligan, 1982; Miller, 1984) are seen as emphasizing sex differences and pointing to the universal (at least in Western culture) essence of being a woman. The debate about the two kinds of positions will be considered in more detail in the context of personality development (chapter 9).

**Radical feminists** have little concern with the debate. They see male domination of women as the most fundamental form of oppression and focus on understanding how men obtain and use power. Those who also are radical lesbians are especially noted for calling attention to men's domination in sexual politics. Note that not all radical feminists are lesbians, and not all lesbians are radical lesbians. Some lesbian feminists are **separatists,** a fourth version of feminism. They want women to be self-sufficient apart from men as representatives of patriarchal society, and they try to isolate themselves from men as much as they can. To the extent that men wish to separate themselves from patriarchal society, they, too, can be separatists; though, in truth, they may have a hard time finding other separatists who accept them. Some feminists are "sometimes separatists." They favor at least some separate activities, such as groups or concerts, or conferences for women only, while not otherwise separating themselves from men.

Although some feminists are called radical and some are not, in a sense any feminist is radical. Being radical means going to the root of the problem and trying to make fundamental changes to eliminate the problem (Steinem, 1984). For women to have real freedom, which all feminists want, there will have to be fundamental changes in society. Feminists differ in exactly how they define the necessary changes and in how they go about working for the changes. Virtually all of them recognize the value of diversity in the efforts. The fifth kind of feminism I will identify is a form adopted by some women of color. Understanding why this form evolved requires consideration of the role of women of color in feminism.

## Feminism and Women of Color

To succeed, the feminist movement must incorporate the diverse perspectives of all women. Minority and majority women share many problems and many joys. Some aspects of women's experiences, however, involve attributes other than being a woman. Race, class, age, and sexual orientation all contribute to diversity among women and cannot be separated from the experience of being a woman. Audre Lorde (1934–1993) described herself as a Black lesbian feminist who was comfortable with the many ingredients of her identity, but she lamented the fact that she was constantly being encouraged to take out one aspect of herself and present it as the meaningful whole. Despite the commonalities of being women, minority women and majority women are likely to have different experiences and interpret even their commonalities within different frameworks (Almquist, 1989; Collins, 1990; Comas-Diaz, 1991; McIntosh, 1988; Smith & Stewart, 1983). Within ethnic minority groups, women have played crucial roles as partners side by side with their husbands and brothers. Contact with whites has disrupted family life, so that minority women have had to struggle to protect their people against the white majority. Should these women, then, align themselves with white women?

Ethnic and racial discrimination pose enormous barriers between minority and white women and between groups of minority women (Almquist, 1989; Comas-Diaz, 1991; Lorde, 1975, 1981/1990). White feminists did come to realize that the women's movement was white and middle class and opened their arms to other women, but often without realizing their own racism and the extent to which it separated them from women of color. They are growing in their understanding of their biases (Allen & Baber, 1992). Writings of women of color and of lesbians have sensitized heterosexual white women to the possible exploitation of women by women. Sheila Ruth (1998), author of a women's studies text, noted how, over the years, she learned from her own work and that of her colleagues:

> I am becoming, for example, keenly aware of my own particularity—a white, middle-class, professional, midwesterner crusted around a working class, Jewish, loner Bronx kid. I understand better what that enables me to say and what I should leave for others to say. . . . I have given up . . . "certitude"; *I know how much I don't know* [italics added]. (p. *x*)

Many women of color are in conflict. The experience of racism makes them hesitate to link with white women, but the experience of sexism puts them in conflict with minority men (Almquist, 1989; Comas-Diaz, 1991; Terrelonge, 1989). African Americans often see the role of uniting African Americans as the primary duty of the women, superseding all other roles, including that of advocating women's own individual liberation. Many African American intellectuals and spokespeople have ignored the issue of sexism because it has been seen as racially divisive.

African American men also experience conflict and strain. Like women, they are influenced by cultural definitions of gender, but they face poverty and racism that interfere with their pursuit of solutions to gender role problems (Clatterbaugh, 1990; Franklin, 1987; Wade, 1995, 1996). African American men accept traditional aspects of the male role (such as being a provider, being ambitious) but also endorse nontraditional aspects (such as spirituality, equalitarianism, emotional sensitivity, family concerns) (Cazenave, 1984). The more nontraditional aspects that African American men see as relevant to their masculinity are thought to have helped sustain the families and communities (Hunter & Davis, 1992). Both African American women and men experience conflict between mainstream—white—definitions of gender and the desire to contribute to the support of their families and communities.

Some women of color are concerned that white women can never understand the full horror of racism or the desperation of intense poverty (Almquist, 1989; Davenport, 1991). Others object to judging white women simply on the basis of their color; they see white women as being victims of racism because they have been oppressed by white men, as have minority groups (Smith & Smith, 1983). Their hope is that women of all groups can work together. Feminist women of color have been energetic in counteracting racism and sexism and in reaffirming their multiple identities (Comas-Diaz, 1991). Some have been clear that they think a feminist consciousness would contribute to the welfare of African Americans, for example, by enabling both women and men to have a deeper understanding of the social problems they face and by eliminating sexism on the interpersonal level within the African American community (Lorde, 1988; Terrelonge, 1989). bell hooks (1984) and Lillian Comas-Diaz (1991) explain that women of color as outsiders have a special vantage point from which to critique and enrich feminist theory and research. Women of color share with white women the experience of oppression by men but, unlike white women, do not have another group of women and men (those of color) to oppress.

Alice Walker (1983), who wrote *The Color Purple* among other books, uses the term **womanist**—what I have called the fifth form of feminism—to define feminism out of African American women's experiences, allowing women to claim their roots in their culture along with their feminism (Comas-Diaz, 1991; Williams, 1987). A womanist is outrageous, courageous, responsible, serious. She loves women and men sexually or nonsexually. She loves dance, the spirit, food, herself. "Womanist is to feminist as purple is to lavender" (Walker, 1983, p. *xi*). Walker defines womanist in terms of personality traits rather than creedal statements; she often uses words in ways that cut beneath the abstractions they so often convey so as to communicate the immediate feelings of women (chapter 16). As a white woman, I feel the concept of womanist challenging me to be fully alive; the concept does not tell me about my beliefs, but about my potential aliveness, and from that aliveness creedal statements may follow.

## Feminism's Influence on the Psychology of Women

The women's movement and feminism have been closely intertwined with the development of psychology of women; psychologists are not immune to their culture, nor are engineers, poets, physicists, or dancers. Feminist ideology led to a reevaluation of psychological theory and research, a questioning of basic assumptions, and an uncovering of ways in which psychology has supported mythology about women (Worell, 1996; Worell & Etaugh, 1994). The people who worked for psychology of women were influenced and inspired by the feminist activities of the 1960s and 1970s; and it was during those times that the most dramatic growth in psychology of women as a field occurred. However, feminist scholarship has acquired autonomy as an intellectual movement and is no longer tightly tied to political feminism (Mednick, 1978).

Perhaps the most important impact of feminism on psychology has been its transforming power. Ellen Kimmel (1989) asked members of the Psychology of Women Division of APA to describe their experiences of feminism. To some extent, responses were as expected: feminism as valuing women, concern with equality of power and seeing the need for change, and gender as a social construct. More interesting were responses that described feminism as a transforming experience: It was "... a lived, conscious, changing experience" (Kimmel, 1989, p. 145). Feminism has a transforming power, "gathering the disparate parts of myself into a whole" (Kimmel, p. 145). Dictionary definitions have their value. Many students reading the first chapter of a text have volunteered, "I didn't think I was a feminist, but ... maybe I am." By the end of the course, many of these students are talking in a different way, suggestive of the transforming experience that many of their teachers have had. Recent evidence supports the observation. Students who had a women's studies course, compared to students in other courses with the same faculty, reported more activism at the end of the course and had continued to be active when measured nine months later (Stake et al., 1994; Stake & Rose, 1994).

***Research Goals***   Feminist psychologists have been critical of psychology while still being committed to it and its growth. The advent of feminism and of psychology of women in the field of psychology has brought important changes in all areas of psychology (O'Connell & Russo, 1991; Worell, 1996; Worell & Etaugh, 1994). Social psychologists Philip Shaver and Clyde Hendrick (1987) described the current wave of feminism as revitalizing academic disciplines. Feminist scholars have attempted to *deconstruct* psychology by analyzing the assumptions about women that have influenced theory, applications, and research. Destruction, however, is not the goal. The goal is to *reconstruct* or *revision* psychology's understanding of women (Bohan, 1990; Crawford & Marecek, 1989).

Much early feminist activity in psychology focused on correcting the biases in a "womanless psychology" (Crawford & Marecek, 1989). Some legitimacy has been gained for previously neglected areas of research about women (Allen & Baber, 1992; Worell, 1996). Among these are women's experiences of mothering, housework, sexual abuse, and employment. In some research areas, women had not been totally forgotten, but the research was seen as confirming stereotypes, so that there was not much need for more attention. Corrections spurred by concern for women have helped round out the field and have eased previous biases. Examples include achievement motivation (chapter 7), menstruation (chapter 6), and women with a paid job (chapter 13).

Most feminists want something more than research that only describes women's lives (Allen & Baber, 1992; Russo, 1995, 1996; Silverstein, 1996; Westkott, 1990). They want research that will help us understand how to facilitate women's well-being and improve women's status as a step toward a more just society (Kahn & Yoder, 1989; Kimmel, 1989; Lott, 1991; Maynard, 1994; Worell, 1996; Worell & Etaugh, 1994). The research goal has been described as research that is *for* women rather than *about* women (Allen & Baber, 1992). Research for women may be about women, but it also may be about men. For example, research on fathering can enhance women's lives (Russo, 1996; Silverstein, 1996). Women's lives may be improved by research on male violence, father abandonment of children, sexual harassment, and mentoring women employees. Male researchers may have easier access to information from men on such issues than women do (Allen & Baber, 1992; Harding, 1987).

***Principles of Feminist Research***  Is feminism appropriate in science? After all, it is an *ism*. It is as appropriate as behavior*ism* or Freudian*ism*. Good feminist science is good science. Feminists do not all think alike, but most accept some basic principles about research that are quite straightforward (Lott, 1991; Peplau & Conrad, 1989; Worell, 1996; Worell & Etaugh, 1994).

◆ First, they accept the principle, shared with philosophers and sociologists of science, that science is not and cannot be fully objective and free of values (Bohan, 1990; Grady, 1981; Kimmel, 1989; Lott, 1991; Peplau & Conrad, 1989; Sherif, 1979; Wallston, 1981; Worell & Etaugh, 1994). Rather than strutting about claiming to be unbiased and chasing dreams of finding the absolute truth, the human beings who are scientists would be ahead if they admitted their biases (if they are aware of them) and, in fact, examined, developed, and espoused their values.

Sociologists of science have long asserted that science and social ideology are interdependent (Merton, 1973; Myrdal, 1969; Tiefer, 1991). Selection of a problem to study is itself a statement that the problem deserves attention. For example, researchers have focused more on "maternal deprivation" than "paternal absence" (note the difference in terminology) on the assumption that a mother's constant attention is necessary for healthy development but a father's is not. Only recently have researchers considered the importance of fathering (Silverstein, 1996; Silverstein & Phares, 1996). Biases are possible at every stage of research, as discussed under Research Considerations, later in the chapter (Sherif, 1987). Scientists often are said to aim for objectivity, but can humans be objective? Should they be? Objectivity can be defined as *inter*subjectivity, not nonsubjectivity (Lott, 1991). This means that "objectivity" is a goal approached through a process of continued verification by others. Knowledge is a set of agreements and those are negotiable (Bohan, 1990).

◆ A second principle accepted by feminist psychologists is that empirical research is valuable. They realize that the methods of psychological research have been misused but still see them as valuable systematic tools. For a while, a dominant position was that feminist research should be qualitative rather than quantitative, because quantitative research is hierarchical (the researcher is in control), it "reduces people to numbers," and women have long been victims of it (Campbell & Schram, 1995; Keller, 1978). Yet, traditional methods have been used to show hidden assumptions that biased conclusions against women (Riger, 1992; White, 1993). The result of the debate has been the general recognition that almost any method can be used for sexist or for feminist purposes (Harding, 1987; Lott, 1985; Peplau & Conrad, 1989; Worell, 1990; Worell & Etaugh, 1994). Feminist psychologists, however, tend to be more open to nontraditional methods (e.g., qualitative methods) than other psychologists are.

◆ Third, feminist psychologists see human behavior as shaped by social, historical, and political forces (Bohan, 1990; Lott, 1991; Peplau & Conrad, 1989; Worell, 1996; Worell & Etaugh, 1994). With the myriad ways that such forces can interact, it may not be possible to discover universal laws of behavior. The aim should be to understand the ways in which social forces, along with biological and intrapsychic ones, affect behavior. Because of the concern with sociocultural forces, psychology of women often is seen as basically social psychology (Kahn & Yoder, 1989; Lott, 1991; Peplau & Conrad, 1989). A majority of women elected president of Division 35 have been social psychologists (Lott, 1991).

◆ Concern with differences among women may be considered a fourth principle of feminist research. Psychology of women has roots in differential psychology—the psychology of individual and group differences. Unfortunately, much research in psychology of women is concerned only with group differences, focusing on how women and men, or boys and girls, differ from each other. That is a step beyond studying only men and generalizing to women, but by itself, it is only a small step: A finding of sex differences is a challenge to continue to investigate the causes and implications of the differences. Sex is a nominal variable: It simply names the two groups of people who are different. Without additional research, we do not know if the names *female* or *male* have any association with the behavior or if the names *Jupiter* and *Mars* would do as well. Carolyn Sherif (1979) likened the variable called sex to a railroad boxcar: "Everyone knows what it is called and what it is used for, but no one knows what is inside" (p. 101). She pointed out that older psychologists were sure that it contained "biology." Modern psychologists do the same, or add culture, or subtract biology, with a result of utter confusion in discussions of sex differences.

There has been some increase in more interesting research studies of within-gender differences: how women differ from each other. This not only is consistent with feminists' concerns about appreciating the diversity of women but also represents a movement toward understanding reasons for differences. Much of the research on individual differences among women analyzes women as differing in masculinity and femininity; this may be a dubious basis for classification (chapter 3) but is thought in some way to point to differences in traditionality of gender role adoption. In other words, not all women are what they are "supposed to be" (i.e., feminine), and they do differ from the more traditional women.

Some research focuses on differences in women's achievement motivation and on how their previous experiences with parents affect their career orientations (chapters 7, 13). Other research calls attention to differences between women who have been sexually abused and those who have not (chapters 15, 16). We have a long way to go before we get to more interesting issues of differences in personality organization, such as the effect of self-esteem or how personality traits and motives are organized and expressed (Ashmore, 1990). What little research there is about women of different ethnic groups still is at the level of group differences.

***Diversity Issues in Research***   Psychology generally has been predominantly about white middle-class men in psychology courses. In turn, psychology of women has been predominantly about white middle-class women in psychology courses, with some attention to professional women in career couples. White is normative (McIntosh, 1988). So far, research does not adequately illuminate the diversity of women's experiences (Caraway, 1991; Reid & Kelly, 1994). Part of the problem is psychology's general neglect of people of color. For example, only 3.6% of journal articles in six APA journals between 1970 and 1989 addressed issues of African Americans (Graham, 1992).

Adding to the problem is the complexity of defining various groups: Women of color are not all alike simply because they are not Caucasians of European descent. The experiences of African American and Hispanic women are not all alike, and within both groups there is diversity. The term *African American* often is used for people who are of dark color but may have their roots in Jamaica, Trinidad, or Haiti, for example. Thus some of these women prefer *Black* as a term of welcome and warmth, unifying them (Hawkins, 1994). *Hispanic* refers to people of Spanish or Latin American descent. Although they share language and many values and customs, those of Puerto Rican and Mexican heritage do not necessarily share experiences and perspectives (Gibson, 1983).

Asian Americans also come from many countries (e.g., China, Philippines, Japan, Vietnam, Korea, Laos). Native Americans and Native Canadians share the experience of being invaded by white Europeans but may have little else in common (LaFromboise et al., 1990). Even when specific groups are studied, there is much variability within the groups (Bronstein & Quina, 1988). Generalizing from one group of women of color to another is hazardous, but because social scientists know so little, the generalizations often are made.

Division 35 has initiated a variety of task forces and committees on specific groups of women of color (Comas-Diaz, 1991; Mednick & Urbanski, 1991). Special journal issues have been devoted to minority women (e.g., Amaro & Russo, 1987; Murray & Scott, 1982; Reid & Comas-Diaz, 1990; Taylor & Smitherman-Donaldson, 1989). Feminist psychotherapists are making intense efforts to become informed about minority viewpoints (chapter 16). Writings of women of color and of lesbians have helped in starting to sensitize other women to the different experiences they have.

Empirical research studies have been slower in coming. Gender research typically fails to include race and ethnic concerns, and studies of ethnic groups often ignore gender issues (Reid & Comas-Diaz, 1990; Reid & Kelly, 1994). When race and gender are studied together in studies of women, we see the error of automatically assuming that "women are women" apart from their ethnic groups. Even when similarities are found, they warrant careful consideration. For example, white women and women of color did not differ in self-ratings on several facets of gender stereotypes (Landrine, Klonoff, & Brown-Collins, 1992). However, the two groups of women differed in how they had defined and interpreted the terms while rating themselves, and furthermore, there were differences among the specific groups of women of color (chapter 3).

Many studies are done with college students. The percentage of minorities in research on college campuses typically is about 8% to 12%, often similar to their representation in the student body. However, the percentage is too small to allow separate analysis and too small to keep any ethnic differences from being overshadowed by the tendencies of the more numerous majority group. Thus, although minority group members do participate in research, it doesn't do much good in understanding similarities and differences between groups (Reid, 1994; Reid & Kelly, 1994).

## Research Considerations

Feminists are particularly concerned with research bias against women. Distortion is not always easily overcome. Even researchers with the best intentions can introduce bias at any phase of the research process. The ideal study is not easy to develop. "The promise of science cannot be realized if . . . certain questions are never asked, or they are asked of the wrong people and in the wrong way, or they are not published because they do not fit accepted theories" (Grady, 1981, p. 629). In this section, we will review some principles of research to help you think more critically about the research described in this book. Your own common sense is a good start, but a few tips can help.

You may think you are only interested in learning about women and not particularly interested in research methodology. However, we cannot be confident in our knowledge unless we evaluate the basis for the data and how the data were collected and interpreted. The examples illustrating research themes are largely about research discussed later in the text, to whet your curiosity about content and to illustrate better the interplay between content and method.

### Preparing for the Research

The first step in research is deciding what the issue is and thinking about it; deciding to study one phenomenon rather than another one is a statement of values. Sometimes the values are plainly practical: A new technique or instrument is available, an advisor suggests a research issue, or some governmental agency or foundation is willing to fund the research (Keller, 1985; Tyler, 1973). A researcher's theoretical predispositions also shape the nature of the problems seen as worthy of study and how the issues are to be studied; not everyone will seek a grant from the National Institutes of Health to study women's depression.

The theory may be a very informal or an implicit one based simply on stereotyped presuppositions (Tiefer, 1991; Wallston & Grady, 1985). Stereotypes and the male perspective often dominate in basic thinking about an issue (Caplan & Caplan, 1994). For example, when spatial abilities or aggression are studied, little attention is given to the "female hormone," while much is made of the "male hormone" (chapters 8, 9). Researchers have typically seen issues of parental employment as mothers' employment causing problems for the children, to the neglect of possible benefits for the children and to the neglect of the consequences of fathers' employment status (chapter 13; Hare-Mustin & Marecek, 1990; Silverstein, 1996).

***Defining the Issue***    How is the issue to be studied? In any research, the constructs (ideas, dimensions, concepts) must be defined. An **operational definition** is a statement of the exact operations used to measure a construct. Most simply, operational definitions make an idea "point-at-able" and tangible so that others may know how a term is being used. Empathy may be measured by self-reports (discussed in the next section) of feelings about others or by physiological measures of responsiveness when listening to the story of another person (chapter 9). Styles of making moral judgments may be measured by having people talk about moral dilemmas that they themselves supply as meaningful or that the researcher supplies (chapter 8). In both of these cases, results vary depending on the operational definition: It is essential to consider the definition in evaluating results. For a more detailed discussion and an example of operationalizing definitions, see Focus on Research 1.1.

***Choosing a Method***   Some operationalizations are based on self-report measures such as interviews, surveys, and paper-and-pencil questionnaires. People tell you what they think of themselves, what they think of others, or how they behave. Other operationalizations are observational; behaviors are observed in a laboratory or in a naturalistic situation. Self-reports sometimes are considered inferior and not to be taken seriously compared to observations. This is an unfortunate bias on the part of psychologists, who, as a group, are very behavioral and have a narrow view of "behavior." Some distortions can occur in self-reports because of people wanting to appear positively (or sometimes negatively). But what is positive to one person may be negative to another, so self-reports are valuable in giving information about how people see themselves or wish to be seen. And sometimes people know themselves quite well; after all, they are with themselves 24 hours a day. To completely dismiss self-reports is to assume that people know nothing about themselves or that they are not willing to tell researchers what they know.

Observations have the advantage of dealing with "what people really do," but they, too, have problems. Just as self-reports are subject to distortion by the person doing the reporting, observational measures also are subject to distortion by the person doing the reporting. Are two children acting aggressively when they romp in the snow? Their behavior is more likely to be rated as "aggression" if they are thought to be girls rather than boys (chapter 9). And observations always occur in a specific setting. The sample of behavior observed in one situation may not be typical—behavior varies with the social context. It is possible to observe behavior in many different situations, but that strains the resources of most researchers.

In short, neither self-reports nor observational methods are perfect, but neither should be dismissed as irrelevant. Instructors and textbook writers are delighted when results from self-report studies match results from observational studies, as they sometimes do (e.g., in studies on self-disclosure, chapter 9), but we do not always have cause for delight.

## Deciding on a Research Design

There are many ways of classifying the designs of research studies. We will discuss three basic designs for research studies with many variations of each. The first of these has the most varied names: **correlational** or **assessment** or **descriptive design.** The

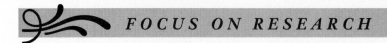

FOCUS ON RESEARCH

### 1.1   Operationalizing Variables: Definitions of Feminism

In college classrooms and the popular press, we often hear that "feminism is dead." With a long and colorful history in the United States, the feminist movement has brought about improvements in women's lives by changing attitudes and laws. Non-sexist language is now encouraged, the notion that women who have been raped caused the attack has been questioned, federal laws prohibit gender discrimination in employment, and laws against sexual harassment are in place in many states. We have created a gender-equitable society in which women and men have the same opportunities, rights, and responsibilities, haven't we? So, feminism has done its job and is no longer needed.

Is this picture really as rosy as it seems? Now we hear about the burnt-out working mom trying to juggle family and work responsibilities; the difficulty of defining, proving, and ending sexual harassment in schools and the workplace; the repeal of affirmative action regulations in some states; and the denial of public funds for abortions for poor women. Perhaps feminism is still a viable concept today. This was the impetus for a study by Linda Jackson, Ruth Fleury, and Donna Lewandowski (1996). These researchers wanted to explore how today's college students, the majority of whom were born after the turbulent years of the women's movement of the 1970s, felt about feminism. How would these young people define the concept? What gender attitudes and personality traits might students who support feminism possess?

In most research projects, one of the first tasks facing the researcher is to define or operationalize the concepts to be studied. The concepts must be identified in terms of specific behaviors or actions that are clearly observable. For example, suppose you have decided to study factors that make people happy. If you approach a potential study participant and ask, "What makes you happy?" the response might be, "What do you mean by happiness?" Only by using operational definitions can researchers accurately gather and discuss information concerning concepts that are internal and private (and some that are external and public), which is much of what psychology is interested in. Happiness might be operationally defined as "the number of smiles per minute," "one's score on the Happiness Scale," or any number of other concrete measures. If possible, the researcher might include several different operational definitions of happiness in the same study and compare people's responses. Each researcher must decide how to operationalize concepts in a study, but rather than being a random, idiosyncratic decision, the choice of operational definitions should be guided by the definitions used by other researchers who have studied the same concepts. By following or building on previous research, each study will be another step in understanding a specific definition of happiness.

In their study of feminism, Jackson, Fleury, and Lewandowski provided operational definitions of several of the abstract concepts they wanted to study. The idea of "support for feminism" was defined simply as one's response on a scale from 1 (strongly oppose) to 5 (strongly support). Two other concepts were also operationally defined by scores on established scales: "Gender attitude" was defined as numerical agreement with certain statements (e.g., "a woman should pay more attention to her family than to her career") taken from the Gender Attitudes Inventory (Ashmore, Del Boca, & Bilder, 1995). "Gender personality traits" were defined as masculinity and femininity scores on the Bem Sex Role Inventory (Bem, 1981).

However, the researchers deliberately did not provide an operational definition for the main concept in their study, that of "feminism." This is a distinct advantage, rather than a flaw, given the purpose of their study. These researchers wanted to know how their college-aged sample conceived of the concept of feminism. So, rather than providing a premade definition of feminism to which participants would react, they asked participants to define what feminism meant to them. Such open-ended questions allow participants to shape a response meaningful to them, as opposed to close-ended questions that force participants to select from a range of presupplied answers. (Questionnaire items that ask participants to respond on a scale of 1 to 5 are examples of close-ended questions.) While open-ended questions have the advantage of allowing greater input on the participant's part and perhaps producing more interesting or explicit information, the researcher must then make sense of this information in some systematic way. Jackson, Fleury, and Lewandowski each acted as coders by reading each participant's definition of feminism and compiling a list of themes common to the definitions. They also noted whether the themes and definitions were favorable or unfavorable. As mentioned in the text discussion of feminism, definitions fell into three categories: 71% were favorable (feminism means demanding equal rights), 6% were unfavorable (feminism means opposing and lashing out at men), and 23% were mixed (feminism means male-bashing and demanding equality). The researchers now had several behaviors that operationally defined feminism and were meaningful to their college participants.

The final results of this research project on feminism showed that the majority of the college samples had a favorable definition of feminism, with women expressing greater support for the concept than men. Women who supported feminism were more egalitarian in their gender attitudes; men who supported feminism were egalitarian only in their attitudes about women in politics. Finally, a woman's gender role (feminine or masculine) was not tied to her support of feminism, but men who scored higher on the Bem scale of femininity expressed greater support for feminism.

JILL BORCHERT ◆

SOURCES: Ashmore, R. D., Del Boca, F. K., & Bilder, S. M. (1995). Construction and validation of the Gender Attitudes Inventory, a structured inventory to assess multiple dimensions of gender attitudes. *Sex Roles, 32,* 753–785. Bem, S. L. (1981). *The Bem Sex Role Inventory: Professional Manual.* Palo Alto, CA: Consulting Psychologists. Jackson, L. A., Fleury, R. E., & Lewandowski, D. (1996). Feminism: Definitions, support, and correlates of support among female and male college students. *Sex Roles, 34,* 687–693.

researcher measures or assesses people as they are, without any attempt to change them, and then describes the people measured, sometimes correlating (co-relating) the measurements. Interviews and surveys asking people what they think about gender roles or how they spend their time at home provide a description of people's attitudes or behavior. The attitudes of women and men might be compared; or gender attitudes and use of time might then be compared within each gender or for both. Or, in a study of the effects of physical maturation on body image, the drawings of young women who have had their first menstrual period could be compared with those who have not (chapter 6). In such cases, nothing has been intentionally done to change the research participants; they are measured, assessed, and described as they are.

The second major design is an **experimental design:** The researcher manipulates the **independent variable** to see what effect there is on another variable, the **dependent variable** (i.e., "dependent" on the manipulation). The researcher is not just describing the way people typically are, because there have been experimental manipulations. The aim is to be able to infer that the independent variable caused the results on the dependent variable. Telling one group of children that a novel toy is for boys and telling another group that it is for girls is an experimental manipulation of toy appropriateness (the independent variable) (chapter 5). Presumably, how the children react to the toy is due to the independent variable of what they were told about the toy. Asking children whether a toy is for boys or for girls would be an assessment of toy appropriateness.

The third major design combines the first two into a **mixed design:** It uses both an assessed variable and a manipulated variable. Giving an experimental manipulation of toy appropriateness—telling children, "These toys are boys' toys, those are girls' toys"—to both boys and girls or to children at different ages would be a mixed design because gender and age are assessed variables.

Experimental studies are often preferred because they represent a more advanced stage of understanding. When two assessed variables are related, we often do not know why. One might cause the other, or both might be caused by a third variable. When children play more with a toy they rate as one for their gender, it might be that personal preference for the specific toy leads them to see the toy as appropriate for their gender and also, independently, leads them to play with it.

Although experiments and controlled laboratory assessments do have advantages, they also have weaknesses. Laboratory situations often involve artificial conditions in which variables normally at work in real life are controlled, so that the effect of the independent variable on the dependent variable can more safely be said to be due to the independent variable. This is a matter of **internal validity**—the study gives an unambiguous answer to the relevant question. However, the result may be that the laboratory situation is so contrived and artificial that it has little relevance to behavior in naturally occurring situations; the study is weak in external validity (Crawford & Marecek, 1989; Sherif, 1979; Worell & Etaugh, 1994).

**External validity** is a matter of the extent to which the results are generalizable (valid) beyond the specific situation and sample. The context affects behaviors in on-going life situations *and* in the situations psychologists devise to measure behaviors. The generalization that people like others who are similar to them better than those who are dissimilar, for example, is shown by research in which the research participants never meet another person; they are given bogus information about how much they agree with the views of the fictitious other (Byrne, 1974). More interesting questions are about how people go about discovering similarities. Putting people alone with a baby or kitten and observing that men are as attentive to the baby or kitten as women are may tell us little about whether a mother or a father is more likely to rush to a crying baby in their home (chapters 9, 12). Research (including experiments) can be done in more naturalistic situations. Even then, results may be suspect. Knowing that men are more likely than women to stop and help a stranger change a tire tells us nothing about everyday helpfulness in a long-term relationship between friends or marriage partners (chapter 9).

Research in psychology of women is more often assessment research than experimental research and often compares women and men. In part, this represents the relative youth of the field. But assessment also is a necessity in that much of what is of interest cannot be or should not be manipulated. To know the effect of teens becoming menstrual or of adult women taking employment, we cannot assign young women or adult women to an experimental group and artificially make them menstruate or require that they gain employment. We have to "take what we can get" and then try to untangle all the naturally occurring factors in order to know the effect of menstruation itself or employment itself. However, we can have more confidence that the results are relevant to people's lives because the confounding factors are part of that world.

## Conducting the Research

***Choosing Subjects***   Who is to participate in the study? Girls? Boys? College students? Adults in midlife? People in a home for the elderly? College students are most often used in psychological research and, as noted previously, are predominantly white. There is nothing wrong with finding out about college students. The problem comes when only college students are used and conclusions are made about people in general (Wallston & Grady, 1985). *The Psychology of Women Quarterly* now has a policy against publishing research when students are used only because they are easy to recruit (Worell, 1990). Some characteristics of women vary by age (chapter 14), and the size of some differences between males and females varies with age (chapters 8, 9).

***Choosing a Comparison Group***   Should women be compared with men, or should women who are highly traditional be compared with those who are not? Should women considering an abortion be compared with women who are not or with men in a relationship with a woman who is (chapter 9)? It is easy to say "both," but unfortunately, researchers often have limited time and funds, so choices must be made. As noted, most comparison groups are men. This itself is not necessarily a bad idea, but there are at least two potential problems. One problem is that it is very easy for a pro-male bias to creep in. Even if the researcher does not succumb to the habit of seeing men's ways as better, the very comparison can suggest that women are not worth studying unless they are compared with men. The second problem is that by comparing "women in general" with "men in general," we are not moving toward understanding the diversity among women and the causes of that. Thus, some feminists have called for more studies involving only women (Lerman, 1986) while noting that comparisons with men can be relevant as well.

***The Researcher***   Researchers are people; research participants are people: The research situation always is an interpersonal one. If researchers know about the hypotheses, their behavior can be subtly affected in ways that make it more likely that the expected results do occur. This phenomenon has been called **experimenter expectancy,** but it can occur in research that is not experimental, so that the more appropriate term is **researcher expectancy** (Rosenthal, 1966, 1967; Rosenthal & Jacobson, 1968). Researcher expectancies are a kind of **self-fulfilling prophecy,** a concept dealt with more in later chapters (chapters 2, 7). What it amounts to is that people's expectations shape their behavior, and their behavior may make it more likely that what they expect to happen does happen. For example, if a teacher assumes that a child is not very bright, the child probably will not do well (chapter 7).

Better studies are performed by "blind" experimenters who do not know the hypothesis and do not know whether they are dealing with a person low or high in dominance, for example. However, researchers do typically know if they are dealing with a woman or a man, a boy or a girl, or a person of color or a white person and often can infer class status. Either because of researcher or subject expectancy, a man doing research with women may get different results from a woman doing the research. Having a researcher of a different ethnic group from the research participants also may affect results. For a look at objectivity in feminist research, see Focus on Research 1.2.

Participants generally want to be good subjects and may shift their behavior knowingly or unknowingly to help out and give the results they think the researcher wants. When this happens, it is attributed to **demand characteristics:** features of a research setting that increase the likelihood of a given result, usually the predicted result (Orne, 1969). Researchers sometimes go to some lengths to disguise the purpose of a study in hopes of reducing demand characteristics. A measure of masculinity-femininity, for example, has unrelated filler items to avoid giving away what the test measures (chapter 3). In contrast, early studies on menstruation accentuated demand characteristics by letting research participants know that the focus of the research was menstruation (chapter 6).

## Results and Interpretations

After data are collected, there is room for bias or simply carelessness in how they are analyzed, how they are interpreted, and whether the results are published or not. When data are found to be **statistically significant,** they are unlikely to have happened by chance; they may or may not be practically important. A statistically significant finding is a reasonable lure for more study—there *is* an effect not likely due to chance, but it may not be particularly meaningful or justify immediate practical application.

What do the data mean? There is room for bias in interpretation of the meaning of the results. Girls and women often report less self-confidence than boys and men do (chapter 7). Does this mean that they are lacking in self-confidence? It may be that boys and men are unrealistically self-confident, while the girls and women are realistic in their self-assessments. When women conform more than men do, the difference often is said to show women's dependence, but it may be that women are more interested in social harmony or that men get defensive in the face of social pressure (chapter 9).

A researcher may elect to try to publish results or not, and then journal editors may elect to publish the results or not. Differences between the sexes generally have been seen as more interesting than lack of differences, and so studies about differences are more likely to be submitted and accepted for publication. The result is the **file-drawer effect:** Nonsignificant results are filed away in a drawer. This means that published research overreports differences and underreports similarities (Unger, 1981). This may be changing (chapter 8). Journals may also reject papers on the grounds that their readership would not be interested; research about women and in areas developed by women often falls under this ax.

Some studies are catchier than others and thus more likely to be picked up by the media (Crawford, 1989). The media seem to be fond of studies reporting gender differences, especially if those differences are said to be linked to biology. A study claiming that there are biological reasons for boys scoring high on math tests captures attention, while studies refuting the claim do not capture attention (chapter 8). Magazine articles are more likely to discuss research suggesting that women's moods change with their menstrual cycle while not discussing the more numerous studies showing no mood change with cycles (Sherif, 1979; chapter 6).

## Living With the Problems

There are many snares in doing and using research. Even a conscientious, nonsexist researcher usually cannot perform the perfect study. Teachers and textbook writers prefer to deal with research areas that have been well developed with lots of research, including replications (a repetition of the study in some way), using many different kinds of methods and different kinds of participants. We want to make some meaningful generalizations for our students and readers. However, many research areas are not well developed. People not engaged in teaching and writing often do not realize the energy that goes into trying to make sense out of some research. We want to say something about what we think is an important experience, but we do not have much of an empirical research base from which to do so. I sometimes write, "The researchers speculated that..." or "If this finding is confirmed..."

More and better research is not just a matter of training professional psychologists. It also is a matter of educating the people who make decisions about how funds for research are to be used, the people who elect those people, and the people who are research consumers—people on the school board or the directors of a community mental health clinic, people setting standards for daycare centers, or people making decisions about whom to hire for a job or how to set up and run a business.

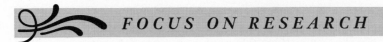

### 1.2    Objectivity in Research: A Case Study of Feminist Psychologists

Usually when we think of science, we conjure up white lab coats, buzzing machines, and laboratory rats. However, it has been said that each of us is an amateur scientist, gathering and processing information to gain an understanding of the world around us. So what is the difference between our activities as amateur scientists and the work of psychologists published in journals and books like this one?

One of the hallmarks of science is objectivity. To be scientific, a conclusion must be based on evidence that is free of personal feelings or opinions. Other people must be able to reach the same conclusions we have reached. In the 19th century when psychology was in its infancy, the study of the mind and of human behavior was modeled after the methods of chemistry, physics, astronomy, and other physical or natural sciences (the so-called hard sciences) that deal with the external, observable world. But psychology attempted to study the internal, hidden world of the mind and therefore was often referred to as a soft science. Not only was its subject matter less observable, but problems of bias were assumed to be unavoidable. After all, how can a human being hope to approach the study of human behavior objectively? Should psychologists therefore study only those people who are different from themselves or those behaviors in which they do not engage? Should psychologists never investigate interesting questions that pop up in their own experiences?

To follow the ideal of scientific objectivity, psychologists have employed the processes of operationalization of concepts and replication of results. While the things psychologists want to study are often internal and hidden (such as feelings, attitudes, and beliefs), they have been made concrete and observable through operational definitions. And what one researcher says happened is never enough to convince us; we must see the same phenomenon replicated by other researchers. In this way psychology has attempted to eliminate the subjective influences of the individual researcher and ensure objective findings.

However, the idea of scientific objectivity in psychology has continued to be questioned, to a large extent by feminist theorists and researchers who wonder if objectivity is truly possible. All people, psychologists included, are raised within a culture and learn certain cultural values. Can these values, along with related stereotypes, biases, and beliefs—the very things psychologists want to study in others—really be put aside by the researcher when designing and conducting a study? As

## *Themes of This Book*

While reading this book and considering the material in your own way, you will be forming your own ideas about what the big messages are. Here, some overlapping

psychologists have confronted this dilemma, they have begun to question just who they should be studying: those "other people" or themselves.

This was the impetus behind Mary Ricketts's study of the perspectives and values feminist psychologists hold about their work. Her thought was that we should know what our own biases are before we attempt to study other people's behavior. As her sample, she chose participants at two conferences in 1985: the Association for Women in Psychology and the Canadian Psychological Association's Section on Women and Psychology. Altogether, 190 conference attendees (184 women and 6 men) completed one survey on their theoretical orientation and a second survey concerning their values. Ricketts considered her research to be a case study of one group of psychologists: feminist psychologists. The members of this group have a shared perspective and common values. Just as with any other group members, this perspective and these values undoubtedly shape the way feminist psychologists do research. A case study is usually thought of as an in-depth study of one or a few specific individuals based on a detailed personal history, family background, and current functioning. Case study findings are usually not generalizable; that is, it isn't known whether the conclusions that can be drawn about an individual can be applied to anyone else. Ricketts has used the case study approach, but she has substituted the unique group of North American feminist psychologists as the focus of study in place of the unique individual. The findings therefore can help us understand only this particular group.

Based on her survey data, Ricketts concluded that the majority of North American feminist psychologists believe in free will, the importance of experiential content, holism, and a qualitative approach. This group also values social activism and focuses on external or social (rather than internal or biological) causes for human behavior. These are the attitudes and beliefs that will color the research conducted by feminist psychologists. Similarly, the research conducted by other psychologists will be colored by their attitudes and beliefs. As we begin to question the objectivity of our science, it is imperative that we have information such as the survey data Ricketts has compiled. Only by turning the focus of the research on the researchers themselves can we understand how our science is less than objective. This doesn't mean we have done bad science; it just means that we must recognize the biases and boundaries of our knowledge.

JILL BORCHERT ◆

SOURCE: Ricketts, M. (1989). Epistemological values of feminists in psychology. *Psychology of Women Quarterly, 13*, 401–416.

organizing themes are offered that appear in varying degrees in varying chapters. They can be summarized as follows:

- ◆ Empirical research is valuable but must be evaluated in its social context.

- Stereotypes hamper both women and men.
- Things are changing but not yet changed.
- Simplest either-or thinking is dangerous.

The first theme is that *empirical research is valuable but must be evaluated in its social context*. The four basic principles of research that feminist psychologists tend to accept are important bases of this book. The feminist acceptance of empirical research as valuable while recognizing that science is not free of values certainly will be evident, along with concern about the social context of behavior and the ways in which women differ from each other. In addition, the book includes the theme that questions about biological factors are appropriate, though there is a history of the misuse of biology in considering women because of social biases influencing the research.

Second is the important point that *stereotypes hamper both women and men*. Both men and women are inhibited in their personal development because of gender-related experiences and expectations. Girls generally are brought up to be feminine and boys to be masculine; they and the adults they become are evaluated against standards of femininity-masculinity even if they do not wish to be. This has been accepted as the "right" way to do things. Unfortunately, evidence about general adjustment and about social adjustment does not support this thinking (chapters 3, 16). Also, when women and men who have been brought up in different ways come together in marriage, they may have difficulty getting along because they see themselves and the meaning of love differently (chapters 10, 11).

A subtheme of this point is that problems for women are exacerbated because of value and power differences intertwined with concepts of femininity and masculinity. The values that society assigns to women, such as caring, warmth, and nurturing, typically are not as socially desirable as those assigned to men, such as aggression, leadership, and dominance (chapter 3): and men are accorded more power simply because they are men. Women have been living in a patriarchal society in which they have less power and status than men do. Women's experiences cannot be understood apart from this.

The book contains numerous examples of the phenomenon of **male as norm**—the "average" as well as the ideal. Women are either ignored ("the invisible woman") or evaluated against male standards. Given that men are right because they are men, when anything goes wrong, women are devalued and blamed—**woman as victim.** Women's bodies often are blamed for the errors attributed to them—their brains are too small (chapter 8), or their raging hormones cause unladylike behavior (chapters 6, 16), or they tempt men to sexual behavior (chapters 11, 15). In many ways, women are defined as bodies. When their bodies are not being blamed for women's supposed inadequacies, their bodies are being evaluated, by both men and the women themselves, for acceptability (chapters 2, 10, 14, 16).

But with all of women's advances in the business and professional world in recent years, haven't things changed? This brings us to a third important theme: *Things are changing but not yet changed*. Or, if you prefer, "Equality is closer than before but not yet achieved," or "Things are improving but not yet ideal." Change as pervasive as

*The social and cultural ideals of the 1950s—the single-earner family and the stay-at-home mom— meant that opportunities for women beyond the home were limited. Today, most women take for granted their right to an equal place in the working world.*

what many of us hope for cannot be achieved overnight, nor even over the 100-plus years since the beginnings of American feminism. For example, there is more attention to strong women in television than previously, but men and stereotypes still prevail (chapter 2). Women's pay is increasing but still is not equal to men's (chapter 13). There is more concern about violence against women than previously, but some women still are reluctant to report rape, and battered wives still cannot count on getting the help they seek (chapter 15). It is important to remember both the successes that have happened and the failures still to be dealt with. Considering only the failures can be discouraging. Considering only the successes can give a false sense of security and reduce vigilance and effort for continued work.

Psychological researchers often report results in terms of the average performance or scores in a particular situation. This is useful in seeing some of the broad principles of human behavior. Yet, it is necessary to consider the individual and the specific situation. Thus, a fourth theme of this book is that *simplest either-or thinking is dangerous.* "Is behavior due to biology or the environment?" It depends on the behavior, the specific biological mechanism of the individual, and the specific environment the individual has experienced. "Are men more aggressive than women?" What form of aggression (e.g., verbal, oral, subtle manipulation) is taking place in what circumstances (e.g., self-defense, defending others)? We do not always know the reason for individual variation or variation from one situation to another. We do know that there are differences both among women and among men in their degree of traditionality with respect to gender roles. Some people are highly conforming to gender roles. Others are much less so (often called androgynous or role flexible, chapter 3); they are less likely to see themselves and other people in either-or terms of masculine (bread-winner) or feminine (reproducer and homemaker) (chapters 3, 5, 13).

Traditionality of gender-typing is the dominant way in which individual differences among women have been studied so far. There has been some attention to differences between employed women and other women, and between ethnic groups, often along with differences in role orientation. Although there are individual differences within ethnic groups, African American people are less likely than whites to make sharp distinctions between what men are like and what women are like. Researchers so far may tell us only about women in general or even about women of color versus white women, but we can remind ourselves of the diversity and distinctiveness of women within any one group.

## Some Final Thoughts: The Past and the Future

Courses in the psychology of women provide women a place where they are heard and attended to. Both women and men may learn about themselves and about the other gender. What is to be learned about the social context that divides women and men is not always pleasant. Women have long faced discrimination and disparagement and continue to do so. In spite of that, many strong women have fought the establishment and may serve as inspiring models for the women of today. Women have accomplished much when they have worked together. Early feminists won the vote for women. Contemporary feminists are working still for other goals of early feminists.

One kind of activity that women have joined together for is scholarly activity in psychology and other disciplines. The aim of psychology of women is to improve scholarly attention to women and thereby improve psychology generally. There has been steady progress in many areas of psychology, though the road to academic utopia is long and hazardous.

In this book you will read about some of the gains that have been made in understanding women and their strengths. Women, like bumblebees, have flown even when the "laws of science" indicated that flight was impossible. If you take the topic seriously, you will come to see things you did not see before. Some of what you come to see may not be very pleasant. But along with the ability to see what is unpleasant often comes the ability to see what is strong and positive about women and men. Learning to see from different perspectives often is accompanied by the willingness to stand up and be counted.

There are many ways of working for humanistic goals in the classroom, the workplace, the family—society at large. All of us, whether we consider ourselves feminists or not, have the opportunity to contribute to a more just society. The aim of my efforts is not to turn every reader into a feminist; it is to contribute to the pool of information and ideas you have for thinking about yourself and the world of which you are a part. Most readers have or soon will have college degrees. That means that you are or will be in a position to use the power of your education to effect societal change. I hope that this book contributes to your understanding of humanity and to your willingness and ability to move our civilization onward, whatever that means to you.

## KEY TERMS

American Psychological
  Association (APA)
sex
gender
feminist
liberal feminist
cultural feminist
radical feminist
separatist
womanist

operational definition
correlational or
  assessment or descriptive
  design
experimental design
independent variable
dependent variable
mixed design
internal validity
external validity

experimenter expectancy,
  researcher expectancy
self-fulfilling prophecy
demand characteristics
statistical significance
file-drawer effect
male as norm
woman as victim

## KEY POINTS

◆ Understanding women requires understanding the cultural context, in which women and men have different experiences.

### Historical Context

◆ There has long been disparagement of women, but many strong women have challenged the system.

◆ Women were relatively prominent in the early years of the APA and are becoming so again. Early women psychologists were concerned with some of the same issues that concern women psychologists today.

◆ The 1970s were important years of growth for the psychology of women.

### Feminism and the Psychology of Women

◆ Few young women consider themselves feminists, although they support the women's movement and describe feminists positively.

◆ The Seneca Falls convention in 1848 is cited as the birth of American feminism. After women attained the vote, there was little feminist activity until 1963.

◆ Many women of color are conflicted about sexism and racism but are contributing to feminism from their own distinctiveness.

◆ Psychology of women has been closely intertwined with feminism, but feminist scholarship is an autonomous intellectual movement. Feminism may be more important as a transforming experience than an ideological creed.

◆ Feminist psychologists recognize that science is not value free, they accept empirical research as valuable, and they see behavior as shaped by social, historical, and political forces; there is concern with women's diversity.

◆ The little research there is combining gender and ethnicity shows both similarities and differences between women of color and majority women.

*Research Considerations*

- Biases may occur at all phases of research, from beginning formulation of the issue through publication. Theories guiding research often have been informal ones based on stereotypes.
- Much research is done in controlled laboratory situations that allow precision and control but may limit meaningfulness of the research.
- The media are likely to attend to studies showing sex differences, especially if they have implications for biology, while neglecting studies that challenge the results. Education of research consumers about research can contribute to better research.

## INTEGRATIVE QUESTIONS

1. Why were the 1970s important in the development of the psychology of women? What are your ideas about why the events of this dynamic decade did not occur earlier or later?

2. What are your own reasons for not being aligned with feminism or for being aligned with it? Which of the five principal varieties of feminism is appealing to you and for what reason?

3. What do you personally have to thank feminists for? Do you have reason to blame them for anything? Why should the history of feminists or women otherwise be important to women?

4. Why should a woman of color be suspicious of feminism? Why should she be interested in it? Does your answer differ for different kinds of women of color?

5. To what extent, if any, does the relevance of feminism to psychology of women mean that psychology of women is "suspect" and cannot be counted on to be a good, "value-free" science?

6. Why should a student who is not a psychology major care about the methods of psychology?

## Chapter 2

# Images and Stereotypes of Women

$T$he broad aim of this chapter is to discuss what stereotypes are and how they work and, particularly, to increase sensitivity to the pervasiveness of stereotyped images of women in public discourse and the impact of that on women's lives. We are bombarded daily with images that reflect and perpetuate stereotypes. The images contribute to the social understandings of gender, shaping the worlds we live in and defining much of what is thought of us and often what we think of ourselves. Although the emphasis here is on gender stereotypes and on ethnicity as it is relevant to gender, my hope is that the sensitization will extend to all groups.

We will consider stereotypes and their self-perpetuating nature and then the stereotypic depictions of women in the media and in language. Stereotyped representations of our social world in the media and language send clear and sharp messages. They tell us how things are and are supposed to be. Children may be more vulnerable to the messages than adults are, but adults are not immune. The dominant message is that men (white men especially) are the norm—both the average and the ideal—against which others (women and minorities) are judged. Women are relatively invisible (unimportant) except as they are physically attractive to and in relationships with men. Some of the messages are relatively blatant, but others are less obvious and influence us in subtle ways.

The following chapter also discusses stereotypes, though from a different perspective. There, we consider more refined psychological measurement of gender stereotypes, variations in their uses, and related concepts of roles and femininity and masculinity.

Before continuing, consider these questions for personal thought:

- ◆ Complete the following sentence: People use stereotypes because . . .
- ◆ Which gender stereotypes do you think are accurate?
- ◆ How does your use of stereotyping compare with that of your parents?

- Have you ever changed your appearance and behavior to please someone else?
- What were your favorite newspaper comics when you were growing up? What are your favorites now? Why?
- What is your favorite television show now? Why? Think back through your past and the kind of shows you liked. Do you see any pattern?
- Do you think that what people watch on television makes a difference in who they are and how they behave?
- How often do you find jokes making fun of women to be funny? Jokes about men? What do you do when you do not find them funny?
- Complete the following sentence: When a student first goes to college, he is likely to . . .

## How Gender Stereotypes Work

The term *stereotype* seems to have been coined by journalist Walter Lippman (1922), who thought about the stereotype machine in use by printers at the time, a curved printing press in which the type was deformed to fit the structure of the press. Lippman went on to define what we now think of as stereotypes as images largely socially determined, which come between our cognitive processes and our perceptions of the world. Stereotypes today are thought of much as Lippman suggested: the images are intended to portray reality, but they can have a deforming or smudging effect that may mislead us about the world.

We use stereotypes because we need to think we understand what is going on; more specifically, we need to think that we know what to expect of others and what they are likely to expect of us. For example, if you "know" that women excel at verbal reasoning, you can explain your own performance at such tasks. Stereotypes are appealing because they help us simplify complex social reality and thus make our social lives easier and more understandable (Cross & Markus, 1993).

Labeling people is the first step in using stereotypes, accompanied by categorization. A woman is labeled as a woman and a mother of four children. What is true, so we think, about women in that category? We use generalizations about people with that label or in that category. "She is very busy." In this case, the generalization likely is correct. However, the woman may have a live-in nanny who is responsible for the children. Or perhaps the children are all grown. A danger of categorization is that not all people in broad categories are like each other, and our assumptions about the people may not be accurate. However, the comfortable feeling the generalization gives may override the issue of accuracy. Generalizations, especially if shared with others, let us feel that we understand a situation or person and therefore are in control.

Thus, a **stereotype** may be defined as a generalization about people on the basis of their group membership, or as a set of beliefs about traits and behaviors of a group of people. **Gender stereotypes** are an organized set of beliefs about the personal attributes of women and of men (Ashmore & Del Boca, 1979, 1981). Some psychologists are now using the concept of schema, with a meaning similar to stereotype. A

**schema** is a knowledge structure of related elements that serves to organize and direct understanding of information (Hamilton, 1979; Hamilton & Sherman, 1994). Schemata (plural) also have been called prototypes, or scripts, and basic cognitive units of personality (e.g., see Cantor & Kihlstrom, 1987).

Some people use stereotypes more than others do. That is, they are more schematic than others; they have a greater readiness to process information on the basis of a particular dimension, although other dimensions are possible and reasonable. It is useful to add that stereotypes are affective as well as cognitive because many people, probably those who are more schematic, have strong feelings about them and get upset if their stereotypes are challenged. Stereotypes often have a prescriptive function as well as a descriptive one—they tell us how things are supposed to be as well as the way they are.

As we will see throughout the book, some stereotypes about women and men do give a relatively accurate picture of reality, but they are limited in their accuracy to a very broad generalization. For example, generally, males are more aggressive than females, but that generalization is simpleminded; there are different kinds of aggression, and there are changes in aggressive behavior over the life span (chapter 9). The problems come when stereotypes are simplistic or erroneous and are assumed to be real instead of photographs of reality. Much of this book is an examination of stereotypic assumptions to discover the limits and qualifications of the generalizations they provide. We will look first at the use of sex as a basis for stereotypes and then consider how stereotypes affect impressions of others and how they affect behavior.

## Sex as a Salient Category

Sex is a primary category in our responses to others because it is highly likely to be used in labeling and categorizing people (Brewer & Lui, 1989; Geis, 1993; Wallston & O'Leary, 1981). Even when sex is irrelevant to our interactions with a person, we feel we need to have the correct label, female or male. Consider your feelings when you see someone on the street and you can't tell for sure whether the person is male or female. Similarly, the first question often asked when a birth is announced is, "Is it a girl or a boy?"

The sex of a person often is noticed and remembered even when it is not relevant and when other information would be more useful. For example, people waiting in a subway station were asked to describe the person who had just sold them a subway token (Grady, 1977). The sex of the seller (female) was mentioned first or second 100% of the time. When sex was mentioned second (25%), race (African American) was mentioned first. If information about sex is missing, people tend to "fill in the gap" and think they remember information about sex. For example, students guessed that an article on politics was written by a man and one on psychology of women by a woman (Paludi & Strayer, 1985). Similarly, articles about physiological psychology were thought to be written by a man and articles about children by a woman (Brannon, 1994).

You might suggest that noticing sex or race and organizing memory on the basis of these categories is simply a way of registering useful information. As reasonable as that sounds, people tend to focus on sex and race even when other information would

*Sex is a a primary category in our social inter-
actions with others. Most of us feel uncomfortable when we can't immediately determine if
someone is male or female.*

be more useful. For example, the task in one study was for one partner to give as few
clues as possible to the other, who had to decide which of a set of photographs was the
"target" selected by the researcher (Grady, 1977). The people in the photographs
varied in sex and race but also in other ways, such as whether or not they were wearing
glasses or a hat. The students giving the clues about the target photo mentioned sex or
race even when information about glasses or a hat would have been more helpful to
their partner in narrowing down the possibilities—thus supporting the notion that
people will attend to race or sex even when that does not help in communicating
information. Noticing sex early activates stereotypes, and stereotypes are hard to
overcome.

## Persistence of Stereotypes

You have probably heard or said, "Seeing is believing!" However, often it is the other
way around—"Believing is seeing." We see what we expect to see (Geis, 1993; Katz,
1996). Stereotypes as cognitive systems or filters or schema guide our attention to
confirming information and structure our memory and interpretation of what was seen
(Hamilton, 1979). When stereotypes are operating, we notice what is relevant to them
and often twist memory and interpretation to fit the stereotyped belief system. Thus,
stereotypes tend to be self-perpetuating, and many times we do not even realize we are
using them or, rather, letting them use us.

***Memory for Stereotypes***    People generally have better memory for information consistent with their stereotypes than they do for irrelevant or inconsistent information
(Cohen, 1981; Liben & Signorella, 1980; Stangor & Ruble, 1989). Highly stereotyped

(schematic) children remembered more traditional than nontraditional pictures. Adults remembered the fact that a woman had not dated in college better when she had been presented as a lesbian than when she had been presented as a heterosexual (Snyder & Uranowitz, 1978). Competence in a role-consistent occupation ("Jane is a good nurse") was remembered better than incompetence, but incompetence in a role-inconsistent occupation ("John is a bad nurse") was remembered better than competence (Cann, 1993). When information does not fit expectations, it often is twisted to accord with stereotypes (Halpern, 1985). Highly schematic children reconstruct and remember nontraditional pictures as being traditional (Signorella & Liben, 1984). When information is forgotten, it is replaced by stereotypical assumptions (Halpern, 1985).

Not only do people tend to remember information that is consistent with stereotypes, they also overestimate the frequency of events that confirm their expectations and underestimate the frequency of events that disconfirm their expectations (Chapman, 1967; Hamilton & Rose, 1980). This phenomenon is called the **illusory correlation** and is present in children as well as adults. For example, children (second and fourth graders) were shown slides of men and women in traditional roles (male firefighter, female nurse), nontraditional roles (male librarian, female carpenter), and neutral roles (male feeding birds, female listening to music); each category was represented an equal number of times (1 or 3) (Meehan & Janik, 1990). Then the children were asked to report whether those slides (plus others not previously presented) had been shown 0, 1, or 3 times. The children estimated traditional pictures as having been presented significantly more often than both the neutral and nontraditional pictures. The same pattern was shown for ninth graders (Sterner & Meehan, 1988) and for college students (Meehan, 1989, unpublished, cited in Meehan & Janik, 1990). In another study, adults overestimated the number of women and men with "gender appropriate" personality traits and underestimated the number with stereotypic traits of the other sex (C. L. Martin, 1987).

*Accuracy and Inaccuracy of Stereotypes*    Because stereotypes simplify reality, the generalizations of a stereotype may give an accurate depiction of a group as a whole but give inaccurate views of individuals (Fiske, 1993). Women and men are different in many ways, as stereotypes tell us, but women are not all alike, nor are men all alike. The categorization of stereotyping can increase the chances of making incorrect assumptions about individuals because of the psychological processes of assimilation and contrast. **Assimilation** involves minimizing the differences within a group and seeing the group members as more similar than they actually are. **Contrast** involves maximizing the differences between groups so that the groups are seen as more different than they really are. Men as a group are taller than women as a group, but the generalization about height operates as a stereotype leading to distortions in judgment about specific individuals; differences in height among women and among men are minimized (assimilation), and differences between women and men are maximized (contrast). Men in photographs were judged to be taller than women even when they were not and even when viewers were told that the photographs had been selected so that for every woman of a certain height, there was a man of the same height (Nelson, Biernat, & Manis, 1990). A warning to avoid stereotyping and a $50 incentive to be accurate did reduce the difference in height judgments given for men and women but by less than 50%—most of the stereotype effect remained. The overestimation of male height is found using photographic targets and judges from kindergarten into adulthood (Biernat, 1993). The only exception is that when seventh graders are targets, people (especially seventh graders) correctly report that girls are taller than boys.

Laboratory "who said what" studies illustrate assimilation, or minimization of differences within groups, in a more social context. In this kind of study, people, usually college students, listen to a conversation and then are asked to identify the person who made specific remarks (Beauvais & Spence, 1987; Cross & Markus, 1993; Frable & Bem, 1985). When viewers made mistakes, the person they identified was typically another person of the same gender and race as the person who actually had made the remark. That is, viewers' memories were organized accurately around the categories of women, men, African American, and white. But, within the groups, the people were interchangeable, suggesting the assimilation that "all those Xs sound alike."

## Self-Fulfilling Prophecy

Another way in which stereotypes tend to be self-perpetuating is that, oftentimes, people "go along with" the stereotypic expectations others hold of them. Like stereotypes in judgments about other people, this often happens nonconsciously; we do not realize what we are doing. The stereotypes are perpetuated by the **self-fulfilling prophecy.** Most simply, this means that people act in ways that make it more likely that their expectation, their "prophecy," comes true. A two-stage process is involved—first, self-presentation, then, behavioral confirmation (Geis, 1993). The idea of the self-fulfilling prophecy was introduced first in the context of two countries preparing for war (Allport, 1958; Merton, 1948). Country A thinks that Country B wants war, so Country A prepares for war—self-presentation. Country B, seeing the preparations of Country A, decides it had best prepare for war. Country A looks at the actions of Country B and gets behavioral confirmation for its view that B wants war.

*Self-Presentation*    Women have been shown to adjust their behavior on the basis of what they think a man expects and is likely to reward—a change of self-presentation (von Baeyer, Sherk, & Zanna, 1981). College women were given information leading them to think that (1) their partner's views about women were either very traditional or very nontraditional and (2) he was either very desirable (tall, Princeton senior, no girlfriend) or undesirable (short, non-Princeton freshman with a girlfriend). Then the women described themselves with respect to their gender-typing on a questionnaire they had also filled out several weeks before. The women thought that the second ratings would be given to the supposed partner.

What was of interest was change in the women's self-depictions. Those who expected a less desirable partner did not change. However, those expecting a highly desirable partner did change their self-presentations markedly toward matching what they thought would be more pleasing to him (Figure 2.1). Then the women took an anagram test (scrambled words to unscramble, such as *kobo, atebl, etshsi*) described to them as a test of intellectual ability, the results of which would be given to their

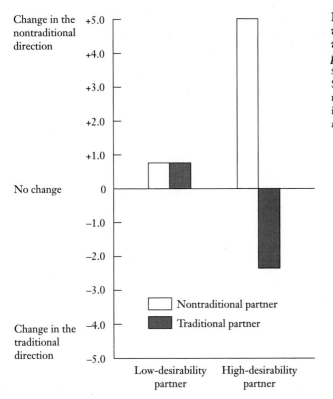

**Figure 2.1** *Changes in women's self-presentations when attributes of a male partner are considered.*
SOURCE: Zanna, M. P., & Pack, S. J. (1975). On the self-fulfilling nature of apparent sex differences in behavior. *Journal of Experimental Social Psychology, 11,* 583–591.

partners. Those women who expected a highly desirable nontraditional partner solved about 20% more anagrams than those who expected a highly desirable traditional partner. Thus, the women modified their self-presentations on the basis of assumptions about a desirable other person. (The anagram solutions are *book, table, thesis.*)

***Behavioral Confirmation***     The second part of the self-fulfilling prophecy—behavioral confirmation—maintains that people's actions produce the behavior they expect in others. How other people react to us shapes our behavior. College men had short talks by phone with women they had been led to believe were attractive or unattractive; photographs had been randomly assigned (Snyder, Tanke, & Berscheid, 1977). Later, judges listened to only the women's side of the conversation. The judges rated as more poised, warm, friendly, sociable, and likable those women thought to be attractive by the men they were talking to. The expectations of the men about the women influenced the women's behavior.

Also relevant is a study in which pairs of students were asked to negotiate division of labor on pairs of tasks that differed in gender role connotations (Skrypnek & Snyder, 1982). Some men thought that their partner was another man, and some thought their partner was a woman; all the men actually were working with a woman. When men thought they were working with men, their partners, who were women, provided behavioral confirmation by selecting masculine tasks (e.g., fixing a light switch). When the men thought they were working with women, the women selected feminine tasks (e.g., decorating a cake). Apparently, because of their expectations, the men behaved in a way that steered their partners (all women) toward certain tasks. The effect carried over to a second phase of the experiment during which the women could initiate interaction about the task.

## Summing Up

Stereotypes help to simplify the processing of information, although they may be misleading. They tend to be self-perpetuating because we are more likely to notice and think we remember information that confirms them. Stereotypes in our culture are perpetuated by many forces; among the most pervasive are the media.

## *Stereotyping in the Media*

The media continually provide stereotypical images of boys and girls, women and men, giving us messages of what people are "supposed to be like." The messages are about activities, occupations, personality attributes, intelligence, and physical appearance. True, sensitivity has increased in recent years, but the changes have been much fewer and smaller than one might suppose. By and large, the media still do not portray the many realities of women's lives, or of men's either for that matter. Some people dismiss the relevance of media, such as TV, with, "Oh, it's just entertainment!" It may be that some adults are not influenced by media, but children learn how to define themselves and their interactions with others from what they see about gender.

The continuing predominant message of the media is that men are the norm, particularly white men. Women are low in visibility and women of color even more so than white women. Women who are present are clustered in a restricted range of roles focusing on home and family, even when they are employed. Also, there is continuing emphasis in diverse forms of media on physical definitions of women as adornments and sex objects.

## Media Forms

The stereotypic themes about women happen in many ways in the various forms of media, all of which are important for different reasons. Comic strips are of special concern for two reasons. First, because they are "only comics" and not to be taken seriously, their effect may be more subtle and undetectable than other forms of media that are more seriously attended to (e.g., editorials). It has been said of cartoons that "of all mass media, comics mirror the American collective subconscious most faithfully (Reitberger & Fuchs, 1972, p. 7). Second, children are likely to have comics read to them and then to read them themselves as they gain reading skills.

Television is credited with being the great socializer in American society, teaching us what is thought important, teaching children how to behave, and teaching immigrants how to assimilate (D. M. Davis, 1990; Furnham & Bitar, 1993; Signorielli, 1989). Almost all households in the United States (98%) have at least one television set (Nielsen Media Research, 1989), and over three fourths of those have more than one (Comstock, 1991; Signorelli, 1991).

The sponsors who pay for media through TV commercials and magazine advertisements do more than inform us about their products or annoy us with interruptions. In some ways, the ads have a bigger impact than the TV shows or magazine articles. In the small amount of time or space they have to get their messages across, sponsors aim for attention-getting devices and situations that are easily identifiable by the audience and in agreement with prevailing cultural values (Furnham & Bitar, 1993). That means they capitalize on stereotypes and reinforce them and do so in catchy ways.

Teens have several forms of media directed toward them, including magazines, MTV and rock videos, and Top 40 radio. Rock music videos have become a pervasive form of entertainment among high schoolers and are a popular choice for college students as well (see Hansen & Hansen, 1988; Sun & Lull, 1986). Boys and men prefer hard-rock music videos, and girls and women prefer soft-rock videos (Toney & Weaver, 1994).

Media are not all the same and do not have the same weaknesses or strengths, but the broad characterizations discussed next stand out across media forms. The studies cited in this discussion generally use the method of **content analysis:** a procedure for analyzing verbal or pictorial material according to dimensions or themes of interest. Coders count the number of times a dimension or theme is relevant. Thus, nonquantitative material is converted to quantitative terms.

## The Invisible Woman

The strongest generalization across media is that the world presented is a white male world. Women are relatively invisible and when seen are presented stereotypically with a limited set of attributes and roles, in the United States and other countries (Mwangi, 1996).

In comics, males, particularly white males, are the most frequent major and minor characters; the few females are predominantly white (Chavez, 1985; D. M. Davis, 1990). African American women are in 10% of Sunday comics (Etter-Lewis, 1988). Even in comics featuring traditional married couples, the women appear less than the men. This was true in 1974, 1984, and 1994 (Brabant, 1976; Brabant & Mooney, 1986, 1997).

From the 1950s through the 1980s, white men have outnumbered women on television by a minimum of two to one (see D. M. Davis, 1990; Signorielli, 1989); the ratio for award-winning TV commercials is similar (Allan & Coltrane, 1996; Mwangi, 1996). There has been one important change: African Americans make up 12.4% of the characters in prime-time dramatic programming (spring, 1987), roughly equal to their representation in the population, with some improvement as well for Hispanics and other minority groups. Yet, the depictions of them, as well as of Hispanics, Asian Americans, and Native Americans when they appear, are stereotypical (Andersen, 1993; Brinson-Pineda, 1985; Chan, 1988; Chow, 1985).

***Girls and Women in Children's Television***    The world presented in children's televi-sion also remains a white male world (Beal, 1994; Feldstein & Feldstein, 1982; Huston, 1983; Levinson, 1981). To make matters worse, television executives made a decision that, starting in fall 1991, all Saturday morning programs would feature dominant male characters with females in a peripheral role if any (Carter, 1991). Their decision was based on the assumption that girls would watch TV with either male or female lead characters, while boys would watch programs only with male leads. The assumption probably is correct, but the girls sometimes watch male-dominated shows only because they have no other option. Girls can be very loyal viewers of programs with a woman as heroine, such as *Wonder Woman, Bionic Woman*, and *Charlie's Angels* (Beal, 1994).

Depictions of girls and women in children's TV shows and in prime-time dra-matic programming are typically stereotyped and traditional (D. M. Davis, 1990; Huston, 1983; McArthur & Eisen, 1976; Signorielli, 1989, 1991; Sternglanz & Serbin, 1974). In children's programming, girls do little but watch or follow the lead of boys, who help them when they get upset (Downs, 1981). What girls do typically does not bring any result or, if there is an outcome, it is punishment (Downs & Gowan, 1980). Similarly, in more than half the fiction in *Seventeen* and *'Teen* magazines for young women, the main character did not actively solve her own problems but depended on someone else to do it for her (Pierce, 1993).

***Men as Experts***    Given the media's view of women, it is no wonder that many ads present men as the experts. In TV ads for children (Ogletree, Williams, Raffeld, Mason, & Fricke, 1987) and for adults (Allan & Coltrane, 1996; Bretl & Cantor, 1988; Furnham & Bitar, 1993), the voice of authority that explains in voice-overs what is going on and what viewers should do is still predominantly (over 90%) a male voice; results are similar (73%) for radio ads (Lont, 1990). One of my students had a short and appropriate summary of what he learned from the television commercials he sur-veyed: Men do not change diapers, but they are experts on how to do it!

Magazine advertisements have increased their representation of women, so that men and women appear in about equal numbers (Bretl & Cantor, 1988). The women, however, continue to be shown in the home more than men are, associated with home products, and in purely decorative roles (Bretl & Cantor, 1988; Courtney & Whipple, 1983; Furnham & Bitar, 1993; Sullivan & O'Connor, 1988). Although radio ads have not been as well researched, studies in England and Australia show that in radio ads as well, women are presented in traditional roles with men as experts (Furnham & Scho-field, 1986; Hurtz & Durkin, 1997).

## Employment and Home Centeredness

The media have increased representations of employed women but often have done so unrealistically by showing them in high-status occupations; the high-status women, however, are not depicted as very concerned about or attentive to their presti-gious jobs.

By 1989, 75% of women shown on television (but only 4% in comics; Chavez, 1985) were employed, while in reality, only 55% of women were employed (Walters

& Huck, 1989). In TV commercials the percentage of women in work settings has been fairly consistent at about 20% since the 1970s, though an increase from the 1950s (Allan & Coltrane, 1996). Employed women originally were cast in a limited number of traditionally female occupations, such as nurses, secretaries, waitresses, and sometimes teachers (Signorielli, 1989). During the 1980s women were in a greater range of professional roles, including lawyers, advertising executives, and news producers; by 1985, a middle-class bias took firm hold as white-collar depictions grew to more than twice those of all other employment categories combined. More women in television have risen to prestigious occupations than have women in real life.

Magazine ads have followed the same pattern. Of women portrayed with occupations, 85% are in roles of business executive, professional, entertainment or sports star, or sales. Professional women on television and in magazines can serve as role models, but constant exposure to professional women may desensitize viewers to the job inequities that still exist and to the lives of women in "women's jobs" (chapter 13). Meanwhile, women in the many low-paying "women's jobs" are getting little confirmation from the media that they exist. The exception is that fiction in magazines is about women in stereotyped occupations (Pierce, 1993).

What kind of role models employed women are is an important issue itself. Professional women on TV, in comics, and in magazine ads are more concerned with family issues than work issues and more identified by heterosexual relationships than men are. They often work from their homes (e.g., *Kate and Allie, The Cosby Show*) or spend more time worrying about men than about any work they may have (*Golden Girls*).

Comic strips provide a good example of the lack of reality in depicting the lives of employed women. Employed wives (*Hi and Lois, For Better or for Worse,* and *Sally Forth*) are more visible and vocal than their traditional counterparts (*Blondie, The Born Loser, Dennis the Menace;* sampled in 1984, before Blondie set up a catering business) (Brabant & Mooney, 1986). In fact, the "modern" wives appear more and speak more than their husbands (Table 2.1). Perhaps that is to be expected of superwomen, as the employed wives were presented as superwomen doing everything except work. Although employed, they still were as likely to be in the home as traditional women were and *more* likely to be shown in child care and home care situations. In addition, the employed women had more time to read (though not material from their briefcases!) and as much leisure as the traditional wives (though far less than their husbands). It should be noted that modern husbands were in the home more than their traditional male counterparts and at about the same rate as their wives.

The message seems to be that women can be wage earners, but they are supposed to be women first—that is, concerned about home and men. This message may feed into the fact that in planning their careers, women are more likely to take account of spouses and families than men are (chapter 13).

## Family Series

Although family and home roles dominate characterizations of women otherwise, women (and minorities) have been underrepresented in family TV series (1947–1990;

**Table 2.1**    Differences Between Traditional and Modern Women and Men as Shown in Sunday Comics

| | Number of appearances (percent) | Number of words spoken | Shown outside home (percent) | Shown inside home (percent) |
|---|---|---|---|---|
| TRADITIONAL COUPLES | | | | |
| Women | 59 | 822 | 28 | 72 |
| Men | 74 | 1573 | 67 | 33 |
| MODERN COUPLES | | | | |
| Women | 80 | 1767 | 32 | 68 |
| Men | 41 | 728 | 34 | 66 |

| | Kinds of activities shown | | | |
|---|---|---|---|---|
| | Home care (percent) | Child care (percent) | Job (percent) | Leisure (percent) |
| TRADITIONAL COUPLES | | | | |
| Women | 15 | 15 | 0 | 28 |
| Men | 14 | 5 | 17 | 55 |
| MODERN COUPLES | | | | |
| Women | 24 | 23 | 16 | 29 |
| Men | 12 | 0 | 12 | 59 |

SOURCE: Mooney, L., & Brabant, S. (1987). Two martinis and a rested woman: "Liberation" in the Sunday comics. *Sex Roles, 17,* (7/8), 409–420.

Moore, 1992). When present, most have been at home, supported by husbands and fathers; the few employed women worked from the home or spent little time away. Attention to single women as parents, women working outside the home, and the feminization of poverty has been rare—the changing roles of women have been largely ignored in the programming. In fact, a general return to the traditional and nuclear family began in the 1980s and continues today (after, for example, *My Three Sons*) (Olson & Douglas, 1997). Series in which the mother does not work outside the home (*Father Knows Best* and *Happy Days*) or, although employed, spends little time away from home (*The Cosby Show, Family Ties, Family Matters*) are well received by current college students.

How are relationships within the home represented? An analysis of selected top-rated family series before and after 1984 (a division point between *Happy Days* and *The Cosby Show*) indicated fluctuations in gender-typed portrayal through the years, but not a trend of continually decreasing male dominance and increasing equality between the parents (Olson & Douglas, 1997). In fact, the trend tended to be curvilinear. On the one hand, college students judged TV spouses as more similar in what they do, more equalitarian, and less dominated by the husband in the later domestic comedies. However, *Home Improvement* (airing 1991 to the present) was seen as portraying low similarity between spouses, low equality, and high dominance. In contrast, *The Cosby Show*

**Table 2.2**  College Student Ratings of Popular Comedy Series on Spouse Similarity, Equality, and Dominance

| Sitcom | Air dates/ Years in Nielsen top 20 | Sex roles of spouses | | |
|---|---|---|---|---|
| | | *Similarity* | *Equality* | *Dominance* |
| Father Knows Best | (1954–1963) (1957–1959) | 2.70(e) | 5.06(d) | 2.95 |
| My Three Sons | (1960–1972) (1960–61, 64–65, 68–70) | 3.08(b) | 5.18(b)(d) | 3.44(b)(d) |
| Happy Days | (1974–1984) (1975–79, 81) | 2.38(c) | 3.56(b)(c) | 4.77(b)(d) |
| The Cosby Show | (1984–1992) (1984–92) | 4.97(b)(d)(f) | 6.47(b) | 2.15(b) |
| Family Ties | (1982–89)  (1984–86) | 4.41(b)(d)(f) | 6.13 | 2.72 |
| Roseanne | (1988–)  (1988–) | 3.31(b)(d)(e) | 5.41(b)(d) | 3.15(b)(d) |
| Family Matters | (1989–)  (1990) | 4.28(b)(d)(f) | 5.89(b)(d) | 3.17(b)(d) |
| Growing Pains | (1985–1992) (1985–88) | 4.67(b)(d)(f) | 6.08(a) | 2.17(c) |
| Home Improvement | (1991–)  (1991–) | 2.16(a) | 3.10(a) | 5.59(a)(d) |

NOTE: Higher numbers reflect higher judgments of the construct. The a is significantly different from b at the .05 level. The c is significantly different from d at the .05 level. The e is significantly different from f at the .05 level.

SOURCE: Olson, B., & Douglas, W. (1997). The family on television: Evaluation of gender roles in situation comedy. *Sex Roles, 36*, 409–427. Based on Tables I, IV, V, and VI.

(airing 1984–1992) received high scores on similarity between spouses' activites, equality, and, along with *Growing Pains*, low ratings for spousal dominance (Table 2.2). *Roseanne* and *Home Improvement* were generally seen in the most negative terms, although both have been in the Nielsen top 20 since their debut. The single-parent series studied, *Grace Under Fire*, was not singled out as being low in family satisfaction or family stability.

## Strong Women

In spite of the continuing stereotyping and unrealistic messages that television gives about women, important changes have occurred. The 1980s can be seen as a decade of "feminization" for network television, but the change is evolutionary, not revolutionary (Walters & Huck, 1989). Television series centered on women are now an established fact (Atkin, Moorman, & Lin, 1991). The most probable explanation is that the expansion corresponds to a period of competition brought on by increased cable services and the Fox Network during the late 1980s (Atkin et al., 1991). Producers became willing to try different things. Also relevant is the fact that women aged 18 years to 49 years became an appealing target for advertisers (Wood, 1990). The trend has continued with shows both short- and long-lived, including *Murphy Brown; Carolyn in the City; Ellen; Sabrina, The Teenage Witch; Xena, Warrior Princess; The Nanny; Suddenly Susan; Grace Under Fire; Cybill; Buffy the Vampire Slayer; ER;* and the *X-Files.*

In addition, women have made advances behind the camera. Diane English produces *Murphy Brown*, Linda Bloodworth produced *Designing Women*, Roseanne Barr produced *Roseanne*, and Beth Sullivan produces *Dr. Quinn, Medicine Woman*. If more women enter the pipeline of television management, what can we expect? We might expect more strong women, to be sure. We might expect programming to open up in

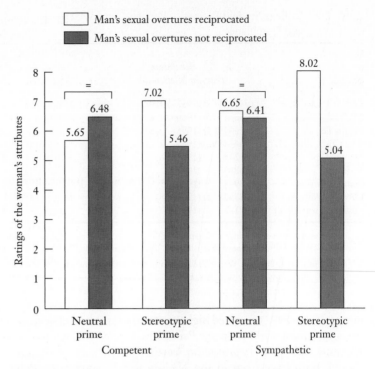

**Figure 2.2** *Judgments about a woman who did or did not reciprocate a man's sexual overtures, judged after viewing neutral or stereotypic videos.*    SOURCE: Hansen, C. H., & Hansen, R. D. (1988). How rock music videos can change what is seen when boy meets girl: Priming stereotypic appraisal of social interactions. *Sex Roles, 19,* (5/6), 287–316.

other ways as well. Both *Designing Women* and *Roseanne* are notable for cross-racial friendships and, along with *Golden Girls,* for heterosexual women having friendships with lesbians and gay men. In May 1997, Ellen announced her lesbianism, the first main character in a prime-time show to do so. Notice that the popular shows by or about women are comedies, with the exceptions of *Murder, She Wrote* and *Dr. Quinn.* Perhaps comedy is a way of creeping toward important issues before we are ready to face them head on (Skill, Robinson, & Wallace, 1987).

## Do the Media Matter?

Does it matter that media give so many stereotypic images? Laboratory and field studies suggest an association between media and attitudes. A variety of experimental laboratory studies has exposed people to media-type material and shown that the presentations influence adults (Geis, Brown, Jennings, & Porter, 1984; Jennings, Geis, & Brown, 1980; Schwartz, Wagner, Bannert, & Mathes, 1987). For example, young women (high school students) had reduced interest in political involvement after having seen advertisements portraying women as homemakers (Schwartz et al., 1987). In another study, college students saw a commercial in which a woman served her husband a TV dinner or the husband served her (Jennings et al., 1980). Women who were shown the nontraditional version later showed more confidence in giving a speech and were less conforming compared with those who were shown the traditional version. Similarly, women who had seen traditional commercials and then wrote about how they would be 10 years later emphasized homemaking over personal achievement (Geis et al., 1984).

What does a TV dinner have to do with giving a speech or planning the future? Nothing directly. But the traditional commercial apparently brought to mind a traditional mind-set or schema. When the man served the woman, the traditional stereotypes were attacked and perhaps gave the women "permission" to have confidence in themselves.

***Effects of Music and Music Videos***   Misogynistic lyrics in both rap and rock music influence judgments of women and men, contributing to an increased acceptance of violence against women (Barongan & Hall, 1995; Johnson, Adams, Ashburn, & Reed, 1995; Johnson, Jackson, & Gatto, 1995). Rock can also influence judgments of a seductive overture and its consequences. Christine Hansen and Ranald Hansen (1988) showed college students stereotypic rock music videos in which women were portrayed as inactive sex objects, or neutral videos in which women were portrayed as friends, mates, or coworkers. After seeing two neutral videos (and one stereotypic one), viewers saw negative connotations in a man's sexual overtures to a woman and saw the woman as more competent and sympathetic when she *rebuffed* the sexual overtures but kept the man's positive regard. In contrast, the viewers who saw two stereotypic rock videos (and one neutral one) considered the man's sexual overtures to be more acceptable and saw the woman as more competent and sympathetic when she *accepted* his overtures rather than refusing them (Figure 2.2).

***Effects of Television***   Some children or adults might be influenced by a single compelling character or program (Beal, 1994), but the effects of viewing for most are likely to be cumulative in ways not tapped in laboratory studies. Field research adds to the conclusion that media have an impact on children and adults. Television viewing by children, ranging from 3 years old through the high school years, is associated with indices such as stereotyping occupational roles; giving sexist responses to questions about the nature of women and men (independence, warmth) and activities (playing sports or cooking); and having notions that "women are happiest at home raising children" and "men are born with more ambition than women" (see Beal, 1994; Signorielli, 1989; Signorielli & Lears, 1992). For example, children who watched more than 25 hours of television a week, compared with those who watched less than 10 hours, thought that boys and men were tough and ambitious, and girls and women were rattle-brained and high-strung (McGhee & Frueh, 1980). Especially for girls (grades 6–10) with a high IQ, TV viewing over a two-year period predicted gender stereotyping a year later (Morgan, 1982).

Among adults (college students and the general population), television viewing is correlated with stereotypical thinking in describing themselves and in describing gender roles; the effect is stronger when the shows watched are stereotypical (Pingree, Starrett, & Hawkins, 1979; Ross, Anderson, & Wisocki, 1982; Signorielli, 1989; Volgy & Schwarz, 1980).

***Is the Relationship Causal?***    Does TV viewing cause increased stereotyping? In experimental situations the short-term impact suggests a causative factor. Also, some researchers were able to take advantage of a natural experiment. They gathered data in a Canadian town just before television became available in the area and again two years later (Kimball, 1986; T. M. Williams, 1986). Children in the town without television initially were less strongly gender-typed than those in comparable communities with television. However, two years after television became available, they were more gender-typed than previously and did not differ from children in other communities.

Overall, it seems that television contributes to stereotyping, but it is foolhardy to blame stereotyping on television alone. Research and theory in the more thoroughly explored area of television and aggression suggest an interaction (e.g., see Eron, 1987)— that is, the more TV people watch, the more stereotypes get embedded and the less they are interacting with real people and perhaps having stereotypes challenged. The more firmly entrenched the stereotypes are, the more comfortable people are seeing those confirmed.

Not all television is one-sided. The more educational, noncommercial television children watch, the fewer stereotypes they have about toys and occupations (Repetti, 1984). Children who watched programs with nontraditional women thought nontraditional occupations were more acceptable for women than other children did (Miller & Reeves, 1976).

Gender stereotyping existed long before television. Nonetheless, evidence suggests that media do contribute to the perpetuation and intensification of stereotypes. An important focus in much media is women's bodies, a topic deserving special consideration.

## The Body Beautiful

The media perpetuate stereotypes about many aspects of women's lives. Women's bodies are especially prominent, suggesting that women are defined through their bodies. The emphasis on attractiveness, thinnness, youthfulness, and sexuality serves to hold up images for women that they cannot match.

### Face-ism and Body-ism

It's hard to miss a gender difference when a woman wearing only underwear is shown with a clothed man. Probably many people miss a less obvious difference, which is, that more of a woman's body than a man's body is shown in the media photographs: Photographs of men are more likely to emphasize the face, a phenomenon called face-ism. Researchers have measured the distance from the top of the head to the lowest part of the chin (used as the numerator) and the distance from the top of the head to

*When a photo of a woman is used in an ad, it is more likely to show her whole body; when a photo of a man is used, it is more likely to show just his face. Researchers suggest that we unconsciously associate instincts and lower functions with the body and intellect and higher faculties with the face or head. Advertising images like this one thus help perpetuate negative stereotypes about women.*

the lowest visible part of the body (the denominator) and calculated an index of face-ism to body-ism (Archer, Iritani, Kimes, & Barrios, 1983). For example, if no face were shown, the index would be .00; if only the face were shown, the index would be 1.00. The higher the ratio, the greater proportion of the photo taken by the face, the greater the face-ism. It turns out that *face-ism* is a male-centered naming that sets up the male as normative—the face-ism of men is the norm as opposed to the body-ism of women—as noted somewhat apologetically by the researchers themselves.

The face-ism index was calculated for photographs of people shown by themselves that were published in issues of three national magazines and two newspapers (*Time, Newsweek, Ms.*, the *San Francisco Chronicle*, and the *Santa Cruz Sentinel*). Excluding *Ms.*, more than 70% of the photographs were of men, and women were more likely to appear in ads than in news stories. On the average, more than half of the photos did not emphasize a woman's face (index of .45 or less), while two thirds of the photos of men were predominantly facial (index of .65 or more). Recent studies show the face-ism higher for whites than for African Americans (Zuckerman & Kieffer, 1994).

Although there has been a general increase in face-ism in news magazines (perhaps because of improved technology), bias continues, even in magazines aimed at women (*Good Housekeeping, Ms.*), and even when status is held constant. The face-ism is higher for whites than for African Americans (Zuckerman & Kieffer, 1994), so that African American women have the lowest face-ism scores (higher body-ism).

The bias is not limited to photos in magazines and newspapers. Paintings from the 17th century show face-ism differences, with differences increasing since then and culminating in the art of the 20th century. The face-ism of whites in portraits is higher than that of African Americans, and African Americans' is higher than that of Native

Americans. College students' drawings also give more prominence to a man's face than to a woman's.

What does it matter? Face-ism is not like more obvious forms of stereotyping, but it may have more power because it operates less consciously (Nigro, Hill, Gelbein, & Clark, 1988). People's inferences about photographed persons varied depending on whether they saw a version of a photograph with facial prominence or a version with some body. Both women and men were rated more favorably on intelligence, dominance, ambition, and physical appearance when shown with facial prominence than when shown with more body. However, the attractiveness of men depended only on their faces, whereas evaluation of women's attractiveness was associated with both faces and bodies (Raines, Hechtman, & Rosenthal, 1990). The researchers suggest that intellect, personality, and character are associated with the face, while weight, physique, and emotion are associated with the body below the face. The different assignment of characteristics may reflect a basic mind-body distinction in which the mind is associated with intellect, will, and decision making while the body is associated with animalistic and earth qualities of emotions and sexuality (as well as defecation) (Lowen, 1967; Ruether, 1984). Thus, the head is emphasized for "good" men and the rest of the body for "bad" women. For further discussion of body focus and how researchers study it, see Focus on Research 2.1.

## Youthfulness and Sexuality

The media continue to emphasize the importance of physical appearance for women and to do so in ways that make it impossible for most women to feel that they "measure up." This itself is bad enough, but some of the specifics making up the definition of *attractive* raise important issues about cultural views of the merit of the female body and of sexuality. What the prevailing cultural view amounts to is that the *adult* woman's body is not good enough. This theme will be demonstrated in several ways in this book. Of immediate relevance is that the adult woman's body must be fixed up in some way to appear young, smooth, thin, and fair of skin and hair—obviously, women of color are at an immediate disadvantage.

The decade of the 1920s—immediately after women attained the legal right to vote and the decade of an important sexual revolution (chapter 11)—was an especially important time during which altering the appearance of the human body became of marked concern. An increasing proportion of magazine ads emphasized the duty of a woman to attend to her appearance in order to keep her husband faithful and the home secure (Basow, 1991; Ewen, 1976). To attain privileges from the patriarchy and keep them, a woman had to attract and please men by being slender, youthful, sensual, and sophisticated (Ewen, 1976; Marchand, 1985). This view evolved as shorter skirts, silk stockings, and briefer bathing suits came in vogue (Basow, 1991). It was as if women's newfound legal and sexual freedom had to be "reined in" to keep them in their place.

*Hairlessness*    Part of the fixing up required of women to appear sexual and youthful was "clean skin." The Gillette Company marketed a safety razor for women in 1924 to keep women's bare necks and underarms "smooth and white" (Adams, 1978). Advertisers did not focus on legs right away (the word *limbs* was used), because legs led to the genital area and were thought too large an area to shave. Legs became of concern in the early 1940s, perhaps because of the shortage of silk stockings due to the war and a bare-legged style, as well as the growing use of the new sheer nylons (Brownmiller, 1984). By the end of the period, most white women removed both leg and underarm hair in order to be considered clean, attractive, and modern (Hope, 1982).

Susan Basow (1991) has speculated that removal of body hair deemphasizes a woman's adult status. It is not until puberty that females (or males) start developing body hair. Lack of hair "demotes" a sexually mature woman to childhood and thus "tames" her sensuality at the same time that her sensuality is on display (Brownmiller, 1984; Freedman, 1986). It also is not until puberty that the typical female develops a belly, and at that time mothers of the past bought daughters corsets, and daughters today start worrying about weight. The result is a curious equation of female attractiveness and sexuality with youth at the expense of adult sexuality.

The message that smooth, hairless skin is part of female attractiveness is so strong that about 80% of women professionals (predominantly white) started to shave because "it was the thing to do" and continue doing so because it is tied up with feeling attractive and feminine (Basow, 1991). The sample was recruited through the National Women's Studies Association and American Psychological Association—groups of women not known for acquiescence to traditional views. Of those few who did not shave their legs, the majority identified themselves as very strong feminists (75.5%) or as not exclusively heterosexual (64.2%). More African Americans than whites keep their leg hair—consistent with the advertising pitch that shaving makes skin "smooth and white."

*Thinness*     The attempted equation of sex with youth is also evident in the presentation of attractive women as thin, although, as just noted, it is normal for girls to gain weight in puberty (chapter 6). Models have become consistently thinner over the years, to a point that they cannot become any thinner. Popular women's magazines and *Playboy* magazine showed a shift toward a thinner ideal shape for women in U.S. culture over a 20-year period, during which the average woman actually was becoming heavier (Garner, Garfinkel, Schwartz, & Thompson, 1980). Later studies of models' and movie stars' measurements show a similar trend (Silverstein, Perdue, Peterson, & Kelly, 1986). In some poses, the model's ribs are obvious. To many people, these women look neither healthy nor attractive.

*Double Standards*     Popular television shows reflect a double standard of attractiveness, revealing that the media consider weight more an issue for women than for men. In a study of 40 of the most popular television programs, few females (5%) were heavy compared with a quarter (25.5%) of the males; more than half the women (69.1%) were rated as thin versus less than a fifth (17.5%) of the men (Silverstein et al., 1986). There was an interesting variation for the very few African American women found (in only 24 series over 35 years) (McLaurin, 1989). While nearly all of the actresses playing employed women were thin and stylish, those playing home-centered roles (e.g., wife, domestic, neighbor) tended to be larger, heavier women. The stylish women typically

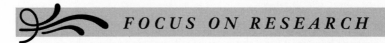

*FOCUS ON RESEARCH*

### 2.1   Using Factor Analysis to Develop a Questionnaire: The Objectified Body Consciousness Scale

Have you ever filled out a questionnaire and wondered how researchers would make sense of the 50 or 100 answers you gave them? When faced with masses of information, researchers often organize them into several groups or "chunks" with common themes. This is the basic idea behind the statistical technique known as factor analysis. Factor analysis is frequently used in the development of multi-item questionnaires.

Nita McKinley and Janet Hyde (1996) created a new questionnaire that measures how women think and feel about their bodies. This scale, the Objectified Body Consciousness Scale, has a twist to it, in that it developed out of a social constructionist view of women's body experiences. The social constructionist view is a staple of feminist theory. This view proposes that, rather than possessing inherent, objective meaning, experiences are given meaning within a cultural context; that is, as a society we subjectively create a reality that fits with our cultural ideals. Our society has a history of viewing women's bodies as the objects of male control and desire. This becomes women's reality, and they, too, adopt an outsider's view of their own bodies. McKinley and Hyde call this "objectified body consciousness," a complex concept that involves several different components. In order to fully understand this concept, we must first break it down into three separate dimensions: body surveillance, internalization of cultural body standards and body shame, and beliefs about responsibility for and control of one's appearance.

The first step in developing the Objectified Body Consciousness Scale was to create a pool of statements that were logically related to each of the three dimensions or subscales. An example statement from the body surveillance subscale reads, "During the day, I think about how I look many times." Statements were constructed so that the reader could indicate her level of disagreement (1=strongly disagree) or agreement (7=strongly agree). There were 69 statements in all: 16 statements dealing with body surveillance, 16 dealing with responsibility and control of one's body, and 37 concerning internalization of cultural standards and body shame. Next, 121 undergraduate women filled out a questionnaire that included all the statements from each of the three subscales.

The second step was to factor analyze the participants' responses to the 69 statements in the questionnaire. First, responses to one statement were compared or correlated with responses to every other statement. A correlation reflects the degree of association or match between a pair of responses. The correlations were then displayed in table format, called a correlation matrix, showing all possible pairs of responses. By looking at the correlations in the matrix, researchers could get a sense of which pairs of statements elicited similar responses and which elicited different responses. This helped them see which statements might be grouped together under a common theme and which were not related. When McKinley and Hyde inspected their correlation matrix, they found that the pattern of correlations sketched three basic themes among the 69 statements. One cluster of statements had to do with observing one's body as an outsider might. A second cluster of statements concerned accepting cultural body standards as if they were of our own making and feeling shame if these standards were not met. The third cluster of statements revolved around the idea that women are personally responsible for their appearance and can control the way they look. If the descriptions of these three clusters sound familiar, they should. They are the same as the three subscales originally proposed by McKinley and Hyde to make up the Objectified Body Consciousness Scale that guided the writing of the original 69 statements. At this point in the analysis, it appeared that the researchers had done a very good job of tapping into the very thoughts, beliefs, and attitudes outlined in their original logic. The correlation matrix supported their logic that statements on the Objectified Body Consciousness Scale fall into three clusters or factors: body surveillance, internalization/body shame, and responsibility/control.

The final step of the factor analysis involved identifying the "fit" between a model and the model to data, the responses women gave to the 69-statement questionnaire. Researchers can take one of two approaches at this point. In one approach, they propose a model based on theory and test how well the data fit this expectation. The other approach is empirical; the model is derived directly from the data and does not rely on the researcher's expectations. No matter which approach is used, this step produces "factor loadings" for the responses on each statement. When a statement loads on a particular factor, that means it fits into that cluster or theme. The preferred outcome for each statement is high loadings on only one factor and low loadings on all other factors. This outcome indicates that the statement is clearly tapping into one aspect (or subscale) of the scale, and that aspect is a distinct and independent part of the overall concept. If statements load on more than one factor, don't load on any factor, or defy logic and load on the wrong factor, then those statements are eliminated from the pool on the assumption that they are poorly written, are confusing to participants, or somehow are not tapping into the concept under study. Of the 69 statements on the Objectified Body Consciousness Scale, 45 were eliminated due to problems with factor loadings. This left 24 statements with a clear loading pattern of 8 statements on each factor or subscale.

Factor analysis gives researchers a way to organize and boil down what may appear to be an overwhelmingly diverse amount of information. It also provides a way to test the logic of questionnaire development in an objective way. While we may set out to ask certain questions of participants, what we ask may not always be interpreted in the way we intend it. Factor analysis allows us to organize and filter information in a way that keeps us on track.

JILL BORCHERT ◆

SOURCE: McKinley, N. M., & Hyde, J. S. (1996). The Objectified Body Consciousness Scale: Development and validation. *Psychology of Women Quarterly, 20(2)*, 181–215.

*Cultural standards strongly influence our perception of physical beauty. Marilyn Monroe, the ideal of the 1950s, was considerably heavier than the ultrathin model of the 1990s.*

were unmarried, childless, and devoted to their jobs. Unlike their male counterparts, they rarely had close relationships at work. To young African American women anticipating work outside the home, to the people who make hiring decisions, and to current professional women, what kind of message does this convey? Not a very positive one.

Cultural images such as those embodied in models affect both men and women. After they saw same-gender models, both women's and men's self-esteem about their bodies decreased (Grogan, Williams, & Conner, 1996). However, the cultural image of women, emphasizing thinness and youth, causes greater havoc on women's satisfaction with themselves. The greater pressure on women than men about physical appearance (Rothblum, 1990) is thought to be associated with women's general lesser satisfaction with their bodies (Lamb, Jackson, Cassiday, & Priest, 1993; Orbach, 1993). About 90% of college-aged women are dissatisfied with their body image (e.g., wanting to lose at least 10 pounds) (Boggiano & Barrett, 1991). The concern about being too fat can start as early as the second grade (DeAngelis, 1990).

Attention to weight is more typical of whites than of women of color, of heterosexuals than lesbians, and of more traditional women than less traditional (Beren, Hayden, Wilfley, & Striegel-Moore, 1997; Gettelman & Thompson, 1993; Jackson, Sullivan, & Rostker, 1988; Thomas & James, 1988). For example, even with higher weight levels, African American women report more positive feelings toward their bodies than do European American women (Harris, 1995). They are less concerned about weight gain and may even wish to gain weight (Wardle & Marsland, 1990). And

African American men prefer heavier women than whites do (Jackson & McGill, 1996; Thompson, Sargent, & Kemper, 1996). However, caution is in order. There is diversity among those women. The kind of ethnic identity is clearly important, and there are concerns about cultural biases in research design and interpretation (Harris, 1995; Jackson & McGill, 1996).

## Other Depictions of Women

Often neglected in discussions of the media's relationship to general cultural thought are humor and educational materials. Humor, like comics, often is overlooked because "it's not serious." People often think of children's and students' books as serious educational material and assume they are accurate and unbiased when in fact both give stereotyped messages.

### Humor

Besides comic strips, discussed previously, popular jokes as well as the one-cell cartoons in magazines also contribute to and reflect societal views of women. Freud's view of humor (tendentious humor specifically) is that it allows the discharge of sexual and aggressive energy in a socially acceptable way. Consistent with his theory, studies have indicated a general preference for humor with sexual or aggressive themes (see Burger, 1997). A mixture of sexual and aggressive themes in material that can be considered sexist appears frequently in cartoons and in widely disseminated jokes (Chavez, 1985; Crawford & Gressley, 1991; Love & Decker, 1989).

Sexism does not necessarily deter either women or men from enjoyment of humor. Although one study found that perceived sexism was negatively related with women's (but not men's) ratings of funniness (Love & Decker, 1989), several studies have shown that women as well as men prefer humor that is disparaging of women over other humor with women involved (see Moore, Griffiths, & Payne, 1987). There are, however, differences as a function of degree of traditionality about women's roles (measured by the Attitudes Toward Women Scale, discussed in the next chapter). College students—both men and women—with less traditional views about women's roles had less preference for sexist humor than did those who scored high on traditionality. This is no surprise. However, even among the nontraditional research participants, the general finding held: Sexist humor was considered funnier than nonsexist humor (Figure 2.3).

On the other side of the coin, feminist humor is not necessarily appreciated by women; college women gave feminist humor lower humor ratings than men did. However, among people over 30 years of age who considered themselves feminists, women appreciated feminist humor more than men did (Stillion & White, 1987). The researchers suggested that feminist humor may disparage men in a way that is threatening to women of college age. Women who identify with feminist values find male-disparaging jokes funnier than female-disparaging jokes (see Stillion & White, 1987).

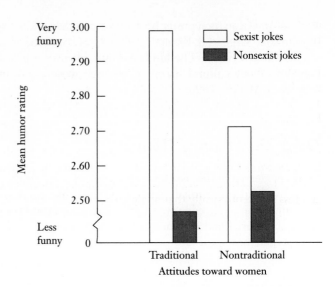

**Figure 2.3** *Appreciation of sexist humor rated by gender and attitudes toward women.* SOURCE: Moore, T. E., Griffiths, K., & Payne, B. (1987). Gender, attitudes towards women, and the appreciation of sexist humor. *Sex Roles, 16,* (9/10), 528.

## Educational Materials

Discussions about the media often overlook books for general reading by children and textbooks. Yet, "texts are important influences that shape us by reflecting the politics and values of our society" (Fox, 1993, p. 656). They define what it means to be female or male in our society, an issue important to children (chapter 5; Turner-Bowker, 1996). Like readers and textbooks for children, textbooks for college students have the chance to challenge stereotypes or to perpetuate them.

***Children's Books***    Problems of women's invisibility and stereotyping in the media are not limited to entertainment but extend into educational materials as well. Girls and women have been relatively invisible in these materials and, when visible, are portrayed in stereotypic ways (Bordelon, 1985; Turner-Bowker, 1996; Weitzman, Eifler, Hokada, & Ross, 1972; Women on Words & Images, 1972). Analyses of storybooks and text-books designed for nearly all age levels give a similar picture as that for television (Beal, 1994; Turner-Bowker, 1996; Weitzman et al., 1972). In general, there have been some changes in these media, but many problems remain.

Since the 1950s the number of representations of females has increased, but there has been little change in how female characters are portrayed (Kortenhause & Demarest, 1993). A study of award-winning books (1984–1994) found an equal number of female and male characters, including in central roles (Turner-Bowker, 1996). However, discrimination continues in terms of greater representation of males in titles and pictures, and differences in how characters are described. Male characters were described in more potent, active, and masculine terms (e.g., great, furious, brave) compared with girls (beautiful, frightened, worthy, sweet, weak, scared). This is consistent with other studies that found males were in dominant, independent, outdoor, heroic, and competitive roles and females in helper, caretaker, dependent, passive, domestic roles (Kortenhause & Demarest, 1993; Weitzman et al., 1972).

Winners of a prestigious award for children's books, the Newbery Medal, have included several with competent, nonstereotypical girls, but of five fiction book winners between 1985 and 1991, three were highly stereotyped (Kinman & Henderson, 1985). In one of the Newbery medal books, a princess pelted a dragon to win a crown but then had to be rescued by a prince, to whom she gave her kingdom! Among children's books in general, there are a few more books about African American girls than previously. In picture books identified as nonsexist, females are more likely than in conventional books to be central characters, independent, and achieving (St. Peter, 1979). However, egalitarianism is not complete; female characters are more emotional and less active physically than male characters (Davis, 1984).

Illustrations in winning books published from 1937 to 1989 showed a larger proportion of female characters using household objects and a larger proportion of male characters using nondomestic objects (Crabb & Bielawski, 1994). There are more female characters in illustrations (other than animals) than previously (1972–1989), but the girls still are not pictured as often as male characters (Purcell & Stewart, 1990). Girls have a somewhat widened range of activities. They are now shown climbing trees, but they get stuck and have to be rescued by boys (McDonald, 1989). The girls, however, are depicted as being very brave while waiting for help to arrive!

*Textbooks*   Women are relatively absent in grade school texts, and their numbers are even lower in high school and college texts. Women are rarely mentioned as important historical figures, government leaders, or scientists. Women's suffrage is presented as a minor advance in the political system (Kirby & Julian, 1981). Only 6% of pictures in science books include adult women. Madam Curie is presented only as a helpmate to her husband, although she won two Nobel Prizes, one after the death of her husband (Donelson & Gullahorn, 1977).

Psychology textbooks have a history of neglecting women as research participants and as scientists, and presenting them stereotypically (APA Publication Manual Task Force, 1975; Denmark, 1982). A more recent analysis of introductory and developmental texts showed women still relatively invisible as major contributors to psychology (Peterson & Kroner, 1992). In addition, girls and women appear less often in illustrations than boys and men and, when shown, are much more likely to be shown as passive and dysfunctional, while males are active, healthy, and competent. Higher level textbooks on research often use sexist language and do not discuss the issues of avoiding sexist bias in research (Campbell & Schram, 1995).

Textbooks "continue to include and perpetuate numerous gender biases and stereotypes" (Peterson & Kroner, 1992, p. 33). These textbooks are the only formal exposure many students will have to what is scientifically known about human behavior. With most of the information presented being about males and with the little attention to women being negative, "Students will have many stereotypes they already hold about women and men reinforced when they should instead be questioning those stereotypes and developing more accurate views of human behavior" (Peterson & Kroner, 1992, p. 34).

## Language About Women

The media constantly remind women of their "place" through the use of language, but the language of everyday interaction is a pervasive and perhaps more important influence on socially constructed images of women. "To understand the importance of linguistic sexism, we must understand the important role language plays in influencing our thoughts and acts through naming, defining, describing, and ignoring" (Henley & Thorne, 1977, p. 202). The dominant message conveyed by language specifically, as for the media generally, is that the male is the norm (Spender, 1990; Thorne & Henley, 1975). Some people consider language issues trivial and "just words," but others find it hard to overlook the insistence with which language structures women's experiences and their realities (Daly, 1974; Spender, 1990).

### Words Describing Women

**Parallel words** are pairs of words, one in feminine form, one in masculine form (Spender, 1990; Thorne & Henley, 1975). They were intended to refer to the same kind of personal roles or attributes of women and men with the connotation of equal value, but they have not worked out that way. Some parallel words to think about are master/mistress, governor/governess, poet/poetess, bachelor/bachelorette (or spinster), steward/stewardess, dame/lord, madame/sir (or master), witch/wizard. Do the words for women really have equal connotations? The suggestion is that they do not. This is because of several features of words about women, whether parallel words or otherwise.

*Infantilization and Trivialization*    As the term suggests, **infantilization** is treating a person as if the person were an infant. Closely related is **trivialization,** or taking away any importance. Words about women often are infantilizations or trivializations (Graham, 1975; Lakoff, 1975; Richardson, 1993; Thorne & Henley, 1975). Calling women *girls* is an example of infantilization and also implies a trivialization of their concerns. Another frequent form of trivialization is referring to women by their first names when men are referred to by their last names and, in some situations, their professional titles.

Stories about sports have been singled out as guilty of girl versus man imagery. Most stories about athletes are about men, but when women are the focus, they are more likely to be referred to by their first names, while men (especially white men) are called by their last names (Messner, Duncan, & Jensen, 1993). In addition, men are described in terms of their strength (sometimes violence), while women are described in terms of their beauty and grace or their small (not really feminine) bodies (Lorber, 1993). Attention to women centers on gymnastics, figure skating, swimming, and diving, with lesser attention to women in basketball, soccer, and lacrosse.

*Baby, dolly, honey, pussycat* are words that can apply to women or children, particularly girls. Adding *ess* or *ette* to masculine words in an attempt to make parallel words tends to connote childlikeness or a cute imitation of the real (male) thing. One faculty woman reported being called a *professorette* (Lips, 1993). Adding the feminine suffix to *governor* removes a woman from the state capitol and places her in the home, caring for children.

## Pejoration and Sexualization

Many words for women started out as equal in connotation to those for men, or at least without demeaning connotations, but over time they became pejorated or sexualized (Ehrlich & King, 1992; Lakoff, 1975; Spender, 1990). **Pejoration** is the process of acquiring negative connotations. **Sexualization** is the process of giving sexual connotations to a person or event that is not itself sexual. Sometimes infantilization or trivialization, pejoration, and sexualization all occur at the same time, and it is a toss-up which to emphasize for any given word, as some of the following examples show.

*Spinster* was originally a respectful term for a woman who was self-supporting because she spun (made fiber into thread or yarn) for a living (Spender, 1990; Thorne & Henley, 1975). *Spinster* was pejorated and sexualized, acquiring negative connotations of the "old maid" or "dried up old maid," clearly with sexual overtones. A *mistress* may be either the woman who is head of a household or a woman having sex outside of marriage (sexualization). Likewise, *dame* and *madame* have double meanings, including sexual ones, which the comparable *lord* and *sir* do not.

To say about a man, "he's a real pro" suggests he is very good at something. To say that a woman is a real pro more often means that she is a prostitute (sexualization as well as pejoration) or is very good at something negative (Lakoff, 1975). Similarly, to say "he is a wizard" means he is extra competent at doing something valuable. Referring to a woman as a witch has mostly negative connotations. It is worth noting that *witch* comes from *wicca* or *wicce*, meaning *wise person* (chapter 17).

Many parallel words are being dropped from general use. Students today may not have heard the terms *steward* and *stewardess*, because those terms have been replaced by *flight attendant*. When *stewardess* was still in use, it often was shortened to *stew*. In those days, the women had to be young, unmarried, and pretty. *Stew* became sexualized and the job trivialized.

***Number of Words About Women***     With trivialization, pejoration, and sexualization, it is no wonder that there are fewer positive words about women than about men (Henley, 1989; Schultz, 1975; Spender, 1990; Stanley, 1977). In addition, there are more slang words about women's bodies than about men's, and many of these reflect sexualization, pejoration, edibility, and even dehumanization: *piece of ass, cunt, meat, cookie, pussie, eating pussie* (Grossman & Tucker, 1997; Kutner & Brogan, 1974; Miller & Swit, 1991). Women of color have specific negative names addressed to them and apparently more than white women, for example, *dark meat, hot tamale, fortune cookie* (Allen, 1984).

Words about chickens are prevalent for women, although a chick is really a young chicken of either sex, or a young child (Eakins & Eakins, 1978). The fowl words applied to women reflect trivialization, pejoration, or sexualization, or a combination. Women are young chicks who get married and have a brood. When they become no spring chick, they start feeling cooped up, go to hen parties, and cackle with the other hens.

They may get mad as an old wet hen and henpeck their husbands. Finally, a woman becomes an old biddy. Her husband may become an old rooster after having been a young cock, but old roosters are still interested in sex, whereas old biddies just want to make trouble. Why the prevalence of fowl language for women? There are no clear answers. It may be because chickens are little, they are around the house in rural communities, and they are killed by women for Sunday dinner; pigs and cows are larger, away from the house, and their slaughter for food is a special occasion for men.

## Women as Exceptional, Decorative, and Relational

When an accomplished person is not a white man, she or he is singled out as an **exception to the rule** or sometimes, for women specifically, as **woman as exception.** Both phrases mean that if such people have done something valuable, they must be singled out, differentiated as exceptions (Luebke, 1989; Thorne & Henley, 1975), because they have violated the standard of white male as norm. Newspaper headlines provide examples: "Grandmother Nabs Thieves," "Female Psychologist Finds...," and "Black Sociologist Says..." When the University of Wisconsin picked a new chancellor, a headline read, "UW Picks Woman Chancellor" (reported by Hyde, 1991). Another headline was "Mayor Picks Woman as Deputy Mayor" ("Mayor Picks Woman," 1991). If the new chancellor or deputy mayor had been a man, it is unlikely that the headlines would have emphasized that.

When a woman is the exception, reporters often assure readers that nonetheless, she still is a woman and does fit her role in some way: She is decorative and **relational.** Regardless of what the news story is about, women are more likely to have their appearance and marital status described than men are (Foreit et al., 1980). When Lynn Yeakel ran against Arlen Specter in a 1992 U.S. Senate election, the *Washington Post* described her silk suit in detail, her haircut, and her husband's profession; halfway through the article, her credentials were discussed. In contrast, an article on Specter discussed his credentials and never mentioned his hair and wardrobe (Bridge, 1993). Articles about Supreme Court justices Sandra Day O'Connor and Ruth Bader Ginsberg focused on issues of the length of the judicial robe to be worn. Vice-presidential candidate Geraldine Ferraro was subjected to newspaper discussions about what kinds of suits and haircuts were appropriate.

Although political candidates of either gender are volunteering information about their families more than they used to (Ogletree, Coffee, & May, 1992), the families of men are not as likely to be presented as a prime definition of the men. The commentary on Top 40 radio stations offers another example of relational woman: Women are referred to primarily by their family roles (wife, mother, daughter, sister) or as women or ladies, while men are referred to as guys, sir, or Mr. (Lont, 1990). The stronger emphasis on relationships for women is evident in the courtesy titles used for women versus men. *Mr.* does not define a man with respect to his marital status, whereas *Mrs.* and *Miss* do. Many women, therefore, prefer *Ms.*, which means *My Self* (McGinley, 1969). The old English word *wif* originally meant a female human being (Gullahorn, 1977). It became *wife*, meaning with a man. Until recently, most marriage ceremonies ended with the pronouncement that the couple were now "man and wife," and she became "Mrs. Somebody-else," while he retained his identity. This practice is fairly recent (Spender, 1990); until the 19th century, *Miss* was a young woman and *Mrs.* was a more mature woman with marital status being irrelevant. There still is debate about why the usage changed. College women who wish to retain or hyphenate their names have more feminist attitudes, have higher scores on instrumentality, and are more likely to be immigrants or women of color; they are more likely to see a strong link between name and identity (Twenge, 1997a).

Whether because of insistence on a relational definition of women or reluctance to recognize women's achievements, professional titles are used less for women than for men (Thorne & Henley, 1975). Or a great deal of emphasis is placed on the woman as exception who has a professional title.

## The Generic Masculine

Perhaps the most pervasive example of differential views of women and men and of male as normative is a form of exclusive language known as the generic masculine. With the **generic masculine,** masculine nouns and pronouns (e.g., *mankind, he, his*) are used, but we are supposed to know that women are included as well as men. "Each student should collect his own books." "All men are created equal." "No man is an island unto himself."

The generic masculine is sometimes ambiguous, sometimes ridiculous, and sometimes misleading (Spender, 1990). There often is no way of knowing whether the masculine reference includes women or denotes only men. "Most congressmen support the bill." Will that be followed by, "Women congressional representatives, however, think otherwise," or a statement suggesting that the women in Congress agree with the men (Matlin, 1991)? Consider the following books: *The Individual and His Religion* (Allport, 1950), *Man Against Himself* (Menninger, 1938), *Man for Himself* (Fromm, 1947), and *The Seasons of a Man's Life* (Levinson, Darrow, Kline, Levinson, & McKee, 1978). Do they deal only with men's concerns or also with women's concerns? Only the last deals exclusively with men, and the authors of that book quickly explain that they studied only men. (Incidentally, all the books seem worthwhile to me; comments about titles are not meant as comments about their quality.)

Just how ridiculous the generic masculine can be is shown by a state law that says, essentially, "No man can be forced to have an abortion against his will" (Key, 1975, cited by Hyde, 1991). While men often do have strong views to be acknowledged about a possible abortion, the law clearly was describing a woman's rights.

***Effects of the Generic Masculine***     The generic masculine can encourage erroneous conclusions. For example, many articles have appeared in the media discussing AIDS among gays, with the possible result that people think of AIDS as a homosexual disease (Hamilton, 1988). A generic interpretation of *gay* is inappropriate because lesbians have the lowest rate of AIDS of any group (and AIDS is not a homosexual disease; chapter 11). The American Psychological Association Committee on Lesbian and Gay Concerns (1991) has advised avoiding *gay* in favor of *lesbian* and *gay male* unless the context makes very clear to whom *gay* refers.

Once again, we must ask whether it matters. The answer is yes, the generic masculine does make a difference (Gastil, 1990; Switzer, 1990). For example, Nancy Henley (1989) reviewed 20 relevant studies of people from 6 years of age on and found that all of the studies showed that people do not think of girls and women as much as they think of boys and men when they see or hear the generic masculine. Relative neglect of women also happens when people themselves use the generic masculine (Hamilton, 1988). For further discussion of this issue and another study, see Focus on Research 2.2.

The impact of the generic masculine was first demonstrated by sociologists who were writing a textbook and used copies of the manuscript in classes (Schneider & Hacker, 1973). For one class, the chapters had generic masculine titles, such as "Urban Man," "Industrial Man," "Political Man." For another class, the titles were "Urban Life," "Industrial Life," "Political Life." The instructors asked students to help by collecting photographs to illustrate the book. Students who had manuscripts with the generic masculine provided more photos of men and of men in positions of power and dominance than did those students who had more inclusive titles. For example, the chapter "Industrial Man" brought submissions of photos of heavy machinery and men doing heavy work, while "Industrial Life" brought submission of photos of inside craft work or scientific and technical work.

This study was followed by laboratory studies with both children and adults. The prevailing model of research involves having people complete sentences or tell stories in response to a sentence with the pronouns *he*, or *he or she*, or the plural *they*. An example for children (first, third, and fifth graders) is "When a kid goes to school, (he, he or she, they) often feels excited the first day." Twelve percent of the stories were about girls when *he* was used—all told by girls (J. S. Hyde, 1984). In contrast, 42% of the stories were about girls when *he or she* was used and 18% when *they* was used. College students responding to "In a large institution, the average student will feel isolated in (his, their, or his or her) introductory class" gave somewhat more stories than children did about women when *his or her* was used (56%); they were even more likely than children to give stories of women in response to *their* (46%) and to *his* (35%) (Moulton, Robinson, & Elias, 1978). Thus college students are more likely to respond about women than children are to *he or she* or *their*. But both college students and children give relatively few stories about girls or women when *he* is used.

Gender differences are not always found in studies of responses to pronoun use, but when they are, girls and women report more imagery of girls and women to *he* and to the gender-inclusive forms than boys or men do (Switzer, 1990). For example, in one study, men gave as much masculine imagery to *he/she* as to *he*; women also gave a lot of masculine imagery to *he*, but very little to *he/she* or *them*. A recurring theme is that when there are differences in stereotyping, men are more stereotyped and male centered.

***Implications of the Generic Masculine***    The generic masculine has implications beyond the immediate imagery. It affects judgments of children and adults and, along with many other factors to be sure, may contribute to lowering girls' self-confidence and limiting their career aspirations (Beal, 1994). For example, children did not consider women as competent as men in being a "wudgemaker" when the generic mascu-line had been used to describe a wudgemaker as when other pronouns had been used (J. S. Hyde, 1984). Judgments of a man's competence did not vary as much as a function of the pronouns used as the judgments of a woman's did—men were good, no matter what the pronoun.

Studies with college students have had similar results. Students read a masculin-ized or gender neutral (*he or she* or no gender-specific words at all) statement about psychologists (Briere & Lanktree, 1983) and then rated the attractiveness of psychol-ogy as a career. Psychology was considered less attractive for women by students who had read the masculinized description than by those who had read the gender netural version.

The generic masculine has been used so extensively that it has left a residue. The result, described by Mykol Hamilton (1991), is "Man = People, People = Man." Hamilton showed that the generic masculine generalizes to *people*, and when *people* is used, subjects assume masculine. Other evidence shows that, in the words of the re-searchers, "The three bears are all boys" (DeLoache, Cassidy, & Carpenter, 1987). For example, mothers were observed looking at books with their young children (18 to 38 months). Even when the characters were treated in a gender neutral way in the book, the mothers referred to 95% of them as males. Similarly, when parents and teachers are explaining a concept with a story about a particular person or animal, they are more likely to use male than female imagery (Women on Words & Images, 1972).

Although elimination of the generic masculine will not immediately reduce the tendency to think of boys and men when girls and women are not specified, the long-term effects will not dissipate as long as the generic masculine continues to be used. The generic masculine may not have the same obvious impact as social, legal, and occupational discrimination. But it is a part of the nonconscious ideology within which those discriminations take place.

Changing long-time habits of thinking and writing is not easy. Some ways of avoiding the generic masculine are given in A Closer Look 2.1 (p. 72). The problem with most writing is that the writer thinks of men and then has to translate the thought to include women as an unequal afterthought. Thus the ultimate solution is to think in gender equal terms in the first place. Robin Lakoff (1975) maintained that gender-related language behaviors cannot be changed by a frontal assault on speech patterns. The deeper issue to be faced is the needed change in social and political inequities. "When that happens, of course, language reform will be moot" (Rubin & Greene, 1991, p. 410).

## *Some Final Thoughts: Why Do We Watch, Listen, and Go Along?*

Most people, whether they mean to or not, are likely to make some stereotyped as-sumptions without realizing it. Stereotypes are easy to use, giving us a quick and easy way to feel that we understand the social world. People use sex as an organiz-ing cue even when it is not useful. Even though some stereotypes provide accurate

## FOCUS ON RESEARCH

### 2.2    Theory-Guided Research: How Sexist Is Our Language?

Language changes constantly; old words die out and new words appear. How long has it been since you heard someone say "groovy"? On the other hand, five years ago, did you know what *cyberspace* was? Our need to express certain ideas pushes us to create and discard words, and this shapes our language. Much of the English language we use today is shaped by the male experience, which makes a great deal of sense when you consider that English grows out of a history of male dominance and male control of resources. Who else would head a company but a chairman? If "all men are created equal," that phrase simply reflects those who held the power to shape a new nation. As women gradually gained recognition and power and moved into positions formerly held only by men, such language was considered to be generic or inclusive of both sexes. Everyone knew that "mankind" meant both men and women. However, many people today consider such male-specific language sexist.

Benjamin Whorf, a psycholinguist, theorized that while our thoughts influence our language, the flip side of the coin also occurs. That is, the words we use and hear shape the way we think. This theory suggests that words like "he," "mankind," and "chairman" lead us to think exclusively of men. This line of reasoning has sparked research into how we process certain words and whether our assumption about generic language is unfounded.

Sik Hung Ng (1990) used a theory of learning and memory to test potential sexist bias in language. We know that the brain codes words both for their specific meaning and for category membership. Thus, the word *poodle* would be coded in terms of the animal's specific characteristics (curly hair, intelligence, pointed snout) as well as in terms of the category "dog." This is true for the word *man* as well. *Man* would be coded in terms of specific characteristics (adult, human) and also in terms of the category "male." But are words such as *he* and *man* assimilated just as easily into the feminine category as the masculine one? Linguistically speaking, are these words truly generic?

The concept of proactive inhibition suggests a way of finding out. Proactive inhibition refers to interference (problems in recall) caused by prior learning when a person is remembering newly learned material. Interference is greatest when the old and new material are similar. Proactive inhibition tells us that memory for a new word will not be as good if one has already memorized other words from the same linguistic category as it would be if the word is different from others one has memorized (belongs

generalizations (men in general are taller than women in general), stereotypes distort perceptions of individuals—women were judged shorter than men even when judges were told that sex would not be a good clue in judging height.

to a different linguistic category). Release from proactive inhibition occurs when the new word is from a different category; the release takes the form of better memory for the distinctive than for the similar word. These twin concepts of proactive inhibition and release from proactive inhibition provide a means for discovering the linguistic category of any word. If the linguistic code for *his* and *man* is truly a masculine one, these words will not be remembered as easily following a list of other masculine words (proactive inhibition) as after a list of feminine words (release from proactive inhibition).

In Ng's study, adolescent girls and boys were randomly assigned to one of two conditions in which they listened to pairs of masculine words (king-Ivan, son-Lewis, boy-Ross) or feminine words (queen-Linda, nun-Mary, girl-Iris). After each list, they heard two additional pairs (man-Robin and his-Chris). Unlike the names in the masculine or feminine lists, both Robin and Chris are unisex names. Will *man* and *his* be as easy to remember after the list of masculine pairs as after the feminine? If so, these words are genuinely generic.

Theory tells us we first need to check for a buildup of proactive inhibition over the initial list of pairs—that is, to look for poorer recall of the last words than the first ones. As expected, this occurred. Next, we need to determine whether proactive inhibition continued for the generic words when they followed the masculine list and whether release from proactive inhibition occurred following the feminine list. Both of these happened as well.

These findings tell us that the words *man* and *his* are coded as masculine words in memory and are not truly generic. Upon hearing the statement "all men are created equal," we do not automatically think of women as well as men. Ng's research helps explain at the cognitive level Benjamin Whorf's contention that the words we use influence our thoughts. In applying these findings to everyday life, Janet Hyde (1984) showed that children rated women's competence at a fictitious occupation of "wudgemaker" lowest when the pronoun *he* was used in a job description. The combination of theoretically based and applied research tells us that our current use of English creates a sexist environment that can be detrimental to women's full acceptance.

JILL BORCHERT ◆

SOURCES: Hyde, J. S. (1984). Children's understanding of sexist language. *Developmental Psychology, 20*, 697–706. Ng, S. H. (1990). Androcentric coding of Man and His in memory by language users. *Journal of Experimental Social Psychology, 26*, 455–464.

---

People often adapt their self-presentations to match stereotypes or adjust their behavior to fit with another person's views and, in turn, get behavioral confirmation. Sometimes, we probably consciously choose to do so because of realistic reasons ("If

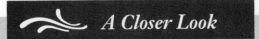

## A Closer Look

### 2.1    Alternatives to Use of the Generic Masculine Pronoun

**Generic masculine form**

If a student decides to do an extra credit project, he is responsible for filling out a form and picking up his form after his instructor has reviewed it.

**Alternatives**

| | |
|---|---|
| Avoid pronouns | Each student doing an extra credit project should explain the plans for the project on the form and then pick up the form after the instructor has reviewed it. |
| Use second person | If you wish to do an extra credit project, you must explain your plans on the form and pick it up after the instructor has reviewed it. |
| Use plural | Students who wish to do an extra credit project are responsible for explaining their plans on the form and picking it up after the instructor has reviewed it. |

**An alternative to avoid**

| | |
|---|---|
| Unnecessary use of pronouns | If a student decides to do an extra credit project, he or she is responsible for filling out the form and then she or he should pick up the form after his or her instructor has reviewed it. |

that's what is needed to get what I want, I'll do it"). However, many times, we are victims of the habits learned over the years of "going along with what is expected" and are not always aware of what we are doing. Well-learned behaviors are hard to change, and stereotyped behaviors are well learned.

It is hard to change stereotyped thinking when all forms of media are continually giving us stereotyped portrayals of both white women and women of color. Women are relatively neglected in the media, and when attended to, they are depicted as concerned about appearance, relationships, and domestic affairs, even if they are professional women. The stereotyping is present even in books for children and textbooks for college-level students. Public presentations of women are particularly likely to convey the message that women are supposed to be thin, white, smooth-skinned (no skin hair showing), and young in appearance. This may demonstrate a defensiveness against women's adult sexuality.

We cannot claim that the media invented gender stereotyping, but evidence clearly shows that they have strong influence on people's thinking. So too does language about women. In everyday interaction as well as the public media, the male is norm, with women either neglected or explained as decorative persons existing because of relationships, or as an exception.

Things are changing on all scores, but they are not yet changed. Men and women are continually voicing objections to the limited depictions of women and of both sexes in minority groups. The voices are audible but not yet clamorous.

In the next chapter we will look at psychologists' specific measurement of stereotypes as they are applied to others and to the self, and some of the implications of having stereotyped attitudes.

## KEY TERMS

| | | |
|---|---|---|
| stereotype | self-fulfilling prophecy | sexualization |
| gender stereotypes | content analysis | exception to the rule, |
| schema | parallel words | woman as exception |
| illusory correlation | infantilization | relational woman |
| assimilation | trivialization | generic masculine |
| contrast | pejoration | |

## KEY POINTS

*How Stereotypes Work*

- Sex is a primary category of responses to people and a frequent focus of stereotypes.
- Stereotypes tend to be self-perpetuating because of their influence on attention, memory, and interpretation of what we see, and because of the self-fulfilling prophecy.

*Stereotyping in the Media*

- In the media generally, women are relatively invisible; when presented, they play limited roles in which they are primarily concerned with the home and relationships with men, and their physical attributes are emphasized.
- Television generally presents girls and women in stereotypical ways, such as needing the help of others and being sexual and subservient.
- Men still are the voice of authority in TV commercials. In magazine advertisements, women and men appear about equally, but women still are associated with home and beauty products or are presented as sexual decorations.
- Popular media have overrepresented employed women and shown women disproportionately in prestigious occupations, as compared to real life, while depicting employed women as having more concern about home and family than about their work.
- TV family series have neglected single women as parents, employed women, and the feminization of poverty. There has been some increase in similarity and equal-

ity between spouses, but it is not a linear increase, as there are signs of preferring mother in the home, though without negation of the single mother. Both laboratory studies and field research show an association between exposure to stereotyped portrayals and gender stereotyping in children and adults.

◆ The 1980s was a decade of feminization in television, in part because of financial reasons and in part because of more women becoming producers. Shows featuring women are more likely to show interracial friendships and friendships with gay men and lesbians. Most are comedies.

◆ In laboratory situations, exposure to stereotyped media is associated with stereotyped behavior and judgments. Field research also shows an association between television exposure and gender stereotyping in children and adults.

◆ Photographs of men focus more exclusively on the face relative to the rest of the body, compared with photographs of women. Facial prominence is associated with more favorable perceptions of the person.

◆ Women and teenagers continue to be told to "fix up" their bodies to be attractive and sexually appealing, including being thin, smooth and hairless, and pale; this amounts to being a *white girl* rather than a white *woman* or a *woman of color.* This emphasis first appeared in the media in the 1920s when women had attained the legal right to vote.

◆ People generally think sexist humor is funnier than other humor involving women, though people with liberal attitudes like sexist humor less than others do. College women may be defensive about feminist humor.

◆ Girls and women appear relatively infrequently in educational materials for students in kindergarten through college; when presented, they are shown stereotypically, as helpless or as helpmates. Introductory and developmental psychology texts continue to perpetuate gender biases and stereotypes instead of providing more accurate views of human behavior.

### Language About Women

◆ Women often are infantilized, trivialized, pejorated, or sexualized by language. When women are presented positively, they are frequently presented as exceptions or in terms of relationships with others. Their professional titles often are not used.

◆ The generic masculine sometimes is ambiguous, ridiculous, or misleading. When exposed to it, people typically "see" or think about males more than females, with some tendency for males to do so more than females. Gender neutral characters often are described as male. Women generally are more concerned about inclusive language than men are.

## INTEGRATIVE QUESTIONS

1. What is your favorite comic or commercial TV show? Why is it your favorite? Analyze it in terms of the themes of media presentations of women.

2. "Media is just entertainment, so relax and enjoy it." What is your response to this statement?

3. Should media present an idealized view of what is possible for women (e.g., prestigious occupations, families with all problems resolved humorously), or should they present reality (e.g., women in low-level jobs, families with ongoing problems)? Describe how the media currently portray women and discuss whether or not this should change.

4. What benefits or problems do you see in the fact that most TV shows about women and about families are comedies?

5. If you wanted to be the idealized sexually attractive woman as depicted by the media, what would you do in order to be that? (Both men and women can answer this question.) What, if anything, do you do now to perpetuate or uphold the image?

6. Do you think that the generic masculine should be avoided? Lay out a plan for implementing your view, whatever it is.

*Chapter 3*

# Gender-Related Views
# of Self and Others

*I*n the previous chapters, we looked at some ways in which the media present gender stereotypes, and we considered evidence that the stereotypes make a difference in people's behavior and judgments. In many ways, that is the practical side of stereotypes—how they play out in everyday life and the media. To describe them, we used broad brush strokes (e.g., men as more important, women as attractive, relational, and home centered). Here, we will look at psychologists' attempts to measure specific aspects of what people have in mind about stereotypes of women and men in general—and about themselves with respect to those stereotypes.

This chapter is concerned with the specific attributes associated with the broad stereotypes. Are there specific data showing that people think men are more important than women, or is it just a media bias? What do people mean when they think of a woman as relational? What role does a woman's attractiveness play in how people react to her?

Psychologists have been concerned both with stereotypes about what women and men in general are like and with the related issue of how people see themselves compared to the stereotyped definitions of masculinity and femininity. A more difficult issue is that of defining the "masculinity" and "femininity" said to underlie the stereotypes of self and others. Why do we use these concepts? What are the implications of using them? We will start the inquiry into such issues by revisiting the topic of stereotypes.

In spite of many changes in women's lives, gender stereotypes are little changed over the recent past. However, they are not monolithic—they do not completely determine our views of ourselves and others. People are not helpless victims of the either-or thinking stereotypes offer. Nor do people necessarily see themselves as completely and only feminine *or* masculine. Considerations of both personal dispositions and social roles are relevant. Cognitive schema theory aims to determine how important traditional views of masculinity and femininity are to individuals in their perceptions of others and themselves. Before continuing, consider these questions for personal thought:

- ◆ How would you describe what most people consider a typical woman? A typical man? Now describe what you personally think is a typical woman. A typical man. How would you describe an ideal woman? An ideal man?
- ◆ Do you consider yourself feminine? Masculine? What do you mean by feminine or masculine?
- ◆ Why do you think stereotypes about women and men got started?
- ◆ Do you think the healthy woman is feminine and only that? Why?
- ◆ Who is more liberal in attitudes about women, men or women? Why? Older or younger people? Why?

## *Gender Stereotypes*

Stereotypes deal with what people are (personality traits), what they do (everyday role behaviors and occupational roles), and what they look like (physical appearance). We begin our discussion with personality traits because of their prominence in definitions and in research on stereotypes and because they provide the basic backdrop for many issues. We then consider them in the context of other components of stereotypes, and we raise some issues, particularly about what components are most important in generating and maintaining stereotypes.

## Some Broad Distinctions

Two broad factors recur in specific descriptions of stereotypes and personally adopted notions of masculinity and femininity. It will be helpful to consider the big picture before the details. In a provocative book, *The Duality of Human Existence* (1966), personality psychologist David Bakan identified two modes of existence or orientation that are present, he assumed, in all life forms. **Agency,** or the **agentic** orientation, is concerned with self-protection, self-aggrandizement, self-assertion, and self-preservation. Agentic values generally are assigned to men. **Communion,** or the **communal** orientation, in contrast, is concerned with group harmony, group participation, cooperation, and group preservation. Communal values generally are assigned to women.

Bakan presents balance and integration of agency and communion as the goal. Agency leads to technological advances but, if it is not mitigated or eased by the communal orientation, also leads to aggression, sexual promiscuity, destruction, death, and evil. Communion unmitigated by agency can lead to lack of self-defense and extreme subjugaton of the self to the demands of the group. Bakan suggested that in other life forms the two orientations naturally work together, but humans in Western civilization have been valuing the agentic over the communal and are in danger because

*In our culture women generally are considered to be more communally oriented—to be concerned with cooperation, group harmony, and group preservation—whereas men are considered to be more agentically oriented—concerned with competition, self-assertion, and self-preservation. Whether communally oriented or not, these women clearly feel joy in each other's company and are not uncomfortable about expressing it.*

of that. Psychologist Carl Jung's position is similar to Bakan's in seeing wholeness and psychological health as a blending of two trends, although culturally one may be emphasized more for one sex than the other rather than being accepted for both.

In a spirit similar to that of personality psychologists, sociologists Talcott Parsons and Robert Bales suggested that there are two necessary roles in groups: The **instrumental** role is concerned with competency and getting the job done. The **expressive** role is concerned with group harmony and keeping the group together so that the job can get done. In well-functioning groups, both roles are filled. Note the similarity of the sociological distinction and the personality distinction. The distinction also has been referred to more simply as "niceness-nurturance" and "potency-strength" (DeLisi & Soundranayagam, 1990).

As discussed in following sections, many psychologists involved with issues about gender stereotypes and roles have suggested that thinking in terms of instrumental or agentic qualities and of expressive or communal qualities instead of masculinity and femininity would help draw attention to basic *human* attributes shared by all. The two sets of attributes are not seen as inherently female or male. They are human attributes that have been differentially assigned so that men are expected to show agency or instrumentality, and women are expected to show communion or expressiveness. In the United States, but not all other countries, men and agency are more valued than women and communion. This means that both women and men are expected to be only "half" of a person, and "women's half" is not valued as much as "men's half."

These recurrent factors, of agency versus communion and the greater valuation of agency, are seen in the detailed studies of stereotypes.

## Themes in Stereotypes

The greater valuation of men as depicted in the media reflects the fact that there are fewer positive words in our language about women than about men (chapter 2). In stereotypes specifically, there are not as many positive words for women as for men. Probably the first major, systematic series of studies on gender stereotypes was in the 1950s (McKee & Sherriffs, 1957, 1959; Sherriffs & Jarrett, 1953; Sherriffs & McKee, 1957). Students selected adjectives that they considered "in general true of women (or men)"; adjectives were considered stereotypic only if both women and men (75% each) agreed in their judgments. The researchers encountered the problem that the number of socially desirable words applied to men outnumbered the number of socially desirable words applied to women by about 2 or 3 to 1. The number of socially undesirable words applied to women outnumbered those applied to men by about 2 or 3 to 1. Other research projects, such as the next two discussed, have had the same result.

One of the projects used the **Adjective Check List (ACL)** (Gough & Heilbrun, 1965), a list of 300 adjectives a person typically selects as being descriptive of self. Using the ACL as a measure of stereotypes, people were asked to indicate the typical characteristics of women and of men (Williams & Bennett, 1975). Studies with college students in 25 countries showed that women were seen as higher in expressive traits (e.g., affectionate, mild, sentimental), and men were seen as higher in traits reflecting activity and strength (adventurous, dominant, independent) (Williams, 1982; Williams & Best, 1982, 1990a). In the United States, of the attributes seen as characteristic of men, 10 were among the most favorable words on the ACL, and 5 were among the most unfavorable. For women, the pattern was reversed—there were 5 favorable and 10 unfavorable adjectives attributed to them (Table 3.1). However, favorability varies across cultures, so that there was no general difference in favorability of adjectives attributed to women and men across the 25 countries.

In another important project, P. S. Rosenkrantz and her colleagues (Rosenkrantz, Vogel, Bee, Broverman, & Broverman, 1968) developed the Sex Role Stereotype Questionnaire of items that both women and men agreed (75% of each) differentiated women from men *and* were seen as *valued* for either women or men. The items were empirically shown to reflect the two independent clusters, or groupings of attributes, postulated by Bakan and by Parsons and Bales. The "warmth-expressiveness" or affective dimension underlying the items valued for women included items such as tactful, gentle, and aware of feelings of others. The "competency" or instrumental dimension underlying the items valued for men included items such as aggressive, independent, and dominant. Although the attributes on the affective dimension were more valued for women, as in the previously mentioned research, there were fewer desirable items for women than for men. The warmth-expressiveness cluster had 12 items, and the competency cluster had 29 (Broverman, Vogel, Broverman, Clarkson, & Rosenkrantz, 1972). Samples are given in Table 3.2.

**Table 3.1**    Favorable and Unfavorable Adjectives
Characteristic of Women and Men

|  | *Favorable* | *Unfavorable* |
|---|---|---|
| ADJECTIVES ASSOCIATED WITH WOMEN | Affectionate<br>Appreciative<br>Attractive<br>Charming<br>Gentle | Affected<br>Complaining<br>Fickle<br>Frivolous<br>Fussy<br>Nagging<br>Prudish<br>Rattlebrained<br>Weak<br>Whiny |
| ADJECTIVES ASSOCIATED WITH MEN | Adventurous<br>Ambitious<br>Confident<br>Courageous<br>Enterprising<br>Independent<br>Logical<br>Rational<br>Realistic<br>Stable | Boastful<br>Coarse<br>Cruel<br>Disorderly<br>Loud |

NOTE: Raters were Euro-American college students, 50 women and 50 men. They were told the research interest was in the typical characteristics of women and men and asked to decide for each of 300 adjectives if it was more frequently associated with men than women or more frequently associated with women than men. The adjectives listed had previously been rated as unfavorable or favorable by another group of students.

SOURCE: Williams, J. E., & Bennett, S. M. (1975). The definition of sex stereotypes via the Adjective Check List. *Sex Roles, 1* (4), pp. 330, 331.

The fact that fewer socially desirable words and more socially undesirable words are associated with women has placed women in a catch-22. If women are "normal" (i.e., they match the stereotypes held for them), they are admitting to more negative attributes than "normal" men do; if they do not admit to more negative attributes, they are not what they should be (previously called "role resistance"). To make matters worse, one of the studies with the Rosenkrantz list showed that the descriptions given by mental health professionals of a "healthy man," but *not* of a "healthy woman," matched their descriptions of a "healthy adult" (chapter 16; Broverman, Broverman, Clarkson, Rosenkrantz, & Vogel, 1970). Women are expected to be less healthy than men! Are women simply devalued, or have we not thought as much about the positive features expected of women as of men? Perhaps both are involved. In any case, we have a demonstration of male as norm (chapter 2) and with it, greater cultural valuation of agency than of communion.

**Table 3.2**   Sample Stereotypic Sex Role Descriptors

*Warmth-expressiveness cluster:*
*feminine pole is more desirable*

| *Feminine* | *Masculine* |
| --- | --- |
| Doesn't use harsh language at all | Uses harsh language |
| Very talkative | Not at all talkative |
| Very tactful | Very blunt |
| Very gentle | Very rough |
| Very religious | Not at all religious |
| Very aware of feelings of others | Not at all aware of feelings of others |
| Very interested in own appearance | Not at all interested in own appearance |
| Easily expresses tender feelings | Does not express tender feelings at all easily |

*Competency cluster:*
*masculine pole is more desirable*

| *Feminine* | *Masculine* |
| --- | --- |
| Not at all aggressive | Very aggressive |
| Not at all independent | Very independent |
| Very emotional | Not at all emotional |
| Very subjective | Very objective |
| Very submissive | Very dominant |
| Very passive | Very active |
| Very illogical | Very logical |
| Feelings easily hurt | Feelings not easily hurt |
| Almost never acts as a leader | Almost always acts as a leader |
| Has difficulty making decisions | Can make decisions easily |

NOTE: Responses were from college students, 74 men and 80 women.

SOURCE: Broverman, I., Vogel, S. R., Broverman, D. M., Clarkson, F. E., & Rosenkrantz, P. S. (1972). Sex role stereotypes: A current appraisal. *Journal of Social Issues, 28*, (2), 59–78.

Perhaps because of the greater valuation of agency and men, *when* there are gender differences in stereotypic beliefs, men's views typically are more stereotypic than women's (Lieblich & Friedman, 1985; McPherson & Spetrino, 1983). It is also clear that men are described in more extreme terms than women, for both personality traits and appearance (Hort, Fagot, & Leinbach, 1990). In addition, men hold themselves to a more rigid standard of masculinity than women hold men to, and to a more rigid standard of conformity than men hold for women. Although there are obvious advantages to being men, as shown throughout this book, there also are psychological

**Table 3.3**    Judgments of Probability That Women and
Men Have Role-Typed Attributes

|  | Women | Men |
|---|---|---|
| TRAIT |  |  |
| Independent | .58 | .78 |
| Competitive | .64 | .82 |
| Warm | .77 | .77 |
| Emotional | .84 | .56 |
| ROLE BEHAVIOR |  |  |
| Financial provider | .47 | .83 |
| Takes initiative with opposite sex | .54 | .82 |
| Takes care of children | .85 | .50 |
| Cooks meals | .83 | .42 |
| PHYSICAL CHARACTERISTICS |  |  |
| Muscular | .36 | .64 |
| Deep voice | .30 | .73 |
| Graceful | .68 | .45 |
| Small-boned | .62 | .39 |

SOURCE: Deaux, K. (1984). From individual differences to social categories:
Analysis of a decade's research on gender. *American Psychologist, 39,* (2),
p. 112.

and physical disadvantages of the male sex role (Brooks-Harris, Heesacker, & Mejia-Millan, 1996). Attempts to change men's attitudes indicate that while men can change attitudes about the male gender role, they are much more resistant to changing their attitudes about their own gender roles or to reducing their fear of femininity. It is hypothesized that the comparatively rigid notions of masculinity lead to comparatively more rigid socialization of boys than of girls, and this then encourages application of more rigid standards to boys and men (chapter 5; Archer, 1984, 1994).

***Changes in Content of Stereotypes***    With all the recent attention to women's issues and activities, and concomitant changes in men's concerns, it is tempting to think that surely stereotypes have changed. But the truth is that clear stereotypes still exist with very little change in the specific content, according to studies from 1957 to 1990 in the United States and in other countries (Bergen & Williams, 1991; Bjerke, Williams, & Wathne, 1989; DeLisi & Soundranayagam, 1990; Werner & LaRussa, 1985). There is no evidence that either women or men are now seen as both communal and agentic. The only notable change is some reduction of the imbalance of positivity and negativity because of the addition of some positive attributes in describing women's communal orientation and the addition of some negative ones in describing men's agentic orientation. For example, the original list of 200 adjectives rated by students in 1957 was given again to students at the same university (University of California, Berkeley) in 1978 (Werner & LaRussa, 1985). The favorable adjectives added to the stereotype of women at the later time were nearly synonymous with adjectives also considered stereotypic at the earlier time, for example, considerate, friendly, sincere, cooperative.

The change for men was mainly in the addition of unfavorable elaborations of the agentic orientation, for example, bossy, demanding, show-off, hasty, rude, self-centered. The additions in both cases "heighten and intensify aspects of previously perceived differences" (Werner & LaRussa, 1985, p. 1099). The researchers underscored the fact that men still see men as being more intelligent than women, and that women still see women as being more anxious and neurotic than men.

Alice Eagly and her colleagues (Eagly & Mladinic, 1989; Eagly, Mladinic, & Otto, 1991) also have shown a favorable evaluation of women's communal qualities (e.g., helpful, gentle, kind) while noting that women still are not in advantaged social positions, such as highly paid sectors of the workforce (chapter 13). Women are seen as good people but still unequal to men. Similarly, other researchers found that women were considered likable but incompetent and unworthy of power and prestige (Fiske & Stevens, 1993).

A surface change without fundamental change occurred on the Rosenkrantz list as well (Ruble, 1983). Only *intellectual*, formerly seen as typical of men, dropped out as a stereotypical distinction between men and women (although the study by Werner and LaRussa, 1985, still found that men were seen as more *intelligent*). The ideal woman and ideal man became more alike (different on only 12 rather than 26 items), but the differences that remained were highly stereotypical. Descriptions of women included "cries easily," "gentle," "expresses tender feelings," "neat"; descriptions of men included "not excitable in minor crises," "mechanical aptitude," "acts as leader," "dominant," "good at sports." In short, there has been some greater appreciation of communal traits than previously but no real changes in stereotypes overall.

## Variations on the Basic Themes

Although stereotypes are widely shared beliefs, as with most issues psychologists study, things are not clear-cut either-or matters. This is shown in several ways. First, people do not think that only men can be aggressive or drive trucks, or that only women can be nurturing or take care of children. When people are asked to rate the *probability* that women and men or boys and girls have certain attributes, or to give the percentage of women and men they think do have the attributes, they do not show either-or thinking by giving only 100% or 0% ratings (Allen, 1995; Cota, Reid, & Dion, 1991; Deaux, 1984; C. L. Martin, 1987, 1995). For example, as shown in Table 3.3, there is not absolute certainty that a man is independent, competitive, and muscular, and there is a reasonable *probability* that a woman can have these qualities. Saying that women are seen as *more likely* to be expressive than men is not the same as saying men are not expressive. Further, these comparisons are being made with stereotypes and with self-views, and stereotypes exaggerate gender differences (C. L. Martin, 1987, 1995). There is a lot of overlap in what is considered typical of males and females. People's expectations vary when situations and subtypes are taken into account.

***Situations and Subtypes***   People seem to take the situation into account when responding to a person in the situation, and expectations about women and men vary from one situation to another (Eagly, 1987; Eckes, 1996; Lawrence, Taylor, & Byers,

1996; Lindsey & Zakahi, 1996; Orlofsky & Stake, 1981). For example, both college women and college men thought expressive traits (tenderness, caring, consideration) were expected in a sexual, dating situation in men as well as in women (Farber, 1992; Lawrence, Taylor, & Byers, 1996). Both had lower expectations of instrumentality as well as expressiveness in the classroom than "in general." The stereotypes for men, however, appear more limited across situations (Eckes, 1996; Hort et al., 1990).

People also distinguish subtypes of women and men. Subtypes of women that have been identified include feminist (self-confident, cunning, doesn't show feelings) and housewife (unattractive, obsequious, selfless, no interests of her own), as well as society lady, the maternal type, the vamp, and the secretary (Eckes, 1996; Six & Eckes, 1991). Subtypes of men include career man, the softy, the egoist, the intellectual, the macho, the cool type, and the playboy.

***Social Class and Ethnic Differences***    Stereotypes vary somewhat with social class and ethnicity, although similarity among groups is the rule, and specific differences are not always consistent from study to study (see Lips, 1993; Niemann, Jennings, Rozelle, Baxter, & Sullivan, 1994). Given that stereotypes as researched are defined predominantly by college students (mainly middle-class whites), the similarity is more remarkable than the differences. For example, white respondents described African American and white women of the middle and lower classes as basically consistent with general stereotypes. However, both social class and ethnic group made some difference. African American women of either class, and lower class women of either ethnic group, differed from the "standard" in ways that were not positive (Landrine, 1985; Weitz & Gordon, 1993).

When there are differences in gender stereotypes about African Americans and whites, African Americans are seen by themselves and by whites as less gender stereotyped than whites are. For example, in one study, African American and white undergraduates described themselves and the other group (Jackson & Tate, 1995; Jackson, Tate, & Ingram, 1995). By African American and white descriptions, African American men and women were relatively equal in instrumentality (independent, strong personality) and in expressiveness (affectionate, understanding). White women and men were seen as traditionally different from each other in these respects; the ratings for African Americans were in between the ratings of the white women and white men. The relative lack of gender differences between African American men and women probably reflects less differentiation between provider and homemaker, because the women traditionally have been employed, and may reflect a greater group cohesiveness in response to pressures of discrimination.

Other evidence with other kinds of groups also calls attention to African Americans using gender stereotypes about themselves less than whites do (Cazenave & Leon, 1987; Hatchett & Quick, 1983; Smith & Midlarsky, 1985). Among the specifics are that African Americans see fewer differences between women and men and are less likely than whites to devalue women (Dugger, 1991; O'Leary & Harrison, 1975; Smith & Midlarsky, 1985). For example, the African Americans in a large-scale study did not see women as passive, while white respondents often mentioned women as passive (Smith & Midlarsky, 1985). Lack of passivity is a repeated theme in depictions of African American women.

Although seeing women as less stereotypically feminine, by white standards of femininity, it is important to African Americans that women be feminine. African Americans rated African American women as relatively high in positive aspects of femininity (Jackson & Tate, 1995); they also saw white males as particularly low. African American women are more likely than white women to think that girls should be brought up to be feminine and boys to be masculine. But what is meant by *feminine* is different for the two groups; generally, *feminine* is seen more positively by African Americans. This difference is discussed further later in the chapter.

***Factors in Reduced Use of Stereotypes***     Clearly, strong consensual views or social stereotypes about gender are widely shared, and it would be foolhardy to say that they do not influence behavior and perceptions of other people. However, some people use stereotypes less than others do, and there are situations in which use of stereotypes is relatively minimized.

Education generally is associated with less stereotyping; for example, people who have attended college are less stereotyped than others (Hall & Frederickson, 1979; Morgan & Walker, 1983; Schaninger & Buss, 1986). The middle class tends to be less stereotyped than the working class, but the difference is not large and seems due to educational differences (Ferree, 1980; Schaninger & Buss, 1986). The indices of **socio-economic status (SES),** education, occupation, and income, are not perfectly correlated. A member of a prestigious occupation may have more education but less income than someone with a less prestigious one; some blue-collar workers have college degrees, while some owners of businesses do not. The effect of education may be a general liberalizing one and/or a specific matter of having more accurate information about diversity within groups of people, so that educated people are more likely to assimilate and contrast less (chapter 2).

There is no doubt that information helps reduce stereotypes. In contrast, when people meet in relatively ambiguous situations, such as during their initial interaction, gender stereotypes are particularly likely to be influential in forming perceptions (Deaux & Major, 1987; Lindsey & Zakahi, 1996).

The pull to use stereotypes may be offset by relevant information. **Individuating information** points to the identity of a person as a person rather than as simply a member of a group; it generally lowers stereotyping, though it is not clear that stereotyping can be easily overcome (Kunda & Sherman-Williams, 1993). College students judged the aggression of a male construction worker and a housewife equally when given information about the situation in which the aggression occurred. Without the individuating information, the judges made stereotyped assumptions about the situation of aggression and judged the construction worker to be more aggressive. They assumed the construction worker decked a coworker who had been taunting him or punched a man sitting at his favorite seat at lunch, while they assumed the housewife was disciplining a son who had hit his brother or who had tracked mud on the carpet. (After spanking the child, she apologized.) When reasons for aggression were equated, judgments of the two were equal.

Individuating information may not always work to overcome stereotypes. Stereotypes can be activated *before* the information is received and the information itself interpreted stereotypically. For example, we may know that someone is "sensitive," but

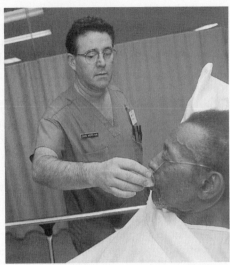

*The components of gender stereotypes tend to clump together, so that we think of people in a given occupation as having certain personality traits, physical characteristics, and role behaviors. We are forced to examine our assumptions when our expectations aren't met, such as when we encounter a male nurse or a female soldier.*

other people are likely to have different interpretations of "sensitive" and to make different inferences about other attributes of the person depending on whether the person is a man or a woman. Considering the varying components of stereotypes can help shed light on this point and help put concern about personality traits in perspective.

## Components of Gender Stereotypes

When people have information about a person other than that the person is a woman or a man, they use the information. However, a lurking problem is that they may use the information stereotypically. Kay Deaux and her colleagues see four components of gender stereotypes (Deaux, 1984; Deaux & Lewis, 1983, 1984). *Personality traits* (e.g., emotional expressiveness, self-confidence) have received most of our attention so far. The other components are *role behaviors* (e.g., child care, household repairs), *occupations* (e.g., nurse, construction worker), and *physical appearance* (e.g., small and graceful, tall and broad shouldered). Two basic issues are relevant: Do these components go together in shaping perceptions? Which component is the most important?

Regarding the first issue, people do assume the components go together to some extent (Deaux & Lewis, 1984). Being given information about a person on one dimension influences assumptions about what the person probably is like on other dimensions and contributes more to shaping views than knowing only that the person is a woman or a man (Deaux, 1984). For example, a woman described as an athlete was assumed more masculine in appearance and in personality traits than a woman not described that way. A man described as being kind and helpful was assumed to have feminine role behaviors and physical characteristics. People respond to information other than that a person is male or female, but stereotypes about what goes with what in broad masculine and feminine clusters still operate. The study showed correlations between ratings on the varying components ranging from .3 to .5. These are not high enough to suggest that people think in all-or-none categories, but they are high enough to suggest stereotypic patterns.

Which component is more important than others? Deaux's research showed that information about physical appearance led to stronger stereotyping than did information about personality attributes, roles, or occupations. A relatively limited amount of information about physical characteristics (presented verbally) was far more influential in subsequent judgments than gender label or information about other components of stereotypes (Deaux & Lewis, 1984). Also relevant is that physical attributes are just as important as psychological attributes to college students giving their own definitions of masculinity-femininity (Jackson, 1985). Other researchers have used photographs (only of women) instead of verbal descriptions of appearance to demonstrate the importance of appearance (Freeman, 1987). Women's physical attractiveness was more important in making judgments about their role behaviors than information about their traits. Curiously, the *most* attractive women were judged the *most* feminine and the *least* likely to do housework. Women face a double bind: They are supposed to be attractive and feminine, but housework is a woman's job!

## Origins of Gender Stereotyping

The current importance of physical appearance in making judgments does not necessarily mean that the other components of stereotypes are irrelevant or that appearance is responsible for the onset of the stereotypes. Alice Eagly (1987; Eagly & Steffen, 1984, 1986) has advocated a **social role theory** that says stereotypes have emerged and have been sustained because the social roles that women and men fill are different: The roles engender different attributes. Women have been more likely than men to be homemakers and child raisers, while men have been more likely than women to be breadwinners. Communal traits seem especially useful for raising children and agentic ones for providing resources. Or, to put it another way, agency does the job of ensuring family physical survival, while communal traits keep the family together socio-emotionally. Eagly proposes that there are personality differences between women and men and that those come largely (not entirely) from the fact that women and men typically have occupied the different social roles. In addition, the different social roles encourage the perception of differences in personality traits. Thus, there is a kernel of truth in the stereotypes. Although Eagly was concerned with gender stereotyping, the theory is not limited to gender: Any group that dominates in an occupational category is expected to be stereotyped.

In support of her views, Eagly demonstrated that research participants saw both women and men as more agentic and less communal when they were presented as full-time employees than when they were presented as homemakers. For part-time versus full-time or no employment, the differences for women were as expected, with increasing agency and decreasing communion as the descriptions ranged from homemaker to part-time worker to full-time employee (Eagly & Steffen, 1986). Part-time employed men were considered less agentic and less communal than those who were homemakers, perhaps because of an assumption that men employed part-time want a full-time job but are unable to get it.

Thus, it seems that social roles, employed or homemaker, lead to some stereotyped assumptions about agentic and communal personality traits. In reality, more men than women tend to be employed full-time (though the gap is decreasing, chapter 13), a fact that encourages people to think that being a woman or a man is responsible for the traits stereotypically assumed for women and for men. People seem especially likely to form stereotypes from occupational differences when there are also biological distinctions between the occupational groups (Hoffman & Hurst, 1990).

How did the division of labor between the sexes get started? One explanation is that, in earlier times at least, women had to be available to nurse their infants, placing constraints on their mobility (Hoffman & Hurst, 1990; Williams & Best, 1982). Hunting and fighting fell to the men more or less by default. Additionally, from the point of view of group survival, exposing men rather than women to dangerous activities is preferable because a group can lose most of its men and still reproduce at an acceptable rate. A man can sire a number of children in a short period of time; a woman needs 9 months to bring the man's contribution to fruition.

Today it is clear that social roles and personality traits are assumed to be related. As long as the genders are occupationally segregated as they still are (chapter 13), we may see a continuation of stereotypes about personality as well as occupational skills. People tend to think women and men are "destined" for different jobs; as long as they are in the different jobs, women and men will be thought of as having the different attributes relevant for those jobs.

It may be that division of labor and related assumptions (whether factual or not) about personality traits initiated the stereotypes, but physical appearance may be as important or more important for their continuance. Physical appearance may be the most potent source of the current operation of stereotypes in interpersonal perceptions (Deaux & Lewis, 1984; Freeman, 1987). In many initial encounters, we only see a person's physical appearance and do not have information about the person's occupation or specific traits. Physical information "becomes an obvious base on which to form judgments . . . and misjudgments" (Freeman, 1987, p. 67). Self-fulfilling prophecies (chapter 2) may start operating before we obtain other information, thus perpetuating gender stereotypes (Deaux & Lewis, 1984; Kunda & Sherman-Williams, 1993).

## Femininity and Masculinity

So far we have focused on stereotypes or beliefs about differences between the "typical" woman and the "typical" man. Now we consider concepts of femininity and masculinity from the perspective of the self-concept—to what extent do people see characteristics that are gender-typed as characteristic of them (Lewin, 1984; Williams

& Best, 1990b)? Do women incorporate societal views of femininity and men the view of masculinity? Is femininity "just natural" for a woman because she is a woman? Is femininity an asset for her? Can she be both feminine and masculine? What has been called M-F research addresses such issues.

## M-F Measurement

Anne Constantinople (1973), in one of the important papers of the 1970s (chapter 1), brought out some ways in which theory and research about femininity (F) and masculinity (M) had long been very fuzzy. Early psychologists thought of F and M as whatever distinguished females from males. This approach involved (1) the assumption of an equivalency between physical makeup and psychosocial makeup and (2) the related assumption that following gender stereotypes is normal—"it's just natural" that women should be feminine and men should be masculine. A third assumption was that F and M are opposites. This is a **bipolar** approach, with F at one end and M at the other, so that the more feminine a person is, the less masculine he or she is.

Many early **M-F** tests, as they have been called, were developed simply by choosing items that women and men answered differently in describing themselves. One test was developed by using only men as subjects, on the logic that statements the men did not endorse must indicate femininity—*a gross case of defining women from a male perspective.* The Mf scale of the Minnesota Multiphasic Personality Inventory (Hathaway & McKinley, 1943) was developed on 13 gay men in a psychiatric hospital on the erroneous assumption that gay men are feminine (chapter 10). It was never clear what the scale measured, and the revision (MMPI-2) remains ambiguous (Lewin & Wild, 1991).

*Contemporary Measurement Instruments*     Thanks to Constantinople (1973), psychologists' thinking about M-F became more sophisticated in the 1970s, though many problems remain. Femininity and masculinity are no longer thought of as opposites, nor are they assumed inherently linked to biological sex. Within a few months of each other, two improved instruments for M-F measurement appeared. They share three main features that distinguish them from previous instruments. First, both provide measures of F and of M on separate **unipolar** dimensions (low to high), so that F and M are not opposites; a person can be high on both F and M, or low on both. Second, both use a social rather than biological criterion of M-F, so that M-F is not tied to biology. Third, both aim to make the two scales equally desirable, so that feminine people are not forced to say more negative things about themselves than masculine people are.

Janet Taylor Spence, Robert Helmreich, and Judy Stapp (1975; and see Spence, 1991, 1993) developed the **Personal Attributes Questionnaire (PAQ),** based on the measure of stereotypes illustrated in Table 3.2. All items tap traits that are socially desirable for both sexes (i.e., rated by college students as characteristic of the ideal woman and ideal man) but that are considered more typical of one sex than the other. The revised short form is considered a unidimensional measure of expressiveness (rather than femininity) and instrumentality (rather than masculinity) (Cota & Fekken,

**Table 3.4**   Some Feminine and Masculine Items from the Short Form of the Bem Sex Role Inventory (BSRI)

| Feminine | Masculine |
| --- | --- |
| Affectionate | Aggressive |
| Eager to soothe hurt feelings | Defends own beliefs |
| Loves children | Dominant |
| Sensitive to others' needs | Has leadership abilities |
| Understanding | Willing to take risks |

SOURCE: Bem, S. (1980). Bem sex-role inventory professional manual. Palo Alto, CA: Consulting Psychologists Press.

1988; Helmreich, Spence, & Wilhelm, 1981; Spence, 1991; Spence & Helmreich, 1978). Note that while the challenge was to correct for the negativity of stereotypes for women, there are undesirable aspects of both sets of roles (Ricciardelli & Williams, 1995). The negative features have been relatively neglected; research indicates that they are worth additional study. A version of the PAQ, the Extended Personal Attributes Questionnaire (EPAQ), does measure the negativity of femininity and masculinity (Spence, Helmreich, & Holahan, 1979).

Sandra Bem (1974) developed the **Bem Sex Role Inventory (BSRI)** by having college students rate the social desirability of characteristics for women and men. The revised short form of the BSRI F and M scales, like that of the PAQ, describes unidimensional measures of instrumentality and expressiveness that are unrelated to each other (Table 3.4) (Ballard-Reisch & Elton, 1992; Martin & Ramanaiah, 1988; Pedhazur & Tetenbaum, 1979; Spence, 1984). The comparable, parallel scales from the PAQ and BSRI short forms are substantially but not perfectly correlated with each other ($r = .75$ for F, $r = .72$ for M) (Spence, 1991).

The PAQ and BSRI are by far the most widely used instruments for researchers interested in gender-related attributes. There are others, however, which some researchers prefer. One is a measure derived from the Adjective Check List, mentioned previously for its use in measuring stereotypes. As a measure of M-F, people check the adjectives they consider to be characteristic of themselves. Another measure is the PRF ANDRO scale, patterned after the BSRI (Berzins, Welling, & Wetter, 1978). The Fe scale from the California Personality Inventory sometimes is used (Gough, 1987), and the Mf scale of the MMPI-2 (Butcher, Dahlstrom, Graham, Tellegen, & Kaemmer, 1989) is used rarely; both are bipolar. For a look at current investigations into sex role stereotypes, see Focus on Research 3.1.

College women's scores on the scales of both the BSRI and the PAQ have increased over recent years, as have men's to a lesser extent (1973–1995; Twenge, 1997a). The result is a smaller difference between women and men on M than previously but without a comparable change on the F scales.

***The Fourfold Classification***   Spence, Helmreich, and Stapp (1975) suggested a fourfold classification, with people categorized as being above or below the median on F and on M, which is possible with the unipolar measurement of F and M as separate dimensions (Figure 3.1, p. 94). A person who scores high on both dimensions is defined as **androgynous.** A **sex-typed** person is one who scores above the median on one dimension and below on the other, being sex-typed either for one's own sex or for the other sex (cross-sex typed). Someone who is low on both dimensions is considered **undifferentiated.** Bem (1974), who introduced the notion of androgyny into the empirical research literature, originally defined it as being equal on both $(F-M = 0)$, but she adopted this system.

The classification has been useful in many studies but has been criticized for lack of reliability and loss of information (Blanchard-Fields, Suhrer-Roussel, & Hertzog, 1994; Pedhazur & Tetenbaum, 1979; Spence, 1984). A difference of only a few points can switch a person from the undifferentiated category to the androgynous category or to either of the other two categories. Loss of information refers to the fact that a person scoring very low on a scale is categorized as "low"—the same as a person scoring higher but just short of the median cutoff. Some researchers relate the F and M scales separately with other variables, without classifying people into the four categories. Studies with each kind of analysis are mentioned in this and later chapters.

*Ethnic Variation*     Some contradictions exist in what little data there are comparing white groups with African Americans, the most studied of the minority groups. When ethnic differences in self-perceptions are found, generally they are such that African American women are less conventionally feminine than white women; this parallels differences in stereotype descriptions. Victoria Binion (1990) found that African American women are more likely to describe themselves as androgynous (on the PAQ) than in other terms, as predicted because of demanding family roles, socialization practices, and cultural expectations. The distributions of general samples of African American women are similar to those for selected white women who are varsity athletes (Colker & Widom, 1980) or scientists (Spence & Helmreich, 1978).

In contrast, Hope Landrine, Elizabeth Klonoff, and Alice Brown-Collins (1992) found no overall differences in self-ratings on gender role descriptions given by college women who were white or women of color, namely, African American, Latina, and Asian American. The three groups of women of color and white women differed only in how passive they saw themselves—African American women rated themselves as significantly less passive than members of each of the other groups. Recall that both white and African American groups see African American women as less passive than they see white women.

However, an important contribution of this study lies in the fact that the researchers asked the women to indicate what they had in mind when they rated themselves. The four groups of women did not always agree on the specific meanings of the attributes to be rated. More women of color (in *each* of the three groups) saw *assertive* as meaning "say whatever's on my mind" (or "aggressive" for African American women), while white women were more likely to see it as "standing up for myself." For women of color, *assertive* and *passive* were opposites—if a woman saw herself as high on assertiveness, she was likely also to see herself low on passivity. For white

## 3.1  Reliability and Validity: Measuring Sex Roles and Sexism

Most of us, at one time or another, have responded to questionnaires. When we're finished, we may have a pretty good sense of the issues the researcher wanted to investigate, but sometimes we wonder, "What was the point of some of those questions?" Measuring behavior with a questionnaire seems simple, but a badly designed questionnaire can result in inaccurate data and erroneous conclusions.

Linda and Daniel King (1997) were interested in gender role stereotypes. They wanted to know if stereotypes about men and women were declining and if we are moving toward greater acceptance that women and men play equal roles as spouses, parents, and workers. To measure such changes, King and King developed a questionnaire they called the Sex-Role Egalitarianism Scale (SRES).

Every good questionnaire must have two qualities: reliability and validity. Reliability refers to consistency. We expect repeated measurements with the same instrument to yield basically the same results. If your bathroom scale is reliable, the weight it registers for you on Monday and again on Tuesday should not differ much. If you weigh 140 pounds on Monday and 150 pounds on Tuesday, it's likely the scale is unreliable. Questionnaires, like bathroom scales, need to be reliable in their measurement of attitudes, beliefs, or the like.

The reliability of the questionnaire can be established in several ways. Using a single administration of the questionnaire, the researcher can assess the consistency of each participant's responses from item to item by computing a reliability measure called "coefficient alpha." The split-half method of determining reliability is also based on a single administration. Participants complete the questionnaire once; then the questions are randomly split into two equal sets and the two sets of responses compared for consistency. In the test-retest method, participants complete the same questionnaire at two different times. The comparison of the two sets of responses indicates the questionnaire's reliability. A major drawback to the test-retest method is boredom; respondents may not pay as much attention the second time through.

A fourth way to measure reliability is the alternate-forms method, which is the procedure used by King and King to illustrate the reliability of their scale. They created twice as many questions as needed for one scale and randomly divided them into two scales. Respondents then completed version one at one sitting and version two at the second sitting. Since the forms are comparable, comparison of the two sets of answers indicates the consistency of response and the reliability of the overall scale. The various methods of establishing a questionnaire's reliability are equally accepted by researchers.

The second quality a good questionnaire must have is validity. Does the questionnaire measure what it claims to measure? There are several different types of validity. Face validity refers to the appearance and presentation of the questionnaire. A "Survey of Religious Values" should ask questions about religious beliefs, not political issues. Content validity means the questionnaire covers the topic being studied. If we are investigating race relations, our instrument must measure interactions among all ethnic groups in a variety of situations, not just how middle-class African Americans and whites respond to each other. Predictive validity can be demonstrated if the score on the questionnaire can predict some future behavior. College entrance tests such as the ACT or SAT are very good predictors of a student's eventual college performance; these tests demonstrate a high degree of predictive validity.

Construct validity is perhaps the most important type of validity to psychologists. It involves understanding the abstract idea (the construct) being measured by continually seeing how the measures relate to other measures. Construct validity can be broken down into two complementary factors: convergent validity and discriminant validity. Responses to one questionnaire should be related to those on a second questionnaire if the two are measuring similar topics; this is called convergent validity. Conversely, if two questionnaires are measuring two very different topics, scores on each questionnaire should differ from each other; this is called discriminant validity. King and King demonstrated the construct validity of their Sex-Role Egalitarianism Scale by showing that responses on the SRES, which measures gender-role attitudes, were closely related to responses on other gender-role attitude scales, such as the Attitudes Toward Women Scale (Spence & Helmreich, 1972). Although each scale measures a specific attitude domain, we logically expect some relationship between the two domains. This similarity of responses on the two scales illustrates the SRES's convergent validity. On the other hand, people's responses on the SRES were not related to their responses on the Bem Sex Role Inventory (Bem, 1974), which measures one's gender-related traits. This difference shows the discriminant validity of the SRES. This pattern of convergent and discriminant validity supports King and King's claim that the SRES is really measuring what it says it is measuring: gender-role attitudes related to egalitarianism.

It is important that any instrument used to measure behavior be both reliable and valid. These two criteria are connected; a questionnaire or test can be reliable (it measures consistently) without being valid (we may not know what is being measured). However, the instrument cannot be valid if it is not reliable. There are many questionnaires in use today, and the best advice is "respondent beware." Before you place too much stock in your score on any questionnaire, ask about its reliability and validity; both are necessary for a good questionnaire. With the use of techniques such as split-half reliability and convergent and discriminant validity, King and King provided concrete evidence that their scale not only consistently measured our attitudes about egalitarianism in gender roles but also truly measures what it sets out to measure.

JILL BORCHERT ◆

SOURCES: Bem, S. L. (1974). The measurement of psychological androgyny. *Journal of Consulting and Clinical Psychology, 42,* 155–162. King, L. A., & King, D. W. (1997). Sex-Role Egalitarianism Scale: Development, psychometric properties, and recommendations for future research. *Psychology of Women Quarterly, 21,* 71–87. Spence, J. T., & Helmreich, R. (1972). The Attitudes Toward Women Scale: An objective instrument to measure attitudes toward the rights and roles of women in contemporary society. *JSAS: Catalog of Selected Documents in Psychology, 2,* 66–67. (Ms. No. 153.)

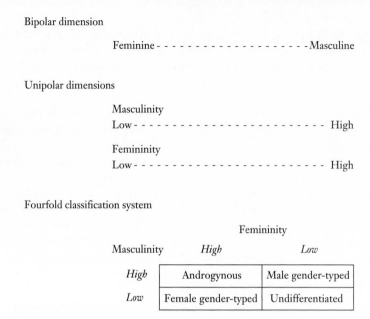

**Figure 3.1** *Conceptions of masculinity-femininity.*

women, there was no relationship between those two attributes. This may be because of different interpretations of the terms: A woman can stand up for herself while still being what the white women considered passive, namely, "laid-back/easygoing."

Another difference of interpretation was of *feminine*. Women of color and white women both tended to see *feminine* as involving traits as well as physical appearance, but women of color more often than white women defined it as involving only traits, with appearance being irrelevant. This is consistent with other evidence indicating that women of color are less likely than white women to show strong concern about stereotypes of feminine attractiveness (chapters 2, 16). Unfortunately, researchers seldom go to the extent these researchers did to uncover cultural differences behind the numbers they analyze. The issue of what is being measured by M-F scales is difficult enough when we do not know what people are thinking as they fill out the instruments.

## Criticisms and Defenses of M-F Research

A bandwagon effect followed the introduction of the BSRI and PAQ, with researchers climbing on board for a piece of the action without thinking about who was driving or where they were going (Mednick, 1989). Thanks in part to that early and careless proliferation of research using the new instruments, even modern M-F research has a bad name among some psychologists. Phyllis Katz (1996) suggested that in the 1980s, "this interesting concept [androgyny] got bogged down in nitpicking" (p. 333). She suggests using the term *flexibility* instead of androgyny. Amid the nitpicking, many questions were raised and appropriately so. Consideration of the criticisms has brought some progress in understanding of androgyny, or flexibility.

*Narrowness*   One criticism of M-F research is that the scales are too narrow to be considered measures of masculinity-femininity. Certainly, the scales are measuring *only* psychological attributes, and those alone cannot be called exhaustive definitions of masculinity-femininity. But whether they are measuring even psychological masculinity-femininity itself is questioned. Although some researchers continue to refer to the scales as M and F measures (Whitley, 1983, 1985), others now clearly consider both the PAQ and BSRI (short forms) to be measures of only gender stereotypic instrumental and expressive traits that are socially desirable for both sexes (Ballard-Reisch & Elton, 1992; Spence, 1991, 1993). It is the ability of the scales to measure abstract general constructs such as masculinity-femininity or of gender role orientation or of gender identity that is questioned.

We have seen already that what African American and white women mean by *feminine* is different. In addition, standard instruments may not measure what white people mean either (Jackson, 1985), and men and women may mean different things by *masculinity* and *femininity* (Blanchard-Fields et al., 1994). In later chapters, expressiveness and instrumentality or agency and communion are typically referred to rather than femininity and masculinity, unless there is some reason to do otherwise, such as because of different measuring procedures or researchers' theories. At a minimum, we must remember that the PAQ and BSRI measure only a "slice" of whatever psychological femininity and masculinity mean in community thought.

*Perpetuation of Stereotypes*   Another criticism of M-F research is that use of the terms feminine and masculine reinforces stereotypes and assumptions that the traits referred to are inherently female and male. This criticism does not necessarily pose a problem if you stop to think about operational definitions. The use of the constructs agentic and communal or instrumental and expressive is a step away from stereotyped notions of biological inherence. Most researchers assume that the dimensions are socially learned aspects of self-image, and they tend to view the instruments simply as indicators of gender relevant aspects of a person's self-concept (Lewin, 1984).

In fact, an advantage of the PAQ and BSRI and the thinking accompanying them is that they provide a way to consider issues related to gender stereotypes that does not pit women against men but enables seeing commonalities between some women and some men in contrast to other women and men. A frequent finding is that both women and men in a category (e.g., androgynous, feminine) behave similarly to each other in a way that differentiates them from people in other categories. For example, androgynous and feminine people—whether women or men—more freely express affection for their partners than do the people in other categories (Antill, 1983; Kurdek & Schmitt, 1986). A related point is that the scales are one way of measuring differences among women (chapter 1). In fact, we will see frequent differences among women as a function of different scores on the PAQ or BSRI.

So far, the concept of androgyny is the closest we have come to studying persons who possess desirable aspects of the gender roles but who are not bound by traditional

*Women of all ages have more liberal, nontraditional attitudes toward women than men do. More so than men, they believe that women should have greater freedom and equality in their roles, rights, and responsibilities. One explanation for these attitude differences is that women believe they have something to gain from a change in the status quo, whereas men believe they have something to lose.*

expectations. Some, however, have suggested that androgyny be considered a transcendence of gender roles rather than equal endorsement of F and M (Block, 1973; Heilbrun, Friedberg, Wydra, & Worobow, 1990; Loevinger, 1976; Rebecca, Hefner, & Oleshansky, 1976; see chapter 5). Early on, Bem (1974) stated that the concept of androgyny contains the seeds of its own destruction, implying that it connotes being "above and beyond" gender-typing; the more androgyny is achieved, the less relevant masculinity and femininity will become.

If Bakan, Jung, and Parsons are correct about the fundamental nature of the orientations they identify, then current M-F measures are a reasonable start. At a minimum, the research has challenged long-held assumptions that women are "supposed to be" one way and men another way, as shown by evidence about adjustment.

## Gender-Typing and Adjustment

Bem originally championed androgynous people as ideal because of their flexibility and ability to respond appropriately across more situations than a sex-typed person could (Bem & Lenney, 1976). This claim immediately attracted a lot of attention because it attacked long-held assumptions. Psychologists and probably most people had long assumed that a person needed to have a role orientation consistent with his or her sex in order to be healthy and happy: A woman should be feminine and a man should be masculine. This is the **traditional** or **congruence model** of adjustment (Whitley, 1983, 1988). Because of the newer conceptualizations of M-F, this view was questioned, and the **androgyny model** was favored: Androgynous people were assumed the healthiest because they possessed a broader range of skills and competencies than individuals with only one set of characteristics (Kelly & Worell, 1977).

A variety of studies have shown a general advantage for both male and female adolescents and adults who are androgynous (see Antill & Cunningham, 1979). For example, androgynous college students (by the short BSRI) more often described themselves in response to a cue, "I am . . ." in positive terms and less often in negative terms (Jackson, 1985). Also, androgynous college students (being female or male did not matter) who experienced a high number of negative events during the 8 weeks of the college quarter did not become more depressed; whereas those who were instrumental or expressive (but not both) did become more depressed with negative life changes; and the expressive students were more inclined to depression than the instrumental students (Roos & Cohen, 1987). Similarly, androgynous students report better health practices than others (Shifren & Bauserman, 1996).

***General Adjustment, Masculinity, and Femininity***   Continuing research strongly supports the **masculinity model:** Masculine people of either gender are assumed to have better general adjustment. Androgynous people, like those classed as masculine, are high in masculinity, and masculinity alone may be the critical element in general adjustment as defined in this culture (Antill & Cunningham, 1979, 1980; Kelly & Worrell, 1977; O'Heron & Orlofsky, 1990; Orlofsky & O'Heron, 1987; Whitley, 1983, 1985, 1988). There are exceptions to be sure, but the general pattern is that, for both women and men, masculinity is a positive correlate for *general* measures of adjustment, such as general self-esteem, lack of depression, and lack of anxiety (Stein, Newcomb, & Bentler, 1992). And, instrumentality at age 12 predicted the adjustment of both women and men when they were ages 31 and 41 (Aubé & Koestner, 1992).

One possible reason for the pattern is that masculine characteristics have broader adaptive significance for a person than feminine characteristics do (Jones, Chernovetz, & Hanson, 1978; Orlofsky & Stake, 1981; Whitley, 1983, 1985, 1988). Another and related hypothesis is that in Western society masculine traits are more highly valued than feminine traits. The relationship of instrumentality, as a part of masculinity, to general adjustment may be due to self-esteem (Feather, 1985; Tennen & Herzberger, 1987; Whitley, 1983, 1985, 1988). It may not be possible to clearly disentangle instrumentality, self-esteem, and culture. Self-esteem is based on having the traits considered important in the culture, and so far in Western cultures, those traits have been ones associated more with the instrumentality ascribed and encouraged for men than with the expressiveness ascribed and encouraged for women.

The role of femininity for general adjustment is less clear. Generally, F is depicted as having minimal or no effect on women's general adjustment (e.g., see Aubé & Koestner, 1992). It is clear that relative lack of femininity is not a problem for women *if* they are high in masculinity—cross-sex-typed women, as well as androgynous women, have scored higher on self-esteem and other adjustment indices than feminine-typed and undifferentiated women (Cook, 1985; Jones et al., 1978; Kelly & Worrell, 1977; Whitley, 1983, 1988). Men, however, do not have as much freedom to deviate from their ascribed role as women do. Cross-sex-typed men appear less well adjusted than sex-typed men, though men are not disadvantaged by femininity if they are high in masculinity as well (Table 3.5; O'Heron & Orlofsky, 1990). This is consistent with the principle noted earlier that role pressures are stronger on males

**Table 3.5**    Depression and Anxiety Scores for Women and Men of Differing Gender Role Categories

|  | Depression | Anxiety |
|---|---|---|
| **WOMEN** | | |
| Androgynous | 4.39 | 37.87 |
| Masculine | 5.55 | 35.95 |
| Feminine | 7.50 | 42.47 |
| Undifferentiated | 8.68 | 44.84 |
| **MEN** | | |
| Androgynous | 5.58 | 37.61 |
| Masculine | 7.28 | 37.61 |
| Feminine | 5.48 | 42.92 |
| Undifferentiated | 11.02 | 48.76 |

NOTE: Participants were college students, 94 men and 141 women. Sex role traits were measured by the long form of the BSRI. Depression was measured by the Beck Depression Inventory, and anxiety was measured by the STAI, assessing the general frequency of anxiety symptoms.

SOURCE: O'Heron, C. A., & Orlofsky, J. L. (1990). Stereotypic and nonstereotypic sex role trait and behavior orientations, gender identity, and psychological adjustment. *Journal of Personality and Social Psychology, 58,* (1), p. 138.

than on females. For a look at another area of adjustment and gender role, see Focus on Research 3.2.

***Putting Femininity and Masculinity in Context***    Many women do not want to be told that they are supposed to be feminine, but neither are they comfortable being told that being feminine is irrelevant or possibly detrimental to their mental health. The challenge is not for women to become like men; it is one of recognizing two basic human tendencies—the agentic and the communal—and the role of each in healthy human development. There is a sense in which women should become more like men, but there is an equally important sense in which men should become more like women. Psychologists have started to see this and to consider positive correlates of femininity.

The **differentiated androgyny model** posits that the relative contribution of M and F will differ according to the facet of self-concept that is relevant to the behavior or situation; researchers should not blindly assume that everything positive is related to androgyny or to masculinity (Kirchmeyer, 1996; Marsh, 1987; Marsh & Byrne, 1991; Orlofsky & O'Heron, 1987). Generally, for both women and men, F is positively associated with measures of social self-esteem, though sometimes M is as well (or more strongly so), presumably because of the self-confidence associated with M (Payne, 1987; Whitley, 1983). Feminine traits contribute to self-perceived effectiveness in and enjoyment of social interaction and to satisfaction with one's interpersonal relationships (Orlofsky & Stake, 1981). They also are more highly related than masculine ones to measures of congeniality and sociability (Orlofsky & O'Heron, 1987) and are of value in increasing meaningful friendships and decreasing loneliness (chapter 10). Attesting to this, heterosexual married couples and lesbian and gay couples are happier if at least one person is high in femininity (Antill, 1983; Kurdek & Schmitt, 1986). And femininity is an asset, along with instrumentality, in some occupations. Among women employed as nurses (Steenbarger & Greenberg, 1990) and those in the field of special education (Eichinger, Heifetz, & Ingraham, 1991), women who were high in both F and M had the least vocational distress and depression. The results likely would be the same for men, given the strong instrumental and interpersonal demands of the professions.

The effects of an attribute, whether M-F or anything else, will vary with the circumstances a person is in, and circumstances, in turn, vary with one's developmental stage (Cunningham & Antill, 1984; Lyons & Green, 1988). What is adaptive in one situation or at one life phase may not be at another. Expressiveness may be useful in a child's world, but it loses relevance to esteem as children, especially girls, grow into adolescence (chapter 5). Adults' scores on F and M measures vary with life stages (chapters 12, 14; e.g., Abrahams, Feldman, & Nash, 1978; Cunningham & Antill, 1984). Women and men generally become more gender-typed in their parenting years, for example, and later become less typed.

## Other Aspects of Thinking About Gender

How are self-concepts of M-F related to other views about gender? Does one large factor explain views about gender in others and in one's self? To understand, we need to look at attitudes and then at the schema theories that try to tie together the varying aspects of gender.

### Attitudes Toward Women

Although there are many measures of attitudes toward women, the most widely used (Beere, 1990; McHugh & Frieze, 1997) is the brief form of the **Attitudes Toward Women Scale (AWS)** (Spence & Helmreich, 1972; Spence, Helmreich, & Stapp, 1973), developed to measure beliefs about women's roles, rights, and responsibilities. Issues relevant to women are not necessarily the same today as they were 25 years ago. Yet the AWS seems to tap a basic underlying dimension of sex role ideology and is correlated with a contemporary measure of affect toward women (Buhrke, 1988; Swim & Cohen, 1997). For a sample of items on one version of the AWS, see A Closer Look 3.1 (p. 102).

***Gender Differences and Change***   In contrast to stereotypes, which have not changed much over the years, attitudes have become more liberal or equalitarian, with women

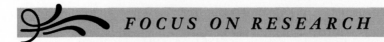

## FOCUS ON RESEARCH

### 3.2    Correlational Research: Uncovering Relationships Between Gender Role and Disturbed Eating

The eating disorders of anorexia and bulimia have generated a great deal of research focusing on the symptoms and treatments for these disorders. However, researchers also want to identify those who are at risk, with an eye toward intervention and prevention. Because it is mainly young women who develop eating disorders, it is logical to wonder if there is something about being female or feminine that is related to developing anorexia or bulimia. We do know that for both men and women masculinity is linked with better general adjustment in several areas of mental health. Is it possible that masculinity is also a factor in avoiding eating disorders?

You probably have noticed that the previous paragraph seems to hedge the connection between gender role and eating disorders, with phrases like "masculinity is linked with . . ." and "femininity is related to . . . ." You won't read that being masculine or feminine *causes* an eating disorder. This language is a giveaway that studies in this area are *correlational*.

Research that categorizes participants into groups based on preexisting qualities (sometimes called status variables), such as masculinity or femininity, is correlational research. In contrast, experimental research relies on randomly placing participants into categories; researchers generally accept that the groups of participants are basically the same before their experimental treatment or exposure. Since the experimental treatment is the only thing that differs between the groups of participants, researchers are in a better position to claim that the treatment *caused* any subsequent changes in participants' behavior.

In correlational research, there is no treatment or exposure. Instead, the participants bring the thing we want to study, their status variable, with them into the study. But along with this status variable may come other life experiences that might systematically influence our findings. The researcher cannot assume that groups of participants categorized according to their status variable are comparable to each other. In other words, researchers have less control over outside factors that might affect participants' behavior. When these outside factors can't be ruled out (controlled), we can't claim with any certainty that the one factor we're interested in (the status variable) caused the change in participants' behavior. The general rule is that correlational research can tell us if two things are related, but it can't tell us if one causes the other.

Sometimes correlational research is the only way we can study certain behaviors. Rita Snyder and Lynn Hasbrouck (1996) wanted to know if women's gender roles and feminist identity, two status variables, were connected to body image and disturbed eating. They could not randomly assign masculine or feminine traits to the women, nor could they randomly hand out different levels of feminist identity. They were forced to approach their research question using a correlational design.

Questionnaires were used to gather information from 71 college women concerning their feminine and masculine traits, how much they identified themselves as feminists, and how they felt about their bodies and eating. Then Snyder and Hasbrouck analyzed the data, which produced several correlation coefficients, symbolized by $r$. Each $r$ illustrates both the direction and the strength of the relationship between two variables. (A variable is some behavior that differs among people and that we are interested in measuring.) The direction of the correlation is noted by a positive or negative sign. A positive sign indicates that as scores on one variable increase, scores on the second variable also increase (think about the relationship between study time and exam grades). A negative sign indicates that as scores on one variable increase, scores on the other decrease (think of the relationship between grades and amount of time spent watching television). The strength of the relationship is indicated by the actual number of the correlation, which can range from .00 (no relationship) to 1.00 (a perfect relationship in which each variable equally affects the other). Snyder and Hasbrouck found that $r = +.34$ for masculine traits and perfectionism (a trait often found among anorexics and bulimics), and $r = +.13$ for feminine traits and perfectionism. While both of these correlations are positive, it is the masculine, not the feminine, gender role that is more strongly linked to one common characteristic of eating disorders, perfectionism—contrary to what we might expect. Snyder and Hasbrouck also found that the stronger a woman's feminist identity, the less concerned she was about being thin ($r = -.28$), and the less dissatisfied she was with her body shape ($r = -.25$). Feminist identity appears to be linked to more positive feelings about one's weight and body.

Even though correlational studies do not allow us to make those much valued cause-and-effect statements, we should not sell them short. Understanding how a woman's traits and identity are related to feelings about her body and possible disordered eating is an important step in understanding a devastating mental illness. Correlational research allows us to investigate status variables that can have a powerful influence in our lives.

JILL BORCHERT ◆

SOURCE: Snyder, R., & Hasbrouck, L. (1996). Feminist identity, gender traits, and symptoms of disturbed eating among college women. *Psychology of Women Quarterly, 20*, 593–598.

*A Closer Look*

### 3.1    Sample Items From the Attitudes Toward Women Scale

On the Attitudes Toward Women Scale, each item is rated on a five-point scale ranging from (1) disagree strongly to (5) agree strongly. The scoring for some items is reversed, so high scores may reflect a more liberal, less traditional, position than low scores.

SAMPLE ITEMS
1. It sounds worse when a woman swears than when a man does.
2. There should be more women leaders in important jobs in public life, such as politics.
3. It is worse to see a drunken woman than a drunken man.
4. A woman should be as free as a man to propose marriage.
5. Women earning as much as their dates should pay for themselves when going out with them.
6. A woman's place is in the home looking after her family rather than following a career of her own.
7. Girls nowadays should be allowed the same freedom as boys, such as being allowed to stay out late.

SOURCE: Nelson, M. C. (1988). Reliability, validity, and cross-cultural comparisons for the simplified Attitudes Toward Women Scale. *Sex Roles, 18,* (5/6), p. 292.

changing more rapidly than men (Spence & Hahn, 1997; Twenge, 1997). The general pattern is that women in all age groups and at all time periods (1972–1995) score significantly more liberal or nontraditional in their attitudes toward women than men do (McKinney, 1987; Nelson, 1988; Spence & Hahn, 1997; Spence & Helmreich, 1978, 1979; Twenge, 1997b). Scores from one study (college students only) are shown in Figure 3.2. Exceptions to women's greater liberality occurred only on two items for college students in 1992 (Spence & Hahn, 1997). Specifically, women were less likely than men to agree that a woman with as much money as her date should share dating expenses and were less likely to agree that a woman should be as free as a man to propose marriage.

The greatest liberality of women has also been shown quite consistently for adolescents of different cultures (e.g., see Basow, 1986; Gibbons, Stiles, & Shkodriani, 1991; Seginer, Karayanni, & Mar'i, 1990). For example, among 11- to 17-year-olds from 46 different countries, attending schools in the Netherlands, girls responded less traditionally than boys did on the adolescent form of the AWS (Gibbons et al., 1991). Adolescents from wealthier, more individualistic countries had more liberal attitudes than those from less wealthy, more collectivist countries (Gibbons et al., 1991). For example, students in the United States were less traditional than those in Fiji (Basow, 1982) and Spain (Pérez-Prada, Shkodriani, Medina, Gibbons, & Stiles, 1990).

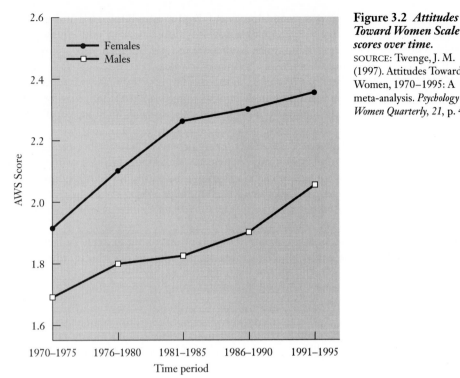

**Figure 3.2** *Attitudes Toward Women Scale scores over time.*
SOURCE: Twenge, J. M. (1997). Attitudes Toward Women, 1970–1995: A meta-analysis. *Psychology of Women Quarterly, 21*, p. 42.

Higher education and incomes have been associated with less traditional attitudes among African Americans in the United States (Binion, 1990; Hershey & Hill, 1978) and among whites in the United States and Britain; but American working-class women are more liberal than comparable British women (Nelson, 1988). With some exceptions, younger people are more liberal than older ones, when comparing people over 40 with those under 40 (Nelson, 1988). High school and college women are more liberal than their mothers, and college men are more liberal than their fathers; high school–age men are most traditional among the men's groups, perhaps reflecting adolescent pressures on them (Spence & Helmreich, 1978, 1979). However, within groups of younger people and within groups of middle-aged adults, age is associated with increasing liberalism. This has been shown for Israeli Jewish adolescents (Seginer et al., 1990); American college students (mostly 18–22 years old; McKinney, 1987); and for married couples studied over a 5-year period (McBroom, 1987).

***Reasons for Gender Differences in Attitudes***    Why are girls and women more liberal than boys and men? The main suggestion has been that girls and women are less invested in maintaining the status quo, in which they have lower status and less free-dom than boys and men. In contrast, boys and men are invested in maintaining the status quo and their greater status and freedom (chapter 10). Thus, girls and women think they have more to gain by a change toward more freedom and equality for women, whereas boys and men think they have more to lose. But men, too, are capable of seeing advantages of more liberalism about gender roles.

The fundamental disparity of views, not always large, is important enough to be a source of tension in dating and then in marriage (chapter 10). With increasing experience in the world, women see more clearly the disadvantages they face and come more to question whether things have to be the way they are. For married women, becoming more liberal was associated with entering new roles, namely, becoming married, becoming a mother, and becoming employed (McBroom, 1987). For men, becoming more liberal was associated with continuing to be married. Perhaps continuing to live with and care for a woman sensitizes men to the pressures on women; it is also true that divorced men are more conservative than divorced women, relative to married men and women (chapter 10).

Attitudes are related to other aspects of perceptions about gender. Because this issue is embroiled in debates about schema, we will consider schema theories first.

## Gender Schema

As discussed in chapter 2, a schema is a framework that serves to organize and direct understanding of information. Being strongly schematic for gender means that a person sorts attributes and behavior into categories related to gender when other cognitive organizations could be useful. The general schematic approach has been shown useful in contributing to understanding of children's gender-typed development (chapter 5) and of adult depression (see Burger, 1997). Its promise for understanding gender in adults is not yet really clear.

***Sandra Bem and Hazel Markus***    There are three major theories about the applicability of gender schema to adults' gender-typing. Each theorist has evidence supporting her position, but the evidence is challenged by others. There is some agreement among the theories, but they differ in important respects. Clearly, some people are more strongly schematic for gender than others. Exactly who is schematic for what is at issue.

Two of the three major theories agree that traditional gender-typed people are gender schematic for material related to their own gender, namely, feminine women for feminine material and masculine men for masculine material. These theories are Sandra Bem's **gender schema theory** and Hazel Markus's **self-schema theory.** They differ on exact predictions for other groups and other kinds of material, and no clear picture can be drawn from the research at this point (Koivula, 1995). For example, Bem predicts that androgynous people will not be schematic for either feminine or masculine material, as if they are above or beyond the notion of gender. Markus predicts that androgynous people will be schematic for both feminine and masculine material, reflecting a view that both aspects of gender are self-relevant to androgynous people. Bem (1981b) reported evidence for her views; Markus (1977) reported evidence for her views. Other researchers have challenged both Bem's and Markus's results (e.g., see Archer & Smith, 1990; Edwards & Spence, 1987; Kite & Deaux, 1986b; Payne, Connor, & Colletti, 1987).

Researchers, however, have shown that people with conventional gender-typing will process information about others more stereotypically (Frable, 1989; Hudak, 1993; Koivula, 1995; Lindsey & Zakahi, 1996). For example, sex-typed individuals attended to the sex of job applicants and devalued women, and sex-typed men were more likely to provide only masculine names in response to the generic masculine. The third major gender schema theory, a multifactorial approach, suggests that Bem and Markus are too simple in their approaches.

*Janet Spence: A Multifactorial Approach*     The third major gender schema theory is based on a **multifactorial approach** in which gender role orientation consists of personality attributes, stereotypes, attitudes, behaviors, social relationships, interests, abilities, values, and so on (Ashmore, 1990; Blanchard-Fields et al., 1994; Di Dio, Saragovi, Koestner, & Aubé, 1996; Edwards & Spence, 1987; Spence, 1984, 1985, 1991, 1993). Janet Spence (1991) suggests that gender role *attitudes* are more predictive than gender-linked personality traits are; the people expected to be schematic are those with strong gender role attitudes and gender stereotypes. In her view, many factors shape gender development, so that the particular sets of gender-relevant characteristics people happen to possess define their *personal* sense of masculinity or femininity. Therefore, no single general instrument, such as the PAQ and BSRI, will tap that (Spence & Sawin, 1985). Research shows the Spence view is productive and useful (Koestner & Aubé, 1995).

Later discussion about the development of gender-typing in children (chapter 5) supports a multifactorial position more than a single factor position. As predicted, individuals high on the AWS and another measure showed more gender clustering than did other subjects. (The other measure was of a tendency to modify behavior in situations with clear gender role demands; Edwards & Spence, 1987.) Conservative views expressed on the AWS are correlated substantially with stereotyped views of women and men in personality traits and role-related behavior. Correlations of both the PAQ and BSRI with AWS are low but sometimes significant, with a pattern suggesting a trend for more liberal attitudes in people with cross-sex-typed traits—that is, high M in women, high F in men (see Spence, 1991).

At best, we can conclude that some people are more schematic or stereotypic than others. The more schematic people are those who are most stereotyped, such as in their views of themselves and/or in their attitudes. More definitive statements about schematic theories are not yet justified by current evidence.

## *Some Final Thoughts: Issues of Femininity and Humanness*

Society has ascribed the communal and expressive dimensions of humanness to women and the agentic and instrumental dimensions to men. With all the activities by and for women of recent years, women and men still are not expected to be agentic as well as communal. An individual still is expected to be only "half human," and the expectations are based on criteria over which individuals have no direct personal control. The half assigned to women is less valued in the United States than the half assigned to men. The differential evaluation contributes to women's greater liberalism and desire to change the status quo. It may also contribute to men's greater concern about their own stereotyping and to holding themselves to rigid standards of masculinity.

The lack of positive evaluation of communion relative to agency is related to adjustment. Attributes expected of men are more strongly associated with general adjustment than those expected of women. Attributes associated with women are related to social relationships, but they are accorded less explicit value than more "manly" aspects of life. When these facts are considered along with the tendency noted in the previous chapter to equate *person* with *man*, it is easy to see how people might think that women are not expected to be "real" people, of equal value to men. Girls are not expected to become women who are as healthy and as human as men are.

The original notion of androgyny, and indeed comments such as those just made, have been criticized as suggesting that women should be more like men. The important message is that both women and men should be "released" to be more fully human. Women can profit from the agency previously claimed only for men. But so, too, can men profit from the communion previously claimed only for women. To forget the interpersonal dimensions of human potential is to see only from the view of male as normative.

Of course, "everyone knows" that people generally are not carbon copies of the stereotyped roles ascribed to them, and, of course, both girls and boys should be free to become all they can be. Yes, but "everyone knows" that the generic masculine refers to women as well as to men, but they are more likely to think of men than of women when seeing or hearing it. Why do people still agree on the basic views of what women are and what men are? Why do the stereotypes persist basically unchanged, with only partially human views of each? Carl Jung suggested that a half person is really a zero, and two zeros do not add up to one. All the more reason for both women and men to develop as much of their human potential as they can.

## KEY TERMS

agency, agentic
communion, communal
instrumental
expressive
Adjective Check List
  (ACL)
socioeconomic status
  (SES)
individuating information
social role theory
bipolar

M-F
unipolar
Personal Attributes
  Questionnaire (PAQ)
Bem Sex Role Inventory
  (BSRI)
androgynous
sex-typed
undifferentiated
traditional or congruence
  model

androgyny model
masculinity model
differentiated androgyny
  model
Attitudes Toward Women
  Scale (AWS)
gender schema theory
self-schema theory
multifactorial approach

# KEY POINTS

## Gender Stereotypes

◆ Stereotypes most often are measured by a trait-adjective method and have more socially desirable traits attributed to men than to women; changes in recent years are few. Men hold themselves to rigid standards.

◆ Stereotypes are not either-or matters but rather probabilistic. Education is associated with reduced stereotyping. There are subtypes of women and of men. African American men and women are seen as differing less from each other than white women and men.

◆ Personality traits, behaviors, occupations, and physical appearance are components of gender stereotypes. Judgments about them are interrelated but not perfectly, so perceived status on one does not necessarily dictate perceived status on another. Attractive women are judged more feminine than others but are seen as less likely to do household tasks.

◆ Judgments about personality characteristics vary with the social role of the person. Eagly suggested that social role division was responsible for the origin of stereotypes.

## Femininity and Masculinity

◆ Psychologists now see femininity and masculinity as two separate dimensions, so that people may be classified as high on both M and F or low on both, or high on one and low on the other.

◆ The most popular M-F measuring instruments, the BSRI and PAQ (short forms), measure only positive personality attributes—specifically, aspects of instrumentality and expressiveness—which are not all there is to masculinity and femininity.

◆ African American women are not as gender-typed as white women. Women of different ethnic groups do not necessarily interpret items on inventories in the same way.

◆ Contemporary gender-typing scales have been used carelessly and are criticized for measuring only part of what is meant by M-F, perpetuating stereotypes, and inviting biological explanations. They provide a way to see individual differences within gender groups and similarities between groups of women and groups of men.

◆ A masculinity model of adjustment is the most supported model for correlates of general adjustment; masculinity is more advantageous for women than femininity is for men. However, for social adjustment, femininity is advantageous for both.

## Other Aspects of Gender

◆ Both women and men have become progressively more liberal in attitudes toward women. However, within all age groups, women are more nontraditional than men, perhaps because of status differences.

◆ There is some evidence that people who are traditionally gender-typed are more schematic in judgments of themselves and others than are people of other categories, about whom degree of schematization is not clear. Spence's theory and evidence suggest that people who are schematic about gender are those with strong role attitudes and stereotypes.

## INTEGRATIVE QUESTIONS

1. Characterize what you mean by femininity and masculinity; compare your views with those of psychologists. Comment on why psychologists should or should not be concerned with femininity and masculinity.

2. To what do you attribute the fact that researchers have recurrently found that there are more socially desirable words describing women than describing men?

3. Considering research and your own observations, to what extent have stereotypes changed over recent years? Why do you think research does or does not match your own views?

4. Consider the most "together" person you know and the least "together" person. Think about those persons in light of your understanding of instrumentality and expressiveness.

5. What are some reasons for men to be generally more stereotyped, conservative, and traditional about gender-typing than women are?

*Chapter 4*

# Biological Foundations of Gender

*T*he boys are outside, playing King of the Mountain, running, and shouting. The girls are inside, playing house, caring for the dolls, and talking to each other. Some people consider such differences in behavior—which they label "masculine" and "feminine"—to be biologically determined. Others consider them a result of experience and environmental influence. The two positions are the core of the so-called nature-nurture debate. People on either side of the debate often have trouble seeing any sense in the other position or any fault in their own position. But, in fact, nature and nurture are closely intertwined, as we will see in this chapter.

The nature-nurture issue is further complicated by the fact that people sometimes assume that biology sets an unalterable destiny. This is not true. Human behavior is very plastic (though the term *elastic* seems more appropriate). Because of our **plasticity,** we are not as biologically fixed or as tied into our biological foundations in some respects as are other species. But expectations often accentuate biological differences. For example, there may be gender differences in infant preferences, but different experiences provided to the infants by the adults around them, based on those adults' expectations, may exaggerate the differences and make biological factors seem more determining than they are. Not only does biology influence experience, but experience can influence biology—a fact that many people miss. The two-way, interactive relationship between biology and experience is referred to as the principle of **reciprocal determinism** (as opposed to biological determinism) (Cacioppo & Bernston, 1992). The perspective that sees biology and experience as reciprocally influential is sometimes referred to as **psychobiological.** In this approach, biological factors are considered but without the claim that biology is more important than experience (Dewsbury, 1991; Lewis, 1990). The terms *biopsychosocial* and *psychosocialbiological* have been used with similar intent (Halpern, 1986). Such approaches take the view that human beings cannot be divided into separate biological, psychological, and social "pieces"; rather, all the pieces work together and influence each other.

In previous chapters we looked at stereotypes and gender roles. In this chapter we consider the biological underpinnings of gender. We look first at prenatal development and consider some basic facts about development. We then consider some unusual cases of development to see if there are lessons to be learned from them about nature-nurture issues. Finally, we consider some aspects of infant behavior that may illustrate the joint action of biological predispositions and the social environment.

Before continuing, consider these questions for personal thought:

◆ Are you a male or a female? How do you know? If you were given a genetic test and found that genetically you are of the other sex than you think you are, how would you feel? Why? What difference would it make to you? To your parents? To your friends?

◆ When you think about differences you have noticed between females and males, are you most likely to think first of "nature" or "nurture"? That is, do you think the differences are due to biology or to experiences after birth? Why do you think what you do?

◆ Have you ever heard slurs or derogatory remarks made about someone who did not fit the mold of what a boy or girl, woman or man, was supposed to look like and be physically—perhaps a boy with a small penis or undescended testes or a girl with wide shoulders or facial hair? Why do you think people who do not conform physically are criticized?

◆ Give yourself a "guided imagery" experience. In your imagination, go through what for you is a typical day, but do so as a member of the other sex. Think concretely and specifically—for example, how does your body feel between the sheets when you wake up, when you bathe and dress, when you go to the bathroom? How do people react to you? How are your confidence and esteem affected? Go through the day from beginning to end. What is your initial reaction on reading this suggestion? Are you willing to try it? Why or why not?

◆ Describe a newborn baby. How do you act with infants? Do your answers differ depending on whether the baby is a boy or a girl? Why?

## Prenatal Development

As late as the 1950s, many experts considered "true sex" (biological sex) and psychological feelings of female or male identity to be determined exclusively by the gonads (ovaries, testes) (Ehrhardt, 1985). In 1945, researcher Albert Ellis had concluded that gender role or gender identity was primarily a matter of rearing (that is, environmental influence) (Ellis, 1945); but it wasn't until the mid-1950s that the research of John Money and John and Joan Hampson (1955a, 1955b) showed that neither gender identity nor female/male behavior was tied solely to biological sex. Their research also helped demonstrate the complexity of biological sex in and of itself. Even at the most basic physical level, sexual definition is not always clear-cut. In addition, there is considerable similarity between female and male development and considerable variability within each kind of development.

**Sexual differentiation** is the set of biological processes that governs the development of an embryo into an individual with female or male physical characteristics. No single factor or event determines sex. Rather, normal sexual development involves a number of steps, which typically occur on an exquisitely timed schedule. For most individuals, development results in consistent sexual characteristics, although there is room for variation at each level. In some cases, however, development results in inconsistent sexual characteristics.

## The Role of Chromosomes and Genes

The only distinct difference between females and males is in terms of the **genetic criterion of sex,** that is, in terms of the chromosomes or genes. Chromosomes are threadlike structures made up of DNA, the material that carries genetic information. Contained on the chromosomes are genes, tiny segments of DNA that control cell functions by making proteins. Most cells of the human body contain 46 chromosomes in 23 pairs. Of the 23 pairs of chromosomes, 22 contain the genetic information for all traits except genetic sex; they are known as autosomes. The 23rd pair, the sex chromosomes, carry the material responsible for genetic sex. Females have two similar sex chromosomes, called XX, while males have dissimilar sex chromosomes, called XY.

The only cells in the human body that do not contain 23 pairs of chromosomes are the reproductive or germ cells—eggs (ova), produced by the ovaries in the female, and sperm, produced in the testes in the male. Egg and sperm cells contain only 23 chromosomes in all, as a result of the cell division process known as meiosis. When an egg and a sperm join in the process of fertilization, the 23 chromosomes in the egg align with the 23 chromosomes in the sperm to produce 23 new pairs, forming the genetic blueprint for a new individual.

The sex chromosome in an egg cell is always an X, but the sex chromosome in a sperm cell can be either an X or a Y. When an X from an egg unites with an X from a sperm, the result, XX, is a genetic female; when an X from the female unites with a Y from the male, the result, XY, is a genetic male. Because a typical woman can contribute only an X and a typical man can contribute either an X or a Y, it is the man who determines the chromosomal sex of the child.

An interesting note about genetic sex is that an XY individual is more vulnerable at every level of development than an XX individual. This vulnerability is evident first in the chromosomes themselves. The X chromosome is large and carries much genetic material, whereas the Y chromosome is small and carries little genetic material. If one X chromosome carries a recessive trait and another X is present, the recessive trait is likely to be countered by a dominant trait on the second X. If the second chromosome is a Y, however, it may not contain a corresponding trait, and the recessive trait will be expressed. Thus, an XY individual is more likely to show recessive traits than an XX individual. Accordingly, more common in males than in females are such recessive sex-linked traits as color blindness, hemophilia, and cerebral sclerosis. Also more common in males are lesser known traits such as webbing between the third and fourth toes, barklike skin, lesions on hands or feet, and hair on the ears.

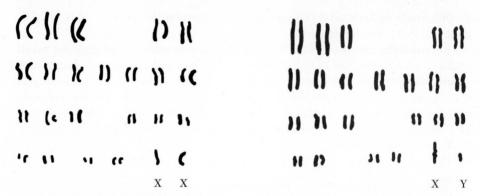

X   X                                              X   Y

*Left: A full set of human female chromosomes, including the female sex chromosomes (XX).*
*Right: Male sex chromosomes (XY).*

The vulnerability of an XY individual is also evident in the sperm (Berk, 1993; Fitzgerald, Strommen, & McKinney, 1977). Although all sperm come from the male, sperm carrying an X chromosome are called female sperm, and sperm carrying a Y chromosome are called male sperm. Male sperm live a shorter time than female sperm. Compensating for this, male sperm swim faster than female sperm, with the result that more XY embryos are conceived than XX embryos. An estimated 125 to 150 XY fetuses are conceived for every 100 XXs, but more XYs are lost both before and after birth. About 25% more XY than XX fetuses are spontaneously aborted (miscarried). More XY fetuses are associated with problem pregnancies generally, and more are stillborn (not alive at birth).

Because there are more XY fetuses to begin with, there are 105 male live births for every 100 female live births. But more male babies die within the first year of life than female babies—35% more for Whites, 22% more for Blacks, assuming ordinary nutrition. When nutrition is impaired or there are other adverse conditions, males are more affected than females. At all ages through the life span, fewer males than females survive. Because more males are conceived and born, however, it is not until a population of individuals born at the same time are in their late 20s or early 30s that the number of women equals and then surpasses the number of men (U.S. National Center for Health Statistics, 1992).

As we shall see when we consider infancy, some psychologists suggest that there is a psychological vulnerability accompanying the physical vulnerability. The physical vulnerability itself may have contributed to the greater valuation of males seen in many patriarchal cultures. Although our forebears did not know about chromosomes, they could observe the sex of aborted fetuses and stillborns as well as the early problems and deaths of sons.

At the genetic level of sexual development, the normal individual is either XX or XY, as we have discussed. The chromosomes constitute the **genotype,** the genetic makeup of the individual. The overt expression of the genotype that develops in the environment is known as the **phenotype.** The genotype is somewhat like the architect's plans for a house; the phenotype is the house that actually is built. The phenotype is highly influenced by additional developments, largely under the control of hormones. With normal development, the phenotype is consistent with the genotype. As stated, males and females are distinctly different only at the chromosomal level. From then on, developmental paths are remarkably similar.

## Development of the Gonads

The Y chromosome seems to do nothing more than direct the development of the gonads, leading to the **gonadal criterion of sex.** Gonads—the ovaries and testes—reproduce the sex cells containing the genetic material for reproduction; they also produce hormones (as do some other organs). In prenatal development, the gonads produce hormones that largely control later development. Both ovaries and testes develop from the same material (the ovotestes or primordial gonad) (Figure 4.1). The material is **unimorphic tissue,** meaning simply that there is one form of it, a form occurring in both XX and XY individuals. One or more genes on the Y chromosome triggers the transformation of the gonadal material into testes (through the TDF, testis-determinism factor) (Crooks & Baur, 1993). Without the presence of the Y chromosome, the outer material of the unimorphic tissue develops into ovaries; with the presence of the Y, the inner material develops into testes.

## The Role of Hormones

Once the ovaries or testes develop, they secrete hormones that control the continuing process of sexual differentiation. This stage is known as the hormonal stage. Testes typically start producing androgens at about 6 weeks. The most important **androgen** is **testosterone:** In later life, it triggers sperm production and influences the sex drive. Ovaries typically start producing estrogen and progesterone at about 12 weeks. **Estrogen** comes to regulate reproductive functions and the development of secondary characteristics; **progesterone** helps regulate the menstrual cycle and sustains pregnancy. Although studies with animals have suggested that ovaries are not necessary for female differentiation (Hood, Draper, Crockett, & Petersen, 1987), there is reason to suggest that estrogen encourages continuing female prenatal development (Fausto-Sterling, 1985, 1989).

It is important to note that both the ovaries and the testes produce both the "male hormones," androgens, and the "female hormones," estrogen and progesterone. In addition, the cortex of the adrenal gland of both males and females secretes small amounts of estrogen and larger amounts of androgen. Thus, the terms male hormones and female hormones are misnomers that accentuate a relative difference into an absolute difference in popular thinking. The differences are in the relative dominance of androgen or estrogen (technically, the ratio of free androgen to estrogen, as the hormones are inactive when they are bound to other substances in the blood) (Hood et al., 1987). Members of both sexes produce both types of hormones. The relative dominance of the "sex hormones" influences later development. This stage is known as the hormonal stage, providing the **hormonal criterion of sex.**

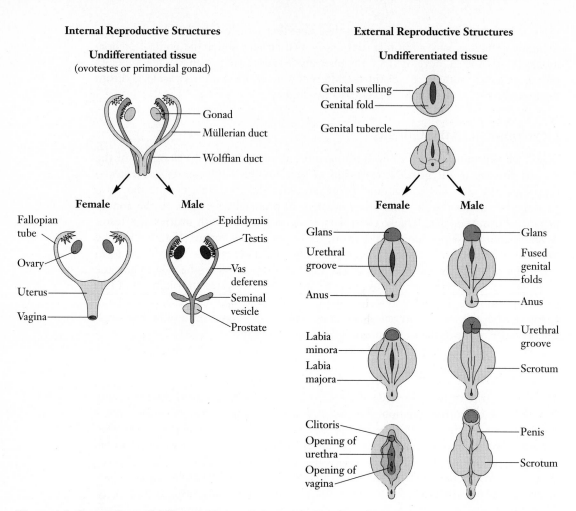

**Figure 4.1** *Prenatal sexual differentiation.* Adapted from Wilson, J. D., George, F. W., & Griffin, J. E. (1981). The hormonal control of sexual development. *Science, 211,* 1280.

## Development of the Internal and External Reproductive Organs

The next stage of sexual development involves development of the **internal reproductive organs** (see Figure 4.1). These organs develop from **dimorphic tissue** (tissue that has two forms), but individuals of each genetic sex have both forms of the tissues. Without androgen, the **Mullerian system** develops into the uterus, Fallopian tubes, and inner third of the vagina. With androgen present, the **Wolffian system** develops into the vas deferens, the seminal vesicles, and the ejaculatory ducts. Also required for typical male development is the **Mullerian-inhibiting substance (MIS),** secreted by the testes. When androgen is present but MIS is not, the Mullerian system develops along with the Wolffian system; this is rare.

**Table 4.1**    Timetable of Prenatal Sexual Differentiation

| Stage | Time | Female | Male |
|---|---|---|---|
| Genetic (genetic sex determined) | Conception | XX | XY |
| Gonadal (gonads develop) | Week 6 (testes); week 12 (ovaries) | Ovaries | Testes |
| Hormonal (hormones produced) | Weeks 7–12 | Absence of testosterone, presence of estrogen | Testosterone |
| Internal reproductive organs (internal structures form) | Weeks 7–12 | Uterus, Fallopian tubes, inner third of vagina | Vas deferens, seminal vesicles, ejaculatory ducts |
| External reproductive organs (external structures form) | Weeks 7–12 | Clitoris, inner and outer labia | Penis, scrotum |

After the internal reproductive organs form, the **external reproductive organs** develop—what can be seen from the outside. The external reproductive systems develop from unimorphic tissue (the genital tubercle). Without androgen, a clitoris develops and the urethral folds stay separated, yielding the inner and outer labia. If androgen is present, a penis and scrotum form. Testes begin forming around the 6th week and ovaries around 12 weeks; experts differ on when development is complete (Halpern, 1986). The timetable of prenatal sexual differentiation is summarized in Table 4.1.

## Female Development: Active or Passive?

Formal and informal discussions and assumptions of prenatal development often suggest that female development is passive: The egg is penetrated by the sperm, which determines whether the individual will be XX or XY; if androgen does not arrive to cause male development, female development occurs by default. The view that male development is active and female development is passive may be because more effort has gone into trying to understand male development (Fausto-Sterling, 1985, 1989; E. Martin, 1987).

Evidence increasingly indicates, however, that female development is an active process of dynamic interchange. There is suggestive evidence that the egg may give signals that affect the likelihood that a female or male sperm will fertilize the egg. The egg reaches out with a tentacle and draws the sperm into the inner area where it then penetrates the top of the head of the sperm and blows it up. As the sperm explodes, its genetic material is distributed throughout the egg (Rabuzzi, 1994). Another reason that female development has been considered passive is that the role of estrogen often is overlooked.

## Brain Differentiation

It is thought that **brain differentiation** is a final stage in prenatal development, and it likely continues for at least a while after birth (Lish et al., 1991; Witelson, 1991).

Testosterone seems to cause specialized receptor cells in the hypothalamus to become insensitive to estrogen; without testosterone, the cells are allowed to become highly sensitive to estrogen (Hood et al., 1987). Prenatal hormones seem to involve an organizational effect, meaning that they permanently influence the central nervous system (Ehrhardt, 1985). They may prime the brain to make it more susceptible or responsive to the events of later life, including, and especially, the effects of hormones at puberty. The later influence of sex hormones is considered activational, suggesting they can activate behavior that was preorganized during earlier development. Activational effects are temporary and reversible.

*Brain Lateralization*    Research has been accumulating since 1974 suggesting that women's and men's brains are organized differently for certain tasks and activities (Bryden, 1979; Harris, 1978; Treadwell, 1987). We must be quick to point out that there is more variability in brain organization from person to person than between women and men (Hahn, 1987; Kimura, 1985). Nonetheless, there are thought to be some general gender differences. The possible gender differences of major concern are in the relative dominance of the left or the right halves, or hemispheres, of the brain.

The extent to which the two hemispheres have specialized functions or are differentially dominant is referred to as **brain lateralization.** A high degree of lateralization means there is a bigger difference between the two halves in terms of their functions and their relative dominance. The more lateralized the two halves, the more asymmetry or hemispheric specialization there is. The less lateralization, the more the two hemispheres are symmetrical or bilateral rather than different from each other. Associated with the notion of lateralization is the idea of amount of communication between the two hemispheres (Harris, 1977). With greater lateralization, there is less communication or more specialization, as if the two hemispheres were saying to each other, "You do your thing and I'll do mine." With greater bilaterality and less lateralization, there is more communication and less specialization, as if the two hemispheres were saying, "Maybe we can help each other."

*Female Symmetry*    There is suggestive evidence that among adults, females have brains that are more symmetrical and more bilateral (or less lateralized) than men's brains, though the generalization is most safely made about right-handed people (Geschwind & Galaburda, 1985a, 1985b; Kimura, 1987). Part of the **corpus callosum,** a bundle of fibers connecting the two hemispheres of the brain, is larger and more developed in females than in males (Figure 4.2) (de Lecoste-Utamsing & Holloway, 1982; Goleman, 1989). Brain scans from living people show that parts of the corpus callosum are up to 23% wider in women than in men and that other connective tissue between the hemispheres also is thicker (Allen, Richey, Chai, & Gorski, 1991). (Previous evidence was from autopsies, and the size of the corpus callosum changes dramatically shortly after death.)

Supporting the idea of greater symmetry in females is the fact that more right-handed females than males use both hemispheres when performing both verbal and spatial tasks. In contrast, more males than females have their verbal abilities primarily in the left hemisphere and their spatial abilities primarily in the right hemisphere. Such general differences may be related to differences in cognitive abilities (chapter 8).

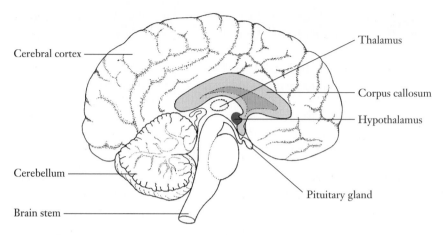

**Figure 4.2** *The brain, viewed through the center, showing the corpus callosum.*
SOURCE: Strong, B., & DeVault, C. (1997). Human sexuality: Diversity in contemporary America (2nd ed.). Mountain View, CA: Mayfield.

Other evidence for greater bilaterality in "female" brains comes from cases of brain injury. For equal amounts and kinds of brain damage, females generally recover more mental functions than males do. This is thought to be because one part of the brain can "take over" better for the damaged part than is true in a more lateralized, asymmetrical brain. More specifically, with damage to the left hemisphere, which is primarily responsible for verbal functions, men typically show decreases in verbal functioning and development of speech disorders and aphasias; with damage to the right hemisphere, men tend to show impairment in nonverbal functions. For women with brain injury, whether the damage is to the right or left hemisphere is not so clearly related to what kinds of cognitive functions are impaired, and recovery is more complete.

***Timing and Source of Brain Organization***   The differences in brain organization, if confirmed by continuing research, are more likely to be influenced by prenatal sex hormones than by genes (Hines, 1982; Hines & Shipley, 1984; Kimura, 1987). However, it is not known whether differences in laterality are present at birth or develop over time. Some authorities believe that differences occur by the preschool years, while others suggest adolescence as the time of maximum differences in laterality. Some brain differences may result from different experiences rather than prenatal hormones. A substantial amount of brain growth occurs under the influence of and in interaction with the environment, giving rise to cultural differences (Hood et al., 1987). For example, the corpus callosum is relatively nonfunctioning at birth and matures gradually; thus, it is responsive to experiential factors. Furthermore, there are cultural differences in laterality likely reflecting different experiences after birth.

Again, the data give two messages. One is that simplistic questions and answers of biology versus experience or nurture versus nature will not suffice. The reality is that there is a complex interplay between nature and nurture at all stages of develop-

## *FOCUS ON RESEARCH*

### 4.1    Animal Research, Ethics, and Generalizability: Do Prenatal Hormones Influence Later Behavior?

What causes our behavior—nature or nurture? Are we preprogrammed by our biology, or do we learn through interacting with our environment? The answer to this perennial question is often a very unsatisfying "it depends." Researchers Sheri Berenbaum, Kristina Korman, and Catherine Leveroni (1995) focused on the biological part of the question: Could our earliest fetal development organize the brain in such a way as to set the stage for behavior when we are children and adults? Their review of past studies led them to focus on prenatal levels of androgen (a category of masculinizing sex hormones that includes testosterone) and cognitive abilities, specifically spatial skills which are involved in tasks such as map reading.

How can we study the effects of prenatal hormones in humans? Berenbaum and her associates noted that the ideal study would alter, in a controlled way, the intrauterine androgen levels of a group of pregnant women. Some fetuses (both female and male) might be exposed to higher-than-normal levels of androgen and some to lower-than-normal levels, while some would experience a normal hormonal uterine environment. After birth, both boys and girls would be raised in an identical social environment, and various behaviors would be measured at set intervals. Any differences in the children's behavior would then have to be due to their different prenatal hormonal levels, as nurture was consistent for all children. Bingo! We would have our answer to that pesky question about biological influences on human behavior.

So, has research like this been done? Would you volunteer your child for such a study? No, probably not. Ethics and morality make studies like this impossible. But rather than abandoning the question, researchers have developed an alternative method: using nonhuman animals as research subjects.

Berenbaum, Korman, and Leveroni report that guinea pigs, mice, rats, rhesus monkeys, and other animals have served as subjects in studies of prenatal hormones. A typical study involves injecting the pregnant mother with the desired amount of hormone during critical periods of fetal development, then observing the behavior of the offspring. In this way, we've found that prenatal hormones affect sexual and dominance behaviors in animals. For example, female guinea pigs whose mothers were injected with testosterone during gestation did not engage in typical female sexual behavior. Instead of the normal receptive behavior, these guinea pigs tried to mount other animals, which is sexual behavior typical of males. It is thought that prenatal hormones

---

ment. The second message is that biology is indeed relevant to phenomena of concern to psychologists. (See Focus on Research 4.1.) The issue is to understand how biology is relevant. Brain structure develops in a social context that can exaggerate or equalize

organize the brain to respond to certain stimuli, which then trigger the particular behavior.

Your first response may be, "Well, great, now we know how prenatal hormones affect some very specific sexually differentiated behaviors in guinea pigs. What does that have to do with humans?" Good question. This is the problem of generalizability that researchers have grappled with for years. Generalizability deals with how well the results of one study apply under different situations. Humans are admittedly much more complex creatures than guinea pigs, and we cannot simply take these results and apply them directly to explain human sexual behavior. Some people have argued that much animal research should not be done because it does not generalize to humans. Others note that at some very basic levels animals and humans do share similar behaviors, so some level of applicability may emerge. They also point out that we may want to know about that animal species for its own sake, regardless of the human connection.

Even if we are able to learn about ourselves and animals through animal research, is it necessary? Animal rights advocates debate animal researchers on this issue. If we cannot ethically involve humans in certain research procedures, should we subject animals to those procedures? Which is more important, avoiding the potential stress and pain the animal subjects experience or gaining the research findings that may benefit humans and reduce human suffering? Currently, researchers have tried to strike a balance by carefully protecting animal subjects while still conducting necessary studies. Both the federal government and the American Psychological Association have written guidelines detailing the use and care of animal subjects. Veterinarians must oversee their housing, feeding, and medical care; researchers and lab assistants must be trained in their handling, and each study must be approved by a review committee that judges the merits of the research.

In their review of previous research, Berenbaum and her associates concluded that animal research provided a firm basis for theorizing about how differences in spatial skills in humans are probably linked to prenatal hormones. As concerned researchers, we must weigh both the negatives and the positives of such research, including issues of generalizability, harm to the animals, and benefits to humans. Ethical researchers realize that care, caution, and humanity must be exercised in relation to animal subjects.

JILL BORCHERT ◆

SOURCE: Berenbaum, S. A., Korman, K., & Leveroni, C. (1995). Early hormone and sex differences in cognitive abilities. *Learning and Individual Differences, 7*, 303–321.

---

sex differences (Hood et al., 1987). "There's nothing about human brains that is so stuck that a different way of doing things couldn't change it enormously" (Juraska, cited in Gorman, 1992, p. 47).

## *How Much Does Biology Matter?*

Part of the fascination with prenatal development has been due to interest in the relative contributions of biology and environment to behavior. This fascination leads to consideration of individuals whose development has not fit the norm, with the hope of understanding the norm as well as the atypical cases. What happens when biological criteria of sex are not consistent with each other? What happens when an individual with physically consistent sexual features is changed in some way? What happens when there is ambiguity? For example, it is not always easy to decide whether a baby has a large clitoris or a small penis. The decision about the neonate's sex can be complicated even more when internal and external organs are not consistent with each other. Surgical corrections of the external genitalia and hormonal treatments may be used to change a baby to one more consistently female or male.

In the rare condition called **true hermaphroditism,** both ovaries and testes develop (either one or two of each or two ovotestes with both ovarian and testicular tissue in the same gland) (Strong & DeVault, 1997; Verp et al., 1992). External genitals are often a mixture of female and male structures. In the more frequent cases of **pseudohermaphroditism,** gonads match chromosomal sex, but internal and external reproductive anatomy is ambiguous or mixed. Cases of pseudohermaphroditism are discussed later in the chapter.

The theoretical hope has been that study of atypical development would help us understand the relative roles of biology and the environment in behavior. However, natural experiments are far from clear, and it is not easy to know what variables are operating in what manner. For example, what are the effects on the parents of knowing their child had surgical or hormonal treatment? John Money indicates that successful sex reassignment requires parental clarity that "our child is a girl (or boy)" and unambiguous rearing with respect to sex. How easy is that for parents to accomplish and for psychologists to measure? And do some parents go overboard in the process of communicating "you are a girl (boy)," so that they put more than usual pressure on the child for behaviors consistent with stereotypic behavior associated with the assigned sex?

Further, if the child learns of the birth condition, what effect does that have on self-perceptions and behavior? If there are siblings who know of the condition, matters become even more complicated. Thus, a wide variety of environmental and physical factors can influence the development of the phenotype, and it is hard to see how studies of atypical conditions can provide clear-cut evidence about biological influences. Nonetheless, such studies are provocative.

### Sex of Assignment, Reassignment, and Rearing

After birth, the first major event affecting our lives as males or females is **sex assignment:** the labeling of an infant as female or male (Money & Ehrhardt, 1972). Parents are likely to be told, "You have a daughter!" or "You have a son!" Thereafter, much of what an individual experiences in the world is determined by social expectations based on the sex of assignment. **Sex of rearing** typically is a result of sex of assignment. What the label means to parents, and then to the child, and how adults rear a daughter or son may vary quite a bit. Exactly what a child experiences as a girl or boy may differ from one family or culture to another, but the label likely is important to the people around the child; sex is an important categorizer, as we saw in chapter 2.

John Money has been very clear in his insistence that sex of assignment and rearing are the important determinants of future development, not chromosomes or prenatal experience (Money, 1975; Money & Ehrhardt, 1972). Sex reassignment, a change of assignment, is thought to be fairly safe within about the first 18 months of life; some extend the time of safety to 2 years. However, there is some reason to be concerned about reassignment earlier than 18 months because infants are learning sex distinctions early and may show gender-typed behavior by then (chapter 5).

Money offered a rather dramatic example of the extent to which nature may be changed by human intervention. The case involved two identical twin boys. During the circumcision of one of them, most of the penis was destroyed. Should the boy go through life with a defective penis? Or should the boy be changed to a girl? The parents decided when the child was 17 months old to raise him as a girl. Initial genital surgery was performed shortly after. Money reported that the girl, although sharing genes and prenatal environment with the brother, developed as a normal girl and showed feminine identity. The case was taken as evidence of the greater importance of sex of assignment and rearing compared with chromosomal sex and prenatal development.

Unfortunately for Money's argument, the picture did not stay so rosy or clear-cut. As a 13-year-old, the girl (former boy)—who did not yet know of the sex reassignment—was seen by psychiatrists not associated with the original project, and problems were evident (Diamond, 1982; Williams & Smith, 1979). She was teased by other children, who called her "cavewoman" and commented on her lack of femininity. She refused to draw a female figure when asked to do so, wanted to be a mechanic, and thought boys have a better life (a view shared with many other girls!). This person, at age 18, requested and then received surgery to reconstruct a penis and scrotum and prefers women as sexual partners (Diamond, 1993). (See Focus on Research 4.2.)

Thus, the case no longer provides the evidence previously claimed that identity is dependent exclusively on learning. However, exactly what we know from this case is up in the air, because the details are not clear (Crooks & Baur, 1993). Perhaps the sex-change operation occurred too late. The parents did not decide on the sex change until the infant was 17 months old, and lack of success with reassignment increases with age. If prenatal development was typically male, as it appears to have been, perhaps the brain was "programmed" as male in ways that became activated as puberty approached. There is no doubt that learning experiences are relevant, as shown by many cases of apparently healthy development following surgical intervention. Whatever may prove to be the ultimate answer, the case does provide a warning against simplistic either-or, biological-environmental, nature-nurture explanations. This is well to keep in mind as we consider some of the other cases of unusual developmental patterns.

## Genetic Variations

Chromosomal errors are fairly common, affecting 1 in 426 children (Nielsen & Wohlert, 1991). The errors include having fewer or more X or Y chromosomes than

### 4.2   Ethical Treatment of Research Participants: Updating a Case Study of Sex Reassignment

One of the most interesting cases regarding sex reassignment is that of the twin boy who, as a result of a circumcision accident at age 8 months, was surgically reassigned as a female. This tragic accident provided a rare opportunity for researchers to study how biology and learning influence our gender-related identity and behavior. Ethics prohibit researchers from performing sex reassignment on physically intact infants as part of a controlled study. To gather their information, researchers must rely on either animal studies or the less frequent human "experiments of nature," such as the circumcision accident. As you might suspect, the chance to study the development of a human infant who had undergone sex reassignment was of enormous importance for the scientific community. However, the interests of science must be weighed against the welfare of the child who will be exposed to the scrutiny of strangers. How do we balance the need for information with the rights of the research participant?

The American Psychological Association has published a list of ethical guidelines that all reputable psychologists must follow in their research. When reading these guidelines, you might first notice the label given to those who take part in the study. They are no longer referred to as "subjects," who provide information and are then dismissed; instead, they are called "participants," who work together with the researcher and without whom the study would not exist. The underlying theme of the ethical guidelines is that research participants must not suffer physical, emotional, or psychological harm or be negatively affected by their experience in any way. They should leave the study in no worse condition and, if possible, in a more enlightened condition than when they entered.

To ensure a particpant's welfare, the guidelines focus on the following basic requirements for any study: voluntary participation, informed consent, and the rights to privacy, confidentiality, and anonymity. Voluntary participation means that people cannot be forced to take part in a study. They must freely choose to enter the study and must be able to quit at any time without penalty. Many studies pay participants for their time or award other compensation, such as extra credit towards a class grade for college participants. It is unethical for the researcher to withhold payment or credit until the participant has completed the study. This is considered coercion and violates the principle of voluntary participation.

Informed consent goes hand and hand with voluntary participation. Each prospective participant must be reasonably informed about what the study will entail before choosing to enter the study. Informed consent involves a written or verbal statement by the researcher that explains to participants how long the study will take, what they will be requested to do or experience, and any potential harm that may result. Informed consent can be problematic; how can you ever have all the information needed to make a truly informed decision? Also, knowledge of the details behind a study may prejudice the participants, causing them to alter their natural responses. The data they then provide may not be an indicator of their true behavior but a reflection of the behavior of people who know what the researchers are looking for. Deception and less-than-fully informed consent may be allowed under some circumstances but never at the expense of the participants' welfare.

Participants have the right to privacy, to confidentiality of their responses or behavior, and to anonymity. When researchers ask a participant to reveal private thoughts on a questionnaire or in an interview or to engage in private behaviors during an observation, this information is a confidential exchange between researcher and participant. Participants have the right to know how this information will be used—if it will be written up in a journal article or presented at a conference. They have the right to request that their data be excluded from the final report of the study. Participants' responses must also be kept anonymous. This is usually achieved by omitting or deleting participants' names or other identifying markers (such as social security numbers) from their responses; most often, participants will be assigned a code number instead. Although this may seem dehumanizing, it is designed to protect the identity of the participant.

Most of the time, psychological research is nonintrusive and carries no threat of harm to the participant. However, some research does deal with sensitive or emotional topics, and protecting participants is especially important. The case study of the child whose penis was destroyed and who was raised as a female illustrates this issue. A team of researchers that included medical and psychological personnel tracked the development of this individual, who is now 34 years old. In addition to this research team, various other personnel have been involved, and in 1980 the British Broadcasting Corporation produced a television report on the case. While developmental reports have been published throughout the years, the identity and location of both the individual and the family have been closely guarded; in current reports he is known only by the pseudonym John. In 1994 and 1995, John agreed to be interviewed by researchers Milton Diamond and H. Keith Sigmundson and to allow the release of his updated story. He hoped that his gender identity struggles would cause researchers to reconsider their acceptance of sex reassignment surgery for infants. Diamond and Sigmundson could only proceed with John's voluntary help based on informed consent and respect for his right to privacy and anonymity. In sensitive cases such as John's, as well as in routine research studies, participants must be treated with dignity and their rights preserved, for participants are the core of any research study.

JILL BORCHERT ◆

SOURCE: Diamond, M., & Sigmundson, H. K. (1997). Sex reassignment at birth: Long-term review and clinical implications. *Archives of Pediatrics and Adolescent Medicine, 151,* 298–304.

typical (Table 4.2). World-class athletes—if they are women—are routinely tested for their chromosomal sex (Lorber, 1994). The purpose of testing is to be sure that women are not "too male" to participate against women, though men are not tested to see if they are "too female" to compete against men. There is no evidence, however, to suggest that chromosomes affect sports ability (Birrell & Cole, 1990). Chromosomes simply do not seem to be as important as hormones. As stated before, the only purpose of the Y chromosome seems to be to stimulate the development of the testes. Two cases serve to demonstrate the relative unimportance of chromosomes by themselves: the XYY individual and the XO individual.

### XYY: "Supermales"

XYY individuals, often called supermales, are unusually tall and may be sterile. At one time it was suggested that they were more aggressive than normal, because they are overrepresented among juvenile delinquents (1 in 14), adult criminals (1 in 12), and the criminally insane (1 in 8) (Jacobs, Brunton, Melville, Brittain, & McClemont, 1965; Jarvik, Klodin, & Matsuyama, 1973). The incidence of XYYs at birth is 1 out of every 1,000 to 3,000 individuals. Although XYYs do have a higher known crime rate than XY males, we cannot conclude that the extra Y causes aggression.

Early studies of XYY individuals were done in institutional settings. A better study, done in Denmark, looked at virtually all young men (ages 28 to 32 years) born in Copenhagen who were within the top 15% of the height distribution (Witkin et al., 1976). Sex chromosomal makeup was assessed for nearly all (90%, 4,139). The 12 XYY men in the sample were compared with 13 men whose genetic sex was XXY, a condition known as Klinefelter's syndrome. Like XYY men, individuals with Klinefelter's syndrome are taller than average, so they provided a control for the effect of size on aggression. But XXY men have some feminization or lack of virilization (smaller penis, wider hips, some breast development, sparse pubic and facial hair, higher pitched voices). The XXY individuals were expected to have committed fewer aggressive acts because of their feminization.

The researchers concluded that chromosomal makeup is not related to criminal activity. Those with low socioeconomic status (SES) were more likely to be convicted of a crime, irrespective of chromosomal makeup. Further, both XXY and XYY men had lower intelligence scores and lower education levels than XY men; perhaps they were more likely to get caught for the crimes they did commit. In addition, the XYY men were not more violent than other men.

### XO: Turner's Syndrome Females

Some individuals have only one chromosome. YO fetuses are thought to occur but to be too vulnerable to survive. **XO** individuals, known as **Turner's syndrome** females, do survive and can lead normal lives. Their external appearance is female, and they are assigned and reared as females, although they have no gonads and so are sterile. They do have a developed Mullerian system, because there was no MIS to inhibit it, but menstruation can occur only with hormone treatment; menstruation is sometimes induced to help the young woman feel more normal.

Turner's syndrome girls are equal to other girls in satisfaction with the female role and in feminine and heterosexual preferences (Ehrhardt, Greenberg, & Money,

**Table 4.2** Genetic and Hormonal Variations in Prenatal Development

| | Chromosomal sex* | Gonads | Internal reproductive structures | External reproductive structures | Secondary sex characteristics | Gender assignment |
|---|---|---|---|---|---|---|
| **GENETIC VARIATIONS** | | | | | | |
| Turner syndrome | Female (45, XO) | Nonfunctioning or absent ovaries | Normal female except for ovaries | Underdeveloped genitals | No breast development or menstruation at puberty | Female |
| Klinefelter syndrome | Male (47, XXY) | Testes | Normal male | Small penis and testes | Female secondary sex characteristics develop at puberty | Male, but frequent gender confusion at puberty |
| "Supermales" | Male (47, XYY) | Testes | Male but may be sterile | Penis and testes | Normal male; tall | Male |
| **HORMONAL VARIATIONS** | | | | | | |
| Androgen-insensitivity syndrome(complete): testicular feminization | Male (46, XY) | Testes, but body unable to utilize androgen (testosterone) | Shallow vagina, lacks normal male structures | Labia | Female secondary sex characteristics develop at puberty; no menstruation; tall | Female |
| Androgen-insensitivity syndrome (incomplete): Reifenstein's syndrome | Male (46, XY) | Testes, but body partially unable to utilize androgen (testosterone) | Partial Wolfian system No Mullerian system | Ambiguous; small penis | Female secondary sex characteristics develop at puberty | Male or female |
| Congenital adrenal hyperplasia | Female (46, XX) | Ovaries | Normal female | Ambiguous, tending toward male appearance; fused vagina and enlarged clitoris may be mistaken for empty scrotal sac and micropenis | Female secondary sex characteristics develop at puberty | Usually male unless condition discovered at birth and rectified by hormone therapy |
| Congenital adrenal hyperplasia | Male (46, XY) | Testes | Normal male | Normal male | Male secondary sex characteristics develop at puberty | Male |
| DHT deficiency | Male (46, XY) | Testes undescended until puberty | Partially formed internal structures but no prostate | Ambiguous; clitoral-appearing micropenis; penis enlarges and testes descend at puberty | Male secondary sex characteristics develop at puberty | Female identity until puberty; majority assume male identity later |

*Chromosomal sex refers to 46, XX (female) or 46, XY (male). Sometimes a chromosome will be missing, as in 45, XO, or there will be an extra chromosome, as in 47, XXY. In these notations, the number refers to the number of chromosomes (46, in 23 pairs, is normal); the letters X and Y refer to sex chromosomes and O refers to a missing chromosome.

SOURCE: Strong, B., & DeVault, C. (1997). Human sexuality: Diversity in contemporary America (2nd ed.). Mountain View, CA: Mayfield.

125

1970; Money & Ehrhardt, 1972). When differences are found, the Turner's syndrome girls show "enhanced femininity," namely, they are less athletic, are engaged in less childhood fighting, and have a greater interest in frilly clothes, jewelry, and perfume. More so than other girls, they have a strong maternal interest together with high career interest (Hines, 1982).

We do not know why an XO pattern should produce both enhanced femininity and high career interest. There is reason to expect parental contribution. Knowing of their daughter's difference, parents might overemphasize feminine traits to encourage similarities with other girls. And, knowing that the girl cannot become a biological mother, the parents may try to develop career-oriented aspirations. An additional consideration is that the typical small stature (under 5 feet) of Turner's syndrome females may be responsible for their reduced outdoor play, since vigorous activity would not likely be reinforced by other children.

## Hormonal Variations

Hormonal variations include both having more or less than the usual amount of a hormone and not being sensitive to a hormone, so that it has no effect (see Table 4.2). Prenatal exposure to high levels of estrogen and progestin has occurred because of hormones given to pregnant women, but few personality differences have been reported and are not related to stereotypical feminine or masculine traits or to the dosages of hormones given the mother. Thus, researchers have not pursued study of these individuals; they have been more concerned with androgen—both its effect and its lack of effect.

*Androgen Insensitivity*   **Androgen insensitivity syndrome (AIS)** is a condition in which XY individuals secrete androgen, but their bodies are not sensitive to it so it has no effect. Insensitivity may be complete or incomplete. With incomplete insensitivity (Reifenstein's syndrome), the Wolffian system is partially developed and the genitalia are ambiguous. The decision about sex assignment can be difficult. When reared as girls, AIS individuals show conventional "girl-type" patterns of behavior. The few who are reared as boys have a very small penis and never completely virilize; they have a masculine identity but are not noted for rivalrous aggression and are hesitant to initiate erotic activity (Money, 1973).

Decisions about sex assignment are easier if the insensitivity, and therefore the feminization, is complete—a condition called testicular feminization. In these cases, neither the Wolffian system nor the Mullerian system develops, because the body is not sensitive to the androgen, which promotes the Wolffian system, but is sensitive to MIS. The infants are externally female and assigned and reared as girls, although they are genetic males. Their breasts develop because of some estrogen from the testes, but, because they do not have ovaries or a Mullerian system, they cannot bear children. The women can have heterosexual intercourse, and evidence indicates that they are good as adoptive mothers (Money & Ehrhardt, 1972). They also tend to be taller than average for women and are drawn to occupations that put a premium on having an attractive female appearance, including modeling, acting, and prostitution. Attractive-

*Fashion modeling is an area that attracts XY individuals with complete androgen insensitivity. Such individuals tend to be tall and thin and have an attractive female appearance, even though they are genetically male.*

ness as a female and the social response that it brings probably contribute to the feminine identity. Cases of complete androgen insensitivity clearly demonstrate that the presence of a Y chromosome does not guarantee life as a man, nor does it rule out life as a woman.

*Androgenization*   Another hormonal variation involves higher-than-usual doses of prenatal hormones. Higher levels of estrogen and progestin do not seem related to stereotypic masculine and feminine behaviors and so have not been studied much. Most research about hormonal overdoses has centered on cases of **androgenization**— excessive prenatal androgen in females. Excessive androgen may occur in either an XX or an XY individual, and it may occur endogenously (for reasons within the individual) or exogenously (for reasons outside of the individual, in this case in the mother). Effects are less severe for exogenous than for endogenous androgenization. Numerous cases of exogenous androgenization occurred in the 1950s when the drug diethylstilbestrol (DES) was given to many women to prevent miscarriage; the drug was a synthetic progestin that apparently converted to androgen (Meyer-Bahlburg et al., 1995; Money & Ehrhardt, 1972). The condition in their children is sometimes called progestin-induced hermaphroditism (PIH).

Endogenous androgenization is exemplified by **adrenogenital syndrome (AG or AGS),** which is often equated with **congenital adrenal hyperplasia (CAH).** (Some authorities use the term AGS to refer to both exogenous and endogenous androgenization.) CAH is a recessive genetic defect in which the adrenal glands of an XX or XY fetus malfunction about the 12th week of prenatal life, with a resulting increase in androgen. (Instead of producing cortisol, the adrenal gland produces progesterone, which converts to a substance similar to testosterone.) Without cortisone therapy, the ongoing high levels of androgen lead to premature puberty (ages 2–3 years) in boys and continuing masculinization in girls. Androgenized boys who are treated tend to have more energy in play and sports than their brothers, who are not androgenized, but are not more aggressive (Ehrhardt & Baker, 1974; Money, 1973). In fact, they are gentle and protective of their smaller peers and are shy and hesitant in relationships with females. Obviously, the extra dose of androgen does not make them domineering "he-men."

Androgenized females have normal female internal organs, which develop before the extra androgen appears, but the external organs, developing after the androgen increase, are male or ambiguous. Androgenized girls may be assigned and reared as either females or males. Before much was known about the syndrome, some individuals were reared as boys, but they experienced physical feminization at puberty, including menstruation.

The general developmental pattern is similar for endogenous and exogenous androgenized females (Ehrhardt & Baker, 1974; Ehrhardt & Money, 1967; Money & Ehrhardt, 1972). They prefer boys' toys and activities but in general not as much as boys do; in research studies they generally score intermediate to boys and girls in control groups (Berenbaum & Snyder, 1995). Although more active and energetic, they are no more aggressive or dominant than other girls and are not likely to pursue sports as a career or as an active hobby (Money & Mathews, 1982). As early as nursery school, they are less interested in feminine toys such as dolls, perhaps because of their activity level (Berenbaum & Hines, 1992). However, they plan on marriage and a family along with a career (as do XO individuals), and they are not unhappy being girls. They prefer simple utilitarian clothing but are willing to dress up when necessary. They are independent and self-reliant, have few personality disturbances, and are good students who are socially mature and easy to get along with. (Although those who participate in research are above average in intelligence, they are not more intelligent than their parents or siblings.) Thus they can be seen as having a healthy integration of conventionally masculine and feminine attributes.

There has been some confusion about the erotic interests of AGS women. Homosexual behavior may be somewhat more common in DES and CAH women, but more evident is that their dreams and fantasies show a greater openness to bisexuality or homosexuality than those of other women (Ehrhardt & Meyer-Bahlburg, 1981; Hurtig & Rosenthal, 1987). Still, the differences are moderate. For example, DES women differed from women in control groups mainly in the degree of bisexuality in imagery that was not expressed in behavior (Meyer-Bahlburg et al., 1995).

Some psychologists conclude that androgenization affects brain development and leads to temperament differences. However, even those psychologists are very quick and clear in pointing out that androgenized females are well within the normal range of typical female development. It should be noted that CAH girls receive on-going cortisone therapy; CAH boys on cortisone therapy also engage in more high-energy activities and rough outdoor activities than other boys (Ehrhardt & Baker, 1974). The high energy level of the girls, like that of the boys, may be due to the

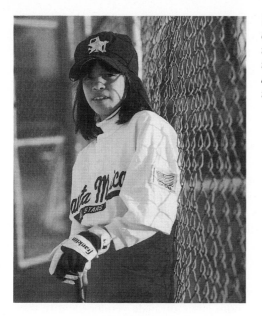

*Young androgenized females—girls who were exposed to excessive androgen prenatally—tend to be more active, although not more aggressive, than normal girls. However, not all "tomboys" are androgenized; many women say they were tomboys as children.*

cortisone (Quadagno, Briscoe, & Quadagno, 1977) rather than the androgenization. And the elevated tomboyishness must be considered cautiously, as 78% of college women and about half (51%) of women generally say that they were tomboys as children (Hyde, Rosenberg, & Behrman, 1977).

Although some experts conclude that parents' and children's attitudes are not likely to be significant factors affecting the tomboyish temperament for either kind of androgenized girl (Ehrhardt & Baker, 1974), others are not so quick to dismiss parents' and daughters' attitudes. Measures of tomboyishness are based on interview data, not on observed behaviors. Probably more important, the appearance of a malelike phallus may have more impact than realized, leading to parental expectations of tomboyish behavior. Many of the girls studied did not have surgical changes until they were well beyond infancy, and some were past 3 years. "The label tomboy may actually precede the appearance of tomboyish behavior if it exists, or it may at least lead to biased perceptions of behavior" (Quadagno et al., 1977, p. 69). Supporting this possibility is the fact that there was evidence of reduced "masculine" play among androgenized individuals born without physical abnormalities, in which cases parents originally did not know of the condition (Hines, 1982).

In sum, it is not clear whether the small differences between androgenized girls and other girls are due to prenatal androgen, to the human response to the condition, or to medication. Determining what is biological and what is social also is an issue with the next anomaly we discuss.

***DHT Deficiency*** Some males are reared as girls and then at puberty start to see themselves as male. These are XY individuals with a genetic deficiency that delays the development of male genitalia. The condition is referred to as **5-alpha** or **DHT deficiency.** (Technically, deficiency of 5-alpha-reductase decreases prenatal production of dihydrotestosterone, DHT, a derivative of testosterone that is necessary for the normal development of male external genitals.) Prenatal androgen levels are normal, and the male internal organs develop normally in these individuals. However, there is severe ambiguity in external genitalia because the testes are undescended at birth, the penis looks like a clitoris, and the partially formed vagina and incompletely formed scrotum look like labia (Ehrhardt, 1985).

Although the condition does exist elsewhere, it came to prominence because of a controversial study in the Dominican Republic (Imperato-McGinley, Peterson, Gautier, & Sturla, 1979). The affected individuals were raised as girls but at puberty, because of testosterone, showed virilization, including deepening of the voice and phallic growth. Their testes descended if they had not done so earlier. Eighteen of these individuals were studied in two small villages; of these, 16 changed their gender role at puberty from female to male. One acknowledged being a male but continued to dress as a female; one kept a female gender identity, married, and sought a sex-change operation. Thus, most made a reversal of roles at puberty and married women.

The researchers concluded that the exposure of the brain to androgen prenatally, early postnatally, and then at puberty has more effect on male gender identity than does sex of rearing. Critics have asked if the individuals really had a female gender identity in childhood and if the rearing was unambiguously female (Baker, 1980; Ehrhardt, 1985; Hood et al., 1987; Strong & DeVault, 1997). The study was done when the individuals were adults, so the data are retrospective, and it is not clear who provided information about the earlier years (Rubin, Reinisch, & Haskett, 1981). Given that the individuals were not genitally normal females at birth, it seems unlikely that those in the surrounding culture did not notice the genital malformation, especially the mothers. This possibility is accentuated because the culture had labels for the condition: *guevedoce* (eggs at 12), *guevote* (penis at 12), and *machihembra* (first woman, then man). The affected children were not seen as normal girls and probably did not behave like most girls of the culture. Indeed, these individuals realized, sometimes between ages 7 and 12 years, that they were different from other girls (Rubin et al., 1981).

The children may have converted to male identity because of social pressure, such as name calling (Hood et al., 1987). And it must be noted that there is a dramatic status difference for men and women in the rural villages of the Dominican Republic (Ehrhardt, 1985). Some of the parents were proud to discover that their daughter was a son!

The possible sociocultural explanation for the identity change is supported by a study of DHT-deficient individuals in New Guinea (the Sambia society of Papua) (Herdt & Davidson, 1988). Researchers in that culture hypothesized that sociocultural factors were primary in encouraging the identity change; they noted that the cultural valuation of the male role made the gender switch very pragmatic. An infertile woman with no breasts and ambiguous genitalia probably could expect to have little chance of a normal marriage or financial support. A change of gender, on the other hand, would bring higher status and economic advantages. These cases as well as other cases of gender change after ambiguous development do show the plasticity of gender and the possibility of gender change (Ehrhardt, 1985; Money, 1968).

## Gender Identity Disorder

People with **gender identity disorder** feel that they are in the wrong kind of body. They have a persistent identification with the other gender, a desire to be (or insistence that they are) of the other sex, and a discomfort with the sex assigned them or the gender role of that sex (American Psychiatric Association, 1994, *Diagnostic and Statistical Manual of Mental Disorders*, 4th ed.) (discussed in chapter 16). These people have been called **transsexuals,** and popularly they often are still referred to by that term. They are not to be confused with **transvestites,** who like to dress in clothes considered appropriate for the other sex but do not wish to be of the other sex (Garber, 1991). When dressed in the clothes of the other sex, transvestites feel excited, while people with gender identity disorder feel comfortable (Crooks & Baur, 1993). Nor are transsexuals to be confused with homosexuals. Males have been thought more likely to have gender identity disorder than females, generally estimated by a factor of at least 3 to 1, but the difference in frequency may be less (Pauly, 1990), and it certainly varies from culture to culture (Strong & DeVault, 1997).

The fact that there are more reported males than females with gender identity disorder is consistent with the general notion that more can go wrong with male development. We must be cautious, however. The greater number of reported males may also reflect society's lower tolerance of a male who deviates from what is expected of him than of a female who deviates from what is expected of her. Girls with gender identity disorder generally experience less ostracism and peer rejection than boys do, at least until adolescence (DSM-IV, 1994). And, given the greater valuation of males, a girl or woman who experiences malelike feelings may not feel there is anything wrong; but a boy or man who experiences femalelike feelings is having experiences consistent with that of the "lesser" sex and therefore may be more likely to feel that "something is wrong with me, I must be in the wrong kind of body" (Unger & Crawford, 1996).

***Causes and Effects***     The etiology of gender identity disorder is not clearly understood, nor is there agreement on the best method of treatment (Arndt, 1991; Bullough, 1991; Lothstein, 1984). There seem to be different patterns of contributing predispositions and different effects of the condition (DSM-IV, 1994). From evidence in other species, some writers emphasize the role of biological factors, such as prenatal hormones affecting brain differentiation (Pauly, 1974). Others suggest adult sex hormones as a factor, but sex hormone levels in transsexuals are comparable with those in other individuals prenatally and in adulthood (Meyer et al., 1986). There is some suggestive but inconclusive evidence about social experiences: Sons may have an unusually strong attachment to mothers and daughters to fathers (Pauly, 1974; Stoller, 1972). Early traumatic experiences in a disturbed family also have been reported (Meyer & Dupkin, 1985).

Some adults report (and their parents report about them) having had discomfort with their genitals along with identification with the other sex as early as 5 or even 2 years of age; these individuals are known as primary transsexuals. For others, signs appear later and more gradually, perhaps in adulthood (secondary transsexuals). Women are more likely than men to report early feelings and preference for cross-gender behavior. Most women report that from their early years they thought of themselves as boys, dressed like boys, preferred boys as friends, liked masculine play, and had no interest in babies or the motherly role. Often they were revolted by their menstruation and sometimes tried to hide their breasts. Of course, these characteristics themselves do not differentiate transsexual girls from many other girls.

Individuals with gender identity disorder often live the heterosexual life expected of them, though some women do not like vaginal penetration. Others have difficulty meeting their sexual needs because they want a heterosexual relationship, but for them the "other sex" (psychologically) has the same genitals as they (Crooks & Baur, 1993). Thus, women want a woman to desire them as she desires a man, and men want a man to desire them as he desires a woman. This can cause problems with would-be lovers, but it does not always: One male lover of a male transsexual commented, "She's a woman, what's between her legs doesn't matter."

***Sex-Change Surgery***    About two thirds of individuals with gender identity disorder live as a member of the other sex without surgery and appear to be relatively happy with their lives (Grimm, 1987). Others request surgery to bring their physical bodies into line with their gender identities (Hausman, 1993). Male-to-female requests have predominated, at about 3 to 1, but the ratio may be dropping. The benefits of surgery are controversial, but there seems to be a trend toward accepting sex reassignment as an option for some people (Beatrice, 1985; Blanchard, Steiner, Clemmensen, & Dickey, 1989; Lindemalm, Korlin, & Uddenberg, 1986; Pauly, 1990). Major determinants of healthy adjustment postoperatively are social support from friends and family members and surgical results that allow the person to pass as a member of the new sex.

Evidence suggests that those who become aware of their incongruence early (primary transsexuals) adjust better than those who discover it later (secondary transsexuals), presumably because of the greater amount of experience in the preferred gender role (Leavitt & Berger, 1990). Results are conflicting about whether a change is easier from male to female or female to male (Strong & DeVault, 1997). The surgery may be easier for the male-to-female change, but more than the body is involved. Achieving a masculine identity by surgery is associated with increased status; changing to a feminine identity is associated with lower status (Blanchard et al., 1989).

Certainly, people can benefit from the change. Many people with gender identity disorder who have had surgery say they feel "out of prison." A former man wrote, "I found that when people took me to be unquestionably a woman, a sense of rightness calmed and satisfied me" (Morris, 1974, p. 130). We do not know why such individuals feel imprisoned and then released with sex change. It is unlikely that hormones alone will provide a sufficient explanation.

## Hormones and Behavior

So far, we have not seen a great deal of evidence justifying the attribution of gender stereotyped behavior or its absence to chromosomes or to prenatal hormones. This does not mean that hormones are irrelevant to human behavior. There are hormonal correlates of behaviors in humans and in other species, but hormonal correlation does not necessarily imply hormonal causation. Both physiological and environmental events may contribute to the same behavior. For example, prenatal androgen may predispose an individual to rough-and-tumble play, but social environmental support is needed for the behavior to continue (Ehrhardt, 1985). On the other hand, the same behavior may develop in an individual with a lower level of prenatal androgens in a more strongly reinforcing environment, and then the hormonal level may change. "The pliability of the human organism is such that *many* pathways during the life course lead to similar behavior sets" (Ehrhardt, 1985, p. 93).

***Some Comments on Aggression***     So far, efforts to understand nature and nurture have been dominated by simplistic answers, often with a one-sided focus on nature. For example, the desire to see nature as causative leads some people to "explain" aggression as a function of testosterone. People often look at other species through an anthropomorphic lens and see what they expect to see—"believing is seeing." Yet there are enormous variations among animal species in overall levels of aggression and in the size of sex differences (Caplan & Caplan, 1994; Hood et al., 1987; Leibowitz, 1975; Sperling, 1991). Seldom mentioned is that female hyenas and female hamsters are more aggressive than males (Hopson, 1987), or that in a variety of primates, high estrogen levels are associated with greater dominance and more aggressive behavior (see Tieger, 1980).

When testosterone is found to be associated with aggression or dominance, the relationship clearly is a two-way street and often varies with the social context (Fausto-Sterling, 1985). For example, male monkeys' testosterone levels fall sharply after they have been defeated (Fedigan, 1982). One variety of fish (cichlids) has three sexes: brightly colored males, pale females, and males that look and act like females (Fernald, cited in Gorman, 1992). When a dominant, sexually active male dies, the sex hormones of the "female-acting" male increase, the color of his scales become bright, and he becomes sexually active. If challenged by a "regular" male who arrives upon the scene, he reverts to paleness and impotence.

We return to the topic of human aggression in chapter 9.

***Androgen in Women: The Social Context and Stress***     Hormone levels in women vary as a function of the social contexts in which they are operating, as indexed by their occupations and gender role orientation. Independent of age, women in professional, managerial, and technical occupations have higher levels of all androgens than women clerical workers and housewives (Purifoy & Koopmans, 1980). It should be noted that to speak only of "androgen" as if it were one hormone is imprecise, although sometimes that is all the published evidence allows. Different androgens seem to be associated with different types of jobs. For example, "people jobs" were found to be associated with certain androgens (androstenedione and some free testosterone), while "thing jobs" were associated with another androgen (testosterone). Testosterone concentration also is higher in women high in need for achievement and autonomy compared to women with lower need in these respects.

To assume that hormones cause different lifestyles is outmoded thinking, however. Ehrhardt (1985) suggests that a relatively high level of prenatal androgen may have predisposed some professional women to activities relevant to achievement and autonomy, and they were in an environment that fostered the predisposition. On the other hand, some or all of the professional women may not have had any unusual hormonal pattern prenatally or pubertally but were socially reinforced for activities related to careers. Then, the demands of the occupation might have increased their androgen production. Thus, again, we see that nature and nurture are intertwined.

Stress is associated with increased testosterone levels in women (see Hood et al., 1987) and has been suggested as responsible for some of the occupational differences in hormonal levels and perhaps in gender-typing. However, it seems simplistic to assume that being a clerical worker or housewife is necessarily less stressful than being in other working situations. It may be powerlessness per se that is associated with lower androgen; different types of stress are associated with different patterns of hormonal secretion (Baucom & Danker-Brown, 1979). These issues are yet to be well researched with respect to women and what women do.

There are some reports of testosterone level differences that seem related to individual differences and to levels of stress, though the kind of stress has not been addressed. For example, in one study, women of varying gender role classifications were found to differ in testosterone levels (Baucom, Besch, & Callahan, 1985). Women who were undifferentiated with respect to gender role orientation (see chapter 3) were the highest in testosterone levels, followed, in order, by androgynous, instrumental ("masculine"), and expressive ("feminine") women. This may seem strange if you think of testosterone as "the male hormone" and equate psychological masculinity with maleness. It is not strange if you consider the increase of testosterone associated with stress; hormones cannot be understood apart from the life of a person in a particular social context.

As noted previously (chapter 3), undifferentiated people are not as high on adjustment measures as are other people. Also, undifferentiated women are dissatisfied with their marriages and are seen negatively even by their close friends (Baucom & Danker-Brown, 1983). Thus, they experience more stress in a general sense. Androgynous and instrumental women have the problem that they are bucking the system, a stressful experience, while expressive women are going along with it. When instrumentality and expressiveness were examined separately, neither alone was associated with testosterone levels: It was the combination of the two kinds of scores that was most relevant.

***Androgens and Personality Differences***   When researchers examined the relationship between testosterone and adjectives checked as self-descriptive on the Adjective Check

List (see chapter 3), they concluded that the pattern of correlation fits the general notion that stress and testosterone level are a function of how individual characteristics interact with a social world (Baucom et al., 1985). Checking adjectives that the authors of the study considered generally unconventional, such as impulsive, sharp-witted, and uninhibited, was positively associated with testosterone. Checking those considered conventional (e.g., civilized, kind, practical) was negatively associated with testosterone. But again we see that the pattern of correlation and interaction is suggestive of relationships rather than conclusive about cause and effect.

***Summing Up***     Hormonal levels cannot be dismissed as irrelevant to human behavior, but we are a long way from understanding their antecedents or consequences. Meanwhile, we must beware the careless ways that hormones often are discussed. Hormones have been cited as "the" cause of a behavior that likely has multiple causes and that may itself "cause" the hormone level. Caution is especially relevant in considering menstruation (chapter 6) and cognitive abilities (chapter 8). For now, the comments of June Reinisch, former head of the Kinsey Institute, will sum up: "There's no question that hormones have an effect. But what does that have to do with the fact that I like to wear pink ribbons and you like to wear baseball gloves? *Probably something, but we don't know what* [italics added]" (cited in Gorman, 1992, p. 51).

# Nature and Nurture in Infancy

Infants are important in and of themselves, of course, but researchers have also been interested in infants for what can be learned from them about biological and environmental contributors to behavior. Again, as with cases of atypical development, answers are neither obvious nor simple. Biology has its effect in a social context. Infants, regardless of sex, may differ from each other for biological reasons, and adults quickly respond to those differences. As a result, two sets of forces, the biological and the social, become intertwined.

There are many similarities between girls and boys. There are also differences, but the differences are not reported consistently (Caplan & Caplan, 1994). In this part of the chapter, we focus on infant capabilities for responding to people. Both male and female infants are biologically prepared to enter the social world and to interact with it and be influenced by it. The people they interact with, however, are likely to have expectations about what girls and boys are "supposed to be like."

## Viability and Competence

One major difference between girls and boys is that girls have greater viability, or ability to maintain life, than boys do. As previously noted, boys are more vulnerable than girls prenatally, and the vulnerability persists. Prenatal death rates from miscarriages and stillbirths are higher for male fetuses, and almost a third more boys than girls die in the first year of life in the United States (Garai & Scheinfeld, 1968; National

Center for Health Statistics, 1992). Male development is more impaired by adverse environmental conditions. Among premature infants with equal incidence and severity of neonatal complications among boys and girls, boys later showed a higher incidence of neurological abnormalities and significantly lower intelligence scores (by 30 months; Cutler, Heimer, Wortis, & Freeman, 1965).

Girls are developmentally older than boys at birth in spite of a slightly shorter gestation (time in the womb)—that is, girls are more physically mature as shown by bone age, the most useful measure of physical maturity (Tanner, 1978a, 1978b). The hardening of girls' bones is 4–6 weeks advanced over that of boys. Given that girls' central nervous systems also may be more mature at birth, there are potentially important implications for interaction with adults.

The lesser viability of males should not overshadow the fact that both male and female infants are capable beings with great potential to process information and respond to people. Babies see, hear, and understand more than most people realize (Friedrich, 1983). Infants as young as 2 months old distinguish between people and objects; they greet people but not objects and are more relaxed with people (see Tronick, 1989). Two aspects of infant competence are particularly relevant to our concerns: their early ability to distinguish between males and females and their early ability to engage in socioemotional interactions.

***Infants' Ability to Distinguish Between Females and Males***    Infants tend to look at their mother when they hear her voice and look at their father when they hear his voice as early as 3½ months, although the effect is more pronounced at 7½ months (Spelke & Owsley, 1979). Infants can discriminate between pictures of male and female faces as early as 5 months of age (Fagan & Shepherd, 1982). A few months later, they also can match voices with pictures (Poulin-Dubois, Serbin, Kenyon, & Derbyshire, 1994). Infants aged 9 to 12 months are more attentive when pictures of males or females presented on a monitor are consistent with the gender of a voice presented at the same time.

Within the second half of the first year of life, infants are learning about sex distinctions. This early awareness may suggest that the "danger" time of sexual reassignment may not be as late as 18 months. However, we do not know what is going on in the infant mind about self-concept with respect to gender, and there is no suggestion that the infants understand gender as adults do. Infants' responsiveness seems based on perceptional characteristics. Women and men generally look and sound different. For example, women use a wider range of frequency in talking to infants; they also increase their voice pitch and variability when talking with infants, though evidence about males on this is mixed (Fernald et al., 1989).

***Sensitivity to the Emotions of Adults***    Infants actively use the emotional expressions of others to understand events and guide their own actions. When 10-month-old infants were placed in a situation in which they thought they faced a "drop-off" (in the "visual cliff"—an apparatus that presents an apparent but not a real drop-off), they looked to their mothers when the apparent depth was ambiguous (Campos, Barrett, Lamb, Goldsmith, & Sternberg, 1983). When mothers exhibited a fearful or angry face, most infants did not cross the apparent danger point. When mothers posed a happy face, most infants would cross. Other adults also have a similar effect. Infants clearly seek from adults affective information to add to their own understanding and even to override their own perceptions—"It looks to me like I might fall if I keep crawling, but Mom says it's OK." The emotional state of others clearly is fundamentally important to the infant (Tronick, 1989).

Infants do not just respond to adults, they also interact with them. During the first year of an infant's life especially, adults need to speak the emotional language that infants understand, and they need to see things from the infant's point of view (Maccoby, 1992). But the infant's ability to initiate and participate in interactions with adults should not be underestimated. Face-to-face interactions between adults and infants as young as 3 months are bidirectional and mutually regulated, rather than regulated only by the adult (Tronick, 1989; Tronick & Cohn, 1989). The principle of **reciprocal socialization** holds that development is not a one-way matter of caregivers influencing infants or of infants influencing caregivers.

If gender is important to adults and infants are responsive to adult expressions, then it is likely that infants are learning something about what the adult world expects of them. There is a great deal of variation from culture to culture in the extent and form of adult responsiveness to infants and in adult expectations of infants (Morelli, Rogoff, Oppenheim, & Goldsmith, 1992). In the United States, parents do respond differently to newborn infants on the basis of sex, though the parental stereotypes may be decreasing (Sweeney & Bradbard, 1988; Karraker, Vogel, & Lake, 1995). In one study, during the first 24 hours after birth, both fathers and mothers of daughters rated their babies as more finely textured and nonattentive than did parents of sons; in relative contrast, the parents of sons rated their newborns as bigger, larger featured, and more attentive than parents of daughters (Rubin, Provenzano, & Luria, 1974). Fathers, but not mothers, rated their daughters as very soft. The groups of girls and boys had been selected to be equal in birth weight and length and in general health.

Parental use of emotional terms and their responsiveness to their infants' emotional expressions also vary with gender of the infant. Infants begin to use emotional terms as early as 13 months (Beeghley, Bretherton, & Mervis, 1986; Ridgeway, Waters, & Kuczaj, 1985). Some evidence suggests that mothers talk about emotions more frequently and at younger ages with daughters than with sons, and over time daughters come to use emotional terms more than sons do (Dunn, Bretherton, & Munn, 1987). Emotional vocabulary is related to children's greater understanding of others' emotions later on (Denham, Zoller, & Couchound, in press).

Mothers seem differentially concerned with anger, pain, and sadness, depending on the infant's gender. In one study mothers tended to ignore their sons' expressions of pain but responded with a knitted brow to their daughters' expressions of pain (Haviland, 1977). However, they responded to sons' expressions of anger with a knitted-brow expression (e.g., "Oh? Tell me about it") but responded to daughters' expressions of anger with an angry expression (e.g., "You shouldn't be angry"). Will sons come to deny pain and daughters to deny anger? We do not know the long-term implications, if any, of the early difference in parental responsiveness, though a parent who responds to infants in these ways likely has expectations that will continue to be

*Babies are born with the ability to interact socially with adults, to "read" and respond to adults' emotions. This means they are also responding to adults' expectations, including unconscious ones, about how they should behave as girls or boys. Research indicates that parents do treat their infants somewhat differently on the basis of the child's sex.*

expressed as the child grows. We know that as the children grow older, mothers also talk more about anger with sons than with daughters (30–35-month-old children) but otherwise use a greater number and variety of emotional words with girls than boys (Fivush, 1989, 1991).

We also know that adults give toys to an infant (e.g., doll, toy football) on the basis of whether they think the infant is a girl or boy (Stern & Karraker, 1989). Parents shape the environment of infants and young children by decorating rooms in stereotypic ways and by providing stereotypic toys (see chapter 5). They also shape it by the nature of their social interactions apart from emotionality.

## Social Responsiveness

Female infants generally are more socially responsive than males in a number of ways (Fitzgerald, 1977; Gatewood & Weiss, 1930; Goldberg & Lewis, 1969; Harris, 1977; Moss, 1967). This may be because of girls' more developmentally advanced state at birth and the implications of that for adults, or it may be for other reasons—such as subtle differences between male and female neonates—that are not yet well understood. For example, newborn girls maintain eye contact longer than boys do. The gaze aversion of boys may be a way to handle the overarousal caused by prolonged eye contact; boys' emotional states build up more rapidly than those of girls (Fagot &

Leinbach, 1987). Girls also have been reported to talk earlier, smile earlier at human faces and voices, show earlier preferences for looking at faces or facelike stimuli, show earlier discrimination of faces, and be more responsive to the cry of another same-sex infant.

The social stimuli of looking and talking may have different effects on male and female infants. Jerome Kagan (1970) presented slides of human faces and taped auditory speech sequences to infants. Although the absolute amount of infant vocalization did not differ between male and female infants, there were differences in what the vocalizations seemed to mean. The boys' vocalizations, accompanied by twisting and moving about, seemed part of a general restlessness, while the girls seemed to be attentive to the social stimuli. For example, a girl who listened attentively to an auditory stimulus was likely to vocalize when it ended, but a boy was not. It is easy to see how a responding adult might assume, "She is paying attention to me, but he is not."

Kagan (1970) proposed that the vocalization and attentiveness patterns were related to the greater maturity of the central nervous system in girls, especially as related to speech functions. He suggested also that mothers spent more time in reciprocal verbalization with daughters, thus connecting vocal responses to human faces; in contrast, mothers used more motoric play with sons. Consistent with this, girls (at 6 months) were more responsive than boys when mothers spoke to them, and they initiated more interactions with the mother than boys did (Gunnar & Donahue, 1980).

It is likely that both female and male infants want social stimulation but differ in what kinds they prefer. Male infants may get some social interaction from the feeding situation that girls get in other situations. Male infants in a variety of cultures have longer feeding times per feeding session and later weaning than females do (Fitzgerald, 1977). The different feeding patterns seem due more to the infant than to the mother. The boys may be "asking" for a calming contact that is particularly important to them. If so, mothers respond.

Mothers are more attentive to male infants than to female infants during the feeding interaction and more attentive to the males they breast-feed than the males they bottle-feed (Walraven, 1974). Breast-feeding may be a highly significant contributor to the attachment relationship for mother and son, while visual and auditory contact may be more important for mother and daughter. What is important for the boy and the girl is that they both do attach to the mother; what is interesting to psychologists is that they may attach in different ways that are yet to be fully studied and understood.

Infant preferences about stimulation may also contribute to the fact that for the first 6 months of life, boys get more proximate stimulation, such as being held, jostled, and tossed up and down; girls receive more distal stimulation, such as being looked at and talked to (Fitzgerald, 1977). For example, African American mothers rubbed, patted, rocked, touched, and kissed their 3-day-old boys more than their 3-day-old girls, but they talked more to their girls (Brown et al., 1975). The greater physical interaction with boys may reflect adult stereotypes, but it also may reflect detection of infant preferences. The influence of infants on adults is shown even more clearly with infant crying and general fussiness.

## Infant Fussiness

Crying is the first way that infants communicate what they need. There seem to be no gender differences in newborn crying. Most of the time, the nature of the crying helps adults see the cause of distress. Researchers have proposed that caregivers' responses to cries play a significant role in the development of infants' communicative competence as well as their personality and cognitive development (see Gustafson & Harris, 1990). Moss (1967) demonstrated the interplay of gender differences in crying and adult responses. Infants were observed in their homes at age 3 weeks and again at age 3 months. At 3 weeks the fussiness of both boys and girls was correlated positively with maternal attentiveness—crying babies were responded to more than others. At 3 months the relationship still was positive for the girls: The more fussy girls got more attention than girls who were less fussy. In contrast, at 3 months the relationship for boys was negative: The more fussy boys got less attention than boys who were less fussy.

Perhaps mothers decided that "boys will be boys" or that boys should learn to "tough it out." Moss, however, suggested that the mothers attempting to calm boy babies were not rewarded as much as were mothers attempting to calm girl babies. Consider the situation of a woman with a new infant. She wants to be a good mother, and she attempts to calm her infant when the infant is upset. In Moss's view, the girls were more likely to reward mothers by calming down, but the boys, who did not calm down, actually gave mothers an aversive stimulus. So, mothers did what anyone is likely to do when recurringly experiencing a negative event—avoid it.

Although interest here is on gender differences, the avoidance of fussy boys is part of a broad pattern. A crying baby causes discomfort in just about anyone, which helps make sure that infants get what they need to survive. Brain-damaged babies and those who have had prenatal and birth complications have particularly aversive cries, and most adults do respond to their cries with extra care. But the cries can be so unpleasant and the infant so difficult to soothe that parents can become frustrated and angry (Berk, 1993). A result is that sick babies are more likely to be abused than healthy ones.

Moss suggested that the boys did not calm down because they were less consolable than girls, perhaps because of a less developed nervous system. In any case, mothers apparently were influenced by their infants—another example of reciprocal socialization. Biological predispositions influence the ways that infants interact in the social world and elicit adult behavior, and the social world may influence how the predispositions are expressed. Clearly, we are a long way from a full understanding of the specifics of the nature-nurture interactions and their implications.

## *Some Final Thoughts: Are the Sexes Really Opposite?*

Who is the "opposite" sex and why are they opposite? The opposite sex may be more like our own than we have realized, and what differences there are may not be fixed by biology. People tend to think of women and men as different physically and psychologically. We saw in chapter 3 that at the psychological level, people are not necessarily feminine or masculine; both women and men can and do score high, or low, on psychological measures of aspects of masculinity and femininity.

In this chapter, we see that at the physical level, people generally are consistently female or male, but males and females are not therefore "opposites." The only clear-cut, either-or difference between typical females and typical males is at the genetic level. Both females and males have both the so-called female and male hormones, and the material for the gonads and internal and external reproductive system is shared by both males and females. Atypical individuals show the extremes of blending of masculine and feminine physical traits that occur in more moderate degrees among typical individuals.

If the body contains, or is, our destiny, it likely is because our social communities make assumptions about what the destiny should be and provide experiences that shape the biological effects and even the course of biological development itself. Androgenized females are often cited as evidence of the importance of the prenatal environment. However, as we have seen, the combination of cortisone therapy and parental labels of their girls as "tomboys" early in life may be more responsible than prenatal androgenization. The case of the identical twin boy whose penis was surgically removed and the cases of 5-alpha boys have been held up as examples of the potency of prenatal development. But they also illustrate the interaction of biology and experience.

In sum, we cannot safely look to prenatal differences or current hormone levels to identify the other sex as the "opposite" sex or to explain differences between women and men. Neither can we proclaim that prenatal experiences and current hormone levels are irrelevant to human behavior. Biological and experiential factors are highly intertwined: We have seen, for example, that brain differentiation may continue after birth, and hormonal levels may vary with circumstances.

Infants of both sexes are prepared "by nature" to interact with the social environment and to obtain support from it, but the social environment is prepared with expectations about what girls and boys are supposed to be like. Both boys and girls come quickly to discriminate between females and males and respond to the emotional cues and behavioral responses given by adults; some of the cues and responses adults give vary with the sex of the infant. If men and women are in any sense opposites or simply different in ways that matter, such differences are more likely due to the social world in which infants and the children they become have to negotiate to get what they want and need. As we will see in the next chapter, the infant, the toddler, and the child are immersed in a social world in which gender is considered of paramount importance.

## KEY TERMS

| | | |
|---|---|---|
| plasticity | psychobiological | genetic criterion of sex |
| reciprocal determinism | sexual differentiation | genotype |

phenotype
gonadal criterion of sex
unimorphic tissue
androgen
testosterone
estrogen
progesterone
hormonal criterion of sex
internal reproductive
  organs, a criterion of sex
dimorphic tissue
Mullerian system
Wolffian system

Mullerian-inhibiting
  substance (MIS)
external reproductive
  organs, a criterion
  of sex
brain differentiation
brain lateralization
corpus callosum
true hermaphroditism
pseudohermaphroditism
sex of assignment
sex of rearing
XO, Turner's syndrome

androgen insensitivity
  syndrome (AIS)
androgenization
adrenogenital syndrome
  (AG or AGS)
congenital adrenal
  hyperplasia (CAH)
5-alpha, DHT-deficiency
gender identity disorder
transsexual
transvestite
reciprocal socialization

## KEY POINTS

### Prenatal Development

◆ Biological and environmental factors are intertwined in their effects on human behavior.

◆ Prenatal sexual differentiation occurs in several stages: genetic, gonadal, hormonal, development of internal reproductive organs, development of external reproductive organs, and probably brain differentiation. For most individuals, the phenotypical sex is consistent with genotypical sex and with other sexual criteria.

◆ Being XX or XY is the only categorical or absolute way males differ from females physically. Males and females both have the same tissue from which gonads, internal reproductive organs, and external reproductive organs develop. The gonads of both males and females secrete both androgens and estrogens. The adrenal cortex also secretes androgens and some estrogen.

◆ Females are more viable than males at all stages of prenatal development and through the early years of life. More males are conceived and born.

◆ Hormones acting prenatally and shortly after birth are thought to have a permanent organizational effect on the brain, while hormones acting later in life have an activational and temporary effect. The brains of females are thought be more bilateral than the brains of males.

### How Much Does Biology Matter?

◆ In many cases of unusual development, assignment and rearing seem more important than biological criteria of sex in affecting the life course. However, reassignment and rearing do not always take precedence over other factors.

◆ Surgical corrections and hormonal therapies can provide consistency in gender when there are anomalies.

◆ Chromosomal variations are not uncommon. XXY males, "supermales," are taller than average but not more aggressive than XY males. Turner's syndrome (XO) females have no gonads and are short in stature but can lead normal lives.

◆ Hormonal variations involve prenatal exposure to abnormal levels of hormones (exemplified by adrenogenital syndrome) or insensitivity to hormonal effects (exemplified by androgen insensitivity syndrome). In 5-alpha or DHT deficiency, a hormonal deficiency delays the development of external reproductive organs in males. The 5-alpha individuals typically change identity and role from female to male during puberty when virilization occurs.

◆ More men than women have gender identity disorder. Some individuals with the disorder live heterosexual lives, while others request a sex change. The causes and appropriate treatment are still debated.

◆ In other species, testosterone and dominance vary with social context. Androgen levels in women vary with occupation and gender role. It is premature to state what personality traits are related to androgen.

## *Infancy*

◆ Females are more physically mature than males at birth and more viable. The female's better developed central nervous system may have implications for interactions with caregivers.

◆ Infants' competence is shown by their early distinctions between males and females, their use of the emotional expressions of others to guide their actions, and their interaction with adults. Adults interact differently with infants, depending on whether the infant is a girl or a boy.

◆ Mothers talk about a greater variety of emotions with daughters than with sons, and they treat sons and daughters differently with respect to anger, pain, and sadness.

◆ Female infants generally are more socially responsive than male infants and more attentive to social stimuli, possibly because of a more developed central nervous system and/or more reciprocal verbalization with adults.

◆ Boy babies appear less consolable than girl babies, so that after 3 months, there is a negative relationship between boys' fussiness and maternal attention.

## INTEGRATIVE QUESTIONS

1. Select any one of the atypical forms of development and make the best case you can for biological determinants for human behavior. Then, critique your own statements from an environmentalist point of view.

2. If you were a parent of a child with inconsistent sexual characteristics, what considerations would you take into account in deciding whether or not to have surgery performed on your child? Do you think parents have the right to make

decisions about surgical and hormonal "corrections" on what nature has made of a child?

3. Consider your interests, hobbies, mannerisms, dress preferences, sexual preferences, and other characteristics. To what extent and in what ways do you think that biological factors might be relevant to these preferences and characteristics? To what extent do you think environmental factors might be relevant?

4. Explain how and why infant behavior is a matter of both the infants' biological predispositions and the social context.

*Chapter 5*

# Development of Gender Role Behavior

Some people consider the development of gender-typed behavior to be "only natural" because they assume that biological differences between females and males result in behavioral differences. Psychologists often acknowledge the possibility of some biological contributors to behavior, but generally they give more weight to experience in shaping behavior. As we saw in chapter 4, the influence of biology is multifaceted, complex, and often strongly mediated by social forces. It is clear that social forces powerfully influence gender-typed development, but we do not yet know the full story of how these forces play out in female and male development. We do not yet know everything about how children develop their notions about gender and their gender-related behaviors.

In this chapter we will explore the current state of knowledge about the development of gender-typing by looking first at research and theory about the early years and the role of parents and peers and then considering the relationship of gender-typing to self-esteem of adolescent women. Finally, we will consider the development of people who do not conform to stereotypes.

Before continuing, consider these questions for personal thought:

- What were your favorite toys when you were a child? Did you ever want to play with a toy considered appropriate for the other sex? With what result?
- Name the first fairy tale or other childhood story that comes to mind. Why does that stand out for you?
- Did you ever wonder what it would be like to be of the other sex than you are? Did you ever want to be of the other sex?
- Think about how your parents treated you when you were younger. Do you think they would have treated you differently had you been of the other sex than you are? What influence do you think your parents had on how feminine and masculine you are?

- What chores were you expected to do as a child? How do you think the chores have influenced you?
- Was your mother employed while you were living at home? How do you think that influenced you?
- When you were an adolescent, what helped you to feel good about yourself? What made you feel not so good about yourself? What did you worry about? As an adolescent, were you looking forward to growing up?
- How do you want to interact with your children? Why? How is that similar to or different from the way your parents interacted with you?

## Facts and Theories About Gender-Typed Development

The degree of gender-typing is a matter of the degree to which an individual is feminine or masculine according to the culture's general views. Two main points are notable about the development of gender-typing in young children. One is how rapidly children take up gender-typed activities and accumulate knowledge of gender stereotypes (Katz, 1996). Until 5 or 6 years of age, most children's views about what girls and women can do and what boys and men can do are very stereotypic and rigid, often more so than the views of their parents. After those early years, as we shall see, the picture is more variable.

A second main point is that gender-typed behavior is more important to adults *for* boys than for girls, and *to* boys themselves than to girls (Messner, 1994; Zucker, Wilson-Smith, Kurita, & Stern, 1995). In other words, parents are more upset by "sissy" sons than by "tomboy" daughters, and the children themselves feel much the same. This may reflect greater valuation of men and of agentic or instrumental values (chapter 3; Feinman, 1981; Urberg, 1982). After the early years, girls tend to hold more relaxed attitudes toward gender role stereotypes than boys do (Katz & Ksansnak, 1994; McAninch, Milich, Crumbo, & Funtowicz, 1996; Signorella, Bigler, & Liben, 1993).

### Some Basic Developmental Events

Gender-typing begins with sex assignment, which, as we saw in chapter 4, typically is made at birth. Many parents do interact differently in some respects with infant girls and infant boys. We also know that some major events, the topics of this section, happen very quickly.

*Self-Labeling and Gender Identity*    Gender identity sometimes is thought of as being a **self-label**, a label of oneself as a girl or as a boy. Self-labeling develops between the ages of 18 months and 3 years (Katz, 1996; Slaby & Frey, 1975; Stipek, Gralinski, & Kopp, 1990; Thompson, 1975; Weinraub et al., 1984). However, much more is involved in gender identity than merely applying the words *girl* or *boy, man* or *woman,* to oneself (see Huston, 1983, 1985; Maccoby, 1988, 1990). It seems better to reserve

**Table 5.1**    Major Landmarks in Gender-Typed Development

| Age | Sex knowledge | Gender stereotype knowledge | Toys, peers, activities |
|---|---|---|---|
| 10 to 18 months | Reassignment OK | | Some toy preference |
| 2 years | | Basic knowledge of activities and occupations | Toy preference<br>Girls show peer preference |
| 18 months to 3 years | 50% self-label at 27 months | | |
| 3 years | Prefer own sex, roles | | Knowledge of toy stereotypes |
| 3 to 5 years | Girls peak at 4 years, boys increase with age | Personality stereotypes used | Boys show peer preference (stronger than girls by age 5) |
| 4 to 5 years | Gender stability<br>Reliably classify others by sex | Occupational stereotypes used<br>Choices for self stereotyped | |
| 5 to 7 years | Gender constancy:<br>50% 5-year-olds,<br>many 7-year-olds,<br>66% 8-year-olds | | |
| 5 to 10 years | | More flexible about trait preference | Increased peer preference |
| 2 to 8 years | Hard to change stereotypes | Hard to change stereotypes | |
| 7 to 11 years | May become more flexible | Girls' occupational choices less stereotyped | |

the term **gender identity** to refer to the implications of the self-label in a person's total understanding of self (Donelson, 1977a). What does a child or adult mean in saying, "I am a girl (woman)," or "I am a boy (man)"? The child acquires knowledge of cultural gender stereotypes and often (not always) adopts the ascribed gender role and comes to match the stereotype to some degree. Gender-typing is a judgment made from the outside, while gender identity is a judgment made from the inside: An individual who feels very feminine may be considered masculine by others.

The degree of match varies from child to child, adult to adult, and from age to age (chapter 14). Not all children or adults are highly stereotyped. Full understanding of gender-typed development requires considering the differences in how people see the implications of their self-label. The many facets of gender-typing do not all occur together, nor are they the same for every individual. Table 5.1 provides an orienting overview.

**Gender preference** is fairly evident by age 3 years. Children typically prefer to be of the sex they are, but the preference is more variable and not as marked for girls as for boys (Abel & Sahinkaya, 1962; Parsons, 1976b). Boys' preference increases with age; girls' preference peaks at 4 years of age and then stabilizes or comes to incorporate some aspects of what is typically thought of as masculine preference (Serbin,

**Table 5.2**   Toy Preference and Toy Identification

| Age | Toy Preference* Girls | | Boys | Toy identification** |
|---|---|---|---|---|
| 2 years | 12.2 | < | 19.1 | 1 |
| 4 years | 17.3 | = | 18.8 | 17 |
| 6 years | 20.9 | = | 21.7 | 20, all |

*Number of times child selected gender-consistent toy, out of 24 pairs.
**Number of children who correctly identified gender-consistent toy, out of 20 children.

SOURCE: Based on data given by Blakemore, J. E. O., LaRue, A. A., & Olejnik, A. B. (1979). Sex-appropriate toy preference and the ability to conceptualize toys as sex-role related. *Developmental Psychology, 15* (3), 339–340.

Powlishta, & Gulko, 1993). For reasons not yet clear, other preferences related to gender-typing often are shown *before* the preference to be what one is.

***Peer and Toy Preference***   **Peer preference** is a preference for children of the same gender, typically accompanied by a negative attitude toward children of the other gender, who become "the other"—children learn to categorize people as "us" versus "them" (Katz, 1996; Martin, 1989; Powlishta, 1990). Girls show the preference at age 2 years and boys about a year later, but boys' preference is stronger than girls' by age 5 (Maccoby, 1988, 1990). A later section discusses peers in more detail.

**Toy preference** means selecting and preferring toys considered (by adults) to be appropriate or role consistent for a girl or a boy. Some infants show toy preference by 12 to 18 months (Caldera, Huston, & O'Brien, 1989; Jacklin, Maccoby, & Dick, 1973; Powlishta, Serbin, & Moller, 1993), and there are reports of 10-month-old girls favoring dolls, even though parents have not encouraged them to do so (Roopnarine, 1986). More typically, toy preference is estimated to be established between 2 and 3 years (Huston, 1983). In one study, toy preference was measured as the number of times the child selected the gender-consistent toy as the one he or she "liked best" out of 24 pairs of toys (Blakemore, LaRue, & Olejnik, 1979). The study also measured toy identification by the number of children out of 20 who correctly identified toys as gender consistent. The results are shown in Table 5.2. Toy preference is stronger earlier for boys than for girls. For example, three fourths of boys, at ages 3 years and 5 years, asked for stereotyped toys for Christmas; only 29% percent of 3-year-old girls, but as many 5-year-old girls (73%) as boys, did so (Robinson & Morris, 1986). Early preference does not seem due to toy differences in size, faces, softness, number of pieces, or moving parts (Maccoby & Jacklin, 1974; O'Brien, Huston, & Risley, 1981).

Toy preference occurs before children have a self-label of their gender and before they can identify the toy as "for boys" or "for girls" (Etaugh & Duits, 1990; Thompson, 1975). Although 2-year-old boys showed toy preference (Table 5.1), only one 2-year-old—a girl—could accurately sort pictures of toys into piles of "girls' toys" and "boys' toys." Stereotyped knowledge of toys is not present until 3 years. Cognitive understanding of toy appropriateness clearly *comes* to be important (Blakemore et al., 1979). Preschoolers showed less interest in and memory for novel gadgets shown in boxes labeled as being for the other sex or both sexes, and they sometimes offered negative comments about those, such as "Yuk, girls!" (Bradbard & Endsley, 1983). As we will see later in this chapter, it is probably important that the children who were interested in the gadgets labeled for the other sex looked to adults for reassurance that it really was OK to be interested in them.

***Stability of Gender Labels***    Although the self-label, gender preference, and peer and toy preference occur early, it takes a while for children to label others accurately. Children younger than 2 years of age had no better than chance accuracy in gender labeling of photographs but had a sharp increase in accuracy during the next half year (Etaugh, Grinnell, & Etaugh, 1989). Still, it is not until about ages 4 or 5 years that most children can label the sex of other people (Rabban, 1950; Thompson & Bentler, 1971). Children who have learned a gender label do show strong preferences for "one of their own" and aversion of "the other." And about half of children who were able to classify according to gender played with more gender stereotyped toys, whereas those who had not, had little toy preference (Fagot & Leinbach, 1989). For most children, classifying gender is not based exclusively or at all on genital differences. Rather, judgments are made on the basis of hair, body type, and clothes more than genitals and breasts (Katcher, 1955; McConaghy, 1979; Thompson & Bentler, 1971). In one study, only 24 of 144 children mentioned genitals as being a primary cue (Thompson & Bentler, 1971).

Children learn whether they are female and male and tend to prefer being that, but for several years they think that being female or male is subject to change (see Huston, 1983). If, as young children think, the definition of sex is a matter of clothing and hairstyle, then it can be changed. Similarly, children also use superficial stereotypes in defining how an African American child can become white and how a white can become a Native American (Aboud, 1988; Wyche, 1991). It takes a while for children to shift the definition from superficial correlates to biological fact.

Also important is that it takes a while for children to understand generic constancy (e.g., that a cat with a face mask of a dog is still a cat; DeVries, 1969). As they begin to climb over this hurdle around age 4 years, children start developing a *relative* certainty or **gender stability** (pseudoconstancy), meaning that they think it likely that a person will not change sex, but they hold out the possibility nonetheless (Brown & Pipp, 1991; Smith, 1987). Although children who have knowledge about genitals may show constancy earlier, they still may think that a girl might develop a penis if she wishes (Frey & Ruble, 1992). By age 5, 50% of children think that they could change their minds about their sex; a girl, for example, might be sure that she could grow up to be a daddy if she wanted to (DeVries, 1969; Kohlberg, 1966).

Gender stability is followed by **gender constancy,** which means that the unchangeability of sex is accepted. Most children seem to have achieved gender constancy by age 7 years, but some (34%) still may not have it at age 8 years. Even before attaining

*Although children know what sex they are by the time they are 3, they do not have the concept of gender constancy—that they will always be the sex they are now—until they are 5 to 7 years old. This boy may believe he can grow up to be a "mommy."*

gender stability or constancy, children are amassing a sizable body of knowledge about gender; after they realize that gender is related to biology, they assume that biology is the reason for different behaviors and interest (Taylor & Gelman, 1991).

***Knowledge of Gender Stereotypes***    Children as young as 2 years are reasonably well informed about gender stereotypes, and their knowledge increases with age (Bauer, 1993; Cowan & Hoffman, 1986; Kuhn, Nash, & Brucken, 1978; Picariello, Greenberg, & Pillemer, 1990; Weinraub et al., 1984). For example, 2-year-olds said that girls like to play with dolls, help mother, talk a lot, ask for help, and never hit (Kuhn et al., 1978). And, when boys grow up, they will be the boss, and girls will clean house. Children learn about personality attributes a little later (3–5 years), possibly because personality attributes are less concrete than activities (Huston, 1983; Intons-Peterson, 1988; Serbin et al., 1993). Children's descriptions of women and girls include "cry a lot," "are quiet and afraid," "thankful," "weak," "gentle," "loving," and "have good manners" (Powlishta, 1990). Children's descriptions of men and boys include "cruel," "strong," "get into fights," "daring," "self-reliant," "talk loudly," and "messy." The more intelligent children have more stereotyped knowledge. Children do become more flexible about traits as they grow (5–10 years) and more flexible about traits than about activities (Trautner, Helbing, Sahm, & Iohaus, 1989). Girls become more flexible than boys, and African American boys become more flexible than white boys (Katz, 1996).

There are social class and ethnic variations in strength of stereotyping and sometimes in the exact content of stereotypes (Huston, 1983; Katz, 1996; Lackey, 1989;

Serbin et al., 1993; Unger, 1979). Generally, children of lower socioeconomic status (SES) are less flexible than middle-class children about personality characteristics of males and females, and middle-class children see more characteristics as shared by women and men than lower SES children do (P. A. Katz, 1987; Romer & Cherry, 1980). Although ethnic differences are not always consistent (P. A. Katz, 1987), white children seem more stereotyped than African Americans (Romer & Cherry, 1980). Studies have found that African American children are somewhat less likely to see men and women stereotypically (Bardwell et al., 1986; Malson, 1983; Price-Bonham & Skeen, 1982). For example, they see women and men as equally expressive emotionally (Romer & Cherry, 1980), and girls especially have less stereotyped views of women than white children do (Gold & St. Ange, 1974; Huston, 1983; Malson, 1983). The reduced stereotyping of African American children is consistent with that of the adults of their culture and may reflect the reduced division of labor in African American culture (chapter 3). Hispanic and European American children do not necessarily differ substantially (Bardwell, Cochran, & Walker, 1986), though Hispanics sometimes seem more stereotyped (e.g., Puerto Ricans; Vázquez-Nuttall & Romero-García, 1989).

At least by kindergarten and probably by age 2 years, most children know stereotypes about occupations and prefer stereotyped occupations for themselves, whether middle class or lower SES, African American or white (Gettys & Cann, 1981; O'Keefe & Hyde, 1983; Serbin et al., 1993). Some children are fairly liberal about what *other* people can be, especially women: Children have an easier time accepting a woman in a man's occupation (e.g., dentistry) than imagining a man in a woman's occupation (e.g., secretarial work) (Labour Canada, 1986). Still, their choices for *themselves* are very stereotypic. Girls say they will be mothers, nurses, and teachers, and boys say they will have active and adventurous futures as policemen or firemen (Looft, 1971; Papalia & Tennent, 1975). Boys are more likely than girls to choose gender-stereotypic jobs for themselves (O'Keefe & Hyde, 1983). Children of more educated parents are less stereotyped about what jobs others can have than are other children, but they, too, are stereotyped about their own occupational choices. Girls, however, become less stereotyped in their choices; 64% of kindergarten girls wanted to enter women's occupations, while only 40% of girls in the eighth grade did. Boys at both ages mentioned only men's occupations.

Maternal employment outside the home cannot be counted on to make a difference in the child's early years, though its effects do increase with the child's age. Preschool girls with employed mothers did not differ from other girls in occupational and toy preferences (Seegmiller, 1980). One 4-year-old girl insisted that women can be nurses but cannot be physicians, although her mother was a physician (Maccoby & Jacklin, 1974). Older girls (aged 5–7) are more likely to choose a less feminine vocation if their mother is in a nontraditional job (Jones & McBride, 1980; Selkow, 1984), and sons' flexibility also increases with the mother's nontraditionality of employment and her employment level (Barak, Feldman, & Noy, 1991; Serbin et al., 1993). As we will see, daughters of employed mothers come to be oriented to nontraditional careers and high achievement.

How are these basic events to be explained? In the following section, we will examine some theories about the development of culturally defined femininity and masculinity. No single theory adequately explains the known facts, though all contribute to our understanding of children from different angles.

## Theories of Gender-Typed Development

Gender-typed development can be seen as a process of change in several domains of human characteristics (Downs & Langlois, 1988; Serbin et al., 1993). One is emotional or affective, as the child forms a bond with particular adults, typically the parent of the same sex. A second is behavioral, referring to gender-typed actions and preferences. The third is a cognitive component of thinking about gender. In other words, people—including children—feel, act, and think. Their feelings, actions, and thoughts are not always consistent.

Three broad theoretical perspectives have been developed to address gender-typing. They tend to emphasize one of the three domains more than the other two. Psychoanalytic theory is primarily concerned with feelings. Social learning theory emphasizes behavior and related preferences. Cognitive developmental theory is concerned with thought processes. The emphases are relative, of course. For example, psychoanalytic theory is cognitive as well as affective, social learning is affective as well as behavioristic, and cognitive developmental theory encompasses behavior and affect. These theories, like those in other areas, differ in what kinds of phenomena fall in their sphere of relevance, so that they are not necessarily competitive, just different. As mentioned earlier, no single theory is accepted as adequately explaining all the facts.

Although each of the major theoretical positions makes very different assumptions about what children are like, they do have some common themes and some common problems (Sedney, 1987). First, they assume that the child lives in a nuclear family with a mother and a father. Further, they emphasize "appropriate" gender-typed development—the development of stereotypic femininity in girls and masculinity in boys—and are not particularly concerned with individual differences among children or in gender-typing beyond childhood. Some of these problems can be addressed with extensions of the theories and must be addressed in view of the within-gender variation now recognized and the changing patterns of American families. A final problem for all is that they assume that gender identity and gender-typing require some sort of internalization or imitation of a same-gendered adult, typically a parent, but gender-related development occurs *earlier* than the postulated special relationship with the same-sex adult that is supposed to encourage gender-typing. Infants' learning about gender may begin much earlier than previously suspected (chapter 4). In spite of the problems, each of the three major theories has something to contribute to our understanding of gender-typing.

## Psychoanalytic Theory

The cornerstone of psychoanalytic theory, of course, is Sigmund Freud (1940/1963, 1933/1965, 1925/1972, 1931/1972). The basic message of Freud's view is that both little girls and little boys *want love and fear the loss of it.* Personality must be understood in a social context of intimate interpersonal relationships (Mitchell, 1975). By the time

Freud got around to systematic attention to gender-typing, he already had some basic tenets of his general theory of personality well entrenched, and those influenced how he approached gender issues: the importance of biology, including sexual and aggressive drives; the importance of early experiences; and the importance of unconscious memories, predominantly including content about early experiences involving sex and aggression.

For gender-typing specifically, the crucial concept is the **Oedipal crisis,** happening around 4 to 6 years of age. The developmental stage during which this crisis occurs is named for an ancient Greek hero, Oedipus, who grew up in an adoptive family and unknowingly killed his biological father and then married his biological mother. Note that the model is a masculine one and Aristotelian in seeing females as deformed males (chapter 1).

*Girls' Development*     Events relevant to gender-typing begin early in life as the mother cares for the infant's needs. Freud's theory of *sexual monism* is that children have the theory that people come in only one sex—their own. Further, the pre-Oedipal girl assumes that her clitoris is a penis. (Reasons for this assumption are not clear, other than Freud's assumption that the penis is the primary organ for a sexual human being.) Like the boy, she has been enjoying stimulation of "the penis," Freud suggests. (It is true that both girls and boys practice genital stimulation very early and learn the word *penis* before any words referring to female genitalia; chapter 11.)

Then, the girl has the profound psychological experience of discovering she does not have a penis; she may have observed males before, but the anatomical specifics were not relevant. The discovery initiates the Oedipal stage and the girl's resulting penis envy. Realizing that she is without a penis, "She is wounded in her self-love by the unfavorable comparison with the boy who is so much better equipped and therefore . . . repudiates her love toward her mother and at the same time often represses a good deal of her sexual impulses in general" (Freud, 1933/1965, p. 126). Her self-deprecation extends to all women, who, like her, are lacking a penis. And she blames mother for not having given her a penis.

The girl shifts her love from mother to father, who has a penis and who may give her a child to compensate for her lack, particularly if the child is a boy. The girl's anxiety about not having a penis leads to love of father. Her sexuality shifts away from her clitoris, which she formerly had actively enjoyed, because it reminds her of her shame: The girl's sexuality comes to be concentrated on the passive, receptive vagina through which the baby may come—the act of thrusting outward of a physical form is thought a symbolic experience of having a penis. Freud was quite clear, however, that the passivity of a healthy woman is only sexual; for example, the act of giving birth is very active. One of his followers, Helene Deutsch, insisted that the passivity should extend through all areas of behavior.

Attachment to father, however, brings problems. Even the most liberal father is not likely to encourage his daughter's overtures for long. Meanwhile, the girl catches on that there is a special relationship between mother and father. Children may not know what goes on beyond the closed parental doors (though they are likely to know more than adults think they do), but they know there is a difference between

*According to Freudian theory, a girl loves her father but shifts her love back to her mother when she realizes she can't compete with her mother on adult terms for her father's love. She learns to identify with her mother and take on a female gender role in order to ensure her parents' love.*

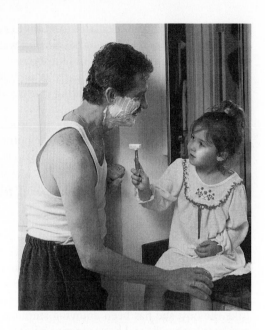

parent-parent and parent-child relationships. Thus, the daughter worries that mother might reject her because she is a rival for the special attachment to father. Although mother deprived her of a penis and does not have one herself, mother still is a loved person who has been giving the girl love and care. Thus, fear of loss of mother's love leads the daughter back to an attachment with mother. She represses her sexual love for father and her aggression toward mother. The girl identifies with mother and by the identification may experience some vicarious enjoyment of father.

The Oedipal stage closes with the identification and the formation of the superego, using the repressed sexual and aggressive energy. Because of repression, the early feelings are not easily available to consciousness. The superego is the internalization of societal standards as *practiced* by the parents as *perceived* by the child. The standards include moral standards and also standards applying to the behavior of women and men. Given the relatively immature stage of cognitive (ego) development at the time, children do not have a clear perception of parental views. Given that the superego is formed with aggressive and sexual energy, it is irrational. As we will see, the girl's anxiety is not so intense as that of the boy, so the repression is not as complete, and there is less sexual and aggressive energy available for superego development. (See Focus on Research 5.1.)

***Boys' Development***    The development of the boy is more straightforward in Freud's theory, perhaps because Freud was thinking from a male perspective and seeing males' bodies as the human norm. The boy, with increasing sexual interest, turns to mother for sexual satisfaction just as he has turned to her for other satisfactions. "By her care of the child's body, she becomes his first seducer" (Freud 1940/1963, p. 90). Like the girl, the boy comes to realize that there is a special relationship between father and mother, and he fears that father will retaliate in some way for his desire for intimacy with mother. Father is contributing to that fear by pressuring the boy to become a "little man" instead of a "mama's boy."

If father is angry at the boy because of the boy's sexual love for mother, it seems reasonable, from a child's point of view, that father will remove the source of the problem, the penis. The boy, like the girl, has been shocked to discover anatomical differences and realizes with horror that he could be deprived of his penis (castration anxiety). Love of mother leads to anxiety. He wants intimacy with mother, but he does not want to lose such a special part of his body. The anxiety causes him to repress his sexual love for mother and his aggression toward father and to identify with father. This brings some uncomfortable distancing from his mother, but it removes the threat to the penis and offers the promise of having a woman (mother) when he grows up. Because the anxiety is more intense for the boy than the girl—losing something he has—the boy's repression is more complete than that of the girl, and more energy is available for the development of the superego.

The dominating patterns are as sketched in the preceding descriptions, but Freud was clear that matters really are more complicated: Both the girl and the boy have sexual interests in both mother and father and fear retribution from the other. The result is that *both* little girls and little boys identify with *both* mother and father and do so in hopes of keeping the love of both mother and father.

*Evaluation*     Freud attempted to define women as well as men within a male-oriented framework: Women are defined physically in terms of what they do not have rather than what they do have. A theorist could build from a biological position, which is important to Freud, and emphasize that women have breasts and a womb and men do not. In fact, some of Freud's followers suggested that womb envy is more important in boys' development than penis envy is in girls' development, or that both boys and girls want each set of genitals (Bettelheim, 1962; Chehrazi, 1986; Erikson, 1950/1963; Horney, 1926). One of those was Karen Horney, who challenged Freud's neglect of social factors in explaining women (chapter 1). She and Clara Thompson (1964/1971), as well as recent theorists (Caplan, 1989; Golombok & Tasker, 1996), have maintained that the penis is important to women only as a *symbol* of male power rather than as a physical organ. Horney, however, did mention that girls may envy the penis as an organ because it makes it easier (and more fun to children) to urinate!

Freud's assumptions about children's anatomical knowledge and their concern with anatomy surpass reality (Bem, 1989; Sherman, 1971). As mentioned earlier, children's distinctions between females and males are not based on genitalia but on outward visible signs. Girls' lack of a penis may be more upsetting to boys than to girls, but evidence of "castration anxiety" in boys and men seems a part of a general body-harm anxiety rather than specific to the penis. Girls show more distaste of the penis than envy of it. After seeing a male cousin in the bath, a little girl said to her mother, "Mommy, isn't it a blessing he doesn't have it on his face?" (Tavris & Wade, 1984).

Two general problems Freud shares with the other two major theoretical positions is that the special relationship with the same-sex parent, called **identification** by Freud, occurs long after the initial appearance of gender-typing (e.g., toy and other

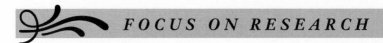

### 5.1    Hypothesis Testing: Erikson's "Inner Space" Theory of Women's Identity

As with many of the early psychological theorists, Erik Erikson's work was heavily influenced by Freud's ideas. Like Freud, Erikson felt anatomy guided psychological development. Erikson proposed that for girls and women, the womb created a positive "inner space" that shaped female experience around internal concerns, such as intimate relationships. For boys and men, the penis formed a sense of "outer space" that focused male psychological development on external concerns, such as finding their place in the larger public sphere. Erikson also incorporated Freud's oral, anal, and phallic stages of development, but gave them a new twist by emphasizing the social rather than the sexual aspects and extending the process of personality development from birth until death, through eight psychosocial stages. Perhaps the most researched of these stages are the two that occur in adolescence and early adulthood: identity and intimacy.

Erikson's sequence of psychosocial stages was based on male experience, which was not uncommon for scientific thought in a male-dominated culture. According to Erikson, adolescent boys deal first with the issue of identity, then with the question of intimacy. The rule for males seems to be, you must know yourself first, before you can share yourself in an intimate relationship. This sequence also fits with boys' and men's experience of anatomically defined "outer space"; their primary motive is to extend themselves, to find their place in the larger world and only then turn inward toward intimate, interpersonal issues. While Erikson proposed an identical sequence of psychosocial stages for both men and women, his insistence that girls' and women's development is shaped by "inner space" suggests that the identity and intimacy stages should be reversed for women. Inner space issues should lead women to first focus on internal, intimate concerns. Identity and one's place in the larger world would then grow out of one's intimate relationships. In other words, as the adolescent girl develops her interpersonal relationships, she comes to know who she is. Are Erikson's proposals correct? How can we test his theory?

A theory is a series of interrelated proposals offered to explain some part of how the world works. To determine whether a theory does a good job in its explanation, we must break each part of the theory down into specific hypotheses (or predictions) and test each one by observing human behavior. If what we see confirms our hypothesis, then the theory that generated that hypothesis is a viable one; it does a good job of explaining that particular slice of life. If our data do not support the hypothesis, then the theory is faulty, and we must rethink it.

The first step in creating a testable hypothesis is to operationally define what we want to measure. In working with Erikson's theory of women's development, researchers S. J. Patterson, I. Sochting, and J. E. Marcia found themselves discussing abstract concepts of inner space and interpersonal context and needed to make these ideas concrete and measurable. Some of the ways they operationalized the interpersonal domain included attitude scores on scales of sexuality, sex roles, the importance of marriage and family, and commitment to others.

Once we have defined our concepts in measurable form, we can create testable hypotheses. These are specific predictions about how the measures relate to each other and often take the form of "if X then Y"—for example, "If one is a woman, then one will hold certain attitudes about sex roles, marriage, family, and commitment." What remains is to gather data with the various measures and compare what we have found to what we thought would happen.

How did the researchers working on Erikson's theory fare with their hypotheses? Did the data they gathered support the prediction that adolescent girls would score higher on measures of interpersonal concerns while adolescent boys would score higher on measures of identity? The question must be answered in two parts. There was no difference found in the overall scores of the young women and men on these measures of intimacy and identity. But some studies have found gender differences in specific domains within the general concept of intimacy. For example, young women have been found to score higher on marriage and family concerns (defined as intimacy issues) than have young men.

The final step in this process is to return to the original theory and assess it in light of the hypothesis tests. As a result of this and other studies, we now know that Erikson's proposed "inner and outer space" and the sequencing of identity and intimacy are ideas that don't contribute much to explaining our lives. These aspects of the theory need to be revised. However, we should not abandon Erikson's entire theory, as data do support the prediction of some differences in the importance young men and women give to intimacy concerns.

Hypothesis testing is a complex and precise process that bit by bit yields answers about a theory. Sometimes the very word *theory* conjures up images of scientific authority and leads to uncritical acceptance on our part, but at other times theories (such as Freud's or Erikson's rather unflattering ideas about women) are automatically discounted and rejected. But no theory should be accepted or rejected out of hand; we must derive concrete, operationally defined hypotheses from each theory, test those hypotheses to determine support (or lack of it) for our predictions, and then reevaluate the theory. Only through hypothesis testing can we have faith that a theory does the best job of describing our world.

JILL BORCHERT ◆

SOURCE: Patterson, S. J., Sochting, I., & Marcia, J. E. (1992). The inner space and beyond: Women and identity. In G. R. Adams, T. P. Gullotta, & R. Montemayor (Eds.). *Adolescent identity formation* (pp. 9–24). Newbury Park, CA: Sage.

gender-related preferences), and there is little relationship between parental attitudes and children's gender-typing. Also, given the importance of a special relationship between two heterosexual parenting figures, it is hard to see Freud's theory covering gender-typing in single-parent families or lesbian families.

It does not seem appropriate, however, to simply dismiss Freud's views as biased and irrelevant. Freud was a keen observer of human behavior. In some respects, he described well, though his explanations for his descriptions can be challenged. In line with modern thinking, Freud maintained that learning was responsible for the development of gender notions; he did not assume that children were born with a male or female identity, but that they developed it in their interpersonal interactions in the culture he was describing (Beal, 1994; Mitchell, 1975). The kind of identity developed was not dependent on the penis or the clitoris but on what children learned from their parents. There is support for his notion that both girls and boys identify with both parents. It follows from Freud's theory of differences in the strength of the superego that girls and women will not be as exclusively feminine as boys and men are masculine. This generally is correct, as noted frequently in this as well as other chapters—gender roles are important to girls but less so than they are to boys. Again, Freud's theoretical explanations may not be appealing, but he correctly saw the phenomena that he tried to explain.

Also because of differences in superego strength, Freud deduced that women are less moral than men. Women, in his view, were swayed by mercy and compassion, which could get in the way of applying abstract rights and principles. Carol Gilligan and others recently have asserted much the same—that women use different principles in making judgments of morality than men do (chapter 8). The difference between Freud and Gilligan is that Freud spoke from a masculinized view of morality and said that women are *less* moral than men; Gilligan's view is that women and men are *equally* moral, but they tend to approach moral issues differently.

Freud was more understanding of women's position in society than generally suspected; for example, he recognized the burden that marriage places on women and the toll of societal teachings on women's sexuality (chapters 10, 11). For the moment, let us end by noting that Freud was aware of the lack of clarity about what masculinity and femininity are, "Pure masculinity and femininity remain theoretical constructions of uncertain content" (Freud, 1925/1972, p. 193). Modern researchers still are debating what femininity and masculinity are and how they should be measured (chapter 3). Further, Freud thought that all people "as a result of their bisexual disposition . . . combine in themselves both masculine and feminine characteristics" (Freud, 1925/1972, p. 193). A major motivation behind contemporary gender role research has been to measure this combination (chapter 3). Freud's theory also provides that because of the development of the ego, an agency capable of rational thinking, gender role stereotypes can be relaxed as an individual grows. An ideal of growth and of therapy for Freud is for the rational ego to gain ascendancy over the irrational superego. Thus, Freud hoped to see a growing person discard the childish, irrational dictates of the superego, replacing them, or at least mediating them, with rationally derived principles.

Psychoanalytic theory is continually evolving. Several contemporary feminists have embraced psychoanalytic theory to illuminate women's experiences (e.g., Bernardez, 1978, 1988; Chodorow, 1978; Dinnerstein, 1977; Gilligan, 1982; Miller, 1976). As yet, these theorists have not had a strong impact on research on gender-typing in the younger years, the primary focus of this chapter. They are discussed elsewhere when their concepts seem more specifically relevant (chapters 9, 16, 17).

## Social Learning Theory

The second major theory relevant to gender-typing is derived from American behaviorism. Behaviorism, as developed by John Watson and then Burrhus Fred Skinner, assumes that it is unnecessary to discuss internal events such as thoughts and feelings; the emphasis is on behavior and observable events in the environment. The application of learning principles to human behavior is called **social learning theory.** When applied to child development, social learning typically refers to the positions of Albert Bandura and Richard Walters (1963) and Walter Mischel (1966). Bandura (1977, 1986, 1989, 1991) and Mischel (1973, 1977, 1979) have increasingly considered internal factors in explaining learning in humans, but the background of behaviorism still is evident. For example, social learning theorists see identification as a useless concept; to them, both imitation and identification describe the same *behavior,* "the tendency of the person to reproduce actions, attitudes or emotional responses exhibited by real-life or symbolic models" (Bandura & Walters, 1963, p. 89).

The social learning position assumes that children get rewarded for behavior consistent with their gender role. Children like rewards and thus "identify with" or become attached to and imitate the same-sex parent to gain more reinforcement. In Freudian theory, children imitate the same-sex parent because of a central motive to keep love; in social learning theory, children imitate the same-sex parent because of a motive to attain rewards or reinforcements.

The most basic mechanism assumed relevant is **reinforcement.** When people, or other organisms, receive reinforcement for a response, the response is likely to increase in frequency. Thus, if Marcia plays with a doll and a parent smiles (a reinforcer), she is likely to play with dolls again. If she plays with her brother's rubber bat and ball and the parent does not smile, playing with them is less likely to happen again. If a parent scowls at her (an aversive stimulus, or punishment), Marcia is likely to play with the bat and ball less often. The effect of the reinforcer (or punishment) can spread through **generalization.** A response reinforced in one situation is likely to appear in other situations (stimulus generalization): Marcia is likely to play with a doll at a neighbor's house or in day care. When one response has been reinforced, other similar responses are likely to be emitted (response generalization)—Marcia is likely to play with doll clothes or wash doll diapers in a toy washing machine.

Generalization has limits, however. The child may not receive reinforcement in all situations or with all similar responses. In such a case, **discrimination learning** takes place: The child learns to discriminate between the conditions under which the response is likely to be followed by a reinforcer and those in which it is not likely to,

*According to social learning theory, children learn gender roles by imitating their same-sex parent and being rewarded for that behavior. A girl takes on a female gender role because she is rewarded for doing so.*

and may be followed by an aversive stimulus. If mother does not mind Marcia playing with "boys' toys," but father does, Marcia will learn not to play with boys' toys when father is around but may continue to do so when only mother is present.

Parents who do allow their children to play with toys of the other gender often find that their own views are not matched by those of other people or by the other children at school. The child may come to discriminate between the liberal safety of home but play only stereotypically at school. Parents may be surprised to see that the impact of peer pressure at school outweighs their own reinforcement at home. For example, one little boy was very attached to a doll his grandmother had made for him. When he went to school for the first time, he took the doll with him. The jeering he experienced from the other boys was so severe that as soon as he got home, he dumped the doll in the garbage. How can one predict whether parents or peers will prevail? With difficulty at best, but as we will see later, peer pressure is quite strong and can, for a while at least, override parental teachings.

***Observational Learning***    The other mechanisms relevant in social learning theory are **observational learning and imitation.** Children learn simply by watching. If they also imitate (perform) the observed behavior, they may receive reinforcement. It is assumed that girls who imitate feminine models and boys who imitate masculine models are rewarded for the imitated behavior. The basic research paradigm used by Bandura and his colleagues in laboratory investigations was to have models act in fairly distinctive ways or make unusual remarks, and then give the observing children a chance to show those same actions. Generally, the models who were more likely to be imitated were those who were warm and nurturing, dominant, or powerful (controlling resources, such as lemonade or nice toys), or who were more skillful than the child (Bandura, Ross, & Ross, 1963a, 1963b; Yando, Seitz, & Zigler, 1978).

The likelihood of imitation is increased if the model is rewarded and decreased if the model is punished. When the model is not rewarded, children nonetheless learn, and they learn as much from punished models as from rewarded ones (Bandura, 1965, 1986). This was demonstrated by first noting what children spontaneously did after the modeling. As expected, they performed more acts observed in a rewarded model than a punished one. However, in the second phase of the study, when offered incentives for showing what else they had learned, it became clear that they had acquired responses from the punished model as well. The model's reward or punishment influenced the likelihood of *performance* but not of *acquisition*. Although not spontaneously imitated immediately, the punished response had been learned and was available for performance. One implication is that because children observe both women and men, they are learning from both and have the responses in their repertoire. What they do depends on what they expect for their actions.

*Evaluation*     Social learning theory seems to be based on straightforward common sense, which has much appeal. Unlike Freudian theory, it has the advantage of **parsimony,** using very few constructs or concepts. By the concept of reinforcement, the theory can address the fact that children show gender-differentiated behavior even before they have a cognitive understanding of gender. The theory also allows for the very quick learning that can happen because of observation.

However, social learning theory is seductively simple. Basically, it sees children as passive recipients of cultural messages (Jacklin & Reynolds, 1993). Children are not little copies of their same-sex parents. Certainly we all know anecdotes of children imitating parents, but many studies do not find correlations between the behavior or attitudes of parents and those of the children (Maccoby & Jacklin, 1974; Sedney, 1987; Smith & Daglish, 1977; Stangor & Ruble, 1987). And, as noted previously, children often are more extreme or stereotypic than the parents. Remember the 4-year-old girl who insisted that women can be nurses but not physicians. The case for the young child's gender-typing being the result of parental reinforcement and modeling is not very compelling.

Social learning *does* occur, but "there also appear to be large gaps in its explanatory power" (Jacklin, 1989, p. 130). For example, children show many responses they have never seen modeled. A particular problem for the theory, as well as for other theories, is that gender-typing happens before it is predicted to happen. In the case of social learning theory, the preference for same-gender models occurs later than predicted, and girls often show more imitation of *both* males and females than boys do (Bussey & Perry, 1982). According to the theory, children attach to the same-gender parent, thus developing gender identity and showing greater imitation of same-gender people. But, until about age 10, children do not prefer a same-sex model over one of the other sex (Maccoby & Jacklin, 1974). However, when *several* models of a given sex perform the same act at the same time, children (3–5 years and 8–9 years) do imitate the same-sex models more than other-sex models *if* the models are not behaving in gender-inconsistent ways (Bussey & Bandura, 1984; Perry & Bussey, 1979). For example, children (3–5 years) matched the choices of models of their own gender if they had seen three women choosing a green Mickey Mouse cap or three men choosing a blue Mickey Mouse cap (Bussey & Bandura, 1984). Such studies indicate that children are making some kind of judgments about the models' behavior that are not well accounted for. The extended theory provides that children form concepts of gender acceptability from the commonalities of repetition and so are more likely to anticipate a reward for imitating the behavior if it is modeled by several of their gender.

A central concept in social learning theory is reinforcement. The definition of reinforcement is circular: A reinforcer is a stimulus that reinforces, namely, it increases the probability of response. The theory does not predict what kinds of events will be reinforcing or when an event that usually has been reinforcing will not control behavior. Two-year-old children may find being given a doll reinforcing, but two years later, that is repulsive to many boys but still reinforcing for many girls. The social learning position does not help us to understand why.

Further, behaviors are said to be under reinforcement control. Yet, children often will not do things for which they would be rewarded. Boys particularly are often reluctant to do what they see as feminine, even if they see another boy or adult man perform the behavior and receive praise (Bussey & Bandura, 1984; Fagot, 1985). Several studies have also shown that children, particularly boys, strongly resist "giving up" a gender-typed behavior in order to obtain reinforcement (see Beal, 1994; Sedney, 1987). In one study, children chose a toy as a prize for participating in research; all chose a gender-typical toy (e.g., truck, necklace). Then, a favorite teacher greatly loved by the children (4- and 5-year-olds) suggested four reasons why the child should trade it for a cross-gender toy (Ross & Ross, 1972). Both boys and girls resisted the suggestions, but boys appeared to be very uncomfortable. They actively argued with the teacher and discredited her advice, saying she was ill or overworked; for example, "Poor teacher, she must have a real bad throat" and, "She has too much to do today" (Ross & Ross, 1972, p. 345).

In short, children have ideas about acceptable behavior that influence receptiveness to reinforcements and attention to models; children's self-reinforcement may be more important to them than the reinforcement given by others. In other words, the gender roles seem to take on a *life of their own*. Social learning positions have difficulty with this. The next position is better on this score.

## Cognitive Developmental Theory

The third major theory that has contributed to our understanding of gender-typing, **cognitive developmental theory,** evolved from Jean Piaget and Barbara Inhelder's work on children's ways of thinking (1956, 1969, 1973). Lawrence Kohlberg (1966) is the dominant pioneer in applying cognitive views to gender development. His original work on children's gender-typing and on the development of moral reasoning (chapter 8) was entirely on boys (and then men). The research was extended to girls and women, but a gender bias can be claimed for some aspects of both theories.

Kohlberg assumes that children have a basic desire to understand the world and be competent in it. Thus, he takes a proactive stance about children: Children "are not passive products of social training" (Kohlberg, 1966, p. 85). Both Freud and social learning theorists have reactive positions, in which the child simply reacts to the environment. At young ages, however, children's ways of dealing with information are different from those of adults because children's thinking is very concrete rather than abstract. In addition, their thinking is **egocentric:** They see from their own perspectives and evaluate others on the basis of their own judgments.

The basic reasoning suggested by Kohlberg is something like "I am good. I am a girl. Therefore, girls are good. Mom is a girl, so Mom is good. I want to be competent in being a girl. So, I will identify with Mom and do what she does." In the child's view, doing girl things is rewarding in and of itself. Children like the love of others (as psychoanalytic theory suggests) and the rewards others give (as social learning theory suggests), but the important rewards are internal ones of seeing themselves as behaving consistently with their gender identities. What is thought to be consistent with the identity is a cognitive judgment by the child. Within this view, children are active participants in their own socialization, a process sometimes called self-socialization (Maccoby & Jacklin, 1974).

More formally, Kohlberg maintained that the first and most important step toward a stable gender identity is a self-categorization or self-label as girl or boy. This self-label then becomes an organizer of information. Cues about the categorization are not genital differences, as emphasized by Freud, but the more easily observable differences in physical size, hairstyle, and clothing. The second major cognitive step is developing a system of values, so that children value what is associated with their own sex (they are egocentric). Then they begin to imitate appropriate behavior and avoid the inappropriate. Third, because of the differential valuing and differential modeling, they develop an identification (or emotional attachment) with the parent of the same sex. The identification leads to additional imitation.

Why is gender singled out by the child as a basis for classification? Some writers have advocated that we teach children to categorize on the basis of other dimensions, such as humanitarianism. The problem with that idealistic suggestion is that children's thinking is concrete. If being a humanitarian were accompanied by concrete, easily visible cues (e.g., being bald), it could be used for categorization. By age 3 years, children also use concrete labels other than sex, including race, body type, height, and age (Powlishta, Serbin, Doyle, & White, 1994). There are many pervasive cues that accentuate gender. The language itself reminds children of gender's importance to adults—the child is expected to learn to use the correct pronouns, for example. Children have many reasons to think that gender is an important distinction in the world they are trying to understand, and minority children are quick to learn minority status as an organizing force.

Because of egocentrism, girls generally prefer to be girls and boys generally prefer to be boys. True, by as early as 3 years old, children do prefer to be of the gender they are and also show scorn for the other gender (Abel & Sahinkaya, 1962; Parsons, 1976b). However, the preference is less strong in girls than in boys. Does Kohlberg's theory apply only to boys, reflecting a bias in its origin? Some writers suggest that the theory does not describe girls well, because the girl's natural ego-centrism is in conflict with the greater power and prestige associated with being male. Children in this culture—a patriarchal one—*are* very responsive to concrete cues of power, competence, prestige, strength, and size. It is not difficult to imagine other cultures in which women's life-giving and milk-producing abilities might be more valued. Here and now, young children are convinced that the best presents come in the biggest boxes. Yet, Kohlberg maintains that the feminine role in this culture has sufficient positive value that girls can channel their efforts at competence into feminine values.

Given children's concern with competence in being a girl or a boy and the importance they attach to the role, the cognitive view explains why the roles take on a life of their own. Conformity to one's role is seen as conformity to the social *moral* order. Given their stage of cognitive development, it is no wonder children are more extreme in their views than are adults, who have more abstract powers and are capable of thinking in terms of gradations rather than either-or categories. You can teach a young child not to put a finger in an empty light bulb socket. You would be ill advised to try to teach the child that it is safe to do so when the switch is off or the fuse is out, but not safe at other times. Young children need clarity in concrete ways they can understand. Sex provides this, as does ethnic group status.

***Evaluation***    All three major positions acknowledge that gender identity is not an inborn part of our senses of self but is developed in a social environment. The proactive stance of Kohlberg's cognitive developmental theory is appealing to many, along with his view that gender role learning is part of more general cognitive developmental processes (Beal, 1994). And the themes of the theory make it easy to see how roles take on a life of their own: Roles help define what it means to be competent. The theory, though emphasizing early years, has clear implications for later development. Stereotypes are expected to become increasingly rigid from 2 to 7 years. However, when children have learned to deal with concrete concepts and understand constancy, rigidity can be reduced. Children continually learn about stereotypes but continually recognize that stereotypes are flexible. They come to understand that gender roles are not inherently tied to physical differences (8–12 years) but see them as helpful in the social system (Kohlberg & Ullian, 1974).

Kohlberg's claim that children do show increased flexibility in middle childhood is questioned, but the fact that the theory provides that gender roles *can* be reduced in rigidity after the early years is appealing to many. Whether or not rigidity is reduced varies with the information children are exposed to about what being a woman or man means. Girls are more likely to become more flexible than boys in several respects, but this may be due to realization of greater cultural status of men than to the reduction of concrete thinking (Martin, 1993; Serbin et al., 1993). As we will see shortly, children can be taught to think about gender roles in more complex ways, and they can be taught to minimize the implications of the meaning of biological differences; as children learn the biological facts about sex differences, they are less likely to use stereotypes.

A weakness in Kohlberg's theory shared with the other major theorists is that the process of internalization of the same-gender parent occurs later than is necessary to explain the development of gender-typed behavior. Kohlberg insisted that children had to identify the sex of others correctly and achieve gender constancy before gender could be a basic organizer. It is not until about 4 or 5 years of age that most children can label the sex of others (Rabban, 1950; Thompson & Bentler, 1971). Many children are not convinced of constancy until around age 6 and some not by then (DeVries, 1969; Kohlberg, 1966). Thus, according to Kohlberg's theory, a stable identity cannot occur until age 6. But, as we have seen, much sex typing has already occurred by then. For example, before gender constancy was fully formed, both African American and white children (4–9 years) had stereotypical preferences (Emmerich & Shepard, 1984).

Kohlberg did acknowledge that some awareness of roles developed before gender constancy was firm but still maintained that with constancy, roles became increasingly important. Many current approaches are modifications or extensions of Kohlberg's work with reduced emphasis on gender constancy and some increased concern with individual differences in flexibility/rigidity.

## Information Processing: Gender Schema Theories

Contemporary psychologists building on Kohlberg's cognitive approach see gender role acquisition in terms of information processing; these theories collectively are called **gender schema theories** (Bem, 1981b, 1984; Levy, 1994a, 1994b; Levy & Carter, 1989; Liben & Signorella, 1987; Markus, Crane, Bernstein, & Siladi, 1982; Martin & Halverson, 1981, 1983; Serbin et al., 1993). The theories generally maintain that what is responsible for gender-typing is gender schema: a generalized readiness to attend to and organize information on the basis of what is considered appropriate for typical females and males (chapter 3). The content and strength of schemas can vary from child to child.

As Kohlberg did, contemporary gender schema theorists emphasize that children with strong schemata are guided by an *internal* motivation to conform to gender-based sociocultural standards as they understand them. Unlike Kohlberg, gender schema theorists do not emphasize gender constancy as necessary for gender role learning, although the exact role of gender constancy is still debatable (Huston, 1983; Stangor & Ruble, 1987). It may be that only gender labeling is necessary for gender schematic processing. Mere recognition of one's sex category "motivates children to be like members of their own group and to learn more of the details for carrying out 'sex-appropriate' behavior" (Martin & Little, 1990, p. 1429). Being members of a group, even a rather arbitrarily defined one, causes adults to develop group cohesion and a spirit of competition with another group. It is little wonder, then, that it is meaningful for children to adopt a group based on what seems so important a category as sex (Powlishta, 1995). Having learned to distinguish between "us and them," children are in a position to make judgments that come "naturally": We are good, they are bad (Katz, 1996).

Preschool and older children have better memory for information consistent with gender role stereotypes than for counterstereotypic information, though the reverse has been reported occasionally (Bauer, 1993; Bigler & Liben, 1992; Levy, 1994a, 1994b; Liben & Signorella, 1993). In addition, children often distort inconsistent information to conform to social roles. One of my students spoke of trying to convince her second graders that her sister is a pilot for a commercial airline. The youngsters persisted in proclaiming the pilot to be a flight attendant, "the lady who brings you food." In laboratory settings, elementary school children commonly distort or forget as much as 50% of counterstereotypic information given them (Cordua, McGraw, & Drabman, 1979). The effects are particularly pronounced for highly schematic children. Children with flexible attitudes show fewer signs of schematic processing, as indicated by their better memory of antistereotypic information (Levy, 1989; Signorella, 1987). They also are less gender-typed in their preferences for activities, occupations, and playmates (Serbin et al., 1993).

During children's early years, strong stereotyping and schematizing may be due at least partially to the fact that many children have trouble classifying on more than one dimension (Bigler & Liben, 1990, 1992). Consider "woman engineer." A child who can classify on only one dimension is likely to have trouble because women are not supposed to be engineers, engineers are men. However, a child with the skill to classify on more than one dimension can classify the person on a sex dimension and on a separate occupational dimension. Children with greater cognitive maturity and advanced classification skills do use less rigid stereotypes than those with less advanced skills (e.g., see Leahy & Shirk, 1984; Serbin et al., 1993; Trautner, Sahm, & Stevermann, 1983). Teaching children cognitive skills to classify on more than one dimension does reduce stereotyping (Bigler & Liben, 1990, 1992). A suggestion is that parents and teachers, not just researchers, can teach children cognitive skills to help them see that sex is not all that is relevant about people.

A major contribution of the information processing approach has been to show that gender acquisition or gender-typing is not one homogenous entity with consistency between all indices of gender-typing and that children are proactive in forming their own views of the meaning of gender. Gender-typing is multidimensional and multidirectional, with different and distinct patterns of development (Berenbaum & Snyder, 1995; Huston & Alvarez, 1990; Serbin et al., 1993; Spence, 1985, 1991; Turner & Gerval, 1995). "The child's acquisition of gender is most accurately compared to an intricate puzzle that the child pieces together in a rather idiosyncratic way" (Hort, Leinbach, & Fagot, 1991, p. 196). Even within the cognitive domain, pieces of the puzzle do not fit together as neatly as theories of a unified gender schema would suggest (Bem, 1981b, 1983).

For example, children (18 months to 4 years) were measured on five cognitive components of gender acquisition: assigning correct gender labels, activity preference, knowledge about typing of objects, memory for gender-related information, and salience of gender in classifying information. To give you an idea of the components, the pictures used to assess gender salience are shown in Figure 5.1. Children were given three choices and asked to select the one that matched two selected by the researcher. The children chose along three dimensions: gender, mood (smiling or frowning), and

Experimenter 1:          Experimenter 2:
"I choose this card."     "I choose this card."

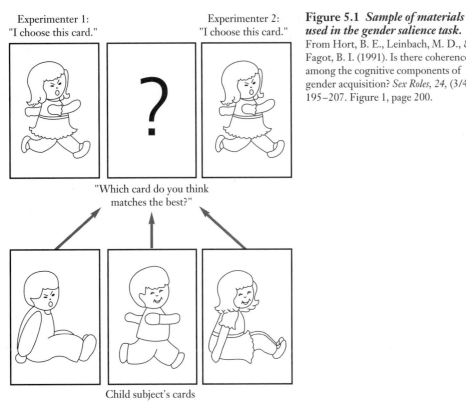

"Which card do you think
matches the best?"

Child subject's cards

**Figure 5.1 *Sample of materials used in the gender salience task.*** From Hort, B. E., Leinbach, M. D., & Fagot, B. I. (1991). Is there coherence among the cognitive components of gender acquisition? *Sex Roles, 24,* (3/4), 195–207. Figure 1, page 200.

activity (running or sitting). Responses were coded as either showing gender salience or not. There was only one significant correlation among all the measures: Children who used gender as a *salient* means of categorization were those who also showed more gender-related knowledge (Hort et al., 1991).

Gender theories also have noted individual differences among children and a greater schematization of boys and among fathers (Bauer, 1993; Katz, 1996; Turner & Gerval, 1995). Further, indices of gender-typing are more strongly related for boys than for girls (see Downs & Langlois, 1988). Children (about 3 years to 6 years) were measured on varying indices in the broad domains of play behavior, identification, and cognition (Downs & Langlois, 1988). Measures *within* each of these domains were more closely related for boys than for girls, and there were more relationships *between* the three domains for boys than for girls. This is consistent with the general principle that girls have more flexibility in their gender behavior than do boys.

Freudian, social learning, and cognitive theorists agree that girls and boys learn what specific attributes are important for girls and boys, men and women, from the world around them. Contemporary cognitive theorists hold a promise of bringing out the complexity and initiative with which children tackle the task of learning what gender is all about.

## Contributors to Stereotyped Development

While children are trying to figure out how to gain love, rewards, and understanding of the world, many forces not only offer information about what they are supposed to do but make rewards and approval contingent on "appropriate" behavior. These forces, which pressure children into assuming ascribed gender roles, are pervasive and effective for many. Big messages are given by the media, parents, and peers. We discussed the role of the media in chapter 2; now we consider the role of parents and peers. (See Focus on Research 5.2.)

## Parental Influence on Gender Roles

In spite of early stereotyped perceptions of newborns (chapter 4), parents do come to respond to the personalities of their children (Lott & Maluso, 1993). Thus, their interactions with children are not based only on sex. In fact, parents treat daughters and sons remarkably alike in many ways; this generally is more true of African American parents than white parents (Katz, 1996; Price-Bonham & Skeen, 1982). However, parents' sex-based distinctions, while relatively few in the context of all parent-child interactions, make a difference. Parents do differentially provide toys, respond to toys and play activities, and assign chores on the basis of the sex of the child (Antill, Goodnow, Russell, & Cotton, 1996; Fagot & Hagan, 1991; Huston, 1983; Lytton & Romney, 1991; Maccoby & Jacklin, 1974). These everyday events turn out to be very influential.

*Toy Selection*   We have seen that toy preference emerges early, often before children can identify themselves as a girl or boy, and before they can cognitively identify the appropriateness of toys as for girls or for boys. It is tempting to suggest that "girls just naturally like dolls." Such a conclusion is dangerous because of the importance of "toy preference" to *adults*. When adults (parents and nonparents) rate the acceptability of play activities for boys and girls, they set narrower boundaries for boys than for girls, and men are more limiting than women are (Fagot, 1974, 1978; Fisher-Thompson, 1990; Martin, 1990). That is, girls are given more latitude than boys in what is acceptable play for them, and women give more latitude to both boys and girls than men do.

Even parents who consider themselves liberal (including those living in a university commune) often provide stereotyped toys, interact stereotypically with their children, and decorate girls' and boys' rooms differently (Barak, Feldman, & Noy, 1991; Fagot, 1974, 1978; Rheingold & Cook, 1975; Weisner, Garnier, & Loucky, 1994; Weitzman, Birns, & Friend, 1985). Observations of the rooms of children 2 years old and younger showed that boys had more sports equipment, tools, and vehicles than girls did; girls had more dolls, furniture, and other types of toys for imitative manipulation (e.g., phones, flowers) (Pomerleau, Bolduc, Malcuit, & Cossette, 1990). Even pacifiers were pink or blue! The girls' bedding, however, was dominantly yellow rather than pink, while the boys' was blue. Degree of stereotyping of rooms is related to the children's stereotyping (children aged 3–5 years of age) (Katz, 1996).

Parental stereotyping about toys is also shown in their responsiveness to children's "wish lists." Children (from preschool through the eighth grade) were more likely to ask for gender-typical toys for Christmas than for atypical toys, but they were less likely to receive the nonstereotypic toys they did ask for.

***Playing With Toys***    Adults not only provide toys for children, they also play with the children and may respond positively or negatively in their play. One-year-old children in working- and middle-class families played essentially equally with soft toys (feminine activities) and vehicles (masculine activities). However, parental tolerance for other-gender play decreased during the second year, at a faster rate for boys than girls (Eisenberg, Wolchik, Hernandez, & Pasternack, 1985; Fagot, 1978; Fagot & Hagan, 1991; Fagot & Leinbach, 1987). Some parents had trouble obeying researchers' instructions to use toys for the other sex when playing with their children; and when playing with an atypical toy, the parents were less enthusiastic than with typical toys (Caldera et al., 1989). Apparently, if children want to play with a happy adult, they should select a stereotyped toy. Children, especially boys, may think that adult approval is contingent on "proper" play. For example, both boys and girls (3–8 years of age) tended to avoid inconsistent toys, and the avoidance increased with age; boys' avoidance was stronger than girls', and boys showed more avoidance when an adult was present than when alone (Hartup, Moore, & Sager, 1963).

Siblings also are relevant to play in ways not yet fully investigated. Interactions with brothers or with sisters can tilt play preferences toward masculine or feminine activities, respectively (Colley, Griffiths, Hugh, Landers, & Jaggli, 1996). The least play stereotyping among school-age children is shown by children who have an older sibling of the other sex (Brody, Stoneman, MacKinnon, & MacKinnon, 1985).

What difference do toys and play habits make? At a minimum, they provide cues to young children about what adults expect at a time when children are trying to figure out what it means to be a girl or a boy. Also of concern are the kinds of activities likely to be associated with the toys and the possible implications for personality and cognitive development (chapters 8, 9). Play is not just a way for children to amuse themselves while waiting to become adults. Play is a way of developing skills and styles of interacting with the world. Girls' toys require passive, sedentary activity, while boys' toys require motor activity and the movement of objects in space. Scooting a toy dump truck and building with logs involve movement in space and learning about objects in space. The nature of boys' play is thought important for development of spatial abilities. There may be implications also for interpersonal styles. When another person, child or adult, is involved in the play, girls' toys elicit close physical proximity and verbal interaction; boys' toys elicit high levels of activity and low physical proximity (Caldera et al., 1989).

***Chores***    Just as parents give toys differentially, they also respond differently to daughters and sons in terms of what they expect them to do as work around the house (Antill, Goodnow, Russell, & Cotton, 1996; Huston, 1983; Huston & Alvarez, 1990; Lytton &

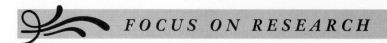

### 5.2    Replication: Kids' Cartoons Carry More Than Comic Messages

Remember Saturday morning cartoons when you were a kid? Each generation seems to have its own set of favorites, and you can almost tell how old people are by the cartoons they remember from their childhood. Have the cartoon characters and the messages they send changed across the years? That might seem like a silly question; after all, they're only lighthearted cartoons. How much social impact can they carry? However, research on observational learning has shown that television in general can be a powerful influence on our thinking and behavior, and cartoons are no exception.

Researchers Teresa Thompson and Eugenia Zerbinos (1995) conducted a literature search, combing through past research for studies on children's cartoons. They found that over the past 20 years many studies had focused on gender representation in cartoons. Triggered by the women's movement, researchers were concerned about gender stereotyping in cartoons and its impact on impressionable children. What those early studies (Mayes & Valentine, 1979; Streicher, 1974) found was not encouraging. There was a great deal of gender stereotyping, with females portrayed as younger, passive, dependent, in need of rescue, and more involved in personal relationships, while males were more violent, emphasized achievement, and played more leading roles in the stories. Noting that women have made some strides toward equality in the past 20 years, Thompson and Zerbinos decided to see if gender equality had arrived in cartoons in the 1990s. They designed a study to update our knowledge in this area by replicating past research.

Replication is a cornerstone of the scientific method. By repeating a study, researchers gain confidence that what happened the first time was not just a fluke or a chance occurrence. In the strictest sense, replication means that the study is repeated step by step with the expectation that the same outcome will occur. This is why it is so important to be precise when writing a research report. Psychology students who are learning the American Psychological Association's style of report writing often complain that this style of writing is dry and boring with little room for creativity, and sometimes they're right! Research reporting relies on clear, precise, and detailed language so that the reader can repeat the study exactly. Unfortunately, strict replication is rarely done. Researchers are eager to break new ground and are often unwilling to replicate their own or others' work, regardless of the contribution this would make to science. But replication does exist in a looser form that allows researchers to expand on a prior study. The researcher can repeat the study with minor changes to see if the

---

Romney, 1991). Girls as young as age 10 are likely to be involved with meal preparation and cleanup, household cleaning, and laundry (Mauldin & Meeks, 1990). Boys are involved with repairs, taking out the garbage, and doing outdoor work. Girls have

same outcome will occur under slightly different conditions. As we build on this type of replication, we can gradually outline the limits of a particular phenomenon. This is the approach to replication taken by Thompson and Zerbinos in their study of cartoons. They applied this form of replication to track changes in cartoon content across time.

After reviewing the literature on previous cartoon studies, Thompson and Zerbinos selected parts of the methodologies of the most important past studies to use in their study. Methodology refers to the mechanics of how the study was run. For example, in this case, methodology would include how the cartoons were selected, what scales were used to evaluate their content, and how the people evaluating them were trained. Thompson and Zerbinos wanted to create a methodology that would be as similar as possible to those used in previous studies. This gave them a basis for comparing the outcome of the new study to prior outcomes—in other words, comparing apples to apples. During 1993, using *TV Guide* listings, the researchers identified and taped 175 cartoon episodes from network and cable stations. Thirty-one college communication majors were trained as coders. Each coder viewed approximately five episodes of the same cartoon series. Coders rated each episode on several different scales, including number of female and male lead and minor characters, their occupations, gender role behaviors, and a variety of personality traits, such as attractiveness, athleticism, and independence.

This evaluation of 1993 cartoons showed that gender stereotypes were alive but perhaps not quite so healthy as they were 20 years ago. Male characters still played more major roles, talked more, achieved more, and were braver than female characters. But, compared to 1970s cartoons, female characters showed more ingenuity and leadership, gave more guidance to others, and were less helpless. Through their work, Thompson and Zerbinos were able to update our knowledge about gender stereotyping in children's cartoons with current data. Then, by replicating past research, they provided a way to compare changes across time. We now know that gender stereotyping in Saturday morning cartoons is still a problem, but positive changes are being made. Children watching today's cartoons are learning a somewhat more balanced perspective on gender roles.

JILL BORCHERT ◆

SOURCES: Mayes, S. L., & Valentine, K. B. (1979). Sex role stereotyping in Saturday morning cartoon shows. *Journal of Broadcasting, 23*, 41–50. Streicher, H. W. (1974). The girls in the cartoons. *Journal of Communication, 24*(2), 125–129. Thompson, T. L., & Zerbinos, E. (1995). Gender roles in animated cartoons: Has the picture changed in 20 years? *Sex Roles, 32*, 651–673.

about 50 minutes less leisure time on a weekday than boys do, just as their mothers are likely to have less leisure time than their fathers (chapter 13). Similar divisions of labor occur in many cultures (Harkness & Super, 1985; Weisner, 1982; Whiting & Whiting,

1975). In lesser developed cultures, women ask both boys and girls to do whatever is needed (Bradley, 1993). But, even so, in middle childhood, boys leave home to do chores with other boys (Whiting & Edwards, 1973).

Although parents are likely to assign chores on gender-typed lines, not all parents do (Weisner et al., 1994). The chores parents assign are related to the toys they give, suggesting the importance (or relative lack of importance) of parents' schemata about gender roles. For example, children who vacuumed or dusted were not limited to stereotypic toys, but no child who was given a girl's toy took out the garbage. Boys who received boys' toys did not do kitchen chores, nor did they vacuum and dust. Apparently, dusting and vacuuming are neutralizing activities! Effects of parental choices about chores for their children, however, may be overridden: Children who watched TV a lot (4 hours or more a day) had the most stereotyped views about what chores should be performed by girls and boys, although their views were not related to the chores they actually performed (Signorielli & Lears, 1992).

## Nontraditional Families

With the increase in mothers' employment and increasing divorce rates, more homes are nontraditional compared with families of the past. In addition, some parents are lesbians or gay men, perhaps attached to another or perhaps not. What is the effect on children's gender-typing?

***Maternal Employment***   Evidence has been very consistent over the past 25 years that children (aged 3 years through adolescence) of employed mothers have less stereo-typed attitudes generally than do children of nonemployed mothers (L. W. Hoffman, 1979, 1989; Huston, 1983; Huston & Alvarez, 1990). Across ethnic groups, the daughters of employed mothers have higher esteem, higher educational aspirations, greater expectancy of careers, and interest in more prestigious occupations than other daughters (Beal, 1994). Given the high likelihood that the daughters will be employed, the daughters will be in a better position to enjoy their work.

Clearly, employed mothers of the past have been modeling unconventional behavior, but something more is probably involved. In families with employed mothers, the mother's or father's attitudes, personalities, and behaviors are likely to differ from those of other parents (Weisner et al., 1994; Willetts-Bloom & Nock, 1994). The greater demands of running the home also may encourage different child-rearing practices and assignment of chores. At a minimum, employed mothers are more likely than other mothers to encourage independence, especially in their daughters.

Correlates of maternal employment are less clear for sons, perhaps reflecting differences in the son's views of their fathers (Beal, 1994). In working-class families, maternal employment may mean to the son that she has to work because the father is a poor provider; the sons show more traditional gender attitudes, perhaps in an attempt to prove that they are and will be a "better man" than the father (Flanagan, 1990; Katz, 1987). In middle-class and wealthy families, in which the sons may assume that mothers work because of desire rather than necessity, the sons, like the daughters, are less stereotyped than sons of women who are primarily homemakers.

***Parental Absence***   Both parents in intact families can be important for gender-typed development, but neither is irreplaceable (Huston, 1983; Jackson, Ialongo, & Stollak, 1986). Children of divorced and intact families differ in some ways, but the size of the overall difference is quite small (Amato & Keith, 1991). The few gender differences are more likely due to differences in parenting styles than any inherent determinant. Girls living with mothers who have not remarried after divorce are likely to have fewer problems than other children of divorce (Grych & Fincham, 1992; Hetherington, 1989; Hetherington, Stanley-Hagan, & Anderson, 1989). This may be a reflection of two factors: (1) the typical mother sees parenting as a more central role than the typical father does, and (2) there is a general deterioration of children's relationships with fathers following divorce (Booth & Amato, 1994; Cooney, 1994).

Boys whose fathers are absent before they are 4 or 5 years old are less aggressive and less likely to engage in rough-and-tumble play than boys from intact homes. The boys are not effeminate, however. For example, they are less likely to play with stereotypical boys' toys, but they prefer neutral toys (e.g., puzzles), not female-typed toys (Brenes, Eisenberg, & Helmstadter, 1985). Exact effects are likely to reflect what the sons learn from mothers and others around them about what being a "real man" means (Beal, 1994). Mothers who are comfortable with rough play have sons more stereotypically masculine than those who are not. Some boys, uncertain about their identity, who grow in groups that emphasize being "tough," develop a compensatory masculinity, including rebellion against authority and avoidance of anything feminine, including involvement with their own children later on (Biller, 1981). Boys in the custody of their fathers are relatively high in maturity, independence, and self-esteem, but they also are less communicative and less overtly affectionate, perhaps because of less exposure to the expressiveness more likely modeled and taught by mothers than by fathers (Hetherington et al., 1989).

Any limits on what parents of either sex teach children in their custody are likely due to social limitations rather than to biological ones (Jackson, Ialongo, & Stollak, 1986). Fathers and mothers may typically encourage different kinds of behaviors, but both father and mother may be capable of stepping in and filling a parental gap, so that a girl develops femininity or a son develops masculinity if that is desired, or either girls or boys develop both femininity and masculinity.

***Lesbian and Gay Parents***   Children of lesbian and gay parents usually adopt the role behaviors typical for their sex, are not confused about their sex, and have no interest in being of the other sex (Flaks, Ficher, Masterpasqua, & Joseph, 1995; Golombok & Tasker, 1996; Patterson, 1992, 1994, 1995). For example, interviewers could not distinguish between children of lesbian mothers and children of single heterosexual mothers (Kirkpatrick, Smith, & Roy, 1981). In short, contrary to psychoanalytic theory and social learning theory, as well as some aspects of social policy, fathers are not necessary for the heterosexuality or the healthy development of children. Even if one assumes that a healthy child must be heterosexual (a dubious assumption), the majority of children from lesbian families are identified as heterosexual, though they may be more likely to explore same-sex relationships if their childhood family was very open and accepting of same-sex relationships (Golombok & Tasker, 1996).

Children who were old enough to observe and remember a transsexual parent going through a sex change also showed no remarkable differences from children raised in more traditional households (Green, 1978). In spite of the evidence of lack of harm to children's social, emotional, or gender role development, there still is strong societal concern about lesbians and gays as parents. Parents of lesbian mothers have gone to court to take custody of their grandchildren away from their daughters.

## Peer Group Culture

Even if parents are not teaching femininity and masculinity, peer groups are, and their influence is tremendous. As gender schema theorists note, children want to be like members of their gender group, and that means differentiating themselves from children of the other group (Katz, 1996). Children develop in segregated groups, with potential implications for later development.

***Peer Preference***    As noted at the beginning of the chapter, girls show a preference for other girls as early as age 2 years, and boys prefer boys by about age 3 years. Preference for association with those of one's own gender leads to **gender segregation.** The segregation is present in preschool and becomes stronger as children grow older (Maccoby, 1988, 1990; Powlishta, 1995; Powlishta et al., 1993; Serbin, Moller, Powlishta, & Gulko, 1991). Nursery school children (4½ years) spent 3 times more time with same-gender peers than with other-gender peers; in children two years older, the differential was more than 10.

Gender is more important than ethnicity when it comes to peer associations; at an integrated school, African American and white boys sat with each other rather than with girls of their ethnic group (Schofield, 1981, 1982). Hearing-impaired children, however, overlook gender differences if they find another child who can sign (Lederberg, Chapin, Rosenblatt, & Vandell, 1986). Otherwise, mixed-sex friendships (typically having started around age 3 years), have to go underground if the children are to avoid teasing by other children (Gottman, 1986). Segregation by sex seems to be cross-cultural but is minimized when there are few children of the same age available (Edwards & Whiting, 1988).

Segregation is greatest in situations that have *not* been structured by adults. Attempts to increase the mixed-sex interaction of preschoolers are short lived and successful only as long as adults are rewarding it (Carpenter & Huston, 1986; Carpenter, Huston, & Holt, 1986; Lockheed, 1986; Katz, 1986). Children seem strongly motivated to practice and maintain gender segregation. Eleanor Maccoby (1988, 1990) notes that individual differences are virtually nil; children who are less strongly gender-typed are as likely to prefer same-gender playmates as are others.

The very act of labeling may increase the tendency to see one sex as "them" and the other as "us" (Katz, 1996). This sets the stage for the use of stereotypes and processes of assimilation and contrast (chapter 3). When forming impressions of unfamiliar girls and boys seen on video, children (ages 8–10) favored their own sex, used stereotypes, exaggerated differences between their own sex and the other (contrast), and exaggerated the similarity within each group (assimilation) (Powlishta, 1995).

**Table 5.3**   Average Ratings for Liking of Peers of Same and Other Gender

| | *Study One* | | | | *Study Two* | | | |
| | | Grades | | | | Grades | | |
| | *K* | *1* | *2* | *3* | *3* | *4* | *5* | *6* |
|---|---|---|---|---|---|---|---|---|
| RATINGS OF GIRLS | | | | | | | | |
| Rated by: | | | | | | | | |
| Girls | 2.52 | 2.59 | 2.60 | 2.62 | 3.86 | 3.67 | 3.54 | 3.73 |
| (Same Sex) | | | | | | | | |
| Boys | 2.20 | 2.19 | 2.15 | 1.93 | 2.52 | 2.17 | 2.67 | 2.37 |
| (Other Sex) | | | | | | | | |
| RATINGS OF BOYS | | | | | | | | |
| Rated by: | | | | | | | | |
| Boys | 2.49 | 2.49 | 2.63 | 2.52 | 3.67 | 3.81 | 3.85 | 3.28 |
| (Same Sex) | | | | | | | | |
| Girls | 2.05 | 1.99 | 2.01 | 1.83 | 2.67 | 2.73 | 2.33 | 2.14 |
| (Other Sex) | | | | | | | | |
| | | 3-point scale | | | | 5-point scale | | |

SOURCE: Hayden-Thompson, L., Rubin, K. H., & Hymel, S. (1987). Sex preferences in sociometric chores. *Developmental Psychology, 23* (4), 558–562. Adapted from Table 1, page 559, and Table 2, page 560.

***Girls' Greater Favoritism to Girls***   Clearly, children's attitudes about peers are not based solely on the peer's actual behavior. Children seem to think that peers of their own gender are good simply because they are of the right gender (Etaugh, Levine, & Mennella, 1984; Martin, Wood, & Little, 1990; Powlishta, 1995; Serbin et al., 1993). However, this gender bias is stronger in girls than in boys: Boys are more positive toward girls than girls are toward boys. In one study, children saw a video of a child, called either Ann or John, engaging in masculine, feminine, or neutral activities, and they were asked to evaluate the child's performance by awarding stars (Olsen & Willemsen, 1978). Both girls and boys gave more stars when the child was presented as one of their own sex, regardless of the nature of the activity. The same-sex bias was stronger for older children than for younger ones and stronger for girls than for boys.

Popularity ratings also demonstrate both preference toward peers of the same gender and a relative favoritism toward girls (Powlishta et al., 1994; Serbin et al., 1993). In one study, children sorted photographs of children in their class into boxes marked "like a lot," "sort of like," and "don't like." In another part of this study, a sociometric rating scale was administered within each classroom, asking children to say how much they liked each of their classmates. Children received higher "like" ratings from peers of their own gender than from those of the other gender, but this was more true of girls than of boys (Table 5.3) (Hayden-Thompson, Rubin, & Hymel, 1987). The positive bias toward the same gender increased from kindergarten through the third grade and then, less markedly, into the sixth grade (Table 5.3). In sum, girls generally liked other girls more than boys liked boys, and overall, girls were liked more than boys were liked.

Girls' greater bias may be due to status differences, because lower status groups sometimes show more in-group favoritism than higher status groups—it's more important to the lower status group to stick together (Turner & Brown, 1978; Van Knippenberg, 1984). Also relevant is that boys frequently dominate mixed-sex interaction and are resistant to girls' attempts to influence them (Charlesworth & Dzur, 1987; Charlesworth & LaFreniere, 1983; Cramer & Skidd, 1992; Maccoby, 1988; Powlishta & Maccoby, 1990). Boys tend to try to get their way through physical means (e.g., shoving another child out of the way) or give direct commands and ignore the polite requests that girls are likely to make. Girls use verbal persuasion and generally try to ease conflict to maintain interpersonal harmony; boys are more concerned with personal status than group harmony and quickly raise issues of dominance (Cramer & Skidd, 1992; Leaper, 1991; Maccoby, 1988; McCloskey & Coleman, 1992; Thorne & Luria, 1986).

Maccoby (1988) concluded that speech is used for social bonding among girls and for an egoistic function among boys. Because of such differences in social styles, girls may dislike boys. Boys also may have reduced favoritism toward boys (relative to girls' favoritism for girls) for the same reason. Both boys and girls are more fearful of boys than of girls, because, as a 6-year-old boy said, "Boys can beat you up more than girls" (Brody, Hay, & Vandewater, 1990, p. 381). Boys sometimes tire of the snakes and snails of their gender and can see some appeal of sugar and spice.

## Peers at Play

Children teach other children, partly through play activities (Funk & Buchman, 1996). By age 3, children reinforce each other for stereotypic play and punish deviations from that (Fagot, 1985; Fagot & Patterson, 1969; MacDonald & Parke, 1986; Moller, Hymel, & Rubin, 1992). Children (by age 10) know that gender norms have exceptions, but they are intolerant of violators (Carter & McCloskey, 1984). Peer approval becomes more associated with boys' gender-typed play than with girls' in later elementary years (Moller, Hymel, & Rubin, 1992). Girls, however, have and give more leeway for deviations than boys do, paralleling adult behavior in this respect (Fagot, 1985). For example, girls playing with hammers are not rejected and left alone as much as are boys playing in the housekeeping area. Girls, however, may see masculine girls as bossy (McAninch, Milich, Crumbo, & Funtowicz, 1996). Children who engage in activities of both genders are criticized but also have some positive interactions.

*Style of Play*    Perhaps more important than content of play is *style* of play. Play is a way in which children express themselves, learn about themselves and each other, and develop styles of interaction that may persist in adult forms (Crombie & Desjardins, 1993; Lever, 1976; Liss, 1983; Moller et al., 1992). In the United States (Maccoby, 1988) and other countries (Whiting & Edwards, 1973), boys' play is more physical and more competitive than girls' play, and more likely to be outside rather than inside (Levy, 1994b). Girls' play with other girls is not passive: Girls (4½ years old) spent more time jumping on a trampoline than boys did, but jumping on another child who was jumping was rare for girls and common among boys

(Maccoby, 1988). Boys playing on the trampoline or with a "Bobo" doll often ended up in good-natured wrestling and mock fighting, while this kind of play was seldom seen among girls.

As boys grow older, their rough-and-tumble play tends to increase along with their activity in large-group competitive games with rules. Boys are almost twice as likely as girls to play competitive games, even when the games are not team sports (Colley et al., 1996; Crombie & Desjardins, 1993; Lever, 1976). Girls' play is more social-cognitive, involving more parallel and constructive play as well as more peer conversations. In girls' games, any competition is indirect: It is against the other girls' scores in jump rope or jacks, for example, rather than being face-to-face confrontation. Girls' games also are less complex and have fewer participants; girls spend more time than boys in play with one other child or in groups of less than five (Crombie & Desjardins, 1993; Vaughter, Sadh, & Vozzola, 1994).

The physicality and competitiveness of boys' play activities may enhance dominance and assertion skills and contribute to the development of the traditional masculine gender role (Moller et al., 1992). Janet Lever (1978) suggested that boys' games give them the opportunity to coordinate with a large number of people, cope with rules and competition, maintain self-control, and experience leadership. Girls' activities emphasize intimacy in a setting of primary human relationships.

*Play and Gender Segregation*   Do differences in play style lead to gender segregation, or does gender segregation foster differences in play style? Some studies have varied the degree of masculinity or femininity and sex and asked children about their preferences (Alexander & Hines, 1994; Zucker et al., 1995). Generally, younger children (4–6 years of age) use sex rather than interests and play styles to decide about liking the other child as a playmate, while older children (7 years of age) prefer other children who have shared interests and play styles (Alexander & Hines, 1994; Martin, 1990). There are suggestions, however, that younger boys prefer girls with masculine styles over boys with feminine styles. It may be that it takes girls longer to experience negative effects of typical masculine play or that boys are simply more stereotypical about play than girls are.

The origins of gender segregation remain controversial. Maccoby (1988, 1990) suggested that biological factors are at work in the different styles of girls and boys, with androgenization of brain organization a possibility (chapter 4). Others suggest that children learn from the adult culture (Caplan & Larkin, 1991; Meyer, Murphy, Cascardi, & Birns, 1991). There may be truth in both positions. A biological contribution may be accentuated by a social world in which children learn from adults that gender is important and that what they do in play is important to adults.

Supporting Maccoby's concern with androgenization is that girls who were exposed to more than usual levels of androgen prenatally—congenital adrenal hyperplasia, CAH, (chapter 4)—preferred boys' toys and boys' activities, though at a lower level than control boys (Berenbaum & Snyder, 1995). It seems that because of their interests, these girls reduce their time with other girls. However, because of female gender identity, the CAH girls, in spite of their activity preferences, still preferred play with girls.

Whatever the reason for gender segregation or for differences in play style, the result is that girls and boys are going their separate ways and developing different modes of social interaction with minimal learning from each other. Then, at adolescence, they are expected to be attractive to those of the other sex, fall in love, get married, and live happily ever after (chapter 10). The pursuit of that ideal is inhibited by the different styles of interpersonal interaction that girls and boys learn. Adults pay high prices for what they did as children. Girls seem to start learning early that who they are, what they are doing, and who they are to be as adults are all relatively undervalued, as seen next.

## Beyond Childhood and Gender-Typing

As we saw in chapter 3, the traditional assumption that feminine women are healthy and adjusted does not have much empirical support. It is relevant to ask about the relationship of gender role orientation and the self-esteem of young women as they grow toward adulthood, and about the development of nonstereotypic behavior.

### Esteem and Gender

Girls' self-esteem and leadership decrease through the school years, with a particular decrease after elementary school (AAUW, 1991; Huston & Alvarez, 1990; Schoeman, Garrison, & Kaplan, 1984). The decrease is largest for white and Hispanic girls and least for African American girls. Two related reasons have been suggested for the decrease. Junior high school seems to be a transition to a more impersonal, masculine environment than previously encountered. And, adolescence is a time of **gender intensification,** when expectations for the young person become more gender specific and pronounced (Douvan & Adelson, 1966; Hill & Lynch, 1985; Huston & Alvarez, 1990). During the teen years, young women are receiving strong but conflicting messages about achievement, popularity, and perhaps about what being an adult woman means: "Be all you can be, but be popular and don't show-up boys." Many teen women feel that they have to choose between meeting the expectations and needs of other people and staying true to themselves. Carol Gilligan and her associates (1990; Brown & Gilligan, 1992; Gilligan, Lyons, & Hanmer, 1990) have demonstrated that young women "go underground." Girls who had been lively, alert, and assertive begin to hold back, question themselves, and deny their feelings. They learn that part of what is expected of them is what some adult women experience as a "silencing of the self" (also see chapter 16). For more on Gilligan's findings, see A Closer Look 5.1.

***Instrumentality and Expressiveness***    Variations in self-esteem are related to gender role adoption, though causation is not clear. As among adults (chapter 3), instrumentality seems beneficial for children and adolescents as well (Markstrom-Adams, 1989). Measures used for young children are not the same as for older children, but there are still indications of the general pattern for preschoolers (Cramer & Skidd, 1992; Jacobs, 1985) and for elementary school children and adolescents (Allgood-Merten &

## A Closer Look

### 5.1 Views of Adolescent Women

Carol Gilligan and her associates, Annie Brown, Nona Lyons, and Trudy Hanmer, as well as many others, have conducted and analyzed a series of in-depth interviews with girls and young women in private and public schools. The most visible of these are the Emma Willard School in Troy, New York, and the Laurel School for girls in Cleveland, Ohio. Although they are private schools, some girls from lower classes attended on scholarships. Most students were white, but girls of color were represented and were not necessarily lower class scholarship students.

The students' own reactions when they heard about the research project were, "What could you possibly learn by studying us?" (Gilligan, 1990, p. 2). They were so used to learning about white males that their attention was diverted from themselves.

> Adolescence is a time of disconnection, sometimes of dissociation or repression in women's lives, so that women often do not remember—tend to forget or to cover over—what as girls they have experienced and known. As the phrase, "I don't know" enters our interviews with girls at this developmental juncture, we observe girls struggling over speaking and not speaking, knowing and not knowing, feeling and not feeling, as we see the makings of an inner division as girls come to a place where they feel they cannot say or feel or know what they have experienced—what they have felt and known. (Brown & Gilligan, 1992, p. 4)

As the girls grow older, they become less dependent on external authorities, less egocentric, more differentiated, responsible, and complex.

> Yet we found that this developmental progress goes hand in hand with evidence of a loss of voice, a struggle to authorize or take seriously their own experience—to listen to their own voices in conversation and respond to their feelings and thoughts—increased confusion, sometimes defensiveness, as well as evidence for the replacement of real with inauthentic or idealized relationships. (Brown & Gilligan, 1992, p. 6)

SOURCES: Brown, L. M., & Gilligan, C. (1992). *Meeting at the crossroads: Women's psychology and girls' development.* Cambridge, MA: Harvard University Press; Gilligan, C., Lyons, N. P., & Hanmer, T. J. (Eds.). (1990). *Making connections: The relational worlds of adolescent girls at Emma Willard School.* Cambridge, MA: Harvard University Press.

Stockard, 1991; Alpert-Gillis & Connell, 1989; Boldizar, 1991; Lamke, 1982a, 1982b; Marsh, Antill, & Cunningham, 1987; Massad, 1981; Wells, 1980).

The picture for expressiveness is more complex. As noted before (chapter 3), the effect of any set of attributes varies with the social environment, and that can vary with age. There are suggestions that attributes considered to be feminine may be advantageous in preschool years but that they progressively lose value as children grow toward understanding the public world of adults rather than the domestic world more familiar to them (Allgood-Merten & Stockard, 1991; Simmons & Blyth, 1987; Cramer & Skid, 1992; Kramer & Melchior, 1990; Rosaldo, 1974). Perhaps because of this, girls' adoption and value of feminine behaviors (their gender preference) generally decrease from preschool into and then through elementary school, while boys' adoption and value of masculine behaviors do not decrease (Boldizar, 1991; Cramer & Skidd, 1992; Katz, 1986; Ruble, Boggiano, Feldman, & Loebl, 1980). Possibly related is that older girls generally are less traditional and more flexible than boys and younger girls, although they may have greater knowledge of gender stereotypes (Katz & Ksansnak, 1994; Signorella et al., 1993).

*Adolescence*    It is particularly interesting that being feminine, as girls are expected to be, becomes irrelevant to girls' self-esteem by the end of elementary school (Allgood-Merten & Stockard, 1991; Boldizar, 1991; Hall & Halberstadt, 1980; Lamke, 1982a; Stein, Newcomb, & Bentler, 1992; Wells, 1980; Worell, 1989). A good illustration of this is provided by a study of children in Grade 4 and in Grades 9 to 12 (Allgood-Merten & Stockard, 1991). Expressiveness and instrumentality were measured by a version of the Children's Personality Attributes Questionnaire (PAQ) (see chapter 3). A sample question on the instrumental (or self-efficacy, as the researchers called it) scale is

1. I do not do well in sports. (reversed)
2. In most ways, I am better than most of the other kids my age.
3. I am often the leader among my friends.
4. When things get tough, I almost always keep trying.

A sample question on the expressiveness (or relational) scale is

1. I am a gentle person.
2. My art work and my ideas are creative and original.
3. I am a very considerate person (thoughtful person).
4. I do not help other people very much. (reversed)

Researchers found that instrumentality was associated with girls' and with boys' esteem: Students scoring higher than others on instrumentality also scored higher on esteem. Expressiveness was related to esteem for *both* girls and boys in Grade 4, but expressiveness was *not* relevant to esteem for girls in Grades 9 to 12. Girls are expected to be expressive, but it is irrelevant to their self-esteem. Boys' esteem was related to their expressiveness—especially in a subsample of boys in a high-achievement group measured both in the earlier years and in high school (Table 5.4).

Adolescence involves a transition from a gender-segregated but relatively egalitarian world of childhood to an unequal world of male dominance in the economic and

**Table 5.4**  Relationship Between Self-Esteem and
Instrumentality and Expressiveness

|  | *Total Sample* | | *Subsample* | |
| --- | --- | --- | --- | --- |
|  | E | I | E | I |
| GIRLS | | | | |
| Grade 4 | .45 | .44 | .44 | .47 |
| Grades 9 to 12 | .07 | .49 | .01 | .71 |
| BOYS | | | | |
| Grade 4 | .34 | .51 | .48 | .43 |
| Grades 9 to 12 | .15 | .42 | .42 | .54 |

NOTE: Entries are Pearson product moment correlations between Expressiveness or Instrumentality and Self-Esteem. All except .01 and .07 are significant at $p < .05$.

The total sample included 607 children in Grade 4 in a predominantly working-class community and 799 teens (Grades 9–12) from a largely middle-class community. The subsample was 52 students, 32 girls and 20 boys, from the working-class sample who were tested first in the 4th grade and later in the 12th grade. They had significantly higher 4th-grade achievement test scores and had mothers with significantly more education than those in the total 4th-grade group.

Self-esteem was measured with the Rosenberg Self-Esteem Inventory.

SOURCE: Allgood-Merten, B., & Stockard, J. (1991). Sex role identity and self-esteem: A comparison of children and adolescents. *Sex Roles, 25* (3/4), 129–139.

political world and in day-to-day interactions (Allgood-Merten & Stockard, 1991). As gender intensification increases and adult standards become more salient, young women may internalize cultural devaluation of what they are supposed to become (Huston & Alvarez, 1990). It is hard to feel good about yourself when caught in a double bind. African American women may experience less devaluation of women and so have less stress, and/or the young women deal with stress better because of strong esteem and ethnic pride.

It is during adolescence that eating disorders are likely to start among young women, and a gender gap emerges, with young women showing more depression and anxiety than young men (Nolen-Hoeksema & Girgus, 1994). More adolescent women than men attempt suicide (chapter 16). Also, some adult women with alcohol problems report having had problems with the transition to adulthood. It has been suggested that something is "profoundly unhealthy about the passage to adulthood for young women" (Allgood-Merten & Stockard, 1991, p. 131). Perhaps the problem is not with the *passage* to adulthood but with *adulthood* itself.

Many young women and men obviously do go through adolescence without psychological problems. Some young people develop into non-gender-typed adults—also termed androgynous or gender flexible—our next topic.

## Adults Who Are Not Gender-Typed

As we have seen, preschoolers may become strongly gender-typed even if parents do not particularly want them to. Both Kohlberg and Freud predicted that with increasing

**Table 5.5**    Loevinger's Ego Development Model Applied to Women's Gender Identity

| Level | Description | Example |
|---|---|---|
| Preconformist Level | Gender roles are seen in egocentric and simple, concrete, visual terms with little or no capacity for abstract ideas. | The man earns the bread, keeps the car running, and drinks beer.<br><br>A man doesn't cry like a woman. |
| Conformist Level | Concern is with incorporating societal views. The conception of gender role identity is simplistic, concrete, and stereotyped. | You're not really a woman until you're married.<br><br>An advantage to being a woman is that women are allowed to be more compassionate and sensitive. |
| Postconformist Level | A. A set of personal beliefs including both agentic and communal concerns about identity. | For women, their identity is wound around their relationships more than their jobs. |
|  | B. Realization of many different points of view. Personal conflicts about roles may be recognized and parts of one's experiences previously denied may be discovered. | I realize now that what I wanted [when I was young] was not maleness but acceptance of my own strengths and powers by other people—the status and consideration granted to the male sex. |

SOURCE: Loevinger, J., *Ego Development*, p. 403. Jossey-Bass, Inc. Publishers, 1976.

cognitive maturity, a growing person could shed some of the early rigidity of gender-typing; social learning theory predicts that the rigidity can be reduced (or reversed) if the reinforcement contingencies change. Mary Anne Sedney (1987) suggests that behavior inconsistent with cultural stereotypes simply takes longer to develop than stereotypic behavior. It may not be until adulthood, when peer pressure may decrease, that people, especially men, become comfortable with behaviors associated with the other gender (Block, 1973; Werrbach, Grotevant, & Cooper, 1990).

Jane Loevinger (1976) has proposed an ego development theory that has been applied specifically to gender role identity (Block, 1973; Costos, 1990; Lasker, 1980). The general developmental pattern is one of increasingly complex perceptions of self and others, specifically, moving from a *preconformist* to a *conformist* and then to a *postconformist* level. People differ in their rate of progress and in their maximum attainment; they do not always outgrow childhood and adolescence cognitively simply because their chronological age keeps increasing. The maximum attainment theorized for gender role identity is to transcend sex and gender distinctions. The stages are illustrated (Table 5.5) by the responses from adult women (average age 27 years; Costos, 1990).

At the preconformist level, gender roles are seen in egocentric and simple, concrete, visual terms, with little or no capacity for abstract ideas such as identity. At the conformist level, concern is with incorporating societal views. The conception of gender role identity is simplistic, concrete, and stereotyped. At the postconformist level, there is more cognitive complexity about gender roles. First, the person has a set of personal beliefs and considers both agentic and communal concerns in personal identity development. Second, at the later part of the postconformist level, the person is aware of many different (and perhaps conflicting) points of view. Personal conflicts about roles may be recognized, and parts of one's experiences previously denied may be discovered. At this highest level, "traditional sex roles have been transcended in favor of a deepened respect for the individual and for seeing men and women as common humanity" (Costos, 1990, p. 729). This seems to be a better definition of androgyny than merely adding together the "feminine" and "masculine" attributes (chapter 3), but it is more difficult to measure. Most research about nonstereotyped people is based on a notion of the mixture of instrumentality and expressiveness.

## Parental Support and Modeling

Parents of individuals who are androgynous or gender flexible have two broad patterns: They are generally positive in their interactions with their children, and they are unconventional. Retrospective and longitudinal evidence are generally consistent about this. **Retrospective studies** ask people to report about the past. **Longitudinal studies** provide information about the same people at two or more different times. The longitudinal data cited here are from the Oakland Growth and Berkeley Guidance Studies (Block, von der Lippe, & Block, 1973), which included extensive studies of children and their parents and follow-up of the children as they grew. The adult children were in their 30s at the time they gave information about gender-typing. Retrospective evidence comes primarily from college students. A study of children (age 3–6 years) also indicates the relevance of the same kind of variables for reducing the gender-typing of children even in the early years (Katz, 1996).

Longitudinal evidence indicates that nonstereotyped adults had a warm and supportive family atmosphere, with parents who were psychologically healthy and emotionally available to the children. Parents were stable, financially secure members of the community, satisfied with their lives and with their marriages; they agreed with each other about discipline and emphasized fairness and responsibility. In contrast, children from families with emotional tension and conflict between parents and children were markedly stereotyped as adults regardless of other aspects of their early home life. It is as if the tension of the home made the security of gender roles attractive.

Both androgynous or flexible women and men recall relatively more love from their fathers and mothers and more parental involvement with and encouragement of their activities than adults of other gender-typings (Jackson et al., 1986; Spence & Helmreich, 1978). Encouragement for instrumentality, achievement, and intellectual curiosity stands out, especially for daughters (Arditti, Godwin, & Scanzoni, 1991; Kelly & Worell, 1976). Traditional children reported the next highest level of parental involvement, while cross-typed and undifferentiated children reported parents with low involvement and encouragement (Jackson et al., 1986; Orlofsky, 1979).

The unconventionality of parents of nonstereotyped adults shown by longitudinal studies included their own lack of stereotyping in personality styles and role behaviors. Parents had some form of sharing responsibility that was unconventional for the time. If parents were loving and supportive but practiced conventional roles, the children became stable adults who were similar to the same-sex parent. Retrospectively, androgynous women were more likely to report mothers with instrumental as well as expressive characteristics (Jackson et al., 1986; Kelly & Worell, 1976). Conversely, women with a more traditional orientation had parents with mainly stereotypic traits and the conventional father-dominant pattern (Lipman-Blumen, 1972).

Having an employed mother has been unconventional for white middle-class children. Thus, white middle-class women who are nonstereotypic are more likely to have employed mothers (DeFronzo & Boudreau, 1979; Hansson, Chernovetz, & Jones, 1977). Working outside the home has been more typical in African American families than in white families (McGoldrick, Garcia-Preto, Hines, & Lee, 1989). Thus, African American girls have been less stereotypic about work than white girls are (Gold & St. Ange, 1974). And, as noted previously, maternal employment has long been a correlate of women's career orientation and choice of nontraditional careers. Will maternal employment continue to be a factor in the development of androgyny? Perhaps. But Sedney (1987) cautions that with the increase in numbers of mothers employed, the context and meaning of maternal employment to the child and to the mother may change. The employed mother will no longer be "special" or different from other mothers, so her employment may be taken for granted by her children. However, the employed mother is still not likely to be around for her children to depend on as much as the nonemployed mother, and she still will be a model of a financial provider. So, there may continue to be differences between the children of employed and nonemployed women.

## Some Final Thoughts: Toward Gender-Free Experience

Children want to be loved and rewarded and to feel that they have some understanding of the social world they live in and their place in it. The adult world has told them that the safest way to achieve those goals is for a girl to be feminine and a boy to be masculine, as defined by adults. The culture gives many messages to children that gender is important, and children quickly learn a great deal about what gender means to adults, although their perceptions may be more extreme and rigid than those of parents. We can see the importance of experience in children's gender-typing, but we do not understand everything (e.g., children show toy preference before they can classify on the basis of sex). Each of three major theories contributes to our understanding. Yet all fall short because they assume the necessity of a critical event (identification with or attachment to a parent, or gender constancy) that happens *after* an amazing amount of gendered learning. Are there features of the child we have overlooked?

Although biological factors have been suggested for differences in play, we do know that the media, parents, and peers teach gender-typing. Parents contribute to gender-typing primarily by selecting stereotypical toys and chores that may shape children's personality and cognitive development. The learning is accentuated in a peer culture in which girls and boys are segregated and their different styles of interaction encouraged.

Probably because of the lesser status of women, adults place somewhat less pressure on girls than on boys to engage in stereotypic behavior. And possibly because of the lesser status, girls show greater bias to girls than boys do to boys. But girls are not necessarily happy with the pressure they do feel nor with what they are expected to become. Girls' self-esteem and gender preference both decline during the school years. The gender intensification of adolescence takes its toll on many young women, as they "go underground."

There may be some biological predispositions for some forms of stereotyped activities, as Maccoby suggests for different play styles. If there are, why do adults feel they have to help nature out? If the roles were "meant to be" for natural reasons, role-consistent behaviors would develop without the pressure. It may be "just natural" or even necessary for children to notice that some people are females and some are males. Sex does provide some concrete cues that children notice and need. Because of their limited cognitive development, it may be natural for children to give more importance to the implications of sex than the parents do—for a while.

Continuing pressures toward gender-typing have their effect, but we must not forget individual differences among parents (and other adults) and among children. Parents with flexible children are warm and accepting in their parenting and they model nonstereotypic behavior in their activities.

In addition, more specifically, adults can encourage more complex thinking to help a child understand that being a woman or a man has no necessary relation to career or educational choices and opportunities. Parents can give their children more of the nonstereotypic toys they request: Most parents probably could survive any trauma of giving their daughter the chemistry set she wants instead of the doll's house they want for her. Parents can encourage both boys and girls to help out around the house with whatever needs to be done, whether it is dusting or taking the garbage out. And parents can attend to the messages they are giving by their own behavior. Love and acceptance between parents and children or between adults need not be contingent upon being feminine or masculine. Humans can be encouraged to become full persons rather than half persons.

## KEY TERMS

self-label
gender identity
gender preference
peer preference
toy preference
gender stability
gender constancy
Freudian theory
Oedipal crisis

identification
social learning theory
reinforcement
generalization
discrimination learning
observational learning,
  imitation
parsimony

cognitive developmental
  theory
egocentric thinking
gender schema theory
gender segregation
gender intensification
retrospective study
longitudinal study

## KEY POINTS

*Facts and Theories About Gender-Typed Development*

- Between infancy and about 6 years is a dynamic time of gender-typed development.

- Toy preference can occur before a child knows what toys are stereotyped or has a self-label, but knowing a toy is for a girl or boy becomes important.

- Young children can be liberal about the occupations for other people but are likely to be stereotyped in their own choice. After kindergarten, girls become more flexible about occupations.

- The big three theoretical approaches to gender-typing have focused on early stereotyped development within nuclear families and do not account for the early age of gender-typing or for individual differences and development within nontraditional families.

- Freudian theory assumes that children want parental love and fear loss of it. In spite of problems with masculinized bias and biological assumptions, some of Freud's descriptions are consistent with modern research and theory.

- Social learning theory assumes that children want rewards. Reinforcement and observation are important, but social learning theory has many weaknesses in accounting for children's gender-typing.

- Kohlberg's cognitive developmental theory emphasizes that not only is conformity with roles important in giving a child a feeling of competence in understanding the world, but it is felt as a moral dictate. The theory accounts for how gender roles take on "a life of their own" and for the possibility of later flexibility, but gender constancy develops *after* strong gender-typing has occurred.

- Contemporary gender schema theory does not assume that gender constancy is necessary for gender-typing. Classification skills to allow flexibility can be taught. Gender-typing is multidimensional, and the many facets are not all related to each other, though they are more related for boys than for girls.

*Contributors to Stereotyped Development*

- Parental differentiation between sons and daughters is strongest for gender-typed toys and play and for chores, but parents give more latitude about play to girls than to boys, and women give more than men. Gender-typed toys may be more important to parents than to children. Giving of toys and assigning chores are related.

- Maternal employment generally has a liberalizing effect on children's gender-typing, especially daughters. Parents of either sex can teach either feminine or masculine behaviors, or both. Children of lesbians or gay men do not differ from children of heterosexuals in gender preferences or identity.

- Gender segregation is strong in childhood, and children show same-gender bias, though the bias is stronger in girls than in boys. This may be because of girls' lesser status and/or because of differences in interaction styles; boys use physical means or direct commands to get their way.

◆ Boys are more physical and competitive in their play, and they play in larger groups in more complex games, often outside. Girls are more verbal and concerned with group harmony. The styles may have implications for adult behavior.

◆ The growing girl's gender adoption decreases and the relevance of expressiveness to her self-esteem decreases while instrumentality stays relevant. Gender differences in psychological problems emerge in adolescence.

◆ The ego development model of gender role identity postulates a pattern of movement from preconformist, to conformist, and then to postconformist, at which point concern with gender roles is transcended.

◆ Parents who are warm and supportive and who are unconventional in some way tend to have children who are flexible in gender roles.

## INTEGRATIVE QUESTIONS

1. What is the evidence for and against a claim that children's toy preferences are due to adults more than to children? What is your own position about toy preference?

2. Take the position of one of the major theories (including gender schema theory) about gender-typing and explain what is known from research about gender-typing in children and adults. As a theorist yourself, coming from that position, you are free to—and invited to—extend or modify the theory as you see necessary.

3. What are the most important ways in which parents teach gender-typing to young children? How does that mesh with what is known about parents of adults who are not gender-typed?

4. Discuss why there is gender bias among children and a greater bias among girls. Do not be limited by what is known about children—think about any comparable phenomena you know of among adults.

5. Why is girls' expressiveness (a component of femininity) not related to their self-esteem as they grow into adolescence? Why is the relationship positive for boys? Does your reasoning about teens apply in any way to adults whom you know?

6. How do your memories of your parents when you were young and your current view of yourself match with the depiction given from research of characteristics of nonstereotyped adults? Have either you or your parents changed in any relevant ways?

7. At what stage do you classify yourself (or someone else you know well) in the gender identity version of Loevinger's ego development model (Table 5.5)? What are your reasons for the classification? How does the classification compare with parental status in the model? If there is a difference from parents, why?

## Chapter 6

# Women's Experiences
# of Menstruation

*A* vital part of coming of age for most adolescent women is the first menstrual period. Thus menstruation is discussed here as a continuation of our exploration of women's early life experiences. Most women continue to menstruate until their late 40s or early 50s; menopause is discussed as part of women's adult development (chapter 14). Although menstruation is a natural event, it is viewed through a set of widely shared negative assumptions. In many ways, women's experiences of menstruation have been taken away from them, to the disadvantage of our understanding of women and of nature. Because of social construction, a natural human experience has been distorted personally, societally, and scientifically.

We will look at cultural perceptions about menstruation that form the mythological framework within which women experience this event and at the implications of puberty for young women. Then we will consider women's general behavior before and during menstruation and how menstruation can be seen as a natural, even joyous, event.

Before continuing, consider these questions for personal thought:

- How did you first hear about menstruation? What did you hear? How did you feel?

- Do you know who was the first girl in your class to menstruate? How did you know, or why do you think you did not know? For women: What was your response when you noticed your first menstrual blood? Who did you tell? What reaction did you get? For men: What have girls or women told you about their menstrual experiences?

- Think back to how your mother or other important women behaved when you were growing up. Were there any cues that it was "that time of the month" for them? What were the cues? How do you think they influenced your views of menstruation?

◆ Did anything change between you and your parents when you went through puberty—when you were growing up?

◆ Were you generally an early maturer or a late maturer? How did that affect your relationship with your friends? Your parents?

◆ Describe your image of the typical premenstrual or menstrual woman.

◆ What would your reaction be if a woman burst energetically into a room and exclaimed, "Wow, I feel great. I'm ovulating!" Or, "Wow, I feel great. I'm menstruating!"

◆ Have you noticed cycles in men that might be due to testosterone fluctuation?

◆ Do women have the same freedom to express anger or irritability as men do?

◆ How could menstruation be considered a joyous experience?

## Perceptions of Menstruation

Blood is a potent symbol. Many religious rituals and sacraments involve blood in some way. Given the importance of blood, people have gone to some lengths to try to understand women's loss of blood once a month. A variety of societies, past and present, have developed myths about menstruation (Abel & Joffe, 1950; Bell, 1990; Ford, 1945; Frazer, 1951; King, 1974; Landers, 1977; Maddux, 1975). *Myths* are stories or beliefs adopted by a group of people to explain their world and their experiences in it. The myths may not make sense by current scientific understanding, but when widely shared, they provide a feeling of comfort and understanding.

The myths about menstruation have been grouped into three broad categories (A Closer Look 6.1). One variety, "protect her," sees the menstruating woman in a highly vulnerable state requiring protection. A second variety, "protect us from her," stems from beliefs in the power of women to pollute and a general devaluation of women (Buckley & Gottlieb, 1988). The touch, the gaze, the presence of a menstruating woman are dangerous to others. Some societies have had menstrual huts for menstruating women, which have often been seen as evidence of the community's desire to protect itself from the women. There is some reason, however, to believe that being in the menstrual hut could be a positive experience. A woman could get away from daily chores for a few days and relax and meditate. Chances are that there were many other women there. Time in the hut was a time of sharing oral history and the secrets of womanhood. It could have been a time of women bonding with each other and growing spiritually. Consistent with this possibility, some American Indians considered menstruation a time of centering and balancing in which the flow washed away impurities; being "on the moon" was a positive experience (Hyde, 1991).

The final broad grouping of menstrual myths is "there is power in the blood." Although menstrual blood might be dirty and dangerous, it does have special powers to heal, to keep dangers away, and even to increase passion. Husbands in New Guinea are especially nice to menstruating wives lest the wives drip blood on them while they are asleep (Rosaldo, 1974).

## A Closer Look

### 6.1    Examples of Myths About Menstruation

#### "Protect Her"

Menstruating women should not go out in the cold, take cold baths, wash their hair, or do heavy housework. If menstrual blood does not flow freely, it will go to the head and cause insanity. Stained napkins are believed to help blood flow, while clean ones reduce blood flow. Since menstrual blood that does not flow freely goes to the head and causes insanity, fresh napkins are not recommended. Wine will help restore the lost blood (and perhaps help women not care so much if their napkins are dirty!).

#### "Protect Us From Her"

A menstruating woman is to be confined to a hammock on a roof or suspended in a dark narrow cage to shut her off from earth and sun so she can poison neither. Menstruating women should not prepare food; bread they bake will not rise; their gaze dulls mirrors and causes knives to lose their sharpness. The gaze of a menstruating woman also causes abortions in animals, her touch withers flowers, her presence blights crops. Cattle will die if she passes over ground where even one drop of menstrual blood has fallen.

#### "There's Power in the Blood"

Weapons forged with a virgin's menstrual blood are especially desired for battle. Menstrual blood is a good treatment for eczema, warts, and malaria. If a woman's periods are slow to come, she can cure her problem by eating bread soaked in the blood of the first menstrual flow of another woman. The passion of a lethargic lover can be increased by putting the first day's menstrual blood in his coffee. One interpretation of the superstition of not walking under a ladder is that a menstruating woman might be on top of it and the unsuspecting walker be touched by the blood.

SOURCES: Abel, T., & N. Joffe, (1950). Cultural background of female puberty. *American Journal of Psychotherapy, 93*, 90–113. Bell, A. R. (1990). Separate people: Speaking of Creek men and women. *American Anthropologist, 92*, 332–345. Ford, C. S. (1945). *A comparative study of human reproduction.* New Haven, CT: Yale University Press. Frazer, J. G. (1951). *The golden bough.* New York: Macmillan. Landers, A. D. (1977). The menstrual experience. In E. Donelson & J. E. Gullahorn (Eds.). *Women: A psychological perspective.* New York: John Wiley. Maddux, H. C. (1975). *Menstruation.* New Canaan, CT: Tobey.

Many of these myths are easy to laugh at. Perhaps it is easier to laugh at others than at ourselves. We, too, have myths.

## Contemporary Views of Menstruation

Myths about menstruation continue, and those of our culture have many similarities to those of other cultures. As late as the 1960s educational consultants for Tampax were asked by high school and college women, "Is it true that menstrual blood is bad blood?" "Will a permanent take during menstruation?" Young women in their 20s said that they could not go to their prom while menstruating because the flowers of the corsage would wilt (Milow, 1983). Some women avoid swimming, shaving, gardening, and biking when they are menstruating (Jurgens & Powers, 1991; Williams, 1983). About half or more of Americans believe that a menstruating woman should not have intercourse (Milow, 1983; Snow & Johnson, 1977). Most Orthodox Jews and Roman Catholics avoid intercourse during menstruation, while less than half of Protestants are likely to do so. Feminist college women are more likely than others to express sexual arousal and have intercourse while menstruating (Hardie & McMurray, 1992).

Menstruation is amazingly underdiscussed, given that women spend about 25% to 35% of their time being premenstrual or menstrual for many years of their lives. About two thirds of Americans think that menstruation should not be mentioned at social gatherings or in the office (Delaney, Lupton, & Toth, 1988; Milow, 1983). Curiously, somewhat more men (38%) than women (27%) think menstruation is an acceptable conversation topic (Milow, 1983). Ads for sanitary supplies were banned from TV and radio until 1972; the word *period* was not used in a TV ad until 1985.

Would menstruation be so negated and neglected if men menstruated instead of women? Gloria Steinem offered some thoughts about this idea in her book *Outrageous Acts and Everyday Rebellions* (1984), saying that if men could menstruate,

> They would brag about how much and how long.
>
> Sanitary supplies would be federally funded and free.
>
> Surveys would show that men did better in sports during their periods.
>
> Women would be considered incapable of mastering any discipline that needs a sense of time, space, and mathematics because they lack the biological gift of measuring the cycles of the moon and planets.

Steinem notes, "The truth is that, if men could menstruate, the power justifications would go on and on."

When menstruation is referred to, euphemisms are likely to be used to dull the effect of what we are talking about. Only 25 of 133 college women reported using the term *menstruation* (Hays, 1987). The term *period* has become relatively standard among college women; 126 of 133 college women used *period*, often along with other expressions, many of which were very negative. Most women who use negative terms also have negative attitudes toward menstruation. "The curse" has been a popular expression, though fortunately falling out of favor with younger adults (Ernster, 1975). Think of the implications: Curses are powerful and negative. The most common euphemisms reported by men were variations of "on the rag" or "flying the flag" (Hays, 1987). When a man is irritable and moody, *he* is said to be "on the rag," or is "ragging." Why is negative imagery about a woman's body used to describe men's negativity? If we must blame the body for negative moods—a practice I'll later challenge—why not use a male reference for a male mood?

In a context in which being a normal woman physically has such negative overtones, it is no wonder that young women have mixed feelings about their first menstruation, the **menarche.** Cynthia Zelman (1991) has provided a humorous but poignant

*A Closer Look*

### 6.2    "Our Menstruation"

"We menstruated simultaneously. We were just sixth-grade girls attending our last year of Chemung Hill Elementary School. We had our first period, *together*. Okay, the actual blood flowed from only one of us upon the great event of our first menstruation, but we shared the experience, most of us unwillingly, some of us traumatically. Collective menstruation it was; like a ritual, like a sacrifice, like a virgin thrown to the gods. We gave something up to get something back; blood for woman-hood. We did not quite understand the event, yet we sensed a monumental purpose. Our menstruation was big . . . (p. 461)

The rest of the afternoon, every girl in the sixth grade kept checking her pants or skirt to see if she was staining blood. It was a fretful afternoon." (p. 467)

SOURCE: Zelman, C. M. (1991, Fall). Our menstruation, for the girls. *Feminist Studies, 17,* (3), 461–467.

statement about the first menstruation (A Closer Look 6.2). Some researchers found that most adult women (18–45 years old) remembered their first experience in some detail (Woods, Dery, & Most, 1983). More than half reported having positive feelings, such as excitement, but more than half also reported negative feelings, such as embarrassment. Younger women now are somewhat more positive than the older women had been, but half are scared and about a third embarrassed (Petersen, 1983). Ambivalence continues.

## Teaching About Menstruation

Instructions to young people about menstruation do not give uniformly positive messages (Whisnant, Brett, & Zegans, 1975). Booklets supplied for hygiene education by makers of menstrual supplies give double messages. On the one hand, the message is that menstruation is a perfectly normal part of development. On the other hand, they say, "Use our products and no one will know you are doing it!" Then there is the curious message a young boy got from advertisements about menstrual supplies: He announced that he wanted a box of tampons for Christmas. "Why?" his astounded mother asked. "Because then I can go horseback riding and swimming and do anything I want to do" (Golub, 1983).

The lack of positive and realistic instruction is unfortunate because adequate preparation is associated with a positive response to menstruation (Brooks-Gunn & Ruble, 1983; Ruble & Brooks-Gunn, 1982). Adolescent girls get more information from the media and peers than from their mothers (Stoltzman, 1986). But some do not get any information. About a third of girls and women in one study did not know what was happening to them when they got their first menstrual period (Sarrell & Sarrell, 1984). When asked what they had wanted as young women first experiencing menstruation, college women said they appreciated the technical information given in schools, but they did not feel prepared for menstruation as a *personal* event (Rierdan, 1983). They wanted to talk about it with an older woman who could acknowledge that their fears and embarrassments were shared with other women. They especially wanted an informed, understanding, accepting mother. The problem, of course, is that many mothers are not comfortable discussing menstruation other than in objective, distant terms. Ignoring the event means the young woman is at the mercy of fears and rumors about an important part of her identity. There are, however, societies in which menarcheal rituals publicize the event, so that the family may enjoy the financial gain of having a young woman who can reproduce (Paige & Paige, 1981).

On the brighter side, there is evidence that people are beginning to celebrate a young woman's first menstrual period (Crooks & Baur, 1993; Washbourn, 1977). The event is acknowledged clearly and openly as cause for celebration. The celebration may involve the mother taking the daughter out to lunch, or having a special celebratory meal for the whole family, or the father sending flowers to the young woman. Parents are encouraged to be sensitive to the desires and feelings of their daughters, because some young women are embarrassed by the attention to the event. Yet, the day may come when greeting cards will be marketed to congratulate a menarcheal young woman, and the first menstrual period will be recognized and supported.

## Biological and Psychological Factors

Menstruation is a biological event to be sure, but it is also a psychological event. The human being is a psychobiological whole (chapter 4). Let us start by considering this important theme at the relatively simple level of what seems to be "purely" physical.

### The Physical Experience

Menstruation is the monthly shedding of the uterine lining in a nonpregnant woman. With menstruation, the body starts preparing again for a pregnancy, developing an egg for potential fertilization and preparing the uterus to receive the fertilized egg. The "average" cycle is calculated as 28 days, though perhaps as few as 16% of women have an average cycle (Willson & Carrington, 1987). The cycle can range from 21 to 40 days (Strong & DeVault, 1997). Fourteen days plus or minus 2 days is the interval between ovulation and the *onset* of menstruation (Willson & Carrington, 1987). Differences in cycle length are due to the phase *before* ovulation, making prediction of ovulation from the preceding cycle difficult.

***The Reproductive Cycle***     The first day of the cycle is set by convention as the onset of bleeding. At this time, estrogen and progesterone levels are at their lowest (Figure 6.1). (Estrogen is the principal hormone regulating female reproductive functions and the development of secondary sex characteristics. Progesterone helps regulate the

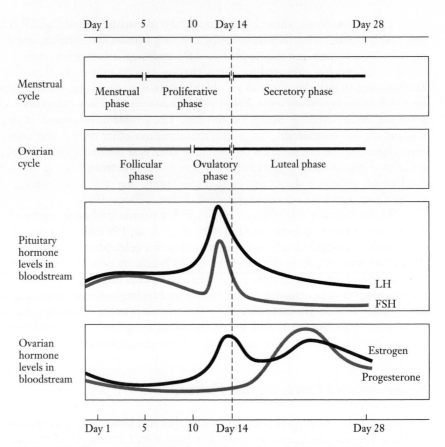

**Figure 6.1** *The menstrual cycle, the ovarian cycle, and hormone levels.*

menstrual cycle and sustain pregnancy.) Because of low estrogen during the period of bleeding, the hypothalamus signals the pituitary gland to release follicle-stimulating hormone (FSH), which causes several follicles (small sacs), each containing an ovum (egg), to start developing in an ovary. FSH also increases the output of estrogen from the ovaries. Estrogen causes the endometrium, the lining of the uterus, to thicken in preparation for a fertilized egg. Several follicles start to mature, but usually only one (the graafian follicle) reaches maturity.

When ovarian estrogen is at its peak, the pituitary depresses FSH and stimulates production of luteinizing hormone (LH), which induces the mature follicle to rupture and release the ovum. This is the time of ovulation, about 14 days before the next period. At the time of rupture, some women experience a twinge or pressure in the lower abdomen (*mittelschmerz*, German for "middle pain"). Cervical mucus secretion becomes clear, slippery, stretchy, and more alkaline, contributing to sperm motility and longevity.

LH causes the ruptured follicle (the portion of the follicle that remains after the egg has matured) to develop into the corpus luteum (literally, "yellow body"), which secretes progesterone and some estrogen. These hormones inhibit the release of FSH and LH and cause the further thickening of the uterine lining in preparation for a fertilized egg. The ovum descends through one of the Fallopian tubes and, if fertilized, becomes embedded in the uterine lining. If it is not fertilized, production of LH and FSH is stopped, so the corpus luteum deteriorates and estrogen and progesterone decrease. The decrease of the hormones causes the shedding of the endometrial cells along with mucus and blood from the broken blood vessels. Menstrual flow, also called menses, usually lasts 2 to 6 days and involves six to eight ounces of discharge (Johnson, 1991). After menstruation is started, the low level of estrogen causes the cycle to start again.

The monthly cycle actually consists of two separate (though obviously related) sets of events, one occurring in the ovaries and the other in the uterus (see Figure 6.1). The ovarian cycle has three phases. During the **follicular phase,** days 1–10, the ovarian follicles are maturing. During the **ovulatory phase,** days 11–14, the follicle wall thins and ruptures, releasing the egg. During the **luteal phase,** days 15–28, the corpus luteum secretes hormones and either deteriorates or, in the event of fertilization, helps to sustain pregnancy until the placenta can take over hormone production.

The uterine or menstrual cycle also has three phases. During the **menstrual phase,** days 1–5, the endometrial wall is shed. During the **proliferative phase,** days 6–14, the endometrium again begins to build up in response to increased estrogen. During the **secretory phase,** days 15–28, either the endometrial cells begin to die or, in the event of fertilization, the endometrium begins to prepare for the fertilized ovum.

*Puberty*    Menstruation is one of many interrelated events of puberty in a young woman. **Puberty** (from the Latin *pubescere*, to be covered with hair) is the general term for the period of rapid physical changes in adolescence during which children reach reproductive maturity (Brooks-Gunn & Petersen, 1983; Golub, 1992; Paikoff & Brooks-Gunn, 1991). The transition from childhood to adulthood in Western societies typically spans ages 12 to 20. Most of the physical changes take place in the first few years, though there are important psychological changes throughout (Wheeler, 1991).

The sequence of events seems to be similar across cultures and ethnicities, although the age at which the events happen may vary. In the United States, African Americans tend to mature earlier than whites, who in turn mature earlier than Asian Americans (Brooks-Gunn & Reiter, 1990; Morrison et al., 1994; Swenson, Erickson, Ehlinger, Carlson, & Swaney, 1989). Generally, when the child is between 8 and 14 years, the hypothalamus triggers events that increase the growth rate of all body tissues and stimulate ovaries and testes. This **growth spurt** may begin as early as 9 years for girls, ending between 14 and 16 years. Boys' spurt usually starts about two years later than girls', typically after age 11, and may continue through the teenage years.

The increased hormone levels cause secondary sex characteristics to develop. In girls, breast development is usually first, with breast buds (a small rose around the nipples) appearing at about 10½ or 11 years, though they may appear as early as 8 years

*The timing of maturation varies greatly. Timing depends on genetic factors (maturation rates of both mother and father), physical factors (amount of body fat, for example), and social factors (such as stress and socioeconomic status).*

or as late as 13 years (Brooks-Gunn, 1988). This is followed shortly by pubic hair and then by axillary hair about two years later. Menarche occurs relatively late in puberty, about 18 months after the growth spurt has reached its peak. The average age of menarche is 12½ years in the United States, about two years after breast buds appear, although a girl may begin menstruation as early as 9 or as late as 17 (Calderone & Johnson, 1989; Zacharias et al., 1976). The labia become enlarged, the vaginal walls become thicker, and the uterus becomes larger and more muscular. Initial cycles may be irregular, and many occur without ovulation (they are anovulatory). In some young women it takes several years for their periods to become regular and predictable (Crooks & Baur, 1993).

## Timing and Occurrence of Menarche and Menstruation

Researchers still do not know exactly what triggers the process of puberty, but we do know that its timing in young women is related to both physical factors and social stress (Beal, 1994). The most frequently cited hypothesis about the physical cause of menarche is that a certain minimum percentage of body fat must be present (Frisch & McArthur, 1974). Girls and boys before pubescence have a similar amount of body fat, but with physical maturity, girls have about twice as much as boys (Warren, 1983). During the growth spurt, girls' body fat increases about 120%. Menarche typically occurs when about one fourth of body weight is fat (Frisch, 1983). About one sixth of young women's body weight is fat at the onset of puberty and about one fourth at menarche.

Another hypothesis supported by research is that skeletal growth must have reached an appropriate level for reproduction (e.g., widened hips) (Tanner, 1978; also see Paikoff & Brooks-Gunn, 1991). For most young women, height and gain in fatty tissue are related. Athletes and dancers who engage in strenuous training frequently have delayed menarche or interrupted menstruation (Frisch, Wyshak, & Vincent, 1980; Gargiulo, Brooks-Gunn, Attie, & Warren, 1987; Warren, 1982, 1983). This has been attributed to their lower levels of fat because of the training, but more than weight may be involved. Girls who mature relatively late are more likely to be interested and talented in sports and dance and tend to be thinner after as well as before puberty.

Genetic factors also influence timing of menarche. There is a correlation between mothers and daughters in cycle length, flow duration, and pain at menstruation. Mothers' and fathers' growth rates have equal effect, so a late maturing girl is as likely to have a late maturing father as a late maturing mother. The average difference in age of menarche for identical twins—who have exactly the same genetic makeup—is 2 months, even if they are reared apart; the firstborn starts first (Marshall & Tanner, 1974). In contrast, twins who share only 50% (fraternal twins) of genetic makeup differ in time of menstrual onset by 8 to 12 months.

Among the environmental factors that affect when puberty occurs are nutrition, stress, exercise, family size, and socioeconomic background (Beal, 1994; Paikoff & Brooks-Gunn, 1991). The average age of menarche is around 16 years in Bangladesh and 18 years in New Guinea. Within industrialized countries, the age has been dropping steadily since 1840. Menarche in the United States occurs about a year and a half earlier than it did in 1905. Girls in higher socioeconomic classes in the same country may have menarche 6 to 12 months earlier than those from poor families, probably because of generally better health and reduced stress (Frisch, 1983; Marshall & Tanner, 1974). But family stress can happen in any social class and may affect menarcheal timing; girls whose family life is very stressed tend to reach puberty earlier than other girls (Belsky, Steinberg, & Draper, 1991; Steinberg, 1988). Early or late menarche may indicate a physical condition that needs attention.

***Amenorrhea***   Menstruation does not always appear when it is expected. If menstruation has never occurred by about age 18 years, the condition is **primary amenorrhea.** The young woman may have a gender anomaly (chapter 4) or important problems needing medical attention (Boston Women's Health Book Collective, 1992; Crooks & Baur, 1993). When menstrual periods stop or become irregular after having occurred previously, the condition is **secondary amenorrhea,** which may have normal or abnormal causes. Secondary amenorrhea is normal during pregnancy and breast-feeding, and it is common in women who have just begun menstruating, those approaching menopause, and those who discontinue birth control pills (Maddux, 1975). Secondary amenorrhea, both with and without a clear medical explanation, and irregularity generally also occur in women who have experienced sexual assault (Golding, 1996). It is more common among athletes than other women, presumably because of the exercise, low body fat, or stress (Loucks & Horvath, 1985; Shangold, 1985). Athletes, however, are advised to have medical evaluations (Shangold, 1980). Amenorrhea may precede or accompany anorexia nervosa (chapter 16).

Stress is a common cause of secondary amenorrhea, but stress also can cause a menstrual period to come early. Stress caused by fear of an unwanted pregnancy gets some women in a vicious cycle. Because they fear pregnancy, menstruation is delayed. Because menstruation is delayed, they become more fearful and stressed, and the period is further delayed. So they get more worried, and on and on.

Psychological concerns about pregnancy also can cause **pseudocyesis:** false pregnancy. A female who is not pregnant shows signs of pregnancy, including amenorrhea and perhaps galactorrhea (milky breast secretions). Not much is known about this condition in humans, but it also occurs in cows, goats, and dogs. Women with pseudocyesis generally are very concerned about pregnancy—either they want it very much or they are very afraid of it. The psyche affects the functions of the pituitary gland via changes in the hypothalamus. There may also be physiological origins, including changes due to chlorpromazine therapy. Cure usually is spontaneous; psychotherapy is not effective.

*Synchrony*    Timing of the cycle also can be affected by whom a woman is associating with. Women living together often menstruate together (Jarrett, 1984; McClintock, 1971). Martha McClintock (1971) studied first-year college students in an all-woman college. Among those women assigned to room together, synchrony in the timing of menstrual periods commonly occurred within 4 months and even more within 6 months. The synchrony was greatest for women who were both roommates and best friends, presumably spending the most time together.

Associating with men also affects the cycle (Vieth, Buck, Gertzlaf, Van Dolfsen, & Slade, 1983). McClintock found that the frequency of menstrual periods varied with how often women dated men. Women who dated more (three or more times a week) experienced shorter cycles than women who dated less (zero to two times a week). Further, some women who did not see men much initially but increased their frequency, reported noticing that their cycles shortened. We do not know exactly what the women did on their dates, but it may not matter for current purposes.

Researchers following up the synchrony effect demonstrated the relevance of **pheromones:** airborne hormones (Cutler, Preti, Krieger, & Huggins, 1986). Women with normal menstrual cycles swabbed their upper lips with perspiration extract from another woman (whom they did not know) or with alcohol. Of those given the perspiration extract, 80% were menstruating in sync with their perspiration donor within three menstrual cycles. A similar study with men as donors of the extract indicated that the effect of association with men also seemed due to pheromones, not to sexual activity (Cutler et al., 1986). Thus, the physical cycle, and puberty itself, does not play out automatically apart from the social context.

## The Psychological Experience

Becoming pubertal has meaning for a young woman's emerging status as an adult, socially and sexually (Beal, 1994; Petersen, 1988). Puberty changes the young woman's body, the expectations others have of her, and her own self-view. The actual body changes are likely to be accompanied by changes in the psychological view of the body—the body image—and this has implications for identity.

As we have seen, menarche typically brings both positive and negative reactions, but embarrassment about physical maturation begins before menarche. Puberty channels children's attention to their own bodies and those of others (Greene & Adams-Price, 1990). Height increase and breast development, which start before menarche, are noticeable to others; they seem to affect psychological functioning more than do the changes that are not visible to others (Petersen, 1988). Sloppy big shirts and sweaters may be the favored garb of fourth and fifth graders because of anxieties about loss of childish bodies (Delaney et al., 1988).

Many girls are teased about breast growth, most often by their parents, and feel embarrassed and angry about the teasing (Brooks-Gunn, 1984). Young women commonly have negative emotions of mild intensity about maturation and the change in body image (Koff, 1983; Koff, Rierdan, & Jacobson, 1981). Puberty seems to affect body image more than it affects other psychological factors (Brooks-Gunn, 1988). Postmenarcheal girls draw themselves with makeup, jewelry, and breasts, in contrast to simpler figures drawn by premenarcheal girls of the same age (Figure 6.2).

The body changes may be associated with the increased self-consciousness girls (primarily white) feel into the high school years (Simmons & Rosenberg, 1975). Advancing pubertal status is related to girls feeling less positive about their bodies, but to boys feeling more positive about theirs (Crockett & Petersen, 1987). This seems due to the fact that boys are evaluated on the basis of how well they perform athletically, while girls are evaluated on the basis of how good they look. The felt self-worth of young teenage women is strongly related to their physical appearance, especially thinness (Kwa, 1994; Powell & Kahn, 1995). This generalization seems more true for white than for African American teens (Tashakkori, 1993). In contrast to whites, African American adolescents have a closer tie between felt closeness with parents and their self-esteem.

Normal female physical maturation brings an increase in fatty tissue, relatively and absolutely, but society values thinness, and media present an unrealistic image of women (Attie & Brooks-Gunn, 1989; chapter 2). It is no surprise, then, that girls (especially white), more than boys, suffer from poor body image and dissatisfaction with weight, feeling that they are too heavy, even though objectively they are normal (see Petersen, 1988). It is during the adolescent years that eating problems become prevalent in young women, and the gender gap in anxiety and depression develops (chapter 16). For teenage girls, body image and self-esteem are highly related; a girl who is unhappy with her body may not see the potential that doing well in school or having rewarding hobbies and friends has for her pride. Attractive girls are more anxious about becoming pubertal than are less attractive girls (Zakin, Blyth, & Simmons, 1984), possibly because they are more likely to define themselves physically.

Both social class and ethnicity affect the young woman's concern about weight. The girl who is most worried about her weight and shows the most decline in self-esteem is likely to be a white girl from an upper-middle-class family (Beal, 1994; Dornbusch, Gross, Duncan, & Ritter, 1987; Martin, 1987). Such a girl is likely to be

**Figure 6.2** *Drawings by premenarcheal and postmenarcheal girls. 1a and 1b were drawn by a premenarcheal girl. 2a and 2b were drawn by a postmenarcheal girl. 3a was drawn by a premenarcheal girl, and 3b was drawn by the same girl postmenarcheally.*    SOURCE: Koff, E. Through the looking glass of menarche: What the adolescent girl sees. In S. Golub, 1983, *Menarche: The transition from girl to woman* (pp. 77–85). Lexington, MA: Lexington Books, D. C. Heath and Co.

most affected by cultural expectations of being thin, beautiful, and "marrying well." In turn, thinness can indicate membership in the elite stratum.

Working-class girls are more likely to expect to be able to support themselves and are less affected by media portrayals of wealthy, thin, white women. African American girls also are likely to be relatively protected from pressures to be thin (Fine & MacPherson, 1992; Hamilton, Brooks-Gunn, Warren, & Hamilton, 1987; Powell & Kahn, 1995). They have a more stable self-image and higher self-esteem than white girls (Simmons & Rosenberg, 1975). African American parents strongly emphasize educational advancement for their daughters and teach them not to accept negative evaluations from others (Comer, 1993; Harris, 1993; Smith, 1982; Ward, 1989). Unfortunately, women of minority groups are becoming more vulnerable to the general societal pressures (chapter 16).

The negative effects of puberty can be diminished or overcome by feeling accepted by peers and by being active (Crockett, Losoff, & Petersen, 1984; Richards, Peterson, Boxer, & Albrecht, 1990). When girls are involved with more after-school activities, including sports, and when they feel more satisfied with sports, they feel more satisfied with their weight and bodies and with themselves (Butcher, 1989; Richards et al., 1990).

Unfortunately, girls' participation in sports declines in the teen years, in large part because the young women are afraid of being seen as "unfeminine." In general, sports and physical activity have been considered a male domain, and in spite of some improvements, not much has changed (see Koivula, 1995). Although physical activity still carries a negative stigma for women (Moore & Gobi, 1995), young women who do participate in athletics do not have a sense of gender role conflict (Miller & Levy, 1996). Those young women who are less traditional (scoring higher on instrumentality measures; chapter 3) are more likely to participate in sports and have better self-esteem than those who are more traditional (Markstrom-Adams, 1989; Marsh & Jackson, 1986; Miller & Levy, 1996).

## Relations With Parents

As noted earlier, puberty and its outward physical signs occur in a social context and influence how people react to young people and, perhaps, how they react themselves. The years of transition into adolescence are a critical time for realignment of family relationships and may affect parents' views about themselves and their parenthood (Hill, 1988; Paikoff & Brooks-Gunn, 1991; Silverberg & Steinberg, 1990). When menstruation begins, young girls expect their parents to treat them more like adults, and to some extent, that happens. Postmenarcheal girls, compared with premenarcheal girls, set more of their own rules and have more liberal time limits (Danza, 1983).

During the pubertal period, the time parents and children spend together, their emotional closeness, and children's yielding to parental decisions all decrease (Montemayor & Hanson, 1985; Paikoff & Brooks-Gunn, 1991; Steinberg, 1988). Many adolescents become hesitant to share feelings because of discomfort discussing pubertal changes (Crockett & Petersen, 1987; Paikoff & Brooks-Gunn, 1991; Zahaykevich, Sirey, & Brooks-Gunn, 1989). They have learned from adults to be uncomfortable with their bodies. Young women are uncomfortable particularly about discussing puberty with fathers; less than 15% tell their fathers about menarche (Brooks-Gunn, 1987; Danza, 1983).

Reduced communication can increase conflict, and conflict with parents does increase during adolescence. However, generally it is less than one might expect and more a matter of bickering and disagreements than a severe rupture of the emotional bonds (Hill & Holmbeck, 1987; Paikoff & Brooks-Gunn, 1991; Petersen, 1988; Santrock, 1990). The potential for mother-daughter conflict during the daughter's early puberty is common, particularly among whites (Brooks-Gunn & Zahaykevich,

*As a girl matures into a young woman, her relationship with her mother changes, particularly when issues of privacy, sexuality, and conflict arise. Parents and children can still be close, however, if they maintain open communication.*

1989; Danza, 1983), though mothers report more conflict and less satisfaction with sons (Hill & Holmbeck, 1987). African American mother-daughter pairs remain close after the daughter's puberty (Fine & MacPherson, 1992). Young white women may direct some of their negative or ambivalent feelings about puberty toward mothers because they think mothers are not sensitive to their need for privacy. Nonetheless, most teens continue to rely heavily on parents for emotional support and guidance (Steinberg, 1987, 1988).

While the girl is facing her sexualization (and perhaps issues of her parents' sexuality) and the ambivalence of femininity (chapter 5), the parents themselves may feel uncomfortable and embarrassed about their child's puberty (Paikoff & Brooks-Gunn, 1991). Some family dynamics may be a matter of parents reliving their own sexuality from younger years (Ferguson, 1977). The father's protectiveness and watchfulness about the daughter's dating increase. In addition, the father may be aware of himself as a sexual being and realize that with his daughter's maturity, cultural taboos about incest become more markedly relevant. Fathers often become more assertive or brusque with postmenarcheal daughters than they were before the daughter's menarche, as if they wanted to establish a psychological distance as well as to control the daughter's life (Hill, 1988).

## Timing of Maturation

The timing of physical maturation clearly affects a young woman's behaviors and feelings (Dubas, Graber, & Petersen, 1991; Paikoff & Brooks-Gunn, 1991; Petersen,

1988). Girls who see themselves as on time feel more attractive and positive about their bodies than others (Tobin-Richards, Boxer, & Petersen, 1983). Being out of sync with one's peers, as either an early or a late maturer, generally has more obvious immediate negative effects for girls than for boys (Simmons & Blyth, 1987; Simmons, Blyth, & McKinney, 1983). Perhaps this reflects the greater tendency to define girls by their appearance, along with the greater sexualization of females and their ambivalence about adulthood.

*Early Maturers*    More research concern has been directed toward early maturing than late maturing girls. The picture is mixed, but problems are evident (Caspi & Moffitt, 1991; Stattin & Magnusson, 1990). Early maturation can bring increased prestige and popularity, especially with boys, but also a feeling of not fitting in. Nearly half (43%) of early maturers (menarche at age 11 years) in one study denied that they had menstruated (Petersen, 1983). Early maturers tend to be larger than others their age (Simmons & Blyth, 1987) and often are dissatisfied with their height and weight and concerned with dieting (Attie & Brooks-Gunn, 1989). (Early maturing females are shorter and heavier than late maturers when pubertal growth is complete; Brooks-Gunn, 1987.) At the same time, they may be losing the support of their old friends and having to make new ones, because girls tend to choose as best friends those who are at a similar level of physical maturation (Brooks-Gunn, Samelson, Wallen, & Fox, 1986; Livson & Peskin, 1980). Early maturing girls tend to associate with friends who are biologically equal but chronologically older than they are (Magnusson, Stattin, & Allen, 1985).

    The early maturing young women, however, are not psychologically and socially ready for the more mature world into which they are drawn (Eichorn, 1976). Because of association with older friends, early maturing women are more likely to date, smoke and drink, have intercourse by age 16, and show a range of antisocial behavior (Crockett & Petersen, 1987; Magnusson, 1988; Simmons, Blyth, Van Cleave, & Bush, 1979). They also have lower self-esteem, less self-confidence, lower school achievement, and more emotional problems than those who are on time or late (Belsky et al., 1991; Simmons & Blyth, 1987). Number of contacts with boyfriends is negatively related to school performance (Feiring & Lewis, 1991). Early maturing girls drop out of school disproportionately; those who stay in school do not have achievement problems in later years.

    The problems of early maturers seem due to dating and the related social expectations and pressures rather than to any inherent effects of early biological maturation. Certainly, earlier sexual activity is not attributable to an earlier sexual drive. According to one study, young women with high rates of dating were likely to have intercourse regardless of their menstrual status (Gagnon, 1983). There is no correlation found between menarche and the onset of masturbation. Further, precocious puberty (6–8 years) is not necessarily associated with early sexual activity.

*Late Maturers*    Late-developing girls may be dissatisfied initially with their appearance and lack of popularity, and their parents may be concerned as well (Paikoff, Brooks-Gunn, & Carlton-Ford, 1991). As they mature, however, these young women are more satisfied with their appearance and more popular than their earlier maturing peers (Simmons & Blyth, 1987). In general, other girls show an increase in behavior problems from ages 13 to 15, but late maturing girls do not (Caspi & Moffitt, 1991). The eventual edge for late maturing females makes sense if it is correct that the transition to adulthood is more problematic for young girls than for young boys. It makes sense also from the perspective of Erik Erikson (1950/1963). Erikson maintained that in complicated societies, young people need a "moratorium"—time to consider the possibilities open to them in the society before forming an identity. The relative advantage of late maturation compared with early maturation is shown also with boys (see Cole & Cole, 1989; Tobin-Richards et al., 1983).

Whether a young woman is an early or late or on-time maturer, she has many years of menstruation ahead of her. What will she be like during her menstrual days?

## Paramenstrual Behavior and Experiences

What are women like premenstrually and menstrually? The term **paramenstrum** frequently is used to refer to the last days before the onset of the menses and the first days of the menses (typically 4 + 4 days). Myths of the danger and power of the blood seem to have formed a strong cognitive and affective background against which menstruation has been seen by many researchers as well as by lay people, to the detriment of women and of our understanding of them. (See Focus on Research 6.1.)

### The Myth of Impaired Performance

Katrina Dalton (1961, 1966), a British physician, reported that paramenstrual women make up a high percentage of women involved in unusual actions, ranging from crashing airplanes and attempting suicide to taking children to emergency clinics for minor colds and sniffles. Other researchers quickly added to the list of unusual things that paramenstrual women presumably do (see Sommer, 1983; Tuch, 1975; Zimmerman & Parlee, 1973). Depending on the behavior in question, about 22% to 54% of women said to be behaving strangely were paramenstrual. When evaluating the claims, however, it is important to be clear about the appropriate base rate against which to compare the percentages. Consider that the paramenstrum conventionally covers 8 days (4 days before and 4 days of menstrual flow), and some women flow for 6 days. A woman may be premenstrual or menstrual 25% to 35% of the time. Thus, if the menstrual cycle has no influence on behavior, 25% to 35% of any woman's behavior of any kind would be expected to fall in the time before and during menstruation. The fact that 22% to 54% of women who show a behavior are paramenstrual may be impressive when compared to zero, but it has a different meaning when compared to 25% or 35%.

There is good reason to think that the associations between the paramenstrum and women's unusual behaviors should not be blamed on the supposedly damaging power of menstrual blood. Women are more likely to be aware of their bodies paramenstrually than at other times and so might be more concerned about their children's health (Tuch, 1975). In addition, claims of unusual behaviors should be evaluated in light of *reciprocal determinism:* causation is not a one-way matter. As noted earlier, stress can affect the menstrual cycle (Parlee, 1982). The stress from having crashed an airplane or attempted suicide could bring the menstrual flow earlier than usual (Horney, 1979). Supporting this notion is the fact that women passengers in car accidents tend to menstruate shortly after the accidents. It is just as plausible to say the accident precipitated the menstrual flow as the paramenstrual state caused the accident.

Notice that no one (as far as I know) has looked to see whether women who are paramenstrual (or in other cycle phases) are more likely to show *positive* behaviors, such as saving a child from a fire, delivering a persuasive speech, or being especially creative. Nor have I heard of measuring the testosterone levels of men who crash planes or wreck cars. Men's testosterone levels do vary, generally being highest in the fall and lowest in the spring (chapter 4). Testosterone levels also have circadian (daily) variation, with highs at 4 a.m. and lows at 8 p.m. June Reinisch (cited in Gorham, 1992) of the Kinsey Institute suggested that if women cannot be trusted because of the recurring monthly cycle, men should be allowed to negotiate peace treaties only in the evenings. The implicit assumption has been that women are victims of a biological cycle but men are not.

The claim that menstruation weakens women so that they cannot work at all or cannot work efficiently is a false assumption for most women. One large study of more than 1000 Air Force pilots in World War II found that the women missed fewer days of flight training than their male counterparts and also that there was no relationship between menstrual phase and flying accidents or grades (Keil, 1982). Sharon Golub (1992) reviewed research on cognitive abilities and the menstrual cycle, from the pioneering work of Leta Holinworth (chapter 1) in 1914 to the present, and found that women did not perform more poorly on cognitive tasks paramenstrually than at other times. And, for women who complain of menstrual symptoms, there is no support for claims of reduced cognitive or motor performance (Golub, 1976; Sommer, 1983; Zimmerman & Parlee, 1973). Yet, when a rare study does find poorer performance paramenstrually, it gets public attention (Kimura & Hamson, 1994). Any particular woman may have impaired performance paramenstrually, but to argue that women should not be surgeons or airline pilots because they menstruate is not warranted.

## Physical Feelings and Moods: Is the Negative Real?

Part of the cultural myth—perhaps a variety of the "protect us" myth—is that paramenstrual women feel miserable, act miserable, and cause misery to all around them. Researchers who have looked for the negative have found it. For example, imagine that you took part in a research study in which you were given an inventory headed "Menstrual Distress Questionnaire" and were asked to rate how you or a woman friend felt during a recent menstrual flow on characteristics such as irritable, depressed, and backaches. Such has been the position of many women and men who have participated in menstrual research using Moos's **Menstrual Distress Questionnaire (MDQ),** one of the most frequently used instruments in menstrual research (Moos, 1968, 1969). (Men participants in menstrual research report on perceptions about women generally or about a specific woman they know.) On the basis of his research, Moos called

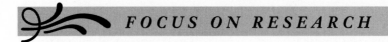

### 6.1    Independent Variables: Are Paramenstrual Symptoms Just in Our Heads?

The laboratory experiment is the classic scientific study. It gives the experimenter the greatest control over factors that might influence the study's outcome, allowing a more precise cause-and-effect interpretation of results. One of the first decisions in designing an experiment is to define the independent variable, also called the manipulated variable or the experimental treatment. One group of participants undergoes this treatment (the experimental group), and their subsequent behavior is compared to that of another group that has not received the treatment (the control group). If the behavior of the two groups differs, it is thought due to the treatment or independent variable.

You might question whether it is possible to design an experiment, with its emphasis on control and manipulation, to study a topic as personal and individual as the experience of premenstrual symptoms. Many research studies of this topic rely on correlational designs, treating a woman's menstrual cycle phase as a status variable—an inherent part of her, much like her age or gender. These studies measure participants' behavior "as is" and uncover associations among variables, but they cannot reach cause-and-effect conclusions. Two researchers, Pamela Klebanov and John Jemmott (1992), were interested in studying women's menstrual expectations, their bodily sensations, and premenstrual symptoms. Rather than employing the usual correlational design, they devised a way to manipulate women's perceptions of their menstrual cycle phase, allowing them to study these factors using an experimental design.

Forty-eight premenopausal women took part in the study. None of the women were pregnant or on birth control pills, and all had regular menstrual cycles. They thought they were participating in a study of their reactions to a new hormonal assay test, the Hormonal Status Test, that could be used to provide information about phases of the menstrual cycle with potential for aiding in birth control decisions.

Klebanov and Jemmott wanted to study how women's expectations of their current menstrual cycle phase influenced their physical symptoms and attitudes toward menstruation. They identified as their independent variable the menstrual cycle phase each woman was in. But remember, an independent variable is one that can be manipulated by the experimenter to create an experimental treatment or situation for the participant. Could Klebanov and Jemmott really manipulate or alter a woman's cycle phase? No, but this study didn't rely on altering the actual biological cycle, but on altering women's *perceptions* of their cycle phase.

In a very medical-looking setting, Klebanov and Jemmott had each woman take the Hormonal Status Test, which involved dipping a strip of chemically treated paper in a sample of the woman's saliva. Ostensibly, the strip would change color in response to hormones in the saliva, and the color would indicate the woman's menstrual cycle phase. In reality, the test was bogus, and all the strips were programmed to turn green. Half the women were informed that green indicated they were "premenstrual" and would begin their periods within 2 to 3 days, while the other half were told that green indicated an "intermenstrual" phase, and they would begin their periods within 7 or 8 days. In this way, the researchers manipulated the cycle phase variable and created two groups of participants whose subsequent behavior they could then compare. In essence, the women who were told they were premenstrual were the experimental group, and those told they were intermenstrual were the control group. The experimental group's treatment was the perception that they were premenstrual, with all the expectations that label carries.

How did Klebanov and Jemmott make sure the women would believe the "results" of this hormone test? The answer lies in their scheduling of the participants to come to the lab for the test. When the women were originally screened prior to being included in the study, they filled out a questionnaire in which, among other things, they reported their menstrual cycle length and the date of the most recent menstruation. This information was then used to schedule each woman (unbeknownst to her) to come to the lab 1 to 7 days before her next expected period. Given this timing, being told she had tested as premenstrual or intermenstrual was believable to these women. To double-check the women's acceptance of their reported cycle phase, the researchers asked each to rate the accuracy of the saliva test; all of the women rated it as accurate, and none expressed any suspicions about the real intent of the study. After this check, participants in both groups completed a health questionnaire indicating any illness symptoms (including premenstrual symptoms) they had experienced in the past 1 to 2 days. They also filled out a questionnaire concerning menstrual attitudes.

Based on the results of their experiment, Klebanov and Jemmott were able to state that the premenstrual label caused women to report more symptoms than did the intermenstrual label. This is strong evidence that the negative expectations associated with the premenstrual phase have a direct effect on women's physical well-being. With ingenuity and careful planning, independent variables can be teased from topics that at first glance do not lend themselves to experimental design.

JILL BORCHERT ◆

SOURCE: Klebanov, P. K., & Jemmott, J. B. (1992). Effects of expectations and bodily sensations on self-reports of premenstrual symptoms. *Psychology of Women Quarterly, 16,* 289–310.

attention to the fact that 30% to 50% of young married women are bothered to some extent by cyclic symptoms; he could have said that 50% to 70% of the women are *not* bothered (Landers, 1977).

Mary Brown Parlee (1974), in one of the important articles of the 1970s (chapter 1), pointed out problems with this kind of research. First, the research setting is high in demand characteristics (chapter 1) that may raise stereotypes about menstruation and concerns about the expectations of the researchers. Variations with the cycle are reported more often when research participants know of the researchers' interest in menstruation than when they do not (Parlee, 1974; Richardson, 1990). The phenomenon is not limited to women's cycles; both women and men overreport symptoms when they think they have an illness. A second problem is that the Moos scales and many others consist mainly or entirely of negative moods or symptoms (McFarlane, Martin, & Williams, 1988). This adds to the demand characteristics and makes it impossible to find evidence of positive feelings (Rossi & Rossi, 1977). In addition, the studies typically have been retrospective, possibly picking up stereotypic memory bias and distortion rather than accurate recall (Parlee, 1974; Ruble, 1977; Ruble & Brooks-Gunn, 1979).

***Correcting the Research***    Researchers today are more careful. A frequent paradigm now is to have women, and sometimes men, rate themselves on a variety of attributes (not just negative ones) every day for a month or more without knowing that the researcher is interested in the menstrual cycle. Sometimes, the same people are then asked to report retrospectively on how they felt during the preceding days. Mood variation sometimes is shown in women at different times of their cycle, but their mood variation is no greater than men's over the same period of time (Alagna & Hamilton, 1986; Dan, 1979; McFarlane et al., 1988; McFarlane & Williams, 1994).

The most frequent finding is that women's daily reports do not show substantial increases in negative moods as menstruation nears. Women's retrospective reports (by the same women recalling the previous days when they were giving daily reports) are more likely to show the "classic" menstrual mood pattern than are day-by-day reports— the retrospective reports presumably are affected by culturally shaped expectations. This has been shown for teenage women, college women, college men reporting about their partners, and for a general sample of adults (Alagna & Hamilton, 1986; Golub & Harrington, 1981; McFarland, Ross, & DeCourville, 1989; McFarlane & Williams, 1994; McFarlane et al., 1988; Parlee, 1982).

In one study both women and men (psychology undergraduates) reported moods and mood stability daily for 60 to 70 days. Then they gave retrospective average ratings for their moods on each day of the week; women also reported for menstrual cycle phases (McFarlane et al., 1988). Women and men did not differ in their reported stability of moods on the daily reports, and women's reports did not vary with phases of the cycle. Of particular interest were the comparisons of retrospective and daily reports. Women retrospectively reported *more* pleasantness during the follicular phase than they had reported on a daily basis and *less* pleasantness during the premenstrual phase; women on oral contraceptives did not differ from others (Figure 6.3). Other researchers found that women also recalled more pain premenstrually and menstrually

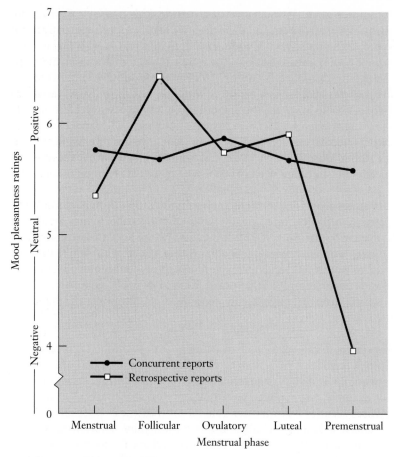

**Figure 6.3** *Comparison of concurrent and retrospective reports of mood pleasantness for phases of the menstrual cycle.*   NOTE: Phases were defined as menstrual, days 1–5; follicular, days 6–12; ovulatory, middle 5 days, i.e., days 13–17; luteal, days 18–24; and premenstrual, days 25–28.   SOURCE: McFarlane, J., Martin, C. L., & Williams, T. M. (1988). Mood fluctuations: Women versus men and menstrual versus other cycles. *Psychology of Women Quarterly, 12,* 201–223.

than they had reported at those times, and they also recalled *less* pain than they had reported between periods (McFarland et al., 1989). Misperceptions of cyclic effects occur in other ways as well. For example, college students recalled more pleasantness for Fridays and Saturdays than they reported day by day (McFarlane et al., 1988).

## Bodily Sensations and Individual Differences

Are we to conclude that retrospective reports are of no value at all and, therefore, that there are no relations between menstrual phase and moods? The answer cannot be an unqualified yes on either issue. Women live in a culture with negative views about women's experiences of menstruation, and their negative expectations apparently influence their retrospective accounts. Yet it is adding insult to injury to suggest that women know nothing of their own bodily sensations. "It seems unlikely that women are complete dupes of socially-produced explanations" (McFarlane et al., 1988, p. 218). The daily report method shows that *on the average*, women do not show cyclic variations (Richardson, 1990). To focus only on the hypothetical "average woman" is to miss those women who might experience strong fluctuations cyclically and have paramenstrual pain. Retrospective reports may be useful when we are interested in individual differences rather than averages. Women's reports of menstrual feelings are influenced by expectations, but they also are influenced by actual feelings (Klebanov & Jemmott, 1992).

Why some women report more menstrual symptoms than others is not clear. Most biological attention has centered on the level of ovarian hormones and given mixed results (Klebanov & Jemmott, 1992). It may not be the level of hormones that distinguishes between women reporting problems and those who don't, but the woman's sensitivity to hormonal levels or cycle fluctuations (Schechter, Bachmann, Vaitukaitis, Phillips, & Saperstein, 1989; Sprock & Yoder, 1997). Or, women may differ in the extent to which they interpret bodily sensations as symptoms (Klebanov & Jemmott, 1992).

***Psychological Correlates*** Evidence is accumulating about psychosocial correlates to bodily distress (Sprock & Yoder, 1997). Menstrual distress seems to be part of a broader distress—women who report distress menstrually also show distress at other times and in other ways. For example, women who have physical discomfort and psychological distress during menses seem to have greater general psychological stress and general health complaints and to take more medication for aches, pains, and illness (Carrie, 1981; Good & Smith, 1980; Paige, 1973). Some researchers found that menstrual distress was related to social anxiety and self-consciousness (Matthews & Carra, 1982). Also, characteristics of women with the most mood changes paramenstrually have included high strung, sensitive, concerned about bodily functions, emotionally unstable, and having trouble understanding human motivation. These personality traits were correlated with mood swings more than with physical symptoms of menstruation.

What causes what is virtually impossible to say. General distress may cause menstrual distress reports, or actual menstrual distress and worry about its coming may cause general distress. Or, a third variable may be involved, leading to both general and menstrual distress: The experience of distress generally or paramenstrually probably varies with the individual woman's specific environment and its particular demands (Heilbrun, Friedberg, Wydra, & Worobow, 1990). Women high in bodily concern, social anxiety, self-consciousness, and so forth, probably feel stressed in a variety of environments. Or, on the other hand, women who generally are stressed may be more likely to show bodily concern, social anxiety, and self-consciousness.

Some early researchers reasoned that the women who were distressed paramenstrually were rejecting their feminine role or were otherwise neurotic (e.g., Coppen & Kessel, 1963). However, many severely neurotic women are free of menstrual symptoms, and women who are not unstable may have severe suffering (Rees, 1953). Studies using the newer gender role scales (chapter 3) do not show any consistent pattern (see Heilbrun et al., 1990).

## Premenstrual Syndrome

Premenstrual syndrome (PMS) is a term used to describe a variety of physical and psychological symptoms that occur systematically with the menstrual cycle and are severe enough to interfere with some aspects of life (Hurt et al., 1992; Schmidt et al., 1991; York, Freeman, Lowery, & Strauss, 1989). This is not an ideal operational definition. The term *premenstrual tension* was used first by R. T. Frank (1931). It was then popularized by Katrina Dalton (1964). PMS is not to be confused with a specific form of painful menstruation (dysmenorrhea), discussed next; the two seldom occur in the same person (Hoffman, 1982).

The best that may be safely said about PMS is that the idea brought menstruation out of the closet. People who would not talk about menstruation before now are willing to talk about it. There are reports that a little more than half (51.7%) of adult women say they have PMS, though few (11.7%) show problems on daily reports (McFarlane & Williams, 1994). However, as we have just seen, PMS is not a well-defined scientific construct. It may be a useful idea to the public but has been of little use to scientists because of the lack of consensus about what it is, what causes it, or how to treat it (Abplanalp, 1983; Gannon, 1988). Descriptions of PMS list from 20 to 200 symptoms (Mitchell, Lentz, Woods, Lee, & Taylor, 1992; Yankauskas, 1990). The list of symptoms possible is extensive, not unique to PMS, and highly variable from woman to woman: For example, they include aggression, depression, tension, irritability, backache, epilepsy, acne, herpes, rage, anxiety, hoarseness, tiredness, and general lowered sense of well-being (Abplanalp, 1983; Gallant, Popiel, Hoffman, Chakraborty, & Hamilton, 1992; Laws, 1985).

Estimates of women suffering from PMS vary from 10% to 95% (T. Adler, 1990a; Golub, 1992). Causative factors are elusive (T. Adler, 1990a, 1990b), and 327 different treatments have been proposed (Eagan, 1983). Research is beginning to clarify effective use of hormones, medications, diet, nutritional supplements, physical activity, esteem building, lifestyle management, and peer support (see Crooks & Baur, 1993).

Premenstrual dysphoric disorder, roughly equivalent to PMS, is considered a psychological disorder (protests about this because of lack of evidence are discussed in chapter 16). The bottom line is, "Women who say they have PMS are saying they have a problem, and it will be important in future studies to try to understand the nature of these problems" (McFarlane & Williams, 1994, p. 365). Here and now, we do not understand the nature of these problems.

## Dysmenorrhea

Painful menstruation is called dysmenorrhea. It is a well-defined construct *not* to be confused with PMS. **Primary dysmenorrhea** usually appears at menarche, with symptoms most noticeable during the first days of the menstrual period. Symptoms include abdominal aching and/or cramping; some women also experience nausea, vomiting, diarrhea, headaches, dizziness, fatigue, irritability, or nervousness (Golub, 1992; Warrington, Cox, & Evans, 1988). It is estimated to occur in 50% to 75% of high school and college-age women and is the leading cause for their missing school or work (Golub, 1992; Warrington et al., 1988).

***Causes of Dysmenorrhea***    The physical cause of dysmenorrhea usually is the overproduction of **prostaglandins,** a type of hormone with a fatty acid base that is found throughout the body. One type of prostaglandin is synthesized in the uterus and stimulates uterine contractions; excessive amounts cause tighter and longer contractions and keep oxygen from reaching the uterus and abdominal muscles (Rome, 1992). Prostaglandins are related to an increase of calcium and a depletion of magnesium and are thought to produce menstrual pain through three mechanisms: increased muscle contraction, decreased uterine blood flow, and increased sensitization of pain fibers (Friederich, 1983). Minor contractions are not noticed, but strong ones cause pain and oxygen deprivation to the uterus (see Boston Women's Health Book Collective, 1992). We do not know why some women have large amounts of prostaglandins, nor why they have them in some cycles but not others. Neither do we know why some women with severe dysmenorrhea do not have elevated prostaglandins (Golub, 1992; Lander, 1988; Warrington et al., 1988).

**Secondary dysmenorrhea** often occurs before or during menstruation. It involves lower abdominal pain that may extend to the back and thighs. Symptoms often are similar to those of primary dysmenorrhea, but the causative factors are different. Possible causes of secondary dysmenorrhea include use of an intrauterine device, pelvic inflammation, obstruction of the cervical opening, and endometriosis. With **endometriosis,** endometrial cells from the uterine lining implant in the abdominal cavity; the implanted tissue can adhere to other tissue, engorge with blood, and cause painful menstruation, lower backache, and pain from pressure during intercourse (Barbieri, 1988). Endometriosis may affect up to 15% of premenopausal women. Treatments are available for the symptoms.

***Treatment of Dysmenorrhea***    Primary dysmenorrhea can be treated with antiprostaglandin medications (Owens, 1984) and may be helped by oral contraceptives, which lead to a lower level of prostaglandins (Marx, 1979). Aspirin, which is much cheaper than prescription drugs, also has been reported to inhibit prostaglandin production and to be helpful in milder cases. Some relief is given by heat, exercise, and diet changes (Budoff, 1983; Golub, 1992; Warrington et al., 1988). Side effects of some drugs are still being investigated, so some women's health groups are hesitant to recommend them (Boston Women's Health Book Collective, 1992).

Research is also needed to understand why placebos sometimes reduce symptoms. **Placebos,** sometimes called sugar pills, are "medications" with no chemical medicinal value. A carefully conducted study of drug effects uses a placebo group to control for any psychological effects of thinking one is taking medication. A careful study is also "blind"—neither the participants nor the researchers making intermediate

*Women need to take time for themselves in order to lead balanced lives. Relaxation and moderation throughout the whole reproductive cycle can help relieve uncomfortable physical and psychological symptoms during menstruation.*

observations are aware of whether a given participant is in the placebo group or in the experimental group receiving the medical treatment.

Placebos do have an effect (T. Adler, 1990a; Lewis, 1992; Rivera-Tovar, Rhodes, Pearlstein, & Frank, 1994). This is not to say that the pain that some women feel is "all in their heads." It is to say that people are psychobiological organisms with complex interactions of the body and the psyche. Placebo effects are frequently found and are not peculiar to women.

## Taking Care Throughout the Cycle

Creating a healthy lifestyle through moderate exercise and proper diet *throughout* the cycle can alleviate some unpleasant symptoms. Specific strategies include increasing fluids and fiber to prevent constipation, decreasing salt intake to help reduce swelling and bloating due to water retention, taking supplements of calcium, magnesium, and B vitamins to help relieve cramps and bloating, and avoiding caffeine, nicotine, and other stimulants (Boston Women's Health Book Collective, 1992). This approach recognizes that menstrual flow is part of a cycle, not separate from other cycle phases. Effective treatment is based on all aspects of a woman's life. One important piece of advice for women is to relax and take time out from the pressures of life for doing things they want to do. Also, if a woman is experiencing pain, keeping a diary of symptoms, stresses, exercise habits, diet, and sleep may help her figure out a plan for herself; or the information may be helpful if she consults a health care professional.

Menstruation is part of a naturally occurring process in physically normal women. If a woman experiences severe pain, something is wrong and should be addressed by a physician. One of my students took this admonition seriously and insisted on medical attention. She had an ovarian cyst promptly operated on. Acceptance of a contemporary cultural myth—that menstruation is supposed to be a painful "curse"—can endanger a woman's life.

## Menstruation as a Natural Event

Acceptance of women's menstrual cycle as a natural event is hampered by a generally negative view of the body and by the greater identification of women with the body and nature. In this part of the chapter, we look at the natural, positive aspects of menstruation and some specific ways in which menstruation has been misused.

### Positive Cyclic Feelings

Concerns about paramenstrual affect and behavior have focused on the negative and blamed problems on "women's raging hormones." Curiously, estrogen and progesterone are at their *lowest* paramenstrually. If the "rage" of hormones is to be held responsible for women's moods, then the focus should be on ovulation, when estrogen is high. At ovulation, however, women report positive, even euphoric, feelings (Rossi & Rossi, 1977). They are active and energetic and have higher self-esteem at ovulation compared to other cycle phases; married women initiate sex with their husbands more frequently at this time. These positive feelings do not occur for women on oral contraceptives. Thus, the term **ovulatory peak** is just as appropriate as the term PMS (see McFarlane et al., 1988).

To add to the puzzle created when research meets stereotypes, women's feelings paramenstrually include positive feelings. Positive moods do not decrease as menstruation approaches, even when negative moods increase (Rossi & Rossi, 1971). Positive and negative feelings are not incompatible; on any one day, people might have a number of positive and a number of negative feelings. Among the positive reports before or during menstruation compared with other cycle phases are feeling dominant and energetic, increased sexual desire, feelings of affection and self-confidence (Alagna & Hamilton, 1986; Chrisler, Johnston, Champagne, & Preston, 1994; Parlee, 1982). When answering retrospectively, women generally underreport the positive moods they had premenstrually.

*A Natural Nuisance*   When given a chance to say something about menstruation that was not negative, 80% of college women highly endorsed a scale of items measuring menstruation as a natural or positive event (A Closer Look 6.3; Brooks-Gunn & Ruble, 1980). Menstruation may be "a pain," but for most women it is of the "pain in the neck" variety more than a physically and psychologically debilitating pain. That is, the dominant negative reaction of college women was that menstruation was bothersome. About two thirds of the women reported no debilitation; only 3% of the women

## *A Closer Look*

### 6.3   Sample Items From the Menstrual Attitude Questionnaire

Participants are asked to rate each item on a 1 to 7 scale, from 1 "Disagree strongly" to 7 "Agree strongly."

#### *Menstruation as a natural event*

1. Menstruation is a recurring affirmation of womanhood.
2. Menstruation allows women to be more aware of their bodies.
3. Menstruation provides a way for me to keep in touch with my body.
4. Menstruation is an obvious example of the rhythmicity which pervades all of life.
5. The recurrent monthly flow of menstruation is an external indication of a woman's general good health.

#### *Menstruation as a bothersome event*

1. Menstruation is something I just have to put up with.

2. Men have a real advantage in not having the monthly interruption of a menstrual period.
3. I hope it will be possible someday to get a menstrual period over with in a few minutes.

#### *Menstruation as a debilitating event*

1. Menstruation can adversely affect my performance in sports.
2. I feel as fit during menstruation as I do during any other time of the month. [Reverse scoring]
3. Women just have to accept the fact that they may not perform as well when they are menstruating.

---

SOURCE: Brooks-Gunn, J., & Ruble, D. N. (1980). The Menstrual Attitude Questionnaire. *Psychosomatic Medicine, 42,* 5. From Table 1, pp. 505–506.

indicated severe pain on a scale measuring debilitation. (This is not to say we should let the "average" detract from the pain of the women who are severely debilitated.)

Compared with college women, people who do not menstruate (men and premenstrual teenage women) and menstrual teens who have not menstruated long underrate the bothersome ways in which menstruation interferes with life, and they overrate the extent to which it is debilitating. The writings of Anne Frank (1952) provide a poignant statement. She wrote that each time she menstruated,

> I have the feeling that in spite of all the pain, unpleasantness, nastiness, I have a sweet secret and that is why, although it is nothing but a nuisance to me in a way, I always long for the time that I shall feel that secret with me again. (p. 117)

In the face of such evidence of relative lack of variation in moods as a function of the cycle, some of you, both women and men, may be reacting much as some researchers reacted: "Yes, but . . ." (McFarlane et al., 1988). The researchers pointed out that some women not prone to irritability or moodiness can reach a point when many problems converge, and an event that otherwise would be minor becomes "the straw that broke the camel's back." It would not be long before the woman herself and those around her concluded that her menstruation caused the uncharacteristic outbursts. Stereotypes of menstruation are strong; events that confirm stereotypes are remembered and are remembered as having occurred more often than they did (illusory correlation, chapter 2). Similarly, behaviors that may not vary in frequency across the cycle may be noted when they occur paramenstrually (Rossi, 1980). Confirming evidence is blown out of proportion and other evidence discounted, including positive feelings and the context of negative behavior.

*Menstrual Joy*    The simple act of taking a Menstrual Joy Questionnaire was enough to increase subsequent reports of positive cycle events (Chrisler et al., 1994). (See Focus on Research 6.2.) It was not just a matter of participants wanting to be "good subjects" in response to demand characteristics of a "joy" questionnaire; they reported more positive correlates of menstruation but did not report fewer negative ones than women who did not take the joy questionnaire first.

Many women do have negative experiences paramenstrually, but they also have joyous ones they have not considered to be a "normal" part of their cycle. After taking the joy questionnaire, about half of college women said they expected a change in their views: They would pay attention to positive concomitants of the menstrual cycle that they had previously ignored, become more aware of their personal fluctuations, enjoy emotional variability, and question why people have negative views of menstruation (Chrisler et al., 1994).

## Misinterpreting the Body

It seems that women are assumed to be physiologically abnormal just because they are women. The abnormality can be invoked whenever necessary to "explain" a number of "faults" that women are thought to show (Fausto-Sterling, 1985). For example, one physical accompaniment of the premenstrual days is the buildup of fluid between cells (called interstitial buildup) (Hatton, 1977). Like other parts of the body, the tear ducts are more full of liquid, so some women feel that they want to cry and may do so. The problem is that they assume crying or feeling like crying means they are depressed. Thinking they must be depressed because they are crying, they cogitate about the possible cause of their depression, and sure enough, they find something to be depressed about. They might avoid this if they attributed the crying feeling to the realistic physical cause, "I feel like crying because my tear ducts are full." Some women relieve or avoid depression by using a calendar to keep track of their cycle so that they do not think their bodily changes are due to depression.

Randi Koeske (1976, 1980, 1983; Koeske & Koeske, 1975) extends this simple example. She maintains that hormonal changes of the cycle are natural ones that women have learned to interpret in predominantly negative ways. In Koeske's studies (Koeske & Koeske, 1975), which have been supported by others (Baines & Slade,

1988), both men and women college students read descriptions of a man, a premenstrual woman, or a non-premenstrual woman—menstrual information was part of general medical information given for each person. The students attributed only negative expressions (e.g., depression, hostility, anger) to a woman's menstrual cycle. Positive behavior premenstrually was seen as due to personality or situational factors. When negative premenstrual behavior was seen as due to biological influences, situational factors were discounted, and the behavior was judged to be more extreme. The behavior was considered more unreasonable and unjustifiable and more indicative of a person who was temperamental, irrational, and immature than when the *same* behavior in the *same* situation was shown by a nonmenstrual woman or by a man.

Koeske suggested that feelings such as hostility and anger are deemed unusual or "out of role" for women and so require special explanation. In contrast, pleasant behavior can be seen more readily as part of a woman's personality or due to the situation she is in. A woman's premenstrual behavior may not be abnormal when compared with a man's behavior. Men's anger may be acceptable as part of "men's nature," but women's anger is unacceptable and is attributed to the cycle, without attempts to detect the reasons for it (Martin, 1987; Taylor, 1988). As noted previously, men have annual and circadian cycles of testosterone, but those are not singled out as reasons to ignore men's aggression or anger or general testiness, nor are they considered reasons to limit men's activities to only certain times of the year or of the day.

If a woman blames her negative behavior only on herself, she is implicitly assuming that there is nothing in the environment that might be eliciting her negative behavior. If she blames herself, she then feels a need to atone and misses the chance to see the problems that are in her environment and may have been there all month long. In this way women confirm stereotypes about the negativity of menstruation, and they confirm the assumption that women have no right to complain. What needs to be addressed is not only views about menstruation but also views about women and their rights to self-expression, assertiveness, and anger.

## The Cost of Menstrual Excuses

Some women may knowingly or unknowingly use menstruation as an excuse for behavior that is not accepted at other times because they feel they cannot be assertive. It has been suggested also that appealing to illness may be the only way out of unwanted sex for some women (Laws, 1985). Whether because of sex or limitations on their expressiveness, more women in one study who said they had menstrual problems than those who said they did not were in a sexual relationship with a man (McFarlane & Williams, 1994). The two groups of women may have differed in sexual drive, or those reporting problems may have considered a low sexual drive (or reluctance to engage in sex) negatively and attributed it to the cycle. For some women, the only time of the month they can express themselves in other than positive ways—"going along" with another person's wishes—is paramenstrually. The problem is that out-of-role behavior paramenstrually is so easily explained away as due to the cycle and not taken seriously.

Menstrual excuses often are honored. College men reported less annoyance when a woman offered a menstrual excuse for negative behaviors than when she

## 6.2   Dependent Variables: Women Report Their Feelings About Menstruation

Have you ever seen one of those television commercials in which a long-haired woman in a gauzy white dress is floating through a flower-filled meadow while the voice-over murmurs about feeling fresh during that "special" time? Ever wonder what in the world was being advertised? Our culture does not deal openly with menstruation, and many of us either avoid the topic or speak of it in euphemisms. Active discussions of menstruation often center around raunchy humor or put-downs. How do women really feel about the biological process that is one of the most remarkable aspects of being female?

Researcher Joan Chrisler and her associates (1994) wondered how women would respond to a positive view of menstruation. They predicted that when menstruation was presented positively, women would report fewer associated unpleasant symptoms and a more positive attitude than when menstruation was presented negatively. Two questionnaires were used to present the topic of menstruation: the Menstrual Distress Questionnaire (MDQ) and the Menstrual Joy Questionnaire (MJQ). As indicated by its name, the MDQ focuses on negative and unpleasant aspects of menstruation and asks about symptoms such as water retention, negative emotions, and pain. The MDQ is one of the most commonly used menstrual questionnaires. In contrast, the MJQ is a new questionnaire that asks questions about the positive aspects of menstruation, including high spirits, self-confidence, creativity, and power. The concepts and the language used by these two questionnaires set the stage for viewing menstruation in two very different ways.

Responses to these two questionnaires are the dependent variables of this study. Behavior (in this case, questionnaire responses) can vary depending on what happens during the study, hence the term dependent variable. Theoretically, a study could have any number of dependent variables. Practically speaking, the number of dependent variables is limited by the participants' willingness to answer questions or react to situations and by how many analyses the researcher has time to do, since each dependent variable produces data that must be measured, analyzed, and interpreted.

Chrisler's study of menstrual attitudes involves two different dependent variables. Some researchers advocate using several *related* dependent variables in order to have multiple measurements of the same behavior. For example, in addition to using a questionnaire to measure women's feelings about menstruation, researchers could use face-to-face interviews, daily journal entries, or direct observation of behavior for evidence of pain, irritability, creativity, and so on. Each related dependent variable picks up on a different aspect of menstrual attitudes and symptoms, and together they produce a more complete picture than any one dependent measure alone. However, using related dependent measures requires a greater investment of time and effort by both the participant and the researcher and isn't always possible. Other important considerations when choosing a dependent measure are reliability (does it produce the same score each time it is used?) and validity (does it measure what it claims to measure?).

After choosing their two dependent measures, Chrisler and her associates were ready to conduct their study. To see whether an emphasis on distress or joy would have an effect on women's responses about menstruation, half of the participants completed the MDQ first and then one week later completed the MJQ. The other half of the participants completed the questionnaires in the reverse order. This procedure is called counterbalancing. It ensures that both questionnaires have an equal chance to influence participants. With this technique we can see if exposure to the first questionnaire influences responses during the second session.

The two dependent variables (responses to the MDQ and MJQ) used in this study call for a special type of analysis called a multivariate analysis of variance, or MANOVA. When the dependent variable is made up of several interrelated responses, such as answers to different statements on a questionnaire or scores on several subscales of a questionnaire, the overlap among the responses can alter the analysis, making it seem that people are responding differently than they actually are. The MANOVA technique corrects this by taking into account the interconnectedness of responses to multiple related items. This was the analysis Chrisler and her group of researchers used to evaluate the questionnaire responses on the MDQ and MJQ.

What did they find? Are women's reported menstrual symptoms and attitudes about menstruation influenced by the positive or negative emphasis placed on the topic? Does it matter which emphasis the woman confronts first? The overall answer is yes. Women's responses were influenced by the slant of the questionnaire, and the first questionnaire seemed to set the tone that carried over to the second session. The researchers reported that women who completed the negatively toned MDQ in the first session were "primed to think of menstruation as a distressing event" and subsequently responded more negatively on the MJQ in session two. Conversely, women who completed the MJQ first subsequently scored higher in session two on items concerning affection, orderliness, excitement, feelings of well-being, and bursts of energy—items that have a more positive slant.

Chrisler and her associates started with what appeared to be a simple research question with two well-defined dependent variables in the form of two menstrual questionnaires. By counterbalancing the presentation of those questionnaires, they were able to expand their research question to include inquiry into carryover effects on women's menstrual attitudes and reported symptoms. The MANOVA analysis of the questionnaire data corrected for the interrelatedness of the items and gave an accurate reading of how the dependent variables were affected by the conditions of the study. The moral of the story is that there is a lot more to a dependent variable than meets the eye.

JILL BORCHERT ◆

SOURCE: Chrisler, J. C., Johnston, I., Champagne, N., & Preston, K. (1994). Menstrual joy: The construct and its consequences. *Psychology of Women Quarterly, 18,* 375–387.

appealed to pain or frustration; but college women generally do not think menstruation justifies antisocial behaviors (Brooks-Gunn & Ruble, 1980; Ruble, Boggiano, & Brooks-Gunn, 1982). For most women, menstruation is bothersome but not debilitating, as noted, so they have little patience with excuses of menstruation. The women who do have debilitating menstruation are more accepting and less blaming of a woman giving menstruation as an excuse for irritability.

At first glance it seems considerate to excuse a paramenstrual woman. However, let's look at it from a larger perspective. As long as menstruation is an excuse for unladylike behavior, people will expect ladylike behavior from women except about one week a month. Then, when women are assertive and expressive, what they say and do will be discounted: "You're just saying that because you are menstruating." Seeing only women as cyclic and seeing menstruation only negatively has the effect of controlling and discounting women and their experiences.

## Some Final Thoughts: Self-Knowledge and Self-Affirmation

Women spend a large part of their adult lives menstruating. Yet, in spite of the scientific understanding of the process now available, many false assumptions continue. These may reflect the general cultural definition of women by their bodies along with the devaluation of women and, perhaps, fear of their birth-giving capacities. The time of first menstruation is not an easy one for many young women, nor is puberty as a whole, as their bodies change and prompt changes in their general self-views. The transition to adulthood is easier if a young woman is a late maturer and if she feels worthwhile.

Menstruating women have been unfairly maligned as showing varying maladaptive behaviors. A relatively small proportion of women (but a large absolute number) do experience paramenstrual disturbance, physically and/or psychologically. Some women have clear physical causes that cannot be explained away as "just a woman's problem." For some women, psychological factors may contribute to physical problems.

The negative societal view of menstruation can act to maximize women's disturbances unnecessarily and to minimize understanding of the natural and even joyous feelings many women do feel with menstruation. Both women and men tend to blame the body for negative behaviors. While trying to excuse women for negative behavior because of menstruation, the excuse-making serves to perpetuate the problem of defining women by their bodies and serves as a reason to dismiss the thoughts and emotions that women express paramenstrually.

We cannot hope to change societal attitudes about menstruation overnight. But menstruating women can help themselves, and others can help them. There is medical information about good nutrition, rest, and exercise that is to be taken seriously, and to do so requires self-knowledge and self-affirmation. Part of self-knowledge is knowing what the body needs and what the feelings are signaling about one's total life. Well-informed and self-affirming women know what their body is saying *throughout* the cycle and respond to the messages.

Self-affirming women can decide that they will not be put down with "You're only saying that because of PMS." Their self-defense will be more believable if they have demonstrated all month long that they are capable of knowing when they object to someone else's behavior and are willing to express themselves. Friends can encourage a woman to affirm herself as a strong woman 4 weeks of the month instead of seeming to be out of character only 1 week a month—even though they themselves may be the targets of her objections!

Finally, self-knowledge and self-affirmation mean recognizing the positive—the natural—of women's experiences: My body is mine and it is good. Some women report a greater harmony with their bodies when they are paramenstrual, which some liken to a spiritual experience. It is as if they make their own psychological "menstrual hut" for sharing with themselves and with other women.

## KEY TERMS

menarche
follicular phase
ovulatory phase
luteal phase
menstrual phase
proliferative phase
secretory phase
puberty

growth spurt
primary amenorrhea
secondary amenorrhea
pseudocyesis
pheromones
paramenstrum
Menstrual Distress
   Questionnaire (MDQ)

premenstrual syndrome
 (PMS)
primary dysmenorrhea
prostaglandins
secondary dysmenorrhea
endometriosis
placebo
ovulatory peak

## KEY POINTS

*Perceptions of Menstruation*

◆ Many societies have had myths about menstruation designed to protect the woman, the group, or to emphasize the power of blood. There are myths in contemporary America as well, and these contribute to young women's ambivalent views about menarche.

◆ Teaching about menstruation is ambiguous. When asked, college women wished that they had experienced more personal sharing about menstruation when they were young. Some families celebrate a daughter's first menstruation.

*Biological and Psychological Factors*

◆ Menarche occurs relatively late in puberty, at 12½ years in the United States. Timing of menarche is influenced by nutrition, general health, stress, and genetic factors.

◆ Stress may cause amenorrhea or may hasten menstrual flow. Pheromones from women are thought to affect the timing of cycles and pheromones from men to affect cycle length.

◆ Adolescent girls often experience a change in body image and concern about weight with puberty; upper-middle-class white adolescents are more affected than others. Negative feelings can be reduced or avoided when girls participate in activities and sports and feel accepted by their peers.

◆ Young people often are not comfortable discussing their maturational changes with parents. Parents themselves may have increased concern about their daughter's and their own sexual feelings.

◆ Early maturing girls are likely to associate with chronologically older youths and to date earlier, but they also are likely to have lower self-esteem and school achievement, and more behavioral problems. Late maturing girls are dissatisfied initially but are better off in the long run.

## Paramenstrual Behavior and Experiences

◆ Evaluations of the rate at which women show unusual behaviors paramenstrually must take into account the length of time a woman spends in the paramenstrum and the fact that the unusual behavior can make the menstrual flow come earlier than usual.

◆ Paramenstrual women do not show impaired work performance.

◆ Weaknesses of past research on menstruation include having demand characteristics, not allowing for the report of positive feelings, and being only retrospective.

◆ When daily reports of mood are taken, there are few signs of negative moods paramenstrually. Retrospective reports typically exaggerate the stereotypical negativity of the paramenstrum and minimize negativity at other cycle phases.

◆ The role of hormones in menstrual distress and strong mood swings is not clear. Women who report strong menstrual distress also show general distress throughout their cycles.

◆ Severe menstrual pain may be due to physical problems needing attention and should not be accepted as "normal for a woman."

## Menstruation as a Natural Event

◆ Women often have strongly positive moods around the time of ovulation and have positive feelings as well as negative ones paramenstrually.

◆ The predominant reactions of college women to menstruation are that it is natural or positive but that it also is a bother. Few report strong debilitation. Confirming evidence of stereotypes is remembered and exaggerated but "thinking joy" can help women break their stereotyped beliefs.

◆ Negative behavior may be seen as out of role for women (but not for men) and attributed to the menstrual state. A woman's paramenstrual feelings may be due to life circumstances that need to be recognized.

◆ Sympathy for a paramenstrual woman may have the unintended effect of controlling and discounting women.

## INTEGRATIVE QUESTIONS

1. Analyze menstruation in the United States in light of the myths of other societies—"protect us," "protect her," "there is power in the blood."

2. Explain why a young girl might not be pleased with her menarche. Assume you are her parent. What can you do to help her? What feelings might you have about yourself as you witness her growth?

3. List reasons for claiming that women are equated with nature and bodies more than men are, to women's disadvantage. If you think it exists, what does the equation tell us about societal views of nature and the human body?

4. Should PMS or the menstrual cycle be considered relevant in cases in which a woman is accused of committing a criminal act? List reasons for and against.

5. "You only feel that way because of your menstrual cycle." Explain how a woman might be relieved by such a comment and how she might be offended by it.

*Chapter 7*

# *Development of Achievement Motivation in Women*

Some people are more concerned about doing well than others are. This is a matter of differences in achievement motivation. Striving to achieve is relevant throughout life and can take many forms. A child may strive to count to 100, a teenager may want to make a varsity sports team and have a good record to get into college, a worker may have a promotion goal, a retired person may want to master a hobby and be a great grandparent. All of these individuals have a standard of excellence they try to meet. Although achievement motivation is a lifelong issue, early experiences in forming behaviors relevant to internal standards of excellence affect many later experiences. Some people develop more concern with achievement standards than others, and some develop more effective ways of pursuing their goals than others. For this reason, in this text, achievement motivation is discussed in the context of early development.

When people in our society think of "achievement," they are most likely to think of the work world, sports, and politics—areas long considered typically masculine. In turn, boys have been encouraged more than girls to develop achievement skills. Some girls and women, nonetheless, have broken social "laws" and risked censure as they have worked toward their goals. Some boys and men are not interested in society's idea of success but are under pressure to strive anyway. Role pressures take their toll on both men and women.

In this chapter we will consider first some of the experiences at school and in the home that shape children's attitudes toward achievement and their skills in working toward achievement goals. Then we look at some of the specific behaviors associated with effective achievement. People who want to achieve may not always do so or, if they do, may waste energy in their pursuits. Finally, we expand the scope of thinking about achievement to show how a research area formerly neglectful of women has been enhanced by attention to women. The broader perspective includes recognizing the environmental forces that have shaped the way women express their achievement concerns. It also includes a newfound recognition that concepts of achievement are relevant in social situations.

Before reading further, consider these questions for personal thought:

- Think of something in the past year that was a success for you and write a description of it. Think of something in the past year that was a failure for you and write a description of it.
- Complete the sentence: "I am proud of myself when . . ." Complete the sentence: "I would be ashamed of myself if . . ."
- When you do not do well on an exam or term paper, what usually is the reason? When you do very well on an exam or term paper, what usually is the reason?
- Does a teacher, parent, or other person stand out in your mind as having had a big effect (positively or negatively) on how you think about your abilities and what you can do in life? Explain.
- Have you ever pretended to be less competent or knowledgeable than you really were? What was the context (e.g., sports, arts, cooking, school courses)? Who were you with? Why did you do that?
- Have you ever felt you had to be "bad" in something in order to be liked, loved, or accepted? For example, being stupid, being a klutz, not being able to boil water?
- "After first term finals, Anne finds herself at the top of her medical school class." Tell a story about this—for example, what is going on in this situation, what will happen to Anne?
- What does *achievement* mean to you?

## Foundations of Achievement Motivation

Children learn a lot in school about who they are, what they can do, and what they can expect from others. What girls learn about their chances for achievement is not as positive as what boys learn, starting with textbooks. Information about textbooks has been considered in chapter 2, but briefly, there still is bias toward male figures, with women underrepresented and misrepresented in children's books and texts.

Girls are also less visible in the classroom, and the bias continues into college. Other factors, such as race and social class, also influence the school environment, but it is the adults—in school as well as at home—who give some of the most potent messages about achievement.

### School Environments

Both girls and boys learn that teaching is a "woman's job" but that the more powerful job of supervising the teaching is a "man's job." In 1990, only 18% of public elementary school principals were women, while 86% of teachers were women; 7% of public high school principals were women, and 47% of teachers were women (U.S. Commerce

Department, 1990). Also, schools with a large percentage of ethnic minority students often have a largely white administration and faculty (Smith, 1987).

The differences make a difference. Minority children may experience a cultural shock when going to school and may encounter discrimination for the first time. Both minority and majority children get a message about gender. Elementary school children in a school with a woman principal were more likely to believe that either women or men could be principals than were children in schools with a man as principal (Paradise & Wall, 1986), and children with men teachers were less stereotyped about teachers' competence than children with women teachers (Mancus, 1992).

Having mostly women as teachers is not necessarily an asset to girls (Mancus, 1992), but neither is having a man as a teacher—both women and men show systematic biases. After all, they are members of a stereotyped culture (Hill, 1991). In fact, with experience, teachers tend to become less influenced by students' gender, and women are likely to have had more teaching experience than men. But the overall picture is not encouraging.

*Girls Are Invisible, Boys Are To Be Taught*    Girls are less visible in the classroom than boys, and what attention they do get is not effective academic instruction. A variety of evidence in research publications ranging from 1972 to 1993 documents this for students in preschool through college (Alvidrez & Weinstein, 1993; AAUW Educational Foundation [AAUW], 1992; Roberts, 1991; Sadker & Sadker, 1985, 1994; Sadker, Sadker, & Klein, 1991). Generally, boys get more attention, both positive and negative, and are more dominant in the classroom (Cherry, 1975; Eccles, 1989; Fagot & Hagan, 1985; Huston, 1983; Sadker & Sadker, 1994; Serbin & O'Leary, 1975; Serbin et al., 1973). Specifically, boys get more effective instructional attention for their academic efforts. They are asked more different kinds of questions and get more feedback, especially positive feedback, about their intellectual abilities.

Boys also get more instruction on how to do things on their own. If a boy speaks without raising his hand, the teacher listens to him; if a girl does, the teacher reprimands her and goes to someone else; if a girl raises her hand, she is less likely to be called on than a boy (Sadker & Sadker, 1985, 1994). If a boy answers incorrectly, the teacher helps him work toward the correct answer or at least encourages his persistence. If a girl errs, the teacher goes on to another student. If a boy gets the correct answer, he is praised ("Excellent!"); if a girl does, it is acknowledged as correct without praise ("OK."). Girls are also less likely than boys to be told whether they were right or wrong (Sadker & Sadker, 1985). Myra and David Sadker (p. 56) provided the following example:

TEACHER:    What's the capital of Maryland? Joel?
JOEL:    Baltimore.
TEACHER:    What's the largest city in Maryland, Joel?
JOEL:    Baltimore.
TEACHER:    That's good. But Baltimore isn't the capital. The capital is also the location of the U.S. Naval Academy. Joel, do you want to try again?

*Girls do not get as much attention in the classroom as boys, especially white, middle-class boys. However, African American girls receive stronger support for academic and occupational achievement from their families than do girls from other groups.*

|  |  |
|---|---|
| JOEL: | Annapolis. |
| TEACHER: | Excellent. Anne, what's the capital of Maine? |
| ANNE: | Portland. |
| TEACHER: | Judy, do you want to try? |
| JUDY: | Augusta. |
| TEACHER: | OK. |

The negative feedback boys get is most often directed toward nonintellectual qualities such as misconduct, low motivation, or messy homework. The negative feedback girls get is more likely to focus on their intellectual inadequacies, while positive feedback to them is for appearance and conduct (Dweck, Goetz, & Strauss, 1980). Girls are taught to comply, and their compliance is rewarded by teachers. Less compliant girls are seen as less competent academically; boys are not rewarded for compliance (Gold, Crombie, & Noble, 1987; Meece, 1987). Teachers consider boys, noncompliant though they are, to be better students generally, and in math especially, and to have a higher potential than girls (Ben Tsvi-Mayer, Hertz-Lazarowitz, & Safir, 1989; Delamont, 1990; Jussim & Eccles, 1992). Teachers also think more often of boys after school hours than they do of girls and have stereotypical views about both.

**Race and Social Class** Both race and social class also influence the school environment (Carr & Mednick, 1988; Comer, 1993; Irving, 1986; Smith, 1987; Wilkinson & Marrett, 1985). The environment supports the efforts of white middle-class boys more than those of other children. Teachers pay less attention to and have lower expectations for the performance of working-class and of minority children than for middle-class and white children (Alvidrez & Weinstein, 1993; Minuchin & Shapiro, 1983; Sadker et al., 1991).

For example, African American girls start out their school experience being more active and interactive than white girls and, initially (kindergarten through second grade), get as much teacher feedback as African American boys. But by later grades (third to fifth), their experiences come to be the same as those of white girls in that they receive less teacher feedback, especially academic feedback, and fewer chances than boys do for answering (AAUW, 1992; Sadker & Sadker, 1994). This can undermine the sense of self-worth that began at home (Comer, 1993). Parents of African American girls do not socialize them to be passive, but the schools mold the girls into the same invisibility of white girls.

Having an African American woman as a teacher is not necessarily advantageous for African American girls, and the picture is not particularly encouraging for African American boys either (Grant, 1985; Irving, 1986; Ross & Jackson, 1991; Taylor, 1979). African American mothers believe that there is a double standard in typical schools, with less challenge given to their children than to white children (Greene, 1990). Parents of the more successful African American children try to offset the bias by stressing to their children the realities of racial barriers, along with ethnic pride and a value of self-development (Harrison, Wilson, Pine, & Chan, 1990).

*Teachers' Assumptions*   Like other people in the society, teachers have developed perceptions and expectations and are not always aware of how those influence their judgments and actions. For example, stereotypes of talkative women are so strong that teachers shown a film of classroom discussion said that girls were more talkative than boys when, in fact, the boys were out talking the girls at a ratio of three to one. Even the teachers active in feminist issues did not spot the bias (Sadker & Sadker, 1985).

Whatever teachers think, for whatever reasons, teachers' assumptions are important. Teacher expectations, grades, the attitudes of other children toward a child, and the child's self-perceptions of competence are all interrelated (Entwisle, Alexander, Pallas, & Cadigan, 1987; Farkas, Grobe, Sheehan, & Shuan, 1990; Phillips, 1984; White & Kistner, 1992). Experimental work has shown that children (selected randomly by researchers) whom the teacher had been led to think were likely to bloom intellectually during the coming year showed an average gain of 15 IQ points during the year; the average gain of the other children was essentially zero (Rosenthal & Jacobson, 1968; Rubovits & Maehr, 1971). The effect presumably was due to subtleties of the teachers' interactions with the "bloomers."

Perhaps in ordinary circumstances (when researchers are not telling them about bloomers), teachers' expectations are based on children's actual ability. Teachers do respond to the reality of ability, but their expectations have an effect apart from the abilities and from the past performance of their students (Jussim & Eccles, 1992). What teachers think of students makes a difference.

*College*    College environments also are not equal for women and for men in terms of textbooks (chapter 2) and in interaction with faculty. Faculty seem important as role models for women and minority students choosing careers, but white men predominate among college faculty and administrators (Basow & Howe, 1980; Fleming, 1984; Gilbert & Evans, 1985). Generally, women's colleges have a higher proportion of women as faculty (Ledman, Miller, & Brown, 1995) and a higher proportion of women graduates who become successful, perhaps because of graduate education (Tidball, 1973, 1976). Curiously, both men and women students feel closer to the women who are faculty than to the men (Tidball, 1973). Between 1974 and 1990 the percentage of women members of college faculties increased only slightly, from 22.5% in 1974–1975 to 27.4% in 1989–1990, with women still underrepresented at the higher ranks in universities (Academe, 1990; National Center for Educational Statistics, 1983). Half of African American faculty are women—but only 4% of faculty are African American (Snyder, 1987).

College faculty pay more attention to men than to women; they call on women less and give women less encouragement for speaking. Women students are interrupted, ignored, and devalued more often than men. Women college teachers encourage more participation and show less bias, with the result that their women students do participate more equally.

*Effects on Girls' Self-Views and Self-Esteem*    With less individualized attention and feedback for performance, girls will have more trouble than boys developing both a realistic view of their abilities and confidence in them. Girls lower their estimates of their abilities more than boys do. As many third-grade girls as boys said they were smart and "know a lot about different kinds of things," but the number of girls saying they were smart decreased from fifth grade to eighth grade (Figure 7.1) (Gold, Brush, & Sprotzer, 1980). In a more recent study, 45% of elementary school girls and 55% of the boys said they were "good at a lot of things"; by high school, only 23% of girls but 42% of boys said that (AAUW, 1992). The decrease is largest for white and Hispanic girls and smallest for African American girls. With strong family and community support, many African American girls do stand up for themselves (Harrison et al., 1990; Jenkins, 1988). This protects their self-esteem but may bring a feeling of distance from the educational system (AAUW, 1992).

Changes in views of competence continue for women in college. At the time of graduation from high school with honors, 21% of the young women and 23% of the young men thought they were far above average in intelligence. By the time they were college sophomores, only 4% of women still thought that, and none did in their senior year (Epperson, 1988). The men's percentages stayed relatively constant.

Students (predominantly white) at all-women's colleges generally fare better, as do African American women at predominantly African American institutions (Chester, 1983; Pascarella, Smart, Ethington, & Nettles, 1987). Minority women at predominantly white institutions suffer from pressures of both racism and sexism (Ethier & Deaux, 1990; Fleming, 1983; Guy-Shaftall & Bell-Scott, 1989; Nieves-Squires, 1991). The women who survive in the typical white college environment are particularly self-reliant and assertive.

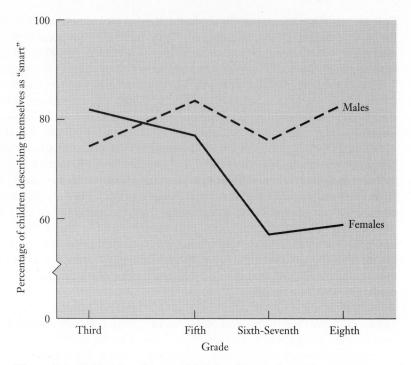

**Figure 7.1** *Children's estimates of their intelligence by grade.*   SOURCE: Gold, A. R., Brush, L. R., & Sprotzer, E. R. (1980). Developmental changes in self-perceptions of intelligence and self-confidence. *Psychology of Women Quarterly, 5,* (2), 231–239. From Table 1, p. 234.

## Parental Expectations for Children

The ways in which parents respond differently to girls and boys about achievement are not so clear as for teachers, but there do seem to be some fairly persistent parental forces at work that inhibit girls' efforts, often paralleling the contributions of teachers. There is general support for the hypothesis that traditional socialization facilitates achievement in boys and inhibits it in girls (Hoffman, 1989; Stein & Bailey, 1973). This is true for African Americans as well as whites (Carr & Mednick, 1988).

Middle-class parents generally value intellectual accomplishments and school achievements both for their sons and for their daughters, but white middle-class parents are likely to have higher expectations and standards for boys' long-range achievements and to expect more disappointment if the goals are not reached by sons than by daughters (Beal, 1994; Entwisle & Baker, 1983; Huston, 1983; Newson & Newson, 1987; Parsons, Adler, & Kaczala, 1982). White, but not African American, college-educated mothers employed in middle-class occupations stressed education for their daughters but did not stress having a career; in fact both white mothers and fathers reacted ambivalently to their daughters' interest in a career (Higginbotham & Weber, 1992).

In relative contrast, poor and working-class parents, and those of minority groups, generally have higher hopes for daughters than for sons. The differences in aspirations for children seem to involve several factors (Beal, 1994). First, girls tend to do better in school (chapter 8) than boys, so that education gives them an avenue for advancement; and, second, some traditionally female jobs are a marked step up the social and economic ladder for poor and working-class parents. Being a secretary, teacher, or nurse may not bring a great deal of pay relative to middle-class standards, but it is a move up into the professional class for some families (Newson & Newson, 1987). Third, ethnic prejudice often is stronger against boys than girls; African American mothers expect that their sons will have more hostility than their daughters from teachers, administrators, and potential employers, although they push their children to do their best regardless of gender (Spencer, Swanson, & Cunningham, 1991).

***Interaction With Daughters***     Generally, children who are taught early to master tasks and to do so independently tend to be more highly motivated to achieve than other children. Traditional socialization techniques do not provide this experience for girls, but we need to remember that "traditional" has a white middle-class meaning that minorities and the working class are more likely to not share.

Parents traditionally do more teaching with their sons than with their daughters and expect boys to learn more than girls (Block, 1983; Dino, Barnett, & Howard, 1984; Frankel & Rollins, 1983). With daughters, parents tend to focus on the interpersonal aspects of the situation, such as how much fun they are having or how nice it is to be doing something together. Fathers generally show more differences than mothers, but mothers are not immune to the bias. For example, in reading bedtime stories to sons, more than to daughters, mothers teach more, as in, "Look, here's a giraffe; can you say 'giraffe'?" (Weitzman, Birns, & Friend, 1985). In addition, mothers discuss social themes more with daughters and autonomous, achievement themes with sons (Fivush, 1993; Flannagan, Baker-Ward, & Graham, 1995).

Differences in how girls and boys are treated are more pronounced in Hispanic mother-child dyads. Hispanic mothers devoted a smaller proportion of their comments to discussing learning-related topics than other mother-child pairs. This is consistent with the general view that Hispanic parents tend to define stereotypical roles more clearly than other parents (Diaz-Guerrero, 1987; Mejia, 1983). Mothers also are very quick to step in to help their daughters, called "anxious intrusion" (Beal, 1994). Both parents are quicker to respond to their daughters' mistakes and requests for help than to their sons', with mothers somewhat more likely to do so than fathers (Rothbart, 1971; Rothbart & Rothbart, 1976). This well-meant protectiveness serves to encourage dependency in girls and to suggest to the girls that they cannot overcome problems through their own efforts.

Parents also generally encourage greater dependency in girls than boys in several other ways (Hoffman, 1977). For example, parents of toddlers are more likely to leave a boy than a girl alone in a room (Fagot, 1978); and they are more likely to supervise and chaperone daughters and to encourage and expect daughters rather than sons to follow them around the house (Fagot, 1974; Goff, 1991; Grusec & Lytton, 1988; Kuczynski & Kochanska, 1990). By elementary school years, boys are allowed to roam over a wider area without special permission, such as coming home after school by themselves, playing in the neighborhood rather than at home, riding buses for more than half an hour, and going to parks, libraries, and other community centers by themselves (Beal, 1994; Newson & Newson, 1987).

Although one reason for the greater restriction on girls is fear of sexual molestation (though boys are not immune to that), parents think their daughters generally are more fragile, frightened, and vulnerable, even though girls are more physically resilient throughout childhood (Kuebli & Krieger, 1991). One result is that boys are more likely to be injured and die from accidents in unsupervised play (Beal, 1994). Another is that girls have less chance for physical harm but suffer the psychological harm of having less chance to develop their self-confidence in coping with unexpected problems in the world outside the home.

Parents, of course, differ. Parents with nontraditional gender views were more likely than those with traditional views to grant earlier independence to daughters (Barnett, 1981). Parents differ also in the chores they assign, and that seems as important for the orientation to achieve as it is for general orientation to gender roles (chapter 5). Encouraging nontraditional attitudes about household duties and about occupational interests was shown important for the development of African American girls' achievement motivation; encouraging traditional attitudes favored boys' achievement motivation (Carr & Mednick, 1988). Parents who are nontraditional about chores are likely to be nontraditional in other ways and to be modeling nontraditional behaviors themselves (chapter 5).

***Effects on Girls' Achievement***    In sum, differences in the way parents treat girls and boys are not huge, but they lean in directions that discourage the development of girls' orientation to achieve, although lower class and minority groups are less likely to do this. The interactions girls of any class or ethnic group have at school do not encourage achievement either. In spite of this, girls still tend to get better grades than boys do.

In other words, girls are achieving, so why be concerned about pressures against girls' achievement? One reason is that girls may be doing well in classes because they are obedient. This is not the same as developing the achievement skills they will need in later life. In addition, they may not be feeling very good about themselves, and they may be achieving at an unnecessary cost of psychic energy. To understand this, we need to look at specific factors involved in effective achievement striving.

## Components of Effective Achievement

David McClelland and his colleagues pioneered research and theory on the motivation to achieve (Atkinson, 1957, 1964; Heckhausen, 1967; McClelland, Atkinson, Clark, & Lowell, 1953). They defined **achievement motivation,** or need for achievement, **nAch,** (following Henry Murray, 1938) as competition with a standard of excellence or the desire to accomplish something difficult—to master objects, people, or ideas— and to do so as rapidly and as independently as possible. More simply, achievement motivation involves goals related to competence (Dweck & Elliott, 1983).

One may compete with or aim for a standard of excellence in many ways, but the McClelland group focused on standards generally relevant to middle-class success, particularly entrepreneurial success. The standards include concerns with academic achievement, intellectual competence, and occupational status and prestige. Despite its original focus on achievement in a relatively narrow sense, the approach has provided a framework for studying a broader array of questions about achievement (Dweck & Elliott, 1983). Men and women, African Americans and whites, are very similar in their concerns about achievement (Crew, 1982; Mednick & Thomas, 1993; Spence & Helmreich, 1983).

Achievement motivation was measured initially with a TAT procedure. The **Thematic Apperception Test (TAT)** was developed by Christiana Morgan and Henry Murray (Morgan & Murray, 1935, 1938/1962). It is a **projective instrument,** which means it presents people with ambiguous stimuli on the assumption that their responses will reveal information not necessarily available on a conscious level. The TAT specifically is a series of ambiguous drawings of people. Research participants typically are asked what is happening, what has led up to the situation, what the main character is thinking, and what will happen. The stories are content analyzed (chapter 2) for achievement themes. With properly developed scoring systems and trained judges, reliability of scoring is relatively high.

The McClelland group demonstrated that the TAT was effective in measuring college men's motivation to achieve. When motivation was aroused by telling the men that the test was important for predicting leadership or intellectual ability, the men told stories with more concern about achievement than when given neutral instructions. Women did not show the increase in achievement imagery when given arousing instructions. Thus, a footnote in a classic book of almost 900 pages (Atkinson, 1958) mentions that because women's data did not fit the predictions, women were not studied any more! The footnote did not mention that women's stories under relaxed conditions were already as high in achievement orientation as were the stories given by men or women under aroused conditions (Stewart & Chester, 1982).

The theory of achievement motivation was long seen as a male theory that did not predict women's behavior very well (Miner, 1980), but continued work has shown that the theory does predict women's behavior (Cooper, 1983; Slade & Rush, 1991). Further, women's orientation to achieve has increased over the years, shown for 1957 to 1976 (Veroff, Depner, Kulka, & Douvan, 1980) and for 1967 to 1981 (Jenkins, 1987), and researchers' interest in women's achievement has increased as well.

The original McClelland approach and then continuing theorizing by Atkinson has identified a number of ways in which high nAch people go about pursuing goals (Atkinson, 1958; Birney, 1968; Heckhausen, 1967; McClelland, 1961; McClelland et al., 1953). There are four basic components in *effective achievement* (called "resultant achievement motivation" by Atkinson): Hope of Success, Hope of Failure, Fear of Failure, and Fear of Success. Efforts to achieve are maximal when Hope of Success (the positive component) is high and all the other components (subtractive) are low. Even with high ability and high desire, people may not achieve, or they may do so at unnecessarily high costs if the subtractive components are high. A Closer Look 7.1 gives a checklist that offers both an overview of research and a practical guide for assessing your effectiveness in using your abilities and energies.

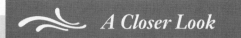 *A Closer Look*

## 7.1    Checklist for Effective Achievement

### Hope of Success

Are you alert to chances to use your skills?

Do you decide to act?

Is your level of aspiration, what you want to accomplish, realistic? Do you know your skills well enough to pick what for you is a moderate level? Do you pick easy tasks or hard ones or moderate ones?

Do you have confidence in meeting your aspirations?

Do you worry too much about negative feedback?

Do you take credit for your successes?

Do you learn from your failures?

Do you let other people's views get in your way?

### Hope of Failure

Do you stand to gain anything by being incompetent in any way?

Do you feel you are accepted better when you goof up than when you do not?

### Fear of Failure

Do you worry a lot about what would happen if you did not accomplish what you set out to?

When you were a child, did adults sometimes let you pull back or get off the hook from tasks or challenges you did not want to face? Why did you want to avoid the task or challenge?

Have you ever felt you were censured more for failure than you were praised for success?

Do you sometimes take the easy way out?

Do you sometimes overestimate what you can do, trying for too hard a challenge?

Do you expect people to sympathize when you fail at something? ("At least you aimed high.")

### Fear of Success

Do you expect any negative consequences for succeeding?

Have you been censured in some way for success?

## Hope of Success

The first major component for effective achievement and the most thoroughly researched is **Hope of Success (HS),** the motive or tendency to approach success. This refers to a marked capacity for experiencing pride with success. People with high HS expect to get a positive outcome for succeeding at a task—they win by winning. It involves, first, seeing a chance to use skills in a meaningful way and deciding to act. If people do not think they have skills whose use will bring reward, they are not likely to use their skills in effective ways. As noted, teachers and parents are less likely to call attention to a girl's skills than to a boy's, and so girls can be hesitant to act on the skills they do have, even if they are aware of having them. The effect of lack of reinforcement for using skills can work backward, so that you simply stop trying and may even "forget" that you have the skills.

To use skills in a meaningful way requires having a realistic or moderate **level of aspiration (LOA or LA):** the specification of exactly how much you want to try to accomplish. How high do you want to try to jump in the high hurdles? How difficult a term paper do you want to tackle? Should you take a hard course or an easier one? For effective achievement, the LOA should be realistic and moderate. Succeeding on an easy task and failing on a hard task do not demonstrate skills. The aspiration of the effective achiever is moderate because there is a good chance for success, but the success is not guaranteed. If success does come, it is evidence of the use of skill. Think of children choosing how close they want to be to the stake in a ring-toss game. Standing close to the stake would be an easy task, with success assured, but it would not demonstrate the child's skills. Standing far away would essentially guarantee failure. That choice also would not demonstrate skills—who could do it from way back there? A medium distance has the most potential for a success that is meaningful—success is possible but not so guaranteed that "just anyone" could do it.

Sometimes the odds are impersonal, objective, and clearly known. Often, the odds are personal and subjective and not clearly known, so that setting an LOA effectively requires a lot of self-knowledge. Do you know enough to take a course without the prerequisite? Are you up to doing an interesting term paper on a subject you've not really thought about before? Are you confident enough to give a short speech to the dorm discussion group? The self-knowledge, however, is likely to depend at least partially on feedback previously received from others. The general pattern of feedback given by teachers to girls is not particularly likely to encourage self-knowledge about abilities, nor confidence about using skills.

*Confidence*    Confidence that one can succeed generally facilitates success. The general finding is that girls and women are not as confident as boys and men (Heatherington et al., 1993; Lenney, 1977). Earlier in the chapter we saw that girls' estimates of their intelligence and being "good at a lot of things" decrease during the school years. Girls and women have been said to be lacking in confidence; often it would be just as true to say that boys and men have too much confidence. Girls have lower expectations than boys on tasks on which they *outperform* boys (Crandall, 1969). Thus girls are unrealistically low and boys unrealistically high. Further, it is the *brightest* girls who most underestimate their chances of success (Stipek & Hoffman, 1980).

If girls who are low in confidence still achieve in school, why should we be concerned about their low confidence? First, it does not feel very good to lack confidence in doing what you are supposed to be doing—being a student! In addition, even when girls are doing well, girls' performance is much more fragile and vulnerable to disruption than boys', and brighter girls are more at risk (Dweck & Elliott, 1983). A final reason for concern is that the girls' underestimations can lead to unrealistically conservative choices as they progress through the school system. The boys' self-confidence, although often unrealistic, can lead them to attempt more tasks, gain practice, and perhaps receive rewards that bolster confidence in the future. The equally

*Women tend to express less confidence than men, especially in traditionally masculine fields, even when they outperform them. Lower expressed confidence levels probably reflect several interacting socialization factors, including the desire to appear modest and noncompetitive.*

able girls may progressively withdraw from efforts to achieve and gradually dwindle in their skills and in their motivation to use them.

In spite of the broad recurring tendency of lower confidence in girls and women than boys and men, women do not always show lower confidence. Women's statements of confidence are more sensitive to the situation than men's. Ellen Lenney (1977) made one of the pioneering contributions of the 1970s (chapter 1) with a detailed analysis illustrating when women are less confident than men and when they are not; her analysis continues to be generally confirmed (Heatherington et al., 1993; Kimball & Gray, 1982; Lenney, 1981, 1983; Stake, 1983).

First, the lower expectancies of success that women state are most marked in areas that seem to be or are labeled as masculine (e.g., science and math) (Carr, Thomas, & Mednick, 1985; Lee, Nelson, & Nelson, 1988; Lenney, 1981; Linn & Hyde, 1989; McMahan, 1982; Stein, Pohly, & Mueller, 1971). This has been shown for African Americans as well as for whites (AAUW, 1992; Carr et al., 1985; Stein et al., 1971). Sometimes men's greater confidence is realistic because of their greater experience in the area, as in video games (Hall, 1990) or economics course material (Basow & Medcalf, 1988). Yet, even when girls and women are making the same grades in "masculine" courses (math, science), they continue to feel less competent and expect lower grades (Ryujin & Herrold, 1989). Women's confidence is not necessarily lower than men's when the task seems relevant to "feminine" skills (e.g., social skills), but men often are as self-confident as women are for feminine tasks. Men's self-confidence does not vary as a function of the task as much as women's. For example, among African American adults recruited in shopping center parking lots, women were less confident about masculine tasks than about feminine or neutral ones, while men were equally confident for all kinds of tasks (Carr & Mednick, 1988).

Second, women's confidence is not lower than men's when there is unambiguous feedback about previous performance (Lenney, 1977). For example, before doing anagrams (Sleeper & Nigro, 1987) or before any examination in an introductory psychology course (Kimball & Gray, 1982), men were more self-confident. After doing some anagrams and getting feedback, or taking the first exam in the course, women and men were equal in confidence. However, what is clear feedback to one person may not be clear to another. As noted, even when young women are making the same or higher grades, they sometimes have lower confidence (Ryujin & Herrold, 1989).

Third, gender differences in self-confidence and in satisfaction with performance diminish or vanish when there is no social comparison (Basow, Smither, Rupert, & Collins, 1989; Clark & Zehr, 1993; Daubman, Heatherington, & Ahn, 1992; Heatherington et al., 1993; Lenney, 1977, 1981, 1983). **Social comparison** means that other people know of one's confidence before doing a task or one's performance on the task. Comparison with others affects women's self-confidence and ratings of their own performance more than it affects men. Unfortunately, in the world outside research laboratories, the relevant domain often is masculine, the feedback can be interpreted in more than one way, and there is social comparison.

***Why Does Social Comparison Matter?*** Several suggestions have been made about why women and men differ in confidence levels (Daubman et al., 1992; Heatherington et al., 1993; Huguet & Monteil, 1995). One is simply that women have been socialized to be less confident, especially in male stereotyped activities and in competitive situations: The developing girl gets many messages that she is not expected to succeed. A second suggestion is that women may state having less confidence than they actually feel—they are *not* really low in confidence but present themselves that way (Heatherington et al., 1993). They may do so to be seen as complying with the feminine gender role mandating "female modesty" and concern for others. An expectation of rewards for feminine self-presentation has some basis in reality. Women seen as modest are seen as feminine; they also are seen as being less competent or professional than an immodest woman (Miller, Cooke, Tsang, & Morgan, 1992; Wiley & Crittendan, 1992). The presence of an audience ordinarily increases concerns about self-presentation, including concerns about behavior consistent with gender roles (Eagly, 1987); thus, others knowing of her confidence would decrease a woman's statements of confidence.

Concern with being feminine might also lead women to understate their confidence out of concern for other people's feelings (Daubman et al., 1992; Major & Adams, 1983) and, specifically, to avoid the possibility of competition (House, 1974). This relational explanation has support (Heatherington et al., 1993). Women in their first semester of college stated a lower expectation for their first semester GPA than comparable men did when they were asked to state the expectation to another, older student who had commented about making a relatively low first term GPA; but women

**Figure 7.2** *Organization of attributions in Weiner's cognitive attribution theory.* SOURCES: Weiner, B. (1979). A theory of motivation for some classroom experiences. *Journal of Educational Psychology, 71,* 3–25. Weiner, B. (1985). An attributional theory of achievement motivation and emotion. *Psychological Review, 92,* 548–573.

|  |  | Locus of Control | |
|  |  | Internal | External |
|---|---|---|---|
| Stability | Stable | Ability: high or low | Task: easy or hard |
|  | Unstable | Effort: high or low | Luck: good or bad |

and men did not differ when the older student had not stated concern (Heatherington et al., 1993).

It may be nice (and feminine!) that women do not want to risk hurting another, but a hidden danger lies in stating low confidence out of concern for others. If you say something often enough, it is easy to come to believe it, and for others to come to believe it as well, thus setting up a self-fulfilling prophecy (chapter 3). Indeed, among French children (10–12 years old), boys performed better and girls performed worse on a task when social comparison was anticipated than when it was not (Huguet & Monteil, 1995). There may be, however, important situational effects yet to be studied (e.g., nature of the task, kind of people involved). Some of the situational factors influencing statements of confidence may also apply to the reasons for success or failure—a matter of attributions.

*Attributions and Personal Responsibility*    For achievement motivation to grow, the person who succeeds must take credit for the success. Taking credit means assuming internal attributions for success—*I* did it! An **attribution** is the assumed meaning or reason for an action or product: "To what do you attribute that?" "What is the reason for that?" According to Bernard Weiner's (1979, 1985, 1990) cognitive attribution theory, people with a high achievement orientation credit their success as due to **internal** reasons: **ability and effort**—"I have the ability and I worked hard." People with a low achievement orientation attribute success to **external** factors: the **task and luck**— "It was an easy exam, and I made some lucky guesses." In contrast, they assume responsibility for failure—"I'm just not smart enough." A person's ability and the difficulty of a task are assumed to be **stable,** while effort and luck are considered **unstable** (Figure 7.2). Weiner later expanded the classification (including a dimension of controllable-uncontrollable), but most relevant research so far has used the original classification.

Effective achievement is thought to involve internal attributions for success and unstable ones for failure. Changing faulty attributions can facilitate achievement. College students who did not do well during their first year of college were persuaded to replace stable attributions (e.g., "I am not a good student") with unstable ones (e.g.,

"People who make low grades the first year often do better from then on"). The students given the new attributions got better grades the next semester and did better when they took the Graduate Record Examination (Wilson & Linville, 1982, 1985).

The predominant response of both women and men is to attribute success to ability, effort, and luck, while failure is seen in terms of task difficulty (Whitley, McHugh, & Frieze, 1986). There are, however, some gender differences along with the similarities (Frieze, Whitley, Hanusa, & McHugh, 1982). Regardless of outcome, men make stronger ability attributions than women do, and women make stronger luck attributions than men do. In addition, when women fail, they cite the difficulty of the task ("too hard") more than men do, while men cite effort ("didn't try") as more relevant than women do (Focus on Research 7.1).

There are numerous group and individual differences, as well as contextual factors, to be explored (Clark, 1993; Cote & Azar, 1997; D'Amico, Baron, & Sissons, 1995). For example, women low in traditionality, high in ability, and high in achievement motivation are more likely than other women to attribute success to internal factors and failure to external ones (Crombie, 1983; Eccles, Adler, & Meece, 1984). Men may be more likely to use ability to explain success on feminine tasks, such as comforting a friend (Clark, 1993). Finally, when women do not feel an obligation to be modest, they seem as likely as men to attribute success to ability (Berg, Stephen, & Dodson, 1981). As mentioned, the factors influencing statements of confidence also may influence attributions. Other people's reactions to a woman's achievement efforts do not encourage effective attributions for women.

***Evaluation of Women's Performance***     Efforts to achieve do not occur in a vacuum. Other people are likely to be observing and making informal comments. Often they judge whether a woman's efforts have been successful or not and make attributions about the reasons for the outcome. The responses of other people can influence a woman's views of her competence, her confidence, her attributions, and her career choices (Rosenthal, 1996).

Are women's and men's achievements equally likely to be considered good? In the "classic Goldberg study," Goldberg (1968) asked college women to evaluate professional essays presented as being by a woman or by a man. The women expressed a bias against women when the articles were in masculine fields (law, city planning). They did not express a bias against men (or against women) when the articles were in feminine fields (primary education, dietetics) or neutral fields (art history, linguistics). The differences in ratings given to women and men said to be authors of the "masculine" articles were small (about 4 points on a 46-point scale), but the study attracted a lot of attention. Many similar studies followed and gave complex and frequently inconsistent results (Durkin, 1987; Nieva & Gutek, 1981; Paludi & Strayer, 1985; Pirri, Eaton, & Durkin, 1995; Swim, Borgida, Maruyama, & Myers, 1989; Top, 1991; Wallston & O'Leary, 1981).

While reviewers continue to find small *overall* differences, they also show some variables that affect judgments and need more attention. Most of the relevant studies have been of college students; how much the results can be generalized to other groups

## FOCUS ON RESEARCH

### 7.1   Longitudinal Research: Why Are You in College?

Here's a scene we've probably all experienced in one form or another. You're at a family gathering and Uncle Ralph is grilling you about being a college student. After all, he points out, going to college is expensive and time consuming, and it doesn't guarantee you'll get a job. So why are you in college? How do you explain your desire to achieve that has led you to college?

Psychologists study attributions to explain why we behave as we do. When events happen in our lives, we try to explain why they occurred—to attribute them to some cause. In turn, the attributions we make influence our subsequent behavior. Attributions can be categorized as internal or external, stable or unstable, and global or specific. If I attribute the A on my test to my overall superior intelligence, I've just made an internal (I did it), stable (my intelligence isn't likely to change), and global (I'm smart at everything) attribution. This attributional pattern is likely to influence my future behavior, as I assume I will continue to succeed at everything I try.

Barbara Bank (1995) wanted to study the attributions college students gave for their decision to seek a bachelor's degree. She focused on two questions: Do the attitudes of college seniors about their college careers reflect the expectations they had as freshmen? Do women and men give the same reasons for seeking a college degree?

In her study, Bank used a longitudinal design, which enables the researcher to test the same group of people at two or more times in their lives. Bank selected two times of measurement, gathering data from a group of students when they entered college as freshmen in 1985 and again in 1989 when they were expected to have graduated. The 1985 questionnaire focused on expectations for finishing college promptly and without interruptions; the 1989 questionnaire gathered information on the reasons the students had sought a bachelor's degree, the importance of the degree to them, and their attributions for their successful or unsuccessful college careers.

Longitudinal research allows researchers to answer unique questions, such as how individuals change over time or how the individual's earlier experience relates to their later behavior. However, this method is not without problems. Several confounds

---

is not clear (Olian, Schwab, & Haberfeld, 1988). Professional white Australian women of a wide age range (20–60 years) did not show bias against women (Pirri et al., 1995), but this does not tell us about people who are not college educated.

When differences in judgment of men's and women's achievements are found, the typical result is that men are evaluated as being better than women (Lott, 1985). The effect of ethnicity is not always clear (Noel & Allen, 1976; Swim et al., 1989). Generally, men and women judges agree in their evaluations, being equally biased or unbiased (Swim et al., 1989; Top, 1991). Exceptions tend to be for women judging women more favorably than men do, but there are some reversals. There is a tendency

(factors that systematically bias the data) can influence the results and make it impossible to be sure what we have really found. Historical events that take place between measurements can influence people's responses. For example, an economic downturn during one's college years could alter original perceptions and behaviors.

Longitudinal research also suffers from the problem of mortality, meaning that participants drop out of the study before it is completed. People move away, die, become too busy to participate, or for some other reason can't be reached for the next round of data collection. As the dropout rate increases, the chance that the remaining participants are a good representation of their group decreases. Bank began her study in 1985 with 495 entering freshmen but was unable to locate 71 of those students four years later. Of the remaining 424 students, 257 returned the 1989 questionnaire. In presenting her study, Bank was very careful to describe in detail the gender, age, ethnicity, and socioeconomic status of her participants to give the reader a clear picture of which student group her findings could apply to, to avoid incorrect generalizations.

With these cautions in mind, what did Bank's study reveal about college students' reasons for seeking a bachelor's degree? First, the data showed that men and women did not give different reasons for going to college, and most importantly, women were no more likely than men to make external attributions for their college success. Instead, Bank found that these women actually tended to take *more* personal credit (make more internal attributions) for their success than did the men. Second, the longitudinal data showed that both female and male students who in 1985 expected uninterrupted schooling and prompt graduation were more likely to complete their degree in four years. Bank notes that overall, these students were confident of their abilities and took personal credit for doing well. A combination of internal attributions and expectations for timely graduation led these students forward to actual college completion on schedule.

JILL BORCHERT ◆

SOURCE: Bank, B. (1995). Gendered accounts: Undergraduates explain why they seek their bachelor's degree. *Sex Roles, 32*, 527–544.

for less bias against women in fields congruent with their gender than in incongruent fields (Swim et al., 1989; Top, 1991). However, a bias against women has been shown even in the field of the psychology of women (Paludi & Bauer, 1983; Paludi & Strayer, 1985). Results are unclear when the field is gender neutral.

The degree of bias against a woman generally is lower the more evidence there is about her qualifications. One kind of information that sometimes reduces biases is evidence of previous success. When paintings had a blue ribbon on them, supposedly from a recent art show, the bias against women did not occur (Pheterson, Kiesler, & Goldberg, 1971). Unfortunately, it often is hard for women to get the blue ribbon, and

## FOCUS ON RESEARCH

### 7.2    Field Research: Out of the Lab and Into the Business Office

Researchers are sometimes accused of living in an ivory tower, producing work that has no relevance to everyday life. It's true that some laboratory experiments create a very artificial environment in which research participants may not act like they normally would. The results of such studies can't be generalized beyond the lab setting. This problem of generalizability or lack of external validity severely limits the usefulness of some lab studies. Field research addresses this very issue.

Field research includes a number of data-gathering methods, such as personal interviews, direct observation, case studies, and participant observation (in which the researcher actually takes part in the lives of the participants during the data gathering). Usually, data gathered in field research is qualitative (behavior described verbally) rather than quantitative (behavior described numerically, such as a rating on a 1–5 scale).

The advantages of field research appealed to researcher Patrice Rosenthal, who studied the attributions managers made about male and female workers and how these attributions might affect the worker's job evaluations (1996). Past research on attribution tells us that compared to men's success, women's success is more likely to be attributed to effort, luck, or ease of the task. Conversely, compared to men's failures, women's failures are more likely to be attributed to lack of ability. So, based on past studies, we would expect women in the workforce to be at a distinct disadvantage if these attributions are used as the basis for promotions or pay raises. However, Rosenthal noted that nearly all the attribution research had been conducted in the laboratory, and she had doubts about its generalizability. Would a manager on the job make the same attributions about his or her actual employees? She decided to take her study into the field, or rather the business office.

Rosenthal went to a health organization and a financial services firm and conducted interviews with 93 managers (44 women and 49 men). Each manager was asked to discuss employees who were successful or unsuccessful in their job performances. In

---

when they get it, other people may explain it away as not really due to the woman's talents—a problem of attributions.

The recurring pattern is that people see ability as important for a man's success—at least if it is a white man who succeeds. Women luck out or try hard—they are considered low on ability (Deaux & Emswiller, 1974; Feldman-Summers & Kiesler, 1974). How traditional the area of achievement is does make some difference in the way women are seen. If a woman succeeds, she is seen as skillful if the task is a feminine one; but if she succeeds on a masculine task, she is considered lucky (Deaux & Emswiller, 1974). The traditionality of the task does not make much difference in how a man's success is viewed, nor in how he sees his own success.

order to compare her findings to those of past quantitative studies, Rosenthal had the manager use a 5-point scale to rate the employees on personal skill and ability, effort, ease of task, and luck or circumstances beyond the employee's control. These ratings indicated the attributions managers made about the employees.

Rosenthal's findings were distinctly different from those of laboratory studies. She discovered that managers of both genders attributed ability and effort as the key to both their female and male employees' job performances, whether those perform-ances were successful or unsuccessful. This study indicates that in the field, managers don't see women workers' successes as due to external factors and their failure as the result of internal personal factors. Instead, men's and women's performances are ex-plained by the same factors, a more equitable situation for the awarding of promotions and pay raises.

How can we reconcile the different conclusions from lab and field studies? Rosenthal notes that in the artificial lab setting, participants who play the roles of manager and employee are most often strangers. Research tells us that we are more likely to rely on stereotypes when judging someone about whom we have little personal knowledge. In the lab studies, managers may make more negative attributions about women (success is due to luck, failure is due to lack of ability) because they are guided by stereotypes. But in a field study the manager has personal knowledge of the em-ployee. Stereotypes lose their power, and managers feel a worker's success or failure on the job is due to her or his internal qualities, including ability, skill, or effort. The conclusions Rosenthal draws from her field study are good news for women workers who, had researchers stayed in the lab, might have worried needlessly about discrimi-nation in job promotion or pay raises.

JILL BORCHERT ◆

SOURCE: Rosenthal, P. (1996). Gender and managers' causal attributions for subordinate performance: A field story. *Sex Roles, 34,* 1–15.

---

When women fail, it is attributed to lack of ability, but men fail because the task is too hard (Cash, Gillen, & Burns, 1977; Etaugh & Brown, 1975; Feather & Simon, 1975). These generalizations are more safely made about whites (as targets and as judges) than about other groups. For example, college students saw a white man's success as a banker as being due to ability; the same success of a white woman and of an African American man and woman was attributed to effort and luck (Yarkin, Town, & Wallston, 1982). In a land where everyone is supposed to be equal, people who are not white men are seen as getting ahead by hard work and luck, and white men are seen as being smarter (Deaux, 1976). For a look at how some of these ideas translate into the business world, see Focus on Research 7.2.

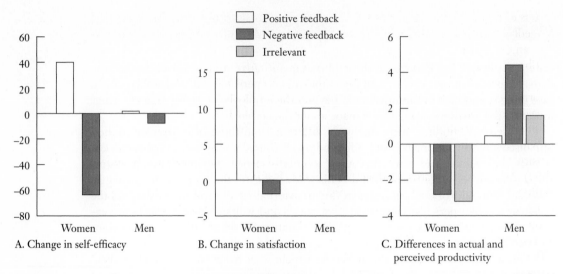

**Figure 7.3** *Gender differences in responsiveness to feedback.*    NOTE: Self-efficacy scores were based on participants' indication of their confidence that they could solve varying numbers of tasks, from 0 (cannot do at all) to 100% (certain can do). Satisfaction scores were based on participants' rating of their satisfaction with their performance, from 0 to 100. Productivity scores were based on discrepancies between participants' estimate of number of tasks they solved and actual number of solved tasks. SOURCE: Roberts, T., & Nolen-Hoeksema, S. (1989). Sex differences in reaction to valuative feedback. *Sex Roles*, *21*, 725–747.

***Responsiveness to Feedback***    A previously neglected aspect of achievement that is likely to prove influential concerns how women and men respond to feedback. Tomi-Ann Roberts and Susan Nolen-Hoeksema have offered provocative evidence from experiments with college students that women are influenced by evaluative feedback in a more straightforward way than men, who are more selective in their responsiveness (Roberts, 1991; Roberts & Nolen-Hoeksema, 1989, 1990). In their studies, college students worked on cognitive tasks (some unsolvable) and at a certain point were given either positive feedback ("You are doing very well. You are above average at this point in the task") or negative feedback ("You are not doing very well. You are below average at this point in the task"). Some students were also given irrelevant feedback ("You have a remarkably steady hand"), and some received no feedback. Whether feedback was positive or negative made significant differences in women's satisfaction with what they had done and their confidence about future performance; in relative contrast, men did not differentially respond to positive or negative feedback in these ways (Figure 7.3). Women also thought that feedback, particularly negative feedback, contained more information relevant to their abilities than did the men. The men did not completely disregard the feedback, but they responded to it in a self-enhancing way. When given negative feedback, the men *overestimated* their productivity relative to both men and women who had been given positive feedback.

Although women lowered their expectations for success more than men after failure, they did not necessarily perform worse nor disparage themselves (similar to the results of other studies, e.g., Eccles et al., 1984). Despite the more direct incorporation of feedback into their self-evaluations, women persisted just as long as men did on the task and did just as well. Women often do well in spite of their responsiveness to feedback, but doing the task is not as satisfying as it might be.

Roberts (1991) suggests that the differences are due partially to differences in the informational value women and men see in the feedback, differences stemming from early experiences. The greater emphasis on independence for boys than for girls enables boys to formulate their own standards of success irrespective of social feedback provided by adults. In contrast, the socialization of girls often results in increasing their sensitivity to the effects of interpersonal interactions and adult feedback (Haddad, 1992). Because the negative feedback boys get in the classroom is not directed at their abilities, boys can attribute it to an irrelevant source, such as a teacher's negative attitude (Dweck, Davidson, Nelson, & Enna, 1978). In contrast, the negative feedback about girls focuses on intellectual inadequacies, making it harder for girls to discount its relevance to their abilities. As with confidence, both sexes may be erring but in different directions—men may underuse feedback from others, while women may overuse it.

## Hope of Failure

A person may be high in Hope of Success but still not be effective in achievement efforts because other components subtract from it. The first subtractive component is **Hope of Failure (HF),** or the motive or tendency to approach failure. People high in HF expect a positive outcome for failure—they win by losing. Not much can be said about HF other than that there is evidence that it exists (Burnstein & Zajonc, 1965; Klinger & McNelly, 1969; Whyte, 1943).

Research about women and HF seems nonexistent. Given that a general incompetence (e.g., "cannot make decisions easily," "excitable in minor crisis"; chapter 3) is part of the role for women, and the media show girls and women being dependent on boys and men (chapter 2), it is not difficult to imagine that some women do feel that they gain acceptance for failure. But in contrast to those women who may hope for failure, many have a marked fear of it.

## Fear of Failure

Except for some people high in HF, it is probably safe to say that no one really enjoys failing, but there are people who are particularly susceptible to negative effects of failure. People with **Fear of Failure (FF),** or the motive or tendency to avoid failure, experience shame from failure—they lose by losing. FF can be measured by negative imagery in TAT stories but more often is measured by self-reports of anxiety, especially test anxiety.

People high in FF avoid situations in which they are called upon to achieve. If that is impossible, they avoid participating in tasks in a way that would expose their feared inadequacies. One way of doing that is to choose a very low or very high level of aspiration instead of a moderate one (Karabenick & Youssef, 1968). With a low

LOA, failure is unlikely. With a high LOA, failure is likely, but the aims were so high that anyone would have failed; with this tactic the person fearing failure may gain some praise for having aimed high. Avoidance of meaningful occasions for achievement brings reduction or avoidance of anxiety, and that reinforces the tendency to avoid putting one's abilities on the line.

Girls tend to be more anxious about failure than boys are, and their anxiety increases during elementary school years more than boys' does (Stein & Bailey, 1973). Jerome Kagan and Howard Moss (1962) found that girls and boys were equal in FF at ages 6 to 8 years. Girls remained relatively stable in the amount of FF as they grew: A young girl high in FF was likely to be high in teen and then early adult years. However, a boy originally high in FF might or might not be high in later years. What apparently happened was that some of the boys who were fearful were encouraged or even shoved into the achievement arena. A boy who avoids is noticed. Socialization pressures push him to deny the anxiety or to control it sufficiently to face the feared challenge, possibly mastering it and gaining rewards that moderate the anxiety. In contrast, a girl who avoids is likely to be neglected rather than encouraged to overcome her fears. She is given the temporary luxury of being allowed to act on her fear and escape the threat of the situation. She pays in the long run.

Fear of failure can lead women to aim beneath their abilities educationally and occupationally without realizing it (Donelson & Gullahorn, 1977). It can also interfere with effectiveness in carrying out the traditional roles of manager of the household, caregiver of children, and partner of a spouse. Kagan and Moss (1962) found that female homemakers who were high in FF were very timid and indecisive in their daily activities. They could not make decisions on their own even within their household and were scared and tense about meeting people.

Fear of failure may develop when parents expect high achievement and do not reward it, but they punish failure (Hill & Eaton, 1977; Teevan & McGhee, 1972). Many parents encourage school achievement in both daughters and sons but may not consider it important enough to reward in daughters.

## Fear of Success

The final component that can subtract from Hope of Success is **Fear of Success (FS or FOS),** a motive or tendency to avoid success. People with FS expect that negative events will follow success—they will lose by winning. Matina Horner (1968, 1972, 1978) predicted that the fear is present in women who are high in achievement orientation and sufficiently high in ability to be capable of achieving (though she slips into suggesting that it is relevant to all women). Her reasoning was that competition against others endangers the affiliative concerns of women. Horner measured FS with a **verbal lead.** The logic of the procedure is the same as with the TAT, but people are given a sentence instead of a picture as a stimulus for telling a story. Horner's now famous verbal lead for women was, "After first term finals, Anne finds herself at the top of her medical school class." Horner gave men a lead about *John* instead of *Anne.*

***Fear of Success Imagery***　　Horner found that 65% of the college women she studied at the University of Michigan showed FS imagery in their stories, compared with only

9% of the men. FS was scored on three themes: (1) fear of loss of femininity, (2) fear of social rejection, and (3) denial. In a typical story, Anne deliberately lowers her academic standing the next term and does all she can to help Carl get his grades up; she drops out of school and marries Carl, who continues in school while Anne raises their family (femininity issue). In other stories, women stressed that Anne was unhappy, aggressive, unmarried, or so ambitious that she used her family, husband, and friends as tools to advance her career (social rejection). Some maintained that Anne was a code name for a fictional person created by a group of students who took turns taking exams and writing papers for the nonexistent Anne (denial) (A Closer Look 7.2).

The women with high fear of success lowered their performance when they were competing with men or with women and shifted their career aspirations to traditionally female areas while in college or dropped out of college (Hoffman, 1977; Horner, 1972). Horner's work captured a lot of attention from people eager to have "the answer" about why women do not achieve as much as men do: The problem with women is they are afraid of success! Therefore, there is nothing wrong with the world. As researchers dived into the issue, it became clear that the problems were not with women but with research about them and with the social context within which women wanted to achieve.

***Critiques of FS***   Although FS has been described as "one of the most theoretically engaging areas of motivational research" (Piedmont, 1995, p. 139), the research has been plagued with theoretical and technical problems. Some researchers have reported that Horner's original analyses were inappropriate, and, when done correctly, show no evidence that women's performance was affected (Zuckerman & Wheeler, 1975).

One problem is that it is not clear what FS is; Horner's original scoring of stories for FS overlaps remarkably with scoring for FF (Piedmont, 1995). Are these fears the same, only packaged differently? Even accepting FS as different from FF, further problems have surfaced.

A major problem is that other researchers have not necessarily found FS high in women and have reported a great deal of variability in how many women and men show FS. Michele Paludi (1984) looked at over 64 studies and found that the median percentage of women showing FS was 49% (with a range from 6% to 93%); the median percentage of men showing FS was 45% (with a range from 7% to 95%). Further, African American women generally show less FS than white women. How much can FS explain about women when its prevalence is so variable? Why should it be considered relevant to women but not to men? Can FS be called a "woman's problem" when there is a lower incidence of it in women (and men) who are androgynous and expressive than in other people (Cano, Solomon, & Holmes, 1984; Sadd, Miller, & Zietz, 1979)? Conflicting results may be partly due to the fact that the competitive situations in the studies were not interesting enough for the participants (Huguet & Monteil, 1995).

Another criticism centers on the procedure. Projective instruments are supposed to be ambiguous to give people a latitude within which to project, but Horner's lead forces people to react to a specific, narrow situation (Tresemer, 1974, 1977). The lead may not elicit material relevant to *personal* perceptions of *personal* success. And, the lead states, "Anne *finds* herself at the *top* . . ." (italics added), suggesting Anne's success

## *A Closer Look*

### 7.2    Sample Stories in Response to "Anne in Medical School"

Stories were created in response to the lead, "After first term finals, Anne finds herself at the top of her medical school class."

#### *Theme: Fear of Social Rejection*

She never saw her friends, never went away. Grades may be important but what good is a good grade if the rest of your life is ruined. After finals Anne always found herself alone, no friends, nothing to do. (College woman)

Ann is an acne-faced bookworm. She runs to the bulletin board and finds she's at the top. As usual she smarts off. A chorus of groans is the rest of the class's reply. (College woman)

#### *Theme: Fear of Loss of Femininity*

Unfortunately Anne no longer feels so certain that she really wants to be a doctor. She is worried about herself and wonders if perhaps she isn't normal. . . . Anne decides not to continue

with her medical work but to take courses that have a deeper personal meaning for her.

#### *Theme: Denial of Reality*

Anne is a code name of a nonexistent person created by a group of medical students. They take turns writing exams for Anne.

#### *Sexual Themes*

There once was a girl named Ann
To make an A was her plan
This chore wasn't easy
but she was so sleazy
She laid the prof and he got queazy.
Now she got her A
And her prof got a lay
And everyone was happy I'd say.
 (College man)

Her jealous boyfriend finished lower than she did got revenge by stealing her birth control pills and Anne became a

---

is a big surprise that she has had nothing to do with. Variations in the cue reduce the incidence of FS stories. For example, when given the lead, "Judy (Joe) has finally gotten what she (he) wanted," very little negative imagery was projected by women (22%) or by men (23%). Also, there was more negative imagery in stories about Anne when she was at the top of the class *or* at the bottom of the class, with minimal negativity for being in the middle (Paludi, 1984). John ranked at the bottom of his class was seen more negatively than Anne at the bottom. Apparently, men but not women are supposed to be at the top, but neither should be at the bottom, especially men.

Perhaps the most basic criticism (in retrospect, to be sure) is the incompleteness of Horner's original design. She had women write stories about Anne and men write stories about John; both were in medical school, a traditional setting for men but not

mother. Her boyfriend caught the next bus out of town and in her great disappointment Anne dropped out of school and jumped off the Bogue St. Bridge. (College man)

She is so overwhelmed she celebrates by letting all the boys lay her as she goes on studying. The future holds for Anne that she will go from whore to prostitute. (10-year-old boy)

### Theme: Idealization of Success

Anne will get the best job in her class. She will become the first nationally recognized female neuro-surgeon. She will become the president of the American Medical Association and cure all rare and common diseases alike. (College woman)

### Theme: Success Against All Odds, Doing It Alone

Of course, Anne was thrilled. She told her boyfriend, her roommates and called her parents. After the excitement died

down she smiled at herself. Yes, she said to herself. People all told me you'll probably get married. No, she decided to forget what others said and plan ahead. I'll be that great surgeon I've always wanted to be. So Anne worked hard and became tops in her field. Despite all chauvinist people who got in her way, she made it. Anne just walked all over them.

She now knows that she's broken the hearts of her male chauvinist fellow students as well as her male chauvinist pig prof. Yea for her. She figures she'll do a fantastic job and land a good internship. And she'll do it all alone—her own perseverance will have paid off.

SOURCES: Horner, M. J. (1968, p. 105). Cited in M. A. Paludi, 1984, Psychometric properties and underlying assumptions of four objective measures of her success. *Sex Roles, 10,* 765–781. Riemer, B. S. (1975). Do women fear success as much as men fear successful women? Unpublished manuscript. Michigan State University, East Lansing, Michigan.

for women. What would happen if women wrote about John and men wrote about Anne? What if Anne and John were at the top of a nursing school class? There are two implications of these issues, namely, men's responses to a woman's success and the domain of success.

*Men's Responses to Women's Success*  If men are negative about a woman's success, perhaps a woman's FS, when it occurs, is a realistic anticipation of censure for success rather than a deep-seated fear of loss of femininity. In fact, men are very negative in their stories about a woman with acknowledged success (Monahan, Kuhn, & Shaver, 1974; Spence, 1974). Boys (10 years old) told stories about Anne with clear hostility, often with rather bizarre deaths and sexual themes. Strange catastrophes caused Anne's

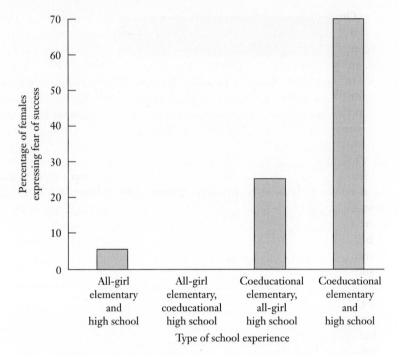

**Figure 7.4** *Responses of female high school seniors to Anne in medical school, showing fear of success as a function of type of school.* SOURCE: Winchel, R., Fenner, D., & Shaver, P. (1974). Impact of coeducation on "fear of success" imagery expressed by male and female high school seniors. *Journal of Educational Psychology, 66,* 726–730.

death and no one went to her funeral, or Anne went from being a whore to a prostitute! (Apparently, there is an important difference between whore and prostitute to the 10-year-old boy who told the story.) College men accepted Anne reasonably well if she was married but not if she was single. The single Anne was seen as a "greasy grind" who succeeded out of loneliness, and then a disaster, illness, or accident ended her life or her career. Women also were more negative to a single than to a married woman, but they did not predict disaster for the single Anne.

Some women do experience men's negative reactions or expect to do so (Horner, 1972; Wang & Creedon, 1989; Weisfeld, Weisfeld, Warren, & Freedman, 1983). One study found that Chicana college women were distressed that their educational achievements might threaten Chicano men (Gonzalez, 1988). The specific threats women felt were that the men would exclude them from political and organizational activities and that college success would cause them to be seen as elitist by the Chicano community. African American women, while generally not as prone as white women to show FS, also have concerns about competition with men and about achievement separating them from their group (Hill, 1994). Type of elementary and high school experience also affects women's fear of success (Figure 7.4).

On the other hand, women (predominantly white) at women's colleges show less fear of success than women at coeducational colleges and universities (Winchel, Fenner, & Shaver, 1974). Women lower in FS may elect to go to women's colleges, or women's colleges may inhibit or deter the development of FS. We do know that the more male students at a college, the lower the achievement of women; and the more women faculty, the higher women's achievement (Tidball, 1973, 1976). Although we do not know the reason, applications to women's colleges have increased over recent years.

*Men's Support of Women*   Although boys and college men in research tell negative stories about a successful Anne, many men actually are supportive of women's achievement concerns (Paludi & Frankell-Hauser, 1986). Horner (1972) offered evidence from her original study not only of the inhibiting effect of women's achievement on some men but of the support (even strongly stated demands) for achievement that some men gave their special women friends—one woman expressed fear of making a C and having to explain such a low grade to her male friend. Also relevant is that fear of success in both white and African American women declines with degree of attachment to a man, from dating to being engaged to being married (Puryear & Mednick, 1974). Similarly, married women returning to college used significantly less fear of success imagery than did the younger unmarried women of typical college ages (Tomlinson-Keasey, 1974). This may be due to their greater maturity and knowing what they wanted or to being married and having a husband's support.

*Traditionality*   Successful women are not invariably seen negatively, nor is it true that successful men are never seen negatively. Just as Anne in medical school is nontraditional, so, too, is John in nursing school. Frances Cherry and Kay Deaux (1978) used a design in which both Anne and John were presented as succeeding in a traditional and untraditional area for their gender, and they had both women and men respond to both kinds of achievement for both Anne and John. Both Anne and John elicited negative imagery when they were in untraditional areas. For both women and men respondents, the least negative imagery was in stories about Anne when she was in nursing school and the greatest when she was in medical school. Similarly, John had more negative stories when he was in nursing school than medical school. Note, however, that half the men told negative stories of Anne in nursing school and nearly half (40%) about John in medical school.

More recent research supports the general finding that women in nontraditional areas are seen more negatively than those in traditional areas, while men have more latitude in occupational choices (Pfost & Fiore, 1990; Yoder & Schleicher, 1996). When Anne succeeded in electrical engineering or electronics, she was accepted as competent at the job, but she was seen as a personal and social deviate—among her deviations was not being feminine. However, John was accepted in nontraditional occupations (nursing, day care). In short, "Undergraduates expect deviation from occupational gender-types in the 1990's to be personally costly for women, but not for men" (Yoder & Schleicher, 1996, p. 171).

Differences in kinds of fear are instructive. For the nontraditional achiever (Anne in medical school, John in nursing school), the themes were fairly typical of a lonely person rejected by peers. In addition, John often was seen as in nursing school only temporarily, until he could get the background to enter medical school. Men's stories about John in medical school emphasized questioning the value of success. In one story, John became a famous doctor and went back home expecting people who had snubbed him in his youth to be impressed, "But no one gives a shit." In short, it seems that when people fear success, women fear criticism and loneliness, while men fear being ignored for success that others do not consider meaningful.

Both women and men can experience fear of success, though perhaps for different reasons. For neither, can the reasons be dismissed as "just your problem." For both, FS calls for attention not only to the social context in which the orientation to achieve develops but also to what are perceived as the consequences of success in the social environment. The next section focuses more on the social context in understanding achievement.

## *Achievement in Broader Perspective*

The basic approach to achievement motivation had a narrow beginning with respect to the kind of achievement studied and the resulting focus on men. Attention is developing now about the social context of expressing urges to achieve. How striving to achieve is expressed varies with the broad social context of the options open to women generally and with the immediate social context of an individual woman's life and her values about the options she has. The focus on social context is one way in which the psychology of women has enhanced research on achievement. Psychology of women also can be credited for an increased attention to the ways affiliation and achievement may work together. In some ways, achievement can be seen as beginning to incorporate both agentic and communal orientations.

### Environmental Options

For a long time it appeared that achievement motivation theory did not predict occupational choices for women, though it did for men. The problem was that the prevailing role norms and social structures and the many other life concerns of women were not taken into account. Sharon Rae Jenkins (1987) found that achievement motivation measured in college for women who graduated in 1967 *did* predict later achievements when the environmental context in which those women chose their careers was considered.

People high in nAch like situations in which there is a moderate probability of success, autonomy with few social demands, and quick, clear feedback about performance (Atkinson, 1981; McClelland, 1961, 1980). Bureaucratic management and entrepreneurial business provide such situations. Previously, those careers were not open to women, and because people highly motivated to achieve tend to adopt cultural standards, such women were less likely than others to seek those careers. Teaching came closer than many other occupations open to women to being attractive to highly motivated women. Teaching is not the most ideal occupation for an achiever because the

*Although some men are threatened by achievement-oriented women, many others expect women to be as motivated as they are. President Clinton clearly supports such achievement-oriented women as Hillary Rodham Clinton, Attorney General Janet Reno, and Secretary of State Madeleine Albright, shown here.*

feedback is not very clear, and there are repeated social obligations. Thus, men highly motivated to achieve were less inclined to select teaching than the comparable women, who had fewer options. Motivation to achieve measured in college did predict women's entry into teaching (acceptable to women) but not into entrepreneurial business careers (not previously acceptable for women).

However, 14 years after graduation, differences showed up between public school and college teachers, reflecting different demands and challenges of the two work settings. Many of the teachers in elementary or high schools were dissatisfied with bureaucracy limiting their autonomy and with routine, repeated success at the same teaching tasks. College teaching, which also involves repeated teaching of the same classes, allows for more creative scholarship, so that there is always room for new challenges and increasing aspirations. As predicted, both college teachers and entrepreneurial businesswomen showed a significant increase in motivation to achieve in the 14 years after college graduation and at that time were higher than other women in achievement motivation.

## The Life Course

It does not take a great deal of insight to suggest that women's need to achieve and the ways it is expressed will vary with the life course. A primary reason for this is the expectation that women will bear and raise children (Frieze, Sales, & Smith, 1991; McClelland, 1985b). For example, shortly after graduation, many women who graduated from college in the 1940s and 1950s were highly motivated to achieve (Baruch, 1967). Ten years later most were not, but the number of women with high scores increased progressively after ten years. The drop in motivation to achieve is assumed to be due to involvement in marriage and motherhood, with an increase when the children are older and the woman feels comfortable returning to her career interests. (Men have not been expected to interrupt their careers because of children.) Women age 50 and beyond often feel a renewed desire to achieve once their children leave home (Paludi & Frankell-Hauser, 1986; chapter 14).

Will the pattern of a drop before a rebound continue as careers for women become more accepted and financially necessary? Any answer is speculative. As women's careers become increasingly important to them personally, they may have a more sustained interest in achievement motivation over the childbearing years. But many will likely continue to have conflicts between career and homemaking activities (chapters 12, 13).

## Affiliation and Achievement

Traditional motivation to achieve and the agentic orientation have been associated with technological advancement (Bakan, 1966). David Bakan feared that the agentic orientation unmitigated by the communal orientation could lead to destructiveness, violence, and, ultimately, evil (chapter 3). Similarly, Janet Spence (1985) has pointed out that the individualism of the traditional models of achievement may be destructive. It may be time to temper individualistic, agentic views of achievement with more communal views. Psychologists are beginning to do this, though they have a long way to go. Much of the thinking about achievement in previous years relied on a view that affiliation and achievement were distinct classes of behavior and that, to women, affiliation was more important than achievement (Travis, Phillippi, & Henley, 1991).

Current thinking is challenging the previous logic pitting achievement against affiliation. For example, it is being increasingly acknowledged that achievement can be pursued in a variety of ways, including affiliative ways (Donelson & Gullahorn, 1977; Spence & Helmreich, 1983; Stein & Bailey, 1973; Travis et al., 1991). A possible interplay of achievement and affiliation is also shown by the fact that motivation for both achievement and affiliation may be explained by the same principles (McClelland, 1985a, 1985b; McClelland, Koestner, & Weinberger, 1989). That is, achieving in interpersonal ways may involve the same variables—aspiration, confidence, fears—as achieving in the more person-centered, entrepreneurial ways.

In the 1950s and 1960s it was popular to dismiss women's motivation to achieve as being motivation to affiliate because women were expressing achievement "only" vicariously. **Vicarious achievement** is gratification of the motive to achieve through other people. It may be that when women teach their children, they are expressing their concerns about achievement as much as their relational concerns. There clearly is reason to see African American women's efforts with their children to be a matter of expressing their achievement concerns.

Both men and women see some of their interpersonal experiences as achievement issues. Cheryl Travis and her colleagues (Travis, Burnett-Doering, & Reid, 1982; Travis, McKenzie, Wiley, & Kahn, 1988; Travis et al., 1991) used a straightforward technique of asking college students to write about something they had done in the last year that was an achievement, or to write about an event in which they fell far short of accomplishing their goals. After each story, the students rated their reported events in varying ways.

In the most recent of these studies, students rated the salience of mastery, personal, and interpersonal themes in the events they had written about (Travis et al., 1991). Mastery was defined as involving skills or tasks in the environment, such as getting grades or a job. The personal dimension involved their own feelings about themselves, their understanding of life, or the kind of person they thought they were. Interpersonal themes—such as agreement, disagreement, liking, interacting—involved relationships with another person or group of persons.

Mastery was rated as salient somewhat more often than the other themes (as one might expect for college students), but a little more than half of the reported events dealt with other themes. A sizable proportion of the events (22%) had personal or interpersonal themes stronger than mastery themes or combined mastery with interpersonal or personal themes (29%). A few events (6%) were high in all three themes. Whether the students were women or men and whether they were telling about success or failure made no significant differences. Mastery, interpersonal, and personal concerns are not antithetical but often are intertwined features of the same event.

## Some Final Thoughts: Helping Yourself and Others

As adult women or men, we cannot undo the past. We cannot turn ourselves into bloomers in the eyes of the teachers we had in our youth. Nor can we undo any parental behavior that discouraged us from trying to achieve to the best of our abilities. We *can* be aware of how the past has influenced us and acknowledge it instead of attributing our behavior to some peculiar quirk that we can do nothing about. We can choose to change.

Effective achievement efforts involve seeing a chance to use skills, aiming for realistic risks, and going for chosen goals with confidence. We can analyze our feelings and actions and try realistically to assess our strengths and weaknesses so that we may use energies more efficiently. When success happens, we can remind ourselves and others that internal attributions are appropriate: "You got a 4.0 on the project because you have the required ability and you worked well in using your talents." Many people have trouble claiming success for themselves, but just getting them to say that they do deserve credit is a start. Encourage yourself and your friends to say that the success was deserved.

Looking at the social context is important in understanding achievement motivation. Is acceptance dependent on being a success? If so, fear of failure may undermine achievement efforts. Are there disadvantages to succeeding? If so, fear of success may undermine achievement efforts. In either case, a woman may choose to keep interpersonal relationships foremost; the important thing is that she choose with awareness of what she is doing. As we have seen, women are more likely than men to have been discouraged in their achievement: They are given messages that they are not expected to achieve, and they are allowed to act on their fear of failure.

Many women have achieved in societally recognized ways, though the number is far less than it should be, and the achievements of many women have been devalued and made at great personal cost. The future looks more positive, as psychologists are coming to recognize that affiliative concerns are relevant to achievement. Perhaps leaders in the workplace may do so as well. More careers are opening up to women (chapter 13), giving women a better chance to choose a career suitable to them. We can predict that this will be beneficial to the development of women's general instrumental or agentic orientation without detriment to expressive, communal concerns. As women become more vocal on the job about their family concerns, men may become more vocal as well, resulting in a tempering of agentic and communal concerns for both women and men.

## KEY TERMS

achievement motivation, nAch

Thematic Apperception Test (TAT)

projective instrument

hope of success (HS)

level of aspiration (LOA or LA)

social comparison

attribution

internal attribution (ability and effort)

external attribution (task and luck)

stable attribution (ability, task)

unstable attribution (effort, luck)

hope of failure (HF)

fear of failure (FF)

fear of success (FS or FOS)

verbal lead

vicarious achievement

## KEY POINTS

*Foundations of Achievement Motivation*

◆ The school environment is not as beneficial for girls as for boys. Girls' esteem decreases through the elementary school years, with larger decreases for whites and Hispanics than for African Americans. The decrease continues into college.

◆ Parents generally value achievements for sons and daughters but have higher expectations and provide more independence and mastery training for sons than for daughters.

### Components of Effective Achievement

- Even when they perform at the same or better levels, girls and women tend to have less confidence than boys and men. Women's self-confidence is not lower than men's when the task is not considered masculine, when there is no social comparison, and when there is unambiguous feedback about previous performance.

- Men tend to use ability to explain success, while women tend to use luck to explain success. Men explain failure as the consequence of lack of effort, and women explain it as owing to the difficulty of the task.

- Other people attribute the success of white men to their ability (even on feminine tasks) and the success of other groups to effort and luck. Women's failure is attributed to their lack of ability and men's to the difficulty of the task.

- College women's responses to feedback are more straightforward, while men tend to show a reaction of self-enhancement. The difference is thought due to childhood experiences of feedback.

- Girls and women are more anxious about failure than are boys and men, in part because they have less encouragement to master their fears. FF affects traditional women's activities as well as their efforts to achieve. FF may develop when children are not rewarded for meeting high parental standards but punished when they do not.

- Horner developed the concept of FS as a relatively stable attribute of personality that leads women to avoid success for fear of losing femininity or of being rejected socially. Her claims have been criticized in several ways.

- Both women and men respond negatively to a verbal lead about a successful woman or man in a nontraditional field. Negativity about a woman is expressed in terms of rejection, while men express negativity about men's success in terms of meaninglessness.

### Achievement in Broad Perspective

- Motivation to achieve predicts women's occupational achievement when social context is considered. Women's achievement motivation has decreased after college graduation and then risen as women get more freedom from family responsibilities. Predictions about whether this will continue in the future are unclear.

- The need to achieve can be expressed in many ways, including personal and interpersonal ways.

## INTEGRATIVE QUESTIONS

1. Considering each of the major components of achievement motivation, discuss how women's tendencies might be explained by early experience with teachers and parents and with other children. Are adults stuck with the effects of their early experience?

2. How are your aims to achieve and your methods of action similar to or different from those of your parents? What differences do you see between each of your parents and yourself in the broad social context and in particular experiences you have had?

3. What area of research about effective achievement is most personally relevant to you in helping you understand something about yourself? Why? Consider any relevant background experiences. What would you like to change and how do you think you can?

4. It is suggested that women may deliberately understate the confidence they feel. Discuss why you think they might do that and the possible implications of women's actions. Do men ever do the same?

5. Take any one example of a personal or an interpersonal event you have experienced and illustrate how HS, HF, FF, and FS may have affected your thoughts and actions. How are the components of effective achievement relevant to your striving in other domains?

*Chapter 8*

# Development of Cognitive Abilities and Moral Reasoning in Women

Girls and women get many messages about their bodies and about their opportunities and chances of achieving. Interwoven with these are specific views about what their brains are capable of—an issue of the development of cognitive abilities. If girls and women were thought mentally able, perhaps their bodies would not be emphasized so much, and their desires to achieve would be taken more seriously. Without a certain level of cognitive ability, achievement is difficult. But without a certain level of concern about achievement, the growing child has reduced incentive to develop cognitive skills. With generally negative messages about competence, there is reduced desire to develop abilities and the achievement skills to use them well. Because gender issues intensify during adolescence, it is a time when young women's views about their bodies, their general competence, and their cognitive abilities are particularly vulnerable.

Cognitive abilities have practical as well as theoretical implications—from who does what around the house to who is offered scholarships and the best career choices to how psychologists understand human development. For example, assumptions about women's abilities are associated with many everyday tasks and influence judgments about who is "supposed" to do what (e.g., "that's a woman's job, this is a man's job"). The everyday jobs include assembling a do-it-yourself bookcase and calling Uncle Frank to explain why he was not told of the family dinner. They include making decisions about who is best able to get the suitcases and other vacation paraphernalia in the car and how to rearrange the room, as well as who will soothe the neighbors' feelings about a recent feud. Personal confidence in doing these things is related to self-concept and to interactions with others. Some tasks, of course, are occupational ones, so that assumptions about women's abilities also have long-term practical implications. Claims of women's deficiencies in some abilities have been used to justify discouraging young women from preparing for, and being hired for, some prestigious occupations.

Gender differences in cognitive abilities, however, typically are fairly small. Nevertheless, they are often exaggerated in professional publications and the public media and are carelessly treated (Grady, 1981). Indeed, some feminist psychologists argue that sex differences in cognitive abilities are not worth attending to (Unger & Crawford, 1989). There are also stereotypes about the cognitive abilities associated with moral reasoning. Claims have been made about women's moral inferiority to men, and some psychological research, later criticized, has seemed to support those claims.

In this chapter we look first at some general principles of thinking about ability differences using the more familiar area of physical abilities. Next we consider evidence about verbal differences, in which girls are assumed superior, and nonverbal and mathematical abilities, in which boys are assumed superior. We look at evidence about environmental and social contributors and practical problems of measuring the abilities. We end with an exploration of moral reasoning.

Before continuing, consider these questions for personal thought:

- What kinds of subjects were you good at and not so good at during early school years? Were there any changes as you progressed through school? How are your college major and career plans related to your past performance in school?

- What kinds of subjects did your parents and teachers expect you to be good at? Not so good? Did their thoughts matter to you?

- What kinds of toys and activities did you like when you were a child? Is that relevant to the kinds of abilities you excel in or do not excel in now?

- Complete the following sentences and think about why you completed them as you did.

  "Girls are good in math and science when . . ."

  "Boys are good in reading and writing when . . ."

- Do you see any reason to think that people generally see women as less moral than men? Why?

- Describe a situation in which you felt you faced a moral dilemma—you were in a tough bind and didn't know quite what to do. How did you resolve it?

- Describe a situation in which a man said one thing was the right thing to do and a woman said that another thing was right. Why do you think they had different views?

## Thinking About Differences in Abilities

In considering abilities, it is important to keep in mind that although averages of groups of females and males may differ statistically, the difference may not be large, and there is always variability around the mean (average). Some people in the low scoring group probably score above the average of the high scoring group, and some people of the high scoring group probably score below the average of the low scoring group. Comparing height provides a simple example: The average man is taller than the average woman, but some women are taller than the average man, and some men are shorter than the average woman.

The study of gender differences took a new turn with the publication of a book by Eleanor Maccoby and Carolyn Jacklin in 1974, *The Psychology of Sex Differences.* Although faulty in some ways (e.g., see Block, 1976; Caplan, 1979; Tieger, 1980), the book awakened psychologists' interest in gender differences. It also set a "minimalist" tone, namely, emphasizing lack of gender differences. There is some speculation (e.g., see Hyde & Linn, 1988) that since the publication of the book, research findings of no difference between the sexes have not gone to the file drawer (chapter 1), as they might have previously, but have been sent to journals and published. Thus, some studies discussed in this chapter are considered by date of publication, as before or after 1974. One kind of criticism of Maccoby and Jacklin's gigantic work involved disagreement with their frequent conclusion of lack of gender difference. However, when there are many studies on an issue and the studies are not always consistent, it is not easy to come up with a conclusion that all will agree with. Since Maccoby and Jacklin's work, meta-analysis has been developed in an attempt to deal with this issue.

## Meta-Analysis

**Meta-analysis** is an objective statistical technique for combining the results from many studies and arriving at an index of the overall or average size of the difference between groups. Some methodologists consider it a necessary step in the advancement of scientific understanding (Hedges & Becker, 1986; Schmidt, 1992). One frequently used index is *d,* which is the difference between two means ($Ma$, $Mb$) divided by the average standard deviation ($s$) of the two groups. *d* tells us how big the difference between the two groups is relative to the variability or spread of scores:

$$d = \frac{(Ma - Mb)}{s}$$

The *d* for each of the studies available is calculated, and the average is then taken. One common convention for evaluating *d* is to consider a *d* of .20 small, a *d* of .50 moderate, and a *d* of .80 large (Cohen, 1988). For purposes of comparison, *d* for gender differences in height is 2.60. Most *d*s for psychological attributes do not approach that level. In this text, $+d$ is used for women having a higher score and $-d$ for men having a higher score; be warned, however, that other works often use a $-d$ to note that females have a higher score.

The development of meta-analysis has been very helpful in providing reminders that the differences that intrigue psychologists and the media often are not very large (Hyde, 1994). Some caution is in order, however (Caplan & Caplan, 1994; Unger & Crawford, 1989). Reviewers still must use judgment in selecting studies and deciding whether different operational definitions (chapter 1) are measuring the same construct. It is possible to group apples and oranges together and not see patterns that may exist either among the apples or among the oranges.

*Being a surgeon requires fine motor skills, something at which women usually excel. However, women's talents in this area are more often channeled into clerical work than into surgery.*

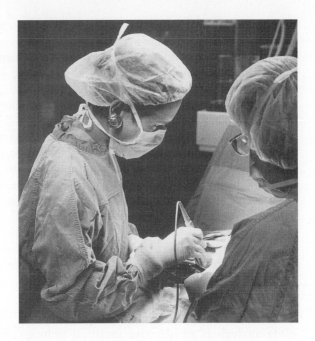

The overall *d* in verbal abilities, for example, may hide the fact that there are differences at some ages but not at others, or for some measures of the ability but not for others. Tests of consistency (homogeneity) can show when the studies grouped together differ from each other in important ways, so that the overall *d* is suspect (Hedges & Becker, 1986). If there are enough studies, the reviewer may be able to make finer distinctions between them. For some areas, it is possible to give an overall *d*, often a small one, and then give larger ones for particular ages, for example.

Let us look quickly at some information on physical abilities to illustrate the principles of thinking about ability differences. These more concrete, familiar examples will provide a foundation for considering some of the cognitive abilities that are a major focus of the chapter.

## Motor Skills

Often, what is called a skill or ability really is a collection of specific skills or abilities, or a family, in which the skills have distinct differences as well as a broad family resemblance that is not always well defined (Caplan & Caplan, 1994). For example, motor skills include skills involving gross movements, large muscle strength, and speed, on the one hand, and finger dexterity and fine motor coordination, on the other. Men generally are better in the former and women in the latter. Finger dexterity and fine motor coordination are needed in sewing and typing, but they are also relevant in surgery. There often is biased interpretation about the implications of actual or presumed differences.

The size of differences in a general skill area varies depending, first, on the specific skill assessed and, second, on the age of the people studied (Linn & Hyde, 1989). For example, $d = -.09$ for the motor skill of balance, while $d = -2.18$ for throwing velocity at age 3 years. For running the 50-yard dash, $d = -.63$ for all ages, but $d = -2.5$ for adolescents and older people. Third, the difference in some abilities varies over time. Male Olympic swimmers are faster than females when compared within the same year, but the record performance of women in 1960 was faster than that of men in 1912. Both men and women have been swimming faster than they used to, but the women have improved more than the men, so that the difference between the women's and men's records has gotten smaller. Now, let us look at a little history before our discussion of specific cognitive abilities.

## Stereotypes in Science

Historically, scientists often have used the cause of objective science in very subjective ways, namely to perpetuate stereotypes. As discussed in chapter 1, science is not free of values. Although science today is less blatantly biased than in the past, there is continuing reason for concern.

Throughout much of Western history, women and people of color have been stereotyped as less intelligent than white men (chapter 1). In the last century, researchers tried to claim biological evidence of white men's superiority by pointing out that women's brains and those of people of color are smaller than white men's brains (Bleier, 1991; Gould, 1980; Russett, 1989; Shields, 1982). Then they realized that if intelligence is only a matter of brain size, elephants would be much more intelligent than white men! Researchers shifted attention to the size of the brain relative to body size. This effort backfired because they found women's brains were actually relatively larger than men's. Concern shifted again, this time to size differences in specific parts of the brain, but that approach gave a hodgepodge of results (Shields, 1975).

In yet another attempt to show white men's biological superiority, the variability hypothesis was introduced. The hypothesis said that men were more variable in intelligence than women so it was understandable that many men were brighter than the average woman. The flip side—that there were a lot of men who were markedly less intelligent than women—was virtually ignored. Although interest in the variability hypothesis diminished, the hypothesis has been continually lurking in research (Shields, 1982).

The measurement of intelligence in a scientific way got off the ground with the pioneering work of Alfred Binet and Theodore Simon in France, who developed the Binet-Simon intelligence test in 1905. The interest in their work spread to the United States, and in 1916 Lewis Terman developed an American version of the test, the Stanford-Binet Scale. At the time, women's issues were in public consciousness because of the issue of women's voting, so intelligence tests were developed to avoid favoritism to men. The tradition of gender fairness has been maintained, and the tests generally are free of gender bias (Dwyer, 1979; Halpern, 1992; Singleton, 1987). Unfortunately, there was no such public consciousness about ethnic differences, so the tests are not equally fair to all ethnic groups; work continues on that problem (Helms, 1992).

## *Verbal Abilities*

Girls and women have been assumed better than boys and men at verbal skills and better at those skills than at other skills (Matlin & Matkoski, 1985). When it was acknowledged that women might be superior in this respect, the suspected superiority was translated into negative interpretations. In the 19th century, women's use of words was seen as responsible for their nearly pathological tendency for lying! People today do not seem to see women as better liars than men, but myths of the past have a way of being translated into current acceptability (chapter 6). A result is dismissal of women's verbal ability into an assumption that women talk more and are more gossipy than men (Caplan & Caplan, 1994). In fact, men actually talk more than women (chapter 9).

## What the Differences Are in Verbal Abilities

The overall gender difference in verbal skills shown by meta-analysis is very small ($d = .11$) and has diminished over recent years (for studies published in 1973 or before, $d = .23$ versus $d = .10$ for later studies) (Hyde, 1994; Hyde & Linn, 1988). Because of variation in the measuring instruments, it is unclear whether the smaller difference in recent years means that males' skills have increased or that females' skills have decreased; some relevant issues will be addressed later. Alternatively, reduction in the file-drawer effect may be responsible.

The size of the difference depends on the specific verbal ability and the age being considered, apart from date of publication (Table 8.1). However, for some specific skills, there are significant differences among the studies that are not accounted for (there is not **homogeneity**). For example, although differences are not large for vocabulary overall, there are differences favoring girls (aged 6 to 10 years, $d = .26$) and young women (aged 19 to 25 years, $d = .23$).

Because they were trying to get general indices, the meta-analysts (Hyde & Linn, 1988) excluded studies of problems in verbal functioning, such as stuttering and dyslexia; males predominate in those studies (Halpern, 1986, 1989). They also excluded studies using the Scholastic Aptitude Test (SAT), for reasons discussed later, and studies of children under 3 years of age.

There are important differences in the younger years and among cultures in ways not yet well depicted by meta-analyses. Girls have a developmental head start in verbal skills (Harris, 1977; Huttenlocher, Haight, Bryk, Seltzer, & Lyons, 1991). They speak sooner and more clearly and, at 18 months, have a larger vocabulary. At about 4 years of age, girls use tenses correctly and use complex constructions such as passive voice; boys take another one or two years to catch up in these areas. Unless they are in underprivileged environments, boys generally start to match girls in late childhood, at ages 11 to 14 years.

Girls read earlier and more thoroughly, though the pattern after early years varies some with age of the children (Harris, 1977) and with the culture (Lummis & Stevenson, 1990). In samples of children in the United States, Taiwan, and Japan, girls in kindergarten and first grade (but not fifth grade) were significantly higher than boys

**Table 8.1**   Gender Differences for Selected Verbal Abilities as a
Function of Age

| Age | All tests | Vocabulary | Reading |
|---|---|---|---|
| 5 years and younger | .13 | .07 | .31 |
| 6–10 years | .06 | .26 | .09 |
| 11–18 years | .11 | .01 | .02 |
| 19–23 years | .06 | .23 | −.03 |
| 26+ years | .20 | .05 | NA |

NOTE: Positive *d*s denote females higher than males; NA = not available.

SOURCE: Hyde, J. S., & Linn, M. C. (1988). Gender differences in verbal ability: A meta-analysis. *Psychological Bulletin, 104*, 53–69. Their Table 6, page 61.

on reading, reading vocabulary, and reading comprehension. More boys than girls are considered to have reading problems and are referred to reading clinics (Finucci & Childs, 1981; Hyde & Linn, 1988; Skinner & Shelton, 1985), but this difference may not be due to boys' greater reading problems. When children were classified as having a reading problem on the basis of a reading score in the bottom 7% for their IQ level, about equal numbers of boys and girls were so classified (Shaywitz, Shaywitz, Fletcher, & Escobar, 1990). Teachers may notice boys with reading problems because of the boys' high activity level and low attentiveness. Girls with reading problems may be neglected because they are quiet, obedient, and compliant, as they are expected to be (chapter 7).

Fewer studies are done on writing ability than reading ability because writing is not easily susceptible to objective testing formats. However, one large-scale five-year study of writing samples of more than 40,000 students from five continents did show that girls get more encouragement in writing and do write better than boys.

## Explanations for the Differences

***Socialization Factors***   Several socialization features clearly contribute to verbal performance. The self-fulfilling prophecy (chapter 2) comes into play here. Children's views about what is acceptable for them influences what they do and who they become. In the United States and some other countries (e.g., Taiwan, Japan), words are seen as feminine (Lummis & Stevenson, 1990). Who teaches reading is a signal to children about the appropriateness of reading for them. In the United States and Canada, girls tend to be better in reading than boys and usually have women teachers. In contrast, in countries where children have men as teachers, such as England, Germany, and Nigeria, boys are equal to or better than girls in reading (Finn, 1980; Johnson, 1973–1974; Nash, 1979). Similarly, the sex of the person giving a reading test is important (Nash, 1979; Shinedling & Pedersen, 1970). In the United States, there are boys who consider reading masculine, and they score higher in reading achievement than do other boys. What it amounts to is that each gender does well when they think it is OK for them to do so. This is a message encountered in the chapter on achievement (chapter 7).

Unfortunately, girls may increasingly think that achievement is inappropriate for them even in the world of words, in which they are expected to be comfortable and competent. Working with longitudinal data, Kathryn Wentzel (1988) found a previously unreported decline from Grade 6 through Grade 10 in girls' standardized test scores (Stanford Achievement Test) in English as well as in mathematics; their classroom grades did not vary with grade level. Boys scored lower than girls on both grades and on standardized tests and did not show systematic changes over grades. Previous researchers had used only cross-sectional samples, showing the expected verbal superiority of girls, and could not see the decline over the grades in girls' performance on standardized tests—girls' scores decreased but still were higher than the boys'. The girls' lack of decline in course grades may be due to their greater comfort with familiar situations relative to novel ones and to a greater caution of girls in taking tests on unfamiliar material. Wentzel maintains that different goals are being tapped by class grades and standardized tests; classroom achievement may reflect social skills and compliance. Could it be that girls see good class performance as OK for them, but "really being smart" is not? Remember also the pressures on adolescent girls, as discussed in previous chapters (chapters 5, 6, 7).

***Biological Explanations*** As yet, biological explanations for differences in verbal abilities, by themselves, are strained, incomplete, and inconsistent. However, some interesting leads and speculations are worth considering (see Caplan, MacPherson, & Tobin, 1985; Halpern, 1986, 1992; Sherman, 1978). Julia Sherman proposed the **Bent Twig hypothesis,** which says that girls get off to a head start that is responsible for any later ability differences. Its name comes from the saying "As the twig is bent, so grows the tree." The head start may be due to more rapid maturation of girls or other biological reasons, or to maternal expectations and encouragement, or to both kinds of factors. (In chapter 4 we saw that adults may respond to and exaggerate biological predispositions of infants.) Whatever the reason, there is a higher verbal interaction between mother and daughter than between mother and son, and girls are more responsive to verbally provided comfort than are boys (chapter 4). Furthermore, when children are toddlers, parents encourage more discussion from daughters than sons about recent events, such as a trip to the zoo (Reese & Fivush, 1993). Thus girls may build up a more positive response to words that leads them to develop a general verbal style of interacting with the world.

Suspected differences in brain lateralization (chapter 4) have been a popular explanation for ability differences. The left hemisphere has been thought more efficient than the right for language functions. Thus, one speculation is that the left hemisphere may develop earlier in female than male infants, giving girls an edge, so that they use language more in processing information (Kimura, 1985; Levy & Reid, 1978; Buffery & Gray, 1972). This could be a reason for the earlier start assumed in the Bent Twig hypothesis. In this biological view, boys develop language ability later than other cognitive abilities so are more susceptible to language disorders.

A competing lateralization approach maintains that females and left-handed males are more likely than right-handed men to be *bilateral* for verbal functions (Levy,

1972; Levy & Sperry, 1970). Evidence both supports and challenges this view (Kimura, 1985, 1987). Recent evidence with advanced technology has indicated that women do process verbal information (analyzing words) more in the right hemisphere, whereas men rely more on the left hemisphere. There is the additional complication that gender differences are much smaller among people with higher verbal IQs (Ojemann, in Gorman, 1992). Obviously, there is more work to be done, and the answers that emerge are not likely to be simple ones.

## Changes Over the Years: The SAT-Verbal

Whatever the reason for differences, small as they are, the issue of diminution in differences over the years has yet to be explained. One potential reason is the fact that the school environment and our culture generally are highly verbal. Whatever biological edge girls might have for verbal material, the environment can compensate for in boys and may have been doing so increasingly. Public school instruction has been highly verbal, giving boys a boost to overcome whatever biological deficiencies they have. "Biological differences" and their implications are not fixed and unaffected by the environment. However, it is unlikely that biological factors can account for the changes in the overall size of $d$ for verbal abilities over the recent years—brains do not evolve quickly.

The SAT-Verbal figures prominently in discussions of changes in gender differences in verbal ability because of its practical importance in decisions about college admission and because gender differences on it have been reversing since 1972, now slightly favoring males ($d = -.11$) (Hyde & Linn, 1988). At least two factors must be considered: test content and who is tested. First, beginning in the early 1970s, when the women's advantage on the verbal section began to wane, adjustments were being made on exam content (Rosser, 1989a, 1989b). Questions on which girls outscored boys were dropped, and questions with science-oriented content were added; the stated aim was to obtain a better balance of scores between the sexes (AAUW, 1992; Mensh & Mensh, 1991).

Second, the sample tested on the SAT is not representative and is biased against women (Halpern, 1989; Hyde & Linn, 1988; Landers, 1989). The SAT is taken by high school seniors who aspire to college in the immediate future. Results cannot be considered generalizable to all young men and women aged about 17 years, or even to all high school students. The less able young people are underrepresented, and these are more likely to be boys than girls: More boys than girls have been put in special classes and are not part of the academic mainstream, and more boys than girls drop out of school because of cultural pressures and perhaps differential job opportunities.

Women who are less prepared have been increasingly likely to take the SAT over the last few decades (Halpern, 1989). They are from families with lower parental income and paternal education and are less likely to attend private school (Ramist & Arbeiter, 1986). Also, more women than men in middle-adult years are likely to be returning to college. They have been out of school for years and are not used to taking timed tests such as the SAT. In short, to draw conclusions from SAT scores (or simply to include them in meta-analyses) is to compare a wide spectrum of young women against a narrower and more selective array of young men.

The gender differences on the SAT are not large. However, they should be considered in terms of their effects, not merely their size (Eagly, 1995; Sadker & Sadker, 1994). Considering the thousands of students involved and the many organizations using tests to award scholarships, the small differences translate into many dollars in scholarship awards across the nation, with young women winning fewer of the dollars than young men do and being more often excluded from elite schools (Rosser, 1987, 1989a, 1989b; Sadker & Sadker, 1994; Verhovek, 1990). When Regents scholarships in New York were based only on the SAT, more than half the awards went to men; when the criterion was changed to one based on both the SAT and class grades, more than half the awards went to women. Yet, the more prestigious Empire State scholarships, requiring higher SAT scores, are given to more boys than girls (Verhovek, 1990). Small differences can translate into big dollars.

In addition, there is the incalculable price of young women's diminished self-esteem, lower career goals, and reduced opportunities in special programs and select colleges (Rosser, 1992). Women can be the losers even when differences are small. A federal court now has ruled that the use of the SAT for awarding scholarships discriminates against girls because it underestimates how well they will do in college (Mensh & Mensh, 1991).

## *Nonverbal Abilities*

While better verbal skills have been associated with women, better nonverbal skills have been associated with men. Public schools have gone to some lengths to compensate for boys' presumed lesser verbal skills but, so far, have not compensated as well for girls' presumed lesser skills in nonverbal ability. As with verbal skills, the size of gender differences is minimal, but the differences can have important implications. As with verbal skills, the exact size of gender differences varies with the specific member of the family of skills. We will look first at a nonverbal skill on which women are superior.

### Perceptual Speed

The general rule that men typically are better than women in nonverbal abilities has one exception. **Perceptual speed** is the ability to pick up details quickly, to shift attention easily, and to compare what is with what should be. Girls exceed boys in this ability by age 5 years, and the difference remains throughout life (Antill & Cunningham, 1982; Feingold, 1988; Gainer, 1962; Miele, 1958). It is difficult to imagine that the difference is due to 5-year-old girls having had more practice than boys with activities relevant to this ability. Males' performance can be improved with training, but females given equal training also improve (Longstaff, 1954).

There is not so much research on this ability as on other abilities. Considering an example of a test that measures this ability (A Closer Look 8.1), you may see that it seems relevant to clerical skills. Surgeons, air traffic controllers, and editors also require the ability. But the "pull" to clerical work has been so strong that perceptual speed has been considered of little social relevance (to people who do not realize how

### A Closer Look

**8.1   Sample Items and Instructions From a Test of Perceptual Speed**

*Instructions:* Compare each line of the COPY at the bottom of the page with the corresponding line of the ORIGINAL at the top. Each *word* or *abbreviation* or *digit* in the copy that is not exactly the same as in the original is one error. In each line, mark every word or abbreviation or figure that is wrong. Then count the errors you have marked in the line and enter the total number in the column at the right. The first line has been done correctly to show you just how to mark and where to enter the total number of errors in the line. Work quickly and accurately.

**ORIGINAL**

| Name | Address | Amount |
|------|---------|--------|
| Dr. Jane Frazier | Madison, Ind. | $7385.96 |
| Mr. Michael Crane | Atlanta, Ga. | 1435.64 |
| Dr. Frank Thompson | Troy, N. Y. | 2537.96 |
| Miss Mary James | Washington, Conn. | 4994.73 |

**COPY**

| Name | Address | Amount | Number of Errors |
|------|---------|--------|------------------|
| Miss Jane Frasier | Madison, Wis. | $7358.96 | 5 |
| Dr. Michael Crane | Atalanta, Ga. | 1434.54 | ____ |
| Dr. Frank Thomson | Troy, N. J. | 2538.96 | ____ |
| Mrs. Marie Jones | Washington, Conn. | 4884.73 | ____ |

SOURCE: General Clerical Test 1944, 1971, 1969. The Psychological Corporation New York. By permission.

much of their lives depends on people with clerical skills). We do not have enough information to generate a meta-analysis or to suggest why the difference exists. In contrast, there is abundant research on spatial skills, on which more men than women characteristically excel.

## Spatial Abilities

More males than females score high on measures of the nonverbal abilities termed spatial skills, and the measured gender differences tend to be larger than for other

The test below is made up of pictures of blocks turned different ways. The block at the left is the reference block and the five blocks to the right are the answer blocks. One of these five blocks is the same as the reference block except that it has been turned and is seen from a different point of view. The other four blocks could not be obtained by turning the reference block. For example:

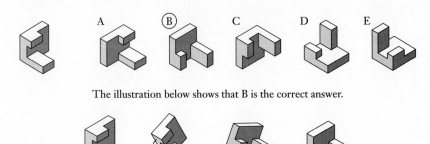

The illustration below shows that B is the correct answer.

**Figure 8.1** *Sample item from a spatial ability test*   SOURCE: Stafford, R. E. (1962). Identical blocks, form AA.

kinds of abilities; the differences generally emerge in adolescence (Cohen & Wilkie, 1979; Halpern, 1992; McGee, 1979; Petersen, 1980). This generalization is most safely made about white people (e.g., see Baughman & Dahlstrom, 1968), though it may apply to other groups as well. Spatial abilities are considered significantly related to high prestige occupations, such as engineering, architecture, and art.

It is somewhat difficult to define spatial abilities in words because spatial abilities are not about words (Caplan & Caplan, 1994). **Spatial abilities** are concerned with thinking about space: They involve the internal reflection of space in thought, or the effective perception and processing of information about objects and their spatial relationships. Spatial abilities deal with nonlinguistic information (Linn & Petersen, 1985). Among everyday examples of spatial abilities are aiming at a target, arranging objects in a specified pattern, imagining how an object would appear if rotated, having a good sense of direction, and trying to fit everything in a car trunk for a vacation when everyone is taking more than needed. They are related also to putting the right wires in the right holes when hooking up the new TV and VCR or CD player, and how the living room would look if the furniture were rearranged.

*Mental Rotation*   Spatial abilities are a family of abilities, and the size of gender differences varies with the specific ability (Voyer, Voyer, & Bryden, 1995). The largest difference is for the visualization task of mental rotation. **Mental rotation** requires turning a two- or three-dimensional object around mentally, imagining how the object would look if rotated (Figure 8.1) (Kimura, 1992). Although the overall $d$ is relatively large ($d = -.73$), there is marked variation from specific test to test (Linn & Petersen, 1986). One task, involving three-dimensional rotation, produces the largest effect ($d = -.94$; Vandenberg version of the Shepard-Metzler mental rotation task); differences are smaller for other tasks ($d = -.26$).

The male advantage is apparent by about age 10 years, the earliest age the ability has been measured reliably (Johnson & Meade, 1987). The high level of concentration required makes it difficult to measure younger children, though it may be that psychologists have not been clever enough to devise valid tests for younger children. Some researchers think that mental rotation is the only kind of spatial ability with enough gender difference to be concerned about. Even women who are good at mental rotation are slower than men (Gallagher, 1989); the greater the rotation required, the greater the time differential (Focus on Research 8.1). Women's scores increase with training, as do men's.

*Spatial Perception*    The next largest difference in spatial abilities occurs for **spatial perception,** which requires locating the horizontal or vertical in spite of distracting information. The principal measure of spatial perception is Herman Witkin's **Rod and Frame test (RFT)** (Figure 8.2, p. 274; Witkin et al., 1954). Subjects sit in a dark room and have the task of adjusting a luminous rod to an erect position. The trick is that the rod is embedded in a luminous frame, which is tilted at varying angles. To the extent that the subject can ignore the distracting frame and set the rod to vertical, she or he is considered **field independent.** If the subject is relatively inaccurate in setting the rod to the vertical, being more influenced by the frame (the field in which the focal figure is situated), she or he is said to be **field dependent.** The Embedded Figures test (EFT) (Witkin, Ottman, Raskin, & Karp, 1971) is a paper-and-pencil test designed as an analogue for the RFT, though the EFT and RFT are not necessarily highly correlated.

The overall $d$ is near moderate ($d = -.44$), but there are important age variations that show an increasing difference with increasing age (Voyer, Voyer, & Bryden, 1995). The gender difference is somewhat less for groups under 12 years of age and for groups 12 to 17 years of age (for both, $d = -.37$), but $d = -.64$ for people over 18 years of age (Linn & Petersen, 1986).

Is it fair to women to say that they are field dependent? First, consider the measurement situation. A woman is led into a dark room, most likely by a male experimenter, and does less well than a man (Haaken, 1988; Sherman, 1978). Then, consider the name. *Dependency* connotes a deficiency, although in his later writings, Witkin (1979) has pointed out that some situations are better approached with a dependent than an independent style. Dependency on the field could be translated accurately as sensitivity to the field. Women could be said to be more *field sensitive* and men more *field insensitive.* Concern about the terminology is not limited to feminists; some neuropsychologists not identified with feminism prefer this terminology (L. J. Harris, 1995, personal communication).

*Spatial Visualization*    The final spatial ability to cover is the one with the smallest gender difference ($d = -.13$) of the three major spatial skills (Linn & Petersen, 1986), and the differences have diminished since 1974 ($d = -.30$ for studies before 1974; $d = -.13$ for later studies). It is called **spatial visualization** and is thought to require both verbal and nonverbal strategies. The **Hidden Figure test (HFT)** is a leading measure. The task is to find an object hidden in a complex scene. There seems to have

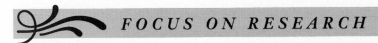

**FOCUS ON RESEARCH**

### 8.1    Interaction Effects: Spatial Abilities Differ in Different Situations

It's a scene right out of the *Twilight Zone*. One average man and one average woman, trapped in a car. He's behind the wheel, she's holding the map. They turn right, left, right again, then turn and retrace their route. Faintly you can hear them:

HE:    This road won't get us to the restaurant. We need to be traveling perpendicular to Main Street.

SHE:    Just wait a minute, I'm all turned around. This map is so disorienting!

Are they caught in a sexist time and motion vortex? Hardly. They're just illustrating the average sex difference in mental rotation, a subset of spatial ability.

Finding a sex difference doesn't mean all members of one gender are whizzes on an ability while all the members of the other gender are hopeless at it. Instead, it means that *on average* one gender will score higher than the other in that domain. Mental rotation tests show a consistent sex difference, with men performing better than women, and this difference is large relative to differences on other spatial abilities. Mental rotation ability appears to be related to the brain organization triggered by prenatal hormones, but is it possible that social factors play a role in this ability? Children do absorb gender stereotypes as they develop and learn what is expected and appropriate for their gender. Such expectations may push boys and men toward developing their mental rotation ability at the same time they inhibit girls and women in this area.

A factorial research design was the approach used by researchers Matthew Sharps, Jana Price, and John Williams (1994) to study this issue. In a factorial design, two or more independent variables, or factors, are completely *crossed*, so that each level of one variable is combined with each level of all the other variables. In Sharps, Price, and Williams's study, the two independent variables were the gender of the participant and the gender stereotyped occupational setting of the mental rotation task (the feminine setting discussed the use of mental rotation in handicrafts and interior decoration and design, while the masculine setting stressed mental rotation in flying military aircraft, navigating naval vessels, and engineering aircraft and propulsion systems).

Factorial designs provide information about the effect of each independent variable alone, called a main effect, and information about the effect of a variable when another variable is present, called an interaction. An interaction exists if the effect of a variable changes when a second variable is present. We might find, for instance, that women perform mental rotation tasks equally well in both gender stereotyped occupational settings, but men perform better in a masculine setting. The existence of an interaction means that we must qualify what we say about a variable. Does the occupational setting make a difference in mental rotation performance? It depends. If the person doing the task is a woman, then no. But if it is a man, the occupational setting influences his performance.

Going back to Sharps, Price, and Williams's experiment, let's see what they did and what they found. Forty college students, 20 women and 20 men, participated. Ten women and 10 men were randomly assigned to the stereotypically masculine occupational setting, while the other half of the female and male participants were assigned to the stereotypically feminine occupational setting. Since the two independent variables both have two categories or levels (participant gender: female, male; occupational setting: masculine, feminine), this specific design layout is referred to as a 2 × 2 (read that "two by two"). This design appears in schematic form below. Each of the four boxes, or cells, contains dependent variable scores from 10 different participants. In this study, the dependent variable is performance on the mental rotation test, so each cell contains 10 of these scores. Basically, the researchers average these 10 scores and compare the four cell averages to see how the independent variables affect the dependent variable.

|  | Gender Stereotypical Occupation | |
|  | Masculine | Feminine |
|---|---|---|
| Participant Gender — Female | | |
| Participant Gender — Male | | |

In their analysis, Sharps and his associates found one main effect and an interaction. There was a main effect of gender, which means that regardless of the occupational setting, women and men performed differently on the test of mental rotation. Not surprisingly, given what we know about gender differences on this ability, the men scored higher than the women. There was no main effect of occupational setting; that is, there wasn't any difference in the performance of the participants assigned to the feminine versus the masculine occupational setting. While the presence or absence of main effects is interesting, it is the interaction that grabs our attention, for here we can see how the two independent variables work in tandem. This study's interaction indicates that men's and women's mental rotation performance differs depending on occupational setting. For women, performance was basically the same in the masculine and feminine settings. But men performed better in the masculine setting than in the feminine setting.

How do the researchers explain this interaction? They suggest that men in our culture are trained to accept and strive for things labeled masculine while rejecting the

*(continued)*

## 8.1    Interaction Effects: Spatial Abilities Differ in Different Situations    *(continued)*

appearance of being feminine. This training motivated men to perform well in the masculine occupational setting but to avoid doing well when that same task was described as part of a feminine occupation. On the other hand, women today are more likely to be androgynously trained, that is, trained to value and excel in both feminine and masculine domains. Thus the gender label of the occupational setting did not influence women's task performance. The factorial design has allowed a more complex look at behavior by combining the effects of two factors on an outcome.

NANCY COBB    ◆

SOURCE: Sharps, M. J., Price, J. L., & Williams, J. K. (1994). Spatial cognition and gender: Instructional and stimulus influences on mental image rotation performance. *Psychology of Women Quarterly, 18*, 413–425.

Error in judgment of the true vertical indicates field-dependence.

Accuracy in judgment of the true vertical indicates field-independence.

**Figure 8.2  *The rod-and-frame apparatus, used to measure field dependence and field independence***   After Witkin et al. (1954). *Personality through perception.* New York: Academic Press.

been an increase in the number of HFT games in Sunday comics, and even on weekday puzzle pages, over the last 20 years or so. The familiarity of the task and practice with it could be responsible for the decreased difference.

## Socialization Experiences

As with verbal abilities, there are strong socialization correlates of the small differences in spatial abilities, and some interesting biological correlates have been suggested as well. Training programs can increase spatial abilities, supporting the role of experience (Vasta, Knott, & Gaze, 1996).

*Freedom, Movement, and Experience*    An important environmental correlate of spatial abilities—perhaps the most important one—is autonomy and freedom of action in the world. Cross-cultural evidence helps demonstrate this point (Berry, 1966; Harris, 1977, 1978; Monroe & Monroe, 1971; Stevenson, Chen, & Booth, 1990; Witkin, 1979). When children have a lot of freedom to roam and there is little status difference between the genders, spatial abilities are high and gender differences minimal. For example, among the Eskimos of the Baffin Island in Canada (before they were moved by the government to a settlement), gender differences were virtually nonexistent, and the people generally were high in field independence (EFT). They were a very mobile people who moved around, following animals in a homogeneous, snowy environment with little variation or contrast. Field independence had survival value in an environment in which people had to distinguish small differences and be able to orient themselves with minimal cues. All group members were valuable, so there was more concern for autonomy for all and less emphasis on women's conformity to narrowed roles than in other cultures. The findings for people living in the desert, also an environment with little variation, are essentially the same.

In contrast, in agricultural communities (the Temme of Sierra Leone), the closer and larger group living arrangement has more social structure and roles, and women and children are firmly controlled by men. Cultural and gender differences in spatial abilities may reflect power and dominance differences, which, in turn, are associated with ecology (Witkin, 1979).

Consistent with cross-cultural evidence, Eleanor Maccoby has maintained that in the United States, girls are insulated from experience. Girls are not allowed as much freedom and mobility in the world as boys are (Block, 1976a, 1976b). Although girls are developmentally more mature than boys, their independence is delayed in terms of not being allowed to play outside unsupervised or visit a friend down the street alone as early as boys are (chapter 7). Boys explore the world and test their mettle in it (Bryant, 1985; Feiring & Lewis, 1987).

*Male Subculture: Toys, Activities, and Sports*    It seems that spatial abilities are developed in the "male subculture" and generally are not taught in the schools (Baenninger & Newcombe, 1989; Vasta et al., 1996). Thus, the schools' emphasis on words may compensate for boys' possible weaknesses in verbal abilities, but they do not compensate for girls' possible weaknesses in spatial abilities.

Men *do* things: They climb up on a roof to fix shingles or a TV antenna, they play with motors and fix gizmos, and toss fishing bobs in the lake. All of these activities help develop spatial skills. The sons learn to do these things as well. Boys' toys provide an introduction to the male subculture. The log set does not assemble itself. A toy vehicle is shoved and propelled across space and its movement in space observed and planned, or misplanned, as it rams furniture legs. The boys' toys also invite physically active play with others. Boys receive more math and spatial games as gifts as well as generally having more experience with spatial activities (Tracy, 1987). Boys who more frequently engaged in ball games and played with blocks, transportation toys, and cube puzzles scored better on field independence than other boys (O'Brien & Huston, 1985; Serbin & Connor, 1979). The typical little girl may face spatial decisions such as where to put her toy stove or how to prop her doll, but, overall, girls' toys do not invite or demand the spatial exploration and manipulation of objects that boys' toys do.

Of course, no law except a slightly crumbling law of public approval says that girls cannot play with "boys' toys" and engage in "boys' activities." The more masculine the ideal or actual self-view and the more masculine-stereotyped activities engaged in, the stronger the spatial skills in both girls and boys, women and men (Baenninger & Newcombe, 1989; Nash, 1975, 1979; Signorella & Jamison, 1986; Signorella, Jamison, & Krupa, 1989; Tracy, 1987). Females' performance on spatial reasoning tests has improved some in the last two generations, possibly because of girls' increased involvement in sports (Feingold, 1988).

Does a propensity to spatial abilities facilitate a more masculine role orientation and activity? Or vice versa? Or are both tendencies generated by a third variable? One study with college students found that self-concept with respect to gender roles (measured with the Bem Sex Role Inventory, BSRI, chapter 3) and spatial activities each had a significant *direct* effect on spatial performance independent of each other (Signorella et al., 1989). The study suggested that it was not a matter of psychological masculinity leading to spatial activities, which, in turn, then leads to better performance on spatial measurements. Nor was it a matter of spatial activities causing a psychological masculinity that then "causes" better spatial performance. The authors of this study called for additional research to explain these findings as well as the differences between women and men in spatial performance that did not seem due to self-concept or activities.

***Measurement Context***   Some gender differences are due to the context of measurement and expectations about the meaning of good performance. It is clear that measures of spatial abilities are not pure measures of cognitive ability (Sharps, Welton, & Price, 1993; Sharps, Price, & Williams, 1994; Focus on Research 8.1). Any test picks up error. Performance is affected by sociocultural expectations about the use of the abilities in different settings (Herrmann, Crawford, & Holdsworth, 1992). When attention is called to the spatial nature of the task, women's performance diminishes and men's increases compared to situations in which no attention is called to spatial ability (on an untimed test). Further, women did better than men on the RFT when they were told that it was a measure of empathy (Naditch, 1976). Measured gender differences in spatial abilities result at least in part from the social context of measurement. The same social contextual variables also may detract from maximal practice and development of the abilities outside the laboratory.

## Biological Correlates

Biological hypotheses about spatial ability concern heredity, brain function, and hormones. Individual differences in spatial ability, like other cognitive abilities, are influenced by heredity (Spuhler & Vandenberg, 1980). However, explaining group differences between males and females genetically requires some special genetic mechanism, which is not clearly understood. Popular for a while was the theory that strong spatial ability was due to a recessive gene on the X chromosome (Bock & Kolakowski, 1973; O'Connor, 1943; Stafford, 1961). There is not sufficient evidence to justify this position (Halpern, 1992; Linn & Petersen, 1985; Sherman & Fennema, 1978), though some authorities think that there is a need for better measurement procedures before conclusions can be made (Linn & Petersen, 1986).

***Brain Functions***    Brain lateralization continues to be studied (Casey, 1996; Casey & Brabeck, 1989; Halpern, 1992, 1994; Levy, 1972). Spatial abilities generally are thought to be located in the right hemisphere. More males than females have their spatial abilities primarily in the right hemisphere and verbal abilities primarily in the left hemisphere. More women than men involve both hemispheres in performing some spatial and verbal tasks.

If women are more bilateral, the left hemisphere may interfere with effective processing of spatial information. That would account for the longer time it takes women who are good on mental rotation and perhaps the larger gender differences on a three-dimensional task than on two-dimensional tasks. (However, one may ask why the greater bilaterality would not interfere with women's verbal ability; Bleier, 1991; Fausto-Sterling, 1992). The longer time would also be accounted for if, for reasons other than bilateralism, girls start relying on words for interaction with the world, as suggested by the Bent Twig hypothesis. In addition, the slower performance might be due to a greater caution on the part of females (Linn & Petersen, 1985).

***Hormones and Spatial Ability***    Hormonal changes associated with puberty have been suggested as responsible for spatial ability differences, but meta-analytic work shows no changes in the size of differences around the time of puberty (Linn & Petersen, 1985, 1986). And it would be dangerous to attribute any differences appearing at puberty exclusively to hormones in light of all the social-psychological dynamics of the adolescent years (chapters 5, 6).

This does not mean that hormones are irrelevant. However, counter to stereotyped intuition, relatively *low* levels of androgen are associated with spatial ability in men and, consistent with stereotypes, with *high* levels in women (Kimura, 1987). When females and males are placed on the same continuum of androgen level, the people in the *intermediate* area do best on spatial tasks (Petersen, 1979). Given that women as a group are relatively lower in androgen and men as a group are relatively higher, the people in the middle are those women with relatively high androgen levels compared with other women and those men with relatively low levels compared with other men. Both boys and girls who were less physically sex-typed than others were better at spatial skills than their peers of more masculine or feminine appearance (Petersen, 1979). The pattern is sufficiently robust that it emerges even with the relatively crude measure of self-ratings of body shapes and also with actual measures of the body.

Other evidence also is consistent with the claim of "moderate is best" with respect to androgen. Men score better on spatial tests in the spring, when androgen levels generally are low, compared with the fall when they are high (chapter 6). Girls androgenized prenatally (chapter 4) are better at spatial skills than other girls, whereas genetic males insensitive to androgen score similarly to physically normal females (Lambert, 1978). Could a similar pattern hold for estrogen—better performance from women when estrogen is low and from men when it is high? Evidence about women is suggestive but far from complete. Women performed much better on measures of mental rotation when estrogen levels were low than when their estrogen levels were high (Gorman, 1992; Kimura, 1989a, 1989b). We do not know about estrogen in men. As is the case for aggression (chapters 4, 9), researchers have been fascinated with "male" androgen to the neglect of "female" estrogen and have been concerned with demonstrating male superiority that somehow has to do with male physical structures or hormones.

## *Mathematics in the Social World*

Mathematics, like spatial ability, is basic in many prestigious occupations and is of concern because of the long-standing view that women are deficient in math. As for verbal and spatial abilities, the gender differences are not as wide as stereotypes suggest, and the differences that do exist do not seem to be necessary ones. However, the differences do indicate a disadvantage for young women because of math (Feingold, 1993).

### What the Differences Are in Mathematical Abilities

The very small difference among the general population ($d = .05$) for mathematical abilities actually favors females. (*General population* means national or classroom samples, but not college or college-bound students or samples selected for lower status or remedial action; Hyde, Fennema, & Lamon, 1990.) The difference has decreased and shifted over the years (for studies published in 1973 or earlier compared to later studies, $d = -.31$ vs. $d = -.14$); studies using the SAT are excluded from most general analyses. Although small, the size of gender differences varies somewhat with ethnicity, being larger among white samples ($d = -.13$), nonexistent for Hispanics ($d = 0.00$) and African Americans ($d = .02$), and favoring women minimally among Asian Americans ($d = .09$).

The overall lack of difference should not overshadow important developmental differences and significant heterogeneity. Of potential importance is the developmental drop in females' ability relative to males'. For general mathematical ability, the very small difference during elementary and middle school years favors girls ($ds = .06, .07$), but the difference is larger in the high school years, favoring boys, ($d = -.29$); the size

*Girls do slightly better in math in elementary and junior high, but boys do better in high school. There are virtually no gender differences in math ability in the general population, but differences increase, favoring males, as the sample becomes more selective. The difference is greatest at highly selective colleges. Many factors—social, developmental, and biological—appear to contribute to this phenomenon.*

of the difference increases more into the young adult years ($d = -.41$ for ages 19 to 25) and beyond ($d = -.59$ for people 26 years old and older) (Table 8.2). Mathematical ability has not been measured before the age of about 4 years, when children generally start counting; girls learn to count earlier than boys. In addition to developmental differences in general ability, there are differences in specific abilities. For computation skills, a small relative advantage for girls in early years ($d = .20$) disappears by high school ($d = 0.0$). Girls and boys are virtually equal at all ages in understanding mathematical concepts ($d$s from $-.07$ to $.02$).

**Table 8.2**  Gender Differences for Selected Math Abilities as a Function of Age

| Age | All tasks | Computation | Concepts | Problem solving |
|---|---|---|---|---|
| 5–10 | 0.06 | 0.20 | 0.02 | 0.00 |
| 11–14 | 0.07 | 0.22 | 0.06 | 0.02 |
| 15–18 | −0.29 | 0.00 | −0.07 | −0.29 |
| 19–25 | −0.41 | NA | NA | −0.32 |
| 26+ | −0.59 | NA | NA | NA |

NOTE: Positive $d$s denote females higher than males; NA = not available.

SOURCE: Hyde, J. S., Fennema, E., & Lamon, S. J. (1990). Gender differences in mathematics performance: A meta-analysis. *Psychological Bulletin, 107*, (2), 139–155.

Gender differences that emerge in mathematical problem solving may tell us something about developmental patterns and, at a practical level, are of concern because of their importance in many careers, such as those in the sciences, engineering, and computer work. Girls and boys are equal in problem solving in elementary school ($d = 0.0$) and middle school ($d = .02$), but girls are behind in high school ($d = -.29$). The gender difference is larger in young adults (aged 19 to 25; $d = -.32$) (Focus on Research 8.2).

The pattern of gender differences in mathematical ability generally and in problem solving specifically is that the size of gender differences increases with the selectivity of the sample. For students headed for college or in colleges that are not highly selective, the difference is larger ($d = -.33$) than for the general population ($d = .05$). The difference is highest for students at highly selective colleges ($d = -.54$) and also is large for samples selected for extreme math precocity ($d = -.41$). The size of the differences varies with the specific math skill. Differences between samples and gender differences are strongest for problem solving, which varies from essentially zero ($d = -.02$) for general samples to $d = -.43$ for highly selected students. Thus the relative disadvantage of females on problem solving increases with age and general ability—the older and brighter women are relatively more disadvantaged.

## Standardized Tests and Course Grades

The disadvantage of women (at least white women) is most marked on the SAT-Math (Rosser, 1989a, 1989b); African American and Hispanic high school women are likely to score higher than the men of their groups, though the patterns of variation among different ethnic and national samples are not always consistent (see Kimball, 1989; Shea, 1994). The SAT-Verbal and SAT-Math tests both give idiosyncratic results that are not always easily explained. The SAT-Math gives larger gender differences on math ($d = -.40$) than expected (overall $d$ for studies excluding the SAT is $-.15$) and seems to measure different mathematical skills than other standardized tests do (AAUW, 1992; Hyde et al., 1990). In addition, the content of items on the SAT-Math has not been balanced for gender differences in interest, although the SAT-Verbal has been.

Among several thousand high school students taking advanced algebra and calculus courses, girls' course grades were higher than boys', but they did not do as well on the SAT (Rosser, 1989a, 1989b). Further, SAT scores underpredict women's college performance (Rosser, 1987; Stricker, Rock, & Burton, 1992). Although women score lower on the tests, they do better in college courses. It has been suggested that this is consumer fraud because it underpredicts the performance of more than half the people who take it (Rosser, 1987, 1992).

Meridith Kimball (1989) agrees with Wentzel (1988), mentioned earlier, in maintaining that course exams and standardized tests are measuring different factors. Girls do as well as or better than boys when they take math courses, and their course performance is relatively stable, while their scores on standardized tests, both verbal and mathematical, decline. In Kimball's view, girls score higher when dealing with familiar situations, such as exams on material covered in courses they have had, whereas boys perform better when dealing with unfamiliar situations, especially on the kinds of problems included on the SAT.

Perhaps because of differences in confidence or of felt pressure to achieve, boys in the United States and Israel seem more likely to take a chance and guess, while girls are more cautious and leave more questions unanswered (Cahan & Ganor, 1995; Kimball, 1989; Linn & Hyde, 1989; Linn & Petersen, 1985). The SAT-Math has been changed so that students must write in answers rather than selecting from provided answers. This *may* reduce the gender differences by preventing boys from capitalizing on guessing. Kimball suggests that girls' strong performance in familiar situations deserves wider publicity. Needless to say, all the problems with the SAT noted in discussion of verbal abilities apply here as well.

## Biological Theories About Mathematical Abilities

It was once thought that mathematical ability was related to spatial skills, so that biological explanations for spatial skills applied to mathematical skills as well. The presumed connection now is questioned or rejected (Chipman, Brush, & Wilson, 1985; Gallagher, 1989; Linn & Petersen, 1986). Concern about biological factors has shifted toward the mathematically gifted specifically. Camilla Benbow and Julian Stanley (1980, 1983) studied very talented junior high school students who were willing to take the SAT-Math (which is designed for high school students). Among these gifted students, boys tended to score 30 points higher than girls, although the boys and girls were not different in SAT-Verbal scores. Benbow and Stanley were interested particularly in the very high scorers among the very able students. Among those scoring 600 or above, boys outnumbered girls 4 to 1. Benbow and Stanley argued that biological factors for mathematical aptitude clearly were implicated because, they claimed, they had ruled out socialization variables. *Note that they did not have any measures of biological variables.* Studies such as this capture public attention because they reinforce implicit assumptions of men's biological superiority. Among the headlines proclaiming the study (as cited by Eccles and Jacobs, 1986):

Are Boys Better at Math? (*New York Times*, December 7, 1980)

Do Males Have a Math Gene? (*Newsweek*, December 15, 1980)

The Gender Factor in Math. A New Study Says Males May Be Naturally Abler Than Females. (*Time*, December 15, 1980)

Male Superiority (*The Chronicle of Higher Education*, December, 1980)

Benbow and Stanley's conclusions have been challenged on several grounds, but the articles objecting to their work have not been widely publicized (Eccles & Jacobs, 1986; Rossi, 1983; Schafer & Gray, 1981). Among the challenges is, first, that the specific phenomenon of greater male representation at the upper levels of math ability is variable (Gallagher, 1989; Lummis & Stevenson, 1990; Tobias, 1982). In one year, 19% of the boys were higher than the highest scoring girl, but in another year, only 0.1% of the boys were higher than the top girl. A second challenge is that it is not clear what differences on the SAT-Math mean. The SAT-Math is not accepted as a pure measure of aptitude (Slack & Porter, 1980). If a problem requires using a quadratic formula, one can miss the problem while still having strong aptitude.

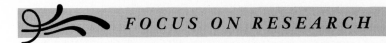

### 8.2    Causal Interpretations of ANOVA Designs: How Girls and Boys Feel About Math and Science

Controversy surrounds the fact that there are far fewer women than men in math and science fields. Is this a case of occupational discrimination? Are women's brains biologically incapable of grasping the cognitive skills needed in these fields? Perhaps our school system is at fault for channeling girls away from math and science courses, or maybe the girls themselves are making academic choices to avoid these classes. What causes such a gender difference? Researcher Melissa Gilbert designed a study to see how fifth- through seventh-grade boys and girls felt about math and science courses and what their attributions for math success and failure were.

Let's dissect the design of Gilbert's study. She identified two independent variables, the students' gender and their year in school. She measured four dependent variables: students' rating of course difficulty, their liking for the course, and their attributions for success and for failure on a math test. The public school student participants were 97 fifth graders, 196 sixth graders, and 68 seventh graders, with all grades just about evenly split between boys and girls. The students filled out the questionnaires in their regular classrooms.

To analyze her data, Gilbert used a statistical technique called analysis of variance (ANOVA). The type of analysis used in a study is not just decided at random when the researcher has data in her hand. Instead, the analysis flows naturally from decisions made earlier in the study. The initial research hypothesis and the way the variables are operationalized sets the stage for the research design and the eventual statistical analysis. Gilbert's use of ANOVA informs the reader that she set up her study as a factorial design in which both independent variables are fully crossed (that is, both boys and girls appear in each of the fifth-, sixth-, and seventh-grade categories). The design of this study can be pictured as a diagram with two columns, each representing one level (male or female) of the first independent variable, gender (see figure). The diagram also contains three rows, each representing one level (fifth, sixth, or seventh) of the second independent variable, year in school. The crossing of these columns and rows produces six cells that represent all possible combinations of the levels of the two independent variables. In Gilbert's factorial design, the cells contained approximately equal numbers of research participants, and participants were assigned to only one cell. The ANOVA procedures then allowed Gilbert to compare six cells' mean scores for each dependent variable. She was then able to determine if, on average, fifth- through seventh-grade boys and girls responded differently regarding their feelings and attributions about math and science.

|  | male | female |
|---|---|---|
| fifth grade |  |  |
| sixth grade |  |  |
| seventh grade |  |  |

Here are Gilbert's conclusions from her analysis. She reports that boys and girls of all three grade levels liked math and science classes equally, but they thought that math got progressively harder from the fifth to the seventh grade. The attributions made by the students regarding success or failure on a math test were remarkably similar for both genders and all three grades. Students tended to attribute their success to studying hard and being good at math and their failure to not studying and the difficulty of the test.

Note that Gilbert's conclusions are not causal in nature. That is, she is careful not to say that being female or male or in the fifth, sixth, or seventh grade caused certain feelings or attributions. Several factors in the study's design determine if it is proper to make a claim of cause and effect. The research participants must be randomly assigned to one of the cells in the factorial design, called treatment groups. This ensures that before the study begins, average scores on the dependent variable as well as any related variables are basically equal across all treatment groups. Participants in each group are then exposed to the designated treatment, which is made up of the combined levels of the independent variables manipulated by the researcher. Gilbert's independent variables, gender and grade in school, are both status variables that can't be manipulated. Participants can't be randomly assigned to be male or female, or fifth, sixth, or seventh graders, so there is no way to be sure that the six cells are equivalent at the start of the study. At the end of the study, even if the groups differ on the dependent variable we cannot claim that these differences are caused by the independent variable. Other characteristics may accompany status variables, and it may be these characteristics that caused the change in the dependent variable.

In her study, Gilbert can report links, relationships, and associations between the independent and dependent variables, but the power to determine cause and effect is

*(continued)*

### 8.2   Causal Interpretations of ANOVA Designs: How Girls and Boys Feel About Math and Science   *(continued)*

lost. This restriction does not make her study any less valuable. While she must be careful not to say that being female or male or being in the fifth, sixth, or seventh grade caused certain behavior, she has found evidence that both girls and boys in these grades have a positive attitude toward math and science and take personal responsibility for succeeding or failing in math. These findings bode well for the eventual disappearance of a gender difference in math and science occupations as this generation approaches adulthood and the world of work.

JILL BORCHERT   ◆

SOURCE: Gilbert, M. (1996). Attributional patterns and perceptions of math and science among fifth-grade through seventh-grade girls and boys. *Sex Roles, 35,* 489–506.

The third and potentially most damaging challenge is that the girls and boys in Benbow and Stanley's sample *did* differ in ways not initially detected. Other researchers uncovered the fact that the boys had received more special training and encouragement from parents and teachers than had the girls and were more likely to have been given math games by parents (Fox, 1981; Fox & Cohen, 1980; Tobias, 1982). In addition, follow-up studies of the talented youth found that family variables (e.g., encouragement for educational and career goals) were important predictors of later achievement, especially for girls (Benbow & Arjmand, 1990). Also relevant is that highly talented students were not automatically included in the study; only those who responded to the invitation to participate did so. The likely effect would be to exclude more of the gifted girls than gifted boys because of gender differences in confidence, especially in gender-inappropriate domains (chapter 7). There may be biological reasons for some differences in mathematics, but the Benbow and Stanley data are not evidence of that.

Another major claim for biological bases of mathematical giftedness (and one appealed to by Benbow and Stanley) was the theory that brain anatomy is altered during fetal life due to excessive testosterone or to an unusual sensitivity to testosterone; this causes a slowing of left brain development and enhancement of right brain development (Geschwind & Behan, 1982; Geschwind & Galaburda, 1985). The result is either mathematical genius *or* learning disorders. However, the hypothesized biological linkages are tenuous and unproven. We do know that socialization variables are related to math performance.

## Attitudes and Math Performance

Numerous considerations from an environmental view have been suggested for boys' better showing on math tests. One of the most obvious considerations is that girls take fewer math courses as soon as the courses become optional, though girls are taking increasingly more math courses now than in previous years (Mitgang, 1988). When controls are made for differences in math background, differences in math scores are diminished but not eliminated (Rosser, 1989). Math courses are not the whole story. Although girls do well in math courses—often better than boys—the attitudes of those around them may make it difficult for them to gain confidence from that success.

Girls are less confident than boys about math and have more negative attitudes and feelings about it; concomitantly, they see math as less valuable than English and have reduced interest in it (Eccles, 1989; Flessati & Jamieson, 1991; Hyde, Fennema, Ryan, Frost, & Hopp, 1990; Kimball, 1989; Spencer, Steele, & Quinn, 1995). When girls succeed in math, they are likely to attribute the success only to effort. For example, elementary and junior high school girls did not expect to do as well as boys on a coming math test. After the test, those girls who had done well attributed their high scores to effort and were not as proud of their success as were the successful boys. The girls who failed were more likely than the failing boys to assume they had low math aptitude and that hard work would not help them do better (Stipek & Gralinski, 1991). Teachers (Fennema, 1990) and parents contribute to this attribution pattern. When daughters succeed in math, parents are likely to see the success as due to effort, while they think that sons succeed because of ability (Yee & Eccles, 1988). This is not likely to increase daughters' confidence nor their achievement motivation (chapter 7).

The adults around them give many other messages to girls suggesting the inappropriateness of girls' interest in success in math (Eccles, Wigfield, Harold, & Blumenfeld, 1993; Jacobs & Eccles, 1992; Jussim & Eccles, 1992). More men than women are teachers of advanced math courses; math textbook materials and games are stereotyped as appropriate for boys more than for girls; teachers have higher expectations for boys' than for girls' math performance; teachers spend more time instructing boys than girls in math courses (Meece, Parsons, Kaczala, & Goff, 1982).

The relative neglect of girls' math ability is poignantly shown in the fact that boys who score high on math achievement tests are more likely to be assigned to high-ability math classes than girls who score equally high (Hallinan & Sorensen, 1987). Parental and teachers' attitudes that math is for boys more than for girls are at a maximum when students are in high school. It is no wonder that the gender difference in students' confidence about math is maximal, though not high, at that time ($d = -.26$). The elaborate study discussed next illustrates more specifically the impact of parents and teachers on girls' views about math.

***The Influence of Adults on Children's Math Performance***   Jacqueline Eccles and Janis Jacobs (1986) studied 164 junior high school students (Grades 7–9) and their parents and teachers for two consecutive years. The girls and boys, almost all from average or above average backgrounds, had equal math grades and math standardized test scores at the start of the study (Time 1) and also reported spending equal amounts of time on math homework. Teachers rated girls' and boys' abilities as equal. What is of interest are influences on performance at Time 2, two years later.

As one might expect, children's perceptions of their ability in math and their anxiety about math predicted their later grades and plans about math (Time 2).

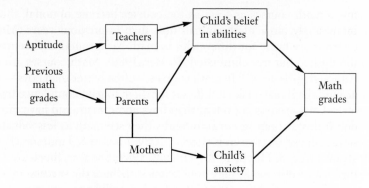

**Figure 8.3** *Influences on child's math grades*    Adapted from Eccles, J. S., & Jacobs, J. E. (1986). Social forces shape math attitudes and performance. *Signs: Journal of Women in Culture and Society, 11,* (21), 367–389.

However, their previous grades were relevant to perceptions of ability and plans *only* to the extent that the grades affected adults' views of the children's ability (Figure 8.3). The adults' confidence was influenced only partially by the children's aptitude and previous grades (Time 1). Math anxiety, like perceptions of ability, was not attributable to performance in the previous math course. Rather, the primary determinant of the children's math anxiety was mothers' belief in the difficulty of math for their children. Math anxiety predicted grades more strongly than past performance did: The connection between anxiety and grades was stronger than the connection between aptitude/achievement and grades. Girls often are higher in math anxiety than boys, as was the case in this study. Anxiety is a key variable for gender differences in math achievement and course enrollment. Given the debilitating effect of anxiety on achievement scores, some of the SAT differences may be due to anxiety.

The problem of girls' mathematical abilities is not that girls are lacking in mathematical abilities. The problem is that adults *assume* girls are less competent in math than boys are. Girls adopt adult views, and the self-fulfilling prophecy (chapter 2) contributes to girls' reduced achievements relative to their potential. The social context shapes individual development. Much the same may be true with respect to our next topic, moral reasoning.

## Moral Reasoning

Moral reasoning, or moral judgment, may seem a vastly different topic from that of the cognitive abilities just discussed. It is discussed here because it is another form of cognitive processing of information in which women have been assumed to be inferior. The leading psychological theory of moral reasoning has been that of Lawrence Kohlberg, a cognitive developmental psychologist, who developed his theory of moral reasoning as well as his theory of gender-typing on males (chapter 5). There has been much recent controversy about gender differences in moral reasoning, which we focus on here, and about related personality issues, discussed in chapter 9.

## Kohlberg's Theory

Kohlberg's (1977, 1984) theory of the development of moral reasoning involves three levels, with two stages in each level. Jane Loevinger's (chapter 5) three levels of ego development are phrased in terms of conformity, and Kohlberg's levels of moral reasoning are phrased in terms of conventionality, but the basic message of the two is the same: The developmental sequence moves from self-centeredness, to becoming socialized, and then to becoming more personalized but at a higher level than previously.

Kohlberg's first level is one of *preconventional* thinking, during which the young child is influenced mainly by self-interest. In Stage 1 the concern is with avoiding punishment for disobedience and in Stage 2, with gaining rewards for obedience. At the second level, the *conventional* level, usually reached in middle childhood, conformity continues to be important but, first, for the sake of having personal ties by being a nice person. (This is Stage 3, also called the good boy-good girl orientation or the morality of interpersonal cooperation.) Then, attention shifts to concern with laws as vital for the social order, so laws are to be obeyed because they are laws (Stage 4).

At the *postconventional* level (also called the principled level), reached in adolescence or adulthood, if at all, morality is based on abstract principles and values, removed from the specific laws of one's own society. Stage 5 is a social contract orientation in which rules are flexible ones to be followed when they bring more good for people. Concern then becomes centered on self-chosen standards of justice that are more important than society's rules and laws (Stage 6). For example, respect for human life is primary and absolute; if stealing is necessary to save another person's life, then so be it.

Kohlberg measured the stages of development using his Moral Judgment Interview. The interview presents, in doll play or in verbal stories, a series of hypothetical moral dilemmas in which a character breaks a rule. The most famous dilemma is about Heinz, a man who does not have the money to buy an expensive drug to save his wife's life and so steals the drug. Should Heinz have done that? Concern is with the reasoning about the action rather than in a particular decision (Colby & Kohlberg, 1986). The theory and measurement procedure were developed on males and then used with females as well.

***Research Findings***     Early studies indicated that women are not as morally advanced as men are. Specifically, the average woman was found to progress only to the stage of making judgments based on obeying rules to gain approval (Stage 3); the average man progressed to the stage of making judgments on the basis of rules to be obeyed (Stage 4). Note that Kohlberg's view is the same as Freud's (chapter 5) in that both see mature morality as a matter of making abstract judgments about moral principles, but women let feelings about people get in the way.

Later work, however, has questioned or even reversed the conclusion of men's superiority in moral reasoning by Kohlberg's definition (Colby & Damon, 1983;

Walker, deVries, & Trevethan, 1988). Education and work experience are important correlates of moral judgment and were not controlled in early studies (Baumrind, 1986; Rest, 1985; Walker, 1984). In one study, among 41 samples of children and adolescents, girls scored higher in 5 and boys in 1 (Walker, 1984). Differences favored men in 4 of 21 studies of adults (ages 21 to 65). There certainly is not strong evidence of males' greater development of moral reasoning.

*A Related Test*    A related measurement procedure is the Defining Issues test, DIT (Rest, 1979). The DIT presents people with moral dilemmas and a list of related issues. They select the issues they judge to be most important in resolving each dilemma. Women consistently score higher than men, though not by large amounts, in samples of junior and senior high school students, college students, and adults ($ds$ = .15, .17, .21, and .28, respectively) (Thoma, 1986). Thus for both the DIT and Kohlberg's procedure, there is a tendency for adolescent girls to obtain slightly higher moral reasoning scores than boys, and the slight edge for women prevails into later years in measurements by the DIT.

## Gilligan's Position

Carol Gilligan (1982), concerned about what at the time appeared to be a lesser showing by women on Kohlberg's measure of moral development, maintained that Kohlberg had a limited view of moral reasoning. In her book, *In a Different Voice*, Gilligan (1982) suggested that there are two equally valid styles or "voices"—justice and care—but Kohlberg did not recognize the morality of care. With a **voice of justice,** which Gilligan thought more likely in men, decisions are made on the basis of abstract rules about what is right or wrong, as valued in Kohlberg's system. In contrast, with a **voice of care,** which Gilligan thought more typical of women, decisions are made on the basis of trying to maximize benefits and minimize losses for all the people involved. The voice of care, of course, is an aspect of the communal orientation, and the voice of justice is an aspect of the agentic orientation (chapter 3).

Unlike Freud and Kohlberg, who saw men's agentic style as superior, Gilligan champions *both* perspectives as equally valid. Although Gilligan sometimes emphasizes gender differences, her critics have overplayed that relative to the big message of her position. Gilligan points out that both women and men can use both justice and care principles and that the two are not contradictory—to be just is not to be uncaring, to be caring is not to be unjust.

Gilligan (1982) aimed to demonstrate her view of women's propensity to the communal view by interviewing women who were facing a real dilemma rather than a hypothetical one, namely, women contemplating abortion. From her results, Gilligan suggested three stages of care reasoning, paralleling Kohlberg's three levels but phrased in terms of care. The first is a stage of self-care (essentially preconventional) in which care centers on one's self because of the need for survival. The second is a stage of caring mainly about other people, seeing goodness as self-sacrifice (essentially conventional). The third involves balancing self-care with care for others (essentially postconventional); to achieve this stage, women need a lot of self-esteem to buck the stereotyped pressures on them to be self-sacrificing.

*Some theorists have proposed that women and men have different moral judgment styles, with women more likely to speak in the voice of "caring" and men in the voice of "justice." It seems more appropriate for both men and women to combine the two voices in their judgments.*

Gilligan's abortion study has been criticized on a number of methodological points (e.g., see Colby & Damon, 1983; Greeno & Maccoby, 1986; Kerber, 1986). Gilligan gives no information about the occupation and education of the women. She scored only by her system, not by Kohlberg's as well. She did not compare the women with men. Research with only women certainly is justified, but Gilligan was making claims about differences between women and men. Nonetheless, the study and the book attracted a lot of attention both inside and outside academia. Many women felt that someone was finally speaking their language and valuing that. *Ms.* magazine selected Gilligan as Woman of the Year in 1984. (The response of feminist psychologists has not been consistently positive, as discussed more in chapter 9.)

## Evidence About the Two Voices

Gilligan's theory instigated a spate of research. The safest thing that can be said is that the two voices *do* exist. Before Gilligan's work, attention to moral reasoning focused on the agentic ideal of rights between separate persons to the neglect of a communal ethic of concern about care of others. Gilligan's basic contribution, that of articulating the communal and expressive dimension of morality, has often been overshadowed by issues of gender differences.

There is evidence both ways about whether or not women and men are different in their moral judgment styles. As so often happens in psychology, different results seem due to different measurement methods: Understanding the differences in methods often throws light on the phenomenon we want to understand. As summarized by Nancy Clopton and Gwendolyn T. Sorell (1993), studies that have found differences between women and men tend to use the respondents' own real-life dilemmas. In contrast, gender differences usually have not been found in studies using hypothetical dilemmas (as Kohlberg did), though there are some exceptions.

This pattern seems to be due to gender differences in the kinds of dilemmas people offer when they offer their own issues. Women raise more issues of personal relationships, including family issues, than men do; men raise more issues of work-related concerns than women do (Pratt, Golding, Hunter, & Sampson, 1988). Further, women tend to rate the dilemmas they give as being more difficult and important than men rate their dilemmas (Ford & Lowery, 1986). For both women and men, care reasoning is found more often in responses to dilemmas with intimate personal content than in responses to abstract, interpersonal dilemmas. Conversely, justice reasoning is used more often in response to highly abstract dilemmas derived from Kohlberg's moral interview format than in responses to standardized dilemmas about intimate or personal matters (Langdale, 1986; Rothbart, Hanley, & Albert, 1986). Thus, gender differences may be due to the kinds of issues raised.

To understand the role of the kind of dilemma discussed, Clopton and Sorell (1993) studied parents and used only dilemmas, both hypothetical and elicited from the parents, about children. Overall, the moral reasoning of mothers and fathers was remarkably similar. The researchers commented on the tenderness, concern, and naturalness of fathers' comments, "as though they only needed to have their attention drawn to an important part of their lives to manifest the care concerns already abundantly present" (Clopton & Sorell, 1993, p. 99). Yet, when men's attention is not drawn to an important part of their lives, the dilemmas they offer tend to be work-oriented.

The pattern suggested is that when thinking about similar problems, women and men may employ similar modes of moral reasoning. Additional work is needed to know whether requiring women to focus on work-related real-life dilemmas will yield responses rich in justice reasoning. The important gender difference may not be in how men and women approach moral issues, but in the kinds of issues that come to mind when thinking of an issue of moral concern (Wark & Krebs, 1996). Clopton and Sorell (1995) have also raised concerns about scoring, because graduate students were able to guess the gender of respondents from the transcripts; yet, men's responses to the dilemma about children were judged the same as women's.

Gilligan's basic thoughts have been extended to apply to differences in styles of learning (Belenky, Clinchy, Goldberger, & Tarule, 1986; Clinchy, 1989; Knight, Elfenbein, & Messina, 1995; Philbin, Meier, Huffman, & Boverie, 1995). *Connected knowing* is a subjective approach in which one attempts to understand others' ideas by taking their perspectives. In relative contrast, *separate knowing* is a style in which one searches or distances the self from the ideas of others and thinks critically and objectively about them. General support is growing for the distinction and for gender differences between the two.

# *Some Final Thoughts: What Can Be Done?*

Women have long been thought inferior to men in many ways, including intellectually and morally. Although many people today are willing to acknowledge women's and men's equal general intelligence, stereotyped assumptions about differences in kinds of abilities continue. Given the apparent attempts to "bring boys up" to girls' levels in verbal abilities and the lack of equal attempts to "bring girls up" to boys' levels in spatial skills and math, it is tempting to worry that the stereotypes of previous centuries are still with us in subtle ways, so that girls' cognitive development is not considered very important. Stereotyped attitudes about gender differences in specific kinds of abilities influence women's and men's career choices, channeling each to traditional jobs for their gender, reinforcing stereotypes, and perpetuating women's lower wages and lesser power occupationally (chapter 13).

Parents and teachers may inadvertently discourage children from experiences that could help develop their abilities. Spatial abilities are developed in ways that have been predominantly male domains. To change this, adults can allow girls some freedom from immediate supervision, and they can provide girls with toys and activities that involve active manipulation of objects. They can avoid teaching that some toys and kinds of play are just for boys. Schools can work to enrich the curriculum for both girls and boys by providing more spatial skill development.

Overall gender differences in mathematical abilities have been decreasing over the years, but there still is cause for concern because of a remaining difference in problem solving specifically and because of the increasing toll taken on young women as they progress into and through high school and then college. Bright college women especially seem victims of negative views of math for women. Part of the problem is biased testing for college admission and awarding of scholarships.

The bigger problems are the attitudes of parents and teachers who do not respond realistically to the mathematical abilities many young girls do have and the climate of classrooms in which young girls are not given the same opportunities as boys for the development of intellectual skills (chapter 7). Girls' achievement in math has little effect on their mothers' and teachers' views of their potential, but the adults' views influence the girls' perceptions of their ability about math and their future plans about it. More recognition of the fact that when girls and college women take math courses they do as well as or better than boys and men could help girls learn to trust their skills and start breaking the stereotype that girls are not good in math.

Women have suffered also from the assumptions that they are morally inferior and need men to keep them from being influenced by compassion for others. Carol Gilligan has suggested that both the abstract style she hypothesizes to be more characteristic of men and the personal style of women are equally valid kinds of moral reasoning. She essentially suggests that the agentic and the communal must balance each other. Her claims, controversial to be sure, have led to researchers realizing that there are two voices, as Gilligan called them. When men are called upon to consider a communal, interpersonal issue, they do show the caring voice. When given hypothetical situations, they tend to use the voice of justice. The differences that do appear seem to be shaped by the social environment and what are said to be proper areas of concern to men or to women, just as different patterns of skill development are shaped by the social environment.

There *may* be biological contributors to the small differences between women and men that exist in cognitive skills and in moral approaches. It is clear that social contextual changes could help both women and men maximize their skill development and their use of both the voices of justice and of care.

## KEY TERMS

| | | |
|---|---|---|
| meta-analysis | mental rotation | spatial visualization |
| *d* | spatial perception | Hidden Figure Test |
| homogeneity | Rod and Frame Test | (HFT) |
| bent twig hypothesis | (RFT) | voice of justice |
| perceptual speed | field dependent- | voice of care |
| spatial abilities | independent | |

## KEY POINTS

◆ The size of gender differences may vary depending on the particular skill within a family of skills, with age of the subjects, and with historical time periods. Scientists often have used biological data to justify claims of white men's superiority.

*Verbal Abilities*

◆ Overall gender differences in verbal abilities are small, favoring females, and have decreased since 1973. The size of the difference varies with age and with specific verbal ability.

◆ Girls' standardized test scores in English and math decline from Grade 6 through Grade 10, although course grades do not vary.

◆ The Bent Twig hypothesis maintains that girls rely on verbal skills early in life, and the tendency to use verbal skills remains. Verbal skills are thought dominantly located in the left hemisphere of the brain (at least for right-handed people). Females may be more left-brain dominant or may be more bilateral for verbal and nonverbal abilities, but many issues are yet to be resolved.

◆ The school environment is highly verbal, which may compensate for whatever inherent verbal inferiorities boys may have relative to girls. The SAT-Verbal now includes items with content of interest to boys. The particular group of people who take the SAT serve to bias results against women. The small SAT differences are sufficient that women get less scholarship money than men.

*Nonverbal Abilities*

◆ Girls are better than boys in perceptual speed from age 5 years, but the skill has not received much attention in research.

◆ The largest gender difference in spatial abilities, favoring males, is for mental rotation. The second largest difference is for spatial perception; the difference is larger for people over 18 years of age than for those younger. The smallest gender differences are for spatial visualization.

◆ Autonomy and freedom of action are strong correlates of spatial ability. Spatial skills are taught in a male subculture and thought to be facilitated by play with boys' toys. Self-perceptions of gender roles and kinds of typical activities are each related to spatial performance.

◆ A moderate amount of androgen is associated with better spatial skills. Estrogen may be related as well.

## Mathematics

◆ Overall gender differences in mathematics for the general population are essentially zero. However, a relative advantage of males in general math ability and problem solving increases with age and selectivity of sample.

◆ The SAT-Math has not been balanced for interest in content of items. Females generally earn equal or better grades in math courses than males do but score lower on standardized tests, especially the SAT-Math.

◆ Girls generally have less positive attitudes toward math than boys do, especially in high school, although their grades in math are equal to or better than boys' grades. Teachers' and parents' views about children's math ability predict future math performance.

## Moral Reasoning

◆ Data originally suggested that women reach a lower level of moral reasoning development than men do, but better research shows a slight edge for females in adolescence and perhaps early adulthood.

◆ Carol Gilligan maintained that women and men tend to use different forms of moral reasoning, both equally valid. Research shows that two voices do exist, but gender differences are not clear, perhaps because of method differences.

## INTEGRATIVE QUESTIONS

1. Name the three most creative women and three most creative men you can think of, either famous people or people you know. What do they have in common? Why do you consider them creative (what about them has contributed to their creativity)? If you have difficulty in thinking of three people of each gender, consider why.

2. Assume that you meet a person who insists that women just are not as smart as men, in either verbal or nonverbal ways. If you thought that a rational presentation of facts would be appropriate, what would you say?

3. Why should small gender differences in cognitive abilities be of concern? Consider both theoretical issues of skill development and practical issues.

4. In what kinds of cognitive abilities are you relatively strong or weak? Try to understand why, thinking of possible biological factors, your teachers and experiences in schools, and your parents.

5. If both women and men can use both the justice and the care voices, explain how Gilligan and later researchers have helped in understanding anything about women.

*Chapter 9*

# Personality and Social Behaviors

$A$re women less aggressive and more peaceful than men? Are they more helpful and caring? Do women speak more gently than men? Are women "soft" and communal and men "hard" and agentic? In short, do women and men "just have different personalities"? You might think that such questions, so long asked, would have clear-cut answers by now. Generally, we will see that there are some gender differences in personality, but the differences are not always large. Further, there are many variations due to age, situation, and experience. Personality psychologists and their close kin, social psychologists, long have been aware of the impact of the environment on personality development and the situational variations that affect how a person responds in any given situation.

Why gender differences occur, when they do, and how the same trait or motive may have different effects within a person are of ongoing concern. Previously, gender differences were either-or matters, with little attention to *why* differences might happen (chapter 1). There has been some progress in understanding differences among women as well as differences between women and men (Burbank, 1994). Situational variations also are receiving attention. Thus we are beginning to appreciate the different ways people may express aggression, leadership, helpfulness, or intimacy because of their previous experiences and the current situation. Women and men probably are much alike while differing in how they express their personal needs and concerns in action.

In this book some facets of personality and social behavior are discussed in other chapters, for example, anxiety in chapters 7 and 16 and self-confidence in chapter 7. Here, we focus on other variables about which there is a reasonable amount of research. To avoid a seemingly endless list of personality variables, the variables are organized under the broad rubrics of agentic and communal traits, but, as we will see, the distinction easily blurs. Both women and men show both agentic and communal orientations. In fact, an important message of this chapter is that traits often thought of as agentic or "masculine" can be expressed communally, in a "feminine" way.

Associated with issues of personality is an important controversy about claims that women are more relational or communal than men are; we will look at that. Finally, communication styles are considered as an important part of women's lives and their interaction with each other and with men.

Before continuing, consider these questions for personal thought:

- Do you think boys and men are more aggressive than girls and women? Why?
- How do you think women handle their anger?
- What is leadership? Are women and men equally good leaders? Do women and men lead in the same ways?
- Is a woman or a man more likely to share with you something intimate and important? Are you more likely to share something intimate with a man or a woman?
- When all is said and done, are women and men different or the same in their personalities and how they interact with people?
- Do women or men talk more? Why? Do women or men smile more? Why? How do you think women and men differ in their verbal and nonverbal communication styles?
- How do you feel when a person of the other gender (not an intimate friend) touches you? When a person of the same gender does?
- Have you noticed differences in the ways men and women typically sit? What are the reasons and effects of any differences you note?

## Agentic Traits and Behaviors

Agentic or instrumental traits (e.g., aggressiveness, leadership) have been researched more extensively than other traits (Buss & Finn, 1987). This may be because they appear early in life, have a clear impact on the environment, and are easier to measure. It may be, of course, that psychologists have thought less about other traits.

Instrumental or agentic traits are thought "masculine" but are important in understanding women in order to show that women are not just passive creatures who let men control the world. Research on need for power shows explicitly how the same attribute can be channeled into different expressions because of different socialization experiences.

### Aggression

Aggression probably is the most frequently studied gender difference. Males have been reported to be more aggressive than females across a variety of cultures, particularly Westernized ones (Björkvist, 1994; Buss & Perry, 1992; Frodi, Macauley, & Thome, 1977; Fry & Gabriel, 1994; Harris & Knight-Bohnoff, 1996b; Maccoby & Jacklin,

1974). This broad generalization must be qualified, however. First, the overall difference, shown by meta-analysis, is moderate ($d = -.48$; Hyde, 1984, 1986). (See chapter 8 for an explanation of meta-analysis.) Second, differences vary with age and the specific methods of defining aggression (e.g., physical, verbal). These variations make aggressiveness more interesting to study (Focus on Research 9.1).

The size of the difference also varies with the kind of measurement (Hyde, 1984). Observational studies of children in natural situations show larger differences than self-reports or reports by parents or teachers, for example. Researchers' observing behavior often is thought superior to reports by the individuals or by others, but this can be questioned—observers may bring stereotypes with them, so that observation is not necessarily "pure" measurement (chapter 1). The stereotyped assumption that boys are more aggressive than girls may lead people to notice and remember aggression in boys. But there is reason also to suspect the opposite—a desensitization effect such that boys' aggressive behavior is seen as normal and somehow not really aggressive, while the same behavior in girls is not normal and therefore considered aggressive. The desensitization effect was demonstrated by showing college students a videotape of two children playing roughly in the snow (Condry & Ross, 1985). The children's gender was disguised by the snowsuits. Students who thought they were watching two boys rated the children's actions as less aggressive than those who thought they were watching a boy and a girl or two girls. If the results are typical, it means that boys' relative aggression is underestimated. The same may be true of men (chapter 15).

Aggressive behavior is more frequent in children age 6 years or less than in older people; so, too, are gender differences in aggressive behavior greater in the young children ($d = -.58$; Hyde, 1984) than in college students ($d = -.27$). The pattern is the same when comparing adolescents (14 years or older) to adults (Eagly & Steffen, 1986). Some age comparisons are tenuous, however, because of differences in how aggression is measured. Studies of preschoolers typically measure physical aggression in natural situations; studies of college students most often measure physical aggression as the amount of electric shock given (or thought to be given) to a stranger in a laboratory setting. However, self-reports of adults over a large age span (21 to 60 years) indicate a decline with age as well as with education, for both women and men (Harris & Knight-Bohnoff, 1996a, 1996b).

As mentioned earlier, the size of gender differences varies with the kind of aggression. Gender differences are greater for physical aggression than for verbal, psychological aggression (Eagly & Steffen, 1986; Harris & Knight-Bohnoff, 1996b). Among college students, men scored much higher than women on self-reported measures of physical aggression ($d = -.89$), somewhat higher on verbal aggression ($d = -.44$), and just a little higher on hostility ($d = -.19$) (Figure 9.1, p. 300; Buss & Perry, 1992). However, differences are larger on other measures of hostility (Woodall & Matthews, 1993).

Men also are more likely than women to describe physically aggressive behavior when they report their own dreams and intentions, as well as their usual behavior (Frodi et al., 1977). The differences in fantasy are apparent in preschool years. Stories told by boys involve more aggressive behavior and attempts to master situations through the use of aggressive activity (Libby & Aries, 1989). Stories told by girls have

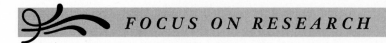

## FOCUS ON RESEARCH

### 9.1   Meta-Analysis: Gender Differences in Personality Traits

We hear a lot about gender differences in cognitive abilities, such as math skills, and in social behaviors, such as empathy or helping. These differences between the sexes capture people's attention and generate many research studies. Alan Feingold, a Yale University graduate student, set about exploring a third area, gender differences in personality traits, that has received less attention. Personality traits are stable patterns of thought, feelings, and actions. Feingold speculated that personality traits may be one of the causes of social behavior, so gender differences in one domain might echo gender differences in the other. To make his exploration as thorough as possible, Feingold used the statistical technique of meta-analysis to assess what we know about gender differences in personality traits.

Feingold first looked at gender difference reviews that had been done by other researchers. Published in 1974, Maccoby and Jacklin's major compilation of sex differences included some studies of personality traits. Their review used the narrative method, in which the researcher groups studies by topic (e.g., anxiety, dominance, nurturance), lists whether each study reported a gender difference or not, and tallies up the counts in each category to decide whether an overall gender difference exists for that topic. The narrative method can produce biased results since each study is given equal weight (one tally each) despite differences such as number of participants, the magnitude of the gender difference, and the overall diversity of participants' responses.

In 1984, Judith Hall undertook another review of the gender difference research in personality traits from 1975 to 1983. She used the quantitative statistical technique of meta-analysis. This technique is an improvement over the narrative method, because it computes an effect size (often reported as $d$) for each study that weights the study's finding and then averages these $d$s across all studies to reach an overall conclusion about the size and consistency of the gender difference (see chapter 8).

Alan Feingold used meta-analysis to update our knowledge of gender differences in the personality traits of self-esteem, anxiety, assertiveness, and locus of control. (Locus of control refers to people's beliefs about internal versus external responsibility for events. Someone with a belief in internal locus of control thinks that a person's own behavior affects what happens; someone with a belief in external locus of control thinks that what happens is due to luck, fate, or powerful others.) Feingold also wanted to compare what we know now against the reviews by Maccoby and Jacklin and Hall. He located 68 studies on these four traits published between 1958 and 1974 that had been used by Maccoby and Jacklin, and he conducted one meta-analysis. Then he searched through the same journals that Hall had used in her 1984 meta-analysis and found 42 studies on the four traits published between 1984 and 1992. Using these studies, he conducted a second meta-analysis, replicating Hall's original work. Now Feingold had conclusions from three meta-analyses: his reevaluation of Maccoby and Jacklin's 1974 narrative review, Hall's 1984 work, and his own 1994 replication of Hall's work using updated studies. These three meta-analyses formed the basis for comparing gender differences in self-esteem, anxiety, assertiveness, and locus of control during three periods over the last three decades.

Let's look at the personality traits one at a time. The effect size ($d$) will be reported for each meta-analysis in chronological order, that is, the reevaluation of Maccoby and Jacklin's 1974 review, Hall's 1984 analysis, and the 1994 replication of Hall's study. For self-esteem, the effect sizes, indicating the size and direction of the gender difference, were $d = .10$ (1974), $d = .12$ (1984), and $d = .16$ (1994). (Feingold uses $+d$ to indicate that men, on average, score higher on that trait and $-d$ to indicate that women score higher.) For anxiety, the effect sizes in chronological order were $d = -.31$, $-.32$, and $-.15$. For assertiveness, $d = .20$, $.12$, and $.17$. For locus of control, $d = .07$, $.24$, and $.08$, indicating that men are more internal and women more external on locus of control.

First, let's interpret the size and direction of the individual effect sizes for the traits. As indicated by the numerical value of the $d$s, while they favor men, the gender differences for self-esteem, assertiveness, and locus of control are small. These differences are consistent and real, but there is much more overlap than difference in these four areas of women's and men's personalities. The effect sizes for anxiety are somewhat larger, showing that women score higher on anxiety, but still indicate a fairly small gender difference.

The next part of the interpretation deals with changes in effect size over time. The effect sizes for all three meta-analyses are most consistent for self-esteem and assertiveness. The 1994 anxiety effect size is only half the size of that of the 1974 and 1984 analyses. On the surface, this drop in effect size could appear to be a true change in the gender difference. However, Feingold speculated that the drop in effect size was due to the inclusion of studies on social anxiety, a trait for which there is little gender difference; the 1974 and 1984 studies dealt mainly with general anxiety and do show a gender difference favoring women. To check his speculation, Feingold ran a separate meta-analysis including only studies of general anxiety from the 1994 analysis; this produced a $d = -.26$, which is consistent with the $d$s from 1974 and 1984. The original change in effect size across time illustrates how important it is for the researcher to clearly define the topic and only include studies that meet that criteria in the meta-analysis.

Feingold was also concerned by the inconsistent effect sizes for internal locus of control, which shows basically no gender difference in the 1974 and 1994 data but favors women in the 1984 meta-analysis. In reviewing the studies included in the 1984 locus of control category, he found that when locus of control was measured by questionnaire, women scored higher, but when this trait was measured by behavioral

*(continued)*

### 9.1    Meta-Analysis: Gender Differences in Personality Traits
### *(continued)*

observation, men scored higher. The inclusion of more studies using the questionnaire method in the 1994 analysis apparently artificially tipped the gender difference in favor of women. Again, careful record keeping helped avoid a misinterpretation of the findings.

These three meta-analyses show that across time, men have been slightly more assertive and women somewhat more anxious than the other gender. However, neither gender appears to have much of an edge in self-esteem or internal locus of control. This study of gender differences in personality traits across time illustrates that in the hands of a careful researcher, meta-analysis can be a powerful tool.

JILL BORCHERT ◆

SOURCES: Feingold, A. (1994). Gender differences in personality: A meta-analysis. *Psychological Bulletin, 116*, 429–456. Hall, J. A. (1984). *Nonverbal sex differences: Communication accuracy and expressive style.* Baltimore: Johns Hopkins University Press. Maccoby, E. E., & Jacklin, C. N. (1974). *The psychology of sex differences.* Stanford, CA: Stanford University Press.

**Figure 9.1** *Gender differences in reported forms of aggression.*
SOURCE: Buss, A. H., & Perry, M. (1992). The Aggression Questionnaire. *Journal of Personality and Social Psychology, 63,* (3), 452–459. Figure based on conversion of data in Table 3, p. 455.

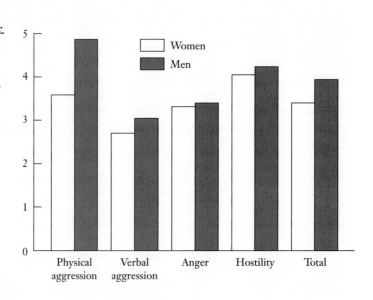

more friendly figures who offer help. At the other end of the age spectrum, men are more involved in violent crimes (not included in the meta-analyses) than women are (e.g., see Lore & Schultz, 1993). Many more women than men are raped and live with an abusive partner (chapter 15). Most men are like most women in that they have not committed rape or abuse, but the proportion of men to women at the upper end of the violence distribution seems great.

***When Women and Girls Are Aggressive*** The broad patterns for greater physical aggressiveness by boys and men than by girls and women cannot be denied. But we cannot therefore conclude that girls and women simply are not aggressive. To do so would ignore facts and contribute to stereotypes that perpetuate men's power over women (White & Kowalski, 1994). Situational variations suggest that girls and women have a higher *threshold* for aggressive behaviors—it takes more for their aggression to be released (Burbank, 1994).

The perceived appropriateness and safety of the potential aggression make a difference. The best predictor of gender difference in aggression is belief about the consequences of aggression (Björkvist, 1994; Björkvist, Osterman, & Lagerspetz, 1994; Eagly & Steffen, 1986). People who believe that aggression might be dangerous to themselves or who believe they would feel guilt or anxiety about hurting someone else are less likely to behave aggressively. Women and girls hold both beliefs more than men and boys do (Boldizar, Perry, & Perry, 1989; Brody, Lovas, & Hay, 1995; Perry, Perry, & Weiss, 1989).

In some circumstances, a woman's aggressiveness toward a man may be dangerous because of differences in physical size and strength and other forms of men's power. Females may learn early in life to avoid physical aggression against men and probably to avoid direct verbal aggression that could easily lead to physical aggression. Adding to the threat of physical violence is the fact that men often have more power for nonphysical retaliation. The punishment women fear also includes being seen as deviant and pathological because women's aggression is seen as irrational, emotional, and inappropriate (Campbell, 1993).

The negative consequences women often fear also are internal ones. Girls and women seem to have anxiety and guilt about aggression, and perhaps empathy for victims, which inhibit the expression of aggression. Boys tend to minimize the suffering of the victim and to think that aggression will make them feel better about themselves (Boldizar et al., 1989; Perry et al., 1989). In laboratory studies using electric shock, women report more guilt and anxiety over the suffering they think they are causing the victim (Eagly & Steffen, 1986). However, women were just as aggressive as men in playing a video game (e.g., dropping a bomb on the other person's target) when they were relatively anonymous, but they were less so when the opponent was sitting close.

Clear provocation apparently overrides women's anxiety and guilt. Gender differences are less likely when people are provoked (Frodi et al., 1977; White, 1983; Zur & Morrison, 1989). In short, gender differences in aggression likely are reflecting differences in willingness to express physical aggression rather than in the potential for being aggressive. Much of women's aggression is indirect.

Indirect aggression, often called **covert or relational aggression,** can be highly effective in harming another while providing relative safety for the aggressor (Björkvist, 1994). It involves social manipulation such as gossiping, trying to win others to one's side, excluding from groups, and sabotaging another's performance. Indirect

*Television character Xena, Warrior Princess, is powerful enough to express anger and hostility through physical force. Real women may develop indirect methods of aggression because physical or other direct aggression is dangerous for them.*

aggression requires a certain amount of social knowledge and skill, so it does not clearly appear until late childhood and increases dramatically around age 11, especially among girls (Björkvist, Lagerspetz, & Kaukiainen, 1992). Several studies have found this kind of aggressiveness to be higher in (or at least more typical of) girls and women than boys and men (Björkvist, 1994; Björkvist & Niemela, 1992; Björkvist et al., 1994; Crick & Grotpeter, 1995; Giancola & Zeichner, 1995). This gender difference, like the difference for physical aggression, exists across non-Western and Western cultures (Fry, 1993; Hines & Fry, 1994; Olson, 1994). Adult aggression is more likely to be indirect and verbal than direct and physical, but physical aggression is prevalent and the search for causes continues.

***Biological Explanations***   When behavioral differences are found between groups known to be biologically different in some way, it is tempting to attribute the behavioral differences to biology at the cost of overlooking the role of social control. Of all the differences between females and males, aggression is thought most likely to be due to biological factors (e.g., see Maccoby & Jacklin, 1974, 1980). The biological underpinnings, however, are not clear, while it is clear that environmental differences are relevant (e.g., see Tieger, 1980). The aggressive behavior of humans and of other species—including the lowly laboratory rat—is highly susceptible to environmental control (Lore & Schultz, 1993).

We saw some of the weaknesses in appealing to studies of other species for explanations of human aggression in chapter 4. These include the neglect of species in which females are more aggressive (such as hyenas and hamsters) and the neglect of the positive relationship of estrogen with dominance and aggressive behavior. Males are not necessarily the daring, aggressive protectors. Among baboons, some males issue warnings when danger threatens and then conveniently place themselves along an escape route or flee into the relative safety of the trees (Leibowitz, 1975). This hardly supports a view of "male the protector." Also typically neglected are findings about the use of indirect aggression, such as shown in female chimpanzees and great apes (Björkvist, 1994).

In humans, the relationship between aggressive behavior and testosterone levels in both women and men is confusingly complex (Björkvist, 1994). For example, prisoners with a violent crime history prior to prison had higher levels of testosterone than men convicted of crimes of lesser violence (Kreuz & Rose, 1972; Tieger, 1980). However, the prisoners who were considered "fighters" in prison were no higher in testosterone than the "nonfighters." Among veterans with little education and low income, testosterone levels were related to more delinquent behavior while growing up and while in military service; the relationship was not found in the other veterans (Dabbs & Morris, 1990).

Testosterone has been associated with irritability and impatience in teenage boys (Olweus, Mattsson, Schalling, & Low, 1980) and in hockey players' reported tendency to fight when other players threaten them (Scaramella & Brown, 1978). However, three out of four studies in which androgens were injected into men found no increased aggression (Björkvist, 1994). When relationships are found between hormone levels—which fluctuate markedly over time—and aggression, they are very modest. The studies that do suggest a connection between testosterone and aggression may receive undue attention because they are in line with the stereotype of the aggressive male and the subordinate female (White & Kowalski, 1994).

*Social Variables*    Even if testosterone predisposes an individual to aggressive behavior, aggression in human and other species is subject to control by the social situation (Lore & Schultz, 1993). Among humans, levels of aggressive behaviors vary greatly from culture to culture (Mead, 1935; Sanday, 1981; Whiting & Edwards, 1973), and equalitarian cultures have virtually no aggression (e.g., Vanatinai, a small island society off New Guinea; Lepowsky, 1994). Cultural dictates can overwhelm any genetic or hormonal influences on aggressive behavior (Bower, 1991; Fry, 1988).

In the United States, as well as in many other countries, differences between genders in experience must be considered. First is the fact that aggressiveness is a *predominant* part of the male role and passivity a part of the female role; it is unladylike for girls and women to act aggressively (Eagly, 1987). Many male activities, such as team sports and military service, encourage aggressive behavior. Children's television is full of males modeling aggression (chapter 2). Boys expect less parental disapproval of aggression and more concrete benefits of getting what they want from another child (Perry et al., 1989). Boys do get more rewards but also more punishment for aggressive behavior, even at the toddler stage (Fagot & Hagan, 1985; Hyde & Schuck, 1977;

Maccoby & Jacklin, 1974; Serbin, O'Leary, Kent, & Tronick, 1973; Tieger, 1980). At the same time, boys are encouraged indirectly to disobey adults ("boys will be boys") and to become proficient in fighting (Tieger, 1980). The attention of punishment itself may be reinforcing.

Clearly, many men come to control whatever aggressive propensities they have. Paula Caplan and Jeremy Caplan (1994) point out that it is rather demeaning to men to assume that they cannot control or take responsibility for their urges. If men were powerless to control their aggressive drives, one would expect society to have imposed some control, such as having a taboo against men being on the streets after dark. Instead, the claim of stronger drives in men has worked to justify their aggression (White & Kowalski, 1994). The claim has been based on biology when facts show the enormous relevance of socialization.

## Anger

Closely associated with aggression is anger. Anger need not be expressed aggressively, but people are more likely to behave aggressively when angry than when not. Feminist psychotherapists have noted that women have problems experiencing and expressing anger (e.g., see Bernardez, 1978, 1988; Collier, Kuiken, & Enzle, 1982; H. G. Lerner, 1985; Miller, 1983). Anger has not been well studied empirically, perhaps because it is an emotion or passion, while aggression is an action (Averill, 1982). We do know, however, that mothers respond differently to an infant's anger on the basis of sex of the infant (chapter 4) and that mothers communicate to young children (3-year-olds) that anger is not an appropriate emotional reaction for girls (Fivush, 1989).

Some studies show that females report less anger than males, others that the anger experienced is equal. More clear is that females and males differ in their primary response to anger. Among fourth and fifth graders, boys more than girls report physical expressions of anger, such as hitting, kicking, and punching. Girls were more likely to report that they sulk and pout (Buntaine & Costenbader, 1997). What children did to get over being angry also varied: Boys were more likely to do something physical, while girls were more likely to report spending quiet time alone as well as talking about it (Table 9.1). Teenagers (11 to 15 years old) report similar differences in dealing with anger (Whitesell, Robinson, & Harter, 1991). Boys in this age group also report dealing with anger by hitting and yelling; girls say they would talk with the person with whom they were angry, get away from the situation, or try to distract themselves.

Evidence with college students indicates some inhibitions on the expression of anger by women and by feminine-typed individuals of either gender, as reported on an aggression questionnaire (A Closer Look 9.1) (Buss & Perry, 1992; Kopper & Epperson, 1991). College women report as much anger as men do but report less aggression and hostility (Figure 9.1). Expressive (feminine) people of either gender have been reported comparatively low on the trait of anger and on outward expression of anger (anger-out) but high on the tendency to suppress anger (anger-in) and try to control it. In contrast, instrumental (masculine) people expressed higher levels of anger and reported more outward expression of anger. Androgynous people appeared less likely to see situations as anger provoking, less likely to respond with anger, more likely

**Table 9.1**  Percentage of Boys and Girls Showing Different
Expressions of Anger

| *How do you usually show that you're angry?* | *Male* (n = 273) % | *Female* (n = 249) % |
|---|---|---|
| Scream and yell | 19.4 | 19.7 |
| Sulk and pout | 23.4 | 32.1 |
| Don't show it | 29.3 | 25.7 |
| Physically Hit, kick, punch, etc. | 15.0 | 6.4 |
| Other | 12.8 | 16.1 |

| *How do you usually get over being angry?* | *Male* (n = 276) % | *Female* (n = 263) % |
|---|---|---|
| Talking about it | 10.9 | 20.5 |
| Spending quiet time alone | 28.3 | 52.9 |
| Doing something physical | 44.2 | 12.9 |
| Other | 16.7 | 13.7 |

SOURCE: Buntaine, R. L., & Costenbader, V. K. (1997). Self-reported differences in the experience and expression of anger between girls and boys. *Sex Roles, 36*, 625–637. Their Table III, p. 632.

to control the experience and expression of anger, but relatively unlikely to suppress anger when they felt it.

In sum, while females (at least younger ones) generally get as angry as often as males, they may differ in how they respond to the anger. Women's direct expression of anger, particularly if directed toward men, is seen as strident, unfeminine, and sexually unattractive (as well as dangerous), though women's anger is "permitted" when they are defending children or helpless adults. Lack of expression of anger can lead to repression of anger (not being aware of it). This can result in losing touch with one's feelings, leading to a state of "silencing the self" and turning anger inward in self-defeating behaviors (chapter 17).

## Leadership

Stereotypes tell us that women are deficient when it comes to agentic leadership as well as in aggression. However, numerous situational differences affect women's display of aggression and of leadership. Women's leadership is often not recognized as leadership. Leadership is in the eyes of the beholder as much as or more than in the behavior of the leader; beholders expect men but not women to be leaders. For example, in newly formed mixed-gender groups, men are more likely to emerge as leaders,

### A Closer Look

## 9.1    Sample Items on an Aggression Questionnaire

PHYSICAL AGGRESSION

Once in a while I can't control the urge to strike another person.

Given enough provocation, I may hit another person.

If I have to resort to violence to protect my rights, I will.

VERBAL AGGRESSION

When people annoy me, I may tell them what I think of them.

My friends say that I'm somewhat argumentative.

ANGER

Some of my friends think I'm a hothead.

Sometimes I fly off the handle for no good reason.

HOSTILITY

At times I feel I have gotten a raw deal out of life.

Other people always seem to get the breaks.

I sometimes feel that people are laughing at me behind my back.

Items are rated on a scale of 1 (extremely uncharacteristic of me) to 5 (extremely characteristic of me).

SOURCE: Buss, A. H., & Perry, M. (1992). The Aggression Questionnaire. *Journal of Personality and Social Psychology, 63*, (3), 452–459. Items selected from Table 1, p. 454.

and women are likely to encounter resistance if they attempt to assume leadership (McGlashan, Wright, & McCormick, 1995). Men are more likely to become leaders even when the group members are told that they all have been selected on the basis of equal ability (Eagly & Karau, 1991; Lockheed & Hall, 1976). Men's relatively easier access to leadership cannot be attributed to their greater personal dominance: when a high-dominant woman is paired with a low-dominant man, he assumes leadership 50% of the time (Fleischer & Chertkoff, 1986; Nyquist & Spence, 1986).

The tendency to assume that men are leaders is so strong that a woman in a leadership position needs many situational cues to indicate that she is in fact the leader (Porter & Geis, 1981; Porter, Geis, & Jennings, 1983). For example, a woman can overcome her invisibility as leader if she sits at the head of the table, begins the discussion, talks more, contributes more new ideas, and supports the ideas suggested by other people—when she is a "superleader" (Offerman, 1986). In one study, even when they made the same contributions to group discussions, women leaders were responded to with more frowns and fewer smiles than men were; the more the woman leader talked, the more unfavorable the facial expressions other group members showed—both women and men (Butler & Geis, 1990). The researchers attributed the groups' reactions to the fact that the woman was seen as violating role and status expectations by taking on leadership; the man who was leading was behaving as expected. Women, however, can and do become leaders.

*Variations in Status and Leadership Styles*     Women can become leaders when their status is increased above the ordinary—it is not enough that women are only *equally* competent (Lockheed & Hall, 1976). For example, women became leaders when the task of the group was to decide how to spend $10,000 on a wedding (a "feminine" task); men became leaders when the group had to decide how to invest $10,000 (a "masculine" task) or how to spend the money on entertainment items (a "neutral" task) (Wentworth & Anderson, 1984). This parallels the facts that men's confidence varies less as a function of the task than women's does, and that men are seen as being more competent on a variety of tasks than women are (chapter 7). Consistently, the differential likelihood of a woman becoming a leader on the feminine tasks (60 versus 40) is much less than that for a man becoming a leader on a masculine task (89 versus 11). In addition, women have to work harder to have leadership; women's participation rates were more strongly associated with leadership ratings than men's were.

The studies mentioned so far are about newly formed groups in the laboratory. They illustrate the initial operation of stereotypes about women's leadership skills and thus show what women have to overcome. Do women have leadership skills that come to be appreciated? Yes. In groups that have worked together for a while, gender recedes in importance (Goktepe & Schneier, 1989). Women and men are a lot alike when they are equal in experience and status in organizations (Eagly & Johnson, 1990; Korabik, Baril, & Watson, 1993; Powell, 1988). But there are differences still.

Although leadership is discussed here as an agentic quality—as it is most commonly accepted—leadership can be communal. Men who emerge as leaders in newly created groups become leaders because of their task-oriented, more agentic behaviors (Eagly & Johnson, 1990; Eagly & Karau, 1991). Women are slightly more likely than men to become social leaders, a communal orientation, but communal leadership is not as readily recognized as leadership (Eagly & Karau, 1991).

Even when women are the "official" task leaders (agentic), they are somewhat more likely than men are to use a communal way of going about getting the job done (Eagly & Johnson, 1990). **Democratic leadership,** somewhat more typical of women ($d = .22$), allows others to participate in making decisions. **Autocratic leadership** discourages the participation of subordinates. Women's relatively greater use of the democratic style may be adaptive because the autocratic, direct power style that men can use well is incongruent with women's role. The slight general tendency to devalue women leaders becomes stronger when women behave directively or are in "masculine" contexts and when men are evaluating them (Eagly, Makhijani, & Klonsky, 1992). Unfortunately, most positions of leadership are "masculinized" ones in which women face status incongruity.

The overall difference in women's and men's styles is consistent with the fact that same-gender groups and mixed-gender groups tend to function differently (Maccoby & Jacklin, 1987; Paikoff & Savin-Williams, 1983). Mixed-gender and groups of only men tend to develop a linear hierarchy with a strong leader and a clear pecking order.

In relative contrast, groups of only women tend to be less linear and less structured but more cohesive; leadership is likely to rotate or be shared (Donelson, 1984; Paikoff & Savin-Williams, 1983).

## Power Motivation and Responsibility

According to traditional views, women do not want power and should not have it, whether it is the power of aggressiveness or of leadership or simply the power of influencing people (Jenkins, 1994; Miller, 1991). The truth is that some women do enjoy power and use it in societally constructive ways (Jenkins, 1994; McAdams, 1994). The **power motive,** or **need for Power (nPow),** is defined as a concern with having impact on others, arousing strong emotions in others, or maintaining reputation and prestige (Winter, 1973, 1988). People high in nPow strive to wield power and to feel stronger, more masterful, and more influential than other people—an agentic attribute on the surface, but one that may be used communally. Power need not be used manipulatively for self-aggrandizement. For example, need for power is high in clerics and college instructors, who, one presumes, want to make a positive impact in other people's lives.

The need for power is one of the needs described in Henry Murray's work and, like need for achievement, can be measured by the TAT (chapter 7). Among college students, power motivation is correlated with leadership in formal organizations, such as holding office in student government or being dormitory counselors. Among working-class women and men, power motivation is associated strongly with holding office in volunteer organizations (McClelland, 1975; Winter & Stewart, 1978). There are no gender differences in level of power motivation, in white or African American people, from junior high school through adulthood (Winter, 1988).

What is interesting about power motivation for our purposes is that it is a good example of how the same motive may be expressed differently in women and men and have different effects in their lives. Women high in the need for power are more satisfied with their marriages and have a lower divorce rate than other women (McAdams, 1994). Those who are well educated tend to marry very successful men. In contrast, men who are highly oriented to power have more difficult and less stable intimate relationships with women; they have more sexual partners, tend to oppress and abuse women, and divorce at a higher rate than other men. One researcher suggested that power-oriented men may have basic concerns of a "feminine evil" so that the men want to hurt women before they are hurt by women (McAdams, 1994).

Also, men's need for power predicts "profligate, impulsive" behavior, such as drinking, drug use, physical and verbal aggression, gambling, and exploitative sexuality. Women generally are lower in such profligate behaviors; when women do show such behaviors, the acts are not related to need for power. Why?

The answer seems to involve early experiences, including the different kind of chores girls and boys are likely to have (chapter 5). David Winter (1988) speculated from cross-cultural evidence that children having chores related to the family's welfare (e.g., child care, food preparation) might channel the need for power in prosocial ways; gender differences in expression of power concerns might be because women are more

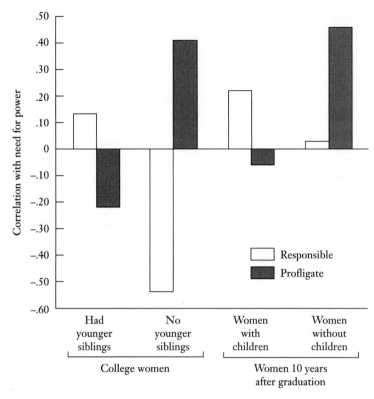

**Figure 9.2** *Correlations with need for power for college women with and without younger siblings and for women 10 years after graduation with and without children.* NOTE: *Measures used for college women:* Responsible power: office holding, canvassing for organization. Profligate power: number of sexual partners, frequency of LSD use, frequency of arguments or verbal fights, fantasied hostility toward high-status other. *Measures used for college graduates:* Responsible power: power-related career, holding office in organization, involvement in organizations or political activity. Profligate behaviors: "hobbies," "activities," or "life style" checked as high point of 10 years since college. SOURCE: Winter, D. G. (1988). The power motive in women—and men. *Journal of Personality and Social Psychology, 54,* (3), 510–519. Based on selected data, Tables 2, 3, p. 516.

likely than men to have had such training. His reasoning was supported. The studies of college students in the United States, which he reanalyzed, did not have information about taking care of children, but they did have information about the presence of younger children. For both college women and men who had a younger sibling, need for power was related to responsible behavior (e.g., office holding), whereas among those without a younger sibling, need for power was related to profligate behaviors. Among people who have graduated from college, both men and women, having children affects the expression of power; data for women are depicted in Figure 9.2, and the men's data were similar. Women and men who have had similar experiences (younger siblings, children) are similar in their expressions of their power orientation. More of this kind of work is needed.

Winter (1988) pointed out that there is much concern about protecting society from the bad effects of profligate power (one could say "unrestrained agency"). He suggested that early training in responsible tasks of family welfare (notably child care and food preparation, but by extension less sexual differentiation in all family chores and socialization) might help direct power motives into responsible, socially useful channels.

## Communal Traits and Behaviors

While roles for men prescribe agentic or instrumental traits, roles for women prescribe communal or expressive traits. The agentic traits of aggression and leadership are associated to some extent with men, but it is not so clear that the communal traits are as strongly associated with women. This may be because women simply do not show the traits expected of them as strongly as men do. However, the relative lack of clear differences in communal traits may be because psychologists who may be more agentic than communal do not make the effort to measure communal traits.

### Empathy

A fundamental part of our emotional lives, empathy provides a link between the feelings of one person and those of another. Definitions vary, but a general definition is that empathy means being sensitive and responsive to the feelings of others (Levenson & Ruef, 1992). Empathic feelings arise when a person values another's welfare and perceives the other to be in need (Batson, Turk, Shaw, & Klein, 1995). There is much less research on empathy than there is on aggression. This sometimes is said to be justified because aggression is a social problem, as it certainly is. However, empathy can inhibit aggression (Dovidio, Allen, & Schroeder, 1990; Miller & Eisenberg, 1988). Why is empathy not a social issue?

Women are thought to be sensitive, caring, and understanding. Gender differences are not always found; when they are, they show girls and women more empathic (Eisenberg & Lennon, 1983). But the operational definitions of empathy influence whether or not differences are found and the size of differences. The biggest differences occur on self-report measures (e.g., "I tend to get emotionally involved with a friend's problems"). All studies surveyed using this method found large differences. Obviously, women and men see themselves differently, or they want to give differing presentations of themselves. Self-reports of empathy are related positively with reported expressiveness and negatively with reported instrumentality (Foushee, Davis, & Archer, 1979; Jose, 1989; Jose & McCarthy, 1988).

Gender differences are not so consistent when methods other than self-reports are used. One method is asking people about their reactions to emotional situations simulated in the laboratory or presented on videotape. Only moderate differences are found in reports of concern for or feeling the same emotion as the protagonist, or in describing the feelings or plans of characters in a story or picture (Brehm, Powell, &

Coke, 1984; Eisenberg & Lennon, 1983). Measures of physiological response to another person's distress also give only moderate evidence of greater female than male sensitivity to others' feelings. It is true that adult women are judged by others as feeling the emotions of others more than men do (Doherty, Orimoto, Singelis, Hatfield, & Hebb, 1995).

One component of empathy is sensitivity to nonverbal cues about another person's feelings. For this component of empathy, research is fairly consistent in showing that girls and women are more accurate in decoding or interpreting nonverbal cues to know what a person is feeling from only looking at a picture or hearing tone of voice; the differences are greater for visual than for auditory cues (Brody & Hall, 1993; Eisenberg & Lennon, 1983; Hall, 1978, 1984; Rosenthal & DePaulo, 1979). One exception is that females are less accurate than males at detecting anger (Rotter & Rotter, 1988; Shields, 1995), consistent with reduced parental attention to anger in girls (Fivush, 1989; chapter 4). Men who are training for or working in occupations requiring interpersonal sensitivity, however, are as good as women at decoding nonverbally expressed emotions (Rosenthal, Archer, DiMatteo, Kowumaki, & Rogers, 1974).

Expectations about empathy vary with status as well as gender role (Stinson & Ickes, 1992). Low-status people are likely to pay attention to and learn the meaning of the nuances of the behaviors of high-status people (Snodgrass, 1985). Supporting this are findings of greater nonverbal sensitivity among African Americans than among whites (Gitter, Black, & Mostofsky, 1972). A case has been made that caring, which involves empathy, is a critical component of African American culture (Collins, 1989). Are women more likely to attend to men than men are to attend to women? Evidence discussed later (chapter 16) indicates that both husbands and wives agree that wives understand husbands better than vice versa.

## Nurture

Closely related to empathy is nurture—empathy lets you know when nurture is needed. Nurture promotes growth or development. Nurture as studied by psychologists usually is about responsiveness to infants or young children. This restricted view of nurture is unfortunate because nurture has an appropriate role in adult relationships, and self-nurture is valuable as well (Donelson, 1984). Women bear and nurse infants, so it has been tempting to think that they are naturally better able to nurture. The stereotype of women's greater nurture is applied to Chicana women (Mirande & Enriquez, 1979), African American women (McCray, 1980), poor women (Belle, 1984), and white middle-class women (Rich, 1976).

Social expectations clearly are related to nurturing behavior. The big picture is much the same as for empathy: Results about gender differences vary with the method of measurement used (Berman, 1980; Watson, Biderman, & Sawyer, 1994). There are large gender differences on self-report measures. Self-presentation associated with status may be operating.

Gender roles may affect how people present themselves in self-reports or behavior (Berman, 1976). For example, some evidence indicates that boys may learn to withhold nurturing behavior. Boys and girls at age 3 years were equal in approaching a young infant and showing affection. However, by age 5 years, boys showed more interest in a kitten and puppy than in an infant, but the girls' behavior was unchanged. In another study, children (aged 5 ) were asked to pose for photographs with an infant (Reid, Tate, & Berman, 1989). Girls stood closer to, smiled at, and touched the baby more than boys did; the difference was greater when girls were asked to play the role of a mother and boys to play the role of a father.

Do boys grow up to be men who do not care about infants? Not necessarily. Few studies (3 of 27) show women being more responsive than men in playing with a baby, child, or animal (Berman, 1980). Similarly, the physiological responses of women and men when looking at a baby are equal. But do findings from research settings generalize to other situations? The answer is not clear. New fathers can be just as likely as mothers to hold, rock, talk to, and smile at their babies and are equally adequate in bottle-feeding them (Parke & Sawin, 1976). On the other hand, new mothers paid more attention to a baby who was not their own compared with men, other women who did not have children, and women who were pregnant (Feldman & Nash, 1978). Also, men often report difficulties interacting with infants but not with older children (chapter 12).

Men may be as physiologically responsive to infants as women and as likely to attend to infants or animals when left with them in a laboratory situation. In the context of their own homes, however, they are relatively unlikely to perform necessary maintenance of their children, though they do play with them (chapters 12, 13). In cultures in which both girls and boys are expected to help with infant care, gender differences in nurture are minimal (Whiting & Edwards, 1973, 1988). In cultures in which girls are socialized more toward infant care than boys are, gender differences in nurture are greater, emerging between ages 7 and 11 years.

The importance of gender-based expectations about the care of the young is clear, but some researchers do not rule out the relevance of biology (although most psychologists do not accept a broad concept of maternal instinct). The higher androgens prenatally in androgenized girls (chapter 4) has been cited as the reason for their lesser interest in dolls and babies (Ehrhardt, 1985; Hines, 1982), but this research has problems (chapter 4). A more potentially promising line of research deals with hormones in the mother during pregnancy and birth that may make nurturing behaviors easier to acquire (Talan, 1986). Any gender difference seems to be in ease of developing the caring skills and quickness of response in providing the care (Beal, 1994).

## Helping Others

Consistent with the stereotype that women are more nurturing and empathic is the view that they are helpful. Girls have a reputation among adults for being more helpful than boys (Radke-Yarrow, Zahn-Waxler, & Chapman, 1983; Zarbatany, Hartmann, Gelfand, & Vinciguerra, 1985). But adult ratings of children's helpfulness may be distorted (Hartshorne & May, 1928; Shigetomi, Hartmann, & Gelfand, 1981). Both girls and boys know that girls are "supposed to be" more helpful and their responses may be shaped accordingly, especially when adults are present (O'Bryant & Brophy, 1976).

*Although women are believed to be more helpful, men prove more helpful in experimental situations, perhaps due to the particular circumstances in which help is needed (such as changing a tire). In long-term, real-life helping situations, women provide much more help than men do.*

When actual behavior is studied in experimental situations, there are no consistent differences, or the differences favor men (Eagly & Crowley, 1986; Pilavin & Unger, 1985). Much of the evidence, however, is about helping strangers in short-term emergency situations, such as when a man has apparently collapsed on the subway, a hitchhiker wants a ride, or someone has a flat tire (Belansky & Boggiano, 1994). The greater helpfulness of men in these situations is not surprising. Many of the situations pose risks for women and call upon competencies more typical of men than of women (e.g., changing a flat tire); even stooping to help a stranger pick up pencils in an elevator makes women vulnerable. When students were asked to predict their helpfulness in varying situations (situations actually studied previously), women's predictions of helpfulness were lower when they saw the situation as more dangerous for them and when they saw themselves as less competent (Eagly & Crowley, 1986). Women and men are equally likely to help by mailing a stamped letter left in a phone booth—helping that is not dangerous and requires little specific competence.

The method of using strangers needing short-term help in studying helping behavior has the advantage of being methodologically efficient (chapter 1). It has the disadvantage of not telling us much about people's helpfulness in the ordinary circumstances of their lives with friends and family who may need help on a long-term basis (Eagly & Crowley, 1986). When helpfulness is listening to a friend talk about a problem, women report more helpfulness than men do (Belansky & Boggiano, 1994). When it is defined as doing housework or taking care of children or caring for ageing parents, there is ample evidence of women's greater helpfulness (chapters 12, 14). Women and men may help in different ways, depending upon what they have been taught to be comfortable with (Beal, 1994).

## Compliance

Gender stereotypes give a picture of women as more compliant or easily influenced by other people than men are. The compliance attributed to women is seen negatively as women being dependent and wishy-washy, without conviction; an equally logical possibility is that the compliance is an attempt to preserve group harmony (Eagly & Wood, 1985). The stereotypes have a core of accuracy, but it does not extend far. Girls are more obedient to their parents and teachers than boys are, but boys are more susceptible to peer pressure than girls are (Hetherington, Cox, & Cox, 1976; Maccoby & Jacklin, 1974, 1987; Serbin et al., 1990). Are girls, then, more compliant?

Among adults, there is a trend for women to be more compliant than men, but it is a small difference and subject to much variation with the specific circumstances, particularly if status is involved. African American women seem less easily influenced and more assertive than white women, perhaps reflecting their generally higher esteem and/or lesser concern with white stereotypes (Adams, 1980, 1983).

When women do "go along with" someone else, factors such as gender roles and status differences are likely to be involved. Lower status people tend to conform more than higher status ones, particularly when others are present (Eagly, 1983, 1987; Eagly & Chrvala, 1986; Eagly & Wood, 1982, 1985). Similarly, when there is group pressure and when they are being observed in the laboratory, women go along with others' views more than men do (Eagly & Chrvala, 1986; Eagly, Wood, & Fishbaugh, 1981). Gender differences are slightly larger when there is group pressure to conform ($d = .32$) than when a single person is exerting the influence ($d = .26$) (Eagly & Carli, 1981). In contrast, when participants are not being observed or there is no pressure for conformity, women are no more likely to conform than men are, suggesting that the differences are more at the level of behavioral expression than at the level of a genuine change of viewpoint. This may reflect the relevance of gender roles and women's relatively lower status. It may also reflect women's greater responsiveness to contextual factors or concern with preserving group harmony, as may be the case with reported self-confidence (chapter 7).

What is thought of as women's conforming tendency might sometimes be better described as a nonconforming tendency of men (Eagly et al., 1981). Men who expected their views to be known to others in the group (public condition) stated less opinion change than men who did not expect the group to know (private condition). In the public condition, men distanced themselves from the group by keeping their own opinions apart from the group and also by seeing the other members as insincere; women's opinion change and ratings of the sincerity of others did not vary by condition. The gender difference is consistent with the gender role prescription that men are to be "independent" and "not easily influenced" (chapter 3). The relevance of roles is shown also in the fact that both men and women who are high in instrumentality conform less than those who are high in expressiveness (Bem, 1975; Brehony & Geller, 1981; Maslach, Santee, & Wade, 1987). Men's relative resistance to influence may be to protect status. Women's relative compliance may be to avoid the censure that a person of low status might experience for lack of compliance.

## Intimacy

Communal traits focus on interpersonal relationships. Women are slightly, but relatively consistently, higher in intimacy motivation (McAdams, 1994). **Intimacy motivation** is a recurrent preference for experiences of warm, close, and communicative interaction with others. Emphasis is on the quality of the relationship (a communal, "being" orientation; McAdams & Bryant, 1987). Although intimacy is correlated with affiliation, affiliation emphasizes gaining or restoring relationships (an agentic, "doing" orientation).

According to analyses of thousands of TAT stories, written mostly by undergraduates, women do score higher than men on motivation for intimacy. Differences are similar with elementary school children. People high in intimacy motivation have more friendly conversations, smile and make more eye contact during conversations, value close one-to-one interchanges, and promote group harmony and cohesiveness rather than dominance by one or two people. They also are rated by their acquaintances as particularly sincere, natural, loving, not dominant, and not self-centered.

As with the need for power, correlates of the need for intimacy are not all the same for women and men. High-intimacy women, compared with low-intimacy women, are generally happy in life and satisfied with their work, family, and leisure (McAdams & Bryant, 1987). In relative contrast, high-intimacy men are not necessarily happier and more satisfied than low-intimacy men. The men high in intimacy, however, do report less life strain, less uncertainty, and fewer psychophysical symptoms than the other men do (e.g., physical ill health, substance abuse). The researchers suggested that high-intimacy women, given more freedom by stereotype, see themselves as involved in a rich interpersonal network. For men, intimacy provides a secure base from which to act with the agentic assurance expected of them, so that they feel less strain and uncertainty than do other men. Again, we see how social experiences and expectations shape the ways that people express their needs.

## Self-Disclosure

Central for high-intimacy people is talking about their private feelings and listening to friends talk about theirs. Sidney Jourard (1971), in a small but important book called *The Transparent Self*, developed the notion of self-disclosure as important for mental health. **Self-disclosure** is the willingness to make one's self known—to reveal personal, intimate information about one's self to selected others. Jourard saw self-disclosure as a sign of a healthy personality and as a necessity for growing. And, as we will see in chapter 10, self-disclosure is important in developing relationships and in minimizing loneliness. Gender roles and status differences free women and inhibit men with respect to self-disclosure. Women who disclose to a new acquaintance are seen more positively than men making the same disclosures (Chelune, 1976; Derlega & Chaikin, 1976; Kleinke & Kahn, 1980).

Both self-reports and behavioral measures show that women generally are more self-disclosing than men; the gender difference did not diminish in the 30 years between 1960 and 1990 (Dindia & Allen, 1992; Dolgin, Meyer, & Schwartz, 1991). Gender differences have been shown for preadolescents, young adults, and older adults. As with most generalizations, this one is tempered by other factors. Differences in self-disclosure vary not only with gender, but also with status, gender role, target of disclosure, content of disclosure, and context or purpose of the interaction (Leaper, Carson, Baker, Holliday, & Myers, 1995). Subordinate people are more likely to disclose than dominant ones (Henley, 1973, cited in Hacker, 1981). It has been suggested that men consciously withhold emotional expression from others in order to maintain power (Sattel, 1976). Androgynous people seem more willing to disclose than those high in only expressiveness or instrumentality; perhaps they have both the desire to disclose and the confidence to do so without fear of being seen as weak (Shaffer, Pegalis, & Cornell, 1991; Sollie & Fischer, 1985).

The target of disclosure (the person being revealed to or not) makes a difference (Dindia & Allen, 1992). Women disclose more to women than men do to men ($d = .31$). But men disclose more to women than to men, and neither women nor men disclose as much to men as to women ($d = .08$) (chapter 10). When the two people are related (friend, parent, spouse), women disclose more than men do (self-report, $d = .21$; observation, $d = .23$).

Another major qualification concerns the content of disclosure, separately and in combination with the target (Dolgin et al., 1991; Shaffer et al., 1991). Although Jourard had in mind relatively intimate information, researchers have expanded the range of topics they consider. Women are more likely than men to disclose on intimate topics (e.g., fears, hopes), as Jourard suggested, but women and men disclose relatively equally on nonintimate topics (e.g., sports, politics) (Snell, Belk, Flowers, & Warren, 1988; Sollie & Fischer, 1985). Women talk about their feelings for themselves and others, whereas men discuss "topical" issues.

## Separate and Connected Selves

In chapter 8 we considered the issue of different styles of moral judgment, prompted principally by the work of Carol Gilligan. Gilligan's analysis of moral judgment also has important implications for social behaviors and personality differences between women and men. In fact, Gilligan (1986) calls attention to Piaget's (1932/1965) observation that without relationships with other people, there would be no moral necessity. Gilligan noted that the voice of justice may be due to having a **separate self**—one defined apart from others. In contrast, the voice of care may be associated with a **connected self**—one defined in terms of relational connectedness with others.

Gilligan suggests that because women are likely to have a connected self, they are anxious about achievements that can threaten affiliation; because men are likely to have a separate self, they are anxious about affiliation that can threaten their separateness. Susan Pollak and Gilligan (1982) had people write stories in response to TAT cards depicting achievement or affiliation situations. Women gave more violent stories about the achievement pictures than about the affiliation pictures, while the reverse was true for men; overall, more men than women wrote stories with violence (51% versus 22%) (Focus on Research 9.2). (The study was criticized, Benton et al., 1983, on methodological grounds, but later work with improved methodology upheld the substance of the original claim, Helgeson & Sharpsteen, 1987.) Pollack and Gilligan suggest that women are likely to be upset with the threat of separation and men by the threat of closeness.

Broad generalizations are difficult to test, and no single study can suffice. Some research does suggest women's greater relationality or connectedness, such as women's intimacy motivation and openness in verbal self-disclosure and nonverbal expressiveness of emotions. Particularly provocative is a study using a novel technique. With the method of **autophotography,** people are asked to describe how they see themselves by providing photographs "that tell who you are" (Ziller, 1990). The kinds of photos they present are related to objective measures (e.g., shy people are less likely than others to include pictures of other people). In the study college women included more pictures of themselves with others and of people smiling, people touching, and groups of people in their autophotographic essays; they also included more pictures of children, parents, grandparents, conversations with friends, and people holding pets (Clancy & Dollinger, 1993). Relative to women, men had more photos of themselves alone and more photos involving physical activity and motor vehicles; women and men were equally likely to include one photo of their car, but men were more likely to offer two or more photos of the car. The researchers concluded that their results, together with those of other methods, provided strong evidence that women define themselves in socially connected terms, whereas men describe themselves in terms of separateness from others.

Other work does not highlight a difference between women and men so much as a difference between the separate and connected styles, which can be characteristic of either women or men. A paper-and-pencil measure of Gilligan's concepts about relationship styles shows a variety of personality correlates (A Closer Look 9.2, p. 320) (Pearson et al., in press). Although women's higher scores than men's on the Connected Self measure and lower ones on the Separate Self are statistically significant, the average differences typically are too small to be of much theoretical interest (Brouwer, 1995). More interesting are the personality differences associated with the two styles. For example, the Connected Self scale is related positively to nurture and negatively to assertiveness/autonomy and to anger; the direction of the correlations is reversed for the Separate Self scale.

In sum, there is evidence that the two moral voices Gilligan described, the voice of justice and of care, do exist (chapter 8) and that concepts of connected or relational self (e.g., communal) relative to separate self (e.g., agentic) are meaningful. On both scores, some studies claim strong gender differences, but others do not. All the studies considered here are with people in the United States. In the United States a high value is placed on independence relative to interdependence compared to other cultures (e.g., groups in Africa and Asia), in which interdependence is highly valued (Markus &

## FOCUS ON RESEARCH

### 9.2    Projective Measures: Are Fantasies of Danger and Aggression Linked to Gender?

Picture a couple sitting quietly beside a river. The spires of a town rise in the distance. What thoughts run through their minds in this peaceful setting? Homicide? Betrayal? Death? Stabbing? Rape?

Impossible?

Yet when college men were asked to tell a story about a scene such as the one above, one quarter spoke of violent acts such as these; very few women did. What are we to make of this violent imagery—or its absence?

Explanations of gender differences in aggression have typically assumed that women repress "normal" levels of aggression, that is, the levels seen in men. Susan Pollak and Carol Gilligan (1982) suggest another explanation for this gender difference. They suggest that differences in aggression reflect the way individuals of either sex perceive social realities. Men and women alike will respond with violence when they perceive danger, but each perceives danger in different settings.

Men are socialized to be independent and self-sufficient. Settings that limit their independence by involving them in emotional connections with others can challenge their sense of self. Will men see danger in situations that involve affiliation? Women are socialized to be interdependent and form relationships with others. Will women perceive danger in situations in which they are isolated from others? Would settings of competitive achievement arouse fears of isolation by setting women apart from the group?

Deep-seated feelings such as reactions to danger are often difficult to observe and measure. Pollak and Gilligan used a projective measure—the Thematic Apperception Test (TAT)—to get at these feelings. This measure consists of a series of ambiguous drawings; subjects are asked to tell a story about each. It is assumed that they will project themselves into the situation they are describing and actually tell about their own thoughts and feelings.

Projective measures such as the TAT give a rich, complex record of an individual's feelings. Often the individual is unable to verbalize these feelings and may even be unaware of them. Since individuals respond to their perceptions of events rather than

---

Kitayama, 1991). We do not know whether gender differences in those cultures are minimized or even reversed relative to this culture. In this culture, much controversy surrounds the claims of women's connected self, and we address this next.

## Women's Communal Orientation: A Controversy

Carol Gilligan built on Jean Baker Miller's (1976) thoughts in *Toward a New Psychology of Women* and Nancy Chodorow's (1978) thoughts as laid out in *The Reproduction of*

to the events themselves, projective measures have an additional advantage in that they let us see these perceptions.

Projective measures have a number of disadvantages as well. Extensive training is required before one can interpret the responses. Reliability and validity for these measures are frequently low; that is, the measure does not necessarily give the same "reading" each time it is used and may not always tap what it was designed to measure. These problems are common with subjective measures such as the TAT, in which there is always a danger that the investigator may be reading his or her own feelings into the interpretation of the subject's answers.

Pollak and Gilligan used two TAT cards that portrayed affiliation and two that portrayed individual achievement. Women and men college students wrote stories about all four cards. When the investigators analyzed the stories, they found that men wrote many more violent stories about the affiliation cards than the achievement ones—more than three times as many. The opposite pattern emerged for women; nearly three times as many violent stories were written in response to the independent achievement cards as to the affiliation ones.

These findings support the hypothesis that men and women perceive danger in different settings. More specifically, the very relationships women seek in order to protect themselves from isolation—a setting they regard as dangerous—are the ones that males perceive as threatening, because they involve connection with others.

Do the writers in our society produce short stories, novels, and scripts that reflect these gender-specific fears? Or have changing sex roles spelled the end to this particular gender difference? Think about the most recent movies or television programs you've seen. When was the last time the heroine chose her career over love or the hero walked away from fame and success to start a family? What are the chances that movies or programs with outcomes like these are critical successes? Movie and television writers may not have read Pollak and Gilligan's study, but they know how to make money by creating situations that appeal to our basic perceptions of life.

NANCY COBB AND MICHAEL WAPNER ◆

SOURCE: Pollak, S., & Gilligan, C. (1982). Images of violence in Thematic Apperception Test stories. *Journal of Personality and Social Psychology, 42,* 159–167.

*Mothering.* Miller maintained that women have developed valuable affiliative (communal) qualities that have been unrecognized and devalued but are necessary for transforming the world into a more human place.

Chodorow (1978) extended Miller's work by elaborating the different experiences daughters and sons have with their mothers. Daughters do not need to separate from mothers to be "feminine" and so never fully separate. Therefore, they come to define themselves as connected to or continuous with other people. Boys, in order to

## A Closer Look

### 9.2    Sample Items on Connected Self and Separate Self Scales

SAMPLE ITEMS FROM THE CONNECTED/
RELATIONAL SELF SCALE

Activities of care that I perform expand both me and others.

Doing things for others makes me happy.

Those about whom I care deeply are part of who I am.

Relationships are a central part of my identity.

SAMPLE ITEMS FROM THE SEPARATE-
OBJECTIVE SELF SCALE

I cannot choose to help someone else if it will hinder my self-development.

Loving is like a contract: if its provisions aren't met, you wouldn't love the person any more.

People who don't work hard to accomplish respectable goals can't expect me to help when they're in trouble.

In my everyday life I am guided by the notion of "an eye for an eye and a tooth for a tooth."

The feelings of others are not relevant when deciding what is right.

Respondents answer items on a 5-point scale from 1 = "Not like me at all" to 5 = "Very much like me."

SOURCE: Pearson, J. L., Reinhart, M. A., Strommen, E. A., Donelson, E., Barnes, C., Blank, L., Cebollero, A. M., Cornwell, K., & Kamptner, L. Connected and separate selves: Development of an inventory and initial validation. In press, *Journal of Personality Assessment*.

---

be "masculine," must separate from the mother. They do not necessarily know what it means to be masculine, but they know it is not feminine and that mother is a woman. So, they become concerned about becoming separate and are anxious about affiliation. Women, not having their relational needs fully met by men who have lesser relational needs, seek relationships with children—they "reproduce mothering." Chodorow advocated greater sharing of parenting to enable separate *and* relational mothers *and* fathers to nurture children with both separate and relational styles.

The writings of women (primarily psychotherapists) at the Stone Center for Developmental Services and Studies at Wellesley College have similar themes (e.g., see Miller, 1991; Surrey, 1991). The Stone Center group has espoused the positive value of women's relationality and explored its implications for diverse issues of power, violence, depression, lesbianism, eating, and almost anything of relevance to women.

Gilligan, Miller, Chodorow, and the Stone Center group aim to bring relationality and connectedness—long associated with women—into prominence for recognition and value. They do not think that women have the communal concerns because of inherent reasons. Experiences after birth, including those related to child rearing and social status, are seen as responsible. Their work has inspired a lot of empirical and theoretical activity, including books on women's cognitive development (Belenky et al., 1986), on educational philosophy (Noddings, 1984), and on theories about war

(Eshtain, 1987). People in disciplines other than psychology have been more receptive than those within psychology, and many of the critics have been very vocal.

*Criticisms*   Although Gilligan, Miller, Chodorow, as well as the Stone Center group, have been inspirations for many, their position, dubbed the "different voice/women's special nature" position (Mednick, 1989), is not without criticism by women psychologists (Hare-Mustin & Marecek, 1988; Lott, 1991; Mednick, 1989; Wallston, 1987; Westkott, 1990). One major criticism is that these writers are augmenting the stereotyped view that women and men are different. In so doing, they are selling out to men by idealizing traditional femininity, which often has served patriarchal values. Defenders can claim that the critics are selling out to men by not being willing to champion the values long identified with women. The critics also resist the suggestion that mothers use their children to meet their own needs for relationship (Westkott, 1990).

A related criticism is that emphasis on women's special nature (e.g., the voice of care) invites a claim of universalism—that all women are alike because they are women, to the neglect of the variety of their experiences. It is true that, so far, differences among women—and among cultures—have not been well attended to. The potential to address differences among women is present, however, in that the claimed gender differences are seen as due to gender differences in child-rearing experiences and in power differences.

Critics also maintain that the "different voice/women's special nature" position diverts scholarship and action away from the social foundations of power inequity. Power inequities do merit attention. People in dominant positions tend to support rules, control, and the justice approach. Those in subordinate positions often appeal to mercy, sympathy, and understanding, as in the care approach. Thus the Gilligan-type approach may not apply to all cultures outside or inside the United States (universalism is not appropriate).

In considering the pros and cons of championing the relational style, it may help to remember that concern with a sense of a relationship in the full healthy human has a long history in personality theory. For Karen Horney (chapter 1) a healthy person shows a natural, spontaneous balance between three orientations: a communal orientation ("moving toward people"), along with an introversion orientation ("moving away from people"), and an agentic orientation ("moving against people"). For Erich Fromm (1956/1974) healthy people relate to other people with productive reason and productive love, which contribute to the growth of others as well as self. Erik Erikson (1950/1963) stated his agreements with Sigmund Freud's comment that the prime abilities of the healthy person are to love and to work. This is a sample of the long precedent for seeing healthy human beings—men or women—as combining the care of communion and the work and self-protectiveness of agency.

## Communication

Much of social interaction involves communication; some people contend that gender differences in communication patterns are more important than other differences. Communication patterns can reflect and perpetuate gender role expectations and status differences. As always, there are frequent situational variations depending on the context.

## Verbal Communication

Stereotypes tell us that women are continually talking (Kramer, 1977; Tannen, 1990). In truth, men talk more than women in natural and in laboratory settings, in mixed-gender groups, and even when talking to a tape recorder. More generally, men show their dominance and status by controlling conversation: Men talk more often (more utterances), talk longer, interrupt more, and control the topic more (Aires, 1976, 1982; Busk, 1982; Haas, 1979; Hall, 1984; Henley, 1977; Lakoff, 1975; Mayo & Henley, 1990; Spender, 1990). When men are not sure what they want to say or cannot find the right words, they "hold the floor" by mumbling, "Um" or "Ah." In contrast, women simply stop talking (Frances, 1979; Hall, 1987). Women also stop talking when they are not being listened to or are continually interrupted. Many professional women report that their suggestions are disparaged or ignored and then listened to and rewarded when made by a man shortly afterwards.

Similarly, women are likely to be interrupted by men: Men interrupt more than women do and interrupt women more than they interrupt men (Busk, 1982; Carli, 1990; Hall, 1984; McMillan, Clifton, McGrath, & Gale, 1977; McMullen, 1992; Smith-Lovin & Brody, 1989; Stewart, Cooper, & Friedley, 1986; Zimmerman & West, 1975). When men attempt to interrupt men, they are less successful than when attempting to interrupt women (Smith-Lovin & Brody, 1989). The few times that women interrupt men, it is to express agreement or encouragement—"Yeah," "Mm-hmm," "Right"—which is hard to consider an interruption because it is an interruption giving men encouragement to keep talking (Thorne & Henley, 1975).

Robin Lakoff (1973, 1975) proposed a number of **sex markers** that distinguish women's speech from men's. She contended that assertive speech is a domain of power denied to women but available to men. It is not clear, however, that the markers denote lack of power rather than social-emotional concerns. For example, one sex marker is a **tag question,** or simply, **tag:** a short phrase at the end of a declaration that turns a statement into a question. "That was a great movie, *wasn't it*?" Women use at least twice as many tags as men (Carli, 1990; McMillan et al., 1977). Tags can be seen as indicating indeterminacy, but they may also reflect interpersonal sensitivity and warmth (McMillan et al., 1977). A related phenomenon is the use of rising intonation at the end of a statement, turning it into a question, currently called *upspeak*.

Other markers do tend to suggest more clearly a weakening of speech (A Closer Look 9.3). Do the other markers differentiate the speech of women and men? Evidence is not totally consistent, probably because of differences in measurement context (Carli, 1990; Quina, Wingard, & Bates, 1987; Simkins-Bullock & Wildman, 1991). An important variable is status.

If women's speech is tentative because of status differences, then status characteristics other than gender should also affect language. This has been shown among romantic couples, parents and children, and strangers: The more powerful or dominant person of either gender is more likely to interrupt successfully, and the less pow-

## *A Closer Look*

### 9.3   Sex Markers in Language Use

**Hedges** are adverbs that weaken the strength of a statement, such as *sort of, perhaps, maybe, you know, whatever,* or *like,* for example, "Drinking and driving is *like* dangerous."

**Disclaimers** are used to avoid being put on the line, for example, "*I may be wrong, but I'm sure I saw him this morning*," "*I'm not an expert in that area,* but. . . ."

**Indirect statements** (imperatives stated as questions) blunt the force of what may be intended as a command, for example, "Have you tried the other desk?" relative to "Try the other desk."

**Intensifiers** are used to provide emphasis but may not be powerful, such as "Drinking and driving is *so* dangerous." What does *so* contribute to the statement? *Very, really, awfully,* and *truly* also are frequently used intensifiers.

**Modal constructions** express doubtfulness about an event that has taken or will take place, using the modal class or words such as *can, could, should, may, might,* for example, "I think I might have said that Joe was seen leaving the apartment" when the speaker has previously stated that Joe was seen leaving the apartment.

**Lengthened requests** extend a simple request beyond necessity, as in, "I would appreciate it very much, that is, if you don't mind, I was wondering if maybe you might be willing to feed the cat while I'm gone."

Other markers include overgeneralization, hypercorrect grammar, and superpolite forms.

---

SOURCES: Lakoff, R. (1975). *Language and woman's place.* New York: Harper & Row. McMillan, J. R., Clifton, A. K., McGrath, D., & Gale, W. S. (1977). Women's language: Uncertainty or interpersonal sensitivity and emotionality? *Sex Roles, 3,* (6), 545–559.

---

erful is more likely to use tags and a supportive language style (Carli, 1990; Dovidio, Brown, Heltman, Ellyson, & Keating, 1988; Kollock, Blumstein, & Schwartz, 1985; Simkins-Bullock & Wildman, 1991). Furthermore, if women's speech is tentative because of status differences, women should be more tentative in mixed-gender groups than same-gender groups. This has been found as well (Carli, 1990; McMillan et al., 1977). College women used more tentative language overall than men. And, showing the importance of status, the gender differences were larger in mixed-gender dyads than same-gender dyads (there were no gender differences within same-gender dyads).

*Effectiveness of Speech Styles*   A separate issue from whether or not women and men differ in their use of speech is that of the effectiveness of the kinds of speech used. Speech styles considered "feminine" and those considered "masculine" are differentially perceived and differentially effective whether the speaker is a woman or a man; men, however, sometimes have an advantage just by being men. Linda Carli (1990) found that speakers (two of each sex) who spoke tentatively were judged less confident, powerful, competent, intelligent, and knowledgeable. However, there were two interesting variations. First, men had an edge just by being men: Men were judged more knowledgeable than women. Second, women's assertiveness was seen differently by women and men. Women who heard an assertive woman were more influenced by her speech and found her more trustworthy than those who heard a tentative woman. In contrast, men who heard a tentative woman were more influenced and found her more trustworthy than those who heard an assertive woman—even though tentative women were considered *less* knowledgeable and competent than assertive women (Figure 9.3). Similarly, men, more than women, were more influenced by the general likableness of women speakers than of men speakers (Carli, LaFleur, & Loeber, 1995). Both men and women rated tentative speakers as less confident, powerful, and intelligent.

Why would men be influenced by tentative women they consider relatively low in knowledge and competence? Carli suggested that the assertive women violated expectations, causing men to resist their arguments. Supporting this is the fact that men rated tentative women as more trustworthy and likable than the assertive women. Women gave assertive women higher marks on these dimensions than they gave to tentative women. Carli raised the issue that women may know what is going on. Thus they may use tentative language as a subtle influence strategy to cope with their low status in mixed-sex interactions. Before low-status people can get their ideas heard, they must demonstrate that they have no desire to compete for status (Meeker & Weitzel-O'Neill, 1985). Tentative women are getting their ideas heard by communicating, "I know my place." However, in so doing, they are perpetuating stereotypes and status differences.

It should be noted that the people were in an experimental situation with strangers. Whether or not the results about influence would generalize to work situations or ongoing interpersonal relationships remains to be shown. It may be that over the long haul, men would see reasons to trust and like a woman for reasons other than that she "knows her place."

***Choice of Words and Pitch***    Men use more slang and hostile verbs than women do (Gilley & Collier, 1970). Women use more polite and supportive words (Haas, 1979; Thorne & Henley, 1975), though this varies with status (Jay, 1992; Kemper, 1984; Selnow, 1985; Siderits, Johannsen, & Fadden, 1985). Women are more likely than men to use grammatically correct speech and to articulate correctly (Haas, 1979; Kramer, 1974; Thorne & Henley, 1975). For example, women are more likely to pronounce *ing* with a *g* rather than as *in* (Shuy, 1969).

Another difference in speech is that men have only three distinctive levels of pitch, whereas women have an additional one, the highest one. This enables women to communicate a broader range of emotions than men, so that women more readily communicate surprise, cheerfulness, and politeness (Brend, 1971; McConnell-Ginet, 1978; Smith, 1985). Raising their pitch also makes women seem less threatening. Unfortunately, women may overuse their higher pitch (Gallaher, 1992). In a society that

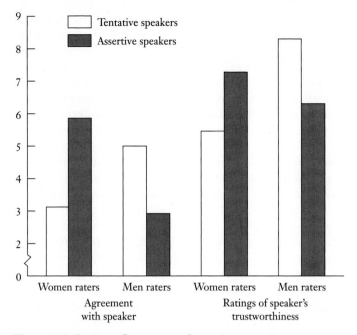

**Figure 9.3** *Ratings of women speakers using tentative or assertive styles.* NOTE: A persuasive message of about 500 words was prepared concerning charging a bus fare for campus. The assertive form did not include tag questions, hedges, or disclaimers; the tentative version did. Two women and two men each rehearsed two versions of a message until they were able to present them in a relaxed, informal manner, giving eight different speeches. Each research participant (60 women, 60 men, all undergraduates) heard only one version. After listening to the speech, participants rated their opinion on the topic on an 11-point scale ranging from complete disagreement (1) to complete agreement (11). They then rated the speaker on 11-point scales for knowledgeability, interest, confidence, power, competence, trustworthiness, likability, intelligence, and tentativeness. SOURCE: Carli, L. L. (1990). Gender, language, and influence. *Journal of Personality and Social Psychology, 59,* (5), 941–951. Based on Table 2, p. 948, and Table 4, p. 949.

has negative connotations about emotionality, the additional high pitch seems to contribute to women's speech being seen as overly emotional and childlike (Stoppard & Grunchy, 1993). Women are not victims of their vocal cords and can learn to control their pitch to communicate what they *want* to communicate. With nonverbal communication as well, women can choose what they wish to communicate.

## Nonverbal Communication

Nancy Henley (1977; Mayo & Henley, 1981) was one of the first to suggest that nonverbal communication is even more influential than verbal language in maintaining a power differential between women and men. Nonverbal communication parallels verbal communication in that women's style often is not as forceful and dominant as the style more characteristic of men. And, as with verbal communication, the differences may reflect status differences or women's greater social-expressiveness. Women generally show more submission or warmth nonverbally, while men show more dominance, though this is more characteristic of whites than of African Americans (Frieze & Ramsey, 1976; Halberstadt & Saitta, 1987). Androgynous people are likely to show a blend of the two broad styles of nonverbal behavior (LaFrance & Carmen, 1980).

***Facial Expressions***   An important aspect of women's generally greater deference nonverbally is through facial expressions. Women smile more than men when talking in same-gender or mixed-gender pairs, when listening to recorded conversations, when criticizing children, when photographed, and when greeting strangers (Deutsch, LeBaron, & Fryer, 1987; Dovidio et al., 1988; Halberstadt & Saitta, 1987). The difference shown by a meta-analysis is fairly large as gender differences go ($d = .60$) (Hall, 1984). The difference apparently develops during adolescence and is more pronounced between traditionally gender-typed men and women than between androgynous women and men (Halberstadt & Saitta, 1987).

Perhaps women smile because they are happier than men? This does not seem to be so. Women generally, more than men, expect others to respond negatively toward them if they do not express positive emotions (Graham, Gentry, & Green, 1981; Stoppard & Grunchy, 1993). Their expectations are well founded: Women, but not men, were rated more negatively (e.g., colder, less happy, more tense) when a description of them was accompanied by a photograph without a smile than when it was accompanied with a smile (Deutsch et al., 1987). In addition, smiling and laughing are associated with nervousness and self-consciousness, social tension and approval seeking, as well as with friendliness (Frances, 1979; Halberstadt & Saitta, 1987; Hall, 1984; Hall & Halberstadt, 1986).

Girls apparently learn to show positive facial and vocal behavior even when having negative feelings, such as when receiving a disappointing gift (Davis, 1995). Children (first and third graders) were given a disappointing gift or an attractive one; in one condition, they were asked to play a game and try to trick an experimenter by looking like they were happy with the gift. Both boys and girls withheld negative expressions more when playing a game than in a spontaneous condition, but boys still showed more negative responses with the disappointing gift than girls did. When playing the game, girls showed no more negativity with the disappointing gift than the desirable one, and less than boys in the spontaneous condition. The researchers suggested that girls have more practice in hiding disappointment and so are better skilled at hiding negative emotions.

Although women smile when they do not feel happy and may hide their disappointments, they otherwise are more open in revealing themselves through facial expressions (Buck, 1977; Gallaher, 1992; Hall, 1984). Just as women are more open verbally, they are more open nonverbally, so that they encode better than men: Their feelings can be more accurately read from their faces. Facial expressiveness is one of the largest gender differences found ($d = 1.01$). The lack of consistent gender differences in children suggests that the pattern is part of learning one's gender roles. This is supported by the fact that facial expressiveness is more closely related to gender role adoption than to sex (Zuckerman, DeFrank, Spiegel, & Larrance, 1982). Expressiveness can be an asset; but in many situations not letting others know what you think is beneficial.

***Personal Space***     The invisible bubble around each person that is not to be invaded is known as **personal space** (LaFrance & Mayo, 1978). Women generally use less personal space than men and are given less space by other women and by men (Baxter, 1970; Sussman & Rosenfeld, 1982). Women are approached more closely than men are and react less negatively to close physical spaces (Freedman, 1980). For example, women seated themselves an average of 4.6 feet from another woman but 8.5 feet from a man (Wittig & Skolnick, 1978). The gender differences are moderately large for women approaching others ($d = .54$) and larger for others approaching women ($d = .86$) (Hall, 1984). Why are women approached more closely? Is it a matter of invasion of women's space being acceptable? Or that women are thought to be more warm and friendly? Research has not solved this issue.

Body posture and movement is a way of claiming space and displaying status (Leffler, Gillespie, & Conaty, 1982). Men take up more space with their bodies, just as they take more "verbal space." Women keep their postures closer, occupy less space, and look more tense; men look relaxed and tend to sprawl out (Davis & Weitz, 1981; Goffman, 1979; Hall, 1984; Mehrabian, 1968). Men, and "masculine" people generally, are more expansive, such as sitting with legs wide apart and having elbows and hands away from the body (Gallaher, 1992). Women's posture is not necessitated by narrow skirts: Similar differences occur in countries with no restricting clothing (Frieze & Ramsey, 1976). Women who are low on expansiveness are seen more favorably, whereas men gain more favor by being relatively high in expansiveness (Gallaher, 1992). Women's style may be considered more polite and refined or "civilized," but men communicate, "I am here and I have a right to be—see me." Women communicate, "Do I have a right to be here? Please don't notice me."

***Touch and Gaze***     Touch is an important way of invading personal space, either for friendly or for other purposes. Touch can express status, or warmth and solidarity, or sexual interest, or threat (Jourard, 1966). Henley (1977; Mayo & Henley, 1981) proposed that men, because of higher status, are freer than women to touch others; women, because of lower status, are more likely than men to be touched by others. Consistent with her views, researchers have shown that touch is associated with status (Leffler et al., 1982; Major & Heslin, 1982; McKenna & Denmark, 1978). Whether because of status or other reasons, in public, nonintimate settings (e.g., shopping malls), though not in art galleries, a bar, or airports, women are more likely than men to be touched, and men are more likely than women to touch (Major, Schmidlin, & Williams, 1990).

Age matters as well as settings. In younger couples (judged to be under 30) the men touched the women, whereas in older couples the women touched the men (Hall & Veccia, 1990, 1991). Roles may permit or require gestures of possessiveness by

*Sociologist Janet Lee Mills demonstrates what happens when women and men violate our expectations about male and female body language. A woman (left) in a typical male pose—unsmiling, arms behind head, leg crossed at knee—appears shocking. A man (right) in a typical female pose—smiling, head tilted, hands folded in lap, ankles crossed—appears ridiculous.*

younger men, who likely are in less developed relationships, or the younger women may touch less to avoid being too forward or seeming too committed. In more developed relationships, roles may permit or require gestures of possession by women.

Touch is more likely in mixed-gender pairs than same-gender pairs by about three to one (Major et al., 1990). Within same-gender white pairs, women touched women more than men touched men, perhaps a physical equivalence to women's greater verbal self-disclosure to each other. Patterns for African Americans are generally similar except that African American men touch each other as much as women touch women, perhaps showing the greater connectedness of African American men. The few mixed-race touches are equally likely to be initiated by either race.

It probably is important to keep in mind that the observations were made in public places, and presumably the pairs were friends. Warmth and intimacy or sexual intent may be primary in young adult mixed-gender touch in such circumstances. Apparently there are no observational studies in work settings (Hall & Veccia, 1990), where patterns may not be the same.

"Although touch can be the most intimate form of expression, it can also be the most hostile" (Major et al., 1990, p. 641). A touch can be appropriate in one situation but not in another; psychologists have not yet codified the subtleties. Concern about harassment in the workplace and between adults and children and teachers and students has increased fear about touch. Unwanted touch is a form of harassment, but people are becoming afraid of using touch to communicate care. Public school teachers have lamented the fact that they are afraid of touching children while feeling that children want adult warmth. All in all, touch has intense interpersonal meanings— meanings of care without harm and meanings of harm without care. It would be a shame to lose the show of care because of fear about harm.

A parallel issue is gaze: making eye contact. Gaze can be considered a visual touch. Like touch, it can communicate a variety of meanings, from friendship or love, to an invitation for interaction, to threat; the meaning often varies with status (Dovidio, 1988). Girls and women consistently gaze more at their conversational partners than boys and men do (Hall, 1987; Hall & Halberstadt, 1986). Mothers and infants gaze at each other as much as adult lovers do. People gaze at women more than they gaze at men, just as women's physical space is invaded more than men's, with or without physical touch. The smoothness of interpersonal interactions varies with the appropriate use of personal space, touch, and gaze, and it is not always easy to know what will be considered appropriate.

## Agency and Communion in Communication

Agency in moderation can be effective in getting a job done but in excess can be destructive or even evil (chapter 3). Verbal and nonverbal communication styles thought more characteristic of men can be assertive and forceful. When extreme they are arrogant, rude, and demeaning to other people. Communication styles thought more characteristic of women can be polite, friendly, warm, and expressive. When extreme they are deferent, incompetent, and self-deprecating. In some situations a woman might choose to communicate assertiveness, but in others she might see warmth as more important. The point is that women can examine their communication patterns and choose to use them rather than being used by them, being victims of habit. And more flexibility in gender role socialization and reduction in power differences could enhance the ability of men and of women to be assertive without being arrogant and to be warm without being deferent—agency and communion working together.

## *Some Final Thoughts: Playing the Game and Changing It*

Stereotypes have some truth to them, but they do not capture the richness and complexity of behavior and certainly not the potentials open to women. If research on gender differences only perpetuates stereotypes (or only disconfirms them), psychologists are not doing their job well. But psychologists are increasingly showing situational variations in behavior and are making headway in seeing developmental antecedents.

The situational variations tell us something about the experiences of women and point to the potential of change. Women and low-status people are supposed to be warm, polite, and caring and are not supposed to be "uppity." Expectations of others can get in a woman's way, such as when her leadership is resisted and when she is seen negatively because she is not smiling. Women know the expectations about them and may consider those, perhaps implicitly or nonconsciously, when deciding how to act in a specific situation. However, when women bend to the situational constraints caused by stereotypes, they perpetuate stereotypes. Will this go on and on?

There are wide individual differences among women and among their responses to situational variations. The effects of situational variations tell us that not all women are "stuck" with gender conformity and low-status behavior, though some women may be more stuck than others. Further, women are relatively flexible. As situations change, they can change. They also have the ability to help the situations change.

There are wide individual differences among men. It is clear that men are not stuck with agentic behaviors to the neglect of communal ones. Many men do learn to control their aggressive behavior, they can channel their strength into helpfulness for others, and they can show their feelings in self-disclosure to women and in their concerns about children. Suggestions that men should be more involved in infant and child care, as fathers and as teachers, have come from several directions.

Some psychologists maintain that women are more relational than men are; others fear that such claims perpetuate the stereotypes that have kept women in the service of men. Perhaps if the relational, communal qualities identified with women had value equal to the instrumental, agentic qualities identified with men, women's relationality would not make them vulnerable to men's power, because men's power would be mitigated by communal concerns. And women would have power as well.

## KEY TERMS

covert or relational
  aggression
democratic leadership
autocratic leadership
power motive, need
  for power (nPow)

intimacy motivation
self-disclosure
separate self
connected self

autophotography
sex markers
tag question, or tag
personal space

## KEY POINTS

*Agentic Traits*

◆ Males behave more aggressively than females, but the size of the gender difference varies with age and measurement method. Women's aggressive behavior increases when they do not feel danger, anxiety, or guilt for the potential aggression or empathy for the victim. From 11 years on, covert aggression becomes typical.

◆ Other species are highly variable in level of aggression and in sex differences in aggression. Contributing to human gender differences in aggression are gender roles and the reward and punishment boys receive for aggression.

◆ Women and feminine people experience anger but are less likely than men and masculine people to express it outwardly in aggression.

◆ Men are more likely than women to become leaders in newly formed groups unless the task is seen as a feminine one. Women are more likely to be unrecognized social leaders and to use a democratic style; women are criticized for directive leadership.

◆ Women and men are equal in motivation for power, but the motive is expressed in different behaviors, apparently because of differences in having responsibility for care of younger children.

## Communal Traits

◆ For both empathy and nurture (defined as responsiveness to infants or children), gender differences are maximal for self-report measures and less for other methods. Very young boys are as nurturing of a young infant as girls are, but seem to unlearn the nurturing. Girls and women are better at decoding than boys and men are.

◆ Men are more helpful to strangers in emergency situations than women are, apparently because of women's perceptions of danger and lack of ability to help in the situations psychologists have studied. The generalizability of these studies is questioned.

◆ Women are somewhat more compliant than men, probably because of status and roles; men seem unusually resistant to pressures to comply.

◆ Women are higher than men in intimacy motivation, and there are gender differences in correlates of the motivation. Women also self-disclose more on intimate topics than men do, and both women and men are more likely to disclose to women than to men.

◆ Studies using the TAT procedure and the autophotographic procedure suggest a more communal style in women than in men. Studies with a paper-and-pencil measure show that the separate and relational styles are differentially related to personality variables.

◆ Controversy surrounds the claims by the "different voice" theorists that women are more communal; these theorists do not claim that the differences are biologically based. Important issues to the critics include the presumed claim of universalism and perpetuation of stereotypic personality traits to the detriment of changing the power differential between women and men.

## Communication

◆ Men control conversation by controlling the topic, interrupting women, talking more often and longer, and ignoring women. Women are more likely to use tentative speech in mixed-gender groups than in same-gender groups.

◆ Speakers (women or men) using feminine speech are seen as less competent than those using masculine speech. But men are more influenced by a tentative woman than an assertive one, while the reverse is true for women.

◆ Women are more likely than men to use grammatically correct speech and to articulate correctly. Women overuse the high pitch that they have, contributing to the view of women as emotional.

◆ Women smile more than men but not because they are happier. Girls apparently learn early to withhold negative affect. Women are more expressive facially, so that their emotional expressions are more easily detected (decoded).

◆ Women are given and claim less personal space than men, and their space (especially younger women's) is more likely to be invaded, including by touch and by gaze. Little is known of touch in the workplace. Touch may express care, status, or threat. Contemporary concerns about inappropriate touch are inhibiting the use of touch to show care.

## INTEGRATIVE QUESTIONS

1. Briefly list the ways in which you think you are different from the "average" person of the *other* gender (10 ways will suffice!). First, compare your list against the personality traits or needs discussed so far in this text. Then, think about why you are this way and discuss in light of this chapter.

2. Think of a time about which you are willing to say, "Yes, I really behaved aggressively then." What triggered your aggression? How was that situation different from others in which you might have acted aggressively but did not? How did you express your aggression? If you cannot think of a time when you were aggressive, do you think that is because you have not been in situations that might trigger aggression?

3. Under what circumstances is a woman accepted as a leader? What variables influence the perception of leadership?

4. You are in a department store and hear a baby crying. What is your first response? What do you think you would do? Analyze in terms of gender differences and situational differences in empathy, nurture, and helpfulness.

5. What advantages and disadvantages for women do you expect if the Gilligan et al. position is proven correct? Incorrect?

6. Analyze how status differences can cause gender differences in communication.

7. Discuss several ways in which agency and communion can be blended in the same actions. You might think of how the traits discussed as agentic can be expressed communally and how those discussed as communal can be expressed agentically.

*Chapter 10*

# Women's Relationships
# with Friends and Lovers

$O$ur lives intertwine with those of other people, starting in infancy and continuing into the last years of life. Both women and men need and enjoy relationships, but they often have different expectations of them. This is not surprising in view of their different experiences with peers (chapter 5). The kinds of relationships that get most attention are romantic heterosexual ones. As important as those are to many women, friendships also are important. And women's joys and problems in heterosexual and lesbian romantic relationships can be better understood when considered in the broader context of women's relationships generally.

In this chapter we first consider friendships. Then we consider heterosexual dating and cohabitation, marriage and divorce, and lesbian relationships. Kin relationships are discussed later (chapter 14).

Before continuing, consider these questions for personal thought:

◆ Who was your best friend when you were a child? Why? What made that person rather than others a "best friend"? When you were a teenager, what did you expect of your best friend? How does that compare with what you expect now?

◆ Do you have a good friend of the other gender? If so, what differences are there between your friendships with those of your own gender and those of the other gender? If not, why not?

◆ When are you lonely? Why are you lonely?

◆ Do you want to be married? Why? Have you ever dreamed of a big wedding?

◆ Why do you think some women choose never to marry a man? What messages did you get when you were growing up about women who do not marry?

◆ Describe your view of the ideal marriage partner for you. Do you think your actual marriage partner will be (or is) a good match with your ideal? What are the differences, if any, and likely reasons for them?

- ◆ Why do you think people get divorced? Under what circumstances would you consider divorce?
- ◆ If you are heterosexual, do you know any lesbians? Could you be good friends with a lesbian? Describe your view of what lesbians are like. If you are lesbian, are any of your good friends heterosexual? How are heterosexual women and lesbians similar or dissimilar as good friends?
- ◆ How important do you think sex is in lesbian relationships?

## *Friendships*

Relationships play an important role in the development of children's social competence, language, self-knowledge, and knowledge of the world (Hartup, 1989; Hartup & Sancilio, 1986; Newcomb & Bagwell, 1995). Relationships with adults ideally provide protection and security for the emergence of basic social skills; then, friendships with peers enable development of social skills (Costin & Jones, 1992). However, what is important to girls and boys about friendship differs, and the differences in styles of relationships beginning in early life seem to have long-term implications for adult relationships.

### Patterns of Friendships in Early Life

Ideas about what friendship is vary with age and with gender. Young children (3–4 years old) essentially equate friend with playmate and "someone who likes you" (Berk, 1993). Sharing as well as playing becomes important to children 4–7 years old. Gender segregation emerges during this time, causing mixed-gender friendships to dissipate or go underground; girls and boys generally go their separate ways with minimal interaction and little chance to learn about each other (chapter 5). Friends generally also are of the same age, race, and social class, though about half of children in integrated schools have at least one friend of another race (Berk, 1993). During middle childhood (8–10 years old), being able to count on the friend becomes important. Girls expect more closeness in relationships than boys do and so are likely to be more selective than boys, having fewer friends and making friends less rapidly (Berndt, 1986). Girls generally have intimate friendships in which they share feelings, exchange presents and compliments, and have long talks about likes and dislikes, triumphs and embarrassments (Johnson, 1996). Boys are more likely to have larger groups of friends and to play physical, competitive games—a pattern that continues into adolescence.

Friends take on intensified importance in adolescence as a source of advice, anchoring, and self-confirmation, with increased emphasis on intimacy, mutual understanding, and loyalty (Johnson, 1996; Reisman, 1990). Adolescents are capable of self-awareness and self-criticism and need the help of friends in understanding and accepting themselves; they have to deal with changes in body image (chapter 6), new sexual feelings, and their general in-between status of being neither a child nor an adult (Strommen, 1977). As was true from preschool days on, friends are likely to be of the same gender and similar in many other ways (Focus on Research 10.1).

*Sharing secrets, confiding in one another, and spending time with one or two special friends are more typical of girls' friendships than of boys' friendships. Girls have fewer but closer friends than boys, who spend more time playing physical games with larger groups.*

Adolescent girls in the United States and other countries have more psychologically intimate relationships involving emotional closeness, trust, sensitivity, and security than boys do (Blyth & Traeger, 1988; Buhrmester & Furman, 1987; Reisman, 1990). Loyal friendships with a confidant help the young women to negotiate the transition to sexuality and to deal with identity issues. Friendships are intense and prone to jealousy under this heavy load. By age 17 or 18 years, the young women have begun to establish an identity, have more familiarity with their impulses, and are more comfortable with young men (Douvan & Adelson, 1966). Friendships with other young women can become less intense and more playful, but sharing important confidences still is important. Adolescent women come to expect that the interpersonal sensitivity and mutual trust they experience with other young women will happen in relationships with men as well.

Because of the young men's social history, the women do not always get what they want from them. Adolescent men do have close friends, but generally their friendships are less intimate than girls' friendships. For example, 35% of boys in one study said the communication in their best friendships was guarded, distant, and superficial, while only 5% of girls said that (Youniss & Smollar, 1986). Androgynous boys, however, equal girls in same-gender intimacy (Jones & Dembo, 1989). Boys are likely to have friendships within a group of other boys, a continuation of the large play groups of boys in childhood. Like women, they expect friends to provide help in times of trouble. The trouble the boys expect is with adult authority. The group also provides

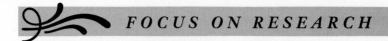

## FOCUS ON RESEARCH

### 10.1   Internal and External Validity: Gang Girls and Their Gangs

*What makes a gang member is that you live in that environment and at some time, in some place, you're going to get into it because you're going to be with a homegirl or a friend who gets into a fight so you're going to have to back her up. (Harris, 1994, p. 293)*

Friendship. Loyalty. Trust. Girls in gangs.

In Los Angeles County alone there are more than 600 gangs with approximately 100,000 members. Gangs, once restricted to low-income inner-city neighborhoods, now stretch into surrounding suburban neighborhoods and schools. Mexican American adolescents make up an increasing number of gang members in the suburbs surrounding Los Angeles, with females actively forming girl gangs. *Cholas*, as these girls are called, operate within a strict subculture in which gang membership brings power, esteem, and a sense of identity. Gang members are most active in their early teens, but even as adults many continue to identify themselves by gang membership.

Mary Harris (1994) wanted to understand the world of Mexican American gang girls from their perspective. Accordingly, Harris interviewed 21 current and former gang girls in the suburbs of Los Angeles, sometimes individually and at other times in groups, asking what motivated them to join a gang and how they felt about their gang activities. She conducted these interviews in different settings—in parks, on street corners, in neighborhood centers, and in their homes. This straightforward technique of simply approaching individuals in the daily contexts of their lives and asking them to recount their experiences produced a dramatic and moving account of human behavior.

Harris found a strong group cohesion and an unwavering loyalty to the gang. When asked their reasons for joining, for instance, these girls spoke of their sense of belonging as well as their need for group support:

> BENITA: All it really is that you want to be a Chola because you see the other girls that want to be a Chola and it looks as if they have fun and everything. You want to put the make-up on like them too.

> RESELDA: You can belong as long as you can back up your s--- and don't rat on your own homegirls or back away. If you don't back them up and you run we'll jump that girl out because she ain't going to take care of nothing. All she wants is our backup and our support but she ain't going to give us none of hers, so what's the use of her being around. She has to be able to hold up the hood. (Harris, 1994, pp. 292–293)

These girls also spoke of their gangs as a family; for many, loyalty to the gang came first. Most gang members derived their status, self-esteem, identity, and sense of belonging from the gang, which substituted for weak support from family and the absence of any real connections to school:

> RESELDA: I used to hate my dad because of what he did to my mom. I grew up with this hatred and anger. . . . A lot of them do come from families that are messed up. A lot of girls, like they ain't got backup in their families. If they get into a gang they got more backup. They've got more girls to really hang around with. . . . They ain't got too much love in the family. So they don't care what's going on. If their family don't care, she don't care. Nothing's going right in her house so what should she care about what's going on out there. (Harris, 1994, p. 294)

As powerful and clearly worthwhile as research such as this is, there can be problems. Harris conducted her interviews in the girls' homes and neighborhood settings, at times having several members of a gang present for a single interview. An advantage in this is that the girls were most likely to be comfortable, and hence candid, when in familiar settings or with their friends. A problem, however, is that one cannot be sure that what they said about their experiences was not influenced by the presence of other gang members or even by their knowledge that, though alone with Harris, their remarks might be overheard. It is possible, in other words, that they may have been less willing to admit to conflicts about belonging to a gang or to other feelings under such conditions. In short, there was more than one possible explanation for some of the findings. When research does not provide an unambiguous answer to the question it was designed to address, we say that it lacks internal validity.

A second type of validity is external validity. Does the answer we get apply only to the people we have observed, or can we generalize the findings to others? Just how representative are the findings? Can we assume that we have an accurate picture of the life of female gang members all over Los Angeles? California? The United States? This is a problem of external validity. The impression we get of gang life can be totally valid for these girls (a question of internal validity) and yet be largely invalid for other gangs (a question of external validity). External validity can also be affected by the very conditions that are necessary to achieve internal validity. Had Harris attempted to experimentally control for some of the factors that might affect the way gang girls responded in these interviews, such as by conducting individual interviews on a university campus away from neighborhood influences, she might have obtained data that were unrepresentative of the way these girls would normally have responded, or might not even have been able to interview any gang girls at all.

NANCY COBB WITH MICHAEL WAPNER ◆

SOURCE: Harris, M. G. (1994). Cholas, Mexican-American girls, and gangs. *Sex Roles, 30,* 289–301.

protection against the fear of homosexuality that could arise if a boy had only one or two special friends. The basic patterns continue into adulthood.

## Same-Gender Friendships in Adulthood

Friendships continue to be important past high school years (Hammersla & Frease-McMahan, 1990; Johnson, 1996). The differences in styles of relationships present in earlier years continue into adulthood and in many ways extend into marriage (Wood, 1996). The differences are not always large but are quite consistent, making for a robust gender difference. However, before looking at the differences, let us comment quickly on some general points to keep in mind (Basow, 1992).

First, the gender differences may be more extreme in white groups than in African American groups; too little is known about other minorities to comment. African Americans may have less pronounced gender differences because the men are more intimate than white men, and the women have greater attachment to families than white women do. In addition, racism generates a climate of care for one's own group that does not have a parallel in white groups (Hill, 1994).

Second, some gender differences vary with gender role orientation: Androgynous and expressive ("feminine") men are more similar to women than to other men in their friendship styles. Given the androgyny of lesbians and gay men (discussed in the final section of this chapter), gender differences likely are more characteristic of heterosexual people than of lesbians and gay men. Third, differences may be smaller in college groups than older groups (Fox, Gibbs, & Auerback, 1985).

As in earlier years, women's friendships with other women tend to be one to one, intimate, and conversational; this seems true of both working-class and middle-class women of varied ethnic groups (Johnson, 1996). Women's friendships with women have been characterized as expressive, communal, or "face-to-face," while men's friendships are seen as instrumental, agentic, or "side-by-side" (Reisman, 1990; Wright & Scanlon, 1991). Women talk with each other, men do things together. Women's friendships in this and other countries generally are emotionally richer, more complex, more holistic, and more likely than those of men to involve psychological intimacy, which includes sharing confidences and emotional supportiveness (e.g., see Jones, Bloys, & Wood, 1990; Reisman, 1990; Veniegas & Peplau, 1997; Wright, 1989; Wright & Scanlon, 1991). However, the distinction between expressiveness and instrumentality must not be overdrawn, nor should the orientations be seen as opposing. Although women's friendships are more expressive than men's, they are not necessarily less instrumental—women do enjoy doing things together and helping each other on tasks (Duck & Wright, 1993; Monsour, 1992).

*Men's Friendships*    Men continue to associate with other men in groups focusing on structured activities, such as playing tennis, and special purposes, such as fixing a car, which provide boundaries for what will happen (Jones et al., 1990; Mazur & Oliver, 1987). Self-disclosure is less likely to be expected in these situations. However, sharing activities can be a way of showing socioemotional concerns (Wood, 1994). One man used the phrase, "Closeness in the Doing," as the title of an article on men's friendships

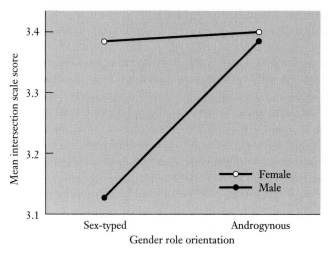

**Figure 10.1 *Depth of friendship interaction as a function of gender roles.*** NOTE: Participants were classified for gender role orientation and then completed an involvement scale for each of three friends, rating 23 interactions on a 5-point scale from 1, for not at all likely, to 5, for extremely likely. Categories of interactions were joint activity, self-disclosure, other-enhancement, other-disparagement, norm regulation, and physical contact. The overall probability rating across all items is thought to indicate level of interpersonal involvement. SOURCE: Barth, R. J., & Kinder, B. N. (1988). A theoretical analysis of sex differences in same-sex friendships. *Sex Roles, 19,* (5/6), 349–363. Figure 1, p. 357. Information passim.

(Inman, 1996), and men do report feeling emotionally close to their men friends (Veniegas & Peplau, 1997). Men also indicate that they would like to discuss feelings and show affection and tenderness toward their men friends more often than they actually do (Reisman, 1990). Androgynous men report more involvement in their relationships (Figure 10.1; Barth & Kinder, 1988), a greater ease of communication and self-disclosure than gender-typed males do, and a disclosure level comparable to gender-typed and androgynous women (Jones et al., 1990; Siavelis & Lamke, 1992).

Men's friendships with men give them less self-affirmation and emotional support than women's friendships with women (Johnson, 1996; P. H. Wright, 1985; Wright & Bergloff, 1984). Men are less likely to feel close and related to the friend, to feel they know the friend and are known by him (Buhrke & Fuqua, 1987). Among college seniors, men rated their interactions with their best male friend as less meaningful than women rated theirs with their best female friends, especially on measures of intimacy and self-disclosure (Elkins & Peterson, 1993; Reis, 1986).

*Challenges to Women's Friendships*    Although women value friendships with other women, they may let a variety of barriers stand in the way of making and keeping friends (Basow, 1992; O'Connor, 1992). Men may unknowingly or knowingly interfere with women's friendships with each other. Unmarried women can feel that another woman is a competitor for men's attention and may call off plans with a woman to accept attention from a man (Strommen, 1977). The most common reason for break-ups of women's friendships in college is dating or marriage (Rose, 1983). The man may be jealous or suspicious of time spent with another woman "just talking," or the woman may feel she "just doesn't have time anymore" (Donelson, 1984; Huyck, 1982). The rejected friend may feel hurt or frustrated; if these feelings are not expressed and resolved, they can damage the relationship (Eichenbaum & Orbach, 1988).

Women with children do not have much time or energy left over after meeting family commitments (Inman, 1996; West, Anderson, & Duck, 1996). Mothers may meet other mothers in the car pool, but developing these acquaintances into friendships takes time. Some findings show that it is time well spent. Married women, especially working-class women, are particularly self-disclosing with the friends they do have, and married women's friendships are more closely related to their general well-being than are those of single women (Goodenow & Gaier, 1986; Hacker, 1981). Religious organizations and activities can help some women get friendship support—families understand taking time for religious obligations better than they understand friendship with a particular other woman.

Race and the cultural differences it often brings also can be a barrier, though some women overcome barriers because of their shared commitments (e.g., religion, work, feminism, lesbianism) (Houston, 1994; Lamphere, 1985; McCullough, 1992). Homophobia is not quite as strong in women as in men, or about women as about men, but nonetheless can deter friendships between women (Pharr, 1988). Particularly if one woman is a lesbian, sexual issues must be clarified.

A final challenge to women's friendships is society's deprecatory view of women, which some women themselves have internalized, so that they do not see the point of spending time with women. Some women do not trust women, whom they consider "gossipy" and not very interesting (Strommen, 1977). With the increase in feminist concerns, women's value of women's friendships has increased; most professional women try to develop same-gender friendships more than mixed-gender ones (Johnson, 1996; Sapadin, 1988). Most professions now have networks of women supporting each other. Women's groups can provide a feeling of an extended family (Donelson, 1984). They give social support and promote feeling good about one's self (Leavy & Adams, 1986).

## Mixed-Gender Friendships in Adulthood

Both women and men have and value friendships with people of the other gender, particularly if they are not married or if they are college students (Swain, 1992; West et al., 1996; Wright & Scanlon, 1991). What do women and men get out of mixed-gender friendships? Generally, it is a matter of getting from the other gender what they do not get from their own. Women enjoy men's companionship without the psychological intensity of their friendships with women; like men, women value having the different perspective of an "insider's view" on how people of the other gender see things (Swain, 1993; Werking, 1994b; Wood, 1994). Also, men are status symbols.

Men value friendships with women because women give them what other men are not so likely to—intimacy and closeness, emotional support, a feeling of acceptance, and relationships with therapeutic value (Elkins & Peterson, 1993; Hammersla & Frease-McMahan, 1990; Reis, 1986). Men generally are more open and self-disclosing to women than to men (Reisman, 1990; Wright & Scanlon, 1991). Men are more likely than women to say that someone of the other gender is a close friend and to look to her for emotional intimacy and support. The woman often is a romantic partner as well. Women in England (Crawford, 1977) and in the United States (L. Rubin, 1983) are more than twice as likely as men to name a close friend other than their spouse (Reisman, 1990).

Like friendships between women, mixed-gender friendships have many societally imposed barriers. This is regrettable because the development of friendships between women and men may be a necessary step in breaking down gender stereotypes through personal contact on equal grounds (Basow, 1992). Boys and girls often come to believe that people of the other gender are somehow significantly different from people of their own gender (Rotenberg, 1984, 1986). The more stereotyped the individual, the less likely a friendship with someone of the other gender (Jackson, 1983; Lavine & Lombardo, 1984). The lower status of women also can inhibit the development of mixed-gender friendships as it does friendships between women.

A large barrier is sexuality (West et al., 1996). The idea of a mixed-gender relationship without sex is hard for many to grasp; indeed, sexual feelings must be dealt with in most mixed-sex friendships. Lesbians need clarity about the role of sex in their friendships, both with women and with men. Given the barriers possible between women and between women and men, some people are more lonely than they need to be, as single people and as married people.

## Loneliness

Loneliness has been defined as a feeling of deprivation and dissatisfaction produced by a discrepancy between the kind of social relations we want and the kind we have (Brehm, 1992). It is not a matter of being with someone or not. We are not necessarily lonely when we are by ourselves, and we can be lonely if we are with someone who is not giving us what we want.

Women report more loneliness when the word *lonely* is used in the measuring instrument (e.g., the NYU Loneliness Scale; Rubinstein & Shaver, 1982), for example, "How often do you feel lonely?" (Borys & Perlman, 1985). Men get higher loneliness scores when the word *lonely* is *not* used in the questionnaire (e.g., the revised UCLA Loneliness Scale; Russell, Peplau, & Cutrona, 1980). These questionnaires contain wording such as "No one really knows me well" or "I am no longer close to anyone." Men pay a higher price for admitting loneliness than women do: Undergraduates evaluated a lonely person more negatively when the person was said to be a man (Borys & Perlman, 1985). Women have more freedom than men do to admit loneliness (Brehm, 1992) but are less likely to feel lonely (Reis, 1986). What loneliness they do feel does not vary with whether or not they are in a romantic relationship. As noted previously, men usually rely on a romantic partner for emotional support and sharing confidences, so men without a partner are more lonely than men with partners.

Our society places tremendous importance on the value of romantic relationships and marriage. Perhaps we should value friendship equally or more and encourage both women and men to develop their potentials for friendships. College students who had reduced loneliness through their first year at college had a greater emphasis on friendship than on romance; the reverse was true for those whose loneliness continued (Cutrona, 1982). Perhaps we also should value solitude as a time in which to grow, enjoy ourselves, and get to know what we really want and are willing to give to others (Brehm, 1992). Societal pressures encourage people to think that they have to be coupled, but if we *must* have other people to be happy, we are placing a terrible burden on them and on ourselves.

## *Heterosexual Dating Relationships*

Although boys and girls have been subjected to different experiences and "trained" in vastly different forms of peer relationships, they nonetheless are supposed to be attracted to each other in adolescence and to work progressively toward selecting a mate with whom they can live comfortably the rest of their lives. Early years of dating are not always very helpful on this score.

The **dating ritual** is a cultural scenario that prescribes behavior designed to reduce some of the stress of heterosexual dating (Alksnis, Desmarais, & Wood, 1996; Huston & Schwartz, 1996). The "good date" is fun to be with, easy to talk to, has a good sense of humor, and is not moody or too serious (Strommen, 1977). The script for dating and being a good date is based on well-learned gender roles, and dating often is not done to get to know the other person but to impress peers of one's own gender (Buhrmester & Furman, 1987; Rose & Frieze, 1989, 1993). Thus the structure of a good date provides for a safe, pleasant time but may interfere with the development of mature intimacy and honesty. As teens move toward early adulthood, they do become more concerned about the attributes of a date as a potential partner.

### Traits Desired in a Partner

***Physical Attractiveness***    Both women and men initially prefer a maximally attractive partner but eventually settle in relationships with a partner about equal to their own attractiveness (Baumeister, Wotman, & Stillwell, 1993; Gonzales & Meyers, 1993). However, the physical attractiveness of the other gender generally is more important to men than to women (Davis, 1990). As early as the ninth grade, boys emphasize good looks in describing the ideal woman, whereas girls emphasize interpersonal traits in describing the ideal man (Stiles, Gibbons, & de la Garza-Schnellmann, 1990). More than is true for men, women's attractiveness is correlated with their dating popularity and their spouses' marital satisfaction (Berscheid, Dion, Walster, & Walster, 1971; Jackson, 1992). Men are attracted to a body type that is thinner than average for women, though African American men are more accepting of larger bodies in women than white men are (Thompson, Sargent, & Kemper, 1996). However, both white and African American women overestimate the extent to which men value thinness, and men exaggerate women's attraction to men with large physiques (Cohn & Adler, 1992; Fallon & Rozin, 1985; Kemper et al., 1994; Thompson et al., 1996).

Why do men emphasize physical appearance? What do women emphasize if not physical appearance? David Buss (1988, 1989, 1991; Buss & Barnes, 1986) proposed a psychobiological or evolutionary account of mate selection based on the assumption that the aim of both women and men—or any life form—is to have their genes passed on. Men, then, are predicted to look for a mate likely to be able to produce a maximum of healthy offspring, namely, an attractive, young, and healthy woman. Women are predicted to look for mates who can provide for them and their offspring, namely, strong and dominant men; in humans, earning power and education are cues of being able to provide. A variety of evidence in this and other countries shows the importance of women's physical attractiveness and relative youth to men and the importance to women of a man's financial prospects and dominance (Regan & Sprecher, 1995.

Whatever the reason for the preferences, both women and men seem to know the other's preferences and shape their tactics for attracting potential mates accordingly (Buss, 1988; Child, Low, McCormick, & Cocciarella, 1996). For example, new brides reported that they had tried to attract their future husbands by wearing stylish clothes, makeup, and jewelry and by being clean and well groomed (Buss, 1988). Grooms said that on early dates they had shown off new possessions and let it be known that they made a lot of money. Ads in the personal columns reflect similar gender differences (Focus on Research 10.2). Heterosexual women, but not lesbians, mention their own attractiveness and the financial status of desired partners; heterosexual men mention the desire for an attractive partner and their own financial solidity (Bailey, Gaulin, Agyei, & Gladue, 1994; Child, Low, McCormick, & Cocciarella, 1996; Davis, 1990; Gonzales & Meyers, 1993; Greenlees & McGrew, 1994; Sprecher, Sullivan, & Hatfield, 1994). This pattern has changed little over recent years (1986–1991) but, if anything, has become accentuated (Willis & Carlson, 1993).

***Other Considerations in Choosing Partners***     Women's interest in the financial prospects of potential partners and men's in physical attractiveness are tempered by other criteria. For example, college women were influenced by a man's income only when responding to a group of men with a predominance of socially desirable personality traits (Desrochers, 1995). Educated young people today are conscious of the other gender's expectations, and the expectations may have expanded or even changed (de Weerth & Kalma, 1995; Peres & Meivar, 1986). For example, in one study, college men expressed their tenderness and cooking abilities; women stressed knowing a lot and being oriented to a prestigious occupation while deemphasizing culinary abilities.

Overall, women and men say remarkably similar things when asked about what they want in meaningful relationships or in a marriage partner. In fact, women and men in the same culture are similar in terms of preference for a mate, suggesting that any culture teaches both women and men what is valuable in that culture; cultural differences are larger than gender differences (Buss et al., 1990). In the United States both college and noncollege students say they want a good companion who is affectionate, kind, considerate, loving, dependable, understanding, loyal, interesting to talk with, and honest, and has a good sense of humor (Buss & Barnes, 1986; Fehr, 1993; Goodwin, 1990; Peplau, 1983; Sedikides, Oliver, & Campbell, 1994).

In one research study, the three characteristics rated most highly by both college women and college men for a meaningful relationship were honesty, fidelity, and

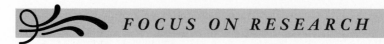

*FOCUS ON RESEARCH*

### 10.2    Ethics and Deception: Love and Rejection in the Personal Ads

Handsome, athletic, SM, broad shoulders, 6', 32, cab driver. Seeks woman for lasting relationship.

Successful, financially secure, SF, intelligent attorney, 30, average appearance. Seeks man for serious relationship.

The popularity of personal ads is a recent phenomenon. Heterosexuals, homosexuals, and bisexuals, single, married, and divorced, teens, grandparents, and every age group in between—all use personal ads to attract partners for every possible relationship, from one-hour anonymous trysts to marriage. Welcome to dating in the 1990s.

The question of who responds to what type of ads and how they make that response intrigued sociologist Erich Goode (1996). Focusing on heterosexual dating, Goode hypothesized that attractiveness and financial resources are two of the most important "commodities" in a dating partner, and not surprisingly, these qualities are often the first things mentioned in a personal ad. Goode wanted to know if women and men responded differently to such ads; that is, are men and women looking for the same thing in an advertised dating partner, and if interested, what type of a response do they make? Is there a gender difference in men's and women's personal ad dating strategies?

How did Goode answer these questions? He used a straightforward approach: He put ads in the personal columns of several newspapers and magazines. Four different ads were used, varying the gender, attractiveness, and occupational/financial success of the individual who ostensibly placed the ad (beautiful waitress, average-looking female lawyer, handsome male cab driver, average-looking male lawyer). The actual participants in the study were the people who responded to the ads.

And respond they did! Goode received 987 written replies to the four ads, 908 of them from men responding to the women's ads (668 of those men wrote to the beautiful waitress; 240 wrote to the successful, average-looking female lawyer). In comparison, 79 women responded to the men's ads (64 to the successful, average-looking male lawyer, 15 to the handsome cab driver). Goode concluded that men are more likely to respond to personals, and they are more influenced by attractiveness. Women, on the other hand, are much less likely to respond, but when they do, they are more influenced by occupational or financial success.

Goode then read each response letter to determine what the participant's dating strategy was. Men were twice as likely to answer more than one ad and to put little effort into their response letters, in some cases simply sending a business card or a xerox of a generic, all-purpose letter. Goode used a sociobiological interpretation for these findings: Men "cast a wide net" for attractive, youthful, fertile women for sex and procreation; women were more selective in their search for financially successful men with access to resources that would ensure the survival of their children. Each of these behaviors increases the likelihood that women and men will produce children and that the species will survive.

This was an interesting, informative, and quite creative study. But was it ethical? The people who responded thought the ads were real and they had a chance of dating the ad writer. Were they disappointed or upset when they received no reply? Did this experience alter their lives in some way? These questions remain unanswered because we don't know what happened to these people.

Goode used deception to conduct this study. He not only withheld the true reason for the study from the participants, but they did not even know they were taking part in a study. Deception studies are not uncommon, but they pose an ethical dilemma. To safeguard participants' rights, APA ethical guidelines require that researchers obtain informed consent from each participant before the study begins and maintain voluntary participation throughout the study (participants can withdraw from the study at any time, without penalty). Deception interferes with both of these ethical guidelines. If the prospective participant does not know the real reason for the study, how can she or he make an informed decision to begin or to continue participation?

Despite these problems, APA guidelines do allow the use of deception in research studies, if certain requirements are met. Researchers must justify their use of deception by showing that alternate methods are not available, that the scientific, educational, or applied value of the study warrants using deception, and that participants are informed of the true nature of the study as soon as possible. This last requirement involves debriefing the participants either orally or in writing, or both, and allowing time for participants to ask questions and express their feelings. Some researchers advocate telling participants why the deception was necessary and reassuring them that anyone would have been taken in. When deception is used, this kind of debriefing can help participants feel less "used" and more comfortable with their experience.

Before beginning any study, but particularly one in which deception is used, the researcher should conduct a cost-benefit analysis. Costs include not only the expenses of time and money but the price paid in participant well-being. Benefits can be thought of as increases in useful knowledge. The costs of deception must be weighed against the study's expected benefits. Researchers struggle with the issue of deception, but it may lead to important new information about human behavior that cannot be obtained in any other way.

JILL BORCHERT ◆

SOURCE: Goode, E. (1996). Gender and courtship entitlement: Responses to personal ads. *Sex Roles, 34*, 141–169.

personality (Table 10.1) (Nevid, 1984). However, differences in the importance of physical appearance still were shown. College women reported a relatively greater emphasis on personal characteristics, while men emphasized physical characteristics more than women did. Gender differences were pronounced when considering what is wanted in a person for a sexual relationship, though women did not neglect physical traits for such a relationship. Women's and men's similarities and differences in their views about what love is all about reveal additional differences in their socialization and role expectations.

## Attitudes About Love

Although women and men are much alike in some ways when it comes to attitudes about love and kinds of love feelings, research has shown some recurring differences (Baumeister et al., 1993). Both women and men value **dyadic attachment,** which essentially is "nest building" or "coupling" with an emphasis on being together and sharing (e.g., "Spending as much time together as possible," "Being able to talk about my most intimate feelings"; Cochran & Peplau, 1985). However, women value equalitarianism and autonomy in relationships more than men do (e.g., "Each of us being able to have our own career," "Having a supportive group of friends as well as my romantic/sexual partner"). The researchers speculated that men assumed they would have autonomy, but women did not assume they also would. As we will see shortly, differences in concern about equalitarianism and autonomy have important implications for dating and marital relationships.

Women tend to have more pragmatic attitudes about love, while men tend to have more idealistic and romantic as well as cynical attitudes (Dion & Dion, 1973; Hendrick & Hendrick, 1995, 1996; Rubin, Peplau, & Hill, 1981). A pragmatic attitude involves analyzing a relationship in terms of a "shopping list" of criteria presumed necessary for a successful relationship (Lee, 1973). Much of the research on attitudes about love is based on descriptions by Lee (1973) and measured in an instrument developed by Hendrick and Hendrick (1996); sample items are shown in A Closer Look 10.1. Men's tendency to idealism is shown in thinking that true love lasts forever, while women think that most people could love any one of several people. Perhaps because of their idealism, men are more cynical than women. The differences are not large, but the patterns are relatively consistent over different kinds of data for American college students (Brehm, 1992). As part of their idealism, men report that they recognize love earlier and fall in love more quickly (Hill, Rubin, & Peplau, 1976; Walster, Walster, & Berscheid, 1978). With this approach, men may be in for a sharper letdown if things do not work out, so they become cynical.

Although men are more idealistic, they also feel more ludic (Hendrick & Hendrick, 1986, 1995, 1996). Ludic behavior is playful enjoyment of a game; with a ludic attitude, sex is a pleasant pastime—playfulness without serious involvement (e.g., "I have sometimes had to keep my partner from finding out about other partners"; Hendrick & Hendrick, 1996). Perhaps because of men's ludic orientation, they are less likely than women to feel that they have been exploited sexually in love affairs that do not work out (Baumeister et al., 1993).

**Table 10.1** Importance of Characteristics in a Romantic Partner in Meaningful Long-Term Relationships and in Sexual Relationships in Heterosexual Women and Men

*Want in meaningful long-term relationship—women and men*

| | Women | | Men | |
|---|---|---|---|---|
| | Rank | Score | Rank | Score |
| Honesty | 1 | 4.89 | 1 | 4.68 |
| Fidelity | 2 | 4.83 | 3 | 4.60 |
| Personality | 3 | 4.82 | 2 | 4.65 |
| Warmth | 4 | 4.80 | 5 | 4.49 |
| Kindness | 5 | 4.80 | 6 | 4.49 |
| Tenderness | 6 | 4.77 | 8 | 4.36 |
| Sensitivity | 7 | 4.75 | 4 | 4.51 |
| Gentleness | 8 | 4.73 | 10 | 4.31 |
| Character | 9 | 4.70 | 7 | 4.41 |
| Patience | 10 | 4.56 | 9 | 4.31 |

*Want in sexual relationship—women*

| | Women | |
|---|---|---|
| | Rank | Score |
| Attractiveness | 1 | 4.51 |
| Sexuality | 2 | 4.46 |
| Warmth | 3 | 4.42 |
| Personality | 4 | 4.41 |
| Tenderness | 5 | 4.39 |
| Gentleness | 6 | 4.36 |
| Sensitivity | 7 | 4.24 |
| Kindness | 8 | 4.23 |
| Build/Fig | 9 | 4.22 |
| Character | 10 | 4.30 |

*Want in sexual relationship—men*

| | Men | |
|---|---|---|
| | Rank | Score |
| Build/Fig | 1 | 4.53 |
| Sexuality | 2 | 4.36 |
| Attractiveness | 3 | 4.31 |
| Facial | 4 | 4.25 |
| Buttocks | 5 | 4.09 |
| Weight | 6 | 4.07 |
| Legs | 7 | 4.02 |
| Breath | 8 | 3.94 |
| Skin | 9 | 3.92 |
| Breasts | 10 | 3.79 |

NOTE: Characteristics were rated on a 5-point scale.

SOURCE: Nevid, J. S. (1984). Sex differences in factors of romantic attraction. *Sex Roles, 11,* (5/6), Adapted from Tables I and II, p. 405.

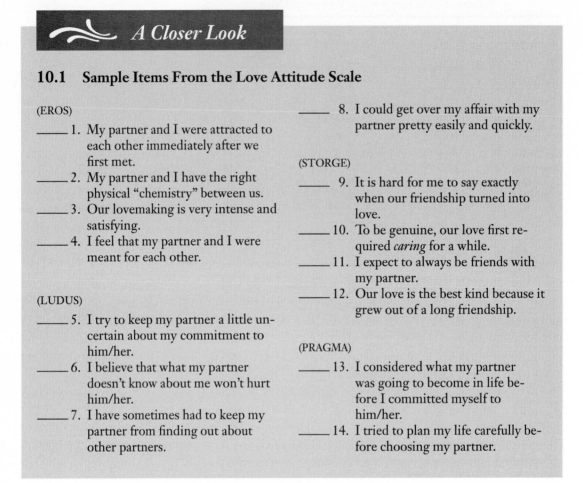

## A Closer Look

### 10.1   Sample Items From the Love Attitude Scale

(EROS)

_____ 1. My partner and I were attracted to each other immediately after we first met.

_____ 2. My partner and I have the right physical "chemistry" between us.

_____ 3. Our lovemaking is very intense and satisfying.

_____ 4. I feel that my partner and I were meant for each other.

(LUDUS)

_____ 5. I try to keep my partner a little uncertain about my commitment to him/her.

_____ 6. I believe that what my partner doesn't know about me won't hurt him/her.

_____ 7. I have sometimes had to keep my partner from finding out about other partners.

_____ 8. I could get over my affair with my partner pretty easily and quickly.

(STORGE)

_____ 9. It is hard for me to say exactly when our friendship turned into love.

_____ 10. To be genuine, our love first required _caring_ for a while.

_____ 11. I expect to always be friends with my partner.

_____ 12. Our love is the best kind because it grew out of a long friendship.

(PRAGMA)

_____ 13. I considered what my partner was going to become in life before I committed myself to him/her.

_____ 14. I tried to plan my life carefully before choosing my partner.

Men and women are equally concerned with erotic or passionate love, as well as altruism (Hendrick & Hendrick, 1987, 1996). Women score higher in storge (friendship love), but storge seems quite high in college men as well as women; friendship love was the most frequently mentioned theme in written accounts of relationships. In spite of gender differences in love styles, the basic structure of belief systems about love is roughly similar (Hendrick & Hendrick, 1996). Because of, or in spite of, their similarities and differences, women and men often have satisfying dating relationships with each other.

## Relationship Satisfaction

Happiness, commitment, and love are all related to satisfaction and longevity of dating relationships. People in love differ from others in that they are higher in erotic love

_____ 15. In choosing my partner, I believed it was best to love someone with a similar background.

_____ 16. A main consideration in choosing my partner was how he/she would reflect on my family.

(MANIA)

_____ 17. When things aren't right with my partner and me, my stomach gets upset.

_____ 18. If my partner and I break up, I would get so depressed that I would even think of suicide.

_____ 19. Sometimes I get so excited about being in love with my partner that I can't sleep.

_____ 20. When my partner doesn't pay attention to me, I feel sick all over.

(AGAPE)

_____ 21. I try to always help my partner through difficult times.

_____ 22. I would rather suffer myself than let my partner suffer.

_____ 23. I cannot be happy unless I place my partner's happiness before my own.

_____ 24. I am usually willing to sacrifice my own wishes to let my partner achieve his/hers.

For each statement:

1 = Strongly disagree with the statement
2 = Moderately disagree with the statement
3 = Neutral—neither agree nor disagree
4 = Moderately agree with the statement
5 = Strongly agree with the statement

SOURCE: Hendrick, C., & Hendrick, S. (1996). Gender and the experience of heterosexual love. In J. T. Wood (Ed.), *Gendered relationships*. Mountain View, CA: Mayfield.

and agapic love (altruistic love) and lower in ludic love (Hendrick & Hendrick, 1988). You probably did not need to read a textbook to think this. Psychologists are trying to add to the understanding of what is involved in this commonplace observance. Similarity between the partners clearly is a correlate of relationship satisfaction. Among the relevant similarities identified are age, interests, sexual attitudes, backgrounds, ideas about marriage, educational aspirations, physical attraction, and intelligence (Hill et al., 1976). For some groups, similarity in religion is important (Markstrom-Adams, 1991).

A particularly important kind of similarity in dating relationships and later in marriage is agreement about gender role behaviors, especially concerning dual-career marriages (Peplau, Rubin, & Hill, 1976, 1977). Couples mismatched on this issue were less satisfied with the relationship while they were together and were more likely to break up within a year than those with shared attitudes (41% versus 26%). Similarly, egalitarianism is related to dating couples' commitment and to marital satisfaction

(Grauerholz, 1987). Entering into considerations of equality are issues of self-disclosure and the man's self-esteem.

Men seem to like to disclose to women and are more likely to disclose to their romantic partners. Both women and men in dating relationships are more satisfied with the relationship the more they disclose to each other (Hendrick, Hendrick, & Adler, 1988) and the more expressive of love their partner is (Siavelis & Lamke, 1992). The college men's self-esteem was related to women's satisfaction with the relationship, while college women's self-esteem was not related to men's satisfaction. The relationship between the man's self-esteem and woman's satisfaction probably reflects continuing assumptions of male power (Peplau & Campbell, 1989). A man with healthy self-esteem and personal security is in a better position to avoid insisting upon having dominant control. He also may be in a better position to share feelings and share the general work of developing and maintaining the relationship—what many consider "women's work." Happiness, commitment, and love are all higher when each partner is seen as contributing equally to keeping the relationship going (Fletcher, Fincham, Cramer, & Heron, 1987). The equality does not always happen or may not be enough.

## When It's Over

Contrary to stereotypes, women are somewhat more likely to initiate breakups of dating relationships than men are and to cite more problems in the relationship than men do; this pattern tends to be true of divorce as well (Hill et al., 1976; Rubin et al., 1981). Relative absence of the characteristics that contribute to relationship satisfaction are typical of relationships that break up. For example, couples that broke up within a few months after initial research participation had not cared and shared as much when first studied as those who stayed together (Hendrick et al., 1988; Simpson, 1987). Even couples who care may discover important differences that interfere with developing a durable relationship. Lack of similarity is a reason for dissolution of relationships. Other general reasons for breaking up include desire to be independent, meeting someone else, and parental pressure; about three quarters of women and men stated boredom as a reason (Hill et al., 1976).

In deciding about ending a relationship, people consider what needs are being satisfied in the relationship and at what cost (Drigotas, Rusbult, & Caryl, 1992). Couples that have broken up have reported no increase over time in rewards, satisfaction, investment, and commitment—the relationship was not growing, it was not going anywhere (Simpson, 1987). Gratification of needs through the relationship is more relevant than commitment to whether or not a relationship dissolves. Thus people may be committed to a relationship, but if their needs are not being well met, breakup becomes more likely, especially when there is optimism about finding a better partner (Simpson, 1987).

Also contrary to stereotypes, when one person is more upset with the breakup, it is more likely the man than the woman (Hill et al., 1976; Rubin, Peplau, & Hill, 1981). Occasionally, no difference is reported (Simpson, 1987). Women more readily than men accept the fact that love has died and the relationship is over—they are more

*When a relationship breaks up, a woman can still count on her friends for support. Because men get more emotional support from women than from men, a man who loses his primary relationship with a woman may feel emotionally isolated.*

practical. They use more active, healthy coping styles to deal with what depression they have (Mearns, 1991). Men are more likely to say they are depressed, lonely, or unhappy. It is hard for them to believe that the relationship really is over—they are idealistic and romantic. For men, a feeling that the breakup came out of the blue probably contributes to their distress. To the extent that women are more sensitive to nuances of relationships, they are more likely to have seen problems even if they do not initiate the breakup (Drigotas & Rusbult, 1992; Jacobson, Follette, & McDonald, 1982; Rubin et al., 1981). A woman might have tried to avert the breakup in ways the man, with his idealism, did not pick up on; and men do not detect meanings from nonverbal cues as well as women do (chapter 9). To the woman, the breakup seems gradual, to the man it seems abrupt. She has been preparing for it in ways he has not.

In addition, dissolution of a romantic relationship may be easier for women because of the interpersonal support they have. As discussed in the earlier section on friendship, men get support from relationships with women that they typically do not get from other men, whereas women typically do get the support they need from other women. The man who experiences a breakup of a romantic relationship likely loses a bigger chunk of his interpersonal life than a woman loses. This is not to say that women do not also experience a significant loss, and for some the loss is more devastating than for others.

Some women are prone to extreme distress at the breakup of a relationship; women with unrestricted views about sex were found to have more pronounced, longer, more intense distress at breakup than did other people (Simpson, 1987). *Unrestricted* in this context includes greater sexual activity in the past and anticipated for the future—more casual attitudes about sex. At first glance, it might seem that a woman with such views about sex could shrug off a breakup. My students tell me that the "unrestricted" women they know seem to want love and are crushed when they "give their body" and do not get love (the unrestricted women were more likely to have had sex with their partners than were restricted women). This possibility is consistent with Karen Horney's (1937) view that intense preoccupation with sex is driven by a desperate search for love and security. In addition, women generally are more likely than men to use sex as a signal of love and in hopes of winning love (chapter 11). Some women have a greater need for love than others do, and when this need is not met, their pain is intense.

## Cohabitation

An alternative to regular dating and to marriage that is being chosen by increasing numbers of couples is **cohabitation**—living together without marriage. Cohabitation has increased almost 60 times over the last 25 years (Cavanaugh, 1990). The U.S. Department of Census in 1980 added a category for **persons of the opposite sex sharing living quarters (POSSLQs**—pronounced "possel-cues"). According to the 1990 census, about 3% of the U.S. population and 12% of the Canadian population were in cohabiting relationships (Saluter, 1994; Stout, 1991). (Note the restriction to mixed-sex partners.) For young couples not previously married, cohabitation is considered a delay of marriage rather than a permanent replacement for it (Blumstein & Schwartz, 1983; DeMaris & Leslie, 1984). For older couples, it may be in place of marriage. Previously divorced people may cohabit rather than risk the possibility of another failed marriage; widowed people may fear losing a spouse's pension if they remarry, or fear that they would be threatening their children's inheritance (Brehm, 1992).

Some couples want to enjoy each other without the pressure of taking on the demanding roles of wife and husband (Brehm, 1992). Yet decision making, division of labor, communication, and relationship satisfaction do not appear to differ between cohabiting and married couples (Blumstein & Schwartz, 1983; Murstein, 1986; Yllo, 1978). Cohabiting couples may be more equalitarian in sharing of household work but are likely to become traditional if they marry (chapter 12). Yet, cohabiting couples are more abusive than married or dating couples (chapter 15).

Young people sometimes cite as an advantage of cohabitation finding out if they will be compatible in marriage. What are the marital outcomes? "Easing into marriage" via cohabitation does not seem better than "jumping into it" (Brehm, 1992). Some researchers find no differences (White, 1989), but the most frequently reported result is that married partners who previously cohabited are *less* happily married and have more divorces than those who did not (Bennett, Blanc, & Bloom, 1988; Newcomb, 1987). For example, 53% of first marriages preceded by cohabitation failed within 10 years compared with 28% of marriages in which the couple had not lived together before marriage (Riche, 1988; data from the National Survey of Families and Households).

Why is cohabitation associated with poorer marital outcomes? Heterosexual cohabiting couples are less committed to the relationship than are married couples and gay and lesbian couples (Kurdek & Schmitt, 1986a, 1986c). The lowered commitment might be associated with personal inclinations that existed before the cohabitation or developed during cohabitation (Newcomb, 1987). Another possibility is that cohabitation may start a "relational clock" running before the "I do's" are said (Brehm, 1992). That is, there may be a time at which problems in any relationship develop, and for cohabiting couples, the process starts before the marriage license is signed. But, with or without legal recognition, marriage still is a popular choice among Americans.

## *Marriage and Divorce*

Many married couples are happy together, sharing, playing, respecting each other, and working out problems, throughout their adult lives. Unfortunately for others, the early years of gender-typed socialization and different styles of social interaction with peers have effects they do not overcome, so they stay together in distressed marriages or they get divorced.

### Who Gets Married

About 95% of Americans are legally married at some time in life, a rate surpassing the rates in most European countries and rates in the 19th century in the United States. However, the general marriage rates have been declining, so that some authorities predict that a 90% proportion is likely for coming years (Norton & Moorman, 1987; Rogers & Thornton, 1985). Another change is that the median age of first marriage has increased during the century to 24.1 for women and 26.3 for men in 1991 (Figure 10.2). The age of those who marry early (by age 19) has remained remarkably stable (Cherlin, 1981), but those who marry later are marrying later than ever. For example, the percentage of people never married has increased for those under 40 and decreased for those over 40. In 1993 U.S. Census figures showed that about 23% of American women and 31% of American men had never been married (U.S. Bureau of Census, 1993), a doubling since 1970 (Saluter, 1994). Previously, more African American women delayed marriage during the young years but generally ultimately married at a rate similar to whites (Norton & Moorman, 1987). Now there is some evidence that white and African American marriage patterns are diverging; about 35% of African American women have not yet married by age 34, and estimates are that about 25% will never marry (Dickson, 1993). Women of Hispanic origin are similar to non-Hispanic white women in entry into first marriages.

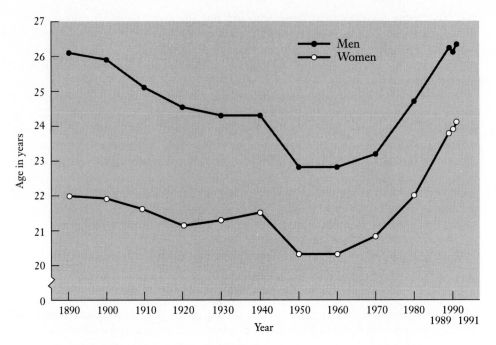

**Figure 10.2** *Change in Median Age of Marriage in the United States, 1890–1991.*
SOURCE: Department of Commerce, Bureau of Census.

People give many reasons for marrying: love, companionship, sex, children, financial security. Women of the past often considered marriage financially necessary and romantic love an extra. As recently as the mid-1960s, only about one fourth of women thought romantic love was necessary for marriage, while two thirds of men did (Kephart, 1967). As entering the labor force has become a more acceptable option for women, the number of women seeing romantic love as necessary has increased to four fifths, the same as for men (Simpson, Campbell, & Berscheid, 1986). Being a wage earner gives women both the freedom to stay single and the freedom to marry for love rather than for financial necessity—it puts women in a better position to *choose* marriage if they wish.

## Single Women

Some women choose not to marry. In the recent past, remaining single was not considered a desirable option, so that marriage was not really a choice. A prominent cultural definition of happiness was "escape from being an 'old maid'" (Bernard, 1973, p. 55). Most young women (90%–95%) still expect to marry and to have children (Machung, 1986). However, being a single woman is seen more and more as a reasonable option, although some negative attitudes persist (Anderson & Stewart, 1994; Seccombe & Ishii-Kuntz, 1994).

Jessie Bernard (1973) called the women who do not marry the "cream of the crop" (and men who do not marry the "bottom of the barrel," at least in terms of marriageability). Single women are better educated than other women and more likely to have well-paid jobs (Braito & Anderson, 1983; Faludi, 1991; Gigy, 1980; Glick & Spanier, 1980; Kelly, 1982). Of employed women, 88% of those who have always been single have college or graduate education compared with 40% of married women (Gigy, 1980). In part, this reflects the **marriage gradient:** the tendency for women to marry men who are older, more educated, or of a higher social class than they. The more education and earning potential a woman has, the fewer men to "marry up" with (Townsend, 1987; Townsend & Levy, 1990). The marriage gradient, however, is not all that is involved. With increased education and income, a woman is in less need of marriage (Spitze, 1988; Townsend & Levy, 1990). Some women stay single because of concerns that marriage and career are incompatible (Allen, 1989). Others may postpone marriage and then discover that they do not need it for happiness. It is not a matter of becoming "reconciled" to single life but rather of discovering its benefits and enjoying them (Donelson, 1977b).

Single adults develop social patterns based on friendships as well as kinships and typically cannot be considered lonely or socially isolated (Essex & Nam, 1987; Rubinstein, 1987; Seccombe & Ishii-Kuntz, 1994). African American single women are particularly likely to get support from family members as well as from women friends and work colleagues (Brown & Gary, 1985; Denton, 1990). Single women and married women generally are similar in life satisfaction and in personal adjustment (Gigy, 1980). When they do differ, single women are better off, such as being higher in self-esteem, more assertive and poised, and less depressed (chapter 16; Faludi, 1991). Obviously, many single women are quite happy and so also are many married women.

## Happy Marriages

Young married couples are extremely happy (Campbell, 1975; Hatfield & Rapson, 1993). Most couples, however, report that disappointment sets in (Hatfield & Rapson, 1993). Often there is a steady drop in marital satisfaction during the first 20 years of marriage and then a rebound when children leave home (chapter 12; Levenson, Carstensen, & Gottman, 1994). Nonetheless, some marriages are happier than others.

Happily married people tend to have some or all of the following characteristics: They are well educated, they married past their teens, they were well-acquainted before marriage, their parents are happily married, and they have good communication and conflict resolution skills as well as relatively egalitarian habits (Birchler, 1992; Cate & Lloyd, 1992; Kurdek, 1991a, 1993; Levenson et al., 1994). Happily married people have a closeness they can count on because there is commitment to each other and to the relationship along with high regard for each other. They respect and nurture each other and feel that they can rely on each other (Antill, 1983; Bee, 1987; Kelly & Burgoon, 1992; Kobak & Hazan, 1991). The closeness or intimacy so important to marital satisfaction includes the emotional intimacy of expressing feelings (Merves-Okin & Amidon, 1991) as well as spiritual intimacy (Hatch, James, & Schumm, 1986). When both members of a couple (heterosexual, lesbian, gay) are expressive (androgynous or "feminine"), they see themselves as happier than do couples in which one or both partners are low on expressive traits (Antill, 1983; Bradbury & Fincham, 1988; Peterson, Baucom, Elliott, & Farr, 1989). A basic similarity, such as in education, background, intelligence, and values, also facilitates sharing (Diamond, 1986; Kurdek, 1991a). With marked dissimilarity, there likely is some status difference that impairs a feeling of equality. High education and self-esteem are thought advantageous in resolving conflict and being prepared for the fading of the idealistic romanticism of the early phases of marriage (Belsky & Rovine, 1990; Kurdek, 1991a).

Young adults, middle-aged adults, and older adults are remarkably consistent in their views of what is important in a happy love relationship. In a study of married couples nominated by their friends as having a satisfying love relationship, women and men agreed that the most important characteristics of their relationship were emotional security, respect, and communication (Reedy, Birren, & Schaie, 1981). The other characteristics, in order, were help and play behaviors, sexual intimacy, and loyalty (Figure 10.3). Not all marriages are as happy as those of this study, however; marriage comes in many different forms.

## Kinds of Marriage: His and Hers

Jessie Bernard (1973) proposed that there are two psychological marriages for every legal one—his and hers, and his likely is more satisfying than hers. Although there are exceptions, generally, men state more satisfaction with their marriages than women do (Fowers, 1991; Suitor, 1991; Wood, Rhodes, & Whelan, 1989). But unrewarding marriages take a greater toll on women than on men (Helson, Mitchell, & Moane, 1984). His and her marriages differ in two major realms of interaction: issues of equality and of the expressions of love and care. Most women are not getting what they want in these areas of interaction (Shek, 1995).

***Issues of Equality***    Lack of equality characterizes most marriages (Cooper, Chasson, & Zeiss, 1985; Finlay, Starnes, & Alvarez, 1985; Fowers, 1991); their basic structure is an unequal one, causing more stress on wives than on husbands. Husbands generally believe in innate roles more than wives do and generally are more traditional and less equalitarian than wives are (Mirowsky & Ross, 1987; Peplau & Gordon, 1985). We have seen that lack of agreement about gender role issues is related to dating dissatisfaction and breakup. It is relevant in marriage as well: Distressed couples have a greater gap in views about equality than nondistressed couples do (Fowers, 1991). Women are gaining more power in marriages because of their employment, but they generally earn less than men and so still have less power as well as less physical strength and less power from gender roles (Blumstein & Schwartz, 1983; Hatfield & Rapson, 1993; Steil & Weltman, 1991). Lesbians are less concerned about financial differences than other couples are (chapter 13).

The most common kind of marriage is a **modern marriage:** The wife is employed by choice but still does the housework and possibly child care in addition to her paid job (Breuss & Pearson, 1996; Hochschild, 1989; Ross, Mirowsky, & Huber, 1983; Schwartz, 1994; Steil & Weltman, 1991). Still fairly rare, though thought to be increas-

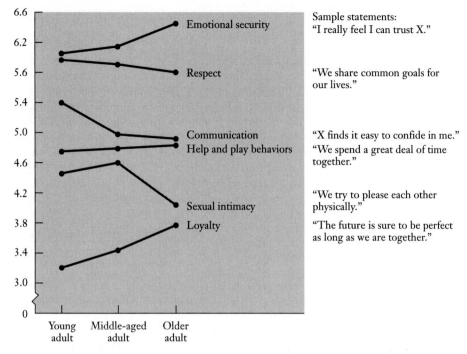

**Figure 10.3** *Importance of components of love for happily married people of different ages.*
NOTE: Young = 28.2 years; middle-aged = 45.4 years; older = 64.7 years.   SOURCE: Reedy, M. N.,
Birren, J. E., & Schaie, K. W. (1981). Age and sex differences in satisfying love relationships across the
adult life span. *Human Development, 24,* 52–66. Figure 1, p. 60.

ing, are fully **equalitarian marriages:** The wife is employed by choice, and duties are
shared (Schwartz, 1994). Couples in equalitarian marriages have lower distress and
higher satisfaction than people in any of the other forms of marriage (Gray-Little &
Burks, 1982; Ross et al., 1983; Schwartz, 1994). These couples have more intimacy,
companionship, mutual respect, mutual understanding, and better communication,
and they put their relationship first (Schwartz, 1994). **Traditional marriages,** in which
the wife does not work outside the home but the husband does, provide psychological
benefits for the husband and for the wife *if* it is her choice not to be employed (Fitzpatrick, 1988; Peplau, 1983). Women are most depressed when they are not employed
but would prefer to be (Benin & Neinstedt, 1985).

The only type of marriage in which the husband has distress because of the
marriage structure, and the one with highest distress for the wife as well, is called the
**traditional desired marriage:** The wife is responsible for housework and children and
is employed but not by choice (Rosen, 1987; Ross et al., 1983). Neither husband nor
wife benefits from this arrangement (Ulbrich, 1988).

A special comment must be made about the concept of "Black Matriarchy," the
notion that African American women rule the family, as claimed in the Moynihan
Report. That does not seem to apply to all African American families (Gary, 1986;
McAdoo, 1993). In fact, among middle-class African Americans in the Baltimore area,

the families come close to the equalitarian model (McAdoo, 1993), with both husbands and wives contributing equally to decisions about the family.

***Expressing Care and Love***    The relationship styles of friendships extend into marriage, with men emphasizing doing things and women emphasizing saying things and sharing feelings (Wills, Weiss, & Patterson, 1974). Lillian Rubin (1983) referred to wives and husbands as "intimate strangers." Their long history of different communication styles (Breuss & Pearson, 1996; Wood, 1996) means women and men like to talk about different things. Women generally enjoy discussing feelings and personal issues as well as sharing the details of the day. In contrast men feel less skillful at sharing feelings and see daily details as superfluous (Wood, 1996).

Women may be tempted to see men's relative lack of interest in personal talk as a rejection of intimacy. Across all social classes, self-disclosure is more important to women than to men, though African American men in early marriage are more disclosing than white men (Oggins, Veroff, & Leber, 1993). Many men who liked to self-disclose when they were dating seem to clam up in marriage. Thus women carry the responsibility for the emotional work of the relationship with a man who is not sharing his own thoughts and feelings (Miller, 1973; Weiss, 1975). This does not mean that men do not love their wives, but their general style of showing love is different from women's (Cancian, 1985; Rubin, 1976, 1983).

As they do in friendship, men show care by acting. One husband was surprised when he washed his wife's car as a sign of affection and his wife did not see that as an act of affection. Francesca Cancian (1985) is concerned that love and intimacy are defined in a feminized fashion and suggests that the feminized definition is likely to make the typical husband feel threatened and controlled by women's push for more intimacy. Talking about the relationship feels to the husband like taking a test his wife made up and he will fail. He reacts with withdrawal, she pressures more for sharing, he withdraws more. Expanding the view of love to include instrumental activities would allow more recognition of men's expressions of love and would also allow housework done by either women or men to be seen as acts of love.

## Communication and Conflict

Conflict and differences of opinion are bound to happen in any relationship, including happy marriages. Good relationships and not-so-good ones differ not so much in the amount of conflict as the way in which disagreement is dealt with (Langhinrichsen-Rohling, Smutzler, & Vivian, 1994; Peterson, 1983). People in satisfying marriages reinforce their partner, show humor and willingness to negotiate and compromise, and attribute positive events to their partner (Aida & Falbo, 1991; Fincham & Bradbury, 1993). In contrast, dissatisfied couples put their partner down and generally express negative views and emotions (Gottman & Levenson, 1992; Levenson & Gottman, 1985).

Equalitarian heterosexual couples, and lesbians generally, are likely to be fairly direct about their concerns: They say what they are concerned about and discuss it, without the need of coercive techniques (Falbo & Peplau, 1980; Gottman, 1979). In marriages with power differences, both women and men engage in game-playing and do so in different ways (Cataldi & Reardon, 1996). It appears that traditional expressive, interpersonally oriented women use more manipulative tactics, including regression, debasement, and the silent treatment. Perhaps because of higher status, men assume they will get their way, so they do not feel the need for a great deal of manipulation. They are, however, willing to use their charm. Because of lower status, women assume that they will not get their way and so use the strategies of people lower in power, such as pouting, crying, withdrawing affection, dropping hints, flattering, and pleading (Howard, Blumstein, & Schwartz, 1986). The tactics sometimes work (the woman is implicitly admitting that she knows "her place" of lesser power) (chapter 9), but they also contribute to views of women as indirect and manipulative—which they are when they have to be because of lesser status.

Status differentials also contribute to the frequent **demand/withdraw pattern:** One person pressures the other, who then withdraws, prompting greater pressure and then more withdrawal (Christensen & Heavey, 1990). Typically, the woman demands and complains and the man withdraws, as in the previously mentioned case of women wanting to talk (Cancian, 1985; Christensen & Heavey, 1990). It might be tempting to think that women are just whiny complainers, but this does not seem an appropriate conclusion. The issue is one of status. Women, with lesser status and power, are the ones more likely to want change. Men, with more power, are more likely to have a vested interest in the status quo. When the tables are turned and men want a change, the pattern reverses: Men demand and women withdraw.

Dynamics of the demand/withdraw pattern were shown in a study of parents who were asked to discuss two issues of child rearing, one on which the mother wanted a change and one on which the father wanted a change (Christensen & Heavey, 1990). The wife-demand/husband-withdraw pattern (a gender difference) was more frequent than the opposite. However, the kind of issue being discussed also was important, supporting the view that power differences contribute to the pattern. Both the husbands and the wives were more likely to demand when discussing a change they wanted and more likely to withdraw when discussing a change the partner wanted. Some couples do not manage to avoid the continual demand/withdrawal spirals or the game playing of inequality. Or, for other reasons, they simply decide that the marriage is not worth the effort to keep it together.

## Divorce

The divorce rate in the United States is greater than in any other industrialized country (Costello & Stone, 1994). The rate more than doubled between 1960 and 1981 (Cherlin, 1981). African American couples are about twice as likely to divorce as white couples, probably because of differences in income and stress (Price & McKenry, 1988). Although the divorce rate may be stabilizing or declining (Bumpass, Castro-Martin, & Sweet, 1991; Norton & Moorman, 1987), estimates are that between 40% and 50% of marriages taking place now in the United States and Canada will end in divorce (Gorlick, 1995; Kitson, 1992; Norton & Moorman, 1987; Price & McKenry, 1988). Over one third of divorces happen within less than 5 years of marriage, with the highest proportion within 3 years of marriage (National Center for Health Statistics, 1991, in Kurdek, 1993).

There are no convincing explanations for why the divorce rate increased, but several factors have been suggested (Chase-Lansdale & Hetherington, 1990). Today, people expect many kinds of satisfactions and excitements from each other. A spouse is to be friend, lover, and caregiver, and the marriage can be dissolved simply if it is dull. Some people see women's employment *leading* to increased divorce rates, while others see women's increasing employment as a *response* to the risk of divorce (Spitze, 1988). Certainly, women's rapid movement into the labor force has led to changed relationships between women and men, reducing women's economic dependence on men while increasing the strain women experience (Bianchi & Spain, 1986; Finlay et al., 1985; Price & McKenry, 1988). As women's income increases, so, too, does their likelihood of divorce (Cherlin, 1979; Kelly, 1982). The women's movement may have helped some women see that they do not have to stay in an unsatisfactory marriage. Finally, there is the practical point that changes in divorce laws have made divorce simpler and less expensive in recent years.

Most people who divorce after a first marriage do remarry (Ihinger-Tallman & Pasley, 1987; Norton & Moorman, 1987). Generally, remarriage rates are higher for men than for women, although the rates for both have been declining since 1980 (Chase-Lansdale & Hetherington, 1990). Women with high incomes or high education have the lowest remarriage rates; men with high incomes or education have the highest remarriage rates (Glick & Lin, 1986; White, 1979). People in second marriages report about the same level of satisfaction as those in first marriages (and men more so in both), but the divorce rate for second marriages is somewhat higher than for first marriages (Cherlin, 1981; Ihinger-Tallman & Pasley, 1987).

The factors associated with distressed marriages are the same ones that predict divorce: having children before marriage, early age of marriage (especially before 20), frequent disagreements, relative lack of education and money, and lack of equality, similarity, good communication, and commitment (Glen & Supanic, 1984; Kitson, 1992; Kurdek, 1993; McGonagle, Kessler, & Gotlib, 1993; Norton & Moorman, 1987). High frequency of attending religious services is related to lower divorce rates, but divorce rates for conservative Protestant denominations are relatively high; rates for Protestants generally are higher than for Catholics or Jews. Further, the divorce rate is higher in people whose parents divorced. The children of divorced parents tend to marry at young ages. White women especially seem to have a lower commitment to marriage, so that any marital failure has reduced importance (Glen & Kramer, 1987).

*Why Divorce?*    Typically, one person wants to terminate the relationship more than the other does because the cost of marriage is greater than the satisfactions (Kelly, 1982; Levinger, 1976). As in dating relationships, people weigh the satisfactions against the costs of the relationship, and the person wanting an end is more likely to be the woman than the man (Gray & Silver, 1990; Kelly, 1982; Kitson, 1992; Spanier & Thompson, 1983); an exception is that after age 55, men are the leading initiators. As in dating relationships, women seem to be more attuned than men to relationship difficulties and become dissatisfied sooner than their partners (Blumstein & Schwartz,

**Table 10.2**   Percentage of Women and Men Giving
Selected Reasons for Divorce

| | Percentage of | |
|---|---|---|
| | Women | Men |
| Communication problems | 69.7 | 59.3 |
| Basic unhappiness | 59.9 | 46.9 |
| Incompatibility | 56.4 | 44.7 |
| Emotional abuse | 55.5 | 24.7 |
| Financial problems | 32.9 | 28.7 |
| Sexual problems | 32.1 | 30.2 |
| Spouse alcohol abuse | 30.0 | 5.8 |
| Spouse infidelity | 25.2 | 10.5 |
| Physical abuse | 21.7 | 3.6 |
| In-laws | 10.7 | 11.6 |
| Children | 8.9 | 4.4 |
| Religious differences | 8.6 | 6.5 |
| Mental illness | 5.0 | 6.9 |
| Spouse drug abuse | 3.9 | 1.4 |
| Own infidelity | 3.9 | 6.2 |
| "Women's lib" | 3.0 | 14.5 |
| Own alcohol abuse | .9 | 9.4 |
| Own drug abuse | .3 | 1.1 |

SOURCE: Cleek, M. G., & Pearson, T. A. (1985). Perceived causes of
divorce: An analysis of interrelationships. *Journal of Marriage and the
Family, 47*, 179–183. Table 3, p. 181.

1983; Gray & Silver, 1990; Huston & Ashmore, 1986; Kitson, 1992). No matter who
initiates it, the decision for divorce is a difficult one finally made after months or even
years of thinking about it.

Communication difficulties were the largest single reason for divorce cited both
by women and by men in a sample of over 600 people (Cleek & Pearson, 1985). Other
prominent difficulties for both women and men were basic unhappiness and incompatibility, though more women than men cited these (Table 10.2). Given their basic
backgrounds, the exact meaning of communication difficulties, basic unhappiness, and
incompatibility differs between women and men (Kelly, 1982). Women are more likely
than men to say that they felt unloved (66% versus 37%). The major complaint of men
(53%) was that their wives neglected their needs and wishes; in turn, a major complaint
of women was that they were criticized by husbands. A survey sponsored by *Cosmopolitan* magazine showed that women also complain of emotional and verbal abuse and
the husband's self-centeredness and distance (A Closer Look 10.2).

***Effects of Divorce***   Divorce may be the best answer for some problematic marriages,
but it is not an easy answer (Albrecht, Bahr, & Goodman, 1983; Bradbury & Fincham,
1990; Kelly, 1982; Kitson, 1992). Divorced people say that they had underestimated
the pain that the divorce would cause (Wallerstein & Kelly, 1980). Time does not

*A Closer Look*

## 10.2   Examples of Women's Final Reasons for Divorce

"When I found myself considering suicide as an alternative to staying married."

"When I realized that my husband, who had many hobbies, didn't consider me one of them . . ."

"When our marriage counselor asked, 'If he made all the changes you want, would that be enough?' and I realized the answer was no."

"When, after watching his father beat me for twenty years, our oldest son was jailed for domestic violence."

"When after having sex I would run to the bathroom and throw up."

"When my next-door neighbor played a tape for me of my husband having such loud sex with another woman that it could be heard through the wall."

From a *Cosmopolitan* magazine survey published in the July 1991 issue, compiled from the responses of more than 20,000 women to a questionnaire.

necessarily heal. Neither time since separation (studied up to 36 years) nor whether or not a new partner was found necessarily changed people's views about divorce (Gray & Silver, 1990).

Divorce is second only to the death of a spouse in the stress it causes (Bursik, 1991a; Holmes & Rahe, 1967) and may produce a greater variety of long-lasting negative effects (Nock, 1981). The effects seem more severe for men than for women, at least for the short term (Price & McKenry, 1988). Divorced people are overrepresented in groups of psychiatric patients, alcoholics, and suicide victims; men are 50% more likely to commit suicide than women after divorce. Problems may have existed before the divorce (and perhaps precipitated it), but authorities tend to agree that divorce is traumatic for most people (Schaie & Willis, 1991).

Divorced women are likely to face a drop in financial status, probably contributing to greater long-term problems for women (Gorlick, 1995; Morgan, 1991; Price & McKenry, 1988). Most women get very little if any money from their former husbands, even if they are awarded child support (Arendell, 1987; Price & McKenry, 1988; Waldman, 1992). Estimates about women's drop in income vary from 30% to 73% (Duncan & Hoffman, 1991; Morgan, 1991; Weitzman, 1985). Only half of women who are supposed to get child support do so (Waldman, 1992). Divorced women often are forced to take low-paying unstable jobs. This puts a strain on the woman and on her children, who are likely to be living with her (Chase-Lansdale & Hetherington, 1990; Hetherington, 1989).

Traditional women in traditional marriages may have more problems adjusting than more equalitarian women (Weitzman, 1985). But for perhaps as many as a third of women, divorce causes little pain. Although divorce is not pleasant, some people do have positive feelings about it and optimism about a new chance for life, with increased psychological growth (Rice, 1994; Schwartz, 1994). Five years after divorce, most people approved of their divorce, even if they initially had been opposed (Wallerstein & Kelly, 1980). Divorced women often report greater closeness to their children than previously (Gorlick, 1995). Also, divorced women, like widows (chapter 14), often report discovering personal strengths (53% of women versus 15% of men) they did not know they had (Brown & Fox, 1979). Women studied at less than 8 months after separation and then 1 year later showed psychological growth over the year (Bursik, 1991a, 1991b). The amount of development was not related to age—older women as well as younger women showed growth. Many women profit psychologically from divorce and grow personally afterward.

## Lesbian Relationships

This chapter started with the topic of friendship. In many ways it is ending with the same topic, because lesbian relationships closely resemble best friendships with the addition of an erotic component (Peplau, 1981, 1982; Rothblum, 1994b). What is more distinctive and important to lesbians about their involvement with a significant other or with other lesbians as friends is not the commonality of a sexual preference for women as much as it is a shared outlook about relationships. The issue of why they became lesbians will be addressed in the following chapter on sexuality. Here, the focus is on relationships. That involves issues of gender roles.

### Gender Roles

People often confuse gender identity (one's understanding of being female or male), gender role behavior (how one behaves), and sexual orientation (choosing a romantic partner) and assume that these components are stereotypically consistent (Peplau & Gordon, 1983a). The truth is that most lesbians feel very much like women. The view that a woman who prefers women over men must be masculine in identity and behavior and that gay men are feminine reflects the **inversion theory** derived from Freudian theory—homosexuals have inverted their gender identity (Ellis, 1915). Unlike some later Freudians, however, Freud did not necessarily think that homosexuals had any problem to be cured (chapter 11). Inversion theory has been discounted by researchers but still is part of popular thinking. Beliefs shape what people "see" (Kite & Deaux, 1987). When told that some women shown in photographs were lesbians, college students rated those women as more masculine than did students told the women were heterosexual. Conversely, students thought women with masculine faces (as rated by others) were more likely lesbians than women with feminine faces (Dunkle & Francis, 1990).

*Lesbians tend to be less gender-typed and stereotypical in their dress and demeanor than are heterosexual women. These women are less likely than a heterosexual couple to play out any kind of gender roles in their relationship, despite stereotypes of "butch" and "femme" roles.*

Lesbians are less stereotypically feminine in personality traits than heterosexual women, but they cannot be considered masculine. Lesbians are more instrumental than heterosexual women but not less expressive (Dancey, 1992; Kurdek, 1987); they also see their ideal woman and ideal man as balanced in terms of instrumentality and expressiveness (Hellwege, Perry, & Dobson, 1988). The lack of gender-typing in views of self and others is paralleled by their style in interpersonal relationships.

In spite of the general belief that lesbians are masculine and gay men are feminine, there also persists a widespread belief that in same-gender relationships, one person "plays the role of the man" and one "plays the role of the woman," called a **butch-femme stereotype** (Huston & Schwartz, 1996; Peplau & Gordon, 1983b). Most lesbians have in fact rejected roles and do not identify as butch or femme (Peplau, 1981, 1982; Peplau & Gordon, 1982; Reilly & Lynch, 1990; Schreurs, 1993). They see the absence of role playing as a major advantage of their lifestyle, and lesbian couples generally engage in less role playing than heterosexual couples or gay men (Blumstein & Schwartz, 1983; Kurdek & Schmitt, 1986b, 1986c).

It is true, however, that newcomers and older lesbians may play butch-femme roles (Martin & Lyon, 1972; Peplau, 1981). A lesbian who has just "come out" may dress as a "butch" in an attempt to identify herself to other lesbians. Lesbians have grown up in a strongly sex-typed world, just as other people have, and they sometimes enter lesbianism on the assumption that the lesbian community also is structured on the basis of traditional sex roles. With time, however, they come to realize that roles are not necessary. Older lesbians who came out in the 1950s or before may use butch-femme roles and simply keep doing what they have always done (Boston Women's Health Book Collective, 1992; Cardell, Finn, & Marecek, 1981; Peplau, 1981).

It is also true that some women, especially those of lesser education and the working class, describe themselves as butch or femme (Weber, 1996). However, what they mean by butch and femme is very different from the heterosexual concept of playing a role. These lesbians tend to define butch as freedom to reject and femme as freedom to accept some stereotypical feminine behaviors in dress, demeanor, and occupational pursuits. Some heterosexual women also reject stereotypic feminine behaviors. They have been called tomboys, a term that does not have the pejorative connotation that butch does.

## Primary Relationships

Contrary to stereotyped views, lesbians and gay men generally prefer a stable love relationship with one person (Bell & Weinberg, 1978; Peplau, 1982, 1996; Peplau, Veniegas, & Campbell, 1996). Nearly half, and perhaps many more, lesbians are in steady relationships (estimates range from 45% to 80%), though they are not necessarily living with the partner. Results from studies of lesbians and gay men must be considered cautiously because it is difficult to obtain a representative sample of members of a hidden population (Berger, 1982; Peplau, 1981); young, well-educated, middle-class whites who are at least somewhat open about their sexual orientation tend to be overrepresented in research samples.

The duration of primary relationships of lesbians varies tremendously, as is true for heterosexual relationships. Some lesbians find the right woman the first time and stay with her for life; most have experienced serial monogamy. The average length of lesbian relationships for professional women was found in one study to be 5.4 years (Eldridge & Gilbert, 1990). As noted in the previous section, over one third of divorces occur within the first 5 years of marriage, predominantly within the first 3 years. Given the pressures on married couples to stay together and on lesbian couples to separate (Gonzales & Meyers, 1993), the strengths of lesbian relationships are more evident than the weaknesses (Peplau, Veniegas, & Campbell, 1996).

Marriage between two people of the same sex is not legally recognized, but many lesbian and gay couples want a ceremony. The Metropolitan Community Church, serving primarily gays and lesbians, performs holy unions to give the spiritual significance of marriage for same-gender couples. Some ministers of mainstream Protestant groups also perform ceremonies for same-gender couples.

The basic values and concerns lesbians have about relationships are remarkably similar to those of heterosexual women (Clunis & Green, 1993; Kurdek, 1991b; Peplau, 1981; Schreurs, 1993). Women generally place greater importance than men do on egalitarianism and on emotional expressiveness. Thus there is likely to be more similarity between women partners on these issues than between heterosexual partners (Kurdek & Schmitt, 1987). Lesbians are more likely than heterosexual women to be in an equal power relationship (Caldwell & Peplau, 1984; Eldridge & Gilbert, 1990; Kurdek, 1993; Kurdek & Schmitt, 1986c; Steil, 1994).

Lesbian, gay, and heterosexual couples (at least those who volunteer for research) have intense feelings of respect and affection (Cardell et al., 1981; Kurdek & Schmitt, 1986a, 1986c; Peplau, 1981). When group differences are found, lesbians have greater satisfaction with their relationships than other groups (Kurdek, 1988a; Metz, Rosser, & Strapko, 1994). For lesbians, as for happy heterosexual couples, sexual intimacy is not as important as other forms of sharing (Eldridge & Gilbert, 1990; Hurlbert & Apt, 1993). Emotional intimacy was most strongly correlated with relationship satisfaction, followed by intellectual intimacy, recreational intimacy, sexual intimacy, and social intimacy.

Relationships are hard work, and the conflicts normally faced are similar in any kind of couple. One major problem for all was summed up by Letitia Peplau (1981), "All partners in close relationships must somehow deal with how much intimacy and independence are desirable and how the two are to be reconciled" (p. 33). Lesbian couples are sometimes thought to be enmeshed with each other (because of societal forces against them) to the detriment of independence and relationship satisfaction. However, empirical research indicates that intimacy is not contradictory to independence and is related to relationship satisfaction (Schreurs & Buunk, 1996).

In addition, lesbians, like heterosexuals, have conflicts about money, sex (including the issue of monogamy), and the demands on time and energy that employment makes. Lesbian and gay couples are more likely than heterosexual couples to be interracial, so that there is more likelihood of cultural conflicts (Garcia, Kennedy, Pearlman, & Perez, 1987; Sang, 1989). For any couple, social support can be important and may be more needed in lesbian than in heterosexual couples.

## Social Support

Lesbians and gay men are bucking tradition and therefore face abuse and discrimination, making social support particularly necessary (Bolla, 1990, Cage, 1993; Herek, 1994; von Schulthess, 1992).

*Hardships*   As many as 94% of lesbians and gay men report having been targets of verbal abuse or threats, and as many as 24% report physical attacks because of their sexual orientation (Berrill, 1992; Herek, 1994). *Gayism* (prejudice toward lesbians and gay men), sexism, and racism tend to go together and to be associated with authoritarianism and traditionalism generally (Haddock, Zanna, & Essex, 1993; Harry, 1995; Kurdek, 1988b; Seltzer, 1992; Stark, 1991). Generally, men are more homophobic than women (Kite & Whitley, in press; Whitley & Kite, 1994, 1995). And generally, gay men are more targeted for prejudice than lesbians are (Kite, 1992; Preston & Stanley, 1987). Having contact with a homosexual, especially with one of equal or higher status, lowers prejudice (Herek & Glunt, 1993; Price, 1994).

Lesbians are legally vulnerable in many ways (Ettelbrick, 1991). Courts have allowed people to be fired on the basis of sexual orientation, though some cities have protective laws (Blank & Slipp, 1994; Leonard, 1994; Martin & Lyon, 1972). In most states, lesbianism is a cause for preventing a woman from having custody of her children from a marriage, though lesbians may conceive their own children (chapter 12).

Minority lesbians have the problem of being a minority within a minority (Espin, 1987). They have a deep sense of tradition but a strong commitment to their lesbianism as well (Smith, 1991). Leota Lone Dog (1991) reported that it was lonely enough to be an Indian in Manhattan and Brooklyn, but to be lesbian as well was frighteningly lonely. Paula Gunn Allen (1981/1984) wrote that "The lesbian is to the American Indian what the Indian is to the Caucasian—invisible" (1984, p. 84). This is in spite of a long tribal history of acceptance of lesbianism as respectable (though perhaps frightening) because it was seen as destined by nonhuman entities. African Americans also seem to try to avoid recognition of lesbianism, but unlike Native Americans, they consider it a violation of nature (Joseph & Lewis, 1981). There are complexities, however. Some African Americans are very liberal, and gay men (with money) are acceptable, while women without money—or children—are less so (Seltzer, 1992; hooks, 1989).

Chicana lesbians do not serve men and so are marginalized within their own culture as well as outside it (Gaspar de Alba, 1993). D. M. Espin, a Cuban-born lesbian, wrote that being a Cuban and a lesbian were equally important to her and having to choose between them would be very painful. If she had to choose, she would choose living among lesbians but would still want expression of her Latin culture (Espin, 1987). Puerto Rican families in the United States have been increasingly accepting of lesbians, and as in other families, women are more likely to accept a lesbian family member than men are (Hildago, 1984). Some Asian American families think that members of their group cannot be gay; when a Korean woman told her parents that she was a lesbian, their response was that it could not be true because being gay is a white disease (Pamela H., 1989).

In spite of their double burden, minority lesbians are able to draw on their strength as minorities. Adrienne Smith (1991), stating that "First of all I'm Jewish, the rest is commentary," pointed out that her Jewish experiences helped her to understand and grow with her lesbianism. The similarities she saw between the "Jewish character" and the "lesbian character" were that both involved a deep sense of community or of family, an awareness of fighting for their lives, and ultimately, the sheer joy of being what one is. For her, coming out as a lesbian and as a Jew went hand in hand as she claimed the uniqueness of her own identity within both groups.

***Sources of Support***    Lesbians generally do receive beneficial social support, and support is related to better adjustment and happiness (Berger, 1990). However, the support is not necessarily from family (Kurdek, 1988c; Leavy & Adams, 1986; Raphael & Robinson, 1980/1984). Cohabiting lesbians and gay men report more support from friends and partners than from family members and coworkers (Kurdek, 1988c;

Kurdek & Schmitt, 1987); heterosexual adults report equal support from friends and family members (Griffith, 1985).

Some family members do have continuing difficulty accepting the fact that one of their family has deviated from the expected (Blumstein & Schwartz, 1983). Positive input from one partner's family can compensate for the lack of acceptance by the other family (Kurdek, 1988). Some parents are accepting from the beginning in ways their children may not realize. One mother, finally being told of her daughter's preference for women, said, "Thank goodness you finally told me. I thought you didn't trust me!" Other parents are stunned at first but, after the initial shock, can accept and value the lives of their children as they see that their child is happy and is a responsible and contributing member of their community. As one parent put it, "You do good work and you have wonderful friends" (Warshow, 1991, p. 82). Parents are capable of growth above stereotypic thinking. The organization **Parents and Friends of Lesbians and Gays** (called **P-FLAG**) offers support to people grappling with a loved one's sexual orientation and also provides active support for the lesbian and gay communities.

Particularly notable about lesbian support is that lesbian friendship systems serve as an extended family, giving a sense of continuity and history (Esterberg, 1996; Cruikshank, 1992; Sang, 1989; Weston, 1991). For many women, it is the friendship network and the style of relationship with a partner that defines what lesbianism means to them.

## Some Final Thoughts: Women, Communion, and Growth

Relationships play an indispensable role in personal growth. Children learn and develop in the context of interpersonal relationships. Adolescent friendships seem especially important in helping young people develop their identities, their sexuality, and their views about their adulthood. Friendships continue to be important in adulthood and throughout life. Friendships with women (or perhaps with androgynous or feminine individuals) seem to offer both women and men general therapeutic value as well as more opportunities for self-disclosure, for gaining deeper knowledge of themselves and others, and for trust.

Women are becoming more free to express their agency or instrumentality as well as their communion or expressiveness. Research on heterosexual and lesbian couples shows the value of equalitarianism in relationships. That equality is not likely if one or both partners are highly gender-typed. Some men are prepared for equalitarianism because of self-esteem, maturity about intimacy, or a background favoring expressiveness. Others grow into it because of their openness to growth and the teaching of their wives and women friends.

Women have led the way in developing interpersonal relationships and communal sharing. Men have been learning to overcome the strong gender role barriers that previously have inhibited them. Personality theorist Carl Jung suggested many years ago that both women and men can learn from each other how to develop aspects of themselves previously buried—*if* they value those neglected traits and want to grow.

## KEY TERMS

dating ritual
dyadic attachment
cohabitation
persons of the opposite
  sex sharing living
  quarters (POSSLQs)

marriage gradient
modern marriage
equalitarian marriage
traditional marriage
traditional desired
  marriage

demand/withdraw pattern
inversion theory
butch-femme
Parents and Friends of
  Lesbians and Gays
  (P-FLAG)

## KEY POINTS

*Friendships*

◆ Girls have fewer but closer friends than boys, from childhood through adolescence, when supportive friends are especially needed.

◆ Gender differences in friendship styles may be more extreme in white samples than in African American samples, and in heterosexual than in homosexual samples.

◆ Friendships between women generally are expressive, communal, and face-to-face, with an emphasis on disclosure and support. Friendships between men generally are instrumental, agentic, or side-by-side, emphasizing doing things together in structured situations with minimal disclosure. But women's friendships also are instrumental, and men gain support from shared activities.

◆ People value friendships with people of the other gender. Men tend to get from friendships with women the intimacy and support women get from other women.

◆ Women are less lonely than men and are less dependent on a romantic relationship in avoiding loneliness.

*Heterosexual Dating Relationships*

◆ For meaningful relationships and marriage, men and women want much the same thing, but a partner's physical appearance is more important to men than to women, and a partner's financial success is more important to women.

◆ Both women and men value dyadic attachment, but women more than men favor equalitarianism. Men tend to be more idealistic and romantic about love but also more ludic and cynical; women tend to be more pragmatic. Women and men are both concerned with passionate love and friendship love.

◆ Similarities, especially about gender role issues, are important in dating satisfaction, as are the amount of disclosure by each partner and men's self-esteem.

◆ Women are more likely than men to initiate the breakup of dating relationships and are less distressed by it, possibly because they see problems in the relationship before the man sees them. However, some women with unrestricted views about sex are highly distressed by breakups.

◆ Cohabitation has increased in all age and socioeconomic groups. There is no evidence that cohabitation is associated with happier marriages.

## Marriage Relationships and Divorce

◆ Americans have married at high rates, but the rate may be declining and people are marrying at later ages. Women see romantic love as necessary for marriage more than they have in the past. Women who stay single generally are better educated than other women and generally are not lonely or maladjusted.

◆ People in happy marriages have mutual understanding, respect, and concern, and many similarities. Emotional intimacy and security, and communication are important for younger as well as older couples.

◆ Men generally are less equalitarian than women, and most marriage structures favor men. Important factors affecting marital happiness are equalitarianism and expressions about love. Equalitarian marriages generally are happier. Better understanding of the differences between the ways men and women express love would benefit both men and women.

◆ Dissatisfied married couples communicate differently than satisfied couples. Women's tactics are influenced by their lower status.

◆ The rate of divorce is higher in the United States than other industrialized countries. Remarriage rates, typically higher for men than for women, are declining. The divorce rate is highest for couples who marry young, are not well educated, have low income, and whose parents divorced.

◆ Women are more likely to initiate divorce than men and list more reasons for divorce. Dominant reasons for divorce are communication problems, unhappiness, and incompatibility. Women particularly mention feeling unloved and criticized; men mention being neglected.

◆ Both women and men are distressed by divorce, although most come to see it as a good thing, and women especially may become stronger than before. Women are likely to have a drop in income and men an increase.

## Lesbian Relationships

◆ Lesbians and gay men are more likely than heterosexuals to be androgynous and to have androgynous ideals for other people. Lesbians generally reject role playing.

◆ Lesbians as well as heterosexual women value emotional expressiveness and equalitarianism in close relationships and are more likely to have these qualities. Lesbian relationships are comparable to heterosexual ones in intensity of care and respect for the partner and in the importance of emotional intimacy.

◆ Lesbians and gay men are subject to discrimination and abuse but do get social support for dealing with that. Lesbian and gay communities provide the support of an extended family.

## INTEGRATIVE QUESTIONS

1. Analyze your friendship patterns as a child and an adolescent and relate them to your current patterns in friendship and romantic relationships. Forecast what you

will be like as a marital partner, or, if already married, analyze your marital relationship in light of your past relationships.

2. Make the best case you can that the basic psychobiological or evolutionary view explains gender patterns in friendships, dating, and marriage. What do you see as weak about your case?

3. Consider the characteristics of happily married people. How do traditional socialization practices and the media affect the likelihood of a happy marriage? If you know a couple happily married for more than 5 years, you may focus your answer on them.

4. Both women and men cite "communication" as a reason for divorce. Why should we expect communication to be a problem?

5. Compare and contrast marriages and lesbian primary relationships.

6. Discuss the gender differences in friendship, dating, and marriage in light of the butch-femme distinction. To what extent do your ideas help you to understand why heterosexuals assume that lesbians play butch-femme roles?

7. Why do you think equalitarianism should be more important to women than to men? What are the effects of different attitudes about it?

# Chapter 11

# *Women's Sexuality*

*A* woman's body is *her* body. She has the right to have her own feelings about it and to make her own decisions about what she does with her body. This simple fact of nature becomes obscured in cultural views of sexuality and often in scientific thought. Women are told how to evaluate their bodies; they continually get confusing and negative messages about their sexuality and themselves. A woman is considered a sex object who is supposed to please men sexually but not to have her own sexual needs. If she enjoys sex, her satisfaction is thought to be the achievement of a male partner; if she enjoys sex too much, she is a slut. If she does not enjoy sex, something is wrong with her. Cultural attitudes have made women's bodies a battlefield in a struggle for power.

Many women have been struggling to reclaim their bodies and themselves in recent years. Women's issues are very much intertwined with the politics of sexuality; body, psyche, and social environment are intermingled at every stage of development (Daniluk, 1993; Naus, 1987). The fact that many women enjoy their sexuality and grow with it is testimony to the resiliency of women.

In this chapter we discuss sexuality as a basic human experience and focus on how societal attitudes have affected women's sexual experiences. The following chapter deals with issues of reproduction, including birth control, teenage pregnancy, and abortion. A later chapter (chapter 15) deals with sexual violence.

Before continuing, consider these questions for personal thought:

- ◆ Are you a sexual being? All of the time or only some of the time? Would you like to feel like a sexual being more or less often?

- ◆ Were you sexually active as a child? What sexual activities, if any, did you engage in?

- ◆ What specific needs do your sexual activities satisfy or frustrate? What do you say to yourself when you are sexually satisfied? When you are sexually frustrated?

- What does sexual liberation mean to you? Do you feel sexually liberated?

- How much sex can a woman have and still be a "good" person? How much sex can a man have and still be a "good" person?

- List all the reasons you can think of why a woman might be heterosexual. Now list all the reasons why a woman might be a lesbian.

- How would you feel if your family and friends thought (correctly or incorrectly) that you had sexual relations with someone of the same sex? With someone of the other sex? What difference does the sex of the other person make?

- Who is more sexual, men or women? What do you mean by being sexual?

## Development of Sexuality in the Early Years

In popular thought sexuality is not important until puberty. But much has gone on in the early years that shapes later experiences, and those early experiences often detract from healthy sexuality, especially for women. Learning about one's body and therefore about sexuality begins in infancy. Adults handling a child can communicate their attitudes about the human body (Delora & Warren, 1971; Masters & Johnson, 1975; Strong & DeVault, 1997). Unfortunately, many parents give negative messages about sexuality instead of responding sensitively to their curious and sensual children. Through nonverbal and then verbal cues, adults can communicate that "the body is not nice," "sex is not nice." Masters and Johnson wrote in one of their books on human sexuality:

> The degree of discomfort may vary—embarrassment for some, shame for others, guilt for the rest—but the children have absorbed from the adult world the idea that the human body is indecent. . . . And while looking or being looked at is bad enough, worse by far is touching or being touched. (1975, p. 245.)

### Childhood Sexuality

Infant sexuality is normal, and childhood sexual activities are more common than often supposed. Our society is more prohibitive and punitive about childhood sexuality than many others are. Ford and Beach (1951) documented cultures that encourage, or at least tolerate, childhood activities such as genital exhibition and manipulation of genitals, and observation of adult copulation. In such societies, early sexual experience typically is considered beneficial and necessary for healthy sexual maturation.

In spite of the comparative restrictiveness in U.S. culture, children do express their normal sexual curiosity about their own and their peers' bodies (Ford & Beach, 1951; Golden, 1987; Strong & DeVault, 1997). And they start much earlier than commonly supposed. Ultrasound pictures show that male fetuses have penile erection in the womb (see Reinisch, 1990). Newborns show sexual arousal in the first months of

*Parents give important messages to their children about sex and their bodies. They convey their own attitudes in how they touch, what words they use to name the genitals, and how they talk about the body. These parents are creating a loving and positive climate for their baby.*

life (Calderone, 1983; Kinsey, Pomeroy, & Martin, 1948; Kinsey, Pomeroy, Martin, & Gebhard, 1953; Montauk & Clasen, 1989).

Infants may show genital response when being nursed, cuddled, or bathed (Kaplan, 1974; Reinisch, 1990). These pleasurable experiences are thought to be important for affection and intimacy later in adulthood. With the development of hand movements, infants explore their bodies and discover the pleasure of genital stimulation. Toddlers cuddle, kiss, and look at each others' genitals (Reiss, 1986). Most parents of 6- and 7-year-olds reported that their daughters (76%) and sons (83%) had some play with friends or siblings, including "playing doctor" and simulating intercourse (Kolodny, 1980). Sex play is at its highest between ages 6 and 10. During this time, children are in gender-segregated groups so are likely to be exploring children of their own sex. This sexual exploration is not predictive of sexual orientation.

Children do not necessarily understand that adults see their games as sexual or unnatural. Sexologist Mary Calderone (1983) stated that a child's body belongs to him or her, and each child should have the right to experience pleasure with it. A hundred years ago, parents forced children to wear straitjackets or metal mittens to bed or buckled them in "genital cages" to prevent their sexual play (Reinisch, 1990). Doctors prescribed castration and clitoridectomy for children who persisted in genital exploration. Less drastically, Dr. John Kellogg introduced corn flakes in 1898 to help maintain health, which he believed would reduce sexual desire (Degler, 1981). Parents no longer use straitjackets or expect cereal to reduce sexual feelings. But their reaction to children's sexuality nonetheless may amount to putting the children in a psychological straitjacket (Reinisch, 1990).

## Negative Messages to Girls

Girls get more negative messages about their bodies than boys do, and women see their bodies more negatively than men see theirs (McKinley & Hyde, 1996). One reason is anatomical. Because of the close physical association between the anus, ure-thral opening, and the vaginal opening, the guilt, shame, and embarrassment girls learn from adults about elimination can extend to the genitals and lead them to see their genitals as unclean (Reinisch, 1990).

The language parents use contributes to girls' anatomical confusion and shame (Reinisch, 1990). Parents sometimes use vague references for girls' genitals, such as "down there" or "your bottom." Other parents make the negative message clear by referring to the genitals as "shames," "dirties," or "nasties." Parental terms for sons' genitals may not be anatomically accurate, but common terms such as "peenee," "peter," or "weenee" are linguistically or figuratively related to penis (Reinisch, 1990). Even those parents who are relatively open and liberal may refer to all fe-male genitals as vagina, instead of using more accurate terms differentiating the vagina from the vulva, clitoris, labia, urethra, and anus. Both girls and boys are likely to learn the word *penis* before any name for female genitals (Gartrell & Mosbacher, 1984).

Girls may develop negative attitudes about their bodies also because of **conceal-ment rituals,** which teach them to conceal their genitals and chests (Gullahorn, 1977a). Girls as young as 2 years old wear bikini bras to cover the "breasts" on a tiny chest as flat as that of boys. They are taught to sit with legs together, while boys can sprawl their legs apart. Little boys taunt little girls with threats to expose their "unmentionables," as shown by the childhood taunt, "Janie, Janie, fine and fair; I can see your underwear." Protection from viewing of women's underwear and genitals is shown also by the stalls in public restrooms for women's urination, relative to the urinals in men's restrooms.

## Self-Gratification

Language and concealment rituals contribute to shame and girls' lack of knowledge about their bodies. This may be related to girls' lower rate of stimulation of their genitals relative to boys'. I prefer to avoid the term *masturbation* for two reasons. Students are quick to point out the strong negative feelings that it elicits. More impor-tant is that the word has no sexuality in it! We speak of heterosexuality and homosex-uality, but the common term for enjoying one's sexuality by oneself does not acknowledge the activity as sexual. It is as if sex is not real sex unless it is shared with someone else. My favorite substitute is autosexuality (*auto* meaning "self"), and this term is used by some experts (Strong & DeVault, 1997). But more frequently used alternatives are **self-gratification, self-pleasure,** and **autoeroticism.** All terms point to the sexuality of one person.

***Gender Differences***    Girls particularly are told, "Don't touch yourself down there" (Strong & DeVault, 1997). According to adults' reports of themselves as children, fewer girls than boys participate in autosexual activities, and when they do, they start later (Hunt, 1974; Janus & Janus, 1993; Kinsey et al., 1953). Although self-gratification among girls is increasing, gender differences continue to be significant (Leitenberg, Detzer, & Srebnik, 1993; Michael, Gagnon, Laumann, & Kolata, 1994). A meta-analysis of studies of sexual attitudes and behaviors found the largest gender difference ($d = -.96$) for self-gratification (Oliver & Hyde, 1993). Although self-gratification seems more acceptable at colleges (Atwood & Gagnon, 1987), about twice as many men as women (e.g., 65% versus 30%) engage in it, and men do so at about three times the frequency of women (Adams, 1986; Davidson & Darling, 1986; Lottes, 1993).

By middle adulthood, about two thirds of women and nearly all men report having experienced self-gratification; exact percentages vary with age, education, and religion (Janus & Janus, 1993). Whatever the comparison, at all ages, men engage in autoeroticism more than women do (Atwood & Gagnon, 1987; Janus & Janus, 1993). African Americans and Latinos are less accepting of autosexuality than whites are, though acceptance is increasing (Wilson, 1986). It may be that women simply do not find self-gratification as pleasurable as men do. But women more than men are socialized to associate sex with romance, relationships, and emotional intimacy (Leitenberg et al., 1993).

***Effects of Gender Differences***    Do the differences in self-pleasuring make a difference? There is reason to think so. When enjoying self-gratification, boys are learning how their bodies work and what gives them pleasure (Strong & DeVault, 1997). Girls are not learning how their body works and are not enjoying it as much. One sex educator spoke of self-gratification as a way to become "*pleasantly at home* [italics added] with your own sexual organs" (Hamilton, 1978, p. 33). Girls who do not become pleasantly at home with their bodies are more likely to have trouble sharing bodily pleasures later in life. Women without previous self-gratification experiences have less positive attitudes toward sexuality and, when married, are less likely to be orgasmic or take longer before having an orgasm (Hite, 1976; Kelly, Strassberg, & Kircher, 1990; Kinsey et al., 1953; Wakefield, 1988).

Adding to the problem is that girls who have not enjoyed their bodies sexually have their first sexual experience with someone else, usually a boy. The young woman may learn from this experience that "*he* gives me my sexual pleasure" and perhaps even that "*my* body is *his*." This is **erotic dependence**: a reliance on someone else for erotic feelings (Hyde, 1991). The dependence of women on men for sexual pleasure feeds the notion of **male as expert.** With this notion, the man is assumed to be more knowledgeable about sexuality than the woman is, and therefore, he is the leader who knows the "right way to do it" (Strong & DeVault, 1997). The young woman is set up to believe that if she does not enjoy a particular sexual activity, it must be her fault since the man knows more about sex than she does. The assumption that men are the experts is considered a leading cause of sexual problems. It also means that women and men are "strangers in the night" (Keen, 1991)—one aspect of the continuing problems that result from women and men talking different languages.

# Heterosexual Attitudes and Activities

Girls and boys are told they are not supposed to be sexual. Then at adolescence, they are to "prove themselves" by being heterosexually attractive. This is hard on youths who are attracted to others of their own sex (Hersch, 1991) and is not easy for any. Adolescents are supposed to follow a **sexual script:** a cultural blueprint specifying the roles to be enacted in sexual interaction (Strong & DeVault, 1997). Cultural models of sexuality are based on male experience, so the scripts are heterosexual ones based on the dichotomies of gendered thinking (Rothblum, 1994b). The script maintains the **double standard of sexuality,** which, like the double standard generally, holds that men are dominant, superior, valued, and free. Although not as pervasive as it used to be (Sprecher & McKinney, 1993), the expectation holds that men are sexually active because they are thought to have a higher sex drive; women are to be virgins until they enter a stable relationship, preferably marriage (Lottes, 1993; Oliver & Sedikides, 1992). There is a built-in problem: Men are expected to be heterosexually active, but their potential partners, women, are not.

The script given to women is more confusing and potentially more psychologically damaging than that given to men. Women have described their sexual development as a process of splitting of self from body in early years, reaching a peak at puberty (Daniluk, 1993). After years of discouragement about sexuality, a young woman becomes a sex object who is expected to attract young men (Laws & Schwartz, 1977); she is to be a seducer, a siren, an enticer. But once she has attracted a young man, she is supposed to refuse him. Her behavior contributes to images of women as asexual, frigid, manipulative, and even destructive of men.

Within the cultural script, women are considered responsible for both men's and their own behavior; men are responsible for neither. Women are bifurcated into two types: the **madonna** and the **whore** (or the **princess** and the **prostitute**) (Ussher, 1989; Wyatt & Riederle, 1994). There have been changes in views about sexuality, but the double standard is still present (McConaghy, 1993).

## Sexual Revolutions

Ira Reiss (1960) maintains that the first and the *real* sexual revolution was in the decade of the 1920s, when rapid changes in society had uprooted young people and left them somewhat disillusioned and in rebellion against Victorian morals (Banner, 1984). Women felt a new confidence and daring after finally attaining the vote. Young women were "flappers" living for fun and freedom, wearing skimpy bathing suits, and talking about sex. However, the sexuality of the young then was person-centered rather than unrestrained: It was frequency of intercourse with fiancees that increased (Banner, 1984). The sexual liberation of the 1960s was a continuation of the 1920s (Reiss, 1960). In both attitudes and behavior, women became and are becoming more like men, but the similarities are not sufficient to say that a single standard prevails (Lawson, 1988; Lottes, 1993; Moffat, 1989). There is convergence between women and men, but there continues to be a difference that matters.

*A major cultural script for adolescent women is to be attractive and seductive but to refuse sexual overtures. What message do you think this young woman is sending? What message do you think she thinks she is sending?*

***Gender Differences in Attitudes***    Overall, college women are moderately conservative in their sexual attitudes, and college men are moderately permissive (Table 11.1; Hendrick, Hendrick, Slapton-Foote, & Foote, 1985). The gender differences are not marked, but they are consistent (Simpson & Gangestad, 1991). Contemporary sexual scripts increasingly recognize women's sexuality and are more relationship oriented than male centered, though women still do not have full sexual equality (Strong & DeVault, 1997).

The views of college men and women are also converging with respect to attitudes about the behavior expected or desired in sexual relationships (Lawrence, Taylor, & Byers, 1996). The men think the ideal man is more expressive than they themselves are, and the women think the ideal woman is more instrumental than they themselves are. They both think the ideal sexual partner is less traditional than they themselves are.

***Sexual Activity***    As with attitudes, the sexual behavior of women is becoming more like that of men, but women are still more conservative than men. Increasing numbers of women and men have had premarital heterosexual intercourse and have been doing so with more partners and at increasingly earlier ages (Bishop & Lipsitz, 1990; Cate &

**Table 11.1**   Scores for Women and Men on Selected Items From a Sexual
Attitudes Scale

|  | *Men* | *Women* |
|---|---|---|
| *Men More Permissive, Not Excessively* | | |
| I do not need to be committed to a person to have sex. | 2.34 | 3.82 |
| Casual sex is acceptable. | 2.29 | 3.49 |
| I would like to have sex with many partners. | 2.63 | 4.19 |
| Sex is a sacred act. | 3.34 | 2.74 |
| *Both Relatively Permissive Premarital* | | |
| Premarital sex is OK under most circumstances. | 2.10 | 2.85 |
| It is all right to have a limited amount of premarital sex. | 2.13 | 2.65 |
| Sex is permissible only within marriage. | 4.17 | 3.50 |
| Unlimited premarital sexual experience is fine. | 2.61 | 3.51 |
| *Extramarital Sex Opposed* | | |
| Extramarital affairs are OK if one's partner doesn't know. | 4.11 | 4.58 |
| Extramarital affairs are unacceptable. | 2.39 | 1.87 |

1 = strongly agree

5 = strongly disagree

SOURCE: Hendrick, S., Hendrick, C., Slapton-Foote, M. J., & Foote, F. H. (1985). Gender differences in sexual attitudes. *Journal of Personality and Social Psychology, 48,* (5), 1630–1642. Excerpts from Table 1, p. 1634.

Lloyd, 1992; Janus & Janus, 1993; Reinisch, Sanders, Hill, & Davis, 1992; Reiss, 1990; Sprecher & McKinney, 1993; Tanfer & Schoorl, 1992). The increase is attributable in part to an increase in effective contraception, legally available abortion, and changing gender roles. In addition there has been a dramatic increase in the number of unmarried men and women over age 18 (Cate & Lloyd, 1992). The increase in sexual activity generally has been steeper for women than for men, but women still are less active sexually than men.

Average age of first intercourse now seems essentially the same for women and men who are in college (17 years plus/minus .2; Lottes, 1993; Reinisch et al., 1992). However, there are variations among ethnic groups (Strong & DeVault, 1997). African American teenagers generally initiate sexual intercourse earlier than whites or Latinos do. Whites narrow the gap by the late teens and, in fact, come to have more partners and more frequent intercourse than young African American women do (Centers for Disease Control [CDC], 1991). The percentage of college women who have had premarital intercourse is as high as 85% in some universities, compared with about 25% in 1925. The number of premarital partners has increased from about 1 for women (often the man they later marry) and 6 for men, to 4 for women and 10 for men, as measured at one university (Whitley, 1988).

***Differences Among Women***   Women with the highest education report the most sexual experience (both heterosexual and homosexual) before marriage; this is in part because education usually increases the length of premarital adulthood (Janus & Janus,

**Table 11.2**   Women's Sexual Experience as a Function of Gender Role Identity

|  | "Masculine" High I/Low E | "Feminine" Low I/High E | Androgynous High I/High E | Undifferentiated Low I/Low E |
|---|---|---|---|---|
| Had intercourse | 75% | 68% | 54% | 40% |
| Number of partners | 3.1 | 1.7 | 1.4 | 1.3 |
| Had oral sex | 80% | 70% | 74% | 54% |
| Nervous | 2.3 | 2.6 | 3.8 | 3.5 |
| Age of first intercourse | 16.8 | 16.5 | 17.1 | 17.7 |
| Number of orgasms per month | 2.2 | 2.8 | 1.6 | 0.7 |
| Orgasm from any source | 78% | 81% | 66% | 52% |

I = instrumental
E = expressive

SOURCE: Leary, M. R., & Snell, W. E., Jr. (1988). The relationship of instrumentality and expressiveness to sexual behavior in males and females. *Sex Roles, 18*, 509–522.

1993). Also, those who have a high career commitment generally are less likely to have intercourse (Thornton & Camburn, 1989). Latinas, with a strong tradition of Roman Catholicism, strongly endorse virginity for women (Espin, 1992). Religious involvement may cause lower sexual activity, but it also may be true that youths with permissive attitudes feel uncomfortable with their religious institutions (Thornton & Camburn, 1989).

Especially relevant to themes of this book is gender role adoption. Sexual activities vary with the gender role of college women but not of men, probably because men receive such an intense message about sexual activity (Leary & Snell, 1988). Women who scored above the median on instrumental traits and below the median on expressive traits (a "masculine" group) were most likely to have had intercourse (75%), to have had a greater number of partners (3.1), and to have had oral sex (80%) (Table 11.2). Women who were above the median on expressiveness and below on instrumentality ("feminine") had their first intercourse at an earlier age (16.5 years) and more orgasms per month (2.8), and they were more likely to have had orgasm by any means, including but not limited to intercourse (81%). The researchers speculated that the findings about the expressive group of women indicated their willingness to "go along" with the desires of their male partners. Undifferentiated women were the least active by any measure, and androgynous women were in between the highs and lows on each measure.

## Sexually Transmitted Diseases

***AIDS and Women***   With sexual activity comes the possibility of **sexually transmitted diseases (STDs).** STDs are the nation's most frequently reported infections (Meyer, 1996). The most dramatic and most publicized STD is **acquired immunodeficiency syndrome (AIDS),** a fatal, incurable viral disease spread by direct contact with infected blood, semen, and vaginal secretions. AIDS is caused by **human immu-**

**nodeficiency virus (HIV),** which destroys the white blood cells that ordinarily fight diseases.

AIDS was once dubbed the "homosexual's disease"—a case of the misleading nature of the generic masculine (chapter 2), because lesbians have the lowest incidence of any group. And, increasingly, AIDS is a concern for heterosexual men and women (CDC, 1993). The rate of new AIDS cases is increasing more rapidly among women— especially minority women—and children than among men (CDC, 1994). Seventy-five percent of American women who have been diagnosed with AIDS are African American or Latina (CDC, 1996). HIV is the leading cause of death for African American women aged 25–44 and the third leading cause of death for all American women in this age group. It is projected that the numbers of women with AIDS will equal the number of men by 2010 (Strong & DeVault, 1997). In addition, women with AIDS don't live as long following diagnosis as men, perhaps because the disease follows a different course and may be missed by physicians until later stages. Women generally have been excluded from clinical trials for HIV and AIDS treatment, though there has been recent improvement. Still, there has been little progress in addressing the need for prevention of infection among women (Amaro, 1995; Strong & DeVault, 1997) (Focus on Research 11.1).

The AIDS scare has affected heterosexual behavior, but not much (Cora-Bramble, Bradshaw, & Sklarew, 1992; Fisher & Fisher, 1992; Metzler, Noell, & Biglan, 1992; Wendell, Onorato, McCray, Allen, & Sweeney, 1992). Most teenagers and college students do not seem to think that they can contract AIDS, even when they are reasonably knowledgeable about the disease (Andre & Bormann, 1991; Sugarman, 1991; Tucker & Cho, 1991). Only about half of sexually active teens and college students use condoms (Centers for Disease Control and Prevention, 1995; Crawford, 1990), and there has been little change in the sexual activity reported by college students (Carroll, 1988; Crawford, 1990). Men are more risky in their behavior than women (Poppen, 1995; Stokes, McKirnan, Doll, & Burzette, 1996).

*Other STDs*    Although AIDS receives the most publicity, other STDs are more prevalent; they also raise the risk for contracting HIV (Aral & Holmes, 1991). In addition, they often are asymptomatic in women and may cause permanent damage before they are detected. Possible effects include pelvic inflammatory disease, infertility, arthritis, cervical cancer, and complications during pregnancy and delivery (Boston Women's Health Book Collective [BWHBC], 1992; Strong & DeVault, 1997).

Estimates are that almost 13 million new cases of STDs occur annually, most (65%) in people under 25 (Cowley & Hager, 1993; Hatcher et al., 1994). One quarter are teens (Russell, 1997). The incidence of nearly every STD is on the rise or at a stable high level. For example, the number of new cases of gonorrhea has decreased since it peaked in the late 1970s, but about 400,000 new cases are still reported each year (Insel & Roth, 1998).

More recently recognized STDs—especially chlamydia, genital warts, and herpes—are called the "new epidemics" (BWHBC, 1992). **Chlamydia** is the most common bacterial STD in the United States today, affecting over 4 million people a year and up to 35% of all sexually active women; it is the most difficult for which to

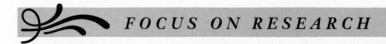

### *FOCUS ON RESEARCH*

## 11.1   Sampling: African American Women and AIDS Prevention

AIDS has been recognized as a major health threat in the United States not only for the gay male community but also for heterosexuals. HIV infection via heterosexual sexual contact is increasing, and minority women are at particular risk. While African American women are only 12% of all women in the United States, they make up 52% of women diagnosed with AIDS, and almost one third of these women contracted the HIV virus through heterosexual contact. Concern is growing over the need to develop prevention programs aimed at at-risk African American women, but for these programs to be effective, what kinds of issues should they focus on? One way to find out is to locate at-risk women and ask them for their input.

Sampling is the process of choosing observations for inclusion in the study. Once the researcher has defined what is to be measured, she must decide how that data will be obtained. If she wants to observe children's play behavior, should she write down every move each child makes over the entire play time? Or if the study concerns teens' attitudes about premarital sex, exactly which teens should she contact? Obviously, the researcher can't include every possible observation or person in the study, as this population is theoretically infinite. However, in order to construct general theories of human behavior, we need to have information about this population. Sampling allows us to learn about the population by drawing a representative subgroup, a sample, from the population. If the sample is drawn at random, we can be reasonably certain that it is representative of the population. This is because in random sampling, each person or event in the population has an equal chance of being chosen for the sample. As the size of the sample grows, it increasingly approximates the characteristics of the population from which it was drawn. Consequently, the behavior measured in a representative sample can be said to reflect behavior in the population; this quality makes random sampling a type of probability sampling.

Sometimes random sampling just isn't feasible or may not be the best way to create a sample. The next two options discussed here are called nonprobability sampling techniques; they do not produce representative samples. If it is hard to locate participants for a study, the "snowball sampling" technique might be used; each participant is asked to supply the names of several other prospective participants who are then contacted by the researcher. Some research topics are more conducive to "judgmental sampling," in which the researcher selects the sample based on knowledge of the population and the aims of the study.

In their investigation of how to create an AIDS prevention program for African American women, the research team headed by Mindy Fullilove (1990) tackled the problem of sampling by using a variation of the judgmental sampling technique. The researchers wanted to set up focus groups in which African American heterosexual lower- and working-class women and teens met for two hours to discuss important sexual issues in their lives. Once the participant criteria (age, sexual orientation, etc.) were set, knowledgeable community leaders were asked to identify participants they judged to be representative members of the defined subgroup. Each prospective participant was then approached and included in a discussion group after she gave informed consent; all who were solicited agreed to participate, but many of the teens did not show up for their discussion group.

Fullilove and her research team stressed that those who participated did not make up a representative sample of all African American heterosexual women and teens who come from lower- or working-class backgrounds. Remember that the purpose of their research was to establish the basic issues on which to ground an AIDS prevention program for at-risk African American females. Given the sensitive nature of the group discussions, the researchers wanted to ensure that participants would feel comfortable discussing sexual issues and would engage in productive dialogue. This was why they based their sample selection on suggestions made by community leaders, who had more personal knowledge of the prospective participants than did the researchers. Had their research topic been different, say, for example, African American women's attitudes about AIDS and safe sex practices, then the issue of representativeness would be of greater importance and random sampling would be a more appropriate way to select participants.

What did Fullilove and her associates learn from the teens and women who participated in the discussion groups? Several key issues faced by African American women in sexual relationships were uncovered. The sexual double standard leaves African American women with less power and respect and consequently less ability to negotiate safe sex in their sexual relationships. In addition, the dramatic increase in African American male unemployment is closely tied to the increasing imbalance in the number of marriageable men and the decline in the stability of adult relationships, including sexual partnerships. This translates into a greater number of short-term sexual partners and greater risk of HIV infection. Armed with this information, Fullilove and her research team suggest that an AIDS prevention program must help African American women develop explicit strategies for sexual communication, focusing on ways to negotiate with men the conditions under which they will engage in sexual activity.

JILL BORCHERT ◆

SOURCE: Fullilove, M. T., Fullilove, R., Haynes, K., & Gross, S. (1990). Black women and AIDS prevention: A view towards understanding the gender rules. *Journal of Sex Research, 27,* 47–64.

test (BWHBC, 1992; CDC, 1995; Hatcher et al., 1994; Lippman, 1995). Like chlamydia, **gonorrhea** is caused by a bacterium; both diseases can be treated with antibiotics. However, untreated chlamydia or gonorrhea in women can lead to **pelvic inflammatory disease,** a serious infection of the uterus, oviducts, and pelvic cavity that can cause infertility and ectopic pregnancy.

**Genital warts,** caused by infection with the **human papillomavirus (HPV),** is the most common STD for which treatment is sought at student health services (Insel & Roth, 1998). HPV infection causes a precancerous cervical condition and is believed to be responsible for 70% to 80% of cervical cancers worldwide. **Genital herpes,** another viral infection, is caused by the **herpes simplex virus (HSV).** Two types of herpes simplex viruses, HSV-1 and HSV-2, cause oral herpes (cold sores) and genital herpes. HSV-1 infection, the usual cause of oral herpes, is extremely common, with over 90% of adults having been exposed; 10% to 20% of adults have been exposed to HSV-2, the usual cause of genital herpes. (Both types of virus can cause either oral or genital sores, and crossover can occur as a result of oral-genital contact.) There is no permanent cure for either genital warts or herpes; infected individuals carry the virus for life. Women with either disease need to make sure they get regular Pap tests.

**Syphilis,** a bacterial infection, can be treated with antibiotics in its early stages, but it can cause blindness, central nervous system damage, or death if left untreated. New syphilis cases are currently at their lowest since 1957, but certain groups, especially African Americans, have much higher rates than the population average (Insel & Roth, 1998).

There still is a social stigma attached to STDs that may affect the quality of medical care, especially for women and even more for poor women and women of color (BWHBC, 1992). No method is 100% effective in avoiding STDs, but the Boston Women's Health Book Collective recommends using condoms (male or female), the diaphragm, and spermicides. Women should also have regular Pap tests and STD screenings to avoid the complications that can result from undiagnosed or asymptomatic infections.

Women may know about the dangers of STDs but not act responsibly to prevent them. Concern about personal safety is not part of the sexual script. At a romantic moment it is difficult to ask, "Do you have a disease?" And for some women, raising the issue poses the risk of challenging male power (Wyatt & Riederle, 1994). Women who want to claim their bodies as their own and who want to reduce the chance of STDs must be assertive in insisting on safer sex.

> The topic [of STDs, AIDS] can become a focus for questioning the relative importance of one's self-worth, and the question may be "Am I important enough *to me* to want safety at the risk of being rejected by a man?" (Cochran & Mays, 1989, p. 534)

The cultural messages given to women make it hard for many women to feel important enough to themselves to protect their physical health. Women's attention in sex is still focused more on their partner than on themselves (Wyatt & Riederle, 1994).

## Affection and Sex

Feelings of affection and closeness are more strongly associated with women's sexual activity (both heterosexual and homosexual) than with men's (Blumstein & Schwartz, 1983; Laumann, Gagnon, Michael, & Michaels, 1994; Quadagno & Sprague, 1991; Randolph & Winstead, 1988; Whitley, 1988b). Most women want a close relationship before having a sexual relationship and are more likely than men to report enjoyment of intercourse only when there is commitment in the relationship (Clark & Hatfield, 1989; McCabe, 1987; Randolph & Winstead, 1988). For example, about two thirds (67%) of college women (and 21% of men) said that emotional involvement is always necessary for them to participate in sexual intercourse (Lottes, 1993). Nearly all college women (94%) said they would feel guilty or anxious about a one-night stand; about half (57%) of the men did. Lesbians are more like heterosexual women in sex attitudes than they are like gay or heterosexual men in that they value the emotional relationship (Blumstein & Schwartz, 1983; Markowitz, 1991; Schreurs, 1993).

Although gender differences in the association of sex and love are found recurringly, it must be noted that many men do prefer sex within a meaningful relationship, and it probably is these men (as well as other women for some women) with whom women have mutually enabling relationships in which they feel validation and acceptance (Daniluk, 1993). More men said they would feel guilty or anxious after a one-night stand than said they would feel comfortable/relaxed or satisfied (57% versus 43%; Lottes, 1993). And more than half of college men and women who were asked their private wishes reported the wish to have one satisfying sexual relationship in life (Ehrlichman & Eichenstein, 1992).

The general gender difference in relevance of affection to sex is shown also in patterns of extramarital involvement (Glass & Wright, 1985; Janus & Janus, 1993). Women are less likely than men to have an extramarital relationship (e.g., about a quarter of women, a third of men; Janus & Janus, 1993), but when women do, the role of affection is more prominent than for men. First, women are more likely than men to report an extramarital involvement that is emotional with *no sex*, while more men than women report a relationship with sex and *no emotion* (Glass & Wright, 1985). Second, women are more likely than men to report unhappy marriages (about two thirds versus about a half) (Glass & Wright, 1985; Hunt, 1969). Apparently, women seek emotional expression and confirmation in extramarital relations more than men do.

## Problems of Liberation

It is now more acceptable for a woman to acknowledge her sexuality than it used to be, but many women find that liberation has brought a new problem: the old rules have changed—but not completely—and it is not really clear what the new rules are. Women report having trouble making decisions, such as, "If I wait too long, he loses interest, but if I don't wait long enough, he thinks I'm easy." When they do have sex, it may not be meaningful for the women.

Some women had early sexual experiences characterized by respect and caring: "I really feel blessed that I was introduced to sex in such a positive way, in such a loving way" (Daniluk, 1993, p. 61), and many other women come to have such an experience.

However, the social scripts do not make such early experiences typical. Most women do not report that their early experiences of intercourse were exhilarating or romantic (Daniluk, 1993; Wolfe, 1980). Most recall first or early experiences as painful, upsetting, disappointing, shameful, or isolating, or as leading to no particular reaction. "Sex was . . . a lot of fear and hurt"; "I always felt very lost and alone, how ironic, I couldn't find anything remotely intimate about it" (Daniluk, 1993, p. 61). "I'm still asking myself, Is this what all the fuss is about?" (Wolfe, 1980, p. 255).

Many women feel that sexual liberation has a male bias (Moffat, 1989; Wolfe, 1981). It has undermined their right to say no and not added much to the right to say yes. Previously, when "good girls" said "No," no was accepted. Now, women who refuse a man's overtures are subject to taunts of frigidity, lack of liberation, or of being a lesbian (Janus & Janus, 1993; Wolfe, 1981). Men sometimes take a woman's refusal of sex as a personal rejection, and some women worry more about men's hurt feelings than about their own wishes. When women were asked to react to scenarios in which a woman refused a man's sexual advance, the most common reaction was concern that she had hurt the man's feelings (Muehlenhard & Schrag, 1991). Women, wishing to prove they are OK and not wanting to risk hurting men, sometimes agree to sex when they really do not want to. They also fear that if they do not have sex, they'll be sitting at home alone. A result has been many women having sex when they do not want it and a general trivialization of sexuality (Lawrence et al., 1996; Wolfe, 1980; Wyatt & Riederle, 1994).

## Lesbian Behavior and Identity

Integrating sexuality with one's self-view is hard on women generally. For some women, the issue is intensified by being attracted sexually to other women, but they do manage to overcome the obstacles and to enjoy their sexuality and their lives otherwise. Who are the women who prefer a woman as a sexual partner? This is not a simple question. Some theoretical views may help set the perspective.

Some theorists, including Freud (1905/1953) and Ford and Beach (1951), have suggested that bisexuality is the human predisposition, but cultural pressures channel sexuality toward heterosexuality. The famous anthropologist Margaret Mead (1972) characterized her ideal society as one in which people were homosexual in their youth, heterosexual while having and rearing children, and then homosexual again after child rearing was over. Ancient Greeks saw heterosexuality as appropriate for having a family but considered homosexual relationships (between men) a superior spiritual and intellectual expression of love.

Kinsey conceptualized sexual expression on a 7-point continuum, from 0 for exclusively heterosexual behavior to 6 for exclusively homosexual behavior; mixtures of male and female partners were intermediate. By using the concept of a continuum, Kinsey was trying to convey that differences between people are quantitative, not qualitative—the differences are ones of degree rather than of kind. Further, an individual's rating can change over time; people can move along the continuum (Reinisch, 1990). It is recognized increasingly that lesbianism and heterosexuality do not represent a clear-cut dichotomy and that for some people, sexual orientation can change (Parker & De Cecco, 1995).

## Patterns of Behavior

Being a lesbian is not a simple matter of who one has sex with. Having had a heterosexual experience does not prevent a woman from being a lesbian, and being a lesbian does not preclude a woman from attraction to or sexual involvement with a man (Blumstein & Schwartz, 1976; Huston & Schwartz, 1996; Kitzinger & Wilkinson, 1995). A recent Kinsey Institute study of a group of lesbians from across the United States found that nearly half (43%) of those who *always* referred to themselves as lesbians had sex at least once with a man since age 18 (Reinisch, 1990).

Very few women (3%) have had sexual relations *only* with women (Hunt, 1974; Kinsey et al., 1953; Kitzinger & Wilkinson, 1995). More (10%–28%) have had some sexual contact with another woman, usually more than one experience (Dreyer, 1982; Hunt, 1974; Janus & Janus, 1993; Kinsey et al., 1953; Wolfe, 1980). The incidence of lesbian experience (and heterosexual experience, as noted previously) typically increases with education, career orientation, and being single. Education may bring a more open attitude about sexuality as well as delayed marriage, thus increasing the time during which a woman may find another woman who interests her. But it should not be assumed that women who are or have been married to a man have not had sexual involvement with another woman or that all highly educated single women have.

Even more women (up to 40%) are open to the possibility of sexual relations with a woman than have had such experience. Sex with other women is a common fantasy (Friday, 1991). Having feelings for a woman does not necessarily lead to the behavior of having sex with a woman. Having had homosexual feelings or experiences does not necessarily make a woman a lesbian. What, then, defines a lesbian?

What is meant by lesbian varies widely from woman to woman. The best definition I know of is that a lesbian is a woman who says she is a lesbian. Some define being a lesbian as being a **woman-identified woman**—a woman whose life is focused in important ways around women (Boston Lesbian Psychologies Collective, 1987; Golden, 1987; Miller, 1982; Radical Lesbians, 1970). Similarly, lesbians have been depicted as women who get their primary emotional support, not necessarily sexual, from women (Matlin, 1993; Radical Lesbians, 1982). Some definitions do include sexual attachment as well as psychological and emotional attachment (Miller, Jacobsen, & Bigner, 1982). Some other definitions are given in A Closer Look 11.1. Before continuing on the issue of lesbian definitions, we need to pause and comment on bisexuality.

## Bisexuality

It is even more difficult to define bisexuality than lesbianism, and some of the women referred to above as lesbians are considered by some to be "really" bisexual. Technically, a **bisexual** is a person who can enjoy sexual activity with members of both sexes or who recognizes a desire to do so without necessarily acting upon the desire

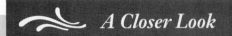

## 11.1    Some Definitions of Lesbianism

[A lesbian is] a woman who loves women, who chooses women to nurture and support and to create a living environment in which to work creatively and independently, whether or not her relations with these women are sexual. (Cook, quoted in Golden, 1987, p. 10)

Sometimes when I talk positively about being a lesbian, heterosexual friends say they hear me criticizing their choice to be with men. That's not true. For me, part of what's essential in being a lesbian is caring for other women, and this includes women who have made choices other than mine. (Cited in BWHBC, p. 177)

Being a lesbian for me is about the joy and wonder of loving women. It means being women-identified, making women my priority. It is a way of life, so much more than a matter of who I want to sleep with. (Cited in BWHBC, p. 177)

[A lesbian is] a woman who has sexual and erotic-emotional ties primarily with women or who sees herself as centrally involved with a community of self-identified lesbians whose sexual and erotic-emotional ties are primarily with women and who is herself a self-identified lesbian. (Ferguson, quoted in Golden, 1987, p. 21)

A Lesbian is the rage of all women condensed to the point of explosion. (Radicalesbians, 1973, cited in Golden, 1987)

Lesbian is a label invented by the Man to throw at any woman who dares to be his equal, who dares to challenge his prerogatives . . . , who dares to assert the primacy of her own needs. (Radicalesbians, 1969, cited in Kitzinger, 1987, p. 43)

---

SOURCES: Boston Women's Health Book Collective. (1992). *The new our bodies, ourselves: A book by and for women.* New York: A Touchstone Book.

Golden, C. (1987). Diversity and variability in women's sexual identities. In the Boston Lesbian Psychologies Collective (Eds.), *Lesbian psychologies: Explorations and challenges.* Urbana, IL: University of Illinois Press.

Kitzinger, C. (1987). *The social construction of lesbianism.* London: Sage.

---

(MacDonald, 1981). Thus, *technically,* many women who identify as lesbian are bisexual. Behavior and identity are not necessarily consistent. Some people acknowledge a basic bisexuality of openness to either sex but identify primarily as lesbian or heterosexual (Riemer, 1995); less than half (38%) of the members of a bisexual organization reported having sexual experience with women and men equally (Schuster, 1988).

Women who label themselves as bisexual often have the problem of not being accepted by heterosexuals or by lesbians (Brown, 1997; Fox 1991). Many heterosexuals, including scientific researchers (Van Wyk & Geist, 1995), are caught up in either-or thinking and do not know what to do with such women (Schuster, 1988). Many lesbians feel such women are copping out and are scared or unwilling to identify with lesbians. However, things may change. More organizations now have the words "lesbian, gay, and bisexual" in their titles, so that the bisexual identity may become more acceptable in the lesbian community. Current evidence, however, is not encouraging on this point (Brown, 1997).

## Development of a Lesbian Identity

Researchers have reported all combinations and sequences of identity and behavior as well as changes in each over the life cycle (Blumstein & Schwartz, 1976; Coleman, 1985; Dixon, 1985; Golden, 1987; Nichols, 1990; Reinisch, 1990). Women have asserted that they are lesbian while being with a male lover; some assert they are heterosexual while being with a female lover. Some have declared themselves clearly lesbian and then married a man. Some went from heterosexuality to homosexuality back to heterosexuality; some went from homosexuality to heterosexuality to homosexuality. Clearly, identity and behavior are both fluid for some people.

What determines the identity? One's self-view is a major determinant, but self-view can vary, and this often involves changes in interpersonal relationships in some way. Theorists trying to understand development of lesbian identity often maintain that association with a woman lover and/or a lesbian community is crucial in forming a lesbian identity (Bell & Weinberg, 1978; Krieger, 1982; Riemer, 1995; Troiden, 1988; Weeks, 1985). Although not all researchers accept this degree of specificity, many do maintain that identity must be placed in a social psychological context (Cox & Gallois, 1996; Eliason, 1996). For example, researchers have found that the label an individual uses varies with the **reference group**—those people the individual associates with and whose perspectives she or he shares. Sexual behavior or desire is not always consistent with the reference group and the label used about preference.

***Theories About Sexual Preference***     Psychologists have tried to find out what affects sexual preference, but without much success (Focus on Research 11.2). Much of the attempt to understand the development of lesbianism has been shaped by Freudian and social learning theory (chapter 5). Freud (1905/1953) thought that people were innately bisexual but, with typical development (though a troubled one of family trauma), establish a heterosexual orientation. Failure to resolve the Oedipal situation (chapter 4) is responsible for a same-sex orientation: The girl does not shift her dominant identification back to the mother and retains interest in her clitoris instead of shifting it to the vagina. It is an inversion theory that lesbians are masculine in identity and gay men are feminine, a theory proven erroneous (chapter 10). Because of Freud's assertion that most people do not completely resolve the Oedipal situation, it follows that a "homosexual component" is present in most people in varying degrees (i.e., homosexual feelings are typical). Although he maintained that same-sex orientation is a case of "arrested development," Freud saw nothing wrong with it and did not advise therapy to "cure" it (Freud, 1960). Unfortunately, many Freudians have automatically equated "arrested development" with pathology, even though that position is not supported by Freud himself nor by evidence.

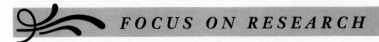

## FOCUS ON RESEARCH

### 11.2    Matched-Subjects Design: Sexual Orientation of Children Raised by Lesbian and Heterosexual Mothers

How much, if at all, do parents influence the sexual orientation of their children? How likely is it, in other words, that a child's sexual orientation will be affected by the sexual orientation of the parents? Or do sexual preferences reflect, in large measure, a roll of the genetic dice?

Recent research with gay men who had twin brothers (Bailey & Pillard, 1991) and with lesbians who had twin sisters (Bailey, Pillard, Neale, & Agyei, 1993) found that a monozygotic twin sibling is significantly more likely to also be homosexual than is a same-sex dizygotic twin sibling. This finding suggests a genetic link to homosexuality, since monozygotic twins have identical genetic makeups, developing as they do from the same fertilized ovum, but dizygotic twins are no more similar genetically than any other two siblings, developing as they do from two separate ova. It can be argued, then, that one's genetic makeup significantly influences one's sexual orientation.

Social cognitive theory, on the other hand, argues that modeling by the same-sex parent is an important determinant of gender development. Accordingly, family environment, as provided by the sexual orientation of parents, should be an important influence on the sexual orientation of the children.

Previous research on the development of sexual orientation in children has been limited to heterosexual families. Critical comparisons of the sexual preferences of adult children raised by homosexual versus heterosexual parents have been lacking. Susan Golombok and Fiona Tasker (1996) corrected this deficiency by investigating the sexual preferences of children raised by lesbian mothers compared to the preferences of children raised by single heterosexual mothers.

Golombok and Tasker contacted 27 lesbian mothers and 27 heterosexual mothers when their children were approximately 9 years old. The children were contacted again fourteen years later when they were approximately 23 years old to determine the influence of being raised by a lesbian or heterosexual mother. Simple? Yes, as long as one controls for other variables that might be related to sexual orientation, such as the presence or absence of a father in the home and the mother's age and social class. First, Golombok and Tasker made sure that children in each of the two types of families were raised in homes in which the father was absent, the homes differing only in the sexual orientation of their mothers. This father-absent criteria is a control variable; it is set by the researchers to be the same for all participants. The researchers also used matching to eliminate the impact of the mother's age and social class on the child's sexual orientation.

To match subjects on some variable, researchers first need to rank the subjects in each sample according to the matching variable—say, social class—and then draw from the two samples pairs of subjects that are at approximately the same level of the variable. Using this procedure, researchers can be sure that the two groups will be equivalent regarding the matching variable. If social class is related to sexual orientation, it will be equated for the two groups of children, those of lesbian and heterosexual mothers. Thus, any difference between the groups in sexual orientation cannot be due to social class.

Matching carries an additional advantage. It reduces the amount of unexplained variability in the groups. This variability, termed random error, is due to the fact that people are individuals and don't all act the same. But when two participants are matched on a variable such as social class or age, they're likely to act more similarly than two people of different social classes or ages. By reducing random error through matching, researchers can more easily see the effects of the variable of interest, in this case, the mother's sexual orientation. Another way to describe this advantage is to say that matched designs are more sensitive, or better able to detect differences due to the treatment, than those in which subjects are randomly assigned to groups.

Matching sounds like such a good idea that one has to wonder why investigators don't use this method all the time. Yet like other procedures, it has disadvantages. The most serious drawback is a statistical one concerning the adjustment used when determining the significance of the tests that evaluate the research outcome.

In designs that do not match subjects, the test of significance is based on the total number of participants; in matched-subjects designs this number is cut in half because the design deals with pairs of participants. This statistical adjustment makes it harder to declare a significant finding; that is, it takes a greater difference between the two groups' behavior (the dependent variable) in order to say that the groups are significantly different. Thus, the advantages and disadvantages of the matched-subjects design offset each other. The design's greater sensitivity to treatment effects does not automatically lead to significant findings, as the significance test requires a larger between-groups difference than in unmatched designs. Nevertheless, when researchers are careful to match participants on a variable that is highly correlated with the dependent variable they want to measure, the matched-subjects design can be the best choice to reduce unexplained variability and detect meaningful differences between groups.

Matched designs are slightly more time consuming to conduct than are those involving random assignment of participants. Researchers must first measure the matching variable, then rank participants before they can be assigned to conditions. Extra expense may also be involved. A more serious disadvantage than either of these is the threat to external validity that occurs when participants who can't be matched must be excluded from the study. Any loss of participants can affect the representativeness of the sample and the researchers' ability to generalize their findings to the population from which the sample was drawn.

*(continued)*

## 11.2    Matched-Subjects Design: Sexual Orientation of Children Raised by Lesbian and Heterosexual Mothers    *(continued)*

What does Golombok and Tasker's matched-subjects design tell us about the influence of lesbian and heterosexual mothers on the sexual orientation of their children? First, adult children of both mothers reported equivalent levels of same-sex attraction; however, those raised by lesbian mothers were slightly more willing to consider the possibility of a homosexual relationship. In regard to the adult children's reported sexual orientation, the researchers found that the majority of participants identified themselves as heterosexual, and this was not influenced by being raised by a lesbian or heterosexual mother.

NANCY COBB   ◆

SOURCES: Bailey, J. M., & Pillard, R. C. (1991). A genetic study of male sexual orientation. *Archives of General Psychiatry, 48,* 1089–1096.

Bailey, J. M., Pillard, R. C., Neale, M. C., & Agyei, Y. (1993). Heritable factors influence sexual orientation in women. *Archives of General Psychiatry, 50,* 217–223.

Golombok, S., & Tasker, F. (1996). Do parents influence the sexual orientation of their children? Findings from a longitudinal study of lesbian families. *Developmental Psychology, 32,* 3–11.

---

Social learning theory (chapter 5) maintains that lesbians have had aversive experiences with males, such as having been punished for early heterosexual sex play, or have had rewarding experiences with females or exposure to pornographic pictures of women. Research does not support this view (Bell, Weinberg, & Hammersmith, 1981; Morin, 1977; Reinisch, 1990). Many lesbians have had positive experiences with men, and many heterosexual women have had negative experiences with men.

Simone de Beauvoir's (1961) existential position emphasizes choice and responsibility for choices. In her view, because of the pressures toward heterosexual choices, a woman who chooses lesbianism is more likely than one who chooses heterosexuality to be making an authentic choice. A lot of feminist writing does portray heterosexuality as oppressive, suggesting women with heterosexual desire are not authentic (Dworkin, 1987; Joseph & Lewis, 1981). Such positions see lesbianism as normal behavior but do little to help explain why some women make the choice and others do not; they also demean women who are genuinely comfortable with heterosexuality.

Some research has focused on trying to discover unusual patterns of relationships between lesbians and their mothers or fathers during younger years. No clear pattern has been shown (Bell et al., 1981). Retrospective studies are problematic because parents' current attitudes toward lesbianism can color lesbians' recollection of earlier events. When differences between early experiences of lesbians and heterosexual women are found, they are not consistent and not large (Wolff, 1971). For example, one study found that more lesbians than heterosexual women recalled their mothers as having been negligent—10% versus zero. The difference is statistically significant, but what is the meaning? What about the 90% of lesbians whose mothers were not seen as negligent?

Retrospective studies of childhood activities seem more promising (Bailey & Zucker, 1995; Bell et al., 1981). However, nonconformity in childhood gender activities is related to adult same-sex behavior more strongly for males than females, and we are a long way from knowing why the association occurs. We must also remember that only 33% of heterosexual women (and 20% of lesbians) say that they were highly feminine when they were growing up, and up to 78% of college women report that they were tomboys (Hyde, Rosenberg, & Behrman, 1977).

*Biological Approaches*     Several biological views about the genesis of homosexuality, dealing with hormones, genetic foundations, and brain structures, have been advanced; so far the research is inadequate and does not present convincing results (Byne & Parsons, 1993; De Cecco & Parker, 1995; Fausto-Sterling, 1995; McGuire, 1995). Much of the concern of researchers continues to be with male behavior, and much of the research guiding thoughts about human sexual behavior has used laboratory rats. For example, the sexual behavior of rats can be manipulated by hormonal treatments, but major differences have not been found in circulating testosterone levels between heterosexuals and either lesbian or gay men (Ellis & Ames, 1987; Money, 1988). Evidence from rats also has been used to suggest the relevance of brain structures (parts of the hypothalamus) that typically are larger in males than females. But the size of the comparable area in humans does not vary with sexual orientation (Swaab & Fliers, 1985). The most famous study about brain structures (LeVay, 1991) did not study any lesbians and was plagued by a number of method errors, including not being clear about which men had same-sex experiences and which had not, and not accounting for the difference in onset of AIDS (Byne & Parsons, 1993).

We cannot say that there are no biological bases predisposing a person to heterosexual or homosexual behavior. We can say that no biological factors have been identified in any proven way. This may be because biological approaches so far have been very simplistic (Byne & Parsons, 1993; De Cecco & Parker, 1995; Fausto-Sterling, 1995; McGuire, 1995). For example, some reviewers concluded that "Conspicuously absent from most theorizing on the origins of sexual orientation is *an active role of the individual constructing his or her identity* [italics added] (Byne & Parsons, 1993, p. 236). They propose an interactional model in which genes or hormones predispose personality traits that influence how a person interacts with the environment, and those interactions with the environment may influence the particular sexual experiences or identity a person finds comfortable.

Also in a spirit of interaction, Michael Storms (1981) more specifically proposed that same-sex sexual preference results when the sex drive matures earlier than usual, when social relations are dominantly with same-gender friends, until about age 12. The strong sex drive typically emerges around the ages of 12 to 15 when teens are associating with those of the other sex. Consistent with Storms' theory, lesbians do mature sexually earlier than heterosexual women (Goode & Haber, 1977; Saghir & Robins, 1973). Also consistent with the theory is the fact that more men than women are exclusively homosexual in behavior; males' sex drive generally emerges earlier than females' drive. We do not yet know all the aspects of personality development that influence sexual orientation.

## Varieties of Sexuality

Clearly, we do not really know much about the genesis of lesbianism or of heterosexuality (Eliason, 1995; Gooren, Fliers, & Courtney, 1990). Researchers have assumed that heterosexual behavior is "just natural" and therefore not in need of explanation. Freud (1905/1953), often criticized for "biology is destiny," actually had a constructionist view—that heterosexuality as a norm is a social construction. He thought that heterosexuality needed explanation and was not a self-evident fact based on a chemically founded attraction. Preliminary research indicates that most heterosexual college students accepted a heterosexual identity imposed upon them by society, religion, gender, or parents' expectations; others had not really thought about it; others were actively questioning their sexuality (Eliason, 1995). Men who had thought about their sexual identity had committed to heterosexuality largely on the basis of rejecting a gay identity. On the other hand, women decided that heterosexuality suited their lives at the time, though being a lesbian or bisexual was an option (Eliason, 1995). The few people of color in the sample often pointed out that race was a more salient identity for them than sexuality, suggesting that sexuality may play a different role in overall identity than for whites.

It might make sense to assume that bisexuality is natural and then focus on the complex and various ways individuals develop heterosexual, homosexual, or bisexual identities. Then we could better appreciate diversities in each group. There probably is not one "homosexuality" but many "homosexualities," just as there is not one "heterosexuality" but many "heterosexualities" (Bell, 1974; Eliason, 1995). Certainly, there are many ways of being a lesbian and therefore many routes into it (Reinisch, 1990; Riemer, 1995). Some lesbians may be highly predisposed to same-sex behavior by factors of biology or early experience. Others may be more influenced by events in adolescence. Still others clearly are influenced by events in their adult lives. These women may be similar in some underlying ways not yet known. Researchers so far have lumped all lesbians together (apparently assuming that lesbianism is defined as women wanting sex with a woman) and tried to discover what went wrong with them. This is the same thing that has happened continually in the history of studying women—scientists have assumed that "women are all alike and something is wrong with them."

It may be necessary first to articulate the varieties of lesbians. Lesbians in England were invited to tell their own stories (Kitzinger, 1987). From their stories, five factors or clusters were apparent and may provide a preliminary typology of lesbians. The first type included women who happily embraced their lesbianism and felt personally fulfilled by it. A second type "fell into lesbianism" by falling in love with a person who happened to be a woman; lesbianism came by definition. They felt that they could have been heterosexuals if they had fallen in love with a man. The third type felt they were "born that way" and made no big deal of it. They accepted the label of lesbian but did not define themselves solely in terms of it. The fourth type discovered lesbianism through radical feminism; they saw being a lesbian as part of the feminist struggle. They rejected heterosexuality because they saw it as an aspect of oppression. The final type considered lesbianism "a cross to bear"; in this group are those who sometimes are ashamed of being lesbian and would prefer to be heterosexual.

As developed so far, this is a crude typology leaving many questions unanswered. It has the advantage of making explicit the fact that lesbians are not all alike and probably cannot be explained by any single existing theory. Lesbians generally are very similar to heterosexual women. As suggested in the previous chapter, lesbianism may be more a matter of preferences about interpersonal relationships than it is of preferences about the specific sex of the person with whom one shares sexual intimacies.

## Women's Sexual Responsiveness

One of the many ways in which women have been misunderstood and misrepresented is through the claim that they are not interested in "real" sex. "Real" sex usually means genital activity leading to orgasm by heterosexual intercourse (Rothblum, 1994b). In contrast, women are depicted as interested only in romance and love. Heterosexual and lesbian women do associate love with sex more closely than men generally do, as we have seen, but this does not mean that they are not interested in genital satisfaction. Women's supposed lack of interest in genital activity is based on erroneous assumptions about their fantasies and about women's sexual functions and potential.

### Erotica and Fantasies

Women do not have as much experience with explicit erotic material as men have (Fisher & Byrne, 1978; Griffitt, 1987; Kinsey et al., 1953). But that does not tell us much about women's sexuality, because adult bookstores and movies actually are adult *male* bookstores and movies, and pornography is demeaning to women (chapter 15). Laboratory research shows that women and men both can be aroused by romantic-erotic and purely erotic stories and movies (Fisher, 1983; Griffitt, 1987; Heiman, 1975). However, imagination may be best (Byrne & Lamberth, 1971). Sexual fantasies are common during daydreams, self-pleasuring, and sexual activities with a partner, and by and large they have a positive contribution (Ellis & Symons, 1990; Hunt, 1974; Knafo & Jaffe, 1984; Strong & DeVault, 1997; Sue, 1979).

Women are said to be more interested in romance than "real" sex because they have more diffuse romantic fantasies than men do (Barclay, 1973), giving only general pictures such as "They made love, and it was wonderful." However, there are important individual differences among women as well as situational variations. Women high in sex guilt do report fewer and less explicit fantasies than women low in sex guilt, for example, "Thoughts of an imaginary lover or stranger enter my mind" (Moreault & Follingstad, 1978). The lack of explicitness seems due to an inhibition about "letting go" rather than lack of knowledge. When given "permission" (through prompts of explicit fantasies as examples), these women's fantasies were like those of the low-guilt women in elaboration of details.

Fantasies of being overtaken also are more typical of women high rather than low in sex guilt and of women generally rather than men generally. The so-called **rape fantasies** have been misused to claim that women want forcible sex. The problem with the logic is that a woman is in control of her fantasies (Gold, Balzano, & Stamey, 1991)—her fantasized "rapist" is not going to do anything she does not want him to do. However, by giving him the lead role in her fantasy, she absolves herself of guilt. In view of the dominant societal teaching that "good women are not sexual," it is no wonder that women who feel guilty about their sexuality displace responsibility for their sexuality. Men also have "rape fantasies," but women do not assume that men want women to force them to sex (Friday, 1980).

## Sexual Responses

In this section we look first at a widely used sexual response model and then consider controversies about women's orgasms. Lest you conclude that orgasm is nothing but a bunch of physical responses that scientists study and argue about, consider first the comments in A Closer Look 11.2, and then note the similarities of comments made by women and men.

Masters and Johnson (1966) studied couples having sex in the laboratory while being monitored physiologically. From their results, they emphasize the physiological similarities between women and men in the four phases of their model of the sexual response cycle: excitement, plateau, orgasm, and resolution. (Other authorities use a different model.) Underlying most biological activities during sexual arousal are myotonia and vasocongestion (Strong & DeVault, 1997). **Myotonia** is increased muscle tension throughout the body, shown in voluntary flexing and involuntary contractions; examples are facial grimaces, contractions of hands and feet, and muscular spasms during orgasm. **Vasocongestion** is the engorgement of body tissues with blood. During sexual arousal, the arteries expand to allow increased flow of blood to organs and tissues, but the veins do not expand sufficiently to allow the blood to flow back out. The result is a congestion or buildup of blood in superficial and deeper tissues, for example, a woman's labia, clitoris, and nipples and a man's penis.

During the excitement phase, muscle tension increases and there is some increase in heart rate and blood pressure and engorgement (Figure 11.1; A Closer Look 11.3). Sexual tension continues to mount during the plateau phase. Women develop the "orgasmic platform," a term Masters and Johnson used for the marked engorgement of the outer third of the vagina. The plateau is followed by orgasm, particularly for men; women, however, may reach the plateau without a following orgasm if stimulation is not effective. The pattern is the same for all forms of sexual behavior, whether alone or with someone of the same or the other sex.

During resolution, the sexual systems return to their nonexcited state, beginning immediately after orgasm if there is no additional stimulation. Men, but not women, typically enter a refractory period, a physiologically imposed "shutdown phase" when additional sexual arousal is unlikely. Because of their relative lack of a refractory period,

## A Closer Look

### 11.2  Women's and Men's Comments About Intercourse and Orgasm

#### Reasons for Having Intercourse

Can you tell which comment is by a woman and which is by a man?

A. "Intercourse makes me happy. I express myself oftentimes better physically. I have lots of love to give, and it's one way that is a better avenue of expressing my feelings for others."

B. ". . . to enjoy myself physically, for experimentation, fun, and to get to know someone better."

A is somewhat more typical of women than of men, and B is more typical of men. However, Person A is a man and Person B is a woman.

#### Personal Descriptions of Orgasms

Can you tell which descriptions are by women and which are by men?

A. When I am aroused, I get warm all over, and I like a lot of holding and massaging of other areas of my body besides my genitals. After time passes . . . I prefer more direct manual stroking.

B. When I am sexually aroused, my whole body feels energized. Sometimes my mouth gets dry, and I may feel a little lightheaded. I want to have all of my body touched and stroked, not just my genitals.

C. When aroused I feel very excited and I fantasize a lot. Then all of a sudden, a warm feeling comes over me, and it feels like a thousand pleasure pins are being stuck into my loins all at the same time.

D. It's like an Almond Joy, "indescribably delicious." The feeling runs from the top of my head to the tips of my toes as I feel a powerful surge of pleasure. It raises me beyond my physical self into another level of consciousness, and yet the feeling seems purely physical. What a paradox! It strokes all over, inside and out. I love it simply because it's mine and mine alone.

E. An orgasm to me is like heaven. All my tensions and anxieties are released. You get to the point of no return, and it's like an uncontrollable desire that makes things start happening.

F. Having an orgasm is like the ultimate time I have for myself. I am not excluding my partner, but it's like I can't hear anything, and all I feel is a spectacular release accompanied with more pleasure than I've ever felt doing anything else.

Women gave descriptions A, E, and F. Men gave descriptions B, C, and D. Notice that both A (a woman) and B (a man) refer to wanting parts of the body other than genitals to be touched. Notice that both D (a man) and F (a woman) refer to orgasm as a very private experience. Notice also that D (a man) and E (a woman) suggest a religious or mystic experience.

---

SOURCE: Crooks, R., & Baur, K. (1990). *Our sexuality* (4th ed.). Redwood City, CA: Benjamin/Cummings.

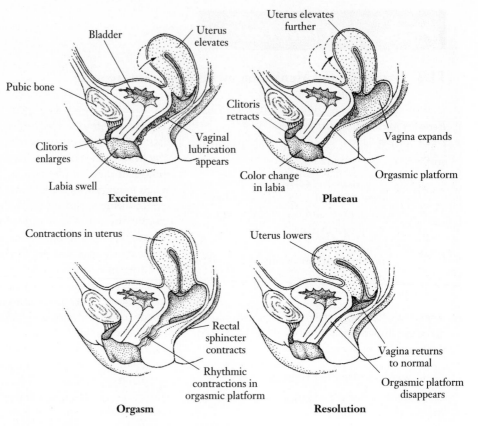

Figure 11.1 *Stages of sexual response in women.*

most women can have **multiple orgasms** (or **sequential orgasms**) if stimulation is continued, meaning more than one orgasm in a short time interval. Any woman capable of regular orgasms will generally be capable of as many as six orgasms within a few minutes if properly stimulated (Masters & Johnson, 1966). Some young men do have multiple orgasms, and most men may be more capable of them than they realize (Comfort, 1972). Many heterosexual women generally do not have more than one orgasm, in part because their partners do not continue providing stimulation past their own orgasm. Women giving themselves pleasure and those who have sex with other women are much more likely than those having sex with men to reach orgasm initially and then to continue to other orgasms (Athanasiou, Shaver, & Tavris, 1970; Masters & Johnson, 1966).

## Issues About Women's Orgasms

Although we know some of the basics of the physiology of women's orgasmic response, there is continuing controversy about what women's orgasms "really" are like—or

## A Closer Look

### 11.3 Phases of the Sexual Response

In the *desire phase* there are fantasies about sexual activity and the desire to have activity.

In the *excitement phase* there is a subjective sense of sexual pleasure. Both women and men experience muscle tension and moderate increases in heart rate and blood pressure. A woman experiences vasocongestion in the pelvis, vaginal lubrication and expansion, and swelling of the external genitalia; "sex flush" (pink or red rash on the chest or breasts) and nipple erection are more common in women than men. Men experience penile tumescence and erection. This phase may last from less than a minute to several hours.

During the *plateau phase* that Masters and Johnson distinguish, sexual tension continues to mount until the peak that leads to orgasm. Heart rate and blood pressure continue to rise, breathing is faster, sex flushes and genital coloration become more noticeable. Muscle tension builds up and may include involuntary contractions and spasms in the plateau and then the orgasmic phase.

The plateau phase for women includes what Masters and Johnson call the development of the orgasmic platform, the engorgement of the outer third of the vagina. It typically lasts only a few seconds to several minutes. Some women try to prolong this state of tension for greater arousal and then more intense orgasm.

The phase of *orgasm* is when sexual pleasure peaks and sexual tension is released. There is increased pelvic congestion with a feeling of pressure, and increased blood pressure, heart rate, and hyperventilation. Rhythmic contractions often occur, followed by decreased congestion and a feeling of emotional or physical release. Women have contractions (not always subjectively experienced) of the wall of the outer third of the vagina. Men have a sensation of ejaculatory inevitability, followed by ejaculation of semen. For both, the anal sphincter rhythmically contracts.

Orgasm is the shortest phase of the response cycle, lasting only a few seconds, though women's orgasms tend to be slightly longer than men's. Women may reach the plateau level without the following release of orgasm. This is most likely during penile-vaginal intercourse when the man reaches orgasm first or when effective manual or oral clitoral stimulation is replaced with penile penetration.

*Resolution*, the final phase of the cycle, involves a return to the nonexcited state. There is a sense of muscular relaxation and general well-being. During this phase, men typically are physiologically refractory to future erection and orgasm; women, in contrast, can respond to additional stimulation almost immediately.

NOTE: Masters and Johnson do not list the desire phase. The American Psychiatric Association does not include the plateau phase.

SOURCE: Based on the American Psychiatric Association. (1994). *Diagnostic and statistical manual of mental disorders* (4th ed.), DSM-IV. Washington, DC: American Psychiatric Association, pp. 493–494; Masters, W. H., & Johnson, V. E. (1966). *Human sexual response.* Boston: Little, Brown.

*should* be like. Freud started things off by distinguishing between **vaginal** and **clitoral orgasms.** He considered the clitoris a stunted penis, so that enjoyment of clitoral stimulation is an experience of "masculine" sexuality in a young girl that in the course of development must give way to the more mature, "feminine," orgasm of vaginal stimulation (chapter 5). Masters and Johnson see no basis for defining different types of women's orgasms, but Freud may have been trying to point to a distinction that does exist in some way.

Josephine and Irving Singer (1972) maintain that women have three types of orgasm. They suggest that what Masters and Johnson studied was the **vulval orgasm** characterized by contractions of the orgasmic platform; this does not require coitus. Singer and Singer pointed to women's comments about different emotional feelings with orgasm. But some emotional aspects of orgasm may disappear when the partners are being observed in a laboratory, so that all orgasms would look alike.

A **uterine orgasm** occurs only with vaginal penetration and depends largely on the pleasurable effects of uterine displacement and contact of the penis with the cervix. As described by the Singers, it does not involve contractions of the orgasmic platform, but it does involve breathing changes. A gasping breathing precedes an involuntary breath-holding response developing after tension in the diaphragm has built up. Orgasm happens at the moment when the breath is explosively exhaled. There is an immediate feeling of relaxation and sexual satiation, typically followed by a refractory period. The uterine orgasm, of course, is essentially the same as Freud's vaginal orgasm. A **blended orgasm** combines features of the first two types. There are contractions of the orgasmic platform, as with vulval orgasm, but with the breathing changes and following satiation of uterine orgasm. The Singers, unlike Freud and many "how-to" books, did not claim that one type of orgasm is better than another.

To add to the pressure some women feel, another kind of orgasm has been proposed, though apparently similar to the uterine orgasm. Ernest Grafenberg (1950) noted the erotic significance of an area in the vagina since called the **Grafenberg-spot** or **G-spot.** It is a fairly large area, about the size of a dime during arousal, of the lower anterior wall of the vagina and the underlying urethra and surrounding glands (Heath, 1984; Ladas, Whipple, & Perry, 1982). It has been thought similar to the male prostate (Heath, 1984; Mallon, 1984). One reason for the fascination is that G-spot orgasms are sometimes accompanied by ejaculation of fluid from the urethral opening. Chemical analysis of the discharge suggests that the ejaculate is not simply urine (though it may have traces of urine) but resembles semen (Darling, Davidson, & Conway-Welch, 1990; Perry & Whipple, 1981; Zaviacic et al., 1988). Understanding of the role and significance of the G-spot is far from complete, and some sexologists are dubious about it. Some sexologists advise that if women want to explore their G-spot, go ahead—but they caution against treating G-spot orgasm as a "new sexual achievement to be relentlessly pursued" (Crooks & Baur, 1993, p. 175).

> There is no single correct, definitive, or supremely normal kind of female orgasm. Since women differ in so many aspects of their being, one should expect variability in their modes of sexual satisfaction as well. (Singer & Singer, 1972, p. 265)

People can feel happy without laughing and sorrow without crying. Women can feel sexual pleasure without the external signs others might expect of them.

## Do Women Have a Higher Sex Drive?

In the popular current view, men "naturally" have a stronger sex drive than women do. The view that women have a stronger drive has a much longer history than the view that men do (A Closer Look 11.4). It was not until the 1840s and 1850s that women's sexuality started being played down or virtually denied (Degler, 1981). Women more than men seem responsible for this new view, because they thought minimizing their sexuality would be a way to reduce pregnancies and achieve autonomy within marriage as well as moral superiority over men in a society concerned about the evils of sex (Cott, 1977).

> Sexuality was the primary source of women's subordination to men; it was the force that brought men and women together into marriage, the very institution in which the subordination of women to men was most clearly accomplished. (Degler, 1981, p. 258)

In the latter part of the 19th century, minimizing their sexuality was a way for women to gain personal freedom. The types of bondage that women suffer and the specific actions they see as useful for loosening the bonds vary with the times. For the young women of the 1920s, claiming some of their sexuality back was a demand for freedom. Young women at the end of the 20th century are pursuing the freedoms claimed by their great-grandmothers, but what constitutes freedom also varies with the times. Today, women seem to want to claim their sexuality within the context of affection and with recognition that their sexuality is only part of what they are.

The view that women are less sexual than men has been challenged since the 1960s. (Sherfey, 1966). Masters and Johnson speculate that the societal minimization of women's sexuality has served to "neutralize women's biophysical superiority" to bring a "psycho-sexual-social balance between the sexes" (Masters & Johnson, 1970, pp. 219–220). Women's greater tendency to multiple orgasms is one reason for the suggestion that women's sexuality has been minimized. Also relevant is that the clitoris is the site of a woman's sexual pleasure and is the only organ that has no known function other than sexual pleasure. One can point also to the fact that so many women enjoy their sexuality in spite of all the social pressures against it.

***Patterns of Orgasmic Responses***    The different experiences of men and women prevent drawing any firm answers about who is more sexual, and such an issue is not likely to promote mutual understanding. What can be said is that the pattern of sexual development of women and men is different. Data about reported sexual activities and desires and orgasmic responsiveness indicate that the male drive peaks in the late teens or early 20s and then decreases rather sharply, while women's drive peaks later and decreases relatively slowly (Kaplan & Sager, 1971); women's peak may be as late as the mid-40s (Reinisch, 1990). For example, women's orgasmic response is faster and more

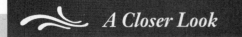

*A Closer Look*

## 11.4    Historical Views of Women's Sexual Drive

The view that women have a strong sexual drive has a long history. The Roman poet, Ovid, believed that women's lust was uncontrollable (Heilbrun, 1973). He recounted the story of Teiresias who had been both a woman and a man. When asked by Jove and Juno which sex enjoyed lovemaking more, Teiresias agreed with Jove that women had the greater pleasure; Juno became upset and struck him blind, so he became known as the blind prophet of Thebes.

The ancient Hebrews assumed that sexual desire was at least equal, and both wife and husband had a mutual obligation to satisfy each other. The Book of Women, compiled in the 12th century by the physician and rabbi Maimonides, spelled out the details of wives' conjugal rights, taking account of the demands of husbands' jobs. For example, a healthy husband with an easy job was to attend to his wife every night, while one who studied the Torah would be weakened from the study, so his wife could expect sex only once a week.

Women in the Middle Ages and preindustrial Europe were thought more capable of sexual pleasure than men (Degler, 1983). The witchcraft persecution of the 15th and 16th centuries coincided with the belief that women were sexually more desirous than men. Women in Elizabethan England were considered highly lusty. The early Puritans who settled in this country had an implicit assumption that men were the more fragile and heart-centered sex and women were the stronger, more bodily oriented sex who must stop and realize how fragile men were. One man was excommunicated from the church (and therefore ostracized from the community) because he refused to have sex with his wife (Ryan, 1983).

Frank recognition of women's sexual needs and the old idea that women are insatiable lingered on at least until the middle of the 19th century (Degler, 1980). Marriage manuals admonished women to control their passions while warning men that their wives had a right to sex. The man's role in sex was to excite the woman to orgasm; the clitoris rather than the vagina was acknowledged as the principal source of excitement. Menopause was not seen as ending women's sexual passion, which was thought to continue to an extreme age.

SOURCES: Degler, C. N. (1981). *At odds: Women and the family in America from the revolution to the present.* Oxford: Oxford University Press.

Heilbrun, C. (1973). *Toward a recognition of androgyny.* New York: Harper & Row.

Ryan, M. P. (1983). *Women in America: From colonial times to the present* (3rd ed.). New York: Franklin Watts.

consistent in the 40s than in the teens or 20s. In addition, more older women (aged 36 to 57) than younger ones (aged 22 to 35) reported that the primary motivation for sex was physical pleasure (43% versus 22%). In contrast, the number of men stating physical pleasure as primary was less among the older group than the younger one (36% versus 44%) (American Health and Psychology Today Service, 1990).

Why does the apparent orgasmic difference exist? There are no clear answers (Reinisch, 1990). Hormonal levels are high in both sexes during puberty. The answer may be more a matter of psychology than biology. Many women may have to lose learned inhibitions and come to trust their partners in order to enjoy their sexuality.

***Speed and Intensity of Orgasm*** Part of the learning for some women and their partners involves developing appreciation of effective stimulation and of the woman's right to request that. Part of the cultural stereotype of women not being as sexual as men is that it takes women longer than men to reach orgasm. But women and men reach orgasm in the same length of time when they are pleasing themselves—about 2 to 4 minutes (Masters & Johnson, 1966). Oral or digital manipulation of the genitals by a partner comes next. The relative effectiveness of these methods is seen as due to the better stimulation of the clitoris, the most sensitive of the female genitals and the transmitter of sexual desire. The woman on top of a man is quicker for the woman than the man on top. When the woman is on top, she has freedom to move her body for optimum pleasure and does not have the weight of a person likely to be heavier than she is on top of her. Women take longer to reach orgasm in the most common position: the missionary position of man on top.

Of all the varieties of couples studied by Masters and Johnson (1979), only heterosexual women consistently expressed dissatisfaction with their sexual activity and less intense arousal and orgasms. Masters and Johnson considered lesbian couples the best lovers. Kinsey et al. (1953) previously had noted that consistency of orgasms was greater in lesbians than in heterosexual women.

Does this mean that a woman must have a woman as lover to experience orgasmic satisfaction? No, not at all. It does mean that heterosexuals may learn something from lesbians. Lesbians put less emphasis on having orgasm as an achievement and more emphasis on communication than the typical heterosexual couple does (Masters & Johnson, 1979). Lesbians have explicitly genital activity less than other couples do, particularly as the relationship develops (Blumstein & Schwartz, 1983; Clunis & Green, 1993; Schreurs, 1993). But during the day they have more ongoing physical contact not specifically genital (Schreurs, 1993) and are more aroused and satisfied with the genital activity they do have (Iasenza, 1992). The picture suggested is that lesbians are more casual about orgasm but enjoy it more intensely than heterosexuals. Orgasm as a goal that makes genital contact meaningful may be more characteristic of, and more damaging to, younger heterosexuals. As people develop into middle age and then the older years, they continually find ways to enjoy sexual pleasure.

## Sexuality in Older Women

Many people think that sex and old age "just don't go together" (Crooks & Baur, 1993; Reinisch, 1990; Schaie & Willis, 1991; Starr, 1987; Strong & DeVault, 1997). This reflects society's overemphasis on the notions that sex is only for attractive young adult partners achieving an orgasm and that age brings a dignity that is incompatible with sex (Barrow & Smith, 1992; Diamond & Karlen, 1980). When older people express affection physically in public, they are either scorned or desexualized—"Isn't that

*Sexual interest does not necessarily decline as people age. In fact, for some, physical and emotional intimacy becomes an increasingly fulfilling part of life.*

cute!"—as if they were 5-year-olds instead of mature adults. The insistence that older people are not to be sexual is institutionalized in many nursing homes (Crooks & Baur, 1993; Strong & DeVault, 1997). Married couples often cannot sleep in the same room, and unmarried people are required to have supervision when visiting people of the other sex. The problem is even more acute for lesbians and gay men (Kehoe, 1988; Kelly & Rice, 1986).

Past studies showed a decrease in sexual interest as people age (Strong & DeVault, 1997). More recent studies indicate that, in spite of some physiological changes (e.g., reduced lubrication, erection), sexual interest and enjoyment often remain strong. People 65 or older report as much total sexual activity as those aged 18 to 26 (Janus & Janus, 1993). For both age groups, about half of women and men reported sexual activities "daily" or "a few times a week." Not all of the activities were with another person. Autosexuality becomes increasingly important as people grow older (Cogen & Steinman, 1990), although sexual activity with another person also continues. Over half of a sample of married people and 24% of those over 76 years of age had intercourse within the previous month, typically four times; genders and ethnic groups did not differ (Marsiglio & Donnelly, 1991). Among a group of healthy people aged 80 to 102, 30% of the women and 62% of the men reported having intercourse (Bretschneider & McCoy, 1988). When declines do happen, they are due more to cultural than biological reasons (Kellett, 1991).

The quantity of genital activity may decrease, the intensity of orgasm may decrease, but the overall quality of sexual relations seems to increase with age for both heterosexual and homosexual women and men (BWHBC, 1992; Cole & Rothblum, 1991; Kimmel, 1978; Rubin, Peplau, & Hill, 1981). Increased concern for quality involves increased experimentation with a variety of genital and nongenital activities (Bachman, 1991; Brecher, 1984; Reinisch, 1990). Older people come to value any activity that feels good to both partners (Starr, 1987) and sometimes seek sex therapy to enhance their sexual lives (LoPiccolo, 1991; Schiavi, 1990).

Older women who stay exclusively heterosexual face the problem of a reduced pool of potential partners because they are more likely to have had their spouse die than men are, and older men often seek younger women. Women have several options. Some women choose a younger man as a partner. Others consider women as sexual partners (Doress & Siegal, 1987). A woman of 60 said that if her husband died, her sexual satisfactions would come from herself or from other women because her relationship with her husband was so wonderful, she couldn't imagine a relationship with another man (BWHBC, 1992). However, it is not easy for older women to find the right woman partner. Older lesbians, like younger ones, are not inclined toward casual sex and generally prefer women of similar ages as partners (Raphael & Robinson, 1980/1984). Of lesbians aged 60 to 86, about half had had no sexual contact in the past year (Kehoe, 1988). Some women enjoy several options. One woman of 60 discovered her sexuality in several ways:

> I thought my life was over when my husband of 35 years died two years ago. I have learned so much in that time. I learned to masturbate. I had my first orgasm. I had an "affair." I have established intimate relationships with women for the first time in my life. (Cited in Crooks & Baur, 1993, p. 469)

Older women do have to face health problems that may affect their sexual activities. So, too, do some younger women, but all are sexual beings with rights to fulfillment.

## Women With Chronic Illness and Physical Disabilities

It is often assumed that women and men, whether heterosexual or homosexual, with chronic illnesses or physical disabilities do not have sexual feelings or cannot act upon them if they do have them (Lew-Starowicz, 1994). These people are subject to **ableism,** a belief that not being physically "normal" prevents them from being able to feel or do anything that other people do. Women more than men are victims of the expectations that they be physically attractive. They become double victims when their bodies do not have the same shape or functions as the bodies of other women (Asch & Fine, 1988; Fine & Asch, 1988a, 1988b; Fisher & Galler, 1988).

Fewer women with disabilities are married than men with disabilities (49% versus 60%) (Asch & Fine, 1988). If a member of a married couple incurs a disability after marriage, a woman is more likely to stay with her disabled husband than a man is to stay with his disabled wife. Women who are physically challenged often are seen by men and by women as "an asexual object" (BWHBC, 1992; Crooks & Baur, 1993).

Certainly, people with disabilities have obstacles other people do not, such as equipment (e.g., artificial limb) and some reduced sensations. Some also feel guilt because their bodies do not meet cultural ideals. Some may have reduced body experiences, but this does not diminish sexual desire nor pleasure from sexual activities (Strong & DeVault, 1997). Even some people who are terminally ill continue to have sexual interests and, depending on the specific circumstances, may have sexual relations (Laury, 1987). Sensitivity and open communication can allow a couple, whether lesbian or heterosexual, to find ways to experience sexual pleasure in spite of disabilities (Lenz & Chavez, 1981; Shaul et al., 1978). Less is known about lesbians with disabilities than about heterosexuals with them (Fine & Asch, 1988b). There are some lesbian illness-support groups; more such groups would be useful (BWHBC, 1992).

## Sexual Problems

Sexual problems are relatively common among heterosexual couples and probably among lesbians (Ende, 1986; Spencer & Zeiss, 1987). Even many happily married women and men (77% and 50%, respectively) report some kind of problem (Ubell, 1984), as do gay men and lesbians (Nichols, 1987). According to a review of studies, nearly half of women and men reported occasional or frequent lack of desire, problems with arousal or orgasm, and painful intercourse (Spector & Carey, 1990). Sexual problems seem relatively "normal":

> I know, all of your buddies are functioning perfectly and never have a problem. If you really believe that, I have a nice piece of ocean-front property in Kansas I'd like to talk to you about. (Zilbergeld, 1992)

***Physiological and Psychological Factors***    Physiological factors can play a role in sexual problems, often in combination with psychological factors (Bancroft, 1992). A woman with a problem can ask for medical tests to find out if there is physiological involvement. Lack of vaginal lubrication may be due to low estrogen or to feelings of indifference or anger about sex. Pain when an object is inserted into the vagina can be caused by lack of lubrication, endometriosis, or strong involuntary contractions of the muscles, sometimes as a conditioned response to fear, conflict, or pain, sometimes caused by a traumatic sexual experience (Kaplan, 1987; Nadelson, 1978).

Sexologists agree, however, on the large role of psychological factors in sexual problems (Crooks & Baur, 1992; Strong & DeVault, 1997). The negative learning in childhood, discussed at the beginning of this chapter, and the ongoing conflicting messages women receive are thought to be major contributors to sexual problems (Carson & Butcher, 1992; Crooks & Baur, 1993; Masters & Johnson, 1970; Masters, Johnson, & Kolodny, 1992; McCabe, 1994; Simpson & Ramberg, 1992). Although lesbians, as just discussed, have been declared "better lovers," they too have grown up in the same general culture and are susceptible to many of the same general pressures as heterosexual women (Clunis & Green, 1993).

Specific sexual problems can occur at any phase of the sexual cycle: lack of interest in sexual activity (inhibited sexual desire); low desire with fear of sex (sexual aversion); lack of vaginal lubrication (inhibited sexual excitement or Hypoactive Sexual Desire, HSD); painful intercourse (dyspareunia); involuntary vaginal contractions (vaginismus); premature orgasm; and lack of orgasm after arousal, lubrication, and enjoyment (anorgasmia), although orgasm may be faked. The incidence of specific disorders varies by ethnic groups (Laumann et al., 1994). For example, African American women (45%) are more likely than Latinas (35%) and whites (31%) to report lack of interest in sex but are more likely (20% versus 18% and 8%) to report climaxing too early (Laumann et al., 1994).

***Social-Psychological Factors***     The double standard and specifically the assumption that the man is expert have the effect of placing women in a position in which many feel they do not have the right to straightforward sexual expression and placing men in the position of having to perform and prove their manliness (Hawton, Catalan, & Fagg, 1991; Levine, 1992; Masters & Johnson, 1970). Coupled with this is the sex-equals-coitus model of heterosexual relationships that may reduce the eroticism experienced by men and women (Crooks & Baur, 1993). Heterosexuals seem to be focusing on the performance and product—more and bigger orgasms—at the expense of the process of finding out and enjoying what is pleasing. Lesbians are less likely to be caught up in the Big-O game, but they are not immune to negative messages, and in any couple, one person may have more power than another and claim greater expertise about sexuality (Brown, 1986; Clunis & Green, 1993).

Negative messages may lead to women being indifferent or angry about sex and going along with sex as an obligation to try to please their partner; this can cause inhibited sexual desire or excitement with a partner but not necessarily in solitary activities (Brown, 1986; Clunis & Green, 1993; Kaplan, 1987; O'Carroll, 1991; Rosen & Leiblum, 1987). Some women enjoy sexual contact but do not have orgasms: They are **anorgasmic.** Anorgasmia (also called orgasmic dysfunction, inorgasmia, and preorgasmia) is the most common dysfunction women report to sex therapists (Spector & Carey, 1990). Most often, the women do not have adequate stimulation, though physical problems are sometimes (5%) involved. Habitual lack of orgasm (global, lifelong, or primary anorgasmia) may be due to fear, anger, guilt, or anxiety that may prevent women from letting go into an orgasmic response they see as "not ladylike." The pressure to have an orgasm to prove that she and her partner are OK can inhibit the desperately sought orgasm.

It is estimated that 5% to 10% of women in the United States have never experienced orgasm (Hite, 1976; Kaplan, 1974; Kinsey et al., 1953; Spector & Carey, 1990). Other women become anorgasmic (secondary anorgasmia) or are anorgasmic only in specific situations (situational anorgasmia). Some experts consider anorgasmia so common that it probably should not be considered a disorder (Carson & Butcher, 1992; Hyde, 1990). Women who are not orgasmic, however, are still sexual; most rate their sexual experiences positively (Raboch & Raboch, 1992). Lesbians are less likely to report lack of orgasm than decreased sexual desire (Nichols, 1987).

Because of pressures to "do it right" (have an orgasm) and please the partner, women may fake an orgasm, which about two thirds of heterosexual women (and a third of men) do (Darling & Davidson, 1986; Strong & DeVault, 1997). Faking can lead to a vicious cycle, as the partner is likely to continue acting as before, while the faker feels pressure to continue faking to avoid revealing the previous deception. The pursuit of more and bigger orgasms has become an all-consuming pastime—a focus on the specific product or orgasm.

Many women and some men are at a great disadvantage from having experienced childhood and/or adult sexual abuse (Masters, Johnson, & Kolodny, 1992; Vandewiel, Jaspers, Schultz, & Gal, 1990). Childhood abuse is thought to be the childhood experience with the greatest negative impact on adult sexuality. Sexually abused children experience sex for the first time in the absence of consent, equality, respect, trust, and safety, and they are robbed of the chance to explore their sexuality in their own way in a manner appropriate for their age (Maltz, 1991). Sexual experience becomes associated with emotional and physical pain. Flashbacks can interrupt whatever pleasures later come in adult sexuality (McCarthy, 1992). When there is little or no memory of the abuse, there still may be symptoms the person cannot understand (Golden, 1988). Childhood abuse, and the question of memories of it, is discussed more fully in chapter 15.

## Sex Therapy

A prevailing model of sex therapy, which may be followed both informally and formally, is the PLSSIT model: Permission, Limited information, Specific Suggestions, and Intensive Therapy (Annon, 1976). Therapy can come in many forms—friends who can listen and genuinely share their own problems, a lover who enjoys the body of a woman who may not like her body herself, books, and even television shows all can help (Crooks & Baur, 1993). They all can give *permission* that it is OK to be sexual, to want more sexual enjoyment, and to have some difficulties in that pursuit. Formal therapy does the same in a more focused and systematic way. In addition, therapists offer *limited information* (only about the specific issue) and give *specific suggestions* or "homework," such as self-gratification exercises in which a woman can learn what she enjoys (Heiman & LoPiccolo, 1988; LoPiccolo & Stock, 1986). Exercises in which partners touch each other for pleasure but not for sexual arousal are excellent ways to learn about the eroticism of many areas of the body and are recommended as an ongoing practice (Crooks & Baur, 1990; Masters & Johnson, 1970). Kegel (1952) exercises involve strengthening the muscles along the sides of the vaginal entrance to increase the sensitivity of the vaginal area; they are a matter of contracting muscles as if trying to stop urination. Reading books can also help (Barbach, 1976; Heiman & LoPiccolo, 1988).

Insight therapy can be valuable to help understand unconscious conflicts with possible childhood origins (Kaplan, 1974, 1983). In contrast, systems theory is based on the idea that the problems are serving important functions in the current relationship—the current interpersonal system (LoPiccolo, 1989). For example, inhibited sexual desire may help maintain some separateness in an otherwise overly close relationship. The therapist looks for the function the problem is filling and tries to get the couple to work toward a more satisfactory resolution of the underlying problem.

Success rates vary with the specific problem; success rates approaching 90% or more for some dysfunctions have become routine (Carson & Butcher, 1992).

Finally, it should be noted that a common recommendation is that women practice self-gratification to explore and become comfortable with their own bodies (Barbach, 1975; Heiman & LoPiccolo, 1988; LoPiccolo & Stock, 1986). With this experience, women can become "at home" with their bodies and experts at knowing what pleases them. They can "own" their bodies, their sexuality, their selves, and be in a better position to share when and if they choose to do so (Dodson, 1987). Thus we end on the same theme with which we began: A woman's body is *her* body.

## Some Final Thoughts: Claiming Freedom, "Our Bodies, Our Selves"

Women's sexuality is clouded with confusing and negative dictates about what women are supposed to be like. Sexual scripts have made women's natural sexuality seem unnatural. Girls are not encouraged to get to know their bodies or to be at home with them as their own; at adolescence they are expected to use their bodies to attract suitors and then to refuse the would-be lovers. Women's bodies are glorified as sex objects to be used to provide pleasure to men on demand. Women themselves have not been encouraged to enjoy their own bodies.

With the sexual revolution of the 1960s, women gained more freedom for sexual experience, but the freedom in many ways was only skin-deep. Women want sex with affection, caring, and commitment, and they often share sexually as an expression of caring for men who may not share their views. Pressures of liberation cause many women to have sex when they do not want it in order to prove that they are OK (e.g., not frigid or lesbians). But women who have sex with too many men still are whores rather than madonnas, prostitutes rather than princesses. How much is too much? Men do not have to face that question—whatever men do is "normal."

The problems and inhibitions extend into relationships. Part of the problem is lack of communication between heterosexual partners, together with the double standard and the related expectations that men are the experts on sex. Another part is due to views that real sex is coitus and that orgasm is to be achieved as a sign of sexual success. But what is the "right" orgasm for a woman? Men's orgasms are not analyzed and codified, but women's have to be debated to be sure women are getting what other people consider the most pleasure.

In spite of everything, many women do manage to develop ownership of their bodies, their selves, and their sexuality. The Boston Women's Health Book Collective aptly chose *Our Bodies, Ourselves* as the title for their book. The success of the book indicates the appeal of the title and the meaning that women found in its content. Women of the past sought freedom in their ways. New times call for new ways. Today, women need to resist pressure to become "liberated" as defined by others; they have the opportunity to define their own sexual freedom. Contemporary women are searching for and claiming their lives, their bodies, and their freedoms as their own. The prospect of what can be accomplished is promising.

## KEY TERMS

concealment rituals
self-gratification, self-
   pleasure, autoeroticism
erotic dependence
male as expert
sexual script
double standard of
   sexuality
madonna-whore, princess-
   prostitute
sexually transmitted
   diseases (STDs)
acquired
   immunodeficiency
   syndrome (AIDS)

human immunodeficiency
   virus (HIV)
chlamydia
gonorrhea
pelvic inflammatory
   disease
genital warts
human papillomavirus
   (HPV)
genital herpes
herpes simplex virus
   (HSV)
syphilis
woman-identified woman
bisexual

reference group
rape fantasies
myotonia
vasocongestion
multiple (or sequential)
   orgasms
vaginal orgasm
clitoral orgasm
vulval orgasm
uterine orgasm
blended orgasm
Grafenberg-spot, G-spot
ableism
anorgasmic

## KEY POINTS

### Development of Sexuality in the Early Years

◆ Adults give infants and children many negative messages about their bodies and
   sexuality. Girls are more likely to develop body shame than boys are.

◆ The relative lack of self-gratification for girls and women is thought to lead to
   sexual dysfunctions because of lack of body knowledge and body ownership.

### Heterosexual Attitudes and Activities

◆ Marked change in premarital sexual behavior took place in the 1920s and 1960s.
   Sexual attitudes became more permissive than formerly, but the double standard
   and gender differences still remain. Increasing numbers of people have sex before
   marriage, but men are still more sexually active than women.

◆ STDs are increasing in frequency. Concern about AIDS has had relatively little
   impact on heterosexual activities.

◆ Women more strongly associate affection and closeness with sex than men do,
   though many men also want sex with love. Women tend to feel that sexual liberation has reduced their right to say no, while they still are criticized for saying yes.

### Lesbian Behavior and Identity

◆ A lesbian is not defined solely by sexual behavior; many women are technically
   bisexual but identify themselves as heterosexual or lesbian. Sexual behavior and
   identity do not necessarily match, and both may change over the life span.

◆ There are no satisfactory theories of the "cause" of lesbianism or of heterosexuality. This may be because there are many varieties of lesbianism, just as there are
   many varieties of heterosexuality.

## *Women's Sexual Responsiveness*

◆ Both women and men are aroused by erotic stories. Women high and low in sex guilt differ in their spontaneous fantasies. Women's fantasies of being overpowered are not evidence of a desire to be raped; men also have "rape fantasies."

◆ There is a great deal of psychological and physiological similarity between women and men in sexual responsiveness; women, however, are more likely to have multiple orgasms. Kinds of women's orgasms are still debated.

◆ The view that women are more sexual than men has a long history. Women are less likely than men to have orgasms in coitus but take the same amount of time to have orgasms as men with self-gratification.

◆ Lesbians communicate better than heterosexuals and are less concerned with orgasm as a goal, although they are more consistently orgasmic and enjoy sexuality more than heterosexual women.

◆ Older people are interested in sex and engage in a variety of sexual activities. Women with chronic illness and disabilities have sexual feelings and want sexual expressions.

◆ Sexual problems are relatively common in women and in men, but more women than men have never had orgasm or do so only rarely. Negative cultural attitudes about sexuality are a leading contributor to sexual problems, as is sexual abuse.

◆ Sex therapy, informal or formal, typically includes giving permission to be sexual, offering information, making suggestions for developing responsiveness, and increasing knowledge. Self-gratification experiences are recommended for women.

## INTEGRATIVE QUESTIONS

1. Summarize the prevailing sexual messages given by society. Explain why these messages are given and the effects of them. You may use yourself as a focal point for discussion if you wish.

2. Select any one (or combination of) sexual problems and construct a theoretical model of how that problem develops. If you wish, focus on someone you know or a hypothetical "typical person."

3. Discuss why you think researchers have been fascinated with searching for (a) "the" causes of homosexuality, especially biological causes, or (b) "the" best female orgasm.

4. Use the typology of lesbians discussed in the chapter and apply it to heterosexual women. Characterize the women of each type. Does it make sense in understanding heterosexual women? What other types do there seem to be?

5. Evaluate the claim that women are more sexual than men and the related claim that societal scripts are designed to hide this fact. Is this an issue that matters?

6. "Old people are not interested in sex because they are mature and dignified." What does this view, shared by many, tell us about societal views of sexuality?

It might help in considering how you feel to think that your grandparents or great-grandparents might be sexually active.

7. "The saying 'knowledge is power' helps to explain why women are socialized to have little information about sex and their bodies" (Wyatt & Riederle, 1994, p. 623). Evaluate this statement. For example, do you agree that women have little information? Does "someone" not want women to have the power of their bodies? If so, who? why?

## Chapter 12

# *Women's Decisions About Reproductive Experiences*

$O$ne indisputable difference between women and men is that women can bear children and men cannot. This fact is at the center of many biological and social issues. Women face decisions, risks, and challenges because of their childbearing capacities, whether they are married or single, lesbian or heterosexual. Women have long sought ways to control their reproductive potential by avoiding having children; they have also long sought ways to have children. There is so much politicalization and medicalization of childbearing issues that it sometimes is hard to remember the individuality, the desires, the experiences of the women whose lives are on the line as they attempt to make their own decisions.

In this chapter we look at women's attempts to prevent childbirth, their decisions and feelings about pregnancies, and the nature of childbirth. We also look at the implications of having a baby. Do women enjoy having a baby? Are they "natural" mothers? Is mothering as good an experience as it could be for women?

Before continuing, consider these questions for personal thought:

- ◆ What would you view as an ideal form of birth control? Is that available? Why or why not?
- ◆ What do you think about a woman who buys condoms?
- ◆ Under what circumstances, if any, would you have an abortion or want your partner or sister to? Under what circumstances would you be strongly opposed?
- ◆ Do you want to have children? Why?
- ◆ Can people without children be happy? What are the advantages and disadvantages of having or not having children?
- ◆ What do you say to yourself when you see a pregnant woman?

◆ Have you ever felt blue when you finally got something you had been want-ing, such as a good grade on a time-consuming special project, a great job, a special new outfit, or a pet?

◆ How long do you think parenting lasts?

## *Attempts To Prevent Pregnancy and Childbirth*

Women throughout history have sought to regulate reproduction by preventing con-ception, often in ways that seem strange today (McLaren, 1990). A frequently used method has been a **pessary:** material placed over the cervix to prevent sperm from reaching the uterus. Women have used leaves, gum arabic, grasses, cork, honey, and dung from a camel, crocodile, or elephant (Newman, 1972). Women have also used **douches**—liquids used to wash out the vagina—of vinegar, lemon juice, and boric acid.

Early Egyptians used condoms as decorations, and then condoms were made of skins and used for contraception; in the 18th century adventurer Giovanni Casanova used condoms made of animal membranes tied with a ribbon at the base of the penis. Condoms became available in rubber in the 1840s. The diaphragm was developed in the 1880s. Modern technology has advanced birth control procedures, but current procedures still do not meet the needs of all women, and many women use procedures that are ineffective.

### Effective Contraceptive Methods

**Sterilization** is the most widely used preplanned method of birth control and is *vir-tually* 100% effective (Boston Women's Health Book Collective [BWHBC], 1992; Gold & Richards, 1994; Insel & Roth, 1998). The procedure for women is **tubal ligation:** The Fallopian tubes are cut and/or blocked so that the eggs cannot enter them. The procedure for men is **vasectomy:** The vas deferens is cut or blocked so sperm cannot mix with seminal fluid. Although there have been some successes with reversing sterilizations, the procedures should be considered permanent. The greatest increase in use of sterilization has been for middle-class couples in which the wife is 35 to 44 years old and there is at least one child. Although sterilization of men generally is safer and considerably less expensive than sterilization of women, sterilization of women is somewhat more frequent.

Women in the United States and elsewhere are not always given a choice about sterilization by their physicians (BWHBC, 1992; Dreifus, 1975). Victims usually are poor, African American, Puerto Rican, Chicana, or Native American women who have been pressured into consent during labor or childbirth, told they would lose benefits otherwise, or not told that the procedure is irreversible. White middle-class women also have been abused by physicians who refuse to sterilize them if they have no children.

Birth control pills, or oral contraceptives, are the next most widely used method of preplanned contraception in the United States and are used increasingly worldwide

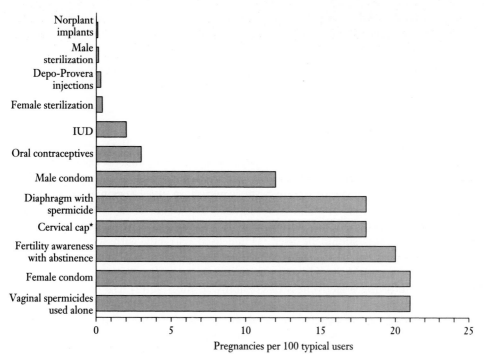

*For women who have given birth, the failure rate of the cervical cap increases to 36%.

**Figure 12.1** *Failure rates of contraceptive methods during the first year of use.*    SOURCE: Insel, P., & Roth, W. (1998). *Core concepts in health* (8th ed.). Mountain View, CA: Mayfield.

(Dawson, 1990). They are used primarily by younger women and by white women more than others. Most users (82%) are under 30; women aged 20 to 24 are the largest group of users (Gold & Richards, 1994; Kash, 1984). Although safer now than when first introduced, birth control pills still pose serious health risks for some women and are not to be used indefinitely by any. The most widely used pills now are combination pills with both estrogen and progestin (BWHBC, 1992). The theoretical failure rate (using the procedure as it should be used) is 0.1%, but the actual failure rate (as it is used) is 3% (Figure 12.1).

The most effective form of contraception in use today is the Norplant implant. It consists of six flexible, matchstick-sized capsules placed under the skin of the upper arm. Norplant implants provide a steady dose of progestin for up to 5 years. Another progestin-only contraceptive is Depo-Provera, administered as an injection and effective for about 12 weeks. The intrauterine device (IUD), a tiny plastic device inserted into the uterus, is an effective but not well understood contraceptive. Many IUDs have been withdrawn from the market because of lawsuits, and only about 2% of all American women currently use them (Insel & Roth, 1998). Norplant, Depo-Provera, and IUDs offer effective, convenient contraception, but all can pose health risks and must be provided by a physician.

Barrier methods of contraception include the male condom, the female condom, the diaphragm, and the cervical cap. To be effective, they must all be used with spermicidal cream or jelly.

Male condoms are the third most commonly used form of birth control. They have the advantages of being easily available and providing protection against STDs as well as pregnancy. Condoms of good quality have a theoretical failure rate of about 2% when used correctly, but the actual failure rate is 12% (Insel & Roth, 1998). A number of precautions are needed for most effective use. They must be fresh (check the expiration date on the package) and made of latex (men who are allergic to the latex can use a lambskin condom under a latex one). They must be put on after arousal and before penetration. Preliminary fluid from the penis can contain sperm, increasing with the number of ejaculations in a short period of time. Sperm from a previous ejaculation may still be on the penis if it is inserted a second time without a condom. Oil-based lubricants such as Vaseline and some lotions weaken condoms, so only water-based lubricants should be used. When used correctly with spermicide and in combination with a diaphragm, male condoms are virtually 100% effective (BWHBC, 1992).

In spite of the effectiveness of condoms, at most about half of sexually active young people use them, and many do so only sporadically, although they know of the effectiveness of condoms (Baldwin, Whiteley, & Baldwin, 1990; Campbell, Peplau, & DeBro, 1992; DeBro, Campbell, & Peplau, 1994). Worry about STDs does not necessarily increase condom use (chapter 11).

Abstinence is the most effective form of birth control and has been used for centuries. Sexual love need not involve penile penetration, even between heterosexuals. Many couples also practice fertility awareness methods, involving abstinence during the fertile phase of the woman's menstrual cycle. The fertile phase is calculated using the calendar, body temperature measurements, or observation of changes in vaginal mucous secretions. Using this method requires more knowledge, attention, and motivation than most of the other methods.

The chance of a sexually active woman who uses no contraceptive method becoming pregnant within a year is 85% (Jones & Forrest, 1992). Some couples use methods that are relatively ineffective. Estimates are that about half of sexually active high school and college students do not use effective procedures (Whitley, 1988). Ineffective methods used by younger people include withdrawal and douching.

## Lack of Contraceptive Use

Why do so many people risk an unwanted pregnancy by not using effective birth control procedures? Why do they risk getting a sexually transmitted disease by not using condoms? A variety of answers have been suggested, and the reasons for one woman may not be the same as for another. Money is a consideration for some as well as the embarrassment of going to a physician. Lack of information is an obvious possibility. Many myths contribute to young people's sense of invulnerability. False beliefs include the notion that a woman cannot get pregnant if the couple has intercourse standing up, if they have intercourse only occasionally, if it is the first time the woman has had intercourse, if she is breast-feeding a baby, if she is having her menstrual period, or if the man ejaculates outside her vagina. Acting on any of these beliefs can result in an unwanted pregnancy.

It is not clear that sex education courses necessarily improve contraceptive use (Furstenberg, Brooks-Gunn, & Chase-Lansdale, 1989; Hayes, 1987; Vinovskis, 1988). People will not use contraceptives if they do not know about them, but just knowing about them is not enough. Knowing the technicalities does not always translate into action.

Young people learn a lot about sexuality from the unrealistic portrayals in the media (Vinovskis, 1988). Love scenes do not show the woman providing a condom, going to the bathroom to insert a diaphragm, or commenting about the pill. Contraceptives are not part of our cultural image of "making love." Men often say that a condom reduces their pleasure, and some women place the man's pleasure over their own safety (Campbell et al., 1992). Men also are concerned, more than women, about the embarrassment of condom use.

Perhaps the most basic reason for lack of contraceptive use is resistance to acknowledging sexuality, particularly women's sexuality (chapter 11). For a woman to be "prepared" is a statement that she is a sexual human being. She may fear that being prepared will be seen as taking the initiative away from the man and communicating that she is "fast" (Wyatt & Riederle, 1994). In Europe, where the sexuality of young people is accepted, youths have low rates of teen pregnancy in spite of high rates of sexual activity (Furstenberg et al., 1989).

The result of American attitudes is that the young women who get pregnant are likely those who have negative attitudes toward sexuality and who are the more traditional young women. They are lower in self-esteem, assertiveness, and internal control, and higher in femininity and in guilt and anxiety about sex (Adler, 1981; Chilman, 1986; Gerrard, 1987; Gerrard, McCann, & Geis, 1984; Ireson, 1984; Morrison, 1985). Religious youths are less likely to have premarital sex than others, but when they do have sex they are less likely to use contraceptives (Miller & Bingham, 1989; Thornton & Camburn, 1989).

## Abortion

Just as they have tried to prevent conception, women also have long attempted abortion (Francke, 1982). Over 5000 years ago, women in China drank quicksilver in oil or swallowed 14 live tadpoles in an effort to end a pregnancy. Russian women squatted over pots of boiling onions, and the women of some Indian tribes climbed up and down coconut palms, striking their stomachs against the trunks. Greeks and Romans considered abortion acceptable (Francke, 1982). Until the late 1800s, women healers in the United States and Western Europe provided abortions (BWHBC, 1992). Today, skilled village abortionists in Thailand, Malaysia, and the Philippines continue traditional massage techniques of abortion.

There are different kinds of abortion. Not all are desired. **Spontaneous abortions** or **miscarriages** occur without a human decision. About 20% to 30% of embryos that implant on the uterine wall are aborted spontaneously, most within the first

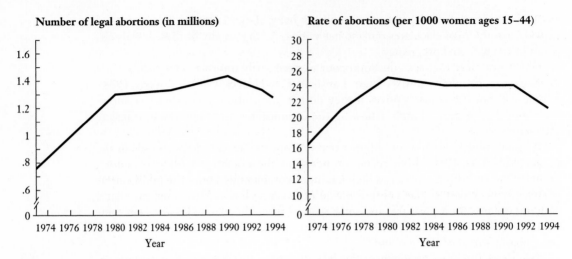

**Figure 12.2** *Abortion rates in the United States.*    SOURCES: Alan Guttmacher Institute. Centers for Disease Control and Prevention. (1997). Abortion surveillance: Preliminary data—United States, 1994. *Morbidity and Mortality Weekly Report,* *45* (51): 1123–1127.

3 months of pregnancy (Salisbury, 1991). About three fourths of women are not aware of the miscarriage (Beck et al., 1988). In contrast, **induced abortions** involve an explicit decision to use medical means to induce or cause an abortion. Induced abortions can be **therapeutic** if, for example, there is a defect in the fetus or a physical or psychological health risk for the mother; these are not considered elective. When the induced abortion is **elective,** the decision is not because of the medical condition of the mother or the fetus. Most public concern is about these elective abortions.

In the United States, nearly 30% of pregnancies were ended by elective abortion in the 1980s (Adler et al., 1992; Russo, Horn, & Schwartz, 1992). The number of legal abortions rose steadily from 1973, when abortions were legalized, leveled off around 1980, and decreased in the early 1990s (Figure 12.2). Still, nearly half (47%) of American women will have had an abortion by age 45 (Gold, 1990).

Legal abortions are the most common surgical procedure in the country and are 3 times safer for a woman than tonsillectomies and 12 times safer than childbirth (Bishop, 1989; Hayler, 1979). The longer the pregnancy has lasted, the more dangerous the procedure and the longer the recovery. More than 90% of all abortions are performed at less than 13 weeks of gestation (Tietze & Henshaw, 1986; Tietze, Forrest, & Henshaw, 1988). Less than 1% are performed at more than 20 weeks, and most of those are because of a fetal defect (Henshaw, Koonin, & Smith, 1991). At the time of maximum danger for abortion, the third trimester of pregnancy, abortion is no more dangerous than delivery—approximately 1 in 10,000 women die (BWHBC, 1992; Wilcox et al., 1988).

Women of all childbearing ages, classes, races, and religions elect abortions, but the majority of those are young (especially 18 or 19), white, poor, and unmarried (Adler et al., 1992; Henshaw et al., 1991; Russo et al., 1992). Although more white women than women of color elect abortion, a greater *proportion* of women of color have abortions, and more Hispanics have abortions than non-Hispanic whites. The differences are thought due to different rates of unintended pregnancies rather than to attitudes about abortion (Russo et al., 1992). Catholic women are as likely to obtain an abortion as other women, and about 16% of all abortions are obtained by born-again and Evangelical Christians (Henshaw & Silverman, 1988).

**Making Decisions**     Decisions about abortion are complex and not undertaken lightly even by pro-choice women (Lemkau, 1988; Russo et al., 1992). Married women and Catholic women have somewhat more difficulty making the decision than other women do (Osofsky, Osofsky, & Rajan, 1973). Reasons for abortion do not differ much across ethnic and racial groups when age, employment status, student status, and parental status are controlled (Torres & Forrest, 1988). What do women consider in deciding about abortion?

Carol Gilligan (1997; chapter 9) concluded that women approach the possibility of abortion with a concern about all the people involved. Other researchers also demonstrate women's concerns about their responsibility to the potential child, their partner, and themselves (Miller, 1992; Russo et al., 1992; Torres & Forrest, 1988). Lack of financial resources to afford a baby and concerns about interpersonal relationships are prominent for minor and adult women. Minors are especially concerned about ability to care for a child, while married mothers are more likely to feel that they are past their childbearing stage, perhaps because of physical problems (Table 12.1; Russo et al., 1992). In short, "A substantial number of women's reasons for abortion reflect responsibilities to others or outside circumstances, aspects of women's realities that sometimes are lost in abortion policy debates" (Russo et al., 1992, p. 193).

**Effects of Abortion Decisions**     The psychological effects of abortion vary because there are many reasons for pregnancy and for terminating it. Women who have a spontaneous abortion or a therapeutic abortion are especially vulnerable to negative effects; they have been lumped inappropriately with women choosing elective abortions in meta-analyses showing harmful effects of abortion (Adler et al., 1992). These women often report dismay at the careless responses of other people, "Oh well, you can try again." Most *can* have a successful pregnancy, but that does not ease their mourning at the death of a loved one (Salisbury, 1991).

In contrast, legal elective induced abortion, particularly in the first trimester, is stressful but not traumatic for most women, as shown in studies done shortly after the abortion and up to 8 years later (Adler et al., 1992; Mueller & Major, 1989). Some of the stress of abortions is caused by having to acknowledge an unwanted pregnancy and decide what to do (Adler, 1992; Cohan, Dunkel-Schetter, & Lydon, 1993). Once the decision is made, abortion is a relatively short-term stressor. The most frequently reported feelings after an abortion are relief and happiness, though often the woman will feel sadness and regret just before the abortion, which supportive friends need to realize (Adler et al., 1992; Dagg, 1991; Lemkau, 1988).

Some women, however, are more likely to have negative results than others (Adler, 1992; Adler et al., 1992; Lemkau, 1988; Major & Cozzarelli, 1992). Important

**Table 12.1** Percentages of Five Groups of Abortion Patients Giving Various Reasons for Abortion

| Reasons | Unmarried minors | Unmarried adults | | Married adults | |
|---|---|---|---|---|---|
| | Nonmothers (261) | Mothers (480) | Nonmothers (852) | Mothers (204) | Nonmothers (46) |
| I. INTERNAL REASONS | 77.8 | 51.5 | 60.7 | 55.9 | 34.8 |
|   A. Not ready for child rearing | 75.9 | 23.8 | 48.5 | 21.1 | 34.8 |
|     1. Too young/not mature enough to raise another child | 61.3 | ■ | 16.1 | ■ | ■ |
|     2. Can't take the responsibility | 33.3 | 22.3 | 35.8 | 18.6 | 34.8 |
|   B. Childbearing completed | ■ | 17.9 | ■ | 39.7 | ■ |
|   C. Desire to avoid single parenthood | 5.0 | 18.1 | 21.4 | ■ | ■ |
|   D. Health | ■ | ■ | ■ | 10.8 | 6.5 |
|     1. Physical problems | ■ | ■ | ■ | 7.8 | 6.5 |
| II. EXTERNAL REASONS | 70.0 | 71.3 | 77.2 | 66.7 | 89.1 |
|   A. General situational factors | 38.3 | 14.8 | 33.6 | 10.3 | 21.7 |
|     1. Education related | 36.8 | 5.2 | 22.7 | ■ | 13.0 |
|     2. Job related/would interfere | 8.8 | 7.1 | 15.0 | 6.9 | 13.0 |
|   B. Fetus related | 6.5 | 8.1 | 11.2 | 11.8 | 23.9 |
|     1. Prescription medication | ■ | ■ | ■ | 5.4 | 15.2 |
|     2. Diagnosed fetal defect | ■ | ■ | ■ | ■ | 6.5 |
|   C. Partner related | 11.9 | 24.0 | 19.0 | 17.2 | 28.3 |
|     1. Partner not ready/wants abortion | 5.0 | ■ | ■ | ■ | 15.2 |
|     2. Relationship may break up/has broken up | ■ | 7.7 | ■ | 5.9 | 10.9 |
|   D. Social disapproval of others | 13.8 | ■ | 9.3 | ■ | ■ |
|     1. Doesn't want others to know pregnant | 10.7 | ■ | 8.5 | ■ | ■ |
|   E. Other responsibilities/other children need me | ■ | 18.5 | ■ | 17.2 | ■ |
|   F. Cannot afford to have a baby | 28.4 | 40.0 | 44.2 | 34.3 | 41.3 |

NOTE: Participants were 1900 abortion patients recruited from 30 abortion facilities in all four regions of the United States in 1987–1988. The table is based on the women's spontaneous answers on a questionnaire to the request to "describe briefly why you are choosing to have an abortion now . . . starting with the most important [reason] first."

Analysis based on data set reported in Torres, A., & Forrest, J. D. (1988). Why do women have abortions? *Family Planning Perspectives, 20*, 169–176.

SOURCE: Russo, N. F., Horn, J. D., & Schwartz, R. (1992). U.S. abortion in context: Selected characteristics and motivations of women seeking abortions. *Journal of Social Issues, 48* (3), 183–202. Table 4, p. 195.

factors are the woman's coping skills, her attitudes about abortion generally, her reasons for becoming pregnant and the clarity of her decision to terminate the pregnancy, and social support from her parents or sexual partner. If the pregnancy began in a relationship that ends, the woman is more likely to have negative feelings, more about the relationship than the abortion. Delays in deciding to have an abortion may indicate a desire to have the child (Lemkau, 1988). Negative feelings often can be lessened through counseling to enhance the woman's coping abilities (Mueller & Major, 1989).

*Teenage mothers are in danger of remaining at a low socioeconomic level and becoming dependent on welfare. However, such problems can be alleviated with strong family, medical, and community support. If this young mother achieves her academic goals, she and her child will have better prospects for the future.*

Some women do not want their pregnancy to continue, but they do deliver and rear the child. What is the effect on their children? Predictions for individual children cannot be made, but there is considerable evidence that, on the whole, unwantedness in pregnancy is related to children's educational performance, quality of adult relationships, and overall psychosocial development (David, 1992).

## Teenage Pregnancy

For every 100 unmarried young women aged 15 to 17 years old, 3.78 gave birth in 1992 (Whitmier, 26 October, 1994; data from National Center for Health Statistics). This was a drop from 1991 (3.87), though still higher than 1986 (3.05). Birth rates for 18- and 19-year-olds have increased steadily. Babies born to teen mothers are more likely to be premature and have elevated risks for mortality and neurological handicaps (Rhodes, Fischer, Ebert, & Meyers, 1993).

## Decisions About Pregnancy

After an initial shock of realizing that they are pregnant, the teen women who decide to deliver a child become increasingly committed as mothers (Roosa, Fitzgerald, & Crawford, 1985). Family and friends also typically are upset initially but come to offer support. Decisions about what to do about an unplanned pregnancy are influenced by many factors not yet well studied. Among them are academic goals, relationships with the baby's father, perceived family support for rearing the child, and how many family members or peers have become young parents or have had abortions (Fox, 1982; Furstenberg et al., 1989).

The rate of pregnant teens offering their children for adoption has remained relatively constant for African Americans at 1% (between 1973 and 1988), while it has declined among whites from 19% to 3% (Sobol & Daly, 1992). African Americans have never had widespread use of *formal* adoption because of a norm that care of a child outside the family is a violation of family values (Stokes & Greenstone, 1971); informal adoption among kin has been a long-standing practice (Hill, 1977). At least 40% of teenage pregnancies are terminated by abortion (Hayes, 1987; National Center for Health Statistics, 1992, in Gold & Richards, 1994). Younger teens are more likely to choose abortion than older ones, and whites more than African Americans (Furstenberg et al., 1989). Teens who choose abortion or adoption tend to come from families of higher socioeconomic status and to have higher academic ambitions than those who keep their children (Furstenberg et al., 1989; Sobol & Daly, 1992).

## Effects of Early Childbirth

Effects of having a child at an early age on educational, economic, and marital futures of single mothers are generally negative, although it is difficult to untangle the effects of early childbirth from the effects of the previous and ongoing environment of the young mother (Hayes, 1987; Whitehead, 1993). For example, teenage mothers are more likely to drop out of high school even when compared to other women of similar socioeconomic background and academic aptitude (Kantrowitz, 1990; Mott & Marsiglio, 1985). It is an open question whether dropping out is due to childbearing or to a lower academic commitment that could have precipitated the pregnancy. Adolescent fathers also have a higher dropout rate than other youths whether or not they marry their pregnant partner (Marsiglio, 1986).

Early childbearing does predict long-term welfare dependency. The majority of young mothers, however, both African American and white, who use welfare during early parenthood do become employed when the youngest child reaches school age. Young mothers who achieve academic goals, manage fertility, and marry become indistinguishable from women who delay childbearing. Those who do not have any of these three "buffers" resemble the stereotype of the chronic welfare mother.

Any effects of being born to a teenage mother are difficult to evaluate because the children are likely to grow up in disadvantaged neighborhoods and in unstable families (Roosa et al., 1985). By adolescence the children of teenage mothers have markedly lower achievement and higher misbehavior than children of older mothers

(Brooks-Gunn & Furstenberg, 1986). However, there are success stories: If the young mother had continued her education and entered a stable marriage by the time her child became an adolescent, the teenage child had superior school performance compared with children whose mothers had not made these changes.

## Public Policy Issues

The little current research there is suggests that social intervention programs can be useful in decreasing early undesired pregnancies and increasing the success of young mothers who want to have their children when they are young, but the programs are costly (Rhodes et al., 1993). Contraceptive and family planning services can reduce early childbearing. Prenatal care programs for teens who do become pregnant, followed by parenting education programs, can be effective (Brooks-Gunn & Furstenberg, 1987; Rhodes et al., 1993). Teens who receive educational assistance have better prospects of economic self-sufficiency and not having many children. Child care services are the services most frequently requested by adolescent mothers and the most likely to be unavailable (Clewell, Brooks-Gunn, & Benasich, in press; Furstenberg et al., 1989).

## *Pregnancy and Birth*

Many women do want motherhood and do enjoy it. They probably would enjoy it more if there were not so many societal dictums designed to tell them what they should be feeling and doing as mothers. It was not until the Industrial Revolution that American society prescribed the ideal of mother and child as enclosed together in the home and that motherhood became internalized as a basic category of feminine identity (Lesser, 1991). The "instructions" to women today reflect this change and have been identified in varying ways: **motherhood mystique** (Harris, 1979); the **institution of motherhood** (Rich, 1976); the **motherhood mandate** (Russo, 1979). The meaning of all is essentially the same. There is a set of social stereotypes that tells women that being a mother is their ultimate fulfillment. Women should have at least two children and be joyously responsible for their development into adulthood; it is mother's fault if the children do not become successful (Caplan, 1989; Ganong & Coleman, 1995; Shields, Steinke, & Koster, 1995).

    The number of births and the birth rate in the United States peaked in 1957 (4,308,000, 2.53 births per 100 population), and then dropped until the late 1970s, when an increase began. A recent high was reached in 1990 (4,179,000, 1.67), with some decrease into 1992 (4,084,000, 1.59 per 100 population) (U.S. National Center for Health Statistics, 1994). There have been two kinds of shifts in patterns of births. One is that births to women aged 15 to 29 have *decreased*, and births to women 30 to 44 years old have *increased* since the post–World War II years and even since 1980 (Grindstaff, 1996). A second change is that more women without a husband are giving birth: In 1990, 28% of all births were to unmarried women (versus 10.7% in 1970, 3.9% in 1950). Women of all ages, at all levels of education, in all races, and in all areas of the country are choosing nonmarital births (Census Bureau, Fertility of American Women, June 1992). Although the highest rates of unwed mothers still are among the young women with less education, the greatest increases are for those who are older and with more education. For example, the number of single women with some college who gave birth nearly doubled in a decade (1982 to 1992).

Reasons for the increase in nonmarital births are unclear. One suggestion is that fewer men can provide the financial *and* emotional support a pregnant woman wants. The women would rather rely on parents and other kin—or on themselves—than risk an unstable marriage just to have a child. In addition, with changing views about women, being a single mother has become more acceptable. For lesbians, technology plus the number of heterosexual women having babies without marriage are relevant; they have choices about motherhood and can elect birth by artificial insemination (BWHBC, 1992; Lesser, 1991).

## Deciding To Be a Parent

There is no shortage of theories on why women want babies. Some have insisted that the desire is part of the essential nature of woman (Shields et al., 1995). Freud (chapter 5) thought that having a baby, especially a male one, was a compensation for not having a penis, and followers of Freud have intensified his views. For example, Helene Deutsch (1944) thought the development of a woman's entire personality was directed toward motherhood. Erik Erikson (1968) pointed to the design of women's bodies and said that without a baby, a woman feels empty and unfulfilled: Menstruation is the crying of the womb because there is no pregnancy. Even Karen Horney (1931/1967), who criticized Freud for lack of attention to cultural factors (chapters 1, 5), thought that women had an instinctual desire for children.

Other writers reject such views. Nancy Chodorow (1978) has theorized that the "reproduction of mothering" is due to the fact that women are the chief caregivers of children and a daughter's bond with the caregiver is not broken as a son's is (chapter 9). The daughter, as a wife, then has greater relational needs than her husband has and pursues those through motherhood. For Chodorow, the "mother instinct" is not instinctual but a result of women's greater participation in child care.

Questioning the "instinct" to be a mother from a different perspective, Jessie Bernard (1973) asked, if wanting children is instinctive, why are so many socialization forces directed at being sure that girls want to grow up and have babies? We can ask also, why have women tried so many means to prevent conception and to terminate pregnancies? Why did women use their moral power in the last century to reduce the risk of pregnancy (chapter 11)?

***Thinking About Children***    If wanting children is "just natural" for women, it also is "just natural" for men, and both women and men have ideas about why and when they want children. Most people—men as well as women—want children and expect to have them. At least 90% of college students say they want children (Gerson, 1980; Shields & Cooper, 1983). Among the reasons women give for wanting children are to experience life's full meaning; to have a chance for growth, stimulation, and pride; to

**Table 12.2**  College Students' Reasons for Wanting Children

| Reason | Percentage |
|---|---|
| Expand oneself; child to carry on name or physical characteristics | 48.29 |
| Achieve adult status or social identity | 47.92<br>55.6 Women, 32.1 Men |
| Establish a family for oneself | 45.25 |
| Fun and stimulation of child | 32.7 |
| Be able to influence or control someone | 23.19 |
| Morally correct | 19.39 |
| Social comparison or competition | 8.0 |
| Sense of accomplishment or creativity | 6.3 |
| Economic benefit | 4.55 |

NOTE: Participants were 179 undergraduate women and 94 undergraduate men. Average age was 19.25 years. The percentages of women and men endorsing a reason are not different unless separate percentages are given.

SOURCE: Gormly, A. V., Gormly, J. B., & Weiss, H. (1987). Motivations for parenthood among young adult college students. *Sex Roles, 16,* 31–39. Data taken from text, pp. 33–36.

make someone in one's own image; to please husbands; to experience pregnancy; to provide nurture and guidance (Lott, 1983; Unger 1979). More specifically, more than half of college students said they wanted to expand themselves, achieve adult status, and establish a family (Table 12.2; Gormly, Gormly, & Weiss, 1987). Less than 10% of the students cited a sense of accomplishment or creativity, although people who have had children consider their children a prime creative accomplishment.

College students also have ideas about when they want to become parents. Basically, they want financial and marital stability and an emotional readiness to settle down. Women have been expected to avoid or interrupt their careers to have a child, while that has not been expected of men. Thus more women than men consider achievement goals and getting to know their spouse (Table 12.3). Of course, some women do not want children or do not care to plan their lives around the biological clock.

## Women Without Children

Women without children have been given a number of labels: "barren" (something is wrong with them), "childless" (defined as something they are not), and "child-free" (defined as something they are, but in a way some see as demeaning to children and to women with children). The difficulty in finding an adequate term for women without children illustrates the pervasiveness of the motherhood mandate and definitions of women through their reproductive system.

Previously, women who did not have children were seen as selfish and maladjusted; in spite of some changes, it is not clear that there is as yet a fully "acceptable"

**Table 12.3**    College Students' Considerations About When
To Have a Child

| Consideration | Percentage |
|---|---|
| Financial stability | 62.36 |
| Marital stability | 49.43 |
| Emotionally ready to settle down | 35.6 |
| After achieving career goals | 21.67 |
| | 29 Women, 4.8 Men |
| After getting to know spouse | 15.59 |
| | 19 Women, 4.8 Men |
| Physically able and right age | 11.79 |
| Complete education | 9.13 |
| Don't know, fatalistic | 6.08 |
| | 3.4 Women, 11.9 Men |
| When I need a challenge, to escape boredom | 1.90 |
| By mistake | 0.38 |
| Depending on world or environmental event | 0.38 |

NOTE: Participants were 179 undergraduate women and 94 undergraduate men. Average age was 19.25 years. The percentages of women and men endorsing a consideration are not different unless separate percentages are given.

SOURCE: Gormly, A. V., Gormly, J. B., & Weiss, H. (1987). Motivations for parenthood among young adult college students. *Sex Roles, 16*, (1/2).

place for them in society (Baruch, Barnett, & Rivers, 1983; Roosa et al., 1985). There also still is concern about having only one child in a family because an only child has been assumed to be maladjusted, self-centered, and unlikable. Research shows that the few differences between only children and others favor only children, especially for achievement motivation (Falbo & Polit, 1986; Polit & Falbo, 1987).

***No Children by Choice***    Some women decide fairly early not to have children (Houseknecht, 1979). Others postpone childbearing, and perhaps marriage as well, and finally decide that they prefer not to have children and, perhaps, not a husband (chapter 10). Both these kinds of women tend to be high in autonomy and achievement orientation and do not show the personal nor marital maladjustment previously thought true of them. These women tend to be more satisfied and more successful in their careers than those with children (Doherty & Jacobson, 1982; Gerson, Alpert, & Richardson, 1984), and their marriages generally are happier (Roosa et al., 1985; White & Booth, 1986). Women at midlife, with or without children, are equally happy (Baruch et al., 1983; Houser, Beckman, & Beckman, 1984).

***Not by Choice: Infertile Couples***    At least 10% of all U.S. married couples in which the woman is of childbearing age seek treatment for infertility each year (Pearson, 1992). Infertility usually is defined as the lack of conception after a year of sexual intercourse without contraceptives; 40% to 50% of infertile couples do eventually conceive and deliver a child (Abbey, Andrews, & Halman, 1991; BWHBC, 1992). Demand for fertility services has increased dramatically both because of improved technology and because of an increase in fertility problems attributed to delayed child-bearing, sexually transmitted diseases, exposure to environmental toxins, and increased use of intrauterine devices and abortion.

Infertile people typically report anxiety, depression, and stress; they feel inade-quate and defective, not quite whole (Abbey et al., 1991; Forrest & Gilbert, 1992; Wright et al., 1991). Some women report feeling "hollow"; some men feel that they are "shooting blanks." Some infertile couples grieve the loss of children not to be born. Couples often are very dependent on each other for social support because they do not tell anyone about the infertility. This can either strengthen the marital relation-ship or put a strain on it and possibly lead to divorce (Berg & Wilson, 1991; Roosa et al., 1985).

Infertile women have both sorrows and benefits because of the lack of children. Half of infertile women think infertility is the most upsetting experience in their lives, compared with only 15% of infertile men (Abbey et al., 1991). Women considered infertile for 5 years reported lower overall levels of well-being and said life was less interesting, emptier, and less rewarding than women who were mothers or women who had chosen not to have children (Callan, 1987). However, the infertile women, like the women who chose not to have children, were more pleased than mothers with the amount of freedom and flexibility in their lives. Infertile women who are still married tend to be very happy with their marriages, perhaps because there are benefits of not having children or because the relationship has been strengthened by sharing the pain (Stiglitz, 1990). Weaker marriages may have already dissolved, or the couples were less willing to volunteer for research. Obtaining representative samples of infer-tile couples is difficult.

Infertile couples now have a number of options (Roosa et al., 1985; Strong & DeVault, 1997), including artificial insemination, in vitro fertilization, surrogate moth-ers, and adoption. Of these options, infertile couples, particularly white, highly edu-cated, middle-class couples, have primarily chosen adoption (Roosa et al., 1985).

In contrast to the first half of the 20th century, the demand today for healthy newborns exceeds supply, in spite of the fact that adoption is prohibitively expensive for many couples. Birth control, abortion, and single women keeping their children minimize the pool. The result has been that children or adolescents previously consid-ered unadoptable because of age, disabilities, or race are being placed in adoptive homes. Thus "problems" of modern times have extended the potential of adoption to children who are not beautiful, healthy, blue-eyed infants.

## Feelings During Pregnancy

Women commonly are thought to be a picture of radiant bliss during pregnancy, although plagued by the annoyance of moodiness, morning sickness, and, for some, the unremitting desire for dill pickles and ice cream. Studies that follow women through planned pregnancies do not support the notion of pregnancy either as a time of emotional turmoil or psychological distress nor as a time of heightened self-actualization and well-being (Striegel-Moore, Goldman, Garvin, & Rodin, 1996; Wille, 1995). Pregnant women do not necessarily feel particularly radiant, and many become increasingly concerned about what they see as their unattractive bodies (Ussher, 1989). In addition, modern science has had the unintended effect of giving women many things to worry about lest they harm the fetus and show themselves to be incompetent mothers. Women are to avoid alcohol, tobacco, cats, cat litter, and many environmental agents containing teratogens (agents that cause birth defects) (BWHBC, 1992). It is suggested also that pregnant women avoid electric blankets and hot tubs.

Although a group of physical symptoms are commonly reported in pregnancy, variations occur from woman to woman and often in the same woman from pregnancy to pregnancy (Lips, 1985). Psychological feelings depend to a large extent on whether the pregnancy is wanted, the woman's physical condition, economic considerations, and the support of partners, relations, and friends.

Some of the characteristic feelings of pregnancy vary with the stage of pregnancy (Focus on Research 12.1) (Striegel-Moore et al., 1996). Feelings of anxiety and sometimes depression and fatigue are relatively common during the first trimester (Leifer, 1980; Sherman, 1971). Chances of spontaneous abortion are greatest then, so women who want the child are concerned about maintaining the pregnancy. The second trimester is the most enjoyable time. The final trimester is not very pleasant for most women. The expectant mother is heavy with the growing fetus. She has trouble with simple tasks, such as getting out of a chair, and her body does not feel like *her* body. And, she starts worrying about the delivery and the health of the child.

Cultural attitudes toward pregnant women range from overprotection to scorn (Taylor & Langer, 1977). A pregnant woman is likely to be infantilized (chapter 3; Walton et al., 1988); she is called a "little mother" as people try to take care of her, and people she hardly knows pat her abdomen. At the same time, cultural ambivalence about women's sexuality (chapter 11) can lead to negative attitudes toward pregnant women. A woman is supposed to be a mother, but she is not supposed to be sexual (Ussher, 1989).

## Preparation for Childbirth and Delivery

Giving birth has not always been as comparatively safe as it now is. In the past, pregnant women often prepared themselves for death during childbirth or worried about the death of their children (Clinton, 1982; Moran, 1980; Ulrich, 1980). Medical technology has improved tremendously, but pregnant women still experience fears, such as those expressed by Robin Morgan, a contemporary feminist:

> I was prey to deep almost archetypal feelings that I must be ready for the possibility of losing the child—or of dying, myself, in childbirth. No matter how "modern" we become, it will take still more time and consciousness . . . before the imprint of a million ghosts dead in childbirth will be erased from the secret thoughts of a pregnant woman. (1978, p. 50)

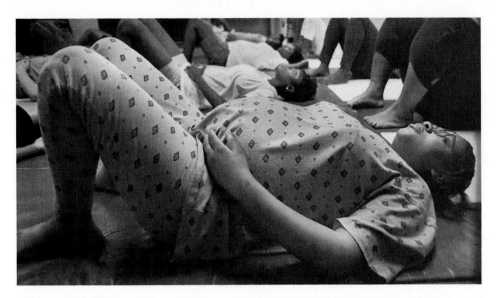

*Childbirth classes help women cope with the experience of birth by providing knowledge, relaxation techniques, and social support. These women are likely to be more satisfied with their birth experience than are women who did not take classes.*

To help women prepare for and participate in childbirth, many varieties of childbirth classes are available. The term *natural* for the birth has fallen into disfavor because of the implications that other methods, especially those using anesthesia, are unnatural. The important point to feminists is that women have a say in the medication given to them (Entwisle, 1985). All programs try to erase the idea that birth is a painful ordeal requiring extensive medical intervention. Most draw on the ideas of Grantly Dick-Read and Bernard Lamaze. Their ideas focus on educating the woman for childbirth and reducing or eliminating pain so she can be conscious and participate in the birth process. They both also stress social support in the training and in labor and delivery. Neither excludes anesthesia if the woman wants it.

Women who have had birth classes have more positive attitudes toward labor and delivery. They have shorter labor, feel less pain, need less medication, and have greater satisfaction with the birth experience (Hetherington, 1990; Hyde, 1990; Kennell, Klaus, McGrath, Robertson, & Hinkley, 1991; Lindell, 1988). Perhaps women who expect a positive experience enroll in classes. However, evidence about coping with stressors generally shows the benefits of features associated with preparatory classes: relaxation, knowledge about what is going on, sense of control, and social support.

Labor is called labor because it is hard work. The hard work is accentuated by the infantilizing and often demeaning conditions frequently a part of giving birth. Although things are changing, a woman giving birth is still placed under physician control (likely male) and given orders by strangers who assure her that they will take

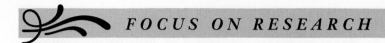

### 12.1    Within-Subjects Design: Pregnancy Changes Both Body and Mind

Pregnancy. According to some women, the best time of their lives. According to others, the worst time. When women share their pregnancy experiences there are stories of morning sickness, the first kick, backaches, and that "glow." What is the true picture of pregnancy?

As the text notes, while there is a great deal of variability in the way individual women experience their pregnancies, there are also some commonalities across the three trimesters. Some evidence indicates that for many women, physical symptoms (nausea, vomiting, fatigue, dizziness) and psychological symptoms (anxiety, depression) ebb and flow depending on the trimester of the pregnancy. In reviewing what is known about physical and psychological changes during pregnancy, a research team headed by Ruth Striegel-Moore found several gaps in our understanding.

Most of the studies were based on women's retrospective reports; that is, the women relied on their memories to give an after-the-fact report of their experiences. Studies that did ask women to record their symptoms as they occurred often began with the first trimester, so there was no pre-pregnancy baseline against which to compare later symptoms.

Striegel-Moore and her research team (1996) designed a study to correct these problems. They gathered physical and psychological information on each woman before she became pregnant and then interviewed her about a wide range of specific symptoms during each of the trimesters of her pregnancy. In addition, the study gathered the same information across 9 months from a control group of women who were not pregnant.

These investigators used a within-subjects or repeated-measures design in a portion of their study. In a within-subjects design, each participant serves in every group or condition, and data are gathered from the same person on more than one occasion. The pregnant and nonpregnant women all participated in a structured interview that was repeated four times at 3-month intervals. This design can be compared with a between-subjects design, in which each participant would serve in only one condition; that is, each woman would be interviewed only once, and a different group of women would be recruited for each of the four scheduled interview times. Within-subjects designs are economical, requiring fewer participants because the same participants react to all conditions. This design is also more sensitive, in that it has a greater ability to detect differences across the conditions. Within-subjects designs are sensitive because by using the same participants in all conditions, they reduce the random variability that comes from individual differences. We expect that the behavior of the same person in different situations should be more consistent than the behavior of two different people in different situations; the result is less "noise" in the data and a clearer picture of differences across the conditions.

Despite these important advantages, this type of design has several serious disadvantages. One is the risk of carryover effects, in which the effect of one experience is still present when the participant moves into the next experience; this carryover can alter the effect of that second experience. In this example, a woman who had a difficult first trimester may carry that negative feeling into the second trimester, making it hard to get a true reading of her symptoms in this second stage of pregnancy. Because of potential carryover effects, some topics simply cannot be studied using a within-subjects design. For example, administering 5-, 15-, and 30-mg doses of a new drug with lasting effects to the same participants over time would not reveal which dosage was the most effective, as each new treatment would be affected by the prior treatment.

In addition to carryover effects, within-subjects designs can have order effects. These reflect systematic changes in performance over time due to factors such as fatigue, boredom, practice, and so on. In some studies, order effects can be controlled through counterbalancing, which presents each condition an equal number of times in each order, thus balancing any effects due to order across all conditions. Counterbalancing was not possible in the study on pregnancy; it would be an amazing researcher who could have some women in the study experience the third trimester before the first, or the baseline before the second trimester! In this study, as in learning studies, order effects are not a problem, as this progression over time is exactly what we want to study. For some studies, both carryover and order effects introduce the potential for confounding. Confounding exists when the difference between treatments or conditions can be explained in more than one way, that is, when a study lacks internal validity.

What did Striegel-Moore and her associates find in their study of pregnancy? They were able to track the occurrence of a variety of physical symptoms from baseline across 9 months of pregnancy. For example, heartburn rose steadily over time to become a major symptom in the third trimester, while nausea peaked drastically in the first trimester and returned to baseline and equaled levels for nonpregnant women by the third trimester. The psychological symptom of moodiness increased for pregnant women during the first trimester but was nearly equal to baseline and nonpregnant control levels during the rest of the pregnancy. The investigators stress that these findings apply only to women who have planned their pregnancies; nonetheless, this within-subjects study, which includes a control group and baseline measures, gives an added dimension to our knowledge of pregnancy.

JILL BORCHERT ◆

SOURCE: Striegel-Moore, R. H., Goldman, S. L., Garvin, V., & Rodin, J. (1996). A prospective study of somatic and emotional symptoms of pregnancy. *Psychology of Women Quarterly, 20,* 393–408.

care of her. Women lie on their backs with their feet in stirrups; that means working against gravity, but it is easier for the physician. Preparatory classes do not necessarily give a woman the control she might have envisioned. In the end, babies are said to be "delivered by physicians" rather than birthed by their mothers. The experience of labor is emotional and physically draining. When things go well, it can be a peak experience (Lips & Morrison, 1986). When there are complications, it can be frightening and painful.

*Modern Couvade*    Some expectant fathers, perhaps as many as 1 out of 5 (Enoch, Trethowan, & Barker, 1967; Trethowan, 1972), experience the **couvade syndrome:** a man showing some physical symptoms of pregnancy, such as nausea and vomiting, appetite change, abdominal pain and swelling, and labor pains. It is speculated that the man envies or is very anxious about his wife's pregnancy. *Couvade* is derived from the French verb *couver*, "to brood" or "hatch." **Couvade rituals** in some cultures provide that the husband takes to his bed when the woman does; he simulates labor and delivery with attendant care from others (Frazer, 1951). He may envy his wife's creativity and seek to bond with the child. Couvade is thought to lure evil spirits away from the woman, help the woman in her labor, and announce that the man is indeed the father (Parke, 1981).

Such ideas seem quaint and amusing, but the modern procedures of our culture may work for the same ends in a more technological way. It has now become relatively common for fathers to participate in childbirth classes and to be present during childbirth (Grossman, Eichler, & Winickoff, 1980; Lips, 1982b). Sharing the experience of pregnancy with their wives allows men to share more of the creativity of life and draws them closer to their wives (Lips, 1982c; Lips & Morrison, 1986). Fathers who participate in delivery seem more involved with their newborns, but the desire to participate seems more important than the participation itself (Entwisle, 1985). Some men who participate see the birth of their child as the most thrilling and profound event of their lives. In spite of the sharing, however, the fact remains that the mother and father can share the experience only up to a point. Birth happens within or from a woman's body, not a man's.

*Cesarean Deliveries*    Some women are told that their baby must be removed through an incision made in the abdominal wall and uterus, by a **cesarean delivery** or **C-section.** Cesarean birth may be recommended because the fetal head is too large for the mother's pelvic structure, because of maternal illness, herpes in the vaginal tract, fetal distress during labor, or the fetus being turned so that the feet rather than the head would come out first (a breech birth). Cesarean births can save the lives of women and their infants, although they may be overused, as discussed below. With changed procedures (incision low and horizontal rather than vertical), women now can have a VBAC (pronounced "vee-bak")—vaginal birth after cesarean. Women who have a cesarean delivery need a longer time to recover and may have negative reactions to the labor and delivery experiences (Entwisle, 1985), but they come through psychologically in fine shape (Padawer, Fagan, Janoff-Bulman, & Strickland, 1988; Reilly, Entwisle, & Doering, 1987).

Children delivered by cesarean procedures may have an advantage, principally because of more positive parental response and greater parental involvement, especially by fathers (Entwisle & Alexander, 1987). During the early weeks after delivery, the mother cannot move around much, so the father has to be involved. The early parental attitudes and behaviors may set a tone that carries over into the child's later years. Parents (about half African American and half white) thought that their cesarean-born children had more ability to do schoolwork, compared with parents of children not born by C-section; and the cesarean-born children themselves expected and attained higher marks than did other children. It would be nice to think there are means other than cesarean deliveries to enhance parents' appreciation of their new infant and fathers' involvement with their infants.

## The Medicalization of Childbirth

Modern medicine has been a mixed blessing for women. In the past, childbirth was a woman's activity occurring in the home, typically with the woman's sister or mother or a midwife to help. During the 19th century, male doctors gradually gained control of childbirth among the upper and middle classes, a control considered by some as due more to political and economic than to scientific reasons (BWHBC, 1992). Working-class women continued to work until delivery and use midwives. Although midwives often had safety records superior to those of physicians, physicians pleaded with legislators to outlaw midwifery.

Today, most births in the United States (but not in all other Western countries) occur in a hospital—a place for sick people designed to facilitate the work of the obstetrician, not the pregnant woman (Mead, 1975). In 1900, 5% of babies in the United States were born in hospitals; by the late 1960s, 95% were (BWHBC, 1992). The positive side of this is that modern technology has dramatically lowered the rates of death of mothers and their newborns. In the United States in 1915, about 100 newborns out of every 1000 died within a year; almost 7 out of every 1000 new mothers died. By 1991, infant deaths had been reduced to less than 8.9 of 1000; no more than 1 woman of 10,000 (7.9) giving birth died from causes related to pregnancy, childbirth, or after-birth complications. It should be noted, however, that the rate for minorities is about three times higher than that for whites (15.6 versus 5.8; U.S. National Center for Health Statistics, 1994).

It should also be noted that the United States lags behind other nations in reducing infant mortality, and the lag is increasing: The United States ranked 7th in the 1950s and 21st in 1991. America's poor are at greatest risk (Children's Defense Fund, 1989, 1991). Other countries take extra precautions to provide for pregnant mothers and then for their infants (Wegman, 1991).

The negative side of modern medicine is that there may be an unnecessary medicalization of childbirth in the United States. Even participatory childbirth classes have been seen as an intrusion into women's experience of birthing (BWHBC, 1992). More drugs and technologies are now used in "normal" births in America than anywhere else in the world (Wertz, 1980). These can reduce unnecessary pain, but some not only prolong labor by decreasing the woman's ability to push the baby through the birth canal but also decrease a woman's awareness of the experience of birth. Drugs also may decrease the baby's heart and respiration rates.

The United States is also criticized for having the highest rate of cesarean deliveries of Westernized countries (Berk, 1993). The rate of C-section deliveries in the United States has increased markedly, from about 5% in 1955 to a quarter of deliveries in 1987 (Silver & Wolfe, 1989; Taffel, Placek, & Kosary, 1992). Some say the increase is due to better use of medical technology; others think cesarean deliveries are aggressive medical interventions that are used more than twice as much as necessary, perhaps because of fear of malpractice suits (Korte & Scaer, 1990; O'Driscoll, Foley, MacDonald, & Stronge, 1988; Public Citizen Health Research Group in AP report, January 29, 1989). This is but one aspect of a continuing controversy: Are the advances of medical science being used to benefit women? Or are women being used by medical science? Or both?

## The Experience of Motherhood

When the first baby arrives, parenthood can be a beautiful, exhilarating experience, and parents often speak of their deep feelings about their infants (Gieve, 1989). However, becoming a parent the first time also can be frightening, hassling, anxiety provoking. Mothers' tasks are made more difficult by the motherhood mystique because their experiences do not always match what they think they are *supposed* to feel (Hoffnung, 1989; Shields et al., 1995). An important decision for women is how they will respond to motherhood. Will they evaluate themselves against unrealistic ideals, or will they allow themselves to experience their motherhood as it is?

### Negative Postpartum Reactions

Many women have negative feelings in the days or months after giving birth, often called **postpartum depression.** The severity of depression and the frequency vary tremendously. What is popularly called **baby blues** or **maternity blues,** usually within a week of delivery, is experienced by 50% to 80% of mothers (McGrath, Keita, Strickland, & Russo, 1990). The woman is emotional, sad, ready to cry, and worried about lack of maternal feelings or frightened by the responsibility, and perhaps guilty at not feeling like the perfect mother. She also may miss being pregnant, feeling hollow inside. As one woman put it, "It took a while to accept the fact that this baby was the same one I'd carried for so long" (BWHBC, 1992, p. 476). The blues typically fade in a few days as the new mother gains confidence and reassurance from others (Berk, 1993).

A few women experience stronger depression, perhaps including some thoughts of violence to the child or to the self (Ziporyn, 1992). Early relief is essential for the sake of the child as well as the mother (Cohn, Campbell, Matias, & Hopkins, 1990). Rest, time away, or talking with someone who understands, whether a friend or a therapist, can break the depression (Steiner, 1990).

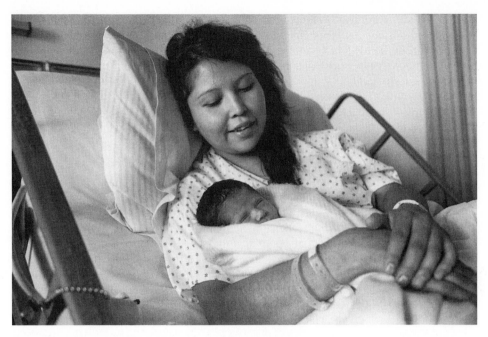

*For this mother, exhaustion has given way to euphoria with the birth of her baby. In the weeks ahead, however, she may feel depressed, frightened, or overwhelmed by her new responsibilities. Some post-partum emotions may be influenced by rapid shifts in hormone levels.*

More severe and more rare, occurring for less than 1% of newly delivered women, is a postpartum mood episode with psychotic features (DSM-IV, 1994). This is a serious breakdown in the ability to cope—a break with reality, often including hallucinations telling the woman to kill the child or delusions that the child is possessed. There may be periods of relative calm and clarity, but getting professional help is strongly advised because the problems often return quickly.

Why do some women become depressed after giving birth? As recently as the 1950s, people thought that women who had any depression, even the mild baby blues, were rejecting motherhood (BWHBC, 1992). This no longer is thought to be the case, but why some women have these feelings is not completely clear. Most post-partum mood disturbances are transient and may be related to the changes in estrogen levels, with possible involvement of thyroid and pituitary functions (Hamilton, 1989; Sprock & Yoder, 1997). Because women who have had severe menstrual problems are more likely to experience postpartum depression, it may be that there is a small group of women whose depression is due to unusual sensitivity to hormonal changes (Cutrona, 1982).

Postpartum depression may not be qualitatively different from reactions to other stressors (Sprock & Yoder, 1997). A new mother does experience stress, such as the stress of delivery, of being awakened repeatedly at night, and of being generally run-down (Gjerdingen & Chaloner, 1994; Hopkins, Campbell, & Marcus, 1987). In a culture that idealizes motherhood, such stressors may be experienced as a negative statement about one's competence at being a mother (Cutrona & Troutman, 1986). Reactions to the stressors also will vary with the woman's temperament, optimism or pessimism, and previous life history (Sprock & Yoder, 1997).

Fears of the sudden changes that responsibility for the child brings, a responsibility similar to but greater than the responsibility some people report when they get a new pet, may also play a part. Another factor probably relevant for childbirth is the tendency for people to become depressed after a major event. One's life previously has been organized around pursuing a goal, with much psychic and physical energy channeled toward it. When the event finally occurs, psychobiological shock and fatigue set in, which can be interpreted as depression. The psyche needs a rest.

Supporting the case for the involvement of psychological factors is that postpartum depression has been reported in new fathers (Liebenberg, 1969; McEwen, 1985) and in adoptive mothers (Melges, 1968). In one study, 89% of women who gave birth reported symptoms of postpartum depression and so did 62% of fathers (Zaslow & Pedersen, 1981). Any links between the hormones and depression are complex ones imbedded in a social context of ongoing life concerns. An important aspect of the social context is transition to parenthood, and some of the difficulties of the transition contribute to women's low moods.

## Transition to Parenthood

Parents often are shocked by the changes in their lives that a newborn demands (Entwisle, 1985). The baby books may be lying all around, but none seems to have the answer needed at the moment. Some babies are harder to care for than others. Having an infant who is not fussy and sleeps through the night from an early age is more likely associated with parental satisfaction than having an infant who seems to be constantly awake and crying, though the impact is greater on mothers than on fathers (Tomlinson, 1987; Wright, Henggeler, & Craig, 1986).

Becoming a parent is an important shift in adult development and takes time; the more time given to the transition *before* birth, the better the adjustment afterward (Mebert, 1991). Preparation is not just a matter of getting the nursery ready but, more importantly, of seeing oneself as a mother or father and being prepared for the work of parenthood (Ruble, Hackel, Fleming, & Stangor, 1988). Decline in marital satisfaction is most likely in couples who have not planned for parenthood realistically or who have not followed through on their plans (Belsky & Rovine, 1990; Moss, Bolland, Foxman, & Owen, 1986).

New parents generally are poorly prepared for infant care and are overly optimistic about their ability (Entwisle & Doering, 1981, 1988). Most men have had little or no experience with infants but generally think their wives know enough. The truth is that more than half of their wives say they have had *no experience at all* in caring for young infants (Entwisle, 1985). When the reality of the baby hits, it is no wonder that both mothers and fathers rate themselves as less competent parents than they had expected to be (Fleming, Ruble, Flett, & Shaul, 1988; Reilly, 1981; Ruble et al., 1988).

Because they don't seem to be meeting cultural expectations, many women feel incompetent as mothers and experience anger, frustration, envy, or panic (Fleming, Ruble, Flett, & Wagner, 1990; Gieve, 1989; Reilly et al., 1987; Ruble et al., 1990). While few women require treatment for postpartum depression, many have milder forms of ongoing depression, including tearfulness, irritability, and feelings of inadequacy; these experiences may increase up to 16 months after delivery (Fleming et al., 1990).

Ongoing difficulties for new mothers are lack of help and the resulting fatigue and limitation on personal freedom (Entwisle, 1985). In heterosexual couples with the father present, gender roles generally become more traditional after the birth of the first child, even when there had been sharing before (Cowan & Cowan, 1988; McHale & Huston, 1985; Palkovitz & Copes, 1988; Rossi, 1988). Men as well as women reported that wives were doing considerably more and the husbands considerably less of the housework and child care after a baby arrived than they had expected (Hackel & Ruble, 1992). Fathers do spend more parenting time when the mother is employed, though not necessarily by much (Darling-Fisher & Tiedje, 1990).

Mothers and fathers still assume different parenting roles. Fathers maintain their roles as primary providers of the infants' material needs (e.g., they work more hours). Mothers are still the primary caregivers for infants, shown by parental reports and observational data (Focus on Research 12.2). Similarly, both mothers and fathers reported that the mother was a better caretaker than the father, though mothers rated fathers higher than fathers rated themselves (Wille, 1995).

Estimates of the amount of time fathers spend with infants range from less than a minute a day to over three hours (Lips, 1993). The time fathers spend, however, is more likely to be playing with the baby than soothing, feeding, changing, dressing, or cleaning the baby. Men tend to help by taking care of older children when the mother is caring for an infant (Shapiro, 1979). Alice Rossi (1988) concluded that, for instinctual reasons, men have difficulty acquiring the skills needed to comfort infants but can interact effectively when children are old enough to walk and talk. However, others have criticized her claim of an instinctual basis (e.g., M. McClintock, 1979).

*Fathering as a Feminist Issue*    Many feminists contend that fathering is a feminist issue, as indicated in a special issue of the *Psychology of Women Quarterly* (Silverstein & Phares, 1996a). Fathers typically are underrepresented in research in spite of their importance (Silverstein & Phares, 1996b). Women's continual movement toward economic equality may contribute to increases in the number of mother-headed families, but some experts guess that a modified version of the nuclear family will become the model family structure in the future (Silverstein, 1996). The changes may involve men becoming more responsive to the needs of women and more involved in child care. At the present, men are generally not very involved in child care, even if they hold equalitarian attitudes (Duindam & Spruijt, 1997). Individually, however, they range from the traditional (hardly any care work within the home) to the very caring father (who does at least as much as his wife).

What lies behind the difference in fathers' behavior? Research suggests different feelings of competence in caring for infants (Wille, 1995). Although this may be the

### 12.2    Direct Observation: How Moms and Dads Parent Infants

As you're sitting in the restaurant, enjoying your dinner, you hear a low wail begin, rise to a crescendo, and break into sobbing. What on earth? Glancing across the room to see what all the fuss is about, you spot a young woman and man desperately trying to quiet an infant. They console, entreat, cajole, all to no avail. Finally, mom picks the infant up and walks out into the lobby, rocking and cooing. "Ah," you chuckle, "The joy of being a parent," and heave a sigh of relief that it's not *your* child.

What do we know about the parenting roles of mothers and fathers? Traditionally, mothers have been the primary caretakers of children, especially young children. Fathers have traditionally been cast as the breadwinners who provide for the child's material needs but are not involved in daily care. These traditional roles have been challenged in the last generation as mothers of young children have entered the labor force and taken on the provider role. To a lesser extent, fathers have been urged to become more involved and active in their children's upbringing. Have these changes led mothers and fathers to revise their parenting roles? This is the question posed by researcher Diane Wille.

Wille knew she could easily gather information from parents using the traditional questionnaire method, but she also knew this kind of self-report had some disadvantages. How could she be sure that what parents said they did was actually what they did? Sometimes, people give what they feel are appropriate or acceptable answers or answers they think will make them look good in the eyes of the researcher. These answers don't always reflect their true behavior. This problem of social desirability can produce skewed responses. As an alternate way of gathering information, Wille used direct observation. She trained observers who conducted home visits with 70 families. During each visit two observers first gathered information on the mother's and father's parenting roles through an interview and questionnaires. Then, for the next 2 hours, the family was encouraged to go about their normal routine while the two observers coded parental interactions with the infant.

Wille found that the information gathered through observation, interview, and questionnaire confirmed each other. Parenting roles were still defined by the gender of the parent, with mothers spending more time in care and play with the infant and fathers working more outside the home. However, when mothers were employed in the labor force, fathers took on more child care responsibility.

Direct observation, as the term suggests, involves directly observing behavior as it unfolds in a situation, classifying and coding it. Coding systems allow researchers to categorize behaviors. Instead of recording everything parents do, for instance, researchers record only specific behaviors. In her study, Wille used a minute-by-minute coding scheme with seven categories: who interacted with the infant (mother or father) and the type of interaction (play, caretaking, or holding); the last category was that of no interaction. This coding system translates observations into quantitative data and makes it easier to detect relationships. The researchers decide on the behaviors to be coded before the study begins. Frequently, observers work from a checklist. As each type of behavior occurs, they simply note its occurrence. Soon, patterns emerge showing the frequency of different types of behavior in different settings or with different people.

Observing behavior directly has a number of advantages. When observations are carried out in a natural setting, such as in Wille's research, there is increased external validity of the research, or the likelihood that the behavior being observed is representative of the way people actually behave in that setting. The use of a coding system increases the reliability of the observations, or the degree to which the two observers working independently of each other agree in their observations. Additionally, some of the problems inherent in questionnaire research, such as selective memory, are eliminated.

Observation does have its disadvantages, however, and one of the most serious of these is reactive behavior. Knowing one is being observed can change one's behavior. The researcher who records reactive behavior may learn a great deal about how the participant acts when being observed but nothing about the participant's normal behavior. Part of this reactivity may have to do with social desirability, as the participant "puts on a good face" for the researcher. Might the parents in Wille's study have played the role of model parents while the observers were there? It's possible. Researchers need to be sure to have observations of adequate length so the participants get used to the situation and gradually resume normal activity. Another disadvantage is the possibility of observer bias. Even when working with an explicit coding scheme, observers bring their own expectations into the situation and may unconsciously attend to certain behaviors and overlook others.

A less serious disadvantage is the time-intensive nature of direct observation. As mentioned, observers must be trained to use the coding scheme accurately, and this takes time. The actual data collection also takes more time in a natural setting than in the laboratory. In a sense, one stands in a stream of behavior with a net, ready to catch (record) certain specimens of interest—but there is no way to speed up the rate at which the behaviors flow by.

JILL BORCHERT ◆

SOURCE: Wille, D. E. (1995). The 1990s: Gender differences in parenting roles. *Sex Roles, 33*, 803–817.

result of instinctual reasons, as Alice Rossi (1988) has suggested, many conclude that it is due to lack of existing explicit training and general gender role training. Fathers do feel more confident and spend more time in infant care if they have had training (McBride, 1990; Parke & Tinsley, 1987).

Women are also calling for a redefinition of fathering and reconstruction of the masculine role (Silverstein, 1996). The request is that fathering come to imply nurturing as well as providing. If connection with others became part of the gender role for men, masculinity would become less oppressive for men as well as for women. Parenting would become less oppressive for women as well. Both women and men could connect more comfortably with their infants, as Chodorow requested. Women's requests parallel those of some men, who want a release from the structures of the male role to become more parental and nurturing (Silverstein, 1996). Some men also want to emphasize that intimacy, care, and connection are parenting skills, not just mothering skills.

Feminists also call attention to what we can learn from gay men about nurturant fathers (Silverstein, 1996). Some gay men stay married to the child's mother, others divorce but have child custody, and still others become stepfathers. Gay fathers, compared to heterosexual fathers, are somewhat less traditional in overall parenting approach because they place more emphasis on nurture than on being a provider. Other researchers find no difference between gay and heterosexual fathers in motivation to become parents, level of involvement with children, or level of intimacy with them (Bigner & Jacobsen, 1989).

## Women's Self-Views as Mothers

Women may or may not have an instinct to have children, but they typically develop strong attachments to their infants, as perhaps fathers would if they were more involved in everyday care. Mothers' attachment to their infants and their feelings of competence grow from before pregnancy into postpartum months (Ruble et al., 1990). In spite of the depression and self-criticism they may have, mothers come more and more to focus on their infants, feel close to them, positive about them, and pleased with their development; they are increasingly involved, protective, and traditional in their mothering roles (Fleming et al., 1990). Mothers also become anxious or irritated about the infant not sleeping or nursing well, infant fussiness, and so on. They find that they are less of a "fun" mom than they had expected to be while not being any more knowledgeable about being a mother. Still, the predominant feeling reported by most mothers when discussing the infant was an increasing sense of well-being.

Mothers are people, however, and concerned about aspects of their lives other than motherhood. The price for their increased investment and delight in their infants and children is paid in various ways. One study found that mothers on maternity leave from employment became mildly depressed or guilty as they thought of returning to employment (when the baby was 3 months) and came to resent the time required to care for a child (by 16 months) (Fleming et al., 1988).

In spite of many delights, child care can be aversive, demanding, and boring. Children's whining, crying, and hitting are not pleasant stimuli (Patterson, 1980).

Mothers at home become more socially bored than they had been when pregnant (e.g., "My life lacks variety," "I wish I could socialize more"; Ruble et al., 1990). Mothers who are at home with children all day become desperate for adult talk and are interested in even the most mundane tales of their partner's work associates, including what everyone ate at lunch or what kind of outfit the boss wore.

Within these broad patterns, there are attitudinal and social class differences in women's experience with parenting and with their expectations and ambitions about their own motherhood; working-class women are likely to be more traditional than middle-class women (Hackel & Ruble, 1992). Traditional women (as measured on the Personality Attributes Questionnaire, chapter 3) had more positive feelings when they were doing proportionally *more* child care relative to expectations; their work may validate their basic values about the traditional nature of marriage and of being a woman (Reilly, Entwisle, & Doering, 1987). In contrast, less traditional women's satisfaction with motherhood was associated with doing *less* child care than they had anticipated and, concomitantly, their spouses doing more child care than other spouses (McHale & Huston, 1985). Traditional women are likely to have married traditional men, but it is likely that the women's attitudes expressed on a day-to-day basis are relevant as well. Traditional women, whose husbands do not help as much, may be clinging to the child care role as a major sphere of expertise and feel guilty for giving up any aspect of the traditional mothering role (Reilly et al., 1987).

Class differences or attitudinal differences also may affect women's shift to the role of mother (Reilly, 1981; Reilly et al., 1987). Working-class mothers seem to step into a role which for them is new but nonetheless is a well-defined role they accept. Middle-class women, who tend to define roles in less stereotypical ways, take time to define the mothering roles in their own ways. They seem to make the transition to motherhood more slowly, but they do make it and share some of the more traditional women's concerns about motherhood as they continue in the role of mother.

## Motherhood as Change

Becoming a mother requires a redefinition of one's identity. Mothers abandon their own interests because of necessary service to the child: "Sometimes I feel lost in the shuffle, confused . . . as if I lost identity" (Lopata, 1971, p. 192). Responsibilities and the time demands of children tie many women down and constrict their personal worlds: "The demands of the children take time and I have less time for myself. . . . I wish I would get out more" (Lopata, 1971, p. 195). The labor required for the child changes other social roles. One has to learn to be satisfied with not being a spotless housekeeper but still being exhausted. The relationship with the husband changes because of fatigue. Many women continue to doubt their effectiveness as mothers and are confused about what proper child rearing is; they have difficulty understanding what children need. Spending time with children is stressful, and spending time *only* with children is associated with lower self-esteem (Wells, 1988).

Children sound like a big pain, and, indeed, they are. However, they are a pain with benefits and joys (A Closer Look 12.1). Although a mother's identity is lost at least temporarily or must be reshaped, women recognize some of the changes as

# ROSE IS ROSE ® by Pat Brady

ROSE IS ROSE reprinted by permission of United Features Syndicate.

positive ones away from selfishness and childishness toward greater maturity. And, when asked, "What are the satisfactions of the homemaker's role?" women spoke of having children, seeing them grow up, and feeling proud of them (Lopata, 1971). Children were more important than any other satisfaction, including general family relations, husband and a happy marriage, and home itself.

## *Some Final Thoughts: What Happened To Women's "Natural Ability"?*

The natural experience of birth has been mystified, politicized, and medicalized to the point that women have to use effort to get any sense of control over their bodies. The naturalness of perpetuating the species has been so clouded in social issues that the women involved often are lost in the shuffle.

Lack of use of effective contraceptives is due in part to the view that a sexual woman is somehow bad, so that it is "better" if she is swept off her feet into pregnancy than if she assumes responsibility for herself as a sexual human being. The result is children having children and having abortions. Should money be spent to avoid the problems of early childbearing? There are differences of opinion.

Abortion is an option chosen by women across the spectra of age and social class but is chosen more by young unmarried women than by others. Should money be spent to provide abortions for women who want to avoid the problems likely to occur in their lives and in their children's lives? Again, there are differences of opinion.

The social issues associated with reproduction should not obscure the fact that most people do want babies and are having them increasingly. Prenatal care and delivery have become more sophisticated medically, with the result that fewer lives are lost, both of infants and of mothers, than in years past. Yet the United States is behind other countries in prevention of infant deaths, and is criticized for medicalizing childbirth with an overuse of drugs and cesarean deliveries.

## A Closer Look

### 12.1    The Joys—and Pains—of Parenthood: Comments From New Parents

"I had heard about the negatives—the fatigue, the loneliness, loss of self. But nobody told me about the wonderful parts: holding my baby close to me, seeing her first smile, watching her grow and become more responsive day by day. How can I describe the way I felt when she stroked my breast while nursing or looked into my eyes or arched her eyebrows like an opera singer; the intensity almost frightened me. For the first time I cared about somebody else more than myself, and I would do anything to nurture and protect her." (Cited in BWHBC, 1992, p. 488)

A father writes,

I feel somehow that I have finally joined the human race. (Greenburg, 1986, p. 92; cited in Crooks & Baur, 1990, p. 401)

His presence helped me to break out of my adult world in which everything was ordered and set, and allowed me to experience the world of childhood, where everything is free and spontaneous. Past memories, long since forgotten, of earlier years and relationships with my own family would surface, effortlessly, to my awareness. It was if Johnathan was the door, the entryway, to my experiencing a new and different aspect of myself. At the same time, I felt even more intimately connected to him. (Greenburg,

1986, p. 7; cited in Crooks & Baur, 1990, p. 402)

"After the baby was born, *she* became the focus of everyone's attention, and I was reduced to the role of caretaker. People would come up and say, 'What a lovely baby,' and *never even look me in the eye* [italics added]. I was proud of my baby, but I felt a nonperson myself. I wanted to say, 'I'm the one who cleans up the messes and gets up at night. Pay attention to me, too!'" (Cited in BWHBC, 1992, p. 484)

"We may feel angry at ourselves, our partner or our babies when we are particularly exhausted or isolated, or when we are not the perfect mothers we expected to be. Anger does not fit in with our fantasies about motherhood. Neither does grief, frustration, panic, jealousy. But they happen. Acknowledgment is the first step in dealing with our feelings." (BWHBC, 1992, p. 484)

SOURCES: Boston Women's Health Book Collective. (1992). *The new our bodies, ourselves* (2nd ed.). New York: Simon & Schuster.

Crooks, R., & Baur, K. (1993). *Our sexuality* (5th ed.). Redwood City, CA: Benjamin/Cummings.

Greenburg, D. (1986). *Dan Greenburg's confessions of a pregnant father.* New York: Macmillan.

The motherhood mystique tells us that women are "naturally" good at parenting, but facts tell us that most women are not well prepared for infant care. Women have little confidence in their ability to be good parents and receive little social support and recognition for their attempts. Because motherhood is so idealized in our society, it is no wonder that many women are unnecessarily frustrated and self-critical.

Nonetheless, many women do survive and thrive as mothers, and their children thrive as well. We need more attention to how so many women deal so well with pregnancy, childbirth, and parenthood. Similarly, some men are supportive of mothers and contribute to caregiving, and it would be useful to understand what makes them more nurturing. If men participated more in child care, everyone would benefit. Men would be in a better position to enjoy their children more. So would women.

## KEY TERMS

pessary

douche

sterilization

tubal ligation

vasectomy

spontaneous abortion,
  miscarriage

induced abortion

therapeutic abortion

elective abortion

motherhood mystique,
  institution of
  motherhood,
  motherhood mandate

couvade syndrome,
  couvade rituals

cesarean delivery,
  C-section

postpartum depression

baby blues, maternity
  blues

## KEY POINTS

*Attempts to Prevent Pregnancy*

- Sterilization is the most widely used effective method of birth control, followed by the pill. Diaphragms used with condoms and spermicide also are effective and provide protection against STDs. Embarrassment and lack of money and knowledge deter the use of contraceptives but highly relevant is the reluctance to admit that women are sexual.

- Most women who elect legal abortions think carefully about responsibility to others and do not show adverse psychological effects, though there are risk factors. Children of mothers who wanted to abort them are comparatively more likely to have a variety of problems, continuing into adulthood.

- Most pregnant teen women are unmarried. Negative effects for the young mother and her child are nearly eliminated if the mother completes school, marries, and has few children. Programs to prevent teen pregnancy and to help mothers and children are promising but expensive.

*Pregnancy and Birth*

- Birth rates have increased in recent years; women under 30 are having fewer babies, and women over 30 are having more. More women of all ages, classes, and races are having babies without being married.

- Both women and men want children and think about timing of their first child.

- Women who elect not to have children are not maladjusted or unhappy with their marriages. Infertile wives are more upset than their husbands or infertile men with lack of a child. The need for and success of fertility clinics have increased. Adoption is expensive and time consuming; more children previously considered "un-adoptable" are being adopted.

- Pregnant women do not necessarily feel positive throughout pregnancy, nor do others react to them only positively. The second trimester, however, seems to be the most enjoyable time.

- Childbirth classes, generally based on the Dick-Read or Lamaze method, aim to inform women about birth, to help them actively participate in it, and to give them social support; neither method precludes anesthesia. There are demonstrated positive benefits of the classes.

- Cesarean deliveries sometimes are necessary, but the United States is criticized for having more than other countries do. Parents of cesarean infants are more positive toward their children than other parents are.

- Death rates of infants and new mothers have dramatically decreased over the years, but the United States lags behind other countries in reducing infant mortality. More drugs and technologies are now used in "normal" births in the United States than anywhere else.

## Motherhood After Birth

- Some women have mild or severe depression postpartum. Hormonal involvement is unclear, but several social and psychological stresses clearly are involved.

- Transition to parenthood is best begun before birth, but parents generally are poorly prepared for infant care. The motherhood mandate and the demands of infant care lead to negative feelings for many mothers. With the birth of the first child, women do more child care and housework than they or their husbands had expected.

- Women become increasingly attached to their infants and increasingly see themselves as mothers. Traditional and nontraditional mothers differ in how they feel about the work of child care, and middle-class women may take more time in adopting the role of mother than working-class women.

- Motherhood is a continuing challenge. Mothers have relatively lower self-esteem when they are with children only. Being a mother involves a shift of identity and abandonment of personal interests, but mothers doubt their competence as mothers. Still, motherhood brings a sense of responsibility, maturity, and creativity.

## INTEGRATIVE QUESTIONS

1. Examine the notion that women "just naturally" want to have babies. Consider the motherhood mandate, attempts to control reproduction, mothers' responses to parenthood, and anything else that seems relevant.

2. How are society's attitudes about women's sexuality and about the nature of "femininity" associated with birth control procedures, decisions about abortions, feelings during pregnancy, and experiences of motherhood?

3. It is usually assumed that everyone will enjoy parenthood without much consideration of the alternative; some have argued that the motherhood mandate takes away choice. Given that, make the best case you can for why a person might elect not to have children. What advantages and disadvantages do you see for the decision? How does your answer differ for a woman and a man? You may use yourself as an example if you wish.

4. Discuss all the reasons why a mother or a father might experience some postpartum depression. Differentiate as necessary between a mother and a father, but be concerned with similarities as well.

5. Consider the quotes in A Closer Look 12.1, and relevant text material, and discuss how such strongly positive and strongly negative feelings can be responses to the same event of parenthood.

6. Discuss any reasons why you see that couvade rituals should be encouraged or discouraged in American society today.

*Chapter 13*

# Women at Work
## and Working at Home

*A* dramatic social transformation has been under way for some time in our country, bringing changes in women's lives and in their personal relationships. Women increasingly have been entering the paid workforce and are projected to continue doing so. Financial reasons are relevant, but so too is the fact that, contrary to the motherhood mandate (chapter 12), women generally enjoy employment. Employed women's lives are enriched by work experience, despite continuing sexual discrimination and pay disparity and despite women having major responsibility for housework and child care. Whether they are in the workforce or at home full-time, women seem to have unrealistic expectations about what employed people can accomplish at home. These all are issues addressed in this chapter.

Before continuing, consider these questions for personal thought:

- What are your major ambitions in life?
- What are the most important things you consider when thinking about a possible career for yourself? How do you think your background and previous experience have influenced your thoughts about your career?
- If you won the lottery and had enough money for a comfortable life without working for pay, would you choose to be employed? How? Why?
- Why do you think women in general make less money than men in general? Why do you think women make less money than a man in the same job, with the same job title?
- What problems do you see for two people cohabiting or married when both are employed? How does your answer vary depending on whether the two people are two women, two men, or a man and a woman?
- Some men are proud of their wives' employment but still do not contribute to work at home as much as their wives do. Any ideas why?

◆ What are the effects on a child of being in day care? Can a child be better off in day care than at home?

## Women's Employment Interests

More women than ever before are employed or looking for employment (Figure 13.1; 59% in 1994, anticipated to be 63% in 2005 versus 19% in 1900 and 34% in 1950) ("Study: Women increase," 1995; Ries & Stone, 1992). In 1995 76% of women with children under age 18 were employed (versus 38% in 1955), and more than half (62.3%) of women with children under age 6 were employed (versus 18% in 1955) (U.S. Bureau of Labor Statistics, 1996). Accompanying the greater number of women in the labor force is an increase in the level of education many women attain.

### Education and Social Context

In spite of the many negative experiences women have had in classrooms (chapter 7), they are sticking it out and achieving higher levels of education than ever before. Women of majority and minority groups in increasing numbers have graduated from high school (Costello & Stone, 1994). Women became the majority of college students in 1979–1980 and were 55% of students in 1990 (Ries & Stone, 1992). In 1989–1990,

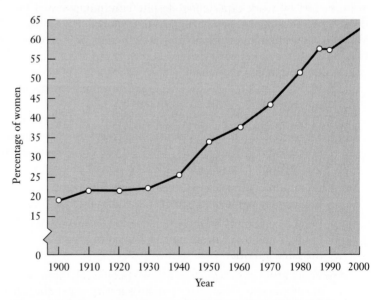

**Figure 13.1 *Percentage of women in the labor force, 1900–2000.***
SOURCE: Department of Commerce, Bureau of the Census, and Department of Labor, Bureau of Labor Statistics. As reported in O. Johnson (Ed.), *1997 Information Please Almanac, The International Authority.* Boston: Houghton Mifflin Company, p. 66.

women received the majority of associate degrees (58%), bachelor's degrees (53%), and master's degrees (52%). The number of women receiving doctoral degrees has steadily increased, but women earned only 37% of doctorates awarded in 1989–1990 (Costello & Stone, 1994).

With more education, women are increasingly entering the professions. Women's representation in fields such as architecture, medicine, economics, law, accounting, and pharmacy has at least doubled since 1972 (Costello & Stone, 1994). Hispanic and Asian/Pacific Islander women made substantial gains in dentistry particularly.

The exact nature of what women want to achieve and do achieve varies tremendously with the social context (Whisler & Eklund, 1986). Social factors restricted the ambitions of the grandmothers and mothers of today's college students. Many women of these generations were satisfied with the fulfillment of family ambition; their main regret was that marriage and family was their only route to satisfaction. Today, mothers are encouraging their college student daughters toward both careers and families. College women have an increased array of options but also often have traditional concerns.

**Careers and Care**    College women are taking their future careers seriously and sharing the pragmatic occupational values that are much more characteristic of men (Bank, 1995; Bridges, 1989, Fiorentine, 1988). At the same time, they are not forsaking the women's traditional values of helping others and being with the family, and they are more influenced by maternal than paternal attitudes (Bridges, 1989; Morinaga, Frieze, & Ferligoi, 1993; Steele & Barling, 1996). It seems that women have several goals simultaneously, whereas men are more single-mindedly focused on a career.

African American women are both more pragmatic *and* more altruistic than white women. They emphasize career advancement, wages, social status, and self-respect more often as important issues in their job choices, but they also have a high degree of commitment to social action, helping people, and helping the family unit economically (Brief & Aldag, 1975; Murrell, Frieze, & Frost, 1991; Simpson, 1984). African Americans tend to teach children a strong work ethic and to encourage perseverance in achieving a higher level than the parents did while being loyal to their heritage (Hill, 1994; McAdoo, 1988, 1989).

Women's family concerns influence their thoughts about careers in ways that men's do not. The majority of adolescent and college women expect to combine career with marriage and motherhood (Machung, 1989; Murrell et al., 1991; Schroeder, Blood, & Maluso, 1992). Both men and women, however, expect that women will play a more prominent role in the family than men will. Accordingly, women's plans about family and work roles are intertwined.

**Conflicts of Traditionality**    For some young women, family is more important than career and may be seen as in conflict with career. Adolescent girls who have a high commitment to marriage and family and who begin dating early tend to have lower occupational aspirations (as well as lower self-esteem) than other girls (chapter 6;

*African American families strongly support education and careers for women, and African American women are both career-oriented and altruistic in their life choices. This young woman may choose a professional field in which she can help others, such as medicine or teaching.*

Danziger, 1983; Holms & Esses, 1988). African American and white women aiming for careers in professions dominated by women rather than by men are more likely to lower their career aspirations because of family plans (Murrell et al., 1991).

The young women aiming for nontraditional occupations have less traditional attitudes about the role of women and generally score higher on instrumentality than other women (Lobel, Agami-Rozenblat, & Bempechat, 1993; Strange & Rea, 1983). They are less likely to state a definite desire for marriage (Sandberg, Ehrhardt, Mellins, Ince, & Meyer-Bahlburg, 1987), or they plan to delay marriage and children (Parsons, Frieze, & Ruble, 1978). They also plan more education than those heading for occupations dominated by women (Murrell et al., 1991). The aim for higher education is more marked among African American women than among white women. African American women's educational aims are consistent with parental teachings (Collins, 1991; Huttman, 1991): Parents stress that some things, including civil rights, can be taken away, but education can never be taken away (Edwards & Polite, 1992). African American parents also are well aware that their children will need more education than white children in order to achieve equally. In sum, college women are thinking seriously about their careers. What can young women expect to get from their planned employment?

## What Women Get From Employment

Most women have to or want to have employment for financial reasons (Lerner, 1994). They may be single women or married women whose husbands do not earn enough for basic necessities or for the extras the couple wants. They may be mothers rearing children with little or no financial help; courts award child care payments to only about half (58%) of women potentially eligible for them, and only about half (51%) of those awarded child support receive the full amount (U.S. Department of Commerce, 1992). Women in lesbian couples, because of their high valuation of an equalitarian relationship (chapter 10), choose to be employed even when it would be practical for one partner not to be employed (Hall with Gregory, 1991).

***Psychological Benefits of Employment***    Employment brings benefits other than financial ones. More than half of employed women, including working-class mothers, say that they would continue working even if they did not have to for financial reasons; the desire to work is stronger for African American women than for white women (DeChick, 1988; "Study: Working moms," 1994). Only a fifth (21%) of employed mothers say they would leave their current jobs to stay home with children. Conversely, about half (56%) of full-time homemakers say they would choose to have a career if they had it to do over again.

Many benefits of paid employment can be summed up quite simply as escape from housework! Women not employed have been said to be susceptible to **housewife's syndrome**—feeling anxious, worried, lonely, worthless. Studies of full-time homemakers stress the negative qualities of housework, including its fragmented, repetitive, and demanding nature, as well as the high isolation and low social rewards associated with the homemaker role (Ferree, 1976; Lopata, 1971; Oakley, 1974; Pleck, 1983).

In contrast, employed women see employment giving them benefits such as chances for mental stimulation, use of skills, self-expression, and interpersonal relationships (Andrisani, 1978; Beckman, 1978; Moore, 1985). Employment outside the home is likely to provide interesting tasks, a general feeling of contact with the world, a feeling of effectiveness, and feelings of accomplishment (Repetti, Matthews, & Waldron, 1989). The general advantage of employment is shown by general psychological correlates.

Numerous studies have found that employed women compared with women who are not employed have better mental and physical health and greater satisfaction with their lives (Amatea & Fong, 1991; Baruch & Barnett, 1986; Coleman & Antonucci, 1983; Grossman & Chester, 1990; Kibria, Barnett, Baruch, Marshall, & Pleck, 1990; Rosen, Ickovics, & Moghadam, 1990; Walker & Best, 1991). We will discuss exceptions to this broad generalization, but for the moment, let's concentrate on the big picture.

The rosy picture associated with employment is not limited to women with prestigious careers but seems to cover the gamut of occupations women have, as shown, for example, in studies of clerks, factory workers, domestics, waitresses, typists, and beauticians (Ferree, 1976; Hiller & Dyehouse, 1987). Employment may be particularly useful to women at crucial transition periods in their lives: Divorced women saw their work as a comforting source of pride and of repair for damaged self-esteem (Crosby, 1990).

Employed women typically feel competent at their jobs, whether working class or professional (Ferree, 1976; Hiller & Dyehouse, 1987). In contrast, many full-time homemakers do not feel competent at doing their job. Homemakers who were bright college educated women (graduated from the University of Michigan with honors 15 to 25 years before the study) were compared with married women on the University of Michigan faculty who had children and with single women on the faculty (Birnbaum, 1975). The homemakers did not feel competent in social skills, traditional housework, or child care. Of the three groups, they had the lowest self-esteem and felt unattractive and lonely, worried about their identity, and missed challenge and creative involvement more often. Some of the characteristics of the unemployed women are suggestive of fear of failure (chapter 7).

Could a selection factor account for the results, with healthier women going into and staying in the labor force? Certainly, health is relevant to employment decisions, but it does not seem responsible for the demonstration of advantages of employment—health may improve with employment (Repetti et al., 1989; Waldron & Jacobs, 1988, 1989).

***Complications of Employment Decisions***    A variety of variables affects whether any particular employed woman has higher happiness or more distress than one who is not employed (Noor, 1996); for example, whether she is doing what she wants to do and is satisfied with that (Baruch & Barnett, 1986; Goldberg & Easterbrooks, 1988; Noor, 1996). Women who are dissatisfied with their main work role, whether a paid job or homemaker, have poorer physical health and shorter life spans than those who are satisfied (Palmore, 1974). Women who do not want employment are not particularly advantaged by lack of employment. For example, women who were not career oriented were not particularly satisfied when they were not employed (Pietromonaco, Manis, & Markus, 1987). Lack of employment by women who want it seems a bigger problem (Stafford, 1984). Mothers (of 1-year-olds) who wanted to be employed but were not were more depressed than women who did not want and did not have employment; those who wanted employment but were at home were in the range of mild depression, while other mothers scored as not depressed (Figure 13.2; Hock & DeMeis, 1990). Similarly, homemakers who are liberal in gender role attitudes (by the Attitudes Toward Women Scale, chapter 3) feel more restricted and more depressed than those homemakers who are traditional in attitudes (Kingery, 1985). (For a look at the interrelationship between psychological distress and marital quality in employed husbands and wives, see Focus on Research 13.1.)

Having children is another factor in psychological effects (Noor, 1996; Pietromonaco et al., 1987). Depression is especially high in employed mothers who have sole responsibility for children and no accessible child care; employed mothers who do have good child care and partners who share child care are low in depression (Reifman, Biernat, & Lang, 1991; chapter 16).

Some women want to work to "get out of the house." Women who are quite happy as homemakers without employment have something in common with employed women—they, too, manage to escape the house (Ferree, 1976). The "happy homemakers" do things outside of the home instead of doing endless chores or watching endless TV, so they do not feel lonely or bored. Also informative is that they feel valued by their husband and other family members for what they do. Criticism and lack of appreciation are frequent complaints of other housewives (including divorcing women, chapter 10), along with social isolation and financial dependence. Having a happy marriage with a husband who is intimate emotionally also reduces depression in full-time homemakers (Vanfossen, 1981).

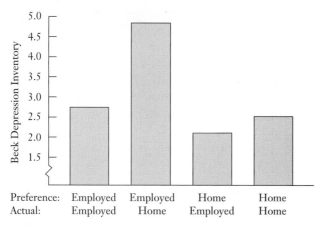

| Preference: | Employed | Employed | Home | Home |
| Actual: | Employed | Home | Employed | Home |

**Figure 13.2 *Depression scores for women varying in preference for employment and actual status.*** NOTE: Data are based on 209 mothers who returned questionnaires at 12 months postpartum and who were married, aged 19 or older, and white. Of these, 87% had been employed during their pregnancy. The mean age was 25.9 years, and mean years of education was 14.33. The depression scores were based on a short form of the Beck Depression Inventory. Mothers who preferred employment but were not employed scored within the mildly depressed range; others scored as not depressed. SOURCE: Hock, E., & DeMeis, D. K. (1990). Depression in mothers of infants: The role of maternal employment. *Developmental Psychology, 26,* (2), 285–291. Figure developed from part of Table 1, p. 288 and information passim.

## Discrimination Issues

Women generally enjoy their employment in spite of the discriminations that lead to pay disparities and personal frustration. **Access discrimination** involves any inhibiting factor that decreases the likelihood of getting a particular job. Differential evaluation of credentials, such as rejecting qualified applicants or offering lower salaries than qualifications warrant, is a form of access discrimination. Other forms start long before applying for a job. Potent are the many background factors that channel girls toward some kinds of employment and away from others; not being encouraged to take math courses in high school is a form of access discrimination. Often, the channeling is done by well-meaning adults who make unwarranted assumptions about girls' personalities and cognitive skills (chapters 8, 9).

Treatment discrimination is differential treatment after being hired; it is typified by slow rates of promotion, assignment to less attractive jobs, low or infrequent raises, and few training opportunities (Terborg & Ilgen, 1975). The distinction between access and treatment discrimination blurs, however. A woman may be hired

### 13.1   Control Variables: Measuring Distress in Dual-Earner Couples

Meet Stephanie and Tom. They are the parents of two children, both are full-time blue-collar workers, and they report a happy marriage.

Next meet Tara and Paul. They have no children, and Tara works as a typist part-time, while Paul has a career as a lawyer. Both report their marriage has been shaky for the last year.

Which of these four people do you think would be most prone to anxiety and depression? In making your educated guess, which factors would you weigh more heavily? Being a parent? Working full-time? The state of the marriage? What about the gender of the person? All of these factors, and more, might be potential contributors to anxiety and depression. The difficulty of studying such a complex problem can be alleviated through the use of control variables.

Control variables are those extraneous factors in a study that are suspected to have an impact on the study's outcome but are not the variables of interest. Researchers must control these variables to keep them from interfering with the studies' final results. Control variables are important in both experimental and correlational designs. Remember that the essence of an experiment is control: By controlling or eliminating the impact of all variables except the independent variable, researchers maximize the chances that the independent variable is the cause of any change in the dependent variable. Two of the most common methods for achieving this control are random selection of participants from the population and random assignment of participants to the experimental and control groups. In this way, all extraneous variables (which include every variable except the independent one) should be evenly distributed among the groups and shouldn't create differences between the groups on the dependent variable. If these variables were not controlled, the experimenter would not be able to make a cause-and-effect interpretation of the relationship between the independent variable and the dependent variable.

Control is also important in correlational designs, although the experimenter has much less physical control over the variables. Because this design uses status variables, participants cannot be randomly assigned to groups, nor can the researcher manipulate treatments. Due to these restrictions, we can never be totally sure that some other variable besides the independent variable has caused the outcome; cause-and-effect interpretations cannot be made. Nonetheless, the more extraneous variables that we are aware of and that can be controlled in this design, the clearer the relationship or association between the two variables of interest will be. The primary way to control variables in a correlational design is through a statistical technique using partial correlation coefficients. Let's take a look at a study that employs this method.

Researcher Rosalind Barnett and her associates (1994) wanted to focus on marriages in which both spouses worked outside the home—"dual-earner couples." Dual-earner couples are becoming the norm in our society, and these researchers wanted to find out if the quality of such marriages was linked with psychological distress, such as anxiety or depression, in the spouses. And, if such distress was present, which spouse, the husband or the wife, was affected? While this seems a simple question, Barnett and her research team knew that, in addition to the quality of the marriage and the gender of the spouse, many other factors in people's lives could also be related to levels of psychological distress. The team decided they needed to control several extraneous variables that fell into two groups: individual-level variables of the person, such as age, education, and occupational prestige, and couple-level variables, such as length of the marriage, household income, and whether the couple had children or not.

Barnett and her associates worked with Massachusetts census lists and randomly contacted 442 dual-earner couples. Both spouses in 300 of these couples agreed to participate; these couples made up the final sample. After gathering information on marital-role quality and psychological distress, researchers asked the couples questions concerning each of the individual- and couple-level control variables. All these data were then analyzed by a procedure that measured the relationship between each control variable and the outcome (in this case, psychological distress scores) and then removed or "partialed out" those associations from the data. For example, our true interest is the relationship between marital-role quality and psychological distress; we hypothesize that as the quality of the marriage decreases, anxiety and depression increase. However, we strongly suspect that having a high-status job might act as a buffer against anxiety and depression; a spouse with a bad marriage but a prestigious job may not feel as much psychological distress as expected. By measuring and removing the relationship between job prestige and psychological distress, we are left with a clearer picture of the relationship between marital-role quality and psychological distress. As we measure and remove the relationship between each control variable and the thing we are trying to predict (psychological distress), we get a clearer view of the relationship between marital-role quality and distress.

Barnett and her team of researchers conducted this partialing-out procedure separately for husbands and wives in their couples sample. The end result revealed that among dual-earner couples there was an association between marital-role quality and psychological distress and that this association was the same for both genders. Spouses who reported more negative marital experiences also reported greater anxiety and depression, and vice versa. The researchers note that this finding runs counter to the stereotype that men are not as affected by marital discord or harmony as are women. When both women and men contribute to the economic support of the household, it appears that the quality of the marriage has a similar impact on the mental health of both spouses.

JILL BORCHERT ◆

SOURCE: Barnett, R. C., Brennan, R. T., Raudenbush, S. W., & Marshall, N. L. (1994). Gender and the relationship between marital-role quality and psychological distress. *Psychology of Women Quarterly, 18,* 105–127.

without access discrimination but then face treatment discrimination on the job that prevents her access to higher jobs in the organization.

## The Jobs Women Have

African Americans and working-class whites traditionally have expected women to be employed as well as to be mothers (Murrell et al., 1991; E. J. Smith, 1982; Thomas & Shields, 1987). In contrast, middle-class whites have tended to see motherhood as basically incompatible with employment (the motherhood mandate, chapter 12) and have channeled daughters toward "women's jobs" only in order to "have something to fall back on" if the worst happens and their daughters have to work for pay. Things are changing, with more mothers encouraging their daughters toward careers, but some of the general patterns of the past are still influential today.

*"Women's Jobs"*    Some occupations are still thought "good for women." These call for use of women's supposed "natural abilities" and allow for molding a woman's life around a man: They involve service to other people, flexibility, and a low status not threatening to men. One aspect of the desired flexibility is being able to stop working for a while for childbearing and then to reenter the labor force. However, interruptions are becoming increasingly unrealistic, as changing technology is affecting many occupations; for example, computer technology changes so rapidly that a year or so off can put a clerical worker behind.

A second aspect of flexibility is geographical mobility. Women are more likely to move because of their spouse's employment than men are, even among professional couples (Biernat & Wortman, 1991). Traditional women's jobs have had relative mobility so that a woman could move with her husband and find a job. More cities have openings for a nurse, teacher, secretary, or beautician than for an expert in medieval literature or for a history professor. Many companies and universities are going to some lengths to find positions for the spouse of someone they wish to hire, but there are limits on how much can be done. For example, a university that wants to hire a man cannot guarantee his wife a judgeship to replace the one she would have to leave for him to join the faculty.

*Gender Segregation*    Although both white women and women of color increasingly are moving into men's jobs, "women's work" is the destination for about two thirds of employed women. There still is **occupational gender segregation:** Women are congregated in some jobs and men in others. In fact, 53% of women and men would have to change occupations to achieve full gender integration (Reskin & Padavic, 1994). African American women previously were more segregated from men than white women were and were segregated from white women as well. Although still concentrated in domestic and service jobs, they have been moving into white-collar jobs at a faster rate than white women have and now are almost equal to white women in representation in those jobs (Betz & Fitzgerald, 1987; Costello & Stone, 1994).

Most of the jobs held predominantly by women are considered **pink-collar jobs,** such as secretarial positions, bookkeeping, sales, or food service. They are low in status, poorly paid, and offer few chances for advancement. Some women choose these jobs, and that must be remembered, but some women take them only because they are available for women. More than one third of the women in the workforce in both Canada and the United States are employed in the clerical sector (Canadian Advisory Council on the Status of Women, 1985; Glenn & Feldberg, 1989). The average secretary is likely to be undercompensated for her skills, which often include mastery of increasingly advancing technology.

Another category of segregated jobs are "women's professions," also called **semi-professions.** These include nursing, social work, elementary school teaching, and librarianship (Etzioni, 1969; Fox & Hesse-Biber, 1984). These professions share with other professions the requirement for advanced education and are recognized as important. However, they do not bring the higher pay, authority, or clear avenues for advancement ordinarily expected of people of their skills and training (Betz & Fitzgerald, 1987).

*Gender Stratification*    When women and men are in the same general kinds of jobs, there still may be **gender stratification.** The numbers of women and men who are bus drivers are approximately equal, but the women are more likely to have part-time work driving school buses, while men drive buses between cities (England & McCreary, 1987). Women are half of college instructors (51%) but are underrepresented (5%) as full professors (Betz & Fitzgerald, 1987).

Women are not safe from biased treatment even in "women's occupations." Men are entering occupations dominated by women at a faster rate than women are entering occupations dominated by men, and men are taking over the more prestigious and well-paid head jobs of women's occupations: Men are overrepresented in senior and administrative positions in public school teaching, social work, and librarianship (Ott, 1989; Spalter-Roth & Hartmann, 1990). However, the lower status of women's jobs is only part of the reason for pay differentials.

## Differential Earnings

Women are earning more than previously but still less than men; this is true among whites, African Americans, and Hispanics (Figure 13.3); disabled women also make less than disabled men (Asch & Fine, 1988; Costello & Stone, 1994). It is not generally known that the lowest point in women's pay in recent history occurred in 1970, when women earned 59.4 cents for every dollar a man made, a regression from nearly 64 cents in 1955. The decrease in 1970 may reflect a backlash against women's activities, perhaps abetted by financial conditions that "just happened to hit women harder." If so, the financial backlash is decreasing. Women's earnings have progressed, so that they got back to the 1955 level in 1985 and increased to 72 cents in 1994. A hopeful sign is that the gap between women and men is lowest for younger workers (Associated Press study, Sex-Based Wage Gap, 1989, February 8). African American women's relative earnings have increased more than white women's, so the gap between white women and African American women has narrowed; African American women earned 79 cents for every dollar a white woman made in 1969 but 92 cents in 1989.

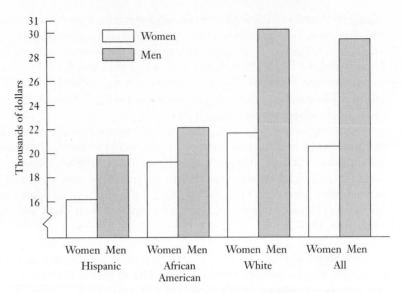

**Figure 13.3** *Median annual earnings by ethnicity and sex, 1991.*
SOURCE: Bureau of the Census. (1992). *Money income of households, families, and persons in the United States, 1991,* Table B-17. As reported in C. Costello & A. J. Stone (Eds.), for The Women's Research and Educational Institute, 1994, *The American woman, 1994-1995: Where we stand.* New York: W. W. Norton. Taken from part of Table 4-3, p. 314.

***Why the Difference?***    Why do the gender differences in pay exist and persist? Differences in abilities cannot account for the disparity (chapter 8). Some of the earnings gap has been attributed to gender segregation and educational differences (Blau & Ferber, 1986; Jacobs, 1989). Men previously had more formal school experience and more vocational training than women. The lower pay of older women may represent in part the previously lower education level of women. However, differential education is not all: Gender and racial discrimination both exist among people with equal education (National Committee on Pay Equity, 1992). It was not until 1989 that women who were *college* graduates made more money than men who were *high school* graduates—and then, by the margin of only $100 a year—and the change was due in part to a decline in income of the men. Among people with college degrees, African American women earned 65%, African American men 76%, and white women 67% of what white men earned (Bovee, 1991).

***Different Classifications: Comparable Worth***    Some of the pay disparity between people of equal education is due to job classifications. The meaning of "equal pay" is fairly clear, but the meaning of "equal work" is less clear (Pinzler & Ellis, 1989). It is easy to say, "They are not doing the same work" because they have different job classifications. A result is that in one state, liquor store clerks make more money than librarians, who are both employed by the state (Hyde, 1991). Being a liquor store clerk requires a high school diploma, while being a librarian requires at least a college degree (it is a profession). But liquor store clerks are predominantly men and librarians are predominantly women. Truck drivers, mostly men, earn more than nurses, mostly women (Lowe & Wittig, 1989).

This kind of gender disparity could be eliminated by using the principle of **comparable worth,** which means requiring equal pay for *comparable* work, not just work that happens to bear the same title (Acker, 1989; Remick, 1984). Jobs requiring similar amounts of education, skill levels, experiences, and supervisory responsibility should be compensated equally, even though the jobs may have different titles. If comparable worth were implemented, librarians would earn more than clerks, and nurses would earn more than truck drivers. On the other hand, dog pound attendants and parking lot attendants, mostly men, would no longer earn more than child care attendants, mostly women (Feldberg, 1984; Jacobs, 1989).

The United States courts do not seem eager to accept the comparable worth principle (Pinzler & Ellis, 1989), but there has been some success with it in Canada (Gunderson, 1989). It is difficult for people who have been conventionally socialized to evaluate the worth of an occupation independent of gender labeling and the associated implicit assumptions about the greater value of men (Baron & Newman, 1990).

*Women and Men With the Same Job*     The greater valuation of men's work is seen also when we look at women and men who are in the same job—women typically make less money than men do, whether the job is in an occupation dominated by women or by men (Table 13.1; U.S. Department of Labor, Bureau of Labor Statistics, 1989, 1993). An exception is that women who are mechanics/repairers earn 105.4% of what men do. The biggest differential is in sales occupations: Women earn 60% of what men do. At all academic ranks, from lecturer to full professor, men earn more than women, and the differential is not due to number of publications (Caplan, 1993; Cohen & Gutek, 1991). Women physicians in 1991 earned less than men even when considering physicians of equal ages and within the same specialty (Council on Ethical and Judicial Affairs, AMA, 1994). In pediatrics, an area stereotypically associated with women's skills of taking care of children, women earn 78% of the hourly wage of men.

The long and short of it all is that the disparity of income is not explained by differences in ability, education, absences, limitations on job hours, work interruptions, or years on the job (Betz & Fitzgerald, 1987; Blau & Ferber, 1986; Corcoran, Duncan, & Hill, 1984; England & McCreary, 1987; Thacker, 1995). Considering all the attempts to understand the variables that could account for the gender disparity, researchers have suggested that men are paid more for what they do simply because they are men (Betz & Fitzgerald, 1987).

*Women's Perception of Discrimination*     Both women and men generally are positive about their jobs, satisfied with them, say they have what they want, what they deserve, and what they had expected to have (Crosby, 1982). Most women realize that women *generally* are discriminated against, but they typically deny that they themselves are. People seem to adopt cognitive strategies that protect them from feeling deprived, a

**Table 13.1**    Women's Median Weekly Earnings Compared to Men's, by Occupation, 1984 and 1992

| | 1984 | | | 1992 | | |
| | Earnings | | Earnings ratio | Earnings | | Earnings ratio |
| Occupation | Female | Male | | Female | Male | |
|---|---|---|---|---|---|---|
| All occupations | 358 | 528 | 67.8 | 381 | 505 | 75.4 |
| Managerial and professional specialty | 512 | 745 | 68.7 | 562 | 777 | 72.3 |
|   Executive, administrative, and managerial | 491 | 770 | 63.9 | 519 | 784 | 66.2 |
|   Professional specialty | 523 | 720 | 72.6 | 587 | 770 | 76.2 |
| Technical, sales, and administrative support | 350 | 541 | 64.6 | 365 | 519 | 70.3 |
|   Technicians and related support | 423 | 605 | 69.9 | 436 | 591 | 73.8 |
|   Sales occupations | 293 | 541 | 54.1 | 313 | 523 | 59.8 |
|   Administrative support, including clerical | 351 | 510 | 68.8 | 364 | 482 | 75.5 |
| Service occupations | 243 | 358 | 67.9 | 248 | 330 | 75.2 |
|   Private household | 180 | —* | — | 177 | —* | — |
|   Protective service | 392 | 509 | 76.9 | 399 | 501 | 79.6 |
|   All other service occupations | 247 | 302 | 81.7 | 248 | 283 | 87.6 |
| Precision production, craft, and repair | 346 | 532 | 65.0 | 336 | 503 | 66.8 |
|   Mechanics and repairers | 444 | 526 | 84.4 | 523 | 496 | 105.4 |
|   Construction trades | —* | 518 | — | —* | 495 | — |
|   Precision production occupations | 331 | 547 | 60.5 | 316 | 520 | 60.8 |
| Operators, fabricators, and laborers | 286 | 428 | 66.9 | 279 | 393 | 71.0 |
|   Machine operators, assemblers, and inspectors | 285 | 444 | 64.1 | 275 | 406 | 67.7 |
|   Transportation and material moving occupations | 347 | 472 | 73.4 | 329 | 436 | 75.5 |
|   Handlers, equipment cleaners, helpers, laborers | 282 | 352 | 80.1 | 279 | 314 | 88.9 |
| Farming, forestry, and fishing | 238 | 280 | 85.0 | 223 | 269 | 82.9 |

*The Bureau of Labor Statistics does not publish median earnings data when the base is less than 50,000 workers.

SOURCES: Bureau of Labor Statistics, *Handbook of labor statistics* August, 1989, Table 43, and *Employment and earnings* January 1993, Table 56. As reported in C. Costello & A. J. Stone (Eds.), for The Women's Research and Educational Institute, 1994, *The American woman, 1994–1995: Where we stand.* New York: W. W. Norton. Table 4-2, pp. 310–311.

phenomenon called the **denial of personal discrimination** (Crosby, 1982, 1984; Crosby, Pullman, Snyder, O'Connell, & Whalen, 1989; Nagata & Crosby, 1991). To acknowledge that one is underpaid means seeing someone as responsible for the injustice; women may resist blaming specific other people for their pay plight. The acknowledgment also brings a risk of being pitied or scorned by others. Behind the denial may be the general socialization through which women as well as men incorporate the view that women are not due very much. The result is that women generally have a lower sense of personal entitlement than do men (Bylsma & Major, 1992; Major, 1989). In laboratory experiments, women work longer, do more work, complete more correct work, and work more efficiently than men for the same amount of pay, and they consider the pay to be fair (Jackson, 1989; Summers, 1988).

Judgments about pay often are based on information from others (Sumner & Brown, 1996). Both college women and men were more influenced about entitlement and satisfaction by information about the pay of others of their own gender (supposedly previous students in the research) than those of the other gender; women also judged their own performance more by the criterion of other women (Bylsma & Major, 1994). Because of structural factors on the job, women in work settings are likely to have only information about other underpaid women (Major & Testa, 1989; Treiman & Hartmann, 1981). Knowledge sometimes can help overcome gender differences in personal entitlement. When college women and men knew that others (with gender neutral names) had been paid higher amounts than they, both felt entitled to more money than those told that others had been paid lesser amounts (Bylsma & Major, 1992). And, those told they had performed well felt they deserved more pay than those told they had performed poorly. Many women in the workplace have not been given clear and fair feedback about their performance and have not had clear access to information about others' pay.

## Differential Evaluation

Both access and treatment discrimination and the resulting pay differentials can happen because of differential evaluation of men's and women's capabilities. Gatekeepers, who decide whom to hire or promote, have long discriminated against women with the same credentials as men. Race interacts with gender in complex ways not yet clear. African Americans tend to be rated lower than whites, but African American women are not always rated the lowest (Greenhaus, Parasuraman, & Wormley, 1990; Nkomo & Cox, 1989; Pulakos, White, Oppler, & Borman, 1989). Physical appearance does make a difference—physical attractiveness is an asset regardless of gender and type of job (Drogosz & Levy, 1996). For women, we know that brunettes rather than blondes and women wearing no cosmetics compared with those who do wear makeup get more favorable evaluations about ability (Kyle & Mahler, 1996). There is an inherent contradiction in these two findings: Fair blondes with feminine makeup are considered pretty, but they are not seen as competent. Gatekeepers also differ in their reactions to a job applicant's general stance (assertiveness, emotionality, rationality) depending on the applicant's gender and the nature of the job (Buttner & McEnally, 1996; Johnson & Scandura, 1994) However, gender issues are in flux (Hartman, Griffeth, Crino, & Harris, 1991; Pazy, 1992).

Complicating the picture is the fact that attitudes are not necessarily translated directly into action. Three examples are particularly relevant. First, concern about not wanting to appear biased can lead to a final judgment that overcomes a bias (Branscombe & Smith, 1990). Undergraduates recommended hiring a white woman rather than a white man and an African American man rather than a white man (other combinations were not tested). However, the numerous intermediary ratings of specific job-related attributes did show bias; the final decision was more under conscious control than the numerous, more subtle intermediate ratings. People can be stereotypically prejudiced, perhaps nonconsciously, but consciously choose to avoid stereotypic final decisions.

In a second case, final decisions can be biased for reasons not related to the candidate. People sometimes make judgments based on self-interest (Katz, 1987; Larwood, Szwajkowski, & Rose, 1988). People who discriminate often think that the boss wants them to. The positive message is that there is hope for change if executives and college administrators establish a climate in which it is clear that those at the top are opposed to discrimination.

The third case points out a danger. Undergraduates who considered a man and a woman as equally deserving of an award gave the award to the man instead of the woman (L'Heureux-Barrett & Barnes-Farrell, 1991). The researchers suggested that the students were bending over backwards to be objective and not give preferential treatment to a woman. We will not have accomplished much by getting people to recognize discrimination against women if they feel they must reward men to show that they are not prejudiced against men. Meanwhile, discrimination occurs without awareness.

***Information Versus Stereotypes***    Most gatekeepers probably think they are making informed decisions about who can do the job, but stereotypes may lead them to assume they have relevant information, such as about cognitive abilities and personal traits (chapters 7, 8; Martell, 1996). For example, people may presume women are not good at math or leadership. The result is discrimination against women or against men when the job is gender-typed (Bronstein, Black, Pfennig, & White, 1986; Glick, Zion, & Nelson, 1988).

When there is clear evidence that a person has the ability to do the job, decisions are likely to be made on that basis (Olian, Schwab, & Haberfeld, 1988; Pazy, 1992; Powell, 1987; Rosenthal, 1996). But relevant information does not always translate into "clear evidence." Information alone does not always override biasing effects of gender stereotypes on work performance assessments (Martell, 1996). Information about job performance can be processed in different ways, such as giving differential attributions (e.g., ability or luck, chapter 7). Also, different criteria may be used for rating performance. If decision makers lack the time, opportunity, or inclination to carefully process information, the likelihood of gender bias is high, including having more liberal standards for men than for women (Martell, 1996). Another limitation of information concerns the amount: How much evidence is enough? Discrimination can take the form of requiring more information about women or minority men, for example, than about white men (Branscombe & Smith, 1990) to override stereotypic assumptions.

However, gender bias can be reduced or reversed when the gatekeepers have been exposed to women doing the job, whether they knew women managers or had wives who were employed (Eskilson & Wiley, 1996; Heilman & Martell, 1986; Pazy, 1992; Taylor & Ilgen, 1981). When men have worked for a woman supervisor, they are not biased in evaluating women's credentials.

***Male/Masculinity Bias***    There remains the problem that the more prestigious and high-paying jobs are likely to be considered masculine, and men and people with masculine traits (women or men) are favored (Glick, 1991; Glick, Wilk, & Perreault, 1995; Hartman et al., 1991; Pazy, 1986). Note that successful women are seen as masculine (Brady, Trafimow, Eisler, & Southard, 1996). Gender often operates as a status characteristic (Ridgeway & Diekema, 1992). Women are placed in a confusing and unreasonable situation. First, women need to be masculine to get the chance to

*Although women are encouraged to dress and act in a "feminine" way on the job, the more feminine they appear, the less competent they are judged to be. With her long earrings and low-cut dress, this woman may be perceived by a prospective employer as less qualified for a job than a woman dressed in a less "feminine" way.*

succeed (Hartman et al., 1991). However, women's masculinity is "not as good as" men's masculinity (or psychological masculinity is not enough to overcome being a woman). And, added to this, women need to be feminine (and men to be masculine) to be accepted as capable (Yoder & Schleicher, 1996). Applicants seen as having masculine traits were preferred for a job thought to need masculine traits, but a woman with masculine traits was discriminated against compared to a man with the same traits (Glick et al., 1988). Conversely, a man with feminine traits was discriminated against relative to a woman with the same traits for a feminine-typed job. Having cross-sex-typed attributes can be a detriment. If a competent (e.g., "masculine") woman is not feminine also, she may be considered "not quite normal" and therefore not fit for the job (Basow, 1990). Lesbians may be singled out because of assumptions that there is something wrong with them (Levine & Leonard, 1984) or that they just will not "fit in" (Shachar & Gilbert, 1983). They often experience discrimination, including being fired, if their personal life becomes known.

Because of the general (white) male/masculinity bias, women and minority men are likely to hit an invisible **glass ceiling** that prevents further progress (Morrison & Von Glinow, 1990; O'Leary & Ickovics, 1991; Stokes, Riger, & Sullivan, 1995). One may encounter the glass ceiling as low as entry-level management jobs or not until higher levels. A prominent case of the glass ceiling at higher levels, and specifically of the necessity for women to be feminine, is that of Ann Hopkins, who was turned down for partnership in a large, prestigious accounting firm (Fiske, Bersoff, Borgida, Deaux, & Heilman, 1991; Sachs, 1989). She clearly had done the job—she had brought

*Ann Hopkins was advised by her employer, the accounting firm Price Waterhouse, that she wasn't "feminine" enough to be promoted to a partnership. She sued the company and won.*

in $40 million in new business, more than the 87 other candidates (all male) nominated for partnership. Most opposition was from those few partners (8 of 32) who had limited contact with her and criticized her "unfeminine" interpersonal skills. They advised her to wear makeup and jewelry and walk more femininely. Her lawsuit progressed to the United States Supreme Court, which ruled that the firm was guilty of gender discrimination because it had treated a woman with an assertive personality in a different way from a man with one. The case is unique because it was the first time the Supreme Court cited psychological evidence on stereotyping in its decision. The evidence was presented by Susan Fiske (Fiske et al., 1991); the American Psychological Association presented a friend-of-the-court brief supporting Fiske's testimony.

## Treatment Discrimination

Even assuming the best—that gatekeepers base hiring and promotion judgments on evidence about performance—there still is ample room for discrimination because of barriers to women being able to use and to develop their competencies. A woman's career path has been called an obstacle course (Ragins & Sundstrom, 1989). By being aware of some of the obstacles, women can be in a better position to try to avoid them or, when that is not possible, to acknowledge them for what they are instead of making things worse by blaming themselves for their lack of advancement (Caplan, 1993).

***Assignments and Resources***   Giving women assignments that are not as conducive to professional development as those given to men and not giving women resources to do the jobs they are given are two important forms of treatment discrimination. First, women may be derailed because of being "good citizens" and "helping out." For example, increased concern about diversity in academia has led to requiring committees to have a woman and a minority; a minority woman "double counts." The women are being "good citizens" by serving on the committees, but their good deeds are done at the expense of their research, which often is the primary basis for promotion decisions. Much the same is true for participation in professional associations (Twale & Shannon, 1996). Women's chief assignments also can be detrimental. The U.S. State Department was found guilty of discrimination against women foreign service officers by giving women jobs below their rank and in less prestigious consular areas, while men had jobs above their ranks and in more prestigious areas (Rowley, 1987).

The second major obstacle to women's advancement is that they are not given the resources they need to do the job. For example, women managers, compared to men, generally are given less authority and power: Women have less control over assets (materials, money, resources), less access to information, and less autonomy and support for their decisions (Denmark, 1993; Kanter, 1977a; Ragins & Sundstrom, 1989). When women are not given the power to do their jobs, they can become frustrated; the same is true for men in such situations (Butler & Geis, 1990; Eagly & Johnson, 1990; Eagly, Makhijani, & Klonsky, 1992).

One way women are deprived of the power of information is by not being part of an influential network (Ragins & Sundstrom, 1989). Most social networks are segregated by gender and race (Ibarra, 1993; Konrad, Winter, & Gutek, 1992), and most people with power are white men; the result is that an **Old (White) Boys' Network** controls power in many organizations. However, gender seems more important than ethnicity in career-related access to relationships with senior managers and personal support from networks (Cianni & Romberger, 1995; Ohlott, Ruderman, & McCauley, 1994). The men with network connections know about job possibilities sooner and have the advantage of being a "friend of a friend," which is particularly important for selection to managerial and high-income positions and to academic positions (Braddock, 1990; Caplan, 1993; Cohen & Gutek, 1991; Ragins & Sundstrom, 1989). Women continually are developing their own networks. As women gain information, power, and solidarity, they are taken more seriously, so that "person" networks are becoming more viable. To get to that point, women have to work together.

*Mentoring and Tokenism*    Women may be disadvantaged by lack of mentoring or by being a token—situations that often go together. A **mentor** gives a special kind of support and information and generally oversees professional growth and socialization that is helpful in entering an occupation (Bahniuk, Dobos, & Hill, 1990; Chao & Gardner, 1992; Goh, 1991; O'Leary & Ickovics, 1991). Mentors often are senior managers, immediate supervisors, or, for graduate students, graduate faculty. Women are likely to have difficulty finding a mentor in fields dominated by men. First, the few women who are in a position to be mentors are likely to be overworked. They are trying to survive and perhaps trying to mentor *all* the younger women. Second, men may worry about possible gossip if they mentor a woman, and they often worry that their mentoring time would be wasted on a woman. The result is that women feel isolated and dissatisfied and do not have the personal support and advantages that men have (Caplan, 1993; Goh, 1991; Ohlott et al., 1994). Helping men to feel more comfortable interacting professionally with women could be useful.

Women often are tokens because they are doing things not commonly done by women in the past. Rosabeth Kanter (1977a, 1977b; Kanter & Stein, 1980) referred to people making up less than 15% of a group as **tokens.** Tokens are both invisible and the center of attention, depending on the whims of the others (Caplan, 1993; Yoder, Aniakudo, & Berendsen, 1996). They are not treated as individuals but as symbols of

## *A Closer Look*

### 13.1    Index of Sexual Harassment

Percentage of working women responding to a *Redbook* survey reporting sexual harassment    88

Percentage of women in the U.S. Navy reporting sexual harassment    90

Percentage of women in the Protestant clergy reporting harassment incidents    77

Percentage of those incidents that involved fellow clergy    41

Percentage of female third-year medical students reporting harassment by residents, interns, and faculty    55

Number of harassment complaints filed with EEOC by women working for elected officials on Capitol Hill in 1991, prior to the Anita Hill case    6,883

Number of harassment complaints filed in 1992, after the Anita Hill case    10,522

SOURCES: Reilly, 1980; Working Women's Institute, 1980; Women Clerics, 1990; Friend, 1990.

the out-group and subjects of gossip. It is no wonder that tokens often feel isolated and powerless (Cota & Dion, 1986; Hans & Eisenberg, 1985). Ironically, they also are seen as exceptions to the rule—"You're different (because you are one of us, when we want you to be)" (Nieva & Gutek, 1981). Thus a woman is supposed to be flattered that she is (sometimes) considered "one of the boys" instead of a woman, and people of color are expected to feel good that the white majority sometimes chooses to try to rob them of their ethnic identities. The form of discrimination may differ for white and African American women (Martin, 1994). White women were seen as having better social relations and more support than African American women (Yoder et al., 1996).

Tokens have several kinds of negative experiences: performance pressures and the stress resulting from their heightened visibility and social isolation. Men, however, may have an easier time as tokens than women do. When men are tokens, they may have some of the same feelings as women, but still may be influential, showing the importance of gender in social status (Craig & Sherif, 1986; Williams, 1992; Yoder, 1991).

***Sexual Harassment***    Whether a woman is a token or one of many women, she may well experience sexual harassment, a form of violence against women (discussed further in chapter 15). Examples of harassment include verbal sexual suggestions or jokes, constant ogling, "accidental" touch, propositions for sex with threats of job loss, and forced sexual relations (MacKinnon, 1979). Sexual harassment is widespread in univer-

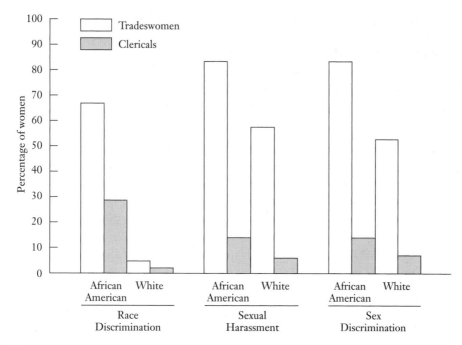

**Figure 13.4** *Discrimination reported by African American and white women in two occupational groups.* NOTE: Data shown are for white and African American skilled trades-women and school secretaries (clericals) reporting sexual discrimination, racial discrimination, or sexual harassment on a lengthy questionnaire. SOURCE: Mansfield, P. K., Koch, P. B., Henderson, J., Vicary, J. R., Cohen, M., & Young, E. W. (1991). The job climate for women in traditionally male blue-collar occupations. *Sex Roles, 25,* (1/2), 63–79. Figure based on Table II, p. 71 and information passim.

sities and in the workplace otherwise, with estimates going up to a minimum of 50% of working women likely to be sexually harassed at some point during their working lives (A Closer Look 13.1; Caplan, 1993; Fitzgerald, 1993; Fitzgerald & Ormerod, 1991; Gruber, 1992; Gutek, 1993; Williams & Cyr, 1992). This is in fact an underestimate because groups at highest risk—women of color and women in nontraditional occupations—are underrepresented in most samples. Women in blue-collar jobs are harassed more than those in pink-collar jobs, and African American women more than white women; African American women also face racial discrimination (Figure 13.4; Martin, 1994; Yoder & Aniakudo, 1995). Lesbians also are subject to taunts and ridicule and physical violence (Levine & Leonard, 1984).

Most women who have been targets of harassment have stress reactions that affect performance: difficulties in concentrating, decreased motivation for work, and negative attitudes toward the job situation (Summers, 1991). Most women are not flattered by the "attention." They are disgusted, angry, intimidated, frightened, frustrated, and embarrassed (Jensen & Gutek, 1982; MacKinnon, 1979). Relatively few women make formal charges because charges take time and money, and the woman risks being seen as a troublemaker (Riger, 1991). Organizations sometimes blame the victim, such as by giving her negative job evaluations, demoting her, or firing her. Obviously, harassment can change a woman's life (Gutek & Koss, 1993).

Harassment has been a continuing problem because it has not yet been fully acknowledged. As one woman speaks out, others often join her. The nationally prominent charges of Professor Anita Hill in the fall of 1991 sensitized many people to the issue. Whether the sensitization remains is yet to be seen.

## *The Women Who Are on the Job*

In spite of all the problems in getting their paid jobs and then performing them, women have long achieved occupationally and are likely to do so in increasing numbers as time goes on. The women who achieve in the job world are likely to have ability, personal strength, and support from others close to them, especially parents.

### Parental Influences

Women who enter fields dominated by men generally have had enriching experiences that lead to a broad view of what women can do (e.g., Angrist & Almquist, 1975; Betz & Fitzgerald, 1987). They generally come from intact families with educated parents and a high rate of maternal employment. They see their parents as having encouraged and supported their career aspirations with less emphasis on marriage. For example, African American women who were lawyers reported that both parents taught them to be autonomous, self-reliant, and economically independent (Simpson, 1984). This kind of evidence is retrospective and subject to the memory distortion of successful daughters; however, it is generally consistent with what is known from studies of children and young adults about the development of androgyny, achievement, and self-esteem (chapters 5, 7).

Much has been made of mothers as models for their daughters' aspirations and rightly so (Focus on Research 13.2; Lerner, 1994; Steele & Barling, 1996). College women (white and African American have been studied) who select pioneering careers (those with few women) are likely to have employed mothers and more highly educated mothers than other college women (Almquist, 1974; Astin, 1978; Betz & Fitzgerald, 1987; Sandberg et al., 1987). Mothers, however, can be important even without a lot of formal education or interesting careers. For example, young African American women without highly educated mothers listed their mothers and grandmothers as special models of strength, endurance, and achievement (Hill, 1994). As important as mothers are, fathers are not to be forgotten. They seem to have a special role in giving "masculine approval" for their daughters to achieve in a "man's way." Aspiring and successful professional women have had particularly close relationships with fathers who encouraged them in nontraditional roles (Hennig & Jardin, 1977), although sometimes it is a brother, boyfriend, or teacher who has given the encouragement (Astin, 1978).

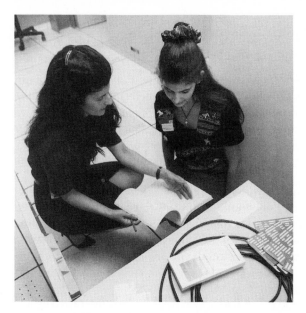

*Women's career aspirations and choices are strongly influenced by the models their mothers provide. This mother, an advisory support specialist at IBM, is showing her 14-year-old daughter how she troubleshoots problems on a computer control unit. Her daughter was in the office as part of the national Take Our Daughters to Work Day.*

As always, there are exceptions. Some women report an internal demand to achieve in spite of disapproving parents (Weitzman, 1979). Also, high achievers have come from lower classes and have had parents without a college education, as shown for women (African American and white) who achieved marked success in business, academia, or government service (Boardman, Harrington, & Horowitz, 1987), achieving women physicians (Mandelbaum, 1978), and politically prominent women (Kelly, 1983). Women from the lower class backgrounds are distinguished from otherwise comparable women of the middle class in having an unusually strong belief in their ability to control their lives—"You can do anything if you put your mind to it." In short, many women have achieved simply because *they decided to do so.*

## Women and Men as Workers

The women who achieve in nontraditional professions are very similar to men in the professions (Eagly, 1987; Kirchmeyer, 1993; Powell, 1988). However, because of the different social contexts in which women and men have grown and the different social environments on the jobs, gender differences do exist. Currently, in business and in academia, women may still need more ability and motivation than men. Women who originally enter a male-dominated field generally are smarter and more motivated than the men in the field are; as the number of women entering the field increases, the gender differential decreases (Jagacinski, 1987). For example, women who entered college engineering programs 10–20 years ago were at the top of their high school classes and had higher SAT scores than the men who entered then. The women attracted to engineering still are very bright. The difference is that now it is not necessary

## 13.2 Path Analysis: Mom's Influence on Daughter's Career Choice

Cathy grew up in a family in which both parents had careers. For as long as she can remember, dinner table discussions involved what had happened at her school that day, at her mother's law office, and on the job site at her father's construction company. Now that Cathy has started her first year at college, she's beginning to think about her own career. Right now she's leaning toward law school and maybe specializing in family law. On hearing this, her mom beams with pride and her dad chuckles about "following in your mother's footsteps."

Just how much influence do parents have on their children's choice of careers? Parents have been known to dictate, sometimes with disastrous results, that children enter the family business or train for a career the parent considers prestigious. On the other hand, some children choose careers that are the exact opposite of, or seem to have no connection to, parental values and desires. If you are a college student, choosing a career is likely to be on your mind. What do you think are the major influences on the career choice you've made or will make very soon?

Researchers Jennifer Steele and Julian Barling were particularly interested in how parental factors influenced young women's career choices (1996). They proposed a model involving several interconnected parental variables that might predict the gender-typed nature of such a career choice. A model is basically an extensive hypothesis that can then be tested for its "fit" to the actual data. No model will provide a perfect fit, but the closer the match between model and data, the more useful that model will be in explaining and predicting behavior. Steele and Barling's model involved maternal and paternal gender role beliefs and role satisfaction, the daughter's perceptions of these maternal and paternal beliefs and level of satisfaction, and the daughter's own gender role beliefs. The researchers hypothesized a system of relationships in which each of these variables contributed to the gender-typed nature of the daughter's career choice.

Couldn't we simply measure these variables in a group of young women and see whether each variable correlated with career choice? We could, but simple correlations only give us information about the relationship of two variables at a time. Steele and Barling's model illustrates a much more complex set of relationships and proposes a causal sequence among the variables. The statistical technique of path analysis allowed them to test this model.

Path analysis is based on correlation, but it involves the use of control variables and time sequencing to establish causal relationships. If a correlation between two variables exists when other theoretically related variables are controlled by the researcher, we can assume (although we can never prove) that a direct causal relationship exists for those variables. Proper time order of variables is also important, and the model must posit a logical sequence in which "earlier" predictor variables precede "later" outcome variables.

As the researcher selects each of the variables and hypothesizes the system of relationships that connected them, the model is created. A path diagram is a visual summary of that model. Steele and Barling created separate models for maternal and paternal influences on the daughter's career choice; the maternal path diagram is illustrated here. As the arrows indicate, daughter's career choice is dependent on her gender role ideology (beliefs), which in turn is dependent on two separate sets of factors. One set is the daughter's perceptions of her mother's satisfaction with her own gender or occupational role, which is shaped by her mother's actual satisfaction. The second set of factors is the daughter's perception of her mother's gender role ideology, which, likewise, is dependent on her mother's actual ideology. The double-ended arrows between maternal role satisfaction and maternal gender role ideology indicate that the two factors are linked but no causal relationship is hypothesized.

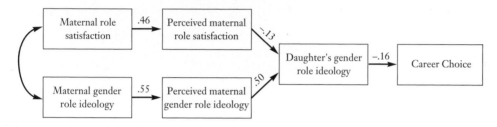

Part of the results of Steele and Barling's path analysis are shown by the correlations next to each arrow. These are called path coefficients and indicate the relationship of the two variables connected by the arrow; they indicate whether the hypothesized relationship was actually found in the data. Path coefficients are not simply a series of separate correlations between two variables; instead, they indicate a relationship between those two variables when all other variables in the model are taken into account. In path analysis, the main focus is on the model itself; while the path coefficients report interesting information about pairs of variables, the most important part of the analysis is how well the entire model represents the data.

Steele and Barling found that the maternal model did, to a significant degree, explain the daughter's career choice; that is, this model provided an appropriate fit to the data. However, the test of the paternal model was not significant, indicating that the father's attitudes did not adequately explain the daughter's career choice. It appears that when young women make occupational decisions, they are more responsive to their mother's influence than their father's. These researchers note that as women continue to enter fields that are currently male dominated and men continue to take on more home and child care responsibilities, jobs and careers are likely to become less gender-typed. Steele and Barling propose that in this version of the future, young women may look to their mothers and fathers equally for career guidance.

JILL BORCHERT ◆

SOURCE: Steele, J., & Barling, J. (1996). Influence of maternal gender-role beliefs and role satisfaction on daughter's vocational interests. *Sex Roles, 34*, 637–648.

*Women did important industrial work during World War II. After the war, they were forced back into the home so their jobs could be offered to returning veterans. The cultural norms that emerged in the 1950s put pressure on women to accept their roles as housewives and mothers.*

that they be markedly brighter than the men competing for the positions. Standards are *not* lowering: The hurdles faced by men and women are becoming equalized.

Women frequently are more committed to their jobs and have more of some of the job-related motivations and traits (Jenkins, 1994; Offermann & Beil, 1992). Women who are managers and business students have shown greater need for power and achievement (chapters 7, 9), with greater value of independence, accomplishment, and the opportunity to use their skills (Beutell & Brenner, 1986; Chusmir, 1984). Similarly, women in middle and upper levels of corporate organizations scored higher than men on autonomy (involving independence, unconventionality, and resistance to domineering authority) (Hatcher, 1991). The choice of a corporate career in a large organization still is a nontraditional choice for women and a traditional one for men. Thus conforming men and nonconforming women may elect this career path. On the other hand, it is possible that successful women managers have had to develop strategies for moving out of the lower status positions to which women are initially assigned (Carbonnel, 1984; Eagly, 1983). To rise to the top, women have to have "something extra," whether they are professionals or blue-collar women.

## Blue-Collar Women

Women are increasingly entering nontraditional blue-collar jobs—becoming carpenters, coal miners, welders, plumbers, electricians, machinists, construction workers (Braden, 1986; Deaux & Ullman, 1983; Martin, 1988; Palmer & Lee, 1990). During World War II, women were an important force in the defense industry; many wanted to stay employed when the war ended but were forced to make way for returning male veterans. Women now are returning to blue-collar jobs, although the proportion of women in the jobs still is low. For example, in 1990, women were only 8.6% of workers in construction-related occupations (International Labour Office, 1991).

More women are entering blue-collar jobs for two main reasons (Palmer & Lee, 1990). First, affirmative action agreements between the federal government and private employers account for much of the change. Second, women have realized that such jobs generally have better pay, fringe benefits, job security, training, and promotional opportunities than do traditionally female-dominated jobs (Bader, 1990; Deaux & Ullman, 1983; Hammond & Mahoney, 1983). Other positive aspects most consistently reported are a sense of accomplishment, autonomy and control over their work, the variety and challenge of the work, and the physicality of the work (Deaux & Ullman, 1983; Ferree, 1987; Mansfield et al., 1991).

Most women entering blue-collar occupations did not expect to do so (Deaux & Ullman, 1983; Martin, 1988). Generally, they started out in other occupations and shifted as the occasion arose, sometimes out of frustration with a current low-paid "feminine" job. Like nontraditional professional women, they benefit from the support and encouragement of friends and family (Houser & Garvey, 1985).

Both blue-collar women and women who are executives are likely to feel lonely on the job (Colwill & Colwill, 1985). Women entering blue-collar positions, however, have problems that exceed those of women in professional and white-collar jobs (Mansfield et al., 1991; Palmer & Lee, 1990). Blue-collar skills often are learned on the job, so that the new woman is likely to have to learn the tricks of the trade from male coworkers. Women in steel plants reported that the men did not teach them the challenging jobs that they taught other men (Deaux & Ullman, 1983). Coworkers and first-line supervisors still typically show some resentment toward women (Meyer & Lee, 1978). Sometimes, there is marked discrimination, and African American trades-women have experienced racial discrimination as well (see Figure 13.4). On the positive side, men who have worked with women previously have better attitudes toward women in the workplace than those who have not (Palmer & Lee, 1990). Men having personal information that a woman *can* do the job pays off for women.

## Career Wives

Some women have demanding careers unrecognized by others: These are **career wives** in a **two-person career.** They are married to a man who needs a second person to contribute to his career, but the second person, a wife, is not paid for her work. The men include corporate executives, politicians, physicians, college presidents and professors, military officers, and clergy. The organizations employing the men think it is their right to get two for the price of one if the man is to succeed.

For some women, considering the times during which they grew to maturity, "hooking up with a good man" was an effective way of working for their own goals (Simonton, 1996). A study of wives of the U.S. presidents shows that their eminence was partially a reflection of their husbands' eminence. However, the woman's reputation was independently determined by her performance as the president's political colleague and her success at establishing her own distinct personality. On the other hand, her reputation was not influenced by her expertise in filling more traditional gender responsibilities.

For other women, being a career wife is an endless grind with few rewards, leading to low self-esteem, loneliness, depression, poor physical health, and substance abuse (Cook, 1987; Kanter, 1977b; Turner, 1986). They are expected to contribute, but their contributions are not recognized and honored. Their lives are controlled without personal reward.

Like other women who are claiming their own lives, career wives are protesting, and organizations are starting to listen to them. For example, wives of clergy have been voicing their desires for their homes not to be an extension of the religious building (Strickland, 1992); former Defense Secretary Casper Weinberger (Moore, 1987) issued an order that a military officer is not to be evaluated negatively because his wife chooses a different career route, namely, her own rather than his!

This change is a step forward for the career wives themselves in claiming their own lives. It also is an important step for the women in the same careers as the husbands of career wives. Women politicians, professors, military officers, and clergy have not had the advantage of a career partner to help them with their jobs and have been disadvantaged because of that. Career wives, by claiming their own freedoms, are giving freedoms to other women as well. Women give to women in many ways.

## Women's Work at Home

Work at home is work and needs to be understood as that. Full-time homemakers have a job that is not valued. Employed women face the challenge of juggling two kinds of work, a challenge accentuated for women with children and no partner who helps in the home. In this final section, we consider the nature of work at home, stresses involving work, and child care.

### Housework Is Her Work

***The Nature of Housework***    Housework is necessary and valuable, but it is not valued as "real" work (Daniels, 1987). Homemakers are more likely to see their work as physically demanding and less likely to see it as mentally demanding, as employed women see their paid work (Grana, Moore, Wilson, & Miller, 1993). Considering modern labor-saving devices such as vacuums, washers for clothes and dishes, and microwave ovens, you might think that the demands on a homemaker have decreased over the years. This is not the case (Szalai, 1972). Sociologist Joann Vanek (1984) has found that women today who are not employed spend as much time doing housework as women did in 1900—more than 50 hours a week. Modern appliances are not *labor saving* but *labor changing* (Robinson, 1980). A change has been that women spend more time than previously in stores and transporting children and husbands. In addition, standards have risen markedly as women aim for perfection for their loved ones (Ferree, 1976; Oakley, 1974; Whitbourne, 1986). A house must be not only clean but well decorated. Homemakers, now, are expected to be "Martha Stewart wanna-bes."

With low status, increasingly high but still unclear standards, lack of support, and never-ending demands of the housework job, it is easy to see how the women doing the job can feel strained and depressed (Crosby, 1982; Ferree, 1976; Oakley, 1974; Schooler, Miller, Miller, & Richtand, 1984). Even among Mexican Americans, who are thought to place a higher value on homemaking for women than non-Hispanic whites, housework is associated with strain, which, in turn, is associated with depression (Golding, 1990). In spite of the strains of housework, there are positive aspects as well (Devault, 1987). Full-time homemakers like the freedom to make their own schedules and enjoy doing things for their loved ones (Baruch, Barnett, & Rivers, 1983; Ferree, 1985, 1987). Employed women also enjoy housework for autonomy and for the feeling of being helpful (Kibria et al., 1990) but often face problems juggling all the demands on them.

Most employed women do not give up the job of homemaker; they work at a paid job all day and then come home to a **second shift,** the work at home (Hochschild, 1989; Weingarten, 1978). They spend about half as much time on housework, their second shift, as nonemployed women do (e.g., 26 hours relative to more than 50 hours a week; Tavris & Wade, 1984). Employed women, however, typically end up with more total work time than unemployed women. Time for travel and dressing for work must be added to the paid work time, so that the average full-time employed woman without children spends about 76 hours a week on work-related activities. Both employed and unemployed wives' time engaged in domestic work increases 5% to 10% with each child; husbands' participation decreases as the family grows larger.

***Help From Husbands***    Married women do not get much help from their husbands, whether the couples are in Yugoslavia or Peru or the United States (Stohs, 1995; Zick & McCullough, 1991). The majority of husbands and wives believe that when the wife is employed, husbands *should* increase their household work, but the beliefs do not translate into action: Women spend more time in household labor, including child care, than men do regardless of women's employment status (Biernat & Wortman, 1991; Lamb, 1987; Wethington & Kessler, 1989). The characteristic finding is that men's time in housework is not particularly affected by the wives' employment. One typical study found that men with employed wives contributed 19 minutes a day more to all home activities than men with nonemployed wives, and those who were fathers spent 24 minutes more per *week* in child care (Douthitt, 1989). American women spend more time and American men spend less time in caring for children (4-year-olds) than parents in other countries (e.g., Belgium, China, Nigeria, Spain; Owen, 1995). Androgynous and expressive men do more household tasks than instrumental men, but their wives still do about twice as much as they do (Gunter & Gunter, 1990). Lack of equity in division of household labor is a leading cause of conflict (Stohs, 1995).

African Americans especially have relatively equalitarian attitudes that men should assist in household tasks and child care duties and that women should share in providing financial support and making family decisions (Cazenave, 1983; Hill, 1972; Johnson, 1981). But division of labor in African American families is gender

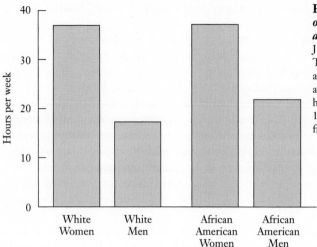

**Figure 13.5 *Time spent on housework, by gender and race.*** SOURCE: Shelton, J., & Shelton, B. A. (1997). The production of gender among black and white women and men: The case of household labor. *Sex Roles, 36,* (3/4), 171–193. Figure developed from Table 1, p. 181.

differentiated, and the women are primarily responsible for maintaining the house and caring for children; for African Americans, as for whites, the women's employment status makes little or no difference (Broman, 1988; Hossain & Roopnarine, 1993; Wilson, Tolson, Hinton, & Kiernan, 1990). African American fathers, however, do more household work than white men and men of other ethnic groups—their activities follow gender lines but less so than other men's. The result is that both white and African American men do less household work than their wives do, but African American men do more than white men, while women of the two groups do essentially the same (John & Shelton, 1997; Figure 13.5).

## The Old and the New

Why is work in the home considered women's work rather than work to be shared by the people who are sharing the home? The answer may lie in two interrelated kinds of suggestions: status and traditionalism. Supporting the view that status makes a difference is the finding that among heterosexual couples, the person who earns more than the other has more financial and overall say-so (Biernat & Wortman, 1991). Also, as the husband's income increases, his child care participation decreases—and he feels better about being a spouse and parent! Similarly, the man in a gay couple who earns more does less housework than his partner does (Blumstein & Schwartz, 1983). Some evidence indicates that only in lesbian couples is wage disparity not accompanied by disparity in housework (Blumstein & Schwartz, 1983). Other evidence indicates that a lesbian who has less money than her partner is uncomfortable (though the more afflu-ent partner is not) and tries to compensate for the inequity by doing more of the household work (Hall with Gregory, 1991).

The power of income, however, does not tell the whole story. As the earnings of wives in academia *increased,* their husbands had *decreased* child care involvement: The women's time in child care increased along with their salaries (Biernat & Wortman,

1991). And, the earnings of wives who were in business were not directly associated with child care. Obviously, money cannot be counted on to give a woman status in her home.

Heterosexual traditionalism seems still present in middle-class and blue-collar families (Crouter, Perry-Jenkins, Huston, & McHale, 1987; Fox & Hesse-Biber, 1984). Earning money and financially providing for the family are intimately bound up with a man's self-respect and his sense of being a good father (chapter 12). Even when husbands are not dissatisfied with their wives' work roles and presumably accept dual careers, they are not necessarily ready to abandon their ownership of the "good provider" role (Mintz & Mahalik, 1996; Staines, Pottick, & Fudge, 1986; Stanley, Hunt, & Hunt, 1986). Heterosexual women support and understand this (Blumstein & Schwartz, 1983). Couples go to great lengths to conceal and to minimize the importance of a high-earning wife's income (Hochschild, 1989; Steil & Weltman, 1991). And, the fact that the husband earned more money than the wife was justification to both husbands and wives for seeing his career as more important than hers (Steil & Weltman, 1991). Yet income disparity was *not* seen as a legitimate reason for placing a higher value on the wife's career when she earned more than her husband did. In addition, wives, but not husbands, who earned more than their spouses reported that they felt greater concerns about arousing competitive feelings.

***Men and Housework***     Housework is undervalued, and many men feel that their masculinity is threatened if they do the undervalued work (Tavris & Wade, 1984). Cohabiting young men often do a sizable share of housework, but the traditionality of being married and then a father is associated with withdrawing from housework (Antill & Cotton, 1988; Rossi, 1985). Housework is not a great deal of fun, and with their greater status, men elect not to participate in it or in the non-fun aspects of child care. Women may not always enjoy housework, but they have been "trained" to do it since childhood, whereas most men have not (chapters 5, 9).

When husbands do household chores, they do not seem to think of themselves as doing their fair share. They do the work "to help," although "it is not my job" (Gunter & Gunter, 1990). Women do what they do because they think "it is my job," or because "it won't get done otherwise." Women often say, "It's easier to do it myself than try to get him to do it." When men do "help out," they have to be reminded to do so. Women have complaints such as, "Yes, he takes the garbage out, but I have to remind him that Tuesday is garbage day." Research confirms this differential in responsibilities. Among a group of professional couples, the husbands were involved in shopping, cleaning, and repair work, but the wives had more responsibility except for repair work (Biernat & Wortman, 1991). Wives also have the responsibility for the hard work of child care; husbands have equal involvement with children only in terms of playing with them (chapter 12).

Men's general resistance to household work is shown in the fact that the more housework and child care men do—African American or white—the less satisfied they are with their marriage and the more they grumble (Baruch & Barnett, 1986; Blumstein & Schwartz, 1983; Broman, 1988; Crouter et al., 1987). In part, men's reduced satisfaction is because they feel resentful about being coerced into the activities by their wives, and wives resent the coercion they feel they must use to get their husbands' help.

Also to be considered are women's concerns about what "a good wife" and "a good mother" are. Men who work little in the home may be feeling that they are doing what they are supposed to be doing. Women who work more than an equal share in the home also may be feeling that they are doing what they are supposed to be doing. The view that housework is women's work may be so deeply ingrained that even women who otherwise are "liberated" may have guilt about taking time away from the home because of their employment; they may reduce guilt and raise self-esteem somewhat through an extra effort of involvement in traditional home activities (Baruch & Barnett, 1986; Lerner, 1994). This was suggested in earlier discussions about the care of infants (chapter 12). Women's guilt about paid work likely is greater in those who work more by choice than by necessity. Those who see a financial necessity for their employment have a "built-in" excuse.

***Guilt by Unrealistic Standards***    The extra work of employed women relative to their husbands may be an attempted atonement but does not seem to remove the guilt. Wives who were professionals generally were more critical of themselves than their husbands were of them and than their husbands were of themselves (Biernat & Wortman, 1991). Women were more likely than men to say they were not the kind of spouse and parent they would like to be and felt guilty about that. They were more bothered than their husbands were about big and small projects around the house, house cleanliness, not having good meals, and finances. In addition, the less child care the wife performed and the more the husband did, the less positive she was with her performance as a spouse. The women were not generally negative; they were generally satisfied with their husbands' contributions and were satisfied with their employment.

Researchers speculated that in judging themselves so harshly, the women were using nonemployed wives and mothers or their own mothers as the standards of comparison. If only because of the amount of time spent in employment, employed women cannot run homes, cook meals, and raise children as their traditional counterparts do. Lifestyles are changing, but new standards are not yet clear and established, much as was suggested for sexuality (chapter 11). "Liberated" women who seek personal expression in employment generally are not using liberated standards for evaluating their housework. This can contribute to stress.

## Stresses and Benefits of Multiple Roles

While multiple roles generally are advantageous, the demands of work and home life do pose role conflicts in lesbians and heterosexual women of all occupations and races; they are more likely to be dealt with by women than by men in heterosexual couples (Crosby, 1982, 1991; Duxbury & Higgins, 1991; Lerner, 1994; Wiersma, 1990). Most research is about heterosexual marriages, but lesbians also struggle with time and energy demands for both work roles and relationship roles (Shachar & Gilbert, 1983).

Although employed life and home life can conflict, often positive as well as negative effects of paid work spill over to life apart from work, and vice versa (Lerner,

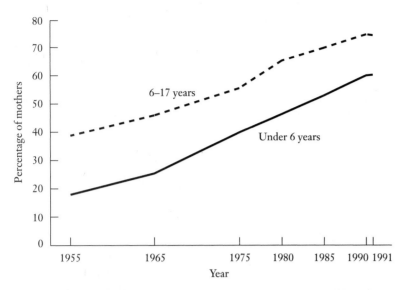

**Figure 13.6** *Percentage of mothers in the labor force, by year and age of youngest child.* SOURCE: "Projections for 2000 from Paula Ries and Anne J. Stone," for the Women's Research and Educational Institute (1992). *The American Woman, 1992–1993: A Status Report.* New York: W. W. Norton & Company, Inc. Table 6-1, p. 308.

1994). The majority of professional women feel that their family lives have positive or neutral effects on their careers and that their work lives have positive effects on their family relationships (Emmons, Biernat, Tiedje, Lang, & Wortman, 1990; Rudd & McKenry, 1986). Friends and family can provide social support and help to keep things in perspective (Amatea & Fong, 1991; Barnett, Marshall, & Singer, 1992). For women who do not have traditional families, social support from friends and having a sense of personal control reduce work stress (Amatea & Fong, 1991). Employers' fears that women's lives apart from work might have a negative impact on work are not well founded (Kirchmeyer, 1993). In fact, women's lives apart from work had less negative impact on their work than men's did. It was suggested that this was due to men's lesser training for homemaking activities, so that they were less able to contain the stresses of home roles.

## Concerns About Children

In spite of the motherhood mandate (chapter 12), as noted earlier, nearly two-thirds (62.3%) of mothers with children under 6 years old were employed in 1995, and the number is expected to increase (Figure 13.6). The question of whether mothers of young children *should* work for pay is essentially irrelevant to modern family life (Silverstein, 1991). Mothers *do* work. The issue is the quality of care for children, and there is much difference of opinion on this. Popular views (only since the late 19th century) hold that mothers' presence is necessary for children's healthy development (Lerner, 1994). Studies showing emotional disorders and intellectual retardation in institutionalized infants contributed to a public outcry against "maternal deprivation" or "maternal absence" (Bowlby, 1951; Spitz, 1965). The negative outcomes were shown later to be due to the disruption of the child's total life circumstances, the lack of later attachment relationships, and inadequate environmental stimulation (Rutter, 1974). Unfortunately, such circumstances seem typical of institutionalization.

***Views About "Maternal Deprivation"***   Some people continue to see women's employment as an issue of maternal deprivation that tugs the conscience still shaped by the motherhood mandate (Scarr, Phillips, & McCartney, 1989; Silverstein, 1991). They do not typically see fathers' employment as an issue of "paternal deprivation" (chapter 12). Attitudes in this respect vary with age and with experience. College students (predominantly white) expect more negative outcomes for children of employed mothers than for children of other mothers, and they expect more negative outcomes than do people who are actually expecting a baby (Bridges & Etaugh, 1994, 1986; Bridges & Orza, 1992, 1993; Etaugh & Study, 1989; Hyde & McKinley, 1993).

There also are differences between white and African American women about the interface between their employment and having children (Bridges & Etaugh, 1994, 1996). Both white and African American people seem to think there are both costs and benefits involved in the maternal employment of mothers of young children. However, white women are relatively concerned about the potential harm for preschool children, while African American women generally expect more positive outcomes of their employment for themselves and their children. African Americans more than whites likely have had a chance to see the positive effects of maternal employment and to integrate their experiences into their personal expectations and general attitudes.

***Day Care and Mother Care***   Critics of day care sometimes write as if employed parents are not parents at all, and as if all women are inherently destined to be good parents (Scarr et al., 1989). Neither assumption, of course, is true. Employed mothers spend about half of their children's waking time with them, considering that they are with them in the evenings, on weekends, and holidays; and, when the child is ill, mothers are likely to stay at home with the child. In addition, employed mothers tend to compensate for their relative absence by increased direct interaction and amount of shared time ("quality time") with their children during nonwork hours (Hoffman, 1989; Moorehouse, 1991).

Motherhood is not instinctual, and parenting is hard work (chapter 12). Not all women who have children, even by choice, are psychologically predisposed to stay at home with their infants. Some of those nonetheless do stay home, perhaps out of a sense of duty (Lerner, 1994). Nonemployed mothers who want to be employed have more problems than other mothers do with relationships with their children, confidence as a mother, depression, and stress (Hock & DeMeis, 1990; Yarrow, Scott, deLeeuw, & Heinig, 1962). Mothers of 12-month-old infants who wanted to be employed but were not were more depressed than other mothers (see Figure 13.2). Employment is especially beneficial for mothers of "difficult" infants (Dienstag, 1987).

Studies with infants as well as older children show that a mother's satisfaction with her employment status relates positively to the quality of mother-child interaction and to various indices of the child's adjustment and abilities. It is not just a matter that a mother with a happy child becomes happy with her job; a mother's job satisfaction predicted her school-aged child's adjustment 2 years later (Guidubaldi, Perry, & Natasi, 1987). A mother's mood does affect her children, even infants. It is to a child's advantage to have a happy mother. "The fantasy that mothers at home with young children provide the best possible care neglects the observation that some women at home full time are lonely, depressed, and not functioning well" (Scarr et al., 1989, p. 1407). Home care cannot be equated with optimal care, nor can child care away from home be equated with deficient care.

***Effects of Day Care***    What are the effects of day care? The quality of child care varies enormously just as the quality of home care does (Scarr et al., 1989). High-quality care is expensive and not only out of reach for low-income parents but a strain on middle-income parents (Lerner, 1994).

Although the research is not without limitations, there is near consensus that child care per se is not a risk factor in children's lives. Rather, poor-quality care and poor family environments produce poor developmental outcomes (Howes, 1990; Lerner, 1994; Scarr et al., 1989; Silverstein, 1991). When infants of employed mothers are insecure in their attachments to their mothers, the insecurity seems due to the fact that the mothers had low desire for motherhood even *before* the birth (Clarke-Stewart & Fein, 1983; Farber & Egeland, 1982). Day care for some children may be advantageous in compensating for poor family environments (Clarke-Stewart, 1989; Vandell & Ramanan, 1991). Mothers themselves think day care is a positive experience for the child, such as by advancing the children's social, language, and learning skills ("Study: Working moms," 1994). Some researchers have concluded that fears about child care are not based on scientifically demonstrated facts, but on socially determined theories about mothers' roles (Scarr et al., 1989).

***Children and Young Adolescents***    Children in self-care (and sometimes those in the care of siblings under 15 years of age) are often called **latchkey children.** For them, as for younger children, it is clear that the family is important (Galambos & Maggs, 1991; Lerner, 1994; Scarr et al., 1989). The type of after-school care per se is less important than the quality of children's experiences with their families. It seems difficult for poor married parents and especially for poor single mothers to provide conditions for their children's optimal development. Alternative care may be especially beneficial in such cases.

For either the poor or the more affluent to benefit from child care services requires first that quality services be available. Surveys show that the quality of child care in the United States (but not European countries) often is low, placing demands on parents to "shop" for child care as carefully as they shop for a new car (Genasco, 1995; Whitmire, 1995). In view of the generally low pay for child care workers, the general low care should be no surprise. Research suggests that for every $1 invested in high-quality early childhood programs, more than $7 is saved through reducing school dropout rates, welfare payments, and juvenile delinquency. For people to benefit from child care requires that parents be freed of the pressures of the motherhood mandate so that they can accept modern necessity without feeling guilty for not being 24-hour-a-day parents. Most adults are not prepared to be parents all day long anyway. It is not clear that either mothers or infants benefit from continual maternal care even in the infant's first year (Scarr et al., 1989).

## Some Final Thoughts: Optimism Amid the Crisis of Change

Many personality theorists (e.g., Freud, Erikson, and Maslow) agree that the healthy *person* is effective in work and love. But traditionally, men have been expected to be experts in work and women have been expected to be experts in love. We currently are in a time of change due to women's increasing employment. It would not be far afield to say that we are in a time of identity crisis, as Erik Erikson used the term. It is an identity crisis about the identity of the family and, particularly, the identities of women and men in heterosexual families. Erikson's concept of crisis implies danger and opportunity. Change brings problems and possible danger by the simple fact that it is a deviation from what people know and have come to expect. But change also brings opportunity.

There is reason for optimism about the changes. Women are climbing higher than before on the career ladder. The more women achieve, the more younger women will envision expanded possibilities for themselves and have women to support them when they enter jobs. The more women there are who do a job well, the more the evaluators, now predominantly men, are likely to give women a fair chance. The more women there are on a job, the more support they can give each other and the more power they can feel and wield, and the more men will respect and assist them. Women still face access and treatment discrimination and glass ceilings, but research demonstrating the hurdles women face is being paid attention to, as shown by the U.S. Supreme Court's decision about Ann Hopkins. There is momentum.

Concerns for women to succeed in business, the professions, and blue-collar work should not overshadow the fact that some women want to be full-time homemakers or pink-collar workers. The important focus is that women feel they have a *choice* about their employed lives and their domestic lives.

Women's increased participation and increased accomplishments in the workforce affect the dynamics in homes. If equality in the workplace and the home is to come, people must adjust their expectations of themselves and of others. They must stop comparing themselves against old standards that are no longer realistic and work to define and practice new standards relevant to current realities. Today, many employed women are overworked as they juggle the demands of being a good employee and of being a good spouse and mother. Meeting today's challenges while preserving and enhancing health and well-being seems to require that both women and men forego the views that men are more competent and valuable than women simply because they are men and that child care and housework are unimportant because they have been the domain of women. Many people hope that both women and men attain support both for work and for love in the workplace and in the home.

## KEY TERMS

housewife's syndrome
access discrimination
treatment discrimination
occupational gender
  segregation
pink-collar job
semi-professions

gender stratification
comparable worth
denial of personal
  discrimination
glass ceiling
old (white) boys' network
mentor

token
career wives, two-person
  career
second shift
latchkey children

## KEY POINTS

### *Women's Employment Interests*

- The percentage of women, including mothers, in the labor force has been increasing. Women's level of education also has increased, and more women are entering professions than in the past.

- Women have become pragmatic about their occupational values, but without a decrease in domestic values or concerns about helping people. Their plans about family and work roles are highly intertwined.

- Many women work because they need or want the money, but they also benefit psychologically from work and feel competent at their work, whereas full-time homemakers often feel incompetent.

### *Discrimination Issues*

- Traditional jobs for women are service oriented, are of low status, and allow flexibility for a woman to fit her job life around a family.

- In 1994 women were earning 72% of what men were earning, an increase over a low in the 1970s. The wage gap is not explained by gender segregation, education differences, or differences in job investment. Women often have a relatively low sense of personal entitlement, often abetted by organizational structures.

- Differential evaluation of competence can occur at the attitudinal or decision level. Gender discrimination is reduced when the job is gender consistent and when there is information that the applicant can do the job. But there is room for bias in the amount of information considered necessary, and there is a continuing male/masculinity bias.

- Women often have fewer professional development opportunities than men and fewer resources to do the jobs they have. They often are excluded from information groups, do not have a mentor, are tokens, and are subject to harassment.

### The Women Who Are on the Job

- High-achieving nontraditional women typically have educated parents who encourage their aspirations. But some women achieve in spite of disapproving or lower class parents. Women who originally entered a male-dominated field were smarter and more motivated than men in the field.
- Women are increasingly entering blue-collar fields because of financial benefits and job enjoyment, but they encounter more adverse situations than those in other jobs; African American women face racial discrimination as well as sexual discrimination and harassment.

### Women's Work at Home

- Full-time homemakers today spend as much time in housework as women did in 1900. Employed women spend less time in housework than other women, but their total time in work activities is greater; they get little help from husbands.
- Traditional heterosexual standards continue, with men concerned about being the breadwinner and women about being the "good wife and mother." Status and money do not explain household inequity in heterosexual couples.
- Employed women face conflicts between their work and family roles, but there is positive as well as negative spillover between work and home life; women's home life has fewer negative effects on their work life than men's home life does.
- Home care cannot be equated with optimal child care, nor can child care away from home be equated with deficient care. Poor family environments are more responsible for poor developmental outcomes than quality day care is.

## INTEGRATIVE QUESTIONS

1. From your knowledge of yourself and your friends, discuss why women and men choose the careers they do. Relate your considerations to chapter themes, including information about the influence of parents and other adults.

2. List and comment on all the reasons you see why a woman should be employed. List and comment on all the reasons you see why a woman should not be employed. What is your ultimate conclusion?

3. A woman you know is about to accept a job in a large corporation. She assumes that there no longer is discrimination against women—after all, she got the job, didn't she! What do you tell her about discrimination and some specifics to watch out for?

4. List and comment on the reasons you can think of why women might be more likely to deny personal discrimination than men are. Then think about what you would do if you realized that you were underpaid—be realistic, what would you *really* do?

5. Select a professional woman, a pink-collar woman, a blue-collar woman, or a career wife whom you know. Or make your own characterization of a "typical"

woman in one of the roles. Discuss the woman in terms of her likely views about career relative to family, her general mental health and life satisfaction, the attitudes of her family and friends, the problems she has on the job and at home. Or, analyze yourself as you are or as you expect to be in terms of these themes.

6. If Alex makes more money than Chris, should Chris do more housework and child care than Alex? Does it matter whether Alex and Chris are of the same sex or different sexes? Does it matter if Alex is a man and Chris a woman, or vice versa?

## Chapter 14

# Adult Development in Women

*W*e have considered many phases of development in the early years, starting with prenatal development and covering issues relevant to childhood, adolescence, and young adulthood. In this chapter we consider selected issues of development past early adulthood into old age and up to death. The United States has not honored its elders as much as some other cultures have. We look at how this influences women's psychological and physical development, how women change as they grow from the 20s to the 30s and on to the older years, and how they see themselves and relate to others.

Women develop psychologically and socially, changing their views of themselves with respect to the world. Yet midlife is more problematic for women than for men because our culture evaluates women more than men on the basis of youthful appearance and childbearing abilities (chapters 2, 10, 12). We will see that most women do not see the loss of children when they leave home as a devastating loss. However, middle-aged women do face some health problems that only women face. As they grow into older adulthood, women continually want and value interaction with other people, and many increasingly become their own person. Because women live longer than men, the joys and problems of development in the older years are increasingly the joys and problems of women.

Before continuing, consider these questions for personal thought:

- ◆ What changes do you expect in yourself over the next 10 years? Over the next 20 years?
- ◆ What do you think is the prime of life for most people? What is related to thinking that life is first-rate for others and for yourself?
- ◆ What is your image of a woman who is menopausal, or "going through the change"?

◆ In what ways, if any, do you think your parents have experienced the depression and upset of the "empty nest syndrome"? Do your mother and father differ in this?

◆ Do you think of your parents as friends? Do you think they think of you as a friend?

◆ How were your relationships with your grandparents different from your relationships with your parents? What do you think you might have given or can give in the future to your grandparents?

◆ What do you think will be the features of your life in later years that will contribute to your general satisfaction with life?

◆ What is the best thing you can see about ageing? The worst?

## *Ageism and the Double Standard of Ageing*

**Ageism** is the belief that a person's worth and abilities are determined by age. This widespread belief includes negative stereotypes, discrimination, and even attempts to avoid contact with older people (Kimmel, 1988; Whitbourne & Hulicka, 1990). U.S. college students listing characteristics of 35-year-old and 65-year-old women and men showed even stronger age stereotyping than gender stereotyping (Kite, Deaux, & Miele, 1991).

Pressures related to ageing are stronger on women than on men because a woman's value often revolves around her youth, her physical attractiveness, and her reproductive abilities. Some women internalize this view more than others. Women who have used their glamour and sexiness to attract men and enhance their self-esteem may find ageing particularly painful (Greenwood, 1992). Ageing for women in this country is seen as highly negative, while there are some advantages for men. Susan Sontag (1979) referred to this as the **double standard of ageing**:

> Competence in most of the activities expected from men, physical sports excepted, increases with age. "Femininity" is identified with incompetence, helplessness, passivity, noncompetitiveness, being nice. Age does not improve these qualities. (p. 464)

A man's wrinkles suggest character and maturity, but what do women's wrinkles suggest? She's "over the hill" or "no spring chicken." Women's femininity is seen as decreasing with age, while men's masculinity is not considered to be affected by age (Deutsch, Zalenski, & Clark, 1986). For example, fewer women over 39 have been nominated for Academy Awards (from 1927 through 1990) than men (27% versus 67%) (Markson & Taylor, 1993). In fact, analysis of films from the 1940s through the 1980s shows that there were fewer women central characters (8%) than men characters (38%) judged as being 35 years of age or older; the pattern was the same for secondary characters (28% of women, 72% of men) (Bazzini, McIntosh, Smith, Cook,

## A Closer Look

### 14.1    Two Views of Older Women

**Whole**
**Woman of the ^ Year.**

Have you ever known a woman named
  "November"?
Neither have I.
Now "May" and "June" and "April" have
  their namesakes—
Ever ask why?

We rarely picture women as autumnal;
Female is spring.
Please, someone, name a newborn girl
  "October"
And hear her sing

Of harvest cut and growth complete and
  fruit mature,
Not just of birth.
Oh, let a woman age as seasons do;
Love each time's worth!

—Miriam Corcoran

Your skins are taut
Your faces smooth
  like fresh plums
My skin is wrinkled
My brow is furrowed
  like a prune
Prunes are sweeter.

—Natasha Josefowitz

SOURCE: Paula B. Doress-Worters and Diana Laskin
Siegal in cooperation with the Boston Women's Health
Book Collective, *The New Our Bodies, Ourselves: Women
Aging with Knowledge and Power.* NY: Touchstone/Simon
& Schuster, 1994, p. xxii; Josefowitz, N. (1984, May).
Plums and prunes. *The Owl Observer*, p. 12.

& Harris, 1997). The women were consistently younger than male characters across all five decades for both central (7.4 years difference) and secondary roles (5.93 years difference). In addition, the relationship between age and negative perceptions (on dimensions such as friendliness, intelligence, goodness) were stronger for women than for men.

Age, like physical attractiveness, may not matter as much to lesbians as to heterosexual women (Davis, 1990; Gonzales & Meyers, 1993). Most of the personal relationship advertisements lesbians write (98%) mention their age, whereas about three fourths of those by heterosexual women do. The heterosexual women are more likely to specify the age of a desired partner (Laner, 1979). Even when a woman is comfortable with her age, others may not be. One woman remarked, "I'm a lot more interesting than I was at twenty-five or thirty-five, but it's a lot harder to get anyone to pay attention" (cited in Doress et al., 1987, p. 81). Women themselves have countered these views by calling attention to the desirability and maturity of later years; some of them are poets with a special gift for expressing what many feel (A Closer Look 14.1).

Important changes are taking place in this country as the number of older people grows and assumes political importance. The AARP (American Association of Retired People) is particularly active and influential. Other organizations serving older people include OWL (the Older Women's League) and SAGE (Senior Action in a Gay Environment). Images of older people are starting to change, perhaps because of their growing numbers and their better health. In a 1991 study, college students attributed some positive characteristics to older women and men—characteristics such as being interesting, experienced, and friendly—although ageism generally was evident (Kite et al., 1991). It is likely to be a while before older people in this country have the respect they do in some other societies. In spite of the ageist pressures on women, women generally grow and develop as interesting people.

## *Personality and Social Development*

Development brings some changes in personality, and people relate to themselves and to the social world in different ways. Life span developmental theorists predict that some aspects of personality change because of the experiences a person is likely to encounter at different times of life. These are **normative changes.** For example, people are likely to change in some ways after the birth of a first baby.

It is not always clear whether changes are normative ones due to development or to cohort effects. A **cohort** is a group of people who have shared experiences because of some similarity among them, such as being born in the same era. For example, the experiences of people born early in this century are very different from the experiences of people born in 1970. What is true of those who were 30-year-olds twenty years ago and have now turned 50 may not be true of today's 30-year-olds when they turn 50. In addition, social clocks affect development (Helson, Mitchell, & Moane, 1984). **Social clocks** are expectations, specific to cohorts, about timing of major events, such as marriage, childbearing, and retirement. For example, the social clock previously held that women would be married and start having children in their early 20s. Recent cohorts have had different social clocks, as more women delay marriage and childbirth. Women do not necessarily follow the social clock, and each woman has her own life course. Still, we can identify issues about adult development within some broad patterns of change that have been shown over decades of life.

### The 20s Into the 40s: Control Issues

Longitudinal studies have demonstrated that people do become more mature and responsible during their 20s (Whitbourne, Zuschlag, Elliot, & Waterman, 1992). The pattern of change has been summed up as a time in which young women are taking control of themselves (Helson & Moane, 1987). Specific changes documented in women include increases in social maturity, self-control, social integration, and conventional femininity (Block, 1971; Freedman & Bereiter, 1963; Helson & Moane, 1987).

Daniel Guttmann (1985) maintains that the **parental imperative** requires gender differentiation of roles and self-concept in preparation for and during the parenting phase, with relaxation of differentiation in the postparental period. Longitudinal data do indicate that conventional femininity increases during a woman's 20s (Helson et al., 1984; Helson & Moane, 1987) and that during the parenting years women are the most stereotypically feminine and men the most stereotypically masculine (Livson, 1976, 1981, 1983).

Parenting can be hard work, requiring a mother to reshape her identity (chapter 10). Women in one study reported a bleak picture of their early 30s. They saw themselves as more disorganized, insufficiently rewarded, resentful, constricted, weak, and lonely. Overall, the 30s seemed to be a time of losing control of one's self (Helson & Moane, 1987). Is that a result of parenting? Some women face identity issues when parenting challenges their views of themselves and their world (chapter 12). Others may face many of the same issues when developing a career past the early, exciting days of "being on the way" professionally. Like mothers, they ask themselves, "Who am I? Is this what I want?"

Those tough early 30s pass, as all experiences and years do. The patterns of change suggested that the women increasingly became the persons they wanted to become (Helson & Moane, 1987). They became more mature and increased their interpersonal and cognitive skills by midlife. As involvement in parenting decreased, involvement in the worker role increased, until at age 42, it was higher than involvement in parenting (Figure 14.1). Most women showed decreased femininity (on the California Personality Inventory; chapter 3) and increased confidence and independence. Yet, by other measures, they showed an increase in attributes that could be seen as mature aspects of expressiveness and interrelatedness: a feeling of commonality with other people, nurture, and affability, with continued increases in complexity of views of self and others. They also became more organized, committed, and more work oriented and effective in their coping skills. More and more, middle-aged women are zestfully exploring the options for development that are continually opening up to women, and they are sending important messages to younger women.

## The Early 50s: Taking More Control

The "flower of youth" is not necessarily the prime of life. There is evidence across a range of societies, primitive and modern, that women's status or freedom from constraint increases when their children become adults (Brown & Kerns, 1985). At that time women have new freedoms, powers, and responsibilities. Valory Mitchell and Ravenna Helson (1990) suggested that the prime of life is in the early 50s. In their 50s most women have launched their children, and life at home becomes simpler. Energy previously directed to children is redirected to partner, work, the community, or self. Generally, health is good and income reaches a peak.

The women Mitchell and Helson (1990) studied graduated from an elite college (Mills College). More women who were predicted to be in their prime (average age of 51) reported their lives as "first rate" than did other women, though the differences among the three middle-aged groups (average ages 46, 51, 56) were not statistically

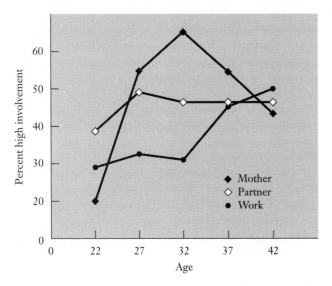

**Figure 14.1** *Percentage of women reporting high levels of involvement in roles of mother, partner, and work.* NOTE: Research participants were two thirds of the senior class (N = 140) at Mills College, a private women's college. Those born between 1936 and 1939 were studied first in 1958 or 1960, when they were 21, and then several times later. The figure shows the percentage (N = 105) of women reporting that they were highly involved in the roles of mother, partner, and/or worker. Highly involved is defined as a rating of 4 or 5 on a 5-point scale for involvement considering interest and time expenditure in the role. SOURCE: Helson, R., & Moane, G. (1987). Personality change in women from college to midlife. *Journal of Personality and Social Psychology, 53*, 176–186. Figure 1, p. 182, and information passim.

significant. The selectiveness of the sample must be kept in mind along with the fact that most of these women were following a white middle-class social clock: We cannot safely generalize the timing of the "prime" to other groups. However, the specific variables associated with seeing life as first rate may be relevant to the life satisfaction of other groups as well.

What factors contributed to a "first-rate" life in the Mitchell and Helson study? Good health and living only with a partner were especially influential, as were feeling financially comfortable (whatever the absolute income) and having high interest in sex, though less than previously. Generally, the women were engaged in the present and felt few negative feelings or need for change. They had an increased sense of autonomy and a joy in living. Although the women in the prime group generally said they had more control over their lives and used that control more than previously for their own wishes, they were not lacking in care of others. Mature care was shown in a sustained interest in family, friends, community, in care for parents, careers, and in caring for themselves. Other research also shows that people in their 50s, as well as those in their

*Many women experience their 50s as the prime of life, a time of freedom and control. This woman may have spent many years raising children and responding to the needs of others; now she has time to listen to her own needs as well.*

70s, see an "others orientation" ("being a caring, compassionate person, and having good relationships") as an important part of life satisfaction (Ryff, 1984). Yet, no time of life is best in all respects. Women in their early 50s regret their losses, accept their limits, and do not have as many intense highs or lows as they had in the past.

We do not know what the effects of delayed motherhood, greater opportunities for women, and greater diversity in social clocks will be. Some specifics may change or become more variable, but the relative pleasure of the 50s may remain. Having a sense of yourself, taking charge of your life, and adjusting to what you cannot control does take time. Although the 50s are being emphasized as a peak time, the self-knowledge, self-control, and self-esteem gained may last and even increase through later years (Diener, 1984); as discussed later in this chapter, people in their 60s and beyond do not just crumple up and die psychologically.

## Traditional Gender Roles

Satisfaction with one's self and one's roles depends in part on congruence with social norms. Norms change with age (Neugarten, Moore, & Lowe, 1965) and with social conditions (Ross, Mirowsky, & Huber, 1983). Nontraditional women who do not find their niche in earlier years generally show psychological growth during middle age (Livson, 1981). Whether this is a normative or a cohort difference is not clear. Cer-

**Table 14.1**   Change in Personality Scale Scores for Women of Different Degrees of
Traditionality, Ages 21 and 43

|  | *Age of women* | *Independence* | *Dominance* | *Self-control* |
|---|---|---|---|---|
| Nonmothers | 21 | 19.00 | 22.88 | 18.58 |
|  | 43 | 21.27 | 25.65 | 20.50 |
| Divorced | 21 | 19.73 | 23.42 | 19.81 |
|  | 43 | 21.84 | 26.65 | 23.38 |
| Neotraditional | 21 | 18.74 | 24.23 | 21.69 |
|  | 43 | 21.23 | 27.03 | 21.94 |
| Traditional | 21 | 19.29 | 22.59 | 24.35 |
|  | 43 | 19.64 | 22.47 | 26.00 |

*Nonmothers:* 17 never married and 12 married without children

*Divorced:* 30 mothers who had divorced, whether or not they had remarried

*Neotraditional:* 35 mothers in intact marriages and in the labor force more than one fifth of the time

*Traditional:* 18 women who were mothers in intact marriages and not engaging in paid work

NOTE: Personality measures are from the California Psychological Inventory (CPI).

SOURCE: Helson, R., & Picano, J. (1990). Is the traditional role bad for women? *Journal of Personality and Social Psychology, 59,* (2), 311–320. From Table 2, p. 316.

tainly, cohorts have experienced different social conditions. Having traditional values was socially rewarded in the 1950s and early 1960s. At that time young women with a traditional feminine orientation were better adjusted, higher in self-esteem, and more confident than their peers (Brown, 1956; Douvan & Adelson, 1966; Marcia, 1980). But such traditional women had lost this lead in psychological strengths by middle age (43 years). Many of the traditional, nonemployed homemakers had become dependent or reserved and generally did not show the gains in independence and dominance shown by other women, namely, employed mothers and women who were not mothers (Table 14.1).

Are differences in the earlier years relative to the present a matter of change in norms (essentially a cohort difference) or a change in what is healthy at different stages of life (essentially a normative change)? Or both? There is no simple answer so far. The effect of any role attribute will vary with its "fit" with the current demands of one's life, and the fit varies with both social norms and age. When being a homemaker is "out of fashion," there may be an increased number of rigid or dependent women in that role than when the role is in "high fashion" (Helson & Picano, 1990).

It is also true that becoming older may require *or* allow more flexibility in role orientation than earlier years do (Cooper, Chasson, & Zeiss, 1985; McGee & Wells, 1982; Rotheram & Weiner, 1983). As women approach the empty nest period, those who do not move toward androgyny tend to be more submissive and dependent during the parenting years, continue a "rigid" femininity during middle age, and are more likely not to be making a healthy adjustment. As noted previously, Mitchell and Helson (1990) found that women with "first-rate" lives reported the importance of an intimate relationship along with a sense of autonomy.

In any case, the relationship between gender role orientation and satisfaction varies with age, but it grows stronger as the years go by. A study of three generations of Mexican American women and men found that less traditional role orientations were positively related to psychological well-being, with the relationship stronger among the older generations (Markides & Vernon, 1984). In another study, androgyny was found to be a better predictor of life satisfaction for older married adults (average age 57 years) than for younger married adults (Blanchard-Fields & Friedt, 1988). (For another look at gender roles, see Focus on Research 14.1.)

Again, it must be emphasized that the effect of any personality style or adoption of gender role characteristics varies both with the age of the woman and with the environment within which the relevant characteristics are displayed (Cartwright & Wink, 1994). Here and now, it appears that traditional gender characteristics are not associated with the personality growth of women as they move into middle age and beyond.

## Body Changes

Just as we develop personally and socially, we also develop physically. Physical development from birth through adolescence is seen as desirable and healthy, but physical development during the adult years is, unfortunately, seen as ageing and something to be avoided, if only it could be. Yet it is just as normal for hair to turn gray and wrinkles to develop during midlife as it is for pubic hair to appear and breasts to develop during puberty. Cultural attitudes favoring youth make the physical changes of adulthood seem negative. Some physical changes, which we discuss here, are relatively specific to women.

### Menopause

Both women and men experience the **climacteric,** a gradual process usually occurring between ages 45 and 65, which includes changes in hormonal output, metabolism, and efficiency of physiological functioning. Some men show fatigue, concentration difficulties, depression, and decreased interest in sex (Kolodny, Masters, & Johnson, 1979). Sexual activity declines, and erection requires more time (Mulligan & Moss, 1991). Women's climacteric has captured more scientific and public attention. It includes an obvious dramatic event, the menopause, popularly called "the change of life" or simply "the change."

**Menopause** is the date of the last menstrual period. But since a woman cannot be sure of which period will be her last, the menopause, practically speaking, is considered to have taken place when 2 years have elapsed since the last menstrual period (Reitz, 1981). The average age of women when they have their final period is about 50, but menopause may occur as early as the late 30s and as late as the late 50s (Beck, 1992; Office of Technology Assessment, 1992). The time before menopause, when the body is becoming ready for the last period, is called the **perimenopause.** During this time most women experience some changes in the regularity, the length, or the amount of their menstrual flow. When the ovaries no longer produce enough hormones to release eggs or build up the uterus, both ovulation and menstruation eventually stop. However, the ovaries usually continue to secrete small amounts of estrogen for 10 years or more after menopause (Boston Women's Health Book Collective [BWHBC], 1992). In addition, when estrogen from the ovaries begins to decline (when a woman is about 25), the adrenal glands gradually take over the production of estrogen.

Negative language about the cessation of menstruation echoes the language used about menstruation itself as "the curse" (chapter 6). Words used about menopause (e.g., *change* of life) reflect a basic identification of women with their ability to reproduce (Chrisler, Torrey, & Matthes, 1990; Zita, 1993). According to *Physicians Weekly*, menopause has a "wake of deadly and debilitating ills" (Kerr, 1992, p. 1). Other references to it include "ovarian failure," "vaginal atrophy," "degenerative changes," and "estrogen starvation." Yet medical people do not refer to "testicular insufficiency" or "senile scrotum" (Reitz, 1981, p. 73).

Research on menopause has paralleled that on menstruation, showing similar methodological biases springing from the underlying view that menstruation and menopause are bad things (chapter 6). A negative biomedical view continues to predominate in the research literature in recent years (1984–1994; Rostosky & Travis, 1996; Focus on Research 14.2, p. 498). Some studies deal only with those women who seek treatment and therefore cannot be expected to be representative (McGrath, Keita, Strickland, & Russo, 1990; Office of Technology Assessment, 1992). Some studies do not distinguish between women who have had surgical menopause (hysterectomy) and natural menopause. Many studies have used measuring instruments that allow women to report only negative experiences, without taking other current life events into account.

***Signs, Not Symptoms***    Symptoms are changes due to illness or disease. Menopause is not an illness or disease. It is a bodily change, with some visible signs (BWHBC, 1992). Cessation of menstrual periods is the only sign that occurs in *all* women. Two other signs are generally but not invariably associated with menopause: hot flashes and vaginal changes (Doress et al., 1987).

**Hot flashes** are sensations of heat due to the irregular dilation and constriction of blood vessels. Skin temperature often rises 4 to 8 degrees, and the body's internal temperature drops because of the lost heat. Hot flashes are related to estrogen decline, but how and why is not clear. They may begin while the menstrual cycles are still regular (Kronenberg, 1990). Some women never have hot flashes, and some women have them off and on as late as their 80s (BWHBC, 1992). Estimates of the percentage of women who experience them range from 24% to 93% (Kronenberg, 1990). The estimated range of women seriously bothered with them is smaller: 10% to 15% (BWHBC, 1992; Doress et al., 1987). Prevalence also varies with culture. For example, women from Western cultures report more hot flashes than Japanese or Indonesian women (Flint & Samil, 1990; Kaufert, 1990).

Though hot flashes are just a nuisance for many women, other women are embarrassed by them, fearing that they are neon signs flashing "the change" to other

## 14.1  Participant Observation: Mexican American Women Reshape Their Roles

As you enter the room you check your pocket; yes, the tape recorder is ready. Scanning the crowd, you see your homework has paid off; from your hairstyle to your shoes, you look like everyone else and will be able to blend in easily. You remind yourself to copy others' body language and match their style of speaking. You want to gain their trust in the hope that they will reveal information important to you.

What is going on here? Are you a social scientist or a secret agent? Actually, this scenario is pretty typical of the participant observation method of research. Participant observation is a type of field research that produces qualitative data, the kind of answers that are not easily transformed into numbers. The researcher tries to become part of the lives of the people under study, spending time or even living with them in their world.

Researcher Norma Williams adopted the participant observation method to study how married Mexican American women shaped their self-identity as wives and workers (1988). Williams wanted to know if the traditional stereotype of the passive Hispanic woman who follows the lead of her husband really reflected today's working-class and professional Mexican American women of early to late middle age. By becoming a participant observer, Williams gained entry into areas of these women's lives and experiences that a questionnaire or a laboratory-based study could not.

In a field study researchers can play various roles, ranging from complete observer, to observer-as-participant, to participant-as-observer, to complete participant. As a complete observer, the researcher is detached, watching the behavior or event from the outside, without becoming a part of it. The researcher may be unobtrusive and unnoticed by the actors, or she may announce her role. (This latter approach is similar to direct observation, except that the data gathered are qualitative.) In the observer-as-participant role, the researcher identifies herself as such and "passes through" the event under study but makes no attempt to truly participate. For example, the researcher studying occupational stress might live at a fire station, go out on calls with the squad, and accompany an injured firefighter to the hospital, but would not participate as a firefighter. In the third option, participant-as-observer, the researcher does take on the role of participant but, at the same time, identifies herself as a researcher. To study the political process, a researcher may work as a campaign volunteer while making no attempt to hide her recording of behavior and events. Finally, the researcher may play the role of complete participant, keeping her identity as a researcher from the people she is studying.

In selecting the appropriate mix of participation and observation, the researcher must weigh ethical considerations and the value of the research. Becoming a complete participant involves deceiving those you are studying, but if the group is closed to outsiders, this may be the only way to gather information. Also, as a participant the researcher may actually change the event or group she is attempting to study. Becoming overinvolved can also bias the information the researcher gathers. On the other hand, if the researcher announces her intentions to the group, people may change their normal behavior, thus invalidating the research. As a complete observer the researcher is unlikely to be privy to inside information and may misinterpret (or miss altogether) important aspects of the event or behavior.

In her study of Mexican American women, Williams chose the observer-as-participant role; she announced her identity as a researcher but participated as a friend in the social lives of the women and their husbands. To do this, she needed to pay particular attention to dress, manners, and social expectations of the working and professional classes in the Mexican American community. Williams notes that she felt strongly about reciprocity in her field work; in return for the rich information her respondents provided, she felt morally obligated to assist them when they asked for her advice.

The information Williams collected revealed that Mexican American women were indeed reshaping their social identities; the professional women had moved farther away from traditional stereotypes than had the working-class women. At one end of the spectrum, Williams identified women who reluctantly maintained their husbands' expectation that they play the traditional role of homemaker and mother while working full-time; these women expressed private concerns about this role, but in the interests of harmony they had not challenged their husbands. At the opposite end of the spectrum were women who considered their careers to be more important than their husbands' needs and expectations. The majority of the women fell in the middle of the spectrum, trying to balance identities as mothers and career women and find a balance between their culture's traditional expectations for women and their own striving for personal identity.

How valid and reliable are data gathered through participant observation methods? Compared to questionnaires and experimental methods, field research appears to tap directly into meaningful behaviors through illustration. When the research provides an unambiguous answer for the question it was designed to address, we say that it shows internal validity. Participant observation also yields fairly good ecological validity: We get a generally accurate picture of how people usually act by observing them in natural settings. However, we must be aware that while the participant-observer tries, to varying degrees, to be unobtrusive, the mere presence of an observer may change the research participants' behavior. The external validity of participant observation or other field study methods can be problematic. This type of validity deals with the generalizability of the findings. Does what Williams learned from her respondents apply to all Mexican American women? The personal relationship of the researcher and the respondents that makes participant observation so unique can also produce results that would not be found with any other researcher or respondents. We can't be sure that the information we've collected is valid for any group other than the one that participated in this study. Despite these disadvantages, participant observations such as Williams' give enormous insight into behaviors and events that are not easily captured by other research designs.

JILL BORCHERT ◆

SOURCE: Williams, N. (1988). Role making among married Mexican-American women: Issues of class and ethnicity. *Journal of Applied Behavioral Science, 24*, 203–217.

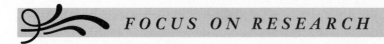

## FOCUS ON RESEARCH

### 14.2   Archival Research: The Meaning of Menopause

Is our Western culture concerned about menopause? It is certainly not a topic most people are comfortable talking about—that is, unless one is a scientist; then it seems to be of utmost importance. In the 10 years between 1984 and 1994, over 9000 science-based journal articles were published on the topic of menopause. That is an average of 900 articles every year, or 75 articles every month, or nearly 20 articles every week. Something important must be going on.

The existence of all of these articles on menopause piqued the curiosity of researchers Sharon Rostosky and Cheryl Travis (1996). Who was so interested in menopause, and what were they saying about it? Combing through the electronic databases for the years 1984–1994, they found that the majority of the articles (9018 to be exact) were published in medical journals; another 227 articles appeared in social science journals. Of this total, 94% dealt with the medical aspects of menopause, mainly hormone replacement; the remaining 6% dealt with social or psychological factors, mainly depression or mood. Overwhelmingly, Rostosky and Travis found, researchers who wrote about menopause took a medical perspective and investigated treatments for this "disorder," which is seen as a deficiency and as problematic for most women.

To answer their question about the historical perspective of menopause research, Rostosky and Travis turned to the existing body of data available through electronic sources. Their investigation is an example of archival research. Other archival sources might be census data, newspapers, marriage records, or letters and diaries; in short, just about any stored records offer information that can be used to answer research questions.

An advantage to archival research is accessibility: The data have already been collected. Another advantage is that many archives, such as the U.S. Census data, are more complete than any data that could be collected in a single research study. Another advantage is that the measures are unobtrusive. Participants do not know they are being studied and therefore do not change their behavior or their answers to questions. Unobtrusive measures are nonreactive: They do not change the behavior they are measuring.

Disadvantages to using archival data also exist. Information may be lost over time. The quality of record keeping can change with time, causing an unsuspecting

people. The flashes may pose health problems for some women—for example, by interfering with sleep. For others, they may be a blessing—one woman reported that she dreaded getting out of bed on a cold winter night to go into a cold bathroom, "Then I had a hot flash, and, all of a sudden, it was very easy to leave my warm bed" (cited in Doress et al., 1987, p. 121). She appreciated her nighttime hot flashes the rest of the winter!

researcher to infer that changes have occurred when in actuality none have. Computers, for example, allow better record keeping by police. As a result, some crimes may appear to have increased, but in actuality it is only being recorded more precisely.

After identifying a source of existing information that could answer their research question, Rostosky and Travis compiled their sample: The "participants" in their research project were the actual studies published between 1984 and 1994. First, the general characteristics of each study were noted, with the discovery that most were medically oriented and had a negative view of menopause.

Next, Rostosky and Travis examined the research methodologies of these studies. They identified a number of methodological flaws that called into question the results of this group of studies, including vague or nonexistent operational definitions of variables, a lack of baseline data, a lack of control groups, and an overgeneralization of findings. While these flaws can be used to challenge the results of the individual studies, taken as a whole, they also challenge the credibility of the medical model of menopause. And yet, despite these biases, Rostosky and Travis note that these studies and the medical model of menopause still have a tremendous impact on our cultural stereotypes of the menopausal experience. This research portrays menopausal women as diseased and deficient, with biological processes that are pathologically different from the "normal" development of men. Confronted by this stereotype held by the public and the medical community, women themselves may weave this negative image into their self-concept. Rostosky and Travis argue for alternative models of menopause that focus on the meaning women themselves give to the normal menopause experience.

Archival research such as this historical investigation of scientific perspectives on menopause makes an important contribution to science. Good research need not include only living participants; sometimes written records provide invaluable information. Rostosky and Travis's investigation allows us to see how the scientific community has viewed menopause in the past; this may generate more studies using archival data or suggest a project involving women's current experiences.

JILL BORCHERT ◆

SOURCE: Rostosky, S. S., & Travis, C. (1996). Menopause research and the dominance of the biomedical model 1984–1994. *Psychology of Women Quarterly, 20,* 285–312.

---

The second common sign of menopause is vaginal change, namely, thinning of the vaginal walls, loss of elasticity, shortening or narrowing of the vagina, and dryness or itching. Again, clear links to estrogen decline are lacking. Many women have vaginal changes long before or long after menopause, or never (BWHBC, 1992). Some women unrealistically fear that menopause will bring an end to sexual activity. In fact, most women (80% in one study, Starr & Weiner, 1981) reported either no change in sexual activity or an improvement in sexual activity. Heterosexual women no longer need concern themselves with pregnancy (Butler & Lewis, 1982; Neugarten, Wood, Kraines, & Loomis, 1968). Pregnancy concerns are not the whole story, though we do not know what the whole story is: About the same percentage of lesbians as heterosexual women report no change or increased sexual appetites (Cole & Rothblum, 1991).

*What Are the "Problems"?*    Part of the cultural myth, and a legacy of the motherhood mystique (chapter 12), is that a woman who can no longer bear children is "over the hill" and, without a useful reproductive system, will have a physical and psychological breakdown. Women themselves do not see it this way. Very few women (5% to 15%) find the signs of menopause severe enough to cause them to seek medical assistance (Brody, 1992). Most women show no difference in number of physical problems from the time before menopause to after and do not consider menopause distressing (Black & Hill, 1984). Generally, evidence does not show increased depression, irritability, or mood swings related to menopause (Matthews, Wing, Kuller, Meilahn, & Kelsey, 1990; Office of Technology Assessment, 1992; Sprock & Yoder, 1997; Strickland, 1988). Women describing their own experiences with menopause often say things such as, "It was nothing" (Martin, 1987), and the majority see it positively because they no longer have the nuisance of menstruation.

Women generally are not more likely to become depressed during menopause than other times (Ballinger, 1990; Sprock & Yoder, 1997). Women who do become depressed at this time have a history of depression (Hunter, 1990) or have multiple worries and role demands. The most marked increases in distress have been associated with social stress, such as that caused by adolescent children, ailing husbands, and ageing parents (McKinlay, McKinlay, & Brambilla, 1987). Probably because of the association with stress and the resources for dealing with it, higher education and social class are associated with lower negative effects (Bart & Grossman, 1978; Lennon, 1987; Office of Technology Assessment, 1992). Generally, life stress is more strongly associated with depression at the time of menopause than menopause itself is. Working-class women, who tend to have physically demanding jobs and few resources, and women who are low in self-esteem and satisfaction with life before menopause are more likely to be distressed (Bart & Grossman, 1978). Surgical menopause (hysterectomy) is more distressing than naturally occurring menopause (McKinlay et al., 1987).

## Hysterectomy

Some women have menopause quickly and earlier than they ordinarily would because they have had a **hysterectomy**—the removal of the uterus—though some women have the procedure after menopause. Nearly 4 in 10 women will have a hysterectomy before they reach age 60 (Office of Technology Assessment, 1992). The average age of women having hysterectomies is about 43 years. Frequently, hysterectomy is done along with **oophorectomy** or **ovariectomy**—removal of the ovaries (National Center for Health Statistics, 1987). Hysterectomy and oophorectomy can be medically necessary and, because of that, sometimes are performed on postmenopausal women as well as premenopausal women. Many argue, however, that hysterectomies are not always necessary or the best treatment (BWHBC, 1992; Doress et al., 1987; Office of Technology Assessment, 1992).

Ironically, many hysterectomies are performed just before menopause, although menopause itself often resolves some problems. Heavy or extended bleeding, for example, can be a sign of approaching menopause in some women, and of course, it ceases in the course of normal menopause. But it is frightening to some women and to their physicians for the realistic reason that in a minority of cases, it may be a sign of cancer (BWHBC, 1992). In addition, the unpredictability of menstrual periods before menopause can be disturbing because of fear of accidental pregnancy; the fewer contraceptive options advisable for older women can add to a woman's susceptibility to have a hysterectomy.

Other countries criticize the United States for the prevalence of hysterectomies. The rate has declined slightly since 1975, but professionals still disagree about its appropriateness (Office of Technology Assessment, 1992). In countries with socialized medicine the rate of hysterectomies is half that in the United States. In the United States, insured women, both rich and poor, have much higher rates of all kinds of surgery than the uninsured (BWHBC, 1992). Surgeons often advise removing the ovaries along with the uterus, "as long as we're in there." Women's groups recommend that healthy ovaries not be removed, because not enough is known about the ovaries' contributions to general health (Doress et al., 1987).

For premenopausal women who want to have children, the loss of the uterus is a dramatic, depressive event; for those not wanting children, it is a relief (Woods, 1984). For both premenopausal and postmenopausal women, many physicians do not warn patients of possible side effects of hysterectomy, such as fatigue, memory loss, loss of sexual feeling, depression, insomnia, and vaginal dryness. A sizable percentage of women who have hysterectomies (33% to 46%) report difficulties with sexual arousal and orgasm, especially if an oophorectomy is also performed (Zussman, Zussman, Sunley, & Bjornson, 1981). The absence of the cervix and uterus deprives some women of sensations that may be important for arousal and orgasm (Morgan, 1991). Removal of the ovaries can reduce sex drive because women's testosterone is mainly produced by the ovaries, and the absence of ovarian estrogen can lead to vaginal dryness. Androgen replacement therapy may be helpful for some women (BWHBC, 1992). Some husbands have difficulties adjusting to their wives' surgery, which, in turn, affect the woman's adjustment to surgery. Thus some women report a deterioration of their sexual relations, but almost as many report improved sexual responsiveness (37% versus 34%).

More women are depressed (70% in one study) after hysterectomy than after other operations (Amath, 1978). There may be physical reasons for the depression yet to be understood, but other possibilities are rage about loss of sexual feeling or from concluding that the surgery was unnecessary. Some women, of course, are pleased with the outcome, especially if cancer was a reality or a possibility (Morgan, 1991). A big message is that women should be informed about possible consequences before they decide that medical intervention is warranted. Getting a second opinion is advised.

*This grandmother has probably "grown shorter" over the years due to osteoporosis. Consuming enough calcium, avoiding nicotine and caffeine, and engaging in weight-bearing exercise can help her granddaughter continue to build bone mass and her daughter retain the bone mass she already has.*

***Bone Loss and Osteoporosis***    Like menopause, the loss of bone tissue is a part of normal physical development (Exton-Smith, 1985). Bone loss begins in the late 30s, accelerates in the 50s for women especially, and slows by the 70s (Avioli, 1982; Heaney, 1982). Women's bone loss, speeded by loss of estrogen, happens at about twice the rate of men's and has more severe consequences because women have less bone than men to start with. Thus, older women are more susceptible to severe bone degeneration— called **osteoporosis**—the leading cause of broken bones in women (Exton-Smith, 1985). It is estimated that at least 65% of women over age 60 and virtually all women over age 90 are affected (Maier, 1988).

Although more women than men are affected by osteoporosis, it is not completely apt to speak of it as a woman's disease. First, as just noted, men also lose bone mass. But because they die earlier than women, most do not live long enough to develop osteoporosis. Second, it is not a woman's disease as much as it is a disease of particular thin white women (Avioli, 1982; Greenwood, 1992). The rate is much greater in whites than in African Americans, apparently because African Americans produce more of the hormone calcitonin. Osteoporosis occurs more often in white women who are fair-skinned, thin, and small-framed. The risk of osteoporosis for women of Hispanic, Mediterranean, or Jewish ancestry is between the low risk of African American women and the high risk of Northern European white women and Asian women. Other risk factors are lack of exercise, deficiencies of calcium and vitamin D, smoking, high-protein diets, and excessive intake of alcohol, caffeine, and sodium (Exton-Smith, 1985). Middle-class women are more likely to be affected than working-class women, perhaps because of more on-the-job exercise in working-class women's jobs. Smoking is thought to interfere with estrogen production ("Bones go up in smoke," 1994). Until recently, the relationship of estrogen to bone loss was not clear, as it was thought that bone tissue had no receptors for estrogen (Maier, 1988). However, recent evidence shows that a different kind of receptor exists than was previously thought (Mosselman, 1997; Moudgil, 1994), and it is now fairly clear that replacing estrogen retards bone loss (Ivey, 1995).

***Hormone Replacement Therapy***    Given some of the effects of menopause, such as osteoporosis and heart attacks, which increase after menopause, replacement of lost estrogen seems to be a good idea. In the 1940s physicians began to use **estrogen replacement therapy (ERT)** rather freely in spite of the lack of adequate research (BWHBC, 1992; Doress et al., 1987). In the 1970s evidence started indicating that ERT increased the risk of endometrial cancer (cancer in the lining of the uterus; chapter 6), gall bladder disease, and possibly breast cancer.

With increased research efforts by pharmaceutical companies, alterations in prescriptions, and evidence about deaths related to osteoporosis, ERT came back in favor in the 1980s. Changes have included prescribing progesterone (generically called progestin or progestogen) in combination with estrogen. The prescription of progesterone and estrogen is known as **hormone replacement therapy (HRT).** At present, determining the "correct" prescription is as much art as science.

No one can say whether any given woman will benefit from HRT. HRT reduces hot flashes and the rate of bone loss, as well as allowing the vaginal walls to remain moist, and it does not increase the risk of endometrial cancer (Ivey, 1995; Rothert, Holmes, Rovner, Schmitt, & Talarzczyk, 1992; Sarrel, 1990). Some authorities say it decreases cardiovascular disease but increases breast cancer (Office of Technology Assessment, 1992). Others point out that for older women generally, the risk of heart disease is considerably greater than the risk of breast cancer and osteoporosis (Brody, 1992).

## Breast Cancer

Breast cancer is not a normal change in women's adult development, but about 1 out of every 9 or 10 American women will develop breast cancer in her lifetime (Cowley, 1990; Kaplan, 1992; Office of Technology Assessment, 1992), and many more women live with the fear of it—it is the second leading form of cancer in women (after lung cancer). An estimated 44,300 deaths from breast cancer occurred in 1996 (American Cancer Society, 1996). The incidence of breast cancer increases rapidly between ages 30 and 50 (Grady, 1988). Minority women are less likely than white women to develop breast cancer, but their death rate has jumped, while that of white women has been relatively constant (Webb, 1994).

Breast cancer is a collective term for at least 15 different types of cancer, each with different growth rates and dangers (Doress et al., 1987). The overall survival rates are constantly increasing, especially with early detection. The overall survival rate within 5 years is 96% if the tumor is localized, 75% if it has spread into nearby regions, and 20% if it has spread to distant areas (American Cancer Society, 1996).

***Risks***    Risk factors for breast cancer include a family history of cancer (principally mother or sister) and the occurrence of a previous cancer (breast or other). Also possibly relevant are late childbearing (after age 30), early menstruation, late menopause, and a history of fibrocystic disease. Very little research has been directed toward risk factors that can be reduced or prevented. There is suggestive evidence that smoking and drinking alcohol reduce the body's ability to fight off cancer (Schatzin et al., 1987; Willet et al., 1987). Even moderate drinking increases the risk, especially among young women; the risk increases with the amount of alcohol consumed.

There is also sufficient information to point to fat intake and environmental toxins as having a causative role (Clorfene-Casten, 1993; National Women's Health Network [NWHN], 1993; Rennie, 1993). Countries with high average fat intake have higher mortality rates from breast cancer than countries with lower fat intake; high amounts of fat are associated with high estrogen levels. Experimental studies in this country have been impeded because of cost and biased assumptions that researchers could not do clean experiments because of faulty reporting by older women and lack of compliance by poor African American women (Rennie, 1993). (One study on nurses received a lot of publicity, but unfortunately the levels of fat intake used to compare "high" and "low" were not appropriate; Rennie, 1993).

Environmental factors also are strongly implicated in breast cancer (Clorfene-Casten, 1993). Women who work in the petroleum and chemical industries have significantly higher rates of breast cancer than the general public, and women living in counties with chemical waste sites have 6.5 times greater rates of breast cancer than women in counties without waste sites. The interests of policy makers, however, are more heavily weighted toward artificially manipulating women's hormones with drugs to prevent breast cancer—a form of blaming the victim.

***Detection***    Regular examinations to detect breast cancer early are crucial (Champion & Miller, 1992; Travis, 1988a), but they are not perfect and are underused. **Breast self-examination (BSE)** is a low-cost detection technique (A Closer Look 14.2). It is not, however, a magic answer. Most breast lumps (75% to 80%) are *not* cancerous, so there is needless worry; on the other hand, cancer may be present years before a breast lump can be detected (Doress et al., 1987; Strong & DeVault, 1997). Nevertheless, starting BSE in the 20s has several advantages, including simply getting in the habit, developing knowledgeability and confidence about how to do it, and getting to know one's breasts. Encouraging women to become comfortable with their bodies is itself enough to recommend it (chapter 11).

Surprisingly few women (about one fourth) take such a relatively simple precaution (Grady, 1988). Research about why so few women examine themselves has not been fruitful; many researchers have turned to exploring intervention procedures. One program trained women and sent monthly postcard reminders, giving rewards such as lottery tickets for BSE (Grady, 1988).

Another way to detect breast cancer is through mammograms—X-rays of the breast to detect lumps for further examination. The efficacy of mammograms is currently debated. So far it seems that women over 50 benefit from them, as shown in lowered death rates of 30% to 50% (BWHBC, 1993; Tabar et al., 1985). Mammography, however, does not affect survival rates for women under 50; this may be because it is less accurate for premenopausal women and because breast cancer may be more aggressive in them (Lavecchia, Negri, Bruzzi, & Franceschi, 1995; NWHN, 1993). Any woman who has had breast cancer is advised to have regular mammograms. Still, mammograms give both false positives and false negatives. Other forms of breast pictures are needed and are being developed (e.g., thermography, ultrasound).

Like BSE, mammography is underused because of fear, pain, cost, anxiety, embarrassment, and lack of strong physician recommendation (Stein, Fox, & Murata, 1991). Physicians are more likely to recommend a mammography to white women than to African American or Hispanic women (23% versus 7%; Gemson, 1990).

*Treatment*     When self-examination or a mammogram lead to a diagnosis of cancer, women have several options. **Lumpectomy** is the surgical removal of a lump along with some surrounding tissue. Radiation therapy takes time and may have negative side effects, though for some women it is desirable (Spletter, 1982). Chemotherapy is effective for some premenopausal women: Drugs are taken orally or injected to try to kill cancer cells in distant parts of the body (Fisher, 1991; Henderson, 1980a, 1980b), but much more research is needed. More research is also needed on hormone therapy to repress or eliminate estrogen in the body. Male hormones and tamoxifen are most commonly used and can give the same effects as surgical removal of the adrenal glands or pituitary gland to limit estrogen production.

**Mastectomy** is the surgical removal of the breast, previously thought to be the only way to deal with breast cancer. From 1970 through 1985 more than one and a half million women in the United States had some kind of mastectomy (Doress et al., 1987). Often, they were given a general anesthetic for a biopsy and awoke to find that one or both breasts had been removed by surgeons who thought time was crucial. Recently, mastectomy has been shown in most cases to be no more effective than removal of the lump only (Fisher et al., 1985a, 1985b; Fisher, 1991). Some women's health groups consider that a radical mastectomy (removal of the breast, underlying muscles of the chest wall, and lymph nodes) is seldom necessary (BWHBC, 1992; Doress et al., 1987).

Women who have a breast removed experience the emotional trauma of losing not just a part of their body but a part associated with sexuality and womanhood; they sometimes are angry, depressed, and grieved, and fear rejection (Kaplan, 1992; Travis 1988a; Woods, 1984). If the woman's relationship with a partner was good before the mastectomy, it is likely to remain so afterwards (Woods, 1984). Although most research has been on heterosexual women, the same is likely true for lesbians. One study found that 75% of women who had lost a breast reported no change or improved health, while 25% reported strong anxiety or depression (Schover, 1991).

Losing part of one's body can be expected to cause grief and a change in body image. Women are advised to recognize this and to recognize how society has emphasized this particular body part in defining womanhood. Is being a woman a matter of

## 14.2   Breast Self-Examination

All women over 20 should practice monthly breast self-examination (BSE) to assist in early detection of breast cancer. Examine your breasts when they are least tender, usually seven days after the start of your menstrual period. If you discover a lump or detect any changes, seek medical attention. Most breast changes are not cancerous.

For a complete BSE, remember these seven P's: positions, perimeter, **palpation,** pressure, pattern, practice with feedback, and plan of action.

1. *Positions.* The first part of BSE is a visual inspection while standing in front of a mirror. Examine your breasts with your arms raised. Look for changes in contour and shape of the breasts, color and texture of the skin and nipple, and evidence of discharge from the nipple. Repeat the visual examination with your arms at your side, with your hands on your hips, and while bending slightly forward.

   The remainder of the examination involves palpation of your breasts. Two positions are possible: *side-lying* or *flat.* The side-lying position is particularly recommended for women with large breasts: Lie on your side and rotate one shoulder back to the flat surface. You will be examining

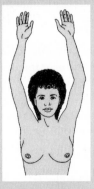

the breast on the side that is rotated back. If you use the flat position, place a pillow or folded towel under the shoulder of the breast to be examined.

2. *Perimeter.* The area you should examine is bounded by a line which extends down from the middle of the armpit to just beneath the breast, continues across along the underside of the breast to the middle of the breastbone, then moves up to and along the collarbone and back to the middle of the armpit. Most cancers occur in the upper outer area of the breast (shaded area).

3. *Palpation.* Use your left hand to palpate the right breast, while holding your right arm at a right angle to the rib cage, with your elbow bent. Repeat the procedure on the other side. Use the pads of three or four fingers to examine every inch of your breast tissue. Move your fingers in circles about the size of a dime. Do not lift your fingers from your breast between palpations. You can use powder or lotion to help your fingers glide from one spot to the next.

4. *Pressure.* Use varying levels of pressure for each palpation, from light to deep, to examine the full thickness of your breast tissue. Using pressure will not injure the breast.

5. *Pattern of search.* Use one of the following search patterns to examine all of your breast tissue:

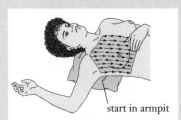

start in armpit

*Vertical Strip:* Start in the armpit and proceed downward to the lower boundary. Move a finger's width toward the middle and continue palpating upward until you reach the collarbone. Repeat this until you have covered all breast tissue. Make at least six strips before the nipple and four strips after the nipple.

*Wedge:* Imagine your breast divided like the spokes of a wheel. Examine each separate segment, moving from the outside boundary toward the nipple. Slide fingers back to the boundary, move over a finger's width and repeat this procedure until you have covered all breast tissue. You may need between 10 and 16 segments.

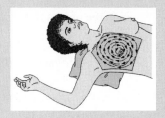

*Circle:* Imagine your breast as the face of a clock. Start at 12 o'clock and palpate along the boundary of each circle until you return to your starting point. Then move down a finger's width and continue palpating in ever-smaller circles until you reach the nipple. Depending on the size of your breast, you may need 8 to 10 circles.

Once you have completed the pattern, perform two additional exams: (1) squeeze your nipples to check for discharge (some women have a normal discharge), and (2) examine the breast tissue that extends into your armpit while your arm is relaxed at your side.

6. *Practice with feedback.* Have your BSE technique checked by your physician or another health care professional. Practice under supervision until you feel comfortable and confident.

7. *Plan of action.* Your personal breast health plan of action should include the following: (1) discuss the American Cancer Society breast cancer detection guidelines with your physician, (2) schedule clinical breast examination, and mammograms as appropriate, (3) do monthly BSEs, and (4) report any changes to your health care professional.

SOURCE: American Cancer Society. (1992, May). *Breast self-examination: A new approach.*

having a lot of estrogen and big breasts? Many women think that there is more to being the person they are.

## Family Relationships Over the Years

The nuclear family typically is considered the core of the family, extending to other people related by blood or marriage. Some people, such as those who are not with a partner or are with a partner of their own sex, build a network of supportive friends, assembling different kinds of families than paired heterosexuals do (Kelly & Rice, 1986). Unfortunately, even less research attention is paid to these families than to those based on blood relationships and marriage. For white and African American women and men (ages 24 to 65), satisfaction with family life and education are important predictors of life satisfaction (Carlson & Videka-Sherman, 1990).

Women are both more and less involved in family than men are. On the one hand, an older woman of a family typically is a **kinkeeper** (Troll, 1984, 1987a). She spreads family news, smooths relationships, and gets family members together. Daughters and granddaughters frequently are "in training" to take over the role, perhaps contributing to bonding between women (Troll, 1984). On the other hand, women have a wider social network outside the family than men do.

### The Empty Nest and Freedom

At some point in a mother's life, she is likely to see her offspring leave home, and the depression thought to occur at this time is part of what is called the **empty nest syndrome.** The terminology connotes loneliness and suggests that women's chief purpose in life is to bring up children, reflecting the motherhood mystique (chapter 10). Curiously, fathers who have been busy in the breadwinner role may regret the missed opportunities to become closer to the departing children (Rubin, 1980). In truth, research generally suggests that mothers whose children have left home are about as happy as or even happier than mothers of the same age with a child still at home (Long & Porter, 1984; Mitchell & Helson, 1990). When children do not leave on time or do not meet expectations, parents have a sense of strain and personal failure (Hagestad, 1984; Hagestad & Neugarten, 1986; Troll, 1985).

***Reactions to the Empty Nest***    The women who do show an empty nest syndrome are "supermothers" who have been highly involved with the mothering role and have few outside interests, because of personal dispositions or cohort effects (Adelmann, Antonucci, Crohan, & Coleman, 1989). For example, women who were in their young adulthood during the 1950s—the height of the feminine mystique (chapter 1)—had more negative reactions than those who were young adults during World War II, when women were in the labor force. Similarly, employed mothers have significantly fewer problems with an empty nest than nonemployed mothers (Frank, Towell, & Huyck, 1985; Powell, 1977).

Some women are content to be full-time mothers for a while but see motherhood as a phase of life rather than as a status defining their identity; they look forward to pursuing interests apart from mothering (Black & Hill, 1984; Long & Porter, 1984). Lillian Rubin (1979) studied 160 women from the working, middle, and professional classes who had given up employment after the birth of their first child. Although some of these women were frightened, lonely, or sad about their children's departure, they were not depressed. In fact, all but one woman felt relief. Most of these women got jobs and reorganized their lives. Rubin thought that the women's movement had helped many women open their eyes to the possibilities for the rest of their lives when the children left home.

This is not to say that women are ecstatic when the nest is empty. There is likely to be some grieving or introspection about a phase of life that is over. Yet, all in all, the evidence suggests that for most women, the time of the empty nest might better be named "freedom phase." One form of freedom is being able to devote more time and energy to the marital relationship, and some traditionally feminine women may, when the children leave, shift their attention and nurturing activities from children to husbands (Frank et al., 1985). Satisfaction with marriage, especially for women, increases after the launching of children (Rollins, 1989; White & Edwards, 1990), but some couples realize that they have not had anything in common except the children and have to reestablish a relationship, live together as "emotionally divorced," or separate and divorce (Fitzpatrick, 1984).

***Adult Children***    After children leave, most parents continue a caring, give-and-take relationship with them. Adolescents and adult children are amenable to adult conversation, they advise parents, and they feel intimate with their mothers especially (Blyth & Foster-Clark, 1987). Most middle-aged parents and their grown-up children see their relationship as positive and strong, though the parents rate the relationship somewhat more positively than their children do (Troll & Bengtson, 1982). Parents tend to see their young adult children as friends and are willing to help out financially when they can. The children benefit also from the parents' experience.

Support goes both ways. Divorcing middle-aged parents are likely to turn to their children and see them as more helpful than other family members (Hagestad, 1984; Hagestad, Smyer, & Stierman, 1984). Mothers are much more likely to seek support from children than are fathers. Many middle-aged mothers decide to go to college because their children urge them to, and middle-aged fathers change some of their ways at the urging of children. Of course, children do not necessarily approve of everything their parents do, and, on the parents' side, fathers sometimes complain about their sons' low achievement and their daughters' poor choice of husbands (Nydegger, 1986). Many families develop DMZs (demilitarized zones)—they have unspoken agreements about avoiding topics they know are potentially inflammatory (Hagestad, 1984).

## Mothers and Daughters

The mother-daughter bond should not be overidealized, but researchers do generally agree that it is the strongest of the parent-child bonds throughout life and the most active and complex (Boyd, 1989; Fischer, 1986; Neugarten, 1968; Troll, 1987b). Although conflicts and many changes occur in the relationship as both mother and daughter develop, the relationship generally becomes increasingly close, empathic, and mutual (Boyd, 1989; Fischer, 1986). Even when there is a gradual deterioration, daughters continue to be interested, concerned, and involved with their mothers.

The life circumstances of both the mother and daughter can influence the relationship (Boyd, 1989; Thompson & Walker, 1984). Distinctively women's experiences such as childbirth and menopause, and even mammograms and pelvic exams, can bring two women close, including mothers and daughters. As the daughter grows, however, she may develop interests that compete in time and energy with the relationship with her mother (Baruch & Barnett, 1983), and marriage can interrupt the mother-daughter attachment (Walker, Thompson, & Morgan, 1987). Nonetheless, evidence suggests what Troll called a "remarkable continuity" in mother-daughter relationships over the first 40 years of life. The final years of life may see an even stronger bonding of the mother and daughter when the mother, as a middle-aged woman, becomes a grandparent to her daughter's children and then, as an older woman, perhaps becomes dependent on her daughter.

## Grandparenthood

Grandparenthood may be a social transition point that marks a change from young adulthood to middle age rather than from middle age to old age (McGreal, 1994). Many women become grandmothers as early as age 40 (Kivnick, 1982) or even in their mid-30s (Burton, 1990). For most parents, becoming a grandparent is an exciting time, though grandparenting styles vary a lot in ways not yet well understood. Women especially appreciate the grandparent role for the pleasure and gratification it provides without the major responsibility for the child (Thomas, 1986a, 1986b). Given the relatively high rates of premarital pregnancy of African American teenagers, some African American grandmothers under age 40 are feeling unwelcome pressure to provide care for grandchildren; the grandparents over 60 value that caregiving role. African American grandparents generally want to live near their grandchildren but not in the same household (Jackson, 1986). Extended families in which child care is provided seem least typical of whites. Native American women (50%) and Latinas (32%) over age 60 are more likely than white women (14%) to report taking care of children (Harris, Begay, & Page, 1989).

Some people wonder whether grandparents or grandchildren "play favorites." Three generations with both male and female members leaves room for much complexity in patterned connections between grandparents and grandchildren. Although some evidence suggests a favoritism for the sons of sons (Baranowski, 1990), more evidence points to the importance of women in the intergenerational linkage (Eisenberg, 1988; Hagestad, 1978). Young adults (18 to 23 years) report closer relationships with their mothers' parents than with their fathers' parents and with grandmothers than with grandfathers; thus they are especially close to maternal grandmothers. Reasons for the patterns found so far are not clear. Do grandmothers encourage more closeness than grandfathers? Do grandmothers feel a special connection through their daughters? Do children extend their attachment to their mother through her to her mother? These issues call for further research, especially in light of changing family patterns.

*Children tend to have closer relationships with their grandmothers than with their grandfathers. With longevity increasing, this woman may even have a relationship with a great-grandchild.*

Divorce poses problems for grandparents as well as for parents (Johnson, 1988). Because of custody arrangements, grandparents may have trouble staying in contact with their grandchildren. Also, grandparents are more likely than previously to live far away from their grandchildren and to live independent lives. Another change is that grandmothers are more likely to be employed than in the past and so have their own interests apart from the family. Such facts may contribute to signs that grandparents are becoming increasingly detached from their grandchildren (Bengtson & Robertson, 1985; Rodeheaver & Thomas, 1986). This is unfortunate in view of what grandparents and grandchildren can give to each other.

Four-generation families are expected to increase as the 21st century comes and people live even longer than they do now. Great-grandchildren may provide psychological support through feelings of family immortality (Doka & Mertz, 1988). Most great-grandparents are proud of their status, although they have a distant relationship with the young (Wentkowski, 1985). Whether older people have great-grandchildren or not, increased longevity brings many women the challenges and joys of the later years.

## The Later Years

As women move through middle age into the later years of life, some things that always have been important retain importance: physical health, financial resources, marriage, sexuality, social relations with kin and friends, and a need for maintaining personal identity. At the same time, illness, widowhood, and living arrangements

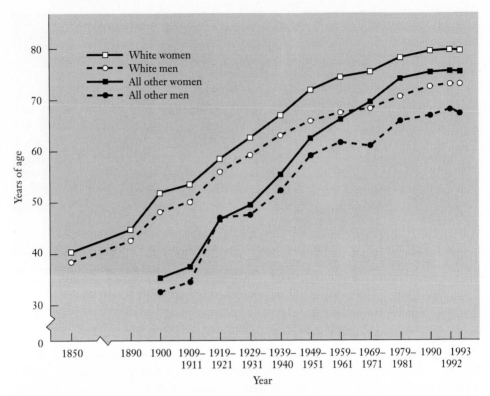

**Figure 14.2** *Differential longevity of women and men over time.*  SOURCE: Department of Health and Human Services, National Center for Health Statistics.

become issues with important implications for interpersonal relationships and personal self-definitions (Szinovacz, 1990).

Older women are the fastest growing segment of the population. What exactly does "older" mean? The most common definition of old age is being 65 and older (Cavanaugh, 1990; Schaie & Willis, 1991). Old people are sometimes divided further into the "young-old" (65 to 74) and the "old-old" (75 and beyond). Chronological age itself is a poor indicator of physical, social, psychological, economic, or mental conditions, but researchers like the convenience.

The number of older adults in the United States has increased steadily over the past century, and the proportion of the elderly is increasing more rapidly for minority groups than for whites (U.S. Bureau of Census, 1992a). There was a tenfold increase in older people between 1900 and 1985, from 3 million to nearly 30 million (Cavanaugh, 1990). By 2030, as the baby boomers reach old age, old people will make up about 17% of the U.S. population. The proportion of old people will increase in other countries as well, including Third World countries.

Older women outnumber older men, and the difference is increasingly pronounced at older ages (Figure 14.2). **Average longevity,** commonly called average life expectancy, refers to the age at which half of the individuals who are born in a particular year will have died. It has increased because of declines in infant mortality rates and better long-term care, and the increase is greater for women than for men. Males' greater vulnerability extends from early life (chapter 4) through older life. Because of increases in longevity, more people are retired and have more years in retirement.

## Retirement

Until 1935, when social security was started, most Americans did not have the retirement now taken for granted (Cavanaugh, 1990; Schaie & Willis, 1991). Women's retirement has not been well studied, perhaps because researchers have assumed that women did not work or that their work was not important to them (Szinovacz, 1990). The relevance of ethnicity to retirement has not been well studied either, although researchers show some ethnic similarities and some differences (Gibson, 1987, 1993).

*Decisions and Planning*   Women retire earlier than men and more often for what are called voluntary reasons (Grambs, 1989; Szinovacz, 1983). Many women are in low-status jobs, but lack of job commitment is not the reason for most women's retirement, though African American women are slightly more likely than men to retire because of job-related experiences (Gibson, 1993). A married woman typically retires because her husband has reached mandatory retirement age, is in poor health, or has sufficient financial assets (Campione, 1987; George, Fillenbaum, & Palmore, 1984; Szinovacz, 1990). Women's retirement is said to be voluntary rather than mandatory, but given the intertwining of lives in a marriage, the man's mandatory or elected retirement may amount to a mandate for the woman. This may be partly why women more often are uncertain about their retirement plans (Lopata & Norr, 1980). The poor health of elderly parents also is relevant because women tend to assume responsibility for parents, as discussed shortly, and may have to retire in order to do so (Szinovacz, 1986/1987, 1989). Marital status and degree of involvement with the role of wife and mother have little overall effect on women's satisfaction with retirement, whereas men who are divorced or widowed are less happy with retirement than those who are married or who never were married (Fox, 1979; Johnson & Price-Bonham, 1980). But women pleased with retirement often are happier with their marriages than before (Higginbottom, Barling, & Kelloway, 1993).

Planning for a typical 50% reduction in income is important in retirement decisions (Atchley, 1988). Women's retirement benefits are only 60% of those of men (Belgrave & Haug, 1987). This is no surprise, in view of women's generally lower pay and frequent absence from the workforce during childbearing years (Hayes, 1995). In addition, until recently, women have received smaller pensions than men in comparable jobs because women are expected to live longer. Even when only professionals are considered, among whites, African Americans, and Puerto Ricans, men have more pension coverage and more generous investment portfolios than women (Behling & Merves, 1985).

*Adjustment to Retirement*   People are generally satisfied with retirement except those with low income, poor health, and little education (Heidbreder, 1972). Within this general trend, women have more trouble adjusting to retirement or looking forward to it and take more time to adapt to it than men (Etaugh, 1993; Gee & Kimball, 1987; Szinovacz, 1983, 1990). This has been shown for people who were teachers and phone company employees (Atchley, 1976) and college faculty and administrators (Anderson, Higgins, Newman, & Sherman, 1978). As you might expect, women who do not want to retire do not adjust as well to retirement (Levy, 1980/1981).

Why do some women have trouble with retirement? There are many possible explanations, some more relevant for some women than others—individual differences are to be considered (Batchelor, 1990). Among these are lack of confidence in building a new way of living, stereotypes of old age, and reduced income. For many married women, the decision to retire is due to their husbands' rather than to their own desires (Gratton & Haug, 1983). Lack of career fulfillment or a sense of incompleteness is relevant for many women (Atchley, 1976). Some women have not been able to achieve as much in their careers as they could have because of moving (or not being able to move) for the sake of their husband's work. Thus they are prone to feeling, "I haven't done everything I could yet." Similarly, women who enter or reenter careers after their children have grown will just be starting to enjoy themselves as career women when their husbands are talking about retirement.

Women who continue their employment after their husbands have retired have lower levels of marital satisfaction than other women (Lee, 1988). This may be because wives do most of the housework, whether or not husbands are retired (chapter 13). If a retired husband continues to do little around the house while his wife is employed, it is easy to understand how her resentment might build up.

Some women may have chosen employment in order to get out of the house in the first place and are not eager to return to it (chapter 13; Vinick & Ekerdt, 1990). In contrast, some women, both previously employed and not, see the home as their domain and are not eager to have a retired husband invading it. At least a third of wives bemoan the fact that their husbands have too much time on their hands and intrude into the wives' household activities (Fengler, 1975). Husbands who have never done housework suddenly become experts on how to vacuum and shop for groceries, and they wonder how their wives have managed to get a meal together when the spices are not alphabetized. These are men who have not planned well for their own retirement and look to their wives for meaning.

Major life transitions are stressful even when they are eagerly anticipated. Women can reduce the stress of retirement by realistically planning about finances and about how to spend their time. Many retired people find volunteer work meaningful, such as in religious, charity, and civic organizations; they enjoy the sense of giving in a meaningful way and find outlets for their leadership and organizational skills as well (Bergquist, Greenberg, & Klaum, 1993). Women as well as men who have been strongly work oriented will find retirement traumatic if they do not find a meaningful substitute for paid work (Atchley, 1975; Lowenthal, 1972). Socializing is appealing to some women, and retired women are more involved in informal social interactions with friends and neighbors than are employed women (Fox, 1977). Women who were making plans for social activities after retirement looked forward to retirement more than other women (Johnson & Price-Bonham, 1980). Among African American retirees, fewer women than men said they missed people at work, but more women than men belonged to clubs and organizations (Jackson & Gibson, 1984). Both women and men enjoy social relationships, but women's pattern of greater interpersonal involvement (chapter 10) extends into the later years.

## Kin and the Social Network

Kin usually become increasingly close over the life span (Troll, 1987a). Research on both elderly African Americans and whites underscores the importance of bonds between adult children and elderly parents (Chatters & Taylor, 1993, 1994). Yet kin are not all there is to the social network of older adults, and having children does not make for greater life satisfaction (Glenn & McLanahan, 1981, 1982). Older people like contact outside of the family, and non-kin are an important source of companionship and practical assistance (Jayakody, 1993; Taylor, Keith, & Tucker, 1993). Some contacts are with friends and neighbors. Some are with others involved in voluntary organizations, including religious organizations: Older adults are more likely to be involved in religious groups than in all other voluntary social groups combined (Chatters & Taylor, 1994; Koenig, 1994). The older people exclusively involved with children and grandchildren have lower morale than those with an ample social life outside the family circle (Lee, 1988; Troll, Miller, & Atchley, 1979).

> It is good to have kin, particularly when you are in need, but it is also good to have friends with whom to share those thoughts and feelings that cannot usually be shared with children or parents. Your parents always remain your parents and your children always remain your children. Even when you are dying, I suspect, you try to represent a model for correct socialization if you are a parent. (Troll, 1987a, p. 760)

Gender differences in the nature of interpersonal relationships (chapter 10) seem to extend into later years (Antonucci & Akiyama, 1987, 1991; Taylor et al., 1993). Women consistently have been shown to have larger and more various networks and a larger variety of people in the network, with each serving several functions. Men's networks are more limited, often consisting of only a wife. Men are most likely to name their wives as their confidants, while women are not so likely to name their husbands (Lowenthal & Haven, 1968; Rubin, 1983). While older married men (aged 50 to 95) relied on their wives for support rather than on children and friends, women consistently reported getting more support than men did from children and friends; the differences were pronounced on "affective support," such as confiding, reassuring, and talking when upset (Antonucci & Akiyama, 1987, 1991). As women age, interpersonal issues come to involve issues about living arrangements.

## Living Arrangements

Abandonment of parents in their old age has been extremely rare (Cavanaugh, 1990; Troll, 1986, 1987). Although a view of the elderly "shoved away" to nursing homes is prevalent, only about 5% of people over 65 live in an institution, but 70% of those are women. Even by age 80, only about 20%, mostly women, are in a nursing home (Russo, 1990). Where are the other elderly? Most live in their own homes or in those of kin. The proportion of older adults living with children has decreased, but this is due largely to an ethic of self-sufficiency, together with the greater financial independence of the elderly, thanks to social security and pension plans (Lee, 1985). Both women and men prefer to live in their own homes, even after the death of a spouse, and are likely to do so until financial or health problems force a change (Markson & Hess, 1980; Troll, 1986). They value their independence and autonomy and do not want to impose on their children (Brody, 1985). Women are more likely to live alone; half (52%) of women over 75 did so in 1991, compared with a fifth (22%) of men (U.S. Bureau of the Census, 1992b).

When the elderly become ill or no longer able to care for their needs independently, they rely heavily on other family members, particularly children, and more so on daughters than sons (Chatters & Taylor, 1993, 1994; Koenig, 1994). Because middle-aged children are concerned about their parents and often about their own children or spouses as well, they have been called the **sandwich generation,** the **caught generation,** or **women in the middle** (Baruch, Barnett, & Rivers, 1983). Single people also can be caught: They are caught between their parents and their work or their own "family," or friendship network, and, in fact, provide more support for elderly parents than do married children (Stoller, 1983). Daughters are more involved than sons in direct caregiving and are just as likely as sons to be involved in managing the care by finding others to provide it (Chatters & Taylor, 1993; Jutras & Veilleux, 1991). Thus the phrase "*women* in the middle" is apt (Brody, 1985, 1990). Daughters of working-class parents are more likely than those of the middle class to be interdependent (Schaie & Willis, 1991; Stueve & O'Donnel, 1984). Middle-class parents and daughters, more than those from the working class, think parents can use services provided by people not in the family. Sons are not necessarily likely to step in if there are no daughters: In families with one child, daughters were more than twice as likely as sons to embrace caregiving (Coward & Dwyer, 1990).

Many elderly people (43%) do not have children living nearby; some (27%) have no living children (O'Bryant, 1988). And caring children often find they cannot meet all the needs of their parents. A nursing home can be the only choice. Some states are investigating the provision of in-home services that would allow older people to live in their own homes longer by providing hot meals, medical care, and help with housework ("Home services for elderly," 1992). The cost in dollars would be much less than the $20,000 to $60,000 now required for a year in a nursing home. The savings in terms of human dignity, freedom, and life satisfaction would be enormous.

When the elderly live with a child, the child is far more likely to be a daughter than a son (Finley, 1989). Older people also often live with a younger sibling, typically a sister (Ikels, 1989). Minority groups seem more likely to have a stronger sense of extended families and to care for older relatives; for example, African American women are twice as likely as white women to have relatives in their homes (Beck & Beck, 1989). Benefits of shared living include shared affection, security of having someone around, and help around the house. On the other hand, when people are used to doing things their own way, conflicts can occur (Cavanaugh, 1990). Living with an elderly person can be particularly burdensome when the older person is sick and needs extensive care.

The parent who is ill is more often the mother than the father, and the caregiver is more often a daughter than a son, though all combinations happen. Issues of ageing are increasingly women's issues. Taking care of a person with health problems is demanding, and even the most devoted loved one can have feelings of depression, resentment, and anger, and guilt about those feelings (Halpern, 1987). Impairment of mental functioning can be especially difficult to deal with. A common mental problem is **dementia:** a family of diseases involving cognitive and behavioral deficits, with some kind of brain damage. Some dementias are due to drugs or malnutrition and are treatable. Alzheimer's disease is the most common and well known example of dementia and is not reversible (Cavanaugh, 1990; Schaie & Willis, 1991). Most people with dementia are women, because of their greater longevity (Butler & Lewis, 1982; Cohen, 1988). Fifteen percent of people over age 65 suffer from dementia (Katzman, 1987), but the incidence increases rapidly with age: Twenty-five percent or more of persons over 85 have dementia. Even so, many people fear dementia needlessly, overreacting to mental or physical mistakes.

The majority of people with dementia (predominantly women) are cared for by family members (predominantly women) (Cavanaugh, 1990), who must change daily routines and watch the continual deterioration of their loved one. Caregivers become fatigued, angered, depressed, and suffer loss of friends and privacy (George & Gwyther, 1986; Gilhooly, 1984). Women who are caregivers often have to quit their jobs (Brody, Kleban, Johnsen, Hoffman, & Schoonover, 1987). Caregivers increasingly have options for relief, but the options are not available everywhere and are not necessarily covered by insurance (Cavanaugh, 1990).

## Widowhood

Women are more likely to lose a spouse to death than men are. Over half of all women over 65 are widows, but only 15% of men are (Cavanaugh, 1990; Schaie & Willis, 1991). The average American woman lives 10 to 18 years after the death of her husband. Most women seem to come to enjoy those years, but others have to deal with poverty and loneliness.

The death is followed by an immediate need for **grief work,** the psychological aspect of dealing with bereavement (Cavanaugh, 1990; Schaie & Willis, 1991). Grief work involves coming to terms with the sorrow, hurt, anger, guilt, confusion, and other feelings that arise after a loss. A woman who has been nursing a sick husband for a long time may feel relief and feel guilty about that. She also may feel anger toward him for endangering his life, toward doctors who "let" him die, or toward clerics who represent a deity who allowed the death. A death that is expected allows for anticipatory grieving, which, if not prolonged, is associated with fewer psychological problems and more rapid recovery after the partner's death (Cavanaugh, 1990; McGloshen & O'Bryant, 1988). In contrast, younger women whose spouses die are likely to face an unexpected death and have had no preparation nor role models for widowhood. Although the immediate impact may be harder on them, after about 18 months, the younger women are reshaping their lives in ways unrealistic for older women. Young widows often come out ahead financially. They receive child support from social security that may exceed what their husbands were providing or what divorced women get.

Financial and legal issues can complicate grief work for many women (Lopata, 1979, 1980). The husband's income or pension may be lost or reduced, in some states bank accounts can be frozen, and there may be large bills from a long illness and the funeral (Barrett, 1977). Because of the nature of social security and private pension plans, as well as their own likely lower wages if they were employed, many widows (40%) are in poverty for at least a while after their husband's death (Morgan, 1989). Some widows are resilient, but others remain depressed and anxious several years later, particularly those who derived their own identities from their husbands (Lopata, 1979, 1980; Wortman & Silver, 1989).

***Social Support and Independence***    Social support plays a crucial role in the grieving process of any partner (Diamond, Lund, & Caserta, 1987; Kalish, 1985, 1987). Lesbians who become widowed because of a partner's death often do not get as much social support as do heterosexuals. In addition, lesbians are legally vulnerable at all stages of life, including the last days (Ettelbrick, 1991). Relatives of a sick partner may "take over" or even deny a woman access to her partner during illness (Doress et al., 1987). If lesbians have not planned well with a lawyer, a surviving partner may find, as relatives legally take over, that assets that had been "ours" become "theirs."

Siblings and kin become more and more important in later adulthood and old age, especially to widows (Anderson, 1984; Cicirelli, 1981, 1986; Ross, Dalton, & Milgram, 1980). A widowed sibling can serve as an "advance role model," by sharing the bereavement and providing evidence that it is possible to survive (McGloshen & O'Bryant, 1988). Sisters seem especially important to women (O'Bryant, 1988). The more siblings, the better women are able to cope, even if they rarely see or call on the siblings for support (Cicirelli, 1980; Diamond, Lund, & Johnson, 1983). Just knowing they are there is important.

Most widows, when faced with the **enforced independence** of living without a husband, come to find that they can handle and even enjoy their more independent lives. The number of women who remarry is lower than that of comparable men. This is due in part to the smaller number of same-age potential marriage partners and the greater social latitude given men to marry someone younger and in part to the fact that many women (75% in one sample; Lopata, 1980) do not want to give up their new-found freedom and independence. Some widows also do not want to care for another sick spouse, and some fear fortune hunters. A cost of the independence is loneliness, a persistent problem for widows but not necessarily as severe as stereotypes suggest (Barrett, 1981; Essex & Nam, 1987). Some women turn their compassion, nurture, and care on themselves (Barrett, 1981); they become their own best friend by responding to their own needs and sharing their own thoughts with themselves. They are not psychologically disturbed; they are energetic, generous women with high self-esteem and joy in living.

***Widows' Needs*** Widows do have instrumental and emotional needs surpassing the needs of most people. After all, a spouse's death is the greatest stress psychologists have measured. Often overlooked is women's need to be needed, which was formerly met by their husbands (McGloshen & O'Bryant, 1988). Older widows (aged 60 to 89) were less lonely when they were in relationships in which they gave as much as they received (Rook, 1987), and they were more likely to have reciprocity with friends than with their children. Widows, like other people, want to be part of a social system in which they participate as givers as well as receivers. Many find that religion offers a chance to give and to receive.

Religion, for several reasons, can be an important means of coping with grief (Ball, 1976/1977; Ellison, 1994; Koenig, 1994; Levin, 1994; McGloshen & O'Bryant, 1988). First, religious involvement is a means of obtaining social contact; that itself is important. Second, participation in charitable activities of religious organizations can be a way of feeling useful. Third, religious involvement for some is important because of belief in a deity (McGloshen & O'Bryant, 1988); religion can give a sense of self-worth and a cognitive framework that can make some stressors seem less threatening (Chatters & Taylor, 1994; Ellison, 1994). Widows' participation in religious-based social activities (not worship) was associated with positive feelings, but not as much as was participation in worship. Religion gives some people a total life perspective, "which conveys some world order and spiritual sense" (Erikson, 1950/1963, p. 232).

Perhaps related to the sense of the spiritual is the phenomenon of the illusion, or sense, of the spouse's presence—physically, visually, auditorially, psychologically, or spiritually (Barrett, 1981; Marris, 1958; Parkes, 1970; Rees, 1971, 1975). Exact experiences vary widely, from verbal conversations with him to writing letters to him, or simply feeling his presence. Estimates of the number of widows in Western countries who have such experiences are around half (47%) or more (60%) (Kalish & Reynolds, 1974; Rees, 1971, 1975); the incidence seems higher in other countries, such as Japan. Many women (69%) feel helped by these experiences, but few (28%) tell anyone other than a researcher about them. Whether or not women have the experience is not related to their degree of social contact or history of depression—these women are by no means ill. They are experiencing a style of widowhood that they realize other people may not understand. And they are relieved to learn that their experiences are relatively common!

## Social Issues

The rapid increase in the number of elderly women means that there is an increasing number of experienced and able people to contribute to society. It also means an increase in social problems such as poverty and physical and psychological health concerns. Although most older people do not see financial problems as major, nearly one quarter of older people are categorized as poor or near poor, with more women than men among the poor (Atchley, 1988; Chen, 1985). The poverty rates for African Americans, Native Americans, and Hispanics are greater than for whites—the women at economic risk in younger years are also at risk in their later years.

*An afternoon hike is a good way for this woman to get some exercise and to spend some time with friends. Like so many older women today, she continues to lead an active life and contribute to the lives of others well beyond her childbearing years.*

In addition, women generally are more likely than men to have chronic diseases and to experience limitations in their activities because of chronic conditions such as arthritis and hypertension (Strickland, 1988). Health care professionals often are biased against women and minorities (Canady, 1994; Tomkins, 1991). African American women are distrustful and even afraid of the health care system because of its inadequate response to their needs (Aguwa, 1994; Edmonds, 1993).

Depressive symptoms and related deficits in self-esteem are prevalent in people over 65, especially among women (Berry, Storandt, & Coyne, 1984; Himmelfarb, 1984; Meeks et al., 1990). Problems with general anxiety are prevalent as well (Bliwise, McCall, & Swan, 1987). Estimating the number of women affected is difficult because many symptoms of physical illness can be similar to symptoms of anxiety or depression—for example, disturbed sleep or appetite, and heart palpitations (Gatz & Smyer, 1992). Older people today tend to consult physicians rather than mental health professionals about their psychological symptoms, and physicians are less likely to refer older adults to mental health services than they are younger adults with equivalent symptoms (Gatz & Smyer, 1992). Thus, relatively few older adults with psychological problems get mental health attention (George, Blazer, Winfield-Laird, Leaf, & Fishbach, 1988). Nursing homes, not prepared to deal with the mentally ill, nevertheless are a major destination for those who are mentally ill (Lair & Lefkowitz, 1990). More than 70% of the chronically mentally ill living in nursing homes are women (Russo,

1990). So far, professionals concerned with mental health and those concerned with ageing have not coordinated their efforts (Gatz & Smyer, 1992).

Future prospects are not bright. Rates of depression in older adults are expected to be much greater in 2020 than in 1990 because successive birth cohorts have *higher* rates of depression (Klerman et al., 1985). And more women will live long enough to develop Alzheimer's disease. Clearly the mental-health-care needs of older adults will grow. Conflicts over who receives government funds—the elderly or other segments of society (e.g., teenage parents and their children; chapter 12)—could become severe (Cavanaugh, 1990).

In spite of the problems of old age to be addressed, most women live active happy lives in their "twilight years" and continue learning, growing, and living. In the process, they make valuable contributions to society as volunteers and simply as interesting people with a vast storehouse of experiences and wisdom.

## Some Final Thoughts: The Development of Ego Integrity

Psychological and physical development doesn't stop after high school and college years. The joys, challenges, and sorrows of childhood, adolescence, young adulthood, middle adulthood are all to be appreciated and understood. So, too, are those of the later years. Although the early child-rearing years can be problematic for mothers, women in middle age seem to start becoming more the persons they had wanted to be. Their relationships with family and friends may change but remain important throughout life.

Kin are more likely to be caregivers of the elderly, with daughters more likely than sons to give the care. Older women have some health problems men do not; both women and men have mental health problems that are not being well served. As more people grow older, conflicts about the use of social resources will increase. It remains to be seen whether the elderly will be valued for who they are and for what they have given and can give to each other and to younger people.

In Erik Erikson's (1980, 1982) theory of personality development, each stage of life poses a crisis (challenge plus danger; chapter 13) to be resolved. Each stage builds upon earlier stages, and it is easier to settle the issues of one stage if those of previous stages have been optimally resolved. The developmental challenge of the last stage of life is to achieve **ego integrity** rather than **ego despair.** Integrity involves feeling whole and coherent, holding together a sense of "I-ness" in spite of physical and cognitive changes. It can be hard to maintain integrity when many familiar aspects of one's life are disappearing—spouse and friends die, the familiar body loses some of its functions, and independence and felt usefulness may dwindle. Such pressures may result in despair—being without hope and seeing no meaning in life.

A person with ego integrity embraces a life well lived. Disappointments are acknowledged, sins confessed, hurts felt. The fruits of previous stages ripen in the woman who accepts her life cycle "as something that had to be and that, by necessity, permitted of no substitutions" (Erikson, 1982, p. 61). What had to be, was, and was satisfying. A researcher who studied very old people in a nursing home commented that "a meaningful past helped make their present suffering more endurable" (Kahn, 1993). The meaningfulness sought by any woman involves a continual process of self-definition. One woman in the nursing home said, "The way I am is what I've been." Development is not complete at age 22, nor at the time of the empty nest, nor at retirement. Each of life's stages brings relatively distinct experiences, but development is continuous, so the experiences of each stage are related to those of the later stages.

Women today have more options at any stage of life than women of the past did. For now, this raises more questions than answers: What will today's women do with the increasing diversity of the choices they have? What will be the impact of their choices in their later years? Will they be comfortable looking back on their lives and saying, "This was *my* life, and a life well lived"? Will they have social support for their choices? Will the knowledge they accumulate over the years be considered more important than their wrinkles? Will a woman's wrinkles come to be a badge of honor? Let us hope the answers reflect positive confirmation of women's lives.

## KEY TERMS

ageism
double standard of
  ageing
normative change
cohort
social clock
parental imperative
climacteric
menopause
perimenopause
hot flashes
hysterectomy

oophorectomy,
  ovariectomy
osteoporosis
estrogen replacement
  therapy (ERT)
hormone replacement
  therapy (HRT)
breast self-examination
  (BSE)
mammogram,
  mammography
lumpectomy

mastectomy
kinkeeper
empty nest syndrome
average longevity
sandwich generation,
  caught generation,
  women in the middle
dementia
grief work
enforced independence
ego integrity, ego despair

## KEY POINTS

◆ This culture has a double standard of ageing, with women being discriminated against more than men.

*Personality and Social Development*

◆ Although they have matured since their early 20s, women in their 30s seem to "lose control of themselves." The 40s are a time of becoming the persons they wanted to become. People tend to show increased traditionalism in role behavior during the parenting years, but the middle years seem to call for, or allow for, more balance of attributes considered masculine and feminine.

◆ The early 50s have been identified as a prime of life, perhaps in part because women are more willing to make choices for themselves while still caring for others.

## Body Changes

◆ Cessation of menstruation is the only sign of menopause occurring for all women; hot flashes and vaginal changes occur for many women. Most women do not show increased physical or psychological problems because of menopause, though there are more negative effects of hysterectomies than of natural menopause. Thin, fair, white women are more prone to osteoporosis than are men and other women.

◆ HRT should be prescribed only after considering a given woman's history and current lifestyle. Although HRT reduces bone loss and hot flashes, it *may* increase the risk of breast cancer and endometrial cancer. It reduces the risk of heart disease and osteoporosis.

◆ The incidence of breast cancer increases after age 30, with women aged 50 and over more at risk than others. Heredity and lifestyle factors are relevant, as are environmental factors. BSE and mammograms can enable early detection, but relatively few women use them. Mastectomy is not always necessary in the treatment of breast cancer.

## Family Relationships Over the Years

◆ Family satisfaction is an important correlate of life satisfaction, but most women and men report the same or greater happiness and marital satisfaction after the last child leaves home compared to when children were at home.

◆ Influence and support between parents and children goes both ways, though mothers tend to look for support from their children more than fathers do. There is some evidence that the mother-daughter bond is the closest of all parent-child bonds.

◆ Becoming a grandparent now is likely to mark a transition from young adulthood to middle age. Grandchildren seem to feel closer to maternal grandparents and to grandmothers than to paternal grandparents and grandfathers.

## The Later Years

◆ Most people enjoy retirement years, but women have more trouble with retirement than men do. Older people typically want and have social support systems, and women have wider systems than men do.

◆ Elderly women are more likely to live alone than men are; parents are more likely to live with a daughter than with a son. Caring for aged people with dementia is hard on caregivers, who are more likely to be women than men.

◆ Women are more likely than men to be widowed because women live longer. Social support is crucial during grief work. Lesbians are less likely to get support than heterosexuals are.

◆ Widowed women are more likely than widowed men not to want remarriage. Siblings, especially sisters, are especially important to widows, and religious involvement is associated with widows' adjustment. Some widows emphasize becoming their own person, and some experience their spouse's presence in varying ways.

◆ Poverty rates are higher for those older people who have suffered discrimination previously—women, particularly minority women.

◆ Older people face problems of poor health but may not be taken seriously in the health care system. The incidence of both depression and dementia in the elderly is expected to increase in coming years. Public debate and controversy about providing resources for elderly people is highly likely.

## INTEGRATIVE QUESTIONS

1. Imagine yourself about to become a parent for the first time (or think back to that time). Think also of what you know about your parents when they became parents. What evidence do you see for or against the parental imperative? To what do you attribute any changes in adults as a function of parenthood?

2. Discuss how your experiences as you develop into old age may be similar to or different from those of current middle-aged and old-aged people (such as your parents or grandparents) because of cohort differences. What role do you see for normative changes in your development?

3. What reasons do you see for the tendency in our culture to (a) give women hormonal treatments to prevent heart disease and osteoporosis, (b) use hysterectomies more than other countries do, (c) assume that women get depressed with the empty nest? You might find it helpful to think also of practices with respect to pregnancy and childbirth.

4. Do you agree that women turn to their adult children for emotional support more than men do? Why? What is the relevance of early childhood experiences? You may use your own experiences as an example or counterexample if you wish.

5. Discuss your experience with your grandparents in light of this chapter's discussion of grandparenting and middle-aged and older people generally. What have you gained from grandparents? What do you think you have given them? Which grandparent do you feel closest to, for what reason?

6. Why do middle-aged and older people want non-kin social support even if they have biological children? Does the answer vary with the attentiveness of the children to their parents?

7. The age period of the 30s has been characterized in the text as a time of "losing control" for women. Compare and contrast that time of life with the period of old age.

8. If you had $100 billion to use on programs for the elderly, teenage pregnancy, prenatal and postnatal care, and health problems of women generally, how would you use the money? Be specific about the percentages going to each cause, the ways in which you would spend the money, and the reasons for your priorities.

## Chapter 15

# Women's Experiences of Violence

"*V*iolence is as American as cherry pie" (H. Rapp Brown, cited in Byrne & Kelly, 1981). In one year, Philadelphia had the same number of homicides as England, Scotland, and Wales combined. There are about 2 million people in Philadelphia and 54 million in the three countries. The general cultural aggression combined with stereotypical gender roles work together to facilitate aggression against women, but aggression against women has been a relatively neglected issue.

> If the leading newspapers were to announce tomorrow a new disease, that over the past year, had afflicted from 3 to 4 million citizens, few would fail to appreciate the seriousness of the illness. Yet, when it comes to the 3 to 4 million women who are victimized by violence each year, the alarms ring softly. (Senator Joseph Biden, 1993, p. 1059)

Men who are not violent with women are those who have resisted the strong pressures toward the aggressiveness of the masculine role. The problem of violence against women cannot be fully understood, let alone solved, by focusing only on the individual men who abuse women. Men are powerful with respect to women, but the power is given to them by society, and they use the power within a social context. "Only by changing the social and cultural institutions that have given rise to the problem can a lasting solution be achieved" (Goodman, Koss, Fitzgerald, Russo, & Keita, 1993, p. 1054).

The APA's first Task Force on Male Violence Against Women conceptualized the many forms of men's violence against women on a continuum (Goodman et al., 1993). All the behaviors involve men's abuse of power (physical strength, economic resources, or employment status) over women who have less power. At one end is men's actual use of physical force; at the other end are coercive behaviors backed by threat of the loss of something of value, such as one's children, a job, or an educational attainment. Thus not all violence is physical violence. Rape is the most dramatic and extreme form of violence against women and the form most researched. Yet the dynamics associated with rape are much the same for child abuse, wife abuse (not necessarily sexual), and abuse of women in the employment world in the form of harassment. Pornography is a cultural statement of the permissibility of men's violence against women at the very least, and at worst it feeds the violence. In this chapter we consider all these issues.

Before continuing, consider these questions for personal thought:

- ◆ Do you think women who have been raped have "asked for it" in any way?
- ◆ How might physical or sexual abuse during childhood affect a person in adulthood?
- ◆ Can you think of reasons you might stay in a relationship in which your partner abused you psychologically or physically? Would your answer be the same if the partner were a spouse?
- ◆ Are you flattered when you know someone is admiring your body?
- ◆ What would you do if a professor offered you a high grade in exchange for a date? What difference, if any, does the gender of the professor make?
- ◆ What similarities and differences do you see between rape and harassment?
- ◆ What do you consider "pornography"? Do you think that seeing porno-graphic material decreases or increases the likelihood of sexual violence?
- ◆ Should pornography be outlawed? What reasons do you see to argue that it should be? That it should not be?

## Rape: The All-American Crime

Susan Griffin (1971) called rape the "All-American crime." The United States has the highest rate of sexual assault of any industrialized country in the world. Rape is the most frequently committed violent crime and most reported of violent crimes, al-though no more than 12% of rapes are reported (National Victims Center, 1992). Not all men rape, but those who do have a profound effect on the lives of women (Griffin, 1971). Susan Brownmiller (1975), in her landmark book, *Against Our Will*, pointed out, "That *some* men rape provides a sufficient threat to keep *all* women in a constant state of intimidation [italics added]" (p. 209). Both Brownmiller and Griffin see rape not as a sexual crime but as an act of terrorism; men feel entitled to sex from women. Women worldwide report living their lives with the threat of sexual violation (Koss, Heise, & Russo, 1994). Men are raped too, but women are raped much more often (90% of rape victims are women), and women will be the focus here (Koss, 1990; Koss, Gidycz, & Wisniewski, 1987). See A Closer Look 15.1 for some comments on rape.

How many women are raped? No answer can be firm. Because relatively few sexual assaults are reported, researchers have used surveys in hopes of counting un-reported rapes. Still, specific estimates vary widely, depending in part on the exact kind of questions asked and the interpersonal dynamics of the interview, as well as the way the sample was recruited and the geographical locale of the sample (DeKeseredy,

## *A Closer Look*

## 15.1   A Comment on Rape

### Rape Poem

There is no difference between being
   raped
and being pushed down a flight of cement
   steps
except that the wounds also bleed inside.

There is no difference between being
   raped
and being run over by a truck
except that afterward men asked if you
   enjoyed it.

There is no difference between being
   raped
and being bitten on the ankle by a
   rattlesnake
except that people ask if your skirt was
   short
and why were you out alone anyhow.

There is no difference between being
   raped
and going head first through a windshield
except that afterward you are afraid
not of cars
but of half the human race.

The rapist is your boyfriend's brother.
He sits beside you in the movies eating
   popcorn.
Rape fattens on the fantasies of the normal
   male
like a maggot in garbage.

Fear of rape is a cold wind blowing
all of the time on a woman's hunched back.
Never to stroll alone on a sand road
   through pine woods,
never to climb a trail across a bald
without that aluminum in the mouth
when I see a man climbing toward me.

Never to open the door to a knock
without that razor just grazing the throat.
The fear of the dark side of hedges,
the back seat of the car, the empty house
rattling keys like a snake's warning.
The fear of the smiling man
in whose pocket is a knife.
The fear of the serious man
in whose fist is locked hatred.

All it takes to cast a rapist is seeing your
   body
as jackhammer, as blowtorch, as adding-
   machine-gun.
All it takes is hating that body
your own, your self, your muscle that
   softens to flab.

All it takes is to push what you hate,
what you fear onto the soft alien flesh.
To bucket out invincible as a tank
armored with treads without senses
to possess and punish in one act,
to rip up pleasure, to murder those who
   dare
live in the leafy flesh open to love.

—Marge Piercy

SOURCE: Piercy, M. (1982). Rape poem. In *Circles on the water.* New York: Knopf.

Schwartz, & Tait, 1993; George, Winfield, & Blazer, 1992; Kahn, Mathie, & Torgler, 1994). A frequently used procedure is to ask women about specific experiences they have had (e.g., "had sex when you did not want to") before asking them if they have been raped.

A frequent estimate is that at least 1 in 4 women have been raped, though some suggest 1 in 3; estimates range from 10% to 50% (Goodman et al., 1993; Koss, 1993; Russell & Howell, 1983). Rape targets are of all races and vary in age from 1-month-old twin infants (boy, girl; "Infant twins assaulted," 1993) to a 92-year-old woman. College women are particularly at risk. Women most at risk for rape are in the early teens to the mid-20s (Russell, 1984a). When racial groups of equal status and life circumstances are compared, white women and African American women are equally likely to be raped, but African American women are more likely than white women to live in circumstances placing them at higher risk (Koss et al., 1987; Russell, 1984a; Wyatt, 1992).

Differences between other ethnic/racial groups are not yet well understood (Hannon, Hall, Kuntz, Van Laar, & Williams, 1995). The rate of rape for Mexican Americans born in Mexico is only one third that for Mexican Americans born in the United States (Sorenson & Siegel, 1992; Sorenson & Telles, 1991). Traditional Mexican culture may include a sense of community that protects its members, but that culture can be eroded when submerged in another culture. Native American women disclose comparatively high rates of rape and Asian American women comparatively low ones (Koss et al., 1987; Russell, 1984a). At this time we do not know if these differences in reports reflect differences in women's readiness to disclose rape or real differences in incidence of rape (Harney & Muehlenhard, 1991).

We do know that African American women are less likely than white women to report assault to authorities (Wyatt, 1991, 1992; Wyatt, Notgrass, & Newcomb, 1990). African American women do not anticipate being protected by predominantly white authorities and institutions. Authorities resist African American women's claims more quickly than they do those of white women. African Americans have lived through a period of American history in which sexual assaults against them were not considered crimes. All of the women of one family were told the story of a relative who was abducted, beaten, raped, and killed (Wyatt, 1992). Being told about the incident was part of the rite of passage into womanhood—rape was something that could happen just because you were black and female. African American women also may fear that a rape report, believed or not, reflects negatively on their group (V. Marsh, personal communication, 1995).

## Kinds of Rape

A typical view of rape is one of a "blitz" rape in which a woman suddenly is attacked by a stranger who has a weapon and threatens her life (Kahn, Mathie, & Torgler, 1994). This kind of rape does happen. Strangers wait for women in dark parking lots and jump out from behind bushes; these rapists are most likely to be reported and prosecuted. It has become clear, however, that there are many fewer of these **stranger rapes** than **acquaintance rapes,** namely, rapes committed by someone the victim knows (typically excluding incest; Lonsway, 1996). At least half of rapes and perhaps more (e.g., 88%) are acquaintance rapes (Bridges, 1991; Lonsway, 1996; Warshaw & Parrot, 1991). Acquaintance rapes also are called **hidden rapes** because they are unlikely to be reported or to bring conviction if they are reported (Muehlenhard, Goggins, Jones, & Saterfield, 1991; Struckman-Johnson, 1991). Acquaintances include men known only casually, steady dates, husbands, and fathers (Koss, Dinero, Siebel, & Cox, 1988).

Some acquaintance rapes are **date rapes,** perpetrated in a dating relationship, occurring anytime from the first date to a time after the couple has had sex together (Patton & Mannison, 1995; Shotland, 1992). It should be noted that about 80% of sexual encounters on dates, both the most recent date and throughout a dating relationship, are encounters wanted by both the man and the woman (Hannon et al., 1995). This is a high percentage, but so, too, is 20%, the percentage of unwanted sexual encounters. Date rape may involve violent physical coercion (or threat of it), but verbal coercion without physical threat is more prevalent and more expected by college women (Cook, 1995). As important as verbal coercion is, however, it typically is not considered in estimates of incidence of rape (Koss et al., 1987; Muehlenhard, 1994a, 1994b; Russell, 1984a), although some writers have inappropriately accused researchers of including verbal coercion in their estimates (Gilbert, 1993; Roiphe, 1993). Verbal coercion is still a form of abuse of men's power over women.

About half of college women in the United States report consenting to sex they did not want (44%, Koss et al., 1987; 55%, Sprecher, Hatfield, Cortese, Potapova, & Levitskaya, 1994). This is a higher percentage than in Russia (32%) and in Japan (27%). U.S. women report feeling overwhelmed by men's continual arguments and pressure (Koss et al., 1987). Men threaten to end the relationship, claim that "everyone does it," imply that the woman is "frigid," make the woman feel guilty, promise love or marriage, threaten bodily self-harm, or plead not to be left with "blue balls" (testicular congestion resulting from sexual arousal without orgasm) (Muehlenhard & Schrag, 1991).

Up to a third of rapes reported to the police are **gang rapes:** rapes by more than one man with one victim (Rozee-Koker & Polk, 1986). The assailants are more likely to be strangers or relatives (39% each) than acquaintances who are not relatives (9%) (Gidycz & Koss, 1990, 1991). Campus gang rapes are relatively common and are usually acquaintance rapes (but not date rapes) occurring during social get-togethers involving alcohol (O'Sullivan, 1991). They occur at all types of institutions, from private religious colleges to large state universities and Ivy League colleges (Ehrhart & Sandler, 1985). Collegiate gang rapes often are not thought of by the men as rape. The rapes sometimes are called "trains." One collegian commented about a campus rape case, "I don't believe she was raped. . . . I believe they ran a train on her" (Pierson, 1984, p. 1B). Gang rape often is a tradition that bonds the men in a group stressing loyalty and sense of superiority (Neimark, 1991; Warshaw, 1988).

## Rape Myths: "But Is It Really Rape?"

People do not seem to like to admit that rape happens and often try to dismiss it as "not really rape." **Rape myths** are generally false attitudes and beliefs that are nevertheless widely and persistently held and that serve to simultaneously deny and justify male sexual aggression against women (Lonsway & Fitzgerald, 1994, 1995). People learn the myths the same way they learn other attitudes, from families and friends, media, dirty jokes, rock videos.

Martha Burt (1980, 1991) grouped rape myths into four broad categories about the victim. The first is that **nothing happened:** There was no sex and no rape. By crying rape, women are thought to be covering up an unwanted pregnancy, getting back at men, or showing wishful thinking. The second group of myths maintains that **no harm was done,** because, for example, "rape is just sex." The claim may be based on a view that the woman already is societally devalued because she has had sex with a man not her husband and so has lost her right to say no. Thus some people do not believe that prostitutes can be raped (Silbert, 1982). Minority women are particularly trapped by these myths because they are stereotyped as sleeping with many men. Divorced women of any group and women who frequent bars also are devalued. The final catch-22 about this myth is that "only bad girls get raped, so if she was raped, she must be a bad girl."

The third group of myths Burt identified remove an incident from the category of real rape by maintaining that **she wanted it,** as in "Come on, Baby, you know you really want it." A husband may ask, "If that's what you wanted, why didn't you come to me?" (Russell, 1975). The closer the prerape situation is to a context in which sex is a possibility, the more difficult it is for people to understand that rape happened; they are unlikely to consider women raped by dates or at a party as having been raped. Perhaps the most devastating idea in this group of myths is the assumption that any healthy woman can resist rape if she really wants to—if she was raped, she really wanted it. With this assumption, the pernicious inherent claim is that there is no such thing as rape. Can you imagine the logic of this myth being applied to a white male stockbroker being robbed of his briefcase? "If he let it happen, it wasn't robbery."

The final group of myths about women is that **she deserved it.** Forced sex is acknowledged to have occurred, but the woman was responsible because she flirted, dressed attractively, teased the man, invited him to her apartment for coffee, or just said hello at the office water fountain. If someone leaves an apartment door unlocked and is burglarized, the crime is acknowledged, even though the victim was careless. In contrast, women are seen to deserve rape if they are in a risky situation they cannot avoid, such as working a late-night shift or hitchhiking when a car breaks down.

Burt also points to interrelated myths about men that reduce the perceptions of their involvement. One is that only crazy men rape, so a sane man cannot be a rapist. A well-dressed, articulate man in a three-piece suit and the "nice guy" around the corner are assumed falsely accused. Second is the myth that rape is the result of men not being able to control their own sexuality, as was presumed when they were teen-agers (chapter 11). In short, women, not men, are seen as responsible for men's actions, unless the men are obviously lunatics. The higher status people, men, are to be excused, while the lower status people, women, are to be blamed. Unfortunately, many women implicitly accept views such as this.

One result of the cultural view of rape is that at least half or more of women with rape experiences do not consider the experiences to be rape (Kahn et al., 1994; Koss &

*Men and women differ greatly in the meanings they attribute to dress, demeanor, and behavior. Some men would interpret this woman's friendly smile and low-cut dress as an invitation to intimacy or a desire for sex.*

Oros, 1982; Muehlenhard & Linton, 1987; Reilly, Lott, Caldwell, & DeLuca, 1992). These women are **unacknowledged rape victims** (Koss, 1985). College women who have been raped by an acquaintance are particularly likely to avoid using the term *rape* (Kahn et al., 1994). Similarly, fewer married women say their husbands have raped them than say that their husbands have used coercion or forced them to have sex (Figure 15.1; Frieze, 1983). Women are reluctant to interpret the actions of the men close to them as violence, and people in general are reluctant to see the violence in rape.

## Judging an Assault

Acceptance of rape myths is critical in judgments about rape (Kopper, 1996). The myths influence the judgments not only of the woman herself but also of other people relevant to her, including her family, officials who work with victims, and jurors who

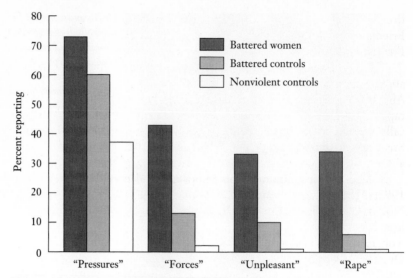

**Figure 15.1** *Women's reports of husband's sexual behavior.*
Pressures: He pressures you to have sex.
Forces: Sex is unpleasant because he forces you to have sex.
Unpleasant: Sex is unpleasant because he makes you do things you do not want to do.
Rape: Husband has raped you.

NOTE: 137 women who had reported physical assaults from their husbands were given a structured interview about violence in their marriages and about marital rape. Each battered woman was matched with a nonbattered woman from the same neighborhood. After interview results were tabulated, it was found that 40 of the comparison women had been physically assaulted by their husbands; these women were considered as a separate "battery comparison or control group."

SOURCE: Frieze, I. H. (1983). Investigating the causes and consequences of marital rape. *Signs: Journal of Women in Culture and Society, 8*, (3), 532–553. Table 2, p. 541.

make legal decisions (Feild, 1978; Kopper, 1996; Lonsway & Fitzgerald, 1994, 1995). The negative reactions of others are associated with the woman's increased psychological symptoms (Ullman, 1996). Judgments often reinforce the myths, adding to the likelihood of continuing distortions in an ever increasing spiral.

Studies of African American, Asian American, Hispanic, and white people have found that men, relative to women, generally accept rape myths more than women do, minimize the seriousness of rape, think women enjoy it, and hold women more responsible (Calhoun & Townsley, 1991; Davis & Lee, 1996; Fischer, 1997; Lonsway & Fitzgerald, 1994; Mori, Bernat, Glenn, Selle, & Zarate, 1995). Both women and men who have had direct exposure to rape (being raped or knowing a victim) have increased sensitivity to rape, with the effect greater for men, perhaps because rape is generally more salient to women (Freetly & Kane, 1995; Hannon et al., 1995).

Traditionality also affects attitudes toward rape, perhaps in conjunction with rape myth acceptance. Women and men with more traditional attitudes toward women's roles are more tolerant of rape and more likely to blame the rape on the victim (Calhoun & Townsley, 1991; Muehlenhard & Falcon, 1990). Still, traditional men rated rape as more justifiable than traditional women did (Muehlenhard, Friedman, & Thomas, 1985). Evidence about ethnicity is not clear (Lonsway & Fitzgerald, 1994).

Characteristics of the woman claiming rape are more important in judgments about rape than other features of the situation, with two important exceptions: First, African American men are more likely to be convicted than white men for a reported rape of a white woman (Brownmiller, 1975; Feild, 1978). Second, stranger rape typically is taken more seriously than date rape (Bridges, 1991; Struckman-Johnson & Struckman-Johnson, 1991). Even in stranger rape, the effect of rape myths is not absent: "If it happened, she wanted it" (Krulewitz & Nash, 1979).

Alcohol consumption is an important and complex issue (Abbey & Harnish, 1995; Abbey, Ross, McDuffie, & McAuslan, 1996; Cook, 1995; Cue, George, & Norris, 1996; Koss, Gidycz, & Wisniewski, 1987; Norris, Nurius, & Dimeff, 1996). At least half (maybe three quarters) of acquaintance rapes involve alcohol consumption. A woman who has been drinking sometimes is seen as a slut, as loose, or as "fair game." Or she may be seen as feeling more sexual, more willing to engage in consensual sexual activities (George, Lehman, Cue, Martinez, & Lopez, in press; Cue et al., 1996). On the other hand, she may be seen as deserving special protection. When only the victim had been drinking, college students were most likely to believe a date rape had happened; when both the man and woman had been drinking, they thought date rape least likely (Abbey & Harnish, 1995; Norris & Cubbins, 1992). If only the man had been drinking, the woman was seen as responsible for what happened. Note that these results are from college students, who generally accept drinking as part of the college scene.

## Women's Experiences of Rape

Women who have experienced rape have given researchers some insight into what they have gone through (Burgess & Holmstrom, 1979; McCombie, 1980; Meyer & Taylor, 1986; Roth & Lebowitz, 1988). The first phase is a realization of a dangerous situation in which rape is likely to happen although denial is attempted: "This couldn't happen to me." This is followed by the rape itself, during which the woman's strongest response is usually fear for her life. Women are often paralyzed physically and cognitively and need reassurance that these reactions are normal (Symonds, 1976). The post-traumatic recoil phase begins immediately after the rape. Women interviewed in hospital emergency rooms tended to be either expressive, showing fear and anxiety, or controlled, showing a calm, subdued facade; no matter what the style, they all expressed the wish that they had reacted faster or fought harder (Burgess & Holmstrom, 1974a, 1974b, 1979). The reconstitution phase, the longest phase, begins as the woman prepares to leave the emergency room or crisis center and may not end for many months or even years. Some women make lifestyle changes to protect themselves from further victimization, such as buying a gun, putting extra locks on the door, or moving out of the area (Ellis, 1983; Russell, 1983a, 1983b; Wyatt et al., 1990).

***Effects of Rape***    Reactions to rape can be considered as post-traumatic stress disorder (PTSD), a form of anxiety disorder (chapter 16). PTSD commonly occurs in people

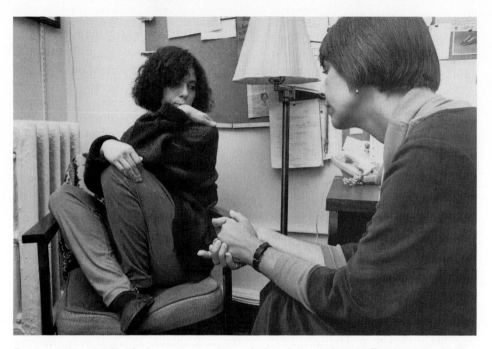

*Post-traumatic stress disorder is common in women who have been raped, with effects lasting months or even years. This woman is likely to experience higher levels of depression and anxiety than women who have not been raped.*

who have survived war and natural disasters (e.g., earthquakes, tornados). Victims suffering from PTSD persistently reexperience the traumatic event in dreams or flashbacks, attempt to avoid stimuli associated with the trauma, and have difficulty concentrating or sleeping. The symptoms may begin immediately or shortly after the traumatic event or may not begin until 6 months or even years later (Halgin & Whitbourne, 1994; Koss & Harvey, 1987). Nearly all (94%) women who went to a trauma center shortly after a rape (within 12 days) met the criteria for PTSD, and nearly half (46%) still did 3 months later (Rothbaum, Foa, Riggs, Murdock, & Walsh, 1992). The traumatic events triggering PTSD contradict beliefs about a just, fair, predictable world: The world suddenly seems out of whack (Janoff-Bulman, 1992; Koss & Burkhart, 1989). Rape is complicated by the interpersonal nature of victimization and the pervasive, malevolent social context of rape (e.g., victimization, blame the woman, rape myths).

Many women continually feel that their rapes have impacts on them, with some feeling the impact after as many as 17 years (Burnam et al., 1988). By itself, time since the rape is not a predictor of the number of current symptoms (George et al., 1992). "Time heals" but not always completely and not on a fixed schedule common to all. Exact consequences of rape vary with circumstances of the rape and with the woman's personality and general level of functioning at the time of the rape. Because of the diversity of such factors and the complexities of their interactions, adaptation is highly idiosyncratic. Cultural differences in the meanings of sexual assault also affect adaptation. The chronic stress of racism seems to exacerbate effects of the stress of sexual assault on menstrual and sexual symptoms of African Americans and Latinas (Golding, 1996). Latinas' extreme concern about women's virginity seems to make them especially vulnerable to sexual problems following sexual assault.

Negative reactions from others, such as being blamed, treated differently, or having someone else take control, are related to poorer self-rated recovery and to more psychological problems (Davis, Brickman, & Baker, 1991). Women are helped by being listened to and believed (Ullman, 1996).

Some initial and lingering effects are quite common. Adolescents and college students who have been victims of stranger and acquaintance rape have higher anxiety and depression scores and more suicide attempts than those who have not been victimized (Gidycz, Coble, Latham, & Layman, 1993; Gidycz & Koss, 1989; Koss, 1988; Koss et al., 1988). Lasting effects include mistrust of men or of people in general, emotional distress, fears of being left alone or being out at night (Wyatt, 1992). Menstrual difficulties and sexual dysfunction can occur (Golding, 1996); some women also become more sexually active, perhaps in an effort to gain mastery over past sexual encounters in which they felt powerless (Koss, Dinero, Seibel, & Cox, 1994).

Although reactions to stranger and acquaintance rape are remarkably similar, some differences have been found. After a stranger rape, the victim is likely to have a strong fear of physical harm and death and a fear of strangers; after acquaintance rape, the victim feels she has been betrayed and humiliated by someone she trusted (Muehlenhard et al., 1991). When the relationship continues, the woman may live in terror, never knowing when the assault may happen again.

***Blame and Survivorship***    A controversial issue about coping with rape is the role of self-blame, a common feeling that can take two forms. **Characterological self-blame** involves maligning one's personality and character in a general and permanent way, for example, "I'm stupid, I'm no good" (and presumably always will be). It is associated with low self-esteem and depression and is detrimental to adjustment (Janoff-Bulman, 1982, 1992). **Behavioral self-blame** is more specific to actions and time, blaming the behavior but not the person, and subject to change (e.g., "Going out alone late at night was not very smart"). This kind of self-blame focuses on errors in judgment that everyone makes from time to time; indeed, the victim may have made a judgment error and the rapist took advantage of her vulnerability. Some researchers (Janoff-Bulman, 1982, 1992) maintain that behavioral self-blame can be an adaptive strategy because it allows women to get some sense of control in their lives: "I did it wrong in the past, but I can do better in the future." Others argue that self-blame is maladaptive. For example, any immediate gain may be offset by long-range negative consequences on self-esteem (Frazier, Klein, & Seales, 1995; Frazier & Schauben, 1994; Katz & Burt, 1988; Koss & Burkhart, 1989).

If the woman seems to feel better with behavioral self-blame, her feelings are to be respected (Diane Wiendersham, personal communication, 1997). During the first several months after rape, the woman must focus all of her psychological and physical energy on emotional survival (Katz, 1991). However, until victims can affirm the reality of victimization—they are not to blame—they cannot complete the emotional process of dealing with rape (Davis & Friedman, 1985; Koss & Burkhart, 1989; Scherer, 1992). Once a woman realizes that she was a victim of an act not under her control, she will be more able to grieve the loss of innocence and the loss of the person she once was. Becoming a true survivor requires the difficult task of getting to know the postrape person she is becoming, affirming that new person, and dealing with themes of meaning and gaining mastery and control (Taylor, 1983). Rape can hardly be called something that is good for women, but it would be a disservice to women to avoid comment on the feelings some have as they turn their victimization into a growth experience and develop improved self-concept and self-direction and control in life (Burt & Katz, 1987; Katz, 1991; Koss & Burkhart, 1989; Nadelson, Notman, & Jackson, 1982; Scurfield, 1985; Veronen & Kilpatrick, 1982; Williams & Holmes, 1981).

## Prevention: More Than Band-Aids

Perhaps the most important message about immediate prevention is overcoming women's sense of invulnerability (Norris et al., 1996). Women tend to think that they can resist victimization, although they know the risks to women in general. Much as with reactions to employment and pay discrimination, they have psychological barriers that put them at risk. With risk of rape, the barriers include fear of embarrassment and concerns about rejection.

Nontraditional women in some ways seem to have fewer barriers and give off cues that reduce the likelihood of attempted rape, and they resist attempts more effectively (Amick & Calhoun, 1987). Research indicates that successful resisters are more autonomous and self-reliant, of larger size and weight, are involved in sports, know self-defense, and have had assertiveness training (Bart, 1980). Such women are less likely to be in an isolated dating situation and more likely to give clear refusals and to use a variety of means to avoid rape. Immediate, varied, and forceful resistance strategies, such as fighting, screaming, fleeing, or pushing the offender away, appear to be more effective for avoiding rape than not resisting but are not used much even when the assailant is a stranger (Bart & O'Brien, 1985; Ullman & Knight, 1993). Pleading, crying, or reasoning are not typically effective. However, there are always exceptions; some men may become more violent with resistance. The woman has to decide how to react, and her decision must be respected. Some programs advise that any strong protest may work, while others recommend avoiding angering the assailant.

Rape prevention programs vary widely but have been characterized generally as confused, scattered, and sporadic (McCall, 1993). They have focused on the immediately practical aim of preventing stranger rapes by recommending that women not go out alone at night, learn self-defense, protest, don't drink, don't go to his apartment, and so on. Yet, in the bigger view, this advice by itself actually reinforces social control over women and the view that women are to blame for rape (Corcoran, 1991). Men rape, and only men can stop rape (Freetly & Kane, 1995). Some schools are starting programs aimed at men (Mahlstedt, 1991; Moses, 1991).

Women, of course, have the legal right to walk alone late at night but not the practical right. Women's groups aim to "Take Back the Night," so that women may have the same real, practical rights as men do. A quiet but firm no should be sufficient, but it is not. Women now say no, but their no is not respected. Until that is changed, rape will happen: Ultimately, prevention of rape requires a change of societal attitudes about aggression generally and about attitudes toward women and men and their relationships. Considering rapists and their attitudes illustrates existing problems. Women's knowledge about men who pose risks may be important in rape prevention programs (Cue et al., 1996).

## Rapists

Rape is primarily a social disease (Russell, 1984a, 1984b). Many men are bitten by the "masculinity bug" but manage to resist the disease it sometimes carries. Others, however, succumb. All the research with those men who do commit rape and those who state predispositions to rape converges to suggest that rape is "an extreme acting out of qualities that are regarded as masculine . . . aggression, force, power, strength, toughness, dominance, competitiveness" (Russell, 1983a, p. 88). In an aggressive culture, being a "real man" is understood by some men to mean being aggressive against women.

A rapist may be of any age, any occupation, any social class, any ethnic group. More convicted rapists (61%) are under 25 than older, and most repeat their offenses (Furby, Weinrott, & Blackshaw, 1989). The larger group of rapists are those who are undetected, especially acquaintance rapists. Although there are many kinds of them, most of the research has been on college men. In one kind of research, college men are asked if they have used any kind of force to have sex with a woman. More than half (59%) report that they have had sex only with mutual consent (Lisak & Roth, 1988; Poppen & Segal, 1988). However, essentially a third (32%) of 2000 college men admitted to having used some degree of physical or emotional coercion to have sex with an unwilling woman, always an acquaintance; none had been reported (Koss, 1985). Some reported physical force, threatened or actual, for intercourse (4%); others reported forced sexual contact without intercourse (5%). The majority of those saying they had been coercive reported extreme verbal pressure (22% of the total sample). Many men who use pressure for sex do not realize that their acts are undesired, because they do not believe women really mean no (Check & Malamuth, 1983; Muehlenhard & Felts, 1987; Shotland & Goldstein, 1983).

Another method of research has men read a description of a sexual assault and rate the likelihood that they would behave like the assailant under similar circumstances if they were sure they would not be caught. From 35% to 60% of college men state some likelihood of having sex with a woman without her consent (Malamuth, 1986, 1989a, 1989b; Osland, Fitch, & Willis, 1996). Men reporting higher ratings also more often report they actually have used force against women, and these men are similar in many ways to men who have been convicted of rape.

Convicted rapists, college men who admit to having used force, and college men stating a likelihood of rape share some features: They are highly gender stereotyped, believe in rape myths, have low opinions of women, and respond to depictions of rape with sexual arousal (Check & Malamuth, 1983; Harney & Muehlenhard, 1991; Lonsway & Fitzgerald, 1994; Osland et al., 1996). These men think that women enjoy

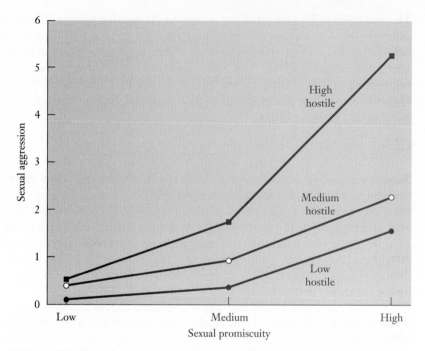

**Figure 15.2** *Sexual aggression as a function of hostile masculinity and sexual activity.* NOTE: Participants were 2652 heterosexual or bisexual college men from a representative sample of the U.S. college population. The sexual activity measure included the age of first sexual intercourse and the number of sexual intercourse partners since the age of 14. Sexual aggression was measured by asking participants to indicate how often since the age of 14 they had ever committed any of 10 coercive acts. Hostile masculinity was measured by three instruments: the Rape Myth Acceptance scale, the Hostility Toward Women scale, and the Negative Masculinity scale.

SOURCE: Malamuth, N. M., Sockloskie, R. J., Koss, M. P., & Tanaka, J. S. (1991). Characteristics of aggressors against women: Testing a model using a national sample of college students. *Journal of Consulting and Clinical Psychology, 59,* (5), 670–681. Figure 2, p. 678.

rape, while other men see rape as an act of violence. College men who rape often try to get their dates high on alcohol or marijuana and tend to use other manipulative techniques such as false statements of love or commitment (Kanin, 1985; Koss & Dinero, 1988). In turn, women do feel more vulnerable when alcohol is used on dates (Cook, 1995; Cue et al., 1996).

Rape is not a matter of sexuality. Violence-prone men do not have a higher sexual drive than other men. If that were the case, men who are more sexually driven would be more likely to engage in both mutually consenting and coercive sex. That is not found. A relatively high level of sexual activity is associated with more sexual aggression only for men high in hostile masculinity; some men are sexually active but are not particularly aggressive (Figure 15.2; Malamuth, Sockloskie, Koss, & Tanaka, 1991).

The measure of hostile masculinity includes general items such as "I am a bossy person," "Most people are out for themselves. I don't trust them very much." Other items focus on women specifically, such as, "I feel upset even by slight criticism by a woman," "I rarely become suspicious with women who are more friendly than I expected" (reverse scoring). The hostile men are likely to have friends who reward aggression toward women (Frank, 1989; Kanin, 1985; Malamuth et al., 1991).

## *Child Sexual Abuse*

Sexual assault of adult women is hard enough to contemplate. Even more difficult to consider is sexual assault of children and adolescents. As in assault on adult women, the assailants are primarily acquaintances who are abusing power, and the assault has long-lasting effects on the victims (Newman & Peterson, 1996).

Definitions vary, but a fairly typical definition of **child sexual abuse** is that it involves both contact and noncontact sexual experiences in which the victim is younger than 18 and the perpetrator is at least five years older (Haugaard & Reppucci, 1988). Exhibitionism by the older person is an example of noncontact abuse. Other definitions specify physical contact. Incest is a specific form of child sexual abuse. A broad definition of incest is "any act with sexual overtones perpetrated by a needed and/or trusted adult, whom a child is unable to refuse" (O'Hare & Taylor, 1983, p. 215). Some researchers use the terms **pedophilia** or **child molestation** for child sexual abuse that is not incest.

Child sexual abuse generally and incest specifically are more likely directed toward a girl than a boy and committed by a man than by a woman, although all combinations of abuse happen (Cutler & Nolen-Hoeksema, 1991). Probably at least one in four women has been abused as a child (Finkelhor, Hotaling, Lewis, & Smith, 1990; Higgins & McCabe, 1994), but estimates vary widely (10%–67%) (Clutter, 1990; Herman, 1981; Herman & Hirschman, 1981; Koss, 1990; Pope & Hudson, 1992; Russell, 1984b). Sexual abuse of children happens in all social strata. Analysis of Bureau of Justice statistics shows that of officially reported cases of sexual abuse of children under age 12 years, very few (4%) of the perpetrators were strangers; more frequent were relatives (46%) and friends and acquaintances (50%) (Bayles, 1995). Molestation by strangers makes news, but incest does not often come to public attention: No more than one in five cases of incest (and perhaps even fewer) is ever reported to the police, and few cases are brought to trial.

The rate of father-daughter incest is not clear from existing research. Father-daughter incest is the most common (20% for girls under age 12) of officially reported incest cases. For women recruited through self-help groups or activities or newsletters for women abused as children, fathers accounted for nearly half (47%) of incest perpetrators; brothers are the next most frequent (31%), followed by others (18%) and stepfathers (9%) (Newman & Peterson, 1996). However, general surveys of more representative samples show that brother-sister and first-cousin contacts are more common than father-daughter contacts (Canavan, Meyer, & Higgs, 1992; Finkelhor, 1979; Hunt, 1974; Stark, 1984). Brother-sister incest without coercion is not necessarily seen negatively by either participant (Finkelhor, 1980; Martinson, 1994). But experience with a much older brother, who often has learned the sexual behavior from other family members who have used power, likely is experienced negatively by a young girl.

## Parents of Incest Victims

The offender in child sexual abuse often is middle-aged, shy, conservative, moralistic, and likely to have superficial relations with other adults, including sexually (Rosenberg & Knight, 1988). Generally poor emotional adjustment is common as well as prior victimization themselves (Johnston, 1987; Seghorn, Prentky, & Boucher, 1987). The biological father who molests his daughter shares many of these traits. In addition, he often is a benign respected member of the community. He is a patriarch who provides for and rules the family rigidly, often in a home in a relatively isolated location (Finkelhor, 1984; Higgins & McCabe, 1994). The daughter, most likely the oldest child, feels overwhelmed by his superior power. The daughter is given a "special" relationship with the father in which he expresses feelings of dependency and nurture, and he does so without fear of the rejection he might receive from a woman (Finkelhor, 1984; Herman, 1981; Justice & Justice, 1979).

The traditional picture of the mother in a family in which father-daughter incest is occurring is that she is a full-time homemaker and ineffective mother who is cold and unaffectionate and isolated from the family and others because of poor health (Goldman & Goldman, 1988). The daughters may hear from their mothers the message, "For my own survival . . . I cannot defend you, and if necessary I will sacrifice you to your father" (Herman & Hirschman, 1981, p. 746). This classical portrait may have been overdrawn, perhaps because daughters not supported by mothers may be more likely to consult psychotherapists, and perhaps because it is simply another way of blaming women for men's sexual behavior. Recent evidence suggests that many (but not all) mothers protect their daughters and reject their husbands when they learn of incest (Crook, 1986), though perhaps few girls (33%) tell their mothers (Newman & Peterson, 1996). Very few survivors, as girls or as adults, blame their mothers or their fathers for the incest, except when the parent was the abuser, especially the father (Table 15.1). For both mother and father, the tendency to blame a parent was correlated with anger toward them only when that parent was the abuser. However, incest victims were higher in anger generally, and more angry at both parents, than were control groups.

Biological fathers are the least likely of father figures to molest their daughters and stepfathers the next least (Finkelhor, 1984; Giles-Sims & Finkelhor, 1984; Gordon & Creighton, 1988). Girls living with father substitutes not married to their mothers are at highest risk of sexual abuse by paternal figures. These men are the youngest of paternal offenders, their relationships to the victims' mothers are of the shortest duration, and their victims are younger (Gordon & Creighton, 1988). The mothers themselves are much younger and may be less effective in protecting their children than are older mothers.

**Table 15.1**   Percentage of Incest Survivors, as Children and Adults,
Holding People Most Responsible for Incest

| Person blamed | By survivor as child | By survivor as adult |
|---|---|---|
| Mother (not abuser) | 5.9 | 2.9 |
| Mother (abuser) | 4.4 | 22.1 |
| Father (not abuser) | 5.9 | 2.9 |
| Father (abuser) | 8.8 | 38.2 |
| Nonparent abuser | 20.6 | 38.2 |
| Self | 54.4 | 5.9 |

NOTE: Percentages exceed 100% because some survivors held more than one person primarily
responsible.

SOURCE: Newman, A. L., & Peterson, C. (1996). Anger of women incest survivors.
*Sex Roles, 34*, 463–491. Table II, p. 469.

## Impact of Child Sexual Abuse

Evidence increasingly shows the devastating effects possible from child sexual abuse
(Beitchman, Zucker, Hood, da Costa, & Akman, 1991; Boyer, 1993; Boyer & Fine,
1992; Frazier & Cohen, 1992; Higgins & McCabe, 1994; Newman & Peterson, 1996).
However, because incest tends to happen in families where other forms of trauma
happen (Newman & Peterson, 1996), it often is difficult to determine what effects are
due to the incest itself. Immediate effects can be shown in cognitive, social, and physical functioning. Psychological effects include a strong sense of shame and guilt, in part
because of the secrecy of the activity: "If it must be kept secret, I must be doing
something bad because parents are good." As children, victims of incest are likely to
blame themselves (see Table 15.1), though they do not blame themselves as adults.
Having a significant person to talk with reduces the severity of the effects, but many
children do not have such a person (Weissberg, 1983). Sexual assaults that occur early
in life may be particularly traumatic because the young girl has fewer coping skills than
an older one (Koss & Burkhart, 1989; Russell, 1986).

There are at least four sets of long-term effects indicated (Browne & Finkelhor,
1986). One is traumatic sexualization—survivors have an unusual concern with sexuality such that they are preoccupied with sex and seek it out, or they avoid sex and men.
The women also may dissociate during sex: They feel that their bodies are sexually
engaged but they themselves are not ("This is not happening to me"). Dissociation
seems related to the high proportion of incest survivors among women who have
multiple personalities (chapter 16) and may be related to the fact that 75% of prostitutes are incest survivors (Weber, 1977). A second effect is a lingering sense of betrayal.
The victims do not trust others or, paradoxically, choose partners who are likely to
betray them. If they do become involved with a trustworthy partner, they are likely to
get rid of that person. A result of these two effects is that many victims have trouble
establishing intimate adult relationships, particularly with men, particularly sexually

(Harter, Alexander, & Neimeyer, 1988; Jackson, Calhoon, Amick, & Maddever, 1990; Janeway, 1981).

Third, incest survivors tend to have low self-esteem together with a sense of powerlessness and victimization (Browne & Finklehor, 1986; Harter et al., 1988; Koss & Dinero, 1989). They have difficulty saying no because, though they felt it and probably said it as children, it was not honored. They may, then, think that being powerless is inevitable and get in situations in which they are likely to be powerless and betrayed (a form of self-fulfilling prophecy; chapter 2). Finally, stigmatization is likely. They feel like dirty, damaged goods. Many incest victims in treatment describe themselves as a witch, bitch, whore, branded, or marked (Herman & Hirschman, 1977). Some other effects follow. Self-mutilation, such as cutting oneself, provides both an awareness of being alive and the punishment felt to be deserved (Bass & Davis, 1988; Herman, 1992).

Given the sense of betrayal, powerlessness, and stigmatization, it is no wonder that women with a history of sexual abuse are more angry, depressed, and anxious than other women; incest victims are more so than other child abuse victims (Cutler & Nolen-Hoeksema, 1991; Newman & Peterson, 1996; Russell, 1986). Nor is it surprising that the incidence of substance abuse is comparatively high among these women (Loftus, Polonsky, & Fullilove, 1994; Russell, 1986).

## Revictimization

The revictimization that plagues some victims of both childhood and adult sexual abuse deserves to be looked at separately. If a girl feels powerless to control what happens to her and feels worthless, the woman she becomes may feel powerless to thwart others who try to harm her. If the woman she is becoming is victimized, the future woman she becomes may feel powerless to thwart others who try to harm her. Victimization predicts further victimization (Chu, 1992; Gidycz et al., 1993; Gidycz, Hanson, & Layman, 1995; Himelein, 1995; Houston & Hwang, 1996; Koss & Dinero, 1989; Mandoki & Burkhart, 1991; Muehlenhard et al., 1991; Wyatt, Guthrie, & Notgrass, 1992). This is not simply a matter of women who have been abused recently being more likely to interpret earlier experiences as abuse. Recent studies with college women show that having been sexually victimized before college predicts victimization during college, even during the first quarter of college.

In these studies college women reported on childhood abuse and abuse during teen years or earlier and then abuse during college (studied over one school quarter, or two or three, or 34 months; Gidycz et al., 1993; Gidycz et al., 1995; Himelein, 1995). The results in all the studies were similar—women victimized at one time are more likely than others to be victimized later.

The later victimization, however, is not inevitable. Melissa Himelein (1995) likened childhood sexual abuse to cancer—as the chance of cancer relapse diminishes with every symptom-free year, so may revictimization be reduced with every aggression-free dating relationship. The previously victimized women at lower risk had a mistrust of dating partners, were less sexually active consensually, and were less likely to use alcohol in dating situations. In Himelein's research, 40% of the women

**Table 15.2**  Scores on Depression and Anxiety of College Women With and Without Abuse History, With and Without Sexual Victimization During a School Term

|  | *Depression* | *Anxiety* |
|---|---|---|
| NONVICTIMS DURING THE QUARTER | 6.47 | 6.70 |
| Without abuse history | 5.19 | 6.03 |
| With abuse history | 7.42 | 8.08 |
| VICTIMS DURING THE QUARTER | 9.97 | 11.29 |
| With abuse history | 10.96 | 12.57 |
| Without abuse history | 9.17 | 9.79 |

NOTE: Participants were undergraduate women who completed measures assessing their victimization prior to age 14, and from age 14 to college, as well as depression and anxiety measures. Depression was measured by the Beck Depression Inventory; anxiety was measured by the Beck Anxiety Inventory. At the end of the academic quarter, they again completed the depression and anxiety measures as well as an assessment of sexual victimization since the beginning of the quarter. Most (82%) were not victimized during the 9-week period of the quarter. However, 3.7% had been raped, and 3.4% were victims of attempted rape. An additional 4.6% and 6.3% were victims of sexual coercion and sexual contact, respectively.

SOURCE: Gidycz, C. A., Coble, C. N., Latham, L., & Layman, M. J. (1993). Sexual assault experience in adulthood and prior victimization experiences. *Psychology of Women Quarterly, 17*, 151–168. Table 2, p. 161 and information passim.

abused in childhood who were revictimized in precollege dating were also victimized in college (32 months later), whereas only 25% of those not victimized in precollege dating were victimized in college. Similarly, Christine Gidycz and her colleagues (1993) found that adolescent victimization was more strongly related to college victimization than childhood victimization was, though adolescent victimization was higher among women abused in childhood than others.

There is a cautionary note. The samples just discussed (college women) are likely to underestimate the prevalence of revictimization, because one result of childhood sexual abuse is school problems, which reduces the likelihood of the young women entering college. Effects even for college women remain. Women with histories of abuse also were more anxious and depressed, whether victimized during the quarter or not. Women victimized during the quarter were more anxious and depressed, whether or not they had a victimization history (Table 15.2).

## "But Was She Really Abused?"

There has been increasing attention in the media to cases of women who say they have recovered repressed memories of child abuse many years after the claimed event. Repression is an unconscious, intentional "holding down" of material, so that it is not easily available to consciousness. Some repression is a common way of coping with traumatic events (Blume, 1990; Briere & Conte, 1993; Fredrickson, 1992). We have no good way of estimating how many women completely repress sexual abuse. Most women (81%) who have some recall of childhood sexual abuse say they have remembered all or part of the abuse throughout their lives, but we do not know how many have no recall (Loftus et al., 1994).

Are the memories that women do have accurate? We cannot know for sure. Children's accounts of sexual abuse generally are remarkably accurate when compared with details given by confessed perpetrators (Schwartz, 1993). With elapsed time, there are changes in exactly what is recalled, but memories of the basic themes of the event remain relatively accurate.

The possibility remains that women who say they have recovered memories of childhood abuse were not abused but have been influenced by the popular media and by therapists' suggestions; however, no one disputes the fact that many women were sexually abused as children (Loftus, 1993; Schwartz, 1993). Knowing that children are abused in higher numbers than previously realized, a therapist may interpret a woman's symptoms in light of that and urge her to become free of her presumed repression (Herman, 1992; Loftus, 1993). Under hypnosis recall can be influenced by suggestions, but recall under hypnosis does not by itself mean the recall is not accurate. Some victims have their fears confirmed when their suspected perpetrators come to the clinic and verify their memories. Other women who suspect that they have been victimized are relieved to discover in hypnosis that they have not been victimized (Schwartz, 1993).

The issue of "false memories" that cause havoc in the lives of the accused cannot be dismissed and clearly calls for more and better research about memory, repression, and hypnosis. However, the issue needs to be considered along with the general societal tendency to dismiss women and their claims of abuse. Rape myths can serve to discount the adult women's charges of rape. A danger with the issue of "false memories" is finding an easy answer to child abuse, namely, a comforting defensive denial of the fact that it exists.

## Battered Women

All states now have laws against spousal abuse, but in spite of this, physical assault between married partners, as well as cohabiting and dating partners, is a serious problem that occurs in all groups within our society (Dobash, Dobash, Wilson, & Daly, 1992; Frieze & McHugh, 1992).

### The Nature of Partner Abuse

Estimates of how many women are beaten vary from 16% (Gelles & Straus, 1990) to one third (Browne, 1993), depending on the people sampled, definitions of aggression, and interaction with the researcher. Abusive men in heterosexual relationships instigate a greater number of aggressive acts than women in lesbian relationships, but the percentage of women who are abused at all may be about the same in the two kinds of relationships (Koss, 1990). Estimates for any group may be underestimates. General surveys do not include very poor, non-English-speaking, hospitalized, homeless, institutionalized, or incarcerated women.

There is disagreement about whether nearly all cases of violence between partners (90%–95%) involve the man as the aggressor (Dobash et al., 1992; Kurz, 1989) or whether women are equally likely to be the aggressors (McNeely & Mann, 1990; Sommers, 1994; Straus & Gelles, 1986, 1990). Part of the issue is definition of assault, for example, slapping or shoving relative to hitting with a fist. It is not disputed that women are far more likely to be injured and need medical care because of abuse than men are (Brush, 1990; Gelles & Straus, 1990). Of women going to emergency rooms in large urban hospitals, many (22% to 50%) go because of abuse (Stark & Flitcraft, 1988).

***Dating Relationships***    Although the main focus here is with wives who are abused, physical aggression in dating relationships also is a social problem and one with dynamics similar to spousal abuse (Pipes & LeBov-Keeler, 1997; Thompson, 1991; White & Koss, 1991). Given that people are dating earlier and getting married later (chapter 10), dating violence likely will become more prevalent. As many as one in four high school students and one half of college undergraduates experience a partner's physical aggression (Levy, 1990; Thompson, 1991). Almost all college women (88%) and men (81%) report being involved in verbal aggression in a heterosexual relationship, as perpetrator or victim (White & Koss, 1991).

Violence occurs in less committed dating relationships, perhaps as a way of testing the strength of the commitment and the degree of love (Cate, Henton, Koval, Christopher, & Lloyd, 1982; Stets & Straus, 1990). However, the abuse seems more likely and more violent as the dating relationship gets more similar to marriage; abuse is higher in cohabiting couples than married or dating couples. Disputes likely are about control issues and involve jealousy, drinking, and sexual refusal (Roscoe & Kelsey, 1986; Sugarman & Hotaling, 1989). The couples often stay together, with some partners thinking the relationship is improved because of the violence ("He wouldn't hit me if he did not love me"). Still, women more than men are emotionally upset by the violence (Makepeace, 1986; Matthews, 1984).

Do violent courtships lead to violent marriages? Of women in violent marriages, up to a half say they had been abused during courtship (Roscoe & Benaske, 1985). Apparently, lack of abuse during courtship is no guarantee that it will not occur during marriage, but its presence during courtship is probably a sign that it will occur in marriage. A predictable cycle is likely in violent dating and marital relationships.

***The Battering Cycle***    In the typical battering cycle, there is an initial time of **tension building**—a time of minor battering, such as verbal abuse and slapping (Walker, 1979, 1989). Fearing that she may leave, he intensifies his attempts at control. Tension escalates until it explodes in an **acute battering incident.** Women often develop an inner sense that tells them when it is coming and that it is coming no matter what they do (A Closer Look 15.2).

In some relationships, the third phase is one of **no tension** in which the man acts as if nothing happened (Dobash & Dobash, 1984; Walker, 1979, 1989). Often,

## *A Closer Look*

### 15.2    Spousal Abuse: "It Didn't Matter What I Did"

Janet had learned to predict when the acute phase was about to happen no matter what she did. She had left her husband, Lewis, several times and each time he persuaded her to return. He often threatened to kill her or himself and she knew he was capable of that.

"The house was strangely quiet. Somehow, I just knew that tonight was going to be the night. It didn't matter what I did. I thought that perhaps I could stave it off. Maybe if I tried just a little bit harder, it would all work out."

She cooked stew, one of his favorite dinners, and set the table with his favorite tablecloth and some candlesticks he had given her as a gift after a previous incident. She also put on a pretty dress he had given her after a previous fight—nice but not too sexy because she did not want to have sex. She knew that it made him feel good for her to use his gifts, though sometimes she did not want to have anything to do with them. He came

home, after having a couple of drinks. She gave him a big hug and kiss and suggested he relax, but he blurted, "No, I'm hungry . . . I want food right now. Now, I want my food."

She went to the kitchen. "All of a sudden, I heard a crashing sound on the floor and footsteps as he came running into the kitchen. I knew there was trouble ahead. 'Why the hell did you put the goddamn candlesticks on the table?' he screamed. 'What's the matter with you? You're so stupid. Don't you know that we save those only for good occasions? What's so good about tonight? Why do you always do things like that? Now your damned tablecloth is ruined. What is it that you have to ruin everything? Don't you like anything that I give you? Can't you keep anything right? You're so stupid. You just can't do anything right.' And on and on he went . . ."

During the meal, Lew screamed at her that the food was lousy and she finally

---

however, this is a period of **loving contrition and reconciliation.** The man begs for forgiveness, promises that he will never abuse again, and showers her with gifts, affection, and charm. He also tends to underplay the violence and claims that the physical harm was her fault ("I pushed her, but she fell against the stove and hurt her head because she is clumsy") but also insists that he was right (Dutton, 1986). The contradictory reactions can be summed up as follows: (1) I did not do it, she did it to herself; (2) I was right to do it; (3) It wasn't that bad; but (4) I feel guilty about it, and I won't do it again.

The husband often enlists family and friends to plead his side of the story so things can return to "normal." Normal means the battering cycle happens all over again. Nonetheless, the third phase reminds the woman that she loves him and makes

told him that if he didn't shut up, she was leaving. "Lew lunged at me and grabbed me, holding me with his left hand, pushing the plate of stew in my face with his right hand. The scalding pain was more than I could bear. I screamed and screamed. He slapped me, kicked me, and pulled my hair until I just didn't know what was happening anymore. I started to run, and he grabbed me and ripped my dress as I was running."

She ran to the bathroom and locked the door, hoping he would not break the lock again as he had done in previous fights. The shouting and screaming stopped. She cleaned herself and put on a bathrobe. Lew had passed out. She cleaned up the mess in the dining room, realizing that things were not going to change. As she was finishing cleaning, Lew got up and was yelling. "I decided, without really thinking, that I'd better get out of the house. I quietly closed the door, took my pocketbook, and started walking." He had sold her car a couple of weeks earlier, saying she didn't really need it. She thought about going to her mother but she lived on the other side of town and Lew had threatened to kill her mother as well as her if she went there. She walked past a police station and went in and asked them to take her to her mother's house. The police never asked her about her bruises.

When she was telling her mother, Lew drove up and told her mother that she was sleeping with other men but he was going to be big-hearted and take her back. She told her mother it was true because she thought Lew would leave her alone if she did. Her mother chastised her and told her to go back to Lew. She went home with Lew and he beat her so badly that she had to go to the doctor the next day. "I explained to the doctor that I had fallen . . . I didn't tell him the truth. I just couldn't. If I did, Lew would only beat me again."

SOURCE: Walker, L. E. (1979). *The battered woman* (pp. 101–105). New York: Harper & Row.

her feel needed, hopeful about the future, and guilty about any thoughts she had about leaving. The time of loving reconciliation (or no tension) stands out as highly rewarding against the background of abuse. The reinforcement increases the likelihood of the cycle occurring again: Violence tends to increase in both frequency and severity if the relationship continues (Okun, 1986; Walker, 1989).

## Abusive Men

Abusive men come from all classes and occupations: They are doctors, professors, police officers, plumbers, car salespeople, and construction workers. Violence is related to the level of family conflict and stress at all education levels (Gelles & Straus, 1979, 1989; Okun, 1986; Straus, Gelles, & Smith, 1990). Levels of violence among African American, Hispanic, and white groups are similar when the groups are equated for employment and socioeconomic class (Coley & Beckett, 1988; Gondolf, 1988a).

Men who typically express stress violently against women have a number of features in common (Walker, 1979). First, they think that husbands should be dominant and are more likely to abuse when they think their authority has been questioned than at other times (Finn, 1986). Second, in spite of their dominance, they are desperately dependent on their wives for nurture (Sperling & Berman, 1991). Because of their dependency and desperation, they are afraid of being abandoned and thus become jealous and suspicious (Holtzworth-Munroe & Anglin, 1991; Okun, 1986). A late dinner is not only a threat to their authority but also a cause for fear that she is seeing another man during the day. Third, the situation is worsened by the fact that abusive men lack skills for prosocial assertion of power, so that they explode in fear and frustration. They are likely to have learned violent expression in their families of origin (Dutton & Strachan, 1987; Sigler, 1989; Walker, 1981). Up to 81% of men who abuse their wives have been abused as children or have seen fathers beat their mothers (Roy, 1982). In turn, up to half (54%) of wife batterers also abuse their children.

Alcohol and other drug problems are related to an increased probability of wife abuse but are not the cause of it (Kantor & Straus, 1990; Leonard & Blane, 1992). Men who are consistently heavy or binge drinkers are more likely to assault their wives than other men are—but most (80%) of these drinkers do not assault their wives at all (Kantor & Straus, 1990). Alcohol can be an indirect cause of violence in that it weakens self-control and provides an excuse—"He wouldn't have done it if he hadn't been drinking" (Hull & Bond, 1986).

What little is known about women who abuse women partners points to their similarities with abusive men. Like men, lesbian batterers use violence to achieve power and dominance in intimate relationships. Like men, they are intensely dependent on the victimized partner. Similarly, substance abuse and exposure as a child to domestic violence facilitate battering (Renzetti, 1992).

## Abused Women

Some people think that women who get into and then stay in an abusive relationship must be **masochists:** people who enjoy pain. Battered women endure pain, but they do not enjoy it (Caplan, 1984). They are no more likely to come from abusive homes than other women are and are less likely to come from abusive homes than their husbands are (33% versus 81%; Roy, 1977). It is unlikely that they suddenly become masochists with marriage. Rather, they enter the marriage with a traditional view of marriage and expect from their husbands the positive experiences they likely had with their fathers (Sigler, 1989). Why do battered women stay? Hope of change, fed by the third stage of the cycle, keeps some women in abusive relationships. Some battered women enter the relationship with low esteem, thinking that no one else would want them (Okun, 1986; Sigler, 1989; Walker, 1981). Probably many other women develop low esteem living with a verbally and physically abusive man. They can become "normal" in as few as 6 months apart from him (chapter 16). Abused women try to deal with the circumstances they are in.

***Active, Not Passive***   Battered women actively try to find ways to deal with their situation. For example, women married to violent men use a wider variety of strategies trying to influence their husbands than wives married to nonviolent men (Aida & Falbo, 1991; Frieze & McHugh, 1992). They increasingly choose actions that have the highest probability of minimizing pain and enhancing survival. When a woman sees that her efforts will no longer protect her or her children, she usually attempts to escape (Walker, 1989).

***Seeking Help***   Most battered women seek help but with little success. Family and friends often reinforce the view that women are responsible for holding marriages together (Frieze, 1986; Sullivan, 1991; Walker, 1989). Women who do receive help from relatives or friends see it as crucial to their being able to leave an abusive relationship (Bowker, 1994; Donato & Bowker, 1984). Battered women also seek help from the community or, if they do not, believe (fairly correctly) that their attempts will not be effective (Sullivan, 1991). The longer and more severe the violence, the more contacts women make (Kalmuss & Straus, 1990; Sullivan & Davidson, 1991; Sullivan, Tan, Basta, Rumptz, & Davidson, 1992).

Without help from the community or acquaintances, women are often left with no financial resources and with increasing fears. Lack of financial resources and fear of revenge are the predominant concerns of both lesbian and heterosexual women (Renzetti, 1992). The concerns are intensified if children are involved (Aguire, 1985; Hofeller, 1982; Sullivan, 1991; Sullivan et al., 1992). The more resources a woman has, the more likely she is to leave the relationship. Women often stay in the relationship because of realistic concerns that the husband may kill her and perhaps the children if she tries to escape (Campbell, 1992; Finkelhor & Yllo, 1985; Sullivan et al., 1992).

## When Abuse Turns to Murder

For every 75 women who kill their husbands, 100 husbands kill their wives (Maxfield, 1989; Wilson & Daly, 1992). The men often hunt down their wives to kill them, whereas wives kill in self-defense and desperation (Dobash et al., 1992). Risk of spousal homicide is greater in interracial couples and increases as age differential increases (Mercy & Saltzman, 1989).

The good news is that since 1976 the overall rate of deaths by boyfriends, husbands, or ex-partners has dropped by 18% (41% for African American women specifically), in spite of a doubling of domestic assault reports (Smith & Loring, 1994). The decline in murders may reflect tougher laws and more aggressive enforcement and an increase in the number of shelters. In spite of the decline, the absolute number of women killed is considerable.

Many women still feel they have to defend themselves and their children by killing the man. The difference between the women who kill their partners and those who do not is not a matter of differences between the women but of differences between the men (Browne, 1987; Dobash et al., 1992). Men who were killed had used alcohol and drugs more often than the comparison group, were generally more violent, abused their children and their wives more often and more severely, and had raped their wives and threatened to kill them more frequently.

In spite of these facts, many more women have been jailed for killing their husbands than have been acquitted. The stories of acquittal get attention because they are the exception to the rule. A man is less likely to receive a murder conviction for murdering his partner than a woman who murders her partner; if he is convicted, he is sentenced to an average of 2 to 6 years, while women are sentenced to 15 to 20 years (Browne, 1987). This pattern suggests the lingering view that women are supposed to have a subordinate status, so that if they object to the subordination and beating, something is wrong with them. In addition, violence by a woman may be seen as more vicious than the same violence by a man because it is inconsistent with what is expected of women (chapter 9). Efforts to help abused women by providing shelters, so that they are less likely to be killed or to kill, have grown over the years.

## Help for Abused Women

The first shelter for women in the United States was Haven House, opened in 1964 in Pasadena, California. It started originally as an alcohol treatment center for women. The term *battering* was not used then, but so many of the women who came had been battered that it became explicitly a shelter for battered women (Barnett & LaViolette, 1993). Other efforts soon followed. There are over 2000 domestic violence programs across the United States; most include shelters. This is not enough. For every woman who receives shelter, three are turned away because of lack of space (Smith & Loring, 1994). Lesbians rarely call shelters because of the fear that they will not be accepted by the heterosexual women (Renzetti, 1992). Most shelters have to rely on scant city or government funds and volunteer gifts. Congress (1984) did pass the Family Violence Prevention and Services Act, providing some funds for victims of domestic violence. A few universities have established shelters for their students and staff.

Shelters provide a place for women to escape, but help is limited and temporary. Many abused women who use shelters do not have the skills to become self-supporting. Cris Sullivan and her colleagues (Campbell, Sullivan, & Davidson, 1995; Sullivan & Davidson, 1991; Sullivan et al., 1992) have developed a project in which trained undergraduates work with women from shelters. Women who worked with advocates were more effective than others in accessing community resources, and their reported quality of life and social support also were higher.

Simply giving battered women self-defense training is like telling them to "take two aspirins and call me in the morning," but the morning does not bring professional attention. More is needed than shelters and help after getting there. Legal and policy reform, along with coordinated community response, is necessary (e.g., see Browne, 1993; Goodman et al., 1993; Reidly & VonKorff, 1991; Syers & Edleson, 1992; United Nations, 1989). (For a look at the role of media violence in disempowering women, see Focus on Research 15.1.)

# Sexual Harassment

Sexual harassment has been likened to rape and called "the little rapes" (Offir, 1982; Popovich, Jolton, Mastragelo, Everton, & Somers, 1995). We have spoken of harassment as a problem women face on the job and given evidence of its prevalence in chapter 13. In this chapter we discuss harassment in terms of violence. Although no experience can be the equivalent of rape, there are similarities among forms of violence, specifically rape and harassment. Both rape and harassment, like battering, are abuses of power, most often by men against women, and the abused person often feels that protests are futile (Abel & Rouleau, 1995; Goodman et al., 1993; Houston & Hwang, 1996). The incidents are not always labeled as what they are, nor are they always reported. Further, recurring differences are found in women's and men's judgments of harassment.

## Reporting and Labeling

A predominant response of women, whether of high school or college age or older, is to try to ignore sexual harassment (Cochran, Frazier, & Olson, 1997; Houston & Hwang, 1996; Riger, 1991). That women do not report the incidents while having reduced tolerance for harassment tells us something about the social context in which women work and about the futility women feel in the face of men's powers. Interestingly, reporting is independent of feminist ideology or experience with harassment (Mazer & Percival, 1989; Saperstein, Triolo, & Heinzen, 1995).

There are costs of being harassed and of reporting the harassment. A large survey of federal employees (U.S. Merit System Protection Board, 1981) found that 20% of women and 18% of men who had experienced harassment made formal complaints. Of those who did, a third found that formal complaint made things worse (Livingston, 1982). When the accused has more power, the complainant is vulnerable to retaliation. Legal actions take time and money, and most employed women do not have much of either (Riger, 1991). Few complainants receive a favorable outcome, and the typical settlements for those few are quite low and unlikely to compensate victims for the emotional and financial stress involved in filing the complaint. On the other hand, not taking action can make a woman feel even more powerless. The fact is that in many organizations women are powerless and victimized. The organizations include academic institutions (Caplan, 1993; Paludi, 1990; Riger, 1991).

Most college students say that they would report harassment, but they actually make reports in comparatively low numbers (estimates range from zero to 30%) (Baker, Terpstra, & Larntz, 1990; Brooks & Perot, 1991; Koss, 1990). Why are reports so low? Students share with employees a fear of not being believed, a distrust of the reporting procedures, and fear of retaliation. Students want to know there is an effective grievance procedure in which they can speak confidentially with a woman staff member who is not in the harasser's department (Metha & Nigg, 1982; Sullivan & Bybee, 1987). Faculty women, harassed by both students and colleagues, also often do not file complaints because they fear damaging their professional advancement

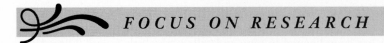

## FOCUS ON RESEARCH

### 15.1    The True Experiment: Media Violence Against Women

What is the formula for a successful Hollywood action blockbuster? Handsome men, beautiful women, mystery, suspense, and inevitably some violence. More often than not, women are the targets of this violence and need to be rescued. There just aren't a lot of strong, resourceful female characters in Hollywood films these days. But there are a lot of women who watch such films. How do women viewers respond to scenes in which females are regularly stalked, chased, abducted, beaten, and raped? Does it change the viewer's self-image? Does she begin to feel more vulnerable herself?

Researchers Penny Reid and Gillian Finchilescu (1995) investigated this question, using an experimental design. The simplest experiment has two groups of participants, one of which, the experimental group, is purposely treated differently than the other, the control group. In all other respects, the two groups are equivalent. If the groups differ afterward on the dependent variable, we can fairly safely assume the difference is due to their treatment, or the independent variable. In order to be confident about this assumption, however, we must be sure that the two groups are the same at the outset. The simplest way to ensure this would be to start with identical groups. But since no two individuals are ever the same in all respects, such a tactic is impossible. An equally good approach is to make sure the groups don't differ in any systematic way. We can accomplish this by assigning individuals at random to either group. If each person has the same chance of being assigned to either group, and if we assign enough people to each, the differences among the people will balance out between the groups. Random assignment will distribute any initial differences more or less evenly between the groups.

Reid and Finchilescu followed this random assignment procedure with 57 college women as their participants. However, they used a special version of the experimental design called a Solomon four-group design. This design combines experimental and control groups with a pretest and a post-test. As the four-group name implies, participants are randomly assigned to one of four groups and treated as follows:

| Group 1 (experimental) | Pretest | Treatment | Post-test |
| Group 2 (control) | Pretest | No treatment | Post-test |
| Group 3 (experimental) | No pretest | Treatment | Post-test |
| Group 4 (control) | No pretest | No treatment | Post-test |

The pretest and post-test are comparable versions of the same questionnaire. The pretest scores help determine if the random assignment procedure worked; if it did, the pretest scores of all four groups should be equivalent. The post-test is the dependent variable; if the independent variable had an effect (in other words, if the treatment worked), we should see a change from pre- to post-test scores, and we should also see a difference between post-test scores of the experimental and control groups.

This design also tells us if giving a pretest has any effect on subsequent behavior; we can compare the post-test scores of the groups that took the pretest against the scores of those that did not have a pretest.

In their study, Reid and Finchilescu used two versions of their Disempowerment Scale as the pre- and post-test. This scale measured feelings of intimidation, fear, safety and protection, control, and competence. Their independent variable was exposure to violent clips from commercial films; the experimental condition used clips of violence toward women, and the control condition used clips of violence toward men. Analysis of the pre- and post-test scores indicated that filling out the Disempowerment Scale before viewing the film clips did not sensitize participants, and the group that viewed the clips of violence against women felt more disempowered on the post-test questionnaire than did the groups that viewed clips of male violence.

Because of their strict experimental design, Reid and Finchilescu can say with great confidence that the increased feelings of disempowerment experienced by women in the experimental groups were caused by exposure to the female-violence clips and not by some other, unaccounted-for factor. One great advantage of an experimental design is its control of confounds. A confound is a factor or variable that the researcher is not aware of that might be responsible for the change in the dependent variable. The presence of confounds severely jeopardizes the researcher's ability to claim that the independent variable is the cause of changes in the dependent variable. Several potential confounds can plague studies, including history effects, which occur when social events that happen during the course of the experiment affect participants' performance on the dependent variable, and selection effects, which occur when participants in one group differ initially from participants in another group. The Solomon four-group experimental design helps identify any history confound by employing a control group; this group's behavior will reflect the history effect alone and can be compared against the experimental group's behavior, which will reflect both history and the experimental treatment. This experimental design also guards against a selection confound in two ways: Random assignment of participants to groups should equate the groups, but the pretest will check this and alert the researcher to any initial group differences in the behavior under study.

How can we use the knowledge that women feel disempowered by watching violence targeted at women? Reid and Finchilescu point out that what is considered entertainment often contains misogynistic violence. Women need to be prepared for this psychological assault in order to counter feelings of vulnerability and disempowerment. Society must also play a role in eradicating such violence by refusing to embrace such films.

JILL BORCHERT ◆

SOURCE: Reid, P., & Finchilescu, G. (1995). The disempowering effects of media violence against women on college women. *Psychology of Women Quarterly, 19,* 397–411.

(Brooks & Perot, 1991; Caplan, 1993; Paludi, 1990). Part of the resistance to reporting, however, results from judgments about what is considered harassment.

Women do not always use the label *rape* when it is justified, nor do they always use the label *harassment* when it is justified. Few university students and faculty say that they have been sexually harassed, but many more say that they have been touched, fondled, and propositioned (5%–10% versus 30%; Brooks & Perot, 1991; Fitzgerald et al., 1988). Part of the reason for the underlabeling is definitional. People generally agree on severe harassment; beyond that, there is vast confusion about what constitutes harassment (Bursik, 1992; Fitzgerald & Ormerod, 1991; Riger, 1991). The more flagrant and frequent the questionable behavior, the more offensive it is seen to be, especially when done by someone with greater power and when physical advances with threats are involved (Brooks & Perot, 1991; Bursik, 1992; Cochran et al., 1997; Riger, 1991). However, harassment by an organizational superior is not the most prevalent type of harassment incident (Gutek, 1985; U.S. Merit System Protection Board, 1981). For example, on college campuses both undergraduates and faculty are more likely to have unwelcome attention from men who are peers, perhaps because there is more interaction with them (Cochran et al., 1997).

## Judgments by Gender

In judging harassment cases, the courts use the reasonable person rule, asking whether a reasonable person would be offended. The problem is that reasonable people may differ in their views (Baker et al., 1990; Katz, Hannon, & Whitten, 1996). Traditionality is an important factor in how people view harassment, as it is in judgments about rape (Dietz-Uhler, 1993; Jensen & Gutek, 1982; Powell, 1986; Valentine-French & Radtke, 1989). Particularly notable is that a reasonable woman and a reasonable man are likely to have different views of what is offensive (Riger, 1991). A recurring finding has been that men see fewer incidents as harassment, consider it less seriously, and are more blaming of women than women are, paralleling the broad gender differences in judgments about rape (Bursik, 1992; Charney & Russell, 1994; Cochran et al., 1997; Murrell & Dietz-Uhler, 1993; Saperstein et al., 1995). However, there are some signs of change. College men agreed with college women in judgments about harassment when the man was a perpetrator and the woman the victim, regardless of whether the two were in a differential or an equal relationship (Katz et al., 1996). In spite of this, we cannot say that gender differences are absent. College women grow less tolerant of harassment as their experience with it increases, while men grow more tolerant (Saperstein et al., 1995). This may reflect men's views that being harassed by a woman is acceptable, because they think of it as flattery or flirtation (Katz et al., 1996; Shea, 1993). Women's views do not change depending on whether a man or a woman is the harasser; but men judge the same act as less likely to be harassing when the perpetrator is a woman than when a man (Figure 15.3; Katz et al., 1996).

Different perceptions of the meaning of behaviors are probably involved when the same event is given different interpretations. Men are more likely than women to think that sexual teasing, looks, or physical contact are flattery, not harassment. They not only think that sexual attentions from a woman are flattering but also are likely

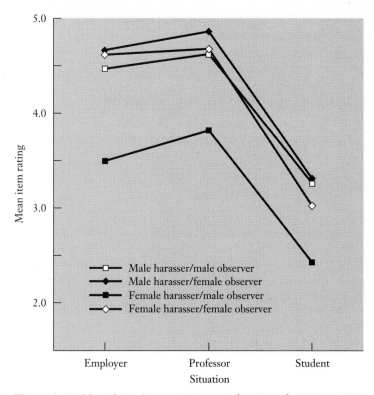

**Figure 15.3** *Mean harassment ratings as a function of group and situation.* NOTE: Participants were 197 undergraduate students, randomly divided into two groups. Participants rated the degree to which they thought sexual harassment occurred in 20 hypothetical interactions in each of three situations using a 7-point sexual harassment scale. In one group, the harasser was a man and the victim a woman; in the other group, the harasser was a woman and the victim a man.

SOURCE: Katz, R. C., Hannon, R., & Whitten, L. (1996). Effects of gender and situation on the allegation of sexual harassment. *Sex Roles, 34,* (1/2), 35–47.

to see women's cues as more sexual and flirtatious than women think they are. This may be why men are more likely to think that women "ask" for the attention (Abbey, 1982, 1991; Abbey & Harnish, 1995; Johnson, Stockdale, & Saal, 1991; Workman & Johnson, 1991).

For example, undergraduate men watching a video interpreted a woman's behavior as sexier than women did, no matter what the level of harassment from a male professor or the woman's response to the harassment (Johnson et al., 1991). The men also saw a female professor with a male student as behaving in more flirtatious, seductive, and sexy ways than women saw her and more so than a professorial man with the same behaviors—men see women as more seductive than they see men. If men see women's behavior more sexually than women do and are not sensitive to variations in a man's behavior, they are more likely to think a woman is "leading them on." The result in men's judgments is that "it is all her fault," a parallel to rape myths.

## Men Inclined to Harassment

Men who are prone to harassment have some similarities with coercive men and indeed report greater likelihood of committing rape than other men do (Pryor, 1987; Pryor & Stoller, 1994). Like coercive men, they have adversarial sex beliefs and highly traditional beliefs about gender roles. They also are authoritarian and have difficulty seeing from another person's perspective, so that they are not likely to understand (or care) that a woman finds their behavior objectionable.

However, the men most prone to harassment are able to control their actions when they have clear messages that the behavior is not appropriate; perhaps their propensity to be traditional and authoritarian leads them to obey orders that come from "higher-ups." Their corrections show that even men inclined to harass are not victims of their so-called instincts. They can let a "voice of authority" take precedence over theirs, just as people may overcome discrimination in hiring when the head people of the organization give a clear message that it is unacceptable (chapter 13).

## *Pornography, Sex, and Aggression*

When considering violence against women, many people raise the issue of pornography as a possible cause. It is not clear that pornography is a direct cause of sexually violent behavior against women. The prevalence of pornography can be seen, however, as a sign of cultural attitudes about men's right to dominate women and in turn contributes to those attitudes. And it is clear that pornography is, at a minimum, an indirect cause of aggression against women.

What is **pornography**? In one view, pornography is *all* sexually explicit material designed to elicit or enhance sexual arousal (Mosher & MacIan, 1994). It might be sexually violent, nonviolent but degrading or dehumanizing, or not degrading and not dehumanizing (Cowan & Campbell, 1994). Another view makes distinctions within the category of sexually explicit material. In this schema, **erotica** is a sexual depiction based on equality and mutual consent. Gloria Steinem (1978, 1980) pointed out that *erotica* comes from the word *eros* and pertains to passionate love or sexual desire; it implies shared pleasure. In contrast, *pornography* comes from the Greek *pornē*, meaning "prostitute." Pornography is sexually explicit material that is degrading or abusive to women and portrayed to endorse the behavior (Longino, 1980; Russell, 1993, 1983d). It is not about sexual love but about dominance and violence. In this view pornography is the antithesis of eroticism and basically is antisexual (Griffin, 1981).

Feminists' objections typically are not about explicit sexual content of mutual desire and consent (erotica) but about the demeaning depiction of women as objects to be used for men's satisfaction (pornography). In view of recent demonstrations that pornography also is racist, feminist concerns are likely to extend to issues of ethnicity and class oppression as well (Focus on Research 15.2; Collins, 1993; Cowan & Campbell, 1994).

Much sexually explicit material is violent or demeaning rather than erotic; it is sexist, racist, and profitable (Cowan & Campbell, 1994). Even MTV and R-rated videotapes have approximately as much violence as X-rated tapes (Donnerstein, Linz, & Penrod, 1987; Jhally, 1991; Rubin, 1990; Yang & Linz, 1990). Depictions of women enjoying force in a nonexplicit sexual context pervade mainstream mass media, including billboard advertisements, fashion magazines, and record covers (Linz, Wilson, & Donnerstein, 1992). Video games targeted for children also highlight force against women.

Demeaning pornography has been considered the media equivalent of rape (Groth & Birnbaum, 1979). Indeed, some of the content of pornography is rape (Campbell, 1993; Giobbe, 1993). Linda Marciano starred as "Linda Lovelace" in the movie *Deep Throat;* she was held prisoner and beaten during the filming of the movie that showed her actually being raped (Blakely, 1985; Lovelace, 1981, 1986; Steinem, 1993). This is not rare (Cowan, Lee, Levy, & Snyder, 1988). Particularly of concern is the unrealistic portrayal, feeding rape myths, of women enjoying force (Mosher & MacIan, 1994; Rapaport & Posey, 1991).

People who defend pornography argue that it allows catharsis, a "harmless draining of sexual fantasies." Catharsis is a Freudian concept (suggested to Freud by a patient, Anna O., actually Bertha Pappenheim, an early noted feminist) that means essentially a cleansing of feelings or "chimney sweeping." The idea is that movies, stories, fantasies, and jokes about "forbidden impulses" such as aggression and sexuality can provide an outlet for those human feelings, so that they are less likely to be directly expressed in actions. Evidence is not totally consistent, but some evidence from other countries (e.g., Denmark, Federal Republic of Germany, Japan) does suggest a cathartic effect (Green, 1987). For example, as pornography became more available in Denmark and Germany, sexual crimes decreased or stabilized; in Japan the most common form of pornography deals with rape, but the rate of rape is one-sixteenth that in the United States.

What works in one culture may not work in another. Data from the United States do not show evidence of a cathartic effect, perhaps because of the greater general level of violence in this country (Russell, 1993, 1983c). Rape is correlated not only with reading magazines such as *Playboy, Penthouse,* and *Hustler* (Koss & Dinero, 1989) but also with reading "outdoor" publications, such as *Field and Stream* and *Guns and Ammo* (Baron & Straus, 1987; Green, 1987). We cannot simplistically conclude that reading such magazines causes men to become rapists, but the evidence discussed next shows that exposure influences attitudes, and attitudes can influence behavior.

## Pornography and Attitudes

It is clear that pornography and media generally have an important indirect effect on sexually aggressive behaviors by affecting attitudes (Check & Malamuth, 1985; Malamuth, 1983, 1986; Malamuth & Briere, 1986; Malamuth & Check, 1985). Attitudes in combination with personality characteristics result in sexually aggressive

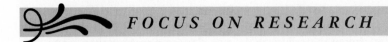

## FOCUS ON RESEARCH

### 15.2    Content Analysis: Pornography Is Sexist and Racist

With the advent of the videocassette industry, more people are renting more movies to view in the comfort of their own homes. Pornographic videocassettes depicting heterosexual activity make up approximately 12% of all rentals, which translates into 395 million X-rated videos rented in one year. This is indeed a growing market.

X-rated videos, characterized by explicit sexuality, fall into three categories. Sexually violent videos show the overt use of threats or force and the infliction of pain. Nonviolent but degrading X-rated videos include objectification, subordination, and inequality between characters maintained through verbal or emotional domination. In both of these categories, male characters are more likely to be the perpetrators of violence or degradation and female characters the targets. The third category of nonviolent and nondegrading X-rated materials are sexually explicit, but the characters participate by choice and mutual consent.

Most researchers have been concerned about the sexual violence and degradation of women in X-rated films. Researchers Gloria Cowan and Robin Campbell (1994) suggested that X-rated materials are not just sexist but racist as well. Pornography is marketed for white men; the fantasy of dominating and exploiting women may well carry over to minority racial groups, particularly African Americans. In the United States, the institution of slavery was intertwined with negative sexual stereotypes about both women and men of African heritage. Are these images a part of today's X-rated films?

The method Cowan and Campbell used in their investigation is a content analysis. This method can be applied to different forms of communication, including books, letters, speeches, songs, television programs, and, as in this case, films. The first task is to operationally define the key variables; from these definitions a list of coding categories is developed. Cowan and Campbell restricted their interest to racially mixed sexual scenes and coded for the presence or absence of the following factors linked to sexism and racism: physical aggression, verbal aggression, inequality, racial stereotyping, intimacy, and submission. Clear and unambiguous coding categories contribute to the internal validity of the study and increase its ability to produce meaningful results. Next, the "participants"—the films themselves—must be randomly selected

---

behavior; the aggression, especially if unpunished and if rewarded by peers, can further affect attitudes. The media may influence the attitudes of people who do not behave violently but voice approval of violence, which may contribute to violent behavior.

Experimental research suggests a causative contribution of pornography to attitudes. Men's exposure to pornography lessens sensitivity to rape and increases acceptance of rape myths, increases reported likelihood of sexual assault, increases sexual callousness toward women, and leads to sexual arousal and rape fantasies (Check &

from the population of X-rated films. Cowan and Campbell's research team visited the adult sections of five local video rental stores and selected at random a total of 54 African American/white interracial X-rated videos.

Perhaps the most important component of a content analysis is the coders or raters. Any time researchers record their observations there is the possibility for researcher bias; the attitudes or experiences of researchers can affect their observations and ultimately skew the results of the study. Employing more than one coder and giving each person identical training in recognizing codable behaviors can help prevent researcher bias and promote accurate and consistent observations. Another way to check that observations are consistent among the coders is to compute the interrater reliability. This is a correlation that measures the agreement between two coders; the higher the correlation, the more the two raters are observing and coding alike and the less their coding is affected by individual bias. A low correlation alerts the researchers that coding categories may need to be more clearly defined or that additional training for coders is required.

Cowan and Campbell conducted two training sessions for the five coders in their study. All coders were female but differed in age, marital status, religious affiliation, race, and past exposure to X-rated materials, thus ensuring different perspectives. Interrater reliability of independently coded scenes was found to be very high. The results of the content analysis showed that both sexism and racism were prevalent in interracial X-rated videos. Women were the victims of men's physical and verbal aggression. Racial sexual stereotypes were present, and both female and male African American characters were portrayed as having lower status than white characters.

How should we interpret these findings? Cowan and Campbell note that their results support the view of some African American feminists that racism and sexism are interwoven issues that together support the white male power base. The researchers note that in the past, pornography has been labeled a woman's or feminist issue; they suggest that pornography should also be labeled a racial issue, to encourage the disempowered groups to take a stand against this medium.

JILL BORCHERT ◆

SOURCE: Cowan, G., & Campbell, R. R. (1994). Racism and sexism in interracial pornography: A content analysis. *Psychology of Women Quarterly, 18,* 323–338.

---

Malamuth, 1985; Donnerstein et al., 1987; Linz, 1985, 1989; Malamuth & Briere, 1986; Senn, 1993). After seeing violent pornographic images, nearly twice as many college men said they would have some likelihood of raping a woman if they knew they would not be caught compared to men without exposure (57% versus 30%; Briere & Malamuth, 1983; Donnerstein, 1983).

Women exposed to depictions of violence against women show increased feelings of disempowerment (Reid & Finchilescu, 1995); they are similarly affected by rap music, which depicts women in sexually subordinate roles (Johnson, Adams, Ashburn, & Reed, 1995). Men also are affected by misogynous rap music, showing a facilitation of sexually aggressive behavior afterwards (Barongan & Hall, 1995).

Apparently, concern should be extended beyond explicitly demeaning pornographic material. Exposure to heavy-metal rock music—irrespective of whether the lyrical content was sexually violent or concerned with religious ideals—increased men's gender role stereotyping and negative attitudes toward women (St. Lawrence & Joyner, 1991).

Of course, individual differences matter—some men are more sexually aggressive to women than others are, and the effects of pornography seem greater for those (Mosher & MacIan, 1994; Rapaport & Posey, 1991). For example, self-reported sexually coercive men were more aggressive against women nonsexually as well as sexually (Malamuth, 1983, 1986). If they had been angered by a woman (supposedly another participant in the research study), they were more aggressive in giving her electric shocks or an unpleasant noise, as part of the experiment, after seeing an aggressive-erotic or an aggressive film in which a woman was physically abused.

In studies in which shock (supposedly) is given by one person, the researcher implicitly gives "permission" for the aggression because the study is a part of "legitimate science." Outside experimental situations, "permission" is given by the general acceptability of male dominance over women.

## What Can Be Done?

Public opinion is divided about whether pornography should be made illegal. Much of the division is along gender lines, with more women (72%) than men (41%) having negative responses to pornography and thinking that laws against pornography should be stricter (Sussman, 1986). The specific responses of women vary, however, as do their views about what should be done (Russell, 1983d; Senn, 1993). Some women dislike pornography because they believe it presents negative images of women while putting forward an unrealistic standard of physical attractiveness for women. Other women see all sexually explicit material as objectionable; they will not have it in their homes, nor will they be involved with male consumers. Still other women do not like such material but are also somewhat grateful that their male partners (who are "sometimes consumers") are not into extremely violent material and that they do not ask to replay the depicted actions in their relationships. These women are relatively satisfied with their marital arrangements but feel pornography is harmful; they focus concerns on children's exposure to it.

Feminists are divided about what should be done (Cowan, 1992; Cowan, Chase, & Stahly, 1989; Russell, 1983d; "Where do we stand," 1994). Some feminists maintain that any restriction of free speech, including that of pornographers, is dangerous and will lead to infringement of individual rights concerning abortion and sexual relationships. Others, such as Catharine MacKinnon (1986, 1987) and Andrea Dworkin (1981; Dworkin & MacKinnon, 1988), maintain that pornography is a form of sex discrimination because it infringes on the civil rights of women. Ordinances supporting this view were passed in Minneapolis and Indianapolis but subsequently declared unconsti-

*Although a direct causal link has not been established between pornography and violence against women, pornography does contribute to a climate in which such violence becomes more acceptable. These protestors' signs offer a number of comments on the effects of pornography.*

tutional or vetoed because the pornographers' right of free speech was seen as more important than the harm to women. The debate continues (Palley, 1994). "When important values, such as individual rights and responsibility to the welfare of others, are pitted against each other, it is clear that . . . some agonizing choices must be made" (Cowan et al., 1989, p. 111).

Some reviewers consider the most promising solution to be one of bypassing the legal and moral issues by focusing on educational interventions aimed at changing beliefs about sexual violence (Linz et al., 1992; Palley, 1994; Stille, 1985). For example, being told of the horrible long-term consequences of rape for the victim reduces the impact of pornography. Another method involves women watching pornography with men (Linz et al., 1992). When college men saw a film with a woman (actually a confederate) who was negative or neutral about the film, the men found the film more embarrassing, upsetting, and degrading to women than did those who watched either with a woman who was positive or without a woman companion. Research about educational interventions is incomplete but is sufficiently promising to be continued. The alternative is to pit people with two equally valid sets of moral and political concerns against each other or, because we are not solving the problem, to pretend the problem does not exist.

## *Some Final Thoughts: Band-Aids and Cures*

Women have been taught to please men and to define themselves through relationships with men; they expect that men will give them protection as well as fulfillment. Yet women are more likely to be victimized by men than by women and by men who are their acquaintances and loved ones than by strangers. The abuse starts in childhood and continues in the dates of young adulthood and in marriages and employment. The more men accept gender stereotyping and rape myths, the more likely they are to be violent with women; the more women accept gender stereotyping and rape myths, the more likely they are to be victimized. Most women not only are uncomfortable being assertive against a man but also resist labeling themselves as victims of men.

Women are advised that to avoid rape they should take self-defense classes, not go out alone late at night, and lock their doors. This advice does little for the children or the abused women who are victims of a trusted loved one behind the locked doors with them. Advice to be assertive and stand up for yourself may escalate a woman's problems on the job instead of solving a harassment problem. Even for women and rape, the advice is good advice in the same way that other symptom treatments are: Take an aspirin when you have a headache, or wash a cut and cover it with a Band-Aid. At some point, it seems wise to wonder why you are having so many headaches or cuts. Assigning women the responsibility to "take care" is treatment of the symptoms of the underlying social disease, not a cure for it. Here and now, women are well advised to take care at night (and when the sun is shining!), but the ultimate aim is to "Take Back the Night," as a feminist saying goes.

The wounds that women experience are due to men's abuse of their power over women, through physical strength, economic resources, or employment status, and simply their status as men. Men could not abuse their power if women were equal in power. But women are being denied their rights. If college women cannot study late at the library or employed women work late and then go home alone and count on safety at home, educational opportunities and vocational opportunities are not equal, nor are women and men equally valued as human beings. When women are "suspect" if they make an accusation, and more so if they are minority women, this is not the land of opportunity for all but the land of opportunity for some men to act upon and perpetuate their greater power.

Erich Fromm (1976/1981), psychologist, social philosopher, and psychoanalyst, wrote that power differential prohibits full human growth. He saw the first rape of a woman as the first act of dominance of one person over another. From there, things went downhill as people became concerned with dominance and power instead of with the productive love and productive work that expresses and generates full human living. Fromm expressed high hopes for the contribution of the women's movement to human growth to the extent that it encourages equality.

Much credit is due the women's movement for raising consciousness about rape, incest, battering, harassment, and pornography. Men as well are participating in increasing awareness of the issues. We have a start toward people working for the fundamental cultural changes necessary to keep women from having the onus of protecting themselves from the violence men are taught to display. That so many women have found ways to survive experiences of rape, child abuse, battering, and harassment is a potent statement of women's strength. That so many men do not victimize women is a statement of their strength in resisting societal definitions of being a man. It is time for changes so that women's strength can be channeled to ends other than surviving abuse and men's strength can be channeled to ends other than abuse or fighting the messages to exert power over women.

It is time for a cure rather than Band-Aids. The cure requires a deep change in societal attitudes about equality as human beings and the differential availability and use of power. It requires a fundamental change in our understanding of what it means to be a woman or a man and how we can best relate to each other.

## KEY TERMS

stranger rape
acquaintance rape, hidden rape
date rape
gang rape
rape myths
"nothing happened" myths
"no harm was done" myths
"she wanted it" myths
"she deserved it" myths

unacknowledged rape victims
post-traumatic stress disorder (PTSD)
characterological self-blame versus behavioral self-blame
child sexual abuse
incest

pedophilia, child molestation
tension-building stage
acute battering incident
no tension, or loving contrition and reconciliation
masochist
pornography
erotica

## KEY POINTS

*Rape*

- The United States has the highest rate of sexual assault of any industrialized country. At least one in four women are raped, but few rapes are reported. Rapes by acquaintances are more frequent than rapes by strangers. As frequent as physical coercion is, verbal coercion is more prevalent.

- Rape myths influence judgments about rape, men's likelihood of committing rape, women's adjustment after rape, and their likelihood of using the word *rape* for their experiences. Stranger rape is taken more seriously than date rape.

- Rape often has an impact for many years; its effects include depression and anxiety, and for women raped by an acquaintance, a feeling of betrayal.

- Self-blame for rape is common and its effects controversial. Becoming a true survivor involves facing evil, grieving for lost innocence, and dealing with themes of meaning, mastery and control, and self-enhancement.

- Convicted rapists, undetected rapists, and men with a likelihood for coercion share many features: strong gender-typing, belief in rape myths, low opinions of women, sexual arousal on viewing depictions of rape. They do not have a higher sex drive than other men.

## Child Sexual Abuse

◆ Child sexual abuse most commonly involves a man and a girl. Father-daughter incest is the most frequent of reported incest cases but brother-sister and cousin-cousin incests occur more frequently.

◆ The father who commits incest is a ruling patriarch. The mother, in the classical picture, is unaffectionate and in poor health. However, many mothers support their daughters when they learn of the incest. Girls living with father substitutes are at highest risk.

◆ Childhood victimization often has immediate and long-term effects: traumatic sexualization, a sense of betrayal and of powerlessness, low esteem, victimization, and stigmatization. Women with childhood victimization are higher in depression and anxiety, more likely to be revictimized, and overrepresented in groups with some mental disorders. Revictimization is not inevitable.

◆ Although most women who were abused as children seem to remember it, some do repress it, and some may have "false memories."

## Battered Women

◆ At least a fourth of wives and at least as many women in dating relationships experience abuse by their partners. Ethnic groups are similar in incidence of family violence when controls are made for income and employment.

◆ Men who batter when stressed are less egalitarian than other men; more likely to come from violent homes; low in verbal assertiveness, self-esteem, and coping skills; and dependent on their wives. Substance abuse often is involved in abuse but cannot be blamed for it.

◆ Many abused women seek help but do not get much. Financial dependency and fear that the husband will kill her or the children if she attempts to escape keep women in the relationship. More men than women kill their intimate partners, but men are less likely to be convicted than women who kill partners.

◆ More shelters for battered women are needed, and more than shelters are needed to enable women's effective functioning out of the shelter.

## Sexual Harassment

◆ Women who are harassed typically have little power and face many personal and financial costs in making a formal complaint.

◆ People typically agree about blatant harassment, but women are more likely than men to label more subtle behaviors as harassment. Men see women as more responsible for harassment than women do, often because men interpret women's behavior as sexual.

## Pornography

◆ The availability of pornography in this country is associated with increased violence. Exposure to pornography affects attitudes, including increasing acceptance of sexual violence and the likelihood of sexual assault and rape fantasies. Sexually coercive men are more sexually responsive to rape depictions than other men are.

◆ More women than men think there should be strict laws against pornography, but there is disagreement among women and among feminists about what should be done.

◆ Educational attempts to reduce the effects of viewing pornography have potential.

## INTEGRATIVE QUESTIONS

1. Discuss the APA's position on violence, e.g., should the meaning of violence be limited to physical violence or conceived more broadly? Why or why not?

2. Outline the reasons why a woman might be reluctant to admit to herself or to her friends and relatives that she has been raped as an adult, she is a victim of childhood sexual abuse, she is a battered woman, she has been harassed. For this question, do not be concerned with formal reporting to authorities. Discuss your outline in terms of the similarities you see and try to explain them.

3. Outline the reasons why a woman who realizes what has happened to her might be reluctant to report to authorities that she has been raped as an adult, she is a victim of childhood sexual abuse, she is a battered woman, she has been harassed. Discuss your outline in terms of the similarities you see and try to explain them.

4. Harassment and pornography in the media have been likened to rape. Is this a trivialization of rape? How are they all similar? How are they different?

5. The author of a column about men in a newspaper said, "The most popular pornography among men involves sexually willing women—women who actively, even hungrily, desire men" (Chethik, 1994, p. 2J). He acknowledges the harm of heavy pornography but encouraged the media to take the best of pornography ("its openness, exploration and celebration of sexuality") and add to it values of equalitarianism and artfulness, along with respect for the power and beauty of sex. Discuss his position. Is this "just another male chauvinist"? Keep in mind definitional issues and what you learned in chapter 11 on sexuality.

6. Outline your program for eliminating violence against women and children. Be specific.

7. Consider any specific instance of violence against women that you know about first hand (you were involved or a close acquaintance was). Analyze it in light of concepts discussed in the text. Point out the differences and similarities of the specific case relative to the text treatment and try to explain.

*Chapter 16*

# *Women's Mental Health*

*W*e have seen throughout this book the pressures of role expectations and of reduced power and status of women. Although many women survive very well and even thrive, the pressures do take a toll. Womanhood as it has been defined stereotypically in our culture is unhealthy. Psychological problems increase in adolescence as young women experience gender role intensification (chapter 5). Women's experiences lead to certain mental health problems, but women's problems have been ignored, trivialized, or overtreated with drugs. Feminists have challenged the mental health system with encouraging results, but much still needs attention.

In this chapter we focus on problems of depression, anxiety disorders, eating problems, alcohol and other drugs, and then consider how women are treated in the mental health system.

Before continuing, consider these questions for personal thought:

- What reason (if any) does the "typical woman" have to be depressed just because she is a "typical woman"?
- What do you do when you are blue? Does it help you get out of the dumps or do you become sadder?
- When you were a child and were scared by something, how did your parents react? How is that relevant to your current fears?
- Have your parents' attitudes about eating influenced your eating habits in any way? How?
- What do you like and dislike about your body? Why? How is your body image related to other images of yourself?
- Is it OK for a "nice young man" to have too much to drink, assuming he doesn't hurt anyone or anything? Is your answer the same for a "nice young woman"?

◆ Is our culture a "drug addictive culture"? What drugs do people around you use? What is your favorite drug, if any?

◆ From what you know now, do you think that women are expected to have psychological disorders?

◆ Would you trust a psychotherapist who wanted to have sex with you for your own good? How about a professor?

## Women's Mental Health Problems

Across all ethnic groups, more women than men use mental health services (Aneshensel, 1992; Conger, Lorenz, Elder, Simons, & Ge, 1993; Gove, 1980; Russo, 1990). Women lead in admissions to private psychiatric hospitals and to general hospitals and in psychological care without hospitalization. Men are predominant in state and county psychiatric hospitals as well as Veteran's Administration hospitals, and so are more likely than women to be hospitalized.

A possibility people often raise to explain women's greater use of mental health services is that women are more likely to admit to problems and seek help. As reasonable as this sounds, evidence does not clearly support it (Amenson & Lewinsohn, 1981; Gove, 1980). There is evidence, however, that men who adhere closely to the traditional masculine role have less favorable attitudes toward seeking psychological assistance than do less traditional men (Wisch, Mahalik, Hayes, & Nutt, 1995).

### Intropunitive and Extrapunitive Reactions

Women's greater use of mental health services seems to be attributable to the ways women and men express their distress. The distinction is not firm and invariable, but many of the disorders that are diagnosed more often in women can be considered intropunitive, and many of those diagnosed more in men are extrapunitive. **Intropunitive** means turning the problem against oneself or punishing oneself—taking it out on yourself. **Extrapunitive** means turning the problem outward in some way, often called acting out. This may involve punishing other people or things—taking it out on others. Among problems more characteristic of women than men are depression and suicidal thoughts, some anxiety problems, and eating disorders (Hraba, Lorenz, Lee, & Pechačová, 1996; Mowbray, Herman, & Hazel, 1992). Among disorders more characteristic of men than of women are antisocial personality, pathological gambling, arson, explosive disorders, and substance abuse—problems generally more physically and sexually threatening and assaultive (Aneshensel, Rutter, & Lachenbruch, 1991; Bennett, Handel, & Pearsall, 1988). Because of differences in how distress is expressed, women are more likely to enter the mental health system, and men are more likely to enter the criminal justice system.

The attention in this chapter is to disorders more often ascribed to women. The standard reference for classification of psychological disorders is the ***Diagnostic*** *and Statistical Manual of Mental Disorders,* originally developed by the American Psychiatric Association in 1952 and now in its fourth version, called **DSM-IV** (1994).

## Depression

Almost everyone gets blue, sad, discouraged, or down in the dumps (a depressive or dysphoric mood) every now and then, but some people are more continuously or severely depressed than others. Depressive symptoms include appetite change, sleep disturbance, low energy level, low self-esteem, concentration difficulties, pessimism, and loss of interest in previously pleasurable activities (DSM-IV, 1994). The symptoms may be moderate (dysthymic disorder) or severe (major depressive episode or disorder). Even the mild depression of normal children and adults can significantly impair functioning in work, school, and social situations and can increase the likelihood of later major depression (Nolen-Hoeksema, 1990; Nolen-Hoeksema & Girgus, 1994).

*Incidence of Depression in Women*   Greater incidence of depression in women than in men in the United States has been shown for African American women, Hispanic women, Native American women, and white women, even when income level, education, and occupation are controlled (Figure 16.1A; McGrath, Keita, Strickland, & Russo, 1990; Mirowsky & Ross, 1995; Robins & Regier, 1991; Weissman et al., 1993). The general pattern is for two to four as many women as men to be considered depressed, whether the depression is defined in terms of an official clinical diagnosis or in terms of reports from predominantly normal women on a self-report scale of depression or in interviews (Nolen-Hoeksema, 1987, 1990; Sprock & Yoder, 1997). Women also have longer periods and multiple episodes of depressed mood (Sargeant, Bruce, Florio, & Weissmann, 1990).

The gender difference becomes apparent in adolescent years (Angold & Worthman, 1993; Lewinsohn, Hops, Roberts, Seeley, & Andrews, 1993; Nolen-Hoeksema & Girgus, 1994). Further, teen women also report more anxiety combined with somatic symptoms (e.g., disordered eating, headaches, breathing difficulties); and these symptoms are highly interrelated, particularly among young women concerned about the limitations placed on women (Silverstein, Caceres, Perdue, & Cimarolli, 1995; Silverstein, Perlick, Clauson, & McKoy, 1993).

The pattern does have some exceptions. No gender differences are found among some elderly groups, probably because depression in men increases substantially with age, whereas depression in women is relatively stable (Blazer, 1993; Nolen-Hoeksema, 1987). Also, college students do not necessarily show the gender difference, though college-aged people not in college do (Faden, 1977; Radloff, 1975).

Another qualification to keep in mind is that depression in men seems to be increasing, so that the gender difference is smaller in younger cohorts than older ones (Weissman et al., 1993). Also, there is a variety of depressions and combinations of depression with other problems, and researchers are only beginning to be sensitive to this issue (Sprock & Yoder, 1997). It may be that women are not higher in "pure" depression but are higher in combinations of depression and anxiety (Joiner & Blalock,

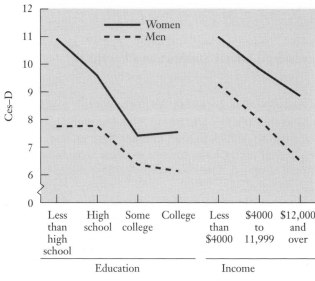

**Figure 16.1A** *Depression scores for women and men by education and income.*

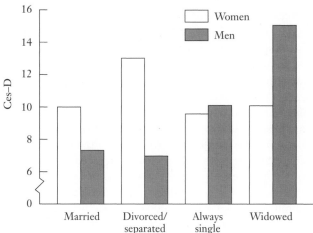

**Figure 16.1B** *Depression scores by gender and marital status.* SOURCE: Radloff, L. (1975). Sex differences in depression: The effects of occupation and marital status. *Sex Roles, 1,* (3), 249–265. Tables III, IV, p. 255.

1995). Different patterns of biological and psychosocial factors may be involved in different forms of depression yet to be identified (Focus on Research 16.1).

***Biological Factors*** Although depression has biological correlates, they have not yet explained gender differences in depression (McGrath et al., 1990; National Institute of Mental Health, 1986; Nolen-Hoeksema, 1987, 1990). Recent publications, however, do suggest that biological factors may contribute to vulnerability or may function as stressors that precipitate depression; in other words, they are not direct causes but work with psychosocial changes and personal dispositions (Sprock & Yoder, 1997).

Determining genetic factors relevant to depression may require considering specific forms of depressive disorders. Some evidence suggests a possible X-linked

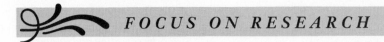

*FOCUS ON RESEARCH*

### 16.1   Multiple Regression: Social Support as a Factor in Depression

Marian wondered why she occasionally felt depressed. After all, she had a wonderful group of friends with whom to share life's ups and downs. She also felt close to her mother and sister, despite the little squabbles that all families have at one time or another. All in all, she counted herself pretty lucky to have so many warm and caring people around her for emotional support. Then why did she have these bouts of depression during which she felt so hopeless?

Research has clearly shown that there is a gender difference in social support, with women having larger social networks, more kin relationships, and more support from same-gender friends than do men. Women's relationships also tend to emphasize intimacy and disclosure more than men's relationships do. All of these factors contribute to an advantage for women in the realm of social support. Paradoxically, women also have higher rates of depression than men. If women are more advantaged in their social relationships, why do more women than men develop depression?

This question led researcher Heather Turner (1994) to develop a study using a multiple regression design. This design is a more complex version of a correlational design. Both procedures involve status assessment or nonmanipulated variables, but a correlation measures the relationship between two variables while multiple regression measures the relationship between a set of predictor variables and one outcome variable. Since very few things in life are related to only one other factor, multiple regression allows researchers to create designs that better reflect the real world, in which several factors are linked to one outcome. Multiple regression is graphically represented by an equation, or model, that specifies the outcome being predicted and the relative contribution of each of the predictor variables, as well as how much of the outcome is due to unknown factors such as chance or measurement error.

There are several types of multiple regression analyses a researcher can use; the choice is dictated by logic and the theory behind the model. Simultaneous multiple regression analyzes the contribution of each predictor variable in the presence of all the rest of the predictors. For example, we would only know the contribution of gender to depression when information about social support, negative interactions, and conflict events are also present. Often, simultaneous regression is used when the researcher is exploring the data but has no basis for thinking one predictor is more important than another. Hierarchical multiple regression allows the researcher to specify the order in

transmission for certain forms of depression and a general genetic foundation for other forms (Winokur, 1991).

Several other biological correlates are being researched (e.g., neurotransmitter, sleep wave patterns, protein and magnesium levels in cerebrospinal fluid, and natural

which the predictor variables are entered into the model. The variable hypothesized to be the most important predictor is entered first, and its relationship to the outcome variable is measured; then the next most important predictor is entered into the analysis, and its impact, in the presence of the first predictor, is measured; and so on, until all predictor variables have been entered and the model is complete. Hierarchical regression is useful when the theory indicates that some variables carry added weight in predicting an outcome.

Heather Turner designed her study in two stages. First she hypothesized that women's advantage in social support could be explained by the number and availability of confidants, the frequency of contact, and the amount of empathy and emotional disclosure in the relationships. She created a model in which these five variables predicted the level of social support; she then conducted a simultaneous multiple regression analysis to test this model. The analysis showed that each of the five variables made a contribution to social support: Women's greater levels of social support are, at least in part, due to having a greater number of available confidants and more empathetic and emotionally disclosing contact with those confidants than men have.

The second stage of Turner's study dealt with her hypothesis concerning depression. She predicted that the combination of gender, lack of social support, and number of negative interactions and conflict events would explain women's higher incidence of depression. The results of the simultaneous multiple regression showed that being female, having less social support, and experiencing more negative interactions and conflict events all worked together to predict greater levels of depression.

What can be learned from Turner's multiple regression analyses concerning factors that contribute to social support and to depression among women? Turner suggests that while women have more social contacts and more emotional involvement with these contacts, there can be a downside to this social support in the form of more exposure to relationship conflict and negative interactions. Our friends and family can provide emotional support and boost us up, but a fight with a close confidant can be a source of stress. Turner also speculates that hearing about a confidant's negative experience can be stressful, even if the incident did not directly involve us. It seems that women pay a price for the close emotional bonds they form with others, and that price may be paid in terms of mental health.

JILL BORCHERT ◆

SOURCE: Turner, H. (1994). Gender and social support: Taking the bad with the good? Sex Roles, *30*, 521–541.

---

killer cells; see Sprock & Yoder, 1997). In short, biological correlates of gender differences in depression cannot be ruled out, though current evidence so far is neither complete nor compelling. There is more agreement about the relevance of psychological and social factors.

*Women's greater social skills and broader support systems may help buffer them from depression. However, women also experience strain from providing social support. If this woman habitually listens to her friend's troubles, she may become vulnerable to depression herself.*

***Psychosocial Factors***   Many researchers trying to understand depression focus on the life circumstances of women (Gove, 1980; Gove & Tudor, 1973; Wu & DeMaris, 1996). A common thread among the risk factors for women's depression and other psychological problems seems to be chronic strain without a sense of control to overcome the strain and to get what is needed for physical survival (e.g., food, safety) or for psychological survival and growth (e.g., love, belongingness, self-esteem). To be blunt, women are more depressed because women's lives bring greater hardship (Wu & DeMaris, 1996). In turn, depressed individuals view events as more stressful and may generate negative events through their behavior (e.g., see Pianta & Egeland, 1994; Simons, Angell, Monroe, & Thase, 1993).

***General Correlates of Depression***   High rates of depression are found among people who are young, poor, less educated, unemployed or in low-status jobs, and ill (Belle, 1990; Golding, 1988; McGrath et al., 1990; Radloff, 1975; Radloff & Monroe, 1978; Russo, 1990; Wu & DeMaris, 1996). Women are more likely than men to live in poverty and to be unemployed (Costello & Stone, 1994). A result is that depression is greatest among young low-income women with young children, particularly those who are divorced or separated, or unemployed (Belle, 1990; Hobfoll, Ritter, Lavin, Hulsizer, & Cameron, 1995). It is not hard to understand why such a woman might be depressed.

The strain of actual or potential violence also contributes to depression (Campbell, Sullivan, & Davidson, 1995; Doyle & Paludi, 1991; Hobfoll, Ritter, Lavin, Hulsizer, & Cameron, 1995; McGrath et al., 1990; Nolen-Hoeksema, 1987, 1990). In one study the rates of depression for African American and white poor young women in the inner city were nearly double that of middle-class samples, particularly for single mothers (Hobfoll et al., 1995). Often overlooked by mental health professionals is the fact that depression is higher in women who have been abused as children, raped, battered, or harassed (chapter 15).

Ethnic minority women are at a particular disadvantage. They are more likely than majority women to be undereducated, living in poverty, and exposed to violence (Belle, 1990). About 150% more African American and Hispanic families headed by women are in poverty than white families headed by women (61% and 60% versus 40%; U.S. Bureau of the Census, 1992). Some minority women, such as Mexicans, Puerto Ricans, and Asians, are recent immigrants and face even more risk from the prejudices of a new culture and its barriers to them (de Snyder, Cervantes, & Padilla, 1990; Leigh, 1994; Loo & Ong, 1982). But being white, middle class, and married is not a guarantee of happiness.

*Traditionality*   Getting married, keeping house, and having children has been portrayed as the ideal for a woman. However, women experience more strain in marriage than men do (Wu & DeMaris, 1996). Marriage conflict is more related to depression and other symptoms of psychological distress in women than in men (Barnett, Brennan, Raudenbush, & Marshall, 1994; McGrath et al., 1990; Radloff, 1975, 1980; Wu & DeMaris, 1996). Marital difficulty is the most common stressor in the 6 months prior to the onset of depression in women.

Women in happy marriages do have lower rates of depression than those in unhappy marriages; but even in happy marriages, wives are more depressed than husbands (Weissman, Bruce, Leaf, Florio, & Holzer, 1991). Divorced women typically are more depressed than married women. This may be because of previous problems with depression and the difficult circumstances they face after the marriage dissolution (chapter 10). Among people without a history of severe depression, men, but not women, have a heightened risk of severe depression immediately following a marital split (Bruce & Kim, 1992). In addition, divorced men are more likely than divorced women to commit suicide and to show other serious psychological disturbances (Price & McKenry, 1988); but evidence from studies of the general population shows lower depression in the men than the women.

When married and single people are considered, the major gender differences in depressive symptoms are among married people, presumably because of differences in role-related strain of women and men (Wu & DeMaris, 1996). Among single people, gender differences are not completely clear. Most studies have shown that women who have always been single are less depressed than single men and generally as psychologically healthy as married men and women, and sometimes more so. However, when divorced people and single parents are included along with always-single people without children, the picture of single people is different. When any unmarried person is considered, recent evidence indicates greater depression in single than married people,

**Figure 16.2** *Gender differences in depression for single and married people.*   SOURCE: Wu, X., & DeMaris, A. (1996). Gender and marital status differences in depression: The effect of chronic strains. *Sex Roles, 34,* 299–319. Their Figure 2, p. 308.

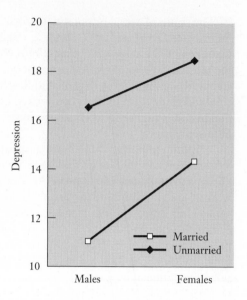

though with less of a gender difference among single people than among married people (Figure 16.2; Wu & DeMaris, 1996). The recent evidence may also signal a widening of the population of single women so that more "postponers" who want marriage are in the pool than in the past.

***Employment***   Although research is not totally consistent about the relationships between employment and depression, the preponderance of research shows that women's employment outside the home generally is associated with less depression than marriage without employment, in part because it insulates women from depression by moderating family stress (Adelmann, 1994; Barnett & Marshall, 1992; Barnett, Marshall, & Singer, 1992; McGrath et al., 1990; Nolen-Hoeksema, 1990; Veiel, 1993). However, recent findings tend to show that role quality is more predictive of women's well-being (Noor, 1996). Also, employment interacts with other factors, such as whether the woman wants employment, the amount of help she gets at home, and quality of child care if she has children (chapter 13). Having a helpful and emotionally supportive partner obviously can assist in allaying depression.

***Relationships***   Many traditional women feel that their sense of self-worth is tied up in relationships and feel responsible for relationships (Miller, 1986). Some writers have called attention to the loss of relationships and feelings of rejection and abandonment as common triggers of depression in women (Donelson, 1977b; Miller, 1986; Pidano & Tennon, 1985; Scarf, 1979). Yet we know that intimate relationships are a stressor for both college men and women (Zuckerman, 1989) and that men are strongly affected by the breakup of dating relationships, divorce, and the death of a spouse (chapter 10). Perhaps more important than the end of a relationship per se are the role of relationships in women's identity and the failure of relationships to meet women's

*Relationships are important to women, but the more a woman defines herself in terms of her relationships, the more likely it is she will experience depression. Staying in touch with her own needs, feelings, and sense of self will help this mother and wife to maintain healthy self-esteem.*

needs. To be dependent on relationships for self-definition is quite a different thing from being your own person with relationships as an important part of who you are. The more women feel defined through other people (e.g., friends, children, husbands), the more depressed they are (Warren & McEachren, 1985). For both single and married women, scores on a measure of Derived Identity (a sense of self that is overly influenced by and dependent upon relationships with significant others) were correlated with depression. Married women had a greater sense of derived identity than single women did and had higher depression scores.

Women can get so caught up in trying to be a "good woman" that they silence themselves to protect relationships that are not satisfying. For some, the silencing starts in early adolescence (Brown & Gilligan, 1992; Gilligan, 1990); for others, the onset may be later. Dana Jack (1991; Jack & Dill, 1992) suggested that women's vulnerability to depression is due to beliefs about how one makes and keeps relationships. She theorized that self-silencing contributes to a drop in self-esteem and feelings of a "loss of self" as a woman continually experiences the self-negation she thinks is required for feminine social behavior. The other person is seen as more important, so the woman judges herself by the standards of the other, puts the other's needs ahead of her own, and withholds expression of feelings to avoid loss of the relationship. Yet the relationship is not satisfying and does not meet the woman's needs for intimacy. In addition, the woman loses her sense of self. She may feel angry and rebellious inside while looking happy on the outside. As you may expect, battered wives scored higher than college students did on a scale measuring silencing of the self.

The theory, however, may apply only to white women. Although African American women score as high as white women on measures of silencing the self and depression, the two are not related for African American women when appropriate controls are made (Carr, Gilroy, & Sherman, 1996).

Women who do not express their needs are not likely to have their needs met. However, even women who do express their needs and who do not feel defined through relationships may not get what they want out of a relationship. Depression often is a communication of despair, "I have needs that you are failing to meet" (Carson & Butcher, 1992, p. 406). Women generally want more psychological intimacy and sharing of feelings than men do (chapter 10; Boggiano & Barrett, 1991). Relative lack of intimacy in a relationship is associated with depression and drinking alcohol in college women (Frank, Jacobson, & Tuer, 1990). Married women, compared with their husbands, feel less understood by their spouses (and their spouses report less understanding), and they rely on their spouses less for emotional help (Barnett & Baruch, 1978; Belle, 1990; Campbell, 1981; McGrath et al., 1990; Vanfossen, 1986). A major predictor of depression for Mexican American women was not having someone to confide in and talk to about important issues. It is difficult to disclose to someone who is not listening (Golding, 1990).

The expressiveness expected of women leads them to be concerned about relationships and is an asset in developing relationships (Arrindell et al., 1997), and thus it is relevant to well-being. But a relative lack of instrumentality to balance the expressiveness may increase vulnerability in relationships as well as susceptibility to stress and upsets from other sources (Arrindell et al., 1997; Hunt, 1993). Expressiveness is associated with giving up control in interpersonal situations and more depression, while instrumentality is associated with assuming control and less depression in women and in men (Sanfilipo, 1994; Sayers, Baucom, & Tierney, 1993).

The generally beneficial effect of instrumentality has been attributed to self-esteem, so some researchers conclude that it is only self-esteem that protects against depression (chapter 3; Feather, 1985; Stoppard & Paisley, 1987; Tennon & Herzberger, 1987; Whitley, 1984). Other researchers attribute the protective effect of instrumentality to the kind of coping associated with it, though that, too, may be related to self-esteem (Brown & Mankowski, 1993; Tennon & Herzberger, 1987).

## Coping With Stress and Sadness

Probably everyone experiences stress of some kind, but we differ in how we experience it and attempt to deal with it. Cognitive and cognitive-behavioral theorists see depression as caused not by the external events but by how we respond to the events (Beck, 1972, 1991; Ellis, 1973; Lazarus & Folkman, 1984). Terminology varies, but the response modes can be seen as **coping:** a process of attempting to resolve difficulties that pose demands for adjustment (Banyard & Graham-Bermann, 1993; Zautra & Wrabetz, 1991).

Coping styles are sometimes seen in terms of a broad continuum of **internalizing-externalizing** approaches, ranging from turning inward toward one's own thoughts and feelings to turning outward away from thoughts and feelings. The broad pattern, with exceptions to be sure, is for women to turn inward and men to turn outward (Levit, 1991), which is consistent with the intropunitive-extrapunitive distinction.

*Stewing and Doing*     One form of internalizing is stewing, or ruminating. A **ruminative style** involves focusing inward on the depressed mood and on the possible causes and consequences of the symptoms (Nolen-Hoeksema, 1987, 1991a, 1991b). Examples of ruminative activities are isolating oneself to think, writing in a diary, or repeatedly telling others how bad one feels. Rumination has several disadvantages: It prevents attention to other life events that could provide positive input, which leads to recall of previous negative experiences and leads to an interpretation of other events in a negative way. A variety of research studies supports the view that rumination does prolong depression and that women are more likely to ruminate than men are (Butler & Nolen-Hoeksema, 1994; Katz & Bertelson, 1993; Nolen-Hoeksema & Morrison, 1991; Nolen-Hoeksema, Morrow, & Fredrickson, 1993; Nolen-Hoeksema, Parker, & Larson, 1994; Thayer et al., 1994).

Why do women ruminate? Certainly, there are sociocultural influences at work. We do know that women, more than men, are advised to ruminate (Ali & Toner, 1996). But the gender difference in coping is part of a more general response style evident in childhood (Gjerde, 1995). Even when in a normal rather than a sad mood, women prefer to think about feelings more often than men do; when women are not sad, the concern with emotions does not cause depression.

One form of externalizing is distraction, or doing something. A **distracting style** involves intentionally distracting oneself from problems through activity. Examples of helpful distractions include engaging in an activity with friends, going to a movie, playing a sport, and working on a hobby that takes concentration. The positive distracting responses have the advantage of leading to other activities that may bring positive experiences to offset the weight of the problem. Some distracting responses are maladaptive, such as reckless driving or drinking. Susan Nolen-Hoeksema (1987, 1990; Morrow & Nolen-Hoeksema, 1990) suggests using distraction first to keep the depression from escalating and then ruminating to understand your feelings and the situation. If you never think about the problem, you are likely to get in the same bad situation again and perhaps come to express your hurt in destructive ways.

*Self-Blame and Other-Blame*     Rumination need not imply self-blame and turning against the self, but it easily can (Epstein, 1992). A general turning inward and self-blame specifically are more characteristic of girls and women than of boys and men (ages 10 through 77; Labouvie-Vief, Hakim-Larson, & Hobart, 1987), and to some extent they are related to degree of gender role adoption (Levit, 1991). Expressive women turn against the self and show more self-dislike and self-blame when depressed than other women do (Cramer & Carter, 1978; Evans, 1982; Oliver & Toner, 1990).

While women (and expressive men) are ruminating, blaming themselves, and thinking about negative events, men (and instrumental women) are using distracting

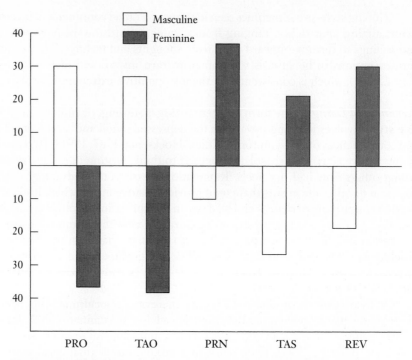

**Figure 16.3** *Relationships between gender role scores and defense scores.*
SOURCE: Levit, D. B. (1991). Gender differences in ego defenses in adolescence: Sex roles
as one way to understand differences. *Journal of Personality and Social Psychology, 61,* (6),
992–999. Figure based on Table 6, p. 996, and information passim.

PRO is projection.

TAO is turning against others (including displacement, identification with the aggressor, and
       aggressive forms of acting out).

PRN is principalization, including intellectualization, rationalization, and isolation of affect.

TAS is turning against self.

REV is reversal, including denial, negation, reaction formation, repression.

styles, blaming others, aggressively acting out, and projecting (e.g., seeing aggression
in others rather than in one's self) (Levit, 1991). The more high school students were
instrumental, the more they used projection and turning against others, and the less
they turned against the self. The more they were expressive, the less they used projection and turning against others and the more they turned against the self (Figure 16.3).

Why do women characteristically develop internalizing styles and blame themselves? Is one style of coping better than the other? The style characteristic of instrumentality and males operates on the external environment but leaves thoughts and
feelings basically unchanged. The style of expressiveness and females may change
thoughts and feelings but leaves the external environment basically unchanged. Either
style in extreme, by itself, is not likely to bring long-term benefits.

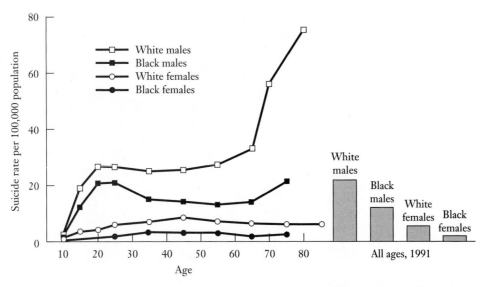

**Figure 16.4** *Suicide rates of African American and white females and males at different ages, 1991.* SOURCE: U.S. National Center for Health Statistics. (1983). *Monthly vital statistics report* and unpublished data. As reported in *The American almanac, 1994–1995, statistical abstract of the United States.* Economics and Statistics Administration and Bureau of the Census. Trade paper edition published 1994 by The Reference Press, Inc., Austin, Texas. Drawn from part of Table 136, p. 101.

NOTE: Missing data for African American women denotes that the figures are too small to meet statistical standards for reliability of a derived figure.

## Suicide

The most extreme form of intropunitiveness is suicide. Depression does not always lead to suicide, and suicide is not always caused by depression, but depression clearly is the most common correlate of suicide (Blazer, Bachar, & Manton, 1986). Many more people think about suicide than attempt it or complete it. The suicide rate is increasing, however, and the increase is sharper for women than for men (Carson & Butcher, 1992; McGrath et al., 1990). Men and white people have higher rates than women and people of color; at all ages, white men have the highest rate and women of color have the lowest rate of completed suicide (Figure 16.4).

If the leading cause of suicide is depression and women are more depressed than men, why do more men than women commit suicide? Women *attempt* suicide about three times as often as men do (Berman & Jobes, 1991). Men complete their suicide attempts up to five times more often than women do. The reason for women's uncompleted attempts relative to men's seems to lie in the methods women use, namely, those that are slower and more prone to error (e.g., sleeping pills, poisons, carbon monoxide in the car, and cutting themselves). These methods allow more time for discovery and rescue. Men tend to use more lethal methods that are quick and sure (e.g., guns, jumping from high places, hanging) (Buda & Tsuang, 1990). The recent increase in women's completed suicides is accompanied by an increase in women's use of the

*Holding a snake may be an unpleasant experience for this young girl, but the experience of confronting fear is an important one for healthy development. Phobias may be more prevalent in women because girls in our culture are not encouraged to overcome their fears, as boys are.*

methods previously the domain of men. Women's depression is real, their attempts at suicide are real, their completed suicides are real. Their anxieties are real as well, though lacking the potential lethal outcomes of depression.

## Anxiety Disorders

At the core of an **anxiety disorder** is an unrealistic, irrational fear so intense as to be disabling. Anxiety disorders are the most common psychiatric disorders in the United States (Neal & Turner, 1991). Women and men suffer equally from anxiety about social situations. Problems of anxiety of special relevance to women are specific phobias and agoraphobia. Like many disorders more typical of women than of men, they tend to appear first in adolescence and early adulthood.

*Specific Fears*   A **specific phobia** is a persistent and disproportionate fear of some specific object or situation, with the recognition by adults that the fear is excessive or unreasonable (DSM-IV, 1994). Common phobias are fear of darkness, snakes, heights, blood, and being alone. If avoidance of the feared object or situation is not possible, the person becomes anxious; when avoidance is possible, anxiety reduction strengthens the response of avoidance. Specific phobias are more frequent in females than in males, though still relatively frequent in males (Myers et al., 1984; Robins et al., 1984).

Experiencing and expressing fears is more consistent with what is expected of girls and women than with what is expected of boys and men, as discussed in chapter 7 about fear of failure. Little boys who are afraid of snakes or animals, like those afraid of achievement situations, are typically urged to master their fears, while little girls are allowed to give in to their fears. The result is that although girls and boys are similar in fearfulness in young years, from adolescence on, females admit to more fears than males do (McFarlane, Allen, & Honzik, 1974). Phobias are generally interpreted as learned fears and typically are not difficult to treat with behavioristic techniques (Halgin & Whitbourne, 1994). The treatment essentially is a corrective for faulty socialization (Fodor, 1982).

*Agoraphobia*    The other phobia of specific concern to women, **agoraphobia** (literally, fear of the market place), is fear of being in situations from which escape would be difficult (or embarrassing) or in which immediate help would be unavailable if something went wrong (DSM-IV, 1994). Agoraphobics usually fear being outside the home alone, being in a crowd, being on a bridge or in an elevator, or traveling. They may even avoid leaving particular parts of the home. The onset of agoraphobia typically is in young adulthood, often shortly after marriage. About 75% or more of the people with agoraphobia are women (Barlow, 1988; Chambless & Goldstein, 1980), and the majority of those (at least 70%) are married (Vose, 1981) and not employed. Because of gender role pressures, men with agoraphobic tendencies cannot afford to stay home; they are likely to self-medicate with alcohol and may end up with severe impairment from alcohol abuse (Barlow & Durand, 1995).

There is reason to think that attempts to understand agoraphobic married women should include the couple, not just the woman (Fodor, 1982; Hafner, 1984, 1988; Hafner & Minge, 1989). Results of a study comparing couples in which the wife was agoraphobic with those in which she was not indicated that the husband may have had an investment in the wife's agoraphobia (Hafner & Minge, 1989). Marital satisfaction in husbands of agoraphobic women was linked with seeing their wives as relatively traditional in gender roles; the association was *reversed* for the husbands of women who were not agoraphobic. The stated desire of agoraphobic wives for employment and some independence may be threatening to their husbands. The interpretation is admittedly speculative but deserves future attention. Agoraphobic women have been cured, but the cures do not always last. It may be that other people are abetting the dependency of agoraphobics so that the interpersonal context must be considered along with the woman herself.

## Dissociative Identity Disorder

Multiple personality disorder is now officially called **Dissociative Identity Disorder (DID)** (DSM-IV, 1994). Women are diagnosed with the disorder up to nine times more often than men (DSM-IV). It is one of several **dissociative disorders,** in which people avoid stress by dissociating or escaping from their central personal identity. Amnesia is another dissociative disorder. With DID some aspects of identity become detached, or dissociated, and a person manifests two or more complete systems of personality. The *alter* personalities (the "detached" ones) usually are strikingly different from the primary (host) personality and seem aimed to help cope with stress (Spiegel & Cardena, 1991). It is common for women with DID to have a male alter who serves as protector. The average number of alters for women is about 15 (8 for men) (DSM-IV, 1994), but Truddi Chase had 92 (Chase et al., 1990; see A Closer Look 16.1). Typically, the alters know of the primary personality and of each other, but the primary personality does not know of the alters.

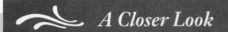

## A Closer Look

### 16.1    Alter Personalities of Truddi Chase

Truddi Chase had a total of 92 separately identifiable personalities. She wrote of her experiences in *When Rabbit Howls* (Chase et al., 1990). Truddi, the main personality, had been "asleep" since age 2, being replaced by "the troops," who were the actual authors of the book. Truddi had been sadistically abused and sexually victimized by her stepfather starting when she was 2 years old. Truddi's mother did not intervene for 14 years. Before treatment, Truddi had continual dizziness, temper tantrums, and periods of blackout and knew nothing of the alter personalities. Currently, Truddi is employed; she is divorced and has one daughter. The treatment of Dr. Robert A. Phillips apparently was successful in achieving a workable integration of the diverse personalities. Truddi's alter personalities included

*Rabbit:* communicates only by howling; this is Rabbit of the book's title.

*Mean Joe:* an 11-foot-tall Protector.

*Miss Wonderful:* a model of human perfection.

*Elvira:* somewhat wild and irresponsible.

*Twelve:* an artistic, sensitive child.

*Black Katherine:* the strong caretaker of Twelve and the other children.

*Sewer Mouth:* a woman who expresses rage in strong language.

*Ean the Irishman:* provides obscure commentary in a thick brogue.

*The Front Runner:* keeps track of the other troops and reports on them.

SOURCE: Chase, T., The Troops for. (1990). *When rabbit howls.* New York: Jove. As reported in R. C. Carson & J. N. Butcher, 1992, *Abnormal psychology and modern life* (pp. 211–212). New York: Harper Collins.

---

The frequency of diagnosis of DID has increased dramatically in recent years (Kluft, 1991). This may be due to clinicians becoming more willing to use the diagnosis, a broadening of the definition, or because of an actual increase in the frequency of the disorder (Halgin & Whitbourne, 1994; Ross, 1989). Whatever the reason, a linkage of DID (as well as amnesia) with childhood abuse is clear (Coons, Bowman, Pellow, & Schneider, 1989; Ross, Heber, Anderson, & Norton, 1989; Wolfe, Gentile, & Wolfe, 1989). In one series of cases, 97% of the patients had some significant trauma, usually sexual or physical abuse; 68% reported incest (Putnam, Guroff, Silverman, Barban, & Post, 1986). The dissociation allows feeling "This is not happening to me" (Kluft, 1991).

## Somatoform Disorders: Somatization and Conversion

Physical problems or complaints with no known medical basis are known as **somatoform disorders** (*soma* means "body"). They are popularly associated with women, but not always correctly. Hypochondriasis is anxiety about the possibility that one has a serious disease; it may emerge at any time of life and is equally likely in women and men (DSM-IV, 1994). Two somatoform disorders more common in women than men are fairly rare and occur most frequently in lower classes. Both typically start in adolescence or early adulthood and bring attention from the medical profession. One is **somatization disorder** (originally called hysteria or Briquet's Syndrome), which involves a seemingly endless list of somatic complaints without medical basis (or with complaints beyond what would be expected). The focus on symptoms may be so pervasive and intense that the woman's identity and interpersonal relations are shaped around the symptoms. Sometimes, only medical personnel (powerful people) care to listen. Some success has been attained with treatment procedures involving development of interaction styles that are not role stereotypic (Barlow & Durand, 1995).

The other somatoform disorder more common in women is **conversion disorder.** Freud popularized the term *conversion hysteria,* using it to note that anxiety from unconscious conflicts was converted into physical symptoms, though there were no underlying physical causes or intentional malingering (Barlow & Durand, 1995). The term *hysterical* has been dropped because of its negative connotations. Common types of conversion are blindness, paralysis, and speech problems. Women's symptoms are more commonly on the left than the right side of the body, for reasons not known (DSM-IV, 1994). Women with conversion symptoms may develop somatization disorder as well, whereas men with the disorder often have features of antisocial personality disorder.

## Food, Alcohol, and Other Drugs

Women stereotypically are defined through their bodies, both in terms of appearance and in terms of reproductive functions (chapters 2, 11, 12). The emphasis on women's bodies also has important implications for what women think of themselves and how they express conflict about gender roles, as well as about how they are seen by health care professionals. In this section we consider issues of food, alcohol, and illicit and prescription drugs.

### Eating Disorders

There may be as many as 7 million American women suffering from eating disorders (Shute, 1992). The overwhelming majority of people affected by eating disorders—at least 90%—are young white females of upper socioeconomic status who are living in a competitive environment (Barlow & Durand, 1995; DSM-IV, 1994). Subgroups of young women for whom thinness is especially important, such as models, athletes, and dancers, show a higher than average incidence of eating disorders (Dunning, 1997; Szymanski & Chrisler, 1990/1991). In the United States the incidence of eating disorders in women has increased steadily over at least the past 30 years and is spreading to diverse groups (Lamb, Jackson, Cassiday, & Priest, 1993; Root, 1990; Strober, 1986). It is suspected that some disorders are undetected in women over 30 (Lamb et al., 1993) and that girls as young as 9 may be affected (Mellin, Scully, & Irwin, 1986).

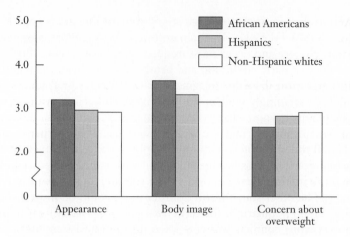

**Figure 16.5  *Body image measures for women of three ethnic groups.***
SOURCE: Cash, T. F., & Henry, P. E. (1995). Women's body images: The results of a national survey in the U.S.A. *Sex Roles, 33*, 19–28. Bar graph developed from part of their Table III, p. 2.

Appearance Evaluation Scale: Seven 5-point items evaluating one's appearance.

Body Areas Satisfaction Scale: Participants give 5-point ratings of dissatisfaction-satisfaction ratings of eight physical areas/attributes (height, weight, hair, face, upper torso, midtorso, lower torso, muscle tone).

Overweight Preoccupation: 5-point ratings of weight vigilance, fat anxiety, current dieting, and eating restraints.

Disturbed eating now is so common in colleges as to be the statistical norm rather than the exception (Mintz & Betz, 1988). Some of the eating problems of college women are transitory, but others may progress into more severe disorders (Thelen, Farmer, Mann, & Pruitt, 1990).

It is fairly clear that a negative body image is linked to eating disorders and other psychological difficulties (Cash & Deagle, 1995; Cash & Grant, in press). Women in the United States have substantial levels of dissatisfaction with their bodies, a dissatisfaction that seems to be increasing (e.g., 1985–1993) (Cash & Henry, 1995). Nearly half of women in a national sample (ages 18 to 70 years) reported negative evaluations of their appearance and a preoccupation with being or becoming overweight. Lesbians generally are more comfortable with their bodies and their age than heterosexual women are. However, college-educated lesbians (predominantly white) embrace a beauty ideal encouraging thinness and fitness, derived from the media and peers, but they also have a basic acceptance of their bodies, derived in sexual relationships (Beren, Hayden, Wilfley, & Striegel-Moore, 1997). African American women are significantly more satisfied with their bodies than Hispanics and whites are (Figure 16.5). African Americans seem to have a broader latitude of acceptance of women's body size, even of women who are heavy (Fallon, Katzman, & Wolley, 1994; Rucker & Cash, 1992). The greater appreciation of a healthy body size has given a relative protection to minority women, but eating disorders do occur and may be growing, not only among African

Americans but among Asian Americans, Native Americans, and Hispanics (Hsu, 1987; Joiner & Kashubeck, 1996; Rosen et al., 1988; Silber, 1986; Smith & Krejci, 1991; Snow & Harris, 1989).

*Bulimia Nervosa*     The hallmarks of **bulimia nervosa,** commonly called bulimia (literally, "ox hunger"), are recurrent episodes of binge eating and inappropriate compensatory methods to prevent weight gain (DSM-IV, 1994). Bulimia was not recognized officially until 1968, but there are references to bulimic behaviors as early as C.E. 130 (Heatherton & Baumeister, 1991). A **binge** is defined as eating an amount of food that is definitely larger than most people would eat in similar circumstances. If you eat too much at a holiday feast, you need not define that as a problematic binge because most people eat too much at such times! Nor is it a binge to snack continually or suddenly get a craving for a particular kind of food. Binge eating is characterized by the abnormality in the amount of food consumed and an initial feeling of lack of control. It typically is done in as much secrecy as possible, done quickly, and with a sense of shame.

     **Inappropriate compensatory behavior** to prevent weight gain is part of bulimia. "Cutting back a bit" after a dietary splurge is not considered inappropriate. A woman with the **purging type** of bulimia regularly engages in self-induced vomiting or the misuse of laxatives, diuretics, or (less frequently) enemas. A woman with the **nonpurging type** uses other compensatory behaviors such as fasting or excessive exercise. Because of the compensatory behaviors, many bulimics maintain normal weight and so conceal their problem; others reveal the problem through obvious extreme weight fluctuations (Barlow & Durand, 1995).

     The rate of bulimia nervosa among adolescent and young adult females is about 1% to 3%; the rate for males is about one tenth of that for females (Collins, Rowland, Salganicoff, & Chait, 1994). Although bulimia is generally less dangerous than anorexia, repeated vomiting can cause the enamel on teeth to erode and can cause life-threatening damage to the throat and stomach, the heart, or the brain (Halmi, 1987; Mitchell, Pyle, & Fletcher, 1991). Bulimia usually is easier to treat than anorexia, through individual and family therapy, support groups, and education about nutrition (Harris, 1991).

*Anorexia Nervosa*     One central feature of **anorexia nervosa,** recognized as a disorder for at least a century, is an intense abhorrence of gaining weight or of becoming fat. Coupled with this is a body image so distorted that the woman has the absurd complaint that she is fat, although she weighs less than 85% of what is normal (DSM-IV, 1994). Some anorexics lose up to 50% of their body weight. Estimates of the rate of the disorder in the United States range from .1% to 5% of the population (Collins et al., 1994; Strober, 1991). About 90% to 96% of anorexics are female (Levine, 1993), with most cases (70% to 90%) developing before 25 years of age (Eckert, 1985). The **binge eating/purging type** of anorexia (or bulimic-anorexic) involves purging after eating small amounts of food *or* after binge eating. For the **restricting type,** weight loss is accomplished by dieting, fasting, or excessive exercise. Binge/purging anorexics seem more similar to normal-weight bulimics than to restricting anorexics (Jackson-

Walker, 1994). In postmenarcheal women, amenorrhea (lack of menstruation; chapter 6) typically follows weight loss; in premenarcheal women, menarche may be delayed. About 5% to 10% of anorexics die of the disorder (Collins et al., 1994; DSM-IV, 1994).

Treatment is difficult because anorexics typically deny their problem. Hospitalization usually is a first step. Behavior modification programs in which anorexics are rewarded for gaining weight are helpful, often combined with family therapy (Gilbert & DeBlassie, 1984). About 30% of treated anorexics fully recover. Others continue to have eating problems in less extreme forms. One third show signs of bulimia (Kreipe, Churchill, & Strauss, 1989). Although bulimia and anorexia are considered distinctive disorders, they are not mutually exclusive: Bulimics may become anorexics, and vice versa (Jackson-Walker, 1994). The distinction between the two is less clear among women at high risk but not yet "clinical cases."

***Causes of Eating Disorders***    Sociocultural influences through idealization of thinness are relevant to the development of both anorexia and bulimia. (Hsu, 1989; Striegel-Moore, 1993). It is easy for adolescent women to believe that if they are slender, they can have all they want in life (Halgin & Whitbourne, 1994; Steiner-Adair, 1986). Nonetheless, to attribute eating disorders only to the thinness ideal is simplistic (Pike, 1995). Most heterosexual adolescent women are concerned about weight and go on diets at some time, but few develop full-blown eating disorders. Biological factors (e.g., deficient norepinephrine and serotonin) cannot be ignored, though direction of causation is not clear.

Why do some women exposed to the messages of "thin is beautiful" develop eating disorders but not others? The final answer is likely to be a complex one, involving families, friendship networks and their concern with issues of weight, and personality variables (Focus on Research 16.2; Pike, 1995). The different theories and speculations have a common focus on the woman's concern about having a sense of personal effectiveness, control and autonomy, and personal expression, including through "masculine" achievement (Pike, 1995). Without this sense of personal efficacy, there is low esteem (Frederick & Grow, 1996).

***Sexual Abuse***    There are reasons to suspect connections between sexual abuse and eating disorders, all of which involve a search for control in some way (Gay, 1993; McFarlane, McFarlane, & Gilchrist, 1988; Root, 1991; Simpson & Ramberg, 1992). The eating problems often are attempts to provide a sense of control over chaotic inner and outer experiences and to numb painful emotions. Also, the attempts to control food intake and purging can be a way to resist taking into the body a foreign substance associated with past abuse. Victims of sexual abuse often believe that they are "bad" and deserve punishment; they achieve control by punishing themselves before others do. Some women attempt to create a sense of safety by protecting themselves with a layer of fat or showing a wish to disappear with a very thin body (Orbach, 1982). They may assume that perpetrators are less likely to abuse a large and powerful or fat and unattractive body and will not be attracted to a childlike or fragile-looking body.

***Family Dynamics and Self-Views***    More research on eating disorders has focused on social dynamics, especially within the family, and resultant feelings of the women about themselves (Dyer & Tiggermann, 1996: Halgin & Whitbourne, 1994). Women with eating disorders have been characterized as having middle-class parents who (1) set high expectations, (2) are overprotective and controlling, and (3) communicate double messages that the daughters are loved but are not to express themselves (Boskind-White & White, 1983, 1986; Humphrey, 1989; Stern et al., 1989). There are indications also that the parents have some marked concern about eating (Jackson-Walker, 1994; Pike, 1995).

The pattern has been extending into lower classes. The daughter tries to be a "good girl"—she tries to meet the high demands and may be an overachiever (Dura & Bornstein, 1989). She also likely is dependent and faces adolescence with little confidence and little sense of personal control of her life (Bornstein, 1992; Schupak-Neubert & Nemeroff, 1993). Faced with their conflict, daughters feel ineffective and afraid of maturity. They also have trouble knowing what they feel (Frank & Jackson-Walker, in press). They have difficulty identifying internal physical states of hunger and satiety and in identifying emotional states (Pike, 1995). As a result, they waver between self-expression and submission (Humphrey, 1989).

All in all, the young women are involved with both parents in a struggle to develop autonomous selfhood and identity (Bornstein, 1992; Jackson-Walker, 1994; McCreery, 1991; Rhodes & Kroger, 1992; Smolak & Levine, 1993). "Who am I expected to be? What do I want to be? Do I have a right to be me? Who am I?" At least part of their confusion involves issues of gender roles and what it means to be a woman relative to what they want for themselves. Women who are dissatisfied with their gender orientation generally desire more masculine characteristics (with or without more feminine traits) and experience more disturbances in eating attitudes and behaviors than those who are satisfied (Johnson & Petrie, 1995).

***Femininity and Denial of Femininity***    Anorexia is an extreme expression of femininity—being thin *and* denying one's own needs—but the anorexic woman devalues femininity and avoids adulthood by defeminizing her body (Boskind-White & White, 1986; Jackson-Walker, 1994; Paxton & Sculthorpe, 1991; Silverstein, Perlick, Clauson, & McKoy, 1990). She may devalue femininity because of the problems it brings for achieving in ways that are considered masculine and bring respect (Bruch, 1978). For example, there are relationships between preferences for slimness, bodily dissatisfaction or disordered eating, striving for intellectual/professional success, desire to be more masculine (e.g., independent, assertive), and beliefs that other people do not consider them to be bright and successful (Johnson & Petrie, 1995; Silverstein et al., 1990; Silverstein et al., 1995). Women for whom intelligence and professional success are important, but being a wife or homemaker is not important, are about twice as likely as other women to report that they eat uncontrollably or that they use purging techniques to control their weight.

In sum, women's bodies become a battleground in a conflict between culturally defined femininity and personal forms of expressiveness that bring respect and reward.

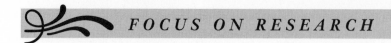

### 16.2   Bias and Blind Controls: Eating Disorders

"You always shut yourself off in your room," her mother said, somewhat angrily.

"I just want to be left alone," she pleaded, the hint of a whine in her voice. The teenager was 17, and her dark eyes communicated a sulky resentment.

The research assistant on the other side of the one-way mirror quickly coded the girl's response: "asserting," "appeasing," "separating," and "interdependent."

"Some message!" he thought, as he watched the family in front of him.

The girl was trim, neither overweight nor underweight. He couldn't tell from her appearance which type of disorder she suffered from; he only knew that this project was about adolescents with eating disorders. For all he knew, she could be a part of the control group, with no disorder at all.

Why keep this graduate student in the dark about the teenager and families he is observing? Why not assume that the more he knows, the better he'll understand and the more accurately he'll record their behaviors? Investigators have found from painful experience that their expectations all too often influence what they see—sometimes even causing them to read things into a person's behavior that just aren't there. Their expectations can lead to researcher bias and systematically alter the results of the study.

Whenever investigators know the conditions of participants, they can bias the outcome of the research, either by interpreting—that is, scoring—the participants' behavior differently or by unconsciously treating participants in that condition differently. If, for example, this graduate student believed that the parents of girls with a certain type of eating disorder were harsh and demanding, he might read hostility into parental remarks even when it wasn't there, or perhaps he would be less friendly with the parents when introducing them to the researcher. The latter difference might lead to tensions in family interactions that otherwise would not be present, thus unintentionally confirming initial expectations.

Investigators can eliminate researcher bias by conducting the experiment "blind." In a single-blind control procedure, such as in the eating disorders study, the

---

Much of the problem may be that women are told that career success is available to them, but they see the many obstacles to that (Silverstein et al., 1993, 1997).

***Disordered Eating in Women of Color***   Although women of color generally may escape the "white woman's" eating problems, the cultural context of women of color does not necessarily protect specific individuals (Root, 1990). People of color live in a *bi*cultural context (Comas-Diaz & Greene, 1994). They are subject to the standards of the dominant culture, particularly when the culture of origin is devalued by the dominant culture (Harris, 1995).

research observer is unaware of the condition of each participant; expectations cannot contribute to any of the observed differences. A single-blind control is adequate in many studies. Some, however, require a double-blind control, in which both participants and researcher are ignorant of each participant's condition. Double-blind controls are frequently used in drug studies in which it is necessary to control for the patients' as well as the doctor's expectations that they will get better if they take an experimental medication. In double-blind drug studies, all participants are given a pill, but half receive a placebo, or sugar pill.

Let's get back to the other side of the one-way mirror in the eating disorders study. Do families of girls with different eating disorders interact in characteristically different ways? Researcher Laura Humphrey (1989) observed 74 adolescent girls with their parents. Sixteen were anorexic, 16 were bulimic, 18 were both anorexic and bulimic, and 24 were normal controls. All of those in the first three categories were patients who had been hospitalized long enough so that one could not distinguish the anorexics by their appearance.

Parents of anorexics were more nurturing and comforting but conversely also more ignoring and neglecting of their daughters than were the parents of bulimics or controls. The anorexic girls were the most submissive of the groups when they were with their parents. Bulimics and their parents were more likely to engage in mutual grumbling and blaming and to exchange disparaging remarks. Interactions of normal controls and their parents were characterized more by helping, protecting, trusting, and simple enjoyment of each other.

These findings underscore the importance of treating the family as a whole as well as working individually with the adolescent when treating eating disorders. Most eating disorders are associated with a pattern of disturbed family interactions.

NANCY COBB ◆

SOURCE: Humphrey, L. L. (1989). Observed family interactions among subtypes of eating disorders using structural analysis of social behavior. *Journal of Consulting and Clinical Psychology, 57,* 206–214.

---

Increased opportunities for "masculine" (white) success are becoming available to women of color, particularly those who conform to dominant white cultural norms (Root, 1990). Both women of color and white women often feel that they must succeed for the sake of their gender. In addition, women of color want to succeed for their families, their group, their minority sisters. Many ethnic families feel responsible for correcting negative images and stereotypes of their ethnic group, so the pressure to be "perfect" may be increasing among ethnic groups (Silber, 1986).

The standards of perfection, of course, are those of the dominant white culture. Women's physical appearance becomes a ticket for acceptance. "The double oppression that women of color encounter—sexism and racism—can, for some individuals, provide the basis for the desperateness that underlies resorting to unhealthy eating and exercise practices" (Root, 1990, p. 529). The women themselves may be hesitant to admit concern about food and weight to researchers, therapists, and even friends, because they feel they are selling out by having a stereotypically white problem. The underlying issues for them as well as for white women seem to involve gender role and the desire for expressiveness and achievement in a white man's world.

## Alcohol Use and Abuse

The number of women, particularly young women, who drink has increased slightly over three decades; problem drinking among women has increased significantly (Matteo, 1988; Rodin & Ickovics, 1990). Women's increased use of alcohol is distressing especially in light of evidence that the physiological consequences of drinking occur more quickly and more severely for women than for men (DSM-IV, 1994; McGrath et al., 1990). Even moderate alcohol use is associated with up to a 50% increase in breast cancer (Collins et al., 1994), and alcohol use also contributes to osteoporosis (chapter 14). Generally, white women are more likely than African American women and Hispanic women to drink at least some (66% versus 54% African American, 35% Mexican American, 34% Puerto Rican, 33% Cuban American) (Leigh, 1994). The minority women who do drink, particularly African American and Native American women, often have even greater health-related problems than white women do (Yandow, 1989).

In spite of the increased use of alcohol among women, alcohol consumption still is more frequent among men than women: The heavier the drinking level being reported, the greater the disproportion of men over women (DSM-IV, 1994; Travis, 1988a). Attempts to explain the gender differential genetically have so far not produced convincing results (Leland, 1982), but the relevance of social psychological variables is clear. Across the social class spectrum, more disapproval, disgust, and revulsion is expressed by both women and men at the intoxication of women than the intoxication of men (Gomberg, 1993a, 1993b; Matteo, 1988; Yandow, 1989). In contrast, men are judged more harshly than women when they express loneliness or depression and are more likely to turn to alcohol or drugs when they have a problem (Borys & Perlman, 1985; Frank et al., 1990; Snell, Belk, & Hawkins, 1987).

***Social Roles***    The same broad societal expectations about what is "proper" that discourage drinking in women also are pressures that can lead women to drink. Research suggests four ways, probably overlapping, that women have developed drinking problems: general gender role pressures, childhood victimization, other early life problems, and midlife stress.

First, alcohol may make it easier for women to feel both what they *are* supposed to feel according to stereotypic expectations and what they *are not* supposed to feel (Bacon, 1974; McClelland, Davis, Kalin, & Wanner, 1972). Alcohol blocks conflict about behaviors and inflates the drinker's self-evaluations (Steele & Josephs, 1990). Expectations about how alcohol will "make" a person behave are as important as the physiological effects, perhaps more so. Thus alcohol can lead people to be more aggressive or more self-disclosing, more amorous or more angry than they would be if they were sober (e.g., see Hull & Bond, 1986; Steele & Southwick, 1985). Under the cover of alcohol, people can express feelings they feel inhibited about when sober— feelings they are supposed to have or those they are not supposed to have.

Women are not expected to express anger, so some women use alcohol to express their anger (Yandow, 1989). Messages to women about their sexuality are confusing (chapter 11), so women may use alcohol to express their sexuality. Because of sexual abuse, some women have a hard time participating in sexual activity unless they are under the influence of alcohol; chemically dependent women have a high rate of childhood victimization (McGrath et al., 1990; Yandow, 1989). Other women also look to alcohol to engage in sexual activity. About half of the women in a national survey indicated that they felt alcohol made sex more pleasurable, decreased sexual inhibitions, and made them feel closer and more open to others (Klassen & Wilsnack, 1986). About a fifth said also that alcohol made them more sexually assertive.

However, alcohol is not a magic route to sexual bliss. Drinking can cause others to see a woman as responsible for sexual interactions she does not want. Many college women (44%) said that they had sex because they had been drinking and wish they had not (chapter 15). Alcohol use puts people at a high risk for undesirable or dangerous consequences, including unprotected sex that can result in pregnancy or STDs or sexual violence (Strong & DeVault, 1997). Even small amounts of alcohol decrease sexual performance, though people may feel less inhibition. Heavy doses of alcohol lead to a vicious cycle, with drinking being both the cause and the effect of impaired sexuality (Klassen & Wilsnack, 1986).

***Early and Later Experiences***   Some women have early experiences other than abuse that predispose them to alcohol use, and they may begin drinking in their teens or 20s. Disruptions in early family life, such as alcoholism in a parent, death of a parent, or divorce, are common in people who develop alcohol problems. Women who are alcoholics are more likely than men who are alcoholics to report such disruptions and also to report feeling rejected and deprived in childhood (Gomberg, 1979; Leland, 1982; Travis, 1988a). Reasons for the differences are not clear but may involve differential responses to problems in relationships and concerns about womanhood.

Childhood and adolescence take a toll on women. Women in their late 40s who were problem drinkers had shown a pattern of emotional dependency, submission, and passivity at adolescence (Filmore, Bacon, & Hyman, 1979). At 15, they were characterized by self-doubt and confusion, fears, rejection of life, distrust of people, and were affiliated with a judgmental and punitive religion. In response to self-doubt and confusion, they attempted to escape into an "ultra femininity." Eating disorders, which typically begin in adolescence and are associated with concerns about femininity, also are highly associated with alcoholism, with a history of eating disorders often leading to later alcoholism (Beary, 1986).

Women with later onset of drinking (in the 30s or 40s) generally had good coping skills previously. They gradually started drinking to deal with depression or suddenly started in response to stress, often one involving relationships (Gomberg, 1979, 1993a,

1993b). Drinking because of negative feelings and in an attempt to cope with or to enhance relationships is the most prevalent type of serious drinking problem among middle-class women (Zucker, 1987), as well as a frequent contributor among college students (Frank, Jacobson, & Tuer, 1990).

Separation or divorce leading to feelings of rejection is a frequent precipitant of alcohol use by middle-aged women (Gomberg, 1993a, 1993b). The effect of divorce and separation appears to be weaker now than in previous generations, probably because there is less of a stigma attached to divorce and less damage to a woman's self-esteem. On the other hand, relationships can be maladaptive and a source of stress. For some women, getting out of a marital relationship is associated with *reduced* drinking. This suggests that the drinking was caused by the unhappiness of the marriage, or that the women were "going along" with the husband in having a drink.

***Treatment Problems***    Treatment approaches for women have been relatively neglected or dominated by sexist attitudes, Betty Ford's Clinic notwithstanding (Bepko & Forth-Finegan, 1991; Cupp, 1994; Karn, 1990; Mondanaro, 1989). Women are reluctant to seek treatment because of role pressures leading to personal denial of the problem, family denial of the problem, and problems of the woman's responsibility for the care of children (Yandow, 1989). Treatment for women needs to include a variety of approaches, including medical services, services to children, and parenting education (Reed, 1985). The need is immense. Alcoholism in women, while less frequent than in men, upsets the homeostasis of the family and community more. "The emotional and financial costs to the children, family and community can hardly be overestimated" (Yandow, 1989, p. 246).

## Drug Use and Abuse

Alcohol is a common form of substance abuse, but other abuse problems can affect women as well. Legal drugs have been more of a problem for women than illegal ones. Generally, about half as many women as men have ever used illegal drugs (opiates, cocaine, hallucinogens, marijuana, hashish) (Fidell, 1982). Women users tend to take lighter or less frequent doses. Some people, of course, experiment with drugs but do not become habitual users. More white women (35%) and African American women (33%) report having used illicit drugs at some point in their lives than do Hispanic women (25%). Slightly more African American women than others use illicit drugs (Horton, 1992).

**Psychotropic drugs** are mind-altering or mood-altering drugs, antidepressants, tranquilizers, and stimulants. Girls and boys and men and women are equally likely to buy over-the-counter versions, such as Compōz and NoDoz (Fidell, 1982). Drugs provided by a physician are a different story. Women have a long history of using "acceptable" drugs. Women more than men are given prescriptions for psychotropic drugs by physicians by a ratio of about 2:1, a ratio that has remained fairly stable for the last 20 years (Biener, 1990; Fidell, 1982; McGrath et al., 1990). This is in spite of the fact that women are not more likely to visit doctors when allowance is made for visits about pregnancy.

The women who use psychotropics on prescription are likely to be older, richer, and more often white than those using illicit drugs. Linda Fidell (1982) notes that ease of contacting sources may be a determinant of what kind of drug, illicit or licit, a person becomes involved with. A physician may be more available for affluent people, but street sources are easier for others to contact.

***Prescription Drugs***     Women may be overmedicated by physicians because they and their problems are not taken seriously. Women who enter the mental health system are more likely to be medicated and given stronger medications than men with the same symptoms (McGrath et al., 1990). If a woman is dealing with a rocky marriage or threats from her boss, it is easier to give her drugs than to listen to her. And a prescription is consistent with the general tendency to blame women's bodies (chapter 6). Why are women so willing to take prescription drugs? Are women overtrusting of physicians (likely to be powerful men) who may not be listening to them in the first place? What is the psychological effect of taking drugs on women's sense of self-control over their lives (Rodin & Ickovics, 1990)? These questions need attention. If women are to be medicated, it seems appropriate to ask that they be included in medical research.

***Women in Drug Research***     Women have been woefully underrepresented in medical research generally (Schroeder & Snowe, 1994). The reason given often is that women's menstrual cycle could affect the results, but there is little resistance to giving the drugs to menstrual women after the drugs are developed. Many studies about drugs exclude women even when women are the primary users of the drugs (Rodin & Ickovics, 1990). For example, women use over 90% of weight-loss pills, but the research about the active agent of those pills (phenylpropanolamine) was done on men (Hamilton, 1986). If women are not included in drug testing, it is no big surprise that women have more side effects from drugs than men do (Rodin & Ickovics, 1990) and that they are helped less by antidepressant drugs than men are (Hamilton, 1986; Raskin, 1974).

The problem is not with drugs themselves. Carefully researched pharmaceutical drugs that are properly used have benefited many people. Problems stem from drug research that does not include women and from using drugs as a "quick cure," saving the health care provider from looking more carefully at the situations of a woman's life and her experiences of it.

***Nicotine and Caffeine***     Nicotine and caffeine are not usually thought of as part of the drug problem, but they are (DSM-IV, 1994). Think of how acceptable it is for a person to say, "I just can't function until I have had my morning cup of coffee." The statement sometimes is accompanied by "and my wake-up cigarette." Caffeine, present in coffee, tea, many soft drinks, chocolate, many over-the-counter medications, as well as some yogurt and ice cream, is a psychoactive substance with effects on mood (Halgin & Whitbourne, 1994; Hughes, Gust, Skoog, Keenan, & Fenwick, 1991). Nicotine also is psychoactive. Both caffeine and nicotine are addictive and can lead to disorders, so that most people have trouble breaking the habit; the frustration of trying to stop the habit intensifies the use of the drugs (Barlow & Durand, 1995). Caffeine and nicotine do not bring the problems associated with alcohol and other drugs, but they contribute to a climate of drug acceptability. (Although smoking cigarettes is falling out of favor, they are only one source of nicotine.) Slightly more men than women smoke, but cigarette smoking is of special concern for women for two reasons: It saps calcium and thus accelerates bone loss, contributing to osteoporosis (as does alcohol) (chapter 14), and it can affect pregnancy (chapter 12).

An increase in women's smoking was associated with an increase in women's deaths from lung cancer (e.g., 1979–1990); about 85% of lung cancer deaths are attributable to smoking. Although more women have breast cancer than lung cancer, white women now are more likely to die of lung cancer than of breast cancer, and African American women are only slightly more likely to die of breast cancer than lung cancer (Collins et al., 1994; Rodin & Ickovics, 1990; Strickland, 1988). Smoking rates have been declining since 1985 for both women and men (Collins et al., 1994; DSM-IV, 1994; Pierce, Giovino, Hatziandreu, & Shopland, 1989). For reasons that are not clear, it is more difficult for women than for men to stop smoking (Gritz, 1984; Waldron, 1991b).

## *Women in the Mental Health System*

Women may be at a disadvantage in the mental health system because they are expected to be unhealthy—with male as norm, females are not normal. Both diagnosis and the ways therapists treat women are at issue (Sprock & Yoder, 1997). Women have successfully challenged the system, but continuing vigilance is necessary.

### The Politics of Diagnosis

Basic conceptions of psychological problems have been criticized for gender bias (Chesler, 1972; Kaplan, 1983; Landrine, 1989; McGrath et al., 1990; Russo, 1984; Wakefield, 1987). There is evidence of a **double standard of mental health,** just as there is a double standard of sexuality and of ageing. Men who act out the masculine role (e.g., being aggressive and unfeeling) are not considered unhealthy, while women who act out the feminine role (e.g., incompetent, anxious) are. As noted in chapter 3, the picture mental health experts give of the healthy adult, gender unspecified, matches that given for the healthy man better than that for a healthy woman (Broverman, Broverman, Clarkson, Rosenkrantz, & Vogel, 1970). Because the normal mature adult is more like a man than like a woman, women are in a catch-22. If they are what experts consider healthy, they are deviating from the gender-typing they are "supposed" to show. If they fit the role prescribed for them, they are not considered healthy adults.

Women in psychology (e.g., see Committee on Women in Psychology, 1985) and psychiatry (e.g., see Kass, Spitzer, Williams, & Widiger, 1989) have had some success in challenging established thinking. A diagnosis that was of long concern was the **Self-Defeating Personality Disorder,** similar to what has been called masochistic personality (chapter 15). Symptoms associated with this disorder (suffering pain, guilt, self-punishment, serving others before self) are commonly associated with being victimized or abused: The diagnosis blamed the victim rather than the perpetrator as the disturbed individual. Yet when battered women are removed from the situation, their symptoms quickly decrease (Committee on Women in Psychology, 1985). Because of strong protests, the classification is not included in the DSM-IV so that victims of abuse now officially are considered normal people who may seek help for problems relating to troubling experiences.

Another example of bias is the inclusion of categories that are named and defined such that men *cannot* have the disorder. **Premenstrual Dysphoric Disorder,** roughly equivalent to what popularly is thought of as PMS (chapter 6; Barlow & Durand, 1995; Laws, 1983; Ussher, 1989), is one example. This disorder is not given full diagnostic status but is in the appendix of the DSM-IV as a disorder needing further study. As discussed in chapter 6, we do not know what PMS is, much less what causes it. Such a diagnostic label can lead people to think women have a serious mental disorder caused by their bodies. Neutral labels such as *periodic affective syndrome* or *cyclic dysphoric disorder* would be more appropriate (Hamilton & Gallant, 1990). Such labels could be applied to men as well and do not assume a specific biological cause.

Further examples of bias can be seen in diagnoses that caricature the traditional feminine role (Landrine, 1988, 1989, 1991). The person with *dependent personality disorder,* for example, has an extreme need to be taken care of, is submissive and clinging, and fears separation (DSM-IV, 1994). People with the diagnosis of *histrionic personality* (formerly called hysterical personality) put on a "show" (the term *histrionic* is from a Latin word meaning "actor"): The DSM-IV describes histrionic personalities as having exaggerated emotions and theatricality, overreacting to minor events, using physical appearance to draw attention to oneself, being influenced by others, behaving seductively or provocatively. Although the general prevalence of these disorders is equal among men and women (Barlow & Durand, 1995), women have been diagnosed with them more than men. Additionally, the disorders themselves resemble the feminine gender role. To understand the implications of a psychological disorder that is similar to a prescribed gender role, consider the impact of such a diagnosis for the male gender role (A Closer Look 16.2).

## Psychotherapy

Since the early 1970s, feminists have spoken loudly and clearly about how women are treated in the mental health system, asserting that psychotherapy has served to keep women in their place—second place (e.g., see Brodsky, 1978; Chesler, 1972; Hare-Mustin, 1983). Psychotherapies often have used an **adjustment model:** The goal is to help a woman adjust to the situation she is in. If she is married and her husband treats her well, any feeling of dissatisfaction is a sign of a problem on her part. If he does not treat her well, she should "adjust" and try harder to please him. The lack of adjustment often is credited to intrapsychic reasons. **Intrapsychic approaches** look within the person (within the psyche), often with assumptions about past experiences, to define and correct the problem. This position emphasizes "What are *you* doing to cause the problem?" and may minimize the external circumstances in which the problems happen. The adjustment model with intrapsychic assumptions increasingly seems

## A Closer Look

### 16.2 When the Tables Are Turned: Seeing Men's Characteristics as Abnormal

Paula Caplan and her colleagues (Caplan, 1991; Pantony & Caplan, 1991) have satirically proposed a diagnosis called "Delusional Dominating Personality Disorder." Symptoms include using power, silence, withdrawal, or avoidance rather than negotiating about interpersonal conflict, and feeling threatened by women who do not disguise their intelligence. Also part of the definition are a need to affirm one's importance by displaying oneself in the company of women who are physically attractive, young, thin, and submissive, and a need for flattery about one's sexual performance or the size of one's genitalia. This disorder occasionally is present in women but more often in men, and is particularly high among leaders of traditional mental health professions, military personnel, executives, and powerful political leaders.

Does this disorder sound silly? If so, it likely is because it describes the stereotypical attitudes and behaviors of powerful and successful people as pathological. Mental health policy is not value neutral but tends to define the behavior of powerful groups as normal and that of other groups as abnormal (Lips, 1993). Researchers have commented that dependency could be defined as letting someone else choose one's underwear, clean one's clothing, cook one's meals, and arrange details of one's social life (Kaplan, 1983; Travis, 1988b). This kind of dependency is sanctioned by society and considered normal for men. Defining that kind of dependency as psychological dependency would mean that men have failed

to separate and need psychological attention. In fact, men are thought to be showing independence by pursuing public activities, while their wives take care of the basics of life and are considered dependent on their husbands. The diagnostic system singles out for scrutiny the ways in which women express dependency but not the ways in which men express dependency.

Marcie Kaplan also proposes an "Independent Personality Disorder" and a "Restrictive Personality Disorder," which "may occur together." The independent disorder involves putting work above relationships, not taking account of others' needs when making decisions, and allowing others to assume responsibility for social life because of an inability to express emotion. Among the symptoms of the restricted disorder are limited expression of emotion and denial of emotional needs, along with constant appearance of self-assurance and being stoic in the face of major events. People with this disorder are seen as distant; engage others to write thank-you notes; and when others introduce topics related to feelings, they change the subject, say nothing, show annoyance, or leave the room.

Adapted from:

Caplan, P. J. (1991). Delusional dominating personality disorder (DDPD). *Feminism and Psychology, 1,* 171–174.

Kaplan, M. (1983). A woman's view of DSM-III. *American Psychologist,* 786–792.

Travis, C. B. (1988b). *Women and health psychology: Mental health issues.* Hillsdale, NJ: Erlbaum.

inappropriate for women as a complete model because we increasingly see that social circumstances have placed women in unhealthy situations: The situations should be changed rather than the woman being expected to adjust to them.

***Gender Bias***   A task force of the American Psychological Association (APA, 1975b) drew attention to the gender bias in psychotherapy and called for sensitization to women and women's issues. To some extent the efforts for correction have been successful, but not completely. Therapists participating in research now use predominantly positive traits of both gender roles to describe healthy persons of each gender (Phillips & Gilroy, 1985). Both healthy women and healthy men are seen as being independent and able to express tender feelings, for example. But therapists still think that the healthy woman cries more and is not quite as competitive as the healthy adult. The reported general reduction in bias may not be because the bias has actually lessened, but because therapists are more reluctant to express their biases than previously.

Sexism does continue in the form of psychotherapists having sexual relations with clients. Less than 1% of clients are estimated to be involved (Williams, 1992), but clients who are involved are likely to experience reduced self-esteem and increased mistrust, depression, guilt, and anger (Bates & Brodsky, 1989). The APA has carefully spelled out that sexual intimacies between therapist and client are unethical in *all* circumstances. Anyone who feels uneasy with a therapist's behavior is advised first to discuss the issue with the therapist. If that does not bring productive results, find a different therapist and think about reporting the offender.

Overall, sexism still exists in the psychotherapy profession, but it is not rampant. Younger therapists are less biased than older therapists, and women are less biased than men. Therapists most likely to be nonsexist are psychologists of either gender who have a large number of women in their practice; those most likely to be sexist are psychiatrists who see relatively few women (Thomas, 1985). Women psychotherapists also tend to be better informed and hold less stereotyped beliefs than their colleagues. Not taking steps to overcome ignorance can be a form of bias.

***Minority Women***   Generally, people of color are less likely to seek services in the mental health system than white people are (Snowden, 1988; Trimble & LaFromboise, 1985; Yamamoto, 1986). Some people do not know the services exist or may have language problems inhibiting their use. Others distrust psychotherapists, particularly white ones. Some cultural groups provide their own psychotherapy through family members and religion, and they resist admitting problems to outsiders. African Americans are likely to turn to family, a minister, or a general physician (Cooper, Crum, & Ford, 1994; Neal & Turner, 1991). If people of color do seek psychological services, they are highly likely to see a white American who probably speaks only English (Greene, 1986).

Psychotherapists' relative ignorance about women is a double problem for women of minority groups, and little has been written about these women (Brown & Root, 1990; Reid & Comas-Diaz, 1990). Psychotherapists who probe the person's past to understand current distress often neglect the relevance of inadequate income, poor housing in dangerous neighborhoods, and sex and racial discrimination. African American psychologists and social workers of both ethnic groups are more sensitive to such problems than white psychologists are (Boyd, 1979). Because of ignorance or insensitivity about gender and racial issues, Latina women (Collier, 1982), African American women (Gray & Jones, 1987), and Asian American women (True, 1990) receive stereotyped advice from professionals that is largely irrelevant to their experiences.

One need for working with minority women is to link psychotherapy with education, health, and social services (Olmedo & Parron, 1981). In one successful example, a child development program was started in San Francisco's Chinatown, combining a drop-in child care program with parent education, counseling, and support services (True, 1990). The program attracts largely immigrant refugee mothers who would be too threatened otherwise to go to a mental health clinic or who cannot leave home without the children.

*Lesbians*    Lesbians are statistically a minority and face a lack of understanding similar to heterosexual women of ethnic minorities. Rates of depression specifically and psychopathology generally for lesbians are comparable to those for heterosexual women, though some typical developmental tasks—"Who am I?" "How am I to act?"—are complicated for lesbians and especially for lesbians of color (Bradford, Ryan, & Rothblum, 1994; Greene, 1994; Kanuha, 1990; Morgan, 1992). Most lesbians who see therapists have personal issues similar to those of heterosexuals, perhaps along with the pressure of discrimination because of their orientation. If a therapist sees sexual orientation as the problem and a lesbian client does not, the therapist is unlikely to offer much help with the problems the client feels. Lesbians' concerns about relationships and how to meet other lesbians may be distorted into issues of personal identity by therapists who are not informed about the social context of lesbians (Rigby & Sophie, 1990). The American Psychiatric Association removed homosexuality from its list of disorders in 1974, but therapists' lack of understanding often continues.

Lesbians do find supportive and knowledgeable therapists; in fact, they use the mental health system and value it more than other women do (Bradford & Ryan, 1987; Cardea, 1985; Hoagland, 1988). The lesbian community places a high value on self-examination and acknowledgment of pain (Morgan, 1992). Arriving at a self-labeled identity as lesbian typically involves much soul searching. Through this process, lesbians may come to value personal growth. Perhaps because of this, lesbians have a more positive view about psychotherapy than heterosexual women, whether or not they personally have used it.

*Varieties of Psychotherapies*    Concern about traditional psychotherapies for women revolves around the extent to which there are inherent assumptions in the system that are detrimental to women. Schools of therapy, such as fulfillment or humanistic therapy (e.g., Rogers, 1959), cognitive and cognitive-behavioral therapy (e.g., Beck, 1991; Ellis, 1973), are not based on theories that are inherently sexist, though of course, any one therapist may be sexist. In contrast, psychoanalytic theory is, at best, highly suspect to many feminists. They see the theory as inherently biased against women and therefore conclude that the related therapy is inherently sexist and incapable of reform

(Hare-Mustin, 1983; Lerman, 1986a, 1986b; Marecek & Kravetz, 1977). Such views must be taken seriously.

However, to dismiss the current psychoanalytic movement as sexist is to do a disservice to the many women and men who are actively engaged in developing psychoanalytic thinking in light of emerging data from research and from their own experiences as therapists and scientists (Karon & Widener, 1995). Half the members of the American Psychological Association's division of psychoanalysis are women (chapter 1). Feminists who fit under the broad psychoanalytic umbrella include Carol Gilligan, Jean Baker Miller, Teresa Bernardez, Nancy Chodorow, Dorthy Dinnerstein, Luise Eichenbaum, and Susie Orbach, to name just a few who have been mentioned in this text.

Nonsexist therapy is encouraged by the APA and may be practiced by a therapist with any theoretical orientation. The principle of **nonsexist therapy** is that women and men should be seen as individuals and treated equally (Marecek & Kravetz, 1977; Rawlings & Carter, 1977; Travis, 1988b). Specifically, therapists should be aware of their own values and knowledgeable about research on the psychology of women; they should avoid gender-biased testing instruments and language and should not use their power to shape women toward stereotypic femininity. Psychotherapists should see clients as individuals and encourage them to make their own decisions, including about sexual preference. Because of their compatibility with feminism, nonsexist therapists often are referred to as feminist therapists, though the connection is not necessarily accurate.

The principles of nonsexist therapy are considered essential in feminist therapy, but **feminist therapy** also incorporates the political values and philosophy of feminism, which can be interwoven with a variety of therapeutic approaches: Feminist therapy is not defined by technique but by values. Perhaps the most basic value is that women's experiences are assumed to be valid and not to be "explained away." Specifically, feminist therapists add to nonsexist therapy the provisions that (1) society is responsible for shaping women's behavior so "the person is political," and (2) therapists should not be more powerful than clients in the therapy relationship (Brodsky, 1980; Greenspan, 1983; Marecek & Kravetz, 1977; Rawlings & Carter, 1977; Travis, 1988b). Feminist therapists assume that women are responsible for their own behavior (as do other therapists) but also that women should recognize the social forces on them and be active agents of social change for themselves and others.

The victimization of all women is considered a universal process affecting all women. Feminist therapists, however, have recognized that they have been seeing women's victimization primarily from the perspective of young, healthy, middle-class white American women (Brown, 1990; Brown & Root, 1990; Rosewater, 1990). Many women are oppressed for reasons other than being women. There is a uniqueness to each individual's victimization experience (Barrett, 1990; Lorde, 1988). "To deny uniqueness would be but another means of victimizing" (Rosewater, 1990, p. 300). Feminists are actively engaged in discovering, valuing, and building upon the diversity of women (Brown & Root, 1990).

Both nonsexist and feminist therapy were inspired by consciousness-raising (C-R) groups—small groups of women with a sense of trust in each other who met to freely discuss their concerns without a leader who makes pronouncements (Brodsky, 1973). A typical experience was the **yeah-yeah experience** of discovering shared experiences: "Yeah, yeah, I've had that experience too!" (Plaskow, 1979), in contrast to hearing, "Yes, but . . . ," as a woman is told why she is wrong. C-R groups did not claim to offer therapy, but they were therapeutic and contributed to the movement for more feminist awareness in psychotherapy. They are a good example of how women have developed their own ways to deal with their problems.

## Some Final Thoughts: Women Will Not Be Silent

There is something profoundly unhealthy about the transition to adulthood for young women in our culture (chapter 5). There is also something unhealthy about the adults young women are expected to become, and what they are expected to become is seen as unhealthy by the culture. In many ways women are treated from an androcentric perspective and their experiences and virtues trivialized, devalued, and demeaned. In the face of gender role expectations and related victimization, some women become anorexic or bulimic, alcoholic, dissociated, depressed, anxious, or suicidal. With lack of affirmation and validation, the voice of any woman can become silenced or distorted into a voice of self-blame and even self-hate. Men face gender role pressures as well, but men's typical expressions of problems are channeled outward against others. Women's dependency on their husbands is considered pathological, but husbands' dependency on their wives is considered normal.

The mental health system also has seen women androcentrically. Feminists have urged important corrections, but problems remain. Women in therapy can be seen as a microcosmic picture of women in current society in that the message they are given is, "You have no reason to complain, if you do complain it is your fault, and we're not going to take it very seriously anyway."

But women have a way of surviving and, like bumblebees, flying. Many women have spoken out and have done much to change things for all. The challenge for women is to refuse to be defined by a role of someone else's choosing and to choose their own way. A further challenge for women is to accept personal responsibility when that is appropriate but to refuse to automatically blame themselves for anything and everything that goes wrong or allow others to do so. To paraphrase a feminist saying, the advice to women is, "Don't put up with being put down."

## KEY TERMS

intropunitive versus
  extrapunitive
*Diagnostic and Statistical*
  *Manual of Mental*
  *Disorders* (DSM-IV)
coping
internalization versus
  externalization

ruminative style versus
  distracting style
anxiety disorder
specific phobia
agoraphobia
Dissociative Identity
  Disorder (DID)
dissociative disorders

somatoform disorders
somatization disorder
conversion disorder
bulimia nervosa: purging,
  nonpurging types
binge
inappropriate
  compensatory behavior

anorexia nervosa: binge
eating/purging,
restricting types
psychotropic drugs
double standard of mental
health

self-defeating personality
disorder
premenstrual dysphoric
disorder
adjustment model
intrapsychic approach

nonsexist therapy
feminist therapy
consciousness-raising
(C-R) groups
yeah-yeah experience

## KEY POINTS

*Women's Mental Health*

◆ Women use mental health services more than men, perhaps because women are
likely to express psychological distress intropunitively, while men are likely to express it extrapunitively.

◆ Women generally are at least two times as likely to be depressed as men are, with
the differential emerging in adolescence. Women are more likely than men to
live in poverty, to experience or fear violence, and to have responsibility for child
care.

◆ Women who have never been married generally are psychologically healthier than
married women are. Employment generally is a psychological benefit for married
women.

◆ Depression is more likely when a woman feels defined through a relationship, feels
she cannot be herself in a relationship, feels she is not heard and understood in a
relationship.

◆ Women (and expressive people) tend to use internalizing responses, including rumination, while men (and instrumental people) tend to use externalizing responses,
including distraction. Girls and women tend to blame themselves, while boys and
men tend to blame others or otherwise express distress externally.

◆ Women attempt suicide more than men do and are completing suicides at an increasing rate.

◆ Women have a higher rate than men of specific phobias and agoraphobia, perhaps
because there is more social support for women to "give in" to their fears. Husbands of agoraphobic women seem to want their wives to be traditional.

◆ DID is more common in women than in men and is triggered by trauma, especially
childhood abuse. Somatization and conversion disorders also are more common in
women, but other somatoform disorders are not.

*Food, Alcohol, and Other Drugs*

◆ Women with anorexia or bulimia may have been victims of childhood abuse and/or
have had troubled relationships with parents in a search for autonomy and control,
leading to conflicts about being a woman.

◆ Although eating disorders are more prevalent in middle-class white women,
women of color also have concerns about acceptance and achievement in a dominantly white society.

◆ Role pressures contribute to women's lesser use of alcohol than men's, but the same role pressures lead to alcohol use in some women, especially for expressing anger and sexuality.

◆ Problems early in life and adolescent confusion predispose some women to begin drinking in their teens or early 20s. Women with later onset of alcoholism started drinking to deal with depression or a sudden stress, often involving relationships.

◆ Both nicotine and caffeine reduce calcium. Lung cancer has surpassed breast cancer as a cause of death for women.

◆ Women use illegal drugs less than men but are more likely to be given prescription psychotropic drugs. Women are underrepresented in drug research.

### Women in the Mental Health System

◆ Although there no longer is a diagnosis for battered women, there is continuing concern about bias against women in the diagnostic system.

◆ Subtle biases that continue in some therapists include dismissal of women's problems and lack of knowledge about women and the social context of their lives. The problem is particularly strong for women of color and lesbians. In spite of this, lesbians value psychotherapy more than heterosexual women do.

◆ Women have worked to encourage the nonsexist therapies now available.

## INTEGRATIVE QUESTIONS

1. Do you agree with the statement "Women are socialized to be depressed"? Why or why not?

2. Discuss the claim that women's lack of control over their lives is responsible for their psychological problems; do not limit yourself to the topic of depression.

3. Explain the connections between women's general personality and response styles, their styles of coping, and the disorders they develop.

4. The text stated that society teaches us that it is OK for women to blame themselves and for men to blame others. To what extent, if any, do you see this supported by general opinion, the diagnostic system, and psychotherapy?

5. Discuss the ways in which women's bodies are seen as responsible for women's problems, both by individual women and by society and the mental health system.

6. How do women cope? Use a broad perspective; do not be limited to concepts of coping styles specifically. Consider all that you know about what women do in the course of dealing with the circumstances of their lives and in helping other women deal with theirs. If you have personal knowledge of poor women or minority women, you may focus on them in relation to text material.

*Chapter 17*

# Challenges, Religion, and Anger

*W*e have examined many facets of women's lives, from conception to old age. Women are born into and grow in a social world that defines and shapes their experiences and development. Many of their experiences have been shaped, and often restricted, by gender roles.

In this chapter we review some of the global messages illustrated by the psychological research described in the text and offer some comments on psychological research about women. One theme of feminist thought is the encouragement of personal involvement and action for social change to correct injustices (Worell & Etaugh, 1994). However, psychological research by itself does not always help or inspire students looking for constructive ways to respond to their frustrations and insights.

In response to that need, I offer discussion of two topics not usually discussed in general books on the psychology of women, namely, religion and anger. Both religion and anger can provide important links between knowledge of psychological facts and social action; both can provide inspiration and insight about the facts and how to act on them. Looking at religion illustrates the diversity of ways that women have joined together to challenge the status quo. Looking at anger illustrates how personal and collective energies have been thwarted or misdirected by gender roles, so that we are weakened in our ability to recognize and use our insights about injustice. Both religion and anger are unpopular topics, but both are important in human life, and both offer opportunities for growth and expression not always recognized.

Before continuing, consider these questions for personal thought:

- What do you consider the most important problems for women generally today? For yourself (whether you are a man or a woman)?
- What kind of gender-related research is of most interest to you personally?

- What role do you think religion has had in defining and enforcing gender roles? If you are religious, what has been the impact of your religion on your own understanding of gender roles?
- What might be the effect on girls and boys of seeing only men as the head clergyperson in synagogue or church?
- What do you think of people who worship a Goddess? Would you (or do you) do it? What is a witch to you?
- How was anger viewed when you were growing up? Do you feel free to express anger now?
- When you think of an angry woman, what is your image? An angry man?
- In what ways can you see anger as necessary and valuable for individual development and social change?

## Challenges: Where We Are Today

Women want "respect for women as full and equal members of the human race" (Pollitt, 1990, p. 12), as noted previously (chapter 1). Contemporary feminists have addressed this desire, as did the feminists of the last century as well as many other unrecognized women over the centuries. As a result, general attitudes about women are more liberal than they used to be (Spence & Hahn, 1997; Twenge, 1997), but women are more liberal than men, and sexism continues.

### Progress

One sign of progress is the greater number of strong women in the media; however, they spring to mind because they are *different* from the ongoing, more numerous stereotypical portrayals of women (chapter 2) and the numerous demeaning and debasing depictions of women in pornography, X- and R-rated videos, and MTV (chapter 16). There is more concern than previously with gender-free or gender-neutral books, toys, and school experiences for children, but the terms *gender free* or *gender neutral* still must be used to distinguish them from the norm (chapters 2, 5).

More occupations are opening for women, but discriminations in pay and opportunities for career development continue (chapter 13). Harassment now is named and acknowledged to exist, but few harassed students and employees take advantage of complaint procedures, in part because of fear of reprisal (chapters 13, 15). Battering also now has a name, and fewer women now are killed by their partners than in previous years, but women's shelters still do not have enough space to accommodate all the women who want shelter (chapter 15). Thanks in part to the popularity of the concept of PMS, it is now recognized publicly that women do menstruate, though the concept often is used to blame women for anything that goes wrong and to prematurely justify a psychiatric diagnosis.

*This woman has many more career options than did her mother or grandmother, but power and prestige still do not come easily to women in our society. Women have to struggle to win and maintain executive positions, and they continue to experience discrimination and harassment.*

## New Problems

It is important to recognize the progress that has been made, but it is also important to recognize where progress has not been made (Katz, 1996; Russo, 1997). Many people assume that with all the activity on behalf of women in the last 30 years, everything is now OK. Overt sexism (as well as racism) may be a thing of the past (see Campbell, Schellenberg, & Senn, 1997), but in many cases it has been replaced by **modern sexism** (Swim, Aikin, Hall, & Hunter, 1995; Yoder & McDonald, 1997) or **neosexism** (Tougas, Brown, Beaton, & Joly, 1995). Modern sexism reflects a conflict between modern values and traditional values; there is a denial of sexism and an espousal of equalitarianism along with negative feelings about women and the belief that women are asking for too much. As with other measures related to sexist beliefs, undergraduate men score higher on measures of these constructs than do women.

Ironically, even women who have poignant personal concerns about their experiences as women, as well as the men who care about them, often seem to assume that their own personal knowledge and experience are somehow isolated from the experiences of women in general. Their experiences may involve feeling ignored in class, being harassed or raped, or being underpaid on the job. Young women are now told that they can "have it all," but they still have to figure out how to mesh employment and marriage, career and parenthood, in ways that young men do not; and they think that the concern is theirs alone rather than one shared with other women. They are responding to the mixture of the new and the old.

New values and expectations about the lives of women have been emerging, but it is not always clear exactly what they are and how they are to operate. So far, the old views fill in the gaps and form the background against which the new are evaluated. Two issues—housework for employed women and sexuality—are good examples of how the old and the new work together in confusing ways. People speak of having an equalitarian marriage, but both the wife and husband speak of him as helping her with the housework, showing the lingering assumption that housework really is her province (chapter 13). Truly equalitarian marriages are rare. Men still have an implicit notion that they should be the major breadwinner, and women still have an implicit notion that they should be the major provider within the home. In spite of their paid jobs, women still seem to measure their household accomplishments against traditional standards not realistic for them.

The sexual liberation of the 1960s brought some acknowledgment of women's sexuality, but many women do not feel liberated (chapter 11). Women now are supposed to be sexual but not on their own terms. Heterosexual women do not necessarily have sex with a man because they want to and do not necessarily enjoy it when they do (Wyatt & Riederle, 1994). They may have sex to avoid "hurting his feelings," but they may be risking their reputation. The line between acceptability and promiscuity is confusingly blurred for women but not for men. Women also often do not insist on use of a condom because their partners do not want to use one, thereby risking their physical health. Heterosexuality still is male oriented.

## Male as Norm, Woman as Victim

Because traditional views coexist with newer ones, there is a continuation of androcentrism: male as norm. Men are assumed to be the experts in sexuality, and "real" sex is defined for many people only as heterosexual intercourse (chapter 11). Even lesbians are influenced by heterosexual definitions, so that "sex" requires genital activity (Rothblum, 1994b). Male as norm also continues in the employment sphere, where masculine assertiveness is needed for powerful positions (but women are supposed to be feminine and charming), and in the related homework arena, where men do not do much work around the house simply because they are men (chapter 13).

Male as norm is seen in interpersonal activities and judgments about them (chapter 15). Rape myths protect men and blame victims. Women's dependency on their husbands is seen as weak at best and pathological at worst, but men's dependency on their wives is considered normal and even an expected right (chapter 16). Men also dominate in conversation and freely interrupt women in what is a form of verbal battering and rape (chapter 9). The persisting view of men as inherently more aggressive than women helps men to maintain a position of power over women (White & Kowalski, 1994).

The other side of the coin is woman as victim. If what men do is right, it must be women's fault if something goes wrong. When women are not promoted, they don't have what it takes, although men may not have given them the chance to show whether they do or not (chapter 13). When girls are ignored in the classroom, it is because they are not assertive, although they are ignored if they raise their hand and criticized if they do not (chapter 7). The fact that young women do not score as high as young men on the SAT-Math is dismissed with, "Girls just are not very good in math," but the lower scores of young men on the SAT-Verbal is seen as a reason to change that test (chapter 8). If a woman does not enjoy sex, it is because women are not as sexual as men. If a woman is raped, she must really want or deserve it (chapter 15). If a woman is beaten by her husband, she must be doing something to upset him.

Many women have internalized their own victimization and blame themselves. Women accept "credit" for achievement failures more readily than men do (chapter 7) and often assume the responsibility and blame for relationships (chapter 16). The tendency of women for intropunitive coping styles, including self-blame, did not develop in a vacuum, nor did the tendency of men for extrapunitive coping styles (chapter 16). It is no wonder that some women learn to punish themselves and some men learn to punish women.

## Attitudes Toward Women's Bodies

Women's bodies are looked at, evaluated, and objectified (Fredrickson & Roberts, 1997). Men sexualize women in many ways, ranging from sexual violence to visual inspection of the body, in which they see a woman's body as separated from her person. This may have important implications for women's sense of shame, anxiety, depression, and varying mental health risks, including eating disorders. Certainly it seems related to how women are treated in the medical and mental health systems.

Because women's bodies are different from men's, it is easy to blame women's bodies for women's behavior. During menstruation and during perimenopause, a woman's body is held more responsible for her behavior than are the social conditions of her life (chapters 6, 14). Women in the United States have hysterectomies and cesarean deliveries at greater rates than women in other countries (chapters 12, 14). Women are more likely than men to be given pills rather than psychotherapy for the same psychological problems (chapter 16). Women are thought not aggressive enough to get ahead because they are deficient in testosterone (chapter 9). Women are defined more than men in terms of the attractiveness of their body and its "reproductive fitness" (chapters 2, 10, 14).

The popular assumption that gender differences are justified or required by nature continues to be used to explain women. People today typically do not state, as Aristotle did, that females are deficient males (chapter 1), but what they do say often reflects that view. The false dichotomy of nature versus nurture enables people to see human behavior as biologically determined apart from the cultural context in which biology develops and expresses itself. This makes it easy to assume implicitly that men have—and deserve—power for biological reasons. An assumption of female superiority would be more justified by a biological view, because the female is biologically more viable than the male (chapter 4). The more important points are that biology and environment should not even be separated, much less pitted against each other, and that biology should not be carelessly assigned responsibility for women's behavior (chapter 1).

## The Maintenance of Gender

Gender is "constituted and maintained through interpersonal processes within a cultural environment" (Gilbert, 1994, p. 541). The interpersonal processes occur within a gendered social structure, and the building blocks of the process and structure are held together by the rewards of acting out the gendered views in interpersonal interactions. For example, by withholding themselves from intimate conversation, men preserve the illusion of being independent and dominant (chapter 10). Women "go along with the game" (Pleck, 1981; Spender, 1985/1990). Women learn to "underfunction" with men to secure a safe place in men's lives (Lerner, 1985). They use the interpersonal strategies of lower status people to try to get what they want (chapter 10). Women are rewarded by men for tentative speech (chapter 9). Some women go so far as to silence themselves (chapter 16). Women learn survival skills to get along with the men in their lives, but in so doing they are reinforcing gender structure.

The gender structure facilitates gender as process (Gilbert, 1994; Unger, 1992). For example, the structure of the employment world has not changed much. Women and men are predominantly in different occupations, and men still earn more than women (chapter 13). Alice Eagly theorized that the division of labor reinforces the assumption that men and women have different personality characteristics, which, in turn, justifies the division of labor (chapter 3). The employment world is making some concessions to family concerns, but women more than men are expected to use benefits such as parental leaves and flexible schedules. Employed mothers are named in our gendered language as "working moms," while employed fathers are simply employed men serious about their careers (Gilbert, 1994). Men do not typically take formal paternity leave when it is offered, but when a baby arrives most do take "a few days off," as labeled by the men themselves and by their coworkers (Pleck, 1993).

People who have low status in a structure learn to be sensitive to the social context. This may be why women's behavior often varies more than men's over different situations (chapter 9). Women want to know when it is acceptable and safe to be themselves and when it is not. Thus, they are more likely to state that they have low self-confidence and to conform with the views of others when other people will know what they are doing than when they are alone (chapters 7, 9). They do not necessarily do this with awareness; often they are simply enacting well-learned behavior.

Race and class are part of societal structure and affect women's lives both in interaction with gender and by themselves. Researchers no longer ignore women of color, but they still tend to see women of color as anomalies. Researchers omit them from studies of the common experiences of women and focus on them in studies of deviant behavior (e.g., teenage pregnancy). White women have become the norm of universal woman. As the norm, their race has been protected from scrutiny, and women of other groups are compared with them. Understanding women's diversity is not just a matter of considering the ethnic memberships of women of color. It also involves understanding how white women's race and ethnicity have affected their views of themselves and of other women.

## Overcoming Gender

When people do not recognize how interpersonal behaviors help maintain the gender structure, they often cannot see why some people object to gender-typing. They may characterize the objectors as advocating that women become like men or that women and men be merged into a "unisex." On the contrary, most women do not accept men as models of the ideal life, nor do they care to emulate men (Freeman, 1975). They want to participate in society, but they also want to be themselves and to question and change society; they object to ascribed roles that limit human development.

A feminist saying is, "Women who want to be like men are not aiming very high." This can be seen as a put-down of men. It also can be seen as a recognition that the current system inhibits the growth and personal expression of both men and women (Freeman, 1976). Gloria Steinem (1995) suggested that if feminist goals were realized, men would live four years longer (chapter 1). A growing body of research shows that men experience strain and conflict because of masculine role pressures (e.g., see McCreary et al., 1996). Change away from gender pressures would most likely not produce a unisex world in which everyone is alike. Rather, we would probably see greater diversity among women and among men than currently is the case.

Can gender differences be reduced or avoided? It is true that young children need concrete categories around which to organize information (chapter 5). However, children are capable of responding to attributes other than gender. In one study, children (ages 6 to 11) who were grouped by the colors red and green, or not separated at all for six weeks, were less likely to see occupations as being only for men or only for women than were children separated by gender. We know that adults raised by loving parents who modeled nonstereotyped behavior are more gender flexible than others (chapter 5), and adults generally move away from strong gender-typing after the parenting years (chapter 14). We do not know that early use of gender categories can be eliminated. We do know that human beings are flexible and adaptive.

It is difficult for some people to imagine a sane and ordered world in which women do not have babies, stay home, and drive the soccer car pool. They have blamed feminism for the breakdown of the family and for a host of other societal problems, including juvenile delinquency, drug abuse, violence against women, male sexual dysfunction, and materialism—an amazing array of powers (Faludi, 1991; Rice, 1994). But feminists do not argue for the abolition of interpersonal support, caring, nurture; nor do they argue that children be allowed to grow without adult teaching and modeling of what the adults consider moral or simply adult behavior. Rather, feminists argue that caring for children and caring for adults are worthwhile human activities that deserve respect. Feminists do not want to destroy human relations; they want to improve them. Two centuries ago, Mary Wollstonecraft pointed out that feminism can lead to more genuine and better relationships:

> Would man but generously snap our chains, and be content with rational fellowship instead of slavish obedience, they would find us more observant daughters, more affectionate sisters, more faithful wives, more reasonable mothers—in a word, better citizens. (1792/1993, p. 121)

In short, feminists seek a better, more just, more caring society through equality between women and men.

## Research Issues

Much of current psychological research relevant to women is concerned with gender differences (Worell, 1995). Some psychologists see the gender differences as generally being too small to be interesting (Hyde & Plant, 1995). But Alice Eagly (1987, 1995) points out that the importance of a difference is a matter not simply of its size but of its consequences in natural settings. For example, the gender difference on the math achievement test of the American College Testing Program is fairly small (accounting for only 5.4% of the variance; McGraw & Wong, 1992). However, that means that if boys and girls were randomly paired, in 63% of the pairings the boy would score higher than the girl. This small difference has had important implications for the distribution of funds for college scholarships.

Other psychologists prefer to avoid questions of gender differences because they see the attributes considered in studies of gender differences as being fixed, stable, and internal; they prefer to approach gender in terms of external interpersonal and institutional matters that affect the distribution of power and privilege (Marecek, 1995). However, attributes are not fixed internal personality traits impervious to the environment. For example, we see age changes in cognitive performance and in indices of masculinity-femininity. And behavior varies across situations, particularly in women, who, apparently more than men, have to learn to modify their behavior as a function of the environment to get desired outcomes.

Gender-difference research can be meaningful when placed in a larger context, and it can be useful when it leads to additional investigations into underlying causes and possible implications (Eagly, 1995). Findings of gender differences that do not lead to further investigation often serve to reinforce the status quo and do not increase our understanding of human development. If some gender differences are biologically influenced, we can profit from knowing that. For example, to the extent that gender differences in spatial abilities are biologically mediated, girls might profit from being taught different ways to approach spatial tasks (Kimura, 1992). To the extent that such gender differences are attributable to experience, professionals could help find ways to give girls more experiences that facilitate high spatial ability. We are in a better position to work for equality if we know reasons for existing gender differences than if we do not (Eagly, 1995).

An important reason for the frequent minimal gender differences is wide variability within gender groups—women differ markedly from each other. When individual differences among women are studied, it is often in terms of gender role traditionality. Indices of traditionality are working class relative to middle class, exclusive homemakers relative to employed women, married women relative to single women, and sometimes heterosexual women relative to lesbians. Gender role instruments (for example, the Personal Attributes Questionnaire, Bem Sex Role Inventory) are not without faults (chapter 3), but they do allow for the measurement of at least part of gender traditionality and provide a way to study differences among women. Measures of attitudes about women may be preferable (as Spence, 1993, has claimed, chapter 3) (McHugh & Frieze, 1997; Spence & Hahn, 1997; Twenge, 1997), but so far they have not been so widely used as the role measures.

If we are to understand women's lives, it may be time to move away from gender per se. People differ from each other in many ways other than gender (e.g., social class, ethnicity), though the implications of those dimensions often interact with gender. What is critical in future research may be to know what is important to women. To discover these areas of concern, psychologists need more freedom for research than they currently have, particularly in their research methods. Research articles are evaluated against methodology criteria that serve to sift out much of what is most informative about women (Reid & Kelly, 1994). An extreme case in point is that one-shot interview studies are not highly regarded in the science of psychology, but such descriptive studies have their place in helping psychologists understand the physical and social worlds that women inhabit. These studies, in which women talk about their experiences, are not the epitome of scientific precision, but they are provocative starting points. If scholars are to understand women, they must at least be free to talk to women, to listen to them, and to watch them in their natural lives.

## Women's Experiences of Religion and Spirituality

Religion is an important part of life for many women and men. When asked for their religious preference fewer than 10% of Americans say they have no religion (Hadaway, 1989). Church attendance has not changed much in the last 50 years, with about 40% of Americans saying they have attended religious services within the last 7 days (e.g., see Chaves, 1989). Their responses may not have been completely true but still indicate the importance of religion.

The current neglect of religion by psychologists may reflect the fact that psychologists are among the least religious of academicians and of psychotherapists (Beit-Hallahmi, 1977; Bergin & Jensen, 1990); they have been said to have an overly narrow professionalism (Jones, 1994). Psychology textbooks generally give relatively little scholarly attention to religion (Kirkpatrick & Spilka, 1989; Lehr & Spilka, 1989).

Psychologists' current views are in marked contrast to the early years of American psychology when many of the leaders of the APA researched religion. Religion went out of favor as Freudianism and behaviorism began to gain prominence in the 1920s, but, like Psychology of Women, it did not disappear from psychology. In 1975

Division 35, Psychology of Women, was established (chapter 1), and a year later Division 36 was founded as Psychologists Interested in Religious Issues, now called Psychology of Religion. Strong appeals have recently been made for acceptance of the idea that science and religion are not mutually exclusive (Jones, 1994).

## Women and Religion

Religion has long been a powerful instrument for both the subordination and the liberation of women. Women are generally somewhat more religious than men on a wide range of measures (Andersen, 1988; Argyle & Beit-Hallahmi, 1975; Batson & Ventis, 1982; Lindsey, 1990). Relative to men, women attend church or synagogue more often, pray more often, report more intense religious experiences, regard religion more favorably, feel closer to God, are more likely to express need for a religious dimension in their daily lives, and are more involved in religious social activities. This pattern has a long history.

*A Bit of History*    The pattern of women's greater religiosity has a long history for a country as young as the United States (A Closer Look 17.1). Women's greater involvement in the Puritan tradition in America was evident by the later part of the 17th century (Dunn, 1980; Moran, 1980). Early Puritan ministers such as Cotton Mather speculated that women's fears of death during their frequent pregnancies, and their fears of children's deaths, made them more susceptible to Divine comfort, a view supported by women's letters and diaries. With immigration, Roman Catholic and Jewish women joined Protestant women in the growing feminization of religion of the 19th century. Women came to be the guardians of spiritual life within the family and responsible for the religious socialization of children (Lindsey, 1990; Sapiro, 1990).

The women themselves gained something besides responsibility, namely, some measure of freedom. First, religion gave women permission for "holy selfishness" (Cott, 1977). As women committed to God, they had a responsibility for attending to their *own* feelings and thoughts, rather than automatically channeling all their concerns into domestic life. Second, with what they believed to be the authority of God on their side, they felt free to be self-assertive and to work for beloved causes (Cott, 1977). This was particularly important in the 19th century when women were largely confined to the domestic sphere and excluded from the public realm. Disapproving husbands and clergy, fearful of what might transpire when women got together, could not well protest against what women proclaimed the will of God and the effectiveness of women's work.

When women act together, they empower themselves and other women, as we saw with C-R groups (chapter 16). Women's religious groups of the 19th century expressed women's piety, their own desire for spiritual growth, and their compassion toward others; they also provided women with an organizational base for developing a sense of sisterhood and articulating feminist concerns (Andersen, 1988). The tradition of women having an impact on communities and society through religious organizations has continued, as has the development of a sense of sisterhood (Sapiro, 1990).

***Current Trends in Gender Roles in Religious Organizations*** The relationship of religious organizations and women is not a completely compatible one, however. Religion has been used to legitimize distinctions based on gender and race (McGuire, 1987; Richardson, 1988). Those religions that are based on literal interpretation of religious texts are generally more supportive of male dominance than others (Chalfant, Beckley, & Palmer, 1987; Renzetti & Curran, 1989). For example, in a national sample, wives in the stricter religions reported weaker support for autonomy within marriage (Wilson & Musick, 1995). In addition, some religions see male dominance as dictated by a higher being (Meadow & Kahoe, 1984). Thus, some forms of religion help perpetuate a cycle of inequality (Focus on Research 17.1, p. 618).

Since the 1960s, both the feminist movement and conservative religion in various forms have become increasingly influential (Steiner-Aeschliman & Mauss, 1996). These movements have often been in conflict, although less conservative religions have been relatively more supportive of feminists' changes, as have been younger cohorts (Kanagy & Driedger, 1996).

Although it is usually assumed that religiosity affects gender ideology, gender role ideology may shape religious beliefs, practices, and experiences (Feltey & Poloma, 1991). Belief in gender equality is associated with decreased belief in orthodox interpretation of religious texts and with decreased personal importance of religion. It is *not* associated with felt closeness with God, whereas gender and age are (women and older people feel closer). As women continue to receive more education, delay childbearing, and enter the labor force, there will probably be an impact on religious views. The feminist movement already has affected religion.

## Division of Labor

***Who Are the Clerics?*** Clergy still are predominantly men (Nesbitt, 1997). The effect of this imbalance is that women in the group do not have a "spiritual supervisor" of their own gender, nor are they made to feel that women are important. This is much the same as in other organizations in which men have the leading positions (e.g., schools, business). In addition, young children often equate the person in the pulpit with God. One child's letter to God starts, "Dear God, are boys better than girls? I know you are one but try to be fair" (quoted in Scanzoni & Hardesty, 1974). Although most clergy are men, new religious groups are often accepting of women; as a group gains stability and acceptance in the community, however, it becomes more male oriented (Barfoot & Sheppard, 1980; Carroll, Hargrove, & Lummis, 1983).

Nevertheless, women have long heard the call and become preachers and then ordained clergy even when they were criticized for doing so (see A Closer Look 17.1). Today the clerical profession, like the professions of law and medicine, has become fairly open to women, though still not without criticism of women who take advantage of that openness (chapter 13). The students at seminaries, law schools, and medical schools now often are about 50% women, and at some the percentage is even higher. From 1977 to 1986 the number of ordained women clergy in the United States

## A Closer Look

### 17.1    Historical Milestones for Women in Religion

1637    Anne Hutchinson excommunicated by the Puritan church in Boston for challenging religious doctrines.

1656    Mary Fisher and Ann Austin, the first Quaker missionaries in America.

1660    Mary Dyer, Quaker missionary, hanged and buried on Boston Commons with no marker. She later came to be considered a martyr, easing anti-Quaker sentiments.

1766    First Methodist congregation in New York City, perhaps the first in the United States, arranged by Barbara Heck, Mother of American Methodism.

1780    A log house inaugurated as a Shaker church by Mother Ann Lee, thought by some to be a female Messiah to complement the male.

1787    Formal recognition given to women as preachers by John Wesley, though he never really approved of the ordination of women.

1788    New Jerusalem established in New York, near Seneca Lake, by followers of the Publick Universal Friend, Jemima Wilkinsen. They aroused the ire of established churches by claiming she was a Messiah.

1810    First sisterhood in America, the Sisters of Charity of St. Joseph's, founded and headed by Mother Elizabeth Bayley Seton. She was canonized in 1975 as the first saint born in the United States.

1812    Society for the Relief of Poor Widows with Small Children founded by Isabella Graham.

1823    Betsy Stockton, first woman to serve as an unmarried woman in a foreign mission field, though she was a domestic helper in a missionary family rather than a missionary herself.

1827    Cynthia Farrar, the first single woman given the designation of missionary.

1832    Maria W. Stewart, first American-born woman to give a public lecture. (Scottish radical Frances Wright was the first woman to speak here publicly, 1829, giving an antislavery and anticlerical speech.) A former servant girl, Stewart felt she had a great work to do in religion. She spoke about freedoms for southern slaves and about the slavery of free blacks in the northeast.

1834    Ursuline convent burned by an anti-Catholic mob.

1836    The Grimke sisters, Sarah and Angelina, first women formally appointed as antislavery agents.

1838    John Humphrey Noyes founded a tiny congregation and developed the idea for the Oneida community in which men had the burden of birth control.

1846    Isaac M. Wise arrived in America to become leader of Reform Judaism and instituted many reforms for women. He championed suffrage and ordination for women but saw neither before he died. He founded Hebrew Union College, 1875, and encouraged women to attend, but none of the women students sought ordination.

1853    Antoinette Brown, first woman ordained in a mainline congregation, the Congregationalist, today largely a part of the United Church of Christ.

1860    Women's society to support single women as missionaries founded by Sarah Doremus, the "Mother of Missions," enabling more single women to go into missionary work.

1860    Seventh-Day Adventist church founded, under the guidance and inspiration of Ellen Gould Harmon White.

1879    The Church of Christ, Scientist, chartered under the leadership of Mary Baker Eddy. Eddy cited 1866 as the year she discovered Christian Science, when she miraculously recovered from what was expected to be a fatal injury.

Late 1880s    The American Baptists and the Disciples of Christ recorded ordination of women, though women were the exception.

1893    National Council of Jewish Women founded.

1911    Hadassah, the women's division of the Zionist Organization of America, founded.

1923    Aimée Semple McPherson dedicated her Angels Temple in Los Angeles as the Church of the Foursquare Gospel.

1956    Ordination of women approved by the United Methodist Church and the United Presbyterian Church, U.S.A.

1964    Ordination of women approved by the Southern Baptist Convention and the Presbyterian Church, U.S.

1968    *The Church and the Second Sex,* a scholarly critique of Catholic Church doctrine influential among Protestant as well as Catholic women, published by Dr. Mary Daly.

1968 and later    A number of Native American women—Luch Covington, Ramona Bennett, Joy Sundberg, Ada Deer—elected as tribal chairs.

*(continued)*

## 17.1    Historical Milestones for Women in Religion    *(continued)*

1970    Ordination of women approved by the Lutheran Church in America.

1972    Sally Preisand, the first woman to be ordained a rabbi.

1976    Ordination of women approved by the Episcopal Church.

1977    Rev. Ellen Barret, first declared lesbian ordained an Episcopal priest.

1977    Rev. Pauli Murray, first African American woman ordained an Episcopal priest.

1979    Rabbi Linda Joy Holtzman, first woman rabbi to head a congregation.

1985    Amy Eilberg ordained, first woman conservative rabbi.

1989    Rev. Barbara Harris, first woman to be bishop in the Anglican Church.

1990    B'nai B'rith International, a fraternal order of Jewish men, voted to admit women as full members while allowing B'nai B'rith Women to continue as a self-governing affiliate with only women as members.

1990    A new version of the Bible introduced for use in major Protestant churches, using contemporary language, eliminating many male-centered terms, and demonstrating sensitivity to issues of race and homosexuality.

1991    Elizabeth Carl, an openly lesbian woman, ordained an Episcopal priest.

1991    A prayer that made sexual equality and environmental concerns part of the official canon of the church approved by the American Presbyterian Church.

doubled, to 21,000, with the greatest increase in the mainline Protestant denominations (see Steiner-Aeschliman & Mauss, 1996). One fourth of those enrolled in Roman Catholic theological schools are women, even though women cannot become priests. In mainline African American denominations, about 4% of the clergy are women, and about 4% of the Jewish rabbis in the United States are women.

Many of the women in seminaries are middle-aged women seeking a second career after a first career in homemaking or other occupations. The experience and ability of the new clergywomen, supplemented by professional theological training, may be a powerful force in fostering egalitarianism between the sexes and generally promoting cooperation, holism, and flexibility in organized religion (Carroll et al., 1983; Ice, 1987). Among clergy as among people in general, men are more conservative than women (Finlay, 1996). In addition, feminist literature has been added to seminary

1992     The United Methodist Church approved a new book of worship with more inclusive ways of referring to God and with prayers drawing on many cultures. Some prayers were to "God our Father and Mother."

1992     The United Presbyterian Church (U.S.A.) adopted a policy discouraging abortion but supporting women's rights to obtain one.

1992     First woman bishop, the Reverend April Urling Larson, elected by the Evangelical Lutheran Church.

1993     Roman Catholic feminists gathered for the third Women-Church conference; they focused on exclusion of women from the ministry, domestic violence, and sexual abuse by the clergy.

1993     Nadeen Bishop, a campus minister at the University of Minnesota, became the first Baptist minister to state publicly that she was a lesbian.

SOURCES:

Costello, C., & Stone, A. J. (Eds.). (1994). *The American woman: 1994–1995*. New York: Norton.

Ries, P., & Stone, A. J. (Eds.). (1992). *The American woman, 1992–1993, a status report*. New York: Norton.

Weidman, J. L. (1985). *Women ministers: How women are redefining traditional roles*. San Francisco: Harper & Row.

*The spirit of Houston: The first national women's conference*. (1978, March). An official report to the president, the Congress and the people of the United States. Washington, D.C. National Commission on the Observance of International Women's Year, U.S. Department of State. Reprinted in S. Ruth (Ed.), 1990, *Issues in feminism* (2nd ed.). Mountain View, CA: Mayfield.

Author's personal files.

curricula, and more women have been appointed to faculties and administrations (Steiner-Aeschliman & Mauss, 1996).

Clergywomen face the same issues that many other professional women do. They have more trouble than men do attaining the more prestigious and lucrative jobs (Andersen, 1988; Briggs, 1995; Nesbitt, 1997; Weidman, 1985). Roman Catholic sisters often do much of the same kind of work that priests do but do not have the full recognition and authority of the priesthood. Often, women are expected to do youth work and counseling, which is seen as women's work, rather than spiritual work with adults. When Protestant or Jewish women do attain a pastorate, they do well. The *experience* of having a clergywoman seems to prove less traumatic to the congregation than the *idea* of having a clergywoman (Weidman, 1985). Laypeople have become more open to ordained women (Steiner-Aeschliman & Mauss, 1996). Like other

## FOCUS ON RESEARCH

### 17.1 Interviews: Can Religious Women Speak Out?

Have you ever felt that you had too much to lose if you spoke your mind? Was it easier to keep silent and not upset those around you? Many researchers, including Carol Gilligan, have delved into this phenomenon of the "lost voice" experienced by young girls and women who are socialized into silencing their thoughts and feelings. How can this happen? Many of our cultural institutions teach us that the appropriate female role is one of nurturance, care for others, and social connectedness. For many girls and women the fear of losing relationships is a powerful force that can stifle not only dissension but even discussion of thoughts and feelings that seem to fall outside the group's norms.

Researchers Jennette Lybeck and Cynthia Neal (1995) found that most of the studies concerning this silencing focused on the socializing influence of school and home environments; very little attention had been paid to religious institutions. As a factor that permeates the lives of millions of American girls and women, what role does religion play in silencing female voices? Does religion help women express their feelings and thoughts, or does it promote silence?

Given the variety of religious attitudes about women's roles, Lybeck and Neal thought the effect might differ depending on the conservatism of the religious organization. They focused their inquiry on two types of Christian churches, drawing their samples from a conservative evangelical congregation that promotes traditional women's roles and a mainline evangelical denomination that supports nontraditional, egalitarian women's roles. They also wanted their study to take a developmental approach, so they recruited female participants from three age groups: 8- to 10-year-olds, 12- to 14-year-olds, and 20- to 30-year-olds. They hypothesized that girls and women from the conservative evangelical church that promotes traditional women's roles would manifest the "lost voice," while those from the egalitarian evangelical congregation would have role models that encouraged expression of their voices. In keeping with their research concern for girls' and women's voices, Lybeck and Neal decided to use face-to-face interviews to gather information from participants.

Interviews, along with questionnaires, are a type of survey research. Surveys rely on self-reports rather than direct observations of behavior, resulting in several important advantages. The researcher can sample a broader range of experience than is permitted by direct observation. Researchers also have access to experiences and behaviors they could not easily observe—attitudes, beliefs, prejudices, and opinions, as well as many private behaviors, such as sexual practices, substance abuse, and family violence.

Interviews provide rich sources of data. Rather than a simple yes or no, they often yield highly personal and complex responses. They are flexible instruments in the hands of skilled interviewers; the use of probes allows the interviewer to follow up on brief responses and gain insights into attitudes and behaviors that would otherwise be missed. The establishment of rapport, a comfortable relationship between the subject and the interviewer, increases the likelihood that the interview will reveal information that otherwise might be withheld.

Interviews can reach individuals who might not respond to a questionnaire. Participants who cannot read, because they are too young or illiterate, can nonetheless respond verbally to an interviewer's questions. Also, many research participants who cannot find the time to fill out and return a questionnaire are willing to be interviewed. Once participants have been reached, the interview format can help ensure that the data they give is valid. A face-to-face interview reduces the number of "don't know" or "no answer" responses commonly found in questionnaires, and the interviewer can clarify confusing or misunderstood questions.

Interviews also have a number of disadvantages. Along with questionnaires, they can suffer from problems of inaccuracy. Untruthfulness, selective memory, intentional or unintentional withholding of information, and distortion due to social desirability or interviewer bias all potentially contaminate the data. Social desirability refers to the tendency of participants to answer questions in a way that helps them "look good" in front of the interviewer. Interviewer bias results when the interviewer's characteristics (e.g., age, gender), opinions, or expectations influence the participant's responses. For example, the interviewer may unintentionally indicate the "correct" answer by accepting some responses but continuing to probe others until they conform to expectations. The interviewer's expectations can also bias the coding or interpreting of responses. Training of interviewers can help, but it cannot totally eliminate problems of bias.

In the interests of reliable data, it is recommended that more than one interviewer be employed in a study. Each interviewer should undergo the same training, which should cover not only what questions to ask, but dress, grooming, and demeanor. Interviewers should be as neutral as possible so that participants respond to the questions, not the interviewer. Also, interviewers in a study should be essentially interchangeable with each other; that is, the participant should respond the same regardless of who the interviewer is. If two different interviewers elicit the same responses, the data are considered more reliable.

The interviews conducted by Lybeck and Neal revealed that regardless of church affiliation, girls between the ages of 8 and 14 reported that they would sacrifice their own opinions and feelings to keep their relationships stable; in other words, they experienced a loss of their voices. When asked how she would handle a disagreement with a friend, one participant made the following comment, typical for this age group: "I would just give in. . . . I would just say, 'it's not worth it,' and probably say 'I'm sorry,' and just give in" (Lybeck & Neal, 1995, p. 7). However, age appears to change this perception, as the group of 20- to 30-year-old women reported feeling freer to express

*(continued)*

### 17.1   Interviews: Can Religious Women Speak Out?   *(continued)*

themselves without fear of losing important relationships; this feeling persisted regardless of church affiliation.

Lybeck and Neal report the only difference between conservative and egalitarian church women appeared in the 20- to 30-year-olds, in relation to their self-perceptions. Women in this age group from the egalitarian church saw their voice as a strength and felt confident in their ability to balance their own needs with the needs of others in their lives. In contrast, the 20- to 30-year old women from the conservative church perceived their voice as more of a weakness, equating the expression of personal needs and opinions with being selfish and disobedient to Christian principles. This group of women struggled with the dichotomy between their personal feelings of independence and identity and the traditional gender roles taught by their church. One participant noted that as an adult woman, it was now easier for her to disagree with others, but, she said, "It's wrong, it's a sin. It's very much a sin to be angry no matter . . . what the result or why or whatever" (Lybeck & Neal, 1995, p. 8). Through their interview method, Lybeck and Neal found that their hypotheses about the role religion plays in suppressing or encouraging girls' and women's voices were only partially supported. Their findings tell us that many women are ready to speak out, but some still feel that it would be wrong.

JILL BORCHERT   ◆

SOURCE: Lybeck, J., & Neal, C. (1995). Do religious institutions resist or support women's lost voice? *Youth & Society, 27,* 4–8.

---

employed women, clergywomen also experience harassment (chapter 15). The problems for clergywomen are often exacerbated if they are also lesbians.

***The Role of Laywomen***   Laywomen active in religious organizations are often expected to manage the kitchen while men manage the budget and the spiritual life of the group. Many religious groups rely heavily on the work of women, but they see women's work as maintenance or background work for the important leadership work of men (Andersen, 1988). Traditional assignment of labor is not limited to traditional religions. In alternative religious movements as well, women's roles involve what is essentially housework and, in some cases, even sexuality (Andersen, 1988; Jacobs, 1984). Women who had voluntarily left some groups (e.g., Hare Krishna, Unification Church) reported that women had the responsibility of soliciting funds and of recruiting new members through their sexual attractiveness. The women who gave these reports left the groups. Many other women face less blatant but perhaps similar discrimination and are in a quandary about what to do.

*A growing number of ordained ministers and rabbis in the United States are women. Such positions offer women the opportunity for leadership, service, and public religious expression.*

## Alternatives and Shared Views

In an unsatisfactory marriage or unpleasant job situation, a woman may accept the situation, request change, or leave. In both cases, many women feel they cannot leave the situation. The alternatives for women dissatisfied with their treatment within their religion are the same. Some women accept their religion's negative attitudes about women as an intrinsic part of their religiousness (Meadow & Kahoe, 1984). They may feel trapped, perhaps believing that their dissatisfaction reflects their own weakness and spiritual failure. Others have left traditional organized religions. Other women have attempted to change their religions. Like feminist scholars generally, in spite of their diversity they have common themes (Christ & Plaskow, 1979; Collins, 1974; Plaskow & Christ, 1989). They accept the principle that history, including religious history, is socially constructed, with women neglected and undervalued. Because of this, they are suspicious of authority and feel free to question it from their own experience.

Another commonality is the development of an organic vision that affirms both body and earth. In much of organized religion, body and earth are devalued. Mind is equated with God and men, intelligence and will, good and sky, while body is associated with women and children, emotions and passion, bad and the earth (Ruether,

1983). Women were "created" (socially constructed) as the rejected part of the male psyche. Feminist theologians, on the other hand, see women positively and emphasize nature and unity. They reject hierarchical images in favor of circular ones. For example, the song "We Are Climbing Jacob's Ladder" has been supplemented with "We Are Dancing Sarah's Circle." Images of birth and rebirth point to the natural cycle of life and unity of life over time.

Exactly how women express these themes varies. **Reformists** choose to remain within their traditional religion and try to reform it. **Revisionists** choose to avoid the mainstream and work for new visions of women's potentialities; the largest group of these are involved with the Goddess movement. The distinctions, however, are not firm, and a person might be a reformist on some issues and a revisionist on others. Similarly, a person may change views over time (Plaskow & Christ, 1989). We look briefly now at the major features of the reformist and revisionist approaches.

## Reformists: Jews and Christians

Jewish, Roman Catholic, and Protestant reformists work within their organized religions on the assumption that the religious are reformable. Reformists do not see themselves as *changing* their religions so much as *purifying* them of a false masculinization that has distorted them. Their efforts include text examination and concern with language and imagery.

*Text Examination*   Text examination involves looking closely at the textual basis of the religion and using modern scholarship to understand the texts instead of relying solely on masculinized interpretations (Fiorenza, 1983). For example, the creation story is not one story but at least two; the one claiming male superiority became the standard (Eisler, 1987; Stone, 1976). Woman is described as a "helpmate," interpreted as meaning that women are to serve men; but when the word for helpmate (*'ezer*) is used elsewhere in Judaic texts, it usually connotes a superior form of help (Mollenkott, 1984; Russell, 1974; Trible, 1973/1979). Phyllis Trible (1973/1979), among others, concludes that the original human was not sexually differentiated and that there is no support for claiming women are inferior to men. She contends also that Eve was more intelligent and responsible than Adam.

Many groups have stories of women being responsible for evil. In Greek legend, Pandora opened a box she was told not to open, and from it flowed all the evils of the world. Theologian Harvey Cox suggests that Eve's "fall" was really the first act of human consciousness and decision making. For those who do not accept such views about Eve, the remark of activist and evangelist Sojourner Truth may be relevant (chapter 1). She suggested that if Eve *alone* turned the world upside down, then women *together* ought to be able to get it right side up again!

*God-Talk*   Much of the early work of reformists concerned language and related imagery about the divine, or "God-talk" (Ruether, 1983); this topic remains controversial among laypeople. The typical language of Christian, Moslem, and Judaic groups refers to the supreme being as male. When religious assumptions are added to the secular concern about the generic masculine, there is a lively issue. It may be helpful to remember that "a God language does not really tell us about God, but it does tell us a considerable amount about *those who use the God language* [italics added]" (Gross, 1979, p. 170).

Both Jewish and Christian analysts of texts agree that Yahweh or God is both male and female and neither male nor female (Mollenkott, 1984; Pagels, 1976; Ruether, 1983; Trible, 1973/1979). They call attention to many examples of female as well as male imagery in the scriptural texts. One example is that the root word for the ideas of compassion and mercy in Hebrew is *rechem*, "womb" (Trible, 1973/1979). In ascribing compassion and mercy to Yahweh, Hebrew thought suggested maternal or womblike qualities. Early texts had many versions in which God was named as unisexual, androgynous, or female, but these were edited and sorted until much of the feminine imagery for God had disappeared from orthodoxy by 200 C.E. (Pagels, 1976).

Reformists today vary in their language, such as using *God-She* as well as *God-He* or speaking of God as both Mother and Father, or as Creator. Many ultimately want a language for the Divine as a liberator who fosters personhood and being. But language habits and related images are hard to transform (Ruether, 1983). The statement "God is neither male nor female; *he* is spirit," illustrates the problem.

***Religious Expressions***    Language and imagery concerns apply also to songs, rituals, and other religious expressions (Emswiller & Emswiller, 1974; National Council of Churches, 1987; United Methodist Church, 1989). Changing words to be inclusive of women (e.g., "Rise Up, Oh Folk of God" instead of "Rise Up, Oh Men of God") is important but by itself is not enough (Collins, 1974; Morton, 1979). Reformists have worked on creating new rituals or reforming old ones; while rituals use words, their power is the *experience* beyond words. Jewish women have been particularly creative in this regard (Gross, 1979; Plaskow, 1979).

Similarly, stories use words but transcend words; a story is an organic whole, a metaphor (Morton, 1979). Telling stories is part of the Jewish and Christian approaches as well as some Eastern approaches (Huie, 1985). In fact, Ellen Umansky (1989) suggested that the most important source of Jewish feminist theology may be *aggada*, Jewish legends and stories which themselves often have been reinterpreted. She tells the story of Sarah, wife of Abraham who thought God wanted him to sacrifice his son, Isaac. She adds Sarah's point of view to the story. In rabbinic legend, Lilith was Adam's first wife, but she could not live with him and flew away, becoming demon of the night. In Plaskow's (1979) version of the story, Eve and Lilith meet and become friends, with a strong bond of sisterhood, causing Adam great concern!

Christian reformists use these Jewish stories and add to them. The story of Mary's pregnancy with Jesus is told from the perspective of an unmarried teenager; the story of the adulteress about to be stoned is told from the perspective of the woman herself (Huie, 1985). Reformists do not see such women's stories as violating the scriptural base but as adding to women's dimensions.

## Revisionists

Some women are not impressed by the reformists' attempts and think that Judaism and Christianity are inherently masculine in structure (e.g., see Christ, 1979; Daly,

1973; Goldenberg, 1979). Many have turned away from their original traditions to Goddess worship; other people have always been aligned with Goddess worship. It has become useful to speak both of the*o*logy (e.g., reformists) and the*a*logy (Goddess people) (Plaskow & Christ, 1989). *Theos* is Greek for a masculine god; *thea* is Greek for goddess.

The most prominent revisionist movement is called by varying names: **Wicca, the Craft,** the New Craft, Witchcraft, the Old Religion, or Paganism or Neo-Paganism (Adler, 1979; Starhawk, 1977/1979, 1982, 1984). Whatever the name, it is a religion of connection with the Goddess. The word *witch* comes from the Old English *wicca* or *wicce*, from a root word (*wic* or *weik*) meaning to bend, turn, or twist (Adler, 1979; Starhawk, 1984). The wicces (pronounced "witches") were the wise women and men of the village who could bend and shape energy; they were healers, counselors, priests, and priestesses. The original meaning of *witch* is a far cry from modern views of ugly hags riding brooms and creating mischief (a strong pejoration; chapter 2). Leading spokeswomen today include Miriam Simos, or Starhawk (1982, 1984), Z (Zsuzsanna) Budapest (1979), and Margot Adler (1979). Witch traditions must be distinguished from Satanism or devil worship—those traditions do exist but are a long way from the modern Craft. Members of Wicca are *not* Satanists. They worship the Goddess, the source of goodness and health, not Satan, the source of evil and destruction.

*The Goddess*    For some members of Wicca, it is important to see the Goddess as the original divine figure (A Closer Look 17.2). Others care only about their experience of the Goddess today. Devotees of the Goddess are not limited to women: Neo-Paganism has always included men.

The Goddess is oriented to the earth, to life, to nature (Starhawk, 1977/1979, 1984). There is no dichotomy between spirit and flesh or between the Divine and the world. The Goddess is a process in nature, in humans, in relations; she is not static and transcendent (e.g., up above) but is immanent (among us). There is only one Goddess (a monotheistic approach), but she has many forms (also a polytheistic approach). She is Mother Earth sustaining all growing things, but she also is a sea shell, a person, a storm.

The great symbol for the Goddess is the moon, which represents the stages in women's lives (Goldenberg, 1979; Starhawk, 1982). The new moon is the Maiden or Virgin (a virgin belongs to herself alone). The full moon is the mature woman, sexual being, mother, giver of life and joy. The waning or dark moon is the old woman, the crone ripe with wisdom, gifts of prophecy, inspiration, and power.

*A Religion of Experience*    The Craft values independence and the deep core of personal strength within that makes each person a unique child of the Goddess. Passion and emotion give depth and color to life. Anger is accepted as a sign that something is wrong and needs to be corrected. The Craft values love most highly: To be a witch is to be a lover of the Goddess and of other human beings. A chief ethical tenet is to harm no one and do as you will (Adler, 1979).

Because the Craft is a religion of experience, the heart of it is ritual rather than beliefs, dogmas, theologies, or scripture (Starhawk, 1984). An essential part of Craft

## A Closer Look

### 17.2    Images of the Divine Female

There is much evidence from the art and artifacts of prehistoric agricultural cultures that the earliest human conception of a divinity was of a Goddess (see Christ, 1983; Eisler, 1987; Ruether, 1983; Starhawk, 1977/1979, 1982, 1984; Stone, 1976). Prehistoric figurines and drawings have been discovered, often with exaggerated breasts, thighs, and buttocks, sometimes pregnant or giving birth. The Goddess is not depicted with symbols of physical power and domination, such as spears or thunderbolts, but with symbols of nature, such as fish, birds, butterflies, bulls, sun, water, and generally emphasizing a unity of all things in nature. Although the societies worshiping the Goddess have been described as matriarchal, there is evidence that they were remarkably equalitarian, with little indication that men were subordinate.

As Judaism and then Christianity spread, many people followed both Goddess traditions and the new religions (Ruether, 1983; Starhawk, 1982, 1984). For example, graves of Israelites show Yahwist and Goddess symbols together. Many early Christian sects thought that God had a female component as well as a male one (Fiorenza, 1979).

It was not until the 16th and 17th centuries that Christians began persecuting "witches"

and Jews. Most victims of witch hunts in Europe and the early American colonies (e.g., Salem) were old widows whose property was coveted, midwives competing with the male medical profession, and freethinkers or simply people who were a problem in the community. With realization that the persecution was becoming unreasonable, belief in witches faded. The tradition of the witches was forgotten except for wild stories of broomstick flights and magic potions. Memory of the Craft faded except within hidden covens. Only in the latter part of the 20th century have witches felt safe enough to begin practicing their religion openly (Starhawk, 1984).

From sources cited in text discussion and from author's unpublished manuscript with representative references, including:

Ruether, R. R. (1981). Women in utopian movements. In R. R. Ruether & R. S. Keller (Eds.). *Women and religion, volume 1. The nineteenth century, a documented history.* Cambridge, MA: Harper & Row.

Walters, R. G. (1978). *American reformers 1815–1860.* New York: Hill and Wang.

Welter, B. (1974). The feminization of American religion: 1800–1860. In *Clio's consciousness raised: New perspectives on the history of women* (pp. 137–157). New York: Harper & Row.

ritual is the raising of power, achieved by chanting, dancing, breathing, and concentrated will (Starhawk, 1977/1979). Rituals are not limited to group activities; they can be done privately as self-affirmations (Z. Budapest, 1977/1979).

## Minorities' Approaches to Spirituality

Minority women have appeal for both reformists and revisionists. We discuss here only Native American and African American views. There are many others that cannot be covered; for example, Nakashima Brock (1989) speaks for the thealogy of Asian American women who seek to reconnect to the sacred in Asian religions. Gloria Anzaldua (1987) writes about how the history of the Goddess was suppressed by patriarchal Aztecs and then by the Spanish Christians.

***Native Americans***    Native Americans' spirituality was not understood by white European colonists who considered the natives to be pagan and godless (Allen, 1986; Parker, 1986; Peterson & Druke, 1983; Sanchez, 1989; Woloch, 1984). The Europeans saw that the natives had no separate place for worship and not even a word for religion. This neglect of religion, so it seemed to the Europeans, was because Native Americans' spirituality was more pervasive than that of the Europeans. Native Americans did not distinguish between the sacred and the profane and considered spirituality applicable to every aspect of life.

Native Americans, like Goddess worshipers, are monotheistic while seeing the Great Being as manifest in all of nature. They include female figures in their creation stories (Parker, 1986). For example, some Native Americans believe that all things come from Thought Woman, the "power of intelligence," also called Earth Mother (Allen, 1986). Earth Mother's power was often linked with the moon; planting and harvesting was shaped around lunar time. Tribal women valued their roles as "vitalizers," with power not only to give birth, but to create and transform.

To tribal people, humans are but one part of the All. All life forms are sacred and to be honored and respected (Ywahoo, 1989). Native Americans prayed for a successful hunt, but they also then thanked the spirit of the bear and asked for forgiveness for the necessity of killing it (Peterson & Druke, 1983). Earth is a living being very much affected by human thought and action in this way of thinking; Euro-Americans waste natural resources because they place humans above the earth (Sanchez, 1989).

***African American Traditions***    African religions have shared much with Native American approaches. The religions Africans brought to America were not a one-day-a-week event, nor were gods only "up there," separated from human life (Genovese, 1974/1976; Levine, 1977). The human being and all things were infused with spirits. A supreme God might preside with the help of many specific gods or spirits. Their religion was one of joy and affirmation of life and human feelings.

Particularly popular with many students are the contemporary writings of Alice Walker and Audre Lorde. In her novel *The Color Purple*, Walker (1982/1989) directly addresses issues about the sex of God and the place of God in the universe: "God is inside you and inside everbody else . . . God is everything . . . God ain't a he or a she, but a It" (p. 103). Sexuality of any kind is a path to God. Of sexual feelings, Walker has the character Shug say, "God love all them feelings. That's some of the best stuff God did" (p. 103). Womanist Walker agrees with feminists that sometimes it is hard to see clearly, "You have to git man off your eyeball, before you can see anything a'tall" (p. 104).

The African American lesbian poet and theorist Audre Lorde (1984) also calls attention to sexuality. She sees the erotic as a spiritual power putting us in touch with the creative energy of the life force. Women have been taught not to trust their feelings; for women to embrace the erotic is to be self-affirming in the face of a racist, patriarchal, and antierotic society. Christian reformists, both women and men, have also emphasized sexuality in theology and generally considered themes from Goddess and ethnic religions (Harrison, 1985; Heyward, 1984; Nelson, 1979). Womanists and feminist reformers are concerned about women's feelings and perspectives, both about sexuality and about another forbidden topic—anger—because conventional religion often has been used to justify widely held prohibitions against women's sexuality and their anger.

## Women's Experiences of Anger

Anger is not a popular topic for general discussion and, like religion, is likely to evoke dispute and disagreement. Because of some mistaken views about anger, most people would rather pretend that anger does not exist, particularly women's anger. Yet it seems appropriate to end a psychology of women textbook with a discussion of anger for at least three reasons. First, there is much to be angry about concerning the demeaning treatment of women that still goes on. Women of color experience anger about racism as well as about sexism (Lorde, 1981/1990). Second, women's anger—and their right to be angry—is not well accepted. When women express anger, they are told that they are angry "only because of PMS," or they are "man-hating feminists," or, at best, they are "just too sensitive." When men express anger on behalf of women, other men may question their sanity or their sexuality. Third, as an emotion, anger has been equated with body and evil in hierarchical thought that has so harmed women.

In this section I will present the view that anger is natural and useful and even necessary for personal growth and societal change. The treatment here is primarily from a theoretical and feminist perspective, particularly that of feminist psychotherapists. More empirical considerations about anger specifically and emotions generally, showing the disapproval of anger that women experience from early ages, were presented in chapters 4 and 9.

Teresa Bernardez (1978), a feminist psychoanalyst, was the first to explore the powerful forces banning women's anger (Lerner, 1985). Other prominent women writing on anger are Jean Baker Miller (1983) and Harriet Lerner (1985). Audre Lorde has provided very potent and insightful comments about anger as well. The topic of women's anger cuts across disciplines, ethnic groups, and classes, and extends into religion. Feminist theologians have written of anger to claim its appropriateness in religious development (e.g., see Harrison, 1985), and people of the Wicca accept anger as an aspect of the Goddess.

## What Is Anger?

People often assume that anger is inevitably accompanied by aggression toward others. This is not so. In fact, when anger is accompanied by aggression, it may be a sign that anger has not been accepted and understood. Because anger is seen as inherently dangerous, we become afraid of our anger and often do not use it constructively.

Anger is a natural reflex to psychological pain. When you inadvertently touch a hot object, you have a natural reflex that prompts you to pull back. The physical pain tells you that something is not right about your relationship with the physical world at that time. Anger is a psychological reflex that tells you that something is not right about your relationships with the psychological world (Focus on Research 17.2). Both pain and anger signal a disturbance in the flow of your relations with the world. "Anger . . . exists for a reason and always deserves our respect and attention" (Lerner, 1985, p. 4). Anger is neither destructive nor constructive; it is an energy that can be expressed in prosocial or antisocial ways. No one blames us for pulling away from a hot object and perhaps uttering a few vocalizations in the process. However, there are cultural prohibitions about the expression of anger. Both women and men have constraints that prevent them from expressing anger and even from knowing when they are experiencing it. The natural response of anger becomes distorted into unnatural expressions.

## Inhibitions on Expressions of Anger

*A Sociological View*    Jean Baker Miller (1983) analyzes anger sociologically in terms of subordinate and dominant groups. Once a group is dominant, it tends to abuse the subordinate group, it restricts the subordinate group's range of actions, and it does not encourage subordinates to full and free expression of their experiences. It also uses stereotypes to characterize subordinates and describes the subordination as normal and natural, and ordained by God or by biology or by both. If the subordinates— "those others"—are angry, something is wrong with them: They are uppity, uncivilized, dumb, or just plain deranged and needing the protection of the dominant group. Direct force is available to keep the subordinates in line in the form of threats of physical violence and of social and economic deprivation.

Subordinates tend to respond to the dominant group's power with supporting and self-protective beliefs. The most basic feeling may be, "I have no right and no cause to be angry." Any hint of anger is met with feelings of weakness and unworthiness. In the face of the dominant group's power, the subordinates' denial of anger promotes survival because anger expressed would bring the anger of the dominant group (Lorde, 1981/1990). A result is that "women have behaved . . . as a caste identifying with their oppressors, internalizing their oppressors' views of them" (Heilbrun, 1979, p. 97).

A woman's anger on her own behalf is seen as a threat to women's femininity, and the support for the ideal of women's behavior is so strong that many women have a hard time realizing that they are angry (Lerner, 1985). If they realize that they are angry, women (and other subordinates) often take their anger as a private, personal experience when the truth is that they share a collective experience (Bernardez, 1988; Lerner, 1985). Domination is maintained by appeal to the stereotypes that women's feelings of anger or bitterness are a sign of their own inferiority, sickness, lack of virtue, or lack of femininity, not the result of their unequal status (Bernardez, 1988; Miller, 1983).

*Like pain, anger is a signal that something is wrong. These women are using their anger at injustice and oppression to work for social change.*

***A Psychodynamic View***    Bernardez (1978, 1988) adds to Miller's views a psycho-dynamic perspective. She theorizes that both girls and boys have an irrational belief in mother's omnipotence: If mother can give life and supply the milk and cookies, she can also end life and cut off the milk and cookies. Thus, both daughters and sons come to fear women's potential destructiveness. The result is that all women are seen as power-ful and in need of restraint. The son grows with a belief in his vulnerability to women. The daughter grows with a belief in her own potential destructiveness. Both attempt to reduce their fears (probably unconsciously) about anger with comforting stereo-typed beliefs that women are only kind, considerate, and loving. This is socially con-structed to mean that women will not be angry except to defend helpless others and will be submissive to men—both men and women can feel protected against women's destructiveness. It is not acceptable for women to be angry about how they themselves are treated or how other women are treated. That is the same as saying that women are not supposed to care about themselves and other women.

## Women's and Men's Anger

Because anger is not feminine, a woman who is angry about how she or other women are treated is seen as sexless and castrating, unloving and unlovable. Language con-demns angry women as shrews, witches, bitches, or hags. Our language does not have an unflattering term to describe men who vent their anger at women (Lerner, 1985). Even *bastard* and *son of a bitch* blame his mother rather than the angry man. Women do not express their anger for fear that it will disrupt relationships and they will not be seen as "nice ladies" (Bernardez, 1988; Lerner, 1985; Miller, 1983). "Since men do

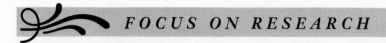

### 17.2    Statistical Tests of Significance: Women Incest Survivors Direct Their Anger

Linda looked over at her therapist. "Yes, I guess I do tend to pick fights with friends and family. I seem to be pretty angry these days." Linda, who as a child had been sexually abused by an uncle, started therapy 4 months ago, but this was the first time the topic of anger had come up. Linda recalled her last conversation with her mother; they had ended up yelling at each other over what seemed to be trivial things. Come to think of it, she'd been pretty angry at her father lately too. "Well," she thought, "I started therapy to work on my self-esteem, but now I wonder where all this anger is coming from." Both Linda and her therapist agree that this should be the focus of next week's session.

Women are often trained to suppress their anger; it is seen as an unfeminine emotion. Anger also disrupts social contact, and for women socialized to value inter-personal relationships, anger is an emotion they cannot afford to voice. What happens, then, to women incest survivors who as adults must deal with their feelings about this violation over which they had no control? Appropriate anger can be a healthy response for these women.

Researchers Amy Newman and Christopher Peterson (1996) wanted to know if anger was a common response of women incest survivors and if so, just who the targets of this anger were. They placed ads in a newsletter and sent out flyers in the community to recruit women who had been sexually abused by a family member as well as women with no history of incest. The research design was a simple questionnaire format. Each woman completed items concerning anger toward mother, father, and the perpetrator of the incest if she or he were other than a parent; the participant's support for feminism; and involvement in psychotherapy.

Newman and Peterson analyzed the women's responses from two different angles. First, working with data from the incest survivor group, they compared anger at mother, anger at father, and anger at the nonparent abuser. Contrary to what we might expect, the three anger ratings differed by less than one unit, regardless of who the abuser had been. In their second analysis, Newman and Peterson looked for relationships between variables. They found small to moderate positive correlations between respondent's anger toward mother and father and respondent's level of feminism, and between anger toward mother and father and involvement in psychotherapy. Now, let's take a look at how Newman and Peterson interpreted the numbers their analyses produced.

With quantitative data, researchers use statistical tests of significance to sort out the importance of a finding. Some common tests are *t*-tests, *F*-tests, and chi-square. Each test is based on probability theory and tells us the likelihood of our results happening simply by chance alone, that is, that our outcomes are a quirk and not dependable. By agreement, researchers set these probabilities at .05 and .01, indicating that only findings that happen by chance as few as 5 times out of 100 or, more strictly, 1 time out of 100, are substantial enough to be called "statistically significant."

Newman and Peterson had two sets of findings to test. First they wanted to know if the three sets of anger ratings for mother, father, and nonparental abuser were different enough to be considered significantly different. The test of the anger ratings indicated they were not significantly different from each other; that is, the differences among the ratings were so small as to have happened by chance more than 5 times out of 100. This in itself is an interesting finding, for it tells us that women incest survivors are about equally angry at both of their parents and the perpetrator, regardless of who inflicted the abuse. Newman and Peterson also conducted significance tests on the correlations between respondents' degree of feminism and their anger toward each parent and between their experience of psychotherapy and their anger toward their parents. Each of these correlations revealed a significant positive relationship between the tested variables. While none of these relationships was exceptionally strong (agreement with feminist ideas correlated with anger at mother, $r = .38$, and with anger at father, $r = .30$, while the experience of psychotherapy correlated with anger at mother, $r = .42$, and with anger at father, $r = .38$), the significant findings indicated these relationships were not likely to have occurred by chance. The researchers had measured relationships that were dependable and consistent.

One last consideration surrounding tests of significance needs to be mentioned. We must distinguish between statistical significance and practical significance. Determining that the probability of a certain outcome is not likely to be due to chance gives us the assurance that we have found something real and consistent. We can depend on this finding occurring again and again, and we can incorporate it into our theories of human behavior. However, this consistent occurrence may involve a behavior that is so unimportant that we say, "So what?" or "Who cares?" For example, the search for gender differences has uncovered many areas of behavior on which women and men differ. What is often pushed to the side in our rush to document differences is that a statistically significant difference does not mean that the difference has value in our daily lives. If we find that, reliably, consistently, and not due to chance, women are more accurate in touching the tip of their tongue to their nose, will this change life as we know it?

Let's take a final look at Newman and Peterson's study of incest survivors and their results. They found no significant differences in survivors' anger at mother, father, or perpetrator. This runs counter to our expectations and shows that, sometimes, a nonsignificant finding can be more interesting than a significant one. These incest survivors appear to hold both parents responsible for not providing protection; anger

*(continued)*

### 17.2    Statistical Tests of Significance: Women Incest Survivors Direct Their Anger    *(continued)*

is not just directed at the mother, who is stereotypically the one responsible for protecting children. Newman and Peterson did find significant correlations between anger at parents and level of feminism and between anger at parents and involvement in therapy. The researchers offer two interpretations of these findings. On the one hand, women who have experienced incest may find that feminist ideas of women's equality and worth and the therapeutic setting give permission to the expression of anger against parents for that childhood violation. Alternatively, the existing anger may make feminism and therapy more attractive coping options when dealing with the aftermath of incest.

JILL BORCHERT  ◆

SOURCE: Newman, A. L., & Peterson, C. (1996). Anger of women incest survivors. *Sex Roles, 34,* 463–474.

not take women's rights seriously, most women also refuse to do so" (Heilbrun, 1979, p. 97). Women's anger with men is turned to anger with the self because a more direct expression would threaten the bond of dependency on men (A Closer Look 17.3).

What are the results of women's lack of expression of anger? Among the specifics that Bernardez (1978) mentions are inhibition in creative work, self-defeating behaviors, pathological submission, self-deprecation. For some, the result is "silencing of the self" (chapter 16), depression, or other psychiatric symptoms. For others, it is often what people fear—an explosion that confirms the view of women as irrational and dangerous (Bernardez, 1978; Lerner, 1985; Miller, 1983). This easily leads to additional inhibition of anger and then to a bigger explosion in a spiraling escalation (Figure 17.1). Although there is something to be angry about, when anger is vented ineffectively, other people do not understand the reasons for the anger and therefore disapprove of it (Lerner, 1985). Some women come to avoid the expression of anger except around the time of menstruation. When anger is expressed only then, women's complaints are especially prone to dismissal (chapter 6).

Men, too, have problems with anger, and those can become women's problems as women become targets of the anger men do not understand. Although men are the dominant group with respect to women, they often are in subordinate positions with respect to other men (Miller, 1983). The pattern starts with the father. Fathers do not tolerate sons' anger with them while often provoking it in sons as young as 1½ years of age (Block, 1978; Gleason, 1975). Fathers frequently spar with their sons and call them "little dumbo" or "peanuthead" but stop playing when the boys become angry and dare to express anger. The boy feels hurt, humiliated, vulnerable, impotent, abandoned, and alone. The result is what Miller calls **deflected anger**—men are deflected from their experiences.

*A Closer Look*

## 17.3 Displeasing Men, Name Calling, and Anger

After the boy at the supermarket had called her those names, Evelyn Couch had felt violated. Raped by words. Stripped of everything. She had always tried to keep this from happening to her, always been terrified of displeasing men, terrified of the names she would be called if she did . . .

. . .

What was this power, this insidious threat, this invisible gun to her head that controlled her life . . . *this terror of being called names?*

She had stayed a virgin so she wouldn't be called a tramp or a slut; had married so she wouldn't be called an old maid; faked orgasms so she wouldn't be called frigid; had children so she wouldn't be called barren; had not been a feminist because she didn't want to be called queer and a man hater; never nagged or raised her voice so she wouldn't be called a bitch . . .

She had done all that and yet, still, this stranger had dragged her into the gutter with the names that men call women when they are angry.

. . .

Then she made herself stop thinking because, all of a sudden, she was experiencing a feeling that she had never felt before, and it scared her. And so, twenty years later than most women, *Evelyn Couch was angry.*

SOURCE: From Flagg, F. (1987). *Fried green tomatoes at the Whistle Stop Cafe.* New York: McGraw-Hill. Selected from pp. 236–237.

The boy is encouraged to be masculine and to *act* aggressively but not to express his *feelings.* He learns to channel his aggression, first into boyhood games and then into the games of business, politics, power, the military. But the boy, and then the man, is hurt when he loses. And the man may fear that his wife will abandon him as his father did. Women can become a scapegoat, a displaced target, for men's anger.

I submit, therefore, that our problems with anger are due to insufficient real experience of anger and insufficient allowance for its direct expression at the time and in the ways in which it could be appropriate—when it need not have the connotations of harm, abuse, or violence. For men, the deflection of anger along with the simultaneous repeated restimulation of aggressive action is the problem. For women, the problem is a situation of subordination, which continually produces anger, along with the culture's intolerance of women's direct expression of anger in any form. (Miller, 1983, p. 7)

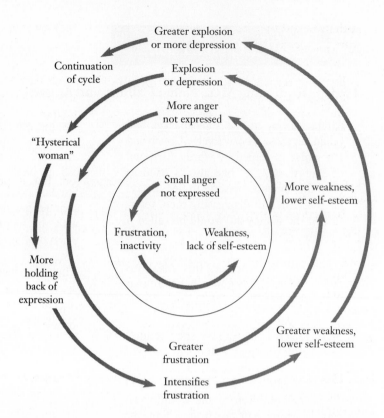

**Figure 17.1** *The cycle of anger.*    SOURCE: Suggested by the words of Miller, J. B. (1983). The construction of anger in women and men. Stone Center Work in Progress No. 83-01.

## The Value and Necessity of Anger

Ultimately, we need to accept anger as a useful emotion so that it can be expressed directly, cleanly, and effectively (Miller, 1983). That will take time. In the meantime, Lorde (1981/1990, p. 174) reminds us, "If I speak to you in anger, at least I have spoken to you." Speaking cleanly and clearly is a start to getting to know each other.

***Anger, Self-Esteem, and Care***    If women are to express anger, they need to realize their sources of strength so they can risk threatening a relationship (Bernardez, 1978, 1988). Some women cannot or will not protest discrimination, or they deny that discrimination exists and then criticize those who do complain: Women who do express anger become scapegoats (Lerner, 1985). "Until women adopt a model for action that sustains the primacy of their own claims, they will not achieve full equality" (Heilbrun, 1979, p. 97). *Anger is the voice of self-respect* (Bernardez, 1978). How can women transform the world if they have no self-respect? How can they care for others if they do not care for themselves?

> For a healthy expression of anger the individual woman needs to grow away from stereotypes of femininity, and to move toward sufficient self-esteem and loving self-regard, the social and emotional support of others, and freedom from fear and social disapproval. This is not an instantaneous conquest. (Bernardez, 1988, p. 9)

Anger is like fertilizer—it may not smell very good, but it promotes growth (Kelschner, 1987).

In the face of some situations, not being angry is not being aware of the world or not being engaged with it. In a potent paper, "The Power of Anger in the Work of Love," feminist theologian Beverly Wildung Harrison (1989) wrote that "anger is a *mode of connectedness to others* and it is always a *vivid form of caring* [italics added]" (p. 220). Anger gives energy to act to correct a wrong one cares about. For Harrison all serious human moral activity, especially action for social change, springs from the power of anger. Lorde (1981/1990) adds that anger is insight: "When we turn from anger we turn from insight, saying we will accept only the designs already known, deadly and safely familiar" (p. 174).

***Hope Has Two Sisters***     At a conference on Third World issues, a minister (Kelschner, 1987) noticed that something was wrong: People were saying the right things, but something was missing. He realized that there was no anger. This reminded him of St. Augustine, who said that *hope has two sisters—anger and courage*. Without anger, there is no impetus or insight to work for change. Without courage, there is no willingness for the work. With both, there is hope.

There is hope for social change if people will use the energy of anger. If you feel angry, what should you do about it? First, try to understand the *specific* reasons for your anger. Otherwise, you may address one kind of issue when you are really angry about another. Second, consider your *priorities*—what problems do you see as most deserving of attention? Third, select those problems most commensurate with *your own resources*—your personality, talents, interests, energies, and capabilities. Finally, *do not sap energy* from what you are doing by feeling guilty about what you are not doing. Know yourself, choose, act upon your decisions.

In short, the answers to "What can I do?" are as varied as people are. We all have different lives, different concerns, different strengths. For one person, simply not laughing at a sexist joke or challenging a sexist comment can be a big step. Another may choose to lead a protest march or organize a sit-in at a topless bar. Some have particular talents in social interaction, and others are adept in the political arena. Feminists of the past provide both models of the diversity of ways of working for change and inspiration for courage (chapter 1). They talked to people, they wrote to public officials and visited governing bodies, they expressed their concerns in publications. They preached and formed organizations. They marched outside brothels and in the streets of the nation's capitol. They met together at Seneca Falls, in each other's homes, and in churches and synagogues. They shared their anger and caring, and they shared their talents and determination. The people of today who are caring enough to be angry are doing the same.

## Some Final Thoughts: The Hope of Anger and Courage

Progress has been made in working toward equality, but many old rules and expectations are with us still, with resulting confusion. The current gender system is oppressive to both women and men, prohibiting each from expressing their full potential for human work and caring.

Anger is the voice of self-respect. Anger can liberate when linked with the courage to feel anger and the courage to act. Women in the last century had to be courageous to stand outside of brothels and record the names of men visiting them. They had to be courageous to protest slavery, treatment of women and the poor, the lack of the vote for women. With their anger and courage, they worked with hope, and they made a difference, though not as big a difference as they wanted. Many people today work with courage and anger, and that brings hope.

Women today are using many of the same modes of expression as their foremothers. Some are working for change within existing organizations, and some are establishing their own groups. Women are bonding in the cause of a feminist transformation of religion; women are encouraging each other to the autonomy that allows and is facilitated by the expression of anger.

Although individual women and the men who support and champion them may not be able to make a big difference, the combined efforts of many people over time will create change. In the words of lyricist Holly Near as sung by Meg Christian,

> Can we be like drops of water falling on the stone
> Splashing, breaking, dispersing in air
> Weaker than the stone by far
> But be aware that as time goes by
> The rock will wear away
> And the water comes again.

### KEY TERMS

| | | |
|---|---|---|
| modern sexism, neosexism | reformists revisionists | Wicca; the Craft deflected anger |

### KEY POINTS

*Challenges: Where We Are Today*

♦ In spite of improvements, many old standards of women's behavior are with us still, with overt sexism being replaced by new forms of sexism and expectations remaining confused (e.g., about housework, sexuality). Views of male as norm and woman as victim continue, with many women internalizing their victimization by blaming themselves. Women's bodies often are associated with objectification and victimization.

◆ Gender-typing is perpetuated through interpersonal processes, social structure, and language. Part of the structure is race, and white women still are seen as universal woman.

◆ Women do not want to be like men; men also have been oppressed by current gendered society.

◆ Research needs to illuminate why the genders do or do not differ and the implications of the differences and similarities, and to clarify reasons for within-gender differences. Researchers need freedom to study women as they are.

## Women's Experiences of Religion and Spirituality

◆ Women are more religious than men by a variety of measures. Women have used freedoms given them by religion in pursuit of their causes as well as personal and feminist development.

◆ Religion has been used to legitimize gender distinctions, but changes in gender role ideology have led to some changes in religion.

◆ Most clergy are men. Clergywomen have the same problems other professional women do and, along with laywomen, still face division of labor in religious organizations.

◆ Reformists work within their traditions, doing work such as examining texts, questioning exclusively masculine images of the Divine, and developing stories and rituals.

◆ People of the Wicca or the Craft worship a Goddess who is immanent in all nature; the moon is a chief symbol. They emphasize the experience of rituals rather than creeds.

◆ Native American and African religions do not distinguish between the sacred and profane. The Divine is monotheistic while being a part of all nature.

◆ Contemporary African American women question the sex of God and see God everywhere. They as well as white theologians are concerned with sexuality and anger (for example, Alice Walker and Audre Lorde).

## Women's Experiences of Anger

◆ Anger is a signal that something is wrong. Anger is less likely to be expressed aggressively when it is accepted and understood.

◆ Jean Baker Miller analyzes inhibitions on the expression of anger in terms of dominance-submission. Teresa Bernardez focuses also on the child's perception of the mother's omnipotence.

◆ Anger in women is expected only in defense of the young and infirm and not on behalf of women themselves. Lack of expression of anger can be damaging to women and lead to ineffective expressions. Men learn to deflect their anger.

◆ Anger has been called the voice of self-respect and seen as necessary for liberation and for showing care. Anger and courage have been called the sisters of hope.

## INTEGRATIVE QUESTIONS

1. Critique the research in psychology of women as presented in this text or in other forms with which you are familiar. What is right about it? What is faulty about it? You may wish to write a letter to journal editors telling them your views on the kind of research you would like to see or to a particular researcher (or group of researchers) about their research.

2. Design one study or series of studies you would like to see done in psychology of women. Make clear why your proposal is important to understanding women and how it compares with other research in the area.

3. Should psychologists be concerned about religion? Should psychologists of women be concerned? Why or why not? What cautions and challenges do you advise?

4. To what extent, and in what ways, is the question "Is God a man or a woman?" a *psychological* issue?

5. Think about what you learned about anger as you were growing up and how you feel and think about it now. Compare that to the analysis given in the text. What are your conclusions?

6. If you are angry about the status of women, what will you do with the anger? What constructive action can you take to remedy the problems you see? Is your anger relevant to your personal growth?

# REFERENCES

AAUW Educational Foundation. (1992). *How schools shortchange girls.* Washington, DC: Author.

Abbey, A. (1982). Sex differences in attributions for friendly behavior: Do males misperceive females' friendliness? *Journal of Personality and Social Psychology, 42,* 830–838.

Abbey, A. (1991). Misperception as an antecedent of acquaintance rape: A consequence of ambiguity in communication between women and men. In A. Parrot & L. Bechholfer (Eds.), *Acquaintance rape: The hidden crime* (pp. 96–112). New York: John Wiley & Sons.

Abbey, A., Andrews, F. M., & Halman, L. J. (1991). Gender's role in responses to infertility. *Psychology of Women Quarterly, 15,* 295–316.

Abbey, A., & Harnish, R. J. (1995). Perception of sexual intent: The role of gender, alcohol consumption, and rape supportive attitudes. *Sex Roles, 32,* 297–313.

Abbey, A., Ross, L. T., McDuffie, D., & McAuslan, P. (1996). Alcohol and dating risk: Factors for sexual assault among college women. *Psychology of Women Quarterly, 20,* 147–169.

Abel, G. C., & Rouleau, J. L. (1995). Sexual abuses. *The Psychiatric Clinics of North America, 18,* 139–153.

Abel, H., & Sahinkaya, R. (1962). Emergence of sex and race friendship preferences. *Child Development, 33,* 934–943.

Abel, T., & Joffe, N. (1950). Cultural backgrounds of female puberty. *American Journal of Psychotherapy, 93,* 90–113.

Aboud, F. (1988). *Children and prejudice.* New York: Basil Blackwell.

Abplanalp, J. M. (1983). Premenstrual syndrome: A selective review. In S. Golub (Ed.), *Lifting the curse of menstruation.* New York: Haworth.

Abrahams, B., Feldman, S. S., & Nash, S. C. (1978). Sex role self-concept and sex role attitudes: Enduring personality characteristics or adaptations to changing life situations? *Developmental Psychology, 34,* 393–400.

Academe. (1990, March-April). Some dynamic aspects of academic careers: The urgent need to match aspirations with compensation, pp. 3–20.

Acker, J. (1989). *Doing comparable work: Gender, class and pay equity.* Philadelphia: Temple University Press.

Adams, D. (1986). Instruction and course content in sex knowledge and attitudes and internal locus of control. *Psychological Reports, 58,* 91–94.

Adams, K. A. (1980). Who has the final word? Sex, race, and dominance behavior. *Journal of Personality and Social Psychology, 38,* 1–8.

Adams, K. A. (1983). Aspects of social context as determinants of black women's resistance to challenges. *Journal of Social Issues, 39,* 69–78.

Adams, R. B. (1978). *King C. Gillette.* Boston: Little, Brown.

Adelmann, P. K. (1994). Multiple roles and psychological well-being in a national sample of older adults. *Journal of Gerontology, 4,* 5277–5285.

Adelmann, P. K., Antonucci, T. C., Crohan, S. E., & Coleman, L. M. (1989). Empty nest, cohort, and employment in the well-being of midlife women. *Sex Roles, 20,* 173–189.

Adler, M. (1979). *Drawing down the moon: Witches, Druids, Goddess-worshippers, and other pagans in America today.* Boston: Beacon Press.

Adler, N. E. (1992). Unwanted pregnancy and abortion: Definitional and research issues. *Journal of Social Issues, 48,* 19–35.

Adler, N. E., David, H. P., Major, B. N., Roth, S. H., Russo, N. F., & Wyatt, G. E. (1992). Psychological factors in abortion. *American Psychologist, 47,* 1194–1204.

Adler T. (1990a, January). Causes, cure of PMS still elude researchers. *APA Monitor,* p. 10.

Adler, T. (1990b, January). Roots of PMS seen as biological. *APA Monitor,* p. 11.

Aeschliman, S., & Mauss, A. L. (1996, March). The impact of feminism and religious involvement on sentiment toward God. *Review of Religious Research, 37,* 248–259.

Aguire, B. E. (1985). Why do they return? Abused wives in shelters. *Social Work, 30,* 350–354.

Aguwa, B. (1994, May 4). African American women distrust health system. *Lansing State Journal,* p. 8B.

Aida, Y., & Falbo, T. (1991). Relationships between marital satisfaction, resources, and power strategies. *Sex Roles, 24,* 43–56.

Aires, E. J. (1976). Interaction patterns and themes of male, female, and mixed groups. *Small Group Behavior, 7,* 7–18.

Aires, E. J. (1982). Verbal and nonverbal behavior in single-sex and mixed-sex groups. Are traditional sex roles changing? *Psychological Reports, 51,* 127–134.

Alagna, S. W., & Hamilton, J. A. (1986). Social stimulus perception and self-evaluation: Effects of menstrual cycle phase. *Psychology of Women Quarterly, 10,* 327–337.

Albrecht, L., Bahr, H. M., & Goodman, K. L. (1983). *Divorce and remarriage.* Westport, CT: Greenwood.

Alexander, G. M., & Hines, M. (1994). Gender labels and play styles: Their relative contribution to children's selection of playmates. *Child Development, 65,* 869–879.

Ali, A., & Toner, B. B. (1996). Gender differences in depressive response: The role of social support. *Sex Roles, 35,* 281–293.

Alksnis, C., Desmarais, S., & Wood, E. (1996). Gender differences in scripts for different types of dates. *Sex Roles, 34,* 321–336.

Allan K., & Coltrane, S. (1996). Gender displaying television commercials: A comparative study of television commercials in the 1950s and 1980s. *Sex Roles, 35,* 185–203.

Allen, B. P. (1995). Gender stereotypes are not accurate: A replication of Martin (1987) using diagnosis vs. self-report and behavioral criteria. *Sex Roles, 32,* 583–600.

Allen, I. L. (1984). Male sex roles and epithets for ethnic women in American slang. *Sex Roles, 11,* 43–50.

Allen, K. R. (1989). *Single women/family ties: Life histories of older women.* Newbury Park, CA: Sage.

Allen, K. R., & Baber, K. M. (1992). Ethical and epistemological tensions in applying a postmodern perspective to feminist research. *Psychology of Women Quarterly, 16,* 1–15.

Allen, L. S., Richey, M. F., Chai, Y. M., & Gorski, R. A. (1991). Sex differences in the corpus callosum of the living human being. *Journal of Neuroscience, 11,* 933–942.

Allen, P. G. (1986). *The sacred hoop.* Boston: Beacon Press.

Allen, P. G. (1989a). The sacred hoop. In J. Plaskow & C. Christ

(Eds.), *Weaving the visions: New patterns in feminist spirituality*. San Francisco: Harper & Row.

Allen, P. G. (1989b). The spirit and the flesh: Sexual diversity in American Indian culture. *The American Indian Quarterly, 13,* 109–111.

Allgood-Merten, B., & Stockard, J. (1991). Sex role identity and self-esteem: A comparison of children and adolescents. *Sex Roles, 25,* 129–139.

Allport, G. (1950). *The individual and his religion*. New York: Macmillan.

Allport, G. W. (1958). *The nature of prejudice*. New York: Doubleday Anchor.

Almquist, E. M. (1974). Attitudes of college men toward working wives. *Vocational Guidance Quarterly, 23,* 115–121.

Almquist, E. M. (1989). The experiences of minority women in the United States: Intersections of race, gender, and class. In J. Freeman (Ed.), *Women: A feminist perspective* (4th ed.). Mountain View, CA: Mayfield.

Alpert-Gillis, L. J., & Connell, J. P. (1989). Gender and sex-role influences on children's self-esteem. *Journal of Personality, 57,* 97–114.

Alvidrez, J., & Weinstein, R. S. (1993). The nature of "schooling" in school transitions: A critical re-examination. *Prevention in Human Services, 10,* 7–26.

Amaro, H. (1995, June). Love, sex, and power: Considering women's realities in HIV prevention. *American Psychologist, 50,* 437–447.

Amaro, H., & Russo, N. F. (Eds.). (1987). Hispanic women and mental health (Special issue). *Psychology of Women Quarterly, 11,* 393–407.

Amatea, E. S., & Fong, M. L. (1991). The impact of role stressors and personal resources on the stress experience of professional women. *Psychology of Women Quarterly, 15,* 419–430.

Amath, J. (1978, December). Hysterectomy and depression. *Obstetrics and Gynecology, 52,* 729.

Amato, P. R., & Keith, B. (1991). Consequences of parental divorce for the well-being of children: A meta-analysis. *Psychological Bulletin, 110,* 26–46.

Amenson, C. S., & Lewinsohn, P. M. (1981). An investigation into the observed sex differences in prevalence of unipolar depression. *Journal of Abnormal Psychology, 90,* 1–13.

American Cancer Society. (1996). *Cancer facts and figures—1996*. Atlanta, GA: Author.

American Psychiatric Association. (1994). *Diagnostic and statistical manual of mental disorders* (4th ed.). Washington, DC: Author.

American Psychological Association Committee on Lesbian and Gay Concerns. (1991). Avoiding heterosexual bias in language. *American Psychologist, 46,* 973–974.

American Psychological Association Publication Manual Task Force. (1975). Report of the task force on sex bias and sex-role stereotyping in psychotherapeutic practice. *American Psychologist, 30,* 1169–1175.

Amick, A. E., & Calhoun, K. S. (1987). Resistance to sexual aggression: Personality, attitudinal and situational factors. *Archives of Sexual Behavior, 16,* 153–163.

Andersen, M. L. (1993). *Thinking about women: Sociological perspectives on sex and gender* (3rd ed.). New York: Macmillan.

Anderson, C. M., & Stewart, S. (1994). The evolution of the sexes. *Science, 257,* 324–326.

Anderson, K., Higgins, C., Newman, E. S., & Sherman, S. R.

(1978). Differences in attitudes toward retirement among male and female faculty and other university professionals. *Journal of Minority Aging, 3,* 51–113.

Anderson, T. B. (1984). Widowhood as a life transition: Its impact on kinship ties. *Journal of Marriage and the Family, 46,* 105–114.

Andre, T., & Bormann, L. (1991). Knowledge of acquired immune deficiency syndrome and sexual responsibility among high school students. *Youth and Society, 22,* 339–361.

Andrisani, P. J. (1978). Job satisfaction among working women. *Signs, 3,* 588–607.

Aneshensel, C. S. (1992). Social stress: Theory and research. *Annual Review of Sociology, 18,* 15–23.

Aneshensel, C. S., Rutter, C. M., & Lachenbruch, P. A. (1991). Social structures, stress, and mental health: Competing conceptual and analytic models. *American Sociological Review, 56,* 166–178.

Angold, A., & Worthman, C. W. (1993). Puberty onset of gender differences in rates of depression: A developmental, epidemiologic and neuroendocrine perspective. *Journal of Affective Disorders, 28,* 145–158.

Angrist, S. S., & Almquist, E. M. (1975). *Careers and contingencies: How college women juggle with gender*. New York: Dunellen.

Annon, J. (1976). *Behavioral treatment of sexual problems: Brief therapy*. New York: Harper & Row.

Antill, J. K. (1983). Sex role complementarity versus similarity in married couples. *Journal of Personality and Social Psychology, 45,* 145–155.

Antill, J. K., & Cotton, S. (1988). Factors affecting the division of labor in households. *Sex Roles, 18,* 531–553.

Antill, J. K., & Cunningham, J. D. (1979). Self-esteem as a function of masculinity in both sexes. *Journal of Consulting and Clinical Psychology, 47,* 783–785.

Antill, J. K., & Cunningham, J. D. (1980). The relationship of masculinity, femininity, and androgyny to self-esteem. *Australian Journal of Psychology, 32,* 195–207.

Antill, J. K., & Cunningham, J. D. (1982). Sex differences in performance on ability tests as a function of masculinity, femininity, and androgyny. *Journal of Personality and Social Psychology, 42,* 718–728.

Antill, J. K., Goodnow, J. J., Russell, G., & Cotton, S. (1996). The influence of parents and family context on children's involvement in household tasks. *Sex Roles, 34,* 215–236.

Antonucci, T. C., & Akiyama, H. (1987). An examination of sex differences in social support among older men and women. *Sex Roles, 17,* 737–749.

Antonucci, T. C., & Akiyama, H. (1991). Convoys of social support: Generational issues. *Marriage and Family Review, 16,* 103–123.

Anzaldua, G. (1987). *Borderlands/La Frontera: The New Mestiza*. San Francisco: Spinsters/Aunt Lute Book Company.

Aral, S., & Holmes, K. (1991). Sexually transmitted diseases in the AIDS era. *Scientific American, 264,* 62–69.

Archer, D., Iritani, B., Kimes, D. D., & Barrios, M. (1983). Faceism: Five studies of sex differences in facial prominence. *Journal of Personality and Social Psychology, 45,* 725–735.

Archer, J. (1984). Gender roles as developmental pathways. *British Journal of Social Psychology, 23,* 245–256.

Archer, J. (1994). Childhood gender roles: Social context and organization. In H. McGurk (Ed.), *Childhood social development*. London: Lawrence Erlbaum.

Archer, J., & Smith, J. (1990, April). *The association between gender scale measures and gender clustering in recall.* Paper presented at the British Psychological Society Convention, Swansea, Wales.

Arditti, J. A., Godwin, D. D., & Scanzoni, J. (1991). Perceptions of parenting behavior and young women's gender role traits and preferences. *Sex Roles, 25,* 195–211.

Arendell, T. J. (1987). Women and the economics of divorce in the contemporary United States. *Signs, 13,* 121–135.

Argyle, M., & Beit-Hallahmi, B. (1975). *The social psychology of religion.* London: Routledge & Kegan Paul.

Aristotle. (1953). *The generation of animals* (Volume 1). (A. L. Peck, Trans.). Cambridge, MA: Harvard University Press.

Arndt, W. B., Jr. (1991). *Genetic disorders and the paraphilias.* Madison, CT: International University Press.

Arrindell, W. A., Vergaram, A. I., Torres, B., Caballo, V. E., Sanderman, R., Calvo, M. G., van der Ende, J., Oosterof, L., Castro, J., Palanzuela, D. L., Zaldívar, F., & Simón, M. A. (1997). Gender roles in relation to assertiveness and Eysenckian personality dimensions: Replication with a Spanish population sample. *Sex Roles, 36,* 79–92.

Asch, A., & Fine, M. (1988). Introduction: Beyond pedestals. In M. Fine & A. Asch (Eds.), *Women with disabilities.* Philadelphia: Temple University Press.

Ashmore, R. D. (1990). Sex, gender, and the individual. In L. A. Pervin, *Handbook of personality: Theory and research.* New York: Guilford Press.

Ashmore, R. D., & Del Boca, F. K. (1979). Sex stereotypes and implicit personality theory: Toward a cognitive-social psychological conceptualization. *Sex Roles, 5,* 219–248.

Ashmore, R. D., & Del Boca, F. K. (1981). Conceptual approaches to stereotypes and stereotyping. In D. L. Hamilton (Ed.), *Cognitive processes in stereotyping and intergroup behavior.* Hillsdale, NJ: Erlbaum.

Ashmore, R. D., Del Boca, F. K., & Bilder, S. M. (1995). Construction and validation of the Gender Attitudes Inventory, a structured inventory to assess multiple dimensions of gender attitudes. *Sex Roles, 32,* 687–693.

Astin, H. S. (1978). Factors affecting women's scholarly productivity. In H. S. Astin & W. S. Hirsch (Eds.), *The higher education of women.* New York: Praeger.

Atchley, R. C. (1975). Adjustments to loss of job at retirement. *Aging and Human Development, 6,* 17–27.

Atchley, R. C. (1976). *The sociology of retirement.* Cambridge, MA: Schenkman.

Atchley, R. C. (1988). *Social forces and aging* (5th ed.). Belmont, CA: Wadsworth.

Athanasiou, R., Shaver, P., & Tavris, C. (1970, July). Sex. *Psychology Today,* pp. 39–52.

Atkin, D. J., Moorman, J., & Lin, C. A. (1991). Ready for prime time: Network series devoted to analysis of theories of coping with stress. *Psychology of Women Quarterly, 17,* 303–318.

Atkinson, J. W. (1957). Motivational determinants of risk-taking behavior. *Psychological Review, 64,* 359–372.

Atkinson, J. W. (Ed.). (1958). *Motives in fantasy, action, and society.* Princeton, NJ: Van Nostrand.

Atkinson, J. W. (1964). *An Introduction to motivation.* Princeton, NJ: Van Nostrand.

Atkinson, J. W. (1981). Studying personality in the context of an advanced motivational psychology. *American Psychologist, 36,* 117–128.

Attie, I., & Brooks-Gunn, J. (1989). The development of eating problems in adolescent girls: A longitudinal study. *Developmental Psychology, 25,* 70–79.

Atwood, J., & Gagnon, J. (1987). Masturbatory behavior in college youth. *Journal of Sex Education and Therapy, 13,* 35–41.

Aubé, J., & Koestner, R. (1992). Gender characteristics and adjustment: A longitudinal study. *Journal of Personality and Social Psychology, 63,* 485–493.

Averill, J. R. (1982). *Anger and aggression: An essay on emotion.* New York: Springer-Verlag.

Avioli, L. V. (1982). Aging, bone and osteoporosis. In S. G. Korenman (Ed.), *Endocrine aspects of aging* (pp. 199–230). New York: Elsevier Biomedical.

Bachman, G. (1991). Sexual dysfunction in the older woman. *Medical Aspects of Human Sexuality,* pp. 42–45.

Bacon, M. (1974). The dependency-conflict hypothesis and the frequency of drunkenness: Further evidence from a cross-cultural study. *Quarterly Journal of Studies on Alcohol, 35,* 863–876.

Bader, E. J. (1990, July/August). Trade unions still exist, racist. *New Directions for Women,* p. M1.

Baenninger, M., & Newcombe, N. (1989). The role of experience in spatial test performance: A meta-analysis. *Sex Roles, 20,* 327–344.

Bahniuk, M. H., Dobos, J., & Hill, S. E. K. (1990). The impact of mentoring, collegial support, and information adequacy on career success: A replication. In J. W. Neuliep (Ed.), *Handbook of replication research in the behavioral and social sciences.* Thousand Oaks: Sage.

Bailey, J. M., Gaulin, S., Agyei, Y., & Gladue, B. (1994). Effects of gender and sexual orientation on evolutionary relevant aspects of human mating psychology. *Journal of Personality and Social Psychology, 66,* 1081–1093.

Bailey, J. M., & Zucker, K. J. (1995). Childhood sex-typed behavior and sexual orientation: A conceptual and quantitative review. *Developmental Psychology, 31,* 43–55.

Bains, G. K., & Slade, P. (1988). Attributional patterns, moods, and the menstrual cycle. *Psychosomatic Medicine, 40,* 469–476.

Bakan, D. (1966). *The duality of human existence.* Chicago: Rand McNally.

Baker, D. D., Terpstra, D. E., & Larntz, K. (1990). The influence of individual characteristics and severity of harassing behavior on reactions to sexual harassment. *Sex Roles, 22,* 305–325.

Baker, S. (1980). Biological influences on human sex and gender. *Signs, 6,* 80–95.

Baldwin, J. I., Whiteley, S., & Baldwin, J. D. (1990). Changing AIDS- and fertility-related behavior: The effectiveness of sexual education. *Journal of Sex Research, 27,* 235–263.

Ball, J. F. (1976/1977). Widow's grief: The impact of age and mode of death. *Omega: Journal of Death and Dying, 7,* 307–333.

Ballard-Reisch, D., & Elton, M. (1992). Gender orientation and the Bem Sex Role Inventory: A psychological construct revisited. *Sex Roles, 27,* 291–306.

Ballinger, C. B. (1990). Psychiatric aspects of the menopause. *British Journal of Psychiatry, 156,* 773–787.

Bancroft, J. (1992). In R. Rosen & S. Leiblum (Eds.), *Erectile disorders.* New York: Guilford Press.

Bandura, A. (1965). Influence of models' reinforcement contingencies on the acquisition of imitative responses. *Journal of Personality and Social Psychology, 1,* 589–595.

Bandura, A. (1977). *Social learning theory.* Englewood Cliffs, NJ: Prentice-Hall.

Bandura, A. (1986). *Social foundations of thought and action: A social cognitive theory.* Englewood Cliffs, NJ: Prentice-Hall.

Bandura, A. (1989). Social cognitive theory. In R. Vasta (Ed.), *Annals of child development: Vol. 6. Six theories of child development.* Greenwich, CT: JAI.

Bandura, A. (1991). Self-regulation of motivation through anticipatory and self-regulatory mechanisms. In R. A. Dienstbier (Ed.), *Nebraska Symposium on Motivation: Vol. 38. Perspectives on motivation.* Lincoln: University of Nebraska Press.

Bandura, A., Ross, D., & Ross, S. A. (1963a). Imitation of film-mediated aggressive models. *Journal of Abnormal and Social Psychology, 66,* 3–11.

Bandura, A., Ross, D., & Ross, S. A. (1963b). A comparative test of the status envy, social power, and secondary reinforcement theories of identificatory learning. *Journal of Abnormal and Social Psychology, 67,* 527–534.

Bandura, A., & Walters, R. H. (1963). *Social learning and personality development.* New York: Holt, Rinehart & Winston.

Bank, B. J. (1995). Gendered accounts: Undergraduates explain why they seek their bachelor's degree. *Sex Roles, 32,* 527–544.

Banner, L. W. (1984). *Women in modern America: A brief history* (2nd ed.). San Diego: Harcourt Brace Jovanovich.

Banyard, V. L., & Graham-Bermann, S. A. (1993). Can women cope? A gender analysis of theories of coping with stress. *Psychology of Women Quarterly 17,* 303–318.

Barak, A., Feldman, S., & Noy, A. (1991). Traditionality of children's interests as related to their parents' gender stereotypes and traditionality. *Sex Roles, 24,* 511–524.

Baranowski, M. D. (1990). The grandfather-grandchild relationship: Meaning and exchange. *Family Perspective, 24,* 201–215.

Barbach, L. (1976). *For yourself: The fulfillment of female sexuality.* Garden City, NY: Doubleday.

Barbieri, R. L. (1988). New therapy for endometriosis. *New England Journal of Medicine, 318,* 512–514.

Barclay, A. M. (1973). Sexual fantasies in men and women. *Medical Aspects of Human Sexuality, 7,* 205–216.

Bardwell, J. R., Cochran, S. W., & Walker, S. (1986). Relationship of parental education, race, and gender to sex role stereotyping in five-year-old kindergartners. *Sex Roles, 15,* 275–281.

Barfoot, C. H., & Sheppard, G. T. (1980). Prophetic vs. priestly religion: The changing role of women clergy in classical pentecostal churches. *Review of Religious Research, 22,* 2–17.

Barlow, D. H. (1988). *Anxiety and its disorders: The nature and treatment of anxiety and panic.* New York: Guilford Press.

Barlow, D. H., & Durand, V. M. (1995). *Abnormal psychology: An integrative approach.* Pacific Grove, CA: Brooks/Cole.

Barnett, R. C. (1981). Parental sex-role attitudes and child-rearing values. *Sex Roles, 7,* 837–846.

Barnett, R. C., & Baruch, G. K. (1978). Women in the middle years: A critique of research and theory. *Psychology of Women Quarterly, 3,* 187–197.

Barnett, R. C., Brennan, R. T., Raudenbush, S. W., & Marshall, N. L. (1994). Gender and the relationship between marital role quality and psychological distress: A study of women and men in dual-earner couples. *Psychology of Women Quarterly, 18,* 105–127.

Barnett, R. C., & Marshall, N. L. (1992). Worker and mother roles, spillover effects and psychological distress. *Women and Health, 18,* 9–40.

Barnett, R. C., Marshall, N. L., & Singer, J. D. (1992). Job experience over time, multiple roles, and women's mental health: A longitudinal study. *Journal of Personality and Social Psychology, 62,* 634–644.

Baron, J. N., & Newman, A. E. (1990). For what it's worth: Organizations, occupations, and the value of work done by women and nonwhites. *American Sociological Review, 55,* 155–175.

Baron, L., & Straus, M. A. (1987). Four theories of rape: A macrosociological analysis. *Social Problems, 34,* 467–489.

Barongan, C., & Hall, G. C. N. (1995). The influence of misogynous rap music on sexual aggression against women. *Psychology of Women Quarterly, 19,* 195–207.

Barrett, C. J. (1977). Women in widowhood: Review essay. *Signs, 2,* 856–868.

Barrett, C. J. (1981). Intimacy in widowhood. *Psychology of Women Quarterly, 5,* 473–487.

Barrett, S. E. (1990). Paths toward diversity: An intrapsychic perspective. In L. S. Brown & M. P. P. Root (Eds.), *Diversity and complexity in feminist therapy.* New York: Harrington Park Press.

Barrow, G., & Smith, P. (1992). *Aging, ageism, and society.* St. Paul, MI: West.

Bart, P. (1980, March). *Socialization and rape avoidance: How to say no to Storaska and survive.* Paper presented at the National Conference on Feminist Psychology, Santa Monica, CA.

Bart, P. B., & Grossman, M. (1978). Menopause. In M. T. Notman & C. C. Nadelson (Eds.), *The woman patient: Medical and psychological interfaces.* New York: Plenum Press.

Bart, P. B., & O'Brien, P. H. (1985). *Stopping rape: Successful survival strategies.* New York: Pergamon.

Barth, R. J., & Kinder, B. N. (1988). A theoretical analysis of sex differences in same-sex friendships. *Sex Roles, 19,* 349–363.

Baruch, G., & Barnett, R. C. (1983). Adult daughters' relationships with their mothers. *Journal of Marriage and the Family, 45,* 601–606.

Baruch, G. K., & Barnett, R. C. (1986). Role quality, multiple role involvement, and psychological well-being in midlife women. *Journal of Personality and Social Psychology, 51,* 578–585.

Baruch, G., Barnett, R., & Rivers, C. (1983). *Lifeprints: New patterns of love and work for today's women.* New York: New American Library.

Baruch, R. (1967). The achievement motive in women: Implications for career development. *Journal of Personality and Social Psychology, 5,* 260–267.

Basow, S. A. (1982). Cross-cultural patterns in achievement orientation: Ethnic group and sex comparisons in Fiji. In R. A. A. Steward (Ed.), *Human development in the South Pacific: A book of readings* (2nd ed.). Suva, Fiji: USP Extension Services.

Basow, S. A. (1986). Correlates of sex-typing in Fiji. *Psychology of Women Quarterly, 10,* 429–442.

Basow, S. A. (1990). Effects of teacher expressiveness: Mediated by teacher sex-typing? *Journal of Educational Psychology, 82,* 599–602.

Basow, S. A. (1991). The hairless ideal: Women and their body hair. *Psychology of Women Quarterly, 15,* 83–96.

Basow, S. A. (1992). *Gender stereotypes and roles* (3rd ed.). Pacific Grove CA: Brooks/Cole.

Basow, S. A., & Howe, K. G. (1980). Role model influence: Ef-

Carson, R. C., & Butcher, J. N. (1992). *Abnormal psychology and modern life* (9th ed.). New York: HarperCollins.

Carter, D. B., & McCloskey, L. A. (1984). Peers and the maintenance of sex-typed behavior: The development of children's conceptions of cross-gender behavior in their peers. *Social Cognition, 2,* 294–314.

Cartwright, L. K., & Wink, P. (1994). Personality change in women physicians from medical student years to mid-40s. *Psychology of Women Quarterly, 18,* 291–308.

Casey, M. B. (1996). Understanding individual differences in spatial ability within females: A nature/nurture interactionist framework. *Developmental Review, 16,* 241–260.

Casey, M. B., & Brabeck, M. M. (1989). Exceptions to the male advantage on a spatial task: Family handedness and college major as a factor identifying women who excel. *Neuropsychologia, 27,* 689–696.

Cash, T. F., & Deagle, E. A. (1995). *The nature and extent of body-image disturbances in anorexia nervosa and bulimia nervosa: A meta-analysis.* Manuscript submitted for publication.

Cash, T. F., Gillen, G., & Burns, D. S. (1977). Sexism and "beautyism" in personnel consultant decision making. *Journal of Applied Psychology, 62,* 301–310.

Cash, T. F., & Grant, J. R. (in press). Cognitive behavioral treatment of body-image disturbances. In V. Van Hasselt & M. Hersen (Eds.), *Sourcebook of psychological treatment manuals for adult disorders.* New York: Plenum Press.

Cash, T. F., and Henry, P. E. (1995). Women's body images: The results of a national survey in the U.S.A. *Sex Roles, 33,* 19–28.

Caspi, A., & Moffitt, T. E. (1991). Individual differences are accentuated during periods of social change: The sample case of girls at puberty. *Journal of Personality and Social Psychology, 61,* 157–168.

Cataldi, A. E., & Reardon, R. (1996). Gender, interpersonal orientation, and manipulation tactic use in close relationships. *Sex Roles, 35,* 205–218.

Cate, C. A., Henton, J. M., Koval, J., Christopher, F. S., & Lloyd, S. (1982). Premarital abuse: A social psychological perspective. *Journal of Family Issues, 3,* 79–90.

Cate, R. M., & Lloyd, S. A. (1992). *Courtship.* Newbury Park, CA: Sage.

Cavanaugh, J. C. (1990). *Adult development and aging.* Belmont, CA: Wadsworth.

Cazenave, N. A. (1983). "A woman's place": The attitudes of middle-class black men. *Phylon: The Atlanta University Review of Race and Culture, 44,* 12–32.

Cazenave, N. A. (1984). Race, socioeconomic status and age: The social context of American masculinity. *Sex Roles, 11,* 639–656.

Centers for Disease Control. (1991). Premarital sexual experience among adolescent women—United States, 1970–1988. *Morbidity and Mortality Weekly Report, 39,* 929–932.

Centers for Disease Control. (1992). The second 100,000 cases of acquired immunodeficiency syndrome—United States. *Morbidity and Mortality Weekly Report, 4,* 28–29.

Centers for Disease Control. (1993, July). HIV/AIDS surveillance. Atlanta, GA: Author.

Centers for Disease Control and Prevention. (1994). Surveillance report: U.S. AIDS cases reported through December 1994. *HIV/AIDS Surveillance Report, 6,* 1–10.

Chalfant, H. P., Beckley, R. E., & Palmer, C. (1987). *Religion in contemporary society.* Palo Alto, CA: Mayfield.

Chambless, D. L., & Goldstein, A. J. (1980). Anxieties: Agoraphobia and hysteria. In A. M. Brodsky & R. Hare-Mustin (Eds.), *Women and psychotherapy: An assessment of research and practice* (pp. 113–134). New York: Guilford Press.

Champion, V. L., & Miller, T. K. (1992). Variables related to breast self-examination: Model generation. *Psychology of Women Quarterly, 16,* 81–96.

Chan, C. S. (1988). Asian-American women: Psychological responses to sexual exploitation and cultural stereotypes. *Women and Therapy, 6,* 16–20.

Chao, G. T., & Gardner, P. D. (1992). Formal and informal mentorships: A comparison of mentoring functions and contrasts with nonmentored counterparts. *Personnel Psychology, 45,* 619–636.

Chapman, L. J. (1967). Illusory correlation in observational reports. *Journal of Verbal Learning and Verbal Behavior, 6,* 151–155.

Charlesworth, W. R., & Dzur, C. (1987). Gender comparisons of preschoolers' behavior and resource utilization in group problem solving. *Child Development, 58,* 191–200.

Charlesworth, W. R., & LaFreniere, P. (1983). Dominance, friendship utilization and resource utilization in preschool children's groups. *Ethology and Sociobiology, 4,* 175–186.

Charney, D., & Russell, R. (1994). An overview of sexual harassment. *American Journal of Psychiatry, 151,* 10–17.

Chase, T., The Troops for. (1990). *When rabbit howls.* New York: Jove.

Chase-Lansdale, P. L., & Hetherington, E. M. (1990). The impact of divorce on life-span development: Short- and long-term effects. In P. B. Baltes, D. L. Featherman, & R. M. Lerner (Eds.), *Life-span development and behavior* (Vol. 10). Hillsdale, NJ: Erlbaum.

Chatters, L. M., & Taylor, R. J. (1993). Intergenerational support: The provision of assistance to parents by adult children. In J. S. Jackson, L. M. Chatters, & R. J. Taylor (Eds.), *Aging in Black America* (pp. 69–82). Newbury Park, CA: Sage.

Chatters, L. M., & Taylor, R. J. (1994). Religious involvement among older African Americans. In J. S. Levin (Ed.), *Religion in aging and health: Theoretical foundations and methodological frontiers* (pp. 196–230). Thousand Oaks, CA: Sage.

Chaves, M. (1989). Secularization and religious revival: Evidence from U.S. church attendance rates, 1972–1986. *Journal for the Scientific Study of Religion, 28,* 464–477.

Chavez, D. (1985). Perpetuation of gender inequality: A content analysis of comic strips. *Sex Roles, 13,* 93–102.

Check, J. V. P., & Malamuth, N. M. (1983). Sex role stereotyping and reactions to depictions of stranger versus acquaintance rape. *Journal of Personality and Social Psychology, 45,* 344–356.

Check, J. V. P., & Malamuth, N. M. (1985). An empirical assessment of some feminist hypotheses about rape. *International Journal of Women's Studies, 8,* 414–423.

Chehrazi, S. (1986). Female psychology. *Journal of the American Psychoanalytic Association, 34,* 111–162.

Chelune, G. J. (1976). Reactions to male and female disclosure at two levels. *Journal of Personality and Social Psychology, 34,* 1000–1003.

Chen, Y. P. (1985). Economic status of the aging. In R. H. Binstock & E. Shanas (Eds.), *Handbook of aging and the social sciences* (2nd ed., pp. 641–665). New York: Van Nostrand Reinhold.

Cherlin, A. (1981). *Marriage, divorce, remarriage.* Cambridge, MA: Harvard University Press.

Cherry, F., & Deaux, K. (1978). Fear of success versus fear of gender-inappropriate behavior. *Sex Roles, 4,* 97–101.

Cherry, L. (1975). The preschool teacher-child dyad: Sex differences in verbal interaction. *Child Development, 46,* 532–535.

Chesler, P. (1972). *Women and madness.* New York: Doubleday.

Chester, N. L. (1983). Sex differentiation in two high school environments: Implications for career development among black adolescent females. *Journal of Social Issues, 39,* 29–40.

Chethik (1994, December 4). The male voice. *Detroit Free Press,* p. 2J.

Child, M., Low, K. G., McCormick, C. M., & Cocciarella, A. (1996). Personal advertisements of male-to-female transsexuals, homosexual men, and heterosexuals. *Sex Roles, 34,* 447–455.

Children's Defense Fund. (1989). *The health of America's children.* Washington, DC: Author.

Children's Defense Fund. (1991). *The state of America's children 1991.* Washington, DC: Author.

Chilman, C. S. (1986). Some psychosocial aspects of adolescent sexual and contraceptive behaviors in a changing American society. In J. B. Lancaster & B. A. Hamburg (Eds.), *School-age pregnancy and parenthood: Biosocial dimensions.* New York: Aldine De Gruyter.

Chipman, S. F., Brush, L. R., & Wilson, D. M. (Eds.). (1985). *Women and mathematics: Balancing the equation.* Hillsdale, NJ: Erlbaum.

Chodorow, N. (1978). *The reproduction of mothering: Psychoanalysis and the sociology of gender.* Berkeley: University of California Press.

Chow, E. (1985). The acculturation experience of Asian American women. In A. G. Sargent (Ed.), *Beyond sex roles* (3rd ed., pp. 238–251). St. Paul, MN: West.

Chrisler, J. C., Johnston, I. K., Champagne, N. M., & Preston, K. E. (1994). Menstrual joy: The construct and its consequences. *Psychology of Women Quarterly, 18,* 375–387.

Chrisler, J. C., Torrey, J. W., & Matthes, M. A. (1990). Brittle bones and sagging breasts, loss of femininity and loss of sanity: The media describe the menopause. In A. M. Voda & R. Conover (Eds.), *Proceedings of the eighth conference of the Society for Menstrual Cycle Research* (pp. 23–35). Salt Lake City: Society for Menstrual Cycle Research.

Christ, C. (1979). Spiritual quest and women's experience. In C. P. Christ & J. Plaskow (Eds.), *Womanspirit rising: A feminist reader in religion.* San Francisco: Harper & Row.

Christ, C. P. (1983). Heretics and outsiders: The struggle over female power in Western religion. *Soundings, 61,* 87.

Christ, C. P., & Plaskow, J. (Eds.). (1979). *Womanspirit rising: A feminist reader in religion.* San Francisco: Harper & Row.

Christensen, A., & Heavey, C. L. (1990). Gender and social structure in the demand/withdraw pattern of marital conflict. *Journal of Personality and Social Psychology, 59,* 73–81.

Chu, J. A. (1992). The re-victimization of adult women with histories of childhood abuse. *Journal of Psychotherapy Practice and Research, 1,* 259–269.

Chusmir, L. H. (1984). Personnel administrators' perception of sex differences in motivation of managers: Research-based or stereotyped? *International Journal of Women's Studies, 7,* 17–23.

Cianni, M., & Romberger, B. (1995). Interactions with senior managers: Perceived differences by race/ethnicity and by gender. *Sex Roles, 32,* 353–373.

Cicirelli, V. G. (1980). Sibling relationships in adulthood: A life span perspective. In L. W. Poon (Ed.), *Aging in the 1980's: Psychological issues.* Washington, DC: American Psychological Association.

Cicirelli, V. G. (1981, August). *Feelings toward siblings in adulthood and old age.* Paper presented at the 89th annual convention of the American Psychological Association, Los Angeles.

Cicirelli, V. G. (1986). Family relationships and care/management of the dementing elderly. In M. Gilhooly, S. Zarit, & E. Birren (Eds.), *The dementias: Policy and management.* Englewood Cliffs, NJ: Prentice-Hall.

Clancy, S. M., & Dollinger, S. J. (1993). Photographic depictions of the self: Gender and age differences in social connectedness. *Sex Roles, 29,* 477–495.

Clark, J., & Zehr, D. (1993). Other women can: Discrepant performance predictions for self and same-sex other. *Journal of College Students Development, 34,* 31–35.

Clark, R. A. (1993). Men's and women's self-confidence in persuasive, comforting, and justificatory communicative tasks. *Sex Roles, 28,* 553–567.

Clark, R. D., & Hatfield, E. (1989). Gender differences in receptivity to sexual offers. *Journal of Psychology and Human Differences, 2,* 39–55.

Clarke-Stewart, K. A. (1989). Infant day care: Maligned or malignant? *American Psychologist, 44,* 266–273.

Clarke-Stewart, K. A., & Fein, G. G. (1983). Early childhood programs. In P. H. Mussen (Ed.), *Handbook of child psychology: Vol. 2. Infancy and developmental psychobiology.* New York: Wiley.

Clatterbaugh, K. C. (1990). *Contemporary perspectives on masculinity: Men, women, and politics in modern society.* Boulder, CO: Westview Press.

Cleek, M., & Pearson, T. (1985). Perceived causes of divorce: An analysis of interrelationships. *Journal of Marriage and the Family, 47,* 179–183.

Clewell, B. C., Brooks-Gunn, J., & Benasich, A. A. (in press). Evaluating child-related outcomes of teenage parenting programs. *Family Relations.*

Clinchy, B. M. (1989). The development of thoughtfulness in college women: Integrating reason and care. *American-Behavioral-Scientist, 32,* 647–657.

Clinton, C. (1982). *The plantation mistress: Women's world in the Old South.* New York: Pantheon Books.

Clopton, N. A., & Sorrell, G. T. (1993). Gender differences in moral reasoning: Stable or situational? *Psychology of Women Quarterly, 17,* 85–101.

Clopton, N. A., & Sorell, G. T. (1995). Concealing respondents' gender in interview transcripts. *Psychology of Women Quarterly, 19,* 147–160.

Clorfene-Casten, L. (1993, May/June). The environmental link. *Ms., iii,* 52–56.

Clunis, D. M., & Green, G. D. (1993). *Lesbian couples: Creating healthy relationships for the 90's.* Seattle, WA: Seal Press.

Clutter, S. (1990, May 3). Gender may affect response and outrage to sex abuse. *Morning Call,* p. D14.

Cochran, C. C., Frazier, P. A., & Olson, A. M. (1997). Predictors of responses to unwanted sexual attention. *Psychology for Women Quarterly, 21,* 207–226.

Cochran, N. A., & Mays, V. M. (1989). Women and AIDS-related concerns. *American Psychologist, 44,* 529–535.

Cochran, S. D., & Peplau, L. A. (1985). Value orientations in heterosexual relationships. *Psychology of Women Quarterly, 9*, 477–488.

Cogen, R., & Steinman, W. (1990). Sexual function and practice in elderly men of lower socioeconomic status. *Journal of Family Practice, 32*, 162–166.

Cohan, C. L., Dunkel-Schetter, C., & Lydon, J. (1993). Pregnancy decision making: Predictors of early stress and adjustment. *Psychology of Women Quarterly, 17*, 223–239.

Cohen, A. G., & Gutek, B. A. (1991). Sex differences in the career experiences of members of two APA divisions. *American Psychologist, 46*, 1292–1298.

Cohen, C. E. (1981). Person categories and social perception: Testing some boundaries of the processing effects of prior knowledge. *Journal of Personality and Social Psychology, 40*, 441–452.

Cohen, D. (1988). Age differences in memory for texts: Production deficiency of processing limitations. In L. O. Light & D. M. Burke (Eds.), *Language, memory, and aging*. New York: Cambridge University Press.

Cohen, D., & Wilkie, F. (1979). Sex-related differences in cognition among the elderly. In M. A. Wittig & A. C. Petersen (Eds.), *Sex-related differences in cognitive functioning* (pp. 145–159). New York: Academic Press.

Cohn, J. E., Campbell, S. B., Matias, R., & Hopkins, J. (1990). Face-to-face interactions of postpartum depressed and nondepressed mother-infant pairs at 2 months. *Developmental Psychology, 26*, 15–23.

Cohn, L. D., & Adler, N. E. (1992). Female and male perceptions of ideal body shapes. *Psychology of Women Quarterly, 16*, 69–79.

Colby, A., & Damon, W. (1983). Listening to a different voice: A review of Gilligan's *In a different voice. Merrill-Palmer Quarterly, 29*, 473–481.

Colby, A., & Kohlberg, L. (Eds.). (1986). *The measurement of moral judgement*. New York: Cambridge University Press.

Cole, E., & Rothblum, E. (1991). Lesbian sex after menopause: As good or better than ever. In B. Sang, J. Warshow, & A. J. Smith (Eds.), *Lesbians at midlife: The creative transformation, an anthology* (pp. 184–193). San Francisco, CA: spinsters book company.

Cole, M., & Cole, S. R. (1989). *The development of children*. New York: Scientific American Books.

Coleman, E. (1985). Bisexual women in marriages. *Journal of Homosexuality, 11*, 87–99.

Coleman, L. M., & Antonucci, T. C. (1983). Impact of work on women at midlife. *Developmental Psychology, 19*, 290–294.

Coley, S. M., & Beckett, J. O. (1988). Black battered women: A review of empirical literature. *Journal of Counseling and Development, 66*, 266–270.

Colker, R., & Widom, C. S. (1980). Correlates of female athletic participation: Masculinity, femininity, self-esteem and attitudes to women. *Sex Roles, 6*, 47–58.

Colley, A., Griffiths, D., Hugh, M., Landers, K., & Jaggli, N. (1996). Childhood play and adolescent leisure preferences: Associations with gender typing and the presence of siblings. *Sex Roles, 35*, 233–245.

Collier, G., Kuiken, D., & Enzle, M. E. (1982). The role of grammatical qualification in the expression and perception of emotion. *Journal of Psycholinguistic Research, 11*, 631–650.

Collier, H. V. (1982). *Counseling women*. New York: Free Press.

Collins, K. S., Rowland, D., Salganicoff, A., & Chait, E. (1994). Assessing and improving women's health. In C. Costello & A. J. Stone (Eds.), *The American woman, 1994–1995: Where we stand, women and health*. New York: Norton.

Collins, M. E. (1991). Body figure perceptions and preferences among preadolescent children. *International Journal of Eating Disorders, 10*, 199–208.

Collins, P. H. (1989). The social construction of black feminist thought. *Signs, 14*, 745–753.

Collins, P. H. (1990). *Black feminist thought: Knowledge, consciousness and the politics of empowerment*. Boston, MA: Beacon Press.

Collins, P. H. (1991). The meaning of motherhood in black culture and black mother-daughter relationships. In P. Bell-Scott, B. Guy-Sheftall, J. J. Royster, J. Sims-Wood, M. DeCosta-Willis, & L. Fultz (Eds.), *Double stitch: Black women write about mothers and daughters*. Boston: Beacon Press.

Collins, P. H. (1993a). The sexual politics of black womanhood. In P. B. Bart & E. G. Moran (Eds.), *Violence against women: The bloody footprints* (pp. 85–104). Newbury Park, CA: Sage.

Collins, P. H. (1993b). Toward an Afrocentric feminist epistemology. In A. M. Jaggar & P. S. Rothenberg (Eds.), *Feminist frameworks: Alternative theoretical accounts of relations between women and men* (3rd ed., pp. 93–103). New York: McGraw-Hill.

Collins, S. (1974). *Another heaven, another earth*. Valley Forge, PA: Judson Press.

Colwill, N. L., & Colwill, H. D. (1985). Women with blue collars: The forgotten minority. *Business Quarterly, 50*, 15–17.

Comas-Diaz, L. (1991). Feminism and diversity in psychology: The case of women of color. *Psychology of Women Quarterly, 15*, 597–609.

Comas-Diaz, L., & Greene, B. (1994). *Women of color: Integrating ethnic and gender identities in psychotherapy*. New York: Guilford Press.

Comer, J. (1993). *African-American parents and child development: An agenda for school success*. Paper presented at the 60th anniversary meeting of the Society for Research in Child Development, New Orleans, LA.

Comfort, A. (1972). *The joy of sex*. New York: Crown.

Committee on Women in Psychology. (1985, October). *Statement on proposed diagnostic categories for DSM-III-R*. Washington, DC: American Psychology Association.

Comstock, G. (1991). *Television and the American child*. San Diego, CA: Academic Press.

Condry, J., & Ross, D. (1985). Sex and aggression: The influence of gender label on the perception of aggression in children. *Child Development, 56*, 225–233.

Conger, R. D., Lorenz, F. O., Elder, G. H., Jr., Simons, R. L., & Ge, X. (1993). Husband and wife differences in responses to undesirable life events. *Journal of Health and Social Behavior, 34*, 71–88.

Constantinople, A. (1973). Masculinity-femininity: An exception to the famous dictum? *Psychological Bulletin, 80*, 389–407.

Cook, E. P. (1985). *Psychological androgyny*. Elmsford, NY: Pergamon Press.

Cook, K. (1987). *Social exchange theory*. Beverly Hills, CA: Sage.

Cook, S. L. (1995). Acceptance and expectation of sexual aggression in college students. *Psychology of Women Quarterly, 19*, 181–194.

Cooney, T. (1994). Young adults' relations with parents: The influence of recent parental divorce. *Journal of Marriage and the Family, 56,* 45–56.

Coons, P. M., Bowman, E. S., Pellow, T. A., & Schneider, P. (1989). Post-traumatic aspects of the treatment of victims of sexual abuse and incest. *Psychiatric Clinics of North America, 12,* 325.

Cooper, K., Chasson, L., & Zeiss, A. (1985). The relation of sex-role self-concept and sex-role attitudes to the marital satisfaction and personal adjustment of dual-worker couples with preschool children. *Sex Roles, 12,* 227–241.

Cooper, P. L., Crum, R. M., & Ford, D. E. (1994). Characteristics of patients with major depression who received care in general medical and speciality mental health settings. *Medical Care, 32,* 15–24.

Cooper, W. H. (1983). An achievement motivation nomological network. *Journal of Personality & Social Psychology, 44,* 841–861.

Coppen, A., & Kessel, N. (1963). Menstruation and personality. *British Journal of Psychiatry, 109,* 711.

Cora-Bramble, D., Bradshaw, M., & Sklarew, B. (1992). The sex education practicum: Medical students in the elementary school classrooms. *Journal of School Health, 62,* 32–34.

Corcoran, C. B. (1991, August). *Sexual assault programs: From victim control to feminist social change.* Paper presented at the annual meeting of the American Psychological Association, San Francisco.

Corcoran, M., Duncan, G. J., & Hill, M. S. (1984). The economic fortunes of women and children: Lessons from the panel study of income dynamics. *Signs, 10,* 232–248.

Cordua, G. D., McGraw, K. O., & Drabman, R. S. (1979). Doctor or nurse: Children's perceptions of sex-typed occupations. *Child Development, 50,* 590–593.

Costello, C., & Stone, A. J. (Eds.). (1994). *The American woman, 1994–1995: Where we stand, women and health.* New York: Norton.

Costin, S. E., & Jones, D. C. (1992). Friendship as a facilitator of emotional responsiveness and prosocial intervention among young children. *Developmental Psychology, 28,* 941–947.

Costos, D. (1990). Gender role identity from an ego developmental perspective. *Sex Roles, 22,* 723–741.

Cota, A. A., & Dion, K. L. (1986). Salience of gender and sex composition of ad hoc groups: An experimental test of distinctiveness theory. *Journal of Personality and Social Psychology, 50,* 770–776.

Cota, A. A., & Fekken, G. C. (1988). Dimensionality of the Personality Attributes Questionnaire: An empirical replication. *Journal of Social Behavior and Personality, 3,* 135–140.

Cota, A. A., Reid, A., & Dion, K. L. (1991). Construct validity of a diagnostic ratio measure of gender stereotypes. *Sex Roles, 25,* 225–235.

Cote, L. R., & Azar, S. T. (1997). Child age, parent and child gender, and domain differences in parents' attributions and responses to children's outcomes. *Sex Roles, 36,* 23–50.

Cott, N. F. (1977). *The bonds of womanhood: Woman's sphere in New England, 1780–1835.* New Haven: Yale University Press.

Council on Ethical and Judicial Affairs, American Medical Association. (1994). Gender discrimination in the medical profession. *Women's Health Issues, 4,* 1–11.

Courtney, A. E., & Whipple, T. W. (1983). *Sex stereotyping in advertising.* Lexington, MA: Lexington Books.

Cowan, C. P., & Cowan, P. A. (1988). *The development of children.* New York: Scientific American Books.

Cowan, G. (1992). Feminist attitudes toward pornography control. *Psychology of Women Quarterly, 16,* 165–177.

Cowan, G., & Campbell, R. R. (1994). Racism and sexism in interracial pornography: A content analysis. *Psychology of Women Quarterly, 18,* 323–338.

Cowan, G., Chase, C. J., & Stahly, G. B. (1989). Feminist and fundamental attitudes toward pornography control. *Psychology of Women Quarterly, 13,* 97–112.

Cowan, G., & Hoffman, C. D. (1986). Gender stereotyping in young children: Evidence to support a concept-learning approach. *Sex Roles, 14,* 11–22.

Cowan, G., Lee, C., Levy, D., & Snyder, D. (1988). Dominance and inequality in X-rated videocassettes. *Psychology of Women Quarterly, 12,* 299–311.

Coward, R. T., & Dwyer, J. W. (1990). The association of gender, sibling network composition, and patterns of parent care by adult children. *Research on Aging, 12,* 158–181.

Cowley, G. (1990, December 10). In pursuit of a terrible killer. *Newsweek,* pp. 62–68.

Cowley, G., & Hager, M. (1993). The politics of the plague (AIDS). *Newsweek, 122,* 62.

Cox, S., & Gallois, C. (1996). Gay and lesbian identity development: A social identity perspective. *Journal of Homosexuality, 30,* 1–30.

Crabb, P. B., & Bielawski, D. (1994). The social representation of material culture and gender in children's books. *Sex Roles, 30,* 69–79.

Craig, J. M., & Sherif, C. W. (1986). The effectiveness of men and women in problem-solving groups as a function of group gender composition. *Sex Roles, 14,* 453–466.

Cramer, P., & Carter, T. (1978). The relationship between sexual identification and the use of defense mechanisms. *Journal of Personality and Social Psychology, 42,* 63–73.

Cramer, P., & Skidd, J. E. (1992). Correlates of self-worth in preschoolers: The role of gender stereotyped styles of behavior. *Sex Roles, 26,* 369–390.

Crandall, V. J. (1969). Sex differences in expectancy of intellectual and academic reinforcement. In C. D. Smith (Ed.), *Achievement related motives in children.* New York: Russell Sage Foundation.

Crawford, I. (1990). Attitudes of undergraduate college students towards AIDS. *Psychological Reports, 66,* 11–16.

Crawford, M. (1977). What is a friend? *New Society, 42,* 116–117.

Crawford, M. (1989). Agreeing to differ: Feminist epistemologies and women's ways of knowing. In M. Crawford & H. Gentry (Eds.), *Gender and thought: Psychological perspectives.* New York: Springer-Verlag.

Crawford, M., & Gressley, D. (1991). Creativity, caring, and context: Women's and men's accounts of humor preferences and practices. *Psychology of Women Quarterly, 15,* 217–231.

Crawford, M., & Marecek, J. (1989). Psychology reconstructs the female: 1968–1988. *Psychology of Women Quarterly, 13,* 147–165.

Crew, J. C. (1982). An assessment of needs among black business majors. *Psychology, 19,* 18–22.

Crick, N. R., & Grotpeter, J. K. (1995). Relational aggression, gender, and social-psychological adjustment. *Child Development, 66,* 710–722.

Crockett, L. J., Losoff, M., & Petersen, A. C. (1984). Perceptions of the peer group and friendship in early adolescence. *Journal of Early Adolescence, 4,* 155–181.

Crockett, L. J., & Petersen, A. C. (1987). Pubertal status and psychosocial development: Findings from early adolescent study. In R. M. Lerner & T. T. Foch (Eds.), *Biological-psychosocial interactions in early adolescence.* Hillsdale, NJ: Erlbaum.

Crombie, G. (1983). Women's attribution patterns and their relation to achievement: An examination of within-sex differences. *Sex Roles, 9,* 1171–1182.

Crombie, G., & Desjardins, M. J. (1993). *Predictors of gender: The Relative importance of children's play, games and personality characteristics.* Biennial conference of the Society for Research in Child Development, New Orleans, LA.

Crook, J. (1986). *Family functioning in families of origin of survivors of father-daughter incest.* Unpublished master's thesis, University of Rhode Island, Kingston.

Crooks, R., & Baur, K. (1993). *Our sexuality* (5th ed.). Redwood City, CA: Benjamin/Cummings.

Crosby, F. J. (1982). *Relative deprivation and working women.* New York: Oxford.

Crosby, F. J. (1984). The denial of personal discrimination. *American Behavioral Scientist, 27,* 371–386.

Crosby, F. J. (1990). Divorce and work life among women managers. In H. Y. Grossman & N. L. Chester (Eds.), *The experience and meaning of work in women's lives.* Hillsdale, NJ: Erlbaum.

Crosby, F. J. (1991). *Juggling.* New York: Free Press.

Crosby, F. J., Pullman, A., Snyder, R. C., O'Connell, M., & Whalen, P. (1989). The denial of personal disadvantage among you, me, and all the other ostriches. In M. Crawford & M. Gentry (Eds.), *Gender and thought* (pp. 79–99). New York: Springer-Verlag.

Cross, S. E., & Markus, H. R. (1993). Gender in thought, belief, and action: A cognitive approach. In A. E. Beall & R. J. Sternberg (Eds.), *The psychology of gender* (pp. 55–98). New York: Guilford Press.

Crouter, A. C., Perry-Jenkins, M., Huston, T. L., & McHale, S. M. (1987). Processes underlying father involvement in dual-earner and single-earner families. *Developmental Psychology, 23.*

Cruikshank, M. (1992). *The gay and lesbian liberation.* New York: Routledge.

Cue, K. L., George, W. H., & Norris, J. (1996). Women's appraisals of sexual-assault risk in dating situations. *Psychology of Women Quarterly, 20,* 487–504.

Cunningham, J. D., & Antill, J. K. (1984). Changes in masculinity and femininity across the family life cycle: A reexamination. *Developmental Psychology, 20,* 1135–1141.

Cupp, A. (1994). *Women and alcoholism.* Unpublished paper, Michigan State University, East Lansing.

Cutler, R., Heimer, B., Wortis, H., & Freeman, A. M. (1965). The effects of prenatal and neonatal complications on the development of premature children at two-and-one-half years of age. *Journal of Genetic Psychology, 107,* 261–276.

Cutler, S. E., & Nolen-Hoeksema, S. (1991). Accounting for sex differences in depression through female victimization: Childhood sexual abuse. *Sex Roles, 24,* 425–438.

Cutler, W. B., Preti, G., Krieger, A., & Huggins, G. R. (1986). Human auxiliary secretions influence women's menstrual cycles: The role of donor extract from men. *Hormones and Behavior, 20,* 463–473.

Cutrona, C. E. (1982a). Nonpsychotic postpartum depression: A review of recent research. *Clinical Psychology Review, 2,* 487–503.

Cutrona, C. E. (1982b). Transition to college: Loneliness and the process of social adjustment. In L. A. Peplau & D. Perlman (Eds.), *Loneliness.* New York: Wiley.

Cutrona, C. E., & Troutman, B. R. (1986). Social support, infant temperament, and parenting self-efficacy: A mediational model of postpartum depression. *Child Development, 57,* 1507–1518.

Dabbs, J. M., & Morris, R. (1990). Testosterone, social class, and antisocial behavior in a sample of 4,462 men. *Psychological Science, 1,* 209–211.

Dagg, P. K. B. (1991). The psychological sequelae of therapeutic abortion—Denied and completed. *American Journal of Psychiatry, 148,* 578–585.

Dalton, K. (1961). Menstruation and crime. *British Medical Journal, 2,* 1752–1753.

Dalton, K. (1964). *The premenstrual syndrome.* Springfield, IL: Charles C. Thomas.

Dalton, K. (1966). The influence of mother's menstruation on her child. *Proceedings of the Royal Society of Medicine, 59,* 1014.

Daly, M. (1973). *Beyond God the Father: Toward a philosophy of women's liberation.* Boston: Beacon.

Daly, M. (1974). Theology after the demise of God the father: A call for the castration of sexist religion. In A. Hageman (Ed.), *Sexist religion and women in the church.* New York: Association Press.

D'Amico, M., Baron, L. J., & Sissons, M. E. (1995). Gender differences in attributions about microcomputer learning in elementary school. *Sex Roles, 33,* 353–385.

Dan, A. J. (1979). The menstrual cycle and sex-related differences in cognitive variability. In M. A. Wittig & A. C. Petersen (Eds.), *Sex-related differences in cognitive functioning, developmental issues.* New York: Academic Press.

Dancey, C. P. (1992). The relationship of instrumentality and expressivity to sexual orientation in women. *Journal of Homosexuality, 23,* 71–83.

Daniels, A. K. (1987). The hidden work of constructing class and community: Women volunteer leaders in social philanthropy. In N. Gerstel & H. Gross (Eds.), *Families and work.* Philadelphia: Temple University Press.

Daniluk, J. C. (1993). The meaning and experience of female sexuality: A phenomenological analysis. *Psychology of Women Quarterly, 17,* 53–69.

Danza, R. (1983). Menarche: Its effects on mother-daughter and father-daughter interactions. In S. Golub (Ed.), *Menarche.* Lexington, MA: Lexington Books.

Danziger, N. (1983). Sex-related differences in the aspirations of high school students. *Sex Roles, 9,* 683–695.

Darling, C., & Davidson, J. (1986). Enhancing relationships: Understanding the feminine mystique of pretending orgasm. *Journal of Sex and Marital Therapy, 12,* 182–196.

Darling, C. A., Davidson, J. K, & Conway-Welch, C. (1990). Female ejaculation: Perceived origins, the Grafenberg spot/area, and sexual responsiveness. *Archives of Sexual Behavior, 19,* 29–47.

Darling-Fisher, C., & Tiedje, L. (1990). The impact of maternal employment characteristics on fathers' participation in child care. *Family Relations, 39,* 20–26.

Darwin, C. (1881/1971). *The descent of man and selection in relation to sex.* London: John Murray.

Daubman, K. A., Heatherington, L., & Ahn, A. (1992). Gender and the self-presentation of academic achievement. *Sex Roles, 27,* 187–204.

Davenport, D. S. (1991). Multicultural gender issues: Special issue: Multiculturalism as a fourth force in counseling. *Journal of Consulting and Development, 70,* 64–71.

David, H. P. (1992). Born unwanted: Long-term developmental effects of denied abortion. *Journal of Social Issues, 48,* 163–181.

Davidson, J. K., & Darling, C. A. (1986). The impact of college-level sex education on sexual knowledge, attitudes, and practices: The knowledge/sexual experimentation myth revisited. *Deviant Behavior, 7,* 13–30.

Davis, A. J. (1984). Sex differentiated behavior in nonsexist picture books. *Sex Roles, 11,* 1–16.

Davis, D. M. (1990). Portrayals of women in prime-time network television: Some demographic characteristics. *Sex Roles, 23,* 325–332.

Davis, M., & Weitz, S. (1981). Sex differences in body movements and positions. In C. Mayo & N. M. Henley (Eds.), *Gender and nonverbal behavior* (pp. 81–92). New York: Springer-Verlag.

Davis, R. C., Brickman, E., & Baker, T. (1991). Supportive and unsupportive responses of others to rape victims: Effects on concurrent victim adjustment, *American Journal of Community Psychology, 19,* 443–451.

Davis, R. C., & Friedman, L. N. (1985). The emotional aftermath of crime and violence. In C. R. Figler (Ed.), *Trauma and its wake: The study and treatment of post-traumatic stress disorder* (pp. 90–111). New York: Brunner-Mazel.

Davis, S. (1990). Men as success objects and women as sex objects: A study of personal advertisements. *Sex Roles, 23,* 43–50.

Davis, T., & Lee, C. (1996). Sexual assault: Myths and stereotypes among Australian adolescents. *Sex Roles, 34,* 787–803.

Davis, T. L. (1995). Gender differences in masking negative emotions: Ability or motivation? *Developmental Psychology, 31,* 660–667.

Dawson, D. (1990). Trends in use of oral contraceptives: Data from the 1987 National Health Interview Survey. *Family Planning Perspectives, 22,* 169.

Deaux, K. (1976). *The behavior of women and men.* Monterey, CA: Brooks/Cole.

Deaux, K. (1984). From individual differences to social categories: Analysis of a decade's research on gender. *American Psychologist, 39,* 105–116.

Deaux, K., & Emswiller, T. (1974). Explanations of successful performance on sex-linked tasks: What's skill for the male is luck for the female. *Journal of Personality and Social Psychology, 29,* 80–85.

Deaux, K., & Lewis, L. L. (1983). Components of gender stereotypes. *Psychological Documents, 13,* 25 (Catalog No. 2583).

Deaux, K., & Lewis, L. L. (1984). Structure of gender stereotypes: Interrelationships among components and gender label. *Journal of Personality and Social Psychology, 46,* 991–1004.

Deaux, K., & Major, B. (1987). Putting gender into context: An interactive model of gender-related behavior. *Psychological Review, 94,* 369–389.

Deaux, K., & Ullman, J. C. (1983). *Women of steel.* New York: Praeger.

de Beauvoir, S. (1961). *The second sex.* New York: Bantam.

DeBro, S. C., Campbell, S. M., & Peplau, L. A. (1994). Influencing a partner to use a condom: A college student perspective. *Psychology of Women Quarterly, 18,* 165–182.

De Cecco, J. P., & Parker, D. A. (1995). The biology of homosexuality: Sexual orientation or sexual preference? *Journal of Homosexuality, 28,* 1–27.

DeChick, J. (1988, July). Most mothers want a job too. *USA Today,* p. D1.

DeFronzo, J., & Boudreau, F. (1979). Further research into antecedents and correlates of androgyny. *Psychology Reports, 44,* 23–29.

Degler, C. N. (1980). *At odds: Women and the family in America from the revolution to the present.* New York: Oxford University Press.

DeKeseredy, W. S., Schwartz, M. D., & Tait, K. (1993). Sexual assault and stranger aggression on a Canadian university campus. *Sex Roles, 28,* 263–277.

Delamont, S. (1990). *Sex roles and the school* (2nd ed.). London: Routledge.

Delaney, J., Lupton, M. J., & Toth, E. (1988). *The curse: A cultural history of menstruation* (Rev. ed.). Urbana: University of Illinois Press.

de Lecoste-Utamsing, C., & Holloway, R. L. (1982). Sexual dimorphism in the human corpus callosum. *Science, 216,* 1431–1432.

DeLisi, R. D., & Soundranayagam, L. (1990). The conceptual structure of sex role stereotypes in college students. *Sex Roles, 23,* 593–611.

DeLoache, J. S., Cassidy, D. J., & Carpenter, C. J. (1987). The three bears are all boys: Mothers' gender labeling of neutral picture book characters. *Sex Roles, 17,* 163–178.

Delora, J. S., & Warren, C. A. B. (1971). *Understanding sexual interaction.* Boston, MA: Houghton Mifflin.

DeMaris, A., & Leslie, G. R. (1984). Cohabitation with the future spouse: Its influence upon marital satisfaction and communication. *Journal of Marriage and the Family, 46,* 77–84.

Denham, S. A., Zoller, D., & Couchound, E. A. (in press). Socialization in preschoolers' emotion understanding. *Developmental Psychology.*

Denmark, F. L. (1982). Integrating the psychology of women into introductory psychology. In C. J. Schere & A. R. Rogers (Eds.), *The G. Stanley Hall Lecture Series* (Vol. 3). Washington, DC: American Psychological Association.

Denmark, F. L. (1993). Women, leadership, and empowerment. *Psychology of Women Quarterly, 17,* 343–356.

Denton, T. C. (1990). Bonding and supportive relationships among black professional women: Rituals of restoration. *Journal of Organizational Behavior, 11,* 447–457.

Derlega, V. J., & Chaikin, A. L. (1976). Norms affecting self-disclosure in men and women. *Journal of Consulting and Clinical Psychology, 44,* 376–380.

de Snyder, V. N. S., Cervantes, R. C., & Padilla, A. M. (1990). Gender and ethnic differences in psychosocial stress and generalized distress among Hispanics. *Sex Roles, 22,* 441–453.

Desrochers, S. (1995). What types of men are most attractive and most repulsive to women? *Sex Roles, 32,* 375–391.

Deutsch, F. M., LeBaron, D., & Fryer, M. M. (1987). What is in a smile? *Psychology of Women Quarterly, 11,* 341–352.

Deutsch, F. M., Zalenski, C. M., & Clark, M. E. (1986). Is there a double standard of aging? *Journal of Applied Social Psychology, 16*, 771–785.

Deutsch, H. (1944). *The psychology of women: A psychoanalytic interpretation* (Vol. 1). New York: Grune and Stratton.

Devault, M. (1987). Doing housework: Feeding and family life. In N. Gerstel & H. E. Gross (Eds.), *Families and work.* Philadelphia: Temple University Press.

DeVries, R. (1969). Constancy of generic identity in the years three to six. *Monographs of the Society for Research in Child Development, 34* (Serial No. 127).

de Weerth, C., & Kalma, A. (1995). Gender differences in awareness in courtship initiation tactics. *Sex Roles, 32*, 717–734.

Dewsbury, D. A. (1991). "Psychobiology." *American Psychologist, 46*, 198–205.

Diamond, M., Lund, D. A., & Caserta, M. S. (1987). The role of social support in the first two years of bereavement in an elderly sample. *Gerontologist, 27*, 599–604.

Diamond, M., Lund, D. A., & Johnson, R. (1983, November). *The role of social support in the first year of bereavement in an elderly sample.* Paper presented at the 36th annual scientific meeting of the Gerontological Society of America, San Francisco, CA.

Diamond, M. A. (1982). Sexual identity, monozygotic twins reared in discordant sex roles and a BBC follow-up. *Archives of Sexual Behavior, 11*, 181–186.

Diamond, M. A. (1993). Some genetic considerations in the development of sexual orientation. In M. Haug, R. E. Whalen, C. Aron, & K. L. Olsen (Eds.), *The development of sex differences and similarities in behavior* (pp. 291–309). Dordrecht: Kluwer Publishing Company.

Diamond, M. A., & Karlen, A. (1980). *Sexual decisions.* Boston: Little, Brown.

Diaz-Guerrero, R. (1987). Historical sociocultural premises and ethnic socialization. In J. S. Phinney & M. J. Rotheram (Eds.), *Children's ethnic socialization: Pluralism and development.* Newbury Park, CA: Sage.

Di Dio, L., Saragovi, C., Koestner, R., & Aubé, J. (1996). Linking personal values to gender. *Sex Roles, 34*, 621–636.

Dickson, L. (1993). The future of marriage and family in black America. *Journal of Black Studies, 23*, 472–491.

Diener, E. D. (1984). Subjective well-being. *Psychological Bulletin, 95*, 542–575.

Dienstag, E. (1986, March). Influences of maternal age and work status on adjustment to parenthood. *Dissertation Abstracts International, 47C*(9–8), 3979–3980.

Dindia, K., & Allen, M. (1992). Sex differences in self-disclosure: A meta-analysis. *Psychological Bulletin, 11*, 106–124.

Dinnerstein, D. (1977). *The mermaid and the minotaur.* New York: Harper & Row.

Dino, G. A., Barnett, M. A., & Howard, J. A. (1984). Children's expectations of sex differences in parents' responses to sons and daughters encountering interpersonal problems. *Sex Roles, 11*, 709–717.

Dion, K. L., & Dion, K. K. (1973). Correlates of romantic love. *Journal of Consulting and Clinical Psychology, 41*, 51–56.

Dixon, J. K. (1985). Sexuality and relationship changes in married females following the commencement of bisexual activity. *Journal of Homosexuality, 11*, 115–133.

Dobash, R. E., & Dobash, R. P. (1984). The nature and antece-dents of violent events. *British Journal of Criminology, 24*, 269–288.

Dobash, R. P., Dobash, R. E., Wilson, M., & Daly, M. (1992). The myth of sexual symmetry in marital violence. *Social Problems, 39*, 71–91.

Dodson, B. (1987). *Sex for one: The joy of self-loving.* New York: Crown.

Doherty, R. W., Orimoto, L., Singelis, T. M., Hatfield, E., & Hebb, J. (1995). Emotional contagion: Gender and occupational differences. *Psychology of Women Quarterly, 19*, 355–371.

Doherty, W. J., & Jacobson, N. S. (1982). Marriage and family. In B. B. Wolman (Ed.), *Handbook of developmental psychology.* Englewood Cliffs, NJ: Prentice-Hall.

Doka, K. J., & Mertz, M. E. (1988). The meaning and significance of great-grandparenthood. *Gerontologist, 28*, 192–197.

Dolgin, K. G., Meyer, L., & Schwartz, J. (1991). Effects of gender, target's gender, topic, and self-esteem on disclosure to best and middling friends. *Sex Roles, 25*, 311–329.

Donato, K. M., & Bowker, L. H. (1984). Understanding the helpseeking behavior of battered women: A comparison of traditional service agencies and women's groups. *International Journal of Women's Studies, 7*, 99–109.

Donelson, E. (1977a). Development of sex-typed behavior and self-concept. In E. Donelson & J. E. Gullahorn (Eds.), *Women: A psychological perspective.* New York: Wiley.

Donelson, E. (1977b). Becoming a single woman. In E. Donelson & J. E. Gullahorn (Eds.), *Women: A psychological perspective.* New York: Wiley.

Donelson, E. (1984). *Nurture.* Philadelphia: Westminster Press.

Donelson, E., & Gullahorn, J. G. (1977). Individual and interpersonal achievement. In E. Donelson & J. E. Gullahorn (Eds.), *Women: A psychological perspective.* New York: Wiley.

Donnerstein, E. (1983). Aggressive pornography: Can it influence aggression toward women? In G. W. Albee, S. Gordon, & H. Leitenberg (Eds.), *Promoting sexual responsibility and preventing sexual problems* (pp. 220–237). Hanover, NH: University Press of New England.

Donnerstein, E., Linz, D., & Penrod, S. (1987). *The question of pornography: Research findings and policy implications.* New York: Free Press.

Doress, P. B., & Siegal, D. L., and the Middle and Older Women Book Project in cooperation with the Boston Women's Health Book Collective. (1987). *Ourselves, growing older: Women aging with knowledge and power.* New York: Simon & Schuster.

Dornbusch, S., Gross, R. T., Duncan, P. D. & Ritter, P. L. (1987). Stanford studies of adolescence using the national health examination survey. In R. M. Lerner & T. T. Foch (Eds.), *Biological-psychosocial interactions in early adolescence.* Hillsdale, NJ: Erlbaum.

Douthitt, R. A. (1989). The division of labor within the home: Have gender roles changed? *Sex Roles, 20*, 693–704.

Douvan, E., & Adelson, J. (1966). *The adolescent experience.* New York: Simon & Schuster.

Dovidio, J. F., Allen, J. L., & Schroeder, D. A. (1990). Specificity of empathy-induced helping: Evidence for altruistic motivation. *Journal of Personality and Social Psychology, 59*, 249–260.

Dovidio, J. F., Brown, C. E., Heltman, K., Ellyson, S. L., & Keating, C. F. (1988). Power displays between women and men in discussions of gender-linked tasks: A multichannel study. *Journal of Personality and Social Psychology, 55*, 580–587.

Downs, A. C. (1981). Sex-role stereotyping on prime-time television. *Journal of Genetic Psychology, 138*, 253–258.

Downs, A. C., & Gowan, D. C. (1980). Sex differences in reinforcement and punishment on prime-time television. *Sex Roles, 6*, 683–694.

Downs, A. C., & Langlois, J. H. (1988). Sex typing: Construct and measurement issues. *Sex Roles, 18*, 87–100.

Doyle, J. A., & Paludi, M. A. (1991). *Sex and gender* (2nd ed.). Dubuque, IA: William C. Brown.

Dreifus, C. (1975, December). Sterilizing the poor. *Progressive*, pp. 13–19.

Dreyer, P. H. (1982). Sexuality during adolescence. In B. B. Wolman (Ed.), *Handbook of developmental psychology* (pp. 559–601). Englewood Cliffs, NJ: Prentice-Hall.

Drigotas, S. M., Rusbult, C. E., & Caryl, E. (1992). Should I stay or should I go: A dependence model of breakups. *Journal of Personality and Social Psychology, 62*, 62–87.

Drogosz, L. M., & Levy, P. E. (1996). Another look at the effects of appearance, gender and job type on performance-based decisions. *Psychology of Women Quarterly, 20*, 437–445.

Dubas, J. S., Graber, J. A., & Petersen, A. C. (1991). A longitudinal investigation of adolescents' changing perceptions of pubertal timing. *Developmental Psychology, 27*, 580–586.

Duck, S., & Wright, P. H. (1993). Reexamining gender differences in same-gender friendships: A close look at two kinds of data. *Sex Roles, 28*, 709–727.

Dugger, K. (1991). Social location and gender-role attitudes: A comparison of Black and White women. In J. Lorber & S. A. Farrell (Eds.), *The social construction of gender* (pp. 38–59). Newbury Park, CA: Sage.

Duindam, V., & Spruijt, E. (1997). Caring fathers in the Netherlands. *Sex Roles, 36*, 149–170.

Duncan, G. J., Hoffman, S. D. (1991). Reconsideration of the economic consequences of marital dissolution. *Demography, 22*, 485.

Dunkle, J. H., & Francis, P. L. (1990). The role of facial masculinity/femininity in the attribution of homosexuality. *Sex Roles, 23*, 157–167.

Dunn, J., Bretherton, I., & Munn, P. (1987). Conversation about feeling states between mothers and their young children. *Developmental Psychology, 23*, 132–139.

Dunn, M. M. (1980). Saints and sisters: Congregational and Quaker women in the early colonial period. In J. W. James (Ed.), *Women in American religion*. Philadelphia: University of Pennsylvania Press.

Dunning, J. (1997, August 3). Eating disorders remain problem for female dancers. *Detroit Free Press*.

Dura, J. R., & Bornstein, R. A. (1989). Differences between IQ and school achievement in anorexia nervosa. *Journal of Clinical Psychology, 45*, 433–435.

Durkin, K. (1987). Social cognition and social context in the construction of sex differences. In M. A. Baker (Ed.), *Sex differences in human performance*. Chichester: Wiley.

Dutton, D. G. (1986). Wife assaulters' explanations for assault: The neutralization of self-punishment. *Canadian Journal of Behavioral Science, 18*, 381–390.

Dutton, D. G., & Strachan, C. E. (1987). Motivational needs for power and spouse-specific assertiveness in assaultive and nonassaultive men. *Violence and Victims, 2*, 145–156.

Duxbury, L. E., & Higgins, C. A. (1991). Gender differences in work-family conflict. *Journal of Applied Psychology, 76*, 60–74.

Dweck, C. S., Davidson, W., Nelson, S., & Enna, B. (1978). Sex differences in learned helplessness: II. The contingencies of evaluative feedback in the classroom, and III. An experimental analysis. *Developmental Psychology, 14*, 268–276.

Dweck, C. S., & Elliot, E. S. (1983). Achievement motivation. In P. H. Mussen (Ed.), *Handbook of child psychology* (4th ed.). New York: Wiley.

Dweck, C. S., Goetz, T. E., & Strauss, N. L. (1980). Sex differences in learned helplessness: IV. An experimental and naturalistic study of failure generalization and its mediators. *Journal of Personality and Social Psychology, 38*, 441–452.

Dworkin, A. (1981). *Pornography: Men possessing women*. New York: Plenum.

Dworkin, A. (1987). *Intercourse*. New York: Free Press.

Dworkin, A., & MacKinnon, C. A. (1988). *Pornography & civil rights: A new day for women's equality*. Minneapolis: Organizing Against Pornography.

Dwyer, C. A. (1979). The role of tests and their construction in producing apparent sex-related differences. In M. A. Wittig & A. C. Peterson (Eds.), *Sex-related differences in cognitive functioning: Developmental issues* (pp. 335–353). New York: Academic Press.

Dyer, G., & Tiggermann, M. (1996). The effect of school environment on body concerns in adolescent women. *Sex Roles, 34*, 127–138.

Eagan, A. B. (1983, October). The selling of premenstrual syndrome. *Ms.*, 26–31.

Eagly, A. (1983). Gender and social influences. A social psychological analysis. *American Psychologist, 38*, 971–981.

Eagly, A. H. (1987). *Sex differences in social behavior: A social-role interpretation*. Hillsdale, NJ: Erlbaum.

Eagly, A. H. (1995). The science and politics of comparing women and men. *American Psychologist, 50*, 145–158.

Eagly, A. H., & Carli, L. L. (1981). Sex of researchers and sex-typed communications as determinants of sex differences in influenceability: A meta-analysis of social influence studies. *Psychological Bulletin, 90*, 1–20.

Eagly, A. H., & Chrvala, C. (1986). Sex differences in conformity: Status and gender-role interpretations. *Psychology of Women Quarterly, 10*, 203–220.

Eagly, A. H., & Crowley, M. (1986). Gender and helping behavior: A meta-analytic review of the social psychological literature. *Psychological Bulletin, 100*, 203–220.

Eagly, A. H., & Johnson, B. T. (1990). Gender and leadership style: A meta-analysis. *Psychological Bulletin, 108*, 233–256.

Eagly, A. H., & Karau, S. J. (1991). Gender and the emergence of leaders: A meta-analysis. *Journal of Personality and Social Psychology, 60*, 685–710.

Eagly, A. H., Makhijani, M. G., & Klonsky, B. G. (1992). Gender and the evaluation of leaders: A meta-analysis. *Psychological Bulletin, 111*, 3–22.

Eagly, A. H., & Mladinic, A. (1989). Gender stereotypes and attitudes toward women and men. *Personality and Social Psychology Bulletin, 15*, 543–558.

Eagly, A. H., Mladinic, A., & Otto, S. (1991). Are women evaluated more favorably than men? *Psychology of Women Quarterly, 15*, 203–216.

Eagly, A. H., and Steffen, V. J. (1984). Gender stereotypes stem from the distribution of women and men into social roles. *Journal of Personality and Social Psychology, 46*, 735–754.

Eagly, A. H., & Steffen, V. J. (1986a). Gender and aggressive behavior: A meta-analytic review of the social psychological literature. *Psychological Bulletin, 100,* 309–330.

Eagly, A. H., & Steffen, V. J. (1986b). Gender stereotypes, occupational roles, and beliefs about part-time employees. *Psychology of Women Quarterly, 10,* 252–262.

Eagly, A. H., & Wood, W. (1982). Inferred sex differences in status as a determinant of gender stereotypes about social influence. *Journal of Personality and Social Psychology, 43,* 915–928.

Eagly, A. H., & Wood, W. (1985). Gender and influenceability: Stereotype versus behavior. In V. O'Leary, R. Unger, & B. Wallston (Eds.), *Women, gender, and social psychology* (pp. 225–256). Hillsdale, NJ: Erlbaum.

Eagly, A. H., Wood, W., & Fishbaugh, L. (1981). Sex differences in conformity: Surveillance by the group as a determinant of male nonconformity. *Journal of Personality and Social Psychology, 40,* 384–394.

Eakins, B. W., & Eakins, R. G. (1978). *Sex differences in human communication.* Boston: Houghton Mifflin.

Eccles, J. S. (1989). Bringing young women to math and science. In M. Crawford & M. Gentry (Eds.), *Gender and thought: Psychological perspectives* (pp. 36–58). New York: Springer-Verlag.

Eccles, J. S., Adler, T., & Meece, J. L. (1984). Sex differences in achievement: A test of alternate theories. *Journal of Personality and Social Psychology, 46,* 26–43.

Eccles, J. S., & Jacobs, J. E. (1986). Social forces shape math attitudes and performance. *Signs: Journal of Women in Culture and Society, 11,* 367–380.

Eccles, J. S., Wigfield, A., Harold, R. D., & Blumenfeld, P. (1993). Age and gender differences in children's self- and task perceptions during elementary school. *Child Development, 64,* 830–847.

Eckert, E. D. (1985). Characteristics of anorexia nervosa. In J. E. Mitchell (Ed.), *Anorexia nervosa and bulimia diagnosis and treatment.* Minneapolis: University of Minnesota Press.

Eckes, T. (1996). Linking female and male subtypes to situations: A range-of-situation-fit effect. *Sex Roles, 35,* 401–426.

Edmonds, M. M. (1993). Physical health. In J. S. Jackson, L. M. Chatters, & R. J. Taylor (Eds.), *Aging in Black America* (pp. 151–165). Newbury Park, CA: Sage.

Edwards, A., & Polite, C. K. (1992). *Children of the dream: The psychology of Black success.* New York: Doubleday.

Edwards, V. J., & Spence, J. T. (1987). Gender-related traits, stereotypes, and schemata. *Journal of Personality and Social Psychology, 53,* 146–154.

Ehrhardt, A. A. (1985). Psychobiology of gender. In A. Rossi (Ed.), *Gender and the life course* (pp. 81–96). Hawthorne, NY: Aldine.

Ehrhardt, A. A., & Baker, S. W. (1974). Fetal androgens, human central nervous system differentiation, and behavior sex differences. In R. Friedman, R. Richart, & R. Vande Wiele (Eds.), *Sex differences in behavior.* New York: Wiley.

Ehrhardt, A. A., Greenberg, N., & Money, J. (1970). Female gender identity and absence of fetal hormones: Turner's syndrome. *Johns Hopkins Medical Journal, 126,* 237–248.

Ehrhardt, A. A., & Meyer-Bahlburg, H. F. L. (1981). Effects of prenatal sex hormones on gender-related behavior. *Science, 211,* 1312–1318.

Ehrhardt, A. A., & Money, J. (1967). Protestin-induced hermaphroditism: IQ and psychosexual identity in a study of ten girls. *Journal of Sex Research, 3,* 83–100.

Ehrhart, J. K., & Sandler, B. R. (1985). *Campus gang rape: Party games?* Washington, DC: Association of American Colleges.

Ehrlich, S., & King, R. (1992). Gender-based language reform and the social construction of meaning. *Discourse and Society, 3,* 151–157.

Ehrlichman, H., & Eichenstein, R. (1992). Private wishes: Gender similarities and differences. *Sex Roles, 26,* 399–422.

Eichenbaum, L., & Orbach, S. (1988). *Between women: Love, envy, and competition in women's friendships.* New York: Viking Penguin.

Eichinger, J., Heifetz, L. J., & Ingraham, C. (1991). Situational shifts in sex role orientation: Correlates of work satisfaction and burnout among women in special education. *Sex Roles, 25,* 425–440.

Eichorn, D. H. (1976). Asynchronizations in adolescent development. In S. E. Drapasten & G. H. Elders (Eds.), *Adolescence in the life cycle: Psychological change and social context.* Washington, DC: Hemisphere.

Eisenberg, A. R. (1988). Grandchildren's perspectives on relationships with grandparents: The influence of gender across generations. *Sex Roles, 19,* 205–217.

Eisenberg, N., & Lennon, R. (1983). Sex differences in empathy and related capacities. *Psychological Bulletin, 94,* 100–131.

Eisenberg, N., Wolchik, S. A., Hernandez, R., & Pasternack, J. F. (1985). Parental socialization of young children's play: A short-term longitudinal study. *Child Development, 56,* 1506–1513.

Eldridge, N. S., & Gilbert L. A. (1990). Correlates of relationship satisfaction in lesbian couples. *Psychology of Women Quarterly, 14,* 43–62.

Eliason, M. J. (1995). Accounts of sexual identity formation in heterosexual students. *Sex Roles, 32,* 821–834.

Eliason, M. J. (1996). Identity formation for lesbian, bisexual, and gay persons: Beyond a "minoritizing" view. *Journal of Homosexuality, 29.*

Elkins, L. E., & Peterson, C. (1993). Gender differences in best friendships. *Sex Roles, 29,* 497–508.

Ellis, A. (1945). The sexual psychology of human hermaphrodites. *Psychosomatic Medicine, 7,* 108–125.

Ellis, A. (1973). *Humanistic psychotherapy: The rational-emotive approach.* New York: McGraw-Hill.

Ellis, B., & Symons, D. (1990). Sex differences in sexual fantasy: An evolutionary psychological approach. *Journal of Sex Research, 27,* 527–555.

Ellis, E. M. (1983). A review of empirical rape research: Victim reactions and response to treatment. *Clinical Psychology Review, 3,* 473–490.

Ellis, H. (1915). *Studies in the psychology of sex: Inversion theory* (3rd ed.). Philadelphia: F. A. Davis.

Ellis, L., & Ames, M. (1987). Neurohormonal functioning and sexual orientation: A theory of homosexuality and heterosexuality. *Psychological Bulletin, 101,* 233–258.

Ellison, C. G. (1994). Religion: The life stress paradigm and the study of depression. In J. S. Levin (Ed.), *Religion in aging and health: Theoretical foundations and methodological frontiers* (pp. 78–121). Thousand Oaks, CA: Sage.

Emmerich, W., & Shepard, K. (1984). Cognitive factors in the development of sex-typed preferences. *Sex Roles, 11,* 997–1007.

Emmons, C. A., Biernat, M., Tiedje, L. B., Lang, E., & Wortman, C. B. (1990). Stress, support, and coping among women professionals with preschool children. In J. Eckenrode & S. Gore (Eds.), *Stress between work and family* (pp. 61–93). New York: Plenum.

Emswiller, S. N., & Emswiller, T. N. (1974). *Women and worship.* New York: Harper & Row.

Ende, J. (1986). Screening for sexual dysfunction. Special Issue: The physician's guide to sexual counseling. *Medical Aspects of Human Sexuality, 20,* 10–14.

England, P., & McCreary, L. (1987). Gender inequality in paid employment. In B. B. Hess & M. M. Ferree (Eds.), *Analyzing gender: A handbook of social science research* (pp. 286–320). Newbury Park, CA: Sage.

Enoch, M. D., Trethowan, W. H., & Barker, J. C. (1967). The couvade syndrome. In M. P. Enoch (Ed.), *Some uncommon psychiatric syndromes.* Bristol: John Wright and Sons.

Entwisle, D. (1985). Becoming a parent. In L. Abate (Ed.), *The handbook of family psychology and therapy* (Vol. 1). Homestead, IL: Dorsey Press.

Entwisle, D. R., Alexander, K. L., Pallas, A. M., & Cadigan, D. (1987). The emergent academic self-image of first graders: Its responses to social structure. *Child Development, 58,* 1190.

Entwisle, D. R., & Baker, D. P. (1983). Gender and young children's expectations for performance in arithmetic. *Developmental Psychology, 19,* 200–209.

Entwisle, D. R., & Doering, S. (1981). *The first birth: A family turning point.* Baltimore: Johns Hopkins University Press.

Entwisle, D. R., & Doering, S. (1988). The emergent father role. *Sex Roles, 18,* 119–141.

Epperson, S. E. (1988, September 16). Studies link subtle sex bias in schools with women's behavior in workplace. *Wall Street Journal,* p. 27.

Epstein, S. (1992). Coping ability, negative self-evaluation, and overgeneralization: Experiment and theory. *Journal of Personality and Social Psychology, 62,* 826–836.

Erikson, E. H. (1950/1963). *Childhood and society* (2nd ed.). New York: Norton.

Erikson, E. H. (1968). *Identity: Youth and crisis.* New York: Norton.

Erikson, E. H. (1980). *Identity and the life cycle.* New York: Norton.

Erikson, E. H. (1982). *The life cycle completed: A review.* New York: Norton.

Ernster, V. L. (1975). American menstrual expressions. *Sex Roles, 1,* 3–13.

Eron, L. D. (1987). The development of aggressive behavior from the perspective of a developing behaviorism. *American Psychologist, 42,* 435–442.

Eshtain, J. B. (1987). *Women and war.* New York: Basic Books.

Eskilson, A., & Wiley, M. G. (1996). The best teacher: Mediating effects of experience with employed women on men managers' responses to subordinates' mistakes. *Sex Roles, 34,* 237–252.

Espin, O. M. (1987). Issues of identity in the psychology of Latina lesbians. In Boston Lesbian Psychologies Collective (Ed.), *Lesbian psychologies: Explorations and challenges.* Urbana: University of Illinois Press.

Espin, O. M. (1992). Cultural and historical influences on sexuality in Hispanic/Latin women. In M. L. Anderson & P. H. Collins (Eds.), *Race, class, and gender: An anthology.* Belmont, CA: Wadsworth.

Essex, M. J., & Nam, S. (1987). Marital status and loneliness among older women: The differential importance of close family and friends. *Journal of Marriage and the Family, 49,* 93–106.

Esterberg, K. G. (1996). Gay cultures, gay communities: The social organization of lesbians, gay men, and bisexuals. In R. C. Savin-Williams & K. Cohen (Eds.), *The lives of lesbians, gays, and bisexuals: Children to adults* (pp. 377–392). Fort Worth, TX: Harcourt Brace.

Etaugh, C. (1993). Women in the middle and later years. In F. L. Denmark & M. A. Paludi (Eds.), *Psychology of women: A handbook of issues and theories* (pp. 213–246). Westport, CT: Greenwood Press.

Etaugh, C., & Brown, B. (1975). Perceiving the causes of success and failure of male and female performers. *Developmental Psychology, 11,* 103.

Etaugh, C., & Duits, T. (1990). Development of gender discrimination: Role of stereotypic and counterstereotypic gender cues. *Sex Roles, 23,* 215–222.

Etaugh, C., Grinnell, K., & Etaugh, A. (1989). Development of gender labeling: Effect of age of pictured children. *Sex Roles, 21,* 769–773.

Etaugh, C., Levine, D., & Mennella, A. (1984). Development of sex biases in children: 40 years later. *Sex Roles, 10,* 911–922.

Etaugh, C., & Liss, M. B. (1992). Home, school, and playroom training grounds for adult gender roles. *Sex Roles, 26,* 129–147.

Etaugh, C., & Study, G. G. (1989). Perceptions of mothers: Effects of employment status, marital status, and age of child. *Sex Roles, 20,* 59–70.

Ethier, K., & Deaux, K. (1990). Hispanics in Ivy: Assessing identity and perceived threat. *Sex Roles, 22,* 427–440.

Ettelbrick, P. L. (1991). Legal protections for lesbians. In B. Sang, J. Warshow, & A. J. Smith (Eds.), *Lesbians at midlife: The creative transition.* San Francisco: spinsters book company.

Etter-Lewis, G. (1988). *Power and social change: Images of Afro-American women in the print media.* Paper presented at the annual meeting of the National Women's Studies Association, Minneapolis, MN.

Etzioni, A. (1969). *The semi-professions and their organization: Teachers, nurses, social workers.* New York: William Morrow.

Evans, G. R. (1982). Defense mechanisms in females as a function of sex-role orientation. *Journal of Clinical Psychology, 38,* 816–817.

Ewen, S. (1976). *Captains of consciousness: Advertising and the social roots of the consumer culture.* New York: McGraw-Hill.

Exton-Smith, A. N. (1985). Mineral metabolism. In C. E. Finch & E. L. Schneider (Eds.), *Handbook of the biology of aging* (2nd ed., pp. 511–539). New York: Van Nostrand Reinhold.

Faden, V. B. (1977). *Primary diagnoses of discharges from nonfederal general hospital psychiatric inpatient units, U.S., 1975 (Mental health statistical note 137).* Rockville, MD: Department of Health, Education, and Welfare Publications.

Fagan, J. F., & Shepherd, P. A. (1982). Theoretical issues in the early development of visual perception. In M. Lewis & L. Taft (Eds.), *Developmental disabilities: Theory, assessment, and intervention.* New York: Medical & Scientific Books.

Fagot, B. I. (1974). Sex differences in toddlers' behavior and parental reaction. *Developmental Psychology, 10,* 554–558.

Fagot, B. I. (1978). The influences of sex of child on parental reactions to toddler children. *Child Development, 49,* 459–465.

Fagot, B. I. (1985). Beyond the reinforcement principle: Another step toward understanding sex role development. *Development Psychology, 21,* 1092–1104.

Fagot, B. I., & Hagan, R. (1985). Aggression in toddlers: Responses to the assertive acts of boys and girls. *Sex Roles, 12,* 341–351.

Fagot, B. I., & Hagan, R. (1991). Observations of parent reactions to sex-stereotyped behaviors: Age and sex effects. *Child Development, 62,* 617–628.

Fagot, B. I., & Leinbach, M. D. (1987). Socialization of sex roles within the family. In B. Carter (Ed.), *Current conceptions of sex roles and sex typing: Theory and research.* New York: Praeger.

Fagot, B. I., & Leinbach, M. D. (1989). The young child's gender schema: Environmental input, internal organization. *Child Development, 60,* 663–672.

Fagot, B. I., & Patterson, G. R. (1969). An "in vivo" analysis of reinforcing contingencies for sex role behavior in the preschool child. *Developmental Psychology, 11,* 563–568.

Falbo, T., & Peplau, L. A. (1980). Power strategies in intimate relationships. *Journal of Personality and Social Psychology, 38,* 618–628.

Falbo, T., & Polit, D. F. (1986). Quantitative review of the only child literature: Research evidence and theory development. *Psychological Bulletin, 100,* 176–189.

Fallon, A. E., & Rozin, P. (1985). Sex differences in perceptions of desirable body shape. *Journal of Abnormal Psychology, 94,* 102–105.

Fallon, P., Katzman, M. A., & Wolley, S. C. (Eds.). (1994). *Feminist perspectives on eating disorders.* New York: Guilford Press.

Faludi, S. (1991). *Backlash: The undeclared war against American women.* New York: Crown Publishers.

Farber, E. A., & Egeland, B. (1982). Developmental consequences of out-of-home care for infants in a low-income population. In E. F. Zigler & E. W. Gordon (Eds.), *Day care: Scientific and social policy issues.* Boston: Auburn House.

Farber, N. (1992). Sexual standards and activity: Adolescents' perceptions. *Child and Adolescent Social Work, 9,* 53–76.

Farkas, G., Grobe, R. P., Sheehan, D., & Shuan, Y. (1990). Cultural resources and school success: Gender, ethnicity, and poverty groups within an urban school district. *American Sociological Review, 55,* 127.

Fausto-Sterling, A. (1985). *Myths of gender: Biological theories about women and men.* New York: Basic Books.

Fausto-Sterling, A. (1989). Life in the XY corral. *Women's Studies International Forum, 12,* 312–331.

Fausto-Sterling, A. (1992). *Myths of gender: Biological theories about women and men* (2nd ed.). New York: Basic Books.

Fausto-Sterling, A. (1995). Animal models for the development of human sexuality: A critical evaluation. *Journal of Homosexuality, 28,* 217–236.

Feather, N. T. (1985). Masculinity, femininity, self-esteem, and subclinical depression. *Sex Roles, 12,* 491–500.

Feather, N. T., & Simon, J. G. (1975). Reactions to male and female success and failure in sex-linked occupations: Impressions of personality, causal attributions, and perceived likelihood of different consequences. *Journal of Personality and Social Psychology, 31,* 20–31.

Fedigan, L. M. (1982). *Primate paradigm: Sex roles and social bonds.* Montreal: Eden Press.

Fehr, B. (1993). How do I love thee? Let me consult my prototype. In S. Duck (Ed.), *Individuals in relationships* (pp. 87–120). Newbury Park, CA: Sage.

Feild, H. S. (1978). Attitudes toward rape: A comparative analysis of police, rapists, crisis counselors, and citizens. *Journal of Personality and Social Psychology, 36,* 156–179.

Feingold, A. (1988). Cognitive gender differences are disappearing. *American Psychologist, 43,* 95–103.

Feingold, A. (1993). Cognitive gender differences: A developmental perspective. *Sex Roles, 29,* 91–112.

Feingold, A. (1994). Gender differences in variability in intellectual abilities: A cross-cultural perspective. *Sex Roles, 40,* 81–92.

Feinman, S. (1981). Why is cross sex-role behavior more approved for girls than for boys? A status characteristic approach. *Sex Roles, 7,* 289–300.

Feiring, C., & Lewis, M. (1987). Perceiving the causes of success and failure of male and female performers. *Sex Roles, 17,* 621–636.

Feiring, C., & Lewis, M. (1991). The development of social networks from early to middle childhood: Gender differences and the relation to school competence. *Sex Roles, 25,* 237–253.

Feldberg, R. (1984). Comparable worth: Toward theory and practice in the United States. *Signs, 10,* 311–328.

Feldman, S. S., & Nash, S. C. (1978). Interest in babies during young adulthood. *Child Development, 49,* 617–622.

Feldman-Summers, S., & Kiesler, S. J. (1974). Those who are number two try harder: The effects of sex on attributions of causality. *Journal of Personality and Social Psychology, 30,* 846–855.

Feldstein, J. H., & Feldstein, S. (1982). Sex differences on televised toy commercials. *Sex Roles, 8,* 581–587.

Feltey, K. M., & Poloma, M. M. (1991). From sex differences to gender role beliefs: Exploring effects on six dimensions of religiosity. *Sex Roles, 25,* 181–193.

Fengler, A. P. (1975). Attitudinal orientations of wives toward their husbands' retirement. *International Journal of Aging & Human Development, 6,* 139–152.

Fennema, E. (1990). Teachers' beliefs and gender differences in mathematics. In E. Fennema & C. G. Leder (Eds.), *Mathematics and gender* (pp. 169–187). New York: Teachers College Press.

Ferguson, L. R. (1977). The woman in the family. In E. Donelson & J. E. Gullahorn (Eds.), *Women: A psychological perspective.* New York: John Wiley.

Fernald, A., Taeschner, T., Dunn, J., Papousek, M., De Boysson-Bardies, B., & Fukui, I. (1989). A cross-language study of prosodic modifications in mothers' and fathers' speech to preverbal infants. *Journal of Child Language, 16,* 477–501.

Ferree, M. M. (1976, September). The confused American housewife. *Psychology Today, 10,* 76–80.

Ferree, M. M. (1980). Working class feminism: A consideration of the consequences of employment. *Sociological Quarterly, 21,* 173–184.

Ferree, M. M. (1985). Between two worlds: German feminist approaches to working class women and work. *Signs, 10,* 517–536.

Ferree, M. M. (1987). She works hard for a living: Gender and class on the job. In B. B. Hess & M. M. Ferree (Eds.), *Analyzing gender: A handbook of social science research* (pp. 322–347). Newbury Park, CA: Sage.

Fidell, L. (1982). Gender and drug use and abuse. In I. Al-Issa (Ed.), *Gender and psychopathology.* New York: Academic Press.

Filmore, K. M., Bacon, S. D., & Hyman, M. (1979). *The 27-year longitudinal study of drinking by students in college, 1949–1976* (Final report to the NIAAA under Contract No. [ADM] 218-76-0015). Berkeley: Social Research Group, University of California.

Fincham, F. D., & Bradbury, T. N. (1993). Marital satisfaction, depression, and attributions: A longitudinal analysis. *Journal of Personality and Social Psychology, 64,* 442–452.

Fine, M., & Asch, A. (Eds.). (1988a). *Women with disabilities.* Philadelphia: Temple University Press.

Fine, M., & Asch, A. (1988b). Epilogue: Research and politics to come. In M. Fine & A. Asch (Eds.), *Women with disabilities.* Philadelphia: Temple University Press.

Fine, M., & MacPherson, P. (1992). Over dinner: Feminism and adolescent female bodies. In M. Fine (Ed.), *Disruptive voices: The possibilities of feminist research* (pp. 175–203). Ann Arbor: University of Michigan Press.

Finkelhor, D. (1979). *Sexually victimized children.* New York: Free Press.

Finkelhor, D. (1980). Sex among siblings: A survey on prevalence, variety and effects. *Archives of Sexual Behavior, 9,* 171–194.

Finkelhor, D. (1984). *Child sexual abuse: New theory and research.* New York: Free Press.

Finkelhor, D., Hotaling, G., Lewis, I. A., & Smith, C. (1990). Sexual abuse in a national survey of adult men and women: Prevalence, characteristics, and risk factors. *Child Abuse and Neglect, 14,* 19–28.

Finkelhor, D., & Yllo, K. (1985). *License to rape: Sexual abuse of wives.* New York: Holt, Rinehart & Winston.

Finlay, B. (June, 1996). Gender differences in attitudes toward abortion among Protestant seminarians. *Reviews of Religious Research, 37,* 354.

Finlay, B., Starnes, C. E., & Alvarez, F. B. (1985). Recent changes in sex-role ideology among divorced men and women: Some possible causes and implications. *Sex Roles, 12,* 637–653.

Finley, N. J. (1989). Theories of family labor applied to gender differences in caregiving for elderly parents. *Journal of Marriage and the Family, 51,* 79–86.

Finn, J. (1986). The relationship between sex role attitudes and attitudes supporting marital violence. *Sex Roles, 14,* 235–244.

Finn, J. D. (1980). Sex differences in educational outcomes. A cross-national study. *Sex Roles, 6,* 9–26.

Finucci, J. M., & Childs, B. (1981). Are there really more dyslexic boys than girls? In A. Ansara, N. Geschwind, A. Galaburda, M. Albert, & N. Gartrell (Eds.), *Sex differences in dyslexia.* Towson, MD: Orton Dyslexia Society.

Fiorentine, R. (1988). Increasing similarity in the values and life plans of male and female college students? Evidence and implications. *Sex Roles, 18,* 143–158.

Fiorenza, E. S. (1979). Feminist spirituality: Christian identity and Catholic vision. In C. Christ & J. Plaskow (Eds.), *Womanspirit rising: A feminist reader in religion.* San Francisco: Harper & Row.

Fiorenza, E. S. (1983). *In memory of her: A feminist theological reconstruction of Christian origins.* Lavergne, TN: Crossroad Publishing Co.

Fischer, G. J. (1997). Gender effects on individual verdicts and on mock jury verdicts in a simulated acquaintance rape trial. *Sex Roles, 36,* 491–501.

Fischer, L. R. (1986). *Linked lives: Adult daughters and their mothers.* New York: Harper & Row.

Fisher, B. (1991). A biological perspective of breast cancer. *CA—A Cancer Journal for Clinicians, 41,* 91–111.

Fisher, B., & Galler, R. (1988). Friendship and fairness: How disability affects friendship between women. In M. Fine & A. Asch (Eds.), *Women with disabilities.* Philadelphia: Temple University Press.

Fisher, B., et al. (1985a). Five-year results of a randomized clinical trial comparing total mastectomy and segmental mastectomy with or without radiation in the treatment of breast cancer. *New England Journal of Medicine, 312,* 665–673.

Fisher, B., et al. (1985b). Ten-year results of a randomized clinical trial comparing total mastectomy and segmental mastectomy with or without radiation in the treatment of breast cancer. *New England Journal of Medicine, 312,* 674–681.

Fisher, J. D., & Fisher, W. A. (1992). Changing AIDS-risk behavior. *Psychological Bulletin, 111,* 455–474.

Fisher, W. A. (1983). Gender, gender-role identification, and response to erotica. In E. R. Allgeier & N. B. McCormick (Eds.), *Changing boundaries.* Palo Alto, CA: Mayfield.

Fisher, W. A., & Byrne, D. (1978). Sex differences in response to erotica? Love versus lust. *Journal of Personality and Social Psychology, 36,* 117–125.

Fisher-Thompson, D. (1990). Adult sex-typing of children's toys. *Sex Roles, 23,* 291–303.

Fiske, S. T. (1993). Controlling other people: The impact of power on stereotyping. *American Psychologist, 48,* 628.

Fiske, S. T., Bersoff, D. N., Borgida, E., Deaux, K., & Heilman, M. E. (1991). Social science research on trial: Use of sex stereotyping research in Price Waterhouse v. Hopkins. *American Psychologist, 46,* 1049–1060.

Fiske, S. T., & Stevens, L. E. (1993). What's so special about sex? Gender stereotyping and discrimination. In S. Oskamp & M. Costanzo (Eds.), *Gender issues in contemporary society* (pp. 173–196). Newbury Park, CA: Sage.

Fitzgerald, H. E. (1977). Infants and caregivers: Sex differences as determinants of socialization. In E. Donelson & J. Gullahorn (Eds.), *Women: A psychological perspective.* New York: Wiley.

Fitzgerald, H. E., Strommen, E. A., & McKinney, J. P. (1977). *Developmental psychology: The infant and young child.* Homewood, IL: Dorsey Press.

Fitzgerald, L. F. (1993). Sexual harassment: Violence against women in the workplace. *American Psychologist, 48,* 1070–1076.

Fitzgerald, L. F., & Ormerod, A. J. (1991). Perceptions of sexual harassment: The influence of gender and academic context. *Psychology of Women Quarterly, 15,* 281–294.

Fitzgerald, L. F., Shullman, S. L., Balley, N., Richards, M., Swecker, J., Gold, Y., Ormerod, A. J., & Weitzman, L. (1988). The incidence and dimensions of sexual harassment in academia and the workplace. *Journal of Vocational Behavior, 32,* 152–175.

Fitzpatrick, M. A. (1984). A topological approach to marital interaction—Recent theory and research. *Advances in Experimental Sociology, 18,* 1–47.

Fitzpatrick, M. A. (1988). *Between husbands and wives: Communication in marriage.* Newbury Park, CA: Sage.

Fivush, R. (1989). Exploring sex differences in the emotional content of mother-child conversations about the past. *Sex Roles, 20,* 675–691.

Fivush, R. (1991). Gender and emotion in mother-child conversations about the past. *Journal of Narrative and Life History, 1*, 325–341.

Fivush, R. (1993). Emotional content of parent-child conversations about the past. In C. A. Nelson (Ed.), *The Minnesota Symposium on Child Psychology: Vol. 26. Memory and affect in development*. Hillsdale, NJ: Erlbaum.

Flagg, F. (1987). *Fried green tomatoes at the Whistle Stop Cafe*. New York: McGraw-Hill.

Flaks, D. K., Ficher, I., Masterpasqua, F., & Joseph, G. (1995). Lesbians choosing motherhood: A comparative study of lesbian and heterosexual parents and their children. *Developmental Psychology, 31*, 105–114.

Flanagan, C. A. (1990). Change in family work status: Effects on parent-adolescent decision-making. *Child Development, 61*, 163–177.

Flannagan, D., Baker-Ward, L., Graham, L. (1995). Talk about preschool: Patterns of topic discussion and elaboration related to gender and ethnicity. *Sex Roles, 32*, 1–15.

Fleischer, R. A., & Chertkoff, J. M. (1986). Effects of dominance and sex on leader selection in dyadic work groups. *Journal of Personality and Social Psychology, 50*, 94–99.

Fleming, A. S., Ruble, D. N., Flett, G. L., & Shaul, D. L. (1988). Postpartum adjustment in first-time mothers: Effects of mood in maternal attitudes and behavior. *Developmental Psychology, 24*, 71–81.

Fleming, A. S., Ruble, D. N., Flett, G. L., & Wagner, V. V. (1990). Adjustment in first-time mothers: Changes in mood and mood content during the early postpartum months. *Developmental Psychology, 26*, 137–143.

Fleming, J. (1983a). Black women in black and white college environments: The making of a matriarch. *Journal of Social Issues, 39*, 41–54.

Fleming, J. (1983b). Sex differences in the educational and occupational goals of black college students. In M. Horner, C. C. Nadelson, & M. T. Notham (Eds.), *The challenge of change* (pp. 297–314). New York: Plenum.

Fleming, J. (1984). *Blacks in college*. San Francisco: Jossey-Bass.

Flessati, S. L., & Jamieson, J. (1991). Gender differences in mathematics anxiety: An artifact of response bias? *Anxiety Research, 3*, 303–312.

Fletcher, G. J. O., Fincham, F. D., Cramer, L., & Heron, N. (1987). The role of attributions in the development of dating relationships. *Journal of Personality and Social Psychology, 53*, 481–489.

Flint, M., & Samil, R. S. (1990). Cultural and subcultural meanings of the menopause. In M. Flint, F. Kronenberg, & W. Utian (Eds.), *Multidisciplinary perspectives on menopause: Annals of the New York Academy of Sciences, 592*, 134–155.

Fodor, I. G. (1982). Gender and phobia. In I. Al-Issa (Ed.), *Gender and psychopathology*. New York: Academic Press.

Ford, C. S. (1945). *A comparative study of human reproduction*. New Haven: Yale University Press.

Ford, C. S., & Beach, F. A. (1951). *Patterns of sexual behavior*. New York: Harper & Row.

Ford, M. R., & Lowery, C. R. (1986). Gender differences in moral reasoning: A comparison of the use of justice and care orientations. *Journal of Personality and Social Psychology, 50*.

Foreit, K. G., Agor, A. T., Byers, J., Larue, J., Lokey, H., Palazzini, M., Patterson, M., & Smith, L. (1980). Sex bias in the newspaper treatment of male-centered and female-centered news stories. *Sex Roles, 6*, 475–480.

Forrest, L., & Gilbert, M. S. (1992). Infertility: An unanticipated and prolonged life crisis. Special Issue: Women and health. *Journal of Mental Health Counseling, 14*, 42–58.

Foushee, H. C., Davis, M. H., & Archer, R. L. (1979). Empathy, masculinity, and femininity. *JSAS Catalogue of Selected Documents in Psychology, 9*, 85 (Ms. No. 1974).

Fowers, B. J. (1991). His and her marriage: A multivariate study of gender and marital satisfaction. *Sex Roles, 24*, 209–221.

Fox, A. (1991). Development of a bisexual identity: Understanding the process. In L. Hutchins & L. Kaahumanu (Eds.), *Bi any other name: Bisexual people speak out*. Boston: Alyson Publications.

Fox, G. L. (1982). *The childbearing decision: Fertility attitudes and behavior*. Beverly Hills, CA: Sage.

Fox, J. H. (1977). Effects of retirement and former work life on women's adaptation in old age. *Journal of Gerontology, 32*, 196–202.

Fox, L. H. (1981). *The problem of women and mathematics*. New York: Ford Foundation.

Fox, L. H., & Cohen, S. (1980). Sex differences in the development of precocious mathematical talent. In L. H. Fox, L. Brody, & G. Tobin (Eds.), *Women and the mathematical mystique* (pp. 94–112). Baltimore: Johns Hopkins University Press.

Fox, M. (1993). Politics and literature: Chasing the "isms" from children's books. *The Reading Teacher, 46*, 654–658.

Fox, M., Gibbs, M., & Auerbach, D. (1985). Age and gender dimensions of friendship. *Psychology of Women Quarterly, 9*, 489–501.

Fox, M. F., & Hesse-Biber, S. (1984). *Women at work*. Palo Alto, CA: Mayfield.

Fox, M. S. (1979). On the diagnosis and treatment of breast cancer. *Journal of the American Medical Association, 241*, 489–494.

Frable, D. E. S. (1989). Sex typing and gender ideology: Two facets of the individual's gender psychology that go together. *Journal of Personality and Social Psychology, 56*, 95–108.

Frable, D. E. S., & Bem, S. L. (1985). If you are gender schematic, all members of the opposite sex look alike. *Journal of Personality and Social Psychology, 49*, 459–468.

Frances, S. J. (1979). Sex differences in nonverbal behavior. *Sex Roles, 5*, 519–535.

Francke, L. B. (1982). *The ambivalence of abortion*. New York: Laurel/Dell.

Frank, A. (1952). *Anne Frank: The diary of a young girl*. Garden City, NY: Doubleday.

Frank, J. G. (1989). *Risk factors for self-reported rape in prisoners and college students*. Unpublished doctoral dissertation, University of South Carolina.

Frank, R. T. (1931). The hormonal causes of premenstrual tension. *Archives of Neurology and Psychiatry, 26*, 1053–1057.

Frank, S., & Jackson-Walker, S. (in press). Family experiences as moderators of the relationship between eating symptoms and personality disturbance. *Journal of Youth and Adolescence*.

Frank, S. J., Jacobson, S., & Tuer, M. (1990). Psychological predictors of young adults' drinking behaviors. *Journal of Personality and Social Psychology, 59*, 770–780.

Frank, S. J., Towell, P. A., & Huyck, M. (1985). The effects of sex-role traits on three aspects of psychological well-being in a sample of middle-aged women. *Sex Roles, 12*, 1073–1087.

Frankel, M. T., & Rollins, J. T. (1983). Does mother know best?

Mothers and fathers interacting with preschool sons and daughters. *Developmental Psychology, 19,* 694–702.

Franklin, C. W., II. (1987). Surviving the institutional decimation of black males: Causes, consequences, and intervention. In H. Brod (Ed.), *The making of masculinities: The new men's studies.* Boston: Allen and Unwin.

Frazer, J. G. (1951). *The golden bough.* New York: Macmillan.

Frazier, P. A., & Cohen, B. B. (1992). Research on the sexual victimization of women: Implications for counselor training. *Counseling Psychologist, 20,* 141–158.

Frazier, P. A., Klein, C., & Seales, L. (1995). *A longitudinal study of causal attributions, perceived control, coping strategies, and post-rape symptoms.* Unpublished manuscript.

Frazier, P., & Schauben, L. (1994). Causal attributions and recovery from rape and other stressful life events. *Journal of Social and Clinical Psychology, 13,* 1–14.

Frederick, C. M., & Grow, V. W. (1996). A mediational model of autonomy, self-esteem, and eating disordered attitudes and behaviors. *Psychology of Women Quarterly, 20,* 217–228.

Fredrickson, B. L., & Roberts, T. (1997). Objectification theory: Toward understanding women's lived experiences and mental health risks. *Psychology of Women Quarterly, 21,* 173–206.

Fredrickson, R. (1992). *Repressed memories: A journey to recovery from sexual abuse.* New York: Simon & Shuster.

Freedman, D. G. (1980). Cross-cultural notes on status hierarchies. In D. R. Omark, F. F. Strayer, & D. G. Freedman (Eds.), *Dominant relations: An ethological view of human conflict and social interactions.* New York: Garland Press.

Freedman, M. B., & Bereiter, C. A. (1963). A longitudinal study of personality development in college alumnae. *Merrill-Palmer Quarterly, 9,* 295–302.

Freedman, R. (1986). *Beauty bound.* Lexington, MA: Lexington Books.

Freeman, H. R. (1987). Structure and content of gender stereotypes: Effects of somatic appearance and trait information. *Psychology of Women Quarterly, 11,* 59–68.

Freeman, J. (1975). *The politics of women's liberation.* New York: Longman.

Freetly, A. J. H., & Kane, E. W. (1995). Men's and women's perceptions of non-consensual sexual intercourse. *Sex Roles, 33,* 785–802.

Freud, S. (1905/1953). Three essays on the theory of sexuality. In J. Strachey (Ed. and trans.), *The standard edition of the complete psychological works of Sigmund Freud* (Vol. 7). London: Hogarth Press.

Freud, S. (1925/1972). Some psychological consequences of the anatomical distinction between the sexes (J. Strachey, Trans.). In P. Rieff (Ed.), *Sexuality and the psychology of love.* New York: Collier.

Freud, S. (1931/1972). Female sexuality (J. Riviere, Trans.). In P. Rieff (Ed.), *Sexuality and the psychology of love.* New York: Collier.

Freud, S. (1933/1965). *New introductory lectures in psychoanalysis* (J. Strachey, Ed. and Trans.). New York: Norton.

Freud, S. (1940/1963). *An outline of psychoanalysis* (J. Strachey, Ed. and Trans.). New York: Norton.

Freud, S. (1960). *Letters of Sigmund Freud* (E. L. Freud, Ed.). New York: Basic Books.

Frey, K. S., & Ruble, D. N. (1992). Gender constancy and the cost of sex-typed behavior: A test of the conflict hypothesis. *Developmental Psychology, 28,* 714–721.

Friday, N. (1980). *Men in love.* New York: Delacorte.

Friday, N. (1991). *Women on top: How real life has changed women's sexual fantasies.* New York: Simon & Schuster.

Friedan, B. (1963/1983). *The feminine mystique.* New York: Dell Publishing.

Friedan, B. (1991, November). The dangers of the new feminine mystique. *McCalls,* pp. 78, 80, 82, 86.

Friedrich, M. A. (1983). Dysmenorrhea. In S. Golub (Ed.), *Lifting the curse of menstruation.* New York: Haworth.

Friend, T. (1990, January 26). Abuse in med school common? *USA Today,* p. 1.

Frieze, I. H. (1983). Investigating the causes and consequences of marital rape. *Signs: Journal of Women in Culture and Society, 8,* 532–553.

Frieze, I. H. (1986, August). *The female victim: Rape, wife battering, and incest.* American Psychological Association Master Lecture, annual meeting of the American Psychological Association, Washington, DC.

Frieze, I. H., & McHugh, M. C. (1992). Power and influence strategies in violent and nonviolent marriages. *Psychology of Women Quarterly, 16,* 449–465.

Frieze, I. H., & Ramsey, S. J. (1976). Nonverbal maintenance of sex roles. *Journal of Social Issues, 32,* 133–141.

Frieze, I. H., Sales, E., & Smith, C. (1991). Considering the social context in gender research: The impact of college students' life stage. *Psychology of Women Quarterly, 15,* 371–392.

Frieze, I. H., Whitley, B. E., Jr., Hanusa, B. H., & McHugh, M. C. (1982). Assessing the theoretical models for sex differences in causal attributions for success and failures. *Sex Roles, 8,* 333–343.

Frisch, R. L., & McArthur, J. (1974). Menstrual cycles: Fatness as a determinant of minimum weight for height necessary for their maintenance or onset. *Science, 185,* 949–951.

Frisch, R. L., Wyshak, G., & Vincent, L. (1980). Delayed menarche and amenorrhea in ballet dancers. *New England Journal of Medicine, 303,* 17–19.

Frodi, A., Macauley, J., & Thome, P. R. (1977). Are women always less aggressive than men? A review of the experimental literature. *Psychological Bulletin, 84,* 634–660.

Fromm, E. (1947). *Man for himself.* Greenwich, CT: Fawcett.

Fromm, E. (1956/1974). *The art of loving.* New York: Harper & Row.

Fromm, E. (1976/1981). *To have or to be?* New York: Harper & Row.

Fry, D. P. (1988). Intercommunity differences in aggression among Zapotec children. *Child Development, 59,* 1008–1019.

Fry, D. P. (1993). *The intergenerational transmission of disciplinary practices and approaches to social interactions.* New York: Garland Press.

Fry, D. P., & Gabriel, A. H. (1994). Preface: The cultural construction of gender and aggression. *Sex Roles, 30,* 165–167.

Funk, J. B., & Buchman, D. D. (1996). Children's perceptions of gender differences in social approval for playing electronic games. *Sex Roles, 35,* 219–231.

Furby, L., Weinrott, M. R., & Blaskshaw, L. (1989). Sex offender recidivism: A review. *Psychological Bulletin, 105,* 3–39.

Furnham, A., & Bitar, N. (1993). The stereotyped portrayal of men and women in British television advertisements. *Sex Roles, 29,* 297–310.

Furnham, A., & Schofield, S. (1986). Sex-role stereotyping in British radio advertisements. *British Journal of Social Psychology, 25*, 165–171.

Furstenberg, F. F., Jr., Brooks-Gunn, J., & Chase-Lansdale, L. (1989). Teenaged pregnancy and childbearing. *American Psychologist, 44*, 313–320.

Furumoto, L. (1980). Mary Whiton Calkins (1863–1930). *Psychology of Women Quarterly, 5*, 55–68.

Gagnon, J. H. (1983). Age at menarche and sexual conduct in adolescence and young adulthood. In S. Golub (Ed.), *Menarche*. Lexington, MA: Lexington Books.

Gainer, W. L. (1962). Ability of the WISC sub-tests to discriminate between boys and girls of average intelligence. *California Journal of Educational Research, 13*, 9–16.

Galambos, N. L., & Maggs, J. L. (1991). Out-of-school care of young adolescents and self-reported behavior. *Developmental Psychology, 27*, 644–655.

Gallagher, S. A. (1989). Predictors of SAT mathematics scores of gifted male and gifted female adolescents. *Psychology of Women Quarterly, 13*, 191–204.

Gallaher, P. E. (1992). Individual differences in nonverbal behavior: Dimensions of style. *Journal of Personality and Social Psychology, 63*, 133–145.

Gallant, S. J., Popiel, D. A., Hoffman, D. M., Chakraborty, P. K., & Hamilton, J. A. (1992). Using daily ratings to confirm premenstrual syndrome/late luteal phase dysphoric disorder: Part I. Effects of demand characteristics and expectations. *Psychosomatic Medicine, 54*, 149–166.

Gannon, L. (1988). The potential role of exercise in the alleviation of menstrual disorder and menopausal symptoms: A theoretical synthesis of recent research. *Women & Health, 14*, 105–127.

Ganong, L. H., & Coleman, M. (1995). The content of mother stereotypes. *Sex Roles, 32*, 495–512.

Garai, J. E., & Scheinfeld, A. (1968). Sex differences in mental and behavioral traits. *Genetic Psychology Monographs, 77*, 169–299.

Garber, L. (1991). *Vested interests*. Boston: Little, Brown.

Garcia, N., Kennedy, C., Pearlman, S. F., & Perez, J. (1987). The impact of race and culture differences: Challenges to intimacy in lesbian relationships. In Boston Lesbian Psychologies Collective (Eds.), *Lesbian psychologies: Exploration and challenge*. Urbana: University of Illinois Press.

Gargiulo, J., Brooks-Gunn, J., Attie, I., & Warren, M. P. (1987). Girls' dating behavior as a function of social context and maturation. *Developmental Psychology, 23*, 730–737.

Garner, D. M., Garfinkel, P. E., Schwartz, D. & Thompson, M. (1980). Cultural expectations of thinness in women. *Psychological Reports, 47*, 483–491.

Gartrell, N., & Mosbacher, D. (1984). Sex differences in the naming of children's genitalia. *Sex Roles, 10*, 869–876.

Gary, L. E. (1986). Predicting interpersonal conflict between men and women: The case of black men. *American Behavioral Scientist, 29*, 635–646.

Gaspar de Alba, A. (1993). Tortillerismo: Work by Chicana lesbians. *Signs, 18*, 956–963.

Gastil, J. (1990). Generic pronouns and sexist language: The oxymoronic character of masculine generics. *Sex Roles, 23*, 629–643.

Gatewood, M. C., & Weiss, A. P. (1930). Race and sex differences in newborn infants. *Journal of Genetic Psychology, 38*, 31–49.

Gatz, M., & Smyer, M. A. (1992). The mental health system and older adults in the 1990s. *American Psychologist, 47*, 741–751.

Gay, P. (1993). The adaptive function of eating disordered symptoms. *Masters and Johnson Reports*, p. 6.

Gee, E. M., & Kimball, M. M. (1987). *Women and aging*. Toronto: Butterworths.

Geis, F. L. (1993). Self-fulfilling prophecies: A social psychological view of gender. In A. E. Beall & R. J. Sternberg (Eds.), *The psychology of gender* (pp. 9–54). New York: Guilford Press.

Geis, F. L., Brown, V., Jennings, J., & Porter, N. (1984). TV commercials as achievement scripts for women. *Sex Roles, 10*, 513–524.

Gelles, R., & Straus, M. (1979). Determinants of violence in the family: Toward a theoretical integration. In W. E. Burr (Ed.), *Contemporary theories about the family* (Vol. 1). New York: Free Press.

Gelles, R., & Straus, M. (1989). *Intimate violence: The causes and consequences of abuse in the American family*. New York: Touchstone.

Gelles, R., & Straus, M. (1990). *Physical violence in American families*. New Brunswick, NJ: Transaction Publishers.

Gemson, D. H. (1990). Screening for breast cancer: Are physicians doing enough? *New York State Journal of Medicine, 90*, 285–286.

Genasco, A. P. (1995, February 15). Child care quality low. *Lansing State Journal*, p. 5B.

Genovese, E. D. (1974/1976). *Roll, Jordon, roll: The world the slaves made*. New York: Vintage Books.

George, L. K., Blazer, D. F., Winfield-Laird, I., Leaf, P. J., & Fishbach, R. L. (1988). Psychiatric disorders and mental health service use in later life: Evidence from the Epidemiologic Catchment Area program. In J. Brody & G. Maddox (Eds.), *Epidemiology and aging* (pp. 189–219). New York: Springer.

George, L. K., Fillenbaum, G., & Palmore, E. (1984). Sex differences in the antecedents and consequences of retirement. *Journal of Gerontology, 39*, 364–371.

George, L. K., & Gwyther, L. P. (1986). Caregiver well-being: A multidimensional examination of family caregivers of demented adults. *The Gerontologist, 26*, 253–259.

George, L. K., Winfield, I., & Blazer, D. G. (1992). Sociocultural factors in sexual assault: Comparison of two representative samples of women. *Journal of Social Issues, 48*, 105–126.

George, W. H., Lehman, G., Cue, K. L., Martinez, L. J., & Lopez, P. A. (1997). Postdrinking sexual inferences: Evidence for linear rather than curvilinear dosage effects. *Journal of Applied Social Psychology, 27*, 629–648.

Gerrard, M. (1987). Sex, sex guilt, and contraceptive use revisited: The 1980s. *Journal of Personality and Social Psychology, 52*, 975–980.

Gerrard, M., McCann, L., & Geis, B. D. (1984). Antecedents and prevention of unwanted pregnancy. In A. U. Rickel, M. Gerrard, & I. Iscoe (Eds.), *Social and psychological problems of women: Prevention and crisis intervention*. Washington, DC: Hemisphere.

Gerson, M. J. (1980, November). Briefcase, baby or both? *Psychology Today, 20*, 30–36.

Gerson, M. J., Alpert, J. L., & Richardson, M. S. (1984).

Mothering: The view from psychological research. *Signs, 9,* 434–453.

Geschwind, N., & Behan, P. (1982). Lefthandedness: Association with immune disease, migraine, and developmental learning disorder. *Proceedings of the National Academy of Sciences, 79,* 5097–5100.

Geschwind, N., & Galaburda, A. M. (1985a). Cerebral lateralization: Biological mechanism, associations, and pathology: I. A hypothesis and a program for research. *Archives of Neurology, 42,* 428–459.

Geschwind, N., & Galaburda, A. M. (1985b). Cerebral lateralization: Biological mechanism, associations, and pathology: II. A hypothesis and a program for research. *Archives of Neurology, 42,* 521–552.

Gettelman, T. E., & Thompson, J. K. (1993). Actual differences and stereotypical perceptions in body image and eating disturbance: A comparison of male and female heterosexual and homosexual samples. *Sex Roles, 29,* 545–562.

Gettys, L. D., & Cann, A. (1981). Children's perceptions of occupational sex stereotypes. *Sex Roles, 7,* 301–308.

Geyer, G. A. (1989, December 8). Is feminism dead? *Providence Journal Bulletin.*

Giancola, P. R., & Zeichner, A. (1995). An investigation of gender differences in alcohol-related aggression. *Journal of Studies on Alcohol, 68,* 675–684.

Gibbons, J. L., Stiles, D. A., & Shkodriani, G. M. (1991). Adolescents' attitudes toward family and gender roles: An international comparison. *Sex Roles, 25,* 625–643.

Gibson, G. (1983). Hispanic women: Stress and mental health issues. *Women and Therapy, 2,* 113–133.

Gibson, R. C. (1987). Reconceptualizing retirement for Black Americans. *Gerontologist, 27,* 691–698.

Gibson, R. C. (1993). The Black American retirement experience. In J. S. Jackson, L. M. Chatters, & R. J. Taylor (Eds.), *Aging in Black America* (pp. 277–299). Newbury Park, CA: Sage.

Gidycz, C. A., Coble, C. N., Latham, L., & Layman, M. J. (1993). Sexual assault experience in adulthood and prior victimization experiences. *Psychology of Women Quarterly, 17,* 151–168.

Gidycz, C. A., Hanson, K., & Layman, M. J. (1995). A prospective analysis of the relationships among sexual assault experiences. *Psychology of Women Quarterly, 19,* 5–29.

Gidycz, C. A., & Koss, M. P. (1989). The impact of adolescent sexual victimization: Standardized measures of anxiety, depression and behavioral deviancy. *Violence and Victims, 4,* 139–149.

Gidycz, C. A., & Koss, M. P. (1990). A comparison of group and individual sexual assault victims. *Psychology of Women Quarterly, 14,* 325–342.

Gidycz, C. A., & Koss, M. P. (1991). The effects of acquaintance rape on the female victim. In A. Parrot & L. Bechholfer (Eds.), *Acquaintance rape: The hidden crime* (pp. 270–284). New York: John Wiley & Sons.

Gieve, K. (1989). *Balancing acts: On being a mother.* London: Virago.

Gigy, L. L. (1980). Self-concept of single women. *Psychology of Women Quarterly, 5,* 321–340.

Gilbert, E. H., & DeBlassie, R. R. (1984). Anorexia nervosa: Adolescent starvation by choice. *Adolescence, 76,* 839–846.

Gilbert, L. A. (1994). Reclaiming and returning gender to context: Examples from studies of heterosexual dual-earner families. *Psychology of Women Quarterly, 18,* 539–558.

Gilbert, L. A., & Evans, S. L. (1985). Dimensions of same-gender student-faculty role model relationships. *Sex Roles, 12,* 111–123.

Gilbert, N. (1993, June 29). The wrong response to rape. *Wall Street Journal,* p. A18.

Giles-Sims, J., & Finkelhor, D. (1984). Child abuse in stepfamilies. *Family Relations, 33,* 407–413.

Gilhooly, M. L. M. (1984). The impact of caregiving on caregivers: Factors associated with the psychological well-being of people supporting a demented relative in the community. *British Journal of Medical Psychology, 57,* 35–44.

Gilley, H. M., & Collier, S. S. (1970). Sex differences in the use of hostile verbs. *Journal of Psychology, 76,* 33–37.

Gilligan, C. (1982). *In a different voice: Psychological theory and women's development.* Cambridge, MA: Harvard University Press.

Gilligan, C. (1986). On *In a different voice:* An interdisciplinary forum: Reply. *Signs, 11,* 324–333.

Gilligan, C. (1990). Teaching Shakespeare's sisters: Notes from the underground of female adolescence. In C. Gilligan, N. P. Lyons, & T. J. Hanmer (Eds.), *Making connections: The relational worlds of adolescent girls at Emma Willard School.* Cambridge, MA: Harvard University Press.

Gilligan, C., Lyons, N. P., & Hanmer, T. J. (Eds.). (1990). *Making connections: The relational worlds of adolescent girls at Emma Willard School.* Cambridge, MA: Harvard University Press.

Giobbe, E. (1993). Surviving commercial sexual exploitation. In D. E. H. Russell (Ed.), *Making violence sexy: Feminist views on pornography* (pp. 37–42). New York: Teachers College, Columbia University.

Gitter, A. G., Black, H., & Mostofsky, D. (1972). Race and sex in the communication of emotion. *Journal of Social Psychology, 88,* 273–276.

Gjerde, P. F. (1995). Alternative pathways to chronic depressive symptoms in young adults: Gender differences in developmental trajectories. *Child Development, 66,* 1277–1300.

Gjerdingen, D. K., & Chaloner, K. M. (1994). The relationship of women's postpartum mental health to employment, childbirth, and social support. *Journal of Family Practice, 38,* 465–472.

Glass, S. P., & Wright, T. L. (1985). Sex differences in types of extramarital involvement and marital dissatisfaction. *Sex Roles, 12,* 1101–1120.

Gleason, J. B. (1975). Fathers and other strangers: Men's speech to young children. In D. P. Dato (Ed.), *Georgetown University roundtable on language and linguistics developmental psycholinguistics: Theory and applications.* Washington, DC: Georgetown University Press.

Glenn, E. N., & Feldberg, R. L. (1989). Clerical work: The female occupation. In J. Freeman (Ed.), *Women: A feminist perspective* (4th ed.). Mountain View, CA: Mayfield.

Glenn, N. D., & Kramer, K. B. (1987). The marriages and divorces of the children of divorce. *Journal of Marriage and the Family, 49,* 811–825.

Glenn, N. D., & Supanic, M. (1984). The social and demographic correlates of divorce and separation in the United States: An update and reconsideration. *Journal of Marriage and the Family, 46,* 563–575.

Glenn, N. D., & McLanahan, S. (1981). The effects of offspring on the psychological well-being of older adults. *Journal of Marriage and the Family, 43*, 409–421.

Glenn, N. D., & McLanahan, S. (1982). Children and marital happiness: A further specification of the relationship. *Journal of Marriage and the Family, 14*, 63–72.

Glick, P. (1991). Trait-based and sex-based discrimination in occupational prestige, occupational salary, and hiring. *Sex Roles, 25*, 351–378.

Glick, P. C., & Lin, S. (1986). Recent changes in divorce and remarriage. *Journal of Marriage and the Family, 48*, 737–748.

Glick, P. C., & Spanier, G. B. (1980). Married and unmarried cohabitation in the United States. *Journal of Marriage and the Family, 42*, 19–30.

Glick, P., Wilk, K., & Perreault, M. (1995). Images of occupations: Components of gender and status in occupational stereotypes. *Sex Roles, 32*, 565–582.

Glick, P., Zion, C., & Nelson, C. (1988). What mediates sex discrimination in hiring decisions? *Journal of Personality and Social Psychology, 55*, 178–186.

Goff, D. M. (1991, April). *Gender differences in expectations for secure attachment behavior.* Paper presented at the biennial meeting of the Society for Research in Child Development, Seattle, WA.

Goffman, E. (1979). *Gender advertisements.* Cambridge, MA: Harvard University Press.

Goh, S. C. (1991). Sex differences in perceptions of interpersonal work style, career emphasis, supervisory mentoring behavior, and job satisfaction. *Sex Roles, 24*, 701–710.

Goktepe, J. R., & Schneier, C. E. (1989). Role of sex, gender roles, and attraction in predicting emergent leaders. *Journal of Applied Psychology, 74*, 165–167.

Gold, A. R., Brush, L. R., & Sprotzer, E. R. (1980). Developmental changes in self-perceptions of intelligence and self-confidence. *Psychology of Women Quarterly, 5*, 231–239.

Gold, A. R., & St. Ange, M. C. (1974). Development of sex role stereotypes in Black and White elementary school girls. *Developmental Psychology, 10*, 461.

Gold, D., Crombie, G., & Noble, S. (1987). Relations between teachers' judgments of girls' and boys' compliance and intellectual competence. *Sex Roles, 16*, 351–358.

Gold, R. B. (1990). *Abortion and women's health.* New York: Alan Guttmacher Institute.

Gold, R. B., & Richards, C. L. (1994). Securing American women's reproductive health. In C. Costello & A. J. Stone (Eds.), *The American woman, 1994–1995: Where we stand, women and health.* New York: Norton.

Gold, S., Balzano, B., & Stamey, R. (1991). Two studies of females' sexual force fantasies. *Journal of Sex Education & Therapy, 17*, 15–26.

Goldberg, P. A. (1968). Are women prejudiced against women? *Transaction, 5*, 28–30.

Goldberg, S., & Lewis, M. (1969). Play behavior in the year-old infant: Early sex differences. *Child Development, 40*, 21–32.

Goldberg, W. A., & Easterbrooks, M. A. (1988). Maternal employment when children are toddlers and kindergartners. In A. E. Gottfried & A. W. Gottfried (Eds.), *Maternal employment and children's development: Longitudinal research.* New York: Plenum.

Golden, C. (1987). Diversity and variability in women's sexual identities. In the Boston Lesbian Psychologies Collective (Eds.), *Lesbian psychologies: Explorations and challenges.* Urbana: University of Illinois Press.

Golden, J. (1988). A second look at a case of inhibited sexual desire. *Journal of Sex Research, 25*, 304–306.

Goldenberg, N. R. (1979). *Changing of the Gods: Feminism and the end of traditional religion.* Boston: Beacon Press.

Golding, J. M. (1988). Gender differences in depressive symptoms: Statistical considerations. *Psychology of Women Quarterly, 12*, 61–74.

Golding, J. M. (1990). Division of household labor, strain, and depressive symptoms among Mexican Americans and non-Hispanic Whites. *Psychology of Women Quarterly, 14*, 103–117.

Golding, J. M. (1996). Sexual assault history and women's reproductive and sexual health. *Psychology of Women Quarterly, 20*, 101–121.

Goldman, R. J., & Goldman, J. D. (1988). The prevalence and nature of child sexual abuse in Australia. *Australia Journal of Sex, Marriage and Family, 9*, 94–106.

Goleman, D. (1989, April 11). Subtle but intriguing differences found in the brain anatomy of men and women. *New York Times*, pp. C1, C6.

Golombok, S., & Tasker, F. (1996). Do parents influence the sexual orientation of their children? Findings from a longitudinal study of lesbian families. *Developmental Psychology, 32*, 3–11.

Golub, S. (1976). The effect of premenstrual anxiety and depression on cognitive function. *Journal of Personality and Social Psychology, 34*, 99–104.

Golub, S. (1983). Menarche: The beginning of menstrual life. In S. Golub (Ed.), *Lifting the curse of menstruation.* New York: Haworth.

Golub, S. (1992). *Periods: From menarche to menopause.* Newbury Park, CA: Sage.

Golub, S., & Harrington, D. M. (1981). Premenstrual and menstrual mood changes in adolescent women. *Journal of Personality and Social Psychology, 41*, 961–965.

Gomberg, E. L. (1979). Problems with alcohol and other drugs. In E. S. Gomberg & V. Franks (Eds.), *Gender and disordered behavior.* New York: Brunner/Mazel.

Gomberg, E. L. (1993a). Women and alcohol: Use and abuse. *Journal of Nervous and Mental Disease, 181*, 211–219.

Gomberg, E. L. (1993b). Alcohol, women and the expression of aggression. *Journal of Studies of Alcohol, 11*, 89–95.

Gondolf, E. W. (1988a). Who are those guys? Toward a behavioral typology of batterers. *Violence and Victims, 3*, 187–203.

Gonzales, M. H., & Meyers, S. A. (1993). "Your mother would like me": Self-presentation in the personal ads of heterosexual and homosexual men and women. *Personality and Social Psychology Bulletin, 19*, 131–142.

Gonzalez, J. T. (1988). Dilemmas of the high-achieving Chicana: The double-bind factor in male/female relationships. *Sex Roles, 18*, 367–380.

Good, P. R., & Smith, B. D. (1980, Summer). Menstrual distress and sex-role attributes. *Psychology of Women Quarterly, 4*, 482–491.

Goode, E., & Haber, L. (1977). Sexual correlates of homosexual experience: An exploratory study of college women. *Journal of Sex Research, 13*, 12–21.

Goodenow, C., & Gaier, E. L. (1986, August). *Best friends: Close reciprocal friendships of married and unmarried women.* Paper presented at the meeting of the American Psychological Association, Washington, DC.

Goodman, L. A., Koss, M. P., Fitzgerald, L. F., Russo, N. F., & Keita, G. P. (1993). Male violence against women: Current research and future directions. *American Psychologist, 48,* 1054–1058.

Goodwin, R. (1990). Sex differences among partner preferences: Are the sexes really very similar? *Sex Roles, 23,* 501–513.

Gooren, L., Fliers, E., & Courtney, K. (1990). Biological determinants of sexual orientation. *Annual Review of Sex Research, 1,* 175–196.

Gordon, M., & Creighton, S. J. (1988). Natal and non-natal fathers as sexual abusers in the United Kingdom: A comparative analysis. *Journal of Marriage and the Family, 50,* 99–105.

Gorlick, C. A. (1995). Divorce: Options available, constraints forced, pathways taken. In N. Mandell & A. Duffy (Eds.), *Canadian families: Diversity, conflict and change* (pp. 211–234). Toronto: Harcourt Brace Canada.

Gorman, C. (1992, January 20). Sizing up the sexes. *Time,* pp. 42–51.

Gormly, A. V., Gormly, J. B., & Weiss, H. (1987). Motivations for parenthood among young adult college students. *Sex Roles, 16,* 31–39.

Gottman, J. M. (1979). *Marital interaction: Experimental investigations.* New York: Academic Press.

Gottman, J. M. (1986). The world of coordinated play: Same and cross-sex friendship in young children. In J. M. Gottman & J. G. Parker (Eds.), *Conservation of friends: Speculations on affective development.* Cambridge, England: Cambridge University Press.

Gottman, J. M., & Levenson, R. W. (1992). Marital processes predictive of later dissolution: Behavior, physiology, and health. *Journal of Personality and Social Psychology, 63,* 221–233.

Gough, H. G. (1987). *California Psychological Inventory, 1987 revised edition.* Palo Alto, CA: Consulting Psychologists Press.

Gough, H. G., & Heilbrun, A. B. (1965). *Adjective Check List manual.* Palo Alto, CA: Consulting Psychologists Press.

Gould, S. J. (1980). *The panda's thumb.* New York: Norton.

Gove, W. R. (1980). Mental illness and psychiatric treatment among women. *Psychology of Women Quarterly, 4,* 345–362.

Gove, W. R., & Tudor, J. (1973). Adult sex roles and mental illness. *American Journal of Sociology, 77,* 812–835.

Grady, K. E. (1977, April). *The belief in sex differences.* Paper presented at the meeting of the Eastern Psychological Association, Boston.

Grady, K. E. (1981). Sex bias in research design. *Psychology of Women Quarterly, 5,* 628–636.

Grady, K. E. (1988). Older women and the practice of breast self-examination. *Psychology of Women Quarterly, 12,* 473–487.

Grafenberg, E. (1950). The role of the urethra in female orgasm. *International Journal of Sexology, 3,* 145–148.

Graham, A. (1975). The making of a nonsexist dictionary. In B. Thorne & N. Henley (Eds.), *Language and sex: Difference and dominance.* Rowley, MA: Newbury House.

Graham, J. W., Gentry, K. W., & Green, J. (1981). The self-presentational nature of emotional expression: Some evidence. *Personality and Social Psychology Bulletin, 7,* 467–474.

Graham, S. (1992). Most of the subjects were White and middle-class: Trends in published research on African Americans in selected APA journals, 1978–1989. *American Psychologist, 47,* 629–639.

Grambs, J. D. (1989). *Women over forty: Vision and realities.* New York: Springer.

Grana, S. J., Moore, H. A., Wilson, J. K., & Miller, M. (1993). The contexts of housework and the paid labor force: Women's perceptions of the demand levels of their work. *Sex Roles, 28,* 295–315.

Grant, A. (1889). Woman's place in nature. *Forum, 7,* 258–263.

Grant, L. (1985). Race-gender status, classroom interaction, and children's socialization in elementary school. In L. C. Wilkinson & C. B. Marrett (Eds.), *Gender influences in classroom interaction* (pp. 57–77). Orlando, FL: Academic Press.

Gratton, B., & Haug, M. (1983). Decision and adaptation: Research in female retirement. *Research on Aging, 5,* 59–76.

Grauerholz, E. (1987). Balancing the power in dating relationships. *Sex Roles, 17,* 563–571.

Gray, B. A., & Jones, B. E. (1987). Psychotherapy and Black women: A survey. *Journal of the National Medical Association, 79,* 177–181.

Gray, J. D., & Silver, R. C. (1990). Opposite sides of the same coin: Former spouses' divergent perspectives in coping with their divorce. *Journal of Personality and Social Psychology, 59,* 1180–1191.

Green, R. (1978). Sexual identity of 37 children raised by homosexual or transsexual parents. *American Journal of Psychiatry, 135,* 692–697.

Green, R. (1987). Exposure to explicit sexual material and sexual assault: A review of behavioral and social science research. In M. R. Walsh (Ed.), *The psychology of women: Ongoing debates.* New Haven, Conn.: Yale University Press.

Greenburg, D. (1986). *Dan Greenburg's confessions of a pregnant father.* New York: Macmillan.

Greene, A. L., & Adams-Price, C. (1990). Adolescents' secondary attachments to celebrity figures. *Sex Roles, 23,* 325–347.

Greene, B. A. (1986). When the therapist is white and the patient is black: Considerations for psychotherapy in the feminist heterosexual and lesbian communities. In D. Howard (Ed.), *The dynamics of feminist therapy.* New York: Haworth Press.

Greene, B. A. (1990). Sturdy bridges: The role of African-American mothers in the socialization of African-American children. In J. P. Knowles & E. Cole (Eds.), *Motherhood: A feminist perspective* (pp. 205–225). New York: Haworth.

Greene, B. A. (1994). Ethnic-minority lesbians and gay men: Mental health and treatment issues. *Journal of Consulting and Clinical Psychology, 62,* 243–251.

Greenhaus, J. H., Parasuraman, S., & Wormley, W. M. (1990). Effects of race on organizational experiences, job performance evaluations, and career outcomes. *Academy of Management Journal, 33,* 64–86.

Greenlees, I. A., & McGrew, W. C. (1994). Sex and age differences in preferences and tactics of mate attraction: Analysis of published advertisements. *Ethology and Sociobiology, 15,* 59–72.

Greeno, C. G., & Maccoby, E. E. (1986, Winter). How different is the "different voice"? *Signs,* pp. 310–311.

Greenspan, M. (1983). *A new approach to women and therapy.* New York: McGraw-Hill.

Greenwood, S. (1992). *Menopause naturally: Preparing for the second half of life.* Volcano, CA: Volcano Press.

Griffin, S. (1971, September). Rape: The all-American crime. *Ramparts,* pp. 26–35.

Griffin, S. (1981). *Pornography and silence.* New York: Harper & Row.

Griffith, J. (1985). Social support providers: Who are they? Where are they met?—and the relationship of network characteristics to psychological distress. *Basic and Applied Social Psychology, 6*, 41–60.

Griffitt, W. (1987). Females, males, and sexual responses. In K. Kelly (Ed.), *Females, males and sexuality: Theories and research* (pp. 141–173). Albany: State University of New York.

Grimm, D. E. (1987). Toward a theory of gender: Transsexualism, gender, sexuality, and relationships. *American Behavioral Scientist, 31*, 66–85.

Grindstaff, C. F. (1996). The costs of having a first child for women aged 33–38, Canada 1991. *Sex Roles, 35*, 137–151.

Gritz, E. R. (1984). Cigarette smoking by adolescent females: Implications for health and behavior. *Women and Health, 9*, 103–115.

Grogan, S., Williams, Z., & Conner, M. (1996). The effects of viewing same-gender photographic models on body-esteem. *Psychology of Women Quarterly, 20*, 569–575.

Gross, R. M. (1979). Female God language in a Jewish context. In C. Christ & J. Plaskow (Eds.), *Womanspirit rising: A feminist reader in religion.* San Francisco: Harper & Row.

Grossman, A. L., & Tucker, J. S. (1997). Gender differences and sexism in the knowledge and use of slang. *Sex Roles, 37*, 101–110.

Grossman, F. K., Eichler, L. S., & Winickoff, S. A. (1980). *Pregnancy, birth, and parenthood.* San Francisco: Jossey-Bass.

Grossman, H. Y., & Chester, N. L. (Eds.). (1990). *The experience and meaning of work in women's lives.* Hillsdale, NJ: Erlbaum.

Groth, A. N., & Birnbaum, H. J. (1979). *Men who rape: The psychology of the offender.* New York: Plenum Press.

Gruber, J. E. (1992). A typology of personal and environmental sexual harassment: Research and policy implications for the 1990s. *Sex Roles, 26*, 447–464.

Grusec, J. E., & Lytton, H. (1988). *Social development.* New York: Springer-Verlag.

Grych, J. H., & Fincham, F. D. (1992). Interventions for children of divorce: Toward greater integration of research and action. *Psychological Bulletin, 111*, 434–454.

Guidubaldi, J., Perry, J. D., & Natasi, B. K. (1987). Growing up in a divorced family: Initial and long-term perspectives on children's adjustment. *Applied Social Psychology Annual, 7*, 202–237.

Gullahorn, J. E. (1977a). Equality and social structure. In E. Donelson & J. E. Gullahorn (Eds.), *Women: A psychological perspective.* New York: John Wiley.

Gullahorn, J. E. (1977b). Sex roles and sexuality. In E. Donelson & J. E. Gullahorn, *Women: A psychological perspective.* New York: Wiley.

Gunderson, M. (1989). Implementation of comparable worth in Canada. *Journal of Social Issues, 45*, 209–222.

Gunnar, M. R., & Donahue, M. (1980). Sex differences in social responsiveness between six months and twelve months. *Child Development, 51*, 252–265.

Gunter, N. C., & Gunter, B. G. (1990). Domestic division of labor among working couples: Does androgyny make a difference? *Psychology of Women Quarterly, 14*, 355–370.

Gustafson, G. E., & Harris, K. L. (1990). Women's responses to young infants' cries. *Developmental Psychology, 26*, 144–152.

Gutek, B. A. (1985). *Sex and the workplace: The impact of sexual behavior and harassment on women, men, and organizations.* San Francisco: Jossey-Bass.

Gutek, B. A. (1993). Sexual harassment: Rights and responsibilities. *Employee Responsibilities and Rights Journal, 6*, 325–340.

Gutek, B. A., & Koss, M. P. (1993). Changed women and changed organizations: Consequences of and coping with sexual harassment. *Journal of Vocational Behavior, 42*, 28–48.

Guttmann, D. (1985). The parental imperative revisited. In J. Meacham (Ed.), *The family and individual development* (pp. 31–60). Basel, Switzerland: Karger.

Guy-Sheftall, B., & Bell-Scott, P. (1989). Finding a way: Black women students and the academy. In C. S. Pearson, D. L. Shavlik, & J. C. Toughton (Eds.), *Educating the majority: Women challenge tradition in higher education.* New York: American Council on Education/Macmillan.

Haaken, J. (1988). Field dependence research: A historical analysis of psychological construct. *Signs, 13*, 311–330.

Haas, A. (1979). Male and female spoken language differences: Stereotypes and evidence. *Psychological Bulletin, 86*, 616–626.

Hackel, L. S., & Ruble, D. N. (1992). Changes in the marital relationship after the first baby is born: Predicting the impact of expectancy disconfirmation. *Journal of Personality and Social Psychology, 62*, 944–957.

Hacker, H. M. (1981). Blabbermouths and clams: Sex differences in self-disclosure in same-sex and cross-sex dyads. *Psychology of Women Quarterly, 5*, 385–401.

Hadaway, C. K. (1989). Identifying American apostates: A cluster analysis. *Journal for the Scientific Study of Religion, 28*, 201–215.

Haddad, Y. S. (1992). The effect of informational versus controlling verbal feedback on self-determination and preference for challenge. *Dissertation Abstracts International, 43* (6-B), 2038.

Haddock, G., Zanna, M. P., & Essex, V. M. (1993). Assessing the structure of prejudice attitudes: The case of attitudes toward homosexuals. *Journal of Personality and Social Psychology, 65*, 1105–1118.

Hafner, R. J. (1984). Predicting the effects on husbands of behavior therapy for wives' agoraphobia. *Behavior, Research, and Therapy, 22*, 227–242.

Hafner, R. J. (1988). The sex role semantic differential. In M. Hersen & A. Bellack (Eds.), *Dictionary of behavioral assessment techniques.* New York: Pergamon Press.

Hafner, R. J., & Minge, P. J. (1989). Sex role stereotyping in women with agoraphobia and their husbands. *Sex Roles, 20*, 705–711.

Hagestad, G. (1978). *Patterns of communication and influence between grandparents and grandchildren.* Paper presented at the World Conference on Sociology, Helsinki, Finland.

Hagestad, G. O. (1984). The continuous bond: A dynamic multigenerational perspective on parent-child relations between adults. In M. Perlmutter (Ed.), *The Minnesota Symposium on Child Psychology: Vol. 17. Parent-child interactions and parent-child relations in child development.* Hillsdale, NJ: Erlbaum.

Hagestad, G. O., & Neugarten, B. L. (1986). Age and the life course. In R. H. Binstock & E. Shanas (Eds.), *Handbook of aging and the social sciences* (2nd ed.). New York: Van Nostrand Reinhold.

Hagestad, G. O., Smyer, M., & Stierman, K. (1984). The impact of divorce in middle age. In R. S. Cohen, B. J. Cohler, & S. H. Weissman (Eds.), *Parenthood: A psychodynamic perspective.* New York: Guilford Press.

Hahn, W. K. (1987). Cerebral lateralization of function: From infancy through childhood. *Psychological Bulletin, 101,* 376–392.

Halberstadt, A. G., & Saitta, M. B. (1987). Gender, nonverbal behavior, and perceived dominance: A test of the theory. *Journal of Personality and Social Psychology, 53,* 257–272.

Halgin, R. P., & Whitbourne, S. K. (1994). *Abnormal psychology: The human experience of psychological disorders.* Fort Worth, TX: Harcourt Brace.

Hall, E. G. (1990). The effect of performer gender, performer skill level, and opponent gender on self-confidence in a competitive situation. *Sex Roles, 23,* 33–41.

Hall, G. S. (1906). The question of coeducation. *Munsey Magazine, 14,* 588–592.

Hall, J. A. (1978). Gender effects in decoding nonverbal cues. *Psychological Bulletin, 85,* 845–857.

Hall, J. A. (1984). *Nonverbal sex differences: Communication accuracy and expressive style.* Baltimore: Johns Hopkins University Press.

Hall, J. A. (1987). On explaining gender differences: The case of nonverbal communication. In P. Shaver & C. Hendrick (Eds.), *Sex and gender* (pp. 177–200). Newbury Park, CA: Sage.

Hall, J. A., & Halberstadt, A. G. (1980). Masculinity and femininity in children: Development of the Children's Personal Attributes Questionnaire. *Developmental Psychology, 16,* 270–289.

Hall, J. A., & Halberstadt, A. G. (1986). Smiling and gazing. In J. S. Hyde & M. C. Linn (Eds.), *The psychology of gender: Advances through meta-analysis* (pp.136–158). Baltimore: Johns Hopkins University Press.

Hall, J. A., & Veccia, E. M. (1990). More "touching" observations: New insights on men, women and interpersonal touch. *Journal of Personality and Social Psychology, 59,* 1155–1162.

Hall, J. A., & Veccia, E. M. (1991). Touch asymmetry between the sexes. In C. L. Ridgeway (Ed.), *Gender, interaction, and inequality.* New York: Springer-Verlag.

Hall, J. L., & Frederickson, W. A. (1979). Sex-role stereotyping, a function of age and education, as measured by a perceptual-projective device. *Sex Roles, 5,* 77–84.

Hall, M., with Gregory, A. (1991). Love and work in lesbian relationships. In B. Sang, J. Warshow, & A. J. Smith (Eds.), *Lesbians at midlife: The creative transition.* San Francisco, CA: spinsters book company.

Hallinan, M. T., & Sorensen, A. B. (1987). Ability grouping and sex differences in mathematics achievement. *Sociology of Education, 60,* 63–72.

Halmi, K. A. (1987). Anorexia nervosa and bulimia. In V. B. Van Hasselt & M. Hersen (Eds.), *Handbook of adolescent psychology.* New York: Pergamon.

Halpern, D. F. (1985). The influence of sex-role stereotypes on prose recall. *Sex Roles, 12,* 363–375.

Halpern, D. F. (1986). A different answer to the question "Do sex-related differences in spatial abilities exist?" *American Psychologist, 41,* 1014–1015.

Halpern, D. F. (1989, August). The disappearance of cognitive gender differences: What you see depends on where you look [Letter to the editor]. *American Psychologist, 44,* 1156–1158.

Halpern, D. F. (1992). *Sex differences in cognitive abilities* (2nd ed.). Hillsdale, NJ: Erlbaum.

Halpern, D. F. (1994). Stereotypes, science censorship, and the study of sex differences. *Feminism and Psychology, 4,* 523–530.

Halpern, R. H. (1987). Age in cross-cultural perspective: An evolutionary approach. In P. Silverman (Ed.), *The elderly as modern pioneers* (pp. 228–252). Bloomington: Indiana University Press.

Hamilton, D. L. (1979). A cognitive-attributional analysis of stereotyping. In L. Berkowitz (Ed.), *Advances in experimental social psychology* (Vol. 12, pp. 53–84). New York: Academic Press.

Hamilton, D. L., & Rose, T. L. (1980). Illusory correlation and the maintenance of stereotypic beliefs. *Journal of Personality and Social Psychology, 39,* 832–845.

Hamilton, D. L., & Sherman, J. W. (1994). Stereotypes. In R. S. Wyer, Jr., & T. K. Srull (Eds.), *Handbook of social cognition: Vol. 2* (2nd ed., pp. 1–68). Hillsdale, NJ: Erlbaum.

Hamilton, E. (1978). *Sex, with love.* Boston: Beacon Press.

Hamilton, J. A. (1986). An overview of the clinical rationale for advancing gender-related psychopharmacology and drug abuse research. *National Institute on Drug Abuse: Research Monograph Series, 65,* 14–20.

Hamilton, J. A. (1989). Postpartum psychiatric syndromes. In B. L. Parry (Ed.), *The Psychiatric Clinic of North America: Vol. 12. Women's disorders* (pp. 89–104). Philadelphia: W. B. Saunders.

Hamilton, J. A., & Gallant, S. J. (1990). Problematic aspects of diagnosing premenstrual phase dysphoria: Recommendations for psychological research and practice. *Professional Psychology: Research and Practice, 21,* 60–68.

Hamilton, L. H., Brooks-Gunn, J., Warren, M. P., & Hamilton, W. G. (1987, December). The impact of thinness and dieting on the professional ballet dancer. *Journal of Medical Problems of Performing Artists, 18,* 117–122.

Hamilton, M. C. (1988). Masculine generics and misperceptions of AIDS risk. *Journal of Applied Social Psychology, 18,* 1222–1240.

Hamilton, M. C. (1991). Masculine bias in the attribution of personhood: People = Male, Male = People. *Psychology of Women Quarterly, 15,* 393–402.

Hammersla, J. F., & Frease-McMahan, L. (1990). University students' priorities: Life goals vs. relationships. *Sex Roles, 23,* 1–14.

Hammond, J. A., & Mahoney, C. W. (1983). Reward-cost balancing among women coal-miners. *Sex Roles, 9,* 17–29.

Hannon, R., Hall, D. S., Kuntz, T., Van Laar, S., & Williams, J. (1995). Dating characteristics leading to unwanted vs. wanted sexual behavior. *Sex Roles, 33,* 767–783.

Hans, V. P., & Eisenberg, N. (1985). The effects of sex-role attitudes and group composition on men and women in groups. *Sex Roles, 12,* 477–490.

Hansen, C. H., & Hansen, R. D. (1988). How rock music videos can change what is seen when boy meets girl: Priming stereotypic appraisal of social interactions. *Sex Roles, 19,* 287–316.

Hansson, R. O., Chernovetz, M. E., & Jones, W., II. (1977). Maternal employment and androgyny. *Psychology of Women Quarterly, 2,* 76–78.

Hardie, E. A., & McMurray, N. E. (1992). Self-stereotyping, sex role ideology, and menstrual attitudes: A social identity approach. *Sex Roles, 27,* 17–37.

Harding, S. (1987). Introduction: Is there a feminist method? In S. Harding (Ed.), *Feminism & methodology.* Bloomington: University of Indiana Press.

Hare-Mustin, R. T. (1983). An appraisal of the relationship between women and psychotherapy: 80 years after the case of Dora. *American Psychologist, 38,* 593–601.

Hare-Mustin, R. T., & Marecek, J. (1988). The meaning of difference: Gender theory, postmodernism, and psychology. *American Psychologist, 43,* 455–464.

Hare-Mustin, R. T., & Marecek, J. (Eds.). (1990). *Making a difference: Psychology and the construction of gender.* New Haven: Yale University Press.

Harkness, S., & Super, C. M. (1985). The cultural context of gender segregation in children's peer groups. *Child Development, 56,* 219–224.

Harney, P. A., & Muehlenhard, C. L. (1991). Factors that increase the likelihood of victimization. In A. Parrot & L. Bechholfer (Eds.), *Acquaintance rape: The hidden crime* (pp. 159–175). New York: John Wiley & Sons.

Harris, B. (1979). Careers, conflict, and children. In A. Roland & B. Harris (Eds.), *Career and motherhood.* New York: Human Sciences Press.

Harris, L. J. (1977). Sex differences in the growth and use of language. In E. Donelson and J. Gullahorn (Eds.), *Women: A psychological perspective.* New York: John Wiley & Sons.

Harris, L. J. (1978). Sex differences in spatial ability: Possible environmental, genetic, and neurological factors. In M. Kinsbourne (Ed.), *Asymmetrical functions of the brain.* Cambridge, England: Cambridge University Press.

Harris, M. B., Begay, C., & Page, P. (1989). Activities, family relationships and feelings about aging in a multicultural elderly sample. *International Journal of Aging and Human Development, 29,* 103–117.

Harris, M. B., & Knight-Bohnoff, K. (1996a). Gender and aggression I: Perceptions of aggression. *Sex Roles, 35,* 1–25.

Harris, M. B., & Knight-Bohnoff, K. (1996b). Gender and aggression II: Personal aggressiveness. *Sex Roles, 35,* 27–42.

Harris, R. T. (1991, March/April). Anorexia nervosa and bulimia nervosa in female adolescents. *Nutrition Today, 26,* 30–34.

Harris, S. M. (1993). The influence of personal and family factors on achievement needs and concerns of African-American and Euro-American college women. *Sex Roles, 29,* 671–689.

Harris, S. M. (1995). Family, self, and sociocultural contributions to body image attitudes of African American women. *Psychology of Women Quarterly, 19,* 129–145.

Harrison, A. O., Wilson, M. N., Pine, C. J., & Chan, S. Q. (1990). *Family ecologies of ethnic minority children.* Washington, DC: American Psychological Association.

Harrison, B. W. (1989a). Making the connections. In J. Plaskow & C. Christ (Eds.), *Weaving the visions: New patterns in feminist spirituality.* San Francisco: Harper & Row.

Harrison, B. W. (1989b). The power of anger in the work of love. In J. Plaskow & C. Christ (Eds.), *Weaving the visions: New patterns in feminist spirituality.* New York: Harper & Row.

Harry, J. (1995). Sports ideology, attitudes toward women, and anti-homosexual attitudes. *Sex Roles, 32,* 109–116.

Harter, S., Alexander, P. C., & Neimeyer, R. A. (1988). Long-term effects of incestuous child abuse in college women: Social adjustment, social cognition, and family characteristics. *Journal of Counseling and Clinical Psychology, 56,* 5–8.

Hartman, S. J., Griffeth, R. W., Crino, M. D., & Harris, O. J. (1991). Gender-based influences: The promotion recommendation. *Sex Roles, 25,* 285–300.

Hartshorne, H., & May, M. A. (1928). *Studies in the nature of character: Studies in deceit.* New York: Macmillan.

Hartup, W. W. (1989). Social relationships and their developmental significance. *American Psychologist, 44,* 120–126.

Hartup, W. W., Moore, S. G., & Sager, G. (1963). Avoidance of inappropriate sex-typing by young children. *Journal of Consulting Psychology, 27,* 467–473.

Hartup, W. W., & Sancilio, M. F. (1986). Children's friendships. In E. Schopler & G. B. Mesiboy (Eds.), *Social behavior in autism.* New York: Plenum Press.

Hatch, R. C., James, D. E., & Schumm, W. R. (1986). Spiritual intimacy and marital satisfaction. *Family Relations: Journal of Applied Family and Child Studies, 35,* 539–545.

Hatcher, M. A. (1991). The corporate woman of the 1990s: Maverick or innovator. *Psychology of Women Quarterly, 15,* 251–259.

Hatcher, R., et al. (1994). *Contraceptive technology* (16th rev. ed.). New York: Irvington.

Hatfield, E., & Rapson, R. L. (1993). *Love, sex, and intimacy: Their psychology, biology, and history.* New York: HarperCollins.

Hathaway, S. R., & McKinley, J. C. (1943). *The Minnesota Multiphasic Personality Inventory.* New York: Psychological Corporation.

Hatton, G. I. (1977). Biology and gender: Structure, sex, and cycles. In E. Donelson & J. E. Gullahorn (Eds.), *Women: A psychological perspective.* New York: John Wiley.

Haugaard, J. J., & Reppucci, N. D. (1988). *The sexual abuse of children.* San Francisco: Jossey-Bass.

Hausman, B. L. (1993). Demanding subjectivity: Transsexualism, medicine, and the technologies of gender. *Journal of the History of Sexuality, 3,* 270–302.

Haviland, J. (1977). Sex-related pragmatics in infants. *Journal of Communication, 27,* 80–84.

Hawkins, B. D. (1994, November 3). An evening with Gwendolyn Brooks. *Black Issues in Higher Education,* pp. 16–21.

Hawton, K., Catalan, J., & Fagg, J. (1991). Low sexual desire: Sex therapy results and prognostic factors. *Behavior Research and Therapy, 29,* 217–244.

Hayden-Thompson, L., Rubin, K. H., & Hymel, S. (1987). Sex preferences in sociometric choices. *Developmental Psychology, 23,* 559–560.

Hayes, C. D. (1987). *Risking the future: Adolescent sexuality, pregnancy, and childbearing: Vol. 1.* Washington, DC: National Academy Press.

Hayler, B. (1979). Abortion. *Signs, 5,* 307–323.

Hays, T. E. (1987). Menstrual expressions and menstrual attitudes. *Sex Roles, 16,* 605–614.

Heaney, R. P. (1982). Age-related bone loss. In M. E. Reff & E. L. Schneider (Eds.), *Biological markers of aging* (pp. 161–167) (NIH Publication No. 82-2221). Washington, DC: U.S. Government Printing Office.

Heath, D. (1984). An investigation into the origins of a copious vaginal discharge during intercourse—"enough to wet the bed"—that is not urine. *Journal of Sex Research, 20,* 194–215.

Heatherington, L., Daubman, K. A., Bates, C., Ahn, A., Brown, H., & Preston, C. (1993). Two investigations of "female modesty" in achievement situations. *Sex Roles, 29,* 739–754.

Heatherton, T. E., & Baumeister, R. F. (1991). Binge eating as escape from self-awareness. *Psychological Bulletin, 110,* 86–108.

Heckhausen, H. (1967). *The anatomy of achievement motivation.* New York: Academic Press.

Hedges, L. V., & Becker, B. J. (1986). *Statistical methods in the meta-analysis of research of gender differences.* Baltimore: Johns Hopkins University Press.

Heidbreder, E. (1972). Factors in retirement adjustment: White-collar/blue-collar experience. *Industrial Gerontology, 12,* 69–72.

Heilbrun, A. B., Jr., Friedberg, L., Wydra, D., & Worobow, A. L. (1990). The female role and menstrual distress: An explanation for inconsistent evidence. *Psychology of Women Quarterly, 14,* 403–417.

Heilbrun, C. (1973). *Toward a recognition of androgyny.* New York: Harper & Row.

Heilbrun, C. (1979). *Reinventing womanhood.* New York: Norton.

Heilman, M. E., & Martell, R. F. (1986). Exposure to successful women: Antidote to sex discrimination in applicant screening decisions? *Organizational Behavior and Human Decision Processes, 37,* 376–390.

Heiman, J. (1975, November). The physiology of erotica: Women's sexual arousal. *Psychology Today,* pp. 90–94.

Heiman, J., & LoPiccolo, J. (1988). *Becoming orgasmic: A sexual growth program for women.* Englewood Cliffs, NJ: Prentice-Hall.

Helgeson, V. S., & Sharpsteen, D. J. (1987). Perceptions of anger in achievement and affiliation situations: An extension of the Pollak and Gilligan versus Benton et al. debate. *Journal of Personality and Social Psychology, 53,* 727–733.

Hellwege, D. R., Perry, K., & Dobson, J. (1988). Perceptual differences in gender ideals among heterosexual and homosexual males and females. *Sex Roles, 19,* 735–746.

Helmreich, R. L., Spence, J. T., & Wilhelm, J. A. (1981). A psychometric analysis of the Personal Attributes Questionnaire. *Sex Roles, 7,* 1097–1108.

Helms, J. E. (1992). Why Is There No Study of Cultural Equivalence in Standardized Cognitive Ability Testing? *American Psychologist, 47,* 1083–1101.

Helson, R. (1972). The changing image of the career woman. *Journal of Social Issues, 28,* 33–46.

Helson, R., Mitchell, V., & Moane, G. (1984). Personality and patterns of adherence and nonadherence to the social clock. *Journal of Personality and Social Psychology, 46,* 1079–1096.

Helson, R., & Moane, G. (1987). Personality change in women from college to midlife. *Journal of Personality and Social Psychology, 53,* 176–186.

Helson, R., & Picano, J. (1990). Is the traditional role bad for women? *Journal of Personality and Social Psychology, 59,* 311–320.

Henderson, C. (1980a). Cancer of the breast—the past decade (medical progress): Part I. *New England Journal of Medicine, 302,* 17–30.

Henderson, C. (1980b). Cancer of the breast—the past decade (medical progress): Part II. *New England Journal of Medicine, 302,* 78–90.

Hendrick, C., & Hendrick, S. S. (1986). A theory and method of love. *Journal of Personality and Social Psychology, 50,* 392–402.

Hendrick, C., & Hendrick, S. S. (1988). Lovers wear rose colored glasses. *Journal of Social and Personal Relationships, 5,* 161–183.

Hendrick, C., & Hendrick, S. (1996). Gender and the experience of heterosexual love. In J. T. Wood (Ed.), *Gendered relationships.* Mountain View, CA: Mayfield.

Hendrick, S. S., & Hendrick, C. (1987). Love and sex attitudes: A close relationship. *Advances in Personal Relationships, 1,* 141–169.

Hendrick, S. S. & Hendrick, C. (1995). Gender differences and similarities in sex and love. *Personal Relationships, 2,* 55–65.

Hendrick, S. S., Hendrick, C., & Adler, N. L. (1988). Romantic relationships: Love, satisfaction, and staying together. *Journal of Personality and Social Psychology, 54,* 980–988.

Hendrick, S. S., Hendrick, C., Slapton-Foote, M. J., & Foote, F. F. (1985). Gender differences in sexual attitudes. *Journal of Personality and Social Psychology, 48,* 1630–1642.

Henley, N. M. (1977). *Body politics: Power, sex, and nonverbal communication.* Englewood Cliffs, NJ: Prentice-Hall.

Henley, N. M. (1989). Molehill or mountain? What we do know and don't know about sex bias in language. In M. Crawford & M. Gentry (Eds.), *Gender and thought.* New York: Springer-Verlag.

Henley, N. M., & Thorne, B. (1977). Womanspeak and manspeak: Sex differences and sexism in communication, verbal and nonverbal. In A. Sargent (Ed.), *Beyond sex roles.* St. Paul, MN: West.

Hennig, M., & Jardin, A. (1977). *The managerial woman.* New York: Anchor Press.

Henshaw, S. K., Koonin, L. M., & Smith, J. C. (1991). Characteristics of U.S. women having abortions, 1987. *Family Planning Perspectives, 23,* 75–81.

Henshaw, S. K., & Silverman, J. (1988). The characteristics and prior contraception use of U.S. abortion patients. *Family Planning Perspectives, 20,* 158–168.

Herdt, G., & Davidson, J. (1988). The Sambia "Turnim-man": Sociocultural and clinical aspects of gender formation in male pseudohermaphrodites with 5-alpha-reductase deficiency in Papua, New Guinea. *Archives of Sexual Behavior, 17,* 33–56.

Herek, G. M. (1994). Assessing heterosexual attitudes toward lesbians and gay men: A review of empirical research with the ATLG scale. In B. Greene & M. Herek (Eds.), *Lesbian and gay psychology: Theory, research, and clinical applications* (pp. 206–228). Thousand Oaks, CA: Sage.

Herek, G. M., & Glunt, E. K. (1993). Interpersonal contact and heterosexuals' attitude toward gay men: Results of a national survey. *Journal of Sex Research, 30,* 239–244.

Herman, J. L. (1981). *Father-daughter incest.* Cambridge, MA: Harvard University Press.

Herman, J. L. (1992). *Trauma and recovery.* New York: Basic Books.

Herman, J. L. & Hirschman, L. (1977). Father-daughter incest. *Signs, 2,* 735–756.

Herman, J. L. & Hirschman, L. (1981). Families at risk for father-daughter incest. *American Journal of Psychiatry, 138,* 967–970.

Herrmann, D. J., Crawford, M., & Holdsworth, M. (1992). Gender-linked differences in everyday memory performance. *British Journal of Psychology, 83,* 221–231.

Hersch, P. (1991, January/February). Secret lives. *Networker,* pp. 37–43.

Hershey, M. R., & Hill, D. B. (1978). Is pollution "a white thing"? Social differences in preadults' attitudes. *Public Opinion Quarterly, 41,* 439–458.

Hetherington, E. M. (1989). Coping with family transitions: Winners, losers, and survivors. *Child Development, 60,* 1–14.

Hetherington, E. M., Cox, M., & Cox, R. (1976). Divorced fathers. *Family Coordinator, 25,* 417–428.

Hetherington, E. M., Stanley-Hagan, M., & Anderson, E. R. (1989). Marital transitions: A child's perspective. *American Psychologist, 44,* 303–312.

Hetherington, S. E. (1990). A controlled study of the effect of prepared childbirth classes on obstetric outcomes. *Birth,* 86–90.

Hidalgo, H. (1984). The Puerto Rican lesbian in the United States. In T. Darty and S. Potter (Eds.). Women-identified women. Palo Alto, CA: Mayfield.

Higginbotham, E., & Weber, L. (1992). Moving up with kin and community: Upward social mobility for Black and White women. Special Issue: Race, class, and gender. *Gender & Society, 6,* 416–440.

Higginbottom, S. F., Barling, J., & Kelloway, E. K. (1993). Linking retirement experiences and marital satisfaction: A mediational model. *Psychology and Aging, 8,* 508–516.

Higgins, D. J., & McCabe, M. P. (1994). The relationship of child sexual abuse and family violence to adult adjustment: Toward an integrated risk-sequelae model. *Journal of Sex Research, 31,* 255–266.

Hill, C. T., Rubin, Z., & Peplau, L. A. (1976). Breakups before marriage: The end of 103 affairs. *Journal of Social Issues, 32,* 147–168.

Hill, J. P. (1988). Adapting to menarche: Familial control and conflict. In M. R. Gunnar & W. A. Collins (Eds.), *Minnesota Symposium on Child Development: 21, Developmental during the transition to adolescence.* Hillsdale, NJ: Erlbaum.

Hill, J. P., & Holmbeck, G. N. (1987). Familial adaptation to biological changes during adolescence. In R. M. Lerner & T. T. Foch (Eds.), *Biological-psychosocial interactions in early adolescence.* Hillsdale, NJ: Erlbaum.

Hill, J. P., & Lynch, M. E. (1985). The intensification of gender-related role expectations during early adolescence. In J. Brooks-Gunn & A. C. Petersen (Eds.), *Girls at puberty: Biological, psychological, and social perspectives.* New York: Plenum Press.

Hill, K. T., & Eaton, W. O. (1977). The interaction of test anxiety and success-failure experiences in determining children's arithmetic performance. *Developmental Psychology, 13,* 205–211.

Hill, N. E. (1994). *Mother-daughter relationships and upward mobility in middle-class African American women.* Unpublished doctoral dissertation, Michigan State University, East Lansing.

Hill, R. (1972). *The strength of Black families.* New York: Emerson-Hall.

Hill, R. B. (1977). *Informal adoption among black families.* Washington, DC: National Urban League, Research Department.

Hill, S. (1991, July 21). Researchers and subtle biases favor boys in science classes. *Boston Sunday Globe,* p. 81.

Hiller, D. V., & Dyehouse, J. (1987). A case for banishing "dual-career marriages" from the research literature. *Journal of Marriage and the Family, 49,* 787–795.

Himelein, M. J. (1995). Risk factors for sexual victimization in dating. *Psychology of Women Quarterly, 19,* 31–48.

Himmelfarb, S. (1984). Age and sex differences in the mental health of older persons. *Journal of Consulting and Clinical Psychology, 52,* 844–856.

Hines, M. (1982). Prenatal gonadal hormones and sex differences in human behavior. *Psychological Bulletin, 92,* 56–80.

Hines, M., & Shipley, C. (1984). Prenatal exposure to diethylstilbestrol (DES) and the development of sexually dimorphic cognitive abilities and cerebral lateralization. *Development Psychology, 20,* 81–94.

Hines, N. J., & Fry, D. P. (1994). Indirect modes of aggression among women of Buenos Aires, Argentina. *Sex Roles, 30,* 213–236.

Hite, S. (1976). *The Hite Report: A nationwide study of female sexuality.* New York: Dell Books.

Hoagland, S. L. (1988). *Lesbian ethics: Toward new value.* Palo Alto, CA: Institute of Lesbian Studies.

Hobfoll, S. E, Ritter, C., Lavin, J., Hulsizer, M. R., & Cameron, R. P. (1995). Depression prevalence and incidence among inner-city pregnant and post-partum women. *Journal of Consulting and Clinical Psychology, 63,* 445–453.

Hochschild, A. (1989). *The second shift: Working parents and the revolutions at home.* New York: Viking.

Hock, E., & DeMeis, D. K. (1990). Depression in mothers of infants: The role of maternal employment. *Developmental Psychology, 26,* 285–291.

Hofeller, K. H. (1982). *Social psychological and situational factors in wife abuse.* Palo Alto, CA: R & E Research Associates.

Hoffman, C., & Hurst, N. (1990). Gender stereotypes: Perception or rationalization? *Journal of Personality and Social Psychology, 58,* 197–208.

Hoffman, J. C. (1982). Biorhythms in human reproduction: The not-so-steady states. *Signs, 7,* 829–844.

Hoffman, L. W. (1977a). Changes in family roles, socialization, and sex differences. *American Psychologist, 32,* 644–657.

Hoffman, L. W. (1977b). Fear of success in 1965 and 1974: A follow-up study. *Journal of Consulting and Clinical Psychology, 45,* 310–321.

Hoffman, L. W. (1979). Maternal employment. *American Psychologist, 34,* 859–865.

Hoffman, L. W. (1989). Effects of maternal employment in the two-parent family. *American Psychologist, 44,* 283–292.

Hoffman, M. L. (1977). Sex differences in empathy and related behaviors. *Psychological Bulletin, 54,* 712–722.

Hoffman, M. L. (1979). Maternal employment: 1979. *American Psychologist, 34,* 859–865.

Hoffman, M. L. (1989). Effects of maternal employment in the two-parent family. *American Psychologist, 44,* 283–292.

Hoffnung, M. (1989). Motherhood: Contemporary conflict for women. In J. Freeman (Ed.), *Women: A feminist perspective* (4th ed.). Palo Alto, CA: Mayfield.

Hogan, J. D., & Sexton, V. S. (1991). Women and the American Psychological Association. *Psychology of Women Quarterly, 15,* 623–634.

Holmes, T. H., & Rahe, R. H. (1967). The Social Readjustment Rating Scale. *Journal of Psychosomatic Research, 11,* 213–218.

Holms, V. L., & Esses, L. M. (1988). Factors influencing Canadian high school girls' career motivation. *Psychology of Women Quarterly, 12,* 313–328.

Home services for elderly. (1992, May 29). *Lansing State Journal,* p. C6.

Hood, K. E., Draper, P., Crockett, L. J., & Petersen, A. C. (1987). The ontogeny and phylogeny of sex differences in development: A biopsychosocial synthesis. In B. Carter (Ed.), *Current conceptions of sex roles and sex typing: Theory and research.* New York: Praeger.

hooks, b. (1984). *Feminist theory: From margin to center.* Boston: South End Press.

hooks, b. (1989). *Talking back: Thinking feminist, thinking black.* Boston: South End.

Hope, C. (1982). Caucasian female body hair and American culture. *Journal of American Culture, 5,* 93–99.

Hopkins, J., Campbell, S., & Marcus, M. (1987). Role of infant-related stressors in postpartum depression. *Journal of Abnormal Psychology, 96,* 237–241.

Hopson, J. L. (1987, August). Boys will be boys, girls will be. . . . *Psychology Today, 21,* 61–65.

Horner, M. S. (1968). *Sex differences in achievement motivation and performance in competitive-noncompetitive situations.* Unpublished doctoral dissertation, University of Michigan.

Horner, M. S. (1972). Toward an understanding of achievement-related conflicts in women. *Journal of Social Issues, 28,* 157–176.

Horner, M. S. (1978). The measurement and behavioral implications of fear of success in women. In J. W. Atkinson & J. O. Raynor (Eds.), *Personality, motivation, and achievement* (pp. 41–70). Washington, DC: Hemisphere.

Horney, J. (1979). Menstrual cycles and criminal responsibility. *Law and Human Behavior, 2,* 25–36.

Horney, K. (1926). The flight from womanhood. *International Journal of Psychoanalysis, 7,* 324–339.

Horney, K. (1931/1967). Premenstrual tension. In H. Kelman (Ed.), *Feminine psychology.* New York: Norton.

Horney, K. (1937). *The neurotic personality of our time.* New York: Norton.

Hort, B. E., Fagot, B. I., & Leinbach, M. D. (1990). Are people's notions of maleness more stereotypically framed than their notions of femaleness? *Sex Roles, 22,* 197–212.

Hort, B. E., Leinbach, M. D., & Fagot, B. I. (1991). Is there coherence among the cognitive components of gender acquisition? *Sex Roles, 24,* 195–207.

Horton, J. A. (Ed.). (1992). *The women's health data book: A profile of women's health in the United States.* Washington, DC: Jacobs Institute of Women's Health.

Hossain, Z., & Roopnarine, J. L. (1993). Division of household labor and child care in dual-earner African-American families with infants. *Sex Roles, 29,* 571–583.

House, W. C. (1974). Actual and perceived differences in male and female expectancies and minimal goal levels as a function of competition. *Journal of Personality, 42,* 493–509.

Houseknecht, S. K. (1979). Timing of the decision to remain voluntarily childless: Evidence for continuous socialization. *Psychology of Women Quarterly, 4,* 81–96.

Houser, B. B., Beckman, S. L., & Beckman, L. J. (1984). The relative rewards and costs of childlessness for older women. *Psychology of Women Quarterly, 8,* 395–398.

Houser, B. B., & Garvey, C. (1985). Factors that affect nontraditional vocational enrollment among women. *Psychology of Women Quarterly, 9,* 105–117.

Houston, M. (1994). When black women talk with white women: Why dialogues are difficult. In A. Gonzales, M. Houston, & V. Chen (Eds.), *Our voices: Essays in culture, ethnicity, and communication.* Los Angeles: Roxbury.

Houston, S., & Hwang, N. (1996). Correlates of the objective and subjective experiences of sexual harassment in high school. *Sex Roles, 34,* 189–204.

Howard, J. A., Blumstein, P., & Schwartz, P. (1986). Sex, power, and influence tactics in intimate relationships. *Journal of Personality and Social Psychology, 51,* 102–109.

Howes, C. (1990). Can the entry into child care and the quality of child care predict adjustment in kindergarten? *Developmental Psychology, 26,* 292–303.

Hraba, J., Lorenz, F. O., Lee, G., & Pechačová, Z. (1996). Gender and well-being in the Czech Republic. *Sex Roles, 34,* 517–533.

Hsu, L. K. G. (1987). Are the eating disorders becoming more common in Blacks? *International Journal of Eating Disorders, 6,* 113–114.

Hsu, L. K. G. (1989). The gender gap in eating disorders: Why are the eating disorders more common among women? *Clinical Psychology Review, 9,* 393–407.

Hudak, M. A. (1993). Gender schema theory revisited: Men's stereotypes of American women. *Sex Roles, 28,* 279–293.

Hughes, J. R., Gust, S. W., Skoog, K., Keenan, R. M., & Fenwick, J. W. (1991). Symptoms of tobacco withdrawal: A replication and extension. *Archives of General Psychiatry, 48,* 52–61.

Huguet, P., & Monteil, J. (1995). The influence of social comparison with less fortunate others on task performance: The role of gender motivations or appropriate norms. *Sex Roles, 33,* 753–765.

Huie, J. R. (1985). Preaching through metaphor. In J. L. Weidman (Ed.), *Women ministers.* San Francisco: Harper & Row.

Hull, J. G., & Bond, C. F., Jr. (1986). Social and behavioral consequences of alcohol consumption and expectancy: A meta-analysis. *Psychological Bulletin, 99,* 347–360.

Humphrey, L. L. (1989). Observed family interactions among subtypes of eating disorders using structural analysis of social behavior. *Journal of Counseling Psychology, 57,* 206–214.

Hunt, M. (1969). *The affair.* New York: World.

Hunt, M. (1974). *Sexual behaviors in the 1970s.* Chicago: Playboy Press.

Hunt, M. G. (1993). Expressiveness does predict well-being. *Sex Roles, 29,* 147–169.

Hunter, A. G., & Davis, J. E. (1992). Constructing gender: An exploration of Afro-American men's conceptualization of manhood. *Gender & Society, 6,* 464–479.

Hunter, M. (1990). Psychological and somatic experiences of the menopause: A prospective study. *Psychosomatic Medicine, 52,* 357–367.

Hunter College Women's Studies Collective. (1983). *Women's realities, women's choices: An introduction to women's studies.* New York: Oxford University Press.

Hurlbert, D. F., & Apt, C. (1993). Female sexuality: A comparative study between women in homosexual and heterosexual relationships. *Journal of Sex and Marital Therapy, 19,* 315–327.

Hurt, S. W., Schnurr, P. P., Severino, S. K., Freeman, E. W., Gise, L. H., Rivera-Tovar, A., & Steege, J. F. (1992). Late luteal phase dysphoria disorder in 670 women evaluated for premenstrual complaints. *American Journal of Psychiatry, 149,* 525–530.

Hurtig, A. L., & Rosenthal, I. M. (1987). Psychological findings in early treated cases of female pseudohermaphroditism caused by virilizing congenital adrenal hyperplasia. *Archives of Sexual Behavior, 16,* 209–223.

Hurtz, W., & Durkin, K. (1997). Gender role stereotyping in Australian radio commercials. *Sex Roles, 36,* 103–114.

Huston, A. C. (1983). Sex-typing. In P. H. Mussen (Series Ed.) and E. M. Hetherington (Vol. Ed.), *Handbook of child psychology: Vol. 4. Socialization, personality, and social development* (4th ed.). New York: Wiley.

Huston, A. C. (1985). The development of sex typing: Themes from recent research. *Development Review, 5,* 1–17.

Huston, A. C., & Alvarez, M. (1990). The socialization context of gender role development in early adolescence. In R. Montemayor, G. R. Adams, & T. P. Cullotta (Eds.), *From childhood to adolescence: A transition period.* Newbury Park, CA: Sage.

Huston, M., & Schwartz, P. (1996). Gendered dynamics in the romantic relationships of lesbians and gay men. In J. T. Wood (Ed.), *Gendered relationships.* Mountain View, CA: Mayfield.

Huston, T. L., & Ashmore, R. D. (1986). Women and men in personal relationships. In R. D. Ashmore & F. K. Del Boca (Eds.), *The social psychology of female-male relations.* New York: Academic Press.

Huttenlocher, J., Haight, W., Bryk, A., Seltzer, M., & Lyons, T. (1991). Early vocabulary growth: Relation to language input and gender. *Developmental Psychology, 27,* 236–248.

Huttman, E. (1991). A research note on dreams and aspirations of Black families. Special Issue: The American dream of family: Ideals and changing realities. *Journal of Comparative Family Studies, 22,* 147–158.

Huyck, M. H. (1982). From gregariousness to intimacy: Marriage and friendship over the adult years. In T. M. Field, A. Huston, H. C. Quay, L. Troll, & G. E. Finley (Eds.), *Review of Human Development.* New York: Wiley.

Hyde, J. S. (1984a). How large are gender differences in aggression? A developmental meta-analysis. *Developmental Psychology, 20,* 722–736.

Hyde, J. S. (1984b). Children's understanding of sexist language. *Developmental Psychology, 20,* 697–706.

Hyde, J. S. (1986). Gender differences in aggression. In J. S. Hyde & M. C. Linn (Eds.), *The psychology of gender: Advances through meta-analysis,* (pp. 51–66). Baltimore: Johns Hopkins University Press.

Hyde, J. S. (1990). *Understanding human sexuality* (4th ed.). New York: McGraw-Hill.

Hyde, J. S. (1991). *Half the human experience* (4th ed.). Lexington, MA: Heath.

Hyde, J. S. (1994). Can meta-analysis make feminist transformations in psychology? *Psychology of Women Quarterly, 18,* 451–462.

Hyde, J. S., Fennema, E., & Lamon, S. J. (1990). Gender differences in mathematics performance: A meta-analysis. *Psychological Bulletin, 107,* 139–155.

Hyde, J. S., Fennema, E., Ryan, M., Frost, L. A., & Hopp, C. (1990). Gender comparisons of mathematics attitudes and affect: A meta-analysis. *Psychology of Women Quarterly, 14,* 299–324.

Hyde, J. S., & Linn, M. C. (1988). Gender differences in verbal ability: A meta-analysis. *Psychological Bulletin, 104,* 53–69.

Hyde, J. S., & McKinley, N. M. (1993). Beliefs about the consequences of maternal employment for children: Psychometric analyses. *Psychology of Women Quarterly, 17,* 177–191.

Hyde, J. S., & Plant, E. A. (1995). Magnitude of psychological gender differences: Another side of the story. *American Psychologist, 50,* 159–161.

Hyde, J. S., Rosenberg, B. G., & Behrman, J. A. (1977). Tomboyism. *Psychology of Women Quarterly, 2,* 73–75.

Hyde, J. S., & Schuck, J. R. (1977, August). *The development of sex differences in aggression.* Paper presented at the meeting of the American Psychological Association, San Francisco.

Iasenza, S. (1992). The relations among selected aspects of sexual orientation and sexual functioning in females. *Dissertation Abstracts International, 52,* 3945.

Ibarra, H. (1993). Personal networks of women and minorities in management: A conceptual framework. *Academy of Management Review, 18,* 56–87.

Ice, M. L. (1987). *Clergy women and their worldviews: Calling for a new age* [Review]. New York: Praeger.

Ihinger-Tallman, M., & Pasley, K. (1987). *Remarriage.* Beverly Hills, CA: Sage.

Ikels, C. (1988). Delayed reciprocity and the support networks of the childless elderly. *Journal of Comparative Family Studies, 19,* 99–112.

Imperato-McGinley, J., Peterson, R. E., Gautier, T., & Sturla, E. (1979). Androgens and the evolution of male-gender identity among male pseudohermaphrodites with 5-alpha-reductase deficiency. *New England Journal of Medicine, 300,* 1233–1237.

Infant twins assaulted by parents. (1993, December 13). *Lansing State Journal,* p. 3B.

Inman, C. (1996). Friendships among men: Closeness in the doing. In J. T. Wood (Ed.), *Gendered relationships* (pp. 95–110). Mountain View, CA: Mayfield.

Insel, P., & Roth, W. (1998). *Core concepts in health* (8th ed.). Mountain View, CA: Mayfield.

International Labour Office. (1991). *Yearbook of labour statistics* (50th ed.). Geneva: Author.

Intons-Peterson, M. J. (1988). *Children's concepts of gender.* Norwood, NJ: Ablex.

Ireson, C. J. (1984). Adolescent pregnancy and sex roles. *Sex Roles, 11,* 189–201.

Irving, J. J. (1986). Teacher-student interactions: Effects on student race, sex and grade level. *Journal of Educational Psychology, 78,* 14–21.

Ivey, D. (1995, January 8). Study cites estrogen value. *Lansing State Journal,* p. 6A.

Jack, D. C. (1991). *Silencing the self: Women and depression.* Cambridge: Harvard University Press.

Jack, D. C., & Dill, D. (1992). The Silencing the Self scale: Schemas of intimacy associated with depression in women. *Psychology of Women Quarterly, 16,* 97–106.

Jacklin, C. N. (1989). Female and male: Issues of gender. *American Psychologist, 44,* 127–133.

Jacklin, C. N., Maccoby, E. E., & Dick, A. E. (1973). Barrier behavior and toy preference: Sex differences (and their absence) in the year-old child. *Child Development, 44,* 196–200.

Jacklin, C. N., & Reynolds, C. (1993). Gender and childhood socialization. In A. E. Beall & R. J. Sternberg (Eds.), *The psychology of gender* (pp. 197–214). New York: Guilford Press.

Jackson, J. (1986). The extended family—Black grandparents: Who needs them? In R. Staples (Ed.), *The Black family: Essays and studies.* Belmont, CA: Wadsworth.

Jackson, J. L., Calhoun, K. S., Amick, A. E., & Maddever, H. M. (1990). Young adult women who report childhood intra-familial sexual abuse: Subsequent adjustment. *Archives of Sexual Behavior, 19,* 211–221.

Jackson, J. S., & Gibson, R. C. (1984). Work and retirement among the Black elderly. In Z. Blau (Ed.), *Current perspectives on aging and the life cycle.* Greenwich, CT: JAI Press.

Jackson, L. A. (1983). The perception of androgyny and physical attractiveness: Two is better than one. *Personality and Social Psychology Bulletin, 9,* 405–413.

Jackson, L. A. (1985). Self-conceptions and gender role: The correspondence between gender-role categorization and open-ended self-descriptions. *Sex Roles, 13,* 549–566.

Jackson, L. A. (1989). Relative deprivation and the gender wage gap. *Journal of Social Issues, 45,* 117–133.

Jackson, L. A. (1992). *Physical appearance and gender: Sociobiological and sociocultural perspectives.* Albany: State University of New York Press.

Jackson, L. A., Fleury, R. E., & Lewandowski, D. A. (1996). Feminism: Definitions, support, and correlates of support among female and male college students. *Sex Roles, 34,* 687–693.

Jackson, L. A., Ialongo, N., & Stollak, G. (1986). Parental correlates of gender role: The relations between parents' masculinity, femininity, and child-rearing behaviors and their children's gender roles. *Journal of Social and Clinical Psychology, 4,* 204–224.

Jackson, L. A., & McGill, O. D. (1996). Body type preference and body characteristics associated with attractive and unattractive bodies by African Americans and Anglo Americans. *Sex Roles, 35,* 295–307.

Jackson, L. A., Sullivan, L. A., & Rostker, R. (1988). Gender, gender role, and body image. *Sex Roles, 19,* 429–442.

Jackson, L. A., & Tate, L. (April–May 1995). *Race, gender and perceptions of gender relevant characteristics.* Paper presented at Midwestern Psychological Association, Chicago.

Jackson, L. A., Tate, L., & Ingram, J. M. (1995). *Race, gender and perceptions of gender-related characteristics.* Unpublished manuscript, Michigan State University, East Lansing, MI.

Jackson-Walker, S. M. (1994). *The implications of separation-individuation difficulties and parent eating preoccupation for disordered eating in late adolescent women.* Unpublished doctoral dissertation, Michigan State University, East Lansing.

Jacobs, E. (1985). Peer intrusions and self-esteem. *International Review of Applied Psychology, 34,* 421–431.

Jacobs, J. (1984). The economy of love in religious commitment: The deconversion of women from nontraditional religious movements. *Journal for the Scientific Study of Religion, 23,* 155–171.

Jacobs, J. A. (1989). *Revolving doors: Sex segregation and women's careers.* Stanford, CA: Stanford University Press.

Jacobs, J. E., & Eccles, J. S. (1992). The impact of mothers' gender-role stereotypic beliefs on mothers' and children's ability perceptions. *Journal of Personality and Social Psychology, 63,* 932–944.

Jacobs, P. A., Brunton, M., Melville, M. M., Brittain, R. P., & McClemont, W. F. (1965). Aggressive behavior, mental subnormality, and the XYY male. *Nature, 208,* 1351–1352.

Jacobson, N. S., Follette, W. C., & McDonald, D. W. (1982). Reactivity to positive and negative behavior in distressed and nondistressed married couples. *Journal of Consulting and Clinical Psychology, 50,* 706–714.

Jagacinski, C. M. (1987). Engineering careers: Women in a male-dominated field. *Psychology of Women Quarterly, 11,* 97–110.

Janeway, E. (1981, November). Incest: A rational look at the oldest taboo. *Ms.,* pp. 61–64.

Janoff-Bulman, R. (1982). Esteem and control bases of blame: "Adaptive" strategies for victims versus observers. *Journal of Personality, 50,* 180–192.

Janoff-Bulman, R. (1992). *Shattered assumptions: Toward a new psychology of trauma.* New York: Free Press.

Janus, S. S., & Janus, C. L. (1993). *The Janus Report on sexual behavior.* New York: Wiley.

Jarrett, L. (1984). Psychosocial and biological influences on menstruation: Synchrony, cycle length, and regularity. *Psychoneuroendocrinology, 9,* 21–28.

Jarvik, L. F., Klodin, V., & Matsuyama, S. S. (1973). Human aggression and the extra Y chromosome: Fact or fantasy? *American Psychologist, 28,* 674–682.

Jay, T. (1992). *Cursing in America.* Philadelphia: John Benjamin.

Jayakody, R. (1993). Neighborhoods and neighbor relations. In J. S. Jackson, L. M. Chatters, & R. J. Taylor (Eds.), *Aging in Black America* (pp. 21–36). Newbury Park, CA: Sage.

Jenkins, A. H. (1988). Black families: The nurturing of agency. In A. F. Coner-Edwards & J. Spurlock (Eds.), *Black families in crisis: The middle class.* New York: Brunner/Mazel.

Jenkins, S. R. (1987). Need for achievement and women's careers over 14 years: Evidence for occupational structure effects. *Journal of Personality and Social Psychology, 53,* 922–932.

Jenkins, S. R. (1994). Structural power and experienced job satisfactions: The empowerment paradox for women. *Sex Roles, 30,* 347–369.

Jennings, J., Geis, L., & Brown, V. (1980). Influence of television commercials on women's self-confidence and independent judgments. *Journal of Personality and Social Psychology, 38,* 203–210.

Jensen, I. W., & Gutek, B. A. (1982). Attributions and assignment of responsibility in sexual harassment. *Journal of Social Issues, 38,* 121–136.

Jensen, J. M. (1990). Native American women and agriculture: A Seneca case study. In E. C. DuBois & V. L. Ruiz (Eds.), *Unequal sisters: A multicultural reader in U.S. women's history* (pp. 51–65). New York: Routledge.

Jhally, S. (1991). *Dreamwork* [Videotape]. The Foundation for Media Education, P.O. Box 2008, Amherst, MA 01004.

Johnson, C. A. (1991). Making sense of dysfunctional uterine bleeding. *American Family Physician, 44,* 149–157.

Johnson, C. B., Stockdale, M. S., & Saal, F. E. (1991). Persistence of men's misperceptions of friendly cues across a variety of interpersonal situations. *Psychology of Women Quarterly, 15,* 463–475.

Johnson, C. E., & Petrie, T. A. (1995). The relationship of gender discrepancy to eating disorder attitudes and behaviors. *Sex Roles, 33,* 405–416.

Johnson, C. L. (1988). Active and latent functions of grandparenting during the divorce process. *Gerontologist, 28,* 185–191.

Johnson, C. L., & Price-Bonham, S. (1980). Women and retirement: A study and implications. *Family Relations, 29,* 380–385.

Johnson, D. D. (1973–1974). Sex differences in reading across cultures. *Reading Research Quarterly, 9,* 67–86.

Johnson, E. S., & Meade, A. C. (1987). Developmental patterns of spatial ability: An early sex difference. *Child Development, 58,* 725–740.

Johnson, F. L. (1996). Friendships among women: Closeness in dialogue. In J. T. Wood (Ed.), *Gendered relationships* (pp. 79–94). Mountain View, CA: Mayfield.

Johnson, J. D., Adams, M. S., Ashburn, L., & Reed, W. (1995). Differential gender effect of exposure to rap music on African American adolescents' acceptance of teen dating violence. *Sex Roles, 33,* 597–605.

Johnson, J. D., Jackson, L. A., & Gatto, L. (1995). Violent attitudes and deferred academic aspirations: Deleterious effects of exposure to rap music. *Basic and Applied Social Psychology, 16,* 27–41.

Johnson, L. B. (1981). Perspectives on Black family research: 1965 to 1978. In H. P. McAdoo (Ed.), *Black families.* Beverly Hills, CA: Sage.

Johnson, N., & Scandura, T. (1994). The effect of mentorship and sex-role style on male-female earnings. *Industrial Relations, 33,* 263–274.

Johnston, W. B. (1987). Child-abuse parents: Factors associated with successful completion of treatment. *Psychological Reports, 63,* 434.

Joiner, G. W., & Kashubeck, S. (1996). Acculturation, body image, self-esteem, and eating-disorder symptomatology in adolescent Mexican American women. *Psychology of Women Quarterly, 20,* 419–435.

Joiner, T. E., Jr., & Blalock, J. A. (1995). Gender differences in depression: The role of anxiety and generalized negative affect. *Sex Roles, 33,* 91–108.

Jones, D. C., Bloys, N., & Wood, M. (1990). Sex roles and friendship patterns. *Sex Roles, 23,* 133–145.

Jones, E., & Forrest, J. (1992). Contraceptive failure rates based on the 1988 NSFG. *Family Planning Perspectives, 24,* 12–19.

Jones, G. P, & Dembo, M. H. (1989). Age and sex role differences in intimate friendships during childhood and adolescence. *Merrill-Palmer Quarterly, 35,* 445–462.

Jones, L. M., & McBride, J. L. (1980). Sex-role stereotyping in children as a function of maternal employment. *Journal of Social Psychology, 111,* 219–223.

Jones, S. L. (1994). A constructive relationship for religion with the science and profession of psychology: Perhaps the boldest model yet. *American Psychologist, 49,* 184–199.

Jones, W. H., Chernovetz, M. E., & Hanson, R. O. (1978). The enigma of androgyny: Differential implications for males and females? *Journal of Consulting and Clinical Psychology, 46,* 298–313.

Jose, P. E. (1989). The role of gender and gender role similarity in readers' identification with story characters. *Sex Roles, 21,* 697–713.

Jose, P. E., & McCarthy, W. J. (1988). Perceived agentic and communal behavior in mixed-sex group interactions. *Personality and Social Psychology Bulletin, 14,* 57–67.

Josefowitz, N. (1984, May). Plums and prunes. *The Owl Observer,* p. 12.

Joseph, G. L., & Lewis, J. (1981). *Common differences: Conflict in black and white feminist perspectives.* Boston: South End Press.

Jourard, S. M. (1966). An exploratory study of body-accessibility. *British Journal of Social and Clinical Psychology, 5,* 221–231.

Jourard, S. M. (1971). *The transparent self* (2nd ed.). New York: Van Nostrand.

Jurgens, J. J., & Powers, B. A. (1991). An exploratory study of the menstrual euphemisms, beliefs, and taboos of Head Start mothers. In D. L. Taylor & F. Woods (Eds.), *Menstruation, health, and illness.* New York: Hemisphere.

Jussim, L., & Eccles, J. S. (1992). Teacher expectations II: Construction and reflection of student achievement. *Journal of Personality and Social Psychology, 63,* 947–961.

Justice, B., & Justice, R. (1979). *The broken taboo: Sex in the family.* New York: Human Sciences Press.

Jutras, S., & Veilleux, F. (1991). Gender roles and care-giving to the elderly: An empirical study. *Sex Roles, 25,* 1–8.

Kagan, J. (1970). Attention and psychological change in the young child. *Science, 170,* 826–832.

Kagan, J., & Moss, H. A. (1962). *Birth to maturity: A study in psychological development.* New York: Wiley.

Kahn, A. S., Mathie, V. A., & Torgler, C. (1994). Rape scripts and rape acknowledgement. *Psychology of Women Quarterly, 18,* 53–66.

Kahn, A. S., & Yoder, J. D. (1989). The psychology of women and conservatism: Rediscovering social change. *Psychology of Women Quarterly, 13,* 417–432.

Kalish, R. A. (1985). The social context of death and dying. In R. H. Binstock & E. Shanas (Eds.), *Handbook of aging and the social sciences* (2nd ed., pp. 149–170). New York: Van Nostrand Reinhold.

Kalish, R. A. (1987). Death and dying. In P. Silverman (Ed.), *The elderly as modern pioneers* (pp. 320–334). Bloomington: Indiana University Press.

Kalish, R. A., & Reynolds, D. K. (1974). Widows view death: A brief research note. *Omega, 5,* 187–192.

Kalmuss, D. S., & Straus, M. A. (1990). Wife's marital dependency and wife abuse. In M. A. Straus, R. J. Gelles, & C. Smith (Eds.), *Physical violence in American families: Risk factors and adaptations to violence in 8,145 families* (pp. 369–379). New Brunswick, NJ: Transaction.

Kanagy, C. L., & Driedger, L. (1996). Changing Mennonite values: Attitudes on women, politics, and peace, 1972–1989. *Reviews of Religious Research, 37,* 342–353.

Kanin, E. J. (1985). Date rapists: Differential sexual socialization and relative deprivation. *Archives of Sexual Behavior, 14,* 218–232.

Kanter, R. M. (1977a). *Men and women of the corporation.* New York: Basic Books.

Kanter, R. M. (1977b). *Work and family in the United States: A critical review and agenda for research and policy.* New York: Russell Sage Foundation.

Kanter, R. M., & Stein, B. A. (1980). *A tale of "O": On being different in an organization.* New York: Harper & Row.

Kantor, G. K., & Straus, M. A. (1990). The "Drunken Bum" theory of wife beating. In M. A. Straus, R. J. Gelles, & C. Smith (Eds.), *Physical violence in American families: Risk factors and adaptations to violence in 8,145 families* (pp. 203–226). New Brunswick, NJ: Transaction.

Kantrowitz, B. (1990, June). High school homeroom. *Newsweek,* pp. 50–54.

Kanuha, V. (1990). Compounding the triple jeopardy: Battering in lesbian of color relationships. In L. S. Brown & M. P. P. Root (Eds.), *Diversity and complexity in feminist therapy.* New York: Harrington Park Press.

Kaplan, H. S. (1974). *The new sex therapy.* New York: Brunner/Mazel.

Kaplan, H. S. (1983). *The evaluation of sexual disorders: Psychological and medical aspects.* New York: Brunner/Mazel.

Kaplan, H. S. (1987). *The illustrated manual of sex therapy.* New York: Brunner/Mazel.

Kaplan, H. S. (1992). A neglected issue: The sexual side effects of current treatment for breast cancer. *Journal of Sex and Marital Therapy, 18,* 3–19.

Kaplan, H. S., & Sager, C. J. (1971). Sexual patterns at different ages. *Medical Aspects of Human Sexuality,* pp. 10–23.

Karabenick, S. A., & Youssef, Z. I. (1968). Performance as a function of achievement motive level and perceived difficulty. *Journal of Personality and Social Psychology, 10,* 414–419.

Karn, E. R. (1990). A comparison of male and female alcoholics' response to treatment process in an outpatient alcoholism treatment center. *Dissertation Abstracts International, 50,* 3156.

Karon, B. P., & Widener, A. J. (1995). Psychodynamic therapies in historical perspective: "Nothing human do I consider alien to me." In B. P. Karon & A. J. Widener (Eds.), *Comprehensive textbook of psychotherapy: Theory and practice.* New York: Oxford University Press.

Karraker, K. H., Vogel, D. A., & Lake, M. A. (1995). Parents' gender-stereotyped preceptions of newborns: The eye of the beholder revisited. *Sex Roles, 33,* 687–701.

Kash, S. D. (1984, January). Birth-control survey. *Ms.,* p. 17.

Kass, F., Spitzer, R. L., Williams, J. B., & Widiger, T. (1989). Self-defeating personality disorder and DSM-III-R: Development of diagnostic criteria. *American Journal of Psychiatry, 146,* 1022–1026.

Katcher, A. (1955). The discrimination of sex differences by young children. *Journal of Genetic Psychology, 87,* 131–143.

Katz, B. L. (1991). The psychological impact of stranger versus non-stranger rape on victims' recovery. In A. Parrot & L. Bechholfer (Eds.), *Acquaintance rape: The hidden crime* (pp. 251–269). New York: Wiley.

Katz, B. L., & Burt, M. R. (1988). Self-blame in recovery from rape: Help or hindrance? In A. W. Burgess (Ed.), *Rape and sexual assault* (Vol. 2, pp. 191–212). New York: Garland.

Katz, D. (1987). Sex discrimination in hiring: The influence of organizational climate and need for approval on decision-making behavior. *Psychology of Women Quarterly, 11,* 11–20.

Katz, P. A. (1986). Modification of children's gender-stereotypical behavior: General issues and research considerations. *Sex Roles, 14,* 591–602.

Katz, P. A. (1987). Variations in family constellation: Effects on gender schemata. In L. S. Liben & M. L. Signorella (Eds.), *Children's gender schemata.* San Francisco: Jossey-Bass.

Katz, P. A. (1996). Carolyn Wood Sherif memorial address: Raising feminists. *Psychology of Women Quarterly, 20,* 323–340.

Katz, P. A., & Bertelson, A. D. (1993). The effects of gender and response style on depressed mood. *Sex Roles, 28,* 509–514.

Katz, P. A., & Ksansnak, K. R. (1994). Developmental aspects of gender role flexibility and traditionality in middle school childhood and adolescence. *Developmental Psychology, 30,* 272–282.

Katz, R. C., Hannon, R., & Whitten, L. (1996). Effects of gender and situation on the perception of sexual harassment. *Sex Roles, 34,* 35–42.

Katzman, R. (1987). Alzheimer's disease: Advances and opportunities. *Journal of the American Geriatrics Society, 35,* 69–73.

Kaufert, P. L. (1990). Methodological issues in menopause research. In M. Flint, F. Kronenberg, & W. Utian (Eds.), *Multidisciplinary perspectives on menopause: Annals of the New York Academy of Sciences, 592,* 114–122.

Keen, S. (1991). *Fire in the belly: On being a man.* New York: Bantam Books.

Kegel, A. (1952). Sexual function of the pubococcygeus muscle. *Western Journal of Surgery, 60,* 521–524.

Kehoe, M. (1988). Lesbians over 60 speak for themselves. *Journal of Homosexuality, 16,* 1–111.

Keil, S. V. W. (1982, April 18). Letter to the editor. *New York Times Magazine,* p. 130.

Keller, E. F. (1978). Gender and science. *Psychoanalysis and Contemporary Thought: A Quarterly of Integrative and Interdisciplinary Studies, 1,* 409–433.

Keller, E. F. (1985). *On the need to count past two in our thinking about gender and science.* BAAS meeting, Glasgow, Scotland.

Kellett, J. M. (1991). Sexuality of the elderly. *Sexual and Marital Therapy, 6,* 147–155.

Kelly, J., & Rice, S. (1986). The aged. In H. Gochros, J. Gochros, & J. Fisher (Eds.), *Helping the sexually oppressed.* Englewood Cliffs, NJ: Prentice-Hall.

Kelly, J. A., & Worell, L. (1976). Parent behaviors related to masculine, feminine, and androgynous sex role orientations. *Journal of Consulting and Clinical Psychology, 44,* 843–851.

Kelly, J. A., & Worell, J. (1977). New formulations of sex roles and androgyny: A critical review. *Journal of Consulting and Clinical Psychology, 45,* 1101–1115.

Kelly, J. B. (1982). *The adult perspective.* In B. B. Wolman (Ed.), *Handbook of developmental psychology.* Englewood Cliffs, NJ: Prentice-Hall.

Kelly, M. P., Strassberg, D. S., & Kircher, J. R. (1990). Attitudinal and experiential correlates of anorgasmia. *Archives of Sexual Behavior, 19,* 165–167.

Kelly, R. M. (1983). Sex and becoming eminent as a political/organizational leader. *Sex Roles, 9,* 1073–1090.

Kelschner, A. (1987). The value of anger. Unpublished sermon, Edgewood United Church, East Lansing, MI.

Kemper, K. A., Sargent, R. G., Drane, J. W., Valois, R. F., Hussey, J. R., & Leatherman, T. L. (1994). Black and white adolescent females' perceptions of ideal body size and social norms. *Obesity Research, 2,* 117–126.

Kemper, S. (1984). When to speak like a lady. *Sex Roles, 10,* 435–444.

Kempton, S. (1970, July). Cutting loose. *Esquire.* (As quoted in Partnow, E. (Ed.). (1993). *The new quotable woman* (p. 493). New York: Penguin.)

Kennell, J., Klaus, M., McGrath, S., Robertson, S., & Hinkley, C. (1991). Continuous emotional support during labor in a U.S. hospital. *Journal of the American Medical Association, 265,* 197–220.

Kephart, W. M. (1967). Some correlates of romantic love. *Journal of Marriage and the Family, 29,* 470–474.

Kerber, L. K. (1986). On *In a different voice:* An interdisciplinary forum: Some cautionary words for historians. *Signs, 11,* 304–310.

Kerr, A. (1992, January 20). A New NIH. *Physicians Weekly, 9,* 1.

Key, M. R. (1975). *Male/female language.* Metuchen, NJ: Scarecrow Press.

Kibria, N., Barnett, R. C., Baruch, G. K., Marshall, N. L., & Pleck, J. H. (1990). Homemaking-role quality and the psychological well-being and distress of employed women. *Sex Roles, 22,* 327–347.

Kimball, M. M. (1986). Television and sex-role attitudes. In T. M. Williams (Ed.), *The impact of television: A natural experiment in three communities.* Orlando, FL: Academic Press.

Kimball, M. M. (1989). A new perspective on women's math achievement. *Psychological Bulletin, 105,* 198–214.

Kimball, M. M., & Gray, V. A. (1982). Feedback and performance expectancies in an academic setting. *Sex Roles, 8,* 999–1007.

Kimmel, D. (1978). Adult development and aging: A gay perspective. *Journal of Social Issues, 34,* 113–130.

Kimmel, D. C. (1988). Ageism, psychology, and public policy. *American Psychologist, 43,* 175–178.

Kimmel, E. B. (1989). The experience of feminism. *Psychology of Women Quarterly, 13,* 133–146.

Kimura, D. (1985, November). Male brain, female brain: The hidden difference. *Psychology Today,* pp. 50–58.

Kimura, D. (1987). Are men's and women's brains really different? *Canadian Psychology, 28,* 133–147.

Kimura, D. (1989a, June). *The effect of exogenous estrogen on motor programming skills in post-menopausal women* (Research Bulletin No. 684). London, Canada: University of Western Ontario, Department of Psychology.

Kimura, D. (1989b, November). How sex hormones boost or cut intellectual ability. *Psychology Today,* pp. 62–66.

Kimura, D. (1992, September). Sex differences in the brain. *Scientific American, 267,* 118–125.

Kimura, D., & Hamson, E. (1994). Cognitive pattern in men and women is influenced by fluctuations in sex hormones. *Current Directions in Psychological Science, 3,* 57–61.

King, S. (1974). *Carrie.* New York: Doubleday.

Kingery, D. W. (1985). Are sex-role attitudes useful in explaining male/female differences in rates of depression? *Sex Roles, 12,* 627–636.

Kinman, J. R., & Henderson, D. L. (1985). An analysis of sexism in Newbury Medal Award books from 1977 to 1984. *Reading Teacher, 38,* 885–889.

Kinsey, A., Pomeroy, W., & Martin, C. (1948). *Sexual behavior in the human male.* Philadelphia: Saunders.

Kinsey, A., Pomeroy, W., Martin, C., & Gebhard, P. (1953). *Sexual behavior in the human female.* Philadelphia: Saunders.

Kirby, D. F., & Julian, N. B. (1981). Treatment of women in high school history textbooks. *Social Studies, 72,* 203–207.

Kirchmeyer, C. (1993). Nonwork-to-work spillover: A more balanced view of the experiences and coping of professional women and men. *Sex Roles, 28,* 531–552.

Kirchmeyer, C. (1996). Gender roles and decision-making in geographically diverse groups: A case for reviving androgyny. *Sex Roles, 34,* 649–663.

Kirkpatrick, L., & Spilka, B. (1989). *Treatment of religion in psychology texts.* Paper presented at the 97th annual convention of the American Psychological Association, New Orleans.

Kirkpatrick, M., Smith, C., & Roy, R. (1981). Lesbian mothers and their children: A comparative survey. *American Journal of Orthopsychiatry, 51,* 545–551.

Kite, M. E., & Deaux, K. (1986a). Attitudes toward homosexuality: Assessment and behavioral consequences. *Basic and Applied Social Psychology, 7,* 137–162.

Kite, M. E., & Deaux, K. (1986b). Gender versus category clustering in free recall: A test of gender schema theory. *Representative Research in Social Psychology, 16,* 38–43.

Kite, M. E., & Deaux, K. (1987). Gender belief systems: Homosexuality and the implicit inversion theory. *Psychology of Women Quarterly, 11,* 83–96.

Kite, M. E., Deaux, K., & Miele, M. (1991). Stereotypes of young and old: Does age outweigh gender? *Psychology and Aging, 6,* 19–27.

Kite, M. E., & Whitley, B. E., Jr. (in press). Sex differences in attitudes toward homosexual persons, behaviors, and civil rights: A meta-analysis. *Personality and Social Psychology Bulletin.*

Kitson, G. C. (1992). *Portrait of divorce: Adjustment to marital breakdown.* New York: Guilford Press.

Kitzinger, C. (1987). *The social construction of lesbianism.* London: Sage.

Kivnick, H. Q. (1982). *The meaning of grandparenthood.* Ann Arbor, MI: UMI Research.

Klassen, A., & Wilsnack, S. (1986). Sexual experience and drinking among women in a U.S. national survey. *Archives of Sexual Behavior, 15,* 363–393.

Klebanov, P. K., & Jemmott, J. B., III. (1992). Effect of expectations and bodily sensations on self-reports of premenstrual symptoms. *Psychology of Women Quarterly, 16,* 289–310.

Kleinke, C. L., & Kahn, M. L. (1980). Perceptions of self-disclosures: Effects of sex and physical attractiveness. *Journal of Personality, 48,* 190–205.

Klerman, G. L., Lavori, P. W., Rice, J., Reich, T., Endicott, J., Andreasen, N. C., Keller, M. B., & Hirschfield, R. M. A. (1985). Birth-cohort trends in rates of major depressive disorder among relatives of patients with affective disorder. *Archives of General Psychiatry, 42,* 689–693.

Klinger, E., & McNelly, F. W., Jr. (1969). Fantasy need achievement and performance. *Psychological Review, 76,* 574–591.

Kluft, R. P. (1991). Multiple personality disorder. In A. Tasman & S. W. Goldinger (Eds.), *Review of psychiatry* (Vol. 10). Washington, DC: American Psychiatric Press.

Knafo, D., & Jaffe, Y. (1984). Sexual fantasizing in males and females. *Journal of Research in Personality, 19,* 451–462.

Knight, K. H., Elfenbein, M. H., & Messina, J. (1995). A preliminary scale to measure connected and separate knowing: The knowing styles inventory. *Sex Roles, 33,* 499–513.

Kobak, R. R., & Hazan, C. (1991). Attachment in marriage: Effects of security and accuracy of working models. *Journal of Personality and Social Psychology, 60,* 861–869.

Koenig, H. G. (1994). Religion and hope for the disabled elder. In J. Levin (Ed.), *Religion in aging and health: Theoretical foundations and methodological frontiers* (pp. 18–51). Thousand Oaks, CA: Sage.

Koeske, R. D. (1976). Premenstrual emotionality: Is biology destiny? *Women and Health, 1,* 11–14.

Koeske, R. D. (1980). Theoretical perspectives for menstrual cycle research. In A. J. Dan, E. A. Graham, & C. Beecher (Eds.), *The menstrual cycle: A synthesis.* New York: Springer.

Koeske, R. D. (1983). *"Curse" is foiled again: Thinking clearly about social and psychological factors in the premenstruation syndrome.* Paper presented at the annual convention of the American Psychiatric Association.

Koestner, R., & Aubé, J. (1995). Multifactorial approaches to the study of gender. *Journal of Personality, 63,* 681–710.

Koff, E. (1983). Through the looking glass of menarche: What the adolescent girl sees. In S. Golub (Ed.), *Menarche: The transition from girl to woman.* Lexington, MA: Heath.

Koff, E., Rierdan, J., & Jacobson, S. (1981). The personal and interpersonal significance of menarche. *Journal of the American Academy of Child Psychiatry, 20,* 148–158.

Kohlberg, L. (1966). A cognitive developmental analysis of children's sex-role concepts and attitudes. In E. E. Maccoby (Ed.), *The development of sex differences.* Stanford, CA: Stanford University Press.

Kohlberg, L. (1977). Moral development: A review of the theory. *Theory into Practice, 16*, 53–59.

Kohlberg, L. (1984). *The psychology of moral development: The nature and validity of moral stages.* San Francisco: Harper & Row.

Kohlberg, L., & Ullian, D. Z. (1974). Stages in development of psychosexual concepts and attitudes. In R. C. Friedman, R. M. Richart, & R. I. Vande Wiele (Eds.), *Sex differences in behavior.* New York: Wiley.

Koivula, N. (1995). Ratings of gender appropriateness of sports participation: Effects of gender-based schematic processing. *Sex Roles, 33*, 543–557.

Kollock, P., Blumstein, P., & Schwartz, P. (1985). Sex and power in interaction: Conversational privileges and duties. *American Sociological Review, 50*, 34–46.

Kolodny, R. (1980, November). *Adolescent sexuality.* Paper presented at the Michigan Personnel and Guidance Association annual convention, Detroit.

Kolodny, R., Masters, W., & Johnson, V. (1979). *Textbook of sexual medicine.* Boston: Little, Brown.

Komarovsky, M. (1953). *Women in the modern world.* (As quoted in Partnow, E. (Ed.). (1993). *The new quotable woman* (p. 348). New York: Penguin.)

Konrad, A. M., Winter, S., & Gutek, B. A. (1992). Diversity in work group sex composition: Implications for majority and minority members. *Research in the Sociology of Organizations, 10*, 115–140.

Kopper, B. A. (1996). Gender, gender identity, rape myth acceptance, and time of initial resistance on the perception of acquaintance rape blame and avoidability. *Sex Roles, 34*, 81–93.

Kopper, B. A., & Epperson, D. L. (1991). Women and anger: Sex and sex-role comparisons in the expression of anger. *Psychology of Women Quarterly, 15*, 7–14.

Korabik, K., Baril, G. L., & Watson, C. (1993). Managers' conflict, management style and leadership effectiveness: The moderating effect of gender. *Sex Roles, 29*, 405–420.

Korte, D., & Scaer, R. (1990). *A good birth, a safe birth.* New York: Bantam.

Kortenhause, C. M., & Demarest, J. (1993). Gender role stereotyping in children's literature: An update. *Sex Roles, 28*, 219–232.

Koss, M. P. (1985). The hidden rape victim: Personality, attitudinal, and situational characteristics. *Psychology of Women Quarterly, 9*, 193–212.

Koss, M. P. (1988). Hidden rape: Incidence, prevalence and descriptive characteristics of sexual aggression and victimization in a national sample of college students. In A. W. Burgess (Ed.), *Sexual assault* (Vol. 11, pp. 3–25). New York: Garland.

Koss, M. P. (1990). Violence against women. *American Psychologist, 45*, 374–380.

Koss, M. P. (1993). Rape: Scope, impact, intervention, and public policy responses. *American Psychologist, 48*, 1062–1069.

Koss, M. P., & Burkhart, B. R. (1989). A conceptual analysis of rape victimization: Long-term effects and implications for treatment. *Psychology of Women Quarterly, 13*, 27–40.

Koss, M. P., & Dinero, T. E. (1988). Predictors of sexual aggression among a national sample of male college students. In V. I. Quinsey & R. Prentky (Eds.), *Human sexual aggression: Current perspectives* (pp. 133–147). New York: New York Academy of Sciences.

Koss, M. P., & Dinero, T. E. (1989). Discriminant analysis of risk factors for sexual victimization among a national sample of college women. *Journal of Consulting and Clinical Psychology, 57*, 242–250.

Koss, M. P., Dinero, T. E., Seibel, C. A., & Cox, S. L. (1988). Stranger and acquaintance rape: Are there differences in the victim's experience? *Psychology of Women Quarterly, 12*, 1–24.

Koss, M. P., Gidycz, C. A., & Wisniewski, N. (1987). The scope of rape incidence and prevalence of sexual aggression and victimization in a national sample of higher education students. *Journal of Consulting and Clinical Psychology, 55*, 162–170.

Koss, M. P., & Harvey, M. R. (1987). *The rape victim: Clinical and community approaches to treatment.* Lexington, MA: Stephen Greene Press.

Koss, M. P., Heise, L., & Russo, N. F. (1994). The global health burden of rape. *Psychology of Women Quarterly, 18*, 509–537.

Koss, M. P., & Oros, C. J. (1982). Sexual experiences survey: A research instrument investigating sexual aggression and victimization. *Journal of Consulting and Clinical Psychology, 50*, 455–457.

Kramarae, C., & Treichler, P. A. (1985). *A feminist dictionary.* Boston: Pandora.

Kramer, C. (1974, February). Women's speech: Separate but unequal. *Quarterly Journal of Speech, 60*, 14–24.

Kramer, C. (1977). Perceptions of female and male speech. *Language and Speech, 20*, 151–161.

Kramer, D. A., & Melchior, J. (1990). Gender, role conflict, and the development of relativistic and dialectical thinking. *Sex Roles, 23*, 553–575.

Kreipe, R. E., Churchill, B. H., & Strauss, J. (1989). Long-term outcome of adolescents with anorexia nervosa. *American Journal of Diseases of Children, 143*, 1322–1327.

Kreuz, I. E., & Rose, R. M. (1972). Assessment of aggressive behavior and plasma testosterone in young criminal populations. *Psychosomatic Medicine, 34*, 321–332.

Krieger, S. (1982). Lesbian identity and community: Recent social science literature. *Signs, 8*, 91–108.

Kronenberg, F. (1990). Hot flashes: Epidemiology and physiology. In M. Flint, F. Kronenberg, & W. Utian (Eds.), *Multidisciplinary perspectives on menopause: Annals of the New York Academy of Sciences, 592*, 52–86.

Krulewitz, J. E., & Nash, J. E. (1979). Effects of victims' resistance, assault outcome and sex of observer on attribution about rape. *Journal of Personality, 47*, 557–574.

Kuczynski, L., & Kochanska, G. (1990). Development of children's noncompliance strategies from toddlerhood to age 5. *Developmental Psychology, 26*, 398–408.

Kuebli, J., & Krieger, E. (1991, April). *Emotion and gender in parent-child conversations about the past.* Paper presented at the biennial meeting of the Society for Research in Child Development, Seattle, WA.

Kuhn, D., Nash, S. C., & Brucken, L. (1978). Sex role concepts of two- and three-year-olds. *Child Development, 49*, 445–451.

Kunda, Z., & Sherman-Williams, B. (1993). Stereotypes and the construal of individuating information. *Personality and Social Psychology Bulletin, 19*, 90–99.

Kurdek, L. A. (1987). Sex role self schema and psychological adjustment in coupled homosexual and heterosexual men and women. *Sex Roles, 17*, 549–562.

Kurdek, L. A. (1988a). Relationship quality of gay and lesbian cohabiting couples. *Journal of Homosexuality, 15*, 93–118.

Kurdek, L. A. (1988b). Correlates of negative attitudes toward homosexuals in heterosexual college students. *Sex Roles, 18,* 727–738.

Kurdek, L. A. (1988c). Perceived social support in gays and lesbians in cohabitating relationships. *Journal of Personality and Social Psychology, 54,* 504–509.

Kurdek, L. A. (1991a). Prediction of increase in marital distress in newlywed couples: A 3-year prospective longitudinal study. *Developmental Psychology, 27,* 627–636.

Kurdek, L. A. (1991b). Correlates of relationship satisfaction in cohabiting gay and lesbian couples: Integration of contextual, investment, and problem-solving models. *Journal of Personality and Social Psychology, 61,* 910–922.

Kurdek, L. A. (1993). Predicting marital dissolution: A 5-year prospective longitudinal study of newlywed couples. *Journal of Personality and Social Psychology, 64,* 221–242.

Kurdek, L. A., & Schmitt, J. P. (1986a). Early development of relationship quality in heterosexual married, heterosexual cohabiting, gay and lesbian couples. *Developmental Psychology, 22,* 305–309.

Kurdek, L. A., & Schmitt, J. P. (1986b). Interaction of sex role self-concept with relationship quality and relationship beliefs in married, heterosexual cohabiting, gay, and lesbian couples. *Journal of Personality and Social Psychology, 51,* 365–370.

Kurdek, L. A., & Schmitt, J. P. (1986c). Relationship quality of partners in heterosexual married, heterosexual cohabiting, and gay and lesbian relationships. *Journal of Personality and Social Psychology, 51,* 710–711.

Kurdek, L. A., & Schmitt, J. P. (1987). Perceived emotional support from family and friends in members of homosexual, married, and heterosexual cohabiting couples. *Journal of Homosexuality, 14,* 57–68.

Kurz, D. (1989). Social science perspectives on wife abuse: Current debates and future directions. *Gender and Society, 3,* 489–505.

Kutner, N. G., & Brogan, D. (1974). An investigation of sex-related slang vocabulary and sex-role orientation among male and female university students. *Journal of Marriage and the Family, 36,* 474–484.

Kwa, L. (1994). Adolescent females' perceptions of competence: What is defined as healthy and achieving. In J. Gallivan, S. D. Crozier, & V. M. Lalande (Eds.), *Women, girls, and achievement.* North York, Ontario: Captus University Publications.

Kyle, D. J., & Mahler, H. I. M. (1996). The effects of hair color and cosmetic use on perceptions of a female's ability. *Psychology of Women Quarterly, 20,* 447–455.

Labour Canada. (1986). *When I grow up: Career expectations and aspirations of Canadian schoolchildren.* Ottawa: Women's Bureau.

Labouvie-Vief, G., Hakim-Larson, J., & Hobart, C. J. (1987). Age, ego level, and the life-span development of coping and defense processes. *Psychology and Aging, 2,* 286–293.

Lackey, P. N. (1989). Adults' attitudes about assignments of household chores to male and female children. *Sex Roles, 20,* 271–281.

Ladas, A., Whipple, B., & Perry, J. (1982). *The G spot.* New York: Holt, Rinehart, & Winston.

LaFrance, M., & Carmen, B. (1980). The nonverbal display of psychological androgyny. *Journal of Personality and Social Psychology, 38,* 36–49.

LaFrance, M., & Mayo, C. (1978). *Moving bodies: Nonverbal communication in social relationships.* Monterey, CA: Brooks/Cole.

LaFromboise, T. D., Heyle, A. M., & Ozer, E. J. (1990). Changing and diverse roles of women in American Indian cultures. *Sex Roles, 22,* 455–476.

Lair, T., & Lefkowitz, D. (1990). Mental health and functional status of residents of nursing and personal care homes (DHHS Publication No. PHS 90-3470). Washington, DC: U.S. Government Printing Office.

Lakoff, R. (1973). Language and woman's place. *Language and Society, 2,* 45–79.

Lakoff, R. (1975). *Language and woman's place.* New York: Harper & Row.

Lamb, C. S., Jackson, L. A., Cassiday, P. B., & Priest, D. J. (1993). Body figure preferences of men and women: A comparison of two generations. *Sex Roles, 28,* Nos. 5/6.

Lamb, M. E. (1987). Introduction: The emergent American fathers. In M. E. Lamb (Ed.), *The father's role: Cross-cultural perspectives.* Hillsdale, NJ: Erlbaum.

Lambert, H. H. (1978). Biology and equality: A perspective on sex differences. *Signs: Journal of Women in Culture and Society, 4,* 97–117.

Lamke, L. K. (1982a). The impact of sex-role orientation on self-esteem in early adolescence. *Child Development, 53,* 1530–1535.

Lamke, L. K. (1982b). Adjustment and sex-role orientation in adolescence. *Journal of Youth and Adolescence, 11,* 247–259.

Lamphere, L. (1985). Bringing the family to work: Women's culture on the shop floor. *Feminist Studies, 11,* 518–540.

Lander, L. (1988). *Images of bleeding: Menstruation as ideology.* New York: Orlando Press.

Landers, A. D. (1977). The menstrual experience. In E. Donelson & J. E. Gullahorn (Eds.), *Women: A psychological perspective.* New York: Wiley.

Landers, S. (1989, April). NY: Scholarship awards are ruled discriminatory. *APA Monitor,* p. 14.

Landrine, H. (1985). Race x class stereotypes of women. *Sex Roles, 13,* 65–75.

Landrine, H. (1988). Depression and stereotypes of women: Preliminary empirical analyses of the gender-role hypothesis. *Sex Roles, 19,* 527–541.

Landrine, H. (1989). The politics of personality disorder. *Psychology of Women Quarterly, 13,* 325–339.

Landrine, H. (1991). *The politics of madness.* New York: Peter Lang.

Landrine, H., Klonoff, E. A., & Brown-Collins, A. (1992). Cultural diversity and methodology in feminist psychology: Critique, proposal, empirical example. *Psychology of Women Quarterly, 16,* 145–163.

Laner, M. R. (1979). Growing older female: Heterosexual and homosexual. *Journal of Homosexuality, 4,* 267–275.

Langdale, C. J. (1986). A re-vision of structural-developmental theory. In G. L. Sapp (Ed.), *Handbook of moral development: Models, processes, techniques, and research.* Birmingham, AL: Religious Education Press.

Langhinrichsen-Rohling, J., Smutzler, N., & Vivian, D. (1994). Positivity in marriage: The role of discord and physical aggression against wives. *Journal of Marriage and the Family, 56,* 69–79.

Laqueur, T. (1990). *Making sex: Body and gender from the Greeks to Freud.* Cambridge, MA: Harvard University Press.

Larwood, L., Szwajkowski, E., & Rose, S. (1988). Sex and race discrimination resulting from manager-client relationships: Applying the rational bias theory of managerial discrimination. *Sex Roles, 18,* 9–29.

Lasker, H. (1980). *Adult development course*. Cambridge, MA: Harvard University, School of Education.

Laumann, E. O., Gagnon, J., Michael, R. T., & Michaels, S. (1994). *The social organization of sexuality*. Chicago: University of Chicago Press.

Laury, G. (1987). Sexuality of the dying patient. *Medical Aspects of Human Sexuality, 21*, 102–109.

Lavecchia, C., Negri, E., Bruzzi, P., & Franceschi, S. (1995). The impact of mammography on breast cancer detection. *Annals of Oncology, 4*, 41–44.

Lavine, L. O., & Lombardo, J. P. (1984). Self-disclosure: Intimate and nonintimate disclosures to parents and best friends as a function of Bem Sex Role category. *Sex Roles, 11*, 735–744.

Lawrence, K., Taylor, D., & Byers, S. (1996). Differences in men's and women's global, sexual, and ideal-sexual expressiveness and instrumentality. *Sex Roles, 34*, 337–357.

Laws, J. L., & Schwartz, P. (1977). *Sexual scripts: The social construction of female sexuality*. Hinsdale, IL: Dryden Press.

Laws, S. (1983). The sexual politics of premenstrual tension. *Women's Studies International Forum, 6*, 19–31.

Laws, S. (1985). Who needs PMT? A feminist approach to the politics of premenstrual tension. In S. Laws, V. Hey, & A. Eagan (Eds.), *Seeing red*. London: Hutchinson.

Lawson, A. (1988). *Adultery*. New York: Basic Books.

Lazarus, R. J., & Folkman, J. (1984). *Stress, appraisal, and coping*. New York: Springer.

Leahy, R. L., & Shirk, S. R. (1984). The development of classificatory skills and sex-trait stereotypes in children. *Sex Roles, 10*, 281–292.

Leaper, C. (1991). Influences and involvement in children's discourse: Age, gender, and partner effects. *Child Development, 62*, 797–811.

Leaper, C., Carson, M., Baker, C., Holliday, H., & Myers, S. (1995). Self-disclosure and listener verbal support in same-gender and cross-gender friends' conversations. *Sex Roles, 33*, 387–404.

Leary, M. R., & Snell, W. E., Jr. (1988). The relationship of instrumentality and expressiveness to sexual behavior in males and females. *Sex Roles, 18*, 509–522.

Leavitt, F., & Berger, J. C. (1990). Clinical patterns among male transsexual candidates with erotic interest in males. *Archives of Sexual Behavior, 19*, 491–505.

Leavy, R. L., & Adams, E. M. (1986). Feminism as a correlate of self-esteem, self-acceptance, and social support among lesbians. *Psychology of Women Quarterly, 10*, 321–326.

Lederberg, A. R., Chapin, S. L., Rosenblatt, V., & Vandell, D. L. (1986). Ethnic, gender, and age preferences among deaf and hearing preschool peers. *Child Development, 57*, 375–386.

Ledman, R. E., Miller, M., & Brown, D. R. (1995). Successful women and women's colleges: Is there an intervening variable in the reported relationship? *Sex Roles, 33*, 489–497.

Lee, A. M., Nelson, K., & Nelson, J. K. (1988). Success estimations and performance in children as influenced by age, gender, and task. *Sex Roles, 18*, 719–726.

Lee, G. R. (1985). Kinship and social support of the elderly: The case of the United States. *Aging and Society, 5*, 19–38.

Lee, G. R. (1988). Marital satisfaction in later life: The effects of nonmarital roles. *Journal of Marriage and the Family, 50*, 775–783.

Lee, J. A. (1973). *The color of love*. Toronto: New Press.

Leffler, A., Gillespie, D. L., & Conaty, J. C. (1982). The effects of status differentiation on nonverbal behavior. *Social Psychology Quarterly, 45*, 153–161.

Lehr, E., & Spilka, B. (1989). Religion in the introductory psychology textbook: A comparison of three decades. *Journal for the Scientific Study of Religion, 28*, 366–371.

Leibowitz, L. (1975). Perspectives on the evolution of sex differences. In R. Reiter (Ed.), *Toward an anthropology of women*. New York: Monthly Review Press.

Leifer, M. (1980a). Pregnancy. *Signs, 5*, 754–765.

Leifer, M. (1980b). *Psychological aspects of motherhood: A study of first pregnancy*. New York: Praeger.

Leigh, W. A. (1994). The health status of women of color. In C. Costello & A. J. Stone (Eds.), *The American woman, 1994–1995: Where we stand, women and health*. New York: Norton.

Leitenberg, H., Detzer, M. J., & Srebnik, D. (1993). Gender differences in masturbation and relation of masturbation experience in preadolescence and early adolescence to sexual behavior and sexual adjustment in young adulthood. *Archives of Sexual Behavior, 22*, 87–98.

Leland, J. (1982). Gender, drinking, and alcohol abuse. In I. Al-Issa (Ed.), *Gender and psychopathology*. New York: Academic Press.

Lemkau, J. P. (1988). Emotional sequelae of abortion. *Psychology of Women Quarterly, 12*, 461–472.

Lenney, E. (1977). Women's self-confidence in achievement settings. *Psychological Bulletin, 288*, 288–292.

Lenney, E. (1981). What's fine for the gander isn't always good for the goose: Sex differences in self-confidence as a function of ability area and comparison with others. *Sex Roles, 7*, 905–924.

Lenney, E. (1983). Sex differences in self-confidence: The influence of comparison to others' ability level. *Sex Roles, 9*, 925–942.

Lennon, M. (1987). Is menopause depressing? An investigation of three perspectives. *Sex Roles, 17*, 1–16.

Lenz, R., & Chavez, B. (1981). Becoming active partners: A couple's perspective. In D. Bullard & S. Knight (Eds.), *Sexuality and disability: Personal perspectives*. St. Louis, MO: Mosby.

Leonard, A. S. (1994, July 25). Fired for being gay. *The New Yorker*, p. 6.

Leonard, K. E., & Blane, H. T. (1992). Alcohol and marital aggression in a national sample of young men. *Journal of Interpersonal Violence, 7*, 19–30.

Lepowsky, M. (1994). Women, men, and aggression in an egalitarian society. Special Issue: On aggression in women and girls: Cross-cultural perspectives. *Sex Roles, 30*, 119–211.

Lerman, H. (1986a). From Freud to feminist personality theory: Getting there from here. *Psychology of Women Quarterly, 10*, 1–18.

Lerman, H. (1986b). *A mote in Freud's eye: From psychoanalysis to the psychology of women*. New York: Springer.

Lerner, G. (1986). *The creation of patriarchy*. New York: Oxford University Press.

Lerner, H. G. (1985). *The dance of anger: A woman's guide to changing the patterns of intimate relationships*. New York: Harper & Row.

Lerner, J. V. (1994). *Working women and their families*. Thousand Oaks, CA: Sage.

Lerner, R. M. (1985). Adolescent maturational changes and psychosocial development: A dynamic interactional perspective. *Journal of Youth and Adolescence, 14*, 355–372.

Lesser, R. (1991). Deciding not to become a mother. In B. Sang, J. Warshow, & A. J. Smith (Eds.), *Lesbians at midlife: The creative transition, an anthology.* San Francisco: spinsters book company.

LeVay, S. (1991). A difference in hypothalamic structure between heterosexual and homosexual men. *Science, 253,* 1034–1037.

Levenson, R. W., Carstensen, L. L., & Gottman, J. M. (1994). The influence of age and gender on affect, physiology, and their interrelations: A study of long-term marriage. *Journal of Personality and Social Psychology, 67,* 56–68.

Levenson, R. W., & Gottman, J. M. (1985). Physiological and affective predictors of change in relationship satisfaction. *Journal of Personality and Social Psychology, 49,* 85–94.

Levenson, R. W., & Ruef, A. M. (1992). Empathy: A physiological substrate. *Journal of Personality and Social Psychology, 63,* 234–246.

Lever, J. (1976). Sex differences in the games children play. *Social Problems, 23,* 478–487.

Lever, J. (1978). Sex differences in the complexity of children's play and games. *American Sociological Review, 43,* 471–483.

Levin, J. S. (1994). Introduction: Religion in aging and health. In J. Levin (Ed.), *Religion in aging and health: Theoretical foundations and methodological frontiers* (pp. xiii–xiv). Thousand Oaks, CA: Sage.

Levine, L. W. (1977). *Black culture and black consciousness: Afro-American folk thought from slavery to freedom.* New York: Oxford University Press.

Levine, M. P. (1993). The role of culture in eating disorders. In D. N. Suggs & A. W. Miracle (Eds.), *Culture and human sexuality.* Pacific Grove, CA: Brooks/Cole.

Levine, M. P., & Leonard, R. (1984). Discrimination against lesbians in the work force. *Signs, 9,* 700–710.

Levine, S. (1992). Intrapsychic and interpersonal aspects of impotence: Psychogenic erectile dysfunction. In R. Rosen & S. Leiblum (Eds.), *Erectile disorders.* New York: Guilford Press.

Levinson, D. J., Darrow, C., Kline, E., Levinson, M., & McKee, B. (1978). *The seasons of a man's life.* New York: Knopf.

Levinson, R. M. (1981). Images of males and females in children's media during the seventies, or Kidvid and Kiddie Lit revisited. *Studies in Popular Culture, 4,* 82–89.

Levit, D. B. (1991). Gender differences in ego defenses in adolescence: Sex roles as one way to understand the differences. *Journal of Personality and Social Psychology, 61,* 992–999.

Levy, B. (1990). Abusive teen dating relationships: An emerging issue for the 90s. *Response to the Victimization of Women & Children, 13,* 5.

Levy, E. (1990). Stage, sex and suffering: Images of women in American films. *Empirical-Studies-of-the-Arts, 8,* 53–76.

Levy, G. D. (1989). Developmental and individual differences in preschoolers' recognition memories: The influences of gender schematization and verbal labeling of information. *Sex Roles, 21,* 305–324.

Levy, G. D. (1994a). High and low gender schematic children's release from proactive interference. *Sex Roles, 30,* 93–108.

Levy, G. D. (1994b). Aspects of preschoolers' comprehension of indoor and outdoor gender-typed toys. *Sex Roles, 30,* 391–405.

Levy, G. D., & Carter, D. B (1989). Gender schema, gender constancy, and gender-role knowledge: The roles of cognitive factors in preschoolers' gender-role stereotype attributions. *Developmental Psychology, 25,* 444–449.

Levy, J. (1972). Lateral specialization of the human brain: Behavioral manifestations and possible evolutionary basis. In J. A. Kiger (Ed.), *The biology of behavior.* Corvallis: Oregon State University Press.

Levy, J., & Reid, M. (1978). Variations in cerebral organization as a function of handedness, hand position in writing, and sex. *Journal of Experimental Psychology: General, 107,* 119–144.

Levy, J., & Sperry, R. W. (1970). Crossed temperature discrimination following section of forebrain neocortical commissures. *Cortex, 6,* 349–361.

Levy, S. M. (1980-1981). The adjustment of the older woman: Effects of chronic ill health and attitudes toward retirement. *International Journal of Aging and Human Development, 12,* 93–110.

Lew-Starowicz, Z. (1994). Problems of disabled persons with a homosexual orientation. *International Journal of Adolescent Medicine and Health, 7,* 233–239.

Lewin, M. (1984). "Rather worse than folly?" Psychology measures femininity and masculinity I: From Terman and Miles to the Guilfords. In M. Lewin (Ed.), *In the shadow of the past: Psychology portrays the sexes.* New York: Columbia University Press.

Lewin, M., & Wild, C. L. (1991). The impact of the feminist critique on tests, assessment, and methodology. *Psychology of Women Quarterly, 15,* 581–596.

Lewinsohn, P. W., Hops, H., Roberts, R. E., Seeley, J. R., & Andrews, J. A. (1993). Adolescent psychopathology: I. Prevalence and incidence of depression and other DSM-III-R disorders in high school students. *Journal of Abnormal Psychology, 102,* 133–144.

Lewis, E. C. (1968). *Developing woman's potential.* Ames: Iowa State University Press.

Lewis, L. L. (1992). PMS and the progesterone controversy. In A. J. Dan & L. L. Lewis (Eds.), *Menstrual health in women's lives.* Urbana: University of Illinois Press.

Lewis, M. (1990). What is psychobiology? *Contemporary Psychology, 35,* 575–577.

L'Heureux-Barrett, T., & Barnes-Farrell, J. L. (1991). Overcoming gender bias in reward allocation: The role of expectations of future performance. *Psychology of Women Quarterly, 15,* 127–139.

Libby, M. N., & Aries, E. (1989). Gender differences in preschool children's narrative fantasy. *Psychology of Women Quarterly, 13,* 293–306.

Liben, L. S., & Signorella, M . (1980). Gender-related schemata and constructive memory in children. *Child Development, 51,* 11–18.

Liben, L. S., & Signorella, M. L. (Eds.). (1987). *Children's gender schemata* (New Directions for Child Development, No. 38). London: Jossey-Bass.

Liben, L. S., & Signorella, M. L. (1993). Gender-schematic processing in children: The role of initial interpretations of stimuli. *Developmental Psychology, 29,* 141–149.

Liebenberg, B. (1969). Expectant fathers. *Child and Family, 8,* 265–277.

Lieblich, A., & Friedman, G. (1985). Attitudes toward male and female homosexuality and sex-role stereotypes in Israeli and American students. *Sex Roles, 12,* 561–570.

Lindell, S. G. (1988). Education for childbirth: A time for change. *Journal of Obstetrics, Gynecology, and Neonatal Nursing, 17,* 108–112.

Lindemalm, G., Korlin, D., & Uddenberg, N. (1986). Long-term follow-up of "sex change" in 13 male-to-female transsexuals. *Archives of Sexual Behavior, 15,* 187–210.

Lindsey, A. E., & Zakahi, W. R. (1996). Women who tell and men who ask: Perceptions of men and women departing from gender stereotypes during initial interaction. *Sex Roles, 34,* 767–786.

Lindsey, L. L. (1990). *Gender roles: A sociological perspective.* Englewood Cliffs, NJ: Prentice-Hall.

Linn, M. C., & Hyde, J. S. (1989, November). Gender, mathematics, and science. *Educational Researcher, 18,* 17–19, 22–27.

Linn, M. C., & Petersen, A. C. (1985). Emergence and characterization of sex differences in spatial ability: A meta-analysis. *Child Development, 56,* 1479–1498.

Linn, M. C., & Petersen, A. C. (1986). A meta-analysis of gender differences in spatial ability: Implications for mathematics and science achievement. In J. S. Hyde & M. C. Linn (Eds.), *The psychology of gender: Advances through meta-analysis* (pp. 67–101). Baltimore: Johns Hopkins University Press.

Linz, D. G. (1985). Sexual violence in the media: Effects on male viewers and implications for society. *Dissertation Abstracts International, 46*(4-B), 1382.

Linz, D. G. (1989). Exposure to sexually explicit materials and attitudes toward rape: A comparison of study results. *Journal of Sex Research, 26,* 50–84.

Linz, D. G., Wilson, B. J., & Donnerstein, E. (1992). Sexual violence in the mass media: Legal solutions, warnings and mitigation through education. *Journal of Social Issues, 48,* 145–171.

Lipman-Blumen, J. (1972). How ideology shapes women's lives. *Scientific American, 226,* 34–42.

Lippman, D. N. (1995, February 12). Women and STDs. *Lansing State Journal,* p. 1A.

Lippman, W. (1922). *Public opinion.* New York: Harcourt.

Lips, H. M. (1982, June). *Symptom-reporting among expectant fathers: A new look at the couvade syndrome.* Paper presented at the annual meeting of the Association for Birth Psychology, Halifax, Nova Scotia.

Lips, H. M. (1985). A longitudinal study of the reporting of emotional and somatic symptoms during and after pregnancy. *Social Science and Medicine, 2,* 631–640.

Lips, H. M. (1997). *Sex & gender: An introduction* (3rd ed.). Mountain View, CA: Mayfield.

Lips, H. M., & Morrison, A. (1986). Changes in the sense of family among couples expecting their first child. *Journal of Social and Personal Relationships, 3,* 393–400.

Lisak, D., & Roth, S. (1988). Motivational factors in non-incarcerated sexually aggressive men. *Journal of Personality and Social Psychology, 55,* 795–802.

Lish, J., Ehrhardt, A., Meyer-Bahlburg, H., Rosen, L., Gruen, R., & Veridiano, N. (1991). Gender-related behavior in development in females exposed to diethylstilbestrol (DES) in utero: An attempted replication. *Journal of the American Academy of Child and Adolescent Psychiatry, 30,* 29–37.

Liss, M. B. (1983). *Social and cognitive skills: Sex roles and children's play.* New York: Academic Press.

Livingston, J. A. (1982). Responses to sexual harassment on the job: Legal. *Journal of Social Issues, 38,* 5–22.

Livson, F. B. (1976). Patterns of personality development in middle-aged women: A longitudinal study. *International Journal of Aging and Human Development, 7,* 107–115.

Livson, F. B. (1981). Paths to psychological health in the middle years: Sex differences. In D. Eichorn, N. Haan, J.

Clausen, M. Honzik, & P. Mussen (Eds.), *Past and present in middle life* (pp. 183–194). New York: Academic Press.

Livson, F. B. (1983). Gender identity: A life-span view of sex role development. In R. Weg (Ed.), *Aging: An international annual: Vol. 1. Sexuality in the later years: Roles and behavior.* Menlo Park, CA: Addison-Wesley.

Livson, N., & Peskin, H. (1980). Perspectives on adolescence from longitudinal research. In J. Adelson (Ed.), *Handbook of adolescent psychology.* New York: Wiley.

Lobel, T. E., Agami-Rozenblat, O., & Bempechat, J. (1993). Personality correlates of career choice in the kibbutz: A comparison between career and noncareer women. *Sex Roles, 29,* 359–370.

Lockheed, M. E. (1986). Reshaping the social order: The case of gender segregation. *Sex Roles, 14,* 617–628.

Lockheed, M. E., & Hall, K. P. (1976). Conceptualizing sex as a status characteristic: Applications to leadership training strategies. *Journal of Social Issues, 32,* 111–124.

Loevinger, J. (1976). *Ego development.* San Francisco: Jossey-Bass.

Loftus, E. F. (1993). The reality of repressed memories. *American Psychologist, 48,* 518–537.

Loftus, E. F., Polonsky, S., & Fullilove, M. T. (1994). Memories of childhood sexual abuse. *Psychology of Women Quarterly, 18,* 67–84.

Lone Dog, L. (1991). Coming out as a Native American. In B. Sang, J. Warshow, & A. J. Smith (Eds.), *Lesbians at midlife: The creative transition, an anthology.* San Francisco, CA: spinsters book company.

Long, J., & Porter, K. L. (1984). Multiple roles of midlife women. In G. Baruch & J. Brooks-Gunn (Eds.), *Women in midlife* (pp. 109–159). New York: Plenum Press.

Longino, H. (1980). What is pornography? In L. Lederer (Ed.), *Take back the night: Women on pornography.* New York: Morrow.

Longstaff, H. P. (1954). Practice effects on the Minnesota Vocational Test for clerical workers. *Journal of Applied Psychology, 38,* 18–20.

Lonsway, K. A. (1996). Preventing acquaintance rape through education. *Psychology of Women Quarterly, 20,* 229–265.

Lonsway, K. A., & Fitzgerald, L. F. (1994). Rape myths: In review. *Psychology of Women Quarterly, 18,* 133–164.

Lonsway, K. A., & Fitzgerald, L. F. (1995). Attitudinal antecedents of rape myth acceptance: A theoretical and empirical reexamination. *Journal of Personality and Social Psychology, 68,* 704–711.

Lont, C. M. (1990). The roles assigned to females and males on non-music radio programming. *Sex Roles, 22,* 661–668.

Loo, C., & Ong, P. (1982). Slaying demons with a sewing needle: Feminist issues for Chinatown's women. *Berkeley Journal of Sociology, 17,* 77–88.

Looft, W. R. (1971). Sex differences in the expression of vocational aspirations by elementary school children. *Developmental Psychology, 5,* 366.

Lopata, H. Z. (1971). *Occupation housewife.* New York: Oxford University Press.

Lopata, H. Z. (1975). Widowhood: Societal factors in life-span disruptions and alternatives. In N. Datan & L. H. Ginsberg (Eds.), *Life-span developmental psychology: Normative life crises* (pp. 217–234). New York: Academic Press.

Lopata, H. Z. (1979). *Women as widows: Support systems.* New York: Elsevier.

Lopata, H. Z. (1980). The widowed family member. In N. Datan & N. Lohmann (Eds.), *Transitions of aging*. New York: Academic Press.

Lopata, H. Z., & Norr, K. F. (1980). Changing commitments of American women to work and family roles. *Social Security Bulletin, 43*, 3–14.

LoPiccolo, J. (1989, April). Sexual dysfunctions: Advances in diagnosis and treatment. Workshop for Oregon Division of The American Association of Marriage and Family Therapy, Portland.

LoPiccolo, J. (1991). Counseling and therapy for sexual problems in the elderly. *Clinics in Geriatric Medicine, 7*, 161–179.

LoPiccolo, J., & Stock, W. E. (1986). Treatment of sexual dysfunction. *Journal of Consulting and Clinical Psychology, 54*, 158–167.

Lorber, J. (1993). Believing is seeing: Biology as ideology. *Gender and Society, 7*, 568–581.

Lorber, J. (1994). *Paradoxes of gender.* New Haven, CT: Yale University Press.

Lorde, A. (1975). *From a land where people live.* (As quoted in Partnow, E. (Ed.). (1993). *The new quotable woman* (p. 48). New York: Penguin.)

Lorde, A. (1981/1990). The uses of anger: Women responding to racism. Keynote address to the National Women's Studies Association Conference, Storrs, CT, 1981. Reprinted in P. C. Hoy II, E. H. Schor, & R. DiYanni. (1990). *Women's voices, visions and perspectives.* New York: McGraw-Hill.

Lorde, A. (1984). *Uses of the erotic: The erotic as power.* Freedom, CA: Crossing Press.

Lorde, A. (1988). Feminism and Black liberation: The great American disease. *The Black Scholar, 10*, 17–20.

Lore, R. K., & Schultz, L. A. (1993, January). Control of human aggression: A comparative perspective. *American Psychologist, 48*, 16–25.

Lothstein, L. (1984). Psychological testing with transsexuals: A 30-year review. *Journal of Personality Assessment, 48*, 500–507.

Lott, B. (1985). The potential enrichment of social/personality psychology through feminist research and vice versa. *American Psychologist, 40*, 155–164.

Lott, B. (1991). Social psychology: Humanist roots and feminist future. *Psychology of Women Quarterly, 15*, 505–519.

Lott, B. (1994). *Women's lives: Themes and variations in gender learning* (2nd ed.). Pacific Grove, CA: Brooks/Cole.

Lott, B., & Maluso, D. (1993). The social learning of gender. In A. E. Beall & R. J. Sternbert (Eds.), *The psychology of gender* (pp. 99–123). New York: Guilford Press.

Lottes, I. L. (1993). Nontraditional gender roles and the sexual experiences of heterosexual college students. *Sex Roles, 29*, 645–669.

Loucks, A. B., & Horvath, S. M. (1985). Athletic amenorrhea: A review. *Medicine & Science in Sports and Exercise, 17*, 56–72.

Love, A. M., & Deckers, L. H. (1989). Humor appreciation as a function of sexual, aggressive, and sexual content. *Sex Roles, 20*, 649–654.

Lovelace, L. (1981). *Ordeal.* New York: Berkley Books.

Lovelace, L. (1986). *Out of bondage.* Secaucus, NJ: Lyle Stuart.

Lowe, R., & Wittig, M. A. (Eds.). (1989). Achieving pay equity through comparable worth. Special issue of the *Journal of Social Issues, 45*.

Lowen, A. (1967). *Love and orgasm.* New York: Signet Books.

Lowenthal, M. F. (1972). Some potentialities of a life-cycle approach to the study of retirement. In F. M. Carp (Ed.), *Retirement.* New York: Behavioral Publications.

Lowenthal, M. F., & Haven, C. (1968). Interaction and adaptation: Intimacy as a critical variable. *American Sociological Review, 33*, 20–30.

Luebke, B. (1989). Out of focus: Images of women and men in newspaper photographs. *Sex Roles, 20*, 121–133.

Lummis, M., & Stevenson, H. W. (1990). Gender differences in beliefs and achievement: A cross-cultural study. *Developmental Psychology, 26*, 254–263.

Lyons, D. S., & Green, S. B. (1988). Sex role development as a function of college experiences. *Sex Roles, 18*, 31–40.

Lytton, H., & Romney, D. M. (1991). Parents' sex-related differential socialization of boys and girls: A meta-analysis. *Psychological Bulletin, 109*, 267–296.

Maccoby, E. E. (1988). Gender as a social category. *Developmental Psychology, 24*.

Maccoby, E. E. (1990). Gender and relationships: A developmental account. *American Psychologist, 44*, 513–520.

Maccoby, E. E. (1992). The role of parents in the socialization of children: An historical overview. *Developmental Psychology, 28*, 1006–1017.

Maccoby, E. E., & Jacklin, C. N. (1974). *The psychology of sex differences.* Stanford, CA: Stanford University Press.

Maccoby, E. E., & Jacklin, C. N. (1980). Sex differences in aggression: A rejoinder and reprise. *Child Development, 51*, 964–980.

Maccoby, E. E., & Jacklin, C. N. (1987a). Gender segregation in childhood. *Advances in child development and behavior, 20*, 239–287.

Maccoby, E. E., & Jacklin, C. N. (1987b). Gender segregation in childhood. In E. H. Reese (Ed.), *Advances in child development.* New York: Academic Press.

MacDonald, A., Jr. (1981). Bisexuality: Some comments on research and theory. *Journal of Homosexuality, 6*, 21–35.

MacDonald, K., & Parke, R. D. (1986). Parent-child physical play: The effects of sex and age of children and parents. *Sex Roles, 15*, 367–378.

Machung, A. (1989). Talking career, thinking job: Gender differences in career and family expectations of Berkeley seniors. *Feminist Studies, 15*, 35–58.

MacKinnon, C. A. (1979). *Sexual harassment of working women: A case of sex discrimination.* New Haven, CT: Yale University Press.

MacKinnon, C. A. (1986). Pornography: Not a moral issue. Special issue: Women and the law. *Women's Studies International Forum, 99*, 63–78.

MacKinnon, C. A. (1987). *Females unmodified: Discourses on life and law.* Cambridge, MA: Harvard University Press.

Maddux, H. C. (1975). *Menstruation.* New Canaan, CT: Tobey.

Magnusson, D. (1988). *Individual development from an interactional perspective.* Hillsdale, NJ: Erlbaum.

Magnusson, D., Stattin, H., & Allen, J. L. (1985). Biological maturation and social development: A longitudinal study of some adjustment processes from mid-adolescence to adulthood. *Journal of Youth and Adolescence, 14*, 267–283.

Mahlstedt, D. (1991, August). *Fraternity violence education project: When men take action.* Paper presented at the meeting of the American Psychological Association, San Francisco.

Major, B. (1989). Gender differences in comparisons and entitlement: Implications for comparable worth. *Journal of Social Issues, 45*, 99–115.

Major, B., & Adams, J. B. (1983). Role of gender, interpersonal orientation, and self-presentation in distributive-justice behavior. *Journal of Personality and Social Psychology, 45*, 598–608.

Major, B., & Cozzarelli, C. (1992). Psychosocial predictors of adjustment to abortion. *Journal of Social Issues, 48*, 121–142.

Major, B., & Heslin, R. (1982). Perception of cross-sex and same-sex nonreciprocated touch: It is better to give than to receive. *Journal of Nonverbal Behavior, 16*, 148–162.

Major, B., Schmidlin, A. M., & Williams, L. (1990). Gender patterns in social touch: The impact of setting and age. *Journal of Personality and Social Psychology, 58*, 634–643.

Major, B., & Testa, M. (1989). Social comparison processes and judgments of entitlement and satisfaction. *Journal of Experimental Social Psychology, 25*, 101–120.

Makepeace, J. M. (1986). Gender differences in courtship violence victimization. *Family Relations, 35*, 383–388.

Malamuth, N. M. (1983). Factors associated with rape as predictors of laboratory aggression against women. *Journal of Personality and Social Psychology, 45*, 432–442.

Malamuth, N. M. (1986). Predictors of naturalistic sexual aggression. *Journal of Personality and Social Psychology, 50*, 953–962.

Malamuth, N. M. (1989a). The attraction to sexual aggression scale: Part I. *Journal of Sex Research, 26*, 26–49.

Malamuth, N. M. (1989b). The attraction to sexual aggression scale: Part II. *Journal of Sex Research, 26*, 324–354.

Malamuth, N. M., & Briere, J. (1986). Sexual violence in the media: Indirect effects on aggression against women. *Journal of Social Issues, 42*, 75–92.

Malamuth, N. M., & Check, J. V. P. (1985). The effects of aggressive pornography on beliefs in rape myths: Individual differences. *Journal of Research in Personality, 19*, 299–320.

Malamuth, N. M., Sockloskie, R. J., Koss, M. P., & Tanaka, J. S. (1991). Characteristics of aggressors against women: Testing a model using a national sample of college students. *Journal of Consulting and Clinical Psychology, 39*, 670–681.

Mallon, R. (1984, October). *Demonstration of vestigial prostatic tissue in the human female.* Paper presented at the annual regional conference of the American Association of Sex Educators, Counselors, and Therapists, Las Vegas.

Malson, M. R. (1983). Black women's sex roles: The social context of a new ideology. *Journal of Social Issues, 39*, 101–113.

Maltz, W. (1991). *The sexual healing journey.* New York: HarperCollins.

Mancus, D. S. (1992). Influence of male teachers on elementary school children's stereotyping of teacher competence. *Sex Roles, 26*, 109–128.

Mandelbaum, D. R. (1978). Women in medicine. *Signs, 4*, 136–145.

Mandoki, C. A., & Burkhart, B. R. (1991). Women as victim: Antecedents and consequences of acquaintance rape. In A. Parrot & L. Bechhofer (Eds.), *Acquaintance rape: The hidden crime* (pp. 176–191). New York: Wiley.

Mansfield, P. K., Koch, P. B., Henderson, J., Vicary, J. R., Cohn, M., & Young, E. W. (1991). The job climate for women in traditionally male blue-collar occupations. *Sex Roles, 25*, 63–79.

Marchand, R. (1985). *Advertising the American dream: Making way for modernity, 1920–1940.* Berkeley: University of California Press.

Marcia, J. E. (1980). Identity in adolescence. In J. Adelson (Ed.), *Handbook of adolescent psychology.* New York: Wiley.

Marecek, J. (1995). Gender, politics, and psychology's ways of knowing. *American Psychologist, 50*, 162–163.

Marecek, J., & Kravetz, D. (1977). Women and mental health: A review of feminist change efforts. *Psychiatry, 40*, 323–329.

Markides, K. S., & Vernon, S. W. (1984). Aging, sex-role orientation, and adjustment: A three-generation study of Mexican-Americans. *Journal of Gerontology, 39*, 586–591.

Markowitz, L. (1991, January/February). Homosexuality: Are we still in the dark? *Networker,* pp. 27–35.

Markson, E. W., & Hess, B. B. (1980). Older women in the city. *Signs, 5*, 127–141.

Markson, E. W., & Taylor, C. A. (1993). Real versus reel world: Older women and the Academy Awards. In N. D. Davis, E. Cole, & E. D. Rothblum (Eds.), *Faces of women and aging* (pp. 157–172). Binghamton, NY: Harrington Park Press.

Markstrom-Adams, C. (1989). Androgyny and its relation to adolescent psychosocial well-being: A review of the literature. *Sex Roles, 21*, 325–340.

Markstrom-Adams, C. (1991). Attitudes on dating, courtship, and marriage: Perspectives on in-group versus out-group relationships by religious minority and majority adolescents. *Family Relations, 40*, 91–96.

Markus, H. (1977). Self-schemata and processing information about the self. *Journal of Personality and Social Psychology, 35*, 63–78.

Markus, H., Crane, M., Bernstein, S., & Siladi, M. (1982). Self-schemas and gender. *Journal of Personality and Social Psychology, 42*, 38–50.

Markus, H. R., & Kitayama, S. (1991). Culture and the self: Implications for cognition, emotion, and motivation. *Psychological Review, 98*, 224–253.

Marris, P. (1958). *Widows and their families.* London: Routledge & Kegan Paul.

Marsh, H. W. (1987). Masculinity, femininity and androgyny: Their relations to multiple dimensions of self-concept. *Multivariate Behavioral Research, 22*, 91–118.

Marsh, H. W., Anhill, J. K., & Cunningham, J. D. (1987). Masculinity, femininity, and androgyny: Relationships to self-esteem and social desirability. *Journal of Personality, 55*, 661–683.

Marsh, H. W., & Byrne, B. M. (1991). Differentiated additive androgyny model: Relations between masculinity, femininity, and multiple dimensions of self-concept. *Journal of Personality and Social Psychology, 61*, 811–828.

Marsh, H. W., & Jackson, S. A. (1986). Multidimensional self-concepts, masculinity, and femininity as a function of a woman's involvement in athletics. *Sex Roles, 15*, 391–415.

Marshall, W. A., & Tanner, J. M. (1974). Puberty. In J. A. David & J. Dobbing (Eds.), *Scientific foundations of pediatrics.* Philadelphia: Saunders.

Marsiglio, W. (1986). Teenage fatherhood: High school accreditation and educational attainment. In A. B. Eister & M. E. Lamb (Eds.), *Adolescent fatherhood.* Hillsdale, NJ: Erlbaum.

Marsiglio, W., & Donnelly, D. (1991). Sexual relations in later life: A national study of married persons. *Journal of Gerontology, 46*, 5338–5344.

Martell, R. F. (1996a). Sex bias at work: The effect of attentional and memory demands on performance ratings of men and women. *Journal of Applied Psychology, 70*, 1939–1960.

Martell, R. F. (1996b). What mediates gender bias in work behavior ratings? *Sex Roles, 35,* 153–169.

Martin, B. A. (1989). Gender differences in salary expectations when current salary information is provided. *Psychology of Women Quarterly, 13,* 87–96.

Martin, C. L. (1987). A ratio measure of sex stereotyping. *Journal of Personality and Social Psychology, 52,* 489–499.

Martin, C. L. (1989). Children's use of gender-related information in making social judgments. *Developmental Psychology, 25,* 80–88.

Martin, C. L. (1990). Attitudes and expectations about children with nontraditional and traditional gender roles. *Sex Roles, 22,* 151–165.

Martin, C. L. (1993). The role of cognition in understanding gender effects. In H. W. Reese (Ed.). *Advances in child development and behavior* (Vol. 23). New York: Academic Press.

Martin, C. L. (1995). Stereotypes about children with traditional and nontraditional gender roles. *Sex Roles, 33,* 727–751.

Martin, C. L., & Halverson, C. F., Jr. (1981). A schematic processing model of sex typing and stereotyping in children. *Child Development, 52,* 1119–1134.

Martin, C. L., & Halverson, C. F. (1983). A schematic processing model of sex typing schemas on young children's memory. *Child Development, 54,* 563–574.

Martin, C. L., & Little, J. K. (1990). The relation of gender understanding to children's sex-typed preferences and gender stereotypes. *Child Development, 61,* 1427–1439.

Martin, C. L., Wood, C. H., & Little, J. K. (1990). The development of gender stereotype components. *Child Development, 61,* 1891–1904.

Martin, D., & Lyon, P. (1972). *Lesbian/woman.* New York: Bantam Books.

Martin, E. (1987). *The woman in the body: A cultural analysis of reproduction.* Boston: Beacon Press.

Martin, H., & Ramanaiah, N. (1988). Confirmatory factory analysis of the Bem Sex Role Inventory. *Psychological Reports, 62,* 343–350.

Martin, S. E. (1988). Think like a man, work like a dog, and act like a lady: Occupational dilemmas of policewomen. In A. Statham, E. M. Miller, & H. O. Mauksch (Eds.), *The worth of women's work: A qualitative synthesis* (pp. 205–224). Albany: University of New York Press.

Martin, S. E. (1994). "Outsider within" the station house: The impact of race and gender on Black women police. *Social Problems, 41,* 383–400.

Martinson, F. M. (1994). *The sexual life of children.* Westport, CT: Bergin & Garvey.

Marx, J. L. (1979). Dysmenorrhea: Basic research leads to a rational therapy. *Science, 205,* 175–176.

Maslach, C., Santee, R. T., & Wade, C. (1987). Individuation, gender role, and dissent: Personality mediators of situational forces. *Journal of Personality and Social Psychology, 53,* 1088–1093.

Massad, C. M. (1981). Sex role identity and adjustment during adolescence. *Child Development, 42,* 1290–1298.

Masters, W. H., & Johnson, V. E. (1966). *Human sexual response.* Boston: Little, Brown.

Masters, W. H., & Johnson, V. E. (1975). *The pleasure bond: A new look at sexuality and commitment.* Boston: Little, Brown.

Masters, W. H., & Johnson, V. E. (1979). *Homosexuality in perspective.* Boston: Little, Brown.

Masters, W. H., Johnson, V., & Kolodny, R. C. (1992). *Human sexuality* (3rd ed.). New York: HarperCollins.

Matlin, M. W. (1991). *The psychology of women* (3rd ed.). New York: Harcourt Brace.

Matlin, M. W. (1993). *Looking into the crystal ball: The psychology of women and gender in the 21st century.* Paper presented at a conference, "Psychology in the 21st Century," York University, Ontario, Canada.

Matlin, M. W., & Matkoski, K. M. (1985). *Gender-stereotyping of cognitive abilities.* Paper presented at the annual meeting of the Eastern Psychological Association, Boston.

Matteo, S. (1988). The risk of multiple addictions: Guidelines for assessing a woman's alcohol and drug use. *Western Journal of Medicine, 149,* 741–745.

Matthews, K. A., & Carra, J. (1982). Suppression of menstrual distress symptoms: A study of Type A behavior. *Personality and Social Psychology Bulletin, 8,* 146–151.

Matthews, W. J. (1984). Violence in college students. *College Student Journal, 18,* 150–158.

Mauldin, T., & Meeks, C. (1990). Sex differences in children's time use. *Sex Roles, 22,* 537–554.

Maxfield, M. G. (1989). Circumstances in supplementary homicide reports: Variety and validity. *Criminology, 27,* 671–694.

Maynard, M. (1994). Methods, practice and epistemology: The debate about feminism and research. In M. Maynard & J. Purvis (Eds.), *Researching women's lives from a feminist perspective* (pp. 10–26). London: Taylor & Francis.

Mayo, C., & Henley, N. (1981). *Gender and nonverbal behavior.* New York: Springer.

Mayor picks woman. (1991, December 28). *Detroit Free Press,* p. 1A.

Mazer, D., & Percival, E. (1989). Ideology or experience? The relationship among perceptions, attitudes, and experiences of sexual harassment in university students. *Sex Roles,* 135–147.

Mazur, E., & Oliver, R. R. (1987). Intimacy and structure: Sex differences in imagery of same-sex relationships. *Sex Roles, 16,* 539–558.

McAdams, D. P. (1994). *The person: An introduction to personality psychology* (2nd ed.). San Diego: Harcourt Brace Jovanovich.

McAdams, D. P., & Bryant, F. B. (1987). Intimacy motivation and subjective mental health in a nationwide sample. *Journal of Personality, 55,* 395–413.

McAdoo, H. P. (1989, November). *Family values and outcomes for children.* Paper presented at conference, One-third of a nation: African American perspectives. African American Family Life: Child rearing and developmental outcomes.

McAdoo, J. L. (1988). Changing perspectives on the role of the Black father. In P. Bronstein & C. P. Cowan (Eds.), *Fatherhood today: Men's changing role in the family.* New York: Wiley.

McAdoo, J. L. (1993). Decision making and marital satisfaction in African American families. In H. P. McAdoo (Ed.), *Family ethnicity: Strength in diversity* (pp. 109–119). Newbury Park, CA: Sage.

McAninch, C. B., Milich, R., Crumbo, G. B., & Funtowicz, M. N. (1996). Children's perception of gender-role-congruent and -incongruent behavior in peers: Fisher-Price meets Price-Waterhouse. *Sex Roles, 35,* 619–638.

McArthur, L. Z., & Eisen, S. V. (1976). Television and sex-role stereotyping. *Journal of Applied Social Psychology, 6,* 329–351.

McBride, A. B. (1990). Mental health effects of women's multiple roles. *American Psychologist, 45,* 381–384.

McBride, S. (1990). Maternal moderators of child care: The role of maternal separation anxiety. *New Directions in Child Development, 49,* 53–70.

McBroom, W. H. (1987). Longitudinal change in sex role orientations: Differences between men and women. *Sex Roles, 16,* 439–452.

McCabe, M. (1987). Desired and experienced levels of premarital affection and sexual intercourse during dating. *Journal of Sex Research, 23,* 23–33.

McCabe, M. P. (1994). Childhood, adolescent, and current psychological factors associated with sexual dysfunction. *Sexual & Marital Therapy, 9,* 267–276.

McCall, G. J. (1993). Risk factors and sexual assault prevention. *Journal of Interpersonal Violence, 8,* 277–295.

McCarthy, B. W. (1992). Sexual trauma: The pendulum has swung too far. *Journal of Sex Education and Therapy, 18,* 1–10.

McClelland, D. C. (1961). *The achieving society.* Princeton, NJ: Van Nostrand.

McClelland, D. C. (1975). *Power: The inner experience.* New York: Irvington.

McClelland, D. C. (1980). Motive dispositions: The merits of operant and respondent measures. In L. Wheeler (Ed.), *Review of personality and social psychology* (Vol. 1, pp. 10–41). Beverly Hills, CA: Sage.

McClelland, D. C. (1985b). How motives, skills, and values determine what people do. *American Psychologist, 40,* 812–825.

McClelland, D. C., Atkinson, J. W., Clark, R. A., & Lowell, E. L. (1953). *The achievement motive.* New York: Appleton-Century-Crofts.

McClelland, D. C., Davis, W. N., Kalin, R., & Wanner, E. (1972). *The drinking man.* New York: Free Press.

McClelland, D. C., Koestner, R., & Weinberger, J. (1989). How do self-attributed and implicit motives differ? *Psychological Review, 96,* 690–702.

McClintock, M. (1979, Summer). Commentary. *Signs, 4,* 703–710.

McClintock, M. K. (1971). Menstrual synchrony and suppression. *Nature, 229,* 244–245.

McCloskey, L. A., & Coleman, L. M. (1992). Difference without dominance: Children's talk in mixed- and same-sex dyads. *Sex Roles, 27,* 241–257.

McCombie, S. L. (1980). *The rape crisis intervention handbook.* New York: Plenum Press.

McConaghy, M. J. (1979). Gender permanence and the genital basis of gender: Stages in the development of constancy of gender identity. *Child Development, 50,* 1223–1226.

McConaghy, N. (1993). *Sexual behavior: Problems and management.* New York: Plenum Press.

McConnell-Ginet, S. (1978). Intonation in a woman's world. *Signs, 3,* 541–559.

McCray, C. A. (1980). The black woman and family roles. In L. Rodgers-Rose (Ed.), *The black woman.* Newbury Park, CA: Sage.

McCreary, D. R., Wong, F. Y., Wiener, W., Carpenter, K. M., Engle, A., & Nelson, P. (1996). The relationship between masculine gender role stress and psychological adjustment: A question of construct validity? *Sex Roles, 34,* 507–516.

McCreery, M. F. (1991). *The role of shame in bulimia nervosa: The female bulimic's perception of interpersonal needs.* Unpublished master's thesis, Michigan State University, East Lansing.

McCullough, M. (1992). *Black and white women's friendships: Claiming the margins.* Unpublished doctoral dissertation, Temple University, Philadelphia.

McDonald, S. M. (1989). Sex bias in the representation of male and female characters in children's picture books. *Journal of Genetic Psychology, 150,* 389–401.

McEwan, C. (1985). Crying the blues: Male postpartum depression explained. *Great Expectations, 14,* 56–59.

McFarland, C., Ross, M., & DeCourville, N. (1989). Women's theories of menstruation and biases in recall of menstrual symptoms. *Journal of Personality and Social Psychology, 57,* 522–531.

McFarlane, A. C., McFarlane, C. M., & Gilchrist, P. N. (1988). Posttraumatic bulimia and anorexia nervosa. *International Journal of Eating Disorders, 7,* 705–708.

McFarlane, J., Allen, L., & Honzik, M. A. (1974). *Developmental study of behavioral problems of normal children.* Berkeley: University of California Press.

McFarlane, J. M., Martin, C. L., & Williams, T. M. (1988). Mood fluctuations: Women versus men and menstrual versus other cycles. *Psychology of Women Quarterly, 12,* 201–223.

McFarlane, J. M., & Williams, T. M. (1994). Placing premenstrual syndrome in perspective. *Psychology of Women Quarterly, 18,* 339–373.

McGee, J., & Wells, K. (1982). Gender typing and androgyny in later life: New directions for theory and research. *Human Development, 25,* 116–139.

McGee, M. G. (1979). Human spatial abilities: Psychometric studies and environmental, genetic, and neural influences. *Psychological Bulletin, 86,* 889–918.

McGhee, P. E., & Frueh, T. (1980). Television viewing and the learning of sex-role stereotypes. *Sex Roles, 6,* 179–188.

McGinley, P. (1969). *Saint-watching.* New York: Viking Press.

McGlashan, K. E., Wright, P. M., & McCormick, B. (1995). Preferential selection and stereotypes: Effects on evaluation of female leader performance, subordinate goal commitment, and task performance. *Sex Roles, 33,* 669–686.

McGloshen, T. H., & O'Bryant, S. L. (1988). The psychological well-being of older, recent widows. *Psychology of Women Quarterly, 12,* 99–116.

McGoldrick, M., Garcia-Preto, N., Hines, P. M., & Lee, E. (1989). Ethnicity and women. In M. McGoldrick, C. M. Anderson, & F. Walsh (Eds.), *Women in families: A framework of feminist theory* (pp. 169–199). New York: Norton.

McGonagle, K. A., Kessler, R. C., & Gotlib, I. H. (1993). The effects of marital disagreement style, frequency, and outcome on marital disruption. *Journal of Personality and Social Relationships, 10,* 385–404.

McGrath, E., Keita, G. P., Strickland, B. R., & Russo, N. F. (1990). *Women and depression: Risk factors and treatment issues.* Washington, DC: American Psychological Association.

McGraw, K. O., & Wong, Y. (1992). A common language effect size statistic. *Psychological Bulletin, 111,* 361–365.

McGreal, C. E. (1994). The family across generations: Grandparenthood. In L. L'Abate (Ed.), *Handbook of developmental family psychology and psychopathology.* New York: Wiley.

McGuire, M. B. (1987). *Religion: The social context.* Belmont, CA: Wadsworth.

McGuire, T. R. (1995). Is homosexuality genetic? A critical review and some suggestions. *Journal of Homosexuality, 28,* 115–145.

McHale, S. M., & Huston, T. L. (1985). The effect of the transition to parenthood on the marriage relationship: A longitudinal study. *Journal of Family Issues, 6,* 409–433.

McHugh, M. C., & Frieze, I. H. (1997). The measurement of gender-role attitudes. *Psychology of Women Quarterly, 21,* 1–16.

McIntosh, P. (1988). *White privilege and male privilege: A personal account of coming to see correspondences through work in women's studies.* Wellesley, MA: Wellesley College Center for Research on Women.

McKee, J. P., & Sherriffs, A. C. (1957). The differential evaluation of males and females. *Journal of Personality, 25,* 356–371.

McKee, J. P., & Sherriffs, A. C. (1959). Men's and women's beliefs, ideals, and self-concepts. *American Journal of Sociology, 64,* 356–363.

McKenna, W., & Denmark, F. L. (1978, March). *Gender and nonverbal behavior as cues to status and power.* Paper presented at the New York Academy of Sciences.

McKinlay, J. B., McKinlay, S. M., & Brambilla, D. J. (1987). The relative contributions of endocrine changes and social circumstances to depression in mid-aged women. *Journal of Health and Social Behavior, 28,* 345–363.

McKinley, N. M., & Hyde, J. S. (1996). The Objectified Body Consciousness Scale: Development and validation. *Psychology of Women Quarterly, 20,* 181–215.

McKinney, K. (1987). Age and gender differences in college students' attitudes toward women: A replication and extension. *Sex Roles, 17,* 353–358.

McLaren, A. (1990). *A history of contraception: From antiquity to the present day.* Cambridge, MA: Basil Blackwell.

McLaurin, P. (1989). *From Beulah to Clair Huxtable: You've come a long way, girl, or have you? The Black woman and television.* Paper presented at the meeting of the International Communications Association.

McMahan, I. (1982). Expectancy of success of sex-linked tasks. *Sex Roles, 8,* 949–958.

McMillan, J. R., Clifton, A. K., McGrath, D., & Gale, W. S. (1977). Women's language: Uncertainty or interpersonal sensitivity and emotionality? *Sex Roles, 3,* 545–560.

McMullen, L. (1992). *Sex differences in spoken langage: Empirical truth or mythic truth?* Paper presented at the annual convention of the Canadian Psychological Association, Quebec City, Canada.

McNeely, R. L., & Mann, R. C. (1990). Domestic violence is a human issue. *Journal of Interpersonal Violence, 5,* 129–132.

Mead, M. (1935). *Sex and temperament in three primitive societies.* New York: Morrow.

Mead, M. (1972). *Blackberry winter: My earlier years.* New York: Washington Square.

Mead, M. (1975). *Male and female.* New York: Morrow.

Meadow, M. J., & Kahoe, R. D. (1984). *Psychology of religion.* New York: Harper & Row.

Mearns, J. (1991). Coping with breakup: Negative mood regulation expectancies and depression following the end of romantic relationships. *Journal of Personality and Social Psychology, 60,* 327–334.

Mebert, C. J. (1991). Dimensions of subjectivity in parents' ratings of infant temperament. *Child Development, 62,* 352–361.

Mednick, M. T. (1978). Psychology of women: Research issues and trends. *New York Academy of Science Annuals, 309,* 77–92.

Mednick, M. T. S. (1989). On the politics of psychological constructs: Stop the bandwagon, I want to get off. *American Psychologist, 44,* 1118–1123.

Mednick, M. T. (1991). Currents and futures in American feminist psychology. *Psychology of Women Quarterly, 15,* 611–621.

Mednick, M. T., & Thomas, V. (1993). Women and the psychology of achievement: A view from the eighties. In F. L. Denmark & M. A. Paludi (Eds.), *Psychology of women: A handbook of issues and theories* (pp. 585–626). Westport, CT: Greenwood Press.

Mednick, M. T., & Urbanski, L. L. (1991). The origins and activities of APA's division of the psychology of women. *Psychology of Women Quarterly, 15,* 651–663.

Mednick, M. T., & Weissman, H. (1975). The psychology of women: Selected topics. *Annual Review of Psychology, 26,* 1–18.

Meece, J. L. (1987). The influence of school experiences on the development of gender schemata. *New Directions for Child Development, 38,* 57–73.

Meece, J. L., Parsons, J. E., Kaczala, C. M., & Goff, S. B. (1982). Sex differences in math achievement: Toward a model of academic choice. *Psychological Bulletin, 91,* 324–348.

Meehan, A. M., & Janik, L. M. (1990). Illusory correlation and the maintenance of sex role stereotypes in children. *Sex Roles, 22,* 83–95.

Meeker, B. F., & Weitzel-O'Neill, P. A. (1985). Sex roles and interpersonal behavior in task-oriented groups. In J. Berger & M. Zelditch, Jr. (Eds.), *Status, rewards, and influence.* San Francisco: Jossey-Bass.

Meeks, S., Carstensen, L. L., Stafford, P. B., Brenner, L. L., Weathers, F., Welch, R., & Oltmanns, T. F. (1990). Mental health needs of chronically mentally ill elderly. *Psychology and Aging, 5,* 163–171.

Mehrabian, A. (1968). Relationship of attitude to seated posture, orientation, and distance. *Journal of Personality and Social Psychology, 10,* 26–30.

Meier, D. E. (1988). Skeletal aging. In B. Kent & R. Butler (Eds.), *Human aging research: Concepts and techniques* (pp. 221–244). New York: Raven.

Mejia, D. (1983). The development of Mexican-American children. In G. J. Powell (Ed.), *The psychosocial development of minority group children.* New York: Brunner/Mazel.

Melges, F. T. (1968). Postpartum psychiatric syndromes. *Psychosomatic Medicine, 30,* 95–108.

Mellin, L. M., Scully, S., & Irwin, C. E. (1986, October). *Disordered eating characteristics in preadolescent girls.* Paper presented at the American Dietetic annual meeting, Las Vegas. Cited in Hesse-Biber, S. (1989). Eating patterns and disorders in a college population: Are college women's eating problems a new phenomenon? *Sex Roles, 20,* 71–89.

Menninger, L. (1938). *Man against himself.* New York: Basic Books.

Mensh, E., & Mensh, H. (1991). The IQ mythology: Class, race, gender, and inequality. Carbondale: Southern Illinois University Press.

Mercy, J. A., & Saltzman, L. E. (1989). Fatal violence among spouses in the United States, 1976–1985. *American Journal of Public Health, 79,* 595–599.

Merton, R. K. (1948). The self-fulfilling prophecy. *Antioch Review, 8,* 193–210.

Merton, R. K. (1973). *The psychology of science: Theoretical and empirical investigations.* Chicago: University of Chicago Press.

Merves-Okin, L., Amidon, E., & Bernt, F. (1991). Perceptions of intimacy in marriage: A study of married couples. *American Journal of Family Therapy, 19,* 110–118.

Messner, M. A. (1994). Ah, ya throw like a girl! In M. A. Messner

& D. F. Sabo (Eds.), *Sex, violence, and power in sports: Rethinking masculinity* (pp. 28–32). Freedom, CA: Crossing Press.

Messner, M. A., Duncan, M. C., & Jensen, K. (1993). Separating the men from the girls: The gendered language of televised sports. *Gender and Society, 7,* 121–137.

Metha, A., & Nigg, J. (1982). Sexual harassment: Implications of a study at Arizona State University. *Women's Studies Quarterly, 10,* 24–26.

Metz, M. E., Rosser, B. R. S., & Strapko, N. (1994). Differences in conflict-resolution styles among heterosexual, gay, and lesbian couples. *Journal of Sex Research, 31,* 293–308.

Metzler, C., Noell, J., & Biglan, A. (1992). The validation of a construct of high-risk sexual behavior in heterosexual adults. *Journal of Adolescence Research, 7,* 233–249.

Meyer, C. B., & Taylor, S. E. (1986). Adjustment to rape. *Journal of Personality and Social Psychology, 50,* 1226–1234.

Meyer, H., & Lee, M. (1978). *Women in traditionally male jobs: The experiences of ten public utility companies.* Washington, DC: U.S. Government Printing Office.

Meyer, J., & Dupkin, C. (1985). Gender disturbance in children. *Bulletin of the Menninger Clinic, 49,* 236–269.

Meyer, S. L., Murphy, C. M., Cascardi, M., & Birns, B. (1991). Gender relationships: Beyond the peer group. *American Psychologist, 46,* 537.

Meyer, W., Webb, A., Stuart, C., Finkelstein, J., Lawrence, B., & Walker, P. (1986). Physical and hormonal evaluation of transsexual patients: A longitudinal study. *Archives of Sexual Behavior, 15,* 121–138.

Meyer-Bahlburg, H. F. L., Ehrhardt, A. A., Rosen, L. R., Gruen, R. S., Veridiano, N. P., Vann, F. H., & Neuwalder, H. F. (1995). Prenatal estrogens and the development of homosexual orientation. *Developmental Psychology, 31,* 12–21.

Michael, R. T., Gagnon, J., Laumann, E. O., & Kolata, G. (1994). *Sex in America: A definitive survey.* Boston: Little, Brown.

Miele, J. A. (1958). Sex differences in intelligence: The relationships of sex to intelligence as measured by the Wechsler Adult Intelligence Scale and the Wechsler Intelligence Scale for Children. *Dissertation Abstracts International, 18,* 2213.

Mill, J. S. (1869/1970). On the subjection of women. In J. S. Mill & H. T. Mill (Eds.), *Essays on sex equality.* Chicago: University of Chicago Press.

Miller, B. C., & Bingham, C. R. (1989). Family configuration in relation to the sexual behavior of female adolescents. *Journal of Marriage and the Family, 51,* 499–506.

Miller, C., & Swit, K. (1991). *Updated words and women: New language in new times.* New York: HarperCollins.

Miller, J. A., Jacobsen, R. B., & Bigner, J. J. (1982). The child's home environment for lesbian versus heterosexual mothers: A neglected area of research. *Journal of Homosexuality, 7,* 49–56.

Miller, J. B. (1976). *Toward a new psychology of women.* Boston: Beacon Press.

Miller, J. B. (1983). *The construction of anger in women and men.* Work in Progress No. 83-01, Stone Center Working Paper Series, Wellesley College, MA.

Miller, J. B. (1986). *Toward a new psychology of women* (2nd ed.). Boston: Beacon Press.

Miller, J. B. (1991). The construction of anger in women and men. In J. V. Jordan, A. G. Kaplan, J. B. Miller, I. P. Stiver, & J. Surrey, *Women's growth in connection: Writings from the Stone Center* (pp. 181–196), New York: Guilford Press.

Miller, J. G. (1984). Culture and the development of everyday social explanation. *Journal of Personality and Social Psychology, 46,* 961–978.

Miller, J. L., & Levy, G. D. (1996). Gender role conflict, gender-typed characteristics, self-concepts, and sport socialization in female athletes and nonathletes. *Sex Roles, 35,* 111–122.

Miller, L. C., Cooke, L. L., Tsang, J., & Morgan, F. (1992). Should I brag? Nature and the impact of positive and boastful disclosures for men and women. *Human Communication Research, 18.*

Miller, M. M., & Reeves, B. (1976). Dramatic TV content and children's sex-role stereotypes. *Journal of Broadcasting, 20,* 35–50.

Miller, P. A., & Eisenberg, N. (1988). The relation of empathy to aggressive and externalizing/antisocial behavior. *Psychological Bulletin, 103,* 324–344.

Miller, W. B. (1992). An empirical study of the psychological antecedents and consequences of induced abortion. *Journal of Social Issues, 48,* 67–93.

Milow, V. J. (1983). Menstrual education: Past, present, and future. In S. Golub (Ed.), *Menarche.* Boston: Lexington Books.

Miner, J. B. (1980). The role of managerial and professional motivation in the career success of management professors. *Academy of Management Journal, 23,* 487–508.

Mintz, L., & Betz, N. (1988). Prevalence and correlates of eating-disordered behaviors among undergraduate women. *Journal of Counseling Psychology, 35,* 463–471.

Mintz, R. D., & Mahalik, J. R. (1996). Gender role orientation and conflict as predictors of family roles for men. *Sex Roles, 34,* 805–821.

Minuchin, P. P., & Shapiro, E. K. (1983). The school as a context of social development. In P. H. Mussen (Ed.), *Handbook of child psychology: Vol. 4. Socialization, personality, and social development.* New York: Wiley.

Mirande, A., & Enriquez, E. (1979). La Chicana: *The Mexican-American woman.* Chicago: University of Chicago Press.

Mirowsky, J., & Ross, C. E. (1987). Belief in innate sex roles: Sex stratification versus interpersonal influence in marriage. *Journal of Marriage and the Family, 49,* 527–540.

Mirowsky, J., & Ross, C. E. (1995). Sex differences in distress: Real or artifact? *American Sociological Review, 60,* 449–468.

Mischel, W. (1966). A social-learning view of sex differences in behavior. In E. E. Maccoby (Ed.), *The development of sex differences.* Stanford, CA: Stanford University Press.

Mischel, W. (1973). Toward a cognitive social learning reconceptualization of personality. *Psychological Review, 80,* 252–283.

Mischel, W. (1977). On the future of personality measurement. *American Psychologist, 32,* 246–254.

Mischel, W. (1979). On the interface of cognition and personality: Beyond the person-situation debate. *American Psychologist, 34,* 740–754.

Mitchell, E. S., Lentz, M. J., Woods, N. F., Lee, K., & Taylor, D. (1992). Methodological issues in the definition of premenstrual syndrome. In A. J. Davis & L. L. Lewis (Eds.), *Menstrual health in women's lives.* Urbana: University of Illinois Press.

Mitchell, J. (1975). *Psychoanalysis and feminism: Freud, Reich, Lang and women.* New York: Vintage.

Mitchell, J. E., Pyle, R. L., & Fletcher, L. (1991). The topography of binge eating, vomiting, and laxative abuse. *International Journal of Eating Disorders, 10,* 43–48.

Mitchell, V., & Helson, R. (1990). Women's prime of life: Is it the 50s? *Psychology of Women Quarterly, 14*, 451–470.

Mitgang, L. (1988, September 20). Flat SAT scores only fuel debate. *Easton Express*, pp. 1, 2.

Moffat, M. (1989). *Coming of age in New Jersey*. New Brunswick, NJ: Rutgers University Press.

Mollenkott, V. R. (1984). *The divine feminine: The biblical imagery of God as female*. Lavergne, TN: Crossroad.

Moller, L. A., Hymel, S., & Rubin, K. H. (1992). Sex typing in play and popularity in middle childhood. *Sex Roles, 26*, 331–353.

Monahan, L., Kuhn, D., & Shaver, P. (1974). Intrapsychic versus cultural explanations of the fear of success motive. *Journal of Personality and Social Psychology, 29*, 60–64.

Mondanaro, J. (1989). *Chemically dependent women*. Lexington, MA: Lexington Books.

Money, J. (1968). *Sex errors of the body: Dilemmas, education, counseling*. Baltimore: Johns Hopkins University Press.

Money, J. (1973). Prenatal hormones and postnatal socialization in gender identity differentiation. In J. K. Cole & R. Dienstbier (Eds.), *Nebraska Symposium on Motivation* (Vol. 21). Lincoln: University of Nebraska Press.

Money, J. (1975). Ablatio penis: Normal male infant sex-reassigned as a girl. *Archives of Sexual Behavior, 4*, 65–72.

Money, J. (1988). *Gay, straight, and in-between: The sexology of erotic orientation*. New York: Oxford University Press.

Money, J., & Ehrhardt, A. A. (1972). *Man and woman, boy and girl*. Baltimore: Johns Hopkins University Press.

Money, J., Hampson, J. G., & Hampson, J. L. (1955a). Hermaphroditism: Recommendations concerning assignment of sex, change of sex, and psychologic management. *Bulletin of the Johns Hopkins Hospital, 97*, 284–300.

Money, J., Hampson, J. G., & Hampson, J. L., (1955b). An examination of some basic sexual concepts: The evidence of human hermaphroditism. *Bulletin of the Johns Hopkins Hospital, 97*, 301–319.

Money, J., & Mathews, D. (1982). Prenatal exposure to virilizing progestins: An adult follow-up study on 12 young women. *Archives of Sexual Behavior, 11*, 73–83.

Monroe, R. L., & Monroe, R. H. (1971). Effects of environmental experience on spatial ability in an East African society. *Journal of Social Psychology, 83*, 3–10.

Monsour, M. (1992). Meanings of intimacy in cross- and same-sex friendships. *Journal of Social and Personality Relationships, 9*, 277–295.

Montauk, S., & Clasen, M. (1989, January). Sex education in primary care: Infancy to puberty. *Medical Aspects of Human Sexuality*, pp. 22–36.

Montemayor, R. & Hanson, E. A. (1985). A naturalistic view of conflict between adolescents and their parents and siblings. *Journal of Early Adolescence, 3*, 83–103.

Mooney, L., & Brabant, S. (1987). Two martinis and a rested woman: "Liberation" in the Sunday comics. *Sex Roles, 17*, 409–420.

Moore, D., & Gobi, A. (1995). Role conflict and perceptions of gender roles. *Sex Roles, 32*, 252–270.

Moore, H. A. (1985). Job satisfaction and women's spheres of work. *Sex Roles, 13*, 663–678.

Moore, M. (1987, October). Commanders barred from interfering in military spouses' careers. *The Washington Post*, p. A6.

Moore, M. L. (1992). The family as portrayed on prime-time television, 1947–1990: Structure and characteristics. *Sex Roles, 26*, 41–61.

Moore, T. E., Griffiths, K., & Payne, B. (1987). Gender, attitudes towards women, and the appreciation of sexist humor. *Sex Roles, 16*, 521–531.

Moorehouse, M. J. (1991). Linking maternal employment patterns to mother-child activities and children's school competence. *Developmental Psychology, 27*, 295–303.

Moos, R. H. (1968). The development of a menstrual distress questionnaire. *Psychosomatic Medicine, 30*, 853–867.

Moos, R. H. (1969, June). *Menstrual Distress Questionnaire: Preliminary manual*. Department of Psychiatry, Stanford University School of Medicine, Stanford, CA.

Moran, G. F. (1980). "Sisters" in Christ: Women and the church in seventeenth-century New England. In J. W. James (Ed.), *Women in American religion*. Philadelphia, PA: University of Pennsylvania Press.

Morelli, G. A., Rogoff, B., Oppenheim, D., & Goldsmith, D. (1992). Cultural variation in infants' sleeping arrangements: Questions of independence. *Developmental Psychology, 28*, 604–613.

Morgan, C. D., & Murray, H. A. (1935). A method for investigating fantasies: The Thematic Apperception Test. *Archives of Neuropsychology and Psychiatry, 34*, 289–306.

Morgan, C. D., & Murray, H. A. (1938/1962). Thematic Apperception Test. In H. A. Murray (Ed.), *Explorations in personality*. New York: Science Editions.

Morgan, C. S., & Walker, A. J. (1983). Predicting sex role attitudes. *Social Psychology Quarterly, 46*, 148–151.

Morgan, K. S. (1992). Caucasian lesbians' use of psychotherapy: A matter of attitude? *Psychology of Women Quarterly, 16*.

Morgan, L. A. (1989). Economic well-being following marital termination: A comparison of widowed and divorced women. *Journal of Family Issues, 10*, 86–101.

Morgan, M. (1982). Television and adolescents' sex-role stereotypes: A longitudinal study. *Journal of Personality and Social Psychology, 43*, 947–955.

Morgan, R. (1978). *Going too far*. New York: Random House.

Morgan, S. (1991). Menopause, hysterectomy and sexuality. In B. Sang, J. Warshow, & A. J. Smith (Eds.), *Lesbians at midlife: The creative transition*. San Francisco: spinsters book company.

Mori, L., Bernat, J. A., Glenn, P. A., Selle, L. L., & Zarate, M. G. (1995). Attitudes toward rape: Gender and ethnic differences across Asian and Caucasian college students. *Sex Roles, 32*, 457–467.

Morin, S. F. (1977). Heterosexual bias in psychological research on lesbianism and male homosexuality. *American Psychologist, 32*, 629–637.

Morinaga, Y., Frieze, I. H., & Ferligoi, A. (1993). Career plans and gender-role attitudes of college students in the United States, Japan, and Slovenia. *Sex Roles, 29*, 317–334.

Morris, J. (1974). *Conundrum*. New York: Harcourt Brace Jovanovich.

Morrison, A. M., & Von Glinow, M. A. (1990). Women and minorities in management. *American Psychologist, 45*, 200–208.

Morrison, D. M. (1985). Adolescent contraceptive behavior: A review. *Psychological Bulletin, 98*, 538–568.

Morrison, J. A., Barton, B., Biro, F. M., Sprecher, D. L., Falkner, F., & Obarzanek, E. (1994). Sexual maturation and obsession in 9- and 10-year-old Black and White girls: The National

Heart, Lung, and Blood Institute Growth and Health Study. *Journal of Pediatrics, 124,* 889–895.

Morrow, J., & Nolen-Hoeksema, S. (1990). Effects of responses to depression on the remediation of depressive affect. *Journal of Personality and Social Psychology, 58,* 519–527.

Morton, N. (1979). The dilemma of celebration. In C. Christ & J. Plaskow (Eds.), *Womanspirit rising: A feminist reader in religion.* San Francisco: Harper & Row.

Moses, S. (1991a, March). Rape prevention "must involve men." *APA Monitor,* pp. 35–36.

Moses, S. (1991b, July). Ties that bind can limit minority valedictorians. *APA Monitor,* p. 47.

Mosher, D. L., & MacIan, P. (1994). College men and women respond to X-rated videos intended for male and female audiences: General and sexual scripts. *Journal of Sex Research, 31,* 99–113.

Moss, H. A. (1967). Sex, age, and state as determinants of mother-infant interaction. *Merrill-Palmer Quarterly, 13,* 19–36.

Moss, P., Bolland, G., Foxman, R., & Owen, C. (1986). Marital relations during the transition to parenthood. *Journal of Reproductive and Infant Psychology, 4,* 57–67.

Mosselman, P. D. (1997). ER-beta: Identification and characterization of a novel estrogen receptor. *FEBS Letters, 392,* 49–53.

Mott, F., & Haurin, R. (1988). Linkages between sexual activity and alcohol and drug use among American adolescents. *Family Planning Perspectives, 20,* 128–137.

Mott, F. L., & Marsiglio, W. (1985). Early childbearing and completion of high school. *Family Planning Perspectives, 17,* 234–237.

Moudgil, V. K. (1994). *Steroid hormone receptors: Basic and clinical aspects.* Boston: Birkhauser.

Moulton, J., Robinson, G. M., & Elias, C. (1978). Sex bias in language use: "Neutral" pronouns that aren't. *American Psychologist, 33,* 1032–1036.

Mowbray, C. T., Herman, S. E., & Hazel, K. L. (1992). Gender and serious mental illness: A feminist perspective. *Psychology of Women Quarterly, 16,* 107–126.

Muehlenhard, C. L. (1994a). Are rape statistics exaggerated? A response to criticism of contemporary rape research. *Journal of Sex Research, 31,* 144.

Muehlenhard, C. L. (1994b). Controversy about rape research and activities. *Journal of Sex Research, 31,* 143.

Muehlenhard, C. L., & Falcon, P. L. (1990). Men's heterosocial skill and attitudes toward women as predictors of verbal sexual coercion and forceful rape. *Sex Roles, 23,* 241–259.

Muehlenhard, C. L., & Felts, A. S. (1987). [An analysis of causal factors for men's attitudes about the justifiability of date rape]. Unpublished raw data.

Muehlenhard, C. L., Friedman, D. E., & Thomas, C. M. (1985). Is date rape justifiable? The effects of dating activity, who initiated, who paid, and men's attitudes toward women. *Psychology of Women Quarterly, 9,* 297–309.

Muehlenhard, C. L., Goggins, M. F., Jones, J. M., & Saterfield, A. T. (1991). Sexual violence and coercion in close relationships. In K. McKinney & S. Sprecher (Eds.), *Sexuality in close relationships* (pp. 155–175). Hillsdale, NJ: Erlbaum.

Muehlenhard, C. L., & Linton, M. A. (1987). Date rape and sexual aggression in dating situations: Incidence and risk factors. *Journal of Counseling Psychology, 34,* 186–196.

Muehlenhard, C., & Schrag, J. (1991). Nonviolent sexual coercion. In A. Parrot & L. Bechholfer (Eds.), *Acquaintance rape: The hidden crime* (pp. 115–128). New York: Wiley.

Mueller, P., & Major, B. (1989). Self-blame, self-efficacy and adjustment to abortion. *Journal of Personality and Social Psychology, 57,* 1059–1068.

Mulligan, T., & Moss, C. R. (1991). Sexuality and aging in male veterans: A cross-sectional study of interest, ability, and activity. *Archives of Sexual Behavior, 20,* 17–25.

Munroe, R. L. (1955). *Schools of psychoanalytic thought: An exposition, critique, and attempt at integration.* New York: Holt, Rinehart and Winston.

Murray, H. A. (1938). *Explorations in personality.* New York: Oxford.

Murray, S. R., & Scott, P. B. (Eds.). (1982). A special issue on black women. *Psychology of Women Quarterly, 6.*

Murrell, A. J., & Dietz-Uhler, B. L. (1993). Gender identity and adversarial sexual beliefs as predictors of attitudes toward sexual harassment. *Psychology of Women Quarterly, 17,* 169–175.

Murrell, A. J., Frieze, I. H., & Frost, J. L. (1991). Aspiring to careers in male- and female-dominated professions: A study of Black and White college women. *Psychology of Women Quarterly, 15,* 103–126.

Murstein, B. I. (1986). *Paths to marriage.* Beverly Hills, CA: Sage.

Myers, J. K., Weissman, M. M., Tischler, C. E., Holzer, C. E., III, Orvaschel, H., Anthony, J. C., Boyd, J. H., Burke, J. D., Jr., Kramer, M., & Stoltzman, R. (1984). Six-month prevalence of psychiatric disorders in three communities. *Archives of General Psychiatry, 41,* 959–978.

Myrdal, G. (1969). *Objectivity in social research.* New York: Pantheon Books.

Nadelson, C. C. (1978). An overview of problems in sexual functioning. In M. T. Notman & C. C. Nadelson (Eds.), *The woman patient: Vol. 1. Sexual and reproductive aspects of women's health care.* New York: Plenum Press.

Nadelson, C. C., Notman, M. T., & Jackson, H. (1982). A follow-up study of rape victims. *Journal of Psychiatry, 139,* 1266–1270.

Naditch, S. F. (1976). Effects of experimental artifact on sex differences in field dependence. *Dissertation Abstracts International, 36,* 5869–5870.

Nagata, D., & Crosby, F. (1991). Comparison, justice, and the internment of Japanese-Americans. In J. Suis & T. A. Wills (Eds.), *Social comparison: Contemporary theory and research.* Hillsdale, NJ: Erlbaum.

Nash, S. C. (1975). The relationship among sex-role stereotyping, sex-role preference and the sex differences in spatial visualization. *Sex Roles, 1,* 15–32.

Nash, S. C. (1979). Sex role as a mediator of intellectual functioning. In M. A. Wittig & A. C. Peterson (Eds.), *Sex-related differences in cognitive functioning* (pp. 263–302), New York: Academic Press.

National Center for Education Statistics. (1983). *Faculty salaries, tenure, and benefits survey.* Washington, DC: Author.

National Center for Health Statistics (1987). *National hospital discharge surveys.* Washington, DC: U.S. Government Printing Office.

National Center for Health Statistics. (1992). As reported in *The 1994 information please almanac.* Boston, MA: Houghton Mifflin.

National Commission on the Observation of International Women's Year. (1978, March). *Spirit of Houston: The first national women's conference* (An official report to the President, the Congress and the people of the United States). Washington, DC: U.S. Department of State.

National Committee on Pay Equity. (1992). The wage gap: Myths and facts. In P. S. Rothenberg (Ed.), *Race, class, and gender in the United States: An integrated study* (2nd ed.). New York: St. Martin's Press.

National Council of the Churches of Christ in the U.S.A. (1987). *An inclusive language lectionary, Readings for year B, Revised.* Division of Education and Ministry of the National Council of the Churches of Christ in the U.S.A.

National Institute of Mental Health. (1986). Women's mental health: Agenda for research. Washington, DC: U.S. Department of Health and Human Services.

National Victims Center. (1992a). *Rape in America: A report to the nation.* Report prepared by the Crime Victims Research and Treatment Center, Medical University of South Carolina, Charleston.

National Victims Center. (1992b, April 23). *Rape in America: A report to the nation.* Arlington, VA: Author.

National Women's Health Network. (1993, May/June). The diet that may save your life. *Ms.*, pp. 47–50.

Naus, P. J. (1987). Sexuality now and in the future. *Sieccan Journal, 2,* 35–44.

Neal, A. M., & Turner, S. M. (1991). Anxiety disorders research with African Americans: Current status. *Psychological Bulletin, 10,* 400–410.

Near, H. (1976). The rock will wear away. Reprinted from "The rock will wear away," lyrics by Holly Near and music by Meg Christian. Hereford Music, Thumbelina Music.

Neimark, J. (1991, May). Out of bounds: The truth about athletes and rape. *Mademoiselle,* pp. 196–199, 244–246.

Nelson, J. B. (1979). *Embodiment: An approach to sexuality and Christian theology.* Minneapolis, MN: Augsburg Publishing House.

Nelson, M. C. (1988). Reliability, validity, and cross-cultural comparisons for the simplified Attitudes Toward Women Scale. *Sex Roles, 18,* 289–296.

Nesbitt, P. D. (1997). Gender, tokenism, and the construction of elite clergy careers. *Review of Religious Research, 38,* 193–210.

Neugarten, B. L. (1968a). The awareness of middle age. In B. L. Neugarten (Ed.), *Middle age and aging: A reader in social psychology.* Chicago: University of Chicago Press.

Neugarten, B. L. (Ed.). (1968b). *Middle age and aging: A reader in social psychology.* Chicago: University of Chicago Press.

Neugarten, B. L., Moore, J. W., & Lowe, J. C. (1965). Age norms, age constraints, and adult socialization. *American Journal of Sociology, 70,* 710–717.

Neugarten, B. L., Wood, V., Kraines, R., & Loomis, B. (1968). Women's attitudes toward the menopause. In B. L. Neugarten (Ed.), *Middle age and aging: A reader in social psychology.* Chicago: University of Chicago Press.

Nevid, J. S. (1984). Sex differences in factors of romantic attraction. *Sex Roles, 11,* 401–411.

Newcomb, A. F., & Bagwell, C. L. (1995). Children's friendship relations: A meta-analytic review. *Psychological Bulletin, 117,* 306–347.

Newcomb, M. D. (1987). Cohabitation and marriage: A quest for independence and relatedness. In S. Oskamp (Ed.), *Social Psychology Annual: 7, Family processes and problems: Social psychological aspects* (pp. 128–156). Beverly Hills, CA: Sage.

Newman, A. L., & Peterson, C. (1996). Anger of women incest survivors. *Sex Roles, 34,* 463–491.

Newman, L. F. (1972). *Birth control: An anthropological view* (Addison-Wesley Modular Publications). Reading, MA: Addison-Wesley.

Newson, J., & Newson, W. (1986). Family and sex roles in middle childhood. In D. J. Hargreaves & A. M. Colley (Eds.), *The psychology of sex roles* (pp. 142–158). New York: Hemisphere.

Ng, S. H. (1990). Androcentric coding of Man and His in memory by language users. *Journal of Experimental Social Psychology, 26,* 455–464.

Nichols, M. (1987). Lesbian sexuality: Issues and developing theory. In Boston Lesbian Psychologies Collective (Ed.), *Lesbian psychologies: Explorations and challenges.* Urbana: University of Illinois Press.

Nichols, M. (1990). Lesbian relationships: Implications for the study of sexuality and gender. In D. P. McWhirter, S. A. Sanders, & J. M. Reinisch (Eds.), *Homosexuality/heterosexuality: Concepts of sexual orientation.* New York: Oxford University Press.

Nielsen, J., & Wohlert, M. (1991). Chromosome abnormalities found among 34,920 newborn children: Results from a 13-year incidence study in Arhus, Denmark. *Human Genetics, 87,* 81–83.

Nielsen Media Research. (1989). *'89 Nielsen report on television.* Northbrook, IL: Author.

Niemann, Y. F., Jennings, L., Rozelle, R. M., Baxter, J. C., & Sullivan, E. (1994). Use of free responses and cluster analysis to determine stereotypes of eight groups. *Personality and Social Psychology Bulletin, 20,* 379–390.

Nietzsche, F. (1886/1966). *Beyond good and evil* (Walter Kaufman, Trans.). New York: Vintage.

Nieva, V. F., & Gutek, B. A. (1981). *Women and work: A psychological perspective.* New York: Praeger.

Nieves-Squires, S. (1991). *Hispanic women: Making their presence on campus less tenuous.* Washington, DC: Association of American Colleges, Project on the Status and Education of Women.

Nigro, G. N., Hill, D. E., Gelbein, M. E., & Clark, C. L. (1988). Changes in the facial prominence of women and men over the last decade. *Psychology of Women Quarterly, 12,* 225–235.

Nkomo, S. M., & Cox, T., Jr. (1989). Gender differences in the upward mobility of black managers: Double whammy or double advantage? *Sex Roles, 21,* 825–839.

Nock, S. L. (1981). Family life-cycle transitions: Longitudinal effects on family members. *Journal of Marriage and the Family, 43,* 703–714.

Noddings, N. (1984). *Caring: A feminine approach to ethics and moral education.* Berkeley: University of California Press.

Noel, R. C., & Allen, M. J. (1976). Sex and ethnic bias in the evaluation of student editorials. *Journal of Psychology, 94,* 53–58.

Nolen-Hoeksema, S. (1987). Sex differences in unipolar depression: Evidence and theory. *Psychological Bulletin, 101,* 259–282.

Nolen-Hoeksema, S. (1990). *Sex differences in depression.* Stanford, CA: Stanford University Press.

Nolen-Hoeksema, S. (1991a). Responses to depression and their effects on the duration of depressive episodes. *Journal of Abnormal Psychology, 100,* 569–582.

Nolen-Hoeksema, S. (1991b). Sex differences in depression and explanatory style in children. *Journal of Youth and Adolescence, 20,* 233–245.

Nolen-Hoeksema, S., & Girgus, J. S. (1994). The emergence of gender differences in depression during adolescence. *Psychological Bulletin, 115*, 424–443.

Nolen-Hoeksema, S., & Morrison, J. (1991). A prospective study of depression and distress following a natural disaster: The 1989 Loma Prieta earthquake. *Journal of Personality and Social Psychology, 61*, 105–121.

Nolen-Hoeksema, S., Morrow, J., & Fredrickson, B. L. (1993). Response styles and the duration of episodes of depressed mood. *Journal of Abnormal Psychology, 102*, 20–28.

Nolen-Hoeksema, S., Parker, L. E., & Larson, J. (1994). Ruminative coping with depressed mood following loss. *Journal of Personality and Social Psychology, 67*, 92–104.

Noor, N. M. (1996). Some demographic, personality, and role variables as correlates of women's well-being. *Sex Roles, 34*, 603–620.

Norris, J., & Cubbins, L. A. (1992). Dating, drinking, and rape. *Psychology of Women Quarterly, 16*, 179–191.

Norris, J., Nurius, P. S., & Dimeff, L. A. (1996). Through her eyes: Factors affecting women's perception of and resistance of acquaintance of sexual aggression threat. *Psychology of Women Quarterly, 20*, 123–145.

Norton, A. J., & Moorman, J. E. (1987). Current trends in marriage and divorce among American Women. *Journal of Marriage and the Family, 49*, 3–14.

Norton, M. B. (1980). *Liberty's daughters: The revolutionary experience of American women, 1750–1800.* Boston: Little, Brown.

Nydegger, C. N. (1986). Asymmetrical kin and the problematic son-in-law. In N. Datan, A. L. Greene, & H. W. Reese (Eds.), *Life-span developmental psychology: Intergenerational relations.* Hillsdale, NJ: Erlbaum.

Nyquist, L., & Spence, J. (1986). Effects of dispositional dominance and sex role expectations on leadership behaviors. *Journal of Personality and Social Psychology, 50*, 377–382.

Oakley, A. (1974). *The sociology of housework.* New York: Pantheon.

O'Brien, M., & Huston, A. C. (1985). Development in sex-typed play in toddlers. *Developmental Psychology, 21*, 866–871.

O'Brien, M., Huston, A. C., & Risely, T. (1981). *Emergence and stability of sex-typed toy preferences in toddlers.* Paper presented at the meeting of the Association for Behavior Analysis, Milwaukee.

O'Bryant, S. L. (1988). Sibling support and older widows' well-being. *Journal of Marriage and the Family, 50*, 173–183.

O'Bryant, S. L., & Brophy, J. E. (1976). Sex differences in altruistic behavior. *Developmental Psychology, 12*, 554.

O'Carroll, R. (1991). Sexual desire disorders: A review of controlled treatment studies. *Journal of Sex Research, 28*, 607–624.

O'Connell, A. N., & Russo, N. F. (Eds.). (1991). Women's heritage in psychology: Origins, development, and future directions. *Psychology of Women Quarterly, 15*, 493–678.

O'Connor, J. (1943). *Structural visualization.* Boston: Human Engineering Laboratory.

O'Connor, P. (1992). *Friendship between women: A critical review.* New York: Guilford Press.

O'Driscoll, K., Foley, M., MacDonald, D., & Stronge, J. (1988). Cesarean section and prenatal outcome: Response from the House of Horne. *American Journal of Obstetrics and Gynecology,* pp. 449–452.

Offermann, L. R. (1986). Visibility and evaluation of female and male leaders. *Sex Roles, 14*, 533–543.

Offermann, L. R., & Beil, C. (1992). Achievement styles of women leaders and their peers: Toward an understanding of women and leadership. *Psychology of Women Quarterly, 16*, 37–56.

Office of Technology Assessment. (1992). *The menopause: Hormone therapy and women's health* (OTA-BP-BA-88). Washington, DC: U.S. Government Printing Office.

Offir, C. W. (1982). *Human sexuality.* New York: Harcourt Brace Jovanovich.

Oggins, J., Veroff, J., & Leber, D. (1993). Perception of marital interaction among Black and White newlyweds.

Ogletree, S. M., Coffee, M. C., & May, S. A. (1992). Perceptions of female/male presidential candidates: Familial and personal situations. *Psychology of Women Quarterly, 16*, 201–208.

Ogletree, S. M., Williams, S. W., Raffeld, P., Mason, B., & Fricke, K. (1987). Female attractiveness and eating disorders: Do children's television commercials play roles? *Sex Roles, 22*, 791–797.

O'Hare, J., & Taylor, K. (1983). The reality of incest. *Women and Therapy, 2*, 215–229.

O'Heron, C. A., & Orlofsky, J. L. (1990). Stereotypic and non-stereotypic sex role trait and behavior orientations, gender identity, and psychological adjustment. *Journal of Personality and Social Psychology, 58*, 134–143.

Ohlott, P. J., Ruderman, M. N., & McCauley, C. D. (1994). Gender differences in managers' developmental job experiences. *Academy of Management Journal, 38*, 46–67.

O'Keefe, E. S. C., & Hyde, J. S. (1983). The development of occupational sex-role stereotypes: The effects of gender stability and age. *Sex Roles, 9*, 481–492.

O'Kelly, C. G., & Carney, L. S. (1986). *Women and men in society. Cross-cultural perspectives on gender stratification.* Belmont, CA: Wadsworth.

Okun, L. (1986). *Woman abuse.* Albany: State University of New York Press.

O'Leary, V. E., & Ickovics, J. R. (1991). Cracking the glass ceiling: Overcoming isolation and alienation. In U. Sekeran & F. Leong (Eds.), *Pathways to excellence: New patterns for human utilization.* Beverly Hills, CA: Sage.

Olian, J. D., Schwab, D. P., & Haberfeld, Y. (1988). The impact of applicant gender compared to qualifications on hiring recommendations: A meta-analysis of experimental studies. *Organizational Behavior and Human Decision Processes, 41*, 180–195.

Oliver, M. B., & Hyde, J. S. (1993). Gender differences in sexuality: A meta-analysis. *Psychological Bulletin, 114*, 29–51.

Oliver, M. B., & Sedikides, C. (1992). Effects of sexual permissiveness on desirability of partner as a function of low and high commitment to relationship. *Social Psychology Quarterly, 55*, 321–333.

Oliver, S. J., & Toner, B. B. (1990). The influence of gender role typing on the expression of depressive symptoms. *Sex Roles, 22*, Nos. 11/12.

Olmedo, E. L., & Parron, D. L. (1981). Mental health of minority women: Some special issues. *Professional Psychology, 12*, 103–111.

Olsen, N. J., & Willemsen, E. (1978). Studying sex prejudice in children. *Journal of Genetic Psychology, 133*, 203–216.

Olson, B., & Douglas, W. (1997). The family on television: Evaluation of gender roles in situation comedy. *Sex Roles, 36*, 409–427.

Olson, E. (1994). Female voices of aggression in Tonga. *Sex Roles, 30*, 237–248.

Olweus, D., Mattsson, A., Schalling, D., & Low, H. (1980). Testosterone, aggression, physical, and personality dimensions in normal adolescent males. *Psychosomatic Medicine, 42*, 253–269.

Orbach, S. (1993). *Hunger strike: The anorectic's struggle as a metaphor for our age.* London: Penguin.

Orlofsky, J. L. (1979). Parental antecedents of sex role orientation in college men and women. *Sex Roles, 5*, 495–512.

Orlofsky, J. L., & O'Heron, C. (1987). Stereotypic and nonstereotypic sex role trait and behavior orientations: Implications for personal adjustment. *Journal of Personality and Social Psychology, 52*, 1034–1042.

Orlofsky, J. L., & Stake, J. E. (1981). Psychological masculinity and femininity: Relationship to striving and self-concepts in the achievement and interpersonal domains. *Psychology of Women Quarterly, 6*, 218–233.

Orne, M. (1969). Demand characteristics and the concept of quasicontrol. In R. Rosenthal & R. L. Rosnow (Eds.), *Artifacts in behavioral research.* New York: Academic Press.

Osland, J. A., Fitch, M., & Willis, E. E. (1996). Likelihood to rape in college males. *Sex Roles, 35*, 171–183.

Osofsky, J. D., Osofsky, H. J., & Rajan, R. (1973). Psychological effects of abortion: With emphasis on immediate reaction and follow-up. In H. J. Osofsky & J. D. Osofsky (Eds.), *The abortion experience.* Hagerstown, MD: Harper & Row.

O'Sullivan, C. S. (1991). Acquaintance gang rape on campus. In A. Parrot & L. Bechhofer (Eds.), *Acquaintance rape: The hidden crime* (pp. 140–156). New York: Wiley.

Ott, E. M. (1989). Effects of the male-female ratio at work: Policewomen and male nurses. *Psychology of Women Quarterly, 13*, 41–58.

Owen, K. (1995, February 21). U.S. moms bear brunt of child care. *Lansing State Journal,* p. 1A.

Owens, P. (1984). Prostaglandin synthetase inhibitors in the treatment of primary dysmenorrhea: Outcome trials reviewed. *American Journal of Obstetrics and Gynecology, 148*, 96–103.

Padawer, J. A., Fagan, C., Janoff-Bulman, R., & Strickland, B. R. (1988). Women's psychological adjustment following emergency cesarean versus vaginal delivery. *Psychology of Women Quarterly, 12*, 25–34.

Pagels, E. H. (1976). What became of God the Mother? *Signs, 2*, 107–119.

Paige, K. E. (1973). Women learning to sing the menstrual blues. *Psychology Today, 7*, 41–46.

Paige, K. E., & Paige, J. M. (1981). *The politics of reproductive ritual.* Berkeley: University of California Press.

Paikoff, R. L., & Brooks-Gunn, J. (1991). Do parent-child relationships change during puberty? *Psychological Bulletin, 110*, 47–66.

Paikoff, R. L., Brooks-Gunn, J., & Carlton-Ford, S. (1991). Effect of reproductive status changes upon family functioning and well-being of mothers and daughters. *Journal of Early Adolescence, 11*, 201–220.

Paikoff, R. L., & Savin-Williams, R. C. (1983). An exploratory study of dominance interactions among adolescent females at a summer camp. *Journal of Youth and Adolescence, 12*, 419–433.

Palkovitz, R., & Copes, M. (1988). Changes in attitudes, beliefs, and expectations associated with the transition to parenthood. *Marriage and Family Review, 6*, 183–199.

Palley, M. (1994). *Sex and sensibility: Reflections on forbidden mirrors and the will to censor.* Hopewell, NJ: Ecco Press.

Palmer, H. T., & Lee, J. A. (1990). Female workers' acceptance in traditionally male-dominated blue-collar jobs. *Sex Roles, 22*, 607–626.

Palmore, E. G. (1974). Predicting longevity: A new method. In E. G. Palmore (Ed.), *Normal aging, II.* Durham, NC: Duke University Press.

Paludi, M. A. (1984). Psychometric properties and underlying assumptions of four objective measures of fear of success. *Sex Roles, 10*, 765–781.

Paludi, M. A., & Bauer, W. D. (1983). Goldberg revisited: What's in an author's name? *Sex Roles, 9*, 387–390.

Paludi, M. A., & Frankell-Hauser, J. (1986). An idiographic approach to the study of women's achievement striving. *Psychology of Women Quarterly, 10*, 89–100.

Paludi, M. A., & Strayer, L. A. (1985). What's in an author's name? Differential evaluations of performance as a function of author's name. *Sex Roles, 10*, 353–361.

Pamela H. (1989). Asian American lesbians: An emerging voice in the Asian American community. In Asian Women United of California (Eds.), *Making waves: An anthology of writings by and about Asian American women.* Boston: Beacon Press.

Pantony, K., & Caplan, P. J. (1991). Delusional dominating personality disorder: A modest proposal for identifying some consequences of rigid masculine socialization. *Canadian Psychology, 32*, 120–135.

Papalia, D. E., & Tennent, S. S. (1975). Vocational aspirations in preschoolers: A manifestation of early sex role stereotyping. *Sex Roles, 11*, 197–199.

Paradise, L. V., & Wall, S. M. (1986). Children's perceptions of male and female principals and teachers. *Sex Roles, 14*, 1–7.

Parke, R. D. (1981). *Fathers.* Cambridge, MA: Harvard University Press.

Parke, R. D., & Sawin, D. B. (1976). The father's role in infancy: A reevaluation. *The Family Coordinator, 25*, 365–371.

Parke, R. D., & Tinsley, B. (1987). Family interaction in infancy. In J. Osofsky (Ed.), *Handbook of infant development* (2nd ed.). New York: Wiley.

Parker, D. A., & De Cecco, J. P. (1995). Sexual expression: A global perspective. *Journal of Homosexuality, 28*, 427–430.

Parker, K. (1986). American Indian women and religion on the southern plains. In R. Ruether & R. Keller (Eds.), *Women and religion in America: Vol. 3. 1900–1968.* San Francisco: Harper & Row.

Parkes, C. M. (1970). "Seeking and finding" a lost object: Evidence from recent studies of the reaction to bereavement. *Social Science and Medicine, 4*, 187–201.

Parlee, M. B. (1973). The premenstrual syndrome. *Psychological Bulletin, 80*, 454–465.

Parlee, M. B. (1974). Stereotypic beliefs about menstruation: A methodological note on the Moos Menstrual Distress Questionnaire and some new data. *Psychosomatic Medicine, 36*, 229–240.

Parlee, M. B. (1982). Changes in moods and activation levels during the menstrual cycle in experimentally naive subjects. *Psychology of Women Quarterly, 7*, 119–131.

Parsons, J. E., Adler, T. E., & Kaczala, C. M. (1982). Socialization of achievement attitudes and beliefs: Parental influences. *Child Development, 53*, 310–321.

Parsons, J. E., Frieze, I. H., & Ruble, D. N. (1978). Intrapsychic factors influencing career aspirations in college women. *Sex Roles, 4*, 337–347.

Parsons, J. F. (1976b). Sex-role choices and peer preference in the middle school years. Unpublished manuscript, Smith College. (Cited in I. H. Frieze, J. F. Parsons, P. B. Johnson, D. N. Ruble, & G. L. Zellman. (1978). *Women and sex roles: A social psychological perspective.* New York: Norton.)

Pascarella, E. T., Smart, J. C., Ethington, C. A., & Nettles, M. T. (1987). The influence of college on self-concept: A consideration of race and gender differences. *American Educational Research Journal, 24*, 49–77.

Patterson, C. J. (1992). Children of lesbian and gay parents. *Child Development, 63*, 1025–1042.

Patterson, C. J. (1994). Families of the lesbian baby boom: Behavioral adjustment, self-concepts, and sex-role identity. In B. Greene & G. Herek (Eds.), *Contemporary perspectives on lesbian and gay psychology, research application* (pp. 156–175). Beverly Hills, CA: Sage.

Patterson, C. J. (1995). Families of the lesbian baby boom: Parents' division of labor and children's adjustment. *Developmental Psychology, 31*, 115–123.

Patterson, G. R. (1980). Mothers: The unacknowledged victims. *Monographs of the Society for Research in Child Development, 45*(5, Serial No. 186), 1–64.

Patton, W., & Mannison, M. (1995a). Sexual coercion in dating situations among university students: Preliminary Australian data. *Australian Journal of Psychology, 47*, 66–72.

Patton, W., & Mannison, M. (1995b). Sexual coercion in high school dating. *Sex Roles, 33*, 447–457.

Pauly, I. (1974). Female transsexualism: Part II. *Archives of Sexual Behavior, 3*, 509–526.

Pauly, I. (1990). Gender identity disorders: Evaluation and treatment. *Journal of Sex Education and Therapy, 16*, 2–24.

Paxton, S. J., & Sculthorpe, A. (1991). Disordered eating and sex role characteristics in young women: Implications for sociocultural theories of disturbed eating. *Sex Roles, 24*, Nos. 9/10.

Payne, F. D. (1987). "Masculinity," "femininity," and the complex construct of adjustment. *Sex Roles, 17*, 359–374.

Payne, T. J., Connor, J. M., & Colletti, G. (1987). Gender-based schematic processing: An empirical investigation and reevaluation. *Journal of Personality and Social Psychology, 52*, 937–945.

Pazy, A. (1986). The persistence of pro-male bias despite identical information regarding causes of success. *Organizational Behavior and Human Decision Processes, 38*, 366–377.

Pazy, A. (1992). Sex-linked bias in promotion decisions. *Psychology of Women Quarterly, 16*, 209–228.

Pearson, L. (1992). The stigma of infertility. *Nursing Times, 88*, 35–38.

Pedhazur, E. J., & Tetenbaum, T. J. (1979). Bem Sex Role Inventory: A theoretical and methodological critique. *Journal of Personality and Social Psychology, 37*, 996–1016.

Peplau, L. A. (1981, March). What do homosexuals want? *Psychology Today*, pp. 28–38.

Peplau, L. A. (1983a). Research on homosexual couples: An overview. *Journal of Homosexuality, 8*, 3–9.

Peplau, L. A. (1983b). Roles and gender. In H. H. Kelley, E. Berscheid, A. Christensen, J. H. Harvey, T. L. Huston, G. Levinger, E. McClintock, L. A. Peplau, & D. R. Peterson (Eds.), *Close relationships* (pp. 220–264). New York: Freeman Press.

Peplau, L. A., & Campbell, S. M. (1989). The balance of power in dating and marriage. In J. Freeman (Ed.), *Women: A feminist perspective*. Mountain View, CA: Mayfield.

Peplau, L. A., & Conrad, E. (1989). Beyond nonsexist research: The perils of feminist methods in psychology. *Psychology of Women Quarterly, 13*, 379–400.

Peplau, L. A., & Gordon, S. L. (1983b). The intimate relationships of lesbians and gay men. In E. R. Allgeier & N. B. McCormick (Eds.), *The changing boundaries: Gender roles and sexual behavior.* Palo Alto, CA: Mayfield.

Peplau, L. A., & Gordon, S. L. (1985). Women and men in love: Gender differences on close heterosexual relationships. In V. E. O'Leary, R. K. Unger, & B. S. Wallston (Eds.), *Women, gender, and social psychology* (pp. 257–292). Hillsdale, NJ: Erlbaum.

Peplau, L. A., Rubin, Z., & Hill, C. T. (1976, November). The sexual balance of power. *Psychology Today*, p. 142.

Peplau, L. A., Rubin, Z., & Hill, R. (1977). Sexual intimacy in dating relationships. *Journal of Social Issues, 33*, 86–109.

Peplau, L. A., Veniegas, R. C., & Campbell, S. M. (1996). Gay and lesbian relationships. In R. C. Savin-Williams & K. Cohen (Eds.), *The lives of lesbians, gays, and bisexuals: Children to adults* (pp. 250–273). Fort Worth, TX: Harcourt Brace.

Peres, Y., & Meivar, H. (1986). Self-presentation during courtship: A content analysis of classified advertisements in Israel. *Journal of Comparative Family Studies, 17*, 19–31.

Pérez-Prada, E., Shkodriani, G. M., Medina, J., Gibbons, J. L., & Stiles, D. A. (1990, May). *Gender role attitudes of adolescents in Iceland, Spain, and the United States.* Paper presented at the annual meeting of the Midwestern Psychological Association, Chicago, IL.

Perry, D. G., & Bussey, K. (1979). The social learning theory of sex differences: Imitation is alive and well. *Journal of Personality and Social Psychology, 37*, 1699–1712.

Perry, D. G., Perry, L. C., & Weiss, R. J. (1989). Sex differences in the consequences that children anticipate for aggression. *Developmental Psychology, 25*, 312–319.

Perry, J. D., & Whipple, B. (1981). Pelvic muscle strength of female ejaculators: Evidence in support of a new theory of orgasm. *Journal of Sex Research, 17*, 22–39.

Petersen, A. C. (1979). Hormones and cognitive functioning in normal development. In M. A. Wittig & A. C. Petersen (Eds.), *Sex-related differences in cognitive functioning: Developmental issues* (pp. 189–214). New York: Academic Press.

Petersen, A. C. (1980). Biopsychosocial processes in the development of sex-related differences. In J. E. Parsons (Ed.), *The psychology of sex differences and sex roles* (pp. 31–55). Washington, DC: Hemisphere.

Petersen, A. C. (1983). Pubertal change and cognition. In J. Brooks-Gunn & A. C. Petersen (Eds.), *Girls at puberty: Biological and psychosocial perspectives.* New York: Plenum Press.

Petersen, A. C. (1988). Adolescent development. *Annual Review of Psychology, 39*, 583–607.

Peterson, C. D., Baucom, D. H., Elliott, J. J., & Farr, P. A. (1989). The relationship between sex role identity and marital adjustment. *Sex Roles, 21*, 775–787.

Peterson, D. R. (1983). Conflict. In H. H. Keller, E. Berscheid, A. Christensen, J. H. Harvey, T. L. Huston, G. Levinger, E. McClintock, L. A. Peplau, & D. R. Peterson (Eds.), *Close relationships.* New York: Freeman Press.

Peterson, J., & Druke, M. (1983). American Indian women and religion. In R. Ruether & R. Keller (Eds.), *Women and religion in America: Vol. 2. The colonial and revolutionary periods: A documentary history.* San Francisco: Harper & Row.

Peterson, S. B., & Kroner, T. (1992). Gender biases in textbooks for introductory psychology and human development. *Psychology of Women Quarterly, 16*, 17–36.

Pfost, K. S., & Fiore, M. (1990). Pursuit of nontraditional occupations: Fear of success or fear of not being chosen? *Sex Roles, 23*, 14–24.

Pharr, S. (1988). *Homophobia: A weapon of sexism.* Little Rock, AR: Chardon.

Pheterson, G. I., Kiesler, S. B., & Goldberg, P. A. (1971). Evaluation of the performance of women as a function of their sex, achievement and personal history. *Journal of Personality and Social Psychology, 19*, 114–118.

Philbin, M., Meier, E., Huffman, S., & Boverie, P. (1995). A survey of gender and learning styles. *Sex Roles, 32*, 485–494.

Phillips, D. (1984). The illusion of incompetence among academically competent children. *Child Development, 55*, 1000–1016.

Phillips, R. D., & Gilroy, F. D. (1985). Sex-role stereotypes and clinical judgments of mental health: The Brovermans' findings reexamined. *Sex Roles, 12*, 179–193.

Piaget, J. (1932/1965). *The moral judgment of the child.* New York: Free Press.

Piaget, J., & Inhelder, B. (1956). *The child's conception of space.* London: Routledge & Kegan Paul. (Original work published 1948)

Piaget, J., & Inhelder, B. (1969). *Psychology of the child.* New York: Basic Books.

Piaget, J., & Inhelder, B. (1973). *Memory and intelligence.* New York: Basic Books.

Pianta, R. C., & Egeland, B. (1994). Relation between depressive symptoms and stressful life events in a sample of disadvantaged mothers. *Journal of Consulting and Clinical Psychology, 62*, 1229–1234.

Picariello, M. L., Greenberg, D. N., & Pillemer, D. B. (1990). Children's sex-related stereotyping of colors. *Child Development, 61*, 1453–1460.

Pidano, A. E., & Tennen, H. (1985). Transient depressive experiences and their relationship to gender and sex-role orientation. *Sex Roles, 12*, 97–110.

Piedmont, R. L. (1995). Another look at fear of success, fear of failure, and test anxiety: A motivational analysis using the five-factor model. *Sex Roles, 32*, 139–158.

Pierce, J., Giovino, G., Hatziandreu, E., & Shopland, D. (1989). National age and sex differences in quitting smoking. *Journal of Psychoactive Drugs, 21*, 293–298.

Pierce, K. (1993). Socialization of teenage girls through teen-magazine fiction: The making of a new woman or an old lady? *Sex Roles, 29*, 59–68.

Piercy, M. (1976). Rape poem. In *Living in the open* (pp. 88–89). New York: Knopf.

Pierson, D. K. (1984, April 1). Mixed bag of reactions follows rape trial verdict. *Lansing State Journal*, pp. 1B–2B.

Pietromonaco, P. R., Manis, J., & Markus, H. (1987). The relationship of employment to self-perception and well-being in women: A cognitive analysis. *Sex Roles, 17*, 467–477.

Pike, K. M. (1995). Bulimic symptomatology in high school girls: Toward a model of cumulative risk. *Psychology of Women Quarterly, 19*, 373–396.

Pilavin, J. A., & Unger, R. K. (1985). The helpful but helpless female: Myth or reality? In V. E. O'Leary, R. K. Unger, &

B. S. Wallston (Eds.), *Women, gender and social psychology.* Hillsdale, NJ: Erlbaum.

Pingree, S., Starrett, S., & Hawkins, R. (1979). *Soap opera viewers and social reality.* Unpublished manuscript, Women's Studies Program, University of Wisconsin–Madison.

Pinzler, I. K., & Ellis, D. (1989). Wage discrimination and comparable worth: A legal perspective. *Journal of Social Issues, 45*, 51–65.

Pipes, R. B., & LeBov-Keeler, K. (1997). Psychological abuse among college women in exclusive heterosexual dating relationships. *Sex Roles, 36*, 585–603.

Pirri, C., Eaton, E., & Durkin, K. (1995). Australian professional women's evaluations of male and female written products. *Sex Roles, 32*, 691–697.

Plaskow, J. (1979). The coming of Lilith: Toward a feminist theology. In C. P. Christ & J. Plaskow (Eds.), *Womanspirit rising: A feminist reader in religion.* San Francisco: Harper & Row.

Plaskow, J., & Christ, C. P. (Eds.). (1989). *Weaving the visions: New patterns in feminist spirituality.* San Francisco: Harper & Row.

Plato. (1955). *The Republic* (H. D. P. Lee, Trans.). Baltimore: Penguin.

Pleck, J. H. (1981). Men's power with women, other men, and society: A men's movement analysis. In R. A. Lewis (Ed.), *Men in difficult times: Masculinity today and tomorrow.* Englewood Cliffs, NJ: Prentice-Hall.

Pleck, J. H. (1983). Husbands' paid work and family roles: Current research issues. In H. Z. Lopata & J. H. Pleck (Eds.), *Research on the interweave of social roles: Vol. 3. Families and jobs.* Greenwich, CT: JAI Press.

Pleck, J. H. (1993). Are "family-supportive" employer policies relevant to men? In J. C. Hood (Ed.), *Work, family, and masculinities.* Beverly Hills, CA: Sage.

Polit, D. F., & Falbo, T. (1987). Only children and personality development: A quantitative review. *Journal of Marriage and the Family, 49*, 309–325.

Pollak, S., & Gilligan, C. (1982). Images of violence in Thematic Apperception Test stories. *Journal of Personality and Social Psychology, 42*, 159–167.

Pollit, K. (1990). *Reasonable creatures: Essays on women and feminism.* New York: Knopf.

Pomerleau, A., Bolduc, D., Malcuit, G., & Cossette, L. (1990). Pink or blue: Environmental gender stereotypes in the first two years of life. *Sex Roles, 22*, 359, 367.

Pope, H. G., & Hudson, J. I. (1992). Is childhood sexual abuse a risk factor for bulimia nervosa? *American Journal of Psychiatry, 149*, 455–463.

Popovich, P. M., Jolton, J. A., Mastragelo, P. M., Everton, W. J., & Somers, J. M. (1995). Sexual harassment scripts: A means to understanding a phenomenon. *Sex Roles, 32*, 315–335.

Poppen, P. J. (1995). Gender and patterns of sexual risk taking in college students. *Sex Roles, 32*, 545–555.

Poppen, P. J., & Segal, N. J. (1988). The influence of sex and sex role orientation on sexual coercion. *Sex Roles, 19*, 689–701.

Porter, N. P., & Geis, F. L. (1981). Women and nonverbal leadership cues: When seeing is not believing. In C. Mayo & N. M. Henley (Eds.), *Gender and nonverbal behavior* (pp. 39–61). New York: Springer-Verlag.

Porter, N. P., Geis, F., & Jennings (Walstedt), J. (1983). Are women invisible as leaders? *Sex Roles, 9*, 1035–1049.

Poulin-Dubois, D., Serbin, L. A., Kenyon, B., & Derbyshire, A.

(1994). Infants' internal knowledge about gender. *Developmental Psychology, 30,* 436–442.

Powell, A. D., & Kahn, A. S. (1995). Racial differences in women's desire to be thin. *International Journal of Eating Disorders, 17,* 191–195.

Powell, B. (1977). The empty nest, employment, and psychiatric symptoms in college-educated women. *Psychology of Women Quarterly, 2,* 35–43.

Powell, G. (1986). Effects of sex role identity and sex on definitions of sexual harassment. *Sex Roles, 14,* 9–19.

Powell, G. N. (1987). The effect of sex and gender on recruitment. *Academy of Management Review, 12,* 731–743.

Powell, G. N. (1988/1993). *Women and men in management.* Newbury Park, CA: Sage.

Powlishta, K. K. (1990). *Intergroup processes and sex-role development.* Paper presented at the University of Waterloo Conference on Child Development, Waterloo, Ontario.

Powlishta, K. K. (1995). Gender bias in children's perceptions of personality traits. *Sex Roles, 32,* 17–28.

Powlishta, K. K., & Maccoby, E. E. (1990). Resource utilization in mixed-sex dyads: The influence of adult presence and task type. *Sex Roles, 23,* 223–240.

Powlishta, K. K., Serbin, L. A., Doyle, A., & White, D. R. (1994). Gender, ethnic, and body type biases: The generality of prejudice in childhood. *Developmental Psychology, 30,* 526–536.

Powlishta, K. K., Serbin, L. A., & Moller, L. C. (1993). The stability of individual differences in gender typing: Implications for understanding gender segregation. *Sex Roles, 29,* 723–737.

Pratt, M. W., Golding, G., Hunter, W., & Sampson, R. (1988). Sex differences in adult moral orientation. *Journal of Personality, 56.*

Preston, K., & Stanley, K. (1987). "What's the worst thing . . . ?" Gender-directed insults. *Sex Roles, 17,* 209–219.

Price, D. (1994, August 8). Surprise advocate for gays. *Liberal Opinion,* p. 5.

Price, S. J., & McKenry, P. C. (1988). *Divorce.* Newbury Park, CA: Sage.

Price-Bonham, S., & Skeen, P. (1982). Black and white fathers' attitudes toward children's sex roles. *Psychological Reports, 50,* 1187–1190.

Pryor, J. B. (1987). Sexual harassment proclivities in men. *Sex Roles, 17,* 269–290.

Pryor, J. B., & Stoller, L. M. (1994). Sexual cognition processes in men high in the likelihood to sexually harass. *Personality and Social Psychology Bulletin, 20,* 163–169.

Pulakos, E. D., White, L. A., Oppler, S. H., & Borman, W. C. (1989). Examination of race and sex effects on performance ratings. *Journal of Applied Psychology, 74,* 770–780.

Purcell, P., & Stewart, L. (1990). Dick and Jane in 1989. *Sex Roles, 22,* 177–185.

Purifoy, F. E., & Koopmans, L. H. (1980). Androstenedione, T and free T concentrations in women of various occupations. *Social Biology, 26,* 179–188.

Puryear, G. R., & Mednick, M. S. (1974). Black militancy, affective attachment, and the fear of success in black college women. *Journal of Consulting and Clinical Psychology, 42,* 263–266.

Putnam, F. W., Guroff, J. J., Silverman, E. K., Barban, L., & Post, R. M. (1986). The clinical phenomenology of multiple personality disorder: Review of 100 recent cases. *Journal of Clinical Psychiatry, 47,* 285–293.

Quadagno, D., & Sprague, J. (1991, June). Reasons for having sex. *Medical Aspects of Human Sexuality, 52.*

Quina, K. L., Wingard, J. A., & Bates, H. G. (1987). Language style and gender stereotypes in person perception. *Psychology of Women Quarterly, 11,* 111–122.

Quinn, S. (1987). *A mind of her own: The life of Karen Horney.* New York: Summit Books.

Rabban, M. (1950). Sex role identification in young children in two diverse social groups. *Genetic Psychology Monographs, 42,* 81–158.

Raboch, J., & Raboch, J. (1992). Infrequent orgasms in women. *Journal of Sex and Marital Therapy, 18,* 114–120.

Radke-Yarrow, M., Zahn-Waxler, C., & Chapman, M. (1983). Children's prosocial dispositions and behavior. In P. H. Mussen (Series Ed.) and E. M. Hetherington (Vol. Ed.), *Handbook of child psychology: Vol. 4. Socialization, personality, and social development* (pp. 469–545). New York: Wiley.

Radloff, L. S. (1975). Sex differences in depression: The effects of occupation and marital status. *Sex Roles, 1,* 249–267.

Radloff, L. S. (1980). Risk factors for depression: What do we learn from them? In M. Guttentag, S. Salasin, & D. Belle (Eds.), *The mental health of women.* New York: Academic Press.

Radloff, L. S., & Monroe, M. K. (1978). Sex differences in helplessness with implications for depression. In L. S. Hansen & R. S. Rapoza (Eds.), *Career Development and the counseling of women.* Springfield, IL: Thomas.

Ragins, B. R., & Sundstrom, E. (1989). Gender and power in organizations: A longitudinal perspective. *Psychological Bulletin, 105,* 51–88.

Raines, R. S., Hechtman, S. B., & Rosenthal, R. (1990). Nonverbal behavior and gender as determinants of physical attractiveness. *Journal of Nonverbal Behavior, 14,* 253–267.

Ramist, L., & Arbeiter, S. (1986). *Profiles, college-bound seniors, 1985.* New York: College Entrance Examination Board.

Randolph, B., & Winstead, B. (1988). Sexual decision making and object relations theory. *Archives of Sexual Behavior, 17,* 389–409.

Rapaport, K. R., & Posey, C. D. (1991). Sexually coercive college males. In A. Parrot & L. Bechhofer (Eds.), *Acquaintance rape: The hidden crime* (pp. 217–228). New York: Wiley.

Raphael, S., & Robinson, M. (1980/1984). The older lesbian: Love relationships and friendship patterns. *Alternate Lifestyles, 3,* 207–229.

Raskin, A. (1974a). Age-sex differences in response to antidepressant drugs. *Journal of Nervous and Mental Disease, 159,* 120–130.

Raskin, A. (1974b). A guide for drug use in depressive disorders. *American Journal of Psychiatry, 131,* 181–185.

Rawlings, E. T., & Carter, D. K. (1977). Feminist and nonsexist psychotherapy. In E. I. Rawlings & D. Carter (Eds.), *Psychotherapy for women.* Springfield, IL: Charles C. Thomas.

Rebecca, M., Hefner, R., & Oleshansky, B. (1976). A model of sex-role transcendence. *Journal of Social Issues, 32,* 197–206.

Reed, B. G. (1985). Drug misuse and dependency in women: The meaning and implications of being considered a special population or minority group. *International Journal of the Addictions, 20,* 13–62.

Reedy, M. N., Birren, J. E., & Schaie, K. W. (1981). Age and sex differences in satisfying love relationships across the adult life span. *Human Development, 24,* 52–66.

Rees, L. (1953). Psychosomatic aspects of the premenstrual tension syndrome. *Journal of Mental Science, 99,* 62.

Rees, W. D. (1971). The hallucinations of widowhood. *British Medical Journal, 4,* 37–41.

Rees, W. D. (1975). The bereaved and their hallucinations. In B. Schoenberg et al. (Eds.), *Bereavement: Its psychosocial aspects.* New York: Columbia University Press.

Reese, E., & Fivush, R. (1993). Parental styles talking about the past. *Developmental Psychology, 29,* 596–606.

Regan, P. C., & Sprecher, S. (1995). Gender differences in the value of contributions to intimate relationships: Egalitarian relationships are not always perceived to be equitable. *Sex Roles, 33,* 221–238.

Reid, P., & Finchilescu, G. (1995). The disempowering effects of media violence against women on college women. *Psychology of Women Quarterly, 19,* 397–411.

Reid, P. T. (1994). The real problem in the study of culture. *American Psychologist, 49,* 524–525.

Reid, P. T., & Comas-Diaz, L. (1990). Gender and ethnicity: Perspectives on dual status. *Sex Roles, 22,* 397–408.

Reid, P. T., & Kelly, E. (1994). Research on women of color: From ignorance to awareness. *Psychology of Women Quarterly, 18,* 477–486.

Reid, P. T., Tate, C. C., & Berman, P. W. (1989). Preschool children's self-presentations in situations with infants: Effects of sex and race. *Child Development, 60,* 710–714.

Reidly, R., & VonKorff, M. (1991). Is battered women's help seeking connected to the level of their abuse? *Public Health Reports, 106,* 360–364.

Reifman, A., Biernat, M., & Lang, E. L. (1991). Stress, social support, and health in married professional women with small children. *Psychology of Women Quarterly, 15,* 431–445.

Reilly, M. E., Lott, B., Caldwell, D., & DeLuca, L. (1992). Tolerance for sexual harassment related to self-reported sexual victimization. *Gender and Society, 6,* 122–138.

Reilly, M. E., & Lynch, J. M. (1990). Power-sharing in lesbian partnerships. *Journal of Homosexuality, 19,* 1–30.

Reilly, P. J. (1980). *Sexual harassment in the Navy.* Unpublished master's thesis, Naval Postgraduate School, Monterey, CA.

Reilly, T. W. (1981). *Modeling the effect of women's self-evaluations in parenting role.* Unpublished doctoral dissertation, Johns Hopkins University, Baltimore.

Reilly, T. W., Entwisle, D. R., & Doering, S. G. (1987, May). Socialization into parenthood: A longitudinal study of the development of self-evaluations. *Journal of Marriage and the Family, 49,* 295–308.

Reinisch, J. M. (1990). *The Kinsey Institute new report on sex: What you must know to be sexually literate.* New York: St. Martin's Press.

Reinisch, J. M., Sanders, S. A., Hill, C. A., & Davis, M. Z. (1992). High-risk sexual behavior among heterosexual undergraduates at a midwestern university. *Family Planning Perspectives, 24,* 116–121.

Reis, H. T. (1986). Gender effects in social participation: Intimacy, loneliness, and the conduct of social interaction. In R. Gilmour & S. Duck (Eds.), *The emerging field of personal relationships.* Hillsdale, NJ: Erlbaum.

Reisman, J. M. (1990). Intimacy in same-sex friendship. *Sex Roles, 23,* 65–82.

Reiss, I. L. (1960). *Premarital sexual standards in America.* New York: Free Press of Glencoe.

Reiss, I. L. (1986). *Journey into sexuality: An exploratory voyage.* Englewood Cliffs, NJ: Prentice-Hall.

Reitberger, R., & Fuchs, W. (1972). *Comics: Anatomy of a mass media.* Boston: Little, Brown.

Reitz, R. (1981). *Menopause: A positive approach.* London: Unwin.

Remick, H. (Ed.). (1984). *Comparable worth and wage discrimination.* Philadelphia: Temple University Press.

Rennie, S. (May-June 1993). Prevention: Drugs vs. diet. *Ms., 2,* 38.

Renzetti, C. M. (1987). New wave or second stage? Attitudes of college women toward feminism. *Sex Roles, 16,* 265–277.

Renzetti, C. M. (1992). *Violent betrayal: Partner abuse in lesbian relationships.* Newbury Park, CA: Sage.

Renzetti, C. M., & Curran, D. J. (1989). *Women, men, and society: The sociology of gender.* Boston: Allyn and Bacon.

Repetti, R. L. (1984). Determinants of children's sex stereotyping: Parental sex-role traits and television viewing. *Personality and Social Psychology Bulletin, 3,* 457–468.

Repetti, R. L., Matthews, K. A., & Waldron, I. (1989). Effects of paid employment on women's mental and physical health. *American Psychologist, 44,* 1394–1401.

Reskin, B. F., & Padavic, I. (1994). *Women and men at work.* Thousand Oaks, CA: Pine Forge Press.

Rest, J. R. (1979). *Development in judging moral issues.* Minneapolis: University of Minnesota Press.

Rest, J. R. (1985). Morality. In J. H. Flavell & E. Markmaa (Eds.), *Cognitive development.* New York: Wiley.

Rheingold, H. L., & Cook, K. V. (1975). The contents of boys' and girls' rooms as an index of parents' behavior. *Child Development, 46,* 459–463.

Rhodes, B., & Kroger, J. (1992). Parental bonding and separation-individuation difficulties among late adolescent eating disordered women. *Child Psychiatry and Human Development, 22,* 249–263.

Rhodes, J. E., Fischer, K., Ebert, L., & Meyers, A. B. (1993). Patterns of service utilizations among pregnant and parenting African American adolescents. *Psychology of Women Quarterly, 17,* 257–274.

Ricciardelli, L. I., & Williams, R. J. (1995). Desirable and undesirable gender traits in three behavioral domains. *Sex Roles, 33,* 637–655.

Rice, J. K. (1994). Reconsidering research on divorce, family life cycle, and the meaning of family. *Psychology of Women Quarterly, 18,* 559–584.

Rich, A. (1976). *Of woman born: Motherhood as experience and institution.* New York: Norton.

Richards, M. H., Boxer, A. M., Petersen, A. C., & Albrecht, R. (1990). Relation of weight to body image in pubertal girls and boys from two communities. *Developmental Psychology, 26,* 313–321.

Richardson, J. T. E. (1990). Questionnaire studies of paramenstrual symptoms. *Psychology of Women Quarterly, 14,* 15–42.

Richardson, L. (1988). *The dynamics of sex and gender: A sociological perspective.* New York: Harper & Row.

Richardson, L. (1993). Gender stereotyping in the English language. In L. Richardson & V. Taylor (Eds.), *Feminist frontiers III* (pp. 44–50). New York: McGraw-Hill.

Riche, M. F. (1988). The postmarital society: In the 1990s, marriage will be an optional lifestyle. *American Demographics, 10,* 22–27.

Ricketts, M. (1989). Epistemological values of feminists in psychology. *Psychology of Women Quarterly, 13,* 401–416.

Ridgeway, C. L., & Diekema, D. (1992). Are gender differences status differences? In C. L. Ridgeway (Ed.), *Gender, interaction, and inequality.* New York: Springer-Verlag.

Ridgeway, D., Waters, E., & Kuczaj, S. A. (1985). Acquisition of emotion-descriptive language: Receptive and productive vocabulary norms for ages 18 months to 6 years. *Developmental Psychology, 21,* 901–908.

Riemer, B. A. (1995). *Lesbian identity formation and the softball environment.* Unpublished doctoral dissertation, Michigan State University, East Lansing.

Rierdan, J. (1983). Variations in the experience of menarche as a function of preparedness. In S. Golub (Ed.), *Menarche.* Lexington, MA: Lexington Books.

Ries, P., & Stone, A. J. (1992). *The American woman, 1992–1993: A status report.* New York: Norton.

Rigby, D. N., & Sophie, J. (1990). Ethical issues and client sexual preference. In H. Lerman & N. Porter (Eds.), *Feminist ethics in psychotherapy.* New York: Springer.

Riger, S. (1991). Gender dilemmas in sexual harassment policies and procedures. *American Psychologist, 46,* 497–505.

Riger, S. (1992). Epistemological debates, feminist voices: Science, social values and the study of women. *American Psychologist, 47,* 730–740.

Rivera-Tovar, A., Rhodes, R., Pearlstein, T. B., & Frank, E. (1994). *Premenstrual dysphorias: Myths and reality.* Washington, DC: American Psychiatric Press.

Roberts, T. (1991). Gender and the influences of evaluations on self-assessments in achievement settings. *Psychological Bulletin, 109,* 297–308.

Roberts, T., & Nolen-Hoeksema, S. (1989). Sex differences in reactions to evaluate feedback. *Sex Roles, 21,* 725–747.

Roberts, T., & Nolen-Hoeksema, S. (1990). *Gender differences in construals of and responsiveness to evaluations in an achievement situation.* Unpublished manuscript, Stanford University, Stanford, CA.

Robins, L. N., Helzer, J. E., Weissman, M. M., Orvaschel, H., Gruenberg, E., Burke, J. D., & Regier, D. A. (1984). Lifetime prevalence of specific psychiatric disorders in three sites. *Archives of General Psychiatry, 41,* 949–958.

Robins, L. N., & Rieger, D. A. (Eds.). (1991). *Psychiatric disorders of America: The epidemiologic catchment area study.* New York: Free Press.

Robinson, C. C., & Morris, J. T. (1986). The gender-stereotyped nature of Christmas toys received by 36-, 48-, and 60-month-old children: A comparison between nonrequested and requested toys. *Sex Roles, 15,* 21–32.

Robinson, J. P. (1980). Housework technology and household work. In S. F. Berk (Ed.), *Women and household labor.* Beverly Hills, CA: Sage.

Rodeheaver, D., & Thomas, J. L. (1986). Family and community networks in Appalachia. In N. Datan, A. L. Greene, & H. W. Reese (Eds.), *Life-span developmental psychology: Intergenerational relations.* Hillsdale, NJ: Erlbaum.

Rodin, J., & Ickovics, J. R. (1990). Women's health: Review and research agenda as we approach the 21st century. *American Psychologist, 45,* 1018–1034.

Rogers, C. R. (1959). A theory of therapy, personality, and inter-

personal relationships as developed in the client-centered framework. In S. Koch (Ed.), *Psychology: A study of a science* (Vol. 3). New York: McGraw-Hill.

Roiphe, K. (1993). *The morning after: Sex, fear, and feminism on campus.* Boston: Little, Brown.

Rollins, B. C. (1989). Marital quality at midlife. In S. Hunter & M. Sundel (Eds.), *Midlife myths.* Newbury Park, CA: Sage.

Romer, N., & Cherry, D. (1980). Ethnic and social class differences in children's sex-role concepts. *Sex Roles, 6,* 245–263.

Rook, K. S. (1987). Reciprocity of social exchange and social satisfaction among older women. *Journal of Personality and Social Psychology, 57,* 145–154.

Roopnarine, J. L. (1986). Mothers' and fathers' behaviors toward the toy play of their infant sons and daughters. *Sex Roles, 14,* 59–68.

Roos, P. E., & Cohen, L. H. (1987). Sex roles and social support as moderators of life stress adjustment. *Journal of Personality and Social Psychology, 52,* 576–585.

Roosa, W., Fitzgerald, H. E., & Crawford, M. (1985). Teenage parenting, delayed parenting, and childlessness. In L. L'Abate (Ed.), *The handbook of family psychology and therapy.* Homestead, IL: Dorsey Press.

Root, M. P. P. (1990). Disordered eating in women of color. *Sex Roles, 22,* 525–536.

Root, M. P. P. (1991). Persistent, disordered eating as a gender specific, post-traumatic stress response to sexual assault. *Psychotherapy, 28,* 96–102.

Rosaldo, M. Z. (1974). Women, culture and society: A theoretical overview. In M. Z. Rosaldo & L. Lamphere (Eds.), *Women, culture and society.* Stanford, CA: Stanford University Press.

Roscoe, B., & Benaske, N. (1985). Courtship violence experienced by abused wives: Similarities in patterns of abuse. *Family Relations, 34,* 419–424.

Roscoe, B., & Kelsey, T. (1986). Dating violence among high school students. *Psychology, a Quarterly Journal of Human Behavior, 23,* 53–59.

Rose, S. M. (1983, August). *Friendship termination patterns of college women and men.* Paper presented at the meeting of the American Psychological Association, Anaheim, CA.

Rose, S., & Frieze, I. (1989). Young singles' scripts for a first date. *Gender and Society, 3,* 258–268.

Rose, S., & Frieze, I. (1993). Young singles' contemporary dating scripts. *Sex Roles, 28,* 499–509.

Rosen, E. I. (1987). *Bitter choices.* Chicago: University of Chicago Press.

Rosen, L. N., Ickovics, J. R., & Moghadam, L. Z. (1990). Employment and role satisfaction: Implications for the general well-being of military wives. *Psychology of Women Quarterly, 14,* 371–385.

Rosen, L. W., Shafer, C. L., Dummer, G. M., Cross, L. K., Deuman, G. W., & Maimberg, S. R. (1988). Prevalence of pathogenic weight-control behaviors among Native American women and girls. *International Journal of Eating Disorders, 7,* 807–811.

Rosen, R. C., & Leiblum, S. R. (1987). Current approaches to the evaluation of sexual desire disorders. *Journal of Sex Research, 23,* 141–162.

Rosenberg, R., & Knight, R. A. (1988). Determining male sexual offender subtypes using cluster analysis. *Journal of Quantitative Criminology, 4,* 383–410.

Rosenkrantz, P. S., Vogel, S. R., Bee, H., Brovermen, I. K., &

Broverman, D. M. (1968). Sex role stereotypes and self-concepts in college students. *Journal of Consulting and Clinical Psychology, 32*, 287–295.

Rosenthal, P. (1996). Gender and managers' causal attributions for subordinate performance: A field story. *Sex Roles, 34*, 1–15.

Rosenthal, R. (1966). *Experimenter effects in behavioral research.* New York: Appleton-Century-Crofts.

Rosenthal, R. (1967). Covert communication in the psychological experiment. *Psychological Bulletin, 67*, 356–367.

Rosenthal, R., Archer, D., DiMatteo, M. R., Kowumaki, J. H., & Rogers, P. O. (1974, September). Body talk and tone of voice: The language without words. *Psychology Today, 8*, 64–68.

Rosenthal, R., & DePaulo, B. M. (1979). Sex differences in eavesdropping on nonverbal cues. *Journal of Personality and Social Psychology, 37*, 273–285.

Rosenthal, R., & Jacobson, L. (1968). *Pygmalion in the classroom: Teacher expectation and pupil intellectual development.* New York: Holt, Rinehart, and Winston.

Rosewater, L. B. (1990). Diversifying feminist theory and practice: Broadening the concept of victimization. In L. S. Brown & M. P. P. Root (Eds.), *Diversity and complexity in feminist therapy.* New York: Harrington Park Press.

Ross, C. A. (1989). *Multiple personality disorder: Diagnosis, clinical features, and treatment.* New York: Wiley.

Ross, C. A., Heber, S., Anderson, G., & Norton, G. R. (1989). Differentiating multiple personality disorder and complex partial seizures. *General Hospital Psychiatry, 11*, 54–58.

Ross, C. E., Mirowsky, J., & Huber, J. (1983). Dividing work, sharing work, and in between: Marriage patterns and depression. *American Sociological Review, 48*, 809–823.

Ross, D. M., & Ross, S. A. (1972). Resistance by preschool boys to sex-inappropriate behavior. *Journal of Educational Psychology, 63*, 342–346.

Ross, H. G., Dalton, M. J., & Milgram, J. E. (1980, November). *Older adults' perception of closeness in sibling relationships.* Paper presented at the 33rd annual scientific meeting of the Gerontological Society of America, San Diego, CA.

Ross, L., Anderson, D. R., & Wisocki, P. A. (1982). Television viewing and adult sex-role attitudes. *Sex Roles, 8*, 589–592.

Ross, S. I., & Jackson, J. M. (1991). Teachers' expectations for black males' and black females' academic achievement. *Personality and Social Psychology Bulletin, 17*, 78–82.

Rosser, P. (1989a). *The SAT gender gap.* Washington, DC: Center for Women Policy Studies.

Rosser, P. (1989b, May-June). SATs no gauge of students' abilities. *New Directions for Women,* pp. 1,7.

Rosser, P. (1992). *The SAT gender gap: ETS responds: A research update.* Washington, DC: Center for Women Policy Studies.

Rosser, P., with the staff of the National Center for Fair and Open Testing (1987). *Sex bias in college admissions tests: Why women lose out* (2nd ed.). Cambridge, MA: National Center for Fair and Open Testing.

Rossi, A. S. (1980). Mood cycles by menstrual month and social week. In A. Dan, E. A. Graham, & C. P. Beecher (Eds.), *The menstrual cycle* (Vol. 1). New York: Springer.

Rossi, A. S. (1985). Gender and parenthood. In A. S. Rossi (Ed.), *Gender and the life course.* New York: Aldine.

Rossi, A. S., & Rossi, P. E. (1977). Body time and social time: Mood patterns by menstrual cycle phase and day of week. *Social Science Research, 6*, 273–308.

Rossi, J. D. (1983). Ratios exaggerate gender differences in mathematical ability [Comment]. *American Psychologist, 38*, 348.

Rostosky, S. S., & Travis, C. (1996). Menopause research and the dominance of the biomedical model 1984–1994. *Psychology of Women Quarterly, 20*, 285–312.

Rotenberg, K. J. (1984). Sex differences in children's trust in peers. *Sex Roles, 11*, 953–957.

Rotenberg, K. J. (1986). Same-sex patterns and sex differences in the trust-value basis of children's friendship. *Sex Roles, 15*, 613–626.

Roth, S., & Lebowitz, L. (1988). The experience of sexual trauma. *Journal of Traumatic Stress, 1*, 79–107.

Rothbart, M., Hanley, D., & Albert, M. (1986). Gender differences in moral reasoning. *Sex Roles, 15*, 645–653.

Rothbart, M. K. (1971). Birth order and mother-child interaction in an achievement situation. *Journal of Personality & Social Psychology, 17*, 113–120.

Rothbart, M. K., & Rothbart, M. (1976). Birth order, sex of child, and maternal help-giving. *Sex Roles, 2*, 39–46.

Rothbaum, B. O., Foa, E. B., Riggs, D. S., Murdock, T., & Walsh, W. (1992). A prospective examination of post-traumatic stress disorder in rape victims. *Journal of Traumatic Stress, 5*, 455–475.

Rothblum, E. (1990). Women and weight: Fad and fiction. *Journal of Psychology, 124*, 5–24.

Rothblum, E. D. (1994b). Transforming lesbian sexuality. *Psychology of Women Quarterly, 18*, 627–641.

Rotheram, M. J., & Weiner, N. (1983). Androgyny, stress, and satisfaction: Dual-career traditional relationships. *Sex Roles, 9*, 151–158.

Rothert, M., Holmes, M., Rovner, D., Schmitt, N., & Talarzczyk, G. (1992). *Estrogen replacement therapy.* Washington, DC: National Center for Nursing Research.

Rotter, N. G., & Rotter, G. S. (1988). Sex differences in the encoding and decoding of negative facial emotions. *Journal of Nonverbal Behavior, 12*, 139–148.

Rousseau, J. J. (1762/1966). *Emile* (Barbara Foxley, Trans.). New York: Dutton.

Rowley, J. (1987, March 26). Court: State Department has discrimination against women. *Easton Express,* p. A3.

Roy, M. (1977). *Battered women.* New York: Van Nostrand.

Roy, M. (1982). *The abusive partner.* New York: Van Nostrand.

Rozee-Koker, P., & Polk, G. (1986). The social psychology of group rape. *Sexual Coercion and Assault: Issues and Perspectives, 1*, 57–65.

Rubin, D. I., & Greene, K. I. (1991). Effects of biological and psychological gender, age cohort, and interviewer gender on attitudes toward gender-inclusive/exclusive language. *Sex Roles, 24*, 391–412.

Rubin, J. Z., Provenzano, F. J., & Luria, Z. (1974). The eye of the beholder: Parents' view on sex of newborns. *American Journal of Orthopsychiatry, 44*, 512–519.

Rubin, L. (1976). *Worlds of pain.* New York: Basic Books.

Rubin, L. (1983). *Intimate strangers: Men and women together.* New York: Harper & Row.

Rubin, L. B. (1979). *Women of a certain age: The midlife search for self.* New York: Harper & Row.

Rubin, L. B. (1990). *Erotic wars: What happened to the sexual revolution?* New York: HarperCollins.

Rubin, L. R. (1980). The empty nest: Beginning or ending? In L. A. Bond & J. C. Rosen (Eds.), *Competence and coping in adulthood.* Hanover, NH: University Press of New England.

Rubin, R. T., Reinisch, J. M., & Haskett, R. F. (1981). Postnatal gonadal steroid effects on human behavior. *Science, 211,* 1318–1324.

Rubin, Z., Peplau, L. A., & Hill, C. T. (1981). Loving and leaving: Sex differences in romantic attachments. *Sex Roles, 7,* 821–835.

Rubinstein, C. M., & Shaver, P. (1982). *In search of intimacy.* New York: Delacorte Press.

Rubinstein, R. L. (1987). Never-married elderly as a social type: Reevaluating some images. *The Gerontologist, 27,* 108–113.

Ruble, D. N. (1977). Premenstrual symptoms: A reinterpretation. *Science, 197,* 291–292.

Ruble, D. N., Boggiano, A. K., & Brooks-Gunn, J. (1982). Men's and women's evaluations of menstrual-related excuses. *Sex Roles, 8,* 625–638.

Ruble, D. N., Boggiano, A. K., Feldman, N. S., & Loebl, J. H. (1980). Developmental analysis of the role of social comparison in self-evaluation. *Developmental Psychology, 16,* 105–115.

Ruble, D. N., & Brooks-Gunn, J. (1979). Menstrual symptoms: A social cognitive analysis. *Journal of Behavioral Medicine, 2,* 171–193.

Ruble, D. N., & Brooks-Gunn, J. (1982). A developmental analysis of menstrual distress in adolescence. In R. C. Friedman (Ed.), *Behavior and the menstrual cycle* (pp. 177–216). New York: Marcel Dekker.

Ruble, D. N., Fleming, A. S., Stangor, C., Brooks-Gunn, J., Fitzmaurice, G., & Deutsch, F. (1990). Transition to motherhood and the self: Measurement, stability, and change. *Journal of Personality and Social Psychology, 58,* 450–463.

Ruble, D. N., Hackel, L. S., Fleming, A. S., & Stangor, C. (1988). Changes in the marital relationship during the transition to first-time motherhood: Effects of violated expectations concerning division of household labor. *Journal of Personality and Social Psychology, 55,* 78–87.

Ruble, T. L. (1983). Sex stereotypes: Issues of change in the 1970s. *Sex Roles, 9,* 397–402.

Rubovits, P. C., & Maehr, M. L. (1971). Pygmalion analyzed: Toward an explanation of the Rosenthal-Jacobson findings. *Journal of Personality and Social Psychology, 19,* 197–203.

Rucker, C. E., & Cash, T. F. (1992). Body images, body-size perceptions, and eating behaviors among African-American and white college women. *International Journal of Eating Disorders, 12,* 291–300.

Rudd, N. M., & McKenry, P. C. (1986). Family influences on the job satisfaction of employed mothers. *Psychology of Women Quarterly, 10,* 363–372.

Ruether, R. R. (1981). Women in utopian movements. In R. R. Ruether & R. S. Keller (Eds.), *Women and religion: Vol. 1. The nineteenth century, a documented history.* Cambridge, MA: Harper & Row.

Ruether, R. R. (1983). *Sexism and God-talk: Toward a feminist theology.* Boston: Beacon Press.

Russell, D., Peplau, L. A., & Cutrona, C. E. (1980). The revised UCLA loneliness scale: Concurrent and discriminant validity evidence. *Journal of Personality and Social Psychology, 32,* 472–480.

Russell, D. E. H. (1975). *The politics of rape.* New York: Stein and Day.

Russell, D. E. H. (1983a). The prevalence and incidence of forcible rape of females. *Victimology: An International Journal, 7,* 81–93.

Russell, D. E. H. (1983b). The incidence and prevalence of intrafamilial and extrafamilial sexual abuse of female children. *Child Abuse & Neglect, 7,* 133–146.

Russell, D. E. H. (1983c). Pornography and rape: A causal model. In D. E. H. Russell (Ed.), *Making violence sexy: Feminist views on pornography* (pp. 120–150). New York: Teachers College Press.

Russell, D. E. H. (1984a). *Sexual exploitation: Rape, child sexual abuse, and work place harassment.* Beverly Hills, CA: Sage.

Russell, D. E. H. (1984b). The prevalence and seriousness of incestuous abuse: Stepfathers vs. biological fathers. *Child Abuse and Neglect, 8,* 15–22.

Russell, D. E. H. (1986). *The silent trauma: Incest in the lives of girls and women.* New York: Basic Books.

Russell, D. E. H. (Ed.). (1993a). *Making violence sexy: Feminist views on pornography.* New York: Teachers College Press, Columbia University.

Russell, D. E. H. (1993b). *Pornography: Turning men on to violence against women.* Berkeley, CA: Russell Books.

Russell, D. E. H., & Howell, N. (1983). The prevalence of rape in the United States revisited. *Signs, 8,* 688–695.

Russell, G. (1986). Grandfathers: Making up for lost opportunities. In R. A. Lewis & R. E. Salt (Eds.), *Men in families* (pp. 233–259). Beverly Hills: Sage.

Russett, C. E. (1989). Sexual science: The Victorian construction of womanhood. Cambridge, MA: Harvard University Press.

Russo, N. F. (1979). Overview: Sex roles, fertility, and the motherhood mandate. *Psychology of Women Quarterly, 4,* 7–15.

Russo, N. F. (1984). Women in the mental health delivery system: Implications for research and policy. In L. E. Walker (Ed.), *Women and mental health policy.* Beverly Hills, CA: Sage.

Russo, N. F. (1990). Overview: Forging research priorities for women's mental health. *American Psychologist, 45,* 368–373.

Russo, N. F. (1995). PWQ: A scientific voice in feminist psychology. *Psychology of Women Quarterly, 19,* 1–3.

Russo, N. F. (1996). Editorial: Masculinity, male roles, and the future of feminist psychology. *Psychology of Women Quarterly, 20,* 1–2.

Russo, N. F. (1997). Forging new directions in gender role measurement. *Psychology of Women Quarterly, 21,* i–ii.

Russo, N. F., Horn, J. D., & Schwartz, R. (1992). U.S. abortion in context: Selected characteristics and motivations of women seeking abortions. *Journal of Social Issues, 48,* 183–202.

Ruth, S. (Ed.). (1998). *Issues in feminism: An introduction to women's studies.* (4th ed.) Mountain View, CA: Mayfield.

Rutter, M. (1974). *The qualities of mothering: Maternal deprivation reassessed.* New York: Jason Aronson.

Ryan, M. P. (1983). *Womanhood in America: From colonial times to the present* (3rd ed.). New York: Franklin Watts.

Ryff, C. (1984). Personality development from the inside: The subjective experience of change in adulthood and aging. In P. B. Baltes & O. G. Brim, Jr. (Eds.), *Life-span development and behavior* (Vol. 6). New York: Academic Press.

Ryujin, D. H., & Herrold, A. J. (1989). Cross-sex comparisons: A word of caution. *Sex Roles, 20,* 713–719.

Sachs, A. (1989, May). A slap at sex stereotypes: The Supreme Court clears the way for discrimination suits. *Time,* p. 66.

Sadd, S., Miller, F. D., & Zietz, B. (1979). Sex roles and achievement conflicts. *Personality and Social Psychology Bulletin, 5,* 352–355.

Sadker, M., & Sadker, D. (1985, March). Sexism in the schoolroom of the '80s. *Psychology Today*, pp. 54, 56, 57.

Sadker, M., & Sadker, D. (1994). *Failing at fairness: How America's schools cheat girls*. New York: Scribners.

Sadker, M., Sadker, D., & Klein, A. (1991). The issue of gender in elementary and secondary education. In G. Grant (Ed.), *Review of research in education* (Vol. 17). Washington, DC: American Educational Association.

Saghir, M., & Robins, E. (1973). *Male and female homosexuality*. Baltimore: Williams & Wilkins.

Salisbury, N. (1991). Personal communication. In R. C. Crooks & K. Baur, *Our sexuality* (5th ed.). Redwood City, CA: Benjamin/Cummings.

Saluter, A. F. (1994). *Marital status and living arrangements: March 1993*. Washington, DC: U.S. Government Printing Office.

Sanchez, C. L. (1989). New World tribal connections. In J. Plaskow & C. P. Christ (Eds.), *Weaving the visions: New patterns in feminist spirituality*. New York: Harper & Row.

Sanday, P. R. (1981). *Female power and male dominance: On the origins of sexual inequality*. Cambridge: Cambridge University Press.

Sandberg, D. E., Ehrhardt, A. A., Mellins, C. A., Ince, S. E., & Meyer-Bahlburg, H. F. L. (1987). The influence of individual and family characteristics upon career aspirations of girls during childhood and adolescence. *Sex Roles, 16*, 649–668.

Sanfilipo, M. P. (1994). Masculinity, femininity, and subjective experience of depression. *Journal of Clinical Psychology, 50*, 144–157.

Sang, B. E. (1989). New directions in lesbian research, theory, and education. *Journal of Counseling and Development, 68*, 92–96.

Santrock, J. W. (1990). *Adolescence* (4th ed.). Dubuque, IA: William C. Brown.

Sapadin, L. A. (1988). Friendship and gender: Perspectives of professional men and women. *Journal of Social and Personal Relationships, 5*, 387–403.

Saperstein, A., Triolo, B., & Heinzen, T. E. (1995). Ideology or experience: A study of sexual harassment. *Sex Roles, 32*, 835–842.

Sapiro, V. (1993). *Women in American society: An introduction to women's studies* (3rd ed.). Mountain View, CA: Mayfield.

Sargeant, J. K., Bruce, M. L., Florio, L. P., & Weissman, M. M. (1990). Factors associated with 1-year outcome of major depression in the community. *Archives of General Psychology, 47*, 515–526.

Sarrel, P. M. (1990). Sexuality and menopause. *Obstetrics and Gynecology, 74*(Suppl. 4), 26S–30S.

Sarrell, P. M., & Sarrell, P. (1984). *Sexual turning points: The seven stages of adult sexuality*. New York: MacmillanCoppen.

Sattel, J. (1976). The inexpressive mask: Tragedy or sexual politics? *Social Problems, 23*, 469–477.

Sayers, S. L., Baucom, D. H., & Tierney, A. M. (1993). Sex roles, interpersonal control, and depression: Who can get their way. *Journal of Research in Personality, 27*, 377–395.

Scaramella, T. C., & Brown, W. A. (1978). Serum testosterone and aggressiveness in hockey players. *Psychosomatic Medicine, 40*, 262–265.

Scarf, M. (1980). *Unfinished business: Pressure points in the lives of women*. New York: Ballantine.

Scarf, M. A. (1979). The more sorrowful sex. *Psychology Today, 12*, 44–52, 89–90.

Scarr, S., Phillips, D., & McCartney, K. (1989). Working mothers and their families. *American Psychologist, 44*, 1402–1409.

Schafer, A. T., & Gray, H. W. (1981). Sex and mathematics. *Science, 24*, 231.

Schaie, K. W., & Willis, S. L. (1991). *Adult development and aging* (3rd ed.). HarperCollins.

Schaninger, C. M., & Buss, W. C. (1986). The relationship of sex-role norms to couple and parental demographics. *Sex Roles, 15*, 77–94.

Schatzkin, A., et al. (1987). Alcohol consumption and breast cancer in the epidemiologic follow-up study of the first national health and nutrition examination survey. *New England Journal of Medicine, 316*, 1169–1173.

Schechter, D., Bachmann, G. A., Vaitukaitis, J., Phillips, D., & Saperstein, D. (1989). Perimenstrual symptoms: Time course of symptom intensity in relation to endocrinologically defined segments of the menstrual cycle. *Psychosomatic Medicine, 51*, 173–194.

Scherer, M. (1992). Child abuse in a therapeutic community. *Therapeutic Care and Education, 1*, 151–163.

Schiavi, R. (1990). Sexuality and aging in men. *Annual Review of Sex Research, 1*, 227–249.

Schmidt, F. L. (1992). What do data really mean? Research findings, meta-analysis, and cumulative knowledge in psychology. *American Psychologist, 47*, 1173–1181.

Schmidt, P. J., Nieman, L. K., Grover, G. N., Muller, K. L., Merrimam, G. R., & Rabinow, D. R. (1991). Lack of effect of induced menses on symptoms in women with premenstrual syndrome. *New England Journal of Medicine, 324*, 1174–1179.

Schneider, J., & Hacker, S. (1973). Sex role imagery and the use of generic "man." *Speech Monograph, 38*, 142–145.

Schoeman, V., Garrison, C., & Kaplan, B. (1984). Epidemiology of adolescent depression. *Public Health Review, 12*, 159–189.

Schofield, J. W. (1981). Complementary and conflicting identities: Images of interaction in an interracial school. In S. A. Asher & J. M. Gottman (Eds.), *The development of children's friendships*. New York: Cambridge University Press.

Schofield, J. W. (1982). *Black and white in school*. New York: Praeger.

Schooler, C., Miller, J., Miller, K. A., & Richtand, C. N. (1984). Work for the household: Its nature and consequences for husbands and wives. *American Journal of Sociology, 90*, 97–124.

Schover, L. R. (1991). The impact of breast cancer on sexuality, body image, and intimate relationships. *CA—A Cancer Journal for Clinicians, 41*, 112–125.

Schreurs, K. M. G. (1993). Sexuality in lesbian couples: The importance of gender. *Annual Review of Sex Research, 4*, 49–66.

Schreurs, K. M. G., & Buunk, B. P. (1996). Closeness, autonomy, equity, and relationship satisfaction in lesbian couples. *Psychology of Women Quarterly, 20*, 577–592.

Schroeder, K. A., Blood, L. L., & Maluso, D. (1992). An intergenerational analysis of expectations for women's career and family roles. *Sex Roles, 26*, 273–291.

Schroeder, P., & Snowe, O. (1994). The politics of women's health. In C. Costello & A. J. Stone (Eds.), *The American woman, 1994–1995; Where we stand, women and health*. New York: Norton.

Schultz, M. (1975). The semantic derogation of women. In B. Thorne & N. Henley (Eds.), *Language and sex difference and dominance*. Rowley, MA: Newbury House.

Schupak-Neubert, E., & Nemeroff, C. (1993). Disturbances in identity and self-regulation in bulimia nervosa: Implications for a metaphorical perspective of "body as self." *International Journal of Eating Disorders, 13,* 335–347.

Schuster, R. (1988). Sexuality as a continuum: The bisexual identity. In Boston Lesbian Psychologies Collective (Eds.), *Lesbian psychologies* (pp. 56–71). Urbana: University of Illinois Press.

Schwartz, M. F. (1993). False memory blues: An editorial. *The Masters and Johnson Report, 3.*

Schwartz, N., Wagner, D., Bannert, M., & Mathes, L. (1987). Cognitive accessibility of sex role concepts and attitudes toward political participation: The impact of sexist advertisements. *Sex Roles, 17,* 593–601.

Schwartz, P. (1994). *Peer marriage.* New York: Free Press.

Scurfield, R. M. (1985). Post-trauma stress assessment and treatment: Overview and formulations. In C. R. Figler (Ed.), *Trauma and its wake: The study and treatment of post-traumatic stress disorders* (pp. 219–256). New York: Brunner/Mazel.

Seccombe, K., & Ishii-Kuntz, M. (1994). Gender and social relationships among the never-married. *Sex Roles, 30,* 585–603.

Sedikides, C., Oliver, M. B., & Campbell, W. K. (1994). Perceived benefits and costs of romantic relationships for women and men: Implications for exchange theory. *Personal Relationships, 1,* 5–21.

Sedney, M. A. (1987). Development of androgyny: Parental influences. *Psychology of Women Quarterly, 11,* 311–326.

Seegmiller, B. R. (1980). Sex-role differences in preschoolers: Effects of maternal employment. *Journal of Psychology, 104,* 185–189.

Seghorn, T. K., Prentky, R. A., & Boucher, R. J. (1987). Childhood sexual abuse in the lives of sexually aggressive offenders. *Journal of the American Academy of Child and Adolescent Psychiatry, 26,* 262–267.

Seginer, R., Karayanni, M., & Mar'i, M. M. (1990). Adolescents' attitudes toward women's roles. *Psychology of Women Quarterly, 14,* 119–133.

Selkow, P. (1984). Effects of maternal employment on kindergarten and first-grade children's vocational aspirations. *Sex Roles, 11,* 677–690.

Selnow, G. W. (1985). Sex diferences in uses and perceptions of profanity. *Sex Roles, 12,* 303–312.

Seltzer, R. (1992). The social location of those holding antihomosexual attitudes. *Sex Roles, 26,* 391–398.

Senn, C. Y. (1993). Women's multiple perspectives and experiences with pornography. *Psychology of Women Quarterly, 17,* 319–341.

Serbin, L. A., & Connor, J. M. (1979). Sex-typing of children's play preference and patterns of cognitive performance. *Journal of Genetic Psychology, 134,* 315–331.

Serbin, L. A., Moller, L., Powlishta, K., & Gulko, J. (1991, April). *The emergence of gender segregation and behavioral compatibility in toddlers' peer preferences.* Paper presented at the biennial meeting of the Society for Research in Child Development, Seattle, WA.

Serbin, L. A., & O'Leary, K. D. (1975, December). How nursery schools teach girls to shut up. *Psychology Today, 9,* 57–58, 102–103.

Serbin, L. A., O'Leary, K. D., Kent, R. N., & Tronick, I. J. (1973). A comparison of teacher response to the pre-academic and problem behavior of boys and girls. *Child Development, 44,* 796–804.

Serbin, L. A., Zelkowitz, P., Doyle, A., Gold, D., & Wheaton, B. (1990). The socialization of sex-differentiated skills and academic performance: A mediational model. *Sex Roles, 23,* 613–628.

Serbin, L. H., Powlishta, K. K., & Gulko, J. (1993). The development of sex typing in middle childhood. *Monographs of the Society for Research in Child Development, 58.*

Shachar, S. A., & Gilbert, L. A. (1983). Working lesbians: Role conflicts and coping strategies. *Psychology of Women Quarterly, 7,* 244–256.

Shaffer, D. R., Pegalis, L., & Cornell, D. P. (1991). Interactive effects of social context and sex role identity on female self-disclosure during the acquaintance process. *Sex Roles, 24,* 1–19.

Shangold, M. (1980). Sports and menstrual function. *The Physician and Sports Medicine, 8,* 66–70.

Shangold, M. (1985). Causes, evaluation, and management of athletic oligomenorrhea. *Medical Clinics of North America, 69,* 83–85.

Shapiro, E. (1979). *Transition to parenthood in adult and family development.* Unpublished doctoral dissertation, University of Massachusetts, Amherst.

Sharps, M. J., Price, J. L., & Williams, J. K. (1994). Spatial cognition and gender: Instructional and stimulus influences on mental image rotation performance. *Psychology of Women Quarterly, 18,* 413–425.

Sharps, M. J., Welton, A. T., & Price, J. L. (1993). Gender and task in the determination of spatial cognitive performance. *Psychology of Women Quarterly, 17,* 71–83.

Shaul, S., Bogle, J., Hale-Harbaugh, J., & Norman, A. (1978). *Toward intimacy: Family planning and sexuality concerns of physically disabled women.* New York: Human Sciences Press.

Shaver, P., & Hendrick, C. (1987). Editors' introduction. In P. Shaver & C. Hendrick (Eds.), *Sex and gender.* Newbury Park, CA: Sage.

Shaywitz, S. E., Shaywitz, B. A., Fletcher, J. M., & Escobar, M. D. (1990). Prevalence of reading disability in boys and girls. *Journal of the American Medical Association, 264,* 998–1002.

Shea, C. (1994, September 7). "Gender gap" on examinations shrank again this year. *Chronicle of Higher Education,* p. A54.

Shea, M. (1993). The effects of selective evaluation on the perception of female cues in sexually coercive and noncoercive males. *Archives of Sexual Behavior, 22,* 415–432.

Shek, D. T. L. (1995). Gender differences in marital quality and well-being in Chinese married adults. *Sex Roles, 32.*

Sherfey, M. J. (1966). *The nature and evolution of female sexuality.* New York: Random House.

Sherif, C. W. (1979). Bias in psychology. In J. A. Sherman & E. T. Back (Eds.), *The prism of sex: Essays in the sociology of knowledge.* Madison: University of Wisconsin Press.

Sherif, C. W. (1987). Bias in psychology. In S. Harding (Ed.), *Feminism and methodology* (pp. 37–56). Bloomington: Indiana University Press.

Sherman, J. A. (1971). *On the psychology of women: A survey of empirical studies.* Springfield, IL: Charles C. Thomas.

Sherman, J. A. (1978). *Sex-related differences in cognition: An essay on theory and evidence.* Springfield, IL: Charles C. Thomas.

Sherman, J. A., & Fennema, E. (1978). Distribution of spatial visualization and mathematical problem-solving scores: A test of Stafford's X linked hypotheses. *Psychology of Women Quarterly, 3,* 157–167.

Sherriffs, A. C., & Jarrett, R. F. (1953). Sex differences in attitudes about sex differences. *Journal of Psychology, 35,* 161–168.

Sherriffs, A. C., & McKee, J. P. (1957). Qualitative aspects of beliefs about men and women. *Journal of Personality, 25,* 451–464.

Shields, S. A. (1975). Functionalism, Darwinism, and the psychology of women: A study in social myth. *American Psychologist, 30,* 739–754.

Shields, S. A. (1982). The variability hypothesis: The history of a biological model of sex difference in intelligence. *Signs, 7,* 769–797.

Shields, S. A. (1995). The role of emotion, belief, and values in gender development. In N. Eisenberg (Ed.), *Social development* (pp. 212–232). Thousand Oaks, CA: Sage.

Shields, S. A., & Cooper, P. E. (1983). Stereotypes of traditional and nontraditional childbearing roles. *Sex Roles, 9.*

Shields, S. A., Steinke, P., & Koster, B. A. (1995). The double bind of caregiving: Representation of gendered emotion in American advice literature. *Sex Roles, 33,* 467–488.

Shifren, K., & Bauserman, R. L. (1996). The relationship between instrumental and expressive traits, health behaviors, and perceived physical health. *Sex Roles, 34,* 841–864.

Shigetomi, C. C., Hartmann, D. P., & Gefland, D. N. (1981). Sex differences in children's altruistic behavior and reputations for helpfulness. *Developmental Psychology, 19,* 434–437.

Shinedling, M., & Pedersen, D. M. (1970). Effects of sex of teacher versus student on children's gain in quantitative and verbal performance. *Journal of Psychology, 76,* 79–84.

Shotland, R. L. (1992). A theory of the causes of courtship rape: Part 2. *Journal of Social Issues, 48,* 127–143.

Shotland, R. L., & Goodstein, L. (1993). Just because she doesn't want to doesn't mean it's rape: An experimentally based causal model of the perception of rape in a dating situation. *Social Psychology Quarterly, 46,* 220–232.

Shute, J. (1992). *Life-size.* Boston: Houghton Miflin.

Shuy, R. W. (1969). *Sex as a factor in sociolinguistic research.* Paper presented at the meeting of the Anthropological Society of Washington. (Available from Educational Resources Information Clearinghouse, No. ED027522.)

Siavelis, R. L., & Lamke, L. K. (1992). Instrumentalness and expressiveness: Predictors of heterosexual relationship satisfaction. *Sex Roles, 26,* 149–159.

Siderits, M. A., Johannsen, W. J., & Fadden, T. F. (1985). Gender, role, and power: A content analysis of speech. *Psychology of Women Quarterly, 9,* 439–450.

Sigler, R. T. (1989). *Domestic violence in context.* Lexington, MA: Lexington Books.

Signorella, M. L. (1987). Gender schema: Individual differences and context effects. In L. S. Liben & M. L. Signorella (Eds.), *Children's gender schemata.* London: Jossey-Bass.

Signorella, M. L., Bigler, R. S., & Liben, L. S. (1993). Developmental differences in children's gender schemata about others: A meta-analytic review. *Developmental Review, 13,* 147–183.

Signorella, M. L., & Jamison, W. (1986). Masculinity, femininity, androgyny, and cognitive performance: A meta-analysis. *Psychological Bulletin, 100,* 207–229.

Signorella, M. L., Jamison, W., & Krupa, M. H. (1989). Predicting spatial performance from gender stereotyping in activity preferences and in self-concept. *Developmental Psychology, 25,* 89–95.

Signorielli, N. (1989). Television and conceptions about sex roles: Maintaining conventionality and the status quo. *Sex Roles, 21,* 341–360.

Signorielli, N. (1991). Adolescents and ambivalence toward marriage: A cultivation analysis. *Youth Society, 23,* 121–149.

Signorielli, N., & Lears, M. (1992). Children, television, and conceptions about chores: Attitudes and behaviors. *Sex Roles, 27,* 157–170.

Silber, T. J. (1986). Anorexia nervosa in blacks and Hispanics. *International Journal of Eating Disorders, 5,* 121–128.

Silbert, M. H. (1982). Prostitution and sexual assault: Summary of results. *International Journal of Biosocial Research, 3,* 69–71.

Silver, M., & Wolfe, S. (1989). *Unnecessary cesarean sections: How to cure a national epidemic.* Washington, DC: Citizens Health Research Group.

Silverberg, S. B., & Steinberg, L. (1990). Psychological well-being of parents with early adolescent children. *Developmental Psychology, 26,* 658–666.

Silverstein, B., Caceres, J., Perdue, L., & Cimarolli, V. (1995). Gender differences in depressive symptomatology: The role played by "Anxious Somatic Depression" associated with gender-related achievement concerns. *Sex Roles, 33,* 621–633.

Silverstein, B., Carpman, S., Perlick, D., & Perdue, L. (1990). Nontraditional sex role aspirations, gender identity conflict, and disordered eating among college women. *Sex Roles, 23,* Nos. 11/12.

Silverstein, B., Perdue, L., Peterson, B., & Kelly, E. (1986). The role of the mass media in promoting a thin standard of bodily attractiveness for women. *Sex Roles, 14,* 519–523.

Silverstein, B., Perlick, D., Clauson, J., & McKoy, E. (1993). Depression combined with somatic symptomatology among adolescent females who report concerns regarding maternal achievement. *Sex Roles, 28,* 637–653.

Silverstein, L. B. (1991). Transforming the debate about child care and maternal employment. *American Psychologist, 10,* 1025–1032.

Silverstein, L. B. (1996). Fathering is a feminist issue. *Psychology of Women Quarterly, 20,* 3–37.

Silverstein, L. B., & Phares, V. (1996a). Expanding the mother-child paradigm: An examination of dissertation research 1986–1994. *Psychology of Women Quarterly, 20,* 39–53.

Silverstein, L. B., & Phares, V. (Eds.). (1996b). Fathering as a feminist issue. Special section. *Psychology of Women Quarterly, 20,* 1–77.

Simkins-Bullock, J. A., & Wildman, B. G. (1991). An investigation into the relationships between gender and language. *Sex Roles, 24,* 149–160.

Simmons, R. G., & Blyth, D. A. (1987). *Moving into adolescence: The impact of pubertal change and school context.* New York: Aldine De Gruyter.

Simmons, R. G., Blyth, D. A., & McKinney, K. L. (1983). The social and psychological effects of puberty on white females. In J. Brooks-Gunn & A. C. Petersen (Eds.), *Girls in puberty.* New York: Plenum Press.

Simmons, R. G., Blyth, D. A., Van Cleave, E. F., & Bush, D. M. (1979). Entry into early adolescence: The impact of school structure, puberty, and early dating on self-esteem. *American Sociological Review, 44,* 948–967.

Simmons, R. G., & Rosenberg, F. R. (1975). Sex, sex-roles, and self-image. *Journal of Youth and Adolescence, 4,* 229–258.

Simons, A. D., Angell, K. L., Monroe, S. M., & Thase, M. E. (1993). Cognition and life stress in depression. *Journal of Abnormal Psychology, 102,* 584–591.

Simonton, D. K. (1996). Presidents' wives and first ladies: On achieving eminence within a traditional gender role. *Sex Roles*, *35*, 309–336.

Simpson, G. (1984). The daughters of Charlotte Ray: The career development process during the exploratory and establishment stages of black women attorneys. *Sex Roles*, *11*, 113–139.

Simpson, J. A. (1987). The dissolution of romantic relationships: Factors involved in relationship stability and emotional distress. *Journal of Personality and Social Psychology*, *53*.

Simpson, J. A., Campbell, B., & Berscheid, E. (1986). The association between romantic love and marriage: Kephart (1967) twice revisited. *Personality and Social Psychology Bulletin*, *12*, 363–372.

Simpson, J. A., & Gangestad, S. W. (1991). Individual differences in sociosexuality: Evidence for convergent and discriminant validity. *Journal of Personality and Social Psychology*, *60*, 870–883.

Simpson, W. S., & Ramberg, J. A. (1992). Sexual dysfunction in married female patients with anorexia and bulimia nervosa. *Journal of Sex and Marital Therapy*, *18*, 44–54.

Singer, J., & Singer, I. (1972). Types of female orgasms. *Journal of Sex Research*, *8*, 255–267.

Singleton, C. H. (1987). Sex roles in cognition. In D. J. Hargreaves & A. M. Colley (Eds.), *The psychology of sex roles* (pp. 60–91). New York: Hemisphere.

Six, B., & Eckes, T. (1991). A closer look at the complex structure of gender stereotypes. *Sex Roles*, *24*, 57–71.

Skill, T., Robinson, D., & Wallace, S. P. (1987). Portrayals of families on prime-time TV: Structure, type, and frequency. *Journal of Broadcasting*, *64*, 367.

Skinner, P. H., & Shelton, R. L. (1985). *Speech, language, and hearing: Normal processes and disorders* (2nd ed.). New York: Wiley.

Skrypnek, B. J., & Snyder, M. (1982). On the self-perpetuating nature of stereotypes about women and men. *Journal of Experimental Social Psychology*, *18*, 277–291.

Slaby, R. C., & Frey, K. S. (1975). Development of gender constancy and selective attention to same-sex models. *Child Development*, *46*, 849–856.

Slack, W., & Porter, D. (1980). Training, validity, and the issue of aptitude: A reply to Jackson. *Harvard Educational Review*, *50*, 392–401.

Slade, L. A., & Rush, M. C. (1991). Achievement motivation and the dynamics of task difficulty choice. *Journal of Personality and Social Psychology*, *60*, 165–172.

Sleeper, L. A., & Nigro, G. N. (1987). It's not who you are but who you're with: Self-confidence in achievement settings. *Sex Roles*, *16*, 57–69.

Smith, A. J. (1991). First of all I'm Jewish, the rest is commentary. In B. Sang, J. Warshow, & A. J. Smith (Eds.), *Lesbians at midlife: The creative transition, an anthology*. San Francisco: spinsters book company.

Smith, A., & Stewart, A. J. (1983). Approaches to studying racism and sexism in black women's lives. *Journal of Social Issues*, *39*, 1–15.

Smith, B., & Smith, B. (1983). Across the kitchen table: A sister to sister dialog. In C. Moraga & G. Anzaldua (Eds.), *This bridge called my back: Writings by radical women of color*. New York: Kitchen Table: Women of Color Press.

Smith, E. J. (1982). The black female adolescent: A review of the educational, career, and psychological literature. *Psychology of Women Quarterly*, *6*, 261–288.

Smith, G. J. (1985). Facial and full-length ratings of attractiveness related to the social interactions of young children. *Sex Roles*, *12*, 287–288.

Smith, J. E., & Krejci, J. (1991). Minorities join the majority: Eating disturbances among Hispanic and Native American youth. *International Journal of Eating Disorders*, *10*, 179–186.

Smith, P. A., & Midlarsky, E. (1985). Emotionally derived conceptions of femaleness and maleness: A current view. *Sex Roles*, *12*, 313–328.

Smith, P. K. (1987). Exploration, play and social development in boys and girls. In D. J. Hargreaves & A. M. Colley (Eds.), *The psychology of sex roles* (pp. 118–141). New York: Hemisphere.

Smith, P. K., & Daglish, L. (1977). Sex differences in parent and infant behavior in the home. *Child Development*, *48*, 1250–1254.

Smith, P. M. (1985). *Language, the sexes, and society*. New York: Basil Blackwell.

Smith, R., & Loring, M. T. (1994). The trauma of emotionally abused men. *Psychology: A Journal of Human Behavior*, *3*, 1–4.

Smith-Lovin, L., & Brody, C. (1989). Interruptions in group discussions: The effects of gender and group composition. *American Sociological Review*, *54*, 425–435.

Smolak, L., & Levine, M. (1993). Separation-individuation difficulties and the distinction between bulimia nervosa and anorexia nervosa in college women. *International Journal of Eating Disorders*, *14*, 33–41.

Snell, W. E., Jr., Belk, S. S., Flowers, A., & Warren, J. (1988). Women's and men's willingness to self-disclose to therapists and friends: The moderating influence of instrumental, expressive, masculine, and feminine topics. *Sex Roles*, *18*, 769–776.

Snell, W. E., Jr., Belk, S. S., & Hawkins, R. C., II. (1987). Alcohol and drug use in stressful times: The influence of the masculine role and sex-related personality attributes. *Sex Roles*, *16*, 359–373.

Snodgrass, S. E. (1985). Women's intuition: The effect of subordinate role upon interpersonal sensitivity. *Journal of Personality and Social Psychology*, *49*, 146–155.

Snow, J. T., & Harris, M. B. (1989). Disordered eating in Southwestern Pueblo Indians and Hispanics. *Journal of Adolescence*, *12*, 329–336.

Snow, L. F., & Johnson, S. M. (1977). Modern-day menstrual folklore. *Journal of the American Medical Association*, *237*, 2736–2739.

Snowden, L. R. (1988). Ethnicity and utilization of mental health services: An overview of current findings. In *Proceedings: Oklahoma Mental Health Research Institute, 1988 Professional Symposium*. Oklahoma City: Oklahoma Mental Health Research Institute.

Snyder, M., Tanke, E. D., & Berscheid, E. (1977). Social perception and interpersonal behavior: On the self-fulfilling nature of social stereotypes. *Journal of Personality and Social Psychology*, *35*, 656–666.

Snyder, M., & Uranowitz, S. W. (1978). Reconstructing the past: Some cognitive consequences of person perception. *Journal of Personality and Social Psychology*, *36*, 941–950.

Snyder, T. D. (1987). *Digest of education statistics*. Washington, DC: Department of Education.

Sobol, M. P., & Daly, K. J. (1992). The adoption alternative for pregnant adolescents: Decision making, consequences, and policy implications. *Journal of Social Issues*, *48*, 143–161.

Sollie, D. L., & Fischer, J. L. (1985). Sex-role orientation, intimacy of topic, and target person differences in self-disclosure among women. *Sex Roles*, *12*, 917–929.

Sommer, B. (1983). How does menstruation affect cognitive competence and psychophysiological response? *Women & Health, 8,* 53–90.

Sommers, C. H. (1994). *Who stole feminism? How women have betrayed women.* New York: Simon & Schuster.

Sontag, S. (1979). The double standard of aging. In J. H. Williams (Ed.), *Psychology of women: Selected readings* (pp. 462–478). New York: Norton.

Sorenson, S. B., & Siegel, J. M. (1992). Gender, ethnicity, and sexual assault: Findings from a Los Angeles study. *Journal of Social Issues, 48,* 93–104.

Sorenson, S. B., & Telles, C. A. (1991). Self-reports of spousal violence in a Mexican-American and non-Hispanic white population. *Violence and Victims, 6,* 3–15.

Spalter-Roth, R., & Hartmann, H. (1990). *Raises and recognition: Secretaries, clerical workers and the union wage premium.* Washington, DC: Institute for Women's Policy Research.

Spanier, G. B., & Thompson, L. (1983). Belief and distress after marital separation. *Journal of Divorce, 7,* 31–49.

Spector, I., & Carey, M. (1990). Incidence and prevalence of the sexual dysfunctions: A critical review of the empirical literature. *Archives of Sexual Behavior, 19,* 389–408.

Spelke, E. S., & Owsley, C. J. (1979). Intermodal exploration and knowledge in infancy. *Infant Behavior and Development, 2,* 13–27.

Spence, J. T. (1974). The Thematic Apperception Test and attitudes toward achievement in women: A new look at the motive to avoid success and a new method of measurement. *Journal of Consulting and Clinical Psychology, 42,* 427–437.

Spence, J. T. (1984). Masculinity, femininity, and gender-related traits: A conceptual analysis and critique of current research. In B. Maher & W. Maher (Eds.), *Progress in experimental personality research: Vol. 13. Normal personality processes.* Orlando, FL: Academic Press.

Spence, J. T. (1985a). Achievement American style: The rewards and costs of individualism. *American Psychologist, 40,* 1285–1295.

Spence, J. T. (1985b). Gender identity and implications for concepts of masculinity and femininity. In T. B. Sonderegger (Ed.), *Nebraska Symposium on Motivation: Vol. 32. Psychology and gender* (pp. 59–96). Lincoln: University of Nebraska Press.

Spence, J. T. (1991). Do the BSRI and PAQ measure the same or different concepts? *Psychology of Women Quarterly, 15,* 141–165.

Spence, J. T. (1993). Gender-related traits and gender ideology: Evidence for a multifactorial theory. *Journal of Personality and Social Psychology, 64,* 624–635.

Spence, J. T., & Hahn, E. D. (1997). The Attitudes Toward Women Scale and attitude change in college students. *Psychology of Women Quarterly, 21,* 17–34.

Spence, J. T., & Helmreich, R. (1972). The Attitudes Toward Women Scale: An objective instrument to measure attitudes toward the rights and roles of women in contemporary society. *Catalog of Selected Documents in Psychology, 2,* 66–67.

Spence, J. T., & Helmreich, R. L. (1978). *Masculinity and femininity: Their psychological dimensions, correlates, and antecedents.* Austin: University of Texas Press.

Spence, J. T., & Helmreich, R. L. (1979). Comparison of masculine and feminine personality attributes and sex role attitudes across age groups. *Developmental Psychology, 15,* 583–584.

Spence, J. T., & Helmreich, R. L. (1983). Achievement-related motives and behaviors. In J. T. Spence (Ed.), *Achievement and achievement motives* (pp. 10–74). San Francisco: Freeman.

Spence, J. T., Helmreich, R. L., & Holahan, C. K. (1979). Negative and positive opponents of psychological masculinity and femininity and their relationships to self-reports of neurotic and acting out behaviors. *Journal of Personality and Social Psychology, 37,* 1673–1682.

Spence, J. T., Helmreich, R. L., & Stapp, J. (1973). A short version of the Attitudes Toward Women Scale (AWS). *Bulletin of the Psychonomic Society, 2,* 219–220.

Spence, J. T., Helmreich, R. L., & Stapp, J. (1975). Ratings of self and peers on sex role attributes and their relations to self-esteem and conceptions of masculinity and femininity. *Journal of Personality and Social Psychology, 32,* 29–39.

Spence, J. T., & Sawin, L. L. (1985). Images of masculinity and femininity: A reconceptualization. In V. O'Leary, R. Unger, & B. Wallston (Eds.), *Sex, gender and social psychology.* Hillsdale, NJ: Erlbaum.

Spencer, M. B., Swanson, D. P., & Cunningham, M. (1991). Ethnicity, ethnic identity, and competence formation: Adolescent transition and cultural transformation. *Journal of Negro Education, 60,* 366–387.

Spencer, S., Steele, C., & Quinn, D. (1995). *Psychological mediators of stereotype vulnerability.* Paper presented at the annual convention of the American Psychological Association, New York City.

Spencer, S., & Zeiss, A. (1987). Sex roles and sexual dysfunction in college students. *Journal of Sex Research, 23,* 338–347.

Spender, D. (1985/1990). *Man made language.* Glascow: Harper Collins Manufacturing.

Sperling, M. B., & Berman, W. H. (1991). An attachment classification of desperate love. *Journal of Personality Assessment, 56,* 45–55.

Sperling, S. (1991). Baboons with briefcases: Feminism, functionalism, and sociobiology in the evolution of primate gender. *Signs, 17,* 1–27.

Spiegel, D., & Cardena, E. (1991). Disintegrated experience: The dissociative disorders revisited. *Journal of Abnormal Psychology, 100,* 366–378.

Spirit of Houston, The: The first national women's conference. An official report to the President, the Congress and the people of the United States. (1978, March). Washington, DC: National Commission on the Observance of International Women's Year, U.S. Department of State. Reprinted in S. Ruth (Ed.). (1990). *Issues in feminism* (2nd ed.). Mountain View, CA: Mayfield.

Spitz, R. A. (1965). *The first year of life.* New York: International Universities Press.

Spitze, G. (1988). Women's employment and family relations: A review. *Journal of Marriage and the Family, 50,* 595–618.

Spletter, M. (1982). *A woman's choice: New options in the treatment of breast cancer.* Boston: Beacon Press.

Sprecher, S., Hatfield, E., Cortese, A., & Potapova, E. (1994). Token resistance to sexual intercourse and consent to unwanted sexual intercourse: College students' dating experiences in three countries. *Journal of Sex Research, 31,* 125–132.

Sprecher, S., & McKinney, K. (1993). *Sexuality.* Newbury Park, CA: Sage.

Sprecher, S., Sullivan, Q., & Hatfield, E. (1994). Mate selection preferences: Gender differences examined in a national sample. *Journal of Personality and Social Psychology, 66,* 1074–1080.

Sprock, J., & Yoder, C. Y. (1997). Women and depression: An

update on the report of the APA task force. *Sex Roles, 36,* 269–303.

Spuhler, K. P., & Vandenberg, S. G. (1980). Comparison of parenting-offspring resemblance for specific cognitive ability. *Behavior Genetics, 10,* 413–418.

Stafford, I. P. (1984). Relation of attitudes toward women's roles and occupational behavior to women's self-esteem. *Journal of Counseling Psychology, 31,* 332–338.

Stafford, R. E. (1961). Sex differences in spatial visualization as evidence of sex-linked inheritance. *Perceptual and Motor Skills, 18,* 428.

Staines, G. L., Pottick K. J., & Fudge, D. A. (1986). Wives' employment and husbands' attitudes toward work and life. *Journal of Applied Psychology, 17,* 118–128.

Stake, J. E. (1983). Ability level, evaluative feedback, and sex differences in performance expectancy. *Psychology of Women Quarterly, 8,* 48–58.

Stake, J. E., Roades, L., Rose, S., Ellis, L., & West, C. (1994). The women's studies experience: Impetus for feminist activism. *Psychology of Women Quarterly, 18,* 17–24.

Stake, J. E., & Rose, S. (1994). The long-term impact of women's studies on students' personal lives and political activism. *Psychology of Women Quarterly, 18,* 403–412.

Stangor, C., & Ruble, D. N. (1987). Development of gender role knowledge and gender constancy. In L. S. Liben & M. L. Signorella (Eds.), *New directions for child development: Children's gender schemata* (pp. 155–165). San Francisco: Jossey-Bass.

Stangor, C., & Ruble, D. N. (1989). Stereotype development and memory: What we remember depends on how much we know. *Journal of Experimental Social Psychology, 25,* 18–35.

Stanley, J. (1977). Gender marking in American English. In A. P. Nilsen (Ed.), *Sexism and language.* Urbana: University of Illinois Press.

Stanley, S. C., Hunt, J. G., & Hunt, L. L. (1986). The relative depiction of husbands in dual-earner households. *Journal of Family Issues, 7,* 3–20.

Starhawk. (1977/1979). Witchcraft and women's culture. In C. Christ & J. Plaskow (Eds.), *Womanspirit rising: A feminist reader in religion.* San Francisco: Harper & Row.

Starhawk. (1982). *Dreaming the dark.* Boston: Beacon Press.

Starhawk. (1984). Immanence: Uniting the spiritual and political. In J. U. Kalven & M. I. Buckley (Eds.), *Women's spirit bonding.* New York: Pilgrim Press.

Stark, E. D. (1984). The battering syndrome: Social knowledge, social therapy and the abuse of women. *Dissertation Abstracts International, 45*(1-A), 307.

Stark, E. M., & Flitcraft, A. (1988). Violence among intimates: An epidemiological review. In V. B. Van Hasselt, R. L. Morrison, A. S. Bellack, & M. Hersen (Eds.), *Handbook of family violence* (pp. 293–317). New York: Plenum Press.

Stark, L. P (1991). Traditional gender role beliefs and individual outcomes: An exploratory analysis. *Sex Roles, 24,* 639–650.

Starr, B. (1987). Sexuality and aging. In M. P. Lawton & G. L. Maddox (Eds.), *Annual review of gerontology and geriatrics* (Vol. 5). New York: Springer.

Starr, B., & Weiner, M. (1981). *The Starr-Weiner report on sex and sexuality in the mature years.* New York: McGraw-Hill.

Stattin, H., & Magnusson, D. (1990). *Pubertal maturation in female development.* Hillsdale, NJ: Erlbaum.

Steele, C. M., & Josephs, R. A. (1990). Alcohol myopia: Its prized and dangerous effects. *American Psychologist, 45,* 921–933.

Steele, C. M., & Southwick, L. (1985). Alcohol and social behavior: 1. The psychology of drunken excess. *Journal of Personality and Social Psychology, 48,* 18–34.

Steele, J., & Barling, J. (1996). Influence of maternal gender-role beliefs and role satisfaction on daughters' vocational interests. *Sex Roles, 34,* 637–648.

Steenbarger, B. N., & Greenberg, R. P. (1990). Sex roles, stress, and distress: A study of person by situation contingency. *Sex Roles, 22,* 59–68.

Steil, J. M. (1994). Supermoms and second shifts: Marital inequality in the 90's. In J. Freeman (Ed.), *Women: A feminist perspective* (5th ed., pp. 149–161). Mountain View, CA: Mayfield.

Steil, J. M., & Weltman, K. (1991). Marital inequality: The importance of resources, personal attributes, and social norms on career valuing and the allocation of domestic responsibilities. *Sex Roles, 24,* 161–179.

Stein, A. H., & Bailey, M. M. (1973). The socialization of achievement orientation in females. *Psychological Bulletin, 80,* 345–366.

Stein, A. H., Pohly, S. R., & Mueller, E. (1971). The influence of masculine, feminine, and neutral tasks on children's achievement behavior, expectancies of success, and attainment values. *Child Development, 42,* 195–207.

Stein, J. A., Fox, S. A., & Murata, P. J. (1991). The influence of ethnicity, socioeconomic status, and psychological barriers on the use of mammography. *Journal of Health and Social Behavior, 32,* 101–113.

Stein, J. A., Newcomb, M. D., & Bentler, P. M. (1992). The effect of agency and communality on self-esteem: Gender differences in longitudinal data. *Sex Roles, 26,* 465–483.

Steinberg, L. (1987). Impact of puberty on family relations: Effects of pubertal status and pubertal timing. *Developmental Psychology, 23,* 451–460.

Steinberg, L. (1988). Reciprocal relation between parent-child distance and pubertal maturation. *Developmental Psychology, 24,* 122–128.

Steinem, G. (1978, November). Erotica and pornography: A clear and present difference. *Ms.,* pp. 53–54, 75–76.

Steinem, G. (1980). Erotica and pornography: A clear and present difference. In L. Lederer (Ed.), *Take back the night* (pp. 115–118). New York: Morrow.

Steinem, G. (1984). *Outrageous acts and everyday rebellions.* New York: Signet Books.

Steinem, G. (1993). The real Linda Lovelace. In D. E. H. Russell (Ed.), *Making violence sexy: Feminist views on pornography* (pp. 23–31). New York: Teachers College Press, Columbia University.

Steinem, G. (1994). *Moving beyond words.* New York: Simon & Schuster.

Steinem, G. (1995, August). Keynote address. Presented at the meeting of the American Psychological Association, New York.

Steiner, M. (1990). Postpartum psychiatric disorders. *Canadian Journal of Psychiatry, 35,* 89–95.

Steiner-Adair, C. (1986). The body politic: Normal female adolescent development and the development of eating disorders. *Journal of the American Academy of Psychoanalysis, 14,* 95–114.

Steiner-Aeschliman, S., & Mauss, A. L. (1996). The impact of feminism and religious involvement on sentiment toward God. *Review of Religious Research, 37,* 248–259.

Stern, J., & Karraker, K. H. (1989). Sex stereotyping of infants: A review of gender labeling studies. *Sex Roles, 20*, 501–522.

Stern, S., Dixon, K., Jones, D., Lake, M., Nemzer, E., & Sansone, R. (1989). Family environment in anorexia nervosa and bulimia. *International Journal of Eating Disorders, 8*, 25–31.

Sterner, P. J., & Meehan, A. M. (1988, February). *Gender stereotypes and memory for the frequency of gender-related events.* Paper presented at the fourth annual University of Scranton Psychology Research Conference, Scranton, PA.

Sternglanz, S. H., & Serbin, L. A. (1974). Sex role stereotyping in children's TV programs. *Developmental Psychology, 10*, 710–715.

Stets, J. E., & Straus, M. A. (1990). The marriage license as a hitting license: A comparison of assaults in dating, cohabiting and married couples. In M. A. Straus, R. J. Gelles, & C. Smith (Eds.), *Physical violence in American families: Risk factors and adaptations to violence in families* (pp. 227–241). New Brunswick, NJ: Transaction Publishers.

Stevenson, H. W., Chen, C., & Booth, J. (1990). Influences of schooling and urban-rural residence on gender differences in cognitive abilities and academic achievement. *Sex Roles, 23*, 535–551.

Stewart, A. J., & Chester, N. L. (1982). Sex differences in human and social motives: Achievement, affiliation, and power. In A. J. Stewart (Ed.), *Motivation and Society* (pp. 172–218). San Francisco: Jossey-Bass.

Stewart, L. P., Cooper, P. J., & Friedley, S. A. (1986). *Communication between the sexes: Sex differences and sex-role stereotypes.* Scottsdale, AZ: Gorsuuch Scarisbrick.

Stiglitz, E. (1990). Caught between two worlds: The impact of a child on a lesbian couple's relationship. *Women & Therapy, 10*, 99–116.

Stiles, D. A., Gibbons, J. L., & de la Garza-Schnellman, J. (1990). Opposite-sex ideal in the U.S.A. and Mexico as perceived by young adolescents. *Journal of Cross-cultural Psychology, 21*, 180–199.

Stille, R. G. (1985). Rape myth acceptance and hostility toward women: Antecedents, prediction of rape proclivity and effects on perception of a realistic rape portrayal. *Dissertation Abstracts International, 45*(12-B, Pt. 1), 3964.

Stillion, J. M., & White, H. (1987). Feminist humor: Who appreciates it and why? *Psychology of Women Quarterly, 11*, 219–232.

Stinson, L., & Ickes, W. (1992). Empathy accuracy in the interactions of male friends versus male strangers. *Journal of Personality and Social Psychology, 6*, 787–797.

Stipek, D., & Gralinski, J. H. (1991). Gender differences in children's achievement-related beliefs and emotional responses to success and failure in mathematics. *Journal of Educational Psychology, 83*, 361–371.

Stipek, D. J., Gralinski, J. H., & Kopp, C. B. (1990). Self-concept development in the toddler years. *Developmental Psychology, 26*, 972–977.

Stipek, D. J., & Hoffman, J. M. (1980). Children's achievement-related expectancies as a function of academic performance histories and sex. *Journal of Educational Psychology, 72*, 861–865.

St. Lawrence, J. S., & Joyner, D. J. (1991). The effects of sexually violent rock music on males' acceptance of violence against women. *Psychology of Women Quarterly, 15*, 49–63.

Stohs, J. H. (1995). Predictors of conflict over the household division of labor among women employed full-time. *Sex Roles, 33*, 257–275.

Stokes, J., & Greenstone, J. (1971). Helping black grandparents and older parents cope with childrearing: A group method. *Child Welfare, 50*, 691–701.

Stokes, J., Riger, S., & Sullivan, M. (1995). Measuring perceptions of the working environment for women in corporate settings. *Psychology of Women Quarterly, 19*, 533–549.

Stokes, J. P., McKirnan, D. J., Doll, L., & Burzette, R. G. (1996). Female partners of bisexual men: What they don't know might hurt them. *Psychology of Women Quarterly, 20*, 267–284.

Stoller, E. P. (1983). Parental caregiving by adult children. *Journal of Marriage and the Family, 45*, 851–858.

Stoller, R. (1972). Etiological factors in female transsexualism: A first approximation. *Archives of Sexual Behavior, 2*, 47–64.

Stoltzman, S. M. (1986). Menstrual attitudes, beliefs, and symptom experiences of adolescent females, their peers, and their mothers. *Health Care for Women International, 7*, 97–114.

Stone, M. (1976). *When God was a woman.* New York: Dial Press.

Stoppard, J. M., & Grunchy, C. D. G. (1993). Gender, context, and expression of positive emotion. *Personality and Social Psychology Bulletin, 19*, 143–150.

Stoppard, J. M., & Paisley, K. J. (1987). Masculinity, femininity, life stress, and depression. *Sex Roles, 16*, 489–496.

Storms, M. D. (1981). A theory of erotic orientation development. *Psychological Review, 88*, 340–353.

Stout, C. (1991). Common law: A growing alternative. *Canadian Social Trends, 23*, 18–20.

St. Peter, S. (1979). Jack went up the hill . . . but where was Jill? *Psychology of Women Quarterly, 4*, 256–260.

Strange, C. C., & Rea, J. S. (1983). Career choice considerations and sex role self-concept of male and female undergraduates in nontraditional majors. *Journal of Vocational Behavior, 23*, 219–226.

Straus, M., & Gelles, R. (1986). Societal change and change in family violence from 1975 to 1985 as revealed by two national surveys. *Journal of Marriage and the Family, 48*, 465–479.

Straus, M. A., & Gelles, R. J. (1990). How violent are American families? Estimates from the National Family Violence Resurvey and other studies. In M. A. Straus & R. J. Gelles (Eds.), *Physical violence in American families.* New Brunswick, NJ: Transaction Publishers.

Straus, M. A., Gelles, R. J., & Smith, C. (Eds.). (1990). *Physical violence in American families: Risk factors and adaptation to violence in 8,145 families.* New Brunswick, NJ: Transaction Publishers.

Stricker, L., Rock, D., & Burton, N. (1992). Sex differences in SAT predictions of college grades. New York: The College Board.

Strickland, B. R. (1988). Sex-related differences in health and illness. *Psychology of Women Quarterly, 12*, 381–399.

Strickland, W. J. (1992). Institutional emotion norms and satisfaction: Examination of a career wife population. *Sex Roles, 26*, 543–550.

Striegel-Moore, R. (1993). Etiology of binge eating: A developmental perspective. In C. G. Fairburn & G. T. Wilson (Eds.), *Binge eating* (pp. 144–172). New York: Guilford Press.

Striegel-Moore, R. H., Goldman, S. L., Garvin, V., & Rodin, J. (1996). A prospective study of somatic and emotional symptoms of pregnancy. *Psychology of Women Quarterly, 20*, 393–408.

Strober, M. (1986). Anorexia nervosa: History and psychological concepts. In K. D. Brownell & J. P. Foreyt (Eds.), *Handbook of eating disorders*. New York: Basic Books.

Strober, M. (1991). Family-genetic studies of eating disorders. *Journal of Clinical Psychiatry, 52*, 9–12.

Strommen, E. A. (1977). Friendship. In E. Donelson & J. Gullahorn (Eds.), *Women: A psychological perspective*. New York: Wiley.

Strong, B., & DeVault, C. (1997). *Human sexuality: Diversity in contemporary America* (2nd ed.). Mountain View, CA: Mayfield.

Struckman-Johnson, C. (1991). Male victims of acquaintance rape. In A. Parrot & L. Bechholfer (Eds.), *Acquaintance rape: The hidden crime* (pp. 192–213). New York: Wiley.

Struckman-Johnson, D., & Struckman-Johnson, C. (1991). Men and women's acceptance of coercive sexual strategies varied by initiator gender and couple intimacy. *Sex Roles, 25*, 661–676.

Study: Women increase in labor force. (1995, March 11). *Detroit Free Press*.

Study: Working moms love busy lives. (1994, April 14). *Lansing State Journal*, p. 7C.

Stueve, A., & O'Donnel, L. (1984). The daughters of aging parents. In G. Baruch & J. Brooks-Gunn (Eds.), *Women in midlife*. New York: Plenum Press.

Sue, D. (1979). Erotic fantasies of college students during coitus. *Journal of Sex Research, 15*, 299–305.

Sugarman, D. B., & Hotaling, G. T. (1989). Dating violence: Prevalence context and risk markers. In M. A. Pirog-Good & J. E. Stets (Eds.), *Violence in dating relationships*. New York: Praeger.

Suitor, J. J. (1991). Marital quality and satisfaction with the division of household labor across the family life cycle. *Journal of Marriage and the Family, 53*, 221–230.

Sullivan, C. M. (1991, August). Battered women as active help-seekers. *Violence Update, 1*, 1.

Sullivan, C. M., & Davidson, W. S., II. (1991). The profusion of advocacy services to women leaving abusive partners: An examination of short-term effects. *American Journal of Community Psychology, 19*, 953–960.

Sullivan, C. M., Tan, C., Basta, J., Rumptz, M., & Davidson, W. S., II. (1992). An advocacy intervention program for women with abusive partners: Initial evaluation. *Journal of Community Psychology, 21*, 309–332.

Sullivan, G. L., & O'Connor, P. J. (1988). Women's role portrayals in magazine advertising: 1958–1983. *Sex Roles, 18*, 181–188.

Sullivan, M., & Bybee, D. I. (1987). Female students and sexual harassment: What factors predict reporting behavior? *Journal of National Association of Women Deans and Counselors, 50*, 11–16.

Sullivan, M. W., Lewis, M., & Alessandri, S. M. (1992). Cross-age stability in emotional expressions during learning and extinction. *Developmental Psychology, 28*, 58–63.

Summers, R. J. (1991). Determinants of judgments of and responses to a complaint of sexual harassment. *Sex Roles, 25*, 379–392.

Summers, T. P. (1988a). Examination of sex differences in expectations of pay and perceptions of equity in pay. *Psychological Reports, 62*, 491–496.

Summers, T. P. (1988b). An investigation of sex differences in job satisfaction. *Sex Roles, 18*, 679–689.

Sumner, K. E., & Brown, T. J. (1996). Men, women and money: Exploring the role of gender, gender-linkage of college major and career-information sources in salary expectations. *Sex Roles, 34*, 823–839.

Sun, S. W., & Lull, J. (1986). The adolescent audience for music videos and why they watch. *Journal of Communication, 29*, 116–124.

Surrey, J. L. (1991). The "self-in-relation": A theory of women's development. In J. V. Jordan, A. G. Kaplan, J. B. Miller, I. P. Stiver, & J. Surrey (Eds.), *Women's growth in connection: Writings from the Stone Center*. New York: Guilford Press.

Sussman, B. (1986, March 22). Pornography concerns women more than men. *Easton Express*, p. A4.

Sussman, N. M., & Rosenfeld, H. M. (1982). Influence of culture, language, and sex on conversational distance. *Journal of Personality and Social Psychology, 42*, 66–74.

Swaab, D., & Fliers, E. (1985). A sexually dimorphic nucleus in the human brain. *Science, 228*, 1112–1115.

Swain, S. O. (1992). Men's friendships with women: Intimacy, sexual boundaries, and the informant role. In P. M. Nardi (Ed.), *Men's friendships*. Newbury Park, CA: Sage.

Sweeney, J., & Bradbard, M. R. (1988). Mothers' and fathers' changing perceptions of their male and female infants over the course of pregnancy. *Journal of Genetic Psychology, 149*, 393–404.

Swenson, I., Erickson, D., Ehlinger, E., Carlson, G., & Swaney, S. (1989). Fertility, menstrual characteristics, and contraceptive practices among white, black, and Southeast Asian refugee adolescents. *Adolescence, 25*, 647–654.

Swim, J. K., Borgida, E., Maruyama, G., & Myers, D. G. (1989). Joan McKay versus John McKay: Do gender stereotypes bias evaluation? *Psychological Bulletin, 105*, 409–429.

Swim, J. K., Aikin, K. J., Hall, W. S., & Hunter, B. A. (1995). Sexism and racism: Old-fashioned and modern prejudices. *Journal of Personality and Social Psychology, 68*, 199–214.

Swim, J. K., & Cohen, L. L. (1997). A comparison between the attitudes toward women and modern sexism scales. *Psychology of Women Quarterly, 21*, 103–118.

Switzer, J. Y. (1990). The impact of generic word choices: An empirical investigation of age- and sex-related differences. *Sex Roles, 22*, 69–82.

Syers, M., & Edleson, J. I. (1992). The combined effects of coordinated criminal justice intervention in woman abuse. *Journal of Interpersonal Violence, 7*, 490–502.

Symonds, M. (1976). The rape victim: Psychological patterns of response. *American Journal of Psychoanalysis, 36*, 27–34.

Szalai, A. (Ed.). (1972). *The use of time*. The Hague, Netherlands: Mouton.

Szinovacz, M. E. (1983). Beyond the hearth: Older women and retirement. In E. W. Markson (Ed.), *Older women: Issues and prospects*. Lexington, MA: Lexington Books.

Szinovacz, M. E. (1986/1987). Preferred retirement timing and retirement satisfaction in women. *International Journal of Aging and Human Development, 24*, 301–317.

Szinovacz, M. E.(1989). Decision-making on retirement timing. In D. Brinberg & J. Jaccard (Eds.), *Dyadic decision-making* (pp. 286–310). New York: Springer.

Szinovacz, M. E. (1990). Women and retirement. In B. B. Hess & E. W. Markson (Eds.), *Growing old in America* (4th ed.) New Brunswick, NJ: Transaction Publishers.

Szymanski, L. A., & Chrisler, J. C. (1990/1991). Eating disorders, gender role, and athletic activity. *Psychology, 27 & 28*(1), 20–29.

Tabar, L., et al. (1985, April 13). Reduction of mortality from breast cancer after mass screening with mammography. *Lancet*, 829–832.

Taffel, S., Placek, P., & Kosary, C. (1992). U.S. cesarean section rates, 1990: An update. *Birth, 19,* 21–22.

Talan, J. (1986, December 9). Tracking the chemistry of the motherhood instinct. *Morning Call,* p. D2.

Tanfer, K., & School, J. J. (1992). Premarital sexual careers and partner change. *Archives of Sexual Behavior, 21,* 45–68.

Tannen, D. (1990). *You just don't understand: Women and men in conversation.* New York: Morrow.

Tanner, J. M. (1978a). *Educational and physical growth.* New York: International Universities Press.

Tanner, J. M. (1978b). *Fetus into man.* Cambridge, MA: Harvard University Press.

Tashakkori, A. (1993). Gender, ethnicity, and the structure of self-esteem: An attitude theory approach. *Journal of Social Psychology, 133,* 479–488.

Tavris, C., & Wade, C. (1984). *The longest war: Sex differences in perspective* (2nd ed.). San Diego: Harcourt Brace Jovanovich.

Taylor, D. (1988). *Red flower: Rethinking menstruation.* Freedom, CA: Crossing Press.

Taylor, D. A., & Smitherman-Donaldson, G. (Eds.). (1989). And ain't I a woman: African American women and affirmative action. *Sex Roles, 21,* 1–12.

Taylor, M. C. (1979). Race, sex and the expression of self-fulfilling prophecies in a laboratory teaching situation. *Journal of Personality and Social Psychology, 37,* 897–912.

Taylor, M. G., & Gelman, S. A. (1991, April). *Children's beliefs about sex differences: The role of nature vs. nurture.* Paper presented at the biennial meeting of the Society for Research in Child Development, Seattle, WA.

Taylor, M. S., & Ilgen, D. R. (1981). Sex discrimination against women in initial placement decisions: A laboratory investigation. *Academy of Management Journal, 24,* 859–865.

Taylor, R. J., Keith, V. M., & Tucker, M. B. (1993). Gender, marital, familial, and friendship roles. In J. S. Jackson, L. M. Chatters, & R. J. Taylor (Eds.), *Aging in Black America* (pp. 21–36). Newbury Park, CA: Sage.

Taylor, S. (1983). Adjustment to threatening events: A theory of cognitive adaptation. *American Psychologist, 38,* 1161–1173.

Taylor, S. E., & Langer, E. J. (1977). Pregnancy: A social stigma. *Sex Roles, 3,* 27–35.

Teevan, R. C., & McGhee, P. E. (1972). Childhood development of fear and failure motivation. *Journal of Personality and Social Psychology, 21,* 345–348.

Tennen, H., & Herzberger, S. (1987). Depression, self-esteem, and the absence of self-protective attributional biases. *Journal of Personality and Social Psychology, 52,* 72–80.

Terborg, J. R., & Ilgen, D. R. (1975). A theoretical approach to sex discrimination in traditionally masculine occupations. *Organizational Behavior and Human Performance, 13,* 352–376.

Terrelonge, P. (1989). Feminist consciousness and black women. In J. Freeman, *Women: A feminist perspective* (4th ed.). Mountain View, CA: Mayfield.

Thacker, R. A. (1995). Gender influence tactics, and job characteristics preferences: New insights into salary determination. *Sex Roles, 32,* 617–638.

Thayer, R. E., Newman, R. J., & McClain, T. M. (1994). Self-regulation of mood: Strategies for changing a bad mood, raising energy, and reducing tension. *Journal of Personality and Social Psychology, 67,* 910–925.

Thelen, M., Farmer, J., Mann, L., & Pruitt, J. (1990). Bulimia and interpersonal relationships: A longitudinal study. *Journal of Counseling Psychology, 37,* 85–90.

Thoma, S. J. (1986). Estimating gender differences in the comprehension and preference of moral issues. *Developmental Review, 6,* 165–180.

Thomas, C. (1985). The age of androgyny: The new views of psychotherapists. *Sex Roles, 13,* 381–392.

Thomas, J. L. (1986a). Age and sex differences in satisfaction with grandparenting. *Journal of Gerontology, 4,* 417–423.

Thomas, J. L. (1986b). Gender differences in satisfaction with grandparenting. *Psychology and Aging, 1,* 215–219.

Thomas, V. G., & Shields, L. C. (1987). Gender influences on work values of black adolescents. *Adolescence, 22,* 37–43.

Thompson, C. M. (1964/1971). On women. In M. R. Green (Ed.), *Interpersonal psychoanalysis.* New York: Mentor.

Thompson, E. H., Jr. (1991). The maleness of violence in dating relationships: An appraisal of stereotypes. *Sex Roles, 24,* 261–278.

Thompson, L., & Walker, A. J. (1984). Mothers and daughters: Aid patterns and attachment. *Journal of Marriage and the Family, 46,* 313–322.

Thompson, S. H., Sargent, R. G., & Kemper, K. A. (1996). Black and white adolescent males' perceptions of ideal body size. *Sex Roles, 34,* 391–406.

Thompson, S. K. (1975). Gender labels and early sex role development. *Child Development, 46,* 339–347.

Thompson, S. K., & Bentler, P. M. (1971). The priority of cues in sex discrimination by children and adults. *Developmental Psychology, 5,* 181–185.

Thorndike, E. L. (1906). Sex in education. *Bookman, 23,* 211–214.

Thorne, B., & Henley, N. (1975). Difference and dominance: An overview of language, gender, and society. In B. Thorne & N. Henley (Eds.), *Language and sex: Difference and dominance.* Rowley, MA: Newbury House.

Thorne, B., & Luria, Z. (1986). Sexuality and gender in children's daily worlds. *Social Problems, 33,* 176–190.

Thornton, A., & Camburn, D. (1989). Religious participation and adolescent sexual behavior and attitudes. *Journal of Marriage and the Family, 51,* 641–653.

Tidball, M. E. (1973). Pespective on academic women and affirmative action. *Educational Review, 17,* 73–389.

Tidball, M. E. (1976). Of men and research: The dominant themes in American higher education include neither teaching nor women. *Journal of Higher Education, 54,* 130–135.

Tiefer, L. (1991). A brief history of the Association for Women in Psychology, 1969–1991. *Psychology of Women Quarterly, 15,* 635–649.

Tieger, T. (1980). On the biological basis of sex differences in aggression. *Child Development, 51,* 943–963.

Tietze, C., Forrest, J. D., & Henshaw, S. (1988). United States of America. In P. Sachdev (Ed.), *International handbook on abortion.* New York: Greenwood.

Tietze, C., & Henshaw, S. K. (1986). *Induced abortion: A world review, 1986* (6th ed.). New York: Alan Guttmacher Institute.

Tobias, S. (1982). Sexist equations. *Psychology Today,* pp. 14–17.

Tobin-Richards, M. H., Boxer, A. H., & Petersen, A. C. (1983). The psychological significance of pubertal change: Sex differences in perceptions of self during early adolescence. In J. Brooks-Gunn & A. C. Petersen (Eds.), *Girls at puberty* (pp. 127–154). New York: Plenum Press.

Tomkins, W. (1994, February 22). Surgeon decries care bias: Forum explores diversity issue. *Lansing State Journal,* p. 5C.

Tomlinson, P. S. (1987). Spousal differences in marital satisfaction during transition to parenthood. *Nursing Research, 36,* 239–243.

Tomlinson-Keasey, C. (1974). Role variables: Their influence of female motivational constructs. *Journal of Counseling Psychology, 21,* 232–237.

Toney, G.T., & Weaver, J. B., III. (1994). Effects of gender and gender role self-perceptions on affective reactions to rock music videos. *Sex Roles, 30,* 567–583.

Top, T. J. (1991). Sex bias in the evaluation of performance in the scientific, artistic, and literary professions: A review. *Sex Roles, 24,* 73–106.

Torres, A., & Forrest, J. D. (1988). Why do women have abortions? *Family Planning Perspectives, 20,* 169–176.

Tougas, F., Brown, R., Beaton, A. M., & Joly, S. (1995). Neosexism: Plus ça change, plus c'est pareil. *Personality and Social Psychology Bulletin, 21,* 842–849.

Townsend, J. M. (1987). Sex differences in sexuality among medical students: Effects of increasing socioeconomic status. *Archives of Sexual Behavior, 16,* 427–446.

Townsend, J. M., & Levy, G. D. (1990). Effects of potential partners' physical attractiveness and socioeconomic status on sexuality and partner selection. *Archives of Sexual Behavior, 19,* 149–164.

Tracy, D. M. (1987). Toys, spatial ability, and science and mathematics achievement: Are they related? *Sex Roles, 17,* 115–138.

Trautner, H. M., Helbing, N., Sahm, W. B., & Iohaus, A. (1989). *Beginning awareness-rigidity-flexibility: A longitudinal analysis of sex-role stereotyping in 4- to 10-year-old children.* Paper presented at the meeting of the Society for Research in Child Development, Kansas City, MO.

Trautner, H. M., Sahm, W. B., & Stevermann, I. (1983). *The development of sex-role stereotypes and classificatory skills in children.* Paper presented at the biennial meeting of the International Society for the Study of Behavioral Development, Munich, Germany.

Travis, C. B. (1988a). *Women and health psychology: Biomedical issues.* Hillsdale, NJ: Erlbaum.

Travis, C. B. (1988b). *Women and health psychology: Mental health issues.* Hillsdale, NJ: Erlbaum.

Travis, C. B., Burnett-Doering, J., & Reid, P. T. (1982). The impact of sex, achievement domain and conceptual orientation on causal attributions. *Sex Roles, 8,* 443–454.

Travis, C. B., McKenzie, B., Wiley, D., & Kahn, A. (1988). Sex and achievement domain: Cognitive patterns of success and failure. *Sex Roles, 19,* 509–525.

Travis, C. B., Phillippi, R. H., & Henley, T. B. (1991). Gender and causal attributions for mastery, personal, and interpersonal events. *Psychology of Women Quarterly, 15,* 233–249.

Treadwell, P. (1987). Biologic influences on masculinity. In H. Brod (Ed.), *The making of masculinities: The new men's studies.* Boston: Allen & Unwin.

Treiman, D. J., & Hartmann, H. I. (1981). *Women, work and wages: Equal pay for jobs of equal value.* Washington, DC: National Academy Press.

Tresemer, D. W. (1974). Fear of success: Popular but unproven. *Psychology Today, 7,* 82–85.

Tresemer, D. (1977). *Fear of success.* New York: Plenum Press.

Trethowan, W. H. (1972). The couvade syndrome. In J. G. Howells (Ed.), *Modern perspectives in psycho-obstetrics.* New York: Brunner/Mazel.

Trible, P. (1973/1979). Eve and Adam: Genesis 2–3 reread. In C. Christ & J. Plaskow (Eds.), *Womanspirit rising: A feminist reader in religion.* San Francisco: Harper & Row.

Trimble, J. E., & LaFromboise, T. (1985). American Indian and the counseling process: Culture, adaptation, and style. In P. Pederson (Ed.), *Handbook of cross-cultural mental health services* (pp. 127–134). Beverly Hills, CA: Sage.

Troiden, R. (1988). *Gay and lesbian identity: A sociological analysis.* New York: General Hall.

Troll, L. E. (1984). *Old ways in new bodies: Handing down kinkeeping.* Paper presented at the annual meeting of the Gerontological Society of America, San Antonio, TX.

Troll, L. E. (1985). *Early and middle adulthood* (2nd ed.). Monterey, CA: Brooks/Cole.

Troll, L. E. (1986). *Family issues in current gerontology.* New York: Springer.

Troll, L. E. (1987a). Gender differences in cross-generation networks. *Sex Roles, 17,* 751–765.

Troll, L. E. (1987b). Mother-daughter relationships through the life span. *Applied Social Psychology Annual, 7,* 284–305.

Troll, L. E., & Bengtson, V. (1982). Intergenerational relations throughout the life span. In B. B. Wolman (Ed.), *Handbook of developmental psychology* (pp. 890–911). Englewood Cliffs, NJ: Prentice-Hall.

Troll, L. E., Miller, S., & Atchley, R. (1979). *Families of later life.* Belmont, CA: Wadsworth.

Tronick, E. Z. (1989). Emotions and emotional communication in infants. *American Psychologist, 44,* 112–119.

Tronick, E. Z., & Cohn, J. F. (1989). Infant-mother face-to-face interaction: Age and gender differences in coordination and the occurrence of miscoordination. *Child Development, 60,* 85–92.

True, R. H. (1990). Psychotherapeutic issues with Asian American women. *Sex Roles, 22,* 477–486.

Tuch, R. H. (1975). The relationship between a mother's menstrual status and her response to illness in her child. *Psychosomatic Medicine, 37,* 388–394.

Tucker, V., & Cho, C. (1991). AIDS and adolescents. *Postgraduate Medicine, 89,* 49–53.

Turner, H. A. (1994). Gender and social support: Taking the bad with the good. *Sex Roles, 30,* 521–541.

Turner, J. (1986). Exchange theory. In J. Turner (Ed.), *The structure of sociological theory.* Chicago, IL: Dorsey Press.

Turner, J., & Brown, R. (1978). Social status, cognitive alternatives and intergroup relations. In H. Tajfel (Ed.), *Differentiation between social groups.* London: Academic Press.

Turner, P. J., & Gerval, J. (1995). A multidimensional study of gender typing in preschool children and their parents: Personality, attitude, preferences, behavior, and cultural differences. *Developmental Psychology, 31,* 759–772.

Turner-Bowker, D. M. (1996). Gender-stereotyped descriptors in children's picture books: Does "Curious Jane" exist in the literature? *Sex Roles, 35,* 461–488.

Twale, D. J., & Shannon, D. M. (1996). Professional service involvement of leadership faculty: An assessment of gender, role, and satisfaction. *Sex Roles, 34,* 117–126.

Twenge, J. M. (1997a). Attitudes toward women, 1970–1995: A meta-analysis. *Psychology of Women Quarterly, 21,* 35–51.

Twenge, J. M. (1997b). "Mrs. His Name"; Women's preference for married names. *Psychology of Women Quarterly, 21,* 417–429.

Tyler, L. (1973). Design for a hopeful psychology. *American Psychologist, 28*, 1021–1029.

Ubell, E. (1984, October 28). Sex in America today. *Parade*, pp. 11–13.

Ulbrich, P. M. (1988). The determinants of depression in two-income marriages. *Journal of Marriage and the Family, 50*, 121–131.

Ullman, S. E. (1996). Social reactions, coping strategies, and self-blame attributions in adjustment to sexual assault. *Psychology of Women Quarterly, 20*, 505–526.

Ullman, S. E., & Knight, R. A. (1993). The efficacy of women's resistance strategies in rape situations. *Psychology of Women Quarterly, 17*, 23–38.

Ulrich, L. T. (1980). Virtuous women found: New England ministerial literature, 1668–1735. In J. W. James (Ed.), *Women in American religion*. Philadelphia: University of Pennsylvania Press.

Umansky, E. (1989). Creating a Jewish feminist theology. In J. Plaskow & C. Christ (Eds.), *Weaving the visions: New patterns in feminist spirituality*. San Francisco: Harper & Row.

Unger, R. K. (1979). *Female and male: Psychological perspectives*. New York: Harper & Row.

Unger, R. K. (1981). Sex as a social reality: Field and laboratory research. *Psychology of Women Quarterly, 5*, 645–653.

Unger, R. K. (1989). *Representations: Social constructions of gender*. Amityville, NY: Baywood.

Unger, R. K., & Crawford, M. (1989). Methods and values in decisions about gender differences (Review of Alice H. Eagly, *Sex differences in social behavior: A social role interpretation*). *Contemporary Psychology, 34*, 122–123.

Unger, R., & Crawford, M. (1996). *Women and gender: A feminist psychology* (2nd ed). New York: McGraw-Hill.

United Methodist Church. (1989). *United Methodist Hymnal: Book of United Methodist worship* (6th ed.). Nashville, TN: United Methodist Publishing House.

United Nations (1989). *Violence against women in the family*. New York: Author.

Urberg, K. A. (1982). The development of the concepts of masculinity and femininity in young children. *Sex Roles, 6*, 659–668.

U.S. Bureau of the Census. (1992a). *Current population reports. Statistical abstracts of the United States*. Washington, DC: U.S. Government Printing Office.

U.S. Bureau of the Census. (1992b). *Marital status and living arrangements, March 1992*. Washington, DC: U.S. Government Printing Office.

U.S. Bureau of the Census. (1992c, August). *Current population reports* (Series P-60, No. 181). *Poverty in the United States: 1991*. Washington, DC: U.S. Government Printing Office.

U.S. Bureau of the Census. (1992d). *Money income of households, families, and persons in the United States, 1991*, Table b-17. Washington, DC: U.S. Government Printing Office.

U.S. Bureau of the Census. (1993). *We the American . . . women*. Washington, DC: U.S. Government Printing Office.

U.S. Department of Labor, Bureau of Labor Statistics. (1989, August). *Handbook of labor statistics*. Washington, DC: U.S. Government Printing Office.

U.S. Department of Labor, Bureau of Labor Statistics. (1993a). Current population survey, 1992 annual averages. Unpublished tabulations. Washington, DC: U.S. Government Printing Office.

U.S. Department of Labor, Bureau of Labor Statistics. (1993b,

January). *Employment and earnings*. Washington, DC: U.S. Government Printing Office.

U.S. Merit System Protection Board, Office of Merit Systems Review and Studies. (1981). *Sexual harassment in the federal work place: Is it a problem?* Washington, DC: U.S. Government Printing Office.

U.S. National Center for Health Statistics. (1992). Monthly vital statistics reports and unpublished data. *Statistical abstracts of the United States*. Austin, TX: Reference Press.

U.S. National Center for Health Statistics. (1994). Vital statistics of the United States (annual), *Monthly vital statistics report*, and unpublished data. *Statistical abstracts of the United States, 1994–1995*. Austin, TX: Reference Press.

Ussher, J. M. (1989). *The psychology of the female body*. New York: Routledge.

Valentine-French, S., & Radtke, H. L. (1989). Attributions of responsibility for an incident of sexual harassment in a university setting. *Sex Roles, 21*, 545–555.

Vandell, D. L., & Ramanan, J. (1991). Children of the national longitudinal survey of youth: Choices in after-school care and child development. *Developmental Psychology, 27*, 637–643.

Van de Wiel, H. B. M., Jaspers, J. P. M., Schultz, W. C. M., & Gal, J. (1990). Treatment of vaginismus: A review of concepts and treatment modalities. *Journal of Psychosomatic Obstetrics and Gynecology, 11*, 1–18.

Vanek, J. (1984). Housewives as workers. In P. Voydanoff (Ed.), *Work and family: Changing roles of men and women*. Palo Alto, CA: Mayfield.

Vanfossen, B. E. (1981). Sex differences in the mental health effects of spouse support and equity. *Journal of Health and Social Behavior, 22*, 130–143.

Van Knippenberg, A. F. M. (1984). Intergroup differences in group perceptions. In H. Tajfel (Ed.), *The social dimension: Vol. 2. European developments in social psychology*. Cambridge, England: Cambridge University Press.

Van Wyk, P. H., & Geist, C. S. (1995). Biology of bisexuality: Critique and observations. *Journal of Homosexuality, 28*, 357–374.

Vasta, R., Knott, J. A., & Gaze, C. E. (1996). Can spatial training erase the gender differences on the water-level task? *Psychology of Women Quarterly, 20*, 549–567.

Vaughter, R. M., Sadh, D., & Vozzola, E. (1994). Sex similarities and differences in types of play in games and sports. *Psychology of Women Quarterly, 18*, 85–105.

Vázquez-Nuttall, E., & Romero-García, I. (1989). From home to school: Puerto Rican girls learn to be students in the United States. In C. T. Garcia Coll & M. de Lourdes Mattei (Eds.), *The psychosocial development of Puerto Rican women* (pp. 60–83). New York: Praeger.

Veiel, H. O. (1993). Detrimental effects of kin support network on the course of depression. *Journal of Abnormal Psychology, 102*, 419–429.

Veniegas, R. C., & Peplau, L. A. (1997). Power and the quality of same-sex friendships. *Psychology of Women Quarterly, 21*, 279–297.

Verhovek, S. H. (1990, March 4). Girls win 51.3% in New York scholarship program. *New York Times*, p. 23.

Veroff, J., Depner, C., Kulka, R., & Douvan, E. (1980). Comparison of American motives: 1957–1976. *Journal of Personality and Social Psychology, 39*, 1249–1262.

Veronen, L. J., & Kilpatrick, D. G. (1982, November). *Stress* inoculation training for victims of rape: Efficacy and differential findings. Paper presented at the Association for Advancement of Behavior Therapy, Los Angeles.

Verp, M., Harrison, H., Ober, C., Oliveri, D., Amarose, A., Lindgren, V., & Talerman, A. (1992). Chimerism as the etiology of a 46,XX/46,XY fertile true hermaphrodite. *Fertility and Sterility, 57,* 346–349.

Vieth, M. J., Buck, M., Gertzlaf, S., Van Dolfsen, P., & Slade, A. (1983, August). *Exposure to men influences the occurrence of ovulation in women.* Paper presented at the 91st convention of the American Psychological Association, Anaheim, CA.

Vinick, B. H., & Ekerdt, D. J. (1990). The transition to retirement: Responses of husbands and wives. In B. B. Hess & W. Markson (Eds.), *Growing old in America* (4th ed., pp. 305–317). New Brunswick, NJ: Transaction.

Vinovskis, M. A. (1988). *An "epidemic" of adolescent pregnancy?* New York: Oxford University Press.

Volgy, T. J., & Schwarz, J. E. (1980). Television entertainment programming and sociopolitical attitudes. *Journalism Quarterly, 57,* 150–155.

von Baeyer, C. L., Sherk, D. L., & Zanna, M. P. (1981). Impression management in the job interview: When the female applicant meets the male "chauvinist" interviewer. *Personality and Social Psychology Bulletin, 7,* 45–51.

von Schulthess, B. (1992). Violence in the streets: Anti-lesbian assault and harassment in San Francisco. In G. M. Herek & K. T. Berrill (Eds.), *Hate crimes: Confronting violence against lesbians and gay men* (pp. 65–75). Newbury Park, CA: Sage.

Vose, R. H. (1981). *Agoraphobia.* London: Faber.

Voyer, D., Voyer, S., & Bryden, M. P. (1995). Magnitude of sex differences in spatial abilities: A meta-analysis and consideration of critical variables. *Psychological Bulletin, 117,* 250–270.

Wade, J. C. (1995). Middle-class African American men's gender role perceptions and gender role conflict: The influence of cultural desirability. *Journal of African American Men, 1,* 217–228.

Wade, J. C. (1996). African American men's gender role conflict: The significance of racial identity. *Sex Roles, 34,* 17–33.

Wakefield, J. C. (1987). Sex bias in the diagnosis of primary orgasmic dysfunction. *American Psychologist, 42,* 464–471.

Wakefield, J. C. (1988). Female primary orgasmic dysfunction: Masters and Johnson versus DSM-III-R on diagnosis and incidence. *Journal of Sex Research, 24,* 363–377.

Waldman, S. (1992, May 4). Deadbeat dads. *Newsweek,* pp. 46–52.

Waldron, I. (1991b). Patterns and causes of gender differences in smoking. *Social Science and Medicine, 32,* 989–1005.

Waldron, I., & Jacobs, J. (1988). Effects of labor force participation on women's health: New evidence from a longitudinal study. *Journal of Occupational Behavior, 30,* 977–983.

Waldron, I., & Jacobs, J. A. (1989). Effects of multiple roles on women's health: Evidence from a national longitudinal study. *Women and Health, 15,* 3–19.

Walker, A. (1982/1989). God is inside you and inside everybody else. In J. Plaskow & C. Christ (Eds.), *Weaving the visions: New patterns in feminist spirituality.* San Francisco: Harper & Row.

Walker, A. (1983). *In search of our mothers' gardens.* New York: Harcourt Brace Jovanovich.

Walker, A., Thompson, L., & Morgan, C. S. (1987). Two generations of mothers and daughters: Role position and interdependence. *Psychology of Women Quarterly, 11,* 195–208.

Walker, L. E. (1979). *The battered woman.* New York: Harper & Row.

Walker, L. E. (1981). Battered women: Sex roles and clinical issues. *Professional Psychology, 12,* 81–91.

Walker, L. E. (1989). Psychology and violence against women. *American Psychologist, 44,* 695–702.

Walker, L. J. (1984). Sex differences in the development of moral reasoning: A critical review. *Child Development, 55,* 677–691.

Walker, L. J., deVries, B., & Trevethan, S. D. (1988). Moral stages and moral orientation in real-life and hypothetical children. *Child Development, 58,* 842–858.

Walker, L. O., & Best, M. A. (1991). Well-being of mothers with infant children: A preliminary comparison of employed women and homemakers. *Women and Health, 17,* 71–89.

Wallerstein, J. S., & Kelly, J. B. (1980). *Surviving the breakup: How children and parents cope with divorce.* New York: Basic Books.

Wallston, B. S. (1981). What are the questions in the psychology of women? A feminist approach to research. *Psychology of Women Quarterly, 5,* 597–617.

Wallston, B. S. (1987). Social psychology of women and gender. *Journal of Applied Social Psychology, 17,* 1025–1050.

Wallston, B. S., & Grady, K. E. (1985). Integrating the feminist critique and the crisis in social psychology: Another look at research methods. In V. E. O'Leary, R. K. Unger, & B. S. Wallston (Eds.), *Women, gender and social psychology* (pp. 7–34). Hillsdale, NJ: Erlbaum.

Wallston, B. S., & O'Leary, V. E. (1981). Sex makes a difference: Differential perceptions of women and men. In L. Wheeler (Ed.), *Review of personality and social psychology* (Vol. 2, pp. 9–41). Beverly Hills, CA: Sage.

Walraven, M. (1974). *Mother and infant cardiac responses during breast and bottle feeding.* Unpublished doctoral dissertation, Michigan State University, East Lansing, MI.

Walsh, M. R. (1985). The psychology of women course: A continuing catalyst for change. *Teaching of Psychology, 12,* 198–203.

Walster, E., Walster, G. W., & Berscheid, E. (1978). *Equity: Theory and research.* Boston: Allyn & Bacon.

Walters, H. F., & Huck, J. (1989, March). Networking women. *Newsweek,* pp. 48–55.

Walters, R. G. (1978). *American reformers 1815–1860.* New York: Hill and Wang.

Walton, M. D., Sachs, D., Ellington, R., Hazelwood, A., Griffin, S., & Bass, D. (1988). Physical stigma and the pregnancy role: Receiving help from strangers. *Sex Roles, 18,* 323–331.

Wang, T. H., & Creedon, C. F. (1989). Sex role orientations, attributions for achievement, and personal goals of Chinese youth. *Sex Roles, 20,* 473–486.

Ward, J. V. (1989). Racial identity formation and transformation. In C. Gilligan, N. P. Lyons, & T. J. Hanmer (Eds.), *The relational world of adolescent girls at Emma Willard School.* Cambridge, MA: Harvard University Press.

Wardle, J., & Marsland, L. (1990). Adolescent concerns about weight and eating: A social-developmental perspective. *Journal of Psychosomatic Research, 34,* 377–391.

Warren, L. W., & McEachren, L. (1985). Derived identity and depressive symptomatology in women differing in marital and employment status. *Psychology of Women Quarterly, 9,* 151–160.

Warren, M. (1982). Onset of puberty later in athletic girls. *Medical Aspects of Human Sexuality, 4,* 77–78.

Warren, M. P. (1983). Physical and biological aspects of puberty. In J. Brooks-Gunn & A. C. Petersen (Eds.), *Girls at puberty* (pp. 3–28). New York: Plenum Press.

Warrington, C. S., Cox, D. J., & Evans, W. S. (1988). Dysmenorrhea. In E. A. Blechman & K. W. Brownell (Eds.), *Handbook of behavioral medicine for women*. Oxford, England: Pergamon.

Warshaw, R. (1988). *I never called it rape*. New York: Harper & Row.

Warshaw, R., & Parrot, A. (1991). The contribution of sex-role socialization to acquaintance rape. In A. Parrot & L. Bechholfer (Eds.), *Acquaintance rape: The hidden crime* (pp. 73–82). New York: Wiley.

Warshow, J. (1991). How lesbian identity affects the mother/daughter relationship. In B. Sang, J. Warshow, & A. J. Smith (Eds.), *Lesbians at midlife: The creative transition*. San Francisco: spinsters book company.

Washbourn, P. (1977). Becoming woman: Menstruation as spiritual challenge. In C. Christ & J. Plaskow (Eds.), *Womanspirit rising: A feminist reader in religion*. San Francisco: Harper & Row.

Watson, P. J., Biderman, J. D., & Sawyer, S. M. (1994). Empathy, sex role orientation, and narcissism. *Sex Roles, 30*, 701–723.

Webb, J. (1994, September 28). Breast cancer more often fatal to black women. *Lansing State Journal*, p. B1.

Weber, E. (1977, April). Sexual abuse begins at home. *Ms.*, pp. 64–67.

Weber, J. C. (1996). Social class as a correlate of gender identity among lesbian women. *Sex Roles, 35*, 253–270.

Weeks, J. (1985). *Sexuality and its discontents*. London: Routledge & Kegan Paul.

Wegman, M. E. (1991). Annual summary of vital statistics, 1990. *Pediatrics, 88*, 1081–1092.

Weidman, J. L. (1985). *Women ministers: How women are redefining traditional roles*. San Francisco: Harper & Row.

Weiner, B. (1979). A theory of motivation for some classroom experiences. *Journal of Educational Psychology, 71*, 3–25.

Weiner, B. (1985). An attributional theory of achievement motivation and emotion. *Psychological Bulletin, 92*, 548–573.

Weiner, B. (1990). Attribution in personality psychology. In L. A. Pervin (Ed.), *Handbook of personality: Theory and research*. New York: Guilford Press.

Weingarten, K. (1978). The employment pattern of professional couples and their distribution of involvement in the family. *Psychology of Women Quarterly, 3*, 43–52.

Weinraub, M., Clemens, L. P., Sockloff, A., Etheridge, T., Gracely, E., & Myers, B. (1984). The development of sex role stereotypes in the third year: Relationships to gender labeling, gender identity, sex-typed toy preference, and family characteristics. *Child Development, 55*, 1493–1503.

Weisfeld, C. C., Weisfeld, G. E., Warren, R. A., & Freedman, D. G. (1983). The spelling bee: A naturalistic study of female inhibition in mixed-sex competition. *Adolescence, 18*, 695–708.

Weisner, T. S. (1982). Sibling interdependence and child caretaking: A cross-cultural view. In M. Lamb & B. Sutton-Smith (Eds.), *Sibling relationships: Their nature and significance across the lifespan* (pp. 305–327). Hillsdale, NJ: Erlbaum.

Weisner, T. S., Garnier, H., & Loucky, J. (1994). Domestic tasks, gender equalitarian values and children's gender typing in conventional and nonconventional families. *Sex Roles, 30*, 23–54.

Weiss, R. S. (1975). *Marital separation*. New York: Basic Books.

Weissberg, M. P. (1983). *Dangerous secrets*. New York: Norton.

Weissman, M. M., Bland, R., Joyce, P. R., Newman, S., Wells, J. E., & Witchen, H. U. (1993). Sex differences in rates of depression: Cross-national perspectives. *Journal of Affective Disorders, 29*, 77–84.

Weissman, M. M., Bruce, M. L., Leaf, P. J., Florio, L. P., & Holzer, C. (1991). Affective disorders. In L. N. Robins & D. A. Reiger (Eds.), *Psychiatric disorders of America: The epidemiologic catchment area study*. New York: Free Press.

Weisstein, N. (1968). Psychology constructs the female. In M. H. Garskoff (Ed.), *Sexism in a sexist society*. New York: Bantam.

Weitz, R., & Gordon, L. (1993). Images of black women among Anglo college students. *Sex Roles, 28*, 19–34.

Weitzman, L. J. (1979). *Sex role socialization*. Palo Alto, CA: Mayfield.

Weitzman, L. J. (1985). *The divorce revolution: The unexpected social and economic consequences of divorce law reforms for women and children in America*. New York: Free Press.

Weitzman, L. J., Eifler, D., Hokada, E., & Ross, C. (1972). Sexrole socialization in picture books for preschool children. *American Journal of Sociology, 77*, 1125–1150.

Weitzman, N., Birns, B., & Friend, R. (1985). Traditional and nontraditional mothers' communication with their daughters and sons. *Child Development, 56*, 894–898.

Wells, A. J. (1988). Variations in mothers' self-esteem in daily life. *Journal of Personality and Social Psychology, 55*, 661–668.

Wells, K. (1980). Gender-role identity and psychological adjustment in adolescence. *Journal of Youth and Adolescence, 9*, 59–73.

Welter, B. (1974). The feminization of American religion, 1800–1860. In M. S. Hartman & L. W. Banner (Eds.), *Clio's consciousness: New perspectives on the history of women*. New York: Harper & Row.

Wendell, D., Onorato, J., McCray, E., Allen, D., & Sweeney, P. (1992). Youth at risk: Sex, drugs, and human immunodeficiency virus. *American Journal of Diseases of Children, 146*, 76–81.

Wentkowski, G. (1985). Older women's perceptions of great-grandparenthood: A research note. *Gerontologist, 25*, 593–596.

Wentworth, D. K., & Anderson, L. R. (1984). Emergent leadership as a function of sex and task type. *Sex Roles, 11*, 513–524.

Wentzel, K. R. (1988). Gender differences in math and english achievement: A longitudinal study. *Sex Roles, 18*, 691–699.

Werking, K. J. (1994a). Hidden assumptions: A Critique of existing cross-sex friendship research. *Personal Relationship Issues, 2*, 8–11.

Werking, K. J. (1994b). *Barriers to the formation of close cross-sex friendship*. Paper presented at the 1994 International Network on Personal Relationships Conference, Iowa City, IA.

Werner, P. D., & LaRussa, G. W. (1985). Persistence and change in sex-role stereotypes. *Sex Roles, 12*, 1089–1100.

Werrbach, G. B., Grotevant, H. D., & Cooper, C. R. (1990). Gender differences in adolescents' identity development in the domain of sex role concepts. *Sex Roles, 23*, 349–362.

Wertz, D. (1980). Man-midwifery. In H. B. Holmes, B. Hoskins, & M. Gross (Eds.), *Birth control and controlling birth: Women-centered perspectives*. Clinton, NJ: Humana Press.

West, L., Anderson, J., & Duck, S. (1996). Crossing the barriers to friendship between men and women. In J. T. Wood (Ed.), *Gendered relationships* (pp. 111–130). Mountain View, CA: Mayfield.

Westkott, M. C. (1990). On the new psychology of women: A cautionary view. *Feminist Issues, 16*, 3–18.

Weston, K. (1991). *Families we choose: Lesbians, gays, kinship.* New York: Columbia University Press.

Wethington, E., & Kessler, R. C. (1989). Employment, parental responsibility, and psychological distress: A longitudinal study of married women. *Journal of Family Issues, 10*, 527–546.

Wheeler, M. (1991). Physical changes of puberty. *Endocrinology and Metabolism Clinics of North America, 20*, 1–14.

Where do we stand on pornography? (1994, January/February). *Ms.*, pp. 32–41.

Whisler, S. C., & Eklund, S. J. (1986). Women's ambitions: A three-generational study. *Psychology of Women Quarterly, 10*, 353–362.

Whistnant, L., Brett, E., & Zegans, L. (1975). Implicit messages concerning menstruation in commercial educational materials prepared for young adolescent girls. *American Journal of Psychiatry, 132*, 815–820.

Whitbourne, S. (1986). *The me I know: A study of adult identity.* New York: Springer.

Whitbourne, S. K., & Hulicka, I. M. (1990). Ageism in undergraduate psychology texts. *American Psychologist, 45*, 1127–1136.

Whitbourne, S. K., Zuschlag, M. K., Elliot, L. B., & Waterman, A. S. (1992). Psychosocial development in adulthood: A 22-year sequential study. *Journal of Personality and Social Psychology, 63*, 260–271.

White, A. (1979). Sex differentials in the effects of remarriage on global happiness. *Journal of Marriage and the Family, 41*, 869–876.

White, J. M. (1989). Reply to comment by Trussell & Rao: A reanalysis of the data. *Journal of Marriage and the Family, 51*, 540–544.

White, J. W. (1983). Sex and gender issues in aggression research. In R. G. Geen & E. I. Donnerstein (Eds.), *Aggression: Theoretical and empirical reviews: Vol. 2. Issues in research.* New York: Academic Press, 1–26.

White, J. W. (1993, September). Feminist contributions to social psychology. *Contemporary Social Psychology, 17*, 74–78.

White, J. W., & Koss, M. P. (1991). Courtship violence: Incidence in a national sample of higher-education students. *Violence and Victims, 6*, 247–256.

White, J. W., & Kowalski, R. M. (1994). Deconstructing the myth of the nonaggressive woman: A feminist analysis. *Psychology of Women Quarterly, 18*, 487–508.

White, K. J., & Kistner, J. (1992). The influence of teacher feedback on young children's peer preferences and perceptions. *Developmental Psychology, 28*, 933–940.

White, L., & Booth, A. (1986). Children and marital happiness. *Journal of Family Issues, 7*, 131–147.

White, L. K., & Edwards, J. N. (1990). Emptying the nest and parental well-being: An analysis of national panel data. *American Sociological Review, 55*, 235–242.

Whitehead, B. (1993, April). Dan Quayle was right. *The Atlantic Monthly*, pp. 47, 50, 52, 55, 58, 60–62, 64–66, 70–72, 74, 77, 80, 82.

Whitesell, N. R., Robinson, N. S., & Harter, S. (1991). *Types and effectiveness of coping strategies employed by young adolescent males and females in anger-provoking situations.* Paper presented at the biennial meeting of the Society for Research in Child Development, Seattle, WA.

Whiting, B., & Edwards, C. P. (1973). A cross-cultural analysis of sex differences in the behavior of children aged 3 through 11. *Journal of Social Psychology, 91*, 171–188.

Whiting, B., & Edwards, C. P. (1988). *Children of different worlds: The formation of social behavior.* Cambridge, MA: Harvard University Press.

Whiting, J., & Whiting, B. B. (1975). *Children of six cultures: A psychocultural analysis.* Cambridge, MA: Harvard University Press.

Whitley, B. E., Jr. (1983). Sex-role orientation and self-esteem: A critical meta-analytic review. *Journal of Personality and Social Psychology, 44*, 765–778.

Whitley, B. E., Jr. (1985). Sex-role orientation and psychological well-being: Two meta-analyses. *Sex Roles, 12*, 207–225.

Whitley, B. E., Jr. (1988a). Masculinity, femininity, and self-esteem: A multitrait-multimethod analysis. *Sex Roles, 18*, 419–431.

Whitley, B. E., Jr. (1988b). The relation of gender-role orientation to sexual experience among college students. *Sex Roles, 19*, 619–638.

Whitley, B. E., Jr., & Kite, M. E. (1994). *Mediators of sex differences in attitudes toward homosexuality: Two meta-analyses.* Paper presented at the meeting of the Midwestern Psychological Association, Chicago.

Whitley, B. E., Jr., & Kite, M. E. (1995). Sex differences in attitudes toward homosexuality: A comment on Oliver and Hyde (1993). *Psychological Bulletin, 117*, 146–154.

Whitley, B. E., Jr., McHugh, M. C., & Frieze, I. H. (1986). Assessing the theoretical models for sex differences in sexual attributions of success and failure. In J. S. Hyde & M. C. Linn (Eds.), *The psychology of gender: Advances through meta-analysis.* Baltimore: Johns Hopkins University Press.

Whitmire, R. (1995, February 6). Many child centers don't measure up. *Detroit News*, p. A2.

Whyte, W. G. (1943). *Street corner society: The social structure of an Italian slum.* Chicago: University of Chicago Press.

Wiersma, U. J. (1990). Gender differences in job attribute preferences: Work-home role conflict and job level as mediating variables. *Journal of Occupational Psychology, 63*, 231–243.

Wilcox, A., Weinberg, C., O'Connor, J., Baurd, D., Schlatterer, J., Canfield, R., Armstrong, G., & Nisuls, B. (1988). Incidence of early loss of pregnancy. *New England Journal of Medicine, 319*, 189–194.

Wiley, M. G., & Crittenden, K. S. (1992). By your attributions you shall be known: Consequences of attributional accounts for professional and gender identities. *Sex Roles, 27*, 259–276.

Wilkinson, L. C., & Marrett, C. B. (Eds.). (1985). *Gender influences in classroom interaction.* Orlando, FL: Academic Press.

Wille, D. E. (1995). The 1990s: Gender differences in parenting roles. *Sex Roles, 33*, 803–817.

Willet, W. C., et al. (1987). Moderate alcohol consumption and the risk of breast cancer. *New England Journal of Medicine, 316*, 1174–1180.

Willetts-Bloom, M. C., & Nock, S. L. (1994). The influence of maternal employment on gender role attitudes of men and women. *Sex Roles, 30*, 371–389.

Williams, C. L. (1992). The glass escalator: Hidden advantages for men in the "female" professions. *Social Problems, 39*, 253–267.

Williams, D. S. (1987). *Christianity and crisis.* New York: Williams.

Williams, J. E. (1982). An overview of findings from adult sex stereotype studies in 25 countries. In R. Rath, H. S. Asthana, D. Sinha, & J. B. H. Sinha (Eds.), *Diversity and unity in cross-cultural psychology.* Lisse, Netherlands: Swets and Zeitlinger.

Williams, J. E., & Bennett, S. M. (1975). The definition of sex stereotypes via the Adjective Check List. *Sex Roles, 1,* 327–337.

Williams, J. E., & Best, D. L. (1982). *Measuring sex stereotypes: A thirty-nation study.* Beverly Hills, CA: Sage.

Williams, J. E., & Best, D. L. (1990a). *Measuring sex stereotypes: A multination study* (Rev. ed.). Newbury Park, CA: Sage.   •

Williams, J. E., & Best, D. L. (1990b). *Sex and psyche: Gender roles and self viewed crossculturally.* Beverly Hills, CA: Sage.

Williams, J. E., & Holmes, K. A. (1981). The second assault: Rape and public attitudes. Westport, CT: Greenwood Press.

Williams, K. B., & Cyr, R. R. (1992). Escalating commitment to a relationship: The sexual harassment trap. *Sex Roles, 27,* 47–72.

Williams, L. R. (1983). Beliefs and attitudes of young girls regarding menstruation. In S. Golub (Ed.), *Menarche.* Lexington, MA: Lexington Books.

Williams, M. H. (1992). Exploitation and inference: Mapping the damage from therapist-patient sexual involvement. *American Psychologist, 47,* 412–423.

Williams, N. (1988). Role making among married Mexican-American women: Issues of class and ethnicity. *Journal of Applied Behavioral Science, 24,* 203–217.

Williams, P., & Smith, M. (1979). *Interview in the First Question* [Film]. London: British Broadcasting System Science and Features Department.

Williams, T. M. (Ed.). (1986). *The impact of television: A natural experiment in three communities.* Orlando, FL: Academic Press.

Willis, F. N., & Carlson, R. A. (1993). Singles ads: Gender, social class, and time. *Sex Roles, 29,* 387–404.

Wills, T. A., Weiss, R. L., & Patterson, G. R. (1974). A behavioral analysis of the determinants of marital satisfaction. *Journal of Consulting and Clinical Psychology, 42,* 802–811.

Willson, J., & Carrington, E. (1987). *Obstetrics and Gynecology* (8th ed.). St Louis, MO: Mosby.

Wilson, J., & Musick, M. (1995). Personal autonomy in religion and marriage: Is there a link? *Reviews of Religious Research, 37,* 3–18.

Wilson, M. I., & Daly, M. (1992). Who kills whom in spouse killings? On the exceptional ratio of spousal homicides in the United States. *Criminology, 30,* 189–215.

Wilson, M. N., Tolson, T. F. J., Hinton, I. D., & Kiernan, M. (1990). Flexibility and sharing of childcare duties in black families. *Sex Roles, 22,* 409–425.

Wilson, P. (1986). Black culture and sexuality. *Journal of Social Work and Human Sexuality, 4,* 29–46.

Wilson, T. D., & Linville, P. W. (1982). Improving the academic performances of college freshmen: Attribution therapy revisited. *Journal of Personality and Social Psychology, 42,* 367–376.

Wilson, T. D., & Linville, P. W. (1985). Improving the performance of college freshmen with attributional techniques. *Journal of Personality and Social Psychology, 49,* 287–293.

Winchel, R., Fenner, D., & Shaver, P. (1974). Impact of coeducation on fear of success imagery. *Journal of Educational Psychology, 66,* 726–730.

Winokur, G. (1991). *Mania and depression: A classification of syndrome and disease.* Baltimore: Johns Hopkins University Press.

Winter, D. G. (1973). *The power motive.* New York: Free Press.

Winter, D. G. (1988). The power motive in women—and men. *Journal of Personality and Social Psychology, 54,* 510–519.

Winter, D. G., & Stewart, A. J. (1978). The power motive. In H. London & J. E. Exner (Eds.), *Dimensions of personality.* New York: Wiley.

Wisch, A. R., Mahalik, J. R., Hayes, J. A., & Nutt, E. A. (1995). The impact of gender role conflict and counseling technique on psychological help seeking in men. *Sex Roles, 33,* 77–89.

Witelson, S. (1991). Neural sexual mosaicism: Sexual differentiation of the human temporo-parietal region for functional asymmetry. *Psychoneuroendocrinology, 16,* 131–153.

Witkin, H. A. (1979). Socialization, culture and ecology in the development of group and sex differences in cognitive style. *Human Development, 22,* 358–372.

Witkin, H. A., Lewis, H. B., Hertzman, M., Machover, K., Meissner, P. B., & Wapner, S. (1954). *Personality through perception.* New York: Academic Press.

Witkin, H. A., Mednick, S. A., Schulsinger, F., Bakkestrom, E., Christiansen, K. O., Goodenough, D. R., Hirschorn, K., Lundsteen, C., Owen, D. R., Philip, J., Rubin, D. B., & Stocking, M. (1976). Criminality in XXY and XYY men. *Science, 193,* 547–555.

Witkin, H. A., Ottman, P., Raskin, E., & Karp, S. (1971). *Manual for Embedded Figures Test.* Palo Alto, CA: Consulting Psychologists Press.

Wittig, M. A., & Skolnick, P. (1978). Status versus warmth as determinants of sex differences in personal space. *Sex Roles, 4,* 493–503.

Wolfe, L. (1980, September). The sexual profile of that Cosmopolitan girl. *Cosmopolitan,* pp. 254–265.

Wolfe, L. (1981). *The Cosmo Report.* New York: Arbor House.

Wolfe, V. V., Gentile, C., & Wolfe, D. A. (1989). The impact of sexual abuse on children: A PTSD formulation. *Behavior Therapy, 20,* 215–228.

Wolff, C. (1971). *Love between women.* New York: Harper & Row.

Wollstonecraft, M. (1792/1967). *A vindication of the rights of woman.* New York: Norton.

Woloch, N. (1984). *Women and the American experience.* New York: Knopf.

Women clerics find sexual harassment. (1990, December 1). *Washington Post,* p. C12.

Women in Words & Images. (1972). *Dick and Jane as victims.* Princeton, NJ: Author.

Women's Programs Office (1991). *Graduate faculty interested in psychology of women.* Washington, DC: American Psychological Association.

Wood, D. B. (1990, December 12). How TV treats women. *Christian Science Monitor,* p. 12.

Wood, J. T. (1994). *Gendered lives: Communication, gender, and culture.* Belmont, CA: Wadsworth.

Wood, J. T. (1996). Gender, relationships, and communication. In J. T. Wood (Ed.), *Gendered relationships.* Mountain View, CA: Mayfield.

Wood, W., Rhodes, N., & Whelan, M. (1989). Sex differences in positive well-being: A consideration of emotional style and marital status. *Psychological Bulletin, 106,* 249–264.

Woodall, K. L., & Matthews, K. A. (1993). Changes and stability of hostile characteristics: Results from a 4-year longitudinal study of children. *Journal of Personality and Social Psychology, 64,* 491–499.

Woods, N. F. (1984). *Human sexuality in health and illness* (3rd ed.). St. Louis, MO: Mosby.

Woods, N. R., Dery, G. K., & Most, A. (1983). Recollections of menarche, current menstrual attitudes, and perimenstrual symptoms. In S. Golub (Ed.), *Menarche: The transition from girl to woman* (pp. 87–97). Lexington, MA: Lexington Books.

Worell, J. (1989). Sex roles in transition. In J. Worell & F. Danner (Eds.), *The adolescent as decision-maker: Applications to development and education* (pp. 245–280). San Diego, CA: Academic Press.

Worell, J. (1990). Feminist frameworks: Retrospect and prospect. *Psychology of Women Quarterly, 14,* 1–5.

Worell, J. (1996). Invited address: Opening doors to feminist research. *Psychology of Women Quarterly, 20,* 469–485.

Worell, J., & Etaugh, C. (1994). Transforming theory and research with women: Themes and variations. *Psychology of Women Quarterly, 18,* 443–450.

Working Women's Institute (1980). *Sexual harassment on the job: Questions and answers.* (Available from 593 Park Ave., New York, NY 10021)

Workman, J. E., & Johnson, K. K. P. (1991). The role of cosmetics in attributions about sexual harassment. *Sex Roles, 24,* 759–769.

Wortman, C. B., & Silver, R. C. (1989). The myth of coping with loss. *Journal of Consulting and Clinical Psychology, 57,* 349–357.

Wright, J., Bissonnette, F., Duchesne, C., Benoit, J., Sabourin, S., & Girard, Y. (1991). Psychosocial distress and infertility: Men and women respond differently. *Fertility and Sterility, 55,* 100–108.

Wright, L. (December, 1985). I want to be alone. *Texas Monthly,* pp. 164, 166, 168.

Wright, P. H. (1985). The Acquaintance Description Form. In S. F. Duck & D. Pearlman (Eds.), *Understanding personal relationships: An interdisciplinary approach.* London: Sage.

Wright, P. H. (1989). Gender differences in adults' same- and cross-gender friendships. In R. G. Adams & R. Blieszner (Eds.), *Older adult friendship: Structure and process.* Newbury Park, CA: Sage.

Wright, P. H., & Bergloff, P. J. (1984). *The Acquaintance Description Form and the study of relationship differentiation.* Paper presented at the Second International Conference on Personal Relationships, Madison, WI.

Wright, P. J., Henggeler, S. W., & Craig, L. (1986). Problems in paradise? A longitudinal examination of the transition to parenthood. *Journal of Applied Developmental Psychology, 7,* 277–291.

Wright, P. H., & Scanlon, M. B. (1991). Gender role orientations and friendship: Some attenuation, but gender differences abound. *Sex Roles, 24,* 551–567.

Wu, X., & DeMaris, A. (1996). Gender and marital status differences in depression: The effect of chronic strains. *Sex Roles, 34,* 299–319.

Wyatt, G. E. (1991). Child sexual abuse and its effects on sexual functioning. *Annual Review of Sex Research, 1,* 249–266.

Wyatt, G. E. (1992). The sociocultural context of African American and white American women's rape. *Journal of Social Issues, 48,* 77–93.

Wyatt, G. E., Guthrie, D., & Notgrass, C. M. (1992). Differential effects of women's child sexual abuse and subsequent sexual revictimization. *Journal of Consulting and Clinical Psychology, 60,* 167–173.

Wyatt, G. E., Notgrass, C. M., & Newcomb, M. (1990). Internal and external mediators of women's rape experiences. *Psychology of Women Quarterly, 14,* 153–176.

Wyatt, G. E., & Riederle, M. H. (1994). Reconceptualizing issues that affect women's sexual decision-making and sexual functioning. *Psychology of Women Quarterly, 18,* 611.

Wyche, K. F. (1991). *The development of concerns of race, ethnicity and gender in children from diverse racial ethnic groups.* Paper presented at the biennial meeting of the Society for Research in Child Development, Seattle, WA.

Yamamoto, J. (1986). Japanese American identity crisis. In E. E. Brody (Ed.), *Minority group adolescents in the U.S.* Baltimore: Williams & Wilkins.

Yando, R., Seitz, V., & Zigler, W. (1978). *Imitation: A developmental perspective.* Hillsdale, NJ: Erlbaum.

Yandow, V. (1989). Alcoholism in women. *Psychiatric Annals, 19,* 243–247.

Yang, N., & Linz, D. (1990). Movie ratings and the contingent of adult videos: The sex violence ratio. *Journal of Communication, 40,* 28–42.

Yankauskas, E. (1990). Primary female syndromes: An update. *New York State Journal of Medicine, 90,* 295–302.

Yarkin, K. L., Town, J. P., & Wallston, B. S. (1982). Blacks and women must try harder: Stimulus persons' race and sex attributions of causality. *Personality and Social Psychology Bulletin, 8,* 21–30.

Yarrow, M. R., Scott, P., deLeeuw, L., & Heinig, C. (1962). Child-rearing in families of working and nonworking mothers. *Sociometry, 25,* 122–140.

Yee, D. K., & Eccles, J. S. (1988). Parent perceptions and attributions for children's math achievement. *Sex Roles, 19,* 317–333.

Yllo, A. (1978). Nonmarital cohabitation. *Alternative Lifestyles, 1,* 37–54.

Yoder, J. D. (1991). Rethinking tokenism: Looking beyond numbers. *Gender and Society, 5,* 178–192.

Yoder, J. D., & Aniakudo, P. (1995). The responses of African American women firefighters to gender harassment at work. *Sex Roles, 32,* 125–137.

Yoder, J. D., Aniakudo, P., & Berendsen, L. (1996). Looking beyond gender: The effects of racial differences on tokenism perceptions of women. *Sex Roles, 35,* 389–400.

Yoder, J. D., & McDonald, T. W. (1997). The generalizability and construct validity of the modern sexism scale: Some cautionary notes. *Sex Roles, 36,* 655–663.

Yoder, J. D., & Schleicher, T. L. (1996). Undergraduates regard deviation from occupational gender stereotypes as costly for women. *Sex Roles, 34,* 171–188.

York, R., Freeman, E., Lowery, B., & Strauss, J. (1989). Characteristics of premenstrual syndrome. *American College of Obstetricians and Gynecologists, 73,* 601–605.

Youniss, J., & Smollar, J. (1986). *Adolescent relations with mothers, fathers, and friends.* Chicago: University of Chicago Press.

Ywahoo, D. (1989). Renewing the sacred hoop. In J. Plaskow & C. Christ (Eds.), *Weaving the visions: New patterns in feminist spirituality.* San Francisco: Harper & Row.

Zahaykevich, M., Sirey, J. A., & Brooks-Gunn, J. (1989). Mother-daughter individuation during early adolescence. Unpublished manuscript. Cited in J. Brooks-Gunn, & M. Zahaykevich. Parent-daughter relationships in early adolescence: A development perspective. In K. Kreppner & R. Lerner (Eds.), *Family systems and life-span development*. Hillsdale, NJ: Erlbaum.

Zakin, D. F., Blyth, D. A., & Simmons, R. G. (1984). Physical attractiveness as a mediator of the impact of early pubertal changes for girls. *Journal of Youth and Adolescence, 13*, 439–450.

Zanna, M. P., & Pack, S. J. (1975). On the self-fulfilling nature of apparent sex differences in behavior. *Journal of Experimental Social Psychology, 11*, 583–591.

Zarbatany, L., Hartmann, D. P., Gelfand, D. M., & Vinciguerra, P. (1985). Gender differences in altruistic reputation: Are they artifactual? *Developmental Psychology, 21*, 97–101.

Zaslow, M. J., & Pedersen, F. A. (1981). Sex role conflicts and the experience of childbearing. *Professional Psychology, 12*, 47–55.

Zautra, A. J., & Wrabetz, A. B. (1991). Coping success and its relationship to psychological distress for older adults. *Journal of Personality and Social Psychology, 61*, 801–810.

Zaviacic, M., et al. (1988). Concentration of fructose in female ejaculate and urine: A comparative biochemical study. *Journal of Sex Research, 24*, 319–325.

Zelman, C. M. (1991). Our menstruation for the girls. *Feminist Studies, 17*, 461–467.

Zick, C. D., & McCullough, J. L. (1991). Trends in married couples' time use: Evidence from 1977–78 and 1987–88. *Sex Roles, 24*, 459–487.

Zilbergeld, B. (1992). *Male sexuality*. Boston: Little, Brown.

Ziller, R. C. (1990). *Photographing the self*. Newbury Park, CA: Sage.

Zimmerman, D. H., & West, C. (1975). Sex roles, interruptions and silences in conversations. In B. Thorne & N. Henley (Eds.), *Language and sex: Difference and dominance* (pp. 105–129). Rowley, MA: Newbury House.

Zimmerman, E., & Parlee, M. B. (1973). Behavioral changes associated with the menstrual cycle: An experimental investigation. *Journal of Applied Social Psychology, 3*, 335–344.

Ziporyn, T. (1992, February). Postpartum depression: True blue? *Harvard Health Letter, 17*, 1–3.

Zita, J. N. (1993). Heresy in the female body: The rhetoric of menopause. In J. C. Callahan (Ed.), *Menopause: A midlife passage* (pp. 59–78). Bloomington: University of Indiana Press.

Zucker, K. J., Wilson-Smith, D. N., Kurita, J. A., & Stern, A. (1995). Children's appraisals of sex-typed behavior in their peers. *Sex Roles, 33*, 703–725.

Zucker, R. A. (1987). The four alcoholisms: A developmental account of the etiologic process. In P. C. Rivers (Ed.), *Nebraska Symposium on Motivation: Vol. 34. Alcohol and addictive behavior*. Lincoln: University of Nebraska Press.

Zuckerman, D. M. (1989). Stress, self-esteem, and mental health: How does gender make a difference? *Sex Roles, 20*, 429–444.

Zuckerman, M., DeFrank, R. S., Spiegel, N. H., & Larrance, D. T. (1982). Masculinity-femininity and encoding of nonverbal cues. *Journal of Personality and Social Psychology, 42*, 548–556.

Zuckerman, M., & Kieffer, S. C. (1994). Race differences in faceism: Does facial prominence imply dominance? *Journal of Personality and Social Psychology, 66*, 86–92.

Zuckerman, M., & Wheeler, L. (1975). To dispel fantasies about the fantasy-based measure of fear of success. *Psychological Bulletin, 82*, 932–946.

Zur, O., & Morrison, A. (1989). Gender and war: Reexamining attitudes. *American Journal of Orthopsychiatry, 59*.

Zussman, L., Zussman, S., Sunley, R., & Bjornson, E. (1981). Sexual response after hysterectomy-oophorectomy: Recent studies and reconsideration of psychogenesis. *American Journal of Obstetrics and Gynecology, 140*, 725–729.

# CREDITS

## Text and Illustrations

**Chapter 2** p. 45 Fig. 2.1 Zanna, M. P. & Pack, S. J., 1975. On the self-fulfilling nature of apparent sex differences in behavior. *Journal of Experimental Social Psychology, 11*, 583–591. Used with permission of Academic Press, Inc. p. 50 Table 2.1 Mooney, L., & Brabant, S., 1987. Two martinis and a rested woman: "Liberation" in the Sunday comics. *Sex Roles, 17*, (7/8), 409–420. Used with permission of Plenum Publishing Corporation. p. 51 Table 2.2 Olson, B., & Douglas, W., 1997. The family on television: Evaluation of gender roles in situation comedy. *Sex Roles, 36*, 409–427. Based on Tables I, IV, V, and VI. Used with permission of Plenum Publishing Corporation. p. 52 Fig. 2.2 Hansen, C. H., & Hansen, R. D., 1988. How rock music videos can change what is seen when boy meets girl: Priming stereotypic appraisal of social interactions. *Sex Roles, 19*, (5/6), 287–316. Used with permission of Plenum Publishing Corporation. p. 62 Fig. 2.3 Moore, T. E., Griffiths, K., & Payne, B., 1987. Gender, attitudes towards women, and the appreciation of sexist humor. *Sex Roles, 16*, (9/10), 528. Used with permission of Plenum Publishing Corporation.

**Chapter 3** p. 80 Table 3.1 Williams, J. E. & Bennett, S. M., 1975. The definition of sex stereotypes via the Adjective Check List. *Sex Roles, 1*, (4), pp. 330–331. Used with permission of Plenum Publishing Corporation. p. 81 Table 3.2 Broverman, I., Vogel, S. R., Broverman, D. M., Clarkson, F. E., & Rosenkrantz, P. S., 1972. Sex role stereotypes: A current appraisal. *Journal of Social Issues, 28*, (2), 59–78. Used with permission of Blackwell Publishers. p. 82 Table 3.3 Deaux, K., 1984. From individual differences to social categories: Analysis of a decade's research on gender. *American Psychologist, 39*, (2), 112. Copyright © 1984 by the American Psychological Association. Used with permission. p. 90 Table 3.4 Bem, S., 1980. Bem sex-role inventory professional manual. Palo Alto, CA: Consulting Psychologists Press. Used with permission from Mind Garden, Inc. p. 98 Table 3.5 O'Heron, C. A., & Orlofsky, J. L., 1990. Stereotypic and nonstereotypic sex role trait and behavior orientations, gender identity, and psychological adjustment. *Journal of Personality and Social Psychology, 58*, (1), 138. Copyright © 1990 by the American Psychological Association. Used with permission. p. 102 A Closer Look 3.1 Nelson, M. C., 1988. Reliability, validity, and cross-cultural comparisons for the simplified Attitudes Toward Women Scale, *Sex Roles, 18*, (5/6), 292. Used with permission of Plenum Publishing Corporation. p. 103 Fig. 3.2 Twenge, J. M., 1997. Attitudes Toward Women, 1970–1995: A meta-analysis. *Psychology of Women Quarterly, 21*, 42. Reprinted with the permission of Cambridge University Press.

**Chapter 4** p. 114 Fig. 4.1 Adapted from Wilson, J. D., George, F. W., & Griffin, J. E., 1981. The hormonal control of sexual development. *Science, 211*, 1280. Copyright © 1981 American Association for the Advancement of Science. Used with permission.

**Chapter 5** p. 167 Fig. 5.1 Hort, B. E., Leinbach, M. D., & Fagot, B. I., 1991. Is there coherence among the cognitive components of gender acquisition? *Sex Roles, 24*, (3/4), 195–207. Figure 1, p. 200. Used with permission from Plenum Publishing Corporation. p. 175 Table 5.3 Hayden-Thompson, L., Rubin, K. H. & Hymel, S., 1987. Sex preferences in sociometric chores. *Developmental Psychology, 23*, (4), 558–562. Adapted from Table 1, p. 559 and Table 2, p. 560. Copyright © 1987 by the American Psychological Association. Adapted with permission. p. 181 Table 5.4 Allgood-Merten, B., & Stockard, J., 1991. Sex role identity and self-esteem: A comparison of children and adolescents. *Sex Roles, 25*, (3/4), 129–139. Used with permission from Plenum Publishing Corporation. p. 182 Table 5.5 Loevinger, Jane, *Ego development*, p. 403, Jossey-Bass, Inc. Publishers, 1976. Copyright © 1976 Jossey-Bass, Inc., Publishers. Used with permission.

**Chapter 6** Box 6.2 p. 192 Zelman, C. M., *Our Menstruation*, vol. 17, no. 3, Fall 1991, 461–467. Used with permission of the publisher, Feminist Studies, Inc., c/o Department of Women's Studies, University of Maryland, College Park, MD 20742. Fig. 6.2 p. 200 Koff, E., 1983 Through the looking glass of menarche: What the adolescent girl sees. In S. Golub, ed., 1983, *Menarche: The transition from girl to woman*, pp. 77–86, Lexington Books, Lexington, MA. Used with permission of Sharon Golub. p. 209 Fig. 6.3 McFarlane, J., Martin, C. L., & Williams, T. M., 1988. Mood fluctuations: Women versus men and menstrual versus other cycles. *Psychology of Women Quarterly, 12*, 211–223. Reprinted with the permission of Cambridge University Press. p. 215 A Closer Look 6.3 Brooks-Gunn, J., & Ruble, D.N., 1980. The Menstrual Attitude Questionnaire. *Psychosomatic Medicine, 42*, 5. From Table 1, pp. 505–506. Copyright © 1980 Williams & Wilkins. Used with permisson.

**Chapter 7** p. 230 Fig. 7.1 Gold, A. R., Brush, L. R. & Sprotzer, E. R., 1980. Developmental changes in self-perceptions of intelligence and self-confidence. *Psychology of Women Quarterly, 5*, (2), 231–239. From Table 1, p. 234. Reprinted with permission of Cambridge University Press. p. 238 Fig. 7.2 Weiner, B., 1979. A theory of motivation for some classroom experiences. *Journal of Educational Psychology, 71*, 3–25. Weiner, B., 1985. An attributional theory of achievement motivation and emotion. *Psychological Review, 92*, 548–573. Copyright © 1979, 1985 by the American Psychological Association. Used with permission. p. 244 Fig. 7.3 Roberts, T., & Nolen-Hoeksema, S., 1989. Sex differences in reaction to valuative feedback. *Sex Roles, 21*, 725–747. Used with permision from Plenum Publishing Corporation. p. 250 Fig. 7.4 Winchel, R., Fenner, D., & Shaver, P., 1974. Impact of coeducation on "fear of success" imagery expressed by male and female high school seniors. *Jour-

stand differences. *Journal of Personality and Social Psychology*, 61, (6), 992–999. Based on Table 6, p. 996. Copyright © 1991 by the American Psychological Association. Used with permission.

**Chapter 17**  p. 636 Lyrics from The Rock Will Wear Away are used with permission of Holly Near.

## *Photos*

**Chapter 1**  p. 8, © The Image Works Archives; p. 16, © Topham/The Image Works; p. 35L, © Corbis-Bettmann; p. 35R, © Pickerell/The Image Works

**Chapter 2**  p. 42, © Michael Newman/PhotoEdit; p. 55, © Mickey Pfleger/Photo 20-20; p. 60L, © Topham/The Image Works; p. 60R, © PhotoEdit

**Chapter 3**  p. 78, © Stephanie Diani/Photo 20-20; p. 86L, © Robert Ullmann/Design Conceptions; p. 86R, © Steve Rubin/The Image Works; p. 96, © Alan Carey/The Image Works

**Chapter 4**  p. 127, © Spencer Grant/Stock Boston; p. 129, © David Young-Wolff/PhotoEdit; p. 138, © David Young-Wolff/PhotoEdit

**Chapter 5**  p. 150, © Francene Keery/Stock Boston; p. 154, © Bachmann/Photo 20-20; p. 160, © Myrleen Ferguson/PhotoEdit

**Chapter 6**  p. 196, © David Young Wolff/PhotoEdit; p. 202, © Michael Newman/PhotoEdit; p. 213, © Esbin-Anderson/Photo 20-20

**Chapter 7**  p. 227, © David Young-Wolff/PhotoEdit; p. 236, © Gale Zucker/Stock Boston; p. 253, © Agence France Presse/Corbis-Bettmann

**Chapter 8**  p. 262, © Jean-Claude Lejeune/Stock Boston; p. 279, © Tony Freeman/PhotoEdit; p. 289, © Richard Hutchings/PhotoEdit

**Chapter 9**  p. 302, © David Young-Wolff/PhotoEdit; p. 313, © David Young-Wolff/PhotoEdit; p. 328, Courtesy Janet Mills, Ph.D.

**Chapter 10**  p. 335, © Jeff Greenberg/The Image Finders; p. 351, © David K. Crow/PhotoEdit; p. 364, © Mark Richards/PhotoEdit

**Chapter 11**  p. 374, © Bachmann/PhotoEdit; p. 378, © Phil Kingsley/The Image Finders; p. 404, © Joel Gordon

**Chapter 12**  p. 421, © Joel Gordon; p. 429, © Jacque Brund/Design Conceptions; p. 435, © Joel Gordon

**Chapter 13**  p. 450, © Tom McCarthy/PhotoEdit; p. 463, © Jonathan Selig/Photo 20-20; p. 464, © Cynthia Johnson/Time Magazine; p. 469, © McLaughlin/The Image Works; p. 472, © Archive Photos/Lambert

**Chapter 14**  p. 492, © Joel Gordon; p. 502, © Jean-Claude Lejeune/Stock Boston; p. 511, © Tom McCarthy/PhotoEdit; p. 520, © David Young-Wolff/PhotoEdit

**Chapter 15**  p. 531, © Reuters/Corbis-Bettmann; p. 534, © Joel Gordon; p. 561, © Barbara Alper/Stock Boston

**Chapter 16**  p. 572, © R. Lord/The Image Works; p. 575, © Joel Gordon; p. 580, © Christopher Brown/Stock Boston

**Chapter 17**  p. 605, © Bob Daemmrich/Stock Boston; p. 621, © H. Gans/The Image Works; p. 629, © Joel Gordon

# INDEX

Page numbers in **boldface** denote key terms in text.